NINTH EDITION
GLOBAL EDITION

Elementary and Middle School Mathematics

Teaching Developmentally

John A. Van de Walle
Late of Virginia Commonwealth University

Karen S. Karp
University of Louisville

Jennifer M. Bay-Williams
University of Louisville

With Contributions by
Jonathan Wray
Howard County Public Schools

Pearson

Harlow, England • London • New York • Boston • San Francisco • Toronto • Sydney • Dubai • Singapore • Hong Kong
Tokyo • Seoul • Taipei • New Delhi • Cape Town • Sao Paulo • Mexico City • Madrid • Amsterdam • Munich • Paris • Milan

Executive Acquisitions Editor: Meredith Fossel
Series Editorial Assistant: Maria Feliberty
Executive Development Editor: Linda Bishop
Vice President, Director of Marketing: Margaret Waples
Senior Marketing Manager: Christopher Barry
Program Manager: Maren Beckman
Project Manager: Christina Taylor
Project Manager, Global Edition: Purnima Narayanan
Senior Acquisitions Editor, Global Edition: Sandhya Ghoshal
Senior Project Editor, Global Edition: Daniel Luiz
Manager, Media Production, Global Edition: M. Vikram Kumar
Senior Manufacturing Controller, Production, Global Edition: Trudy Kimber
Editorial Production Service: MPS North America LLC
Manufacturing Buyer: Deidra Skahill
Electronic Composition: Jouve
Interior Design: Diane Lorenzo
Cover Image: © CristinaMuraca/Shutterstock

Credits and acknowledgments borrowed from other sources and reproduced, with permission, in this textbook appear on appropriate page within text or on page C-1.

Pearson Education Limited
Edinburgh Gate
Harlow
Essex CM20 2JE
England

and Associated Companies throughout the world

Visit us on the World Wide Web at:
www.pearsonglobaleditions.com

© Pearson Education Limited 2015

The rights of John A. Van de Walle, Karen S. Karp, and Jennifer M. Bay-Williams to be identified as the authors of this work have been asserted by them in accordance with the Copyright, Designs and Patents Act 1988.

Authorized adaptation from the United States edition, entitled Elementary and Middle School Mathematics: Teaching Developmentally, 9th edition, ISBN 978-0-13-376893-0, by John A. Van de Walle, Karen S. Karp, and Jennifer M. Bay-Williams, published by Pearson Education © 2016.

ISBN 10: 1-292-09769-8
ISBN 13: 978-1-292-09769-5

British Library Cataloguing-in-Publication Data
A catalogue record for this book is available from the British Library.

10 9 8 7 6
20 19 18

Typeset in Janson Text LT Std Roman by MPS North America LLC.

Printed in Malaysia (CTP-VVP)

About the Authors

John A. Van de Walle

The late John A. Van de Walle was a professor emeritus at Virginia Commonwealth University. He was a leader in mathematics education who regularly offered professional development workshops for K–8 teachers in the United States and Canada focused on mathematics instruction that engaged students in mathematical reasoning and problem solving. He visited many classrooms and worked with teachers to implement student-centered math lessons. He co-authored the *Scott Foresman-Addison Wesley Mathematics K–6* series and contributed to the original Pearson School mathematics program *enVisionMATH*. Additionally, John was very active in the National Council of Teachers of Mathematics (NCTM), writing book chapters and journal articles, serving on the board of directors, chairing the educational materials committee, and speaking at national and regional meetings.

Karen S. Karp

Karen S. Karp is a professor of mathematics education at the University of Louisville (Kentucky). Prior to entering the field of teacher education she was an elementary school teacher in New York. Karen is the volume editor of *Annual Perspectives in Mathematics Education: Using Research to Improve Instruction* and is the co-author of *Developing Essential Understanding of Addition and Subtraction for Teaching Mathematics in Pre-K–Grade 2, Discovering Lessons for the Common Core State Standards in Grades K–5*, and *Putting Essential Understanding of Addition and Subtraction into Practice Pre-K–Grade 2*. She is a former member of the board of directors for the National Council of Teachers of Mathematics (NCTM) and a former president of the Association of Mathematics Teacher Educators. She continues to work in classrooms with teachers of students with disabilities.

Jennifer M. Bay-Williams

Jennifer M. Bay-Williams is a mathematics educator at the University of Louisville (Kentucky). Jennifer taught elementary, middle, and high school in Missouri and in Peru, and continues to work in classrooms at all levels with students and with teachers. Jennifer has published many articles on teaching and learning in NCTM journals. She has also authored and co-authored numerous books, including *Developing Essential Understanding of Addition and Subtraction for Teaching Mathematics in Pre-K–Grade 2, Math and Literature: Grades 6–8, Math and Nonfiction: Grades 6–8, Navigating through Connections in Grades 6–8*, and *Mathematics Coaching: Resources and Tools for Coaches and Other Leaders*. She is on the board of directors for the National Council of Teachers of Mathematics (NCTM) and previously served on the Board of Directors for TODOS: Equity for All and as secretary and president for the Association of Mathematics Teacher Educators (AMTE).

About the Contributor

Jonathan Wray is the technology contributor to *Elementary and Middle School Mathematics, Teaching Developmentally* (6th–9th editions). He is the instructional facilitator for Secondary Mathematics Curricular Programs in the Howard County Public School System. He is the president of the Association of Maryland Mathematics Teacher Educators (AMMTE) and past president of the Maryland Council of Teachers of Mathematics (MCTM) and serves as manager of the Elementary Mathematics Specialists and Teacher Leaders (ems&tl) Project. He has been recognized for his expertise in infusing technology in mathematics teaching and was named an Outstanding Technology Leader in Education by the Maryland Society for Educational Technology (MSET). Jon is also actively engaged in the National Council of Teachers of Mathematics (NCTM), serving on the Emerging Issues and Executive Committees. He has served as a primary and intermediate grades classroom teacher, gifted/talented resource teacher, elementary mathematics specialist, curriculum and assessment developer, grant project manager, and educational consultant.

Brief Contents

Contents

SECTION I   Teaching Mathematics: Foundations and Perspectives

The fundamental core of effective teaching of mathematics combines an understanding of how students learn, how to promote that learning by teaching through problem solving, and how to plan for and assess that learning on a daily basis. Introductory chapters in this section provide perspectives on trends in mathematics education and the process of doing mathematics. These chapters develop the core ideas of learning, teaching, planning, and assessment. Additional perspectives on mathematics for students with diverse backgrounds and the role of technological tools are also emphasized.

SECTION II   Development of Mathematical Concepts and Procedures

This section serves as the application of the core ideas of Section I. Here you will find chapters on every major content area in the pre-K–8 mathematics curriculum. Numerous problem-based activities to engage students are interwoven with a discussion of the mathematical content and how students develop their understanding of that content. At the outset of each chapter, you will find a listing of "Big Ideas," the mathematical umbrella for the chapter. Also included are ideas for incorporating children's literature, integrations with the mathematical practices, and formative assessment notes. These chapters are designed to help you develop pedagogical strategies and to serve as a resource for your teaching now and in the future.

CHAPTER 8
Developing Early Number Concepts and Number Sense   166

CHAPTER 9
Developing Meanings for the Operations   191

CHAPTER 10
Developing Basic Fact Fluency   218

CHAPTER 11
Developing Whole-Number Place-Value Concepts   246

CHAPTER 12
Developing Strategies for Addition and Subtraction Computation   271

CHAPTER 13
Developing Strategies for Multiplication and Division Computation   301

CHAPTER 14
Algebraic Thinking, Equations, and Functions   323

CHAPTER 15
Developing Fraction Concepts   363

CHAPTER 16
Developing Fraction Operations   395

CHAPTER 17
Developing Concepts of Decimals and Percents   427

CHAPTER 18
Ratios, Proportions, and Proportional Reasoning   453

CHAPTER 19
Developing Measurement Concepts   477

Preface

All students can learn mathematics with understanding! It is through the teacher's actions that every student can have this experience. We believe that teachers must create a classroom environment in which students are given opportunities to solve problems and work together, using their ideas and strategies, to solve them. Effective mathematics instruction involves posing tasks that engage students in the mathematics they are expected to learn. Then, by allowing students to interact with and productively struggle with *their own mathematical ideas* and *their own strategies,* they will learn to see the connections among mathematical topics and the real world. Students value mathematics and feel empowered to use it.

Creating a classroom in which students design solution pathways, engage in productive struggle, and connect one mathematical idea to another is complex. Questions arise, such as, "How do I get students to wrestle with problems if they just want me to show them how to do it? What kinds of tasks lend themselves to this type of engagement? Where can I learn the mathematics content I need in order to be able to teach in this way?" With these and other questions firmly in mind, we have several objectives in the ninth edition of this textbook:

1. Illustrate what it means to teach mathematics using a problem-based approach.
2. Serve as a go-to reference for all of the mathematics content suggested for grades pre-K–8 as recommended in the Common Core State Standards (CCSSO, 2010) and in standards used in other states, and for the research-based strategies that illustrate how students best learn this content.
3. Present a practical resource of robust, problem-based activities and tasks that can engage students in the use of significant mathematical concepts and skills.
4. Report on technology that makes teaching mathematics in a problem-based approach more visible, including links to classroom videos and ready-to-use activity pages, and references to quality websites.

We hope you will find that this is a valuable resource for teaching and learning mathematics!

NEW to this Edition

We briefly describe new features below, along with the substantive changes that we have made since the eighth edition to reflect the changing landscape of mathematics education. The following are highlights of the most significant changes in the ninth edition.

Blackline Masters, Activity Pages and Teacher Resource Pages

More than 130 ready-to-use pages have been created to support the problems and Activities throughout the book. By accessing the companion website, which lists the content by the page number in the text, you can download these to practice teaching an activity or to use with K–8 students in classroom settings. Some popular charts in the text have also been made into printable resources and handouts such as reflection questions to guide culturally relevant instruction.

Activities at a Glance

By popular demand, we have prepared a matrix (Appendix D) that lists all Section II activities, the mathematics they develop, which CCSS standards they address, and the page where they can be found. We believe you will find this an invaluable resource for planning instruction.

Self-Assessment Opportunities for the Reader

As we know, learners benefit from assessing their understanding along the way especially when there is a large amount of content to comprehend. To support teacher learning, each chapter begins with a set of learning outcomes that identify the goals of the chapter and link to Self-Check quizzes. Self-Checks fall at the end of every major text section. Also, at the end of each chapter the popular Writing to Learn section now has end-of-chapter questions.

Expanded Lessons

Every chapter in Section II has at least one Expanded Lesson linked to an Activity. You may recognize some of these from the Field Experience Guide. These lessons focus on concepts central to elementary and middle school mathematics and include (1) NCTM and CCSSO grade-level recommendations, (2) adaptation suggestions for English language learners (ELLs) and students with special needs, and (3) formative assessment suggestions.

Increased Focus on Common Core State Standards for Mathematics and Mathematical Practices

What began in the eighth edition is even stronger in the ninth edition. The CCSS are described in Chapter 1 along with other standards documents, and the Standards for Mathematical Practices are integrated into Chapter 2. In Section II, CCSS references are embedded in the text and every Activity lists the CCSS content that can be developed in that Activity. Standards for Mathematical Practice margin notes identify text content that shows what these practices look like in classroom teaching.

Reorganization and Enhancement to Section I

If you are a seasoned user of this book, you will immediately note that Chapters 2 through 4 are dramatically different. Chapter 2 has Activity Pages for each of the tasks presented and the chapter has been reorganized to move theory to the end. Chapter 3 now focuses exclusively on worthwhile tasks and classroom discourse, with merged and enhanced discussion of problems and worthwhile tasks; the three-phase lesson plan format (*before*, *during*, and *after*) has been moved to the beginning of Chapter 4. Chapter 4, the planning chapter, also underwent additional, major revisions that include (1) adding in the lesson plan format, (2) offering a refined process for planning a lesson (now eight steps, not ten), and (3) stronger sections on differentiating instruction and involving families. Chapter 4 discussions about ELLs and students with special needs have been moved and integrated into Chapter 6. Chapter 7, on technology, no longer has content-specific topics but rather a stronger focus on emerging technologies. Content chapters now house technology sections as appropriate.

Major Changes to Specific Chapters

Basic Facts (Chapter 10)

There are three major changes to this chapter. First, there is a much stronger focus on assessing basic facts. This section presents the risks of using timed tests and presents a strong collection of alternative assessment ideas. Second, chapter discussions pose a stronger developmental focus. For example, the need to focus first on foundational facts before moving to derived facts is shared. Third, there is a shift from a focus on mastery to a focus on fluency (as described in CCSS and in the research).

Developing Strategies for Addition and Subtraction (Chapters 11 and 12)

In previous editions there was a blurry line between Chapter 11 on place value and Chapter 12, which explored how to teach students to add and subtract. Although these topics overlap in many ways, we wanted to make it easier to find the appropriate content and corresponding activities. So, many components formerly in Chapter 11 (those that were explicitly about strategies for computing) have been shifted to Chapter 12 on addition and subtraction. This resulted in 15 more activities in Chapter 12, seven of which are new.

Fraction Operations (Chapter 16)

Using learning trajectories and a developmental approach, the discussion of how to develop meaning for each operation has been expanded. For example, the operation situations presented in Chapter 9 are now connected in Chapter 16 to rational numbers. In particular, multiplication and division have received much more attention, including more examples and activities. These changes are in response to the many requests for more support in this area!

Developing Concepts of Data Analysis (Chapter 21)

Look for several important changes in Chapter 21. There are 12 new activities that emphasize topics in CCSS. There also is more discussion on the shape of data, variability, and distribution. And, there is a notable increase in middle grades content including attention to dot plots, sampling, bivariate graphs, and, at the suggestion of reviewers, mean absolute deviation (MAD).

Additional Important Chapter-Specific Changes

The following substantive changes (not mentioned above) include

> **Chapter 1:** Information about the new NCTM *Principles to Actions* publication with a focus on the eight guiding principles
>
> **Chapter 2:** A revised and enhanced Doing Mathematics section and Knowing Mathematics section
>
> **Chapter 3:** A new section on Adapting Tasks (to create worthwhile tasks) and new tasks and new authentic student work
>
> **Chapter 4:** Open and parallel tasks added as ways to differentiate
>
> **Chapter 5:** A more explicit development of how to use translation tasks to assess students' conceptual understanding
>
> **Chapter 6:** Additional emphasis on multi-tiered systems of support including a variety of interventions

Chapter 7: Revisions reflect current software, tools, and digital apps as well as resources to support teacher reflection and collaboration

Chapter 8: Addition of Wright's progression of children's understanding of the number 10 and content from the findings from the new Background Research for the National Governor's Association Center Project on Early Mathematics

Chapter 9: An expanded alignment with the problem types discussed in the CCSS document

Chapter 13: Expanded discussion of the written records of computing multiplication and division problems including lattice multiplication, open arrays, and partial quotients

Chapter 14: A reorganization to align with the three strands of algebraic thinking; a revamped section on Structure of the Number System with more examples of the connection between arithmetic and algebra; an increased focus on covariation and inequalities and a decreased emphasis on graphs and repeating patterns, consistent with the emphasis in CCSS

Chapter 15: Many fun activities added (with manipulatives such as Play-Doh, Legos, and elastic); expanded to increase emphasis on CCSS content, including emphasis on number lines and iteration

Chapter 17: Chart on common misconceptions including descriptions and examples

Chapter 18: Major changes to the Strategies section, adding tape diagrams and expanding the section on double number lines; increased attention to graphing ratios and proportions

Chapter 19: An increased focus on converting units in the same measurement system, perimeter, and misconceptions common to learning about area; added activities that explore volume and capacity

Chapter 20: The shift in organizational focus to the four major geometry topics from the precise van Hiele level (grouping by all level 1 components), now centered on moving students from level to level using a variety of experiences within a given geometry topic

Chapter 22: Major changes to activities and figures, an expanded focus on common misconceptions, and increased attention to the models emphasized in CCSS-M (dot plots, area representations, tree diagrams)

Chapter 23: A new section on developing symbol sense, expanded section on order of operations, and many new activities

What You Will Find in This Book

If you look at the table of contents, you will see that the chapters are separated into two distinct sections. The first section consists of seven chapters and covers important ideas that cross the boundaries of specific areas of content. The second section, consisting of 16 chapters, offers teaching suggestions and activities for every major mathematics topic in the pre-K–8 curriculum. Chapters in Section I offer perspectives on the challenging task of helping students learn mathematics. Having a feel for the discipline of mathematics—that is, to know what it means to "do mathematics"—is critical to learning how to teach mathematics well. In addition, understanding constructivist and sociocultural perspectives on learning mathematics and how they are applied to teaching through problem solving provides a foundation and rationale for how to teach and assess pre-K–8 students.

You will be teaching diverse students including students who are English language learners, are gifted, or have disabilities. In this text, you will learn how to apply instructional strategies in ways that support and challenge *all* learners. Formative assessment strategies, strategies for diverse learners, and effective use of technological tools are addressed in specific chapters in Section I (Chapters 5, 6, and 7, respectively), and throughout Section II chapters.

Each chapter of Section II focuses on one of the major content areas in pre-K–8 mathematics curriculum. It begins with identifying the big ideas for that content, and also provides guidance on how students best learn that content through many problem-based activities to engage them in understanding mathematics. Reflecting on the activities as you read can help you think about the mathematics from the perspective of the student. As often as possible, take out pencil and paper and try the problems so that you actively engage in *your learning* about *students learning* mathematics. In so doing, we are hopeful that this book will increase your own understanding of mathematics, the students you teach, and how to teach them well.

Some Special Features of This Text

By flipping through the book, you will notice many section headings, a large number of figures, and various special features. All are designed to make the book more useful as a long-term resource. Here are a few things to look for.

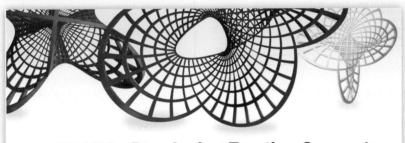

CHAPTER

15

Developing Fraction Concepts

LEARNER OUTCOMES

After reading this chapter and engaging in the embedded activities ar
able to:

15.1 Describe and give examples for fractions constructs.

15.2 Name the types of fractions models and describe activities

15.3 Explain foundational concepts of fractional parts, including i
and connect these ideas to CCSS-M expectations.

15.4 Illustrate examples across fraction models for developing th

15.5 Compare fractions in a variety of ways and describe ways to

15.6 Synthesize how to effectively teach fraction concepts.

Fractions are one of the most important topics students need to understand in order to be successful in algebra and beyond, yet it is an area in which U.S. students struggle. NAEP test results have consistently shown that students have a weak understanding of fraction concepts (Sowder & Wearne, 2006; Wearne & Kouba, 2000). This lack of understanding is then translated into difficulties with fraction computation, decimal and percent concepts, and the use of fractions in other content areas, particularly algebra (Bailey, Hoard, Nugent, & Geary, 2012; Brown & Quinn, 2007; National Mathematics Advisory Panel, 2008). Therefore, it is absolutely critical that you teach fractions well, present fractions as interesting and important and commit to helping students understand the big ideas.

 BIG IDEAS

◆ For students to really understand fractions, they must experien
constructs, including part of a whole, ratios, and division.

◆ Three categories of models exist for working with fractions—ar
length (e.g., $\frac{3}{4}$ of an inch), and set or quantity (e.g., $\frac{1}{2}$ of the cla

◆ Partitioning and iterating are ways for students to understand t
especially numerators and denominators.

◆ Equal sharing is a way to build on whole-number knowledge to i

◆ Equivalent fractions are ways of describing the same amount b
fractional parts.

◆ Fractions can be compared by reasoning about the relative size
and reasoning are important in teaching understanding of fract

◀ **Learning Outcomes [NEW]**

To help readers know what they should expect to learn, each chapter begins with learning outcomes. Self-checks are numbered to cover and thus align with each learning outcome.

◀ **Big Ideas**

Much of the research and literature espousing a student-centered approach suggests that teachers plan their instruction around big ideas rather than isolated skills or concepts. At the beginning of each chapter in Section II, you will find a list of the key mathematical ideas associated with the chapter. Teachers find these lists helpful to quickly envision the mathematics they are to teach.

Self-Check Prompts [NEW] ▶

To help readers self-assess what they have just read, a self-check prompt is offered at the end of each significant text section. After answering these quiz questions online and submitting their responses, users can review feedback on what the correct response is (and why).

You may decide instead to break the shape up into two rectangles and ask the student to find the area of each shape and combine. Then have the student attempt the next shape without the modification—you should always lead back to the original task. However, if you decide to begin with rectangular regions and build to compound shapes composed of rectangles, you have *scaffolded* the lesson in a way to ramp up to the original task. In planning accommodations and modifications, the goal is to enable each student to successfully reach your learning objectives, not to change the objectives. This is how equity is achieved—by reaching equal *outcomes*, not by equal treatment. Treating students the same when they each learn differently does not make sense.

Complete an Accommodation or Modification Needs table to reflect on how you will plan for students in your classroom who have special needs. Record the evidence that you are adapting the learning situation.

 Complete Self-Check 6.1: Mathematics for ALL Students

 Providing for Students Who Struggle and Those with Special Needs

One of the basic tenets of education is the need for individualizing the content taught and the methods used for students who struggle, particularly those with special needs. Mathematics learning disabilities are best thought of as cognitive differences, not cognitive deficits (Lewis, 2014). Students with disabilities often have mandated individualized education programs (IEPs) that guarantee access to grade-level mathematics content—in a general education classroom, if possible. This legislation also implies that educators consider individual learning needs not only in terms of *what* mathematics is taught but also *how* it is taught.

Prevention Models

In many areas, a systematic process for achieving higher levels performance for all students includes a multitiered system of support frequently called response to intervention (RtI). This

---

Connecting Fractions and Decimals   **409**

Activity 17.2   CCSS-M: 4.NF.C.6; 5.NBT.A.1; 5.NBT.A.2; 5.NBT.A.3a

Shifting Units

Give students a collection of paper base-ten pieces created from Base-Ten Materials, or base-ten blocks. Ask them to pull out a particular mix—for example, a student might have three squares, seven strips, and four "tinies." Tell students that you have the unit behind your back; when you show it to them, they are to figure out how much they have and to record the value. Hold up one of the units. Observe what students record as their value. Ask students to accurately say their quantity aloud. For ELLs and students with disabilities, it is particularly important that you write these labels with the visuals in a prominent place in the classroom (and in student notebooks) so that they can refer to the terminology and illustrations as they participate in the activity. Repeat several times. Be sure to include examples in which a piece is not represented so that students will understand decimal values like 3.07. Continue playing in partners with one student selecting a mix of ... the number.

 ENGLISH LANGUAGE LEARNERS

 STUDENTS with SPECIAL NEEDS

. Each milli- useful

help- Given ealing num- or on

this is onpro- rtion.).

Numbers like 3.2 or 12.1389 do not relate to money and can cause confusion (Martinie, 2007). Students' initial contact with decimals should be more flexible, and so money is not recommended as an initial model for decimals, although it is certainly an important application of

▲ Activities

The numerous activities found in every chapter of Section II have always been rated by readers as one of the most valuable parts of the book. Some activity ideas are described directly in the text and in the illustrations. Others are presented in the numbered Activity boxes. Every activity is a problem-based task (as described in Chapter 3) and is designed to engage students in doing mathematics.

◀ Adaptations for Students with Disabilities and English Language Learners

Chapter 6 provides detailed background and strategies for how to support students with disabilities and English language learners (ELLs). But, many adaptations are specific to a particular activity or task. Therefore, Section II chapters offer activities (look for the icon) that can meet the needs of exceptional students including specific instructions with adaptations directly within the Activities.

---

196   **Chapter 10** Developing Basic Fact Fluency

 FORMATIVE ASSESSMENT Notes. When are students ready to work on reasoning strategies? When they are able to (1) use counting-on strategies (start with the largest and count up) and (2) see that numbers can be decomposed (e.g., that 6 is 5 + 1). Interview students by posing one-digit addition problems and ask how they solved it. For example, 3 + 8 (Do they count on from the larger?) and 5 + 6 (Do they see 5 + 5 + 1?). For multiplication, 3 × 8 (Do they know this is 3 eights? Do they see it as 2 eights and one more eight?). ■

 Complete Self-Check 10.1: Developmental Phases for Learning the Basic Facts

Teaching and Assessing the Basic Facts

This section describes the different ways basic fact instruction has been implemented in schools, followed by a section describing effective strategies.

Different Approaches to Teaching the Basic Facts

Over the last century, three main approaches have been used to teach the basic facts. The pros and cons of each approach are briefly discussed in this section.

Memorization. This approach moves from presenting concepts of addition and multiplication straight to memorization of facts, not devoting time to developing strategies (Baroody, Bajwa, & Eiland, 2009). This approach requires students to memorize 100 separate addition facts (just for the addition combinations 0–9) and 100 multiplication facts (0–9). Students may even have to memorize subtraction and division separately—bringing the total to over 300

Formative Assessment Notes ▶

Assessment should be an integral part of instruction. Similarly, it makes sense to think about what to be listening for (assessing) as you read about different areas of content development. Throughout the content chapters, there are formative assessment notes with brief descriptions of ways to assess the topic in that section. Reading these assessment notes as you read the text can also help you understand how best to assist struggling students.

Creating Graphs

Students should be involved in deciding how they want to represent their data, but they will need to be introduced to what the options are and when each display can and cannot be used.

The value of having students actually construct their own graphs is not so much that they learn the techniques, but that they are personally invested in the data and that they learn how a graph conveys information. Once a graph is constructed, the most important activity is discussing what it tells the people who see it. Analyzing data that are numerical (number of pockets) versus categorical (color of socks) is an added challenge for students as they struggle to make sense of the graphs (Russell, 2006). If, for example, the graph has seven stickers above the five, students may think that five people have seven pockets or seven people have five pockets.

Creating graphs requires care and precision, including determining appropriate scales and labels. But the reason for the precision is so that an audience is able to see at a glance the summary of the data gathered on a particular question.

 Standards for Mathematical Practice
MP6. Attend to precision.

TECHNOLOGY Note. Computer programs and graphing calculators can provide a variety of graphical displays. Use the time saved by technology to focus on the discussions about the information that each display provides! Students can make their own selections from among different graphs and justify their choice based on their own intended purposes. The graphing calculator puts data analysis technology in the hands of every student. The TI-73 calculator is designed for middle-grade students. It will produce eight different kinds of plots or graphs, including pie charts, bar graphs, and picture graphs, and will compute and graph lines of best fit. The Internet also offers opportunities to explore different graphs. Create a Graph (NCES Kids

 Standards for Mathematical Practice
MP5. Use appropriate tools strategically.

◀ **Standards for Mathematical Practice Margin Notes [NEW]**

Connections to the eight Standards of Mathematical Practice from the Common Core State Standards are highlighted in the margins. The location of the note indicates an example of the identified practice in the nearby text.

▲ **Technology Notes**

Infusing technological tools is important in learning mathematics, as you will learn in Chapter 7. We have infused technology notes throughout Section II. A technology icon is used to identify places within the text or activity where a technology idea or resource is discussed. Descriptions include open-source (free) software, applets, and other Web-based resources, as well as ideas for calculator use.

192 Chapter 9 Developing Meanings for the Operations

REFLECTIONS ON CHAPTER 9

WRITING TO LEARN

Click here to assess your understanding and application of chapter content.

1. Make up a compare story problem. Alter the prob to provide examples of all six different possibilities compare problems.

2. Explain how missing-part activities prepare students mastering subtraction facts.

3. Make up multiplication story problems to illustrate difference between equal groups and multiplicative c parison. Then create a story problem involving ra area or arrays.

4. Why is the use of key words not a good strategy to te children?

FOR DISCUSSION AND EXPLORATION

RESOURCES FOR

LITERATURE CONNECTIONS

There are many books with stories or pictures concern collections, the purchase of items, measurements, and so that can be used to pose problems or, better, to stimulate c dren to invent their own problems. Perhaps the most wic mentioned book in this context is *The Doorbell Rang* by Hutchins (1986). You can check that one out yourself, as as the following suggestions.

Bedtime Math *Overdeck (2013)*

This book (and accompanying website) is the author's tempt to get parents to incorporate math problems into nighttime (or daytime) routine. There are three levels of ficulty, starting with problems for "wee ones" (pre-K), tle kids" (K–2), and "big kids" (grade 2 and up). Each problems revolves around a high-interest topic such as r coasters, foods, and animals. Teachers can use these probl in class for engaging students in all four operations.

One Hundred Hungry Ants *Pinczes (1999)* View One Hundred Angry Ants (https://www.youtube.com/watch?v=kmdSUHPwJtc)

A Remainder of One *Pinczes (2002)*

These two books, written by a grandmother for her gra child, help students explore multiplication and divis

◀ **End of Chapter Resources**

The end of each chapter includes two major subsections: *Reflections*, which includes "Writing to Learn" and "For Discussion and Exploration," and *Resources*, which includes "Literature Connections" (found in all Section II chapters) and "Recommended Readings."

Writing to Learn [ENHANCED]. Questions are provided that help you reflect on the important pedagogical ideas related to the content in the chapter. Actually writing out the answers to these questions in your own words, or talking about them with peers, is one of the best ways for you to develop your understanding of each chapter's main ideas.

For Discussion and Exploration. These questions ask you to explore an issue related to that chapter's content, applying what you have learned. For example, questions may ask you to reflect on classroom observations, analyze curriculum materials, or take a position on controversial issues. We hope that these questions will stimulate thought and cause spirited conversations.

Literature Connections. Section II chapters contain great children's literature for launching into the mathematics concepts in the chapter just read. For each title suggested, there is a brief description of how the mathematics concepts in the chapter can be connected to the story. These literature-based mathematics activities will help you engage students in interesting contexts for doing mathematics.

Recommended Readings. In this section, you will find an annotated list of articles and books to augment the information found in the chapter. These recommendations include NCTM articles and books, and other professional resources designed for the classroom teacher. (In addition to the Recommended Readings, there is a References list at the end of the book for all sources cited within the chapters.)

Supplements for Instructors

Qualified college adopters can contact their Pearson sales representatives for information on ordering any of the supplements described below. These instructor supplements are all posted and available for download (click on Educators) from the Pearson Instructor Resource Center at www.pearsonglobaleditions.com/vandewalle. The IRC houses the following:

- **Instructor's Resource Manual** The Instructor's Resource Manual for the ninth edition includes a wealth of resources designed to help instructors teach the course, including chapter notes, activity suggestions, and suggested assessment and test questions.
- **Electronic Test Bank** An electronic test bank (TB) contains hundreds of challenging questions as multiple-choice or short-answer questions. Instructors can choose from these questions and create their own customized exams.
- **PowerPoint™ Presentation** Ideal for instructors to use for lecture presentations or student handouts, the PowerPoint presentation provides ready-to-use graphics and text images tied to the individual chapters and content development of the text.

Acknowledgments

Many talented people have contributed to the success of this book, and we are deeply grateful to all those who have assisted over the years. Without the success of the first edition, there would certainly not have been a second, much less nine editions. The following people worked closely with John on the first edition, and he was sincerely indebted to Warren Crown, John Dossey, Bob Gilbert, and Steven Willoughby, who gave time and great care in offering detailed comments on the original manuscript.

In preparing this ninth edition, we have received thoughtful input from the following mathematics teacher educators who offered comments on the eighth edition or on the manuscript for the ninth. Each reviewer challenged us to think through important issues. Many specific suggestions have found their way into this book, and their feedback helped us focus on important ideas. Thank you to Jessica Cohen, Western Washington University; Shea Mosely Culpepper, University of Houston; Shirley Dissler, High Point University; Cynthia Gautreau, California State University in Fullerton; Kevin LoPresto, Radford University; Ryan Nivens, East Tennessee State University; Adrienne Redmond-Sanogo, Oklahoma State University; and Douglas Roebuck, Ball State University. We are indebted to you for your dedicated and professional insight.

We received constant and valuable support and advice from colleagues at Pearson. We are privileged to work with our development editor, Linda Bishop, whose positive demeanor and upbeat responses on even the tightest of deadlines was most appreciated. Linda consistently offered us sound advice and much encouragement. We are also fortunate to work with Meredith Fossel, who has helped us define the direction of this edition, and helped us with the important decisions that would make the book a better product for pre-service and in-service teachers. We also wish to thank the production and editing team at MPS North America LLC, in particular Katie Watterson, who carefully and conscientiously assisted in preparing this edition for publication. Finally, our sincere thanks goes to Elizabeth Todd Brown, who helped write some of the ancillary materials.

We would each like to thank our families for their many contributions and support. On behalf of John, we thank his wife, Sharon, who was John's biggest supporter and a sounding board as he wrote the first six editions of this book. We also recognize his daughters, Bridget (a fifth-grade teacher in Chesterfield County, Virginia) and Gretchen (an associate professor of psychology and associate dean for undergraduate education at Rutgers University–Newark). They were John's first students, and he tested many ideas that are in this book by their sides. We can't forget those who called John "Math Grandpa": his granddaughters, Maggie, Aidan, and Gracie.

From Karen Karp: I would like to express thanks to my husband, Bob Ronau, who as a mathematics educator graciously helped me think about decisions while offering insights and encouragement. In addition, I thank my children, Matthew, Tammy, Joshua, Misty, Matt, Christine, Jeffrey, and Pamela for their kind support and inspiration. I also am grateful for my wonderful grandchildren, Jessica, Zane, Madeline, Jack and Emma, who have helped deepen my understanding about how children think.

From Jennifer Bay-Williams: I am forever grateful to my supportive and patient husband, Mitch Williams. My children, MacKenna (12 years) and Nicolas (9 years), along with their peers and teachers, continue to help me think more deeply about mathematics teaching and learning. My parents, siblings, nieces, and nephews have all provided support to the writing of this edition.

Most importantly, we thank all the teachers and students who gave of themselves by assessing what worked and what didn't work in the many iterations of this book. In particular for the ninth edition, we thank teachers who generously tested activities and provided student work for us: Kimberly Clore, Kim George, and Kelly Eaton. We continue to seek suggestions from teachers who use this book so please email us at teachingdevelopmentally@gmail.com with any advice, ideas, or insights you would like to share.

Pearson would like to thank the following people for their work on the Global Edition:

Contributor:
Somitra Kumar Sanadhya, C.R. Rao Advanced Institute for Mathematical Sciences

Reviewers:
Santanu Bhowmik, Pathways World School, Aravali
Pranab Sarma, Assam Engineering College
B.R. Shankar, National Institute of Technology Karnataka, Surathkal

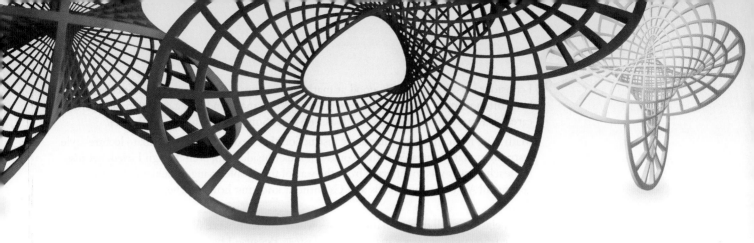

CHAPTER

1

Teaching Mathematics in the 21st Century

LEARNER OUTCOMES

After reading this chapter and engaging in the embedded activities and reflections, you should be able to:

1.1 Summarize the factors that influence the teaching of mathematics.

1.2 Describe the important documents that are a part of the movement toward a set of shared expectations for students.

1.3 Explore the qualities needed to learn and grow as a professional teacher of mathematics.

Someday soon you will find yourself in front of a class of students, or perhaps you are already teaching. What general ideas will guide the way you will teach mathematics? This book will help you become comfortable with the mathematics content of the pre-K–8 curriculum. You will also learn about research-based strategies for helping students come to know mathematics and be confident in their ability to do mathematics. These two things—your knowledge of mathematics and how students learn mathematics—are the most important tools you can acquire to be successful.

 ## Becoming an Effective Teacher of Mathematics

Before we get started, think back to when you were in pre-K–8 classrooms as a student. What are your remembrances of learning mathematics? Here are some thoughts from in-service and pre-service teachers of whom we asked the same question. Which description do you resonate with?

> I was really good at math in lower elementary grades, but because I never understood why math works, it made it very difficult to embrace the concepts as I moved into higher grades. I started believing I wasn't good at math so I didn't get too upset when my grades reflected that. *Kathryn*

> As a student I always felt lost during mathematics instruction. It was as if everyone around me had a magic key or code that I missed out on getting. *Tracy*

> I remember math being very challenging, intimidating, and capable of making me literally sick to my stomach. Math was a bunch of rules and formulas I was expected to memorize, but not to understand. *Mary Rebekah*

I consider myself to be really good at math and I enjoy mathematics-related activities, but I often wonder if I would have been GREAT at math and had a completely different career if I cared about math as much as I do now. Sometimes I feel robbed. *April*

Math went from engaging, interactive instruction that I excelled at and loved, to lecture-style instruction that I struggled with. I could not seek outside help, even though I tried, because the teacher's way was so different from the way of the people trying to help me. I went from getting all As to getting low Bs and Cs without knowing how the change happened. *Janelle*

Math class was full of elimination games where students were pitted against each other to see who could answer a math fact the fastest. Because I have a good memory I did well, but I hated every moment. It was such a nerve-wracking experience and for the longest time that is what I thought math was. *Lawrence*

Math was never a problem because it was logical, everything made sense. *Tova*

As you can see these memories run the gamut with an array of emotions and experiences. The question now becomes, what do you hope your students will say as they think back to your mathematics instruction? The challenge is to get all of your students to learn mathematics with understanding and enthusiasm. Would you relish hearing your students, fifteen years after leaving your classroom, state that you encouraged them to be mathematically minded, curious about solving new problems, self-motivated, able to critically think about both correct and incorrect strategies, and that you nurtured them to be a risk takers willing to try and persevere on challenging tasks? What will your legacy be?

As part of your personal desire to build successful learners of mathematics, you might recognize the challenge that mathematics is sometimes seen as the subject that people love to hate. At social events of all kinds—even at parent–teacher conferences—other adults will respond to the fact that you are a teacher of mathematics with comments such as "I could never do math," or "I can't even balance my checking account." Instead of dismissing these disclosures, consider what positive action you can take. Would people confide that they don't read and hadn't read a book in years? That is not likely. Families' and teachers' attitudes toward mathematics may enhance or detract from students' ability to do math. It is important for you and for students' families to know that mathematics ability is not inherited—anyone can learn mathematics. Moreover, learning mathematics is an essential life skill. You need to find ways of countering these statements, especially if they are stated in the presence of students, pointing out that it is a myth that only some people can be successful in learning mathematics. Only in that way can the chain of passing apprehension from family member to child, or in rare cases teacher to student, be broken. There is much joy to be had in solving mathematical problems, and you need to model this excitement and nurture that passion in your students.

Your students need to ultimately think of themselves as mathematicians in the same way as many of them think of themselves as readers. As students interact with our increasingly mathematical and technological world, they need to construct, modify, communicate or integrate new information in many forms. Solving novel problems and approaching circumstances with a mathematical perspective should come as naturally as reading new materials to comprehend facts, insights, or news. Consider how important this is to interpreting and successfully surviving in our economy and in our environment.

The goal of this book is to help you understand the mathematics methods that will make you an effective teacher. As you dig into the information your vision and confidence will grow.

 ## A Changing World

In his book *The World Is Flat* (2007), Thomas Friedman discusses the need for people to have skills that are lasting and will survive the ever-changing landscape of available jobs. These are specific categories within a larger group that are called "untouchables" as regardless of the shifting landscape of job options—they will be successful in finding jobs. He is the one who defined these broad categories—such as math lover. Friedman points out that in a world that is digitized and surrounded by algorithms, math lovers will always have career opportunities and options. This is important as science, technology, engineering, and math (STEM) jobs, because of a skills gap, take more than twice as long to fill as other jobs in the marketplace (Rothwell, 2014). This is also aligned with the thinkers who believe students need to not just be college ready but innovation ready (Wagner, 2012).

Now it becomes the job of every teacher of mathematics to prepare students with skills for potential careers and develop a "love of math" in students. Lynn Arthur Steen, a well-known mathematician and educator, stated, "As information becomes ever more quantitative and as society relies increasingly on computers and the data they produce, an innumerate citizen today is as vulnerable as the illiterate peasant of Gutenberg's time" (1997, p. xv).

The changing world influences what should be taught in pre-K–8 mathematics classrooms. As we prepare pre-K–8 students for jobs that possibly do not currently exist, we can predict that there are few jobs for people where they just do simple computation. We can also predict that there will be work that requires interpreting complex data, designing algorithms to make predictions, and using the ability to approach new problems in a variety of ways.

As you prepare to help students learn mathematics for the future, it is important to have some perspective on the forces that effect change in the mathematics classroom. This chapter addresses the leadership that you, the teacher, will develop as you shape the mathematics experience for your students. Your beliefs about what it means to know and do mathematics and about how students make sense of mathematics will affect how you approach instruction and the understandings and skills your students take from the classroom.

Factors to Consider

For more than two decades, mathematics education has constantly undergone change. There have been significant reforms that reflect the technological and informational needs of our society, research on how students learn mathematics, the importance of providing opportunities to learn for all students, and ideas on how and what to teach from an international perspective. Just as we would not expect doctors to be using the exact same techniques and medicines that were prevalent when you were a child, teachers' methods are evolving and transforming via a powerful collection of expert knowledge about how the mind functions and how to design effective instruction (Wiggins, 2013).

There are several significant factors in this transformation. One factor is the public or political pressure for change in mathematics education due largely to information about student performance in national and international studies. These large scale comparisons of student performance continue to make headlines, provoke public opinion, and pressure legislatures to call for tougher standards backed by testing. The pressures of testing policies exerted on schools and ultimately on teachers may have an impact on instruction. These studies are important because international and national assessments provide strong evidence that mathematics teaching *must* change if our students are to be competitive in the global market and able to understand the complex issues they must confront as responsible citizens.

National Assessment of Education Progress (NAEP). Since the 1960s, at regular intervals, the United States gathers data on how fourth-, eighth-, and twelfth-grade students are doing in mathematics on the NAEP. These data provide an important tool for policy makers and educators to measure the overall improvement of U.S. students over time in what is called the "Nation's Report Card." NAEP uses four achievement levels: below basic, basic, proficient, and advanced, with proficient and advanced representing substantial grade-level achievement. The criterion-referenced test is designed to reflect the current curriculum but keeps a few stable items from 1982 for purposes of comparison (Kloosterman, Rutledge, & Kenney, 2009b). In the most recent assessment in 2013, less than half of all U.S. students in grades 4 and 8 performed at the desirable levels of proficient and advanced (42 percent in fourth grade and 35 percent in eighth grade) (National Center for Education Statistics, 2013). Despite encouraging gains in the NAEP scores over the last 30 years due to important shifts in instructional practices (particularly at the elementary level) (Kloosterman, Rutledge, & Kenney, 2009b), some U.S. students' performance still reveals disappointing levels of competency.

Trends in International Mathematics and Science Study (TIMSS). In the mid-1990s, 41 nations participated in the Third International Mathematics and Science Study, the largest study of mathematics and science education ever conducted. Data were gathered in grades 4, 8, and 12 from 500,000 students as well as from teachers. The most widely reported results revealed that U.S. students performed above the international average of the TIMSS countries at the fourth grade, below the average at the eighth grade, and significantly below average at the twelfth grade (National Academy Press, 1999; U.S. Department of Education, 1997).

TIMSS studies were repeated often with the most recent in 2011 in which 57 countries participated. For details, please visit the TIMSS website. The 2011 TIMSS found that U.S. fourth and eighth graders were above the international average but were significantly outperformed at fourth-grade level mathematics by education systems in Singapore, Republic of Korea, Hong Kong, Chinese Taipei, Japan, Northern Ireland, Belgium, Finland, England, and the Russian Federation and outperformed at the eighth-grade level by education systems in Republic of Korea, Singapore, Chinese Taipei, Hong Kong, Japan, Russian Federation, Israel, and Finland.

One of the most interesting components of the study was the videotaping of eighth-grade classrooms in the United States, Australia, and five of the highest-achieving countries. The results indicate that teaching is a cultural activity and, despite similarities, the differences in the ways countries taught mathematics were often striking. In all countries, problems or tasks were frequently used to begin the lesson. However, as a lesson progressed, the way these problems were handled in the United States was in stark contrast to high-achieving countries. Analysis revealed that, although the world is for all purposes unrecognizable from what it was 100 years ago, the U.S. approach to teaching mathematics during the same time frame was essentially unchanged (Stigler & Hiebert, 2009). Other countries incorporated a variety of methods, but they frequently used a problem-solving approach with an emphasis on conceptual understanding and students engaged in problem solving (Hiebert et al., 2003). Teaching in the high-achieving countries more closely resembles the recommendations of the National Council of Teachers of Mathematics, the major professional organization for mathematics teachers, discussed next.

National Council of Teachers of Mathematics (NCTM). One transformative factor is the professional leadership of the National Council of Teachers of Mathematics (NCTM). The NCTM, with more than 80,000 members, is the world's largest mathematics education organization. This group holds an influential role in the support of teachers and an emphasis on what is best for learners. Their guidance in the creation and dissemination of standards for curriculum, assessment, and teaching led the way for other disciplines. For an array of resources, including the Illuminations component which consists of a set of exciting instructional experiences for your students, visit the NCTM website.

 Complete Self-Check 1.1: A Changing World

 # The Movement toward Shared Standards

The momentum for reform in mathematics education began in earnest in the early 1980s. The main impetus was a response to a need for more problem solving as well as the research of developmental psychologists who identified how students can best learn mathematics. Then in 1989, NCTM published the first set of standards for a subject area in the *Curriculum and Evaluation Standards for School Mathematics.* Many believe that no other document has ever had such an enormous effect on school mathematics or on any other area of the curriculum.

NCTM followed in 1991 with a set of standards for teaching that articulated a vision of teaching mathematics for all students, not just a few. In 1995, NCTM added to the collection the *Assessment Standards for School Mathematics,* which focused on the importance of integrating assessment with instruction and indicated the key role that assessment plays in implementing change (see Chapter 5). In 2000, however, NCTM released *Principles and Standards for School Mathematics* as an update of its original standards document. Combined, these documents prompted a revolutionary reform movement in mathematics education throughout the world.

As these documents influenced teacher practice, ongoing debate continued about the U.S. curriculum. In particular, many argued that instead of hurrying through several topics every year, the curriculum needed to address content more deeply. Guidance was needed in deciding what mathematics content should be taught at each grade level and, in 2006, NCTM released *Curriculum Focal Points*, a little publication with a big message—the mathematics taught at each grade level needs to be focused, provide depth, and explicitly show connections.

In 2010, the Council of Chief State School Officers (CCSSO) presented the Common Core State Standards, which are grade-level specific standards which incorporate ideas from *Curriculum Focal Points* as well as international curriculum documents. A large majority of U.S. states adopted these as their standards. In less than 25 years, the standards movement transformed the country from having little to no coherent vision on what mathematics should be taught and when, to a more widely shared idea of what students should know and be able to do at each grade level.

In the following sections, we discuss three significant documents critical to your work as a teacher of mathematics.

Principles and Standards for School Mathematics

The *Principles and Standards for School Mathematics* (NCTM, 2000) provides guidance and direction for teachers and other leaders in pre-K–12 mathematics education. This is particularly true in states and regions where they have developed their own standards.

The Six Principles. One of the most important features of *Principles and Standards for School Mathematics* is the articulation of six principles fundamental to high-quality mathematics education. These principles must be blended into all programs as building excellence in mathematics education involves much more than simply listing content objectives.

The Equity Principle. The strong message of this principle is there should be high expectations and intentional ways to support all students. All students must have the opportunity and adequate support to learn mathematics regardless of their race, socioeconomic status, gender, culture, language, or disability. This principle is interwoven into all other principles.

The Curriculum Principle. The curriculum should be coherent and built around "big ideas" in the curriculum and in daily classroom instruction. We think of these big ideas as "important" if they help develop other ideas, link one idea to another, or serve to illustrate the discipline of mathematics as a human endeavor. Students must be helped to see that mathematics is an integrated whole that grows and connects across the grades rather than a collection of isolated bits and pieces.

The Teaching Principle. What students learn about mathematics depends almost entirely on the experiences that teachers provide every day in the classroom. To provide high-quality mathematics education, teachers must (1) understand deeply the mathematics content they are teaching; (2) understand how students learn mathematics, including common misconceptions; and (3) select meaningful instructional tasks and generalizable strategies that will enhance learning.

The Learning Principle. This principle is based on two fundamental ideas. First, learning mathematics with understanding is essential. Mathematics today requires not only computational skills but also the ability to think and reason mathematically to solve new problems and learn to respond to novel situations that students will face in the future. Second, students *can* learn mathematics with understanding. Learning is enhanced in classrooms where students are required to evaluate their own ideas and those of others, make mathematical conjectures and test them, and develop their reasoning and sense-making skills.

The Assessment Principle. Ongoing assessment highlights the most important mathematics concepts for students. Assessment that includes ongoing observation and student interaction encourages students to articulate and, thus, clarify their ideas. Feedback from daily assessment helps students establish goals and become more independent learners. By continuously gathering data about students' understanding of concepts and growth in reasoning, teachers can better make the daily decisions that support student learning. For assessment to be effective, teachers must use a variety of assessment techniques, understand their mathematical goals deeply, and have a research-supported notion of students' thinking or common misunderstandings.

The Technology Principle. Calculators, computers, and other emerging technologies are essential tools for learning and doing mathematics. Technology permits students to focus on mathematical ideas, to reason, and to solve problems in ways that are often impossible without these tools. Technology enhances the learning of mathematics by allowing for increased exploration, enhanced representation, and communication of ideas.

The Five Content Standards. *Principles and Standards* includes four grade bands: pre-K–2, 3–5, 6–8, and 9–12. The emphasis on preschool recognizes the need to highlight the critical years before students enter kindergarten. There is a common set of five content standards throughout the grades:

- Number and Operations
- Algebra
- Geometry
- Measurement
- Data Analysis and Probability

Each content standard includes a set of goals applicable to all grade bands followed by specific expectations for what students should know at each grade band. Although the same five content standards apply across all grades, you should not infer that each strand has equal weight or emphasis in every grade band. Number and Operations is the most heavily emphasized strand from pre-K through grade 5 and continues to be important in the middle grades, with a lesser emphasis in grades 9–12. This is in contrast to Algebra, which moves from an emphasis related to number and operations in the early grades and builds to a strong focus in the middle and high school grade bands.

The Five Process Standards. The process standards refer to the mathematical processes through which pre-K–12 students acquire and use mathematical knowledge. The process standards should not be regarded as separate content or strands in the mathematics curriculum, rather, they are integral components of all mathematics learning and teaching. The five process standards and ways you can develop these elements in your students can be found in Table 1.1.

Members of NCTM have free online access to the *Principles and Standards* and nonmembers can sign up for 120 days of free access to the full document on the NCTM website under the tab Standards and Focal Points.

Common Core State Standards

As noted earlier, the dialogue on improving mathematics teaching and learning extends beyond mathematics educators. Policymakers and elected officials considered previous NCTM standards documents, international assessments, and research on the best way to prepare students to be "college and career ready." The National Governors Association Center for Best Practices and the Council of Chief State School Officers (CCSSO) collaborated with other professional groups and entities to develop shared expectations for K–12 students across states, a focused set of mathematics content standards and practices, and efficiency of material and assessment development (Porter, McMaken, Hwang, & Yang, 2011). As a result, they created the Common Core State Standards for Mathematics (CCSS-M) which can be downloaded for free at http://www.corestandards.org/math. At this time more than 40 states, Washington, D.C., four territories, and Department of Defense Schools have adopted the Common Core State Standards. This represents the largest shift of mathematics content in the United States in more than 100 years. A few states did not opt to participate in the adoption of the standards from the start of their development and at this time others are still deciding their level of participation or reevaluating their own standards against CCSS-M.

TABLE 1.1 THE FIVE PROCESS STANDARDS FROM *PRINCIPLES AND STANDARDS FOR SCHOOL MATHEMATICS*

Process Standard	How Can You Develop These Processes in Your Students?
Problem Solving	• Start instruction with a problem to solve—as problem solving is the vehicle for developing mathematical ideas. • Select meaningful mathematical tasks. • Set problems in a situation to which students can relate. • Use a variety of strategies to solve problems. • Have students self-assess their understanding of the problem and their strategy use.
Reasoning and Proof	• Have students consider evidence of why something is true or not. • Create opportunities for students to evaluate conjectures—do they hold true? • Encourage students to use logical reasoning to see if something always works or their answers make sense. • Demonstrate a variety of ways for students to justify their thinking through finding examples and counterexamples to use in a logical argument.
Communication	• Invite students to talk about, write about, describe, and explain their mathematical ideas as a way to examine their thinking. • Give students opportunities to share ideas so that others can understand and actively discuss their reasoning. • Share examples of student work, so students can compare and assess others' thinking. • Present precise mathematical language and notation so that the word usage and definitions can act as a foundation for students' future learning.
Connections	• Emphasize how mathematical ideas explicitly connect to students' prior mathematical knowledge and future learning. • Assist students in developing the relationships between the mathematics being learned and real world contexts and in other subject areas.
Representation	• Encourage students to use multiple representations to explore relationships and communicate their thinking. • Create opportunities for students to move from one representation of an mathematical concept or idea to another to add depth of understanding. • Provide problems where students can use mathematical models to clarify or represent a situation.

Source: Adapted with permission from NCTM (National Council of Teachers of Mathematics). (2000). *Principles and standards for school mathematics.* Reston, VA: NCTM. Copyright 2000 by the National Council of Teachers of Mathematics. All rights reserved.

The document articulates an overview of *critical areas* for each grade from K–8 to provide a coherent curriculum built around big ideas. These larger groups of related standards are called *domains*, and there are eleven that relate to grades K–8 (see Figure 1.1).

The Common Core State Standards go beyond specifying mathematics content expectations to also include Standards for Mathematical Practice. These are "'processes and proficiencies' with longstanding importance in mathematics education" (CCSSO, 2010, p. 6) that are based on the underlying frameworks of the NCTM process standards and the components of mathematical proficiency identified by NRC in their important document *Adding It Up* (National Research Council, 2001). Teachers must develop these mathematical practices in all students (CCSSO, 2010, pp. 7–8) as described briefly in Table 1.2. A more detailed description of the Standards for Mathematical Practice can be found in Appendix B.

Kindergarten	Grade 1	Grade 2	Grade 3	Grade 4	Grade 5	Grade 6	Grade 7	Grade 8
Counting and Cardinality								
	Operations and Algebraic Thinking					Expressions and Equations		
	Number and Operations in Base Ten					The Number System		
	Measurement and Data					Statistics and Probability		
	Geometry							
			Number and Operations—Fractions			Rations and Proportional Relationships		Functions

FIGURE 1.1 Common Core State Standards domains by grade level.

TABLE 1.2   THE STANDARDS FOR MATHEMATICAL PRACTICE FROM THE COMMON CORE STATE STANDARDS

Mathematical Practice	K–8 Students Should Be Able to:
Make sense of problems and persevere in solving them.	• Explain what the problem is asking. • Describe possible approaches to a solution. • Consider similar problems to gain insights. • Use concrete objects or drawings to think about and solve problems. • Monitor and evaluate their progress and change strategies if needed. • Check their answers using a different method.
Reason abstractly and quantitatively.	• Explain the relationship between quantities in problem situations. • Represent situations using symbols (e.g., writing expressions or equations). • Create representations that fit the problem. • Use flexibly the different properties of operations and objects.
Construct viable arguments and critique the reasoning of others.	• Understand and use assumptions, definitions, and previous results to explain or justify solutions. • Make conjectures by building a logical set of statements. • Analyze situations and use examples and counterexamples. • Justify conclusions in a way that is understandable to teachers and peers. • Compare two possible arguments for strengths and weaknesses to enhance the final argument.
Model with mathematics.	• Apply mathematics to solve problems in everyday life. • Make assumptions and approximations to simplify a problem. • Identify important quantities and use tools to connect their relationships. • Reflect on the reasonableness of their answer based on the context of the problem.
Use appropriate tools strategically.	• Consider a variety of tools and choose the appropriate tool (e.g., manipulative, ruler, technology) to support their problem solving. • Use estimation to detect possible errors and establish a reasonable range of answers. • Use technology to help visualize, explore, and compare information.
Attend to precision.	• Communicate precisely using clear definitions and appropriate mathematical language. • State accurately the meanings of symbols. • Specify appropriate units of measure and labels of axes. • Use a level of precision suitable for the problem context.
Look for and make use of structure.	• Identify and explain mathematical patterns or structures. • Shift viewpoints and see things as single objects or as comprised of multiple objects. • Explain why and when properties of operations are true in a context.
Look for and express regularity in repeated reasoning.	• Notice if patterns in calculations are repeated and use that information to solve problems. • Use and justify the use of general methods or shortcuts by identifying generalizations. • Self-assess as they work to see whether a strategy makes sense, checking for reasonableness prior to finalizing their answer.

Source: Based on Council of Chief State School Officers. (2010). *Common Core State Standards*. Copyright © 2010 National Governors Association Center for Best Practices and Council of Chief State School Officers. All rights reserved.

Watch this video (https://www.youtube.com/watch?v=5s0rRk9sER0) to get a good overview of the CCSS-M from teachers and authors. Additionally, the Illustrative Mathematics Project website provides tools and support for the Common Core State Standards. It includes multiple ways to look at the standards across grades and domains as well as provides task and problems that will illustrate individual standards.

Learning Progressions. The Common Core State Standards were developed with strong consideration given to building coherence through the research on what is known about the development of students' understanding of mathematics over time (Cobb & Jackson, 2011). The selection of topics at particular grades reflects not only rigorous mathematics but also what is known from current research and practice about learning progressions which are sometimes referred to as *learning trajectories* (Clements & Sarama, 2014; Confrey, Maloney, & Corley, 2014; Daro, Mosher, & Corcoran, 2011; Maloney, Confrey, Ng & Nickell, 2014). It is these learning progressions that can help teachers know what came before as well as what to expect next as students reach key points along the (Corcoran, Mosher, & Rogat, 2009) road to learning mathematics concepts. These progressions identify the interim goals students should reach on the pathway to desired learning targets (Daro, Mosher, & Corcoran, 2011). Although these paths are not identical for all students, they can inform the order of instructional experiences which will support movement toward understanding and application of mathematics concepts. There is a website for the "Progressions Documents for the

Common Core Math Standards" where progressions for the domains in the Common Core State Standards can be found.

Assessments. The initial idea was to have new summative assessments developed through two major consortia, Partnership for Assessment of Readiness for College and Careers (PARCC) and Smarter Balanced Assessment Consortium, are developing assessments which will align to the *Common Core State Standards*. These assessments will focus on both the grade-level content standards and the standards for mathematical practice. This process is being put into place to eliminate the need for each state to develop unique assessments for the standards, a problem that has existed since the beginning of the standards era. Yet, there are states developing their own approaches to end-of-year assessment as well.

Principles to Actions

NCTM has developed a publication that capitalizes on the timing of the adoption of the Common Core State Standards to explore the specific learning conditions, school structures, and teaching practices which will be important for a high quality education for all students. The book uses detailed classroom stories and student work samples to illustrate the careful, reflective work required of effective teachers of mathematics through 6 guiding principles (see Table 1.3). A series of presentations (webcasts), led by the authors of the publication, explore several of the guiding principles and are available on the *Principles to Actions* portion of the NCTM's website.

TABLE 1.3 THE SIX GUIDING PRINCIPLES FROM THE *PRINCIPLES TO ACTIONS*

Guiding Principle	Suggestions for Classroom Actions That Align with the Principles
Teaching and Learning	• Select focused mathematics goals. • Use meaningful instructional tasks that develop reasoning, sense making, and problem solving strategies. • Present and encourage a variety of mathematical representations that connect the same ideas or concepts. • Facilitate student discussions and conversations about important mathematical ideas. • Ask essential questions that are planned to be a catalyst for deeper levels of thinking. • Use a strong foundation of conceptual understanding as a foundation for procedural fluency. • Encourage productive struggle—as it is a way to deepen understanding and move toward student application of their learning. • Generate ways for students to provide evidence of their thinking through discussions, illustrations, and written responses.
Access and Equity	• Establish high expectations for all students. • Provide supports targeted to student needs (equity not equality). • Provide instructional opportunities for students to demonstrate their competence in different ways—creating tasks with easy entry points for students who struggle and extension options for those who finish quickly. • Identify obstacles to students' success and find ways to bridge or eliminate those barriers. • Develop all students' confidence that they can do mathematics. • Enhance the learning of all by celebrating students' diversity.
Curriculum	• Build connections across mathematics topics to capitalize on broad themes and big ideas. • Look for both horizontal and vertical alignment to build coherence. • Avoid thinking of a curriculum as a checklist or disconnected set of daily lessons.
Tools and Technology	• Include an array of technological tools and manipulatives to support the exploration of mathematical concepts, structures, and relationships. • Think beyond computation when considering the integration of technology. • Explore connections to how technology use for problem solving links to career readiness.
Assessment	• Incorporate a continuous assessment plan to follow how students are performing and how instruction can be modified and thereby improved. • Move beyond test results that just look at overall increases and decreases to pinpoint specific student needs. • Consider the use of multiple assessments to capture a variety of student performance. • Encourage students to self-assess sometimes by evaluating the work of others to enhance their own performance. • Teach students how to check their work.
Professionalism	• Develop a long-term plan for building your expertise. • Build collaborations that will enhance the work of the group of collaborators as you enhance the performance of the students in the school. • Take advantage of all coaching, mentoring and professional development opportunities and be a life-long learner. • Structure in time to reflect on and analyze your instructional practices.

Pause & Reflect

Take a moment now to select one or two of the six guiding principles that seem especially significant to you and are areas in which you wish to develop more expertise. Why do you think these are the most important to your teaching? •

 Complete Self-Check 1.2: The Movement toward Shared Standards

An Invitation to Learn and Grow

The mathematics education described in this book may not be the same as the mathematics content and the mathematics teaching you experienced in grades K–8. As a practicing or prospective teacher facing the challenge of teaching mathematics from a problem solving approach, this book may require you to confront some of your personal beliefs—beliefs about what it means to *do mathematics*, how one goes about *learning mathematics*, how to *teach mathematics*, and what it means to *assess mathematics*. Success in mathematics isn't merely about speed or the notion that there is "one right answer." Thinking and talking about mathematics as a means to sense making is a strategy that will serve us well in becoming a society where all citizens are confident in **their ability to do math** (https://www.youtube.com/watch?v=0gW9g8Ofi8A).

Becoming a Teacher of Mathematics

This book and this course of study are critical to your professional teaching career. The mathematics education course you are taking now as a pre-service teacher or the professional development you are experiencing as an in-service teacher will be the foundation for much of the mathematics instruction you do in your classroom for the next decade. The authors of this book take that seriously, as we know you do. Therefore, this section lists and describes the characteristics, habits of thought, skills, and dispositions you will need to succeed as a teacher of mathematics.

Knowledge of Mathematics. You will need to have a profound, flexible, and adaptive knowledge of mathematics content (Ma, 1999). This statement is not intended to scare you if you feel that mathematics is not your strong suit, but it is meant to help you prepare for a serious semester of learning about mathematics and how to teach it. The "school effects" for mathematics are great, meaning that unlike other subject areas, where students have frequent interactions with their family or others outside of school on topics such as reading books, exploring nature, or discussing current events, in the area of mathematics what we do in school is often "it" for many students. This adds to the earnestness of your responsibility, because a student's learning for the year in mathematics will likely come only from you. If you are not sure of a fractional concept or other aspect of mathematics content knowledge, now is the time to make changes in your depth of understanding and flexibility with mathematical ideas to best prepare for your role as an instructional leader. This book and your professor or instructor will help you in that process.

Persistence. You need the ability to stave off frustration and demonstrate persistence. Dweck (2007) has described the brain as similar to a muscle—one that can be strengthened with a good workout! As you move through this book and work the problems yourself, you will learn methods and strategies that will help you anticipate the barriers to students' learning and identify strategies to get them past these stumbling blocks. It is likely that what works for you as a learner will work for your students. As you conduct this mental "workout," if you ponder, struggle, talk about your thinking, and reflect on how these new ideas fit or don't fit with your prior knowledge, then you will enhance your repertoire as a teacher. Remember as you model these characteristics for your students, they too will begin to value perseverance more than speed. In fact, Einstein did not describe himself as intelligent—instead he suggested he was just someone who continued to work on problems longer than others. Creating opportunities for your students to productively struggle is part of the learning process (Stigler & Hiebert, 2009).

Positive Disposition. Prepare yourself by developing a positive attitude toward the subject of mathematics. Research shows that teachers with positive attitudes teach math in more successful ways that result in their students liking math more (Karp, 1991). If in your heart you say, "I never liked math," that mindset will be evident in your instruction (Beilock, Gunderson & Levine, 2010; Maloney, Gunderson, Ramirez, Levin & Beilock, 2014). The good news is that research shows that changing attitudes toward mathematics is relatively easy (Tobias, 1995) and that attitude changes are long-lasting (Dweck, 2006). Additionally math methods courses have been found to be effective in reducing mathematics anxiety (Tooke & Lindstrom, 1998). Expanding your knowledge of the subject and trying new ways to approach problems, you can learn to enjoy doing and presenting mathematical activities. Not only can you acquire a positive attitude toward mathematics, as a professional it is essential that you do.

To explore your students' attitudes toward mathematics consider using the interview protocol provided at the companion website. Here you can explore how the classroom environment may affect their attitudes.

Readiness for Change. Demonstrate a readiness for change, even for change so radical that it may cause disequilibrium. You may find that what is familiar will become unfamiliar and, conversely, what is unfamiliar will become familiar. For example, you may have always referred to "reducing fractions" as the process of changing $\frac{2}{4}$ to $\frac{1}{2}$, but this is misleading as the fractions are not getting smaller. Such terminology can lead to mistaken connections. Did the reduced fraction go on a diet? A careful look will point out that *reducing* is not the term to use; rather, you are writing an equivalent fraction that is simplified or in lowest terms. Even though you have used the language *reducing* for years, you need to become familiar with more precise language such as "simplifying fractions."

On the other hand, what is unfamiliar will become more comfortable. It may feel uncomfortable for you to be asking students, "Did anyone solve it differently?" especially if you are worried that you might not understand their approach. Yet this question is essential to effective teaching. As you bravely use this strategy, it will become comfortable (and you will learn new strategies!).

Another potentially difficult shift in practice is toward an emphasis on concepts as well as procedures. What happens in a procedure-focused classroom when a student doesn't understand division of fractions? A teacher with only procedural knowledge is often left to repeat the procedure louder and slower, "Just change the division sign to multiplication, flip over the second fraction, and multiply." We know this approach doesn't work well if we want students to fully understand the process of dividing fractions, so let's consider an example using $3\frac{1}{2} \div \frac{1}{2} =$ _____. You might start by relating this division problem to prior knowledge of a whole number division problem such as $25 \div 5 =$ _____. A corresponding story problem might be, "How many orders of 5 pizzas are there in a group of 25 pizzas?" Then ask students to put words around the fraction division problem, such as "You plan to serve each guest $\frac{1}{2}$ a pizza. If you have $3\frac{1}{2}$ pizzas, how many guests can you serve?" Yes, there are seven halves in $3\frac{1}{2}$ and therefore 7 guests can be served. Are you surprised that you can do this division of fractions problem in your head?

To respond to students' challenges, uncertainties, and frustrations you may need to unlearn and relearn mathematical concepts, developing comprehensive conceptual understanding and a variety of representations along the way. Supporting your mathematics content knowledge on solid, well-supported terrain is your best hope of making a lasting difference in your students' learning of mathematics—so be ready for change. What you already understand will provide you with many "Aha" moments as you read this book and connect new information to your current mathematics knowledge.

Life-Long Learning, Make Time to Be Self-Aware and Reflective. As Steve Leinwand wrote, "If you don't feel inadequate, you're probably not doing the job" (2007, p. 583). No matter whether you are a pre-service teacher or an experienced teacher, there is always more to learn about the content and methodology of teaching mathematics. The ability to examine oneself for areas that need improvement or to reflect on successes and challenges is critical for growth and development. The best teachers are always trying to improve their practice through the reading latest article, reading the newest book, attending the most recent conference, or signing up for the next series of professional development opportunities. These teachers don't say, "Oh, that's what I am already doing"; instead, they identify and celebrate each new insight. The highly effective teachers never "finish" learning nor exhaust the number of new mental connections that they make and, as a result, they never see teaching as stale or stagnant. An ancient Chinese proverb states, "The best time to plant a tree is twenty years ago; the second best time is today." Explore the self-reflection chart on professional growth available at the companion website to list your strengths and indicate areas for continued growth.

Think back to the quotations from teachers at the beginning of this chapter. Again, what memories will you create for your students? As you begin this adventure let's be reminded of what John Van de Walle said with every new edition, "Enjoy the journey!"

 Complete Self-Check 1.3: An Invitation to Learn and Grow

REFLECTIONS ON CHAPTER 1

WRITING TO LEARN

1. What are the characteristics, habits of thought, skills, and dispositions needed to succeed as a teacher of mathematics? Give a brief explanation for each.

2. What are the six Standards for Mathematical Practice? How do they relate to the Common Core State Standards content expectations?

FOR DISCUSSION AND EXPLORATION

♦ Studies have shown that math education must change if our students are to be competitive in the global market and understand the complex issues they must confront as responsible citizens. Examine a textbook or school mathematics curriculum at any grade level of your choice to find some real-life applications of the topics covered in each chapter. Consider the sociocultural background of your students and think of ways to teach the topics covered in the textbook with motivating real-life examples that the students can connect with easily.

RESOURCES FOR CHAPTER 1

RECOMMENDED READINGS

Articles

Hoffman, L., & Brahier, D. (2008). Improving the planning and teaching of mathematics by reflecting on research. *Mathematics Teaching in the Middle School, 13* (7), 412–417.

This article addresses how teachers' philosophies and beliefs influence their mathematics instruction. Using TIMSS and NAEP studies as a foundation, the authors discuss posing higher-level problems, asking thought-provoking questions, facing students' frustration, and using mistakes to enhance understanding of concepts. They suggest reflective questions that are useful for self-assessment or discussions with peers.

Books

Bush, S. & Karp, K. (2015) *Discovering lessons for the* Common Core State Standards *in grades K–5.* Reston, VA: NCTM.

Bush, S. & Karp, K. (2014) *Discovering lessons for the* Common Core State Standards *in grades 6–8.* Reston, VA: NCTM.

These two books align the lessons in articles in NCTM journals for the past fifteen years with the Common Core State Standards and the Standards for Mathematical Practices. They provide a way to see how the standards play out in instructional tasks and activities for classroom use.

Exploring What It Means to Know and Do Mathematics

LEARNER OUTCOMES

After reading this chapter and engaging in the embedded activities and reflections, you should be able to:

2.1 Describe what it means to do mathematics.

2.2 Design and implement strategies for solving authentic mathematics tasks.

2.3 Illustrate through content examples, what a mathematically proficient student knows and is able to do.

2.4 Compare learning theories related to mathematics, and connect the theories to effective teaching practices.

2.5 Synthesize the important theoretical and content ideas related to learning mathematics.

This chapter explains how to help students learn mathematics. To get at how to help students learn, however, we must first consider what is important *to* learn. Let's look at a poorly understood topic, division of fractions, as an opening example. If a student has learned this topic well, what will they know and what should they be able to do? The answer is more than being able to successfully implement a procedure (e.g., commonly called the "invert and multiply" procedure). There is much more to know and understand about division of fractions: What does $3 \div \frac{1}{4}$ mean conceptually? What is a situation that might be solved with such an equation? Will the result be greater than or less than 3 and why? What ways can we solve equations like this? What illustration or manipulative could illustrate this equation? What is the relationship of this equation to subtraction? To multiplication? All of these questions can be answered by a student who fully understands a topic such as division of fractions. We must lead students to this conceptual understanding.

This chapter can help you. It could be called the "what" and "how" of teaching mathematics. First, *what* does doing mathematics look like (be ready to experience this yourself through four great tasks!) and what is important to know about mathematics? Second, *how* do we help students develop a strong understanding of mathematics? By the end of this chapter, you will be able to draw strong connections between the what and the how of teaching mathematics.

 ## What Does It Mean to Do Mathematics?

Mathematics is more than completing sets of exercises or mimicking processes the teacher explains. Doing mathematics means generating strategies for solving a problem, applying that strategy, and checking to see whether your answer makes sense. Finding and exploring regularity or order, and then making sense of it, is what doing mathematics in the real world is all about.

Doing mathematics in classrooms should closely model the act of doing mathematics in the real world. Even our youngest students can notice patterns and order. For example, post a series of problems and ask first or second graders, "What patterns to you notice?"

$$6 + 7 =$$
$$5 + 8 =$$
$$4 + 9 =$$

Think about the patterns students might notice: the first addend is going down 1, the second one is going up one, and the sums are the same. How might exploring these patterns help students to learn about addition? Also consider the next situation related to multiplication that might be explored by third to fifth graders.

Even $\times$ Even = Even	Always	Sometimes	Never
Odd $\times$ Odd = Even	Always	Sometimes	Never
Odd $\times$ Even = Even	Always	Sometimes	Never

Exploring generalizations such as these multiplication ones provides students an opportunity to learn important relationships about numbers as they deepen their understanding of the operations. With each of these problems, you have the opportunity to have students debate which answer they think is correct and to justify (i.e., prove) their response.

In middle school, students continue to explore more advanced patterns and order, extending to negative numbers and exponents, as well as using variables. You also might ask middle school students to look for patterns comparing two solutions, as in this example:

For a fundraiser, Annie and Mac decided to sell school wristbands. They cost $.75 and they are going to sell them for $2.50. They sold 35 the first day. They each calculate the Day 1 profit differently. Who is correct? Explain.

Annie: $(35 \times 2.50) - (35 \times .75) =$

Mac: $\$1.75 \times 35 =$

In comparing these two strategies for finding profit, students are seeing relationships between the equations and the situations, noticing properties of the operations "in action," and discussing equivalencies (a major idea in mathematics!).

Engaging in the science of pattern and order, as the previous two examples illustrate, is *doing* mathematics. Basic facts and basic skills such as computation of whole numbers, fractions, and decimals are important in enabling students to be able to *do* mathematics. But if skills are taught by rote memorization or isolated practice, students will not learn to *do* mathematics, and will not be prepared to do the mathematics required in the 21st century.

Verbs of Doing Mathematics

Doing mathematics begins with posing worthwhile tasks and then creating an environment where students take risks, share, and defend mathematical ideas. Students in traditional mathematics classes often describe mathematics as imitating what the teacher shows them. Instructions to students given by teachers or in textbooks ask students to listen, copy, memorize, drill, and compute. These are lower-level thinking activities and do not adequately prepare students for the real act of doing mathematics. In contrast, the following verbs engage students in doing mathematics:

collaborate	describe	justify
communicate	develop	predict
compare	explain	represent
conjecture	explore	solve
construct	formulate	use
create	invent	verify
critique	investigate	

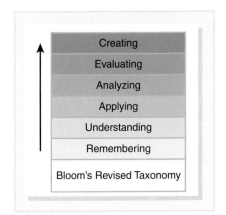

FIGURE 2.1 Bloom's (Revised) Taxonomy (Anderson & Krathwohl, 2001).

Source: Anderson, L.W., & Krathwohl, D. R. (Eds.). (2001). *A taxonomy for learning, teaching, and assessing: A revision of Bloom's Taxonomy of educational objectives: Complete Edition.* New York, NY: Addison Wesley, Longman.

These verbs lead to opportunities for higher-level thinking and encompass "making sense" and "figuring out." These verbs may look familiar to you, as they are on the higher level of Bloom's (revised) Taxomony (Anderson & Krathwohl, 2001) (see Figure 2.1).

In observing a third-grade classroom where the teacher used this approach to teaching mathematics, researchers found that students became "doers" of mathematics. In other words the students began to take the math ideas to the next level by (1) connecting to previous material, (2) responding with information beyond the required response, and (3) conjecturing or predicting (Fillingim & Barlow, 2010). When this happens on a daily basis, students are getting an empowering message: "You are capable of making sense of this—you are capable of doing mathematics!"

 Complete Self-Check 2.1: What Does It Mean to Do Mathematics?

 # An Invitation to Do Mathematics

The purpose of this section is to provide you with opportunities to engage in the science of pattern and order—to *do* some mathematics. For each problem posed, allow yourself to try to (1) make connections within the mathematics (i.e., make mathematical relationships explicit) and (2) engage in productive struggle.

We will explore four different problems. None requires mathematics beyond elementary school mathematics—not even algebra. But the problems do require higher-level thinking and reasoning. As you read each task, stop and solve first. Then read the "Few Ideas" section. Then, you will be doing mathematics and seeing how others may think about the problem differently (or the same). Have fun!

Searching for Patterns

1. *Start and Jump Numbers*

Begin with a number (start) and add (jump) a fixed amount. For example, start with 3 and jump by 5s. Use the Start and Jump Numbers Activity Page or write the list on a piece of paper. Examine the list and record as many patterns as you see.

A Few Ideas. Here are some questions to guide your pattern search:

- Do you see at least one alternating pattern?
- Have you noticed an odd/even pattern? Why is this pattern true?
- What do you notice about the numbers in the tens place?
- Do the patterns change when the numbers are greater than 100?

Don't forget to think about what happens to your patterns after the numbers are more than 100. How are you thinking about 113? One way is as 1 hundred, 1 ten, and 3 ones. But, of course, it could also be "eleventy-three," where the tens digit has gone from 9 to 10 to 11. How do these different perspectives affect your patterns? What would happen after 999?

Next Steps. Sometimes when you have discovered some patterns in mathematics, it is a good idea to make some changes and see how the changes affect the patterns. What changes might you make in this problem?

Your changes may be even more interesting than the following suggestions. But here are some ideas:

- Change the start number but keep the jump number equal to 5. What is the same and what is different?
- Keep the same start number and explore with different jump numbers.
- What patterns do different jump numbers make? For example, when the jump number was 5, the ones-digit pattern repeated every two numbers—it had a "pattern length" of 2. But when the jump number is 3, the length of the ones-digit pattern is 10! Do other jump numbers create different pattern lengths?
  - For a jump number of 3, how does the ones-digit pattern relate to the circle of numbers in Figure 2.2? Are there similar circles of numbers for other jump numbers?
  - Using the circle of numbers for 3, find the pattern for jumps of multiples of 3, that is, jumps of 6, 9, or 12.

Using Technology. Calculators facilitate exploration of this problem. Using the calculator makes the list generation accessible for young children who can't skip count yet, and it opens the door for students to work with bigger jump numbers like 25 or 36. Most simple calculators have an automatic constant feature that will add the same number successively. For example, if you press $3 + 5 =$ and then keep pressing $=$, the calculator will keep counting by fives from the previous answer. This works for the other three operations. Consider demonstrating this with an online calculator or app for the white board so the class can observe and discuss the counting.

Analyzing a Situation

2. Two Machines, One Job

Ron's recycle shop started when Ron bought a used paper-shredding machine. Business was good, so Ron bought a new shredding machine. The old machine could shred a truckload of paper in 4 hours. The new machine could shred the same truckload in only 2 hours. How long will it take to shred a truckload of paper if Ron runs both shredders at the same time?

Use the Two Machines, One Job Activity Page to record your solution to this problem. Do not read on until you have an answer or are stuck. Can you check that you are correct? Can you approach the problem using a picture?

A Few Ideas. Have you tried to predict approximately how much time you think it should take the two machines? For example, will it be closer to 1 hour or closer to 4 hours? What facts about the situation led you to this estimated time? Is there a way to check your estimate? Checking a guess in this way sometimes leads to a new insight.

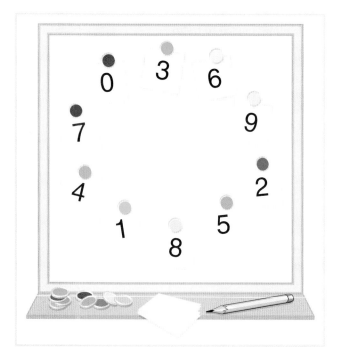

FIGURE 2.2   For jumps of 3, this cycle of digits will occur in the ones place. The start number determines where the cycle begins.

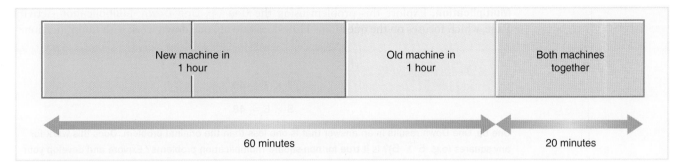

FIGURE 2.3   Cora's solution to the paper-shredding problem.

Some people draw pictures to solve problems. Others like to use something they can move or change. For example, you might draw a rectangle or a line segment to stand for the truckload of paper, or you might get some counters (chips, plastic cubes, pennies) and make a collection that stands for the truckload.

Consider Solutions of Others.   There are many ways to model and solve the problem, and understanding other people's ways can develop our own understanding. The following is one explanation for solving the problem, using strips (based on Schifter & Fosnot, 1993):

> "This rectangle [see Figure 2.3] stands for the whole truckload. In 1 hour, the new machine will do half of this." The rectangle is divided in half. "In 1 hour, the old machine could shred $\frac{1}{4}$ of the paper." The rectangle is divided accordingly. "So in 1 hour, the two machines have done $\frac{3}{4}$ of the truck, and there is $\frac{1}{4}$ left. What is left is one-third as much as what they already did, so it should take the two machines one-third as long to do that part as it took to do the first part. One-third of an hour is 20 minutes. That means it takes 1 hour and 20 minutes to do it all.

As with the teachers in these examples, it is important to decide whether your solution is correct through justifying why you did what you did; this reflects real problem solving rather than checking with an answer key. After you have justified that you have solved the problem in a correct manner, try to find other ways that students might solve the problem—in considering multiple ways, you are making mathematical connections.

Generalizing Relationships

 3. *One Up, One Down*

Addition. When you add 7 + 7, you get 14. When you make the first number 1 more and the second number 1 less, you get the same answer:

$$\uparrow \quad \downarrow$$
$$7 + 7 = 14 \quad \text{and} \quad 8 + 6 = 14$$

It works for 5 + 5 too:

$$\uparrow \quad \downarrow$$
$$5 + 5 = 10 \quad \text{and} \quad 6 + 4 = 10$$

Does this work for any doubles? For what other addition problems does one up, one down work? Why does it work?

Explore this problem using the One Up, One Down: Addition Activity Page. Explore and develop your own conjectures.

Multiplication. Explore this problem using the One Up, One Down: Multiplication Activity Page, which focuses on the question, "How does one up, one down work with multiplication?"

$$\uparrow \quad \downarrow$$
$$7 \times 7 = 49$$
$$8 \times 6 = 48$$

One Up, One Down results in an answer that is one less than the original problem. Does this work for any squares (e.g., 5×5)? Is it true for non-square multiplication problems? Explore and develop your own conjectures.

Explore the multiplication problem, responding to the questions posed. Notice that you are asked to develop conjectures. Developing and testing conjectures are an important aspect of mathematical reasoning (Lannin, Ellis, & Elliott, 2011).

A Few Ideas. Multiplication is more complicated. Why? Use a physical model or picture to compare the before and after products. For example, draw rectangles (or arrays) with a length and height of each of the factors (see Figure 2.4(a)), then draw the new rectangle (e.g., 8-by-6-unit rectangle). See how the rectangles compare.

You may prefer to think of multiplication as equal sets. For example, using stacks of chips, 7×7 is seven stacks with seven chips in each stack (set) (see Figure 2.4(b)). The expression 8×6 is represented by eight stacks of six (though six stacks of eight is a possible interpretation). See how the stacks for each expression compare. Consider working with one or both of these approaches to gain insights and make conjectures.?

Additional Patterns to Explore. Recall that doing mathematics includes the tendency to extend beyond the problem posed. This problem lends itself to many "what if?" questions. Here are a few. If you have found other ones, great!

- Have you looked at how the first two numbers are related? For example, 7×7, 5×5, and 9×9 are all products with like factors. What if the product were two consecutive numbers (e.g., 8×7 or 13×12)? What if the factors differ by 2 or by 3?
- Think about adjusting by numbers other than one. What if you adjust two up and two down (e.g., 7×7 to 9×5)?
- What happens if you use big numbers instead of small ones (e.g., 30×30)?
- If both factors increase (i.e., one up, one up), is there a pattern?

Have you made some mathematical connections and conjectures in exploring this problem? In doing so you have hopefully felt a sense of accomplishment and excitement—one of the benefits of *doing* mathematics.

Experimenting and Explaining

4. *The Best Chance of Purple*

Samuel, Susan, and Sandu are playing a game. The first one to spin "purple" wins! Purple means that one spin lands on red and one spins lands on blue (see Figure 2.5). Each person chooses to spin each spinner once or one of the spinners twice. Samuel chooses to spin spinner A twice; Susan chooses to spin spinner B twice;

(a)

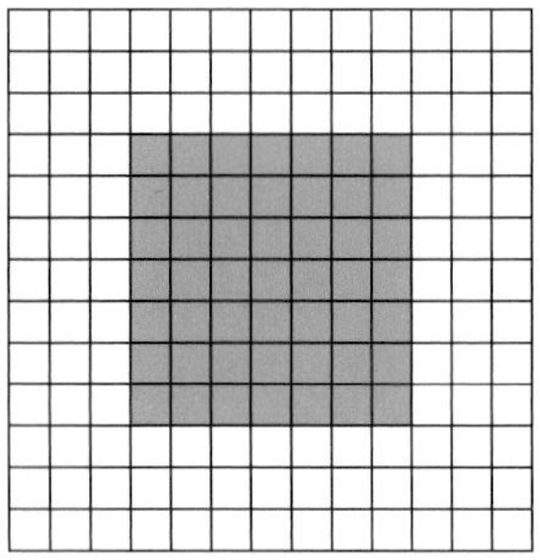

This is 7 × 7 shown as an array of 7 rows of 7.

(b)

This is 7 × 7 as 7 sets of 7.

What happens when you change one of these to show 6 × 8?

FIGURE 2.4   Two physical ways to think about multiplication that might help in the exploration.

and Sandu chooses to spin each spinner once. Who has the best chance of purple? (based on Lappan & Even, 1989)

Think about the problem and what you know. Experiment. Use the Best Chance of Purple Activity Page to explore this problem.

A Few Ideas. A good strategy for learning is to first explore a problem concretely, then analyze it abstractly. This is helpful in situations involving chance or probability. Use a paper clip with the spinners on your Activity Page, or use a virtual spinner (e.g., The NCTM Illuminations website has an Adjustable Spinner).

Consider these issues as you explore:

- Explain who you think is most likely to win and why.
- For Sandu's turn (spinner A, then spinner B), would it matter if he spun B first and then A? Why or why not?
- How might you change one spinner so that Susan has the best chance at purple?

Strategy 1: Tree Diagrams. On spinner A, the four colors each have the same chance of coming up. You could make a tree diagram for A with four branches and all the branches would have the same chance (see Figure 2.6). Spinner B has different-sized sections, leading to the following questions:

- What is the relationship between the blue region and each of the others?
- How could you make a tree diagram for B with each branch having the same chance?
- How can you add to the diagram for spinner A so that it represents spinning A twice in succession?
- Which branches on your diagram represent getting purple?
- How could you make tree diagrams for each player's choices?
- How do the tree diagrams relate to the spinners?

Tree diagrams are only one way to approach this. If the strategy makes sense to you, stop reading and solve the problem. If tree diagrams do not seem like a strategy you want to use, read on.

Strategy 2: Grids. Partition squares to represent all the possible outcomes for spinner A and spinner B. Although there are many ways to divide a square into four equal parts, if you use lines going all in the same direction, you can make comparisons of all the outcomes of one event (one whole square) with the outcomes of another event (drawn on a different square). For two independent events, you can then create lines going the other direction for the second event. Samuel's two spins are represented in Figure 2.7(a). If these two squares are overlapped, you can visually see that two parts (two-sixteenths) are "blue on red" or "red on blue." Susan's probability can be determined by layering the

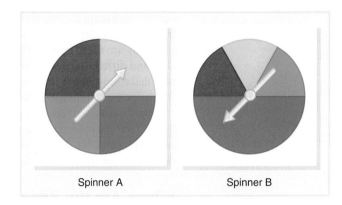

FIGURE 2.5 You may spin A twice, B twice, or A then B. Which choice gives you the best chance of spinning a red and a blue (purple)?

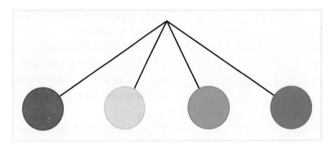

FIGURE 2.6 A tree diagram for spinner A in Figure 2.5.

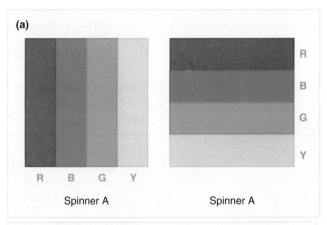

(a)

R   B   G   Y
Spinner A

R
B
G
Y
Spinner A

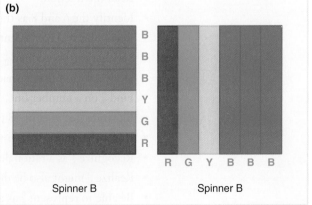

(b)

B
B
B
Y
G
R
Spinner B

R   G   Y   B   B   B
Spinner B

FIGURE 2.7 Grids can illustrate the chance of spinning purple with two spins.

squares in Figure 2.7(b); and Sandu's from layering one square from Figure 2.7(a) with one from Figure 2.7(b).

Why are there four parts for spinner A and 6 parts for spinner B? How is the grid strategy alike and different from the tree diagram? One strategy may make more sense to you, and one may make more sense to another. Hearing other students' explanations and reasoning for both strategies are important in building a strong understanding of mathematics.

Interesting mathematics problems such as the four presented here are plentiful. The Math Forum, for example, has a large collection of classic problems along with discussion, solutions, and extensions. NCTM teacher journals include monthly problems, and readers submit student solutions for these tasks, which appear in an issue a few months later.

Where Are the Answers?

Did you notice that no answers were shared for these four rich tasks? How do you feel about not being able to "check your answer"? You may be wondering if your answer is correct, or if there are other answers. We did this intentionally, because one aspect of becoming mathematically proficient is to be able to rely on one's own justification and reasoning to determine if an answer is correct.

Consider the message students receive when the textbook or the teacher is the source of whether an answer is correct: "Your job is to find the answers that the teacher already has." In the real world of problem solving and doing mathematics, there are no answer books. Doing mathematics includes using justification as a means of determining whether an answer is correct.

 Complete Self-Check 2.2: An Invitation to Do Mathematics

 ## What Does It Mean to Be Mathematically Proficient?

In setting learning objectives for students, we often ask, "What will students know? What will students be able to do?" The previous section addressed what they should be able to do, here we focus on several important points related to what students need to know. An important aspect of knowing is understanding.

Let's go back to fractions as an example. What is important for a student to know about fractions such as $\frac{6}{8}$? What might a fourth grader know about $\frac{6}{8}$? At what point do they know enough that they can claim they "understand" fractions? It is more complicated than it might first appear. Here is a short list of what they might know or be able to do:

- Read the fraction.
- Identify the 6 and 8 as the numerator and denominator, respectively.
- Recognize it is equivalent to $\frac{3}{4}$.
- Say that it is more than $\frac{1}{2}$ (recognize relative size).
- Draw a region that is shaded in a way to show $\frac{6}{8}$.
- Find $\frac{6}{8}$ on a number line.
- Illustrate $\frac{6}{8}$ of a set of 48 pennies or counters.
- Know that there are infinitely many equivalencies to $\frac{6}{8}$.
- Recognize $\frac{6}{8}$ as a rationale number.
- Realize $\frac{6}{8}$ might also be describing a ratio (girls to boys, for example).
- Be able to represent $\frac{6}{8}$ as a decimal fraction.

For any item on this list, how much and what a student understands will vary. For example, a student may know that $\frac{6}{8}$ can be simplified to $\frac{3}{4}$ but not understand that $\frac{3}{4}$ and $\frac{6}{8}$ represent

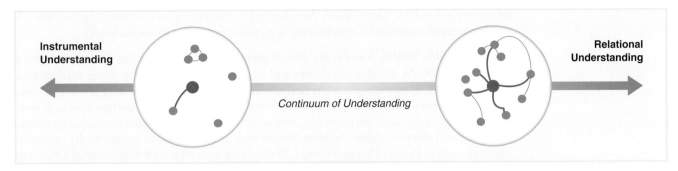

FIGURE 2.8 Understanding is a measure of the quality and quantity of connections that a new idea has with existing ideas. The greater the number of connections to a network of ideas, the better the understanding.

equal quantities, thinking that three-fourths is actually smaller. Or, they may be able to find one fraction between $\frac{1}{2}$ and $\frac{6}{8}$, but not be able to find others or think there is only one fraction between these two fractions.

Understanding can be defined as a measure of the quality and quantity of connections that an idea has with existing ideas. Understanding is not an all-or-nothing proposition. It depends on the existence of appropriate ideas and on the creation of new connections, varying with each person (Backhouse, Haggarty, Pirie, & Stratton, 1992; Davis, 1986; Hiebert & Carpenter, 1992).

Relational Understanding

One way that we can think about understanding is that it exists along a continuum from an *Instrumental understanding*—doing something without understanding (see Figure 2.8) to a *Relational understanding*—knowing what to do and why. These two terms were introduced by Richard Skemp in 1978 and continue to be an important distinction related to what is important for students to know about mathematics.

In the $\frac{6}{8}$ example, a student who only knows a procedure for simplifying $\frac{6}{8}$ to $\frac{3}{4}$ has an understanding near the instrumental end of the continuum, while a student who can draw diagrams, give examples, find equivalencies, and tell the approximate size of $\frac{6}{8}$ has an understanding toward the relational end of the continuum. Here we briefly share three important ways to nurture a relational understanding.

Use and Connect Different Representations. In order for students to build connections among ideas, different representations must be included in instruction, and opportunities must be provided for students to make connections among the representations. Figure 2.9 illustrates a Web of Representations that apply to any mathematical concept. Students who have difficulty translating a concept from one representation to another also have difficulty solving problems and understanding computations (Lesh, Cramer, Doerr, Post, & Zawojewski, 2003). Strengthening the ability to move between and among these representations improves student understanding and retention. For any topic you teach, you can give students the Translation Task Activity Page to complete. You can

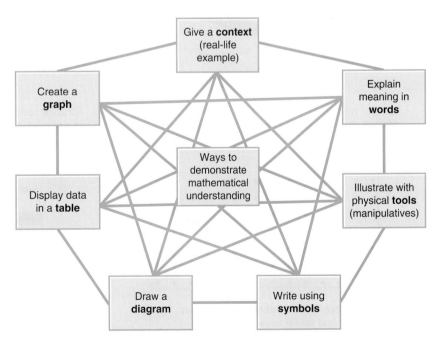

FIGURE 2.9 Web of Representations. Translations between and within each representation of a mathematical idea can help students build a relation understanding of a mathematical concept.

fill out one box and ask them to insert the other representations, or you can invite a group to work on all four representations for a given topic (e.g., multiplication of whole numbers).

Explore with Tools. A *tool* is any object, picture, or drawing that can be used to explore a concept. CCSS-M incudes calculators and manipulatives as tools for doing mathematics (CCSSO, 2010). *Manipulatives* are physical objects that students and teachers can use to illustrate and discover mathematical concepts, whether made specifically for mathematics (e.g., connecting cubes) or for other purposes (e.g., buttons). Choices for manipulatives (including virtual manipulatives) abound—from common objects such as lima beans to commercially produced materials such as Pattern Blocks. Figure 2.10 shows six examples, each representing a different concept, just to give a glimpse (Part II of this book is full of more options). More and more of these manipulatives and others (e.g., geoboards, base-ten blocks, spinners, number lines) are available in a virtual format, for example, on the National Library of Virtual Manipulatives website and the NCTM Illuminations website. Each has a range of manipulatives available.

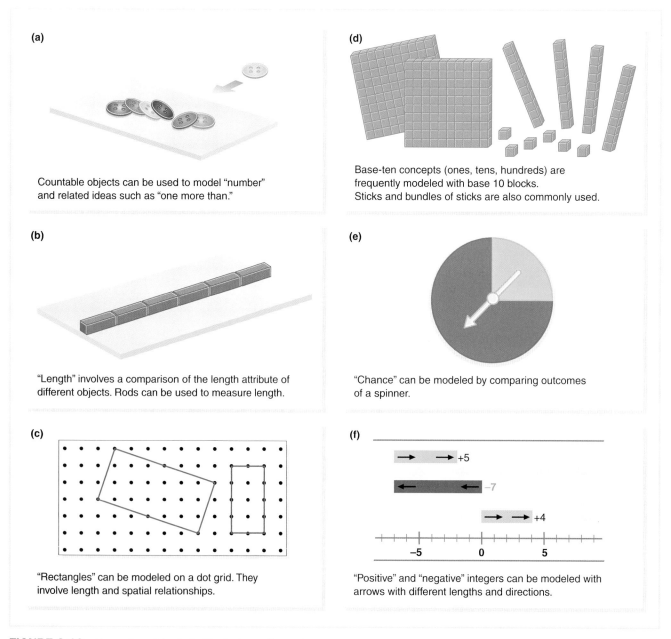

(a)
Countable objects can be used to model "number" and related ideas such as "one more than."

(d)
Base-ten concepts (ones, tens, hundreds) are frequently modeled with base 10 blocks.
Sticks and bundles of sticks are also commonly used.

(b)
"Length" involves a comparison of the length attribute of different objects. Rods can be used to measure length.

(e)
"Chance" can be modeled by comparing outcomes of a spinner.

(c)
"Rectangles" can be modeled on a dot grid. They involve length and spatial relationships.

(f)
"Positive" and "negative" integers can be modeled with arrows with different lengths and directions.

FIGURE 2.10 Examples of tools to illustrate mathematics concepts.

A tool does not "illustrate" a concept. The tool is used to visualize a mathematical concept and only your mind can impose the mathematical relationship on the object (Suh, 2007b; Thompson, 1994). As noted in the What Chance of Purple problem, manipulatives can be a testing ground for emerging ideas. They are more concrete and provide insights into new and abstract relationships. A variety of tools should be accessible for students to select and use appropriately as they engage in doing mathematics (CCSSO, 2010).

Before you continue, consider each of the concepts and the corresponding model in Figure 2.10. Try to separate the physical tool from the relationship that you must impose on the tool in order to "see" the concept.

The examples in Figure 2.10 are models that can show the following concepts:

a. The concept of "6" is a relationship between sets that can be matched to the words *one*, *two*, *three*, *four*, *five*, or *six*. Changing a set of counters by adding one changes the relationship. The difference between the set of 6 and the set of 7 is the relationship "one more than."

b. The concept of "measure of length" is a comparison. The length measure of an object is a comparison relationship of the length of the object to the length of the unit.

c. The concept of "rectangle" includes both spatial and length relationships. The opposite sides are of equal length and parallel and the adjacent sides meet at right angles.

d. The concept of "hundred" is not in the larger square but in the relationship of that square to the strip ("ten") and to the little square ("one").

e. "Chance" is a relationship between the frequency of an event happening compared with all possible outcomes. The spinner can be used to create relative frequencies. These can be predicted by observing relationships of sections of the spinner.

f. The concept of a "negative integer" is based on the relationships of "magnitude" and "is the opposite of." Negative quantities exist only in relation to positive quantities. Arrows on the number line model the opposite of relationship in terms of direction and size or magnitude relationship in terms of length.

While tools can be used to support relational understanding, they can be used ineffectively and not accomplish this goal. One of the most widespread misuses of tools occurs when the teacher tells students, "Do as I do." There is a natural temptation to get out the materials and show students how to use them to "show" the concept. It is just as possible to move blocks around mindlessly as it is to "invert and multiply" mindlessly. Neither promotes thinking or aids in the development of concepts (Ball, 1992; Clements & Battista, 1990; Stein & Bovalino, 2001). On the other extreme, it is ineffective to provide no focus or purpose for using the tools. This will result in nonproductive and unsystematic investigation (Stein & Bovalino, 2001).

Mathematical Proficiency

As you learned in Chapter 1, the standards used in many U.S. states are the CCSS-M (2010). Whether or not your state is one of these, the eight Standards of Mathematical Practice are worthy of attention (See Appendix B). They describe what a mathematically proficient student can do. These are not graduation expectations—these are *daily expectations* for doing mathematics, beginning in kindergarten and continuing throughout school. They are based on research on how students learn that was published by the National Research Council (NRC) in *Adding It Up* (NRC, 2001). Figure 2.11 illustrates these interrelated and interwoven strands. For more on fluency, listen to a past-president of NCTM. Go

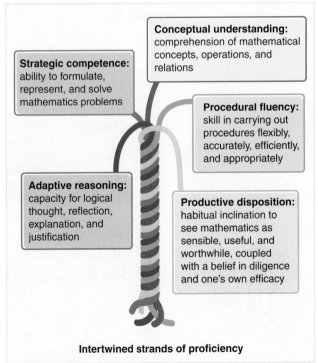

Strategic competence: ability to formulate, represent, and solve mathematics problems

Conceptual understanding: comprehension of mathematical concepts, operations, and relations

Procedural fluency: skill in carrying out procedures flexibly, accurately, efficiently, and appropriately

Adaptive reasoning: capacity for logical thought, reflection, explanation, and justification

Productive disposition: habitual inclination to see mathematics as sensible, useful, and worthwhile, coupled with a belief in diligence and one's own efficacy

Intertwined strands of proficiency

FIGURE 2.11 *Adding It Up* describes five strands of mathematical proficiency.

Source: National Research Council. (2001). *Adding It Up: Helping Children Learn Mathematics*, p. 5. Reprinted with permission from the National Academy of Sciences, courtesy of the National Academies Press, Washington, DC.

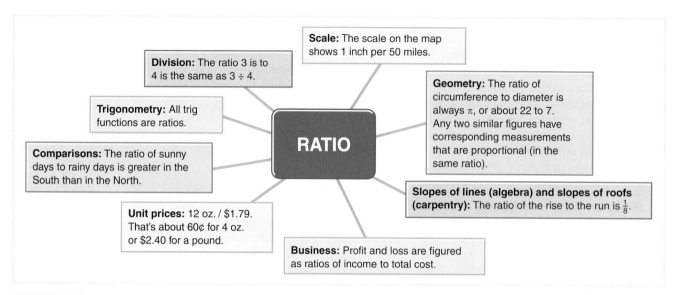

FIGURE 2.12 Potential web of ideas that could contribute to the understanding of "ratio."

to the NCTM website and search for the 2014 Annual Meeting Webcast "President's Session—Fluency . . . It's More Than Fast and Accurate."

Conceptual Understanding. Conceptual understanding is a flexible web of connections and relationships within and between ideas, interpretations and images of mathematical concepts—a relational understanding. Consider the web of associations for ratio as shown in Figure 2.12.

Students with a conceptual understanding will connect what they know about division and numbers to make sense of scaling, unit prices, and so on. Note how much is involved in having a relational understanding of ratio.

Conceptual understanding includes the network of representations and interpretations of a concepts through the use of pictures, manipulatives, tables, graphs, words, and so on (see Figure 2.9). An illustration for ratios across these representations is provided in Figure 2.13.

Procedural Fluency. Procedural fluency is sometimes confused with being able to do standard algorithms correctly and quickly, but it is much bigger than that. Look at the four descriptors of procedural fluency in Figure 2.11. Fluency includes having the ability to be flexible and to choose an appropriate strategy for a particular problem. Let's look at the problem 37 + 28. Younger students might be able to count all (see Figure 2.14(a)), or even start with the larger and count on to reach a total. Eventually skip counting can be used as a more efficient strategy, and students are able to count up by 10s and 1s (see Figure 2.14(b)). At a

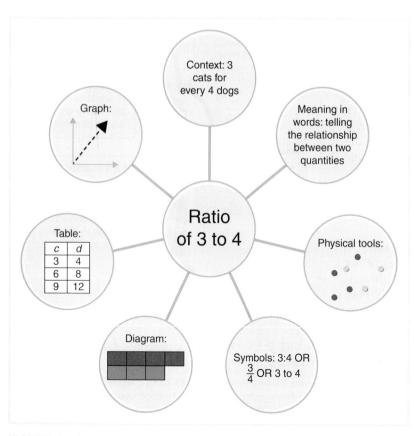

FIGURE 2.13 Multiple representations for ratio of 3 to 4.

higher level of fluency, students are able to select a strategy that is efficient, for example, moving two from the 37 to the 28 to create a benchmark number or adding two on to 28 to add, and then taking it off again (see Figure 2.14(c)). Notice that to use these efficient and appropriate strategies requires a conceptual understanding of place value and addition.

The ineffective practice of teaching procedures in the absence of conceptual understanding (https://www.youtube.com/watch?v=FVKtQwARe6c) results in a lack of retention and increased errors, rigid approaches, and inefficient strategy use (Figure 2.14(d)).

Think about the following problem: $40,005 - 39,996 =$ _____. A student with rigid procedural skills may launch into the standard algorithm, regrouping across zeros (often with difficulty), rather than notice that the number 39,996 is just 4 away from 40,000, and therefore that the difference between the two numbers is 9.

Efficient Strategy: 39,996   40,000   40,005

Developing conceptual understanding alongside procedural proficiency is crucial to becoming mathematically proficient (Baroody, Feil, & Johnson, 2007; Bransford et al., 2000; NCTM, 2014). Visit the companion website for an observation tool that focuses on evidence of mathematical proficiency in a classroom setting.

Perseverance and a Productive Disposition. As the Mathematical Practices and the Strands of Proficiency describe, being proficient at mathematics is not just what you know, but how you go about solving problems. Consider this short list of reflective prompts. Which ones might a proficient student say yes to often?

- When you read a problem you don't know how to solve, do you think, "Cool, something challenging. I can solve this. Let me now think how."?
- Do you consider several possible approaches before diving in to solve?
- Do you have a way of convincing yourself or your peer that it had to be correct?
- Do you recognize a wrong path and try something else?
- When you finish a problem, do you wonder whether it is right? If there are other answers?
- Do you look for patterns across examples and try to see a new shortcut or approach that might work?
- As you work, do you decide to draw a picture, use a calculator, or model the problem with a manipulative?

When students are in classrooms where they are able to do mathematics, these proficiencies develop and students build a stronger understanding of the mathematics they need to know, both the concepts and procedures, and are able to become mathematically proficient.

 Complete Self-Check 2.3: What Does It Mean to Be Mathematically Proficient?

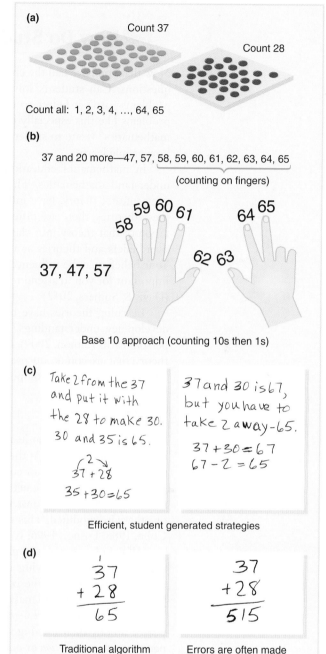

FIGURE 2.14 A range of levels of procedural fluency for $37 + 28$.

How Do Students Learn Mathematics?

Now that you have had the chance to experience doing mathematics, you may have a series of questions: Can students solve such challenging tasks? Why take the time to solve these problems—isn't it better to do a lot of shorter problems? Why should students be doing problems like this especially if they are reluctant to do so? In other words, how does "doing mathematics" relate to student learning? The answer lies in learning theory and research on how people learn.

In mathematics education there is no consensus about what it means to know and understand mathematics. Theories, such as behaviorism, cognitivism, constructivism, and sociocultural theory, have influenced the way in which mathematics is taught. Even within these theories, there are different interpretations of what they mean and what the interpretation of that theory into classroom practice might look like. As a teacher, you rely on your own beliefs and theories as you decide what you think will most help your students learn. Your beliefs may be influenced by theorists and from your own pragmatic experiences. It is important for you to attend to your own beliefs and how they relate to your teaching practice (Davis & Sumara, 2012).

Learning theories have been developed through analysis of students and adults as they develop new understandings. They can be thought of as tools or lenses for interpreting how a person learns (Simon, 2009). Here we describe two theories, constructivism and sociocultural theory, that are commonly used by researchers to understand how students learn mathematics. These theories are not competing and are compatible (Norton & D'Ambrosio, 2008).

Constructivism

Constructivism is rooted in Jean Piaget's work which was developed in the 1930s and translated to English in the 1950s. At the heart of constructivism is the notion that learners are not blank slates but rather creators or constructors of their own learning. Integrated *networks*, or *cognitive schemas*, are both the product of constructing knowledge and the tools with which additional new knowledge can be constructed. As learning occurs the networks are rearranged, added to, or otherwise modified. This is an active endeavor on the part of the learner (Baroody, 1987; Cobb, 1988; Fosnot, 1996; von Glasersfeld, 1990, 1996).

All people construct or give meaning to things they perceive or think about. As you read these words you are giving meaning to them. Whether listening passively to a lecture or actively engaging in synthesizing findings in a project, your brain is applying prior knowledge your existing schemas to make sense of the new information.

Through *reflective thought*—the effort to connect existing ideas to new information—people modify their existing schemas to incorporate new ideas (Fosnot, 1996). This can happen through *assimilation* or *accommodation*. Assimilation occurs when a new concept "fits" with prior knowledge and the new information expands an existing network. Accommodation takes place when the new concept does not "fit" with the existing network, causing what Piaget called *disequilibrium*, so the brain revamps or replaces the existing schema.

Construction of Ideas. To construct or build something in the physical world requires tools, materials, and effort. The tools we use to build understanding are our existing ideas and knowledge. The materials we use may be things we see, hear, or touch, or our own thoughts and ideas. The effort required to connect new knowledge to old knowledge is reflective thought.

In Figure 2.15, blue and red dots are used as symbols for ideas. Consider the picture to be a small section of our cognitive makeup. The blue dots represent existing ideas. The lines joining the ideas represent our logical connections or relationships that have developed between and among ideas. The red dot is an emerging idea, one that is being constructed. Whatever existing ideas, blue dots, are used in the construction will be connected to the new idea, red dot, because those were the ideas that gave meaning to it. If a potentially relevant idea, blue dot, is not accessed by the learner when learning a new concept, red dot, then that potential connection will not be made. For more information on how constructivism applies to mathematics education, the Math Forum offers links to numerous sites and articles.

Sociocultural Theory

In the 1920s and 1930s, Lev Vygotsky, a Russian psychologist, began developing what is now called sociocultural theory. There are many theorical ideas that sociocultural theory shares with constructivism (for example, the learning process as active meaning-seeking on the part of the learner), but sociocultural theory has several unique features. One is that mental processes exist between and among people in social learning settings, and that from these social settings the learner moves ideas into his or her own psychological realm (Forman, 2003).

An important aspect of sociocultural theory is that the way in which information is internalized, or learned, depends on whether it was within a learner's zone of proximal development (ZPD) (Vygotsky, 1978). Simply put, the ZPD refers to a range of knowledge that may be out of reach for a person to learn on his or her own, but is accessible if the learner has support from peers or more knowledgeable others. Researchers Cobb (1994) and Goos (2004) suggest that in a true mathematical community of learners there is something of a common ZPD that emerges across learners and there are also the ZPDs of individual learners.

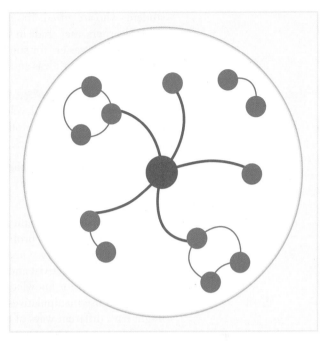

FIGURE 2.15   We use the ideas we already have (blue dots) to construct a new idea (red dot), in the process developing a network of connections between ideas. The more ideas used and the more connections made, the better we understand.

Another major component in sociocultural theory is *semiotic mediation*. Semiotic refers to the use of language and other tools, such as diagrams, pictures, and actions, to convey cultural practices. Mediation means that these semiotics are exchanged between and among people. So, semiotic mediation is the way in which an individual's beliefs, attitudes, and goals affect and are affected by sociocultural practices (Forman & McPhail, 1993). In mathematics, semiotics include mathematical symbols (e.g., the equal sign) and it is through classroom interactions and activities that the meaning of these symbols are developed.

Social interaction is essential for learning to occur. The nature of the community of learners is affected by not just the culture the teacher creates, but the broader social and historical culture of the members of the classroom (Forman, 2003). In summary, from a sociocultural perspective, learning is dependent on the new knowledge falling within the ZPD of the learner who must have access to the assistance, and occurs through interactions that are influenced by tools of mediation and the culture within and beyond the classroom.

Implications for Teaching Mathematics

It is not necessary to choose between a social constructivist theory that favors the views of Vygotsky and a cognitive constructivism built on the theories of Piaget (Cobb, 1994; Simon, 2009). In fact, when considering classroom practices that maximize opportunities to construct ideas, or to provide tools to promote mediation, they are quite similar. Classroom discussion based on students' own ideas and solutions to problems is essential to learning (Wood & Turner-Vorbeck, 2001).

Remember that learning theory is not a teaching strategy—theory *informs* teaching. This section outlines teaching strategies that are informed by constructivist and sociocultural perspectives. You will see these strategies revisited in more detail in Chapters 3 and 4, where a problem-based model for instruction is discussed, and in Section II of this book, where you learn how to apply these ideas to specific areas of mathematics.

Importantly, if these strategies are grounded in how people learn, it means *all* people learn this way—students with special needs, English language learners, students who struggle, and students who are gifted. Too often, when teachers make adaptations and modifications for particular learners, they trade in strategies that align with learning theories and research for methods that seem "easier" for students. These strategies, however, provide fewer opportunities for students to connect ideas and build knowledge—thereby impeding, not supporting, learning.

Build New Knowledge from Prior Knowledge. If you are teaching a new concept, like division, it must be developed using what students already know about equal subtraction and sharing. Consider the following task.

Goodies Toy Store is creating bags with 3 squishy balls in each. If they have 24 squishy balls, how many bags will they be able to make

Here, consider how you might introduce division to third graders and what your expectations might be for this problem as a teacher grounding your work in constructivist or sociocultural learning theory.

From a constructivist and sociocultural perspective, this classroom culture allows students to access their prior knowledge, use cultural tools, and build new knowledge. You might ask students to use manipulatives or to draw pictures to solve this problem. As they work, they might have different ways of thinking about the problem (e.g., skip counting up by 3s, or skip counting down by 3s). These ideas become part of a classroom discussion, connecting what they know about equal subtraction and addition, and connecting that to multiplication and division. Interestingly, this practice of connecting ideas is not only grounded in learning theory, but has been established through research studies.

Recall that making mathematical relationships explicit is connected with improving student conceptual understanding (Hiebert & Grouws, 2007). The teacher's role in making mathematical relationships explicit is to be sure that students are making the connections that are implied in a task. For example, asking students to relate today's topic to one they investigated last week, or by asking "How is Lisa's strategy like Marco's strategy?" when the two students have picked different ways to solve a problem, are ways to be "explicit" about mathematical relationships. Students apply their prior knowledge, test ideas, make connections, compare, and make conjectures. The more students see the connections among problems and among mathematical concepts, the more deeply they understand mathematics.

Provide Opportunities to Communicate about Mathematics. Learning is enhanced when the learner is engaged with others working on the same ideas. The rich interaction in such a classroom allows students to engage in reflective thinking and to internalize concepts that may be out of reach without the interaction and input from peers and their teacher. In discussions with peers, students will be adapting and expanding on their existing networks of concepts.

Create Opportunities for Reflective Thought. Classrooms need to provide structures and supports to help students make sense of mathematics in light of what they know. For a new idea you are teaching to be interconnected in a rich web of interrelated ideas, children must be mentally engaged. They must find the relevant ideas they possess and bring them to bear on the development of the new idea. In terms of the dots in Figure 2.15 we want to activate every blue dot students have that is related to the new red dot we want them to learn. It is through thinking, talking, and writing, that we can help students reflect on how mathematical ideas are connected to each other.

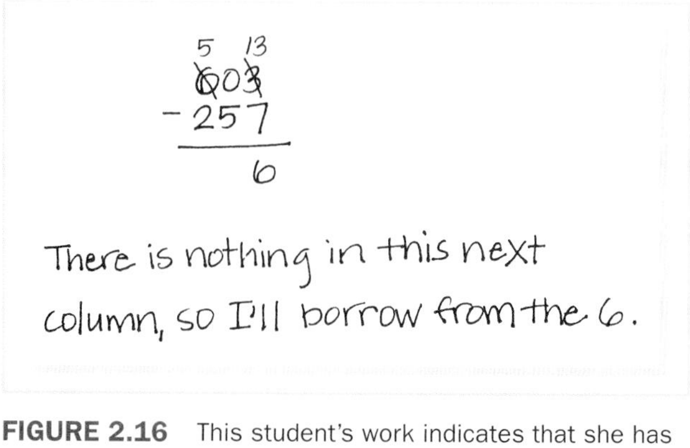

Encourage Multiple Approaches. Encourage students to use strategies that make sense to them. The student whose work is presented in Figure 2.16 may not understand the algorithm she used. If instead she were asked to use her

FIGURE 2.16 This student's work indicates that she has a misconception about place value and regrouping.

own approach to find the difference, she might be able to get to a correct solution and build on her understanding of place value and subtraction.

Even learning a basic fact, like 7×8, can have better results if a teacher promotes multiple strategies. Imagine a class where students discuss and share clever ways to figure out the product. One student might think of 5 eights (40) and then 2 more eights (16) to equal 56. Another may have learned 7×7 (49) and added on 7 more to get 56. Still another might think "8 sevens" and take half of the sevens (4×7) to get 28 and double 28 to get 56. A class discussion sharing these ideas brings to the fore a wide range of useful mathematical "dots" relating addition and multiplication concepts.

Engage Students in Productive Struggle.

Have you ever just wanted to think through something yourself without being interrupted or told how to do it? Yet, how often in mathematics class does this happen? As soon as a student pauses in solving a problem the teacher steps in to show or explain. While this may initially get the student to an answer faster, it does not help the student learn mathematics—engaging in productive struggle is what helps students learn mathematics. As Piaget describes, learners are going to experience disequilibrium in developing new ideas. Let students know this disequilibrium is part of the process. This is also one of the findings mentioned earlier as key to developing conceptual understanding (Hiebert & Grouws, 2007).

Notice the importance of both words in "productive struggle." Students must have the tools and prior knowledge to solve a problem, and not be given a problem that is out of reach, or they will struggle without being productive; yet students should not be given tasks that are straightforward and easy or they will not be struggling with mathematical ideas. When students. even very young students, know that struggle is expected as part of the process of doing mathematics, they embrace the struggle and feel success when they reach a solution (Carter, 2008).

This means redefining what it means to "help" students! Rather than showing students how to do something, your role is to ask probing questions that keep students engaged in the productive struggle until they reach a solution. This communicates high expectations and maximizes students' opportunities to learn with understanding.

Treat Errors as Opportunities for Learning.

When students make errors, it can mean a misapplication of their prior knowledge in the new situation. Remember that from a constructivist perspective, the mind is sifting through what it knows in order to find useful approaches for the new situation. Students rarely give random responses, so their errors are insight into misconceptions they might have. For example, students comparing decimals may incorrectly apply "rules" of whole numbers, such as "the more digits, the bigger the number" (Martinie, 2014). Often one student's misconception is shared by others in the class and discussing the problem publicly can help other students understand (Hoffman, Breyfogle, & Dressler, 2009). You can introduce errors and ask students to imagine what might have led to that answer (Rathouz, 2011). This public negotiation of meaning allows students to construct deeper meaning for the mathematics they are learning.

Scaffold New Content.

The practice of *scaffolding*, often associated with sociocultural theory, is based on the idea that a task otherwise outside of a student's ZPD can become accessible if it is carefully structured. For concepts completely new to students, the learning requires more structure or assistance, including the use of tools like manipulatives or more assistance from peers. As students become more comfortable with the content, the scaffolds are removed and the student becomes more independent. Scaffolding can provide support for those students who may not have a robust collection of "blue dots."

Honor Diversity.

Finally, and importantly, these theories emphasize that each learner is unique, with a different collection of prior knowledge and cultural experiences. Since new knowledge is built on existing knowledge and experience, effective teaching incorporates and builds on what the students bring to the classroom, honoring those experiences. Thus, lessons begin with eliciting prior experiences, and understandings and contexts for the lessons are selected based on students' knowledge and experiences. Some students will not have all the "blue dots" they need—it is your job to provide experiences where those blue dots are developed and then connected to the concept being learned.

Classroom culture influences the individual learning of your students. As stated previously, you should support a range of approaches and strategies for doing mathematics. Students' ideas should be valued and included in classroom discussion of the mathematics. This shift in practice, away from the teacher telling one way to do the problem, establishes a classroom culture where ideas are valued. This approach values the uniqueness of each individual.

Create a Classroom Environment for Doing Mathematics. Classrooms where students are making sense of mathematics do not happen by accident—they happen because the teacher establishes practices and expectations that encourage risk taking, reasoning, sharing, and so on. The list below provides expectations that are often cited as ones that support students in doing mathematics (Clarke & Clarke, 2004; CCSSO, 2010; Hiebert et al., 1997; NCTM, 2007).

1. *Persistence, effort, and concentration are important in learning mathematics.* Engaging in productive struggle is important in learning! The more a student stays with a problem, the more likely they are to get it right. Getting a tough problem right leads to a stronger sense of accomplishment than getting a quick, easy problem correct.
2. *Students share their ideas.* Everyone's ideas are important, and hearing different ideas helps students to become strategic in selecting good strategies.
3. *Students listen to each other.* All students have something to contribute and these ideas should be considered and evaluated for whether they will work in that situation.
4. *Errors or strategies that didn't work are opportunities for learning.* Mistakes are opportunities for learning—why did that approach not work? Could it be adapted and work or is a completely different approach needed? Doing mathematics involves monitoring and reflecting on the process—catching and adjusting errors along the way.
5. *Students look for and discuss connections.* Students should see connections between different strategies to solve a particular problem, as well as connections to other mathematics concepts and to real contexts and situations. When students look for and discuss connections, they see mathematics as worthwhile and important, rather than an isolated collection of facts.

These five features are evident in what teachers do and what students do. You can observe videos, such as Cathy's Class (available at the companion website) to look for these classroom practices, as well as to see the extent to which students are becoming mathematically proficient. You might also visit classrooms or record your own teaching and use the Observation Tool: Classroom Environment for Doing Mathematics, as a way to see how you can establish such an environment in your own classroom.

 Complete Self-Check 2.4: How Do Students Learn Mathematics?

 # Connecting the Dots

It seems appropriate to close this chapter by connecting some dots, especially because the ideas represented here are the foundation for the approach to each topic in the content chapters. This chapter began with discussing what *doing* mathematics is and challenging you to do some mathematics. Each of these tasks offered opportunities to make connections between mathematics concepts—connecting the blue dots.

Second, you read about what is important to know about mathematics—that having relational knowledge (knowledge in which blue dots are well connected) requires conceptual and procedural understanding as well as other proficiencies. The problems that you solved in the first section emphasized concepts and procedures while placing you in a position to use strategic competence, adaptive reasoning, and a productive disposition.

Finally, you read how learning theory—the importance of having opportunities to connect the dots—connects to mathematics learning. The best learning opportunities, according to constructivism and sociocultural theories, are those that engage learners in using their own knowledge and experience to solve problems through social interactions and reflection. This is what you were asked to do in the four tasks. Did you learn something new about mathematics? Did you connect an idea that you had not previously connected?

This chapter focused on connecting the dots between theory and practice—building a case that your teaching must focus on opportunities for students to develop their own networks of blue dots. As you plan and design instruction, you should constantly reflect on how to elicit prior knowledge by designing tasks that reflect the social and cultural backgrounds of students, to challenge students to think critically and creatively, and to include a comprehensive treatment of mathematics.

 Complete Self-Check 2.5: Connecting the Dots

REFLECTIONS ON CHAPTER 2

WRITING TO LEARN

1. How would you describe what it means to "do mathematics"?

2. Select three of the verbs for doing mathematics. For each, think about what it looks like when a student is "doing" it, then explain or draw a picture of what it might look like.

3. Why is conceptual understanding important?

4. Describe how "Two Machines, One Job" may be implemented in a way that reflects constructivist and/or sociocultural learning theory.

FOR DISCUSSION AND EXPLORATION

- Consider the following task and respond to these three questions.
- Some people say that to add four consecutive numbers, you add the first and the last numbers and multiply by 2.
- Is this always true? How do you know? (Stoessiger & Edmunds, 1992)

   a. What features of "doing mathematics" does it have?
   b. What web of ideas do you need to draw on to make sense of the problem?
   c. To what extent does it task have the potential to develop mathematical proficiency?

- Not every educator believes in the constructivist-oriented approach to teaching mathematics. Some of their reasons include the following: There is not enough time to let kids discover everything. Basic facts and ideas are better taught through quality explanations. Students should not have to "reinvent the wheel." How would you respond to these arguments?

RESOURCES FOR CHAPTER 2

RECOMMENDED READINGS

Articles

Berkman, R. M. (2006). One, some, or none: Finding beauty in ambiguity. *Mathematics Teaching in the Middle School, 11*(7), 324–327.

This article offers a great teaching strategy for nurturing relational thinking. Examples of the engaging "one, some, or none" activity are given for geometry, number, and algebra activities.

Carter, S. (2008). Disequilibrium & questioning in the primary classroom: Establishing routines that help students learn. *Teaching Children Mathematics, 15*(3), 134–137.

This is a wonderful teacher's story of how she infused the constructivist notion of disequilibrium and the related idea of productive struggle to support learning in her first-grade class.

Hedges, M., Huinker, D., & Steinmeyer, M. (2005). Unpacking division to build teachers' mathematical knowledge. *Teaching Children Mathematics, 11*(9), 478–483.

This article describes the many concepts related to division.

Suh, J. (2007). Tying it all together: Classroom practices that promote mathematical proficiency for all students. *Teaching Children Mathematics, 14*(3), 163–169.

As the title implies, this is a great resource for connecting the NRC's Mathematics Proficiencies (National Research Council, 2001) to teaching.

Books

Lampert, M. (2001). *Teaching problems and the problems of teaching.* New Haven, CT: Yale University Press.

Lampert reflects on her personal experiences in teaching fifth grade and shares with us her perspectives on the many issues and complexities of teaching. It is wonderfully written and easily accessed at any point in the book.

Mason, J., Burton, L., & Stacey, K. (2010). *Thinking mathematically* (2nd ed.). Harlow, England: Pearson Education.

This classic book is about doing mathematics. There are excellent problems to explore along the way, with strategy suggestions. It is an engaging book that will help you learn more about your own problem solving and become a better teacher of mathematics.

CHAPTER 3

Teaching through Problem Solving

LEARNER OUTCOMES

After reading this chapter and engaging in the embedded activities and reflections, you should be able to:

3.1 Compare different approaches to problem solving in mathematics teaching and learning.

3.2 Describe features of a worthwhile mathematical task, including how to find, adapt, or create one.

3.3 Connect the ideas for creating a worthwhile task to the teaching of concepts and procedures.

3.4 Explain how to engage students in classroom discourse, including classroom discussions and in writing.

3.5 Justify why using worthwhile tasks and classroom discourse are important to the learning of all students.

Imagine yourself in a mathematics classroom. What are students working on? What are they talking about? Likely students will be working on a task carefully selected by the teacher that allows them to engage in doing mathematics. Doing mathematics means that students are engaged in learning mathematics through reasoning and problem solving. *Principles to Actions* (NCTM, 2014) includes reasoning and problem solving as one of eight mathematics teaching practices, explaining that effective teachers engage students in solving and talking about tasks that can be solved in different ways by different students. The first of the CCSS-M (CCSSO, 2010) explains that mathematically proficient students are able to make sense of a situation, select solution paths, consider alternative strategies, and monitor their progress—problem solve. In this chapter, we focus on how to teach through problem solving, including how to select worthwhile tasks and facilitate student engagement (e.g., talking and writing) in those tasks.

 ## Problem Solving

Our understanding of how people learn has changed dramatically in the past two decades (see Chapter 2). And, the world in which we live and work has also changed dramatically. What do you remember about the types of problems or tasks that you were expected to do in school? How were you expected to engage in them? Although it is changing, many students are still given problems in which they are told exactly how to solve them.

Skills needed in the 21st-century workplace are less about being able to compute and more about being able to design solution strategies. These include critical thinking, communication, collaboration, and creativity, as well as being able to use technology (Partnership for 21st Century Skills, n.d.). Students engaged in these inquiry-based or problem-based practices are encouraged to ask: Why? What would happen if? What is another way? How does this way compare to that way? Will this always work? Inquiry is a disposition of openness, curiosity, and wonder (Clifford & Marinucci, 2008; Cochran-Smith & Lytle, 2011). This disposition comes naturally to young students—our goal as teachers is to nurture it, not squelch it.

Teaching for Problem Solving

Schroeder and Lester (1989) refer to this role of problems as teaching *for* problem solving, one of three ways to use problems in learning mathematics. Each is briefly discussed here.

Teaching for problem solving starts with learning the abstract concept and then moving to solving problems as a way to apply the learned skills (explain-practice-apply). For example, students learn the algorithm for adding fractions and, once that is mastered, solve story problems that involve adding fractions.

Teaching *for* problem solving is engrained in mathematics teaching practice: The teacher presents the mathematics, the students practice the skill, and finally, students solve story problems that require using that skill. Unfortunately, this approach to mathematics teaching has not been successful for many students in understanding mathematics concepts. Why? Here are a few reasons:

- It requires that all students have the necessary prior knowledge to understand the teacher's explanations—which is rarely, if ever, the case.
- It communicates that there is only one way to solve the problem, misrepresenting the field of mathematics and disempowering students who naturally may want to try to do it their own way.
- It positions the student as a passive learner, dependent on the teacher to present ideas, rather than as an independent thinker with the capability and responsibility for solving the problem.
- It decreases the likelihood a student will attempt a novel problem without explicit instructions on how to solve it. But that's what doing mathematics is—figuring out an approach to solve the problem at hand.

Some teachers may think that showing students how to solve a set of problems is the most helpful approach for students, preventing struggling while saving time. However, it is the struggle that leads to learning, so teachers must resist the natural inclination to take away the struggle. The best way to help students is to not help too much. In summary, teaching *for* problem solving—in particular modeling and explaining a strategy for how to solve the problem—can actually make students worse at solving problems and doing mathematics, not better.

In the past, we assumed that walking students through a procedure or showing a step-by-step method for solving a particular type of problem was the most helpful approach to learning. However, students learn by *doing* mathematics, engaging in challenging but accessible tasks, and employing their own ideas and strategies.

Teaching about Problem Solving

Students need guidance on *how* to problem solve. This includes the process of problem solving and learning strategies that can help in solving problems—for example, "draw a picture."

Four-Step Problem Solving Process. George Pólya, a famous mathematician, wrote a classic book, *How to Solve It* (1945), which outlined four steps for problem solving. These widely adopted steps for problem solving have appeared and continue to appear in many resource books and textbooks. Explicitly teaching these four steps to students can improve their ability to think mathematically. The four steps are described very briefly in the following list:

1. *Understanding the problem.* First, you must figure out what the problem is about and identify what question or problem is being posed.

2. *Devising a plan.* Next, you think about how to solve the problem. Will you want to write an equation? Will you want to model the problem with a manipulative? (See the next section, "Problem Solving Strategies.")

3. *Carrying out the plan.* This step is the implementation of your selected plan.

4. *Looking back.* This final step, arguably the most important as well as most often skipped, is when you determine whether your answer from step 3 answers the problem as originally understood in step 1. Does your answer make sense? If not, loop back to step 2 and select a different strategy to solve the problem, or loop back to step 3 to fix something within your strategy.

Most recently, the ideas of Pólya have been infused in the Standards for Mathematical Practice, in particular the first practice of making sense of problems and persevering in solving them (CCSSO, 2010). The beauty of Pólya's framework is its generalizability; it can and should be applied to many different types of problems, from simple computational exercises to authentic and worthwhile multistep problems.

Problem Solving Strategies. Strategies for solving problems are identifiable methods for approaching a task. These strategies are "habits of mind" associated with thinking mathematically (Levasseur & Cuoco, 2003; Mark, Cuoco, Glodenberg, & Sword, 2010). Students select or design a strategy as they devise a plan (Pólya's step 2). The following labeled strategies are commonly encountered in grades K–8, though not all of them are used at every grade level.

- *Visualize.* Seeing is not only believing—it is also a means for understanding! Using manipulatives, acting it out, drawing a picture, or using dynamic software are ways to help represent, understand, and communicate mathematical concepts.

- *Look for patterns.* Searching for patterns, including regularity and repetition in everyday, spatial, symbolic, or imaginary contexts, is an important entry point into thinking mathematically. Pattern seeking is an important habit of mind and one of the CCSS-M Mathematical Practices. Patterns in number and operations play a huge role in helping students learn and master basic skills starting at the earliest levels and continuing into middle and high school.

- *Predict and check for reasonableness.* This is sometimes called "Guess and Check," but students are predicting more than they are guessing. This is not as easy as it may sound, as it involves making a strategic attempt, reflecting, and adjusting if necessary. The quantitative analysis (the answer is too small or too big) supports student sense making and is a bridge to algebra (Guerrero, 2010).

- *Formulate conjectures and justify claims.* As students interpret a problem, making conjectures and then testing them can help students solve the problem and deepen their understanding of the mathematical relationships. This reasoning is central to doing mathematics (Lannin, Ellis, & Elliott, 2011).

- *Create a list, table, or chart.* Systematically accounting for possible outcomes in a situation can provide insights into its solution. Students may make an organized list, a table or t-chart, or chart information on a graph. The list, table, or chart is used to search for patterns in order to solve the problem.

- *Simplify or change the problem.* Simplifying the quantities in a problem can make a situation easier to understand and analyze. This can lead to insights that can be applied to the original, more complex quantities in a problem. One way to simplify the problem is to test specific examples. The results of testing examples can provide insights into the structure of the task.

- *Write an equation.* Using or inventing symbols, numbers, notations, and equations are compact ways of modeling a situation. Writing an equation can provide insights into the structure of the problem and be used in solving the task.

Mathematical problem solving is founded in curiosity. The ways of thinking described here become the tools by which students can enter into unfamiliar and novel tasks. These strategies are not distinct, but interrelated. For example, creating a list is a way of looking for patterns. When students employ one of these strategies, it should be identified, highlighted, and discussed. Labeling a strategy provides a useful means for students to talk about their methods, which can help students make connections between and among strategies and representations. Over time, these mathematical ways of thinking will become habits.

It is important not to "proceduralize" problem solving. In other words, don't take the problem solving out of problem solving by telling students the strategy they should pick and how to do it. Instead, pose a problem that lends itself to different ways of thinking and allow students to approach the problem in a way that makes the most sense and is best supported by their own reasoning, such as the example here.

Eight friends met for a skating party. Each friend shook hands once with everyone else. How many handshakes occurred?

Access the companion website for an Activity Page for this task. Without suggesting any strategy, ask students to explore this problem, design a solution strategy, implement it, and be ready to share. The following are common solution strategies:

Visualize by acting it out or drawing a picture:

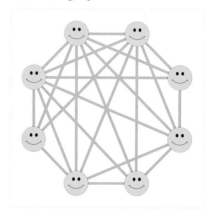

Create a smaller problem and record in a table:

Number of Friends	2	3	4	5	6	7	8
Number of Handshakes	1	3	6	10	15	21	28

Write an equation:

The first friend can shake 7 hands, the next friend only has 6 hands to shake (she already shook hands with the first friend), and so on:

$$7 + 6 + 5 + 4 + 3 + 2 + 1 + 0 = 28$$

During the sharing of results, you can help students understand the strategies they did not use and see connections among the strategies, and you can highlight a particular strategy so that more students are able to use that strategy the next time.

Similar problems can be posed to support the development of these reasoning strategies for example:

1. If six softball teams play each other once in a round-robin tournament, how many games will be needed?

2. How many blocks are needed for the 10th staircase?

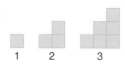

Teaching through Problem Solving

This approach means that students learn mathematics *through* inquiry. They explore real contexts, problems, situations, and models, and from those explorations they learn mathematics. Teaching *through* problem solving might be described as upside down from teaching *for* problem solving—with the problem or task presented at the beginning of a lesson and related knowledge or skills emerging from exploring the problem. For example, in exploring the situation of combining $\frac{1}{2}$ and $\frac{1}{3}$ feet of ribbon to figure out how long the ribbon is, students would be led to discover the procedure for adding fractions.

Mathematical ideas become the outcomes of the problem solving experience rather than elements that must be taught before problem solving (Hiebert et al., 1996, 1997). Furthermore, the process of solving problems is completely interwoven with the learning; children are *learning* mathematics by *doing* mathematics and by doing mathematics they are learning mathematics (Cai, 2010).

Teaching through problem solving acknowledges what we now know about what it means to learn and do mathematics (see Chapter 2). Our knowing is always changing, incomplete, situated in context, and interconnected. What we learn becomes part of our expanding and evolving network of ideas—a network without endpoints. What we learn through problem solving and inquiry can change what we thought we knew before, and can be the basis for asking new questions that can lead to new learning (Thomas & Brown, 2011).

In the last two decades, much more attention has been given to how to use inquiry in teaching and learning mathematics (e.g., Goos, 2004; Jaworski, 2006; Schoenfeld, 1996; Towers, 2010). Teaching through problem solving shifts the focus from learning about mathematics through the teacher's unveiling of a new idea to engaging with mathematics to discover important mathematical concepts. Teaching through problem solving positions students to engage in inquiry. Students:

- Ask questions
- Determine solution paths
- Use mathematical tools
- Make conjectures
- Seek out patterns
- Communicate findings
- Make connections to other content
- Make generalizations
- Reflect on results

Hopefully this sounds familiar. This list reflects the Standards for Mathematical Practice (CCSS-M) and reflects components of being mathematically proficient. Teaching through problem solving is a conceptually focused, process-driven, student-centered approach to instruction. Teachers employ students' creativity, reasoning skills, prior knowledge, and perseverance.

 Complete Self-Check 3.1: Problem Solving

 ## Features of Worthwhile Tasks

In order to create classroom experiences for students where they can engage in learning through inquiry, problems or tasks that have the potential to engage students in this way must be identified or created. Such problems are referred to as "worthwhile tasks" or "rich tasks." As a teacher, you need to know what constitutes a worthwhile task and where to find or create such tasks. A worthwhile task (https://www.youtube.com/watch?v=XI3-52B0V6s) is problematic—it poses a question for which (1) the students have no prescribed or memorized rules or methods to solve and (2) there is not a perception that there is one "correct" solution method (Hiebert et al., 1997). Worthwhile tasks offer boundaries or constraints within which students have the freedom to explore.

A worthwhile task may take on many different forms. It might be clearly defined or open-ended; it may involve problem solving or problem posing; it may include words or be purely symbols; it may take only a few minutes to solve or may take weeks to investigate; it may be real-life or abstract. What makes it a rich task is that it is problematic, in other words, it engages students in figuring out how to solve it. A task can be problematic at first and then become routine as a student's knowledge and experience grows. For example, a story problem such as, "Molly's team has scored 2 goals more than the other team. 8 goals have been scored. What is the score of the game?" could be a rich task to explore in grade 1 or 2, but be "routine" for older or more mathematically advanced students. Here is one for you to try (see also the Missing Numbers Activity Page):

$$10 + \blacksquare = 4 + (3 + \blacktriangle)$$

Find numbers for each shape to make the equation true.

Find more pairs of numbers that will make the equation true.

What do you notice about the numbers for any correct solution?

Is this type of task familiar to you? Do you know what you are going to do to find a solution? If you experienced uncertainty about how to solve it, then this could be nonroutine, and thereby position you to engage in inquiry—a worthwhile mathematical task. On the other hand, this could be a problem that immediately triggers an approach and you go directly to employing that approach. In this case, it may be appropriate practice, but it is not a task that is likely to provide you with new mathematical insights or knowledge.

High Levels of Cognitive Demand

Worthwhile tasks are cognitively demanding, meaning they involve higher-level thinking. Low cognitive demand tasks (also called *routine problems* or *lower-level tasks*) involve stating facts, following known procedures (computation), and solving routine problems. Higher-level thinking tasks, on the other hand, involve making connections, analyzing information, and drawing conclusions (Smith & Stein, 1998). For example, if you ask students to find the area of a rectangle, there is a different level of thinking than if you ask students to create a "blueprint" of a room and to figure the area of the floor. Table 3.1 provides a well-known framework that is useful in helping to determine whether a task is set up to challenge students.

As you read through the descriptors for the low-level and high-level cognitive demand descriptors, you will notice that the low-level tasks are routine and straightforward. In other words, they do not engage students in productive struggle. Conversely, with the high-level (nonroutine) tasks, students not only engage in productive struggle as they work, but they employ problem solving strategies and are challenged to make connections to concepts and to other relevant knowledge.

Multiple Entry and Exit Points

Because your students will likely have a wide range of experiences in mathematics, it is important to use problems that have multiple entry points, meaning that the task can be approached in a variety of ways and has varying degrees of challenge within it. Having multiple entry points can accommodate the diversity of learners in your classroom because students are encouraged to use a variety of strategies that are supported by their prior experiences. Having a choice of strategies can lower the anxiety of students, particularly English language learners, or ELLs (Murrey, 2008). Students are encouraged to engage with the task in a way that makes sense to them, rather than trying to recall or replicate a procedure shown to them.

Tasks should also have multiple exit points, or various ways to express solutions that reveal a range of mathematical sophistication and have the potential to generate new questions. Even though students might initially select an inefficient or less sophisticated approach, as ideas are exchanged during and after the problem is solved, students have opportunities to understand and try out other approaches. As students discuss ideas, draw pictures, use manipulatives, or act out a problem, defend their strategy, critique the reasoning of others, and write about their thinking, they are engaged in higher-level thinking and the teacher is able to gather useful formative assessment data about students' mathematical understanding.

TABLE 3.1   LEVELS OF COGNITIVE DEMAND

Low-Level Cognitive Demand	High-Level Cognitive Demand
Memorization Tasks ● Involve either producing previously learned facts, rules, formulas, or definitions or memorizing ● Are routine—involving exact reproduction of previously learned procedure ● Have no connection to related concepts	**Procedures with Connections Tasks** ● Focus students' attention on the use of procedures for the purpose of developing deeper levels of understanding of mathematical concepts and ideas ● Suggest general procedures that have close connections to underlying conceptual ideas ● Are usually represented in multiple ways (e.g., visuals, manipulatives, symbols, problem situations) ● Require that students engage with the conceptual ideas that underlie the procedures in order to successfully complete the task
Procedures without Connections Tasks ● Specifically call for use of the procedure ● Are straightforward, with little ambiguity about what needs to be done and how to do it ● Have no connection to related concepts ● Are focused on producing correct answers rather than developing mathematical understanding ● Require no explanations or explanations; focus on the procedure only	**Doing Mathematics Tasks** ● Require complex and nonalgorithmic thinking (i.e., nonroutine—there is not a predictable, known approach) ● Require students to explore and understand the nature of mathematical concepts, processes, or relationships ● Demand self-monitoring or self-regulation of one's own cognitive processes ● Require students to access relevant knowledge in working through the task ● Require students to analyze the task and actively examine task constraints that may limit possible solution strategies and solutions ● Require considerable cognitive effort

Source: Adapted from Smith, M. S., & Stein, M. K. (1998). Selecting and creating mathematical tasks: From research to practice. *Mathematics Teaching in the Middle School, 3*(5), 344–350. Reprinted with permission.

Consider the opportunities for multiple entry and exit points in the following kindergarten or first-grade tasks.

TASK 1: [The teacher places a bowl of objects (e.g., toy cars) on the table.] Do we have enough [toy cars] for everyone in the class?

TASK 2: [The teacher gives each student a page with pictures of cars copied in rows (see Do We Have Enough? Activity Page). Do we have enough cars for everyone in the class?

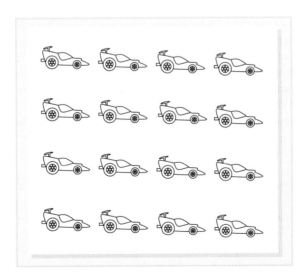

If toy cars (or a cube representing a car) are available, as in the first task, the children are likely to pass them out to see if there are enough cars and miss any opportunity to think mathematically about the situation. The second task is more problematic and can be approached in different ways, providing valuable insights into their thinking. Students might count the cars. As they count, you can observe their thinking: Do they start at the top and count across the rows? Or do they haphazardly count and miss or double-count? Do they count by ones?

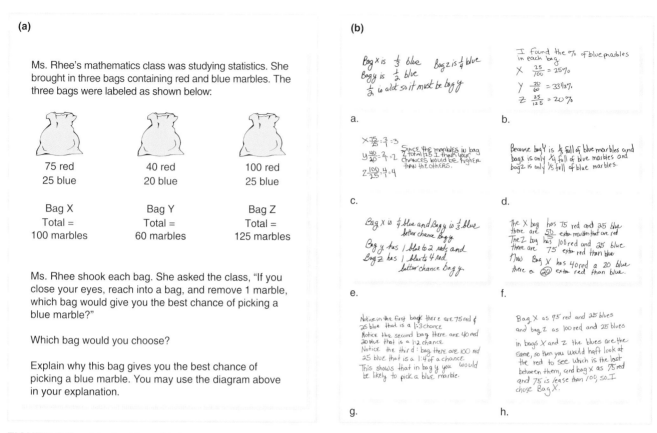

FIGURE 3.1 A task with multiple entry and exit points, as illustrated by the range of student solutions.

Source: Smith, M. S., Bill, V., & Hughes, E. K. (2008). Thinking Through a Lesson: Successfully Implementing High-Level Tasks. *Mathematics Teaching in the Middle School, 14*(3), 132–138. Reprinted with permission.

By twos? By fours? Instead of counting cars, students might count their friends in the class first. Or, students might "assign" a car to each friend, writing names on each car. Counting the cars is just one aspect of the task; students must also decide how that number compares to the number of students in the class. Does a student just know that the number of cars is greater or less than the number of students? Do they represent each child in the class with a counter, and match a counter with a pictured car? Do they look for the two numbers on a hundreds chart or number line to compare? Clearly, the second task offers many more opportunities for all children to engage in the task in a variety of ways.

Figure 3.1(a) provides a high cognitive demand task that has multiple entry and exit points.

 Pause & Reflect

Before studying the solutions in Figure 3.1(b), read the problem, select a strategy and solve it. ●

Figure 3.1(b) illustrates a range of solutions. Student (b) used percentages as a way to compare; student (d) found simplified fractions to compare quantities; student (g) used part-part ratios to reason about the quantities. In addition, several solutions reveal student misconceptions. Notice that in solution (a), the student has recorded part-part ratios, but then is comparing the values as though they are fractions (part-whole) and in solution (f) the student is comparing differences, rather than attending to the multiplicative relationships. During a classroom discussion, the teacher's role is to ensure that the strategies are strategically shared (perhaps sharing some less advanced strategies first or related strategies together). In doing this, students can clear up misconceptions, make connections among the strategies and among mathematical ideas (i.e., ratio, fractions, percents, and probability), and thereby advance their understanding of mathematics (Smith, Bill, & Hughes, 2008).

Relevant Contexts

Certainly one of the most powerful features of a worthwhile task is that the problem that begins the lesson can get students excited about learning mathematics. Compare these two sixth-grade introductory tasks on ratios:

"Today we are going to explore ratios and see how ratios can be used to compare amounts."

"In a minute, I am going to read to you a passage from Harry Potter about how big Hagrid is. We are going to use ratios to compare our heights and widths to Hagrid's."

Contexts can also be used to learn about cultures (such as those of students in your classroom) and connect to other subjects. Children's literature and links to other disciplines are explored here for their potential to engage students in learning mathematics.

Children's Literature. Children's literature is a rich source of problems at all levels, not just primary. Children's stories can be used to create high cognitive demand tasks with multiple entry points. An example of literature lending itself to mathematical problems is the very popular children's picture book *Two of Everything* (Hong, 1993). In this magical Chinese folktale, a couple finds a pot that doubles whatever is put into it. (Imagine where the story goes when Mrs. Haktak falls in the pot!) In a second-grade classroom, the students can calculate how many students would be in their class if the whole class fell in the Magic Pot. Figure 3.2 illustrates different ways that students solved the problem (multiple entry points) and different ways they explained and illustrated how they figured it out (multiple exit points). Notice that the student using the hundreds chart has a wrong answer. The teacher will need to follow up to determine whether this was a copy error or a misconception.

The great thing about literature is that there are often several tasks that can be launched from the story. In this case, the Magic Pot can start doing other unexpected things, like tripling what is put in, or increasing what is put in by 5, and so on—making it a wonderful context for input-output activities to build a foundation for the later study of functions (see Suh, 2007a, and Wickett, Kharas, and Burns, 2002, for more ideas on this book).

In *Harry Potter and the Sorcerer's Stone* (Rowling, 1998), referred to earlier, the lesson is based on the author's description of Hagrid as twice as tall and five times as wide as the average man. Students in grades 2–3 can cut strips of paper that are as tall as they are and as wide as their shoulders are (you can cut strips from cash register rolls). Then they can figure out how big Hagrid would be if he were twice as tall and five times as wide as they are. In grades 4–5, students can create a table that shows each student's height and width and look for a pattern (it turns out to be about 3 to 1). Then they can figure out Hagrid's height and width and see whether they keep the same ratio (it is 5 to 2). In grades 6–8,

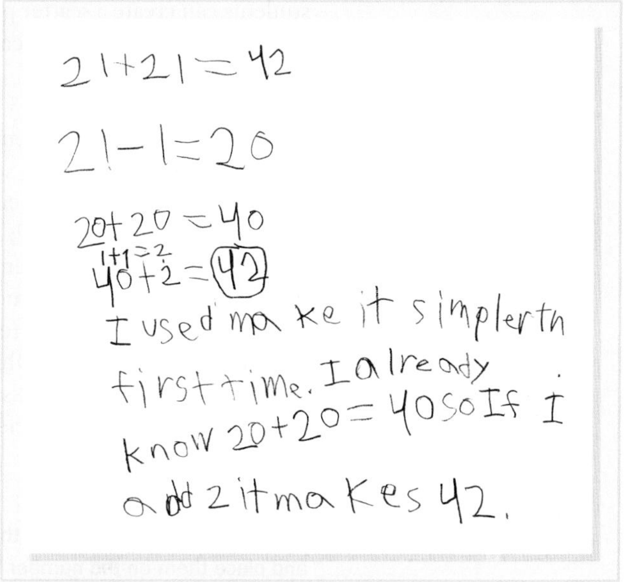
21+21=42
21-1=20
20+20=40
1+1=2
40+2=42
I used make it simplerth first time. I already know 20+20=40 so If I add 2 it makes 42.

Robbie adds tens and ones to solve.

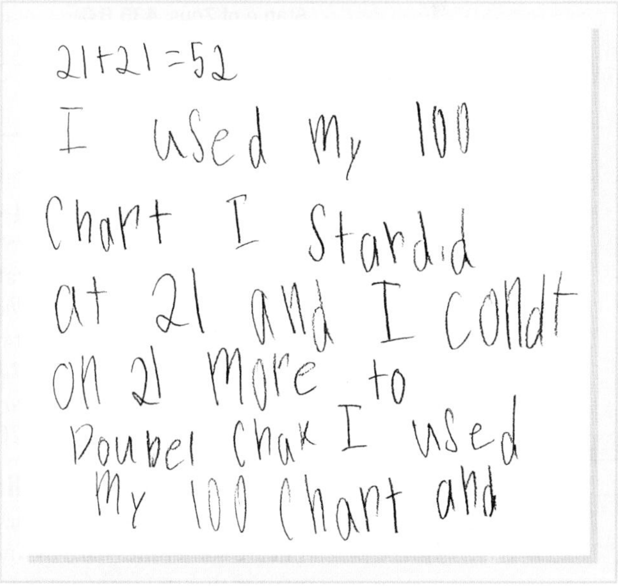
21+21=52
I used my 100 Chart I Stard.d at 21 and I condt on 21 more to Doubel Chak I used my 100 Chart and

Kylee uses a hundreds chart and counts on.

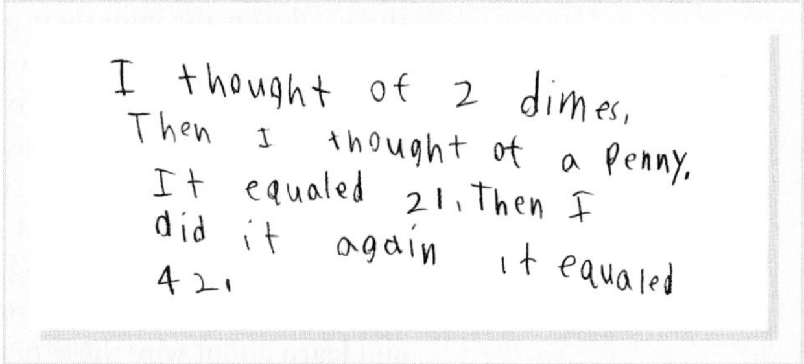
I thought of 2 dimes, Then I thought of a Penny, It equaled 21, Then I did it again it equaled 42,

Benjamin uses the context of money to combine.

FIGURE 3.2 Second graders use different problem solving strategies to figure out how many students there would be if their class of 21 were doubled.

students can create a scatter plot of their widths and heights and see where Hagrid's data would be plotted on the graph. Measurement, number, and algebra content are all embedded in this example.

Whether students are 5 or 13, literature resonates with their experiences and imaginations, making them more enthusiastic about solving the related mathematics problems and more likely to learn and to see mathematics as a useful tool for exploring the world. Several recent teacher resources focus on using nonfiction literature in teaching mathematics (Bay-Williams & Martinie, 2009; Petersen, 2004; Sheffield & Gallagher, 2004). Nonfiction literature can include newspapers, magazines, and the Web—all great sources for problems that have the added benefit of students learning about the world around them.

There are books of lists (e.g., Scholastic Book of Lists (Buckley & Stremme, 2006) and world record books, for example, which provide many great contexts for exploring the world, and comparing world data to your class. Dates can lend to creating number lines. For example, the dates for the seven wonders of the ancient world can be used to explore negative numbers.

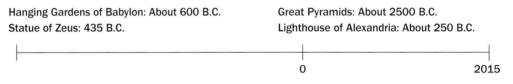

Where on the number line do these wonders of the ancient world go? Can you find the other wonders and place them on the number line?

Hanging Gardens of Babylon: About 600 B.C. Great Pyramids: About 2500 B.C.
Statue of Zeus: 435 B.C. Lighthouse of Alexandria: About 250 B.C.

In Section II, each end-of-chapter resources section includes "Literature Connections," quick descriptions of picture books, poetry, and novels that can be used to explore the mathematics of that chapter. Literature ideas are also found in articles in professional journal articles (e.g., *Teaching Children Mathematics*), textbooks and curriculum resources teacher guides, and books dedicated to using literature to teach mathematics (e.g., *Math Solutions Math & Literature Series, Using Children's Literature to Teach Problem Solving in Math* (White, 2014); *Exploring Mathematics through Literature* (Thiessen, 2004) and *New Visions for Linking Literature in Mathematics* (Whitin & Whitin, 2004)).

Links to Other Disciplines. Finding relevant contexts for engaging all students is always a challenge in classes of diverse learners. Using contexts familiar for all students can be effective but are sometimes hard to find. An excellent source for problems, therefore, is the other subject matter that students are studying. Elementary teachers can pull ideas from the topics being taught in social studies, science, and language arts; likewise, middle school teachers can link to these subjects through their grade-level colleagues. Other familiar contexts such as art, sports, and pop culture can also be valuable.

In kindergarten, students can link their study of natural systems in science to mathematics, for example, by sorting leaves based on color, smooth or jagged edges, feel of the leaf, and shape. Students learn about rules for sorting and can use Venn diagrams to keep track of their sorts. They can observe and analyze what is common and different in leaves from different trees. Sorting and measuring, topics in both mathematics and science, are more concepts to explore with leaves. Older students can find the perimeter and area of various types of leaves and learn about why these perimeters and areas differ.

AIMS (Activities in Mathematics and Science), a series of teacher resource books integrating mathematics and science, has fantastic ideas in every book. In *Looking at Lines* (AIMS, 2001), a middle school AIMS book, students hang paper clips from a handmade balance to learn about linear equations (mathematics) and force and motion (science). Visit the AIMS website for more information.

The social studies curriculum is rich with opportunities to do mathematics. Timelines of historic events are excellent opportunities for students to work on the relative sizes of numbers and to make better sense of history. Students can explore the areas and populations of various countries, provinces, or states and compare the population densities, while in social studies they can talk about how life differs between regions with 200 people living in a square mile and regions with 5 people per square mile.

Evaluating and Adapting Tasks

Throughout this book, in student textbooks, on the Internet, at workshops you attend, and in articles you read, you will find suggestions for tasks that *someone* believes are effective for teaching a particular mathematics concept. Yet a large quantity of what is readily available falls short when measured against the standards of being a worthwhile task. Researchers have found that teachers benefit from using an intentional selection process to help in the selection of worthwhile tasks (Barlow, 2010; Breyfogle & Williams, 2008–2009).

The Task Evaluation and Selection Guide in Figure 3.3 is designed for this purpose—for you to use to ensure that a task you are considering has the maximum potential to help your students learn mathematics. The idea is not to have all the boxes checked off, but to consider to what extent the task you are analyzing meets these criteria. A task could rate very high on the number of problem solving strategies, but miss the mark in terms of being relevant for students, hence you decide to trade out the context for something more interesting. Or, the task is complete with the features and problem solving strategies, but it does not match your mathematical goals for the lesson. You may then alter the task to focus on the mathematics you have selected or save it for when it is a better match.

Just as students become adept at problem solving strategies and can access them without referring to a list of possible strategies, hopefully the ideas on this Task Evaluation and Selection Guide will become part of your problem solving as you decide whether to use a particular task with your students.

Imagine that you are teaching fourth grade and are seeking a worthwhile task for this goal from CCSS-M (this topic is common to grade 4 or 5):

4.G.A.2: Classify two-dimensional figures based on the presence or absence of parallel or perpendicular lines, or the presence or absence of angles of a specified size. Recognize right

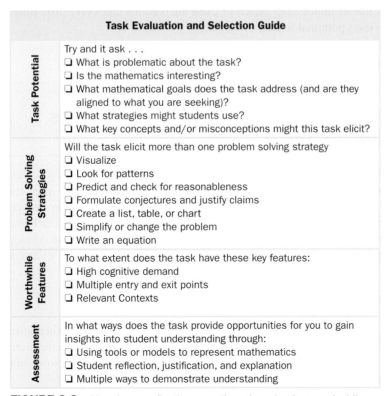

Task Evaluation and Selection Guide	
Task Potential	Try and it ask . . . ❏ What is problematic about the task? ❏ Is the mathematics interesting? ❏ What mathematical goals does the task address (and are they aligned to what you are seeking)? ❏ What strategies might students use? ❏ What key concepts and/or misconceptions might this task elicit?
Problem Solving Strategies	Will the task elicit more than one problem solving strategy ❏ Visualize ❏ Look for patterns ❏ Predict and check for reasonableness ❏ Formulate conjectures and justify claims ❏ Create a list, table, or chart ❏ Simplify or change the problem ❏ Write an equation
Worthwhile Features	To what extent does the task have these key features: ❏ High cognitive demand ❏ Multiple entry and exit points ❏ Relevant Contexts
Assessment	In what ways does the task provide opportunities for you to gain insights into student understanding through: ❏ Using tools or models to represent mathematics ❏ Student reflection, justification, and explanation ❏ Multiple ways to demonstrate understanding

FIGURE 3.3 Use these reflective questions in selecting worthwhile tasks.

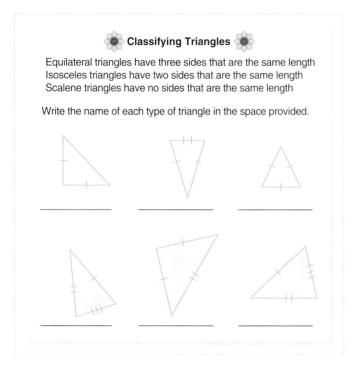

FIGURE 3.4 Example of a categorizing triangles worksheet.

triangles as a category, and identify right triangles. (CCSSO, 2010, p. 32)

You type "classify triangles" into a web search. Hundreds of links and worksheet images appear. Figure 3.4 is a likely replica of what you might find.

 Pause & Reflect

How does this task measure up on the Task Evaluation and Selection Guide? How might you adapt the task so that it rates higher on some of these measures of a worthwhile task? ●

This worksheet appears to match the learning goals, but it does not involve problem solving strategies, or include high-level cognitive demand, multiple entry points, or relevant contexts. How might you adapt this task? One possibility is remove the tick marks telling which sides are the same, distribute just the grid of triangles, letter them, and ask students to write similarities and differences between pairs of triangles. This provides multiple entry points and a high level of cognitive demand. Or, you might only use the list of terms at the top and ask students to identify examples of each in the room or in a picture book. Another option might be to cut out the triangles, ask students to create piles of what they consider the "same" triangles and to put names on their groups. In a later discussion, different possible ways to sort triangles can be discussed and appropriate terminology can be reinforced. Extensions might include asking students, "Can you build two triangles of different sizes that are both isosceles?" "Can you create a triangle with three obtuse angles? Why or why not?" "If a triangle is classified as [right], then which classifications for sides are possible or impossible?" Each of these adaptations takes very little time, and greatly increases the tasks potential to be worthwhile.

✓ Complete Self-Check 3.2: Features of Worthwhile Tasks

Developing Concepts and Procedures through Tasks

In Chapter 2, we discussed the importance of developing mathematical proficiency through conceptual understanding and procedural proficiency. Now that you know more about problem solving and the features of a worthwhile task, we can make a distinction between tasks that specifically target student's proficiency in mathematical concepts and in mathematical procedures (remembering that both are important and interrelated). Students can develop conceptual understanding or procedural proficiency through problem solving. Here we share six examples; the first three focus on concepts, the latter three on procedures.

Concepts

Learning mathematics involves developing rich connections between mathematical ideas. The more connections made, the richer the conceptual network becomes. By considering students' backgrounds and using worthwhile tasks, students can expand their network of connections and develop new mathematical concepts and new ways of thinking. Here are a few examples.

Concept: Partitioning   Grades: K–1

Think about six bowls of cereal placed at two different tables. Draw a picture to show a way that six bowls might be placed at two tables. Can you find more than one way? How many ways do you think there are?

In kindergarten or grade 1, students will likely determine one or two ways to decompose 6 on their own. By sharing the different possibilities, the teacher can ask them if they have found all the possible combinations. As one table grows from 0 to 6 bowls, the other table begins at 6 and shrinks by ones to 0 (seven ways!). Through this task, students can extend their understanding of the concept of partitioning to similar tasks, such as "How many ways can you put 10 stuffed animals into 2 baskets? From these specific examples, they can begin to generalize the pattern that they have noticed and determine how many combinations they will find when any number is partitioned into two parts.

Concept: Fractions Greater Than 1   Grades: 3–5

Place an X on the number line about where $\frac{11}{8}$ would be. Explain why you put your X where you did.

    0   2

Note that the task can be solved in variety of ways—for example, with a ruler or by folding a strip of paper. Students need to justify where they placed their mark. In the follow-up discussion, the teacher will be able to help the class refine ideas about fractions greater than 1 (for example, that 11 eighths are equivalent to a whole and 3 more eighths) and the importance of using benchmarks, in this case 1, to help estimate the relative size of numbers.

Concept: Comparing Ratios and Proportional Reasoning   Grades: 6–8

Jack and Jill were at the same spot at the bottom of a hill, hoping to fetch a pail of water. They both begin walking up the hill, Jack walking 5 yards every 25 seconds and Jill walking 3 yards every 10 seconds. Assuming constant walking rate, who will get to the pail of water first?

Students can engage in this task in a variety of ways. They can represent the problem visually with jumps on a number line or symbolically using a rate approach (determining the number of yards per second for each person). This task focuses on how students are able to compare ratios. By specializing and considering several examples, either in this context or another, students will begin to generalize a procedure for comparing ratios, which is the essence of proportional reasoning. See It's a Matter of Rates Expanded Lesson on the companion website for a full lesson on this task.

Procedures

Some teachers will use teaching *through* problem solving approach for concepts, but not for procedures. This creates a disconnect for students—why wouldn't they use their own strategies for procedures when they were designing strategies for the related concepts? Students can invent their own strategies for doing procedures and this should be valued and encouraged by teachers. (This point is elaborated throughout Section II of this book.) A few examples of tasks that elicit student-invented procedures are shared next.

Procedure: Adding Two-Digit Whole Numbers   Grades: 1–2

What is the sum of 48 and 25? How did you figure it out?

Even though there is no story or situation to resolve, this task is still problematic because students must figure out how they are going to approach the task. (They have not been taught the standard algorithm at this point.) Students might work on the problem using manipulatives, pictures, or mental strategies. After students have solved the problem in their own way, the teacher gathers the students together to hear one another's strategies and solutions (Russell, 1997). This following list contains just some of the approaches created by students in one second-grade classroom:

$4\boxed{8} + 2\boxed{5}$ (Boxed digits "help" them.)

$40 + 20 = 60$

$8 + 2 = 10$ $\boxed{3}$ (The 3 is left from the 5.)

$60 + 10 = 70$

$70 + 3 = 73$

$40 + 20 = 60$

$60 + 8 = 68$

$68 + 5 = 73$

$48 + 20 = 68$

$68 + 2$ ("from the 5") $= 70$

"Then I still have that 3 from the 5."

$70 + 3 = 73$

$25 + 25 = 50$ $\boxed{23}$

$50 + 23 = 73$

Teacher: Where does the 23 come from?

"It's sort of from the 48."

How did you split up the 48?

"20 and 20 and I split the 8 into 5 and 3."

$48 - 3 = 45$ $\boxed{3}$

$45 + 25 = 70$

$70 + 3 = 73$

In a similar way, procedures for other operations on whole numbers, decimals, and fractions can be invented and discussed.

Procedure: Division of Fractions   Grades: 5–7

Anthony is knitting scarves for gifts for his sisters. Each scarf is one yard long and he can knit $\frac{1}{4}$ of a scarf each day. How long will it take him to make 3 scarves?

When students explore this task without the label "division of fractions," they can approach the problem in multiples ways. Leah, Kelly, Jaden and MacKenna (see the companion website) solved the task applying what they knew, including skip counting by fourths (Leah), measurement equivalencies (Kelly), ratios of yards to days (Jaden), and rates of days per yards (MacKenna). To extend their thinking about scarf-making, they were asked what would happen if Anthony decided to use a different pattern and could now make $\frac{3}{4}$ of a yard in one day. A review of their second task shows that they used both their strategies and their answers from the first task in interesting ways. With more experiences with scarf-making with other rates, students can begin to connect to the concept of division and to generalize how solve such problems.

Procedures related to measurements can be taught through worthwhile tasks.

Procedure: Area of a Rectangle   Grades: 3–4

Find the area of the cover of your math book by covering it with color tiles. Repeat for the areas of books of various sizes. What patterns do you notice in covering the book? Is this pattern or rule true for covering any rectangle?

Most formulas can be developed through problem solving. For example, students can look at circular container lids to explore how the diameter relates to the circumference of a circle, or cut parallelograms to create rectangles in order to see how these formulas are related (see Chapter 19 for more on learning measurement through problem solving).

Teaching mathematical concepts and procedures through problem solving helps students go beyond acquiring isolated ideas toward developing a connected and increasingly complex network of mathematical understanding (Boaler, 2002; Cai, 2003, 2010; Carpenter, Franke, Jacobs, Fennema, & Empson, 1998; Lambdin, 2003; Lesh & Zawojewski, 2007).

What about Drill and Practice?

Drill and practice is present to at least some degree in nearly every classroom. Most lessons in traditional textbooks include a long section of exercises, followed by a few story problems, usually only using mathematics taught in that lesson (rather than incorporating and connecting to past ideas). In addition, drill-and-practice workbooks and software programs abound.

A question worth asking is, "What has all of this drill accomplished?" It has been an ever-present component of mathematics classes for decades and yet the adult population is replete with those who almost proudly proclaim "I was never any good at math" and who understand little more about the subject than basic arithmetic. We must rethink the use of drill and practice.

The phrase "drill and practice" slips off the tongue so rapidly that the two words *drill* and *practice* appear to be synonyms—and, for the most part, they have been. In the interest of developing a new or different perspective on drill and practice, consider definitions that differentiate between these terms as different types of activities rather than link them together.

> *Practice* refers to different tasks or experiences, spread over numerous class periods, each addressing the same basic ideas.

> *Drill* refers to repetitive exercises designed to improve skills or procedures already acquired.

 Pause *&* **Reflect**

In essence, practice is what this book is about—providing students with ample and varied opportunities to reflect on or create new ideas through worthwhile tasks. Drill, if it occurs, should happen *after* practice. It is useful to know what benefits we can anticipate from drill and practice. •

Practice. Practice, because it engages students in doing mathematics, has the following benefits (which should sound familiar by now):

- An increased opportunity to develop conceptual ideas and more elaborate and useful connections
- An opportunity to develop alternative and flexible strategies

- A greater chance for all students to understand, particularly students with special needs
- A clear message that mathematics is about figuring things out

It is important to point out that practice can and does develop procedural fluency. The fear that without extensive drill students will not master "basic skills" is not supported by recent research on standards-based curriculum or practices (Stein & Smith, 2010). Students in practice-focused programs perform about as well as students in traditional programs on computational skills and better on problem solving and conceptual understanding.

Drill. Drill can provide students with the following:

- An increased facility with a procedure—but *only* with a procedure already learned
- A review of facts or procedures so they are not forgotten

Limitations of drill include:

- A focus on a singular method and an exclusion of flexible alternatives
- A false appearance of student understanding
- A rule-oriented or procedural view of mathematics

A long-standing, though not research-supported, belief is that students learn through drill. In reality, drill can only help students get faster at what they already know. Drill is not a reflective activity. The nature of drill asks students to do what they already know how to do, even if they just learned it. Drill also has a tendency to narrow the learner's thinking to use one approach rather than select an approach based on the context of the problem.

When students successfully complete a page of exercises, teachers (and students) may believe that this is an indication that they've "got it." Superficially learned procedures are easily and quickly forgotten and confused, in particular by students who struggle with mathematics or students who have disabilities (who are often the target of additional drill). It is no wonder that so many students and adults dislike mathematics. Real mathematics is about sense making and reasoning—it is a science of pattern and order. Students cannot possibly obtain this exciting view of mathematics when constantly being asked to drill on procedures that may not even make sense to them.

When Is Drill Appropriate? In a review of research, Franke, Kazemi, and Battey (2007) report that drill improves procedural knowledge, but not conceptual understanding. But when the number of problems is reduced and time is then spent discussing problems, conceptual understanding can be increased while not diminishing procedural knowledge. The key is to keep drills short and to connect procedures to the related concepts.

When drill is appropriate—for example, recalling basic facts—a little bit goes a long way. Drill, because it is review, is best if limited to 5 to 10 minutes. Devoting extensive time to drilling on a procedure is not effective and can negatively affect students' perceptions, motivation, and understanding.

Drill and Student Errors. As discussed earlier, the range of background experiences that students bring is a challenge for all teachers. For students who do not pick up new ideas quickly, there is a temptation to give in and "just drill 'em." Before committing to this solution, ask yourself these two questions: *Will drill build understanding? What is this telling the child?* The child who has difficulties has certainly been shown a process before. It is naive to believe that the drill you provide will be more beneficial than the drills this child has undoubtedly experienced in the past. Although drill may provide short-term success, it will have little effect in the long run. What children learn from more drill is: "Math is full of rules that I don't understand," which leads to not liking mathematics and believing they are not good at it.

In reality, when a student is making errors on a procedure, it is usually a conceptual issue. Using a medical metaphor, the drill errors are a symptom, not the problem. The problem is typically conceptual, therefore remediation should include dropping back to activities that strengthen the student's conceptual knowledge.

 Complete Self-Check 3.3: Developing Concepts and Procedures through Tasks

Orchestrating Classroom Discourse

To help students become productive mathematical thinkers, teachers must be comfortable with uncertainty, ask key questions, be able to respond to students, probe student thinking, prompt students to reflect on their thinking, and know the difference between productive and nonproductive struggle (Heaton & Lewis, 2011; Towers, 2010). Teachers, themselves, must display dispositions to do mathematics; that is, teachers must be willing to explore, experiment and make conjectures, recognize multiple solution paths, make connections among strategies, and monitor and reflect on their work.

Classroom discourse refers to the interactions that occur throughout a lesson. Learning how to orchestrate an effective classroom discussion is quite complex and requires attention to various elements. The goal of discourse is to keep the cognitive demand high while students are learning and formalizing mathematical concepts (Breyfogle & Williams, 2008–2009; Kilic et al., 2010; Smith, Hughes, Engle, & Stein, 2009). Note that the purpose is not for students to tell their answers and get validation from the teacher.

Classroom Discussions

The value of student talk in mathematics lessons cannot be overemphasized. As students describe and evaluate solutions to tasks, share approaches, and make conjectures, learning will occur in ways that are otherwise unlikely to take place. Students—in particular English language learners, other students with more limited language skills, and students with learning disabilities—need to use mathematical vocabulary and articulate mathematics concepts in order to learn both the language and the concepts of mathematics. Students begin to take ownership of ideas (strategic competence) and develop a sense of power in making sense of mathematics (productive disposition). As they listen to other students' ideas, they come to see the varied approaches in how mathematics can be solved and see mathematics as something that they can do.

In *5 Practices for Orchestrating Productive Mathematics Discussions*, Smith and Stein (2011) identify important teacher moves, beginning with *anticipating* responses to the selected worthwhile task (discussed previously). As students are working, the teacher *monitors*, observing strategies students are using and asking questions, such as:

- How did you decide what to do? Did you use more than one strategy?
- What did you do that helped you make sense of the problem?
- Did you find any numbers or information you didn't need? How did you know that the information was not important?
- Did you try something that didn't work? How did you figure out it was not going to work?

The questions are helping students reflect on their own strategies and helping the teacher determine which strategies to *select* for a public discussion after the lesson. Having selected a range of strategies to be shared, the teacher strategically *sequences* the presentations so that particular mathematical ideas can be emphasized. And, perhaps most importantly, the teacher designs questions and strategies that *connect* strategies and mathematical concepts. These tend to be questions that are specific to the task, but some general questions include:

- How did [Leslie] represent her solution? What mathematical terms, symbols, or tools did she use? How is this like/different from [Colin's] strategy?
- Was there something in the task that reminded you of another problem we've done?
- What might you do the same or differently the next time you encounter a similar problem?

Notice these questions focus on the problem solving process as well as the answer, and what worked as well as what didn't work. A balanced discussion helps students learn how to do mathematics.

TABLE 3.2 PRODUCTIVE TALK MOVES FOR SUPPORTING CLASSROOM DISCUSSIONS

Talk Moves	What It Means and Why	Example Teacher Prompts
1. Revoicing	This move involves restating the statement as a question in order to clarify, apply appropriate language, and involve more students. It is an important strategy to reinforce language and enhance comprehension for ELLs.	"You used the hundreds chart and counted on?" "So, first you recorded your measurements in a table?"
2. Rephrasing	Asking students to restate someone else's ideas in their own words will ensure that ideas are stated in a variety of ways and encourage students to listen to each other.	"Who can share what Ricardo just said, but using your own words?"
3. Reasoning	Rather than restate, as in talk move 2, this move asks the student what they think of the idea proposed by another student.	"Do you agree or disagree with Johanna? Why?"
4. Elaborating	This is a request for students to challenge, add on, elaborate, or give an example. It is intended to get more participation from students, deepen student understanding, and provide extensions.	"Can you give an example?" "Do you see a connection between Julio's idea and Rhonda's idea?" "What if . . . "
5. Waiting	Ironically, one "talk move" is to not talk. Quiet time should not feel uncomfortable, but should feel like thinking time. If it gets awkward, ask students to pair-share and then try again.	"This question is important. Let's take some time to think about it."

Source: Based on Chapin, S., O'Conner, C., & Anderson, N. (2009). *Classroom Discussions: Using Math Talk to Help Students Learn* (2nd ed.). Sausalito, CA: Math Solutions. Reprinted with permission.

In addition to these five teacher actions (anticipating, monitoring, selecting, sequencing, and connecting), you have to make sure that everyone participates in the classroom discussion. In *Classroom Discussions*, a teacher resource describing how to implement effective discourse in the classroom, Chapin, O'Conner, and Anderson (2009) write, "When a teacher succeeds in setting up a classroom in which students feel obligated to listen to one another, to make their own contributions clear and comprehensible, and to provide evidence for their claims, that teacher has set in place a powerful context for student learning" (p. 9). Struggling learners often struggle because they have been denied the opportunity to explore and connect ideas. These authors share five "talk moves" that help a teacher to get students talking about mathematics (see Table 3.2).

The following exchange illustrates an example of discourse with a small group of students discussing how to solve 27 − 19 = ____. The teacher is asking two students (Tyler and Aleah) to reconcile that they got different answers.

> **Tyler:** Well, I added one to nineteen to get twenty. So then I did twenty-seven take away twenty and got seven. But I added one, so I needed to take one away from the seven, and I got six.
> **Teacher:** What do you think of that, Aleah?
> **Aleah:** That is not what I got.
> **Teacher:** Yes, I know that, but what do you think of Tyler's explanation?
> **Aleah:** Well, it can't be right, because I just counted up. I added one to nineteen to get twenty and then added seven more to get twenty-seven. So, I counted eight altogether. Six can't be right.
> **Teacher:** Tyler, what do you think of Aleah's explanation?
> **Tyler:** That makes sense, too. I should have counted.
> **Teacher:** So, do you think both answers are right?
> **Tyler:** No.
> **Aleah:** No. If it was twenty-seven minus twenty, the answer would be seven, because you count up seven. So, if it is nineteen, it has to be eight.
> **Tyler:** Oh, wait. I see something. I did get the seven. . . . ? See, I got the twenty-seven take away twenty is seven. But then . . . ? I see . . . ? it's twenty-seven take away nineteen. I took away twenty! I took away too many so I have to add one to the seven. I get eight, just like Aleah! (Kline, 2008, p. 148)

Although this conversation is with two children, a similar style can be used in whole-class discussions, pushing students to help students make sense of what is correct and incorrect about their strategies.

❙❙ Pause & Reflect

What "talk moves" do you notice in the previous vignette? See if you can identify two. ●

Considerable research into how mathematical communities develop and operate provides us with additional insight for developing effective classroom discourse (e.g., Rasmussen, Yackel, & King, 2003; Stephan & Whitenack, 2003; Wood, Williams, & McNeal, 2006; Yackel & Cobb, 1996). Suggestions from this collection of research include the following recommendations:

- Encourage student–student dialogue rather than student–teacher conversations that exclude the rest of the class. "Juanita, can you answer Lora's question?" "Devon, can you explain that so that LaToya and Kevin can understand what you are saying?" When students have differing solutions, have students work these ideas out as a class. "George, I noticed that you got a different answer than Tomeka. What do you think about her explanation?"
- Encourage students to ask questions. "Pete, did you understand how they did that? Do you want to ask Antonio a question?"
- Ask follow-up questions whether the answer is right or wrong. Your role is to understand student thinking, not to lead students to the correct answer. So follow up with probes to learn more about their answers. Sometimes you will find that what you assumed they were thinking is not correct. And if you only follow up on wrong answers, students quickly figure this out and get nervous when you ask them to explain their thinking.
- Call on students in such a way that, over time, all students are able to participate. Use time when students are working in small groups to identify interesting solutions that you will highlight during the sharing time. Be intentional about the order in which the solutions are shared; for example, select two that you would like to compare presented back-to-back. All students should be prepared to share their strategies.
- Demonstrate to students that it is okay to be confused and that asking clarifying questions is appropriate. This confusion, or disequilibrium, just means they are engaged in doing real mathematics and is an indication they are learning.
- Move students to more conceptually based explanations when appropriate. For example, if a student says that he knows 4.17 is more than 4.1638, you can ask him (or another student) to explain why this is so. Say, "I see *what* you did but I think some of us are confused about *why* you did it that way."
- Be sure *all* students are involved in the discussion. ELLs, in particular, need more than vocabulary support; they need support with mathematical discussions (Moschkovich, 1998). For example, you can use sentence starters or examples to help students know what kind of responses you are hoping to hear and to reduce the language demands. Sentence starters can also be helpful for students with disabilities because it adds structure. You can have students practice their explanations with a peer. You can invite students to use illustrations and actual objects to support their explanations. These strategies benefit not just the ELLs and other students in the class who struggle with language, but all students.

Questioning Considerations

Questions are important in learning about student thinking, challenging conclusions, and extending the inquiry to help generalize patterns. Questioning is very complex and something that effective teachers continue to improve on throughout their careers. Here are some major considerations in questioning that influence student learning.

1. *The "level" of the question.* Questions are leveled in various models. For example, Bloom's Taxonomy revised includes six levels (knowledge, comprehension, application, analysis, synthesis, evaluation), with each one more cognitively demanding than the previous (Anderson & Krathwohl, 2001). Smith and Stein's (1998) *Levels of Cognitive Demand* include two low-level demand categories and two high-level demand categories. Regardless of the taxonomy or specific categories, the key is to ask higher-level questions (see Table 3.1). This is critical if students are to think at higher levels, and yet too few higher-level questions are used in mathematics teaching.

2. *The type of understanding that is targeted.* Both procedural and conceptual understanding are important, and questions must target both. If questions are limited to procedural questions, such as "How did you solve this?" or "What are the steps?" then students will be thinking about procedures, but not about related concepts. Questions focused on conceptual knowledge include, "Will this rule always work?" "How does the equation you wrote connect to the picture?" and "Why use common denominators to add fractions?"

3. *The pattern of questioning.* As Herbel-Eisenmann and Breyfogle (2005) articulate, "Thinking about the questions we ask is important, but equally important is thinking about the *patterns of questions* that are asked" (p. 484). One common pattern of questioning goes like this: teacher asks a question, student answers the question, teacher confirms or challenges answer. This "initiation-response-feedback" or "IRF" pattern does not lead to classroom discussions that encourage all students to think. Another pattern is "funneling," when a teacher continues to probe students in order to get them to a particular answer. This is different than a "focusing" pattern, which uses probing questions to negotiate a classroom discussion and help students understand the mathematics. The talk moves described previously are intended to help facilitate a focusing discussion.

4. *Who is doing the thinking.* You must be sure your questions engage all students! When you ask a great question, and only one student responds, then students will quickly figure out they don't need to think about the answer and all your effort to ask a great question is wasted. Instead, use strategies to be sure everyone is accountable to think about the question you posed. Ask students to "talk to a partner" about the question. Employ the talk tools described in this chapter.

5. *How you respond to an answer.* When you confirm a correct solution rather than use one of the talk moves, you lose an opportunity to engage students in meaningful discussions about mathematics and thereby limit the learning opportunities. Use student answers to find out if other students think the conclusions made are correct, whether they can justify why, and if there are other strategies or solutions to the problem.

How Much to Tell and Not to Tell

One of the most perplexing dilemmas for teachers is how much information and direction to provide to students during mathematical inquiry. On one hand, telling can diminish what is learned and lower the level of cognitive demand in a lesson by eliminating the productive struggle that is key to conceptual understanding (Hiebert & Grouws, 2007). On the other hand, to tell too little can sometimes leave students floundering.

Researchers who have analyzed classroom practices as they relate to student learning suggest, "Information can and should be shared as long as it does not solve the problem [and] does not take away the need for students to reflect on the situation and develop solution methods they understand" (Hiebert et al., 1997, p. 36). They go on to suggest three things that teachers do need to tell students:

- *Mathematical conventions.* The symbols used in representing "three and five equals eight" as $3 + 5 = 8$ are conventions ($+$ and $=$). Terminology and labels are also conventions. As a rule of thumb, symbolism and terminology should be introduced *after* concepts have been developed as a means of expressing or labeling ideas. Sometimes students with disabilities benefit from preteaching on terminology and the meaning of symbols to support their participation in the problem solving process.

- *Alternative methods.* When an important strategy does not emerge naturally from students, then the teacher should introduce the strategy, being careful to introduce it as "another" way, not the only or the best way.

- *Clarification or formalization of students' methods.* You should help students clarify or interpret their ideas and point out related ideas. A student may add 38 and 5 by noting that 38 and 2 more is 40 with 3 more making 43. This strategy can be related to the Make 10 strategy used to add $8 + 5$. The selection of 40 as a midpoint in this procedure is an important place-value concept. Drawing everyone's attention to this connection can help other students see the conclusion, not to mention build the confidence of the students who originally proposed the strategy.

Writing to Learn

Classroom discourse includes oral and written language. Writing improves student learning and understanding (Bell & Bell, 1985; Pugalee, 2005; Steele, 2007). The act of writing is a reflective process and involves students in metacognition. Metacognition (https://www.youtube.com/watch?v=dUqRTWCdXt4) refers to conscious monitoring (being aware of how and why you are doing something) and regulation (choosing to do something or deciding to make changes) of your own thought process. Metacognition is connected to learning (Bransford, Brown, & Cocking, 2000).

Writing plays a critical role in classroom discourse. Writing can serve as a rehearsal for a classroom discussion. It can be difficult for students to remember how they solved a problem. A written record or a predrawn picture can be used for reference during discussions. Writing helps students focus on the need for precise language

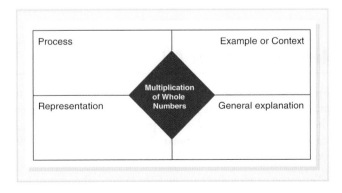

FIGURE 3.5 A student gives an example and explains how to solve $3\frac{1}{2} \div \frac{1}{4}$.

in mathematics and understand that illustrations can support a good explanation. And, a written product provides evidence for you to further analyze student understandings after the lesson (see Chapter 5 for using writing to assess student learning). For example, the student work in Figure 3.5 illustrates how a fifth grader is thinking about division by the fraction $\frac{1}{4}$.

To help elicit better explanations, you might consider the following two possibilities:

- Give students a template to begin their report: "I (We) think the answer is _____. We think this because _____."
- Give the following instruction: "Use words, pictures, and numbers to explain how you got your answer and why you think your answer makes sense and is correct."

Posting different written solutions, just like hearing about solutions, engages students in reflecting on which strategy makes sense. Writing for different audiences can also be valuable. First graders writing to third graders, such as in a pen pal structure, can lead students to explain more and enjoy the process (Lampe & Uselmann, 2008).

Graphic Organizers. Writing can be improved with the use of graphic organizers. Graphic organizers can be used to help students connect representations, as in the template illustrated here.

Process	Example or Context
	Multiplication of Whole Numbers
Representation	General explanation

In each box, students record the problem, explanation, illustration, and the general math concept (Wu, An, King, Ramirez, & Evans, 2009; Zollman, 2009). The requirements for each box can be adapted as needed for the content area; for example, in geometry you may have boxes for characteristics, illustrations, examples and nonexamples.

The I-THINK framework can be used to ensure students are developing metacognitive skills (Lynch, Lynch, & Bolyard, 2013; Thomas, 2006):

Individually think about the task

Talk about the problem.

How can it be solved?

Identify a strategy to solve the problem.

Notice how your strategy helped you solve the problem.

Keep thinking about the problem. Does it make sense? Is there another way to solve it?

Using organizers like the I-THINK framework can help students be more aware of their mathematical thinking and better at communicating that thinking to you, which provides you with better formative assessment data.

Technology Tools in Writing. Take advantage of the following free programs to allow students to write, edit, and submit work to you electronically:

Text Editing (real-time, collaborative writing tools)

- Google Docs and SpreadPages
- Etherpad
- Zoho Docs (includes the ability to use math equations with MathType)

Wikis (free, asynchronous, collaborative website-creation tools)

- PBworks
- Wikispaces (includes the ability to use math equations)
- Wikidot

Blogging Tools

- Blogger
- Tumblr
- WordPress

Web-based tools such as these can be used on a variety of devices in the mathematics classroom, the computer lab, the library, and at home to allow students and teachers to collaboratively draft, read, and edit one another's mathematical ideas. Students who are reluctant to write by hand or in a Word document could be motivated by the more interactive technologies, increasing the likelihood that they will produce quality written explanations.

 Complete Self-Check 3.4: Orchestrating Classroom Discourse

 Problem Solving for All

Teaching through problem solving provides opportunities for all students to become mathematically proficient. This view is supported by NCTM standards and by prominent mathematics educators who have worked extensively with at-risk populations (Boaler, 2008; Diversity in Mathematics Education, 2007; Gutstein, Lipman, Hernandez, & Reyes, 1997; NCTM, 2014; Silver & Stein, 1996). Teaching through problem solving:

- *Focuses students' attention on ideas and sense making.* When solving problems, students are necessarily reflecting on the concepts inherent in the problems. Emerging concepts are more likely to be integrated with existing ones, thereby improving understanding. This approach honors the different knowledge students bring to the classroom.

- *Develops mathematical processes.* Students solving problems in class will be engaged in all five of the processes of doing mathematics—the process standards described by NCTM's *Principles and Standards*: problem solving, reasoning, communication, connections, and representation. These processes move mathematics into a domain that is more accessible, more interesting, and more meaningful.

- *Develops student confidence and identities.* As students engage in learning through problem solving, they begin to identify themselves as doers of mathematics (Boaler, 2008, Cobb, Gresalfi, & Hodge, 2009; Leatham & Hill, 2010). Every time teachers pose a problem-based task and expect a solution, they say to students, "I believe you can do this." When students are engaged in discourse where the correctness of the solution lies in the justification of the process, they begin to see themselves as mathematicians.

- *Provides a context to help students build meaning for the concept.* Providing a context, especially when that context is grounded in an experience familiar to students, supports the development of mathematics concepts. Such an approach provides students access to the mathematics, allowing them to successfully learn the content.

- *Allows an entry and exit point for a wide range of students.* Good problem-based tasks have multiple paths to the solution. Students may solve 42 − 26 by counting out a set of 42 counters and removing 26, by adding onto 26 in various ways to get to 42, by subtracting 20 from 42 and then taking off 6 more, by counting forward (or backward) on a hundreds chart, or by using a standard computational method. Each student gets to make sense of the task using his or her own ideas. Furthermore, students expand on these ideas and grow in their understanding as they hear and reflect on the solution strategies of others. In contrast, the teacher-directed approach ignores diversity, to the detriment of most students.

- *Allows for extensions and elaborations.* Extensions and "what if" questions can motivate advanced learners or quick finishers, resulting in increased learning and enthusiasm for doing mathematics. Such problems can be configured to meet the needs of a range of learners.

- *Engages students so that there are fewer discipline problems.* Many discipline issues in a classroom are the result of students becoming bored, not understanding the teacher directions, or simply finding little relevance in the task. Most students like to be challenged and enjoy being permitted to solve problems in ways that make sense to them, giving them less reason to act out or cause trouble.

- *Provides formative assessment data.* As students discuss ideas, draw pictures or use manipulatives, defend their solutions and evaluate those of others, and write reports or explanations, they provide the teacher with a steady stream of valuable information. These products provide rich evidence of how students are solving problems, what misconceptions they might have, and how they are connecting and applying new concepts. With a better understanding of what students know, a teacher can plan more effectively and accommodate each student's learning needs.

- *Is a lot of fun!* Students enjoy the creative process of problem solving, searching for patterns, and showing how they figured something out. Teachers find it exciting to see the surprising and inventive ways students think. Teachers know more about their students and appreciate the diversity within their classrooms when they focus on problem solving.

When students have confidence, show perseverance, and enjoy mathematics, it makes sense that they will achieve at a higher level and want to continue learning about mathematics, opening many doors to them in the future. In the following chapter, a three-phase lesson format is explained. This lesson structure engages students in learning through problem solving.

 Complete Self-Check 3.5: Problem Solving for All

REFLECTIONS ON CHAPTER 3

WRITING TO LEARN

1. What are the distinctions between the three ways to approach problem solving (teaching *for* problem solving, teaching *about* problem solving, teaching *through* problem solving)?

2. What is meant by multiple entry and exit points? Why are they important?

3. What are high cognitive demand tasks? Why are they important?

4. How can tasks help achieve mathematical proficiency in students? Explain with some examples.

FOR DISCUSSION AND EXPLORATION

♦ Select an activity from any chapter in Section II of this text and apply the Task Evaluation and Selection Guide. What are the task's strengths? Weaknesses? How might you adapt it to enhance the task or make it more relevant for your students?

♦ Getting 100 percent participation in classroom discussions is important and difficult. What strategies might you use to engage everyone in the discussion and to ensure that students are listening to each other and critiquing the reasoning of their peers?

RESOURCES FOR CHAPTER 3

RECOMMENDED READINGS

Articles

Hartweg, K., & Heisler, M. (2007). No tears here! Third-grade problem solvers. *Teaching Children Mathematics, 13*(7), 362–368.

These authors elaborate on how they have implemented the before, during, and after lesson phases. They offer suggestions for supporting student understanding of the problem, ideas for questioning, and templates for student writing. The data they gathered on the response of teachers and students are impressive!

Reinhart, S. C. (2000). Never say anything a kid can say! *Mathematics Teaching in the Middle School, 5*(8), 478–483.

The author is an experienced middle school teacher who questioned his own "masterpiece" lessons after realizing that his students were often confused. This classic article shares a teacher's journey to a teaching through problem solving approach. Reinhart's suggestions for questioning techniques and involving students are superb.

Rigelman, N. R. (2007). Fostering mathematical thinking and problem solving: The teacher's role. *Teaching Children Mathematics, 13*(6), 308–314.

This is a wonderful article for illustrating the subtle (and not so subtle) differences between true problem solving and "proceduralizing" problem solving. Because two contrasting vignettes are offered, it gives an excellent opportunity for discussing how the two teachers differ philosophically and in practice.

Books

Boaler, J., & Humphreys, C. (2005). *Connecting mathematical ideas: Middle school video cases to support teaching and learning.* Portsmouth, NH: Heinemann.

This book offers cases from Cathy Humphreys's classroom based on different content areas and issues in teaching. Each case is followed by a commentary. Accompanying the book are two CDs that provide videos of the cases.

Buschman, L. (2003). *Share and compare: A teacher's story about helping children become problem solvers in mathematics.* Reston, VA: NCTM.

Larry Buschman describes how he makes problem solving work in his classroom. Much of the book is written as if a teacher were interviewing Larry as he answers the kinds of questions you may also have.

Hiebert, J., Carpenter, T. P., Fennema, E., Fuson, K., Wearne, D., Murray, H., Olivier, A., & Human, P. (1997). *Making sense: Teaching and learning mathematics with understanding.* Portsmouth, NH: Heinemann.

The authors of this significant and classic book make one of the best cases for developing mathematics through problem solving.

White, J. (2014). *Using children's literature to teach problem solving in math: Addressing the Common Core in Grade K–2.* New York, NY: Taylor & Francis.

This book is organized around the eight Mathematical Practices (CCSSO, 2010) and offers suggested books and lessons addressing various content topics. Each lesson provides excellent insights into engaging students in learning through problem solving.

4

Planning in the Problem-Based Classroom

LEARNER OUTCOMES

After reading this chapter and engaging in the embedded activities and reflections, you should be able to:

4.1 Explain the features of a three-phase lesson plan format that supports mathematical inquiry and problem solving.

4.2 Design lessons following a planning process focused on mathematical inquiry.

4.3 Describe alternatives to the full-class, three-phase lesson plan.

4.4 Illustrate ways to differentiate instruction to address a range of learners.

4.5 Determine strategies for communicating with and engaging families in mathematics learning.

Designing a lesson that engages students in problem solving looks quite different from a traditional lesson that follows an "explain, then practice" pattern. The mathematical practices such as modeling mathematics, reasoning quantitatively, and looking for generalizations and structure are not developed in a lecture-style lesson. In contrast, in classrooms where learning is assumed to be a complex process and where inquiry and problem solving are emphasized, lessons make use of worthwhile tasks that challenge students' thinking and involve them in communicating and justifying their ideas. Preparing a lesson shifts from preparing an agenda of *what will happen* to creating a "thought experiment" to consider *what might happen* (Davis, Sumara, & Luce-Kapler, 2008). The three-phase lesson format discussed in this chapter and the process for preparing such a lesson are intended to support the creation of lessons that support mathematical inquiry.

 ## A Three-Phase Lesson Format

A three-phase lesson format provides a structure for lessons where students focus on a topic of inquiry, engage in action, and follow up with discussion, reflection, and connections. We refer to these three phases as *before*, *during*, and *after*, referring to students' engagement in a worthwhile task—what happens to set up that inquiry, what happens as they explore, and what happens after the task is solved (see Figure 4.1). In this section, we describe each of the three phases, appropriate teacher actions and interaction within each phase, and examples to illustrate the phase.

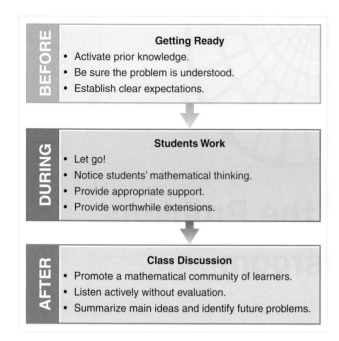

FIGURE 4.1 Teaching through problem solving lends itself to a three-phase structure for lessons.

The *Before* Phase of a Lesson

There are three related agendas for the *before* phase of a lesson:

1. *Activate prior knowledge.* This means both to remind students what they have previously learned and connect to their personal experiences.
2. *Be sure the task is understood.* Students should be able to explain what the task is asking them to do. This does not mean to explain *how* to solve it, just that they understand the task.
3. *Establish clear expectations.* This includes both how they will be working (individually, in pairs or small groups) and what product you expect from them to demonstrate their understanding of the mathematics.

These *before* phase expectations need not be addressed in the order listed. For example, for some lessons you will do a short activity to activate students' prior knowledge for the problem and then present the problem and clarify expectations. Other times, a question might arise from previous work and the lesson may begin by having students brainstorm their own experiences related to the question and what information or tools they need to explore it.

Teacher Actions in the *Before* Phase. What you do in the *before* portion of a lesson will vary with the mathematical goals and the selected task. For example, if your students are familiar with solving story problems and know they are expected to use words, pictures, and numbers to explain their solutions in writing, all that may be required is to read through the problem with them and be sure all understand it. On the other hand, if the task leads to a situation where students need to model it mathematically with a new manipulative or technology, more time may be needed to familiarize students with the tool.

Activate Prior Knowledge. Activate specific prior knowledge related to the mathematical learning goals. What form this preparation activity might take will vary with the topic, as shown in the following three options and examples.

First, some tasks are more accessible if students first explore a related but *simpler task*, as in the perimeter problem (based on Lappan & Even, 1989).

Concept: Perimeter   **Grades: 4–6**

Assume that the edge of a square is 1 unit. Add square tiles to this shape so that it has a perimeter of 18 units.

Instead of beginning your lesson with this problem, you might consider activating prior knowledge in one of the following ways:

• Draw a 3-by-5 rectangle of squares on the board and ask students what they know about the shape. (It's a rectangle. It has squares. There are 15 squares. There are three rows of five.) If no one mentions the words *area* and *perimeter,* you could write them on the board and ask if those words can be used in talking about this figure.
• Provide students with some square tiles or grid paper and say, "I want everyone to make a shape that has a perimeter of 12 units. After you make your shape, find out what its area is." After a short time, have several students share their shapes. Students can also use a virtual geoboard, like the one found at the Math Playground.

Each of these warm-ups uses the vocabulary needed for the focus task. The second activity suggests the tiles as a possible model students may elect to use and introduces the idea that there are different figures with the same perimeter.

The following problem is designed to help students use addition to solve a subtraction problem.

Concept: Subtraction   **Grades: 2–3**

Dad says it is 503 miles to the beach. When we stopped for gas, we had gone 267 miles. How much farther do we have to drive?

Before presenting this problem, you can elicit prior knowledge by asking the class to supply the missing part of 100 after you give one part. Try numbers like 80 or 30 at first; then try 47 or 62. When you present the actual task, you might ask students if the answer to the problem is more or less than 300 miles.

A second way to activate prior knowledge is connect to the students' life experiences. If the problem does not begin with a context you can add one. This helps students see mathematics as relevant and helps them make sense of the mathematics in the problem.

Concepts: Ratios and Statistics   **Grades: 6–7**

Enrollment data for the school provide information about the students and their families—in this case, comparing the whole school to one class.

	School	Class
Siblings		
None	36	5
One	89	4
Two	134	17
More than two	93	3
Race		
African American	49	11
Asian American	12	0
White	219	15
Travel-to-School Method		
Walk	157	10
Bus	182	19
Other	13	0

If someone asked you how typical the class was compared to the rest of the school, how would you answer? Write an explanation of your answer. Include one or more charts or graphs that you think would support your conclusion.

The teacher might begin the task by gathering class data and asking students to compare their own class to the class in the problem. This connects to the students and to the mathematics, as the task requires comparisons. Students might discuss (e.g., think-pair-share) what "typical" means and how they could determine what a typical class is.

Third, estimating or predicting can activate prior knowledge. When the task is aimed at the development of a computational procedure, ask students to estimate the answer. This practice can help students recall the meaning of the operation.

Concept: Multiplication   **Grades: 3–4**

How many small unit squares will fit in a rectangle that is 54 units long and 36 units wide? Use base-ten blocks to help you with your solution. Note that base-ten blocks come in ones (one cube), tens (a row of ten cubes), and hundreds (a ten-by-ten grid). Make a plan for figuring out the total number of squares without doing too much counting. Explain how your plan would work on a rectangle that is 27 units by 42 units.

Be Sure the Task Is Understood. You must always be sure that students understand the problem before setting them to work. It is important for you to analyze the problem in order to anticipate student approaches and possible misinterpretations or misconceptions (Wallace, 2007). Time spent at this stage of the problem solving process is critical to the rest of the lesson. You can ask questions to clarify student understanding of the task; for example, "What are we trying to figure out? Do we have enough information?"and "What do you already know that can help you get started?" The more questions raised and addressed prior to the task, the more engaged students will be in the *during* phase.

Consider a problem-based approach to mastering the multiplication facts. The most difficult facts can each be connected or related to a fact already learned, called a "foundational fact" or "known fact."

Concept: Multiplication Facts   **Grades: 3–4**

Use a known fact to help you solve each of these facts: 4×6, 6×8, 7×6, 3×8.

For this task, it is essential that students understand the idea of using a known fact. They have most likely used foundational facts in addition. You can build on this prior knowledge by asking, "When you learned addition facts, how could knowing $6 + 6$ help you find the answer to $6 + 7$?" and follow up with asking, "What might a known fact be in multiplication?"

In the case of a word problem, like the following one, it is important to help students understand the meaning of the sentences without giving away how to solve the problem. This is particularly important for poor readers and for ELLs.

Concept: Multiplication and Division   **Grades: 3–5**

The local candy store purchased candy in cartons holding 12 boxes per carton. The price paid for one carton was $42.50. Each box contained 8 candy bars that the store planned to sell individually. What was the candy store's cost for each candy bar?

Questions to build background might include: "What is the problem asking? How does the candy store buy candy? What is in a carton? What is in a box? What does that mean when it says 'each box'?" The last question here is to identify vocabulary that may be misunderstood. It is good to first ask students what the problem is asking. Asking students to reread a problem does little good, but asking students to restate the problem or tell what question is being asked helps students be better readers and problem solvers.

Establish Clear Expectations. There are two components to establishing expectations: (1) how students are to work and (2) what products they are to prepare for the discussion.

It is always a good idea for students to have some opportunity to discuss their ideas with classmates prior to sharing their thoughts in the *after* phase of the lesson. When students work in groups, though, there is the possibility of some students not contributing or learning. On the other hand, when students work alone, they have no one to look to for an idea and no chance to talk about the mathematics and practice what they might later share with the whole group. So it is essential to have students be individually accountable and also work together.

One way to address both individual accountability and sharing with other students is a think-write-pair-share approach (Buschman, 2003b). The first two steps are done individually, and then students are paired for continued work on the problem. With independent written work to share, students have something to talk about.

Because teaching through problem solving focuses on processes (strategies) and solutions, it is important to model and explain what a final product might be. One expectation could be a written explanation and/or illustration of the problem. As noted earlier, writing supports student learning in mathematics, and having multiple ways to demonstrate knowledge is important for providing access to all learners (multiple exit points). One effective strategy is to have each student write and illustrate their solution independently, then present the team's solution as a group, with each person sharing a part of the presentation.

The *During* Phase of a Lesson

Once curiosity has been piqued, students engage in mathematical activity alone, with partners, or in small groups to explore, gather and record information, make and test conjectures, and solve the mathematical task. In this *during* phase, students need to have access to tools, such as models, images, diagrams and notation. There are four clear expectations to attend to in this phase:

1. *Let go!* Give students a chance to work without too much guidance. Allow and encourage students to embrace the struggle—it is an important part of doing mathematics.
2. *Notice students' mathematical thinking.* Take this time to find out what different students are thinking, what ideas they are using, and how they are approaching the problem. This is a time for observing, listening, and interacting with students.
3. *Provide appropriate support.* Consider ways to support student thinking (as needed) without taking away their responsibility of designing a solution strategy and solving the problem in a way that makes sense to them.
4. *Provide worthwhile extensions.* Be prepared for students who finish quickly. Anticipate how you might extend their thinking.

Teacher Actions in the *During* Phase. In making instructional decisions in the *during* phase you must ask yourself, "Does my action lead to deeper thinking or is it taking away the thinking?" These decisions are based on carefully listening to students and knowing the content goals of the lesson.

Let Go! Once students understand what the problem is asking, it is time to *let go*. Although it is tempting to rescue students who are feeling frustrated and uncertain in the *during* phase, you need to hold yourself back. Doing mathematics takes time, and solutions are not always obvious. It is important to communicate to students that spending time on a task, trying different approaches, and consulting each other are important to learning and understanding mathematics. When students are stuck, you can ask questions like, "Is this like another task we have done?" "Have you organized the information you have so far?" "What is it about this problem that is difficult?" These questions help students because they support their thinking and help them focus on what is difficult, yet do not tell them how to solve the problem.

Students will look to you for approval of their results or ideas. Avoid being the source of right and wrong. When asked if a result or method is correct, respond by saying, "How can you decide?" or "Why do you think that might be right?" or "Can you check that somehow?" Asking "How can we tell if that makes sense?" reminds students that the correctness of an answer lies in the justification, not in the teacher's brain or answer key.

Letting go also means allowing students to make mistakes. When students make mistakes (and when they are correct), ask them to explain their process or approach to you. They may catch their mistake. In addition, in the *after* portion of the lesson, students will have an opportunity to explain, justify, defend, and challenge solutions and strategies. This process of uncovering misconceptions or computational errors nurtures the important notion that mistakes are opportunities for learning (Boaler & Humphreys, 2005).

Notice Students' Mathematical Thinking. "Professional noticing" means that you are trying to understand a student's approach to a problem and decide an appropriate response to extend that student's thinking in the moment (Jacobs, Lamb, & Philipp, 2010). Consequently, your questions must be based on the students' work and responses to you. This is very different from listening for or leading students toward an answer. As you notice the range of strategies, consider how they are related and in what order you might sequence the sharing of solutions in the *after* phase (Smith & Stein, 2011).

The *during* phase is one of two opportunities you have to find out what your students know, how they think, and how they are approaching the task you have given them. (The other is in the *after* phase.) As students are working, any of the following prompts can help you notice what they know and are thinking:

- Tell me what you are doing.
- I see you have started to [multiply/subtract/etc.] these numbers. Can you tell me why?
- Can you tell me more about . . . ?
- Why did you . . . ?
- How did you solve it?
- How does your picture connect to your equation?
- I am not clear on what you have done here. Will you explain it so I can understand?

By asking questions, you find out where students are in their understanding of the concepts. Don't be afraid to say you don't understand their strategy. When you are open to learning, you help students feel more comfortable with engaging in the mathematics.

Be aware that your actions can inadvertently shut down student thinking and damage self-esteem. "It's easy" and "Let me help you" are two such statements. Think about the message each one sends. If a student is stuck and you say, "It's easy," then you inadvertently say, "You are not very smart or you wouldn't be stuck." Similarly, saying "Let me help you" communicates that you think the student cannot solve the problem without help. The probing questions offered here, in contrast, communicate to students the real messages you want to send: "Doing mathematics takes time and thinking. You can do it—let's see what you know and go from there."

Provide Appropriate Support. If a group or a student is searching for a place to begin, you might suggest some broad strategies (in addition to using the probing questions listed). Jacobs and Ambrose (2008) suggest four "teacher moves" to support student thinking before giving a correct answer:

- Ensure the student understands the task: "What do you know about the problem?" If needed, change the context to a more familiar one so that the student can understand it.
- Change the mathematics to a parallel problem with simpler values. This is something students will eventually do on their own as one of their problem solving strategies.
- Ask students what they have tried: "What have you tried so far?" "Where did you get stuck?"
- Suggest that the student use a different strategy: "Have you thought about drawing a picture?" "What if you used cubes to act out this problem?"

Concept: Percent Increase and Decrease   **Grades: 6–8**

In Fern's Furniture Store, Fern has priced all of her furniture at 20 percent over wholesale. In preparation for a sale, she tells her staff to cut all prices by 10 percent. Will Fern be making a 10 percent profit, less than a 10 percent profit, or more than a 10 percent profit? Explain your answer.

For this task, consider the following suggestions that do not take away student thinking, but provide some starting point:

- "Try drawing a picture or a diagram that shows what 10 percent off and 20 percent more means."
- "Have you tried picking a price and seeing what happens when you increase the price by 20 percent and then reduce the price by 10 percent?"

Notice that these suggestions are not directive, but rather serve as starters. After offering a hint, walk away—this keeps you from helping too much and the student from relying on you too much.

Provide Worthwhile Extensions. There will always be students who finish earlier than their classmates. Early finishers can often be challenged in some manner connected to the problem just solved without it seeming like extra work.

On the surface, some tasks seem simple and students may assume they are done. In this case, use extensions that will strengthen student understanding. For example, consider the area and perimeter task in this chapter. If a student finds one solution quickly, say, "I see you found one way to do this. Are there any other solutions? Are any of the solutions different or more interesting than others? Which of the shapes with a perimeter of 18 has the largest area and which has the smallest area? Does the perimeter always change when you add another tile?"

Questions that begin "What if . . . ?" or "Would that same idea work for . . . ?" are ways to extend student thinking in a motivating way. For example, "Suppose you tried to find all the shapes possible with a perimeter of 18. What could you find out about the areas?" As another example, consider the following task.

Concept: Percent Increase and Decrease   **Grades: 6–8**

The dress was originally priced at $90. If the sale price is 25 percent off, how much will it cost on sale?

This is an example of a straightforward problem with a single answer. Many students will solve it by multiplying by 0.25 and subtracting the result from $90. Ask students, "Could you find another way? Rico solved it by finding 75 percent of 90—does this work? Will it work in all situations? Why?" Or you can extend the use of different representations by asking, "How would you solve it using fractions instead of decimals? Draw me a diagram that explains what you did."

Second graders will frequently solve the next problem by counting or using addition.

Concept: Addition and Subtraction   **Grades: K–2**

Maxine had saved up $9. The next day she received her allowance. Now she has $12. How much allowance did she get?

To extend student thinking, ask, "How would you do that on a calculator?" and "Can you write two equations that represent this situation?" These are ways of encouraging children to connect $9 + ? = 12$ with $12 - 9 = ?$.

The *After* Phase of a Lesson

In the *after* phase of the lesson, your students will work as a community of learners, discussing, justifying, and challenging various solutions to the task they have all just worked on. Ideas generated in the *during* phase must have a chance to "bump against each other" so that mathematical ideas can emerge (Davis & Simmt, 2006, p. 312). The *after* phase is an important time to make drawings, notations, and writing visible to others; to make connections between the ideas that have emerged; and to create spaces for students to take up, try on, and expand on the ideas of others. It is in the *after* phase where much of the learning will occur, as students reflect individually and collectively on the ideas they have explored. It is challenging but critical to plan sufficient time for a discussion. The expectations for the *after* phase require careful consideration of possible student responses, recognition of the responses generated in the *during* phase, and a willingness to be open to unanticipated responses.

1. *Promote a mathematical community of learners.* Engage the class in productive discussion, helping students work together as a community of learners.

2. *Listen actively without evaluation.* Take this second major opportunity to find out how students are thinking—how they are approaching the task.
3. *Summarize main ideas and identify future tasks.* Make connections between strategies or different mathematical ideas and/or lay the groundwork for future tasks and activities.

Teacher Actions in the *After* Phase. Be certain to plan ample time for this portion of the lesson and then be certain to *save* the time. Twenty minutes is not at all unreasonable for a good class discussion and sharing of ideas. It is not necessary for every student to have finished, but all students will have something to share. This is not a time to check answers, but time for the class to share and compare ideas.

Promote a Mathematical Community of Learners. Over time, you will develop your class into a community of learners where students feel comfortable taking risks and sharing ideas, where students and the teacher respect one another's ideas even when they disagree, where ideas are defended and challenged respectfully, and where logical or mathematical reasoning is valued. You must teach your students about your expectations for this time and how to interact respectfully with their peers.

Listen Actively without Evaluation. As in the *during* phase, the goal here is noticing students' mathematical thinking and, in addition, making that thinking visible to other students. When you serve as a member of the classroom community and not as the sole evaluator, students will be more willing to share their ideas during discussions. Resist the temptation to judge the correctness of an answer. When you say, "That's correct, Dewain," there is no longer a reason for students to think about and evaluate the response. Had students disagreed with Dewain's response or had a question about it, they will not challenge or question it because you've said it was correct. Consequently, you will not have the chance to hear and learn from them and notice how they are thinking about the problem. You can support student thinking without evaluation: "What do others think about what Dewain just said?"

Relatedly, use praise cautiously. Praise offered for correct solutions or excitement over interesting ideas suggests that the students did something unusual or unexpected. This can be negative feedback for those who do not get praise. Comments such as "Good job!" and "Super work!" roll off the tongue easily. However, there is evidence to suggest that we should be careful with expressions of praise, especially with respect to student products and solutions (Kohn, 1993; Schwartz, 1996).

In place of praise that is judgmental, Schwartz (1996) suggests comments of interest and extension: "I wonder what would happen if you tried . . . " or "Please tell me how you figured that out." Notice that these phrases express interest and value the student's thinking. For example, if Ethan is sharing his work (see Figure 4.2) to show how many different ways five people could be on the two stories of a house, you can ask Ethan to explain his thinking and ask Ethan and his classmates such things as, "Are all of these ways different?" or "I wonder if there are other ways?" These prompts engage all students in thinking about Ethan's solution and extend everyone's thinking about the problem.

There will be times when a student will get stuck in the middle of an explanation. Be sensitive about calling on someone else to "help out." You may be communicating that the student is not capable on his or her own. Allow ample thinking time. You can offer to give the student time and come back to them after hearing another strategy. Remember that the *after* phase is your window into student thinking (i.e., formative assessment); listening actively will provide insights for planning tomorrow's lesson and beyond.

Summarize Main Ideas and Identify Future Tasks. The main purpose of the *after* phase is to formalize the main ideas of the lesson. In addition, it is the time to reinforce appropriate terminology, definitions, or symbols.

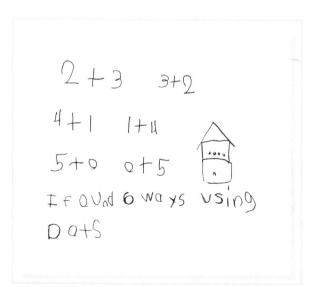

FIGURE 4.2 Ethan shows his thinking about "How many ways 5 people might be on two floors of a house."

If a task involves multiple methods of computing, list the different strategies on the board. These can be labeled with the student's name and an example. Ask students questions that help them understand and see connections between the strategies.

There are numerous ways to share verbally, such as a partner exchange, where one partner tells one key idea and the other partner gives an example. Following oral summaries with individual written summaries is important to ensure that you know what each child has learned from the lesson. For example, exit slips (handouts with one or two prompts that ask students to explain the main ideas of the lesson) can be used as an "exit" from the math instruction. Or be creative—ask students to write a newspaper headline to describe the day's activity and a brief column to summarize it. Many engaging templates and writing starters are available online.

Finally, challenge students to think beyond the current task. Each task is just a specific example of a general category of tasks (Goldenberg & Mason, 2008). Ask students to make conjectures and look for generalizations for addressing related tasks. For example, when comparing fractions, suppose that a group makes this generalization and you display it: *When deciding which fraction is larger, the fraction in which the bottom number is closer to the top number is the larger fraction. Example: $\frac{4}{7}$ is not as big as $\frac{7}{8}$ because 7 is only 1 from 8 but 4 is 3 away from 7.* This is an interesting hypothesis, but it is not correct in all instances. The conjecture needs to discussed in this *after* phase, as a homework activity, or in a subsequent lesson to determine whether it is always right or to find fractions for which it does not work (counterexamples).

 Complete Self-Check 4.1: A Three-Phase Lesson Format

 ## Process for Preparing a Lesson

In Chapter 3, we discussed the selection or creation of worthwhile tasks and so far in this chapter we have discussed the three-phase lesson plan model for implementing worthwhile tasks. In this section we look more closely at the decision making that goes into teaching a three-phase lesson plan. The first column (green) in Figure 4.3 illustrates the multitude of decisions to make prior to planning the actual three-phase lesson. None of these decisions is made in isolation. You might decide to adapt the task based on the mathematics of the task or because of your students' needs. The assessment decisions may relate to the task, the students, or the content goals. Once the content and task decisions are made, the three-phase lesson is ready to be

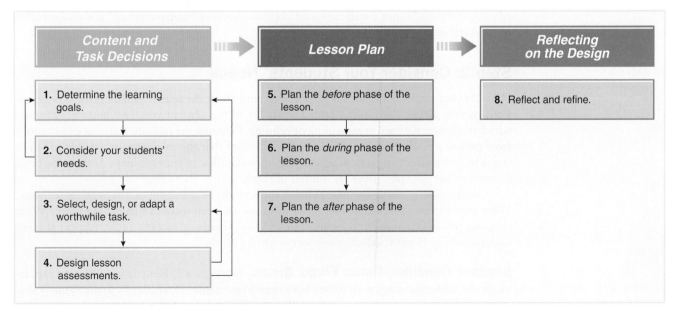

FIGURE 4.3   Eight-step process for planning a lesson.

designed (see purple-shaded steps in Figure 4.3). Once the plan is drafted, it is important to review and finalize the plan, taking into consideration the flow of the lesson, the anticipated challenges, expected responses and misconceptions from students, and the questions or prompts that best support the learner. Each of the considerations in planning a problem-based lesson is briefly discussed next. Within the considerations, an example lesson titled "Fixed Areas Expanded Lesson" is discussed to illustrate how the process is implemented.

Step 1: Determine the Learning Goals

How do you decide what mathematics your students need to learn? Every state has mathematics curriculum standards. Many U.S. states have adopted the *Common Core State Standards* (CCSSO, 2010), which identifies mathematics content by grade level. When planning a lesson, it is important to ask, "What should my students be able to *do* when this lesson is over?" The focus of the inquiry should start with the mathematics content and Mathematical Practices (CCSSO, 2010), rather than just a fun activity or an isolated skill. Thinking about connections across the curriculum will help you plan not only a strong lesson, but a series of lessons that results in a coherent approach to teaching mathematics.

Content Goals: Fixed Areas. One of the big ideas in developing measurement concepts is that area and perimeter are related. As the shapes of regions change, but the area stays the same, the perimeter changes (also true for volume and surface area). In looking at the standards for fourth grade, you read, "Apply the area and perimeter formulas for rectangles in real world and mathematical problems" (CCSSO, 2010). A possible goal for one lesson on this topic is for students to explore the relationship between area and perimeter, specifically that one can change while the other stays the same.

This goal leads to the development of observable and measurable *objectives*. The objectives are the things you want your students to *do* or *say* to demonstrate what they know. There are numerous formats for lesson objectives, but there is consensus that an objective must state clearly what the learner will do.

For example, you might determine the following objectives:

1. Students will be able to draw a variety of rectangles with a given area and accurately determine the perimeter of each.
2. Students will be able to explain relationships between area and perimeter.
3. Students will describe a process (their own algorithm) for finding perimeter of a rectangle.

As a counterexample, "Students will understand that the perimeter can change and the area can stay the same" is not a well-designed objective because "understanding" is not observable or measurable.

Step 2: Consider Your Students' Needs

What do your students already know or understand about the selected mathematics concepts? Perhaps they already have some prior knowledge of the content you have been working on, which this lesson is aimed at expanding or refining. Examine the relevant learning expectations from previous grades and for the next grade. Be sure that the mathematics you identified in step 1 includes something new or at least slightly unfamiliar to your students. At the same time, be certain that your objectives are not out of reach.

Questions to consider include: What context might be engaging to this range of learners? What might students already know about this topic that can serve as a launching point? What misconceptions might need to be addressed? What visuals or models might support student understanding? What vocabulary support might be needed?

Student Considerations: Fixed Areas. Students will likely bring different experiences and understandings even if they have been in the same school, but by grade 4, many students will likely have prior experiences with perimeter and area. Some students may expect that for a given area, there is only one perimeter. The investigation will challenge this expectation.

Also, though students may notice generalizations on how to find area and perimeter, the focus of the lesson should not be on measurement formulas, but on the relationship between area and perimeter.

Step 3: Select, Design, or Adapt a Worthwhile Task

With your goals and students in mind, you are ready to consider what task, activity, or exercise you might use. Chapter 3 provided extensive discussion on what to consider for this step, so it is only mentioned briefly here.

The questions to ask yourself are, "Does the task I am considering address the content goals (step 1) and the needs of my students (step 2)?" "Does the task have potential to engage my students in the Mathematical Practices?" and "Will the task require students to apply problem solving strategies?" If the answers to these questions are yes, the task can become the basis for your lesson. You may still decide on minor adaptations, like adding in a children's book or changing the context, to better connect to your students. If you find the task does not fit your content and student needs, then you will need to either make substantial modifications or find a new task. It is absolutely essential that you do the task yourself. It is only in exploring the task that you can identify possible challenges, anticipate student approaches, and determine the strategies you want to highlight. Teachers who consider ways students might solve the task are better able to facilitate the lesson in ways that support student learning (Matthews, Hlas, & Finken, 2009; Stein, Remillard, & Smith, 2007).

Task Considerations: Fixed Areas. A valuable focus of inquiry is, "What happens to the perimeter when we fix the area, but allow the shape to change?" You might challenge fourth graders to figure out how many rectangles they can create with a given area. This exploration might become the basis for asking, "What rectangles of the same area result in the largest or the smallest perimeter?" You will need to decide what fixed area you wish to use. After exploring, you might decide that for fourth graders 36 square units is a good choice because it results in five different choices, including a square (see Figure 4.4).

By doing the task, the relationship between area and perimeter become more obvious and you notice relationships that help you decide how to focus the discussion in the lesson. For example, you might want to attend to the fact that as shape becomes more square, the perimeter decreases. It might occur to you as you solved the problem that students might wonder whether they should consider 1×36 the same as 36×1 and whether a square is considered a rectangle.

Several contexts are possible for this task. For example, the square tiles could be tables and the perimeter contextualized as how many people can sit around the tables when arranged in different ways. Or, the task could focus on fencing in an area for a pet or a playground.

Step 4: Design Lesson Assessments

Thinking about what you want students to experience and how they are going to demonstrate their understanding of the content goals is an important consideration that occurs early in the planning process. It is important to assess in a variety of ways (see Chapter 5 for extended discussions of assessment strategies). *Formative assessment* allows you to gather information that can be used for adjusting the direction of the lesson midstream or making changes for the next day, as well as informing the questions you pose in the discussion of the task for the *after* phase of the lesson. *Summative assessment* captures whether students have learned the objectives you have listed for the lesson.

Assessment Considerations: Fixed Areas. The essential question for fixed areas is "What happens to the perimeter when we fix the area, but allow the shape to change?" You determined two objectives in step 1.

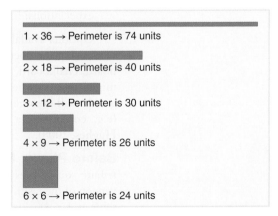

$1 \times 36 \rightarrow$ Perimeter is 74 units

$2 \times 18 \rightarrow$ Perimeter is 40 units

$3 \times 12 \rightarrow$ Perimeter is 30 units

$4 \times 9 \rightarrow$ Perimeter is 26 units

$6 \times 6 \rightarrow$ Perimeter is 24 units

FIGURE 4.4 Possible rectangles with whole number sides and total area of 36 square units.

Objective 1. Students will be able to draw a sufficient variety of possible rectangles for a given area and determine the perimeters.

Assessment.

- In the *during* phase, I will use a checklist to see whether each student is able to create at least three different rectangles with the given area and accurately record the perimeter.
- I will ask each student, "How did you figure out the perimeter of that [pick one] rectangle?"

Objective 2. Students will be able to describe the relationship between area and perimeter.

Assessment.

- In the *during* phase, ask students, "What have you noticed about the relationship between area and perimeter of these rectangles?"
- At the end of the *after* discussion, ask students to complete an exit slip (written summary) to explain the relationship between area and perimeter of a rectangle and to draw pictures to support their explanation.

Objective 3. Students will describe a process (their own algorithm) for finding perimeter of a rectangle.

Assessment.

- In the *during* phase of the lesson, ask, "How are you finding perimeter? Are you seeing any patterns or shortcuts? Explain it to me."
- In the *after* phase, discuss different strategies students used to find the perimeter.

These first four steps in the lesson planning process provide the backbone of your lesson. Once you have a clear sense of these considerations, you can outline the three phases of the lesson. Although the following three phases are listed in order, it is likely you will go back and forth among these phases as you plan.

Step 5: Plan the *Before* Phase of the Lesson

As discussed in the earlier section titled "Teacher Actions in the *Before* Phase," the beginning of the lesson should elicit students' prior knowledge, provide context, and establish expectations. Questions to guide your thinking include:

- Would a simpler version of the task activate prior knowledge, introduce vocabulary, and/or clarify expectations?
- In what ways can you connect the task with previous mathematical experiences, other disciplines, or an interesting current event?
- What presentation strategies and questions will minimize misinterpretations and clarify expectations?

Options available for presenting tasks include having it written on paper, using their texts, using the document camera on a projection device; or posting on an interactive whiteboard, chalkboard, or chart paper. Students need to know (1) the resources or tools they might use; (2) whether they will work independently or in groups; (3) if in groups, how groups will be organized, including assigned roles; and (4) how their work will be presented (e.g., completing a handout, writing in a journal, preparing a team poster) (Smith, Bill, & Hughes, 2008).

Before Phase: Fixed Areas. To elicit past experiences and establish expectations, distribute square tiles to students and ask them to build a rectangle using 12 tiles (a simpler version of the task). Clarify vocabulary (perimeter and area) and expectations (that 3×4 is the same as 4×3).

Decide on a context. For example, with a school play on the horizon, you might use the context of a stage, asking students to think about building a stage that has an area of 36 square meters. Consider questions to raise curiosity like, "Does it matter what the length and width are for the stage floor in terms of how much space we have for doing our play? Would one shape of rectangle be better or worse than another? Find different possibilities and then pick one that will best serve the performers."

Step 6: Plan the *During* Phase of the Lesson

The *during* phase is an opportunity for students to fully engage in the task and for you to learn mathematics alongside your students, to notice what students are thinking, and to provide support and challenges when needed. Carefully prepare prompts that can help students who may be stuck or who may need accommodations that will give them a start without taking away the challenge of the task. Have options of other materials such as geoboards or grid paper. Prepare extensions or challenges you can pose to students.

The *during* phase is your opportunity to interact with individuals or small groups and learn what they know and can do. Students should become accustomed to explaining what they are thinking and doing. This phase is also a time for you to think about which groups might share their work, and in what order, in the *after* phase of the lesson.

During Phase: Fixed Areas. You might make one trip around the room to see that students are actually building a rectangle and recording its dimensions. In the second round, ask the questions you prepared in step 4 for each objective. If students finish early, ask them to consider applying their conjecture of the best dimensions for a stage that is 48 square meters.

Step 7: Plan the *After* Phase of the Lesson

The *after* phase is when you connect the task to the learning goals. Even if the mathematics is obvious to you, students may complete the activity without making the intended connections. That means careful planning of the *after* phase is critical. The following questions should be taken into consideration (Smith, Bill, & Hughes, 2008):

1. How you will organize the discussion to accomplish the mathematical goals (e.g., which solutions will be shared and in what order)?
2. What questions you will ask to help students make sense of the mathematics, make connections to other mathematics, see patterns, and make generalizations?
3. How will you involve all students (over time, not in every lesson)?
4. What evidence are you seeking that will tell you the students understand?

Pay particular attention to the *after* phase of your plan. You can find an excellent task, but if you do not have time to discuss it after students have explored it, students may not be able to formalize their mathematical understandings. Importantly, the point of the *after* phase is not just to hear student solutions, but to compare and analyze those tasks, making connections among the strategies and generalizations about the mathematics. Plan an adequate amount of time for your discussion. A worthwhile problem can take 15 to 20 minutes to discuss.

After Phase: Fixed Areas. First, ask different groups to draw one of their rectangles, with its measurements, on the interactive whiteboard. Second, ask the following questions:

- How did you find the perimeters of these rectangles? (Record different ideas—look for shortcuts and note those responses in words and symbols on the board.)
- What do you notice about the relationship between area and perimeter? (Students should notice that there are a number of possible perimeters for a given area and that the perimeter is smaller when the shape is more "square.")
- If you were the stage architect, which of the rectangles would you pick and why?

After the discussion, you might distribute an exit slip that asks students to explain the second question above to the architect, using illustrations to support the explanation.

Step 8: Reflect and Refine

Steps 5, 6, and 7 result in a tentative lesson plan. The final step is to review this tentative plan in light of the lesson considerations determined in steps 1–4, making changes or additions as needed. In addition, review to see if there are opportunities to press on a mathematical practice or discuss a problem solving strategy.

A well-prepared lesson that maximizes the opportunity for students to learn must be focused and aligned. There is often a temptation to do a series of "fun" activities that seem to relate to a topic but that are intended for slightly different learning goals. First, look to see that three parts of the plan are clearly aligned and balanced: the objectives, the assessment, and the questions asked in the *during* and *after* phases. If the questions are all focused on only one objective, add questions to address each objective or remove the objective that is not addressed.

The quality of your questioning is so critically important to the potential learning that it is a fitting last step. Using your objectives as the focus, review the lesson to see that in the *before* phase you are posing questions that capture students' attention and raise curiosity about how to solve the problem. In the *during* and *after* phases, you are using questions based on the objectives to focus students' thinking on the critical features of the task and what you want them to learn. Research on questioning indicates that teachers rarely ask higher-level questions—this is your chance to review and be sure that you have included some challenging questions that ask students to extend, analyze, compare, generalize, and synthesize. These questions help students more deeply understand the concepts.

Reflect and Refine: Fixed Areas. This lesson is well-aligned, with a worthwhile task (e.g., multiple entry and exit points), a lesson plan that increases in challenge and engages students in mathematical reasoning, and formative assessments aligned to each objective. Higher-level questions based on the objectives are posed to students in the *during* and *after* phases. Some additional questions to have prepared for early finishers or advanced students include the following:

> What if the task involved a fixed perimeter (https://www.youtube.com/watch?v=XI3-52B0V6s)? Would there be different possible areas?

> Which one might an architect prefer for a dance stage rather than a play stage?

> Is a square a rectangle? Use what you know of the characteristics of the shapes to explain.

 Complete Self-Check 4.2: Process for Preparing a Lesson

 # More Options for the Three-Phase Lesson

The basic lesson structure we have been discussing assumes that a class will be given a task or problem, allowed to work on it, and end with a discussion. However, not every lesson is developed around a task given to the whole class. The three-phase format can be applied to other lesson structures, such as mini-lessons and learning centers.

Short Tasks

The three-phase lesson can be applied in as few as 10 minutes. You might plan two or three cycles in a single lesson. Review these short tasks and think about how you might implement a *before*, *during* and *after* design.

Kindergarten	Ms. Joy's class has three fish in their fish tank and Ms. Lo's class has five fish in their fish tank. If we combined the fish, how many would we have?
Grade 2	If you have forgotten the answer to the addition fact 9 + 8, how might you figure it out in your head?
Grade 4	On your virtual geoboard, make a figure that has only one line of symmetry. Make a second figure that has at least two lines of symmetry.

Grade 6	After playing the game "Race" four times, you notice that it took 30 minutes. If this rate is constant, how many games can you play in 45 minutes? In 2 hours?
Grade 8	Write a situation that fits each equation below: $y = 12x$ $y = 30x + 5$

Pose the task to students (*before*). Then, ask students to *think-pair-share*. Students first spend time developing their own thoughts and ideas on how to approach the task (*think*). Then they pair with a classmate and discuss each other's strategies (*pair*). This can occur as a brief *during* phase. After partners have shared, small groups or the whole class can share and compare strategies (*share*). Think-pair-share provides an opportunity to test out ideas and to practice articulating them. For ELLs, students with learning disabilities, and students who tend not to participate, this offers both a nonthreatening chance to speak and an opportunity to practice what they might later say to the whole class.

Learning Centers

A particular topic may lend itself to having students work at different tasks at various classroom locations. Each learning center can emphasize the curriculum goal using different manipulatives, situations, or technology. For example, the concept that a number can be made up of two or more parts is an important relationship for young children to understand (decomposing numbers). To develop this understanding, students need opportunities to create part-part-whole relationships using different objects. A lesson might focus on the number 6 and include four stations, one with counters in two piles, one with cubes creating two towers, one with finding dominoes that equal 6, and one with paper and pencil asking students to find ways two friends can share 6 plums.

The *before* phase is important when using learning centers, as it is still important to elicit prior knowledge, ensure the task is understood, and establish clear expectations. It may include modeling what happens at each center. The *during* phase is still the time where students engage in the task, but they are stopping and rotating to new centers within this phase of the lesson. It is still important to ask questions and even more important to keep track of what strategies students are using and which ones you will later highlight. In the *after* phase, you may decide to focus on one particular center, or you may begin with the center that was the least challenging for students and progress to the one that was most challenging. Or, you may not discuss what was done at each center, but instead ask students to talk about what they learned about the number 6, for example.

Learning centers can also be used for independent work. Even in this case, the three-phase model can be implemented by placing a series of reflective questions for students to use as they participate in the task at the center. A good task for this type of center is one that can be repeated. For example, students might play a game where one student covers part of a known number of counters and the other student names the amount in the covered part. Good technology-supported tasks, especially Internet applications, can be the focus of a learning center. Lessons such as "Fraction Game" on the NCTM Illuminations website are engaging and can played over and over again.

You may want students to work at centers in small groups or individually. Therefore, for a given topic you might prepare four to eight different activities. Place materials for the activity or game (e.g., counters and recording sheets) in a container or folder so that it is easy to pull out for use and to replace for the next group.

Planning three-phase inquiry lessons using worthwhile tasks and ensuring that the lesson meets the needs of all students requires intentional and ongoing effort. Questions are likely to surface. Access the companion website for to access Frequently Asked Questions for problem-based approaches to instruction that includes seven of the most common questions with brief responses. This page may help you as you contemplate how to plan for your students, or consider ways to advocate for teaching through problem solving with other teachers, families, and/or administrators.

 Complete Self-Check 4.3: More Options for the Three-Phase Lesson

Differentiating Instruction

Every classroom contains a range of student abilities and backgrounds. Perhaps the most important work of a teacher is to be able to plan (and teach) lessons that support and challenge *all* students to learn important mathematics. The three-phase lesson plan is highly effective in meeting the needs of a range of learners. Students are asked to make sense of the task (*before*), bring their own skills and ideas to the problem to solve it in their own way (*during*), and then articulate their thinking, as well as hear the thinking of others (*after*). In contrast, in a traditional highly directed lesson, the assumption is made that all students will understand one approach. Students not ready to understand the ideas presented must focus their attention on following rules or directions in an instrumental manner (i.e., without a conceptual understanding). In addition to using a problem-based approach, there are specific adaptations that can meet the needs of the diverse learners in your classroom; this is the focus of Chapter 6.

Differentiating instruction means that a teacher's lesson plan includes strategies to support the range of different academic backgrounds found in classrooms that are academically, culturally, and linguistically diverse (Tomlinson, 1999). When considering what to differentiate, first consider the learning profile of each student. Second, consider what can be differentiated across three critical elements:

- *Content* (what you want each student to know)
- *Process* (how you will engage them in thinking about that content)
- *Product* (what they will show, write, or tell to demonstrate what they have learned)

Third, consider how the physical learning environment might be adapted. This might include the seating arrangement, specific grouping strategies, and access to materials.

Content can be differentiated in many ways, including resources or manipulatives used, mathematics vocabulary developed, examples and nonexamples used to develop a concept, and teacher-directed groups used to provide foundations for a new concept (Cassone, 2009).

Process can also be differentiated in various ways. Tomlinson and McTighe (2006) suggest that in thinking about process, teachers think about selecting strategies that build on students' readiness, interests, and learning preferences. In addition, the process should help students learn effective strategies and reflect on which strategies work best for them. Learning centers (discussed previously) and tiered lessons are two ways to differentiate the process. (*Products* are discussed in Chapter 5.)

Open Questions

Many questions in textbooks are closed, meaning there is one answer, and often only one way to get there. Such a task cannot meet the needs of range of learners in the classroom. *Open questions* are broad-based questions that invite meaningful responses from students at many developmental levels (Small, 2012).

One number is about one-half of another. Their product is close to 100. What might the numbers be?

You can take a closed task and make it open—for example, rather than ask students to add 8 + 12, say, "The answer is 20, what is the equation?" You can give "clues" and ask students to write an equation that fits the clues.

Open questions are particularly useful in taking low cognitive demand tasks and turning them into high cognitive demand tasks. Compare these two tasks:

Task A: Write 35,045,011 in scientific notation.

Task B: Write two numbers that are more easily compared when in scientific notation. Write two numbers that are difficult to compare when in scientific notation.

The *after* phase of lessons that include open questions can be rich with debate as students critique the solutions and ideas of their peers.

Tiered Lessons

Tiered lessons include a set of similar problems focused on the same mathematical goals, but adapted to meet the range of learners, with different groups of students working on different tasks. For example, students might all be working on decomposing numbers, but some students are finding ways to decompose 5 into two numbers, some are working on decomposing 8 into two numbers, and some are working on decomposing 8 and also considering more than two addends. The adaptation is not necessarily just to the *content;* it can also be any of the following (Kingore, 2006):

1. *The degree of assistance.* This might include providing examples or partnering students.
2. *How structured the task is.* Students with special needs, for example, benefit from highly structured tasks, but gifted students often benefit from a more open-ended structure.
3. *The complexity of the task given.* This can include making a task more concrete or more abstract or including more difficult problems or applications.
4. *The complexity of process.* This includes how quickly paced the lesson is, how many instructions you give at one time, and how many higher-level thinking questions are included as part of the task.

Consider the following:

Original Task

Eduardo had 9 toy cars. Erica came over to play and brought 8 cars. Can you figure out how many cars Eduardo and Erica have together? Explain how you know.

The teacher distributes cubes to students to model the problem and paper and pencil to illustrate and record how they solved the problem. He asks students to be ready to explain their solution.

Adapted Task

Eduardo had some toy cars. Erica came over to play and brought her cars. Can you figure out how many cars Eduardo and Erica have together? Explain how you know.

The teacher asks students what is happening in this problem and what they are going to be doing. Then he distributes task cards that tell how many cars Eduardo and Erica have. He has varied how hard the numbers are, giving the students who are struggling numbers less than 10 and the more advanced students open-ended cards with multiple solutions.

Card 1 (easier)

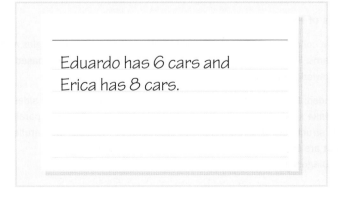

Eduardo has 6 cars and
Erica has 8 cars.

Card 2 (moderate)

Eduardo has 13 cars and
Erica has 16 cars.

Card 3 (advanced)

Eduardo has _ cars and
Erica has _ cars. Together
they have 25 cars. How many
cars might Eduardo have and
how many might Erica have?

In each case, students must use words, pictures, models, or numbers to show how they figured out the solution. Various tools are provided (connecting cubes, counters, and hundreds chart) for their use.

There are (at least) three options for how to organize the use of the task cards. First, the teacher can give everyone the cards in order. Second, the teacher can give students only one card, based on their current academic readiness (e.g., easy cards to those who have not yet mastered addition of single-digit numbers). Third, the teacher can give out cards 1 and 2 based on ability and use card 3 as an extension for those who have successfully completed card 1 or 2. In each of these cases, the teacher will know at the end of the lesson which students are able to model and explain addition problems and plan the next lesson accordingly. Notice that this tiered lesson addresses both the complexity of the task and complexity of the process (instructions are broken down by first starting with the no-numbers scenario).

The following example illustrates how to tier a lesson based on how much *structure* is provided (some are more open-ended than others), yet all tasks focus on the same learning goal of identifying properties of parallelograms.

Topic: Properties of Parallelograms   **Grade: 5–6**

Students are given a collection of parallelograms, including squares and rectangles as well as nonrectangular parallelograms. The following tasks are distributed to different groups based on their learning needs and prior knowledge of quadrilaterals:

- Group A, open ended: Explore the set of parallelograms. Measure angles and sides using your ruler and protractor. Make a list of the properties that you think are true for every parallelogram.
- Group B, slightly structured: Use your ruler and protractor to measure the parallelograms. Record any patterns that are true for all of the parallelograms related to:
    Sides Angles Diagonals

- Group C, highly structured: Explore the parallelograms to find patterns and rules that define the shapes as parallelograms. Use a ruler to measure the sides and a protractor to measure the angles. First, sort the parallelograms into rectangles and nonrectangles.

  1. What pattern do you notice about the measures of the *sides* of all the parallelograms in the *nonrectangle* set?

     What pattern do you notice about the measures of the *sides* of all the parallelograms in the *rectangle* set?
  2. What pattern do you notice about the measures of the *angles* of all the parallelograms in the *nonrectangle* set?

     What pattern do you notice about the measures of the *angles* of all the parallelograms in the *rectangle* set?

Parallel Tasks

Parallel tasks, like tiered lessons, involve students working on different tasks all focused on the same learning goal. With parallel tasks, the focus is on choice (Small, 2010, 2012). Giving a choice increases student motivation and helps students become more self-directed learners (Bray, 2009; Gilbert & Musu, 2008).

Topic: Scientific Notation   **Grade: 8**

Select one of the numbers below and represent it at least four different ways.

3,500,000,000   0.0035

Choices can be embedded within stories:

Topic: Subtraction   **Grades: 2–3**

Eduardo had {12, 60, 121} marbles. He gave Erica {5, 15, 46} marbles. How many marbles does Eduardo have now?

An adaptation for fractions can include pairing the choices, with option a being more challenging than option b (Phelps, 2012).

Topic: Addition   **Grades: 5–6**

Camila is making trail mix. She puts in some raisins and ___ cups of nuts. In total she has ____ cups of trail mix. How many cups of raisins did she put in the trail mix?

$$\text{a. } \tfrac{3}{4}, 1\tfrac{1}{2} \quad \text{b. } \tfrac{5}{8}, 2\tfrac{1}{4}$$

Students selecting (1) are working with fourths and halves; in (2) are working with fourths and eighths. In both cases they are considering adding fractions with like-sized parts. This story is also written with a missing addend (called start unknown). As you will learn in Chapter 9, it is important to have the unknown value in different parts of the story (not just the result). Parallel tasks provide choice, and students tend to choose the numbers that provide the greatest challenge without being too difficult. What they choose, therefore, also provides useful formative assessment data.

Flexible Grouping

Allowing students to collaborate on tasks provides support and challenges, increasing their chance to communicate about mathematics and build understanding. Collaboration is also an important life skill. Students feel that working in groups improves their confidence, engagement, and understanding (Nebesniak & Heaton, 2010). *Flexible grouping* means that the size and makeup of small groups vary in a purposeful and strategic manner. In other words, sometimes students are working in partners because the nature of the task best suits two people; other times they are in groups of four because the task has enough tasks or roles to warrant a larger team. Also, groups can be selected based on the students' academic abilities, language needs, social dynamics, and behavior. It is often effective to use mixed-ability (heterogeneous) groups, strategically placing struggling learners with more capable students who are likely to be helpful.

Groups may stay the same for a full unit so that the students become skilled at working with one another. If students are seated with their groups in clusters of four, they can still pair with one person from their group when the task is better suited for pairs.

Regardless of whether groups have two or four members or whether you have grouped by mixed ability (heterogeneous) or similar ability (homogeneous), the first key to successful grouping is *individual accountability*. That means that while the group is working together on a product, individuals must be able to explain the process, the content, and the product. Although this may sound easy, it is not.

Second, and equally important, is building a sense of *shared responsibility* within a group. At the start of the year, it is important to do team building activities and to set the standard that all members will participate and that all team members are responsible to ensure that all members of their group understand the process, content, and product. Good resources for team building activities (though there are many) include *Team Building Games on a Shoestring* (a free downloadable collection, all done with shoestrings) (Heck, 2006), *Team Building Activities for Every Group* (Jones, 1999), and *Feeding the Zircon Gorilla and Other Team Building Activities* (Sikes, 1995).

One strategy that ensures individual accountability and shared responsibility is a jigsaw grouping technique. In this strategy, students are placed in a home group and then go to an expert group to become an expert on something, returning to their home group to share what they've learned. Although this was originally designed to cover large amounts of narrative material, it can be effectively used in mathematics, especially to emphasize different representations (Cleaves, 2008). As Cleaves describes, students go to expert groups to explore a problem (e.g., how three different people save money). In each group, the problem is presented with a different representation: graphs, tables, situations, or story. Students analyze the situation in the expert group and then return to their home group to share and compare the different representations and solutions.

You must consistently reinforce individual accountability and shared responsibility. When a member of a small group asks you a question, your response should be not to answer the question but to pose a question to the whole group to find out what they think. Students will soon learn that they must use teammates as their first resource and seek teacher help only when the whole group needs help. Also, when observing groups, rather than ask Angela what she is doing, you can ask Bernard to explain what Angela is doing. Having all students participate in the oral report to the whole class builds individual accountability. Letting students know that you may call on any member to explain what they did is a good way to be sure all group members understand what they did. Additionally, having students individually write and record their strategies and solutions is important. The more you use these strategies and others like them, the more effectively groups will function and the more successfully students will learn the concepts.

Avoid ability grouping! As opposed to differentiation, ability grouping means that groups are formed and those needing more support in the low group are meeting different (lesser) learning goals than students needing less support in the high group. Although this may be well-intentioned, it only puts the students in the low group further behind, increasing the gap between more and less dependent students and significantly damaging students' self-esteem. Visit the companion website to access details some of the negative effects of ability grouping.

Complete Self-Check 4.4: Differentiating Instruction

Planning for Family Engagement

Teaching mathematics developmentally, addressing the increased content demands articulated in the Common Core State Standards Initiative (CCSSO, 2010), and ensuring that students are mathematically proficient requires everyone's commitment. Parents know the importance of mathematics for their child's future. They participate in their child's learning by doing such things as supporting homework, volunteering at the school, and meeting with teachers, even if they may recall unpleasant experiences or difficulties with mathematics from their own schooling. Understanding that memories of mathematics classes are not always pleasant for parents and appreciating their support prepares us to suitably identify for parents the mathematics goals that students should be experiencing in the 21st century. This is important because research has found that positive parent emotions lead to positive student emotions, and positive student emotions are connected to better performance (Else-Quest, Hyde, & Hejmadi, 2008).

Communicating Mathematics Goals

Every year parents need opportunities to get information directly from the leaders and teachers in the school about their child's mathematics program, including the kind of instruction that might differ from what they experienced in their own schooling. For example, even if your school has been engaged for several years in implementing a mathematics program that reflects the NCTM *Principles to Actions* or the Common Core State Standards, the curriculum will still be new to the parents of your students. Without such opportunities for communication, parents may draw their own conclusions about the effectiveness of the mathematics curriculum, develop frustrations and negative opinions about what is happening in their child's classroom or school, and communicate this apprehension to other parents. Table 4.1 highlights common questions parents ask about problem-based mathematics programs. Providing a forum for parents highlights the importance of the subject and gives parents confidence that your school is a great place for preparing their children for middle school and beyond.

Be proactive! Don't wait for concerns to arise. Strategies include engaging parents in family math nights, positive homework practices, and sharing where to find mathematics-related resources for their children.

TABLE 4.1   PARENT QUESTIONS RELATED TO MATHEMATICS TEACHING AND LEARNING

Category	Types of Questions
Pedagogy	• Why isn't the teacher teaching? (And what is the point of reinventing the wheel?) • Are children doing their own work when they are in groups? Is my child having to do the work of children who don't understand the work? • Why is there so much reading and writing in math class? • Why is my child struggling more than before?
Content	• Is my child learning the basic skills? • Why is my child learning different ways (than I learned) for doing the operation? • Will my child be on track of Algebra I in eighth grade? Ninth grade? • Where are the math topics I am used to seeing and why are there topics I never learned? • Is my child learning mathematics or just doing activities?
Evidence	• Is there any evidence that this approach or curriculum is effective? • Will my child do better on state/national standardized tests with this new approach? • Will this prepare my child for middle school, high school, college, and beyond?
Understanding	• Why is mathematics teaching changing? • How can I help my child [with homework; to be successful]? • Where can I learn more about the *Common Core State Standards*?

Source: From Bay-Williams, J. M., & Meyer, M. R. (2003). What Parents Want to Know about Standards-Based Mathematics Curricula. *Principal Leadership,* 3(7), 54–60. Copyright 2003 National Association of Secondary School Principals. www.principals.org. Reprinted with permission.

Family Math Nights

You can showcase your mathematics program by including a math component in a back-to-school night, discussing it in a PTA meeting, or a hosting a Family Math Night. Critical to this plan is providing opportunities for parents to be learners of mathematics so they experience what it means to *do mathematics* (just like their children) as well as to address their questions about the mathematics program.

Engage in Doing Mathematics. The heart of a Family Math Night is having positive experiences doing mathematics! When choosing mathematical tasks to use with parents, be sure the tasks focus on content that really matters to them and relates to what they already know is a part of the mathematics curriculum. Figure 4.5 contrasts two kindergarten problems focused on decomposing numbers with connections to supporting basic fact mastery. Tasks and activities throughout this book are also ideal for a Family Math Night.

 Pause & Reflect

What distinctions do you notice between the two tasks in Figure 4.5? What is valued as "doing mathematics" in both of the problems? •

The potential each of these problems has to support and challenge children in making sense of mathematics should be made explicit during a discussion with parents. After giving parents time to do both tasks and discussing solution strategies (as you would with students), ask participants to consider the learning opportunities in the two contrasting tasks. Ask questions such as these:

What skills are being developed in each problem?

Which problem gives more opportunity to make connections between mathematics and the real world?

Which task would your child be most motivated to solve? Why?

Help parents identify the depth of the mathematics in the worthwhile task. For example, in grades K–2 children are building important foundations of number and operations through algebraic reasoning—looking for patterns, reasoning, and generalizing. Share the Common Core State Standards Mathematical Practices and focus on the goal of having students becoming mathematically proficient as described in those standards. Ask parents "Where do you see these proficiencies being supported in the two tasks we did?"

Talk about Learning through Inquiry. When parents ask questions that point to their belief that mathematics is best learned through direct instruction—just as they learned it—remind them of the experience parents had in *doing* mathematics with the parking lot task.

TASK 1:

Find the answer to these equations. Use counters or draw pictures to show your work.

$1 + 5 =$ _____ $\qquad\qquad$ $0 + 6 =$ _____

$3 + 3 =$ _____ $\qquad\qquad$ $2 + 4 =$ _____

TASK 2:

The parking lot has only blue and red cars. There are 6 cars parked. How many blue and how many red cars might be in the parking lot? Find as many ways as you can. Draw a picture and write an equation for each answer.

Extensions: Can you find all of the ways to have 6 red and blue cars in the parking lot? How many ways can you find to have a total of 5 cars? How many ways can you find to have a total of 7 cars? Do you see a pattern?

FIGURE 4.5 Two tasks to explore at a kindergarten or first-grade Family Math Night.

Point to the difference between being *shown* how to do something (e.g., this is how you add, now practice this) and *developing* an understanding of something (e.g., How many different ways can you partition 6? How do you know if you have found all the ways?). You can help parents identify the skills and concepts that are developed through these two experiences. Ask, "In what ways are children learning about addition? About subtraction? How do the different ways support eventual mastery of the basic facts?" Point out that skills are still important, and children benefit by generating their own procedures. Encourage families to engage in inquiry at home. Give them a task to take home. The Family Math Take-Home Planning Guide can help you prepare such a task.

Describe Your Role. In an inquiry-based classroom, parents may not think the teacher is "teaching." Explain your role in *organizing* (selecting a worthwhile task), *facilitating* (setting up and monitoring the task and student engagement with the task), and *questioning* (asking questions in each lesson phase to help students make connections or to deepen their understanding).

Justify the Use of Cooperative Groups. Parents may wonder about their child working in cooperative groups because this may differ from their own mathematics learning experiences. You can justify the use of cooperative groups in a variety of ways:

1. *Share the one-page parent overview from the NCTM Families Ask department titled "Cooperative Learning" (Coates & Mayfield, 2009).* Families Ask, a feature posted on the NCTM website and published in *Mathematics Teaching in the Middle School*, provides over 20 excellent discussions on a range of topics appropriate for parents in elementary and middle school.
2. *Include a feature in your parent newsletter.* Early in the year, you can feature cooperative learning, addressing its importance across content areas. In mathematics, this can include the following benefits: hearing different strategies, building meaning, designing solution strategies, and justifying approaches, all of which are essential to building a strong understanding of mathematics and important life skills.
3. *Send home letters introducing math units of study.* If you are about to teach a unit on adding and subtracting fractions, a letter can help parents know the important aspects of the content. This is a great time to mention that students will work in groups so that they can see different ways to solve tasks.
4. *Do a cooperative learning mathematics activity at a Family Math Night.* Use a task that lends itself to assigning roles to different members of the group and won't take long to solve. Have parents work with two or three others to solve the task.
5. *Invite parents to assist in a mathematics group assignment.* Seeing firsthand the dialogue and thinking that happens in cooperative groups can go a long way in illustrating how valuable cooperative groups can be!

Advocate for Use of Technology. Parents may be avid users of technology, yet still have concerns about their child using calculators and computers if they have not mastered their basic facts. Even though research overwhelmingly finds that students using calculators achieve at least as much as those not using calculators, calculators are widely blamed for students' lack of reasoning and sense making. Reassure parents that students will learn the basic facts and procedures and that a calculator can support that learning. The calculator is used when it is *appropriate* to support the mathematical goals of the day. For example, students can use calculators when the goal is learning volume, not when the goal is learning how to multiply. Mastery of basic facts should *not* be a prerequisite to using a calculator. Instead, students (and teachers) should be making good decisions about whether a calculator supports or detracts from solving a particular problem (and learning the intended mathematics).

Provide Support for Problem Solving. Teaching parents how to help their children has also been found to make a difference in supporting student achievement (Cooper, 2007). Parents value school mathematics, but they associate mathematics with skills and seatwork (Remillard & Jackson, 2006). It is your job to help them understand the broader goals of mathematics. Real mathematics involves more word problems and far fewer "naked number" skill problems. Skills that can be executed on a $1 calculator are less necessary in the 21st-century workplace, but number sense, reasoning, and being able to solve real problems is absolutely essential. Provide parents with a card that includes reading strategies for helping their child interpret story problems, such as the one featured in Figure 4.6.

Parents may worry when they see their child struggle with a single mathematics problem because they may believe that fast means successful. But faster isn't smarter. Cathy Seeley's book with this same title (2009) is a great read on this topic written for families, educators, and policymakers. Seeley offers 41 brief messages, many of which can address parent questions about mathematics (e.g., "A Math Message to Families: Helping Students Prepare for the Future"). Explain that engaging in productive struggle is one of the two most effective ways teachers can develop conceptual understanding in students (the other is making connections between mathematical ideas) (Hiebert & Grouws, 2007).

Address Concerns about Procedures. Students should be using strategies that make sense to them, and this applies to the procedures such as dividing whole numbers. Yet parents may think that they are not learning the standard algorithms. Point out that the skills are still there, they just look different because they are presented in a way based on understanding, not just memorization. Second, explain that standard algorithms are one technique, but mathematically proficient students must have access to multiple strategies so that they can select the most efficient strategy in any given situation. Pose examples, such as these:

$$69 + 47 = \underline{\quad}$$

$$309 - 288 = \underline{\quad}$$

$$487 + 345 = \underline{\quad} + 355$$

Ask for volunteers to share the ways that they thought about the problems. For the subtraction problem, for example, the following might be shared:

- 300 take away 288 is 12, then add the 9 back on to get 21
- 288 up to 300 is 12 and up 9 more is 21
- 309 to 300 is 9, then down to 290 is 10 more (19), and then to 288 is 2 more (21)

These invented strategies, over numerous problems, reinforce place-value concepts and the relationship between addition and subtraction. Noticing that these values are both near 300 helps select a strategy. Point out that this bird's-eye view of the problem (looking at it holistically first, then deciding how to solve it) is important in being "good" at mathematics.

Homework Practices

You may have heard parents say, "I am not good at math" or "I don't like solving math problems." Parents may feel this way and, given the research just described, it is particularly important to redirect parents to portray mathematics in a positive light. For example, "Even though math can be hard, stick with it and you will figure it out." Teaching parents how to help their children has also been found to make a difference in supporting student achievement (Cooper, 2007).

Homework can be a positive experience for students, families, and the teacher. Take the following recommendations into consideration when thinking about the homework that you will assign to your students:

Mimic the Three-Phase Lesson Model. Complete a brief version of the *before* phase of a lesson to be sure the students understand the homework before they go home. At home, students complete the *during* phase. When they

Solving Math Story Problems—Try These Strategies:

- Read problem aloud.
- Paraphrase what the story is about.
- Discuss math vocabulary.
- Find and write the question.
- Draw a picture of the problem.
- Act out the problem (have fun!).
- Use household items to illustrate the problem.

FIGURE 4.6 A note card for parents to help their child solve story problems.

return with the work completed, apply the sharing techniques of the *after* phase of the homework. Students can even practice the *after* phase with their family if you encourage this through parent or guardian communications.

Use a Distributed-Content Approach. Homework can address content that has been taught earlier in the year as practice, that day's content as reinforcement, or upcoming content as groundwork. Interestingly, research has found that distributed homework that combines all three components is more effective in supporting student learning (Cooper, 2007). The exception is students with learning disabilities, who perform better when homework focuses on reinforcement of skills and current class lessons.

Promote an "Ask-Before-Tell" Approach with Parents. Parents may not know how best to support their child when he or she is stuck or has gotten a wrong answer. One important thing you can do is to ask parents to implement an "ask-before-tell" approach (Kliman, 1999). This means that before parents explain something, they should ask their child to explain how he or she did it. The child may self-correct (a life skill), and if not, at least the parent can use what they heard from their child to provide targeted assistance.

Provide Good Questioning Prompts for Parents. Providing guiding questions for parents or guardians supports a problem-based approach to instruction as they help their children. Figure 4.7 provides a teacher-made bookmark with guiding questions that can be emailed to parents, used as a bookmark in their text, or taped into homework journals.

Invite parents into your mathematics lessons. If parents can witness firsthand your questioning and the many ways that problems can be solved, they will have a vision of how they can support learning at home. For example, they may notice that you encourage students to select their own strategy and explain how they know it works. Parents will also pick up on the language that you are using and will be able to reinforce that language at home.

Resources for Families

Parents will be a better able to help to their child if they know where to find resources. The Internet can provide a wealth of information, but it can also be an overwhelming distraction. Help families locate good places to find math support. First, check whether your textbook provides websites with online resources for homework. These resources can include tutorials, video tutoring, connections to careers and real-world applications, multilingual glossaries, podcasts, and more. Second, post websites that are good general resources. Here are some examples:

- *Figure This! Math Challenges for Families.* This NCTM resource has a teacher corner and a family corner. It offers outstanding resources to help parents understand standards-based mathematics, help with homework, and engage in *doing* mathematics with their children. It was originally designed for middle school, but the family corner provides general guidance and many of the challenges now address content in grades 3 through 5 (e.g., on fractions). It is also available in Spanish.
- *National Council of Teachers of Mathematics (NCTM) Family Resources Website.* This frequently updated site connects families to help with homework, current trends in mathematics, and resources.
- *Math Forum Website.* This site includes many features for teachers and families. For example, "Ask Dr. Math" is a great homework resource because students can write in their questions and get answers fairly quickly. Parents may also want to read or participate in Math Discussion Groups, read about Key Issues for the Mathematics Community, or download some of the very interesting problems posted here.
- *HCPSS Family Mathematics Support Center.* This site, developed by the Howard County Public School System (MD) helps families gain a better understanding of their child's mathematics program; refresh or build understanding of new (or unfamiliar) math concepts, skills, and practices;

Math Thinking Bookmark

When stuck on a math problem, ask:

- What do you need to figure out?
- What is the problem about?
- What words are confusing? What words are familiar?
- Did you solve problems like this one in class today?
- What have you tried so far? What else can you try?
- Can you make a drawing or chart to help you think about the problem?
- What terminology or processes do you use in your class?
- Does your answer make sense?
- Is there more than one answer?
- How might you check your answer?

FIGURE 4.7 Sample bookmark with questions for parents to help their children with homework.

and provides additional support and practice opportunities for students, as needed throughout the school year.

There are also great websites for specific content. For example, Conceptua Math has excellent digital tools for exploring fraction operations. Share these sites with families as you introduce new units.

Seeing Mathematics in the Home. In the same way that families support literacy by reading books with their children or pointing out letters of the alphabet when they encounter them, families can and should support numeracy. Because this has not been the practice in many homes, it means you have the responsibility to help parents see the connection between numeracy and everyday life. Kliman (1999) offers some excellent suggestions, which include asking parents to share anecdotes and find mathematics in the books they read, have scavenger hunts, and create opportunities during household chores. Prepare an engaging letter to families that shares suggestions, such as the examples in the Math-at-Home Letter for Pre-K–2, the Math-at-Home Letter for Grades 3–5, and the Math-at-Home Letter for Grades 6–8.

Adults constantly use estimation and computation in doing everyday tasks. If you get parents to talk about these instances with their children, imagine how much it can help students learn about mathematics and its importance as a life skill.

Involving *All* Families

Some families are at all school events and conferences, whereas others rarely participate. However, all families want their children to be successful in school. Parents who do not come to school events may have anxiety related to their own school experiences, or they may feel complete confidence that the school and its teachers are doing well by their child and that they do not need to participate. In some cultures, questioning a teacher may be perceived as disrespectful. Rodríguez-Brown, a researcher on Hispanic families, writes, "It is not that Latino parents do not want to support their children's learning. . . . [They] believe that it is disrespectful to usurp the teachers' role" (2010, p. 352).

Try to find ways to build a strong rapport with all families. Some strategies to consider include the following:

1. *Honor different strategies for doing mathematics.* Although this is a recommendation in standards documents, it is particularly important for children from other countries because they may have learned different ways to do the operations (Civil & Planas, 2010).
2. *Communicate with positive notes and phone calls.* Be sure to find a way to compliment each student's mathematical thinking (not just a good score on quiz) at some point early in the school year.
3. *Host informal gatherings to discuss mathematics teaching and learning.* Having regular opportunities to meet with the parents allows for the development of rapport and trust. Consider hosting events in out-of-school facilities. Schools in high-poverty communities have found that having parent events at a community center or religious institution brings in families that are reluctant to come into a school.
4. *Incorporate homework that involves the family.* When a student brings in homework that tells about his or her family and you provide positive feedback or a personal comment, then you are establishing a two-way communication with the family via homework.
5. *Translate letters that are sent home.* If you are doing a class newsletter for families or a letter describing the next mathematics unit, make an effort to translate the letter into the native language of the families represented in your class. If you cannot do this, consider having the first class session include a component in which students write to their families about what they are about to do. Ask them to write in their parents' first language and to include visuals to support their writing. Ask parents to respond (in their language of choice). This is a great practice for helping students know what they need to learn, and it communicates to families that they are an important part of that learning.
6. *Post homework on your webpage.* For parents that are not native speakers of English, posting problems on your site makes it easier for them to take advantage of online translations.

Although these translations may not be perfectly accurate, they can aid in helping parents and students understand the language in the problems.

For more suggestions, see Chapter 6 and read the NCTM Research Brief titled "Involving Latino and Latina Parents in Their Children's Mathematics Education" (Civil & Menéndez, 2010).

 Complete Self-Check 4.5: Planning for Family Engagement

REFLECTIONS ON CHAPTER 4

WRITING TO LEARN

1. What are advantages of using a three-phase lesson plan model? How does it compare to how you learned mathematics?

2. You are planning for a three-phase lesson on partitioning fractions (grade 2). Describe what you will do prior to actually planning the lesson.

3. You find a task for partitioning fractions: Using dotted grid paper, draw 4-by-4 squares. Then draw lines to show fourths. Find as many ways as you can. How might you develop a three-phase lesson around this task?

4. What are the important aspects you would consider while deciding what to differentiate? Explain one of these aspects with an example.

5. How can you teach parents to help their children study mathematics?

FOR DISCUSSION AND EXPLORATION

◆ Examine a textbook for any grade level. Look at a lesson and determine two or three objectives or big ideas covered in the chapter. Is the task worthwhile? Does it meet your students' needs? What assessments might you use? Collaboratively discuss all eight steps in the lesson planning process (see Figure 4.3).

◆ Take a major topic for a particular grade level (e.g., multiplication for grade 3). How can families be involved in supporting this learning goal? Consider the ideas discussed in the chapter, as well as online resources that can be used.

RESOURCES FOR CHAPTER 4

RECOMMENDED READINGS

Articles

Holden, B. (2008). Preparing for problem solving. *Teaching Children Mathematics, 14*(5), 290–295.

This excellent "how to" article shares how a first-grade teacher working in an urban high-poverty setting incorporated differentiated instruction. Holden describes how she prepared her classroom and her students to be successful through six specific steps.

Williams, L. (2008). Tiering and scaffolding: Two strategies for providing access to important mathematics. *Teaching Children Mathematics, 14*(6), 324–330.

Using a second-grade fraction lesson and a third-grade geometry lesson as examples, Williams shares how they were tiered, and

then how scaffolds, or supports, were built into the lesson. A very worthwhile article.

Focus Issue: Differentiation (October 2012). *Teaching Children Mathematics.*

This issue has a wonderful collection of articles with pragmatic suggestions for differentiating instruction.

Book

Litton, N. (1998). *Getting your math message out to parents: A K–6 resource.* Sausalito, CA: Math Solutions Publications.

Litton is a classroom teacher who has practical suggestions for communicating with family members. The book includes chapters on parent conferences, newsletters, homework, and family math night.

Creating Assessments *for* Learning

LEARNER OUTCOMES

After reading this chapter and engaging in the embedded activities and reflections, you should be able to:

5.1 Differentiate between formative and summative assessment.

5.2 Describe three important methods for assessing student understanding.

5.3 Analyze the kinds of rubrics and their uses.

5.4 Describe how writing can be used in assessment.

5.5 Explain the value of student self-assessment.

5.6 Identify ways that tests can be used in the classroom to enhance learning.

5.7 Explore ways to show evidence of and communicate about student learning with grades that shape instructional decisions.

What ideas about assessment come to mind from your personal experiences? Tests? Quizzes? Grades? Studying? Anxiety? All of these are common shared memories. Now suppose that you are told that the assessments you use should be designed to help students learn and to help you teach. How can assessment do those things?

 ## Integrating Assessment into Instruction

The Assessment Principle in *Principles and Standards* (2000) and NCTM's position statement (2013) stress two main ideas: (1) Assessment should enhance students' learning, and (2) assessment is a valuable tool for making instructional decisions. This aligns with the distinction between assessment *of* learning, where students are only evaluated on what they know at a given moment in an effort to home in on what they don't know, and assessment *for* learning, where students are continually evaluated so that instruction can be targeted to gaps and their learning is improved over time (Black & Wiliam, 1998).

Assessment is not separate from instruction and in fact should include the critical mathematical practices (CCSSO, 2010) and processes (NCTM, 2000) that occur in the course of effective problem-based instructional approaches. The typical end-of-chapter or end-of-year test of skills may have value, but it rarely reveals the type of data that can fine-tune instruction so that it is tailored to improving the performance of individual students. In fact, Daro, Mosher, and Corcoran (2011) state that "the starting point is the mathematics and thinking the student brings to the lesson, not the deficit of mathematics they do not bring" (p. 48). Stiggins (2009) goes further to suggest that students in the upper elementary grades should be informed partners in understanding their progress in learning and how to enhance their growth in understanding concepts. They should begin to use their own assessment results to move forward as learners as they see that "success is always within reach" (p. 420). Using carefully selected assessment tasks allows us to integrate assessment into instruction and make it part of the learning process.

Assessments usually fall into two major categories: summative or formative. *Summative assessments* are cumulative evaluations that might generate a single score, such as an end-of-unit test or the standardized test that is used in your state or school district. Although the scores are important for schools and teachers, they do not often help shape teaching decisions on particular topics or identify misunderstandings that may block future growth.

On the other hand, *formative assessments* are used to check the status of students' development during instructional activities, to preassess, or to attempt to identify students' naive understandings or misconceptions (Hattie, 2009; Popham, 2008; Wiliam, 2008). When implemented well, formative assessment dramatically increases the speed and amount of student learning (Nyquist, 2003; Wiliam, 2007; Wilson & Kenney, 2003) by providing targeted feedback to the student and using the results and evidence collected to improve instruction—either for the whole class or individual students. Meaningful feedback from (not to) the students as to what they know and where they make errors or have misconceptions is one of the most powerful influences on achievement (Hattie, 2009). The data you collect will inform your decision making for the next steps in the learning progression. As Wiliam states, "To be formative, assessment must include a recipe for future action" (2010, slide 41).

Wiliam goes on to note three key processes in formative assessment: (1) Identify where learners are; (2) identify the goal for the learners; and (3) identify a path to reach the goal. Let's look at example of this process. A third-grade class was asked to solve the following word problem: "If Lindy has 34 shells in her collection and Jesse has 47, how many shells are in both collections?" Immediately the teacher observes one student quickly jotting down a straight line on the paper, making a hash mark with a 34 underneath and using small arcs to jump up four times to 74, then making one jump of six and another jump of one and indicating 81 with a hash mark (see Figure 5.1). Another student selects from a collection of base-ten materials in the center of the table, models each number, groups the tens together, then combines the ones and trades 10 of the ones for an additional ten piece, getting 81 as an answer. Observing a different student, the teacher notes he is using counters but is counting by ones. First he counts out the 34, then the 47, and then recounts them all to reach 78 (miscounting along the way). The information gathered from observing these three students reveals very different paths the teacher should take for the next steps. This teacher is at the first step in Wiliam's three key processes, noting where students are in their learning. Moving into the second step, the teacher notes that one student should move to more challenging tasks, whereas the other two students need to move closer to the CCSS standard of representing and solving addition and subtraction problems within 100 through more targeted instruction.

If summative assessment could be described as a digital snapshot, formative assessment is like streaming video. One is a picture of what a student knows captured in a single moment of time; the other is a moving picture that demonstrates active student thinking and reasoning. In this video (https://www.youtube.com/watch?v=kPf0nQFfv50), Dylan Wiliam discusses strategies that support formative assessment. In the following pages we will focus on formative assessment approaches that include Piaget's three broad categories of formative assessments: observations, interviews, and tasks (Piaget, 1976).

What Is Assessment?

The term *assessment* is defined in the NCTM *Assessment Standards* (see Table 5.1) as a way to collect evidence about students' content knowledge, flexibility in applying that knowledge, and disposition or attitudes toward mathematics (NCTM, 1995). Note that "gathering evidence" is more than just giving a test or quiz. If you restrict your view of assessment to tests and quizzes, you will miss seeing how assessment can "make learning visible" (Hattie, 2009, p. 173) and thereby help students grow.

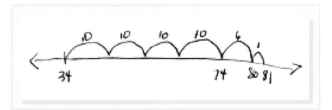

FIGURE 5.1 A student uses an empty number line to add 34 + 47.

TABLE 5.1 THE NCTM ASSESSMENT STANDARDS

Mathematics	• Base assessments on the essential concepts and skills as defined by state or local standards
	• Develop assessments that encourage the application of mathematics to real-world situations
	• Focus on significant and meaningful mathematics
Learning	• Incorporate assessment as an integral part of instruction and not an isolated singular event at the end of a unit of study
	• Inform students about important content by emphasizing those ideas in your instruction
	• Base future instruction on evidence of students' strengths or gaps of understanding
Equity	• Respect the unique qualities, experiences, and expertise of all students
	• Maintain high expectations for students while recognizing their individual needs
	• Incorporate multiple assessment approaches, including accommodations and modifications for students with disabilities
Openness	• Establish with students the expectations for their performance
	• Give attention not only to answers but also to the thinking processes students used
	• Provide examples of responses that do and do not meet expectations for student discussion
Inferences	• Reflect on what students are revealing about what they know
	• Use multiple assessments (e.g., observations, interviews, tasks, tests) to draw conclusions about students' performance
	• Establish a rubric that describes the evidence needed and the value of each component used for scoring
Coherence	• Match your assessments with both the objectives of your instruction and the methods and models used in your instruction
	• Ensure that assessments are a reflection of the desired expectations
	• Develop a feedback loop that allows you to use the assessment results to inform your instruction

Source: Adapted *Assessment Standards for School Mathematics*, copyright © 1995 by the National Council of Teachers of Mathematics. Reprinted with permission.

What Should Be Assessed?

The broader view of assessment requires that appropriate assessment of students' mathematical proficiency (National Research Council, 2001) reflects the full range of mathematics: concepts and procedures, mathematical processes and practices, and even students' disposition to mathematics.

Conceptual Understanding and Procedural Fluency. Good assessments provide students with the opportunity to demonstrate how they understand essential concepts in more than one way. For example, you can assess students as they complete an activity, observing as students discuss and justify—in short, while students are doing mathematics—and gain information that provides insight into the nature of the students' understanding of that idea. You can also ask for more detail, something often not possible on tests.

Procedural fluency should also be assessed. This includes understanding the procedure—if a student can compute with fractions yet has no idea of why he needs a common denominator for addition but not for multiplication, then the procedure has not been "mastered" to the extent it must be for a student to have procedural fluency.

Strategic Competence and Adaptive Reasoning. Truly understanding mathematics is more than just content knowledge. The skills represented in the five process standards of *Principles and Standards* and the eight Standards for Mathematical Practice from the *Common Core State Standards* should also be assessed. One way to communicate to students that the processes/practices are important is to craft a list of rubric statements about doing mathematics that your students can understand so they recognize what you expect. Here are several examples that can be used for individual work, group work, or discussions:

Problem Solving

• Works to make sense of and fully understand problems before beginning
• Perseveres to demonstrate a variety of strategies
• Assesses the reasonableness of answers

Reasoning

- Justifies solution methods and results
- Recognizes and uses counterexamples
- Makes conjectures and/or constructs logical progressions of statements based on reasoning

Communication

- Explains ideas in writing using words, pictures, numbers/equations, graphs, tables (depending on grade level)
- Analyzes the thinking of others
- Uses precise language, units, and labeling to clearly communicate ideas

Connections

- Makes connections between mathematics and real contexts
- Makes connections between mathematical ideas

Representations

- Uses representations such as drawings, graphs, symbols, and models to help think about and solve problems
- Moves between models
- Explains how different representations are connected

These statements should be discussed and explicitly modeled with your students to help them understand that these are valuable behaviors. Share weak and strong examples of student work with the class to help all students see how to improve.

Productive Disposition. Collecting data on students' ability to persevere, as well as their confidence and belief in their own mathematical abilities, is also an important assessment. This information is most often obtained with observation, self-reported assessments, interviews, and journal writing. Information on perseverance and willingness to attempt problems is available to you every day when you use a problem-solving approach.

 Complete Self-Check 5.1: Integrating Assessment into Instruction

 # Assessment Methods

There are three basic methods for using formative assessment to evaluate students' understanding: observations, interviews, and tasks (Piaget, 1976). *Tasks* refers to written products and includes performance-based tasks, writing (e.g., journal entries, student self-assessments), and tests. Here we will discuss each basic method in depth.

Observations

All teachers learn useful bits of information about their students every day. When the three-phase lesson format suggested in Chapter 3 is used, the flow of evidence about student performance increases dramatically, especially in the *during* and *after* portions of lessons. If you have a systematic plan for gathering this information while observing and listening to students during regular classroom instruction, at least two very valuable results occur. First, information that may have gone unnoticed is suddenly visible and important. Second, observation data gathered systematically can be added to other data and used in planning lessons, providing feedback to students, conducting parent conferences, and determining grades.

Depending on what information you may be trying to gather, several days to two weeks may be required to complete a single observation for each student on how they are progressing on a standard. Shorter periods of observation will focus on a particular cluster of concepts or skills or on particular students. Over longer periods, you can note growth in mathematical processes or practices, such as problem solving, modeling, or reasoning. To use observation effectively, you should take seriously the following maxim: *Only try to collect data on a reasonable number of students in a single class period.*

For example, students may be playing a game in which each child draws a domino, adds the two parts and compares it to the other child's total, with the higher amount scoring a point. As students play, the teacher is observing the way in which students are adding the two parts of the domino and how they use numbers. Some students count every dot on the domino. Others will use a counting-on strategy (the student sees four dots on one side and counts on from four to tally the total number). Some will recognize certain patterns immediately without counting. Others may be unsure whether 12 beats 11. Data gathered from asking questions about and listening to a pair of students work on an activity or an extended project provide significant insights into students' thinking (Petit & Zawojewski, 2010). Especially if used for grading, it is important to keep dated written anecdotal notes that can be referred to later.

Anecdotal Notes. One system for recording observations is to write short notes either during or immediately after a lesson in a brief narrative style. One possibility is to have a card for each student taped on the top edge of a clipboard (see Figure 5.2). Another is to write anecdotal notes on an electronic table and store them in a spreadsheet or in a multicolumn table that documents students' use of mathematical practices. In any case, focus your observations on about five students a day. The students selected may be members of one or two cooperative groups or a group previously identified as needing additional support.

Checklists. To cut down on writing and help focus your attention, an individual checklist with several specific processes, mathematical practices, or content objectives can be devised and duplicated for each student (see Figure 5.3). As you can see, there is a place for comments that should focus on specifics about students' conceptual understandings and achievement of big ideas. For example, you will probably find a note such as "is beginning to see how multiplication facts can be related, such as using 10×7 to think about 9×7" more helpful than "knows the easy multiplication facts but not the hard ones."

Another Observation Checklist involves listing all students in a class on one to three pages (see Figure 5.4). Across the top of the page are specific abilities or common misconceptions to look for. (These can be based on learning progressions or trajectories.) Pluses and minuses, checks, or codes can be entered in the grid. A full-class checklist is more likely to be used for long-term objectives. Topics that might be appropriate for this format include problem solving strategies, strategic use of representations or tools, and such skill areas as basic fact fluency or computational estimation. Dating entries or noting specifics about observed performance is also helpful.

Questioning. Observations do not have to be silent. Probing into student thinking through the use of questions can provide helpful data and more insights to inform instruction. As you circulate around the classroom to observe and evaluate students' understanding, your use of questions is one of

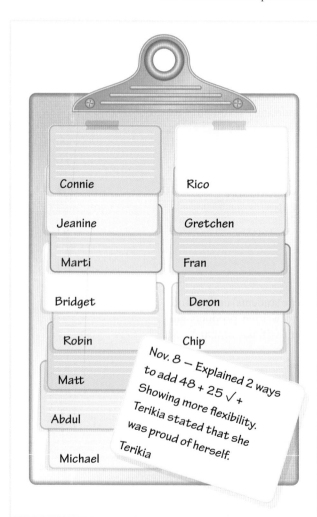

FIGURE 5.2 Preprinted cards for observation notes can be taped to a clipboard or folder for quick access.

the most important ways to formatively assess in each lesson phase. Keep the following essential questions in mind as you move about the classroom to prompt and probe students' thinking (print off these Question Probes to carry with you):

- What can you tell me about [today's topic]?
- How can you put the problem in your own words?
- What did you do that helped you understand the problem?
- How does this problem remind you of another problem we've done?
- Did you find any numbers or information you didn't need? How did you know that the information was not important?
- How did you decide what to do?
- How did you decide whether your answer was right?
- Did you try something that didn't work? How did you figure out it was not going to work?
- What is something you did in this problem that you could use to help you solve other problems?
- Can you show that idea with [a model, a sketch, an equation]?

Getting students accustomed to responding to these questions (as well as familiar with asking questions about their thinking and the thinking of others) helps prepare them for the more intensive questioning used in more formal interviews. Also, challenging students who are secure with their answers or thinking helps them focus on their reasoning.

Interviews

Diagnostic interviews are a means of getting in-depth information about an individual student's knowledge and mental strategies about concepts. The interview is usually a one-on-one investigation of a student's thinking about a particular

NAME: Sharon V.

FRACTIONS	NOT THERE YET	ON TARGET	ABOVE AND BEYOND	COMMENTS
Understands numerator/denominator		✓		
Area models		✓		Used pattern blocks to show 2/3 and 3/6
Set models	✓			
Uses fractions in real contexts	✓			
Estimates fraction quantities		✓		Showing greater reasonableness
PROBLEM SOLVING				
Understands problem before beginning work		✓		Stated problem in own words
Is willing to take risks	✓			Reluctant to use abstract models
Justifies results				

FIGURE 5.3 A focused checklist and rubric can be made for each student.

Topic:	Not There Yet	On Target	Above and Beyond	Comments
Mental Computation Adding 2-digit numbers	Can't do mentally	Has at least one strategy	Uses different methods with different numbers	
Names				
Lalie		✓ 3-18-09 3-21-09		
Pete	✓ 3-20-09	✓ 3-24-09		Difficulty with problems requiring regrouping
Sid			✓ + 3-20-09	Flexible approaches used
Lakeshia		✓		Counts by tens, then adds ones
George		✓		
Pam	✓			Beginning to add the group of tens first
Maria		✓ 3-24-09		Using a posted hundreds chart

FIGURE 5.4 A full-class observation checklist can be used for long-term or short-term objectives.

concept, process, or mathematical practice that lasts from three to ten minutes. The challenge of diagnostic interviews is that they are assessment opportunities, not teaching opportunities. It is hard to hear students making errors and not respond immediately. Instead, the interviews are used to listen to students' descriptions of their strategies and probe their understanding with the purpose of discovering both strengths and gaps,

These interviews, although often labor intensive, are rich assessments that provide powerful evidence. In each interview, a student is given a problem and asked to verbalize his or her thinking at points in the process. Sometimes students self-correct a mistake but, more frequently, teachers can unearth a student's misunderstanding or reveal what strategies students have mastered. When teachers focus on errors and identify common pitfalls they can build greater sophistication in students' conceptual understanding (Bray & Santagata, 2014).

The problems you select should match the essential understanding for the topic your students are studying. In every case, have paper, pencils, and a variety of materials available—particularly those models and materials you have been using during your instruction. It is often useful to have a scoring guide or rubric available to jot down notes about emerging understandings, common methods you expect students to use, or common misunderstandings that may come to light.

Examples of diagnostic interviews include asking students: Which is greater, $\frac{7}{8}$ or $\frac{7}{7}$? Or you could ask a student to look at the following: Are the two numbers circled the same?

In each case, the task should be aligned to recent work (such as the comparison of two possibly confusing fractions) or your attempts to pinpoint underlying foundational gaps in understanding (as in the potential for thinking that the sixes are the same rather than representing 6000 and 60). Also, see some sample interview options, including a Sample Interview for Primary Grades, a Sample Interview for Intermediate Grades, and/or Student Observation and Interview: Learning through Problems.

Diagnostic interviews have the potential to provide information that you simply cannot get in any other way. Think of interviews as a formative assessment tool to be used for only a few students at a time, not for every student in the class. You can briefly interview a single student while the rest of the class is working on a task or rotating through learning stations. For example, if the whole class is working in groups, you can explain to them that you will be interviewing some students to better understand their thinking. Teachers also work with a student at an interactive whiteboard and record the whole conversation and any written work.

The most obvious reason to consider an interview with a particular student is that you need more information about how he or she is mentally constructing concepts or using a procedure. In fact, these dialogues can be considered intensive error analysis. Follow-up instruction will be more successful if you can pinpoint why a student is having difficulty before you try to fix the problem.

A second reason for conducting an interview is to gather information to assess the effectiveness of your instruction. In an examination of hundreds of research studies, Hattie (2009) found that the feedback that teachers received from students on what they knew and did not know was critical in improving students' performance. That is precisely what diagnostic interviews are designed to do!

For example, are you certain that your students have a good understanding of place value, or are they just completing exercises according to rote procedures? Let's look at an actual classroom situation.

Ms. Marsal was working with George, a student with disabilities who was displaying difficulty with calculating multidigit numbers. George also exhibited unreasonable estimates to computations, in some cases thinking the answer to a problem would result in tens when it was in the hundreds. To get George to reveal where his thinking was in terms of what he understood and where some gaps might be, Ms. Marsal planned a diagnostic interview. Using an adaptation of a task modeled at a conference presentation (Griffin & Lavelle, 2010), she asked George to write the number that goes with 3 ones, 1 hundred, and 5 tens as written on a paper and shown here.

3 ones   1 hundred   5 tens

Although base-ten materials were on the table, they went untouched. George responded by writing 315 (writing in the order he heard the numbers, without attention to the place values). As is necessary in these interviews, Ms. Marsal resisted the temptation to immediately correct him, and instead probed further by asking George to take out 3 ones, 1 hundred, and 5 tens using the base-ten materials. Showing fluency with the values of base-ten materials, George took out the correct amounts and placed them on the table, but in the order given in the problem, not in place-value order. Then, when offered a place-value mat, George said, "I get it," and placed them in the correct positions. When asked to write the number that corresponded with the materials, George wrote the number (153), as seen in Figure 5.5. Ms. Marsal asked why he had two different answers and which number he thought was correct. George quietly pondered and then pointed to the second number (153) and said, "This one is right; I think you were trying to trick me."

FIGURE 5.5 Student work on place value.

Although this interview revealed that the student had a good grasp of the value of the base-ten materials, it also revealed that there were lingering gaps in his understanding of the place-value concepts. Yet, this is a case in which the diagnostic interview was an actual learning experience. Notice that the teacher linked the assessment to the classroom instruction through the use of concrete materials and the structured semiconcrete support of the place-value mat. This connection provided a way for the student to think about the actual size of the number rather than just the individual digits. In addition, the cognitive dissonance caused by the difference in the two numerical outcomes—one responding to just the words alone and the other with concrete materials—enabled more connected ideas to emerge. Planning could then begin for future instruction based on actual evidence from the student.

There is no one right way to plan or structure a diagnostic interview. In fact, flexibility is a key ingredient. You should, however, have an overall plan that includes an easier task and a more challenging task in case you have misjudged your starting point. Also, did you notice that the teacher in the vignette had instructional materials ready for the student to use? Be sure you have materials available that match those students have used during instruction and that could provide insights into what the student understands. Also be prepared with some probing questions. Here are a few to consider:

- How would you explain this to a second grader (or your younger sister)?
- Can you draw a picture to help you think about this problem?
- Can you explain what you just did?
- What does this [point to something on the paper] stand for?
- Why did you solve it that way?
- Can you show me what you are thinking with the [materials such as fraction pieces, counters, hundreds chart, and so on]?
- Why do you think you got two different answers? Which one do you think is correct?
- If you tried to do this problem again, which approach would you try first?

In each case, it is important to explore whether the student can use models to connect actions to what he or she wrote or explained earlier.

Consider the following suggestions as you implement your diagnostic interview:

- **Avoid revealing whether a student's answer is right or wrong.** Often facial expressions, tone of voice, or body language can give a student clues that the answer is correct or incorrect. Instead, use a response such as "Can you tell me more?" or "I think I know what you are thinking."
- **Wait silently for the student to give an answer.** Give ample time to allow the student to think and respond. Only then should you move to rephrasing the question or probing for a better understanding of the student's thoughts. After the student gives a response (whether it is accurate or not), wait again! This second wait time is even more important because it encourages the student to elaborate on his or her initial thought and provide more information. Waiting can also provide you with more time to think about the direction you want the interview to take.
- **Remember that you should not interject clues or teach.** The temptation to help is sometimes overwhelming. Watch and listen. Your goal is to use the interview not to teach but to find out where the student is in terms of conceptual understanding and procedural fluency.
- **Let students share their thinking freely without interruption.** Encourage students to use their own words and ways of writing things down. Interjecting questions or correcting language can be distracting to the flow of students' thinking and explanations.

The benefits of the diagnostic interview become evident as you plan instruction that capitalizes on students' strengths while recognizing possible weaknesses and confusion. Also, unlike large-scale testing, you can always ask another question to find out why a student is taking an incorrect or unexpected path. You may also discuss results of interviews with colleagues to gain shared insights (Stephan, McManus, & Dehlinger, 2014). These insights are invaluable in moving students to mathematical proficiency, as there is perhaps no better method for developing instruction that supports student understanding than having students explain their thinking and a team of teachers sharing a conversation about the evidence.

Tasks

The category of *tasks* refers to a variety of written products, including problem-based tasks, journal entries, student self-assessments, and tests. Good assessment tasks for either instructional or formative assessment purposes should permit every student in the class, regardless of mathematical ability, to demonstrate his or her knowledge, skill, or understanding.

Problem-Based Tasks. *Problem-based tasks* are tasks that are connected to actual problem solving activities used in instruction. Good tasks permit every student in the class to demonstrate their abilities (Rigelman & Petrick, 2014; Smith & Stein, 2011). They also include real-world or authentic contexts that interest students or relate to recent classroom events. Of course, be mindful that English language learners may need support with contexts, as those challenges with language should not overshadow the attention to their mathematical ability.

Problem-based tasks have several critical components that make them suitable for assessment. They:

- Focus on an important mathematics concept or skill aligned to a valued learning expectation
- Stimulate the connection of students' previous knowledge to new content
- Allow multiple solution methods or approaches with a variety of tools
- Offer opportunities for students to correct themselves along the way
- Provide occasions for students to confront common misconceptions
- Encourage students to use reasoning and explain their thinking
- Create opportunities to observe students' use of mathematical processes and practices
- Generate data for instructional decision making as you listen to your students' thinking

Notice that the following examples of problem-based tasks are not elaborate, yet when followed by a discussion, each can engage students for most of a class session (also see Problem-Based Tasks for other tasks to try with students). What mathematical ideas and practices are required to successfully respond to each of these tasks? Will the task help you determine how well students understand the ideas?

Shares   (Grades K–2)

Learning Targets: (1) Solve multistep problems involving the operations. (2) Use models and words to describe a solution.

Leila has 6 gumdrops, Darlene has 2, and Melissa has 4. They want to share them equally. How will they do it? Draw a picture to help explain your answer.

At second grade, the numbers in the "Shares" task should be larger. What additional concepts would be involved if the task were about sharing cookies and the total number of cookies was 34?

The Whole Set   (Grades 3–4)

Learning Targets: (1) Determine a whole, given a fractional part (using a set model). (2) Make sense of quantities and their relationships in a context.

Mary counted 15 cupcakes left from the whole batch that her mother made for the picnic. "We've already eaten two-fifths," she noticed. How many cupcakes did her mother bake?

In the following task, students are asked to think about the thinking of other students. Analysis of "other" students' performances is a good way to create tasks.

Decimals   (Grades 4–5)

Learning Targets: (1) Compare two decimals by reasoning about their size. (2) Analyze and critique the reasoning of others.

Alan tried to make a decimal number as close to 50 as he could using the digits 1, 4, 5, and 9. He arranged them in this order: 51.49. Jerry thinks he can arrange the same digits to get a number that is even closer to 50. Do you agree or disagree? Explain.

This next task is a good example of an open-ended assessment. Consider how much more valuable this task is than asking for the angle measure in the triangle on the left.

Two Triangles   (Grades 7–8)

Learning Targets: (1) Classify two-dimensional shapes into categories based on their properties.
(2) Attend to precision by applying definitions to define categories.

Tell everything you can about these two triangles. Given what you wrote about the two triangles, determine which of the following statements are true: The large triangle is an isosceles triangle; the small triangle is an isosceles triangle; the big triangle has an area of 2 square units; the small triangle has an area of 1 square unit; the large triangle has at least one angle that measures 45 degrees; the small triangle has at least one angle that measures 30 degrees; the two triangles are similar. Explain your thinking.

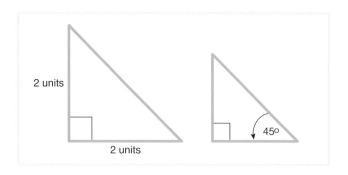

Algebra: Graphing (Grade 8)

Learning Targets: (1) Compare and analyze quadratic functions. (2) Build a logical argument for a conjecture using reasoning.

Does the graph of $y = x^2$ ever intersect the graph of $y = x^2 + 2$? What are some ways that you could test your conjecture? Would your conjecture hold true for other equations in the form of $y = x^2 + b$? Within all quadratic functions of the form $y = ax^2 + b$, when would your conjecture hold true?

Even with a graphing calculator, proving that these two graphs will not intersect requires reasoning and an understanding of how graphs are related to equations and tables.

Much can be learned about students' understanding in a discussion that follows students solving the task individually. Watch this video called My Favorite No (https://www.youtube.com/watch?v=srJWx7P6uLE) to see how a teacher uses students' incorrect answers to develop a conversation about mathematics. Students must develop the habit of sharing, writing, and listening to justifications. In particular, it is important for students to compare and make connections between strategies and debate ideas in order to assist them in organizing their thoughts, thinking about their position, and analyzing the positions of others. This can be developed by forcing students to take a position (e.g., Does the order of factors affect the answer in a multiplication problem?). The resulting discussions will often reveal students' misconceptions and serve as reminders about previous discussions (using ideas that came to the forefront in previous classes) (Barlow & McCrory, 2011).

Translation Tasks. One important option for a task is what we refer to as a *translation task*. Using seven representations for concepts, students are asked to use more than one representation (e.g., words, tools, and numbers) to demonstrate understanding of a single problem. As students move between these representations, there is a better chance that a concept will be formed correctly and integrated into a rich web of ideas.

So what is a good way of structuring a translation task? With use of template based on a format for assessing concept mastery from Frayer, Fredrick, and Klausmeier (1969) (see Figure 5.6) and a Translation Task Activity Page, you can give students a computational equation and ask them to:

Equation/Written Symbols	Story Problem/Real-World Situation
36 + 49 =	
Model/Illustration	Explanation/Meaning of the Operation

FIGURE 5.6   Translation task template with example task.

- Write a word problem that matches the equation
- Illustrate the equation with materials, models, or drawings
- Explain their process of arriving at an answer or the meaning of the operation

In particular, students' ability to communicate how they solved a problem is critical for open-response questions on many summative assessments (Parker & Breyfogle, 2011).

Translation tasks can be used for whole-class lessons or for individual or small-group diagnosis. For example, second-grade children may be given an equation such as $36 + 49 = ?$. Their task could be to draw a model of base-ten materials in the "Model/Illustration" area (younger children could just use manipulatives), describe a story problem or real-world situation in the upper right corner and explain to another person in writing (or scripted or audio recorded by the teacher for younger children) how they solved the addition in the fourth area marked "Explanation/Meaning of the Operation."

Think about using translation tasks when you want to find out more about a student's ability to represent ideas in various forms and explain why these representations are similar or different. Depending on the age of the student, the translation task can start in any section of the template, with the student filling in the other three sections. For example, in the "Word Problem" area, write "One side of the rectangle is 6 cm. The area is 48 cm². How long is the other side?"

One step in the process of moving from teaching tasks to assessment tasks involves the addition of a rubric. The next section will explain how you can create and use both generic rubrics that describe general qualities of performance and topic-specific (or curriculum-based) rubrics that include criteria based on particular lesson objectives.

 Complete Self-Check 5.2: Assessment Methods

 # Rubrics and Their Uses

Problem-based tasks may tell us a great deal about what students know, but how do we analyze and use this information? These assessments yield an enormous amount of information that must be evaluated by examining more than just a simple count of correct answers. A rubric consists of a scale based on predetermined criteria with two important functions: (1) It permits the student to see what is central to excellent performance, and (2) it provides the teacher with scoring guidelines that support analysis of students' work.

It may be helpful to make a distinction between *scoring* and *grading*. *Scoring* compares students' work by established criteria set in advance—many times collected by a rubric. *Grading* is summarizing a student's performance through the accumulation of a variety of scores and data about their understanding of important concepts and skills (Stenmark & Bush, 2001).

In a teaching-through-problem-solving approach, you will often include criteria and performance indicators on your rubrics such as the following:

- Solved the problem(s) accurately and effectively
- Justified and explained strategy use or arguments
- Used logical reasoning
- Expressed a grasp of numerical relationships and structure
- Incorporated multiple representations and/or multiple strategies
- Demonstrated an ability to appropriately select and use tools and manipulatives
- Communicated with precise language and accurate units
- Identified general patterns of ideas that repeat, making connections from one big idea to another

Rubrics are usually built from the highest possible score or level. By describing what an outstanding performance would be on a given standard or learning target (these are called performance indicators, performance level descriptors, or achievement level descriptors), you are then able to set the benchmarks for the other levels.

There are two groups nationally that are building assessments to align with the Common Core State Standards. One is the Partnership for Assessment of Readiness for College and Careers (PARCC) and it has published grade level and subject-specific Performance Level Descriptors (PLDs), which describe what students at specific performance levels should know and be able to do relative to grade-level or course content standards. The PLDs can be found on PARCC's website and can serve as the starting point for developing high quality performance based rubrics for grades 3–8 mathematics. The second group is the Smarter Balanced Assessment Consortium (SBAC) and it has a similar resource on their website called the Achievement Level Descriptors (ALDs). These serve as descriptions of the knowledge, skills, and processes demonstrated by students in each category of performance. These ALDs can be used by various stakeholders to understand the types of knowledge, skills, and processes that students have demonstrated on the SBAC assessments. There are four types of ALDs designed to serve the following purposes: (1) test development and conceptualization (Policy ALDs), (2) item-writing guidance (Range ALDs), (3) cut-score recommendation and standard-setting guidance (Threshold ALDs), and (4) test-score interpretation (Reporting PLDs). See if your local school system is using either and explore these resources.

Generic Rubrics

Generic rubrics identify broad categories of performance instead of specific criteria for a particular task and therefore can be used for multiple assignments. The generic rubric allows a teacher to score performances by first sorting into two broad categories, as illustrated in the four-point rubric shown in Figure 5.7. The scale then allows you to separate each category into two additional levels as shown. A rating of 0 is given for no response, no effort, or for responses that are completely off task. The advantage of the four-point scale is the relatively easy initial sort into "Got It" or "Not There Yet."

Another possibility is to use your three- or four-point generic rubric on a reusable form (see Four-Point Rubric), as in Figure 5.7. This method is especially useful for planning purposes.

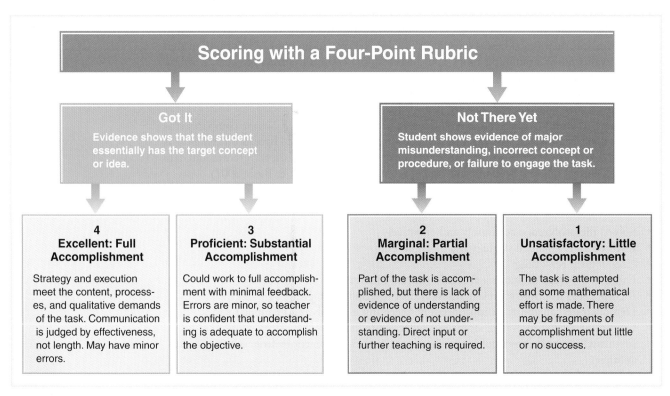

FIGURE 5.7 With a four-point generic rubric, performances are first sorted into two categories. Each performance is then considered again and assigned to a point on the scale.

But there are times when the generic rubrics do not give enough definition of the specific criteria for a particular task. For those instances, a task-specific rubric is helpful.

Task-Specific Rubrics

Task-specific rubrics include specific statements, also known as *performance indicators*, that describe what students' work should look like at each level of the rubric and, in so doing, establish criteria for acceptable performance on that particular task. Initially, it may be difficult to predict what student performance at different levels will or should look like, but your criteria will depend on your knowledge and experience with students at that grade level and your insights about the task or mathematical concept. One important part of setting performance levels is predicting students' common misconceptions or the expected thinking or approaches to the same or similar problems.

To facilitate developing performance levels, write out indicators of "proficient" or "on target" performances before you use the task in class. This self-check will ensure that the task is likely to accomplish your purpose. If you find yourself writing performance indicators in terms of the number of correct responses, you are most likely looking at drill or practice exercises, not the problem-based tasks for which a rubric is appropriate. Like athletes who continually strive for better performances rather than "good enough," students should always recognize the opportunities to excel. When you take into account the total performance (processes, answers, justifications, extension, and so on), it is always possible to "go above and beyond."

Consider use a flexible Anecdotal Notes Rubric (see Figure 5.8) with space for content indicators and another column to jot down names of students who fall in that performance grouping. A quick note or comment may be added to a name.

Pause & Reflect

Consider the task titled "The Whole Set" on page 93. Assume you are creating a task-specific four-point rubric to share with your fourth graders. What indicators would you use for level 3 and level 4 performances? Start with a level 3 performance, then think about level 4. Try this before reading further. ●

Determining performance indicators is always a subjective process based on professional judgment. Here is one possible set of indicators for the "The Whole Set" task:

3. Determines the correct answer or uses an approach that would yield a correct answer if not for minor errors. Explanations and reasoning are weak. Giving a correct result and reasoning for the number eaten but an incorrect result for the total baked would also be a level 3 performance.
4. Determines the total number baked and uses words, pictures, and numbers to explain and justify the result and how it was obtained. Demonstrates a knowledge of fractional parts and the relation to the whole.

Indicators such as these should be shared ahead of time with students. Sharing indicators before working on a task clearly conveys what is valued and expected. In addition, it is important to review the indicators with students after they get their tasks and rubrics. Including examples of correct answers and successful responses (anonymously) will help students understand how they may have done better. Importantly, students need to see models of what a level 4 performance looks like.

FIGURE 5.8 Record names in a rubric during an activity or for a single topic over several days.

What about level 1 and level 2 performances? Here are suggestions for the same task:

2. Uses some aspect of fractions appropriately (e.g., divides the 15 into 5 groups instead of 3) but fails to illustrate an understanding of how to determine the whole. Shows evidence that they don't understand a fraction is a number. (The student may believe it is two whole numbers.)

1. Shows some effort but little or no understanding of a fractional part relative to the whole.

Unexpected methods and solutions happen. Don't box students into demonstrating their understanding only as you thought or hoped they would when there is evidence that they are accomplishing your objectives in different ways. Such occurrences can help you revise or refine your rubric for future use.

At the beginning of the year, discuss your generic rubric (such as Figure 5.7) with the class and post it prominently. When students start to understand what the rubric really means, you might have students self-assess their own work using the generic Four Point Rubric and explain their reasons for the rating.

 Complete Self-Check 5.3: Rubrics and Their Uses

 Writing as an Assessment Tool

As an assessment tool, writing in journals, exit slips, or other formats provides a unique window to students' perceptions and the way a student is thinking about an idea. Even a kindergartner can express ideas in markings on paper and begin to explain what he or she is thinking. Finally, student writing is an excellent form of communication with parents during conferences. Writing shows evidence of students' thinking, telling parents much more than any grade or test score.

When students write about their solutions to a task prior to class discussions, the writing can serve as a rehearsal for the conversation about the work. Students who otherwise have difficulty thinking on their feet now have a script to support their contributions. Call on these more reluctant talkers first so that their ideas are heard and valued. They can also summarize a learning situation through such prompts as:

Concepts and Processes

- "I think the answer is . . . I think this because. . . ." (Some teachers duplicate the problem and have students tape it into the journal.)
- Write an explanation for a new or younger student of why 4×7 is the same as 7×4 and whether this works for 6×49 and 49×6. If so, why?
- Explain to a student in class (or who was absent today) what you learned about decimals.
- If you got stuck today in solving a problem, where in the problem did you have trouble?
- After you got the answer to today's problem, what did you do so that you were convinced your answer was reasonable? How sure are you that you got the correct answer?
- Write a story problem that goes with this equation [this graph, this diagram, this picture].

Productive Dispositions

- "What I like the most (or least) about mathematics is . . ."
- Write a mathematics autobiography. Tell about your experiences in mathematics outside of school and how you feel about the subject.
- What was the most interesting mathematics idea you learned this week?

If you are working with pre-K–1 students, these writing prompts may sound too advanced. However, there are specific techniques for journals in kindergarten and first grade that have been used successfully. To begin the development of the writing-in-mathematics process, use a language experience approach. After an activity, write "Giant Journal" and a topic or prompt on a large flipchart or interactive whiteboard. Students respond to the prompt, and then you write their ideas, adding the contributor's name and even drawings when appropriate, as in Figure 5.9. The "writing" should be a record of something the student has just done and is comfortable with.

 Complete Self-Check 5.4: Writing as an Assessment Tool

 # Student Self-Assessment

Stenmark (1989) notes that when students assess their own progress and growth they are developing an important life-long learning skill. Student self-assessment should not be your only measure of their learning or disposition, but rather a record of how *they perceive* their strengths and weaknesses as they begin to take responsibility for their learning.

You can gather student self-assessment data in several ways, including preassessments that catch areas of confusion or misconceptions prior to formally assessing students on particular content or by regularly using exit slips (index cards or paper slips with a quick question or two) when students are concluding the instructional period (Wieser, 2008). As you plan for the self-assessment, consider what you need to know to help you find better instructional strategies and revised learning targets. Convey to your students why you are having them do this activity—they need to grasp that they must play a role in their mastery of mathematics rather than just focus on completing a task. Encourage them to be honest and candid.

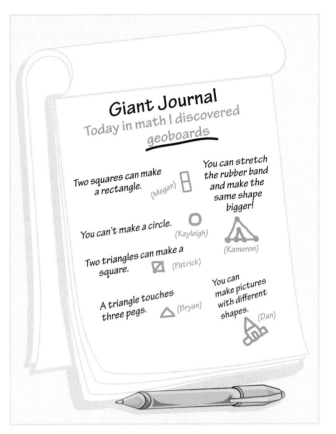

FIGURE 5.9 A journal in kindergarten may be a class product on a flipchart.

An open-ended writing prompt is a successful method of getting self-assessment data:

- How well do you think you understand the work we have been doing on fractions during the last few days? What is still causing you difficulty with fractions?
- Write two of the important things you learned in class today (or this week).
- Which problem(s) on the activity sheet/quiz did you find the most challenging? Which were the easiest?

Another method is to use some form of a questionnaire to which students respond. These can have open-ended questions, response choices (e.g., *seldom, sometimes, often; disagree, don't care, agree*), concept maps, drawings, and so on. Many such instruments appear in the literature (see Whitin, 2007), and many textbook publishers also provide examples. Here are some items you could use to build such a questionnaire:

- I feel sure of myself when I get an answer to a problem.
- I sometimes just put down any answer so I can get finished.
- I like to work on really hard math problems.
- Math class makes me feel nervous.
- If I get stuck, I feel like quitting or going to another problem.
- I am not as good in mathematics as most of the other students in this class.
- Mathematics is my favorite subject.
- Memorizing rules is the only way I know to learn mathematics.
- I will work a long time at a problem until I think I've solved it.

In each case, the self-assessment supports students' movement to be active rather than passive learners. Although it takes additional time to infuse these assessments into the daily schedule, allowing students to take part in the assessment process is motivating and encourages students to monitor and adapt their approaches to learning.

 Complete Self-Check 5.5: Student Self-Assessment

Tests

Tests will always be a part of assessment and evaluation, and like all other forms of assessment, they should match the goals of your instruction. Tests can be designed to find out what concepts students understand and how their ideas are connected. Tests of procedural knowledge should go beyond just knowing how to perform an algorithm and to require the student to demonstrate a conceptual basis for the process. The following examples will illustrate these ideas.

1. Write a multiplication problem that has an answer that falls between the answers to these two problems:

$$\begin{array}{cc} 49 & 45 \\ \times 25 & \times 30 \end{array}$$

2. **a.** In this division exercise, what number tells how many tens were shared among the 6 sets?
   a. Instead of writing the remainder as "R2," Elaine writes "$\frac{1}{3}$." Explain the difference between these two ways of recording the leftover part.

$$6\overline{)296}\,^{49\,R2} \qquad 6\overline{)296}\,^{49\frac{1}{3}}$$

3. On a grid, draw two figures with the same area but different perimeters. List the area and perimeter of each.

4. For each subtraction fact, write an addition fact that helps you think of the answer to the subtraction fact.

$$\begin{array}{cccc} 12 & 9 & 9 & 14 \\ \underline{-3} & \underline{+3} & \underline{-4} & \underline{-7} \\ 9 & 12 & & \end{array}$$

5. Draw pictures of arrows to show why $^-3 + {}^-4$ is the same as $^-3 - {}^+4$.

   If a test is well constructed, much more information can be gathered than simply the number of correct or incorrect answers. The following considerations can help maximize the value of your tests:

1. *Permit students to use calculators.* Except for tests of computational skills, calculators allow students to focus on what you really want to test.

2. *Use manipulatives and drawings.* Students can use models to work on test questions when those same models have been used during instruction to develop concepts. Simple drawings can be used to represent counters, base-ten pieces, fraction pieces, and the like (see Figure 5.10). Be sure to provide examples in class of how to draw the models before you ask students to draw on a test.

3. *Include opportunities for explanations.* Give students the time and space to describe their thinking and their use of strategies.

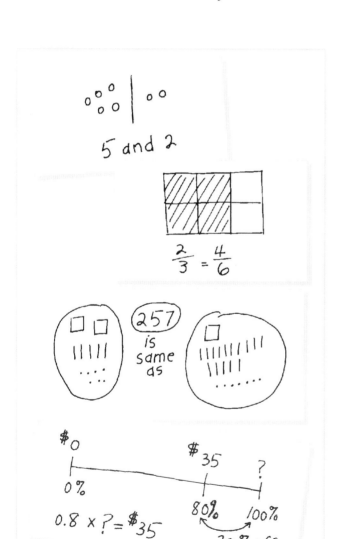

FIGURE 5.10 Students can use drawings to illustrate concepts on tests.

4. *Use open-ended questions.* Tests in which questions have only one correct answer tend to limit what you can learn about what the student has learned.

Another option is to consider quizzes that are done in collaboration with a peer. These "partner quizzes" (Danielson & Luke, 2006) allow for more complex problems, so that students need to talk and are unlikely to want to work on their own. Although some students will work individually first and then discuss the problems, others will discuss along the way. Once they have a partner for a quiz, they will not get that partner again (and no talking to others—only your partner). The teacher comments on and evaluates only one of the team's quizzes and then the partners are able to revise and resubmit. The increased student dialogue and discussion of answers links well to the goal of analyzing the reasoning of others!

Improving Performance on High-Stakes Tests

Many school systems have mandated summative tests in mathematics at every grade from 3 through 8. Although the method of testing and even the objectives to be tested remain up to individual states, now with the adoption of the Common Core State Standards, many states will be sharing end-of-year assessments. These assessments will include performance assessments and not just rely on multiple-choice questions (Sawchuk, 2010).

Whatever the details of the testing program in your particular state, these external tests impose significant pressures on school districts, which in turn put pressure on principals and teachers. External testing that has such consequences is typically referred to as *high-stakes* testing. High stakes make the pressures of testing significant for both students (Will I pass? Will my parents be upset?) and teachers (Will my class meet proficiency levels?). The pressures certainly have an effect on instruction. Because you will likely not be able to avoid the pressures of high-stakes testing, the question becomes, "How will you respond?"

The best advice for succeeding on high-stakes tests is to teach the big ideas in the mathematics curriculum that are aligned with your required standards. Students who have learned conceptual ideas in a manner focused on relational understanding and who have learned the processes and practices of doing mathematics will perform well on tests, regardless of the format or specific objectives. In short, a problem-based approach is the best course of action for raising scores.

 Complete Self-Check 5.6: Tests

 # Communicating Grades and Shaping Instruction

A grade is a statistic used to communicate to others the achievement level that a student has attained in a particular area of study. The accuracy or validity of the grade is dependent on the information used in generating the grade, the professional judgment of the teacher, and the alignment of the assessments with goals and objectives. Determining a grade requires using scores along with other information about a student's work—it is not merely averaging available scores.

For effective use of the assessment information gathered from problems, tasks, and other appropriate methods to assign grades, some hard decisions are inevitable. Some are philosophical, some require school or district policies about grades, and all require us to examine what we value and the objectives we communicate to students and parents.

Among the many components of the grading process, one truth is undeniable: *What gets graded by teachers is what gets valued by students.* Using observations, interviews, exit slips, journals, and rubric scores to provide feedback and encourage a pursuit of excellence must also relate to grades (NCTM, 2014). However, mistakenly converting four out of five on a rubric score to a percentage or three out of four on a rubric to a grade of C can focus the attention on grades rather than the emphasis on learning and striving for excellence (Kulm, 1994). Instead, grading must be based on the performance tasks and other activities for which you assigned rubric ratings; otherwise, students will soon realize that these are not important scores. The grade at the end of the marking period should reflect a holistic view of where the student is now relative to your goals.

The process of grading students using multiple forms of assessment has the potential to enhance your students' achievement. As you develop tools to match your instruction and provide evidence of your students' understanding, also work with colleagues. In small groups or with a grade-level partner, you can share tasks, analyze samples of students' work to try to decipher errors, and engage in discussions about how they have responded to similar student misconceptions. Working as a team to create, implement, and analyze assessments will enrich your ability to select and administer meaningful performance-based questions or tasks and enhance your professional judgment by questioning or confirming your thinking.

For assessments to be useful, teachers must know how to act on the evidence revealed in an assessment or set of assessments to address the learning needs of students (Heritage, Kim, Vendlinski, & Herman, 2009). This includes shifting from one approach or strategy development to another, pointing out examples or counterexamples to students, or using different materials and prompts. Knowing how to shape the next steps in instruction for an individual when the content is not learned is critical if you are going to avoid "covering" topics and move toward student growth and progress. If instead you just move on without some students, "students accumulate debts of knowledge (knowledge owed to them)" (Daro, Mosher, & Corcoran, 2011, p. 48). Take some time to watch Daniel J. Brahier's webinar posted on NCTM's website titled, "Principles to Actions: Actions to Improve Curriculum and Assessment Practices."

Summative assessment scores on high-stakes tests are of little utility in creating instructional next steps to help students progress (Daro, Mosher, & Corcoran, 2011). But the formative assessment described throughout this book can help. Interspersed in Section II of this book are Formative Assessment Notes that suggest ways to assess areas where students struggle; in some cases, including specific activities as follow-up lessons. As you learn more about your students, you will be able to target lessons that will address their naive understandings and misconceptions through the learning supports provided in each chapter.

 Complete Self-Check 5.7: Communicating Grades and Shaping Instruction

REFLECTIONS ON CHAPTER 5

WRITING TO LEARN

1. What is the difference between formative and summative assessment? Give examples of each.
2. Describe the essential features of a rubric. Give three examples of performance indicators.
3. How can you incorporate self-assessment in teaching? How does it help the learning?
4. How does writing serve as a learning tool?
5. What care should be taken by the teacher in the grading process?

FOR DISCUSSION AND EXPLORATION

♦ Examine a few end-of-chapter tests in various mathematics textbooks. How well do the tests assess concepts and understanding? Mathematical processes and practices?

♦ Research studies have shown that testing students during the teaching process enhances their learning of the subject. Collaborate with your grade-peers to devise experiments to evaluate the effectiveness of tests during teaching. Examine the factors in test design that may not lead to significant improvement in learning, and try to think of ways to avoid these pitfalls.

RESOURCES FOR CHAPTER 5

RECOMMENDED READINGS

Articles

Kling, G., & Bay-Williams, J. (2014). Assessing basic fact fluency. *Teaching Children Mathematics, 20*(8), 488–497.

These authors share examples of a variety of formative assessment ideas that include observations, interviews, journaling, and quizzes on the road to fact fluency. They also address the limitations and risks of timed tests.

Walker, E. T., & Molisani, J. (2014). Driving students to performance assessments: What students can do. *Mathematics Teaching in the Middle School, 19*(8), 468–476.

The authors describe a performance assessment that involves applying knowledge about proportion and scale as the students work with matchbox cars. The task, a task-specific rubric, and insights about student learning are shared.

Books

Collins, A. (Ed.). (2011). *Using classroom assessment to improve student learning.* Reston, VA: NCTM.

Using CCSS-M–based examples, this book focuses on formative assessments for middle grades. Emphasizing such strategies as questioning, observation protocols, interviews, classroom discussions, and exit slips, this practical guide is a worthwhile resource.

Wright, R., Martland, J., & Stafford, A. (2006). *Early numeracy: Assessment for teaching and intervention.* London, UK: Paul Chapman Educational Publishers.

This book includes diagnostic interviews for assessing young students' knowledge and strategy use related to number and the operations of addition and subtraction. Using a series of frameworks, the authors help teachers pinpoint students' misconceptions and support appropriate interventions.

CHAPTER 6

Teaching Mathematics Equitably to All Children

LEARNER OUTCOMES

After reading this chapter and engaging in the embedded activities and reflections, you should be able to:

6.1 Differentiate between a modification and an accommodation.

6.2 Describe the components of a multitiered system of support for struggling students and identify successful components of interventions for students with disabilities.

6.3 Explain characteristics of culturally responsive instruction, including how to focus on developing academic vocabulary during mathematics instruction.

6.4 Apply knowledge of working with students who are gifted and talented mathematically.

6.5 Detail ways to implement a gender-friendly classroom.

6.6 Illustrate approaches that are used to develop students' resilience and reduce resistance in learning mathematics.

The NCTM position statement on Access and Equity in Mathematics Education states that we should hold the expectation that all children can reach mathematics proficiency and that high levels performance must be attained regardless of race, ethnicity, gender, socioeconomic status, ability, or linguistic background (NCTM, 2014). Students need opportunities to advance their knowledge supported by teaching that gives attention to their individual learning needs. Students' backgrounds are not only an important part of who they are as people, but who they are as learners—and this background enriches the classroom.

Many *achievement* gaps are actually *instructional* gaps or *expectation* gaps. It is not helpful when teachers set low expectations for students, such as when they say, "I just cannot put this class into groups to work; they are too unruly" or "My students can't solve word problems—they don't have the reading skills." Operating under the belief that some students cannot do mathematics ensures that they won't have ample opportunities to prove otherwise. Instead we suggest you consider Storeygard's (2010) mantra for teachers, which proclaims, "My kids can!"

 ## Mathematics for ALL Students

Teaching for equity is much more than providing students with an equal opportunity to learn mathematics. It is not enough to require the same mathematics courses, give the same assignments, and use the identical assessment criteria. Instead, teaching for equity attempts to attain equal outcomes for all students by being sensitive to individual differences. Equitable instruction comes from having high expectations for all learners as aligned with NCTM's position statement (2014). How you will maintain equal outcomes (high expectations) and yet provide for individual differences (strong support) is challenging. Equipping yourself with an ever-growing collection of instructional strategies for a variety of students is critical. A strategy that works for one student may be completely ineffective with another, even for a student with the same exceptionality. Addressing the needs of *all* means providing access and opportunity for:

- Students who are identified as struggling or having a disability
- Students from different cultural backgrounds
- Students who are English language learners
- Students who are mathematically gifted
- Students who are unmotivated or need to build resilience

You may think, "I do not need to read the section on culturally and linguistically diverse (CLD) students because I plan on working in a school that doesn't have an immigrant population." But demographics continue to shift. Did you know that between 1970 and 2012 the Hispanic population in the United States increased sixfold (Brown, 2014)? In 2012, 13 percent of the U.S. population was born outside of the United States, and within this group there are more individuals who are not citizens than are naturalized citizens (U.S. Census Bureau, 2014).

Or you may think, "I can skip the section on mathematically gifted students because they will be pulled out for math enrichment." But students who are mathematically talented need to be challenged in the daily core instruction, not just when they are participating in a program for gifted students.

The goal of equity is to offer all students access to important mathematics during their regular mathematics instruction in the classroom. Yet inequities exist, even if unintentionally. For example, if teachers do not build in opportunities for student-to-student interaction in a lesson, they may not be addressing the needs of girls, who are often social learners, or English language learners, who need opportunities to speak, listen, and write in small-group situations. It takes more than a desire to be fair or equitable; it takes knowing the strategies that accommodate each type of learner and making every effort to incorporate those strategies into your teaching. "Equity does not mean that every student should receive identical instruction; instead, it demands that reasonable and appropriate accommodations be made as needed to promote access and attainment for all students" (NCTM, 2000, p. 12)*. Take the time to watch, **"Webcast**–Making Math Work for All –A Focus on Equity,"** facilitated by Dr. Robert Q. Berry, III, and available on NCTM's website.

As you work with students' areas of strength, identify opportunities to stretch students' thinking in ways that change unfamiliar experiences to more familiar ones. For example, if you are teaching area and you are discussing plots of land or gardens with students who live in an urban setting, reading a story such as *City Green* (Disalvo-Ryan, 1994) can help make the unknown known. Students can see how a land plot in an urban community can be divided and shared among neighbors. With this approach, all students can experience the background context needed for the task.

There are two paths to making a given task accessible to all students: *accommodation* and *modification*. An *accommodation* is a response to the needs of the environment or the learner; it does not alter the task. For example, you might write down directions for a student instead of just saying them or printing the task in a larger font. On the other hand, a *modification* changes the task, making it more accessible to the student. For example, suppose the task begins with finding the area of a compound shape, as shown here.

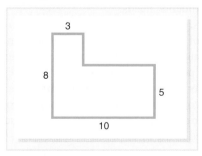

You may decide instead to break the shape up into two rectangles and ask the student to find the area of each shape and combine. Then have the student attempt the next shape without the modification—you should always lead back to the original task. However, if you decide to begin with rectangular regions and build to compound shapes composed of rectangles, you have *scaffolded* the lesson in a way to ramp up to the original task. In planning accommodations and modifications, the goal is to enable each student to successfully reach your learning objectives, not to change the objectives. This is how equity is achieved—by reaching equal *outcomes*, not by equal treatment. Treating students the same when they each learn differently does not make sense.

Complete an Accommodation or Modification Needs table to reflect on how you will plan for students in your classroom who have special needs. Record the evidence that you are adapting the learning situation.

 Complete Self-Check 6.1: Mathematics for ALL Students

 # Providing for Students Who Struggle and Those with Special Needs

One of the basic tenets of education is the need for individualizing the content taught and the methods used for students who struggle, particularly those with special needs. Mathematics learning disabilities are best thought of as cognitive differences, not cognitive deficits (Lewis, 2014). Students with disabilities often have mandated individualized education programs (IEPs) that guarantee access to grade-level mathematics content—in a general education classroom, if possible. This legislation also implies that educators consider individual learning needs not only in terms of *what* mathematics is taught but also *how* it is taught.

Prevention Models

In many areas, a systematic process for achieving higher levels performance for all students includes a multitiered system of support frequently called response to intervention (RtI). This approach commonly emphasizes ways for struggling students to get immediate assistance and support rather than waiting to fail before they receive help. Multitiered models are centered on the three interwoven elements: high-quality curriculum, instructional support (interventions), and formative assessments that capture students' strengths and weaknesses. These models were designed to determine whether low achievement was due to a lack of high-quality mathematics (i.e., "teacher-disabled students") (Baroody, 2011; Ysseldyke, 2002) or due to an actual learning disability. They can also help determine more intensive instructional options for students who may need to have advanced mathematical challenges beyond what other students study.

Response to Intervention. RtI (https://www.youtube.com/watch?v=nkK1bT8ls0M) is a multitiered student support system that is often represented in a triangular format. As you might guess, there are a variety of RtI models developed by school systems as they structure their unique approaches to students' needs.

As you move up the tiers, the number of students involved decreases, the teacher–student ratio decreases, and the level of intervention increases. Each tier in the triangle represents a level of intervention with corresponding monitoring of results and outcomes, as shown in Figure 6.1. The foundational and largest portion of the triangle (tier 1) represents the core instruction that should be used with all students based on a high-quality mathematics curriculum and instructional practices (i.e., manipulatives, conceptual emphasis, etc.) and on progress monitoring assessments. For example, if using a graphic organizer in tier 1 core math instruction, the following high-quality practices would be expected in the three phases of the lesson—*before*, *during*, and *after*:

- *Before*: States lesson purpose, introduces new vocabulary, clarifies concepts from needed prior knowledge in a visual organizer, and defines tasks of group members (if groups are being used)

- *During*: Displays directions in a chart, poster, or list; provides a set of guiding questions in a chart with blank spaces for responses
- *After*: Facilitates a discussion to highlight or make more explicit the significant concepts or skills and then presents summary and list of important concepts as they relate to one another

Tier 2 represents students who did not reach the level of achievement expected during tier 1 instruction. Students in tier 2 should receive supplemental targeted instruction (interventions) using more explicit strategies with systematic teaching of critical skills and concepts, more intensive and frequent instructional opportunities, and more supportive and precise prompts to students (Torgesen, 2002). The NCTM Position Statement on Interventions (2011) suggests that they endorse the use of interventions that increase in intensity as students demonstrate continuing struggles with learning mathematics. Interventions may require "heroic action to preclude serious complications" (Fuchs & Fuchs, 2001, p. 86).

If further assessment reveals students have made favorable progress, the extra interventions are faded and discontinued. But, if difficulties and struggles remain, the interventions can be adjusted in intensity, and in rare cases, students are referred to the next tier of support. Tier 3 is for students who need intensive assistance, which may include comprehensive mathematics instruction or a referral for special education evaluation or special education services. Strategies for the three tiers are outlined in Table 6.1.

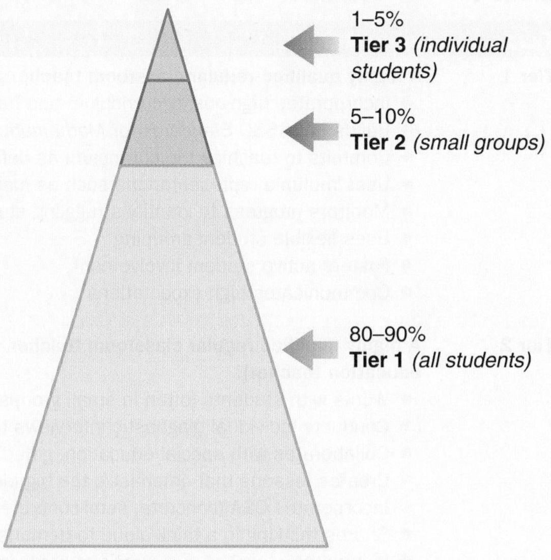

Progress Monitoring. A key to guiding students' movement within tiers is the monitoring of students' progress. One way to collect evidence of student knowledge of concepts is through the use of diagnostic interviews. Diagnostic interviews are described throughout the book in many Formative Assessment Notes. Another approach is to assess students' growth toward fluency in basic facts, an area that is a well-documented barrier for students with learning disabilities (Mazzocco, Devlin, & McKenney, 2008). Combining instruction with short daily assessments proved to be a way to help students not only be better at remembering but better at generalizing to other facts (Woodward, 2006). The collection of information gathered from these assessments will reveal whether students are making the progress expected or if more intensive instructional approaches need to be put into place.

1–5%
Tier 3 *(individual students)*

5–10%
Tier 2 *(small groups)*

80–90%
Tier 1 *(all students)*

Common Features across Tiers

- **Research-Based Practices:** Prevention begins with practices based on students' best chances for success.
- **Data-Driven:** All decisions are based on clear objectives and formative data collection.
- **Instructional:** Prevention and intervention involve effective instruction, prompts, cues, practice, and environmental arrangements.
- **Context Specific:** All strategies and measures selected to fit individual schools, classrooms, or students.

FIGURE 6.1 Multitiered systems of support: Using effective strategies to support all students.

Source: Based on Scott, Terence, and Lane, Holly. (2001). *Multi-Tiered Interventions in Academic and Social Contexts.* Unpublished manuscript, University of Florida, Gainesville.

Implementing Interventions

NCTM has gathered a set of effective, research-based strategies (NCTM, 2007b) for teaching the small subset of students for whom the initial core instruction was not effective (the students needing tier 2 or tier 3 interventions). These strategies include explicit strategy instruction, think-alouds, concrete and visual representations of problems, peer-assisted learning activities, and formative assessment data provided to students and teachers.

Explicit Strategy Instruction. Explicit instruction is characterized by highly structured, teacher-led instruction on a specific strategy. When engaging in explicit instruction you do not merely demonstrate the strategy and have students practice it; instead, you try to illuminate the decision making along the way—a process that may be troublesome for these

TABLE 6.1 INTERVENTIONS FOR TEACHING MATHEMATICS

Tiers	Intervention
Tier 1	**A highly qualified regular classroom teacher:** • Incorporates high-quality curriculum and has expectations for all students to be challenged • Builds in CCSSO *Standards for Mathematical Practice* and NCTM process standards • Commits to teaching the curriculum as defined • Uses multiple representations such as manipulatives, visual models, and symbols • Monitors progress to identify struggling students and students that excel at high levels • Uses flexible student grouping • Fosters active student involvement • Communicates high expectations
Tier 2	**A highly qualified regular classroom teacher, with collaboration from other highly qualified educators (i.e., special education teacher):** • Works with students (often in small groups) in supplemental sessions outside of the core instruction • Conducts individual diagnostic interviews to target strengths and weaknesses • Collaborates with special education, gifted, and English language learner specialists • Creates lessons that emphasize the big ideas (focal points) or themes • Incorporates CSA (concrete, semi-concrete, abstract) approach • Shares thinking in a think-aloud to demonstrate how to make problem solving decisions • Incorporates explicit systematic strategy instruction (i.e., summarizes key points and reviews key vocabulary or concepts prior to the lesson) • Models specific behaviors and strategies, such as how to handle measuring tools or geoboards • Uses mnemonics or steps written on cards or posters to help students follow, for example, the stages of problem solving • Uses peer-assisted learning, in which another student can provide help to a student in need • Supplies families with additional support materials to use at home • Encourages student use of self-regulation and self-instructional strategies such as revising notes, writing summaries, and identifying main ideas • Teaches test-taking strategies and allows the students to use a highlighter on the test to emphasize important information • "Slices back" (Fuchs & Fuchs, 2001) to material from a previous grade to ramp back up to grade-level curriculum
Tier 3	**A highly qualified special education teacher:** • Works one-on-one with students • Uses tailored instruction based on specific areas of weakness • Modifies instructional methods, motivates students, and adapts curricula • Uses explicit contextualization of skills-based instruction

learners without support. In this instructional strategy, after you assess students so you know what to target, you use a tightly organized sequence, from modeling the strategy, to prompting students through the model, to practice. Your instruction uses these teacher-led explanations of concepts and strategies, including the critical connection building and meaning making, that help learners relate new knowledge with concepts they know. Let's look at a classroom teacher using explicit instruction:

As you enter Mr. Logan's classroom, you see a small group of students seated at a table listening to the teacher's detailed explanation and watching his demonstration of equivalent fraction concepts. The students are using manipulatives, as suggested by Mr. Logan, and moving through carefully selected tasks. He tells the students to take out the red "one-fourth" pieces and asks them to check how many "one-fourths" will exactly cover the blue "one-half" piece. Mr. Logan asks, "Is equivalent a word you know?" Then, to make sure students don't allow for any gaps or overlaps in the pieces, he asks them to talk about their reasoning process by asking the question, "What are some things you need to keep in mind as you place the fourths on the half?" Mr. Logan writes their responses on the adjacent board as $\frac{2}{4} = \frac{1}{2}$ and also as "two-fourths is the same as one half" to connect the ideas that they are looking for how many fourth pieces cover one half piece. Then he asks them to compare the brown "eighths" and the yellow "sixths" to the piece representing one-half and records their responses. The students take turns answering these questions out loud. During the lesson Mr. Logan frequently stops the group, interjects points of clarification, and directly highlights critical components of the task. For example, he asks, "Are you surprised that it takes more eights to cover the half than fourths?" Vocabulary words, such as *whole,* numerator, denominator, and equivalent, are written on the "math wall" nearby and the definitions of these terms are reviewed and reinforced throughout the lesson. At the completion of the lesson, students are given several similar examples of the kind of comparisons discussed in the lesson as independent practice.

A number of aspects of explicit instruction can be seen in Mr. Logan's approach to teaching fraction concepts. He employs a teacher-directed teaching format, carefully describes the use of manipulatives, and incorporates a model-prompt-practice sequence. This sequence starts with verbal instructions and demonstrations with concrete models, followed by prompting, questioning, and then independent practice. The students are deriving mathematical knowledge from the teacher's oral, written, and visual clues.

As students with disabilities solve problems, explicit strategy instruction can help guide them in carrying out tasks. First, ask the student to read and restate the problem, draw a picture, develop a plan by linking this problem to previous problems, write the problem in a mathematical sentence, break the problem into smaller pieces, carry out operations, and check answers using a calculator, hundreds chart, or other appropriate tool. These self-instructive prompts, or self-questions, structure the entire learning process from beginning to end. Unlike more inquiry-based instruction, the teacher models these steps and explains components using terminology that is easily understood by students with disabilities—students who did not discover these ideas independently through initial tier 1 or 2 activities. Yet, consistent with what we know about how all students learn, students are still doing problem solving (not just skill development).

Concrete models can support explicit strategy instruction. For example, a teacher demonstrating a multiplication array with cubes might say, "Watch me. Now make a rectangle with the cubes that looks just like mine." In contrast, a teacher with a more inquiry-oriented approach might say, "Using these cubes, how can you show me a representation for 4×5?" Although initially more structured, the use of concrete models in this fashion will provide students with disabilities with greater access to abstract concepts.

There are a number of possible advantages to the use of explicit strategy instruction for students with disabilities. This approach helps you make more explicit the covert thinking strategies that others use in mathematical problem solving. Although students with disabilities hear other students' thinking strategies in the *after* phase of each lesson, they frequently cannot keep up with the rapid pace of the sharing. Without extra time to reprocess the conversation, students with disabilities may not have access to these strategies. More explicit approaches are also less dependent on the student to draw ideas from past experience or to operate in a self-directed manner.

There are some aspects of explicit strategy instruction that have distinct disadvantages for students with special needs, particularly the times students must rely on memory—often one of their weakest skills. There is also a concern that highly teacher-controlled approaches promote prolonged student dependency on teacher assistance. This is of particular concern for students with disabilities because many of them are described as passive learners.

Students learn what they have the opportunity to practice. Students who are never given opportunities to engage in self-directed learning (based on the assumption that this is not an area of strength) will be deprived of the opportunity to develop skills in this area. In fact, the best explicit instruction is scaffolded, meaning it moves from a highly structured, single-strategy approach to multiple models, including examples and nonexamples. It also includes immediate error correction with the fading of prompts to help students move to independence. To be effective, explicit instruction must include making mathematical relationships explicit (so that students, rather than only learning how to do that day's mathematics, make connections to other mathematical ideas). Because making connections is a major component in how students learn, it must be central to learning strategies for students with disabilities.

Concrete, Semi-Concrete, Abstract (CSA) Sequence. The CSA (concrete, semi-concrete, abstract) intervention has been used in mathematics education in a variety of forms for years (Heddens, 1964; Witzel, 2005). Based on Bruner and Kennedy's stages of representation (1965), this model reflects concrete representations that encourage learning through movement or action (enactive stage) to semi-concrete representations of drawings or pictures (iconic) and learning through abstract symbols (symbolic). Built into this approach is the return to visual models and concrete representations as needed or as students begin to explore new concepts or extensions of concepts previously learned. As students share reasoning that shows they are beginning to understand the mathematical concept, there can be a shift to semi-concrete representations. This is not to say that this is a rigid approach that only moves to abstraction after the other phases. Instead, it is essential that there is parallel modeling of number symbols throughout this approach to explicitly relate the concrete models and visual representations to the corresponding numerals and equations. CSA also includes modeling the mental conversations that go on in your mind as you help students articulate their own thinking. Used particularly in a combination with explicit strategy instruction, this approach has met with high levels of success for students with disabilities (Flores, Hinton & Strozier, 2014; Mancl, Miller & Kennedy, 2012; Miller & Kaffar, 2011).

Peer-Assisted Learning. Students with special needs benefit from other students' modeling and support (Fuchs, Fuchs, Yazdian, & Powell, 2002). The basic notion is that students learn best when they are placed in the role of an apprentice working with a more skilled peer or "expert." Although the peer-assisted learning approach shares some of the characteristics of the explicit strategy instruction model, it is distinct because knowledge is presented on an "as-needed" basis as opposed to a predetermined sequence. The students can be paired with older students or peers who have more sophisticated understandings of a concept. At other times, tutors and tutees can reverse roles during the tasks. Having students with disabilities "teach" others is an important part of the learning process, so giving them a chance to explain to a peer or younger student is valuable.

Think-Alouds. When you use a "think-aloud" as an instructional strategy, you demonstrate the steps to accomplish a task while verbalizing the thinking and reasoning that accompany the steps. Remember, don't start where your thinking is; assess and start where the student's thinking is. Let's look at an example. Consider a problem in which fourth-grade students are asked to determine how much paint is needed to cover the walls of their classroom. Rather than merely demonstrating, for example, how to use a ruler to measure the distance across a wall, the think-aloud strategy would involve talking through the steps and identifying the reasons for each step while measuring the space. As you place a mark on the wall to indicate where the ruler ended in the first measurement, you might state, "I used this line to mark off where the ruler ends. How should I use this line as I measure the next section of the wall? I know I have to move the ruler, but should I repeat what I did the first time?" All of this dialogue occurs prior to placing the ruler for a second measurement.

Often teachers share alternatives about how else they could have carried out the task. When you use this metacognitive strategy, teachers try to talk about and model possible approaches (and the reasons behind these approaches) in an effort to make your invisible thinking processes visible to students.

Although you will choose any of these strategies as needed for interventions, your goal is always to work toward high student responsibility for learning. Movement to higher levels of understanding of content can be likened to the need to move to a higher level on a hill. For some, formal stair steps with support along the way is necessary (explicit strategy instruction); for others, ramps with encouragement at the top of the hill will work (peer-assisted learning). Other students can find a path up the hill on their own with some guidance from visual representations (CSA approach). All people can relate to the need to have different support during different times of their lives or under different circumstances, and it is no different for students with special needs (see Table 6.2). Yet, these students must eventually learn to create a path to new learning on their own, as that is what will be required in the real world after formal education ends. Leaving students only knowing how to climb steps with support and then having them face hills without constant assistance from others will not help them attain their life goals.

TABLE 6.2   COMMON STUMBLING BLOCKS FOR STUDENTS WITH DISABILITIES

Stumbling Blocks for Students	What Will I Notice?	What Should I Do?
Trouble forming mental representations of mathematical concepts	• Can't interpret a number line • Has difficulty going from a problem about a garden plot (finding area) to graph or dot paper representation	• Explicitly teach the representation—for example, exactly how to draw a diagram (e.g., partition a number line) • Use larger versions of the representation (e.g., number line or grid paper) so that students can move on or interact with the model
Difficulty accessing numerical meanings from symbols or issues with number sense	• Has difficulty with basic facts; for example, doesn't recognize that $3 + 5$ is the same as $5 + 3$ • Does not understand the meaning of the equal sign • Can't interpret whether an answer is reasonable	• Explicitly teach multiple ways of representing a number showing the variations at the same time • Use a number balance to support understanding of the equal sign • Use multiple representations for a single problem to show how it would appear in a variety of ways (base-ten blocks, illustrations, and numbers) rather than using multiple problems
Difficulty keeping numbers and information in working memory	• Loses counts of objects • Gets confused when other students share multiple strategies during the *after* portion of the lesson • Forgets how to start the problem solving process	• Use ten-frames to help students organize counts • Explicitly model how to use skip counting • Write down ideas of other students during discussions • Incorporate a chart that lists the main steps in problem solving as an independent guide or make bookmarks with questions students can ask themselves as prompts
Lacks organizational skills and the ability to self-regulate	• Misses steps in a process • Writes computations in a way that is random and hard to follow	• Use routines as often as possible or provide self-monitoring checklists to prompt steps along the way • Use graph paper to record problems or numbers • Create math walls as a reference
Misapplies rules or overgeneralizes	• Applies rules such as "Always subtract the smaller from the larger" too literally, resulting in errors such as $35 - 9 = 34$ • Mechanically applies algorithms—for example, adds $\frac{7}{8}$ and $\frac{12}{13}$ and generates the answer $\frac{19}{21}$.	• Always give examples as well as counterexamples to show how and when "rules" should be used and when they should not • Tie all rules into conceptual understanding; don't emphasize memorizing rote procedures or practices

Teaching and Assessing Students with Learning Disabilities

Students with learning disabilities have very specific difficulties with perceptual or cognitive processing that may affect memory; general strategy use; attention; the ability to speak or express ideas in writing; the ability to perceive auditory, visual, or written information; or the ability to integrate abstract ideas. Although specific learning needs and strategies that work for one student may not work for another, there are some general ideas that can help in planning for students with special learning needs. The following questions should guide your planning:

1. What organizational, behavioral, and cognitive skills are necessary for students with special needs to derive meaning from this activity?
2. Which students have significant weaknesses in any of these skills or concepts?
3. How can I provide additional support in these areas of weakness so that students with special needs can focus on the conceptual task in the activity? (Karp & Howell, 2004, p. 119)*.

Each phase of the lesson has specific considerations for students with special needs. Some strategies apply throughout a lesson. The following discussion is not exhaustive but provides some specific suggestions for offering support throughout the lesson while maintaining the challenge.

Structure the Environment

• *Centralize attention.* Move the student close to the board or teacher. Face students when you speak to them and use gestures. Remove competing stimuli.

---

*Karp, K., & Howell, P. (2004). Building Responsibility for Learning in Students with Special Needs, p. 119. *Teaching Children Mathematics*, 11(3), p. 118–126. Reprinted with permission. Copyright © 2004 by the National Council of Teachers of Mathematics. All rights reserved.

- *Avoid confusion.* Word directions carefully and specifically and ask the student to repeat them. Give one direction at a time.
- *Create smooth transitions.* Ensure that transitions between activities have clear directions and that there are limited chances for students to get off task.

Identify and Remove Potential Barriers

- *Help students remember.* Recognizing that memory is often not a strong suit for students with special needs, develop mnemonics (memory aids) for familiar steps or write directions that can be referred to throughout the lesson. For example, STAR is a mnemonic for problem solving: **S**earch the word problem for important information; **T**ranslate the words into models, pictures, or symbols; **A**nswer the problem; **R**eview your solution for reasonableness (Gagnon & Maccini, 2001).
- *Provide vocabulary and concept support.* Explicit attention to vocabulary and symbols is critical throughout the lesson. Preview essential terms and related prior knowledge/ concepts, creating a "math wall" of words and symbols to provide visual cues and connect symbols to their precise meanings.
- *Use "friendly" numbers.* Instead of using $6.13, use $6.00 to emphasize conceptual understanding rather than mixing computation and conceptual goals. Incorporate this technique when computation and operation skills are *not* the lesson objective.
- *Vary task size.* Assign students with special needs fewer problems to solve. Some students can become frustrated by the enormity of the task.
- *Adjust the visual display.* Design assessments and tasks so that there is not too much on a single page. The density of words, illustrations, and numbers on a page can overload students. Find ways to put one problem on a page, increase font size, or reduce the visual display.

Provide Clarity

- *Repeat the timeframe.* Give students additional reminders about the time left for exploring the materials, completing tasks, or finishing assessments. This helps students with time management.
- *Ask students to share their thinking.* Use the think-aloud method or the think-pair-share strategy.
- *Emphasize connections.* Provide concrete representations, pictorial representations, and numerical representations. Have students connect them through carefully phrased questions. Also connect visuals, meanings, and words. For example, as you fold a strip of paper into fourths, point out the part-whole relationship with gestures as you pose a question about the relationship between $\frac{2}{4}$ and $\frac{1}{2}$.
- *Adapt delivery modes.* Incorporate a variety of materials, images, examples, and models for visual learners. Some students may need to have the problem or assessment read to them or generated with voice creation software. Provide written instructions in addition to oral instructions.
- *Emphasize relevant points.* Some students with disabilities may inappropriately focus on the color of a cube instead of the quantity of cubes when filling a prism to measure volume.
- *Support the organization of written work.* Provide tools and templates so students can focus on the mathematics rather than the organization of a table or chart. Also use graphic organizers, picture-based models, and paper with columns or grids.
- *Provide examples and nonexamples.* Show examples of triangles as well as shapes that are not triangles. Help students focus on the characteristics that differentiate the examples from those that are not examples.

Consider Alternative Assessments

- *Propose alternative products.* Provide options for how to demonstrate understanding (e.g., a verbal response that is written by someone else, audio recorded, or modeled with a manipulative). Use voice recognition software or word prediction software that can generate a whole menu of word choices when students type a few letters.
- *Encourage self-monitoring and self-assessment.* Students with disabilities often are not good at self-reflection. Asking them to review an assignment or assessment to explain what was

difficult and what they think they got right can help them be more independent and take greater responsibility for their learning.

- *Consider feedback charts.* Help students monitor their growth by charting progress over time.

Emphasize Practice and Summary

- *Consolidate ideas.* Create study guides that summarize key mathematics concepts and allow for review. Have students develop their own study guides.
- *Provide extra practice.* Use carefully selected problems (not a large number) and allow the use of familiar physical models.

Adapted list reprinted with permission from Karp, K., & Howell, P. (2004). Building Responsibility for Learning in Students with Special Needs. *Teaching Children Mathematics, 11*(3), p. 118–126. Copyright © 2004 by the National Council of Teachers of Mathematics. All rights reserved.

Not all of these strategies will apply to every lesson or every student with special needs, but as you are thinking about a particular lesson and certain individuals in your class, you will find that many of these will allow a student to engage in the task and accomplish the learning goals of the lesson. The Center for Applied Special Technology (CAST) website contains resources and tools to support the learning of all students, especially those with disabilities, through universal design for learning (UDL).

Teaching Students with Moderate/Severe Disabilities

Students with moderate/severe disabilities (MSD) often need extensive modifications and individualized supports to learn mathematics. This population of students may include those with severe autism, sensory disorders, limitations affecting movement, cerebral palsy, processing disorders such as intellectual disabilities, and combinations of multiple disabilities.

Originally, the curriculum for students with moderate or severe disabilities was called "functional," in that it often focused on life-related skills such as managing money, telling time, using a calculator, measuring, and matching numbers to complete such tasks as entering a telephone number or identifying a house number. Now directives and assessments have broadened the curriculum to address the grade-level expectations in the Common Core State Standards or other curriculum policy documents.

At a beginning level, students develop number sense, use measuring tools, compare graphs, explore place-value concepts, use the number line and compare quantities. When possible, the content should be connected to life skills and features of jobs. Shopping skills and activities in which food is prepared are both options for mathematical problem solving. At other times, link mathematical learning objectives to everyday events in a practical way. For example, when the operation of division is studied, figuring how candy can be equally shared at Halloween or how game cards can be dealt would be appropriate. Students can also undertake a small project such as constructing a box to store different items as a way to explore shapes and both length and volume measurements.

Do not believe that all basic facts must be mastered before students with moderate or severe disabilities can move forward in the curriculum; students can learn geometric or measuring concepts without having mastered addition and subtraction facts. Geometry for students with moderate and severe disabilities is more than merely identifying shapes, but is in fact critical for orienting in the real world. Concepts such as parallel and perpendicular lines and curves and straight sides become helpful for interpreting maps of the local area. Students who learn to count bus stops and judge time can be helped to successfully navigate their world.

The handout Activities for Students with Moderate or Severe Disabilities offers ideas across the curriculum appropriate for teaching students with moderate to severe disabilities. Also, look at the Additional Strategies for Supporting Students with Moderate/Severe Disabilities handout for more strategies to modify grade-level instruction and support students with moderate and severe disabilities.

 Complete Self-Check 6.2: Providing for Students Who Struggle and Those with Special Needs

Culturally and Linguistically Diverse Students

We are lucky to be in a country with rich diversity in cultural practices and languages. Students' native languages are not only an important part of their cultural heritage, but of how they think, communicate, and learn. From 1980 to 2012, the number of school-aged children who speak a language other than English at home has risen from 4.7 million to almost 12 million, or about 22 percent of school-aged children (National KIDS COUNT, 2012).

Students from different countries, regions, or experiences, including those who speak different languages, are sometimes viewed as challenges to a teacher or school. Rather, students' varied languages and backgrounds should be seen as a resource in teaching (Gutierrez, 2009). Valuing a person's cultural background is more than a belief statement; it is a set of intentional actions that communicates to the student, "I want to know about you, I want you to see mathematics as part of your life, and I expect that you can do high-level mathematics." In getting to know students, we access their funds of knowledge (the essential knowledge or information students use to survive and thrive) (Gonzáles, Moll, & Amanti, 2005). Instead of teaching English language learners (ELLs) from a deficit model (they have a lack of knowledge and experience), we can connect their experiences at home and with family to those of the mathematics classroom. The more we enhance learning for all students, regardless of their places of birth, the more enriched the opportunities for learning become.

Mathematics is commonly referred to as a universal language, but this is not entirely true; treating mathematics as universal can lead to inequities in the classroom. Conceptual knowledge (e.g., multiplication) is universal. But procedures and symbols are culturally determined. In the United States, for example, 3×4 is interpreted as three groups of four. In other countries it is interpreted as three taken four times. As you will also read in Chapters 12 and 13, there are many algorithms for whole-number operations.

How we do mathematics is also culturally determined. For example, mental mathematics is highly valued in other countries, whereas in the United States, recording every step is valued. Compare the following two division problems from a fourth-grade classroom (Midobuche, 2001):

$$
\begin{array}{r}
495 \\
3\overline{)1485} \\
-12 \\
\hline
28 \\
-27 \\
\hline
15 \\
-15 \\
\hline
0
\end{array}
\qquad
\begin{array}{r}
495 \\
3\overline{)1485} \\
28 \\
15 \\
0
\end{array}
$$

Can you understand the thinking of the first student? If you learned division in the United States, this is likely easy to follow. But, if you learned division in another country, you may wonder why the first solution has so many numbers recorded. Can you follow the second example? It is, in effect, the same thinking process, but the multiplication and related subtraction are done mentally. The critical equity question, though, is not whether you can follow an alternative approach, but how you will respond when you encounter a student using such an approach:

- Will you require the student show their steps, disregarding the way they learned it?
- Will you ask the student to elaborate on how they did it?
- Will you have the student show other students their way of thinking?

The latter two responses communicate to students that you are interested in their way of knowing mathematics.

Culturally Responsive Instruction

Culturally responsive mathematics instruction is not just for recent immigrants; it is for *all* students, including students from different ethnic groups, socioeconomic status, and so on. It includes consideration for content, relationships, cultural knowledge, flexibility in approaches, use of familiar or interesting learning contexts, a responsive learning community, and working in crosscultural partnerships (Averill, Anderson, Easton, Te Maro, Smith, & Hynds, 2009). It is complex. A learning strategy may be highly effective in one setting yet not work in a different setting. Following are four strategies for differentiation that address the specific needs of linguistically and culturally diverse students. Also see Reflection Questions to Guide Teaching and Assessing Culturally Relevant Instruction.

Focus on Important Mathematics. Too often, our first attempt to help ELLs is to simplify the mathematics or remove the language from the lesson. Simplifying or removing language can take away opportunities to learn. Culturally responsive instruction stays focused on the big ideas of mathematics (i.e., based on standards) and helps students engage in and stay focused on the big ideas. For example, in a lesson on perimeter and area of nonstandard shapes, a recording sheet might begin with definitions of each term and then a sketch to illustrate the situation (Murrey, 2008). The teacher can incorporate opportunities for students to share their definitions and to discuss the meaning of the task prior to solving it. In this way ELLs are able to focus on finding the solution.

Make Content Relevant. There are really two components for making content relevant. One is to think about the mathematics: Is the mathematics presented meaningfully and is it connected to other content? Helping students see that mathematical ideas are interrelated will fill in or deepen their understanding of and connections to previously taught content. For example, consider the following problem:

Edwin has some trains. He gives 2 to Marta. Edwin now has 6 trains. How many did Edwin have before he gave some away?

You may recognize that this task connects addition and subtraction, and that the initial value (how many trains Edwin had before he gave any away) is the unknown amount. Although the mathematics is presented in a conceptual and meaningful manner, it is important to connect addition to subtraction, as well as to connect symbols to the situation. For example, one student might use a think-addition approach: "I know that he has 6 now and plus the 2 from Marta means he had 8." Another student might say: "I thought 'what number minus 2 equals 6' and I know that is 8." The symbols that represent the students' thinking are $6 + 2 = ?$ and $? - 2 = 6$, respectively. Having students connect the symbols back to their thinking and to the story helps build strong mathematical connections and understanding of the operations.

Second, making content relevant is also about contexts. What contexts can bring meaning to the mathematics? There are many! Historical or cultural topics abound. Seeing mathematics from various cultures provides opportunities for students to put faces on mathematical contributions (Remillard, Ebby, Lim, Reinke, Hoe, & Magee, 2014). For example, you can introduce the Mayan place-value system as a way to think about how we write numerals and to think more deeply about reasoning about the structure of number (Farmer & Powers, 2005).

Incorporate Students' Identities. Incorporating students' identities in the mathematics they do overlaps with the previous category but merits its own discussion. Students should see themselves in mathematics and see that mathematics is a part of their culture.

Both researchers and teachers have found that telling stories about their own lives, or asking students to tell stories, makes the mathematics relevant to students and can raise student achievement (Turner, Celedón-Pattichis, Marshall, & Tennison, 2009). The Where to Find

Mathematics in Homes and Communities handout provides ideas for finding mathematics relevant to things at home or in the community.

The following teacher's story illustrates one way to incorporate family history and culture by reading *The Hundred Penny Box* (Mathis, 1986). The story describes a 100-year-old woman who remembers an important event in her life for every one of her 100 pennies from different years. Each penny is more than a piece of money; it is a "memory trigger" for her life.

Taking a cue from the book, I asked each child to collect one penny from each year they were alive. Children were encouraged to bring in additional pennies their classmates might need. Then the children consulted with family members to create a penny timeline of important events in their lives. Using information gathered at home, they started with the year they were born, listing their birthday and then recording first steps, accidents, vacations, pets, births of siblings, and so on. Then I asked them to find how many years between certain events or to calculate their age when they adopted a pet or learned to ride a bicycle. I also used these events in the weeks and months to come as subjects of story problems and other mathematics investigations on number lines.

Ensure Shared Power. When we think about creating a positive classroom environment, one in which all students feel as if they can participate and learn, we are addressing considerations related to power. The teacher plays a major role in establishing and distributing power, whether it is intentional or not. In many classrooms the teacher has the power—telling students whether answers are right or wrong (rather than having students determine correctness through reasoning), demonstrating processes for solving problems (rather than give choices for how students will engage in the problem), and determining who will solve which problems (rather than allowing flexibility and choice for students). Instead, establish a classroom environment where everyone feels their ideas are worth consideration. The way that you assign groups, seat students, and call on students sends clear messages about who has power in the classroom. Distributing power among students leads to empowered students.

Each day's lesson provides new opportunities and challenges as you think about how you will make lessons culturally responsive. Table 6.3 is designed to help guide your thinking. If these reflective questions become internalized and are part of what you naturally think about as you plan, teach, and assess, then you are likely to lead a classroom where all students are challenged and supported.

Creating effective learning opportunities for ELLs involves integrating the principles of bilingual education with those of effective mathematics teaching. When learning about mathematics, students may be learning content in English for which they do not know the words in their native language. For example, in studying measures of central tendency (*mean, median,* and *mode*), they may not know words for these terms in their first language, increasing the challenge for learning academic language in their second language. In addition, story problems are difficult not only due to the language but also to the fact that sentence structure in story problems is different from sentences in conversational English (Janzen, 2008). Teachers of English to Speakers of Other Languages (TESOL), a professional organization focused on the needs of ELLs, argues that ELLs need to use both English and their native language to read, write, listen, and speak as they learn content—a position similarly addressed in NCTM standards documents and position statements (2013). The strategies discussed in this section are those appearing most frequently in the literature as critical to increasing the academic achievement of ELLs in mathematics classrooms (e.g., Celedón-Pattichis & Ramirez, 2012; Echevarria, Vogt, & Short, 2008). Table 6.3 offers reflective questions related to instructional planning for and the teaching of ELLs.

Focus on Academic Vocabulary

English language learners enter the mathematics classroom from homes in which English is not the primary language of communication. Although a person might develop conversational English language skills in a few years, it takes as many as seven years to learn "academic

TABLE 6.3 REFLECTIVE QUESTIONS TO FOCUS ON CULTURALLY RESPONSIVE MATHEMATICS INSTRUCTION

Aspect of Culturally Responsive Instruction	Reflection Questions to Guide Teaching and Assessing
The content of the lesson is about important mathematics and the tasks communicate high expectations.	• Does the content include a balance of procedures and concepts? • Are students expected to engage in problem solving and generate their own approaches to problems? • Are connections made between mathematics topics?
The content is relevant.	• How is the content related to students' lives? • In what way is prior knowledge elicited/reviewed so that all students can participate? • How are students asked to connect the mathematics to situations in their own lives? • How are student interests (events, issues, literature, or pop culture) used to build interest, motivation, and meaning?
The instructional strategies communicate the value of students' identities.	• In what ways are students invited to include their own experiences within a lesson? • Do story problems reflect the real experiences of students? • Are individual student approaches presented and showcased so that each student sees their ideas as important to others? • If alternative algorithms are used by students, are they shared with other students as valuable strategies? • Are multiple modes to demonstrate knowledge (e.g., visuals, explanations, models) valued?
The instructional strategies model shared authority for the learning.	• Are students justifying the correctness of solutions? • Are students expected to engage in whole-class discussions where they share and respond to others' ideas? • How are roles assigned so that every student feels that they contribute to the lesson and learn from other members of the class? • Are students given choices in how they solve a problem? In how they demonstrate knowledge of the concept?

language," which is the language specific to a content area such as mathematics (Cummins, 1994). Academic language is harder to learn because it is not used in a student's everyday world.

Honor Use of Native Language. Valuing a student's language is one of the ways you value their cultural heritage. In a mathematics classroom, students can communicate in their native language while continuing their English language development (Haas & Gort, 2009; Moschkovich, 2009; Setati, 2005). For example, a good strategy for students working in small groups is having students discuss the problem in their preferred language. If a student knows enough English, then the presentation in the *after* phase of the lesson can be shared in English. If the student knows little or no English and does not have access to a peer who shares his or her native language, then visuals or pictures, a translator, web-based mathematics glossary, or self-made dictionary can be components of a support system. You may find that bilingual students will *code-switch*—moving between two languages. Research indicates that this practice supports mathematical reasoning because the student is selecting the language from which they can best express their ideas (Moschkovich, 2009).

Certain native languages can support learning mathematical words. Because several languages have their roots in Latin, many math words are similar across languages (Celedón-Pattichis, 2009; Gómez, 2010). For example, *aequus* (Latin), *equal* (English), and *igual* (Spanish) are cognates. See if you can figure out the English mathematics terms for the following Spanish words: *división, hexágano, ángulo, triángulo, álgebra, circunferencia,* and *cubo.* Students may not make this connection if you do not point it out, so explicitly teaching students to look for cognates is important.

Use Content and Language Objectives. Every lesson should begin with telling students what they will be learning. You do not give away what they will be discovering, but you can state the larger purpose of the lesson so that they are better able to make sense of the details when challenged by some of the oral or written explanations. By explicitly including language expectations, students know the language they will be developing alongside the mathematical goals. Here are two examples of dual objectives:

1. Students will analyze properties and attributes of three-dimensional solids. (mathematics)
2. Students will describe in writing and orally a similarity and a difference between two different solids. (language and mathematics)

Explicitly Teach Vocabulary. Intentional vocabulary instruction must be part of mathematics instruction for all students. This includes terms within a lesson and additional opportunities to develop academic language. Examples of these additional opportunities to reinforce mathematical understanding while learning vocabulary include:

- Personal math dictionaries (Kersaint, Thompson, & Petkova, 2009) that link concepts and terms with drawings or clip art
- Graphic organizers that look at multiple ways to help define a term (see Figure 6.2 and activity sheet Vocabulary Reference Card Template)
- Games focused on vocabulary development (e.g., Charades, "$10,000 Pyramid," "Concentration")
- Mathematics word walls, including visuals and translations
- Skits, poems, or songs to address the everyday and mathematical meaning of words in the curriculum (Seidel & McNamee, 2005)

All students benefit from an increased focus on language; however, too much emphasis on language can diminish the focus on the mathematics. It is important that the language support should be *connected* to the selected task or activity. As you analyze a lesson, identify terms related to the mathematics and to the context that may need explicit attention. Consider the following task, released from the 2009 National Assessment of Educational Progress (NAEP) (National Center for Education Statistics, 2011):

Sam did the following problems.

$$2 + 1 = 3$$
$$6 + 1 = 7$$

Sam concluded that when he adds 1 to any whole number, his answer will always be odd.

> **Is Sam correct?** _____
> **Explain your answer.**

In order for students to engage in this task, the terms *even* and *odd* must be understood. Both terms may be known for other meanings beyond the mathematics classroom (*even* can mean level and *odd* can mean strange). "Concluded" is not a math word but must be understood if the student is to understand the meaning of the problem. Finally, you must give guidance on how students will explain their answers—must it be in words, or can they use pictures or diagrams? Offering multimodal communication options is valuable (Moffett, Malzahn, & Driscoll, 2014).

FIGURE 6.2 Vocabulary reference card—place the target word in the center and fill in the other sections.

The vocabulary reference card contains: Description, Visual Representation, Symbols, Related Operation or Concept, with a central oval for the target word.

Pause & Reflect

Odd and *even* are among hundreds of words that take on different meanings in mathematics from everyday activities. Others include *product, mean, sum, factor, acute, foot, division, difference, similar,* and *angle.* Can you name at least five others? ●

Facilitating Engagement during Instruction

Engaging ELLs in classroom activities and discussions is critical. This includes (1) efforts to ensure ELLs understand and have the background for engaging in the focus tasks and (2) building structures for student participation throughout the lesson.

Build Background. Similar to building on prior knowledge, building background takes into consideration native language and culture as well as content (Echevarria, Vogt, & Short, 2008). If possible, use a context and appropriate visuals to help students understand the task you want them to solve. For example, Pugalee, Harbaugh, and Quach (2009) spray-painted a coordinate axis in a field, so that students could build background related to linear equations. Students were given various equations and contexts and had to physically find (and walk to) points on the giant axis, creating human graphs of lines. This nonthreatening, engaging activity helped students make connections between what they had learned and what they needed to learn.

Some aspects of English and mathematics are particularly challenging to ELLs (Whiteford, 2009/2010). Examples include the following:

- The names of teen numbers in English don't correspond to place value. For example, the Spanish word for 16 is an amalgamation of "ten and six" (as opposed to the English reversal of "six ten").
- Teen numbers sound a lot like their decade number—if you say *sixteen* and *sixty* out loud, you will hear how similar they are. Emphasizing the *n* helps ELLs hear the difference.
- Decimal places are hard to distinguish from other place values. Emphasizing the *th* sound helps students differentiate between hundreds and hundredths.
- U.S. measurement systems have unrelated terminology for every new unit and are not organized by base 10. Although this is hard for all learners, having no life experiences with cups, pints, inches, miles, and other customary units adds to the difficulty for ELLs.

When you encounter these situations and others, additional time is needed to build background and draw attention to how you recognize the intended meaning of the words.

Use Comprehensible Input. *Comprehensible input* means that the message you are communicating is understandable to students. Modifications include simplifying sentence structures and limiting the use of nonessential or confusing vocabulary. Note that these modifications do not lower expectations for the lesson. Sometimes unnecessary words and phrases in questions make them less clear to nonnative speakers. Compare the following sets of teachers' directions:

Not Modified: You have an activity sheet in front of you that I just gave out. For every situation, I want you to determine the total area for the shapes. You will be working with your partner, but each of you needs to record your answers on your own paper and explain how you got your answer. If you get stuck on a problem, raise your hand.

Modified: Please look at your paper. [Holds paper and points to the first picture.] You will find the area. What does *area* mean? [Allows wait time.] How can you calculate area? [*Calculate* is more like the Spanish word *calcular,* so it is more accessible to Spanish speakers.] Talk to your partner. [Points to mouth and then to a pair of students as she says this.] Write your answers. [Makes a writing motion over paper.] If you get stuck [shrugs shoulders and looks confused], raise your hand [demonstrates].

Notice that three things have been done: sentences have been shortened, confusing words have been removed, and related gestures and motions have been added to the oral directions. Also notice the wait time the teacher gives. It is very important to provide extra time after posing a question or giving instructions to allow ELLs time to translate, make sense of the request, and then participate.

Another way to provide comprehensible input is to use a variety of tools to help students visualize and understand what is verbalized. In the preceding example, the teacher is modeling the instructions. Effective tools include manipulatives, pictures, real objects, multimedia demonstrations, and diagrams. For example, if teaching volume of rectangular solids, show a one-inch cube and a rectangular container and ask, "How many same-sized cubes will fill this container? As you ask, physically start to move cubes into the container to illustrate. Review relevant terms such as base, length, width, and height by having students help label a container.

Encourage Discourse That Reflects Language Needs. Discourse, or the use of classroom discussion as a means to make sense of the mathematics, is essential for the learning of all students (Cirillo, Steele, Otten, Herbel-Eisenmann, McAneny, & Riser, 2014). But it is particularly important for ELLs who need to engage in productive language (writing and speaking) as well as receptive language (listening and reading).

There are strategies you can use in classroom discourse that help ELLs understand and participate in discussions. For example, *revoicing* is a research-based strategy that helps ELLs hear an idea more than once with the appropriate language applied to the concepts. Because ELLs cannot always explain their ideas fully, rather than just calling on another student, *pressing* for details is important. This pressing, sometimes known as expansion moves (Choppin, 2014), is not just so the teacher can decide whether the idea makes sense; it is so that other students can make sense of the idea (Maldonado, Turner, Dominguez, & Empson, 2009). Because the use of language is particularly important, having opportunities for students to practice phrases through think-pair-share is needed. Finally, remember that students from other countries often solve or illustrate problems differently.

Plan Cooperative/Interdependent Groups to Support Language. The use of cooperative groups is a valuable way to differentiate instruction. Placing an ELL with two English-speaking students may result in the ELL being left out. On the other hand, grouping all Spanish speakers together prevents the students from having opportunities to participate in the mathematics lesson in English. Consider placing a bilingual student in a group with a student with limited English, or place students that have the same first language together with English speakers so that they can help each other understand and participate (Garrison, 1997; Khisty, 1997).

Implementing Strategies for English Language Learners

Attention to the needs of the English language learner must be considered at each step of the instructional planning process. Explore the Guide for Planning and Teaching Mathematics to English Language Learners. In the following example, the teacher uses several techniques mentioned in the guide that provide support for English language learners while keeping expectations high.

Ms. Steimer is working on a third-grade lesson that involves the concepts of estimating length and measuring to the nearest half-inch. The task asks students to use estimation to find three objects that are about 6 inches long, three objects that are about 1 foot long, and three objects that are about 2 feet long. Once identified, students are to measure the nine objects to the nearest half-inch and compare the measurements with their estimates.

Ms. Steimer has a student from Korea who knows very little English and a student from Mexico who speaks English well but is new to U.S. schools. These two students are not familiar with the measurement units of feet or inches and will not have measured using fractions. She takes time to address the language and the increments on the ruler to the entire class. Because the word *foot* has two meanings, Ms. Steimer decides to address that explicitly before launching into the lesson. She begins by asking students what a "foot" is. She allows time for them to discuss the word with a partner and then share their answers with the class. She explains that today they are going to be using the measuring unit of a foot (while holding up the foot ruler). She asks students what other units can be used to measure length. In particular, she asks her ELLs to share what units they use in their countries of origin, having metric rulers to show the class. She asks students to study the ruler and compare the centimeter to the inch by posing these questions: "Can you estimate about how many centimeters are in an inch? In 6 inches? In a foot?"

Moving to the lesson objectives, Ms. Steimer uses a ruler on the document camera and enlarges the image so all students can see the demarcations. Below the ruler she has a snake whose length ends at the $8\frac{1}{2}$ inch mark. Then, she asks students how long the snake is and writes their reply of $8\frac{1}{2}$ inches on the board. Next, she asks students to tear a paper strip that they estimate is 6 inches long. Students then measure their paper strips with rulers to the nearest half inch. Now she has them ready to begin estimating and measuring.

 ## Pause & Reflect

Review Ms. Steimer's lesson. What specific strategies did she use to support ELLs? •

There are several strategies in this example that provide support for ELLs: Discussion of the word *foot* using the think-pair-share technique recognized the potential language confusion and allowed students the chance to talk about it before becoming confused by the task. The efforts to use visuals and concrete models (the ruler and the torn paper strip) and to build on students' prior experience (use of the metric system in Korea and Mexico) provided support so that the ELLs could succeed in this task. Most importantly, Ms. Steimer did not diminish the challenge of the task with these strategies. If she had altered the task, for example, by not expecting the ELLs to estimate because they didn't know the inch very well, she would have lowered her expectations. Conversely, if she had simply posed the problem without taking time to have students study the ruler or to provide visuals, she may have kept her expectations high but failed to provide the support that would enable her students to succeed. Finally, by making a connection for all students to the metric system, she showed respect for the students' cultures and broadened the horizons of other students to measurement in other countries.

Consider a particular lesson you are planning and use the Sheltering a Lesson for English Language Learners planning sheet to record adaptations and instructional strategies that need to be included.

 Complete Self-Check 6.3: Culturally and Linguistically Diverse Students

 # Providing for Students Who Are Mathematically Gifted

Students who are mathematically gifted include those who have high ability or high interest. Some may be gifted with an intuitive knowledge of mathematical concepts, whereas others have a passion for the subject even though they may have to work hard to learn it. Many students' giftedness becomes apparent to parents and teachers when they grasp and articulate mathematics concepts at an age earlier than expected. They are often able to easily make connections between topics of study and frequently are unable to explain how they quickly got an answer (Rotigel & Fello, 2005).

Many teachers have a keen ability to spot talent when they note students who have strong number sense or visual/spatial sense (Gavin & Sheffield, 2010). Note that these teachers are not pointing to students who are speedy with their basic facts, but those who have the ability to reason and make sense of mathematics.

Do not wait for students to demonstrate their mathematical talent; instead, develop it through a challenging set of tasks and inquiry-based instruction (Van Tassel-Baska & Brown, 2007). Generally, as described previously when discussing the RtI model, high-quality core instruction is able to respond to the varying needs of diverse learners, including the talented and gifted. Yet for some of your gifted students, the core instruction proves not to be enough of a challenge. The curriculum should be adapted to consider level, complexity, breadth, depth, and pace (Assouline & Lupkowski-Shoplik, 2011; Johnsen & Sheffield, 2014; Renzulli, Gubbins, McMillen, Eckert, & Little, 2009; Saul, Assouline, & Sheffield, 2010).

There are four basic categories for adapting mathematics content for gifted mathematics students: *acceleration, enrichment (depth), sophistication (complexity),* and *novelty* (Gallagher & Gallagher, 1994; Ravenna, 2008). The emphasis on applying, implementing, and extending ideas must overshadow the mental collection of facts and concepts.

Acceleration. Acceleration recognizes that your students may already understand the mathematics content that you plan to teach. Some teachers use "curriculum compacting" (Reis & Renzulli, 2005) to give a short overview of the content and assess students' ability to respond to mathematics tasks that would demonstrate their proficiency. Allowing students to increase the pace of their own learning can give them access to curriculum different from their grade level while demanding more independent study. But, moving students to higher mathematics (by moving them up a grade, for example) will not succeed in engaging them if the learning is still at a slow pace. Research reveals that when gifted students are accelerated through the curriculum they become more likely to explore STEM (science, technology, engineering, and mathematics) fields (Sadler & Tai, 2007).

Enrichment. Enrichment activities go beyond the topic of study to content that is not specifically a part of your grade-level curriculum but is an extension of the original mathematical tasks. For example, while studying place value both using very large numbers or decimals, mathematically gifted students can stretch their knowledge to study other bases such as base five, base eight, or base twelve. This provides an extended view of how our base-ten numeration system fits within the broader system of number theory. Other times the format of enrichment can involve studying the same topic as the rest of the class while differing on the means and outcomes of the work. Examples include group investigations, solving real problems in the community, writing data-based letters to outside audiences, or identifying applications of the mathematics learned.

Sophistication. Another strategy is to increase the sophistication of a topic by raising the level of complexity or pursuing greater depth of content, possibly outside the regular curriculum or by connecting mathematics to other subject areas. For example, while studying a unit on place value, mathematically gifted students can deepen their knowledge to study other numeration systems such as Roman, Mayan, Egyptian, Babylonian, Chinese, and Zulu. This provides a multicultural view of how our numeration system fits within historical number systems (Mack, 2011). In the algebra strand, when studying sequences or patterns of numbers, mathematically gifted students can learn about Fibonacci sequences and their appearances in the natural world in shells and plant life.

Novelty. Novelty introduces completely different material from the regular curriculum and frequently occurs in after-school clubs, out-of-class projects, or collaborative school experiences. The collaborative experiences include students from a variety of grades and classes volunteering for special mathematics projects, with a classroom teacher, principal, or resource teacher taking the lead. The novelty category includes having students explore topics that are within their developmental grasp but outside the curriculum. For example, students may look at mathematical "tricks" using binary numbers to guess classmates' birthdays or solve reasoning problems using a logic matrix. They may also explore topics such as topology through the creation of paper "knots" called flexagons or large-scale investigations of the amount of food thrown away at lunchtime. A group might create tetrahedron kites or find mathematics in art. Another aspect of the novelty approach provides different options for students in culminating performances of their understanding, such as demonstrating their knowledge through inventions, experiments, simulations, dramatizations, and visual displays.

Noted researcher on the gifted, Benbow (Read, 2014), states that acceleration combined with enrichment is best practice. Then learning is not only sped up but the learning is deeper and at more complex levels.

Strategies to Avoid. There are a number of ineffective approaches for gifted students, including the following:

1. *Assigning more of the same work.* This is the least appropriate way to respond to mathematically gifted students and the most likely to result in students' hiding their ability.
2. *Giving free time to early finishers.* Although students find this rewarding, it does not maximize their intellectual growth and can lead to students hurrying to finish a task.
3. *Assigning gifted students to help struggling learners.* Routinely assigning gifted students to teach students who are not meeting expectations does not stimulate their intellectual growth and can place them in socially uncomfortable or sometimes undesirable situations.
4. *Providing gifted pull-out opportunities.* Unfortunately, generalized gifted programs are often unrelated to the regular mathematics curriculum (Assouline & Lupkowski-Shoplik, 2011). Add-on experiences are not enough to build more complex and sophisticated understandings of mathematics.
5. *Offering independent enrichment on the computer.* Although there are excellent enrichment opportunities to be found on the Internet, the practice of having a gifted students use a computer program that focuses on skills does not engage them in a way that will enhance conceptual understanding and support their ability to justify their thinking.

Sheffield (1999) writes that gifted students should be introduced to the "joys and frustrations of thinking deeply about a wide range of original, open-ended, or complex problems that encourage them to respond creatively in ways that are original, fluent, flexible and elegant" (p. 46). Accommodations, modifications, and interventions for mathematically gifted students must strive for this goal.

 Complete Self-Check 6.4: Providing for Students Who Are Mathematically Gifted

 # Creating Gender-Friendly Mathematics Classrooms

Hyde, Lindberg, Linn, Ellis, and Williams (2008) reveal that in analyzing standardized test scores from more than 7.2 million U.S. students in grades 2–11, there were no differences in math scores for girls and boys. According to Hyde, this shows the positive results of the efforts over the past 20 years to counter the stereotype that math is a subject for boys. But Hyde also wrote that "girls who believe the stereotype wind up avoiding harder math classes."

After high school, more males than females enter STEM fields (Ceci & Williams, 2010). These are critical career fields linked to the economic well-being of any nation. The president of the Society of Women Engineers stated, "Why, while girls comprise 55 percent of undergraduate students, do they account for only 20 percent of engineering majors, and boys remain four times more likely to enroll in undergraduate engineering programs?" (Tortolani, 2007). It remains important to be aware of and address gender equity in your classroom. Some suggest the underrepresentation of females is due to the large proportion of males (4 to 1) at the highest performance levels of such tests as SAT Math (Wai, Cacchio, Putallaz, & Makel, 2010). These high performers are often the population that seeks out STEM careers. In the formative years, we must challenge gender stereotypes for both sexes and create gender-friendly environments for learning mathematics and for stimulating all students' interest in pursuing college majors and careers in mathematics-related fields.

Gender Differences

Although we base any concerns regarding gender differences on test scores, and the debate about the influence of biologically or environmentally determined factors on differences continues (Spelke, 2005), it is in fact the socially and culturally constructed gender differences that educators must examine for change. By finding some of the roots of gender differences in and out of the classroom, we can help create gender-friendly mathematics instruction for boys and girls.

Belief Systems. The belief that mathematics is a male activity persists in our society and is held by both sexes (Cheryan, 2012; Else-Quest, Hyde, & Linn, 2010). Stereotypes that boys are better in math shape girls' self-perceptions and motivations (Nosek, Banaji, & Greenwald, 2002). What may result is a decrease in emerging interest in math. Females report that interest is a very influential factor in their decision to pursue higher-level math courses (Stevens, Wang, Olivarez, & Hamman, 2007), often expressing that they are less proficient than males—even when they perform at similar levels (Correll, 2001). "The relative absence of females in math and science careers fuels the stereotype that girls cannot succeed in math-related areas and thus young girls are, often subtly, steered away from them" (Barnett, 2007). Yet, recent research suggests that the link between confidence and interest may be in the way the subject is taught with more inquiry-oriented approaches favorably influencing females' performance and thinking (Laursen, Hassi, Kogan, & Weston, 2014).

Teacher Interactions. Teachers may not consciously seek to stereotype students by gender; however, the gender-based assumptions of our society may affect teacher–student interactions. According to Janet Hyde, "[b]oth parents and teachers continue to hold the stereotype that boys are better than girls [at math]" (Seattle Times News Services, 2008). Observations of teachers' interactions in the classroom indicate that boys get more attention and different kinds of attention than girls. Boys receive more criticism for wrong answers as well as more praise for correct answers. Boys also tend to get more negative discipline-related attention focusing on self-control and work ethic (Lubienski, Robinson, Crane & Ganley, 2013). Females in math classes often go unobserved, and a study found them to be "quiet achievers" (Clarke et al., 2001). Also, female teachers with math anxiety negatively influence female students' mathematics achievement—even over just a one-year period (Beilock, Gunderson, Ramirez, & Levine, 2010). Yet, females get as good or better grades in mathematics than males (Gallagher & Kaufmann, 2005; Riegle-Crumb, 2006).

What Can You Try?

As already noted, the reasons for girls' and boys' perceptions of themselves vis-à-vis mathematics are partially a function of the educational environment, so that is where we should look for solutions. As a teacher, you need to be aware of your instructional practices and work at ensuring equity for boys and girls. As you interact with students, be sensitive to the following:

- *Equally call on and ask higher-level questions of males and females.* Assess the classroom discourse by tallying the number of questions asked of boys and girls and noting which students ask questions and what kinds of questions they ask.
- *Provide opportunities for students to act out or model mathematical situations or concepts with movements and gestures.* Males show strong spatial abilities (Klein, Adi-Japha, & Hakak-Benizri, 2010; Wai, Lubinski, & Benbow, 2009) and by involving boys (and girls) in visual representations and physical actions you can support mathematics learning.
- *Encourage all students to be active participants.* There are girls and boys who may tend to shy away from involvement, lack motivation, or not be as quick to seek help. So, follow the tenets of this book and use a problem-based approach to instruction. Research demonstrates that using inquiry-oriented instruction reduces the gender gap and, in fact, supports all learners (Laursen, Hassi, Kogan, & Weston, 2014).
- *Use collaboration.* Collaboration can include organized small-group work or whole-class discussions as peers critique each other's reasoning and offer alternative strategies. Collaboration develops communication skills that many males and females need.
- *Attend to the context of problems.* Offer problem situations that explore many student interests, not just a stereotypically gendered topic such as sports.

- *Ensure that there are diverse characters in the children's literature used in mathematics instruction.* Select stories with male and female characters who problem solve and try many strategies (see Karp, Brown, Allen, & Allen, 1998).
- *Discuss STEM careers to increase students' interest in these fields.* Invite family or community members, particularly females who are in what may be perceived as "male oriented" careers, to talk to your class.

 Complete Self-Check 6.5: Creating Gender-Friendly Mathematics Classrooms

 # Reducing Resistance and Building Resilience

There are students who make a decision that they won't be able to learn mathematics, so why try? Teachers need to "reach beyond the resistance" and find ways to listen to students, affirm their abilities, and motivate them. Here are a few key strategies for getting there.

Give Students Choices That Capitalize on Their Unique Strengths. Students often need to have power over events by having a stake and a say in what is happening. Therefore, focus on making classrooms inviting and familiar as you connect students' interests to the content. Setting up situations where these students feel success with mathematics tasks can bring them closer to stopping the willful avoidance of learning mathematics. Schools, like families and communities, are protective support systems that can foster resilience and persistence.

Nurture Traits of Resilience. Benard (1991) suggests there are four traits found in resilient individuals—social competence, problem solving skills, autonomy, and a sense of purpose and future. Use these characteristics to motivate students and help them reach success. Encourage your students to be persistent despite risk and adversity. Get students to think critically and flexibly in solving novel problems. These skills develop strategies that will serve students in all aspects of their lives. Also continue to nurture high levels of student responsibility and autonomy, intentionally fostering a disposition that students can and will be able to master mathematical concepts.

Make Mathematics Irresistible. Motivation is based on what students expect they can do and what they value (Wigfield & Cambria, 2010). The use of games, brainteasers, mysteries that can be solved through mathematics, and counterintuitive problems that leave students asking, "How is that possible?" help generate excitement. But the main thrust of the motivation emerges from you. Teachers need to communicate a passion for the content. Be enthusiastic and show that mathematics can make a difference in students' lives.

Give Students Leadership in Their Own Learning. High-achieving students tend to suggest their failures were from lack of effort and see the failure as a temporary condition that can be resolved with hard work. On the other hand, students with a history of academic failure can attribute their failures to lack of ability. This internal attribution is more difficult to counteract, as students think their innate lack of mathematical ability prevents them from succeeding no matter what they do. So, help students develop personal goals for their learning by asking them to reflect on their performance on a unit assessment, write personal goals for the next unit, or monitor how they are doing on their basic fact memorization and set weekly targets.

 Self-Check 6.6: Reducing Resistance and Building Resilence.

REFLECTIONS ON CHAPTER 6

WRITING TO LEARN

1. How is equity in the classroom different from teaching all students equally?

2. For children with learning disabilities, what are two strategies to modify instruction?

3. What can you do to make your class gender-friendly?

4. Describe a few strategies to reduce resistance to math learning in the class.

5. In the context of providing for the mathematically gifted, what is meant by enrichment? Give an example of how you might add depth to a classroom activity.

FOR DISCUSSION AND EXPLORATION

◆ Think about the difference between "equity" and "equality" of mathematics teaching in a class. Develop some specific methods for equitable mathematics teaching in a socially or culturally diverse class. Discuss this with your peer group to understand what methods should be preferred if you were to use them in such a classroom. Ask for their opinion on why a particular method you envisage may or may not work effectively.

RESOURCES FOR CHAPTER 6

RECOMMENDED READINGS

Articles

Bay Williams, J., & Livers, S. (2009). Supporting math vocabulary acquisition. *Teaching Children Mathematics*, *16*(4), 238–246.

Looking at words used in the mathematics classroom that have multiple meanings (i.e., mean, table), the authors show ways to support ELLs in the classroom.

Hodges, R., Rose, R., & Hicks, A. (2012). Interviews as RtI tools. *Teaching Children Mathematics*, *19*(1), 30–36.

This article emphasizes ways to identify the strengths and weaknesses of students with disabilities and the implication for instruction within an RtI framework.

Iliev, N., & D'Angelo, F. (2014). Teaching mathematics through multicultural literature. *Teaching Children Mathematics*, *20*(7), 452–457.

The authors blend strategies for teaching reading and mathematics for young learners.

Book

Johnsen, S. K., & Sheffield, L. J. (Eds.). (2013). *Using the common core state standards for mathematics with gifted and advanced learners*. Reston, VA: NCTM.

This book is in collaboration with the National Association for Gifted Children and provides examples and strategies for practitioners. Trajectories for talent development are detailed, as are ideas for encouraging creativity and critical thinking.

CHAPTER

7

Using Technological Tools to Teach Mathematics

LEARNER OUTCOMES

After reading this chapter and engaging in the embedded activities and reflections, you should be able to:

7.1 Describe ways in which teachers can combine the strategic use of technology with effective pedagogy to address important mathematics content.

7.2 Describe the benefits and appropriate uses of calculators.

7.3 Describe strategic uses of digital tools within a mathematics program.

7.4 Examine guidelines for selecting and using digital content to support mathematics teaching and learning.

7.5 Examine guidelines for evaluating resources on the Internet and increase an awareness of emerging technologies in mathematics education.

Mathematical technologies refers to digital content accessed via computers, calculators, and other handheld or tablet devices; computer algebra systems (CAS); dynamic geometry software; online digital games; recording devices; interactive presentation devices; spreadsheets; as well as the Internet-based resources for use with these devices and tools. A technology-enabled learning setting is an educational environment supported by mathematical technology tools, communicative and collaborative tools, or a combination of each (Arbaugh et al., 2010). "Tools are the materials, models, and representations that students use to organize and keep track of their thinking as they solve problems" (Ernst & Ryan, 2014, p. 222). Communicative and collaborative tools, sometimes referred to as *nonmathematical technologies* (Cohen & Hollebrands, 2011), encourage synchronous or asynchronous collaboration, communication, and construction of knowledge, and include blogs, wikis, and digital audio or videocasts.

 Tools and Technology

"An excellent mathematics program integrates the use of mathematical tools and technology as essential resources to help students learn and make sense of mathematical ideas, reason mathematically, and communicate their mathematical thinking" (NCTM, 2014, p. 78). Tools and Technology are among the five essential elements of effective school mathematics programs in NCTM's *Principles to Actions: Ensuring Mathematical Success for All*, an emphasis also supported by NCTM's position statement on the role of technology in the teaching and learning of mathematics (NCTM, 2011a). The CCSS *Standards for Mathematical Practice* promote the strategic use of appropriate tools and technology, which include digital applications, content, and resources

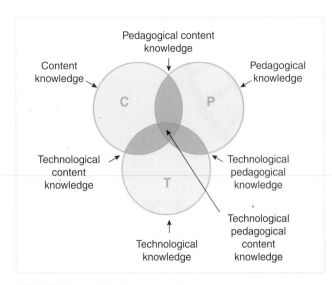

FIGURE 7.1 TPACK framework.

(CCSSO, 2010). Thinking of technology as an "extra" added on to the list of things you are trying to accomplish in your classroom is not an effective approach. According to Fey and his colleagues (2010), "Teachers need to carefully select and design learning opportunities for students where technology is an essential component in developing students' understanding, not where it is simply an appealing alternative to traditional instructional routines" (p. 275). *Instead, technology should be seen as an integral part of your instructional arsenal of tools for deepening student understanding.* It can enlarge the scope of the content students can learn and it can broaden the range of problems that students are able to tackle (Ball & Stacey, 2005; NCTM, 2008).

Pedagogical content knowledge (PCK) is the intersection of mathematics content knowledge with the pedagogical knowledge of teaching and learning (Shulman, 1986)—a body of information possessed by teachers that the average person, even one strong in mathematics, would not likely know. PCK represents the specific strategies and approaches that teachers use to deliver mathematical content effectively to students. Technological, pedagogical, and content knowledge (TPACK) (https://www.youtube.com/watch?v=4gQ2JEho_UA), as shown in Figure 7.1, describes the infusion of technology to this mix (Mishra & Koehler, 2006; Niess, 2008). We suggest that teachers consider technology as a conscious component of each lesson and a regular strategy for enhancing student learning. This chapter's emphasis on the importance of technology in instruction is carried over throughout the content chapters, especially in sections highlighted with the technology icon. Its value becomes evident when technological features embedded in a lesson enhance students' opportunities to learn important mathematics.

Technology-Supported Learning Activities

Grandgenett, Harris, and Hofer (2010–2011) propose seven "genres" of mathematics activities in which teachers can combine the strategic use of technology with effective pedagogy to address important mathematics content. These activities engage learners to consider and make sense of new information, practice various techniques, interpret and explore concepts, produce artifacts and representations, apply mathematics to the real world, evaluate their work and the work of others, and create products and resources. When two or more learning activities are combined and supported by strategic digital technology use, the chance for modeling the complexity of real-world applications of mathematics increases (Checkley, 2006; Fuson, Kalchman, & Bransford, 2005). Table 7.1 provides ways to think about how digital tools, pedagogy, and content can be brought together to engage students in strategic and meaningful uses of technology and to model processes and practices that deepen student understanding.

TABLE 7.1 TECHNOLOGY-SUPPORTED LEARNING ACTIVITIES

Description of Technology Support Activity	Sample Digital Tools/Resources
1. Consider and Make Sense of New Information.	
Gain information from a student or teacher demonstration or presentation activity.	Screencasting (Doceri, Educreations, Explain Everything, Jing, ShowMe, QuickTime), document camera, digital (video) camera, interactive whiteboards, presentation applications (Keynote, PowerPoint, Prezi), video (Animoto, YouTube, School Tube, Teacher Tube, Video), or other media tools
Gather information from reading a passage(s) from a digital or printed text.	Evernote, Notability, Curriculet, E-textbooks, portable document format (pdf) files, text files, websites
Engage in discourse with peers, teachers, or experts related to concepts, processes, or practices.	Edmodo, Google Apps, Math Forum's "Ask Dr. Math," online discussion groups and social networking tools (VoiceThread), Blackboard Collaborate™, GoToMeeting, Google Voice, and Video Chat

Look for, develop, and generalize relationships in patterns and repeated calculations.	Virtual manipulatives, computer algebra systems (CAS), dynamic geometry software (Geometer's Sketchpad, GeoGebra), Illuminations activities, spreadsheets, calculators (including online calculators, such as Desmos)
Select and use online research tools strategically to solve problems and deepen understanding.	Online databases (ERIC, SIRS, World Book, Gale Researcher, Math Forum's MathTools, NROC), web searching, simulations
Strive to understand the characteristics, context, or meaning of problems.	Concept and mind-mapping tools (Freeplane, Inspiration, Kidspiration, Lucid Chart, Popplet)

2. Practice Various Techniques.

Use tools to compute numerous items or large quantities.	Scientific/graphing calculators, spreadsheets, WolframAlpha
Do strategy-based drill and practice.	XtraMath, AAAMath, FASTT Math, MathXL, iFlash, computation apps on handheld/tablet devices
Do strategy-based problem solving puzzles.	Virtual manipulatives, brainteaser websites (First in Math, CoolMath4Kids), online Sudoku

3. Interpret and Explore Concepts.

Make conjectures, develop arguments, and highlight different approaches for solving problems.	Edmodo, Google Apps, screencasts (Doceri, Educreations, Explain Everything, Jing, Show-Me, QuickTime), dynamic geometry software (Geometer's Sketchpad, GeoGebra), widgets (Explore Learning), blogs, podcasts, wikis, concept and mind-mapping tools, online discussion groups and social networking tools (VoiceThread), email
Categorize information to examine relationships.	Concept and mind-mapping tools, databases/spreadsheets, drawing tools
Explain relationships in representations.	2D and 3D animations, online discussion groups and social networking tools (Edmodo, VoiceThread), video (iMovie, Windows Movie Maker, Camtasia 2), Global Positioning Devices (Google Earth), engineering calculation software (Mathcad)
Estimate and approximate values to examine relationships.	Basic/scientific/graphing calculators, spreadsheets, online savings calculators, classroom response systems (clickers)
Examine and interpret a mathematics-related phenomenon.	Dynamic geometry software (Geometer's Sketchpad, GeoGebra), online graphing calculator (Desmos), video sharing communities (YouTube, TeacherTube, SchoolTube, iTunesU), portable data collection devices/tools

4. Produce Artifacts and Representations.

Demonstrate understanding of a mathematical concept, topic, or process.	Interactive whiteboard, online discussion groups and social networking tools (VoiceThread), video (iMovie, Windows Movie Maker, Camtasia 2), document cameras, presentation software (Keynote, PowerPoint, Prezi), podcasts, screencasts (Doceri, Educreations, Explain Everything, Jing, Show-Me, QuickTime)
Produce a written document, journal entry, or report describing a concept, topic, or process.	Word processing application (with Math Type), collaborative editing tools (Google Docs), concept or mind-mapping tools (Freeplane, Inspiration, Kidspiration, Lucid Chart, Popplet), blogs, wikis, social networking tools
Develop a mathematical representation.	Spreadsheets, virtual manipulatives, concept or mind-mapping tools, graphing calculator
Pose a mathematical problem to illustrate a mathematics concept or relationship.	Word processing applications, online discussion groups, social network tools, email

5. Apply Mathematics to the Real World.

Review or select a strategy to solve a problem.	Online help sites (LearnZillion, Math Forum), TI, Casio (calculator), Key Curriculum Press (Geometer's Sketchpad), WolframAlpha online
Apply mathematical knowledge to test-taking situation.	Test-taking and survey software, classroom response systems
Apply a mathematical representation to model a real-world situation.	Spreadsheets, graphing calculators, virtual manipulatives, portable data collection devices/tools

6. Evaluate Student Work and the Work of Others.

Compare and contrast mathematical strategies or determine the most appropriate strategy for particular situations.	Inspiration, Kidspiration
Test a solution and check to see whether it makes sense within the context of a situation.	Scientific/graphing calculator, spreadsheet

(Continued)

TABLE 7.1 *(Continued)*

Description of Technology Support Activity	Sample Digital Tools/Resources
Make conjectures and use counterexamples to build a logical progression of statements to explore and support their ideas.	Geometer's Sketchpad, GeoGebra, Excel, online calculators
Evaluate mathematical work through the use of technology-supported feedback.	Online discussion groups, blogs
7. Create Products and Resources.	
Engage in peer teaching of a mathematics concept, strategy, or problem.	Presentation software (Keynote, PowerPoint, Prezi), interactive whiteboards, video (Animoto, Jing, YouTube, SchoolTube, TeacherTube, Vimeo)
Develop a solution pathway.	Concept or mind-mapping tools, collaborative writing tools (Google docs), wikis, social networking tools
Develop a creative project, invention, or artifact.	Word processor, animation tools, Geometer's Sketchpad, GeoGebra
Create a mathematical process for others to use.	Computer programming, iMovie, Windows Movie Maker, screencasts (Jing, QuickTime)

Source: Adapted from Grandgenett, N., Harris, J., & Hofer, M. (2011). An Activity-Based Approach to Technology Integration in the Mathematics Classroom. *NCSM Journal of Mathematics Education Leadership, 13*(1), 19–28. Reprinted with permission. Copyright 2011, by the National Council of Teachers of Mathematics. All rights reserved.

 Complete Self-Check 7.1: Technology-Supported Learning Activities

 # Calculators in Mathematics Instruction

In its position statement on calculator use in elementary grades, NCTM maintains its long-standing view by stating, "Calculators can promote the higher-order thinking and reasoning needed for problem solving in our information- and technology-based society, and they can also increase students' understanding of and fluency with arithmetic operations, algorithms, and numerical relationships. . . . [T]he use of calculators does not supplant the need for students to develop proficiency with efficient, accurate methods of mental and pencil-and-paper calculation and in making reasonable estimations" (NCTM, 2011, p. 1)*.

Even with the prevalent use of calculators in society and the professional support of calculators in schools, the use of calculators is not always central to instruction in a mathematics classroom, especially at the elementary level. Sometimes educators and students' families are concerned that just allowing students to use calculators when solving problems will hinder students' learning of the basic facts. However, rather than an either–or choice, just as with the use of other digital technologies, there are conditions when students should use technology and other times when they must call on their own resources.

Based on efficiency and effectiveness, students should learn when to use mental mathematics, when to use estimation, when to tackle a problem with paper and pencil, and when to use a calculator. Ignoring the potential benefits of calculators by prohibiting their use can inhibit students' learning. Helping students know when to grab a calculator and when not to use one is one of the Standards of Mathematical Practice (MP5: Use appropriate tools strategically). Having teachers and students engage in a conversation about when to use calculators can expand students' abilities to think about how challenging mathematics must be balanced with the development of their computational skills.

Help families understand that calculator use will in no way prevent students from learning rigorous mathematics—in fact, calculators used thoughtfully and meaningfully enhance the learning of mathematics. Furthermore, families should be made aware that calculators and other digital technologies require students to be problem solvers. Calculators can only calculate

---

*Reprinted with permission from the National Council of Teachers of Mathematics position statement, Calculator Use in Elementary Grades, copyright 2014 by the National Council of Teachers of Mathematics. All rights reserved.

according to input entered by humans. In isolation, calculators cannot answer the most meaningful mathematics tasks and they cannot substitute for thinking or understanding. Sending home calculator activities that reinforce important mathematical concepts and including calculator activities on a Family Math Night are ways to educate families about appropriate calculator use.

When to Use a Calculator

If the primary purpose of the instructional activity is to practice computational skills, students should not be using a calculator. On the other hand, students should have full access to calculators when they are exploring patterns, conducting investigations, testing conjectures, solving problems, and visualizing solutions. Situations involving computations that are beyond students' ability without the aid of a calculator are not necessarily beyond their ability to think about meaningfully.

As students come to fully understand the meanings of the operations, they should be exposed to realistic problems with realistic numbers. For example, young students may want to calculate how many seconds they have been alive. They can think conceptually about how many seconds in a minute, hour, day, and so on. But the actual calculations and those that continue to weeks and years can be done more efficiently on a calculator.

Also include calculators when the goal of the instructional activity is not to compute, but computation is involved in the problem solving. For example, middle-grade students may be asked to identify the "best buy" when there are different percentages off different-priced merchandise. Whether purchasing a digital tablet or getting a deal on ride tickets at the fair, the goal is to define the most economical relationship, given a set of choices, by calculating the various percentage discounts with a calculator. (Visit the companion website for Guidelines in Setting Up a Learning Center and Planning Template.) Calculators are also valuable for generating and analyzing patterns. For example, when finding the decimal equivalent of $\frac{8}{9}, \frac{7}{9}, \frac{5}{9}$, and so on, an interesting pattern emerges. Let students explore other "ninths" and make conjectures as to why the pattern occurs. Again, the emphasis is not to determine a computational solution but instead to use the calculator to help find patterns and seek regularity in repeated reasoning (MP8).

Finally, calculators can be used as accommodations for students with disabilities. When used for instruction that is not centered on developing computation skills, calculators can help ensure that all students have appropriate access to the curriculum to the maximum extent possible.

Benefits of Calculator Use

Understanding how calculators contribute to the learning of mathematics includes recognizing that the "the body of research consistently shows that the use of calculators in the teaching and learning of mathematics does not contribute to any negative outcomes for skill development or procedural proficiency, but instead enhances the understanding of mathematics concepts and student orientation toward mathematics" (NCTM, 2011b, p. 1). This includes handheld and online four-function, scientific, and graphing calculators. A specific discussion of graphing calculators is found later in this chapter.

Calculators Can Be Used to Develop Concepts and Enhance Problem Solving. The calculator can be much more than a device for calculation. As shown in an analysis of more than 79 research studies, K–12 students (with the exception of grade 4) who used calculators improved their "basic skills with paper-pencil tasks both in computational operations and in problem solving" (Hembree & Dessert, 1986, p. 96). Other researchers confirm that students with long-term experience using calculators performed better overall than students without such experience on both mental computation and paper-and-pencil problems (Ellington, 2003; Smith, 1997b; Wareham, 2005).

Although some worry that calculator use can impede instruction in number and operations, the reverse is actually the case, as shown in the following examples. In grades K–1, students who are exploring concepts of quantity can use the calculator as a counting machine. Using the automatic-constant feature (not all calculators perform this in the same way, so check how it works on your calculator) students can count. For example, press the following keys—[0] [+] [1] [=] [=] [=]—to count by ones, pressing the equals key for as long as the count continues. Help students try this feature. The "count by ones" on the calculator can reinforce students' oral counting, identification of patterns, and can even be used by one student to count their classmates as they enter the classroom in the morning. Children's literature with repeated phrases, such as the classic *Goodnight Moon* (Brown, 1947), provides an opportunity for students to count. Students can press the equal sign each time the little rabbit says goodnight in his bedtime routine. At the completion of the book they can compare how many "goodnights" were recorded. Follow-up activities include using the same automatic-constant feature on the calculator with different stories or books to skip-count by twos (e.g., pairs of animals or people), fives (e.g., fingers on one hand or people in a car), or tens (e.g., dimes, "ten in a bed," apples in a tree).

Older students can investigate decimal concepts with a calculator, as in the following examples. On the calculator, $796 \div 42 = 18.95238$. Consider the task of using the calculator to determine the whole-number remainder. Another example is to use the calculator to find a number that when multiplied by itself will produce 43. In this situation, a student can press 6.1 $\boxed{\times}$ $\boxed{=}$ to get the square of 6.1. For students who are just beginning to understand decimals, the activity will demonstrate that numbers such as 6.3 and 6.4 are between 6 and 7. Furthermore, 6.55 is between 6.5 and 6.6. For students who already understand the density of decimals, the same activity serves as a meaningful and conceptual introduction to square roots.

Calculators Can Be Used for Practicing Basic Facts. Students who want to practice the multiples of 7 can press 7 $\boxed{\times}$ 3 and delay pressing the $\boxed{=}$. The challenge is to answer the fact to themselves before pressing the $\boxed{=}$ key. Subsequent multiples of 7 can be checked by simply pressing the second factor and the $\boxed{=}$. The TI-10 (Texas Instruments) and TI-15 calculators have built-in problem solving modes in which students can practice facts, develop lists of related facts, and test equations or inequalities with arithmetic expressions on both sides of the relationship symbol.

A class can be split in half, with one half required to use a calculator and the other required to do the computations mentally. For $3000 + 1765$, the mental math team wins every time. It will also win for simple facts and numerous problems that lend themselves to mental computation. Of course, there are many computations, such as 537×32, where the calculator team will be faster. Not only does this simple exercise provide practice with mental math, but it also demonstrates to students that it is not always effective or efficient to reach for the calculator.

Calculators Can Improve Student Attitudes and Motivation. Research results reveal that students who frequently use calculators have better attitudes toward the subject of mathematics (Ellington, 2003). There is also evidence that students are more motivated when their anxiety is reduced; therefore, supporting students during problem solving activities with calculators is important. A student with disabilities who is left out of the problem solving lesson due to weak knowledge of basic facts will not pursue the worthwhile explorations the teacher plans. That does not excuse them from learning their facts. As we try to increase students' confidence that they can solve challenging mathematics problems, we can expand their motivation to be persistent and stay engaged in the process of thinking about numbers. Again, the strategic use of the calculator is guided by the plans of the teacher and the eventual decision making of the students.

Calculators Are Commonly Used in Society. Calculators are used by almost everyone in every facet of life that involves any sort of exact computation. Students should be taught how to use this commonplace tool effectively and also learn to judge when to use it. Though available on virtually every type of digital device or smartphone, many adults have not learned how to use the automatic-constant feature of a calculator and are not practiced in recognizing common errors that are often made on calculators. Effective use of calculators is an important skill that is best learned by using them regularly in meaningful problem solving activities. Visit the companion website for a video that features John A. Van de Walle discussing the benefits of calculator use.

Graphing Calculators

Handheld and web- or app-based graphing calculators help students visualize concepts as they make real-world connections with data. When students can actually see expressions, formulas, graphs, and the results of changing a variable on those visual representations, a deeper understanding of concepts can result. Graphing calculators are used in upper-elementary classes through high school and beyond, but the most common use is at the secondary level. Because graphing calculators are permitted and in some cases required on such tests as the SAT, ACT, PSAT, AP, and state-mandated high school mathematics exams, it is critical for all students to be familiar with their use.

It is a mistake to think that graphing calculators are only for doing "high-powered" mathematics. The following list demonstrates some features the graphing calculator offers, every one of which is useful within the standard middle school curriculum.

- The display window permits compound expressions such as $3 + 4(5 - \frac{6}{7})$ to be shown completely before being evaluated. Furthermore, once evaluated, previous expressions can be recalled and modified. This promotes an understanding of notation and order of operations. Expressions can include exponents, absolute values, and negation signs, with no restrictions on the values used.
- Even without using function definition capability, students can insert values into expressions or formulas without having to enter the entire formula for each new value. The results can be entered into a list or table of values and stored directly on the calculator for further analysis.
- Variables can be used in expressions and then assigned different values to see the effect on expressions. This simple method helps with the idea of a variable as something that varies.
- The distinction between "negative" and "subtract" is clear and very useful. A separate key is used to enter the negative of a quantity. The display shows the negative sign as a superscript. If $^-5$ is stored in the variable B, then the expression $^-2 - {}^-B$ will be evaluated correctly as $^-7$. This feature is a significant aid in the study of integers and variables.
- Points can be plotted on a coordinate screen either by entering coordinates and seeing the result or by moving the cursor to a particular coordinate on the screen.
- Very large and very small numbers are managed without error. The calculator will quickly compute factorials, even for large numbers, as well as permutations and combinations. For example, $23! = 1.033314797 \times 10^{40}$.
- Statistical functions allow students to examine the means, medians, and standard deviations of large and sometimes complex sets of data. Data are entered, ordered, added to, or changed almost as easily as on a spreadsheet.
- Graphs for data analysis are available, including box plots, histograms, and—on some calculators—circle graphs, bar graphs, and pictographs.
- Random number generators allow for the simulation of a variety of probability experiments.
- Scatter plots for ordered pairs of real data can be entered, plotted, and examined for trends. The calculator will calculate the equations of best-fit, linear, or quadratic functions.
- Functions can be explored in three modes: equation, table, and graph. Because the calculator easily switches from one to the other and because of the trace feature, the connections between these modes become quite clear.
- The graphing calculator is programmable. Programs are very easily written and understood. For example, a program involving the Pythagorean theorem can be used to find the lengths of sides of right triangles.
- Students can share data programs and functions from one calculator to another, connect their calculators to a classroom display screen, save information to a computer and share findings with classmates and the teacher, and download software applications that give additional functionality for special uses.

A popular and full-color graphing calculator, the TI-Nspire™ CX, is used in many classrooms. Student work can be transferred between the TI-Nspire and computer via TI-Nspire Student Software and also via the TI-Nspire™ App for iPad®. A student can explore how changing the width of a rectangle overlaid on an image of an aerial view of a building keeps the perimeter constant but affects the area. The student can simultaneously see the image of the rectangle that they can manipulate to desired dimensions, a table of matching values, and a graph of the resulting area. Rather than toggling from one representation to another, they can all be considered at one time, which strengthens the ability to see patterns. There are even options for writing notes to record discoveries or findings. An increasingly popular graphing calculator is Desmos, a free online tool that can be used on any computer or tablet, has an intuitive interface, uses a series of sliders, and allows the user to add text boxes to graphs, share graphs via email, and more.

These amazing tools are only as useful as the tasks teachers provide for students. Arguments against graphing calculators are similar to those for other calculators—and are equally unsubstantiated. These tools have the potential to provide students with significant opportunities for exploring real mathematics.

Portable Data-Collection Devices

In addition to the capabilities of the graphing calculator alone, portable data-collection devices and probe/sensor tools make these tools even more remarkable. Texas Instruments calls its version the Calculator-Based Ranger 2 motion sensor. Other companies may refer to this device as a computer-based laboratory. Casio's version, the Data Analyzer EA-200, is nearly identical. These devices accept a variety of probes, such as temperature or light sensors and motion detectors that can be used to gather real data. These data can be transferred to the graphing calculator, where they are stored in one or more lists. The calculator can then produce scatter plots or prepare other analyses.

These instruments help students connect graphs with real-world events. They emphasize the relationships between variables and can dispel common misconceptions students have about interpreting graphs (Lapp, 2001). Lapp explains that students often confuse the fastest rate of change with the highest point on the graph or they may erroneously think that the shape of the graph is the shape of the motion (like a bicycle going up the hill is faster—increasing speed—than a bicycle going downhill). The fact that the graph can be produced immediately is a powerful feature of the device that allows these missteps in thinking to be tested and discussed. One of the most exciting aspects of digital sensors and probe software devices involves the application of skills used in science, technology, engineering, and mathematics (STEM) investigations.

 Complete Self-Check 7.2: Calculators in Mathematics Instruction

 Appropriate and Strategic Use of Digital Tools

Many digital tools are designed for student interaction in a manner that extends beyond the physical textbook or a tutor. Some of these programs come in the form of applets or mobile apps. Mathematics applets have been around since the late 1990s and still exist as targeted programs that can be freely accessed and manipulated on the Internet. Commonly referred to as *e-tools* or *virtual manipulatives,* the National Library of Virtual Manipulatives has more than 100 Java applets that address concepts within each content standard and are organized across K–12 grade bands. Mobile apps, emerging and powerful software tools created for use in the mathematics classroom on tablet devices, can be purchased online from mobile app publishers. iOS apps for use on Apple devices can be downloaded from the iTunes App Store. Android apps can be downloaded from Google Play and various other online, third-party app stores.

An e-tool or mobile app can be used somewhat like a physical manipulative; by itself, it does not teach. However, the user of a well-designed tool has a digital "thinker tool" with which to explore mathematical ideas. In the following discussion, the intent is to provide some perspective on the different kinds of input to your mathematics program that instructional technology programs might offer.

Concept Instruction

A growing number of programs make an effort to offer conceptual instruction using real-world contexts to illustrate mathematical ideas. Using problem solving situations, specific concepts are developed in a guided manner to support reasoning and sense making.

What is most often missing in instructional applications is a way to make the mathematics problem based and engage students fully in the conceptual activity. Often when students work on a digital device, there is little opportunity for discourse, conjecture, or original ideas. Additionally, some classrooms are outfitted with interactive whiteboards, but the teacher controls the program on the large display screen with the class watching. Some software even presents concepts in such a fashion as to remove learners from thinking and constructing their own understanding. When prevented from direct contact with digital tools, just as with physical resources, students' understanding can suffer. Some digital resources are best used when one or two students control the program on a large display screen with the class engaged in teacher-guided discussion and analysis. In this way, the teacher and/or students can pose questions and entertain discussions that are simply not possible without the aid of technology. The key is that technology should be used strategically by both teacher and students to improve understanding, promote engagement, and increase mathematical proficiency (NCTM, 2008).

Problem Solving

With the current focus on problem solving, more digital publishers purport to teach students to solve problems through their digital simulations. But problem solving is not the same as solving problems. Thinkport's online mathematics interactives demonstrate good examples of problem solving through gaming simulations. Here the problems are not typical story problems awaiting a computation, but more thoughtful simulations set in real and engaging contexts. DreamBox Learning provides an adaptive, individualized, online program for K–8 students that enables teachers and parents to track student progress on curriculum aligned with the Common Core State Standards, as well as NCTM's and other state and Canadian standards. Innovative tools such as the open number line, snap blocks (algebraic thinking), match and make (number patterns and computation), and quick images (subitizing and cardinality), with corresponding lessons and formative assessment opportunities, are available.

Drill and Reinforcement

Drill programs give students practice with skills that are assumed to have been previously taught. In general, a drill program poses questions that are answered directly or by selecting from a multiple-choice list. Many of these programs are set in gaming formats that make them exciting for students who like video games.

Drill programs evaluate responses immediately. How they respond to the first or second incorrect answer is one important distinguishing feature. At one extreme, the answer is simply recorded as wrong with multiple opportunities to correct it. At the other extreme, the program may branch to an explanation of the correct response. Others may provide hints or supply a visual model to help with the task. Some programs also offer record-keeping features for the teacher to keep track of individual students' progress and/or build specific learning pathways based on the student's correct and incorrect responses.

One feature worth mentioning is differentiated drill, such as is found in *XtraMath*, *FASTT Math* (Scholastic) and *First in Math*® (Suntex International). *XtraMath* is a free online math fact fluency program that is designed to help students pre-assess, keep track of, and master addition, subtraction, multiplication, and division facts in short, daily practice sessions. The subscription-based *FASTT Math* (Fluency and Automaticity through Systematic Teaching with Technology) program works to help all students develop fluency with math facts. In short sessions that are customized for individual learners, the software and web-based versions automatically differentiate instruction based on each student's previous performance. *First in Math*® a subscription-based online game, offers students a self-paced approach to practicing basic math skills and complex problem solving tasks. Each of these programs provide students with the opportunity to earn electronic incentives and move on to more difficult exercises.

 Complete Self-Check 7.3: Appropriate and Strategic Use of Digital Tools

Guidelines for Selecting and Using Digital Resources for Mathematics

There is so much digital content available for teaching mathematics. Some commercially published digital resources can be expensive, so free, open-source content should be used whenever possible. Even though many online tools are free to use, schools must still provide for Internet access and the appropriate hardware devices. In either case, it is important to make informed decisions when investing limited funds.

NCSM (2011), with support from the Council of Chief State School Officers, Brookhill Foundation, and Texas Instruments, has created a free *CCSS-M Curriculum Analysis Tool*, designed to evaluate the extent to which instructional technology resources:

- Integrate technology tools and software in ways to engage students with the Common Core State Standards for Mathematical Practice
- Provide opportunities for teachers and/or students to collaborate and communicate with each other
- Include opportunities to assess conceptual understanding and skill fluency through worthwhile mathematical tasks
- Provide guidance for teacher use of tools and technology that supports and enhances student learning

How digital content is used in mathematics instruction will vary considerably with the topic, the grade level, and the content itself. The CCSS-M Curriculum Analysis Tool can be found on the National Council of Supervisors of Mathematics's website.

Guidelines for Using Digital Content

The following are offered as considerations that you should keep in mind as you select digital content.

- Digital content should contribute to the objectives of the lesson or unit. It should not be used as an add-on or substitute for more accessible approaches.
- For individualized or small-group use, provide specific instructions for using the resource and provide time for students to freely explore or practice.
- Combine online activities with offline activities (e.g., collect measurement data in the classroom to enter into an online spreadsheet).
- Create a management plan for using the digital content. This could include a schedule for use (e.g., during centers, during small-group work) and a way to assess the effectiveness of the resource use. Although some programs include a way to keep track of student performance, you may need to determine whether the tool is effectively meeting the objectives of the specific lesson or unit.

How to Select Appropriate Digital Content

The most important requirement for selecting digital resources is to be well informed about the content and to evaluate its merits in an objective manner.

Gathering Information. One of the best sources of information about digital resources is the review section of NCTM journals or other journals that you respect. Many websites offer reviews on both commercially available digital resources and Internet-based tools. The Math Forum's Math Tools (Drexel University) is one such site.

One important consideration is whether the digital content is accessible for all students, including individuals with disabilities. Can the text be enlarged or highlighted or converted from text to speech? Are the graphics easily recognizable, containing mouse-overs (where the action is written or spoken as the mouse is moved over the image) and not dependent on color for meaning? Can the software be used with a keyboard or on a touchscreen instead of a mouse or trackpad? All these questions are derived from the universal design principles defined at the Center for Applied Special Technology (CAST) website.

TechMatrix is a powerful tool for finding "assistive and educational technology tools and resources to support learning for students with disabilities and their classmates" (National Center for Technology Innovation, 2010). Select mathematics under the heading "Content Area" and take a look at research-based reports, products, and professional development sections related to the use of technology for students with special needs.

When selecting any technology tool or digital resource, it is important to evaluate it appropriately. Try first to get a preview or at least a demonstration version. Take advantage of any offer for free 30-day trial access. Before purchasing, try the digital resource with students in the grade that will be using it. Remember, it is the mathematics content you are interested in, not the game the students might be playing.

Criteria. Think about the following points as you review digital resources (visit the companion website for a rubric on Evaluating Mathware or Websites).

- How will students be challenged to learn better than opportunities without the digital access? Don't select or use a digital tool just to put your students on a digital device. Go past the clever graphics and the games and focus on what students will be learning.
- How are students likely to be engaged with the *content* (not the frills)? Remember that student reflective thought is the most significant factor in effective instruction. Is the mathematics presented so that it is problematic and rigorous for the student?
- How easy is the tool or resource to use? There should not be so much tedium in using the resource that attention is diverted from the content or students become frustrated.
- How does the tool or resource develop knowledge that supports conceptual understanding? In practice programs, how are incorrect answers handled? Are the models or explanations going to enhance student understanding?
- What controls and assessments are provided to the teacher? Are there options that can be turned on and off (e.g., sound, types of feedback or help, levels of difficulty)? Is there a provision for record keeping so that you will know what progress individual students have made?
- Are high-quality user guides or professional development services available? Minimally, the support provided should clearly state how the resource is to operate and provide troubleshooting.
- Is the digital resource equitable in its consideration of age, gender, and culture?
- What is the nature of the licensing agreement? For example, is a site license or district license available? If you purchase a single-user package, it is not legal to install or access the program on multiple computers.
- Be sure that the digital application will run on the computers at your school. The description of system requirements should indicate the compatible platform(s) and the version of the required operating systems. School districts usually have a technology review process to address apps, software, hardware, and network compatibility requirements.

 Complete Self-Check 7.4: Guidelines for Selecting and Using Digital Resources

Mathematics Resources on the Internet

The Internet is a wellspring of information. Instead of using a standard search engine to find mathematics-related information, it is sometimes better to have some places to begin. Several good websites will usually provide more links to other sites than you will have time to search. One source for good technological tools is this book. Throughout each chapter you will find references to digital tools and technology resources. The types of resources you can expect to find include professional information, teacher resources, digital tools, and open-source applications. Here is a list of some recommended online mathematics resources.

Annenberg Learner

This tremendous resource lists free online professional learning activities, including information about all sorts of interesting uses of mathematics in the real world, resources for free and inexpensive materials, and information about funding opportunities.

Center for Implementing Technology in Education (CITEd): TechMatrix

CITEd's TechMatrix is a useful database of technology products that supports instruction in mathematics for students with special needs. Each product evaluation includes a link to the supplier's website.

Illuminations (NCTM)

This is an incredible collection developed by NCTM to provide teaching and learning resources, such as lesson ideas and digital tools, that are intended to "illuminate" *Principles and Standards for School Mathematics*. Also at this site are multimedia investigations for students and links to video vignettes designed to promote professional reflection. In addition, Calculation Nation allows students to explore mathematics topics while playing games with one another over the Web.

Illustrative Mathematics

This website contains free, vetted resources for mathematics teachers with a focus on illustrating standards through tasks, videos, lesson plans, and curriculum modules.

Inside Mathematics

This site features examples of innovative teaching methods, insights into student learning, tools for mathematics instruction that teachers and specialists can use immediately, resources to support the *Common Core State Standards*, and video tours of the ideas and materials on the site.

How to Select Online Resources

The massive amount of information available on the Internet must be sifted through for accuracy and sorted by quality when you plan instruction or when your students gather information or research a mathematics topic. For example, identifying a mathematics lesson plan on the Internet does not ensure that it is effective, as anyone can publish any idea they have on the Web. To use the Web as a teaching toolbox for locating successful mathematics tasks, motivating enrichment activities, or supportive strategies to assist struggling learners, it is better to go to trustworthy, high-quality websites than merely plug a few keywords into a search engine. If you choose to explore webpages, blogs, or wikis (collaboratively created and updated webpages) more broadly, take the elements enumerated in Table 7.2 into consideration. These criteria are critical for your use as a discerning educator and can be adapted or simplified for your students as they evaluate material on the Web. The main topics are adapted from a group of considerations suggested by Smith (1997a).

Emerging Technologies

Emerging technologies refers to the ever-changing landscape of technological tools and advances. In our increasingly technological society, we must help students explore the latest technology-enabled tools with a curious mind and a reasoned approach to learning about the innovation.

TABLE 7.2   EVALUATING RESOURCES ON THE INTERNET

	Criteria	Justification	Evidence/Verification
Authority	• The page should identify authors and their qualifications. • The site should be associated with a reputable educational institution or organization.	• Anyone can publish pages on the Web. You want to be sure that the information is from a reliable source and is of high quality.	• Contact information for the author or organization is easily available. Is there a link to the organization's home page? • Do the authors establish their expertise? • Use the "Who Is" domain research service to identify the author of the site. • Is the URL domain .org, .edu, .gov, .net, or .com?
Content	• The site should match topic of interest. • The materials should add depth to your information.	• The information should be useful facts rather than opinions. • The text should be actual information from an expert and not paraphrased from another site.	• Is it a list of links from other sites? • Are the statements verified by footnotes and research? • Do the authors indicate criteria for including information?
Objectivity	• The site should not reflect a biased point of view. • Authors should present facts and not try to sway readers.	• Websites can try to influence the readers rather than provide independent and evenhanded information sources	• Are there advertisements or sponsors either on the page or linked to the page? • Does the author discuss multiple theories or points of view?
Accuracy	• Information should be free of errors. • Information should be verified by reviewers or fact-checkers.	• Websites can be published without reviewers or accuracy checks.	• Does the page contain obvious errors in grammar, spelling, or mathematics? • Are original sources clearly documented in a list of references? • Can the information be cross-checked through another source? • Are charts, graphs, or statistical information labeled clearly?
Currency	• The site should be current and frequently revised.	• Information is changing so rapidly that pages that are not maintained and up to date cannot provide the reliable information needed. • Currency is a key advantage of the Web over print sources. If there is no evidence of currency, the site loses its potential to add to knowledge in the field.	• Look for dates and updates for the page. • Links should be current and not lead to dead sites. • References should include recent citations. • Photos and videos should be up to date (unless related to a historical topic).
Audience	• The site's target (i.e., whether it is for your own use or the potential use of students in your classroom) should be clear. • The site should detail whether it is a self-created site or has been created by others. • The site should be accessible by all learners, particularly those with disabilities.	• In education, the audience may be students, families, teachers, or administrators. Presenting information for a well-defined audience is critical.	• Check for suggested grade levels or ages. • Check to see that content and hyperlinks to other sites are free of offensive material (including advertisements). • Does the site allow for easy use through menus or search features that help students find information? • What is the reading level of the narrative? • Are there options for students with disabilities? Do they adhere to the principles of universal design by, for example, considering students with visual impairments (by using increased font size, synthesized speech, or a screen reader) or students with hearing impairments (by including captions for video or audio materials)? See CAST's UDL Center online to learn more.

Electronic Textbooks (e-Textbooks). The tight funding in schools, coupled with the success of e-readers such as Amazon's Kindle and Barnes and Noble's Nook and digital tablets such as Microsoft's Surface Tablet and Apple's iPad®, have pressured some schools and districts to reconsider their approach to textbook adoption. This, in turn, has forced textbook publishers to deliver programs that can be customized for districts and viewed using digital devices. For example, Discovery Education's Math Techbook™ Digital Textbook includes inquiry-based lessons, digital tools, and opportunities for formative assessment with targeted feedback. The Math Techbook™ is designed to help students develop a balance of conceptual understanding, procedural fluency, and apply their knowledge to solving real-world problems. Advantages to schools using e-textbooks include integrated formative assessment tools, enhanced and updated lessons using digital media, and the ability to access/store content for multiple disciplines on one device. Challenges include the costs associated with providing mobile hardware access to each student and the need for curriculum redesign, staff training, and improved networking and infrastructure stability (Fey, Hollenbeck, & Wray, 2010).

Whiteboard Mobile Apps and Pencasting. There are several mobile apps that double as digital whiteboards with audio capture capabilities. Students can record and capture their mathematical representations on the screen while sharing their verbal reasoning. These files can be archived and shared electronically via email or the Web. Doceri, Educreations, Explain Everything, and Show Me are just a few of these powerful, free or low-cost apps. The Smartpen (available from Livescribe) allows students and teachers to easily capture written representations and audio recordings and make them accessible to others in digital format. Users need the Livescribe Smartpen, dot paper, and a computer or tablet with which to sync pencasts. Students can revisit and share the animated Smartpen recording on a computer or iOS handheld device/tablet using Evernote, a software suite that archives digital notes and files.

Teacher Blogs. There is a close link between teachers who are reflective practitioners and those who grow to be considered master teachers by their students and peers. No doubt most would also agree that being part of a network of professionals, including learning from and seeking the advice of colleagues and mentors both inside and outside the school building, is critical to success in the teaching profession. The Math Twitter Blogosphere (MTBoS) is a group of mathematics educators from various locations around the world who share in "a passion for our craft, and a desire to get a little bit better each year." The greatest thing about this blogging community is that it is free, open to all interested parties, and is made up of a group of engaging and supportive professionals who freely share advice and resources and often collaborate to develop amazing projects and innovations. Whether you are interested in writing (or just reading) a math blog, you should visit the Math Twitter Blogosphere website or follow the online discussions that take place at #MTBoS on Twitter.

 Complete Self-Check 7.5: Mathematics Resources on the Internet

REFLECTIONS ON CHAPTER 7

WRITING TO LEARN

1. Explain at least three ways that technological tools have affected the mathematics curriculum and how it is taught. Give examples to support your explanation.

2. Describe some of the benefits of using calculators regularly in the mathematics classroom. Which of these seem to you to be the most compelling? What are some of the arguments against using calculators?

3. Give some examples of appropriate and strategic uses of digital tools in mathematics teaching.

4. How can portable data-collection devices be used to improve student understanding of graphs?

5. What kind of information can you expect to find on the Internet that would be useful in teaching mathematics? How can you evaluate the quality of that information?

6. What are some of the emerging technologies? How can you stay abreast of new technologies as they develop?

FOR DISCUSSION AND EXPLORATION

◆ Ask some teachers about their opinions on the use of emerging technologies in the classroom. In which situations can they be more useful than current teaching practices? Do you see any disadvantages in the introduction of more technology in the classrooms? Examine the ways technology could impact future mathematics teaching.

◆ Check out at least three of the tools suggested in Table 7.1. Select one and try it with students. Teach a lesson that incorporates the digital resource as either a teacher tool or student activity.

RESOURCES FOR CHAPTER 7

RECOMMENDED READINGS

Articles

Suh, J. M., Johnston, C. J., & Douglas, J. (2008). Enhancing mathematical learning in a technology-rich environment. *Teaching Children Mathematics (15)*4, 235–241.

The authors share considerations for leveraging technology-enabled learning environments by describing the teacher's role and strategies for increasing equity and access for diverse learners. Benefits of virtual manipulative use are also described.

Thompson, T., & Sproule, S. (2005). Calculators for students with special needs. *Teaching Children Mathematics, 11*(7), 391–395.

This excellent argument for the use of calculators for students who have learning problems that affect their mathematical skill can help counter any objections raised by calculator critics. Included is a framework that is easily used to make decisions about when to allow calculator use that is not only appropriate for students with disabilities, but for every student.

Book

Fey, J., Hollenbeck, R., & Wray, J. (2010). Technology and the mathematics curriculum. *NCTM Seventy-Second Yearbook*. Reston, VA: NCTM.

This book illustrates how teachers can incorporate the effective use of technology to enhance mathematics learning and support effective teaching.

CHAPTER 8

Developing Early Number Concepts and Number Sense

LEARNER OUTCOMES

After reading this chapter and engaging in the embedded activities and reflections, you should be able to:

8.1 Recognize that teaching very young children mathematics involves using a developmental approach in presenting high-quality number activities.

8.2 Demonstrate how to develop children's skills for counting, including subitizing (recognizing a total number of objects in an organized collection) to 3 or 5 without counting each object.

8.3 Plan ways to teach students to compare quantities and describe relationships between numbers.

8.4 Develop ways to connect mathematical ideas to the real-world activities of young learners.

Young children enter school with many ideas about number and these ideas should be built upon to develop new relationships over time. With time and a variety of experiences, children can develop a full understanding of number that will grow into more advanced mathematics concepts. This chapter emphasizes the development of number ideas for numbers up to 20 but also considers the number names and counting sequences up to 100 by ones and tens. These foundational ideas can all be extended to content that enhances the development of number (measurement, data, operations) and content directly affected by how well early number concepts have been developed (basic facts, place value, and computation). Teachers begin, however, by introducing critical big ideas about counting and comparing number quantities to nurture and build young children's conceptual understandings of number concepts and number sense.

 BIG IDEAS

- Counting tells how many things are in a set. When counting a set of objects, the last word in the counting sequence names the quantity for that set (*cardinality*).

- Numbers relate through comparisons of quantities, including greater-than, less-than, and equal-to relationships. These comparisons are made through one-to-one correspondence of objects in sets. The number 7, for example, is three more than 4, two less than 9, composed of 3 and 4, three away from 10, and can be quickly recognized in several patterned arrangements of dots. These ideas about the number 7 extend to composing and decomposing larger numbers such as 17, 57, and 370.

◆ Number concepts are intimately tied to operations with numbers based on situations in the world around us. Application of number relationships to problem solving marks the beginning of making sense of the world in a mathematical manner.

◆ *Number sense* means that you can think about different sized quantities and use numbers and relationships in multiple ways to estimate and solve problems.

Promoting Good Beginnings

Research shows that preschoolers' early mathematical performance establishes a foundation for their future academic success (Frye et al., 2013; Levine et al., 2010). In alignment, the National Council of Teachers of Mathematics' (NCTM's) position statement emphasizes that all children need an early start in learning mathematics (2013). This document provides research-based recommendations to help teachers develop high-quality learning activities for children in the first 6 years of life:

1. Enhance children's natural interest in mathematics and assist them in using mathematics to make sense of their world.
2. Build on children's experience and knowledge, taking advantage of familiar contexts.
3. Base mathematics curriculum and teaching practices on a solid understanding of both mathematics and child development.
4. Use formal and informal experiences in the curriculum and teaching practices to strengthen children's problem solving and reasoning processes.
5. Provide opportunities for children to explain their thinking as they interact with mathematical ideas.
6. Assess children's mathematical knowledge, skills, and strategies through observation and other informal approaches.

 Pause & Reflect

Although all of these recommendations are critical, which two do you think are most important for your own professional growth? ●

In 2009, the National Research Council (NRC) established the Committee on Early Childhood Mathematics to examine research on how mathematics is taught and learned in children's early years. Unfortunately, they identified that in early childhood settings there was a lack of opportunities for learning mathematics, especially as compared to opportunities for language and literacy development. Surprisingly, they also noted that what a 5- or 6-year-old knows about mathematics can predict not only their future math achievement (National Mathematics Advisory Panel, 2008) but also their future reading achievement.

This NRC committee identified three foundational areas in mathematics content for early learners: the number core, the relations core, and the operations core. This chapter begins with the first two core areas; Chapter 9 will provide a focus on the third core in examining the meaning of the operations. Please note that as you develop children's initial abilities in counting, the conversations about number relationships begin. Therefore, the activities and concepts in this chapter are not sequential but coexist in a rich environment of mathematical experiences where children see connections between numbers.

 Complete Self-Check 8.1: Promoting Good Beginnings

The Number Core: Quantity, Counting, and Knowing How Many

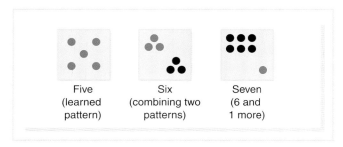

Five
(learned
pattern)

Six
(combining two
patterns)

Seven
(6 and
1 more)

FIGURE 8.1 Recognizing a patterned set.

Families help even 2- and 3-year-olds count their fingers, toys, people at the table, and other small sets of objects. Questions such as "Who has more?" or "Are there enough?" are part of children's daily lives. Evidence indicates that when children have such experiences, they begin to develop understanding of the concepts of number and counting (Baroody, Li, & Lai, 2008; Clements & Sarama, 2014). We therefore include abundant activities to support the different experiences that children need to gain a full understanding of number concepts.

Quantity and the Ability to Subitize

Children explore quantity before they can count. They can identify which cup is bigger or which plate of blueberries has more berries. Soon they need to attach an amount to the quantities to explore them in greater depth. When you look at an amount of objects, sometimes you are able to just "see" how many are there, particularly for a small group. For example, when you roll a die and know that it is five without counting the dots, that ability to "just see it" is called *subitizing*. There are times when you are able to do this for even larger amounts, when you break apart a group of dots shown in a pattern of ten by seeing five in one row and mentally doubling it to get 10. "Subitizing is a fundamental skill in the development of children's understanding of number" (Baroody, 1987, p. 115). Subitizing can be a complex skill that needs to be developed and practiced through experiences with patterned sets.

Many children easily recognize patterned sets of dots on dice due to the many games they have played. Similar instant recognition (subitizing) can be developed for other patterns (see Figure 8.1). Naming these amounts immediately without counting aids in "counting on" (from a known patterned set) or learning combinations of numbers (seeing a patterned set of two known smaller patterns). To support beginning learners in subitizing use 3 objects organized in patterns that are symmetric before moving to numbers such as 5 or more challenging images. Visit the Subitizing Exercise website to help test and develop the speed and accuracy of your ability to subitize.

Good materials to use in pattern recognition activities include a set of dot plates made with paper plates and the sticky dots commonly available in office supply stores (see Figure 8.2). Note that some patterns are combinations of two smaller patterns or a pattern with one or two additional dots. These should be made in two colors. Keep the patterns compact and organized. If the dots are too spread out, the patterns are hard to identify. Explore interactive activities from the Freudenthal Institute for Science and Mathematics Education (FIsme) web-based repository of "Speedy Pictures 1" and "Speedy Pictures 2" where children can practice subitizing and basic addition using flashed images of fingers, dice, beads on a frame, or eggs in a carton holding ten.

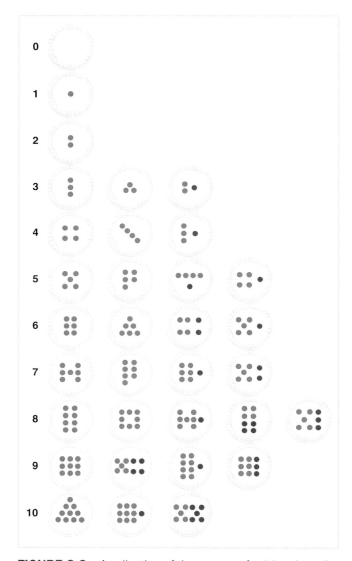

FIGURE 8.2 A collection of dot patterns for "dot plates."

Activity 8.1

CCSS-M: K.CC.B.4

Learning Patterns

Provide each child with 10 counters and a piece of paper or a paper plate as a mat. Hold up a dot plate for about five seconds and say, "Make the pattern you saw on my plate using the counters on your plate. How many dots did you see? What did the pattern look like?" Spend time discussing the configuration of the pattern and how many dots are on the plate. Then show the plate again so children can self-check. Do this with a few new patterns each day. To modify this activity for children with disabilities, you may need to give the child a small selection of premade dot plates. Then instead of creating the pattern with counters, the child finds the matching dot plate.

STUDENTS with SPECIAL NEEDS

Activity 8.2

CCSS-M: K.CC.B.4a; K.CC.B.4b

Dot Plate Flash

Hold up a dot plate for three seconds and say, "How many dots did you see? What did the pattern look like?" Children like to see how quickly they can recognize the pattern and say how many dots. Include easy patterns first, and when needed, show a plate a second time so children can get another look. Add more dots as children's confidence builds. Children can also flash dot plates to each other as a workstation activity.

Instant-recognition activities with dot plates are exciting and can be done in 5 minutes at any time of day and at any time of year.

CCSS Standards for Mathematical Practice

MP7. Look for and make use of structure.

Early Counting

Meaningful counting activities begin with 3- and 4-year-olds, but by the end of kindergarten (CCSSO, 2010), children should be able to count to 100. The counting process cannot be forced, so for children to have an understanding of counting, they must construct this idea. They do so by working through a variety of counting experiences and activities. Only the counting sequence of number words is a rote procedure. The meaning attached to counting is the key conceptual idea on which all other number concepts are developed.

The Development of Verbal Counting Skills. As you have already read, to plan for effective instruction you must identify the knowledge children already possess and build from that point. You will find that there are research-based learning trajectories (also called *learning progressions*) that can help you move to the next step by using the information as a path for your instructional direction. This is very much the case for counting. The counting trajectory (Clements & Sarama, 2014) identifies the overarching goals of counting and how to help a child move to more sophisticated levels of thinking. Table 8.1 is based on this research and is a selection of levels and sublevels identified as benchmarks (pp. 36–46) in the trajectory.

Verbal counting has at least two separate skills. First, a child must be able to produce the standard list of counting words in order: "One, two, three, four. . . ." Second, a child must be able to connect this sequence in a one-to-one correspondence with the objects in the set being counted. Each object must get one and only one count. As part of these skills, children should recognize that each counting number identifies a quantity that is one more than the previous number and that the new quantity is embedded in the previous quantity (see Figure 8.3). This knowledge will be helpful later in breaking numbers apart.

Experience and guidance are major factors in children's development of counting skills. While many children come to kindergarten able to count sets of 10 or beyond, some children may have less background knowledge and may require additional practice. In some cases, use counterexamples to help clarify a number. For example, you can label four blocks as "four" but also consider labeling six blocks as "not four," stating, "That's six blocks, not four blocks." This

TABLE 8.1 LEARNING TRAJECTORY FOR COUNTING

Levels of Thinking	Characteristics
Precounter	Here the child has no verbal counting ability. A young child looking at three balls will answer "ball" when asked how many. The child does not associate a number word with a quantity.
Reciter	This child verbally counts using number words, but not always in the right order. Sometimes they say more numbers than they have objects to count, skip objects, or repeat the same number.
Corresponder	A child at this level can make a one-to-one correspondence with numbers and objects, stating one number per object. If asked "How many?" at the end of the count, they may have to recount to answer.
Counter	This student can accurately count objects in an organized display (in a line, for example) and can answer "How many?" accurately by giving the last number counted (this is called *cardinality*). They may be able to write the matching numeral and may be able to say the number just after or before a number by counting up from 1.
Producer	A student at this level can count out objects to a certain number. If asked to give you five blocks, they can show you that amount.
Counter and Producer	A child who combines the two previous levels can count out objects, tell how many are in a group, remember which objects are counted and which are not, and respond to random arrangements. They begin to separate tens and ones, like 23 is 20 and 3 more.
Counter Backwards	A child at this level can count backward by removing objects one by one or just verbally as in a "countdown."
Counter from Any Number	This child can count up starting from numbers other than one. They are also able to immediately state the number before and after a given number.
Skip Counter	Here the child can skip-count with understanding by a group of a given number—tens, fives, twos, etc.

Source: Based on Clements and Sarama (2014).

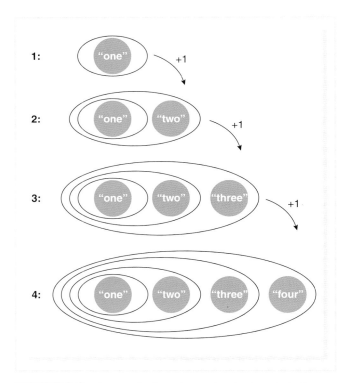

FIGURE 8.3 In counting, each number is one more than the previous number.

Source: National Research Council. (2009). *Mathematics learning in early childhood: Paths toward excellence and equity,* p. 27. Reprinted with permission from the National Academy of Sciences, courtesy of the National Academies Press, Washington, DC.

precision will help children grasp the meaning of a number (Frye et al., 2013).

The size and arrangement of the set are also factors related to success in counting. Obviously, longer number strings require more practice to learn. The first 12 counting words involve no pattern or repetition, and many children do not easily recognize a pattern in the teen numbers. Children learning the skills of counting—that is, matching oral number words with objects—should initially be given sets of blocks or counters that they can move, or pictures of sets that are arranged in an organized pattern for easy counting.

For many children, especially children with disabilities, it is important to have a plan for counting. The children should count objects from left to right, move the objects as they count or point, and touch them as they say each number word out loud. Consistently ask, "How many do you have in all?" at the end of each count.

Meaning Attached to the Counting of Objects.

Fosnot and Dolk (2001) state that an understanding of cardinality and its connection to counting is not a simple task for 4-year-olds. Children will learn *how* to count (matching counting words with objects) before they understand that the last count word stated in a count indicates the amount of the set (how many you have in all) or the set's *cardinality* as shown in Figure 8.4. Children who make this connection are said to have the cardinality principle, which is a refinement of their early ideas about quantity and is required for kindergartners (CCSSO, 2010). Most, but certainly not all, children by age $4\frac{1}{2}$ make this connection (Fosnot & Dolk, 2001).

FORMATIVE ASSESSMENT Notes. Children who count successfully orally may not have attached meaning to their counts. Here is a diagnostic interview that will help you assess a child's thinking. Show a child a card with five to nine large dots in a row so that they can be easily counted. Ask the child to count the dots. If the count is accurate, ask, "How many dots are on the card?" Early on, children may need to count again, but a child who is beginning to grasp the meaning of counting will not need to recount. Now ask the child, "Please give me the same number of counters as there are dots on the card." Here is a sequence of indicators to watch for, listed in order from a child who does not attach meaning to the count to one who is using counting as a tool:

FIGURE 8.4 The child has learned cardinality if, after counting five objects, he or she can answer the question "How many do you have in all?" with "Five."

Does the child not count but instead take out counters and make a similar pattern?

Will the child recount?

Does the child place the counters in a one-to-one correspondence with the dots?

Does the child just count the dots and retrieve the correct number of counters?

Can the child show that there are the same number of counters as dots?

As the child shows competence with patterned sets, move to using random dot patterns. ■

To develop the full understanding of counting, engage children in games or activities that involve counts and comparisons, such as Activity 8.3 Fill the Tower.

Activity 8.3   CCSS-M: K.CC.B.5

Fill the Tower

Children take turns rolling a die and collecting the indicated number of counters. They then place these counters on one of the towers on their Fill the Tower Game Board **Activity Page**. The object is to fill all towers with counters. As an option, require that the towers be filled exactly so that a roll of 5 cannot be used to fill four empty squares. To modify this activity for children with disabilities, use a die with only 2 or 3 (dots or numerals) on the sides. You can increase the number choices on the die when you have evidence that the child is counting accurately. A modification for gifted children is to have them use a die with higher numbers and a game board with larger towers.

STUDENTS with SPECIAL NEEDS

Playing Fill the Tower provides opportunities for you to talk with children about number and assess their thinking. Observe how they count the dots on the die. Ask, "How do you know you have the right number of counters?" and "How many counters did you put in the tower? How many more do you need to fill the tower?"

Regular classroom routines, such as counting how many napkins or snacks are needed at snack time, how many materials are needed for an activity, how many children plan to eat the school lunch, or even simply taking attendance, are additional opportunities for children to engage in purposeful counting. But make sure these activities involve more than the children simply following the teacher's count. Look for ways to make these situations into real problems and discuss children's strategies. You can also count groups of children, as in the video "Mingle and Count," which can be found on the Teaching Channel website. Also, visit the companion website to link to The Find Activity Page that explores children's counting strategies.

Thinking about Zero. Children need to discover the number zero (Clements & Sarama, 2014), particularly as it is a required standard of kindergartners (CCSSO, 2010). Surprisingly, it is not a concept that is easily grasped without intentionally building understanding. Three- and 4-year-olds can begin to use the word *zero* and the numeral 0 to symbolize that there are no objects in the set. With the dot plates discussed previously (see Figure 8.2), use the zero plate to discuss what it means that there is no dot on the plate. We find that because early counting often involves touching an object, zero is sometimes not included in the count. Zero is one of the most important digits in the base-ten system, and purposeful conversations about it and its position on the number line are essential. Activities 8.1, 8.2, and 8.11 are useful in exploring the number zero.

Numeral Writing and Recognition

Kindergartners are expected to write numbers from 0 to 20 in K.CC.A.3 within the counting and cardinality domain (CCSSO, 2010). Helping children read and write the 10 single-digit numerals is similar to teaching them to read and write letters of the alphabet. Neither has anything to do with number concepts. Numeral writing can be engaging. For example, ask children to trace over pages of numerals, make numerals from clay, trace them in shaving cream on their desks, press the numeral on a calculator, write them on the interactive whiteboard or in the air, and so on.

Activity 8.4   CCSS-M: K.CC.A.3

Number Necklaces

Place a necklace (a card with a yarn string) that has a numeral on each card (you can also show the corresponding amount). Initially, show numbers on cards and ask students who are wearing that number to step forward. Now is a good time to show numbers written backwards to highlight how that is not a match to anyone in the room. Then call out different numbers or show different amounts, and students should either step forward or find a peer with the same amount. This game can progress to calling out a number, and then two children who add to that number pair up.

Activity 8.5   CCSS-M: K.CC.B.4; K.CC.B.5

Number Tubs

Give each child four to six closed margarine tubs, each containing a different number of pennies or counters. The child is asked to find a tub with a particular number of counters. First they can estimate. Then after the child looks inside and counts to find the correct tub, add a new twist. Allow the child to label the tubs with sticky notes to show the amount inside. At first, the child may make four dots to represent four counters, but eventually, with encouragement, the numeral will be written. Then the child can recognize the value of writing the numbers in a form that all can understand and that doesn't require recounting.

Activity 8.6   CCSS-M K.CC.B.4c; K.CC.A.2

Line Them Up!

STUDENTS
with
SPECIAL NEEDS

To prepare for this activity, use painters' or electricians' tape on the floor as a number line. Prepare a set of cards with one numeral on each card that represents the sequence of numbers you want the children to investigate (such as 0 through 20 for kindergarten). Mix the cards and place them face down in a pile. Ask a child to take the top card from the pile and place the card on the number line. Have a second child take the next card off the pile and position the card on the line in the appropriate position. As children place their numeral cards, ask questions such as, "How did you know where to place your number?" "Is your number before or after. . . " and "Does your number go on the left or the right of. . . ?" Continue placing the cards until all the cards are placed on the number line in the conventional sequence. Once all the cards are placed, have the children read the sequence forward as well as backward and discuss the need for even spacing. If any number is out of sequence or too closely spaced, see if the children can determine how to correct the order and placement of the cards. You can modify this activity by using smaller sets of easier numbers, longer sequences of larger numbers, or by using number sequences that start at a number other than zero or one.

Perhaps the most common preschool and kindergarten exercises have children match sets with numerals. Children are given pictured sets (e.g., frogs) and asked to write or match the number that tells how many. Alternatively, they may be given a number and told to make a set with that many objects. The website Illuminations from NCTM offers several activities in the "Let's Count to 5" unit, such as Focus on Two, Three in a Set, and Finding Four, where children make sets of zero through five objects and connect number words or numerals to the sets. Songs, rhymes, and activities that appeal to visual, auditory, and kinesthetic learners are included. Explore other activities on the Illuminations website for counting to 10 and 20. When children are successful with these matching-numeral-to-sets activities, it is time to move on to more advanced concepts, such as counting on and counting back.

Counting On and Counting Back

Although the forward sequence of numbers is familiar to most young children, counting on from a particular number and counting back are often difficult skills. In particular, for English language learners, counting back is more difficult (try counting back in a second language you have learned). Eventually, first-graders should be able to start from any number less than 120 and count on from there (CCSSO, 2010). Frequent use of Activities 8.7, 8.8, and 8.9 is recommended.

Activity 8.7   CCSS-M: K.CC.A.1; K.CC.A.2

Up and Back Counting

Counting up to and back from a target number in a rhythmic fashion is an important counting exercise. For example, line up five children and five chairs. As the whole class counts from 1 to 5, the children sit down one at a time. When the target number, 5, is reached, it is repeated; then the child who sat on 5 now stands, and the count goes back to 1 with the children standing up one at a time, and so on, "1, 2, 3, 4, 5, 5, 4, 3, 2, 1, 1, 2 . . . ." Start at numbers other than one. Children find these exercises both fun and challenging.

This last activity is designed to help children become fluent with the number-word sequence in both forward and reverse order, and to begin counts with numbers other than 1. Children will later realize that counting on is adding and counting backward is subtracting. Fosnot and Dolk (2001) describe counting on as a "landmark" on a child's path to number sense.

Activity 8.8   CCSS-M: K.CC.A.2; K.CC.B.5

Counting On with Counters

Give each child 10 or 12 counters lined up left to right. Tell them to count four counters and push them under their left hands or place them out of sight in a cup (see Figure 8.5). Then, pointing to the hidden counters in the hand or cup, ask "How many are there?" (Four.) "So let's count like this: fooour . . . (pronouncing the first number slowly and pointing to their hand), five, six . . . ." Repeat with other numbers of counters under the hand.

Activity 8.9   CCSS-M: K.OA.A.1; 1.OA.B.5

Real Counting On

This game for two requires a deck of cards (numbers 1 to 7), a die, a paper cup, and counters. The first player turns over the top number card and places the indicated number of counters in the cup. Place the card next to the cup as a reminder of how many are inside. The second player rolls the die and places that many counters next to the cup (see Figure 8.6). Together they decide how many counters in all. A Recording Sheet with columns for "In the Cup," "On the Side," and "In All" will support children's organization. Increase to higher numbers in the card deck when children master the smaller numbers. For children with disabilities, keep the number of counters in the cup constant (such as 5) and have them just count on from the number until they are fluent and then move on to the full game.

STUDENTS with SPECIAL NEEDS

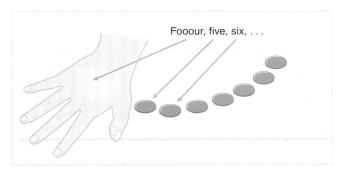

Fooour, five, six, . . .

FIGURE 8.5 Counting on: "Hide four. Count, starting from the number of counters hidden."

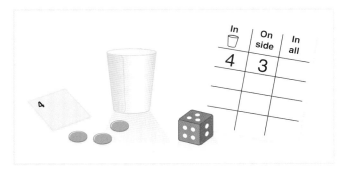

FIGURE 8.6 How many in all? How do children count to tell the total?

Observe how children determine the total amounts in Activity 8.9. Children who are not yet counting on may empty the counters from the cup or will count up from one without emptying the counters. As children continue to play, they will eventually use counting on as that strategy becomes meaningful and useful.

> ✓ Complete Self-Check 8.2: The Number Core: Quantity, Counting, and Knowing How Many

The Relations Core: More Than, Less Than, and Equal To

The concepts of "more," "less," and "same" are basic relationships contributing to children's overall understanding of number. Almost any child entering kindergarten can choose the set that is *more* if presented with two sets that are obviously different in number. In fact, Baroody (1987) states, "A child unable to use 'more' in this intuitive manner is at considerable educational risk" (p. 29). Classroom activities should help children build on and refine this basic notion.

Though the concept of less is logically related to the concept of more (selecting the set with more is the same as *not* selecting the set with less), the concept of *less* proves to be more difficult for children than *more*. A possible explanation is that young children have many opportunities to use the word *more* but may have limited exposure to the word *less*. To help children, frequently pair the idea of *less* with *more* and make a conscious effort to ask "Which is less?" questions as well as "Which is more?" questions. In this way, the concept can be connected with the better-known idea and the term *less* can become familiar.

For all three relationships (more/greater than, less/less than, and same/equal to), children should construct sets using counters as well as make comparisons or choices between two given sets. Conduct Activities 8.10, 8.11, and 8.12 in a spirit of inquiry with requests for children's explanations, such as "Can you show me how you know this group has less?"

Activity 8.10
CCSS-M: K.CC.C.6

Make Sets of More/Less/Same

Provide about eight cards with pictures of sets of **4 to 12** objects (or use large dot cards), a set of counters, word cards labeled *More*, *Less*, and *Same*, and paper plates (or low boxes that can define the work space, to support children with disabilities). Next to each card, have children make three collections of counters: a set that is more than the amount in the picture, one that is less, and one that is the same (see Figure 8.7). Start children who struggle with matching the set that is the same. For children who are ready, use the Relationship Cards Activity Page to place the words and symbols between the quantities.

STUDENTS with SPECIAL NEEDS

Activity 8.11
CCSS-M: K.CC.A.3; K.CC.C.6

Find the Same Amount

Give children a collection of cards with pictures of sets on them, such as Dot Cards 1-6. Have children pick any card in the collection and then find another card with the same amount to form a pair. Continue finding other pairs. This activity can be altered to have children find dot cards that are "less" or "more." Some children with disabilities may need a set of counters with a blank ten-frame to help them "make" a pair instead of finding a pair.

STUDENTS
with
SPECIAL
NEEDS

Activity 8.12
CCSS-M: K.CC.A.3; K.CC.C.6; K.O.A.A.1

More, Less, or the Same

This activity is for partners or a small group. Use the More-or-Less Cards Activity Page, making four to five of each card. Then make two sets of Number Cards to create the two decks of cards shown in Figure 8.8. To play, one child draws a number card, places it face up, and puts that number of counters into a cup. Next, another child draws one of the more-or-less cards and places it next to the number card. For the More cards, the designated number of counters are added to the cup; for the Less cards, counters are removed; and, for Zero cards, no change is made. Children then predict how many counters are in the cup. The counters are emptied and counted and then the game is repeated by drawing new cards. Eventually, the words *more* and *less* can be paired or substituted with *add* and *subtract* to connect these ideas with the arithmetic operations.

 FORMATIVE ASSESSMENT Notes. Observe children as they do these activities. Children whose number ideas are completely tied to counting and nothing more will select cards at random and count each dot. Others will begin by estimating and selecting a card that appears to have about the same number of dots. This demonstrates a significantly higher level of understanding. Also, observe how the dots are counted. Are the counts made accurately? Is each dot counted only once? Does the child touch the dot? A significant milestone (subitizing) occurs when children recognize small patterned sets without counting. Use the activity Okta's Rescue at NCTM's Illuminations website to help students subitize a variety of sets. ■

✓ **Complete Self-Check 8.3(a): The Relations Core: More Than, Less Than, and Equal To**

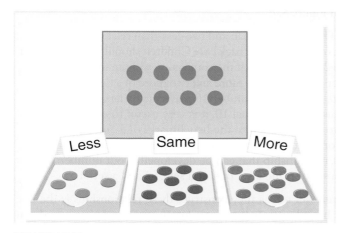

FIGURE 8.7 Making sets that are more, less, and the same.

FIGURE 8.8 Materials to play "More, Less or the Same."

One More / Two More / One Less / Two Less

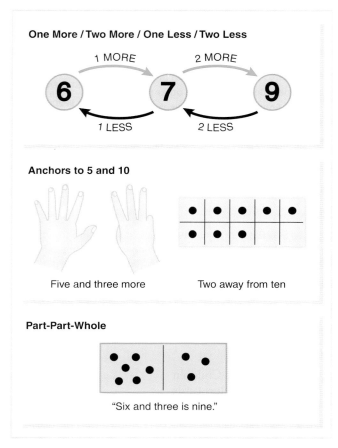

Anchors to 5 and 10

Five and three more   Two away from ten

Part-Part-Whole

"Six and three is nine."

FIGURE 8.9 Three number relationships for children to develop.

Excerpt from *Principles and Standards* reprinted by permission of the National Council of Teachers of Mathematics. Copyright 2000.

Developing Number Sense by Building Number Relationships

Howden (1989) described *number sense* as a "good intuition about numbers and their relationships. It develops gradually as a result of exploring numbers, visualizing them in a variety of contexts, and relating them in ways that are not limited by traditional algorithms" (p. 11). In *Principles and Standards for School Mathematics*, they state, "As students work with numbers, they gradually develop flexibility in thinking about numbers, which is a hallmark of number sense. . . . Number sense develops as students understand the size of numbers, develop multiple ways of thinking about and representing numbers, use numbers as referents, and develop accurate perceptions about the effects of operations on numbers" (NCTM, 2000, p. 80)*.

⏸ Pause & Reflect

You already have seen some of the early foundational ideas about number. Stop now and make a list of all of the important ideas that you think children should *know about* the number 8. Put your list aside, and we will revisit your ideas later. ●

The discussion of number sense begins as we look at the relationships and connections children should make about numbers up to 20. But "good intuition about numbers" does not end with these smaller whole numbers. Children continue to develop number sense as they use numbers in operations, build place-value understanding, and devise flexible methods of computing and making estimates involving large numbers, fractions, decimals, and percents.

Relationships between Numbers 1 through 10

CCSS **Standards for Mathematical Practice**
MP2. Reason abstractly and quantitatively.

Once children acquire cardinality and can meaningfully use their counting skills, they need to expand their collection of ideas about number sense to develop the knowledge needed to work with operations. We want children to move away from counting by ones to solve simple story problems and have the strategies for mastering basic facts by emphasizing the development of number relationships such as those in Figure 8.9:

• *One and two more, one and two less.* The two-more-than and two-less-than relationships involve more than just the ability to count on two or count back two. Children should know that 7, for example, is 1 more than 6 and also 2 less than 9. Visit the companion website for a video of a teacher working on students' understanding of one more and two more of a number.
• ***Benchmarks numbers*** *of 5 and 10.* Because the number 10 plays such a large role in our numeration system and because two fives equal 10, it is very useful to develop relationships for the numbers 1 to 10 connected to the benchmarks of 5 and 10.
• *Part-part-whole relationships.* To conceptualize a number as being composed of two or more parts is the most important relationship that can be developed about numbers. For example, 7 can be thought of as a set of 3 and a set of 4 or a set of 2 and a set of 5.

The principal tool young children will use as they construct these relationships is the one number tool they possess: counting. Initially, you will notice a lot of counting by ones, and you may wonder if you are making progress. Have patience! As children construct new relationships and begin to use more powerful ideas, counting by ones will become less and less necessary.

One and Two More; One and Two Less. When children count, they don't automatically think about the way one number is related to another. Their goal is only to match number words with objects until they reach the end of the count. To learn that 6 and 8 are related by the corresponding relationships of "two more than" and "two less than" requires reflection on these ideas. Counting on (or back) one or two counts is a useful tool in constructing these ideas.

Note that the relationship of "two more than" is significantly different from "comes two counts after." The latter relationship is applied to the string of number words, not to the quantities they represent; it is like the letter *H* coming two after the letter *F*. However, there is no numeric or quantitative difference between *F* and *H*. The quantity 8 would still be two more than 6 even if there were no number string to count. Remember, you want to develop the numeric relationship.

Begin with Activity 8.13, which focuses on the two-more-than relationship.

Activity 8.13   CCSS-M: K.OA.A.2; 1.OA.C.5

Make a Two-More-Than Set

Provide children with six Dot Cards. For each card, children should display a set of counters that is two more than the set shown on the card. Similarly, spread out eight to ten dot cards, and for each card, find a card that is two less than it. (Omit the 1 and 2 cards for two less than, and so on.) Also, see the Expanded Lesson Two More Than/Two Less Than and the Two More Than and Two Less Than Activity Pages.

In activities where children find a set or make a set, they can also select the matching Number Cards that identify the quantity in the set. Children can be encouraged to take turns reading the associated number sentence to their partner. If, for example, a set has been made that is two more than a set of four, the child can say, "Two more than four equals six" or "Six is the same as two more than four." The next activity combines the relationships.

Activity 8.14   CCSS-M: 1.OA.C.5

A Calculator Two-More-Than Machine

Teach children how to make a two-more-than machine. Press 0 $\boxed{+}$ 2 $\boxed{=}$. This makes the calculator a two-more-than machine. Now press any number—for example, 5. Children hold their finger over the $\boxed{=}$ key and predict the number that is two more than 5. Then they press $\boxed{=}$ to confirm. If they do not press any of the operation keys ($\boxed{+}$, $\boxed{-}$, $\boxed{\times}$, $\boxed{\div}$), the "machine" will continue to perform in this way. A digital version of a Two-More-Than Machine is the hundred chart and corresponding calculator applet found on NCTM's website under "Learning about Number Relationships."

Using Benchmark Numbers 5 and 10. Here again, we want to help children relate a given number to other numbers, specifically 5 and 10 to support thinking about relationships with various combinations of numbers. For example, in each of the following expressions, consider how the knowledge of 8 as "5 and 3 more" and as "2 away from 10" can play a role in how a child thinks about $5 + 3, 8 + 6, 8 - 2, 8 - 3, 8 - 4$, and $13 - 8$. For example, $8 + 6$ may be thought of as $8 + 2 + 4$ ("Making 10" strategy). Later, similar relationships can be used in the development of mental computation skills with larger numbers, such as $68 + 7$.

The most common models for exploring the *benchmark* numbers 5 and 10 are Five-Frames and Ten-Frames. The five-*frame* is a 1×5 array and the *ten-frame* is simply a 2×5 array in which counters or dots are placed to illustrate numbers (see Figure 8.10). Each child should have one, positioned horizontally.

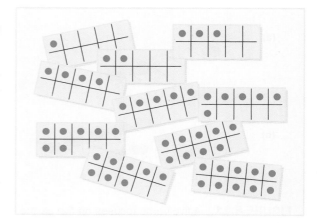

FIGURE 8.10   Ten-frames.

Standards for Mathematical Practice

MP3. Construct viable arguments and critique the reasoning of others.

For pre-K or kindergarten children who have not yet explored a ten-frame, it is a good idea to begin with a five-frame. Provide about 10 counters that will fit in the five-frame sections and try Activity 8.14.

Activity 8.15   CCSS-M: K.CC.C.7; K.OA.A.5

Five-Frame Tell-About

Explain that only one counter is permitted in each section of the Five-Frame. Have children show three on their five-frame, as seen in Figure 8.11(a). "What can you tell us about 3 from looking at your five-frame?" After hearing from several children, try other numbers from 0 to 5. Children may initially place their counters on the five-frame in any manner. For example, with four counters, a child may place two on each end and say, "It has a space in the middle" or "It's two and two." There are no wrong answers with the initial placements. Focus attention on how many more counters are needed to make f. Next, try numbers between 5 and 10. As shown in Figure 8.11(b) , numbers greater than 5 are shown with a full five-frame plus additional counters on the mat but not in the frame. In discussion, focus attention on these larger numbers as 5 and some more: "Seven is the same as five and two more."

Standards for Mathematical Practice

MP7. Look for and make use of structure.

When five-frames have been used for a week or so, consider introducing ten-frames. Play a ten-frame version of a "Five-Frame Tell-About," but soon introduce the following convention for showing numbers on the ten-frame: *Always fill the top row first, starting on the left, the same way you read. When the top row is full, place counters in the bottom row, also from left to right.* This approach will provide structure for seeing a full row in the ten-frame as five without counting, as in Figure 8.10. At first, children may continue to count every counter by ones. But then ask questions such as "What are you looking at in the ten-frame to help you find how many?" and "How does knowing you have a full row help you find how many you have?"

Move children to a problem solving situation by having them create different numbers, as suggested in Activity 8.16.

Activity 8.16   CCSS-M: K.CC.C.6; K.CC.C.7

Number Medley

ENGLISH LANGUAGE LEARNERS

Begin by having all children make the same number on their ten-frame. Then call out or hold up random numbers between 0 and 10. After each number, the children change their ten-frames to show the new number. If working with English language learners (ELLs), consider saying the number in their native language or writing the number. Children can play this game independently by using a prepared list of about 15 random numbers. One child plays "teacher" and the rest use the ten-frames.

(a)

(b)

FIGURE 8.11   A five-frame focuses on five as the benchmark.

Observe that some children doing Activity 8.16 will take all counters off and begin each new number from a blank frame. Others will have learned what each number looks like. And others will soon learn to adjust numbers by adding on or taking off only what is required, often subitizing a row. These strategies of moving from one number to another number more efficiently need to come from the children, not from you. Ask the children, "How do you decide how to change your ten-frame?" Look for opportunities to draw children's attention to how others are making these changes by having children share strategies. With continued practice, all children will grow. Additionally, how children use the ten-frame provides you with insights into their current number concept development; therefore, activities like this one can be used as a diagnostic interview.

To add another dimension to the activity, have the children tell, *before* changing their ten-frames, how many more counters need to be added (addition) or removed (subtraction). For example, if the frame showed 6, and the teacher called out "4," the children would respond, "Subtract two!" and then change their ten-frames accordingly. A discussion of how they know what to do is valuable.

Small ten-frame cards are an important variation of ten-frames and can be made from cardstock. Use the Little Ten- Frames Activity Page, with a set of 20 cards that consists of a 0 card, a 10 card, and two of each of the numbers 1 to 9. The cards allow for simple practice activities to reinforce the 5 and 10 as benchmarks, as in Activity 8.17.

Activity 8.17   CCSS-M: K.CC.B.5

Ten-Frame Flash

ENGLISH LANGUAGE LEARNERS

Flash Little Ten-Frame Cards to the class or a small group and see how quickly the children can tell how many dots are shown. This activity is fast-paced, takes only a few minutes, can be done at any time, and is highly engaging. For ELLs, producing the English word for the number may take more time, so either make pairs with similar language skills, or encourage children to use their preferred language.

Important variations of "Ten-Frame Flash" include:

- Saying the number of spaces on the card instead of the number of dots
- Saying one more than the number of dots (or two more, one less, or two less)
- Saying the "10 fact"—for example, "Six and four equals ten"
- Saying the sum by adding the flashed card to a card they have at their desk (for challenging advanced learners)

Ten-frame tasks are surprisingly challenging for children, as there is a lot to keep in their working memory. Children must reflect on the two rows of five, the spaces remaining, how a particular number is more or less than 5 and how far away it is from 10. Watch this video on working memory (http://www.youtube.com/watch?v=efCq_vHUMqs) to see how much young children have to think about to keep all of these ideas in their working memory. How well children can respond to "Ten-Frame Flash" is a quick diagnostic assessment of their current number concept level. Consider interviews that include the variations of the activity listed. Because the distance to 10 is so important, another assessment is to point to a numeral less than 10 and ask, "If this many dots were on a ten-frame, how many blank spaces would there be?" Or, you can also simply ask, "If I have seven, how many more do I need to equal ten?" There are virtual activities with the five-frames and ten-frames on the NCTM Illuminations webpage with associated games that develop counting and basic computation skills. These activities can be used with individual learners as there is a voice-over option that will ask children questions about the tasks. Also, watch this video called Beyond Fingers (https://www.youtube.com/watch?v=3fTCAicmUWY) to see how a teacher works with a group of kindergartners to explore combinations of ten and some more to make the numbers from 11 to 19 on the ten-frame.

❚❚ Pause & Reflect

Before reading on, gather eight counters. Count out the set of counters in front of you as if you were a 4- or 5-year-old. ●

Part-Part-Whole Relationships. Any child who has learned how to count meaningfully can count out eight objects as you just did. What is significant about the experience is what it did *not* cause you to think about. Nothing in counting a set of eight objects will cause a child to focus on the fact that it could be made of two parts. For example, separate the counters you just counted into two piles and reflect on the combination. It might be 2 and 6, 7 and 1, or 4 and 4. Make a change in your two piles of counters and say the new combination to yourself. Focusing on a quantity in terms of its parts (*decomposing numbers*) has important implications for developing

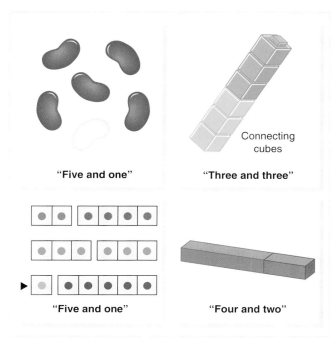

"Five and one"   "Three and three"

"Five and one"   "Four and two"

FIGURE 8.12 Assorted materials for building parts of six.

number sense. Of the three number relationships (Figure 8.9), *part-whole* ideas are easily the most important, and the ability to think about numbers in terms of the *part-part-whole* relationship is a major milestone.

Basic Ingredients of Part-Part-Whole Activities. Most part-part-whole activities focus on a single number for the entire activity. For example, a pair of children might work on breaking apart or building the number 7 throughout the activity. They can either build (*compose*) the designated quantity in two or more parts (this is also known as a "both addends unknown" situation), or else they start with the full amount and separate it into two or more parts (*decompose*). Kindergartners usually begin these activities working on the number 4 or 5. As concepts develop, children extend to numbers 6 to 12.

When children do these activities, have them say or "read" the parts aloud and then write them down on some form of recording sheet (or do both). Reading and writing the combinations serve as a means of encouraging reflective thought focused on the part–whole relationship. Writing can be in the form of drawings, numbers written in blanks (a group of _____ cubes and a group of _____ cubes), or addition equations ($3 + 5 = 8$ or $8 = 2 + 6$). There is a clear connection between part-part-whole concepts and addition and subtraction ideas.

Part-Part-Whole Activities. Activity 8.18 and its variations may be considered the "basic" part-part-whole task.

Activity 8.18
CCSS-M: K.OA.A.3; 1.OA.C.6

Build It in Parts

ENGLISH LANGUAGE LEARNERS

Provide children with one type of material, such as connecting cubes or squares of colored paper. Ask students, "How many different combinations for a particular number can you make using two parts?" (If you wish, you can allow for more than two parts.) Use a context that will be familiar to your children, or consider a piece of children's literature. For example, ask how many different combinations of six hats the peddler in the picture book *Caps for Sale* (Slobodkina, 1938) can wear, limiting the color choices to two and keeping the colors together (i.e., 3 red and 3 blue caps, 4 red and 2 blue, etc.). (Note that the book is also available in Spanish for some ELLs and is it read for students in English in this video, http://www.youtube.com/watch?v=lNptSCKqdfg). Each different combination can be displayed on a small mat. Here are just a few ideas, each of which is illustrated in Figure 8.12.

- **Use two colors of counters, such as lima beans spray-painted on one side (also available in plastic).**
- Make bars of connecting cubes of two different colors. Keep the same colors together on the bar.
- Make combinations using two dot strips—strips of cardstock about 1 inch wide with stick-on dots.
- Make combinations of two Cuisenaire rods connected as a train to match a given amount.
- Use beads on a pipe cleaner or use an arithmetic rack.

CCSS **Standards for Mathematical Practice**

MP8. Look for and express regularity in repeated reasoning.

As you observe children working on the "Build It in Parts" activity, ask them to "read" a number sentence that matches the representation to their partner. Two or three children working together may have quite a large number of combinations, including repeats. Try to encourage them to see a pattern.

Activity 8.19 is a step toward a more abstract understanding of combinations that equal 5 (or other totals). Children can do these mentally or use counters. Allowing options is both a good instructional strategy and a way to see how ready children are for addition.

Activity 8.19

CCSS-M: K.OA.A.3; K.OA.A.5

Two Out of Three

Make lists of three numbers, two of which total the whole that children are focusing on. Here is an example list for the number 5:

2–3–4
5–0–2
1–3–2
3–1–4
2–2–3
4–3–1

With the list on the board, children can take turns selecting two numbers out of the three choices that equal the whole. As with all problem solving activities, children should be challenged to justify their answers.

Missing-Part Activities. An important variation of part-part-whole activities is referred to as *missing-part* activities. In a missing-part activity, children are given the whole amount and use their already developed knowledge of the parts of that whole to tell what the covered or hidden part is. If they are unsure, they simply uncover the unknown part and say the full combination. Missing-part activities provide maximum reflection on the combinations for a number. They also serve as the forerunner to subtraction. With a whole amount of 8 but with only 3 showing, the child can later learn to say and write "8 − 3 = 5."

The next three activities illustrate variations of this important idea of a missing part. For any of these activities, you can use a context from familiar classroom events or from a children's book, such as the animals hiding in the barn in *Hide and Seek* (Stoeke, 1999).

Activity 8.20

CCSS-M: K.OA.A.2

Covered Parts

A set of counters equal to the target amount is counted out, and the rest are put aside. One child places the counters under a margarine tub or piece of cardstock. The child then pulls some counters out into view. (This amount could be none, all, or any amount in between.) For example, if 6 is the whole and 4 are showing, the other child says, "Four and *two* equals six." If there is hesitation or if the hidden part is unknown, the hidden part is immediately shown (see Figure 8.13).

Activity 8.21

CCSS-M: K.OA.A.4

Missing-Part Cards

For each number from four to ten, make missing-part cards on 3-by-9-inch strips of cardstock. Each card has a numeral for the whole and two dot sets with one set covered by a flap. For the number 8, you need nine cards with the visible part ranging from 0 to 8 dots. Children use the cards as in "Covered Parts," saying, "Four and two equals six" for a card showing 6, four dots showing and two dots hiding under the flap.

Activity 8.22

CCSS-M: K.OA.A.1; K.OA.A.2

I Wish I Had

Hold out a bar of connecting cubes, a dot strip, or a dot plate showing six or less and say, "I wish I had six." The children respond with the part that is needed to equal 6. Counting on can be used to check. The game can focus on a single number (especially as a starting point for children with disabilities), or the "I wish I had" number can change each time (see Figure 8.13). Consider adding a familiar context, like "I wish I had six books to read." See the corresponding Expanded Lesson I Wish I Had and the accompanying Two Column Cards Activity Page for this activity.

STUDENTS
with
SPECIAL
NEEDS

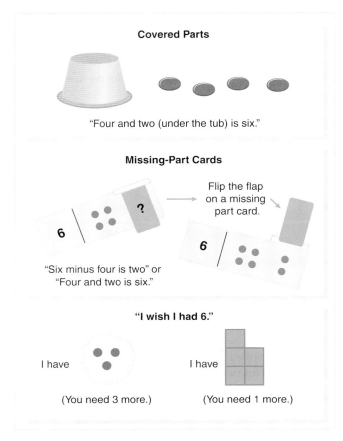

Covered Parts

"Four and two (under the tub) is six."

Missing-Part Cards

Flip the flap on a missing part card.

"Six minus four is two" or
"Four and two is six."

"I wish I had 6."

I have

(You need 3 more.)

I have

(You need 1 more.)

FIGURE 8.13 Missing-part activities.

(a)

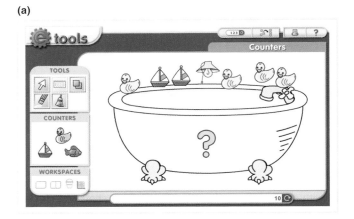

(b)

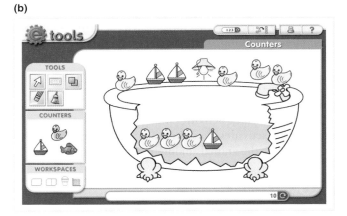

FIGURE 8.14 Scott Foresman's *eTools* software is useful for exploring part-part-whole and missing-part ideas.

Source: Scott Foresman Addison-Wesley Math Electronic-Tools CD-ROM Grade K Through 6. Copyright 2004 Pearson Education, Inc. or its affiliate(s). Used by permission. All rights reserved.

TECHNOLOGY Note. You can also incorporate digital formats for any of the preceding activities. There are lots of ways you can use the computer software to create part-part-whole activities. All that is needed is a program that permits children to create sets of objects on the screen. Look at Scott Foresman's eTools and choose "Counters." Under "workspaces" on the bottom left, select the bucket icon and then pick the bathtub and add boat, duck, or goldfish counters. As shown in Figure 8.14(a), children can stamp different bathtub toys either in the bathtub (unseen) or outside the tub. The numeral on the bathtub shows how many are in the tub, or it can show a question mark (?) for missing-part thinking. The total is shown at the bottom. By clicking on the light bulb, the contents of the bathtub can be seen, as shown in Figure 8.14(b). This program offers a great opportunity to develop both part-part-whole and missing-part concepts. ■

Pause & Reflect

Remember the list you made previously about what children should know about the number 8? Let's refer to it and see if you would add to it or revise it based on what you have read to this point. Do this before reading on. ●

Here is a possible list of the kinds of things that children should learn about the number 8 (or any number up to about 20) while they are in pre-K and kindergarten:

- Count to 8 (know the number words and their order)
- Count 8 objects and know that the last number word tells how many
- Recognize, read, and write the numeral 8 and pair it with an amount of objects
- State more and less by 1 and 2—8 is one more than 7, one less than 9, two more than 6, and two less than 10
- Recognize *patterned sets* for 8 such as

- Relate to the *benchmark numbers* of 5 and 10: 8 is 3 more than 5 and 2 away from 10
- State part-whole relationships: 8 is the same 5 and 3, 2 and 6, 7 and 1, and so on (this includes knowing the missing part of 8 when some are hidden)
- Identify doubles: double 4 equals 8
- State relationships to the real world: my brother is 8 years old; my reading book is 8 inches wide

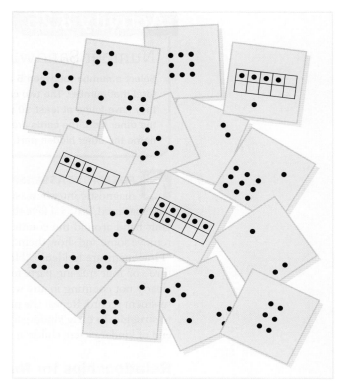

FIGURE 8.15   Dot cards.

Dot Cards as a Model for Teaching Number Relationships. Here we combine more than one of the relationships discussed so far into several number development activities by using the complete set of dot cards. As children learn about ten-frames, patterned sets, and other relationships, the Dot Cards provide a wealth of activities (see Figure 8.15) and help them think flexibly about numbers. The full set of cards contains dot patterns, patterns that require counting, combinations of two and three simple patterns, and ten-frames with "standard" as well as unusual dot placements. These dot cards add another dimension to many of the previous activities and can be used effectively in Activities 8.23, 8.24, and 8.25.

Activity 8.23   CCSS-M: K.CC.C.6

Double War

The game of "Double War" (Kamii, 1985) is played like the War card game, but on each play, both players turn up two dot cards instead of one. The winner is the player with the larger total number. Children playing the game can and should use many different number relationships to determine the winner without actually finding the total number of dots. A modification of this activity for children with disabilities would have the teacher (or another child) do a "think-aloud" and describe her thinking about the dots using relationships as she figures who wins the round. This modeling is critical for children who struggle.

STUDENTS *with* **SPECIAL NEEDS**

Activity 8.24   CCSS-M: K.CC.C.6; K.OA.A.2

Difference War

Deal out the dot cards to the two players as in "Double War," and prepare a pile of about 40 counters. On each play, players turn over one card from the top of the stack. The player with the greater number of dots wins as many counters from the pile as the difference between the two cards. Used cards are put aside. The game is over when the cards or counters run out. The player with the most counters wins the game. This game can also be played so the person with "less" wins the number of counters in the difference. Modify the game for gifted students by having children turn two cards, find the sums, and make the comparisons.

Activity 8.25

CCSS-M: K.OA.A.2; 1.OA.C.6

Number Sandwiches

Select a number between 5 and 12, and have children find combinations of two cards that total that number. The two cards are placed back to back with the dot side facing out. When they have found at least 10 pairs, the next challenge is for the partner to name the number on the other side. The cards are flipped over to confirm. The same pairs can then be used again to name the other hidden part.

FORMATIVE ASSESSMENT Notes. To assess part-whole relationships, use a missing-part diagnostic interview (similar to Activity 8.20). Begin with a number you believe the child has "mastered," say, 5. Have the student count out that many counters into your open hand. Close your hand around the counters and confirm that the child knows how many are hidden. Then remove some and show them in the open palm of your other hand (see Figure 8.16). Ask the child, "How many are hidden?" "How do you know?" Repeat with different amounts removed, trying three or four missing parts for each number. If the child responds quickly and correctly and is clearly not counting in any way, call that a "mastered number" and check it off on the child's assessment record. Repeat the process with the next higher number. Continue until the child begins to struggle. In early kindergarten, you will find a range of mastered numbers from 4 to 8. By the end of kindergarten, children should master numbers through 10 (CCSSO, 2010). ■

Relationships for Numbers 10 through 20 and Beyond

Although pre-K, kindergarten, and first-grade students experience numbers up to 20 and beyond daily, it should not be assumed that they will automatically extend the set of relationships they developed with smaller numbers to numbers beyond 10. And yet these larger numbers play a big part in many counting activities, in basic facts, and in much of what we do with mental computation. In fact, several researchers suggest the movement to number instruction beyond 10 and even beyond 20 as soon as possible sets the stage for developing initial place-value knowledge (Fosnot & Dolk, 2001; Wright, Stranger, Stafford, and Martland, 2006).

Pre–Place-Value Concepts. Recognizing a set of ten plays a major role in children's early understanding of numbers between 10 and 20. When children see a set of six together with a set of ten, they should know without counting that the total is 16. This work with composing and decomposing numbers from 11 through 19 in kindergarten is seen as an essential foundation for place value (CCSSO, 2010).

FIGURE 8.16 A missing-part number assessment. "There are eight in all. How many are hidden?"

Pause & Reflect

Say to yourself, "One ten." Now think about that from the perspective of a child just learning to count to 20! What could "one ten" possibly mean when ten tells me how many fingers I have and is the number that comes after nine? How can it be one of something? ●

Wright and colleagues (2006) outlined a three-level progression of children's understanding of ten:

1. *An initial concept of ten*. The child understands ten as ten ones and does not see the ten as a unit. When children at this level work on a task involving tens, they will count by ones.

2. *An intermediate concept of ten*. The child understands ten as a unit composed of ten ones but relies on materials or representations to help complete tasks involving tens.

3. *A facile concept of ten.* The child solves tasks involving tens and ones without using materials or representations. At this level, children mentally think about two-digit numbers as groups of tens and ones.

The Common Core State Standards suggests that first-graders should know that "10 can be thought of as a bundle of ten ones—called a 'ten'" (CCSSO, 2010, p. 15). The difficulty in children discussing "one ten and six ones" (what's a one?) does not mean that a set of ten should not figure prominently in the discussion of the teen numbers. Initially, children do not see a numeric pattern in the numbers between 10 and 20. Rather, these number names are simply ten additional words in the number sequence. In some languages, the teens are actually stated as 10 and 1, 10 and 2, 10 and 3. But because this is not the case in English, for many children, the teens provide a significant challenge.

Activity 8.26 helps children visualize the idea of ten and "some more."

Activity 8.26

CCSS-M: K.NBT.A.1

Ten and Some More

Use a simple two-part mat and a story that links to whatever counters you are using. Then have children count out ten coffee stirrers onto the left side of the mat. Next, have them put five stirrers on the other side. Together, count all of the stirrers by ones. Chorus the combination: "Ten and five equals fifteen." Turn the mat around: "Five and ten equals fifteen." Repeat with other numbers in a random order, but always keep 10 on the left side of the mat. After playing the game for a while, bundle the 10 stirrers with a rubber band.

Activity 8.26 is designed to teach the numbers in the "teens" and thus requires some explicit instruction. Following this activity, explore numbers through 20 in a more open-ended manner. Provide each child with a Double Ten-Frame mat. In random order, have children show numbers up to 20 on the frames. Have children discuss how counters can be arranged on the mat so that it is easy to see how many are there. At first, not every child will create a full set of 10, but as this idea becomes more popular, they will develop the notion that teens are 10 and some more. Then challenge children to find ways to show 26 counters or even more.

Extending More-Than and Less-Than Relationships. The relationships of one more than, two more than, one less than, and two less than are important for all numbers and are built from children's knowledge of the same concepts for numbers less than 10. The fact that 17 is one less than 18 is connected to the idea that 7 is one less than 8. Children may need explicit support in making this connection.

Activity 8.27

CCSS-M: K.CC.C.6; K.NBT.A.1

More and Less Extended

Project an image of seven counters and ask what is two more, or one less, and so on. Now add a filled ten-frame to the display (or 10 in any pattern) and repeat the questions. Pair up questions by covering and uncovering the ten-frame as in Figure 8.17.

Numbers to 100: Early Introductions. According to the Common Core State Standards, kindergartners are expected to be able to count to 100 (CCSSO, 2010). Therefore, early exposure to numbers to 100 is important. Although it is unlikely that children in kindergarten or first grade will initially have a facile understanding of tens and ones related to place value, they should learn much about the sequence of numbers and the counting patterns to 100, if not beyond.

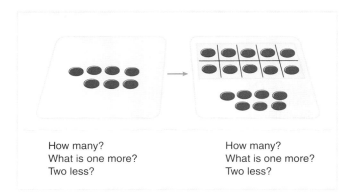

How many?
What is one more?
Two less?

How many?
What is one more?
Two less?

FIGURE 8.17 Extending relationships to the teens.

1	2	3	4	5	6	7	8	9	10
11	12	13	14	15	16	17	18	19	20
21	22	23	24	25	26	27	28	29	30
31	32	33	34	35	36	37	38	39	40
41	42	43	44	45	46	47	48	49	50
51	52	53	54	55	56	57	58	59	60
61	62	63	64	65	66	67	68	69	70
71	72	73	74	75	76	77	78	79	80
81	82	83	84	85	86	87	88	89	90
91	92	93	94	95	96	97	98	99	100

FIGURE 8.18 A hundreds chart.

The hundreds chart (Figure 8.18) is an essential tool for every K–2 classroom. An extremely useful version of the chart is made of transparent pockets into which each of the 100 numeral cards can be inserted. You can hide a number by inserting a blank card in front of a number in the pocket. You can insert colored pieces of paper in the slots to highlight various number patterns. And you can remove some or all of the number cards and have children replace them in their correct location (see Chapter 11 for more ideas and activities). Hundreds Charts can be made on cardstock or a computer version can be found at the NCTM website under E-examples of the Principles and Standards for School Mathematics. This eChart uses a calculator and hundreds chart together so that children can visually see the patterns generated by the calculator.

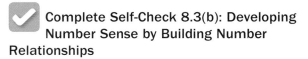 **FORMATIVE ASSESSMENT Notes.** Replacing the number cards or tiles from a blank chart is a good learning center activity for two children to work on together. By listening to how children go about finding the correct locations for numbers, you can learn a lot about how well they have constructed an understanding of the 1-to-100 sequence. ■

 **Complete Self-Check 8.3(b): Developing Number Sense by Building Number Relationships**

Number Sense in Their World

Here we examine ways to broaden early knowledge of numbers. Relationships of numbers to real-world quantities and measures and the use of numbers in simple estimations can help children develop flexible, intuitive ideas about numbers. For example, using the setting of a Toy Shop at the NCTM Illuminations website offers several activities that focus on finding numbers in the real world.

Calendar Activities

The NRC Committee (2009) stated that "using the calendar does not emphasize foundational mathematics" (p. 241). They go on to remind early childhood teachers that although the calendar may be helpful in developing a sense of time, it does not align with the need to develop mathematical relationships related to the number 10 because the calendar is based on groups of seven. Although 90 percent of the classrooms surveyed reported using calendar-related activities (Hamre, Downer, Kilday, & McGuire, 2008), there are significant issues with this work being considered the kind of mathematics instruction that will support young learners in reaching mathematical literacy. The NRC concludes, "Doing the calendar is not a substitute for teaching foundational mathematics" (p. 241). Ethridge and King (2005) suggest that children learn to parrot the response for the predictable questions and they didn't always understand some of the concepts presented. Clements, Baroody, and Sarama (2013) suggest to avoid the inappropriate use of the calendar, as it engages only a few students. The key message is that doing calendar math should be thought of as an "add on" and not take time away from essential pre-K–2 mathematics concepts.

Estimation and Measurement

One of the best ways for children to think of real quantities is to associate numbers with measures of things. Measures of length, weight, and time are good places to begin. Just measuring and recording results will not be very effective unless there is a reason for children to be interested in or think about the result. To help children think about what number might tell how long the desk is or how heavy the book is, it important if they could first write down or tell you an estimate. To produce an estimate is, however, a very difficult task for young children. They do not easily grasp the concept of "estimate" or "about." For example, suppose that you have cut out a set of very large footprints, each about 18 inches long. You would ask, "About how many of the giant's footprints will it take to measure across the rug in our reading corner?" The key word here is *about*, and it is one that you will need to spend a lot of time helping your children understand. To this end, the request of an estimate can be made in ways that help with the concept of "about." For example, the following questions can be used with early estimation activities:

* *More or less than* _____? Will the rug be more or less than 10 footprints long? Will the apple weigh more or less than 20 blocks? Are there more or less than 15 connecting cubes in this long bar?
* *Closer to* _____ *or to* _____? Will the rug be closer to 5 footprints or closer to 20 footprints long? Will the apple weigh closer to 10 blocks or closer to 30 blocks? Does this bar have closer to 10 cubes or closer to 50 cubes?
* *About* _____? (You can even suggest possible numbers as options.) About how many footprints long is the rug? About how many blocks will the apple weigh? About how many cubes are in this bar?

Asking for estimates using these formats helps children learn what you mean by "about." Every child can make a close estimate with some supportive questions and examples. However, rewarding children for the closest estimate in a competitive fashion will often result in their trying to seek precision and not actually estimate. Instead, discuss all answers that fall into a reasonable range. One of the best approaches is to give students ranges as their possible answers: "Does your estimate fall between 10 and 30? Between 50 and 70? Or 100 and 130?" Of course, you can make the choices more divergent until they grasp the idea.

Here are some activities that can help students connect numbers to real situations.

 Standards for Mathematical Practice
MP2. Reason abstractly and quantitatively.

Activity 8.28   CCSS-M: K.MD.A.1

Add a Unit to Your Number

Write a number on the board. Now suggest some units to go with it and ask the students what they can think of that fits. For example, suppose the number is 9. "What do you think of when I say 9 *dollars*? Nine *hours*? 9 *cars*? 9 *kids*? 9 *meters*? 9 *o'clock*? 9 *hand spans*? 9 *gallons*?" Spend time discussing and exploring each unit. Let students suggest other appropriate units. Students from different cultures and ELLs may bring different ideas to this activity and including these ideas is a way to bring their culture into all students' school experiences.

 ENGLISH LANGUAGE LEARNERS

Activity 8.29   CCSS-M: K.MD.A.1

Is It Reasonable?

Select a number and a unit—for example, 15 feet. Could the teacher be 15 feet tall? Could a house be 15 feet wide? Can a man jump 15 feet high? Could three children together stretch their arms 15 feet? Pick any number, large or small, and a unit with which students are familiar. Then make up a series of these questions. Also ask, "How can we find out if it is reasonable or not? Who has an idea about what we can do?" Then have the students select the number and unit.

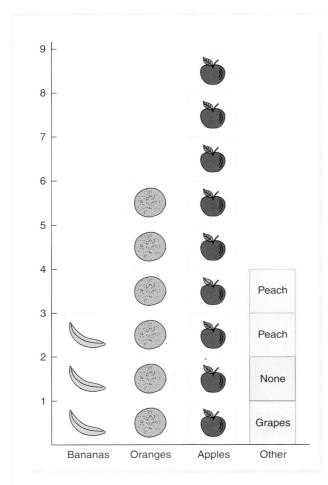

Class graph showing fruit brought for snack. Paper cutouts for bananas, oranges, apples, and cards for "others."

- Which snack (or refer to what the graph represents) is most, least?
- Which are more (less) than 7 (or some other number)?
- Which is one less (more) than this snack (or use fruit name)?
- How much more is _____ than _____ ? (Follow this question immediately by reversing the order and asking how much less.)
- How much less is _____ than _____ ? (Reverse this question after receiving an answer.)
- How much difference is there between _____ and _____ ?
- Which two bars together are the same as _____ ?

FIGURE 8.19 Relationships and number sense in a bar graph.

These activities are problem based in the truest sense. Not only are there no clear answers, but students can easily begin to pose their own questions and explore the numbers and units most interesting to them.

Data Collection and Analysis

Graphing activities are good ways to connect children's worlds with number and relationships. Graphs can be quickly made from any data gathered with children, such as favorites (ice cream flavors, sports teams, pets), number of sisters and brothers, and transportation modes to school. Once students classify and count the number of objects in each category (K.MD.B.3 in the CCSS-M), graphs can be used to share the information. Graphs can be connected to content in other subject areas, such as an investigation of objects that float or sink. Here are some other options for graphs that are linked to children's literature:

- *Chrysanthemum* (Henkes, 2008): create a graph of the length of children's first names (i.e., use categories 3, 4, 5 letters and so on).
- *This is the Way we Go to School* (Baer, 1990): make a graph of the way children come to school
- *We're Going on a Leaf Hunt* (Metzger, 2008): have children collect a leaf from around their home or around the school, create a graph of different types of leaves.
- *3 Little Firefighters* (Murphy, 2003): use children's career aspirations to make a graph (i.e., sort jobs into public service, entertainment, education, and so on)

In the early stages of number development, the use of graphs is primarily for developing number relationships and for connecting numbers to real quantities in the children's environment. The graphs focus attention on tallies and counts of realistic things. Once a simple bar graph is made, it is very important to take the time to ask questions (e.g., "What do you notice about our class and our ice cream choices?"). Equally important, graphs clearly exhibit comparisons between numbers that are rarely made when only one number or quantity is considered at a time. See Figure 8.19 for an example of a graph and corresponding questions. At first, children may be challenged with questions involving differences, but these comparison concepts add considerably to children's understanding of number and are a focus of 1.MD.C.4 in the Common Core State Standards (CCSSO, 2010).

 Complete Self-Check 8.4: Number Sense in Their World

REFLECTIONS ON CHAPTER 8

WRITING TO LEARN

1. What must a child be able to do in order to accurately count a set of objects?

2. What are 3 types of relationships for numbers 1 through 10? Explain briefly what each means, and suggest an activity for each.

3. How can a teacher assess greater-than, less-than, and equal-to relationships?

4. Describe two different ways to develop the idea of associating numbers with real quantities among children. Suggest methods with which the students can relate easily.

FOR DISCUSSION AND EXPLORATION

◆ Examine mathematics teaching literature to find games for building computational fluency in children. Try some of these in your classes. Compare them with the activities in this chapter. What ideas are stressed in these games and activities? How do they differ?

◆ You've noticed that a child you are working with is counting objects with an accurate sequence of numbers words but is not attaching one number to each object. Therefore, the child's final count is inconsistent and inaccurate. What would you plan to help this child develop a better grasp of one-to-one correspondence?

RESOURCES FOR CHAPTER 8

LITERATURE CONNECTIONS

Children's literature abounds with wonderful counting books and visually stimulating number-related picture books. Have children talk about the mathematics in the story. Begin by talking about the book's birthday (copyright date) and how old the book is. Here are a few ideas for making literature connections to concepts for early learners.

10 Little Hot Dogs *Himmelman (2010)*

This predictable-progression counting book highlights 10 dachshund puppies climbing on and off a chair. Children can create their own stories using a mat illustrated with a Chair and move counters representing the puppies on or off. Two children can compare the numbers of dogs on their chairs. Who has more puppies? How many more? How many different ways can you put 6 puppies on the two chairs?

Pete the Cat and his Four Groovy Buttons
Litwin (2012)

Pete is one cool cat who never gets flustered. He starts with four groovy buttons on his shirt, but one by one they pop off and he ends up with zero—or does he? As he counts down,

the numeral is shown, along with the written word and the recording of a related subtraction equation. The story is a perfect lead-in to counting objects and counting backwards. Using a five-frame with buttons can help children model Pete's situation. Listen to *Pete the Cat and his Four Groovy Buttons* at https://www.youtube.com/watch?v=M2YwCgtvnNg

RECOMMENDED READINGS

Articles

Griffin, S. (2003). Laying the foundation for computational fluency in early childhood. *Teaching Children Mathematics, 9*(6), 306–309.

This useful article for assessment lays out five stages of number development with a simple addition story problem task followed by activities to develop number for each stage.

Losq, C. (2005). Number concepts and special needs students: The power of ten-frame tiles. *Teaching Children Mathematics, 11*(6), 310–315.

This article supports struggling learners in the use of a countable and visual model—the ten-frame tile. The ten-frames are positioned vertically to enhance subitizing and provide tools for formative assessment.

Moomaw, S., Carr, V., Boat, M., & Barnett, D. (2010). Preschoolers' number sense. *Teaching Children Mathematics, 16*(6), 333–340.

How can you best assess young learners? This article offers curriculum-based assessments that can capture number sense concepts through gamelike activities.

Books

Dougherty, B., Flores, A., Louis, E., & Sophian, C. (2010). *Developing essential understanding of number and numeration for teaching mathematics in prekindergarten–grade 2.* Reston, VA: NCTM.

This book describes what big mathematical ideas a teacher needs to know about number, how number connects to other mathematical ideas, and how to teach and assess this pivotal topic.

Richardson, K. (2003). *Assessing math concepts: The hiding assessment.* Bellingham, WA: Mathematical Perspectives.

This is one of a series of nine assessment books with diagnostic interviews covering number topics from counting through two-digit numbers. Extensive explanations and examples are provided.

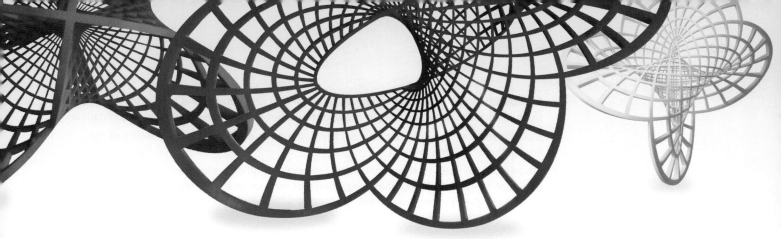

Developing Meanings for the Operations

LEARNER OUTCOMES

After reading this chapter and engaging in the embedded activities and reflections, you should be able to:

9.1 Generalize that teaching about the four operations with whole numbers involves developing meaning through problem structures.

9.2 Demonstrate how to develop children's skills in joining, separating, part-part-whole, and comparison in additive situations where the unknown can be in any position.

9.3 Demonstrate how to develop children's skills in multiplicative situations involving equal groups, comparison, area, and arrays and combinations where the unknown can be in any position.

9.4 Explain how students can apply the properties of the operations as strategies to either add, subtract, multiply, or divide.

9.5 Explain how the remainder in a division problem can be interpreted.

9.6 Describe strategies for solving contextual problems.

This chapter is about helping children connect different meanings, interpretations, and relationships to the four operations of addition, subtraction, multiplication, and division so they can accurately and fluently apply these operations in real-world settings. This is all part of the Operations Core (National Research Council [NRC], 2009), in which students learn to see mathematical situations in their day-to-day lives or in story problems and begin to make models of these situations in words, pictures, models, and/or numbers (e.g. equations). The Operations Core builds and expands on the NRC's Number Core and Relations Core discussed in Chapter 8 and will be extended in the discussion of number sense and place value in Chapter 11. As children learn to connect the big ideas listed below, they can and should simultaneously be developing more sophisticated ideas about number, recognizing ways to think about basic fact combinations, and accurately and fluently applying these operations in real-world situations. This develops *operation sense*.

BIG IDEAS

♦ Addition and subtraction are connected. Addition names the whole in terms of the parts, and subtraction names a missing part.

* Multiplication involves counting groups of equal size and determining how many are in all (multiplicative thinking) or using a representative set as unit in a multiplicative comparison.
* Multiplication and division are related. Division names a missing factor in terms of the known factor and the product.
* Models can be used to solve contextual problems for all operations and to figure out what operation is involved in a problem regardless of the size of the numbers. Models also can be used to give meaning to number sentences.

 ## Teaching Operations through Contextual Problems

Contextual problems are the primary teaching tool that you can use to help children construct a rich understanding of the operations. These contexts activate problem solving strategies (Schwartz, 2013). What might a good lesson that is built around contextual problems look like? The answer comes more easily if you think about children not just solving the problems but also using words, pictures, and numbers to explain how they went about solving the problem and why they think they are correct. Children should solve problems using whatever techniques they wish including whatever physical materials or drawings they feel they need to help them. What is important is that they explain what they did and why it makes sense within the context of the situation. If they are recording their ideas on paper, whatever they put on their paper, whether a written explanation or a drawing they used to help them solve the problem, it should explain what they did well enough to allow someone else to understand it. With the emphasis on children explaining their ideas and reasoning, lessons should focus on two or three problems and the related discussions.

 Complete Self-Check 9.1: Teaching Operations through Contextual Problems

 ## Addition and Subtraction Problem Structures

Let's begin with a look at three categories of problem structures for additive situations (which include both addition and subtraction) and later explore four problem structures for multiplicative situations (which include both multiplication and division). These categories help children develop a schema to separate important information and to structure their thinking. In particular, researchers suggest that students (particularly those with disabilities) should be explicitly taught these underlying structures so that they can identify important characteristics of the situations and determine when to add or subtract (Fagnant & Vlassis, 2013; Fuchs, Fuchs, Prentice, Hamlett, Finelli, & Courey, 2004; Xin, Jitendra, & Deatline-Buchman, 2005). When children are exposed to new problems, the familiar characteristics will assist them in generalizing from similar problems on which they have practiced. Furthermore, teachers who are not aware of the variety of situations and corresponding structures may randomly offer problems to children without the proper sequencing to support their full grasp of the meaning of the operations. By knowing the logical structure of these problems, you will be able to help children interpret a variety of real-world contexts. More importantly, you will need to present a variety of problem types (within each structure) as well as recognize which structures produce the greatest challenge for students.

CCSS **Standards for Mathematical Practice**
MP3. Construct viable arguments and critique the reasoning of others.

CCSS **Standards for Mathematical Practice**
MP7. Look for and make use of structure.

Researchers have separated addition and subtraction problems into structures based on the kinds of relationships involved (Verschaffel, Greer, & DeCorte, 2007). These include *change* problems (*join* and *separate*), *part-part-whole* problems, and *compare* problems (Carpenter, Fennema, Franke, Levi, & Empson, 2014). The basic structure for each of these three categories of problems is illustrated in Figure 9.1.

Depending on which of the three quantities is unknown, a different problem type results. Each of the problem structures is illustrated with the story problems that follow using the number family 4, 8, 12. Note that the problems are described in terms of their structure and interpretation and not as addition or subtraction problems. Contrary to what you may have thought, a joining action does not always mean addition, nor does separate or remove always mean subtraction.

Change Problems

Join/Add to Problems. For the action of joining, there are three quantities involved: an initial or *start amount*, a *change amount* (the part being added or joined), and the *resulting amount* (the total amount after the change takes place). In Figure 9.1(a), this is illustrated by the

Problem Type and Structure with Physical Action Involved: **Change Problems**

	Result Unknown	Change Unknown	Start Unknown
Join (add to) **(a)** 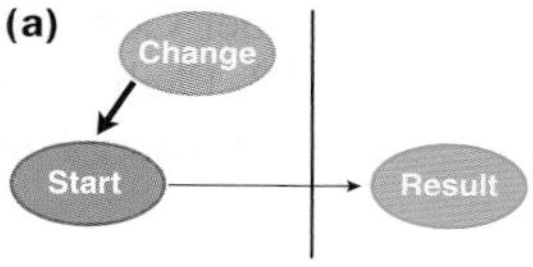 *Change, Start, Result*	Sandra had 8 pennies. George gave her 4 more. How many pennies does Sandra have altogether? $8 + 4 = \square$	Sandra had 8 pennies. George gave her some more. Now Sandra has 12 pennies. How many did George give her? $8 + \square = 12$	Sandra had some pennies. George gave her 4 more. Now Sandra has 12 pennies. How many pennies did Sandra have to begin with? $\square + 4 = 12$
Separate (take from) **(b)** 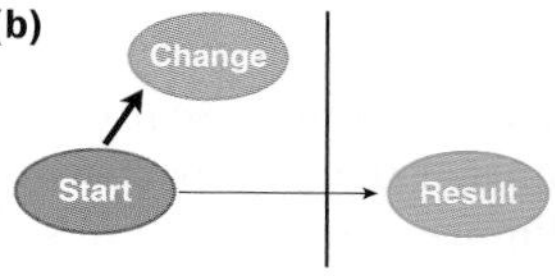 *Change, Start, Result*	Sandra had 12 pennies. She gave 4 pennies to George. How many pennies does Sandra have now? $12 - 4 = \square$	Sandra had 12 pennies. She gave some to George. Now she has 8 pennies. How many did she give to George? $12 - \square = 8$	Sandra had some pennies. She gave 4 to George. Now Sandra has 8 pennies left. How many pennies did Sandra have to begin with? $\square - 4 = 8$

Problem Type and Structure with No Physical Action Involved: **Part-Part-Whole** and **Compare Problems**

	Whole Unknown	One Part Unknown	Both Parts Unknown
Part-Part-Whole **(c)** 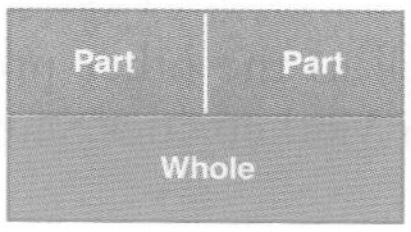 *Part, Part, Whole*	George has 4 pennies and 8 nickels. How many coins does he have? $4 + 8 =$	George has 12 coins. Eight of his coins are pennies, and the rest are nickels. How many nickels does George have? $12 = 4 + \square$ or $12 - 4 = \square$	George has 12 coins. Some are pennies and some are nickels. How many of each coin could he have? $12 = \square + \square$

	Difference Unknown	Larger Quantity Unknown	Smaller Quantity Unknown
	Situations of - How many more?		
Compare **(d)** 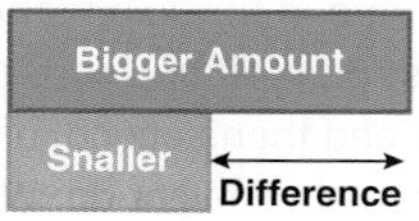 *Bigger Amount, Smaller, Difference*	George has 12 pennies, and Sandra has 8 pennies. How many more pennies does George have than Sandra? $8 + \square = 12$	George has 4 more pennies than Sandra. Sandra has 8 pennies. How many pennies does George have? $8 + 4 = \square$	George has 4 more pennies than Sandra. George has 12 pennies. How many pennies does Sandra have? $\square + 4 = 12$
	Situations of - How many fewer?		
	George has 12 pennies. Sandra has 8 pennies. How many fewer pennies does Sandra have than George? $12 - 8 = \square$	Sandra has 4 fewer pennies than George. Sandra has 8 pennies. How many pennies does George have? $\square - 4 = 8$	Sandra has 4 fewer pennies than George. George has 12 pennies. How many pennies does Sandra have? $12 - 4 = \square$

FIGURE 9.1 Basic structures for addition and subtraction story problem types. Each structure has three numbers. Any one or more of the three numbers can be the unknown in a story problem.

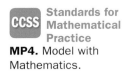

change being "added to" the start amount. See the Join Story Activity Page where students can work with counters and model the problem on the story situation graphic organizer. Visit the companion website to watch a video of a student solving a change unknown addition problem. You will see how she reasons to get the answer using doubles facts she already knows.

Separate/Take From Problems. In *separate problems*, the start amount is the whole or the largest amount, whereas in the *joining problems*, the result is the largest amount (whole). In separate problems, the change is that an amount is being physically removed or taken away from the start value. See the Separate Story Activity Page for a useful graphic organizer.

Part-Part-Whole Problems

Part-part-whole problems also known as *put together and take apart* problems in the Common Core State Standards (CCSSO, 2010), involve two parts that are conceptually or mentally combined into one collection or whole, as in Figure 9.1(c) . These are different from change problems in that there is no action of physically joining or separating the two quantities. In these situations, either the missing whole (total unknown), one of the missing parts (one addend unknown), or both parts (two addends unknown) must be found. There is no meaningful distinction between the two parts in a part-part-whole situation, so there is no need to have a different problem for each part as the unknown. The third situation in which the whole or total is known and the two parts are unknown creates opportunities to think about all the possible decomposition of the whole. This structure links directly to the idea in the Number Core that numbers are embedded in other numbers. Students can break apart 7 into 5 and 2. Each of the addends (or parts) were embedded in the 7 (whole). See Part-Part-Whole Story, an Activity Page for the corresponding graphic organizer.

Compare Problems

Compare problems involve the comparison of two quantities. The third amount in these problems does not actually exist but is the *difference* between the two amounts. Like part-part-whole, comparison problems do not typically involve a physical action. Figure 9.1(d) illustrates the compare problem structure, and the corresponding Compare Story Activity Page can help students model the situation. There are three ways to present compare problems, corresponding to which quantity is unknown (smaller, larger, or difference). For each of these, two examples are given: one problem in which the difference is stated in terms of "how many more?" and another in terms of "how much less?" Note that the language of "more" will often confuse students and thus presents a challenge in interpretation.

You can find more examples of these compare problems as well as the other problem types in the Common Core State Standards (see Table 1 in the CCSS Mathematics Standards Glossary; CCSSO, 2010, p. 88).

 Pause & Reflect

Go back through all of these examples and match the numbers in the problems with the components of the structures in Figure 9.1. For example, which numbers in the Join Problems match to start, change, and result? For each problem, if possible, first print off and copy the graphic organizer Activity Page that goes with that problem structure, and then second, use a set of counters or coins to model (solve) the problem as you think children might do. Write either an addition or subtraction equation that you think best represents the problem as you did it with counters and then compare your equation to the ones in Figure 9.1. ●

As you look back at the equations for each of the problems, you may have written some equations where the unknown quantity is not isolated on the right side of the equal sign. For example, the equation for the join problem with start part unknown is $\square + 4 = 12$. This is referred to as the *semantic* equation for the problem because the numbers are written in the order that follows the meaning of the word problem (see Figure 9.2). When the semantic

Quantity Unknown	Join Problems	Separate Problems
Result Unknown	$8 + 4 = \square$	$12 - 4 = \square$
Change Unknown	$8 + \square = 12$ (semantic) $12 - 8 = \square$ (computational)	$12 - \square = 8$ (semantic) $12 - 8 = \square$ (computational)
Start Unknown	$\square + 4 = 12$ (semantic) $12 - 4 = \square$ (computational)	$\square - 4 = 8$ (semantic) $4 + 8 = \square$ (computational)

FIGURE 9.2 The semantic and computational equations for each of the six join and separate problems in Figure 9.1(a) and (b). Notice that for result-unknown problems, the semantic form is the same as the computational form.

form does not isolate the unknown on one side of the equal sign, an equivalent equation can be written for the same problem. In this case, for $\square + 4 = 12$, the equation we can write is $12 - 4 = \square$. This is referred to as the *computational* form of the equation, which isolates the unknown quantity. It is also the equation you would need to use if you were to solve these equations with a calculator. This may be an efficient way to solve the problem, but children typically begin to think about and model the situation based on the sequence played out in the problem, which is modeled more appropriately by the semantic equation. When the semantic form is not also the computational form, help students see how these equations are equivalent and that there are several ways to represent a situation as an equation. The structure of the equations also may cause difficulty for English language learners (ELLs), who may not initially have the flexibility in creating equivalent equations due to reading comprehension issues with the story situation.

Problem Difficulty

The structure of some problem types is more difficult than others. As stated previously, join and separate with result-unknown problems or the two-parts unknown problems are easier because children can model the physical action or act out the situation. However, the join or separate problems in which the start is unknown (e.g., Sandra had some pennies) are often the most difficult, probably because students attempting to model the problems directly do not know how many counters to put down to begin. Instead, they often use trial and error (Carpenter, Fennema, Franke, Levi, & Empson, 2014) to determine the unknown start amount. Problems in which the change amounts are unknown can also be difficult.

Part-part-whole problems can be difficult for children for two reasons: (1) There is no action to model because the situation describes a conceptual bringing together of quantities, and (2) it is a challenge for children to grasp that a quantity can represent two things at once. For example, if the problem describes three cars and four trucks in a parking lot and asks how many vehicles are in the lot, children have to understand that the cars and trucks are also part of the larger category of vehicles.

Compare problems are often challenging, as the language of "how many more?" often confuses students into adding instead of finding the difference. Many children will solve compare problems as part-part-whole problems without making separate sets of counters for the two amounts. The whole is used as the large amount, one part for the small amount and the second part for the difference. Additionally, children often have more experiences with the relationships of more and greater than, so you need to ensure they have opportunities to think about relationships described using the language fewer and less than. Note that when the larger amount is unknown, stating the problem using the term *more* is easier for children because the relationships between the quantities and the operation more readily correspond to each other. In the smaller unknown situation, stating the problem using the term *fewer* is easier for children for the same reason. Similar to the part-part-whole problems, the lack of a physical action in these situations makes it difficult for children to model or act out these kinds of problems.

Visit the companion website for a video clip of a diagnostic interview of a second-grader named Richard. Note that Richard struggles with both the addition and subtraction problems he is given.

What surprised you in Richard's interview? How might this student struggle to solve problems in a whole class setting? What might be some next steps in Richard's instruction? Now let's look at ideas for supporting the teaching of addition and subtraction.

✓ **Complete Self-Check 9.2(a): Addition and Subtraction Problem Structures**

  ## Teaching Addition and Subtraction

So far, you have seen a variety of story problem structures for addition and subtraction, and you probably have attempted them using counters to help you understand how these problems can be solved by children. Combining the use of situations and models (counters, drawings, number lines, bar diagrams) is important in helping students construct a deep understanding of these two operations. Remember that building the understanding of these operations now will support these operations with larger numbers, fractions, and decimals later on. As you read this next section, note that addition and subtraction are taught at the same time.

Contextual Problems

There is more to think about than simply giving students problems to solve. In contrast with the rather straightforward and brief contextual problems in the previous section, consider the following problem, which the student has solved in Figure 9.3.

Yesterday we were measuring how tall we were. You remember that we used the connecting cubes to make a big train that was as long as we were when we were lying down. Dion and Rosa were wondering how many cubes long they would be together if they lie down head to foot. Dion had measured Rosa, and she was $49\frac{1}{2}$ cubes long. Rosa measured Dion, and he was 59 cubes long. Can we figure out how long they will be end to end?

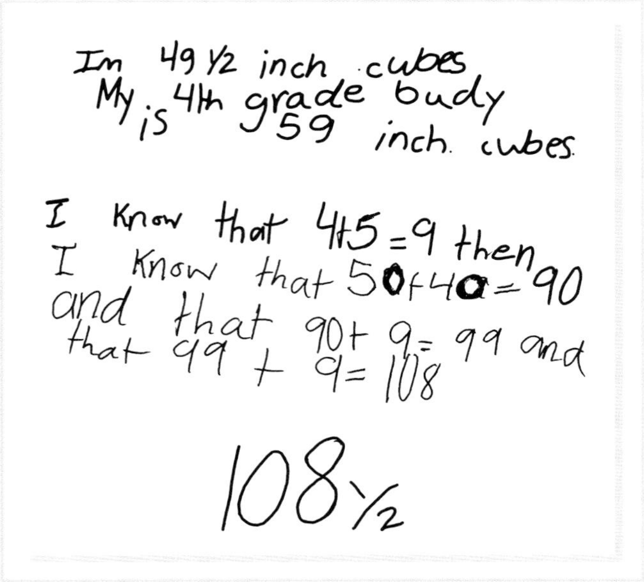

Fosnot and Dolk (2001) point out that in story problems, children tend to focus on getting the answer. "Context problems, on the other hand, are connected as closely as possible to children's lives, rather than to 'school mathematics.' They are designed to anticipate and to develop children's mathematical modeling of the real world" (p. 24). Contextual problems might derive from recent experiences in the classroom; a field trip; a discussion in art, science, or social studies; or from children's literature. Because contextual problems connect to life experiences, they are important for ELLs, too, even though it may seem that the language presents a challenge to them. Some strategies to support comprehension of problems include using a noun-verb word order, replacing terms such as "his/her" and "it" with a name, and removing unnecessary vocabulary words. A visual aid, or actual students modeling this story, would also be effective strategies for ELLs and students with disabilities.

For example, the preceding problem could be rewritten as:

Yesterday, we measured how long you were using cubes. Dion and Rosa asked how many cubes long they are when they lie down

FIGURE 9.3 Student work shows a child's thinking as she calculates the total measurement of Rosa's and Dion's heights.

head to foot. Rosa was $49\frac{1}{2}$ cubes long, and Dion was 59 cubes long. How long are Rosa and Dion when lying head to foot?

Lessons Built on Context or Story Problems. What might a good lesson built around word problems look like? The answer comes more naturally if you think about students not just solving the problems but also using words, pictures, and numbers to explain how they solved the problems and justify why they are correct. In a single class period, focus on a few problems with in-depth discussions rather than a lot of problems with little elaboration. Students should use whatever physical materials or drawings they feel will help them. Whatever they put on their paper should explain what they did well enough to allow someone else to understand their thinking.

A particularly effective approach is having students correct others' written solutions. For example, give the class a set of fictitious students' work with calculations related to a recent school event or other context. By using anonymous work, the students in your class can analyze the reasoning used, assess the selection of the operation, find the mistakes in computation and identify errors in copying numbers from the problem.

CCSS Standards for Mathematical Practice
MP3. Construct viable arguments and critique the reasoning of others.

Choosing Numbers for Problems. The structure of the problem will change the difficulty of the task, but you can also vary the difficulty of the problem by the numbers you choose to use. If a student struggles with a problem, use smaller numbers to see if it is the size of the numbers causing the obstacle. Likewise, you can also intensify the challenge by increasing the size of the numbers. In general, the numbers in the problems should be in accord with the students' number development. According to the Common Core State Standards (CCSSO, 2010), by the end of their respective school years, kindergartners should count as many as 20 objects to answer "how many?" and solve addition and subtraction word problems to 10; first-graders should add and subtract up to 20 and demonstrate fluency up to 10; and second-graders should be able to fluently add and subtract up to 20 using mental strategies. Kindergartners are expected to decompose numbers between 11 and 19 into tens and ones; first-graders are learning about decomposing two-digit numbers up to 100; and second-graders are learning about decomposing three-digit numbers up to 1000. Rather than wait until students develop techniques for computing numbers, use word problems as an opportunity for them to learn about number and computation simultaneously. For example, a problem involving the combination of 30 and 42 has the potential to help first- and second-graders focus on sets of 10. As they decompose 42 into 40 and 2, it is not at all unreasonable to think that they will add 30 and 40 and then add 2 more. The structure of a word problem can strongly influence the type of strategy a student uses to solve multidigit problems. This is especially true for students who have not been taught the standard algorithms for addition and subtraction. You can learn more about *invented strategies* for computation in addition and subtraction in Chapter 12.

Introducing Symbolism. Preschool children initially have no need for the symbols $+$, $-$, and $=$ as they listen and respond to addition and subtraction situations orally. However, by kindergarten and first grade these symbolic conventions are required. To ramp up to this need, whenever young children are engaged in solving story problems, introduce symbols as a way to record what they did as they share their thinking in the discussion portion of a lesson. Say, "You had the whole number of 12 in your problem, and the number 8 was one of the parts of 12. You found out that the unknown part was 4. Here is a way we write that: $12 - 8 = 4$." The minus sign should be read as "minus" or "subtract" but *not* as "take away." The plus sign is easier because it is typically a substitute for "and." Some children may describe a counting-up strategy to find the solution of 4, so also introduce the equivalent equation as $8 + 4 = 12$.

Some care should be taken with the equal sign, as it is a relational symbol not an operations symbol (such as + and −). That can confuse children. The equal sign means "is the same as." However, many children think of it as a symbol that signals that the "answer is coming up." This video (https://www.youtube.com/watch?v=eO3OQI9Jwts) illustrates these misconceptions. Children often interpret the equal sign in much the same way as the = on a calculator: the key you press to get the answer. An equation such as $4 + 8 = 3 + 9$ has no "answer" and is still true because both sides stand for the same quantity. A good idea is to use the phrase "is the same as" in place of or in conjunction with "equals" as you record and read the equal sign in equations. Avoid saying $2 + 2$ "makes" 4. Using a variety of equations, such as $9 = 5 + 4, 6 = 6$, and $3 + 3 = 2 + 4$, is a way to help students understand the meaning of the equal sign, as this knowledge is a CCSS standard for grade 1.

Another approach is to think of the equal sign as a balance; whatever is on one side of the equation "balances" or equals the other side. This will support algebraic thinking in future grades if developed early (Knuth, Stephens, McNeil, & Alibali, 2006). (See Chapter 14 for a detailed look at teaching the equal sign as "is the same as" rather than "give me the answer.")

FORMATIVE ASSESSMENT Notes. Observing how students solve story problems will give you information about your students' understanding of number, strategies they may be using to answer basic facts, and methods they are using for multidigit computation. You must look beyond the answers they get on a worksheet. For example, a child who uses counters and counts each addend and then recounts the entire set for a join-result-unknown problem (this is called *count all*) needs to develop more sophisticated strategies. With more practice, they will count on from the first set. This strategy will be modified to count on from the larger set; that is, for $4 + 7$, the child will begin with 7 and count on, even though 4 is the start amount in the problem. Eventually, students use facts retrieved from memory, and their use of counters fades completely or counters are used only when necessary. Observing children solving problems provides evidence to help you decide what numbers to use in problems and what questions to ask that will focus students' attention on more efficient strategies. ∎

Model-Based Problems

Many students will use counters, bar diagrams, or number lines (models) to solve story problems. These models are thinking tools that help them understand what is happening in the problem and keep track of the numbers and steps in solving the problem. Problems can also be posed using models when there is no context involved.

Addition. When the parts of a set are known, addition is used to name the whole in terms of the parts. This simple definition of addition serves both *action situations* (join and separate) and static or *no-action situations* (part-part-whole).

Each part-part-whole model shown in Figure 9.4 represents $5 + 3 = 8$. Some of these are the result of a definite put-together or joining action, and some are not. Notice that in every example, both of the parts are distinct, even after the parts are combined. These models will be used with larger numbers in grades 3–5, but the structure of the models remains the same. If counters or base-ten materials are used, the two parts should be in different piles, on different sections of a mat, or (in the case of counters) in different colors. For children to see a relationship between the two parts and the whole, the image of the five and three must be kept as two separate sets. This helps children reflect on the action after it has occurred. "These red chips are the ones I started with. Then I added these three blue chips, and now I have eight chips altogether."

The use of *bar diagrams* (also called *strip or tape diagrams*) as semiconcrete visual representations is a central fixture of

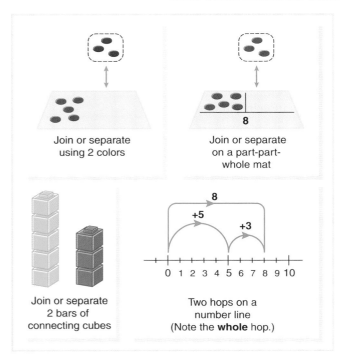

Join or separate using 2 colors

Join or separate on a part-part-whole mat

Join or separate 2 bars of connecting cubes

Two hops on a number line (Note the **whole** hop.)

FIGURE 9.4   Part-part-whole models for $5 + 3 = 8$ and $8 - 3 = 5$.

both Japanese curriculum and what is known as *Singapore mathematics*. As with other tools, these diagrams support students' mathematical thinking by generating "meaning-making space" (Murata, 2008, p. 399) and are a precursor to the use of number lines. Murata states, "Tape diagrams are designed to bring forward the relational meanings of the quantities in a problem by showing the connections in context" (p. 396). You can find online bar diagram tools called "Thinking Blocks" at Math Playground's website and as a free app in the iTunes Store. Thinking Blocks can be used to help students model and solve contextual problems involving operations with whole numbers and fractions.

A *number line* is an essential model, but it can initially present conceptual difficulties for children below second grade and students with disabilities (National Research Council, 2009). This is partially due to their difficulty in seeing the unit, which is a challenge when it appears in a continuous line. A number line is also a shift from counting a number of objects in a collection to length units. There are, however, ways to introduce and model number lines that support young learners as they learn to use this representation (see Figure 9.5). Familiarity with number lines is essential because students in the third grade will use number lines to locate fractions and add and subtract time intervals, fourth-graders will locate decimals and use them for measurement, and fifth-graders will use perpendicular number lines in coordinate grids (CCSSO, 2010).

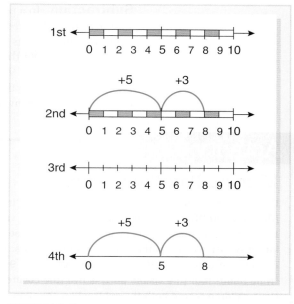

FIGURE 9.5   Sequence of number lines.

A number line measures distances from zero the same way a ruler does. If you don't actually teach the use of the number line through an emphasis on the unit (length), children may focus on the hash marks or numerals instead of the spaces (a misunderstanding that becomes apparent when their answers are consistently off by one). At first, children can build a number path by using a given length, such as a set of Cuisenaire rods of the same color. This will show that each length unit is "one unit," and that same unit is repeated over and over (iterate) to form the number line (Dougherty, 2008). Also, playing board games with number paths helped low-socioeconomic-status students develop a better concept of number magnitude and helped them estimate more accurately on a number line (Siegler & Ramani, 2009). Furthermore, if arrows (hops) are drawn for each number in an expression, the length concept is more clearly illustrated. To model the part-part-whole concept of 5 + 3, start by drawing an arrow from 0 to 5, indicating, "This much is five." Do **not** point to the hash mark for 5, saying, "This is five." Then go on to show the three hops and count "six, seven, eight" (not "one, two, three") to demonstrate the counting-on model and reinforce the mental process. Eventually, the use of a ruler or a scale in a bar graph or coordinate grid will reinforce this model.

There's an interactive number line at the Math Learning Center that helps students visualize number sequences and model strategies for addition, subtraction, multiplication, and division. It can be used to represent sequences of numbers, including whole numbers and multiples of a variety of numbers. An app version of this and other free tools are available for use on a variety of digital devices.

Activity 9.1

CCSS-M: K.OA.A.2; 1.OA.A.1; 1.OA.A.2 and 2.OA.A.1

Up and Down the Number Line

Create a large number line on the floor of your classroom, or display one in the front of the room. (Make sure your line starts with a zero and has arrows at each end of the line.) Use a stuffed animal for hopping, or if the number line is large enough, ask a student to walk the number line. Pose a variety of problem situations and talk about the movement required for each. Start with a context that requires moving a distance, such as the frog hopping away from the lily pad. This emphasizes the spaces (units of length) on the number line and is a wonderful mental image for thinking about the meaning of addition and subtraction.

Subtraction. In a part-part-whole model, when the whole and one of the parts are known, subtraction can be used to name the missing part. If you start with a whole set of 8 and remove a set of 3, the two sets that you know are the sets of 8 and 3. The expression 8−3, read "eight minus three," names the set of 5 that remains (note that we didn't say "take away"). Notice that the models in Figure 9.4 are models for subtraction as well as addition (except for the action). Helping children see that they are using the same models or pictures connects the two operations through their inverse relationship.

Activity 9.2   CCSS-M: K.OA.A.2; 1.OA.A.1; 1.OA.A.2; 2.OA.A.1

Missing-Part Subtraction

Use a situation about something that is hiding, as in the "lift-the-flap" book *What's Hiding in There?* (Drescher, 2008), where animals are concealed in various locations in the woods. Explain to the children that they can model the animals by using a fixed number of tiles placed on a mat. One child separates the tiles into two parts while another covers his or her eyes. The first child covers one of the two parts with a sheet of paper, revealing only the other part (see Figure 9.6[b]). The second child says the subtraction sentence. For example, "Nine minus four [the visible part] is five [the covered part]." The covered part can be revealed for the child to self-check. Have children record both the subtraction equation and the addition equation. ELLs may need sentence prompts such as "_____ minus _____ equals _____."

ENGLISH LANGUAGE LEARNERS

Activity 9.3   CCSS-M: K.OA.A.3; 1.OA.A.1; 1.OA.B.4

Pigs in Cages

Appropriate for the pre-K–1 student, use the book *Guinea Pigs Add Up* (Cuyler, 2010) to think about a growing and changing population of class pets—guinea pigs! There are many options for using this story, such as starting with two addends unknown: "How many ways can you place 10 guinea pigs in two cages?" Use the Activity Page Both Addends Unknown. Another idea is to use the book as a context for missing-part thinking for subtraction. Use the Guinea Pig Problem Activity Page to pose questions to the students about the numbers of pigs in the cage, numbers adopted, and how many are left. Students can use the Cage Mat and the little Guinea Pig Counters Activity Pages and model the problem. Children can pose their own questions and record the appropriate number sentences.

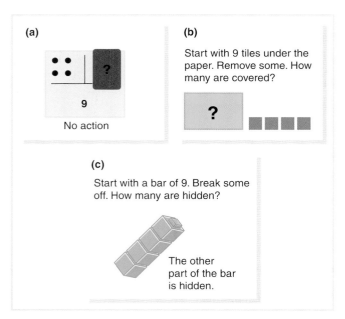

(a)

9

No action

(b)

Start with 9 tiles under the paper. Remove some. How many are covered?

?

(c)

Start with a bar of 9. Break some off. How many are hidden?

The other part of the bar is hidden.

FIGURE 9.6 Models for 9 − 4 as a missing-part problem.

Subtraction as Think-Addition. Note that in Activities 9.2 and 9.3, the situations end with two distinct parts, even when there is a remove action. The removed part remains on the mat as a model for an addition equation to be written after writing the subtraction equation. A discussion of how two equations can be written for the same situation is an important opportunity to connect the operations of addition and subtraction. This is significantly better than the traditional worksheet activity of "fact families" in which children are given a family of numbers such as 3, 5, and 8 and are asked to write two addition equations and two subtraction equations. This often becomes a meaningless process of dropping the numbers into slots without much meaning.

Thinking about subtraction as "think-addition" rather than "take-away" is significant for mastering subtraction facts. Because the tiles for the remaining part or unknown addend are left hidden under the cover, when children do these activities they are encouraged to think: "What goes with the part I see to make the whole?" For example, if the total or whole number of tiles is 9, and 6 tiles are removed from under the cover, the child is likely to think in terms of "6 and what amount add to 9?" or "What goes with 6 to equal 9?" The mental activity is "think-addition" instead of "count what's left." Later, when working on subtraction facts, a subtraction fact such as $9 - 6 = \square$ should trigger the same thought pattern: "6 and what equals 9?"

Comparison Models. *Comparison situations* involve two distinct sets or quantities and the difference between them. Several ways of modeling the difference relationship are shown in Figure 9.7. The same model can be used whether the difference or one of the two quantities is unknown.

Note that it is not immediately clear to students how to associate either the addition or subtraction operations with a comparison situation. From an adult vantage point, you can see that if you match part of the larger amount with the smaller amount, the large set is now a part-part-whole model that can help you solve the problem. In fact, many children do model compare problems in just this manner. But it is a challenge to show students this idea if they do not construct it themselves.

Have students make two amounts (perhaps with two bars of connecting cubes) to show how many pencils are in their backpacks. Discuss the difference between the two bars to generate the third number. For example, if the students make a bar of 10 and a bar of 6, ask, "How many more do we need to match the 10 bar?" The unmatched cubes in the larger bar show that the difference is 4. "What equations can we make with these three numbers?" Have children make up other story problems that involve the two amounts of 10 and 6. Discuss which equations go with the problems that are created.

Properties of Addition and Subtraction

The Commutative Property for Addition. The *commutative property* (sometimes known as the *order property*) for addition means you can change the order of the addends and it does not change the answer. Although the commutative property may seem obvious to us (simply reverse the two piles of counters on the part-part-whole mat), it may not be as obvious to children. Because this property is essential in problem solving (counting on from the larger number), mastery of basic facts (if you know $3 + 9$, you also know $9 + 3$), and mental mathematics, there is value in spending time helping children construct the relationship (Baroody, Wilkins, & Tiilikainen, 2003). First-graders do not need to be able to name the property as much as they need to understand and visualize the property, know why it applies to addition but not subtraction, and apply it (CCSS 1.OA.B.3). But, as a caution, you should always name the property accurately and never use a "nickname" that will confuse the child (and subsequent teachers), such as saying the "ring around the Rosie" property for the commutative property. Those arbitrary names are confusing as students progress. Use the precise terminology.

Schifter (2001) describes students who discovered the commutative property while examining sums to ten. Later, the children were asked whether they thought it would always work. Many students were unsure if it worked all of the time and were especially unsure about it working with large numbers. The point is that children may see and accept the commutative property for sums they've experienced but not be able to explain or even believe that this important property works for all addition combinations. Asking students to think about when properties do (and don't) apply is the heart of mathematics, addressing numeration, reasoning, generalizing, and algebraic thinking.

To help children focus on the commutative property, pair problems that have the same addends but in different orders. Using different contexts helps children focus on the significant similarities in the problems. The following problems are examples.

Counters

Cubes

Difference

Number Line

FIGURE 9.7 Models for the difference between 8 and 5.

Tania is on page 32 in her book. Tomorrow she hopes to read 15 more pages. What page will she be on if she reads that many pages?

The milk tray in the cafeteria had 15 cartons. The delivery person filled the tray with 32 more milk cartons. How many milk cartons are now on the tray?

Ask if anyone notices how these problems are alike. If done as a pair, some (not all) children will see that when they have solved one, they have essentially solved the other. Note that some children will attempt to overgeneralize the commutative property to subtraction. Use contextual situations or story problems to help children confront this misconception.

The Associative Property for Addition. The *associative property* for addition states that when adding three or more numbers, it does not matter whether the first pair is added first or if you start with any other pair of addends. There is much flexibility in addition, and students can change the order in which they group numbers to work with combinations they know. This knowledge is expected of first-graders in the CCSS in Standard 1.OA.B.2 (CCSSO, 2010). For example, knowing this property can help students identify "combinations of ten" from the numbers they are adding by mentally grouping numbers in an order different from just reading the expression from left to right.

Activity 9.4   CCSS-M: 1.OA.B.2

More Than Two Addends

Give students six sums to find involving three or four addends. Prepare these on a page divided into six sections with space to write beneath each sum. Within each, include at least one pair with a sum of 10 or perhaps a double: $4 + 7 + 6, 5 + 9 + 9,$ or $3 + 4 + 3 + 7$. Students should show how they added the numbers. If you are working with students with disabilities, you may need to initially support them in their decision making, suggesting that they look for a 10 or a double and have them underline or circle those numbers as a starting point.

STUDENTS *with* **SPECIAL NEEDS**

Figure 9.8 illustrates a child's thinking. As your children share solutions, there will be some who added using a different order but got the same result. From this discussion, you can help them conclude that they can add numbers in any order. You are also using the associative property, but it is the commutative property that is more important. This is also an excellent number-sense activity because many students will find combinations of ten in these sums or will use doubles. Learning to adjust strategies to fit the numbers is the beginning of the road to computational fluency.

The Zero Property. Story problems involving zero and using zeros in the three-addend sums are also good opportunities to help children understand zero as an identity element in addition or subtraction (see Table 3 in the CCSS Mathematics Glossary, p. 90) Occasionally, children believe that $6 + 0$ must be more than 6 because "adding makes numbers bigger," or that $12 - 0$ must be 11 because "subtracting makes numbers smaller." Instead of making meaningless rules about adding and subtracting zero, build zero into the problem solving routine using contextual situations.

Although these properties are algebraic in nature (generalized rules), they are discussed here because the meanings of the properties are essential to understanding how numbers can be added. Explicit attention to these concepts (build the

CCSS
Standards for Mathematical Practice
MP2. Reason abstractly and quantitatively.

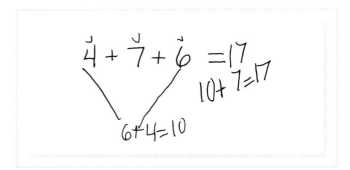

FIGURE 9.8 A child shows how she added using check marks to keep track of numbers used.

terminology over time) will help students become more flexible (and efficient) in how they combine numbers.

 Complete Self-Check 9.2(b): Addition and Subtraction Problem Structures

 # Multiplication and Division Problem Structure

Like addition and subtraction, there are problem structures that will help you as the teacher in formulating and discussing multiplication and division tasks. They will also help your students in generalizing as they solve familiar situations.

Most researchers identify four different classes of multiplicative structures: equal groups, comparison, area (CCSS includes arrays with area), and combinations (see Figure 9.9). Of these, the two structures *equal groups* (the focus in the CCSS third-grade standards) and *multiplicative comparison* (the focus in the CCSS fourth-grade standards), are by far the most prevalent in elementary school (CCSSO, 2010). Arrays begin to be considered in second grade in the CCSS as addition situations with equal groups, and area problems are introduced in the third grade under the CCSS domain of Measurement and Data. Problems with combinations are found in seventh grade in the CCSS when students identify all of the possible outcomes in situations exploring probability.

Equal-Group Problems

In multiplicative problems, one number or factor counts how many sets, groups, or parts of equal size are involved. The other factor tells the size of each set, group, or part. The third number in each of these two structures is the whole or product and is the total of all of the parts. The parts and wholes terminology is useful in making the connection to addition. When the number and size of groups are known, the problem is a *multiplication* situation. When either the group size is unknown (How many in each group?) or the number of groups is unknown (How many groups?), then the problem is a *division* situation. But note that these division situations are not alike. Problems in which the size of the group is unknown are called *fair-sharing* or *partition* division problems. The whole is shared or distributed among a known number of groups to determine the size of each. If the number of groups is unknown but the size of the equal group is known, the problems are called *measurement division* or sometimes *repeated-subtraction* problems. The whole is "measured off" in groups the given size. Use the illustration in Figure 9.9(a) as a reference. Visit the companion website for a video clip of a student demonstrating measurement division as he uses information of the total and the size of each group to find the number of groups (unknown).

Sometimes equal-group problems have been called *repeated-addition* problems, as the equal group is being added over and over. And in fact, multiplication is an efficient way to carry out a repeated-addition situation. This may be an important initial connection for young learners to make, as the multiplication and the repeated addition produce the same results for positive whole numbers. But by the time students are multiplying fractions, this notion falls apart. Additionally, repeated addition is not an efficient way to carry out multiplication—it is just the opposite (try 23 × 57). So, move away from additive thinking to thinking of a multiplier and equal sets as soon as you are able to do so. There is also a subtle difference between equal-group problems and those that might be termed *rate* problems ("If there are four apples per child, how many apples would three children have?"). In a rate problem, students are working with a composed unit (in this case, apples per child).

Comparison Problems

In multiplicative comparison problems, there are really two different sets or groups, as there were with comparison situations for addition and subtraction. In additive situations, the comparison is an amount or quantity difference between the two groups. In multiplicative situations,

Problem Type and Structure with Equal Groups (second set of problems are rate problems)

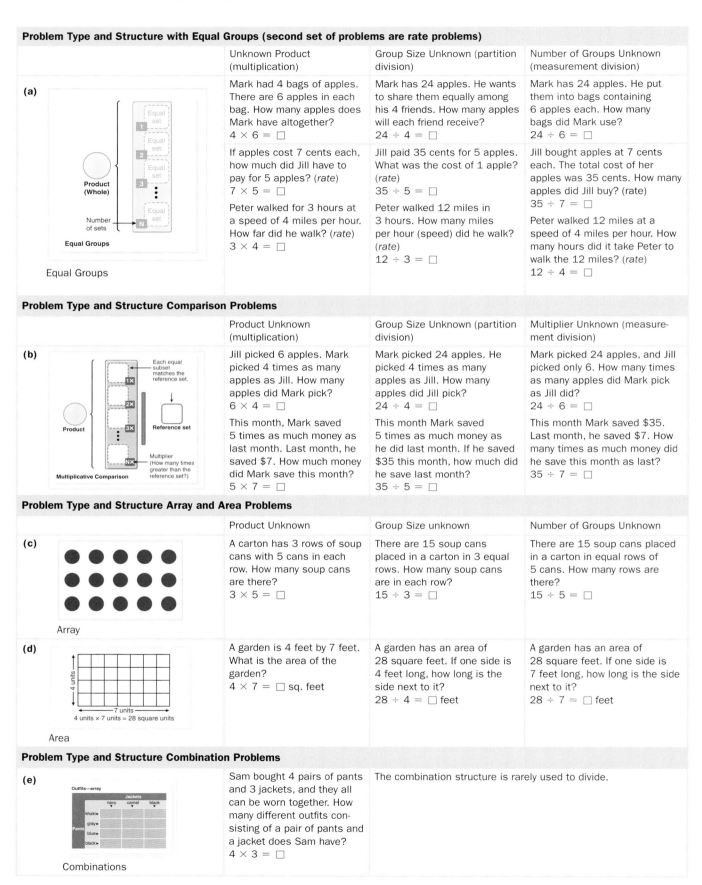

	Unknown Product (multiplication)	Group Size Unknown (partition division)	Number of Groups Unknown (measurement division)
(a) Equal Groups	Mark had 4 bags of apples. There are 6 apples in each bag. How many apples does Mark have altogether? $4 \times 6 = \square$	Mark has 24 apples. He wants to share them equally among his 4 friends. How many apples will each friend receive? $24 \div 4 = \square$	Mark has 24 apples. He put them into bags containing 6 apples each. How many bags did Mark use? $24 \div 6 = \square$
	If apples cost 7 cents each, how much did Jill have to pay for 5 apples? (*rate*) $7 \times 5 = \square$ Peter walked for 3 hours at a speed of 4 miles per hour. How far did he walk? (*rate*) $3 \times 4 = \square$	Jill paid 35 cents for 5 apples. What was the cost of 1 apple? (*rate*) $35 \div 5 = \square$ Peter walked 12 miles in 3 hours. How many miles per hour (speed) did he walk? (*rate*) $12 \div 3 = \square$	Jill bought apples at 7 cents each. The total cost of her apples was 35 cents. How many apples did Jill buy? (rate) $35 \div 7 = \square$ Peter walked 12 miles at a speed of 4 miles per hour. How many hours did it take Peter to walk the 12 miles? (*rate*) $12 \div 4 = \square$

Problem Type and Structure Comparison Problems

	Product Unknown (multiplication)	Group Size Unknown (partition division)	Multiplier Unknown (measurement division)
(b) Multiplicative Comparison	Jill picked 6 apples. Mark picked 4 times as many apples as Jill. How many apples did Mark pick? $6 \times 4 = \square$ This month, Mark saved 5 times as much money as last month. Last month, he saved $7. How much money did Mark save this month? $5 \times 7 = \square$	Mark picked 24 apples. He picked 4 times as many apples as Jill. How many apples did Jill pick? $24 \div 4 = \square$ This month Mark saved 5 times as much money as he did last month. If he saved $35 this month, how much did he save last month? $35 \div 5 = \square$	Mark picked 24 apples, and Jill picked only 6. How many times as many apples did Mark pick as Jill did? $24 \div 6 = \square$ This month Mark saved $35. Last month, he saved $7. How many times as much money did he save this month as last? $35 \div 7 = \square$

Problem Type and Structure Array and Area Problems

	Product Unknown	Group Size unknown	Number of Groups Unknown
(c) Array	A carton has 3 rows of soup cans with 5 cans in each row. How many soup cans are there? $3 \times 5 = \square$	There are 15 soup cans placed in a carton in 3 equal rows. How many soup cans are in each row? $15 \div 3 = \square$	There are 15 soup cans placed in a carton in equal rows of 5 cans. How many rows are there? $15 \div 5 = \square$
(d) Area 4 units × 7 units = 28 square units	A garden is 4 feet by 7 feet. What is the area of the garden? $4 \times 7 = \square$ sq. feet	A garden has an area of 28 square feet. If one side is 4 feet long, how long is the side next to it? $28 \div 4 = \square$ feet	A garden has an area of 28 square feet. If one side is 7 feet long, how long is the side next to it? $28 \div 7 = \square$ feet

Problem Type and Structure Combination Problems

(e) Combinations	Sam bought 4 pairs of pants and 3 jackets, and they all can be worn together. How many different outfits consisting of a pair of pants and a jacket does Sam have? $4 \times 3 = \square$	The combination structure is rarely used to divide.

FIGURE 9.9 The four problem structures for multiplication and division story problems.

the comparison is based on one group being a particular multiple of the other (multiple copies). With multiplication comparison, there are three possibilities for the unknown: the product, the group size, and the number of groups (see Figure 9.9[b]).

 Pause *&* Reflect

What you just read is complex yet important. Stop now and get a collection of about 35 counters and a set of paper plates to model the equal-groups examples starring "Mark." Match the story with the structure model in Figure 9.9(a). How are these problems alike and how are they different? Repeat for "Jill" problems.

Repeat the same process with the comparison problems using a colored plate different from your other plates to represent the reference set. Again, start with the first problem in each set and then the second problem. Reflect on how they are the same and different. ●

Area and Array Problems

What distinguishes *area* (also known as *product-of-measures* problems) from the others is that the product is literally a different type of unit from the two factors. In a rectangular shape, the product of two lengths (length × width) is an area, usually measured in square units. Note in Figure 9.9(d) how different the square units are from the two factors of length: 4 feet times 7 feet is not 28 feet but 28 square feet. The factors are each one-dimensional entities, but the product consists of a *two*-dimensional unit. The study of area will be considered in great depth in Chapter 19 on measurement.

The *array* is a model for an equal-group situation (Figure 9.9[c]). It is shown as a rectangular grouping, with one factor representing the number of rows and the other representing the equal number found in each column. CCSS groups arrays with area rather than with the equal-group problems because arrays can be thought of as a logical lead-in to the row-and-column structure of an area problem.

Although the following multiplicative structure is more complex and therefore not a good introductory point, it is important that you recognize it as another category of multiplicative problem structures.

Combination Problems

Combination problems (also called *Cartesian products*) involve counting the number of possible pairings that can be made between two or more sets (things or events). Students often start by using the model shown in Figure 9.9(e) where one set is the row (pants) and the other the column (jackets). This visual links to the array and the area representations. It is possible—rarely—to have related division problems for the combinations concept. Counting how many combinations of two or more things or events are possible is important in determining probabilities—in seventh grade.

 Complete Self-Check 9.3: Multiplication and Division Problem Structure

 Teaching Multiplication and Division

Multiplication and division are often taught separately, with multiplication preceding division. It is important, however, to combine multiplication and division soon after multiplication has been introduced in order to help children see how these operations have an inverse relationship. In most curricula, these topics are first presented in grade 2 (as suggested by the Common Core State Standards) and then become a major focus of the third grade with continued development in the fourth and fifth grades.

A major conceptual hurdle in working with multiplicative structures is understanding groups of items as single entities while also understanding that a group contains a given number of objects (Blote, Lieffering, & Ouewhand, 2006; Clark & Kamii, 1996). Children can solve the problem, "How many apples in 4 baskets of 8 apples each?" by counting out four sets of eight counters and then counting all. To think multiplicatively about this problem as *four sets of eight* requires children to conceptualize each group of eight as a single item to be counted. Experiences with making and counting equal groups, especially in contextual situations, are extremely useful.

Contextual Problems

When teaching multiplication and division, it is essential to use interesting contextual problems instead of more sterile story problems (or "naked numbers"). However, as with addition and subtraction, there is more to think about than simply giving students word problems to solve. Consider the following problem.

Yesterday, we discovered that it took 7 yards of paper to cover the bulletin board in the school's front lobby. There are 25 more bulletin boards of the same size in the hallways around the school. How many yards of paper will we need if we cover all the bulletin boards in the school hallways?

This problem is based on students' experiences and builds on a known context that all can access. When such a familiar context is used, students are more likely to demonstrate a spontaneous and meaningful approach to solve the problem, as they are connected to it.

The tendency in the United States is to have students solve many problems in a single class period with a focus on getting the answers. But if you change the focus to sense making, solving only a few problems using tools strategically such as physical materials, drawings, as well as equations can be a better approach. Whatever students write on paper, they should explain it in enough detail for another person to follow their thinking. Leave enough space on an activity sheet to encourage multiple strategies—it is amazing how leaving only a small space will just prompt an answer and nothing more.

Symbolism for Multiplication and Division. When students solve simple multiplication story problems before learning about multiplication symbolism, they will most likely begin by writing addition equations to represent what they did. This is your opportunity to introduce the multiplication sign and explain what the two factors mean.

The usual convention in the United States is that 4×8 refers to four sets of eight, not eight sets of four. There is no reason to be so rigid about this convention that you would mark a student as incorrect (particularly because the convention is just the opposite in some countries where they say 4 taken 8 times). The important thing is that the students can tell you what each factor in their equations represents. In vertical form, it is usually the bottom factor that indicates the number of sets or groups. These conventions allow us to communicate clearly about the problem with each other. It also helps to build toward the commutative property of multiplication.

The quotient 24 divided by 6 is represented in three different ways: $24 \div 6$, $6\overline{)24}$, and $\frac{24}{6}$. Students should understand that these representations are equivalent. The fraction notation becomes important at the middle school level. Students often mistakenly read $6\overline{)24}$ as "6 divided by 24" due to the left-to-right order of the numerals. Generally, this error does not match what they are thinking.

Compounding the difficulty of division notation is the unfortunate phrase "goes in to," as in "6 goes into 24." This phrase carries little meaning about division, especially in connection with a fair-sharing or partitioning context. The "goes in to" terminology is simply ingrained in adult parlance; it has not been in textbooks for years. Instead of this phrase, use appropriate terminology with students, such as "How many groups of 6 are in 24?"

Choosing Numbers for Problems. When selecting numbers for multiplicative story problems or activities, there is a tendency to think that large numbers pose a burden to students or that 3×4 is somehow easier to understand than 4×17. An understanding of products or quotients is not affected by the size of numbers as long as the numbers are within

CCSS **Standards for Mathematical Practice**

MP6. Attend to precision.

your students' grasp. A contextual problem involving 14×8 is appropriate for third -graders. When given the challenge of using larger numbers, children are likely to invent computational strategies (e.g., ten 8's and then four more 8's) or model the problem with manipulatives.

Remainders

More often than not in real-world situations, division does not result in a simple whole number. For example, problems with 6 as a divisor will result in a whole number only one time out of six. In the absence of a context, a remainder can be dealt with in only two ways: it can either remain a quantity left over or be partitioned into fractions. In Figure 9.10, the problem $11 \div 4$ is modeled to show the remainder as a fraction.

In real contexts, remainders sometimes have three additional effects on answers:

- The remainder is discarded, leaving a smaller whole-number answer.
- The remainder can "force" the answer to the next highest whole number.
- The answer is rounded to the nearest whole number for an approximate result.

These problems illustrate all five possibilities.

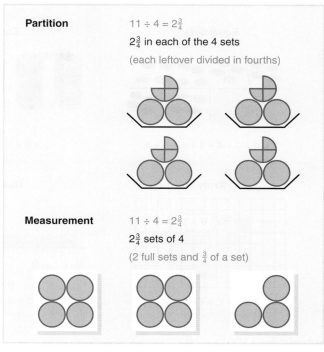

FIGURE 9.10 Remainders expressed as fractions.

---

1. You have 30 pieces of candy to share fairly with 7 children. How many pieces of candy will each child receive?
   Answer: 4 pieces of candy and 2 left over (*left over*)

2. Each jar holds 8 ounces of liquid. If there are 46 ounces in the pitcher, how many jars will that be?
   Answer: 5 and $\frac{6}{8}$ jars (*partitioned as a fraction*)

3. The rope is 25 feet long. How many 7-foot jump ropes can be made?
   Answer: 3 jump ropes (*discarded*)

4. The ferry can hold 8 cars. How many trips will it have to make to carry 25 cars across the river?
   Answer: 4 trips (*forced to next whole number*)

5. Six children are planning to share a bag of 50 pieces of bubble gum. About how many pieces will each child get?
   Answer: About 8 pieces for each child (*rounded, approximate result*)

Students should not just think of remainders as "R 3" or "left over." Addressing what to do with remainders must be central to teaching about division. In fact, one of the most common errors students make on high-stakes assessments is to divide and then not pay attention to the context when selecting their answer. For example, in problem 4 above, answering with $3\frac{1}{8}$ trips doesn't make any sense.

 Pause *&* Reflect

It is useful for you to make up problems in different contexts. See if you can come up with division problems whose contexts would result in remainders dealt with as fractions, rounded up, and rounded down. ●

Model-Based Problems

In the beginning, students will be able to use the same models—sets, bar diagrams, and number lines—for all four operations. A model not often used for addition but extremely important and

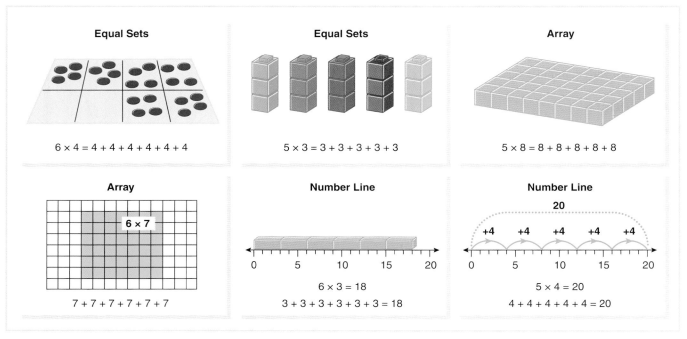

FIGURE 9.11 Models for equal-group multiplication.

widely used for multiplication and division is the array. An *array* is any arrangement of things in rows and columns, such as a rectangle of square tiles or blocks. See the 10×10 Multiplication Array, Blackline Master 16.

To make clear the connection to addition, very early multiplication activities can also include writing an addition sentence for the same model. A variety of models is shown in Figure 9.11.

As with additive problems, students benefit from activities with models to focus on the meaning of the operation and the associated symbolism, such as Activity 9.5.

Activity 9.5
CCSS-M: 4.OA.B.4

Factor Quest

STUDENTS with SPECIAL NEEDS

Start by having students think about a context that involves arrays such as parade formations (see the Literature Connections at the end of the chapter), seats in a classroom, or patches on a quilt. Then assign a number that has several factors— for example, 12, 18, 24, 30, or 36. Have students build as many rectangular arrays as they can (perhaps made from square tiles or cubes). Then have them record their arrays by drawing them on grid paper—see the Factor Quest Activity Page. For each, write the corresponding multiplication equations. For students with physical disabilities who may have limited motor skills to manipulate the materials, you can go to the Factorize applet on the NCTM Illuminations website.

Draw students' attention to the dimensions of the arrays, having them make the connection between the factors in the multiplication expression they have written to the number of rows and columns (the dimensions of the rectangle). Your class will undoubtedly want to decide whether a rectangle that is 3 by 8 should be counted differently from 1 that is 8 by 3. Leave the decision to the class, but take advantage of the opportunity to discuss how 3 rows of 8 are the same amount as 8 rows of 3. Note that if sets rather than arrays are made, 3 sets of 8 look very different from 8 sets of 3. So, as students begin to think about the commutative property of multiplication, arrays provide a helpful representation.

The next activity is an extension of "Factor Quest" in that students look for patterns in the factors they find for numbers, such as the number of factors, the type of factors, the shape of the resulting array, and so on. Rather than assigning numbers that have several factors, this activity suggests including numbers that have only a few factors so that differences between numbers become more distinct.

Activity 9.6 CCSS-M: 4.OA.B.4

Factor Patterns

Tell students that their task is to find all the multiplication expressions and the corresponding rectangular array(s) for several numbers (e.g., **1 through 16 or 10 through 25**). Have enough square tiles available that students can explore all possible arrays. For example, for the number 12, they can build **12 × 1, 6 × 2, 4 × 3**, and the three matching pairs using the commutative property. Then they record their rectangles for a given number on the 1-Centimeter Grid Paper and label each rectangle with the corresponding multiplication expression (e.g., **6 × 2**). This organization helps when students are comparing arrays across different numbers. After identifying the multiplication equations and the rectangular arrays, students are to look for patterns in the factors and arrays. For example, which numbers have the fewest number of arrays and, therefore, the fewest number of factors? Which numbers have only a factor of 1 and itself? Which numbers have arrays that form a square? What can you say about the factors for even numbers? Do even numbers always have two even factors? What about odd numbers? Encourage students to think about why different patterns occur.

Use this activity to explore the numbers that are *prime* (only have a factor of itself and 1) and those that are *composites* (those that can be made with two or more different arrays). Have students continue to consider the patterns that they notice as they classify different numbers into these groupings.

Activities 9.5 and 9.6 can also include division concepts. When students have learned that 3 and 6 are factors of 18, they can write the equations $18 \div 3 = 6$ and $18 \div 6 = 3$ along with $3 \times 6 = 18$ and $6 + 6 + 6 = 18$ (assuming that three sets of six were modeled). Activity 9.7 is a variation of the same activity but focuses instead on division. Having students create word problems to fit what they did with the tiles, cubes, or counters is another excellent elaboration of this activity. Connecting the situation to the materials and to the equation is important in demonstrating understanding.

Activity 9.7 CCSS-M: 3.OA.A.2

Divide and Conquer

Using the context of a story about sharing, such as *Bean Thirteen* (McElligott, 2007), provide children with a supply of counters (beans) and a way to place them into small groups (small paper cups). Have children count out a number of counters to be the whole or total amount and record this number. Next, specify either the number of equal groups to be made or the size of the groups: "Separate your counters into four equal-sized groups," or "Make as many groups of four as is possible." Have children write the corresponding multiplication equation for what their materials show; under that, have them write the division equation. For ELLs, be sure they know what *groups, equal-sized groups,* and *groups of four* mean. For students with disabilities, consider having them start with a partition approach (i.e., separate your counters into three groups), in which they share the counters by placing one at a time into each cup. Explore the Expanded Lesson Divide and Conquer for additional details about this activity.

STUDENTS with SPECIAL NEEDS

ENGLISH LANGUAGE LEARNERS

Be sure to have the class do both situations—the number of equal groups unknown and group size unknown. Discuss with the class how the two situations are different, how each is related to multiplication, and how each is written as a division equation. You can show the different ways to write division equations at this time, such as $13 \div 4$, $4\overline{)13}$, and $\frac{13}{4}$. Do Activity 9.7

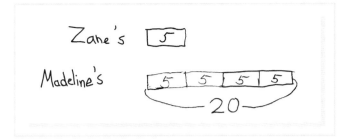

FIGURE 9.12   A student's work shows a model for multiplicative comparisons.

several times. Make sure to include whole quantities that are multiples of the divisor (no remainders) and situations with remainders. Note that it is technically incorrect to write the answer to a problem like 31 ÷ 4 as 7 R 3 because this is not a number (a quotient should be a number). As written, the 3 is not well defined because it is really $\frac{3}{4}$. However, in the beginning, the form 7 R 3 may be the most appropriate.

The activity can be varied by changing the model. Have children build arrays using square tiles or blocks, or draw arrays on square grid paper and present the exercises by specifying how many squares are to be in the array. Then specify the number of rows that should be made (partition) or the length of each row (measurement). How could students model the remainder using drawings of arrays on grid paper? Explore the applet "Rectangle Division" from the National Library of Virtual Manipulatives for an interactive illustration of division with remainders that demonstrates vividly how division is related to multiplication.

When modeling multiplicative comparison problems, consider exploring them with a bar diagram. See Figure 9.12 for a bar diagram related to the following situation:

Zane has five small toy cars. Madeline has four times as many cars. How many does Madeline have?

Activity 9.8   CCSS-M: 4.NBT.B.6

The Broken Division Key

Have students find methods of using the calculator to solve division exercises without using the divide key. "Find at least two ways to figure out 135 ÷ 5 without pressing the divide key." If the problem is put in a story context, one method may actually match the problem better than another. Good discussions may follow different solutions with the same answers. Are they both correct? Why or why not?

Consider ways to explore a broken multiplication key as well.

 Pause & Reflect

Can *you* find three ways to solve 61 ÷ 14 on a calculator without using the divide key? For a hint, see the footnote.*

Properties of Multiplication and Division

There are some multiplicative properties that are useful and thus worthy of attention. The emphasis should be on the ideas and applications rather than the terminology or definitions.

Commutative and Associative Properties of Multiplication. It is not obvious that 3 × 8 is the same as 8 × 3 or that, in general, the order of the numbers makes no difference (the *commutative property*). A picture of 3 sets of 8 objects cannot immediately be seen as 8 piles of 3 objects, nor on a number line are 8 hops of 3 noticeably the same as 3 hops of 8.

The array, by contrast, is quite powerful in illustrating the commutative property, as shown in Figure 9.13(a). Children should build or draw arrays and use them to demonstrate why each array represents two equivalent products. As in addition, there is an *associative property* of multiplication that is fundamental in flexibly solving problems (Ding & Li,

*There are two measurement approaches to find out how many 14's are in 61. A third way is finding 14 times what number is close to 61.

2010). This property allows that when you multiply three numbers in an expression, you can multiply either the first pair of numbers or the last pair and the product remains the same. A context is helpful, so here is an example that could be shared with students. Each tennis ball costs $2. Each can has 3 tennis balls. How much will it cost if we need to buy 6 cans? After analyzing the problem by showing actual cans of tennis balls or illustrations, students should try to consider the problem from two ways: (1) find out the cost for each can and then the total cost, $6 \times (3 \times 2)$; and (2) find out how many balls in total and then the total cost, $(6 \times 3) \times 2$ (Ding, 2010). See Figure 9.13(b).

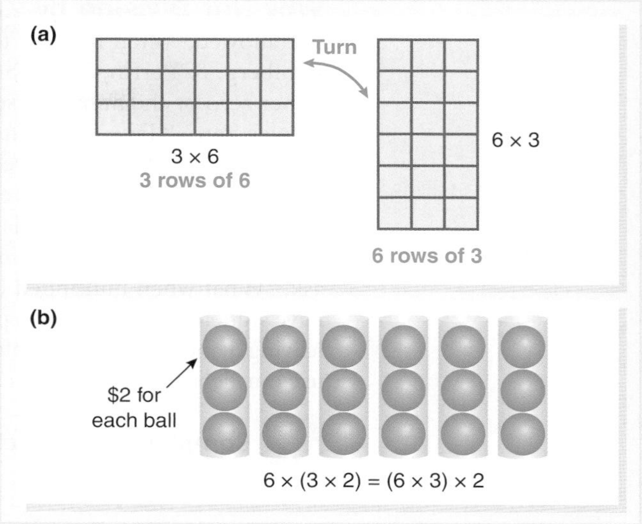

Zero and Identity Properties. Factors of 0 and, to a lesser extent, 1 often cause conceptual challenges for students. In textbooks, you may find that a lesson on factors of 0 and 1 has students use a calculator to examine a wide range of products involving 0 or 1 (423×0, 0×28, 1536×1, etc.) and look for patterns. The pattern suggests rules for factors of 0 and 1 but not a reason. In another lesson, a word problem asks how many grams of fat there are in 7 servings of celery with 0 grams of fat in each serving. This approach is far preferable to an arbitrary rule, because it asks students to reason. Make up interesting word problems involving 0 or 1, and discuss the results. Problems with 0 as a first factor are challenging. Note that on a number line, 5 hops of 0 lands at 0 (5×0). What would 0 hops of 5 be? Another fun activity is to try to model 6×0 or 0×8 with an array. (Try it!) Arrays for factors of 1 are also worth investigating.

Distributive Property. The *distributive property of multiplication over addition* refers to the idea that you can split (*decompose*) either of the two factors in a multiplication problem into two or more parts and then multiply each of the parts by the other factor and add the results. The final product is the same as when the original factors are multiplied. For example, to find the number of yogurts in 9 six-packs, use the logic that 9×6 is the same as $(5 \times 6) + (4 \times 6)$. The 9 has been split into 5 six-packs and 4 six-packs. The concept involved is very useful in relating one basic fact to another, and it is also involved in the development of two-digit computation. Figure 9.14 illustrates how the array model can be used to demonstrate that a product can be broken up into two parts. The next activity is designed to help students discover how to partition factors or, in other words, learn about the distributive property of multiplication over addition.

FIGURE 9.13 A model for the commutative property for multiplication (a), and an illustration of a problem showing the associative property of multiplication (b).

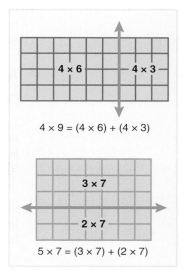

FIGURE 9.14 Models for the distributive property of multiplication over addition.

Activity 9.9

CCSS-M: 3.OA.B.5; 5.OA.A.1

Divide It Up

Supply students with several sheets of centimeter grid paper or color tiles to represent a small garden that will be planted with two different kinds of vegetables. Assign each pair of students a garden plot size, such as 6×8. Garden sizes (products) can vary across the class to differentiate for varying skill levels, or they can be the same. Ask students to find all of the different ways to make a single slice or cut through the garden to divide the plot for the two different vegetables. For each slice, students write an equation. For a slice that results in one row of 8, students would write $6 \times 8 = (5 \times 8) + (1 \times 8)$. The individual equations can be written in the arrays as is shown in Figure 9.14. Although the CCSS suggests grade five students learn about the use of grouping symbols such as parentheses, the full discussion of the order of operations is in the sixth grade (6.EE.A.2c).

Why Not Division by Zero?. Sometimes children are simply told, "Division by zero is not allowed," often because teachers do not fully know how to explain this concept (Quinn, Lamberg, & Perrin, 2008). Some children harbor misconceptions that the answer should be either zero or the number itself. To avoid an arbitrary rule, pose problems to be modeled that involve zero: "Take 30 counters. How many sets of 0 can be made?" or "Put 12 blocks in 0 equal groups. How many are in each group?" or "Can you show me how to share 5 oranges with 0 children?" Then move students toward reasoned explanations (Crespo & Nicol, 2006) that consider the inverse relationship of multiplication and division and take the answer and put it back into a multiplication problem as a check. Then, with the orange problem you would ask, "What when multiplied by 0 produces an answer of 5?" Right, there is no answer. If you have students think of it as repeated subtraction, they would take 0 from the original 5 oranges, leaving 5 and so forth. Therefore, division by 0 is undefined; it just doesn't make sense when we use our definition of division and its inverse relationship to multiplication.

 Complete Self-Checks 9.4b and 9.5: Teaching Multiplication and Division

 # Strategies for Solving Contextual Problems

We have suggested the use of contextual problems or story problems to help children develop meanings for multiplication and division. But often students are at a loss for what to do. Also, struggling readers or ELL students may need support in understanding the problem. In this section, you will learn some techniques for helping them.

Analyzing Context Problems

Consider the following problem:

In building a road through a neighborhood, workers filled in large holes in the ground with dirt brought in by trucks. 638 truckloads of dirt were required to completely fill the holes. The average truck carried $6\frac{1}{4}$ cubic yards of dirt, which weighed 7.3 tons. How many tons of dirt were used to fill the holes?

Typically, in fifth-grade textbooks, problems of this type are found as part of a series of problems revolving around a single context or theme. Data may be found in a graph or chart, or perhaps a short news item or story. Students may have difficulty deciding on the correct operation and are often challenged to identify the appropriate data for solving the problem. Sometimes they will find two numbers in the problem and guess at the correct operation. Instead, students need tools for analyzing problems. At least two strategies can be taught that are very helpful: (1) thinking about the answer before solving the problem, or (2) working a simpler problem.

Think about the Answer before Solving the Problem. Students who struggle with solving word problems need to spend adequate time thinking about the problem and what it is about. In addition, ELLs need to comprehend both the contextual words (like *dirt*, *filled*, and *road*) and the mathematical terminology (*cubic yards*, *weighed*, *tons*, *how many*). Instead of rushing in and beginning to do calculations (believing that "number crunching" is what solves problems), they should spend time talking about (and, later, thinking about) what the answer might look like. In fact, one great strategy for differentiation is to pose the problem with the numbers missing or covered up. This eliminates the tendency to number crunch. For our sample problem given above, it might look like this:

What is happening in this problem? Some trucks were bringing dirt to fill up holes.

Is there any extra information we don't need? We don't need to know about the cubic yards in each truck.

What will the answer tell us? It will give us how many tons of dirt were needed to fill the holes. The answer will be some number of tons.

Will that be a small number of tons or a large number of tons? Well, there were 7.3 tons on each truck, but there were a lot of trucks, not just one. It's probably going to be a lot of tons.

About how many tons do you think it will be? If there were 1000 trucks, it would be 7300 tons. So it will be less than that. But it will be more than half of 7300, so the answer is more than 3650 tons.

Standards for Mathematical Practice

MP1. Make sense of problems and persevere in solving them.

In this type of discussion, three things are happening. First, children are focusing on the problem and the meaning of the answer instead of on numbers. The numbers are not important in thinking about the structure of the problem. Second, with a focus on the structure of the problem, children identify the numbers that are important as well as numbers that are not important. Third, the thinking leads to a rough estimate of the answer and the unit of the answer (tons in this case). In any event, thinking about what the answer tells and about how large it might be is a useful starting point.

Work a Simpler Problem.   The reason that models are rarely used with problems such as the dirt problem is that the large numbers are very challenging to model. Distances in thousands of miles and time in minutes and seconds—data likely to be found in the upper grades—are sometimes difficult to model. The general problem solving strategy of "try a simpler problem" can almost always be applied to problems with unwieldy numbers.

A simpler-problem strategy has the following steps:

1. Substitute small whole numbers for all relevant numbers in the problem.
2. Model the problem (with counters, drawings, number lines, bar diagrams, or arrays) using the new numbers.
3. Write an equation that solves the simpler version of the problem.
4. Write the corresponding equation, substituting back the original numbers.
5. Calculate!
6. Write the answer in a complete sentence, and decide whether it makes sense.

Figure 9.15 shows how the dirt problem might be made simpler. It also shows an alternative in which only one of the numbers is made smaller and the other number is illustrated symbolically. Both methods are effective.

The idea is to provide tools children can use to analyze a problem instead of just guessing which computation to use. It is much more useful to have students do a few problems in which they must use a model or a drawing to justify their solution than to give them a lot of problems in which they guess at a solution but don't use reasoning and sense making.

Caution: Avoid Relying on the Key Word Strategy!   It is often suggested that students should be taught to find "key words" in story problems to use to decide whether to add, subtract, multiply, or divide. Some children are encouraged to use lists of key words with the corresponding operation linked to the word. For example, "altogether" and "in all" mean you should add, and "left" and "fewer" indicate you should subtract. The word "each" suggests multiplication. To some extent, the overly simple and formulaic story problems sometimes found

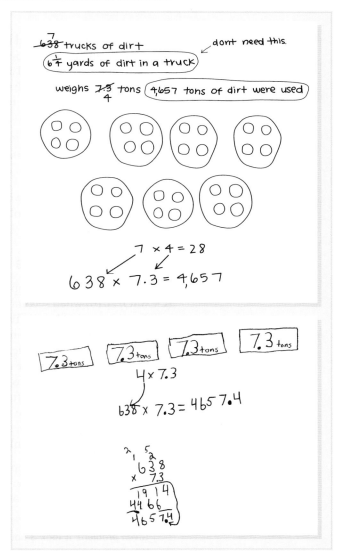

FIGURE 9.15   Two ways students created a simpler problem.

in textbooks reinforce this approach (Sulentic-Dowell, Beal, & Capraro, 2006). When problems are written in this way, it may appear that the key word strategy is effective.

In contrast with this belief, researchers and mathematics educators have long cautioned against the strategy of key words (e.g., Clement & Bernhard, 2005; Kenney, Hancewicz, Heyer, Metsisto, & Tuttle, 2005; Sowder, 1988). Here are four arguments against relying on the key word approach:

1. The key word strategy sends a terribly wrong message about doing mathematics. The most important approach to solving any contextual problem is to analyze it and make sense of it using all the words. The key word approach encourages children to ignore the meaning and structure of the problem and look for an easy way out. Mathematics is about reasoning and making sense of situations. Sense-making strategies always work!

2. Key words are often misleading. Many times, the key word or phrase in a problem suggests an operation that is incorrect. The following problem shared by Drake and Barlow (2007) demonstrates this possibility:

> There are three boxes of chicken nuggets on the table. Each box contains six chicken nuggets. How many chicken nuggets are there in all? (p. 272)

Drake and Barlow found that a student generated the answer of 9, using the words "how many in all" as a suggestion to add 3 + 6. Instead of making sense of the situation, the key word approach was used as a shortcut in making a decision about which operation to select.

3. Many problems do not have key words. A large percentage of problems have no key words. A student who has been taught to rely on key words is then left with no strategy. Here's an example:

> Aidan has 28 goldfish. Twelve are orange and the rest are yellow. How many goldfish are yellow?

4. Key words don't work with two-step problems or more advanced problems, so using this approach on simpler problems sets students up for failure, as they are not learning how to read for meaning.

Multistep Problems

Two-step word problems appear for the first time in the Common Core State Standards (CCSSO, 2010) when second-graders are expected to solve two-step addition and subtraction word problems (2.OA.A.1). Two-step word problems in all four operations are part of the third-grade standards (3.OA.D.8) and multistep problems in all four operations with whole numbers are expected in fourth grade, including problems with remainders that must be interpreted (4.OA.A.3). Fifth-graders use multistep problems with measurement scenarios (5.MD.A.1), and of course, multistep problems continue with a variety of numbers and contexts in middle school and beyond. Yet, children often have difficulty with problems with more than one step. First, be sure children can analyze the structure of one-step problems in the way that we have discussed. The following ideas, adapted from Huinker (1994), are designed to help students see how two problems can be linked together to help think about multistep problems.

1. Give students a one-step problem and have them solve it. Before discussing the answer, have the students use the answer to the first problem to create a second problem. The rest of the class can then be asked to solve the second problem, as in the following example:

> *Given problem:* It took 3 hours for the Morgan family to drive the 195 miles to Washington, D.C. What was their average speed?
>
> *Second problem:* The Morgan children remember crossing the river at about 10:30 a.m., or 2 hours after they left home. About how many miles from home is the river?

2. Make a "hidden question." Repeat the approach above by giving groups different one-step problems. Have them solve the first problem and write a second problem. Then they should write a single combined problem that leaves out the question from the first problem. That question from the first problem is the "hidden question," as in this example:

Given problem: Toby bought three dozen eggs for 89 cents a dozen. How much was the total cost?

Second problem: How much change did Toby get back from $5?

Hidden-question problem: Toby bought three dozen eggs for 89 cents a dozen. How much change did Toby get back from $5?

Have other groups identify the hidden question. Because all students are working on a similar task (be sure to mix the operations), they will be more likely to understand what is meant by a *hidden question*.

3. Pose standard two-step problems, and have the students identify and answer the hidden question. Consider this problem:

The Marsal Company bought 275 widgets wholesale for $3.69 each. In the first month, the company sold 205 widgets at $4.99 each. How much did the company make or lose on the widgets? Do you think the Marsal Company should continue to sell widgets?

Begin by considering the questions that were suggested earlier: "What's happening in this problem?" (*something is being bought and sold at two different prices*). "What will the answer tell us?" (*how much profit or loss there was*). These questions will get you started. If students are stuck, you can ask, "Is there a hidden question in this problem?" While the examples given here provide a range of contexts, using the *same* (and familiar) context across this three-step process would reduce the linguistic demands for ELLs and therefore make the stories more comprehensible—and the mathematics more accessible.

 FORMATIVE ASSESSMENT Notes. One of the best ways to assess knowledge of the meaning of the operations is to have students generate story problems for a given equation or result (Drake & Barlow, 2007; Whitin & Whitin, 2008). Use a diagnostic interview to see whether your students can flexibly think about an operation. Fold a sheet of paper into quarters or use the Translation Task Activity Page based on the work of Shield and Swinson (1996). Give children an expression such as 5×7; ask that they record and answer it in the upper left-hand quarter, write a story problem representing the expression in the upper right quarter, draw a picture (or model) in the lower left section, and describe how they would tell a younger child how to solve this problem in the last section. (For a student with disabilities, the child could dictate the story problem and the description of the solving process while the teacher transcribes.) Students who can ably match scenarios, models, and explanations to the computation will demonstrate their understanding, whereas students who struggle will reveal areas of weakness. Adapt the assessment by giving children the result (e.g., "24 cents") and asking them to write a subtraction problem (or any other appropriate type of problem) that will generate that answer, along with models and word problems written in the remaining quarters. Another option is to use the context from a piece of children's literature to create a word problem that emphasizes the meaning of one of the four operations; each student then has to complete the other three sections. ■

✓ **Complete Self-Check 9.6: Strategies for Solving Contextual Problems**

REFLECTIONS ON CHAPTER 9

WRITING TO LEARN

1. Make up a compare story problem. Alter the problem to provide examples of all six different possibilities for compare problems.
2. Describe some problem types that are often difficult for children. What could be the reasons for this difficulty?
3. Make up multiplication story problems to illustrate the difference between equal groups and multiplicative comparison. Then create a story problem involving rates, area or arrays.
4. Describe a few properties of multiplication and division, and explain how you will introduce them to students.

FOR DISCUSSION AND EXPLORATION

- Some research studies have compared the performance of two student groups on word problems on algebraic concepts. One group was only taught the basic operations while the other group was taught algorithms (specific methods) to solve these problems. It was observed that the group with specific algorithms made more errors in solving problems. Which approach should you use and why?
- See how many different story problem structures (including unknowns in all positions) you can find in a textbook. In the primary grades, look for join, separate, part-part-whole, and compare problems. For grades 3 and up, look for multiplicative structures. Are the various problem structures with unknowns in all positions well represented?

RESOURCES FOR CHAPTER 9

LITERATURE CONNECTIONS

There are many books with stories or pictures concerning collections, the purchase of items, measurements, and so on that can be used to pose problems or, better, to stimulate children to invent their own problems. Perhaps the most widely mentioned book in this context is *The Doorbell Rang* by Pat Hutchins (1986). You can check that one out yourself, as well as the following suggestions.

Bedtime Math *Overdeck (2013)*

This book (and accompanying website) is the author's attempt to get parents to incorporate math problems into the nighttime (or daytime) routine. There are three levels of difficulty, starting with problems for "wee ones" (pre-K), "little kids" (K–2), and "big kids" (grade 2 and up). Each set of problems revolves around a high-interest topic such as roller coasters, foods, and animals. Teachers can use these problems in class for engaging students in all four operations.

One Hundred Hungry Ants *Pinczes (1999)* View
One Hundred Angry Ants (https://www.youtube.com/watch?v=kmdSUHPwJtc)

A Remainder of One *Pinczes (2002)*

These two books, written by a grandmother for her grandchild, help students explore multiplication and division.

The first tells the tale of 100 ants on a trip to a picnic. In an attempt to speed their travel, the ants move from a single-file of 100 to two rows of 50, then four rows of 25, and so forth. This story uses visual representation of arrays and students can be given different sizes of ant groups to explore factors and products. The second book describes the trials and tribulations of a parade formation of 25 bugs. As the queen views the rectangular outline of the parading bugs, she notices that 1 bug is trailing behind. The group tries to create different numbers of rows and columns (arrays), but again 1 bug is always a "leftover" (remainder). Students can be given different parade groups and can generate formations that will leave 1, 2, or none out of the group. Watch A Remainder of One (https://www.youtube.com/watch?v=s4zsaoAlMpM).

RECOMMENDED READINGS

Articles

Clement, L., & Bernhard, J. (2005). A problem solving alternative to using key words. *Mathematics Teaching in the Middle School, 10*(7), 360–365.

This article explores the use of sense making in solving word problems as a replacement for using a key word strategy. The emphasis is on the meanings of the operations as common student misconceptions are analyzed.

Sullivan, A. D., & Roth McDuffie, A. (2009). Connecting multiplication to contexts and language. *Teaching Children Mathematics, 15*(8), 502–512.

This article examines a way to give meaning to multiplication by avoiding the word times *and moving toward collective nouns (e.g., a pride of lions); the students (including students with disabilities) explored photos of real-world groupings and created their own word problems.*

Books

Carpenter, T. P., Fennema, E., Franke, M. L., Levi, L., & Empson, S. (2014). *Children's mathematics: Cognitively guided instruction.* (2nd Edition) Portsmouth, NH: Heinemann.

This is the classic book for understanding word-problem structures for all operations. The structures are explained in detail along with methods for using these problems with students. Videos of classrooms and children modeling strategies are included.

Caldwell, J., Kobett, B., & Karp, K. (2014). *Putting essential understanding of addition and subtraction into practice in grades prekindergarten–2.* Reston, VA: NCTM.

Lannin, J., Chval, K, & Jones, D.. (2013). *Putting essential understanding of multiplication and division into practice in grades 3–5.* Reston, VA: NCTM.

These two books offer the big ideas about how to teach the four operations, including the mathematical content teachers need to know and connections to topics that come before and after these critical ideas.

10

Developing Basic Fact Fluency

LEARNER OUTCOMES

After reading this chapter and engaging in the embedded activities and reflections, you should be able to:

10.1 Describe the phases for developing fluency of the basic facts.

10.2 Contrast different approaches to teaching basic facts, including effective teaching and assessment practices.

10.3 Illustrate strategies for helping students derive addition, subtraction, multiplication, and division facts.

10.4 Describe strategies for reinforcing and remediating basic fact mastery.

Basic facts for addition and multiplication are the number combinations where both addends or both factors are less than 10. Basic facts for subtraction and division are the corresponding combinations. Thus, $15 - 8 = 7$ is a subtraction fact because the corresponding addition parts are less than 10. The goal with basic facts is to develop **fluency.** The Common Core State Standards (CCSSO, 2010) describe this as students being able to (1) flexibly, (2) accurately, (3) efficiently, and (4) appropriately solve problems. Teachers plan their instruction for learning basic facts around "big ideas" related to developing fluency.

 BIG IDEAS

- Students move through three phases in developing fluency with basic facts: counting, reasoning strategies, and mastery (Baroody, 2006). Instruction and assessment must help students through these phases without rushing them.

- Number relationships provide the foundation for strategies that help students remember basic facts. For example, knowing how numbers are related to 5 and 10 helps students master facts such as $3 + 5$ (think of a ten-frame) and $8 + 6$ (because 8 is 2 away from 10, take 2 from 6 to make $10 + 4 = 14$).

- When students are not fluent with the basic facts, they often need to drop back to earlier phases; more drill is not the answer.

Developmental Phases for Learning the Basic Facts

Developing fluency of addition and subtraction concepts begins in kindergarten and continues through grade 2, when students must know their addition facts from memory (i.e., have mastered the facts). Similarly, fluency with multiplication begins in grade 2, with knowing the facts from memory being a goal by the end of grade 3 (CCSSO, 2010).

Developing fluency with basic facts is a developmental process—just like every topic in this book! Flash cards and timed tests are *not* the best way to develop fluency. Instead, focus on number sense (the four components of fluency). Research indicates that early number sense predicts school success more than other measures of cognition, like verbal, spatial, or memory skills or reading ability (Jordan, Kaplan, Locuniak, & Ramineni, 2007; Locuniak & Jordan, 2008; Mazzocco & Thompson, 2005).

Students progress from counting to eventually "just knowing" that $2 + 7$ is 9 or that 5×4 is 20. This developmental progression takes time and many experiences. Arthur Baroody, a mathematics educator who does research on basic facts, describes three phases of learning facts (2006, p. 22):

> *Phase 1: Counting strategies*: Using object counting (e.g., blocks or fingers) or verbal counting to determine the answer. (Example: $4 + 7 = $ ___. Student starts with 7 and counts on verbally 8, 9, 10, 11.)
>
> *Phase 2: Reasoning strategies*: Using known information to logically determine an unknown combination. (Example: $4 + 7$. Student knows that $3 + 7$ is 10, so $4 + 7$ is one more, 11.)
>
> *Phase 3: Mastery:* Producing answers efficiently (quickly and accurately). (Example: $4 + 7$. Student quickly responds, "It's 11; I just know it.")

Figure 10.1 outlines the developmental methods for solving basic addition and subtraction problems.

Phase 1 is primarily addressed in Chapters 8 and 9. This chapter elaborates on Phase 2 and Phase 3.

	Addition	**Subtraction**
Counting	Direct modeling (counting objects and fingers) • Counting all • Counting on from first • Counting on from larger Counting abstractly • Counting all • Counting on from first • Counting on from larger	Counting objects • Separating from • Separating to • Adding on Counting fingers • Counting down • Counting up Counting abstractly • Counting down • Counting up
Reasoning	Properties • $\alpha + 0 = \alpha$ • $\alpha + 1 = $ next whole number • Commutative property Known-fact derivations (e.g., $5 + 6 = 5 + 5 + 1$; $7 + 6 = 7 + 7 - 1$) Redistributed derived facts (e.g., $7 + 5 = 7 + (3 + 2) = (7 + 3) + 2 = 10 + 2 = 12$)	Properties • $\alpha - 0 = \alpha$ • $\alpha - 1 = $ previous whole number Inverse/complement of known addition facts (e.g., $12 - 5$ is known because $5 + 7 = 12$) Redistributed derived facts (e.g., $12 - 5 = (7 + 5) - 5 = 7 + (5 - 5) = 7$)
Retrieval	Retrieval from long-term memory	Retrieval from long-term memory

FIGURE 10.1   The developmental process for basic fact mastery for addition and subtraction.

Source: Henry, V. J., & Brown, R. S. (2008). "First-Grade Basic Facts: An Investigation into Teaching and Learning of an Accelerated, High-Demand Memorization Standard." *Journal for Research in Mathematics Education, 39*(2), p. 156.

FORMATIVE ASSESSMENT Notes. When are students ready to work on reasoning strategies? When they are able to (1) use counting-on strategies (start with the largest and count up) and (2) see that numbers can be decomposed (e.g., that 6 is 5 + 1). Interview students by posing one-digit addition problems and ask how they solved it. For example, 3 + 8 (Do they count on from the larger?) and 5 + 6 (Do they see 5 + 5 + 1?). For multiplication, 3 × 8 (Do they know this is 3 eights? Do they see it as 2 eights and one more eight?). ■

 Complete Self-Check 10.1: Developmental Phases for Learning the Basic Facts

Teaching and Assessing the Basic Facts

This section describes the different ways basic fact instruction has been implemented in schools, followed by a section describing effective strategies.

Different Approaches to Teaching the Basic Facts

Over the last century, three main approaches have been used to teach the basic facts. The pros and cons of each approach are briefly discussed in this section.

Memorization. This approach moves from presenting concepts of addition and multiplication straight to memorization of facts, not devoting time to developing strategies (Baroody, Bajwa, & Eiland, 2009). This approach requires students to memorize 100 separate addition facts (just for the addition combinations 0–9) and 100 multiplication facts (0–9). Students may even have to memorize subtraction and division separately—bringing the total to over 300 isolated facts! There is strong evidence that this method simply does not work. You may be tempted to respond that you learned your facts in this manner; however, as long ago as 1935 studies concluded that students develop a variety of strategies for learning basic facts in spite of the amount of isolated drill that they experience (Brownell & Chazal, 1935).

A memorization approach does not help students develop strategies that could help them master their facts. Baroody (2006) points out three limitations:

- *Inefficiency.* There are too many facts to memorize.
- *Inappropriate applications.* Students misapply the facts and don't check their work.
- *Inflexibility.* Students don't learn flexible strategies for finding the sums (or products) and therefore continue to count by ones.

Notice that a memorization approach works against the development of *fluency* (which includes being able to flexibly, accurately, efficiently, and appropriately solve problems). According to CCSS-M, students should have fluency with addition and subtraction facts (0–9) by the end of second grade and fluency with multiplication and division facts by the end of third grade (CCSSO, 2010). Compare grade-level standards at www.corestandards.org/math.

When taught basic facts via memorization, many struggling learners and students with disabilities continue to use counting strategies because they have not had explicit instruction on reasoning strategies (Mazzocco et al., 2008). In addition, drill can cause unnecessary anxiety and undermine student interest and confidence in mathematics.

Explicit Strategy Instruction. For more than three decades, explicit strategy instruction has been used in many classrooms. Students learn a strategy (e.g., combinations of 10). Students then explore and practice the strategies (e.g., using a ten-frame to see which facts equal 10). Research supports the use of explicit strategy instruction as effective in helping all students learn (and remember) their basic facts (e.g., Baroody, 1985; Bley & Thornton, 1995; Fuson, 1984, 1992; Rathmell, 1978; Thornton & Toohey, 1984).

Explicit strategy instruction is intended to *support* student thinking rather than give the students something new to remember. It is not effective to just memorize (for the same reason that memorizing isolated facts doesn't work). A heavy focus on memorizing strategies results in students with lower number sense (Henry & Brown, 2008). The key is to help students see the possible strategies and then *choose* one that helps them solve the problem without counting. For example, seeing that 6 × 8 can be partitioned into (5 × 8) + (1 × 8). This chapter focuses heavily on strategies for learning the basic facts.

Guided Invention. Guided invention also focuses on strategies, but in a more open-ended manner. It is focused on having students select a strategy based on their knowledge of number relationships (Gravemeijer & van Galen, 2003).

A teacher might post the fact 6 + 7. One student may think of 6 + 7 as "double 6 is 12 and one more is 13." Another student sees it as 7 + 3 (to make 10) and then 3 more. Another student may take 5 from each addend to make 10 and then add the remaining 1 and 2. The key is that each student is using number combinations and relationships that make sense to them.

In *guided invention* the teacher may not explain a strategy, but carefully set up tasks where students notice number relationships. For example, in the 6 + 7 task, the teacher might ask students to place counters in two ten-frames and then think of different ways they can visually move the counters to combine the frames.

> **CCSS** **Standards for Mathematical Practice**
> **MP7.** Look for and make use of structure.

Teaching Basic Facts Effectively

Plan experiences that help students move through the three phases. In discussing student strategies, focus student attention on the methods that move students from phase 1 to phase 2. For example, ask students how they solved 7 + 4. Some will have used counting on (phase 1). Others will use the Making 10 strategy (7 + 3 is 10 and 1 more equals 11). Help the students who are counting on to see the connections to Making 10. To move from phase 2 to recall, continue to provide engaging and diverse experiences where students are using and talking about their strategies. Students will become quicker and eventually will "just know" more and more facts.

Use Story Problems. Research has found that when a strong emphasis is placed on solving problems, students not only become better problem solvers but also master more basic facts than students in a drill program (National Research Council, 2001). Story problems provide context that can help students understand the situation and apply flexible strategies for doing computation.

Some teachers are hesitant to use story problems with English language learners (ELLs) or students with disabilities because of the additional language or reading required, but because language supports understanding, story problems are important for all students. For addition, to work on the Making 10 strategy, you might use this story:

> **CCSS** **Standards for Mathematical Practice**
> **MP1.** Make sense of problems and persevere in solving them.

Rachel had 9 toy ponies in one barn and 6 ponies in another barn. How many ponies did she have altogether?

⏸ Pause & Reflect

How does this problem increase the likelihood that students will develop the Making 10 strategy? ●

The numbers and situation in this story lend to thinking of 9 + 6 as equivalent to 10 + 5 (one pony could be moved to the other barn).

Multiplication stories can focus on array situations. Arrays help students see how to decompose a fact (splitting the rows) and see the commutative property (e.g., 3 × 7 = 7 × 3). For example, consider that a class is working on the 7 facts. The teacher points to the calendar (an array) and poses the following question:

In 3 weeks we will be going to the zoo. How many days until we go to the zoo?

Standards for Mathematical Practice

MP3. Construct viable arguments and critique the reasoning of others.

Suppose that Aidan explains how she figured out 3×7 by starting with double 7 (14) and then adding 7 more. Ask students to explain what Aidan did and why it works.

Explore if doubling could be used for other 7s facts. Ask, "How might doubling help us figure out how many days in 4 weeks (4×7)? Give students time to work in small groups on this question. Students can discover how to think of a single fact as a combination of facts (e.g., that 4×7 is $2 \times (2 \times 7)$ or 7 doubled and doubled again), applying important properties of multiplication. Posing strategy-focused questions followed by a brief discussion of the strategies that students used can improve student accuracy and efficiency with basic facts (Rathmell, Leutzinger, & Gabriele, 2000).

Explicitly Teach Reasoning Strategies. In addition to using story situations, explicitly teach reasoning strategies. A lesson may examine a collection of facts for which a particular strategy is appropriate. For example, students must know their Combinations of 10 addition facts before they are ready to learn the facts that result in numbers greater than 10 (so that they can use this strategy). You can give partners a ten-frame and a deck of cards numbered 0 to 10. One student draws a card and places that many counters on the ten-frame. Without counting, their partner tells how many more to fill the frame (i.e., equal 10). Discuss how to figure out combinations that equal 10. Use other games and activities to be sure all students know their Combinations of 10.

The "big idea" behind teaching reasoning strategies is for students to make use of *known facts* and relationships to *derive unknown facts*. Students might use one of their Combinations of 10 strategies, like $7 + 3$, to solve an unknown fact, like $7 + 5$, noticing that $7 + 5 = 7 + 3 + 2$. Keep this "big idea" in mind as you review each of the reasoning strategies described in this section. Visit the companion website to watch how Connor, Myrna, and Miguel use known facts to solve $6 + \_\_\_ = 13$.

Don't expect to have a strategy introduced and understood with just one lesson or activity. Students need lots of opportunities to make a strategy their own. Start with the most basic strategies and build from there. Plan many activities and make games and interactive activities part of daily work at school and home.

It is a good idea to display reasoning strategies for students to reference. Give the strategies names that make sense so that students know when to apply them (e.g., "Strategy for $\times$ 3s: Double and add one more set. Ex: $3 \times 7 = (2 \times 7) + 7 = 14 + 7 = 21$").

Assessing Basic Facts Effectively

A glance back at Chapter 5 will illustrate many formative assessment strategies: observations, interviews, performance tasks, and writing. Why do we use these strategies? To figure out what students know and what they do not know so that we can design instruction. Why, then, is assessment of basic facts often limited to timed tests? We must do better if we are going to ensure that all students learn their basic facts.

What Is Wrong with Timed Tests? First, timed tests do not assess the four elements of fluency. You gain no insights into which strategies students are using, nor if they are flexible in using those strategies. You have a little insight into how efficient they are, but you don't really know much here either, because they might have used very inefficient strategies for some facts while going quickly through others. So, at best, you get a sense of which facts they are getting correct (accuracy). Second, timed tests negatively affect students' number sense and recall of facts (Boaler, 2012, 2014; Henry & Brown, 2008; Ramirez, Gunderson, Levine, & Beilock, 2013). Third, timed tests are not needed for students to master their facts (Kling, 2011), so they take up time that could be used in meaningful and more palatable learning experiences.

How Might I Assess Basic Fact Fluency? Think about each of the aspects of fluency and ask yourself, "How can I determine if each of my students is able to do that for this set of facts?" Table 10.1 offers a few ideas for each component of fluency (based on Kling & Bay-Williams, 2014).

As you assess, remember there is no one "best" strategy for any fact. For example, $7 + 8$ could be solved using Making 10 or Near-Doubles. The more you emphasize choice, the more

Standards for Mathematical Practice

MP2. Reason abstractly and quantitatively.

TABLE 10.1 EFFECTIVE STRATEGIES FOR ASSESSING BASIC FACT FLUENCY

Aspects of Fluency	Observation	Interview Probes	Writing (Journals or Tests)
Appropriate strategy selection	As they play a game, are they picking a strategy that makes sense for that fact? For example, for 9 + 2 they might count on, but not for 9 + 6.	Nicolas solved 6 + 8 by changing it in his mind to 4 + 10. What did he do? Is this a good strategy? Tell why or why not.	Review the multiplication table. Write which facts are your "toughies." Next to each one, tell a strategy that you want to remember to use.
Flexibility	As for strategy selection, do they pick Making 10 for 9 + 6? Do they notice that 8 × 3 is also 3 × 8?	Solve 6 × 7 using one strategy. Now try solving it using a different strategy.	Explain how you think about these two problems: 13 − 3 = 12 − 9 =
Efficiency	How long does it take to select a strategy? Are they quick to use doubles? Does efficiency vary with certain facts, like facts over 10 (add) or the 7s facts (multiply)?	Go through this stack of cards and sort by the ones you *just know* and the ones you *use a strategy*	Solve these [basic fact] problems (provide a set of 10). If you *just knew* the answer, circle it. If you *used a strategy,* write the strategy's name (e.g., Close Fact).
Accuracy	Which facts are they consistently getting correct?	What is the answer to 7 × 8? How do you know it is correct (how might you check it)?	Review your [3s facts] with your partner. Make a stack of the ones when you were correct and not correct. Record which facts you have "down pat" and which you are still learning.

students will be able to find strategies that work for them, and that will lead to their own fact fluency.

Activity 10.1 is good for assessing students' flexibility and ability to select an appropriate strategy for a fact.

Activity 10.1

CCSS-M: 1.OA.C.6; 2.OA.B.2; 3.OA.B.5; 3.OA.C.7

If You Didn't Know

ENGLISH LANGUAGE LEARNERS

Pose the following task: If you did not know the answer to 8 + 5 (or any fact that you want students to think about), how could you figure it out without counting? Encourage students to come up with more than one way (hopefully using the strategies suggested previously). ELLs and reluctant learners benefit from first sharing their ideas with a partner and then with the class.

The more students are engaged in activities and games, the more chance you have to use observations and interviews to monitor which *strategies* students know and don't know and which *facts* they know and don't know (games are discussed in the Reinforcing Basic Fact Mastery section). Then, you can adapt the games and instruction to address their needs.

 Complete Self-Check 10.2: Teaching and Assessing the Basic Facts

 # Reasoning Strategies for Addition Facts

Recall that basic fact mastery depends on progressing through three phases. The second phase, reasoning strategies, warrants significant attention; too often students are asked to go from counting (phase 1) to memorization (phase 3). Therefore a significant part of this chapter is devoted to what reasoning strategies are important to teach and how to teach them well.

Reasoning strategies for addition facts are directly related to one or more number relationships. In Chapter 8, numerous activities were suggested to develop these relationships. In kindergarten and first grade, significant time should be devoted to decomposing and composing numbers and exploring number combinations (e.g., combinations that equal 5 and combinations that equal 10). In grade 2, students continue to develop reasoning strategies until they know their addition facts from memory. It takes many experiences over many months for students to move from using strategies to just knowing their facts. Note: no memorization needed—just many activities like the one shared here! The first four strategies listed are foundational to the later strategies. Visit the companion website to watch John A. Van de Walle discuss reasoning strategies for addition.

One More Than and Two More Than

Each of the 36 facts highlighted in the following chart has at least one addend of 1 or 2. These facts are a direct application of the one-more-than and two-more-than relationships described in Chapter 8. Being able to count on, then, is a necessary prerequisite to being able to apply this strategy (Baroody et al., 2009).

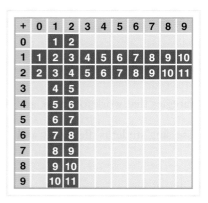

Story problems in which one of the addends is a 1 or a 2 are easy to make up. For example, *Seven children were waiting for the slide. Then 2 more children got in line. How many children were waiting for the slide?* Ask different students to explain how they got the answer of 9. Some will count on from 7. Some may still need to count 7 and 2 and then count all. Others will say they knew that 2 more than 7 is 9. Helping students see the connection between counting on and adding two will help students move from counting strategies to reasoning strategies.

Activity 10.2

CCSS-M: 1.OA.A.1; 1.OA.C.6; 2.OA.B.2

How Many Feet in the Bed?

Read *How Many Feet in the Bed?* by Diane Johnston Hamm. On the second time through the book, ask students how many more feet are in the bed when a new person gets in. Ask students to record the equation (e.g., 6 + 2) and tell how many. Two less can be considered as family members get out of the bed. Find opportunities to make the connection between counting on two and adding two using a number line or ten-frame. For ELLs, be sure that they know what the phrases "two more" and "two less" mean (and clarify the meaning of *foot*, which is also used for measuring). Acting out with students in the classroom can be a great illustration for both ELLs and students with disabilities.

ENGLISH LANGUAGE LEARNERS

STUDENTS *with* **SPECIAL NEEDS**

The different responses will provide you with a lot of information about students' number sense. As students are ready to use the two-more-than idea without "counting all," they can begin to practice with activities such as the following.

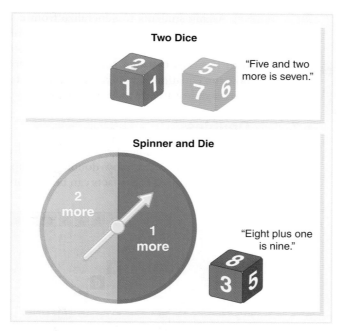

FIGURE 10.2 One-more and two-more activities.

Figure 10.2 illustrates the ideas in Activity 10.3. Notice that activities such as these can be modified for almost all of the strategies in the chapter.

Activity 10.3 CCSS-M: 1.OA.C.5; 1.OA.C.6; 2.OA.B.2

One More Than and Two More Than with Dice and Spinners

Make a die labeled +1, +2, +1, +2, "one more," and "two more." Use with another die labeled 3, 4, 5, 6, 7, and 8 (or whatever values students need to practice). After each roll of the dice, students should say the complete fact: "Four and two more is six." Alternatively, roll one die and use a spinner with +1 on one half and +2 on the other half. For students with disabilities, you may want to start with a die that just has +1 on every side and then another day move on to a +2 die. This will help emphasize and practice one approach. Similarly, in Expanded Lesson Two More Than/Two Less Than, students use dot cards to connect the idea of more and less to adding and subtracting.

STUDENTS *with* **SPECIAL NEEDS**

Adding Zero

Nineteen addition facts have zero as one of the addends. Though adding 0 is generally easy, some students overgeneralize the idea that answers to addition problems are bigger than the addends. They also may have a harder time when the 0 comes first (e.g., $0 + 8$). Use story problems involving zero and use drawings that show two parts with one part empty.

+	0	1	2	3	4	5	6	7	8	9
0	0	1	2	3	4	5	6	7	8	9
1	1									
2	2									
3	3									
4	4									
5	5									
6	6									
7	7									
8	8									
9	9									

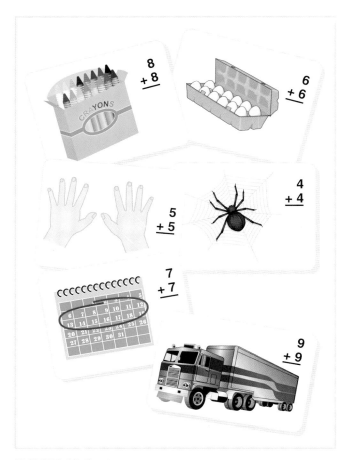

FIGURE 10.3 Situations for doubles facts.

Asking students to generalize from a set of problems is a good way to reinforce reasoning and avoid overgeneralization. You can write about 10 zero facts on the board, some with the zero first and some with the zero second. Discuss how the equations are alike. Ask students to create their own stories and/or to illustrate the problems.

Doubles

There are ten doubles facts from $0 + 0$ to $9 + 9$, as shown here. Students often know doubles, perhaps because of their rhythmic nature. These facts can be anchors for other facts.

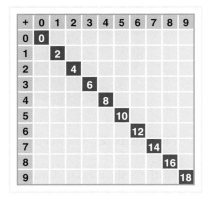

Students with disabilities or difficulties with memorizing can benefit from picture cards for each of the doubles, as shown in Figure 10.3. Story problems can focus on pairs of like addends: "Alex and Zack each found 7 seashells at the beach. How many did they find together?"

Activity 10.4
CCSS-M: 1.OA.C.5; 1.OA.C.6; 2.OA.B.2

Double Magic

A double machine is a fun concept for students and a good connection to algebraic thinking. Read *Two of Everything* (Hong, 1993), a Chinese folktale in which a couple (the Haktaks) find a magic pot that doubles everything that goes into it. Use a plastic cauldron (easily purchased around Halloween) or any container. Visit the companion website to access a recording page for students. Make a set of cards with an "input number" on the front side and the double of the number on the reverse. The card is flipped front to back as it comes out of the pot. You can do this as a whole class, having students write the double on a personal whiteboard, or have students work in partners, with one student flipping the card and the other stating the fact.

Activity 10.5
CCSS-M: 1.OA.C.6; 2.OA.B.2

Calculator Doubles

Students work in pairs with a calculator. Students enter the "double maker" ($2\times$) into the calculator. One student says a double—for example, "Seven plus seven." The other student presses 7, says what the double is, and then press $=$ to see the correct double (14) on the display. The students then switch roles and reset the calculator ($2\times$). For ELLs who are just learning English, invite them to say the double in their native language or in both their native language and English. (Note that the calculator is also a good way to practice $+1$ and $+2$ facts.)

ENGLISH LANGUAGE LEARNERS

Combinations of 10

Perhaps the most important strategy for students to know is the combinations that equal 10. It is a foundational fact from which students can derive many facts (Kling, 2011). Consider story situations such as the following and ask students to tell possible answers.

There are ten boys and girls on the bus. How many girls and how many boys might be on the bus?

The ten-frame is a very useful tool for creating a visual image for students.

6 and 4 is 10.

FIGURE 10.4 Combinations of 10 on a ten-frame.

Activity 10.6   CCSS-M: 1.OA.B.4; 1.OA.C.6; 2.OA.B.2

How Much to Equal 10?

Place counters on one Ten-Frame (see Figure 10.4) and ask, "How many more to equal 10?" This activity can be repeated using different start numbers. Eventually, display a blank ten-frame and say a number less than 10. Students start with that number and complete the "10 fact." If you say, "four," they say, "four plus six equals ten." This can be completed as whole class or with students working with a partner. Students who are still in phase 1 of learning the facts (using counting strategies) or students with disabilities may need additional experience or one-on-one time working on this process.

Making 10

All of the basic facts with sums greater between 11 and 20 can be solved by using the Making 10 strategy. Students use their known facts that equal 10 and then add the rest of the number onto 10. For example, to solve $6 + 8$, a student might start with the larger number (8), see that 8 is 2 away from 10; therefore, they take 2 from the 6 to make 10 and then add on the remaining 4 to get 14. Making 10 is also aptly called Break Apart to Make Ten (BAMT) (Sarama & Clements, 2009) and Up over 10 (the CCSS-M uses the phrase Making 10). Listen to student explanations at the companion website as they use the Making 10 strategy.

+	0	1	2	3	4	5	6	7	8	9
0										
1										
2										11
3									11	12
4								11	12	13
5							11	12	13	14
6						11	12	13	14	15
7					11	12	13	14	15	16
8				11	12	13	14	15	16	17
9			11	12	13	14	15	16	17	18

This reasoning strategy is extremely important and is heavily emphasized in high-performing countries (Korea, China, Taiwan, and Japan) where students learn facts sooner and more accurately than U.S. students (Henry & Brown, 2008). Yet this strategy is not emphasized enough in the United States. A study of California first graders found that this strategy contributed more to developing fluency than using doubles (even though using doubles had been emphasized by teachers and textbooks in the study) (Henry & Brown, 2008).

The Making 10 strategy can also be applied to larger numbers. For example, for $28 + 7$, students can make 30, seeing that $28 + 7 = 30 + 5$. Thus, this reasoning strategy deserves significant attention in teaching addition (and subtraction) facts.

Double Ten-Frame (see Blackline Master 15) can help students visualize the Making 10 strategy. For example, cover two ten-frames with a problem, like $6 + 8$. Ask students to visualize moving counters from one frame (e.g., the one with 6 in it) to fill the other ten-frames (e.g., the one with 8). Ask, "How many moved?" "How many remain in the unfilled frame?" After students have found a total, have students share and record the equations. Activities 10.7 and 10.8 are designed for this purpose.

Activity 10.7
CCSS-M: 1.OA.B.3; 1.OA.C.6; 2.OA.B.2

Move It, Move It

This activity is designed to help students see how to go Making 10. Visit the companion website to access the Activity Page for **Move It, Move It** and a mat with Double Ten-Frame (Blackline Master 15). Flash cards are placed next to the ten-frames, or a fact can be given orally. The students cover each frame with counters to represent the problem ($9 + 6$ would mean covering nine places on one frame and six on the other). Ask students to "move it"—to decide a way to move the counters so that they can find the total without counting. Get students to explain what they did and connect to the new equation. For example, $9 + 6$ may have become $10 + 5$ by moving one counter to the first ten-frame. Emphasize strategies that are working for that student (5 as an anchor and/or Combinations of 10 and/or Making 10).

Activity 10.8
CCSS-M: 1.OA.B.3; 1.OA.C.6; 2.OA.B.2

Frames and Facts

Make Little Ten-Frame Cards and display them to the class on a projector. Show an 8 (or 9) card. Place other cards beneath it one at a time as students respond with the total. Have students say aloud what they are doing. For $8 + 4$, they might say, "Take 2 from the 4 and put it with 8 to make 10. Then 10 and 2 left over is 12." Move to harder cards, like $7 + 6$. The activity can be done independently with the little ten-frame cards. Ask students to record each equation, as shown in Figure 10.5. Especially for students with disabilities, highlight how they should explicitly think about filling in the little ten-frame starting with the higher number. Show and talk about how it is more challenging to start with the lower number as a counterexample.

STUDENTS
with
SPECIAL
NEEDS

Frames and Facts

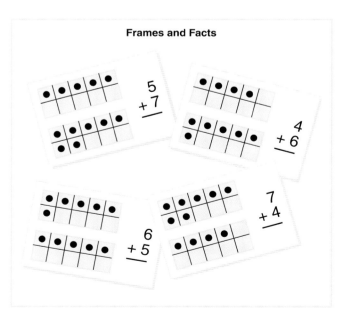

FIGURE 10.5 Frames and facts activity.

Using 5 as an Anchor

The use of an anchor (5 or 10) is a reasoning strategy that builds on students' knowledge of number relationships and is therefore a great way to both reinforce number sense and learn the basic facts. Using 5 as an anchor means looking for fives in the numbers in the problem. For example, in $7 + 6$, a student may see that 7 is $5 + 2$ and that 6 is $5 + 1$. The student would add $5 + 5$ and then the extra 2 from the 7 and the extra 1 from the 6, adding up to 13.

The ten-frames discussed in Chapter 8 can help students see numbers as 5 and some more. And because the ten-frame is a visual model, it may be a strategy that visual learners and students with disabilities find particularly valuable.

Near-Doubles

Near-doubles are also called "doubles-plus-one" or "doubles-minus-one" facts and include all combinations where one addend is one more or less than the other. This is a strategy that uses a known fact to derive an unknown fact. The strategy

Activity 10.9

CCSS-M: 1.OA.B.3; 1.OA.C.5; 1.OA.C.6; 2.OA.B.2

Flash

Project a Double Ten-Frame (Blackline Master 15) on the board. Without letting students see, place counters on each—for example, six on one and seven on the other—so that the top row is full (five counters) and the extras are in the next row of each ten-frame. Flash (uncover) for about three to five seconds and recover. Ask students how many counters they saw. Then uncover and have students explain how they saw it. You can also have students use the Little Ten-Frames to do this activity with partners.

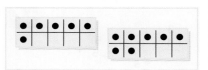

is to double the smaller number and add 1 or to double the larger and then subtract 1. Therefore, students must know their doubles before they can work on this strategy.

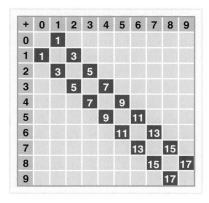

To introduce near-doubles, write a doubles fact and a near-doubles fact right under it, as illustrated here.

$$5 + 5$$
$$5 + 6$$

Ask students how the first equation might help them solve the second equation. Activity 10.10 elaborates on this idea.

Activity 10.10

CCSS-M: 1.OA.B.3; 1.OA.C.6; 2.OA.B.2

On the Double!

Create a display (on the board or on paper) that illustrates the doubles (see Figure 10.6). Prepare cards with near-doubles (e.g., 4 + 5). Ask students to find the doubles fact that could help them solve the fact they have on the card and place it on that spot. Ask students if there are other doubles that could help.

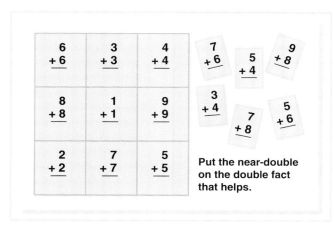

FIGURE 10.6 Near-doubles fact activity.

Near-doubles can be more difficult for students to recognize and therefore may not be a strategy that all students find useful. In that case, do not force it.

 Complete Self-Check 10.3a: Reasoning Strategies for Addition Facts

Reasoning Strategies for Subtraction Facts

Subtraction facts prove to be more difficult than addition. This is especially true when students have been taught subtraction through a "count-count-count" approach; for $13 - 5$, *count* 13, *count* off 5, *count* what's left. As discussed earlier in the chapter, counting is the first phase in reaching basic fact mastery.

Figure 10.1 at the beginning of the chapter lists the ways students might subtract, moving from counting to mastery. Without opportunities to learn and use reasoning strategies, students continue to rely on counting strategies to come up with subtraction facts, a slow and often inaccurate approach. Therefore, spend sufficient time working on the reasoning strategies outlined here to help students move to phase 2 and eventually on to mastery (phase 3).

Think-Addition

As the label implies, in this strategy students use known addition facts to produce the unknown quantity or part of the subtraction (see Figure 10.7). If this important relationship between parts and the whole—between addition and subtraction—can be made, subtraction facts will be much easier for students to learn. As with addition facts, it is helpful to begin with facts that have totals of 10 or less (e.g., $8 - 3$, $9 - 7$) before working on facts that have a total (minuend) higher than 10 (e.g., $13 - 4$).

The value of think-addition cannot be overstated; however, if think-addition is to be used effectively, it is essential that addition facts be mastered first. Evidence suggests that students learn very few, if any, subtraction facts without first mastering the corresponding addition facts. In other words, mastery of $3 + 5$ can be thought of as prerequisite knowledge for learning the facts $8 - 3$ and $8 - 5$.

Story problems that promote think-addition are those that sound like addition but have a missing addend: *join, initial part unknown; join, change unknown;* and *part-part-whole, part unknown* (see Chapter 9). Consider this problem:

Janice had 5 fish in her aquarium. Grandma gave her some more fish. Then she had 12 fish. How many fish did Grandma give Janice?

Notice that the action is *join*, which suggests addition. There is a high probability that students will think, "Five and how many more equals 12?" In the discussion in which you use problems such as this, your task is to connect this thought process with the subtraction fact, $12 - 5$. Students may use an Making 10 strategy to solve this, just as they did with addition facts ("It takes 5 to get to 10 and 2 more to 12 is . . . 7").

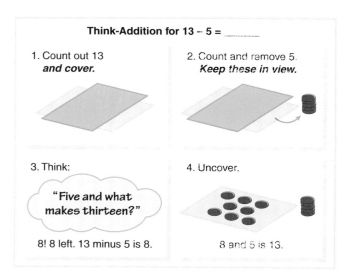

FIGURE 10.7 Using a think-addition for subtraction facts.

Pause & Reflect

Before reading further, look at the three subtraction facts shown here, and reflect on what thought process you use to get the answers. Even if you "just know them," think about what a likely process might be.

$$14 \quad\quad 12 \quad\quad 15$$
$$\underline{-9} \quad\quad \underline{-6} \quad\quad \underline{-6}$$

What stories might you tell that will help students "think addition?" ●

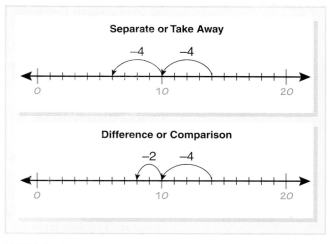

FIGURE 10.8   Down Under 10 illustrated on the number line for 14 – 8.

Down Under 10

There are two ways to think about Down Under 10. The first is to think about it as a "separate" situation. For 14 − 8, the thinking is to first take away 4 to get to 10, then take away 4 more to get the answer of 6. Another way to think about this is as a "comparison," finding the difference" or distance between the two numbers. How far apart are 14 and 8? Jump down 4 to the 10 and two more to the 8—they are 6 apart. These two interpretations are illustrated in Figure 10.8.

Down Under 10 is a derived fact strategy: Students use what they know (that 14 minus 4 is 10) to derive a related fact (14 − 5). Like the Combinations of 10 and Making 10 strategies discussed previously, this strategy is emphasized in high-performing countries but not emphasized enough in the United States (Fuson & Kwon, 1992).

To develop the Down Under 10 strategy, write pairs of facts in which the difference for the first fact is 10 and the second fact is either 8 or 9: 16 − 6 and 16 − 7; 14 − 4 and 14 − 6, and so on. Have students solve each problem and discuss their strategies. If students do not naturally see the relationship, ask them to think about how the first fact can help solve the second. Illustrate on a number line. Use story problems such as these:

Becky walks 16 blocks to school. She has walked 7. How many more blocks does Becky have left? (Separate)

Becky walks 16 blocks to school; Corwin walks 9 blocks. How many more blocks does Becky walk? (Comparison)

Activity 10.11   CCSS-M: 1.OA.B.4; 1.OA.C.6; 2.OA.B.2

Apples in the Trees

Project a Double Ten-Frame (Blackline Master 15) as a display with chips covering the first ten-frame and some of the second (e.g., for 16, cover 10 in the first frame and 6 on the second frame). Tell students some apples have fallen to the ground—you will tell them how many and they will tell you how many are still in the trees. Repeat the activity, asking students to explain their thinking. For ELLs or culturally diverse students, you can change to a context that is familiar or timely.

ENGLISH LANGUAGE LEARNERS

Take from 10

This excellent strategy is not as well known or commonly used in the United States but is consistently used in high-performing countries. It takes advantage of students' knowledge of the combinations that make 10, taking the initial value apart into 10 and ones. This is how it works for $15 - 8$:

(1) Think: 10 + 5
$- 8$

(2) Take from the 10: 10 − 8 = 2

(3) Add 5 back on: 2 + 5 = 7

Try it on these examples:

15 − 8 =   **17 − 9 =**   **14 − 6 =**

If you have students from other countries, they may know this strategy and can share it with others. It can be used for all subtraction facts having minuends greater than 10 (the "toughies") by just knowing how to subtract from 10 and knowing addition facts with sums less than 10.

Activity 10.12

CCSS-M: 1.OA.B.3; 1.OA.B.4; 1.OA.C.6; 2.OA.B.2

Apples in Two Trees

Adapting Activity 10.11, explain that each ten-frame is a different tree. Tell students you will tell them how many apples fall out of the "full" tree and they will tell you how many apples are left (on both trees). Each time, ask students to explain their thinking.

In the discussion of addition and subtraction strategies, you have seen a lot of activities. Activities and games provide a low-stress approach to practicing strategies and working toward fluency. More games and activities for all operations can be found later in this chapter.

 Complete Self-Check 10.3b: Reasoning Strategies for Subtraction Facts

 # Reasoning Strategies for Multiplication and Division Facts

Using a problem-based approach and focusing on reasoning strategies are just as important, if not more so, for developing mastery of the multiplication and related division facts (Baroody, 2006; Wallace & Gurganus, 2005). As with addition and subtraction facts, start with story problems as you develop reasoning strategies.

Understanding the commutative property cuts the basic facts to be memorized in half! For example, a 2×8 array can be described as 2 rows of 8 or 8 rows of 2. In both cases, the answer is 16.

Foundational Facts: 2, 5, 0, 1

For some reason, multiplication is often approached in numerical order (1s, 2s, 3s, . . . up through 9s). (Note: in some settings, multiplications facts go through 10 or even 12, but in the CCSS, basic facts are limited to single-digit factors, which is how they are addressed in this section). A more effective approach is to start with the facts that build on students' strengths and prior knowledge. A good place to start? 2s and 5s! These facts connect to students' experiences with skip counting and addition doubles (Heege, 1985; Kamii & Anderson, 2003; Watanabe, 2006). This work can begin at the end of second grade or at the beginning of third grade. Next, 0s and 1s are foundational facts. Be sure these are understood, not just memorized. The sections here share strategies for helping students learn the foundation facts: 2, 5, 0, and 1. Watch John A. Van de Walle discuss reasoning strategies for multiplication at the companion website.

Twos. Facts that have 2 as a factor are equivalent to the addition doubles and should already be known by students. Help students realize that 2×7 is the same as $7 + 7$. Use story problems in which 2 is the number of sets. Later, use problems in which 2 is the size of the sets, helping students recognize the commutative property of multiplication.

CCSS **Standards for Mathematical Practice**
MP7. Look for and make use of structure.

George was making sock puppets. Each puppet needed 2 buttons for eyes. If George makes 7 puppets, how many buttons will he need for the eyes?

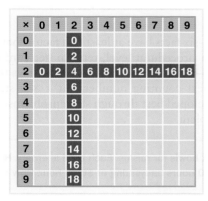

Fives. Practice skip counting by fives. Keep track of how many fives have been counted (If we jump by 5s four times on the number line, where will we land?). Use arrays that have rows with 5 dots. Point out that such an array with six rows is a model for 6×5, eight rows is 8×5, and so on. Time is also a good context for fives because of the way analog clocks are made.

Activity 10.13   CCSS-M: 3.OA.A.1; 3.OA.C.7

Clock Facts

Focus on the minute hand of the clock. When it points to a number, how many minutes after the hour is it? See Figure 10.9(a). Connect this idea to multiplication facts with 5. Hold up a flash card as in Figure 10.9(b), and then point to the number on the clock corresponding to the other factor. In this way, the fives facts become the "clock facts."

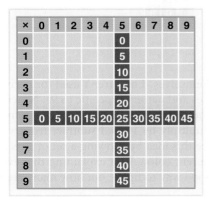

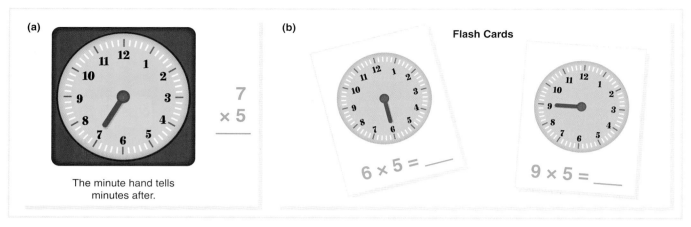

FIGURE 10.9 Using clocks to help learn fives facts.

Zeros and Ones. Thirty-six facts have at least one factor that is either 0 or 1. These facts, though apparently easy on a procedural level, tend to get confused with "rules" that some students learned for addition—for example, the fact $6 + 0$ stays the same, but 6×0 is always zero, or that $1 + n$ is the next counting number, but $1 \times n$ stays the same. The concepts behind these facts can be developed best through story problems. For example, invite students to tell stories to match a problem.

$6 \times 0 =$ ____ . There are six bowls for raisins. Each bowl is empty. How many raisins?

$0 \times 6 =$ ____ . You worked 0 hours babysitting at $6 an hour. How much money did you make?

Avoid rules that aren't conceptually based, such as "Any number multiplied by zero is zero."

Illustrate ones using arrays to show commutativity ($8 \times 1 = 1 \times 8$) and use stories like the ones for zero. With 0 and 1, help students generalize what it means to have $n \times 0$, $0 \times n$, $1 \times n$ and $n \times 1$ without just memorizing these properties.

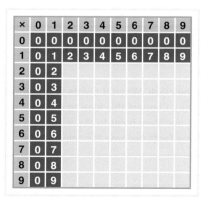

Nifty Nines

CCSS Standards for Mathematical Practice

MP2. Reason abstractly and quantitatively.

Nines are in a category by themselves. They aren't used for deriving the other facts, but there are several reasoning strategies and patterns specific to 9s. Nines can actually be derived from 10s. For example, 7×9 can be found by finding 7×10 and removing one set of 7, or $70 - 7$. Because students often can multiply by 10 and subtract from a decade value, this strategy is effective. You might introduce this idea by showing a set of bars such as those in Figure 10.10 with only the end cube a different color. After explaining that every bar has 10 cubes, ask students if they can think of a good way to figure out how many are yellow.

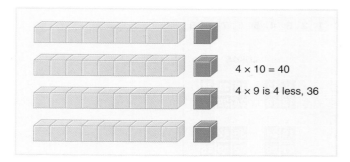

FIGURE 10.10   Using tens to think of the nines.

4 × 10 = 40

4 × 9 is 4 less, 36

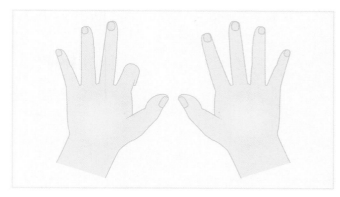

FIGURE 10.11   Nifty nines using fingers to show 4 × 9.

Nines facts have interesting patterns that can help to find the products: (1) the tens digit of the product is one less than the non-nine factor and (2) the sum of the two digits in the product equals 9. For 7 × 9 = 63, the tens digit is one less than 7 and 6 + 3 = 9. Ask students to explore and discover nines patterns and write down patterns they notice.

One less

9 × 7 = 63

Add to 9

×	0	1	2	3	4	5	6	7	8	9
0										0
1										9
2										18
3										27
4										36
5										45
6										54
7										63
8										72
9	0	9	18	27	36	45	54	63	72	81

After discussing all the patterns, ask students how these patterns can be used to figure out a product to a nines fact. Challenge students to think about why this pattern works. (*Warning:* This strategy, grounded in the base-ten system, can be useful, but it also can cause confusion because the conceptual connection is not easy to see.)

A tactile way to help remember the nifty nines is to use fingers—but not for counting. Here's how: Hold up both hands. Starting with the pinky on your left hand, count over for which fact you are doing. For example, for 4 × 9, you move to the fourth finger (your pointer). Bend it down. Look at your fingers: You have three to the left of the folded finger representing 3 tens and six to the right—36! (Barney, 1970). See Figure 10.11.

Derived Multiplication Fact Strategies

The following chart shows the remaining 25 multiplication facts. Notice if students recognize the commutative property, there are only 15 facts to learn. These remaining facts can be learned by using foundational facts. (Note: students must first know their foundational facts!)

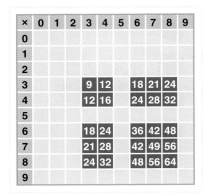

Standards for Mathematical Practice

MP5. Use appropriate tools strategically.

Arrays. Arrays are powerful thinking tools for deriving multiplication facts. Figure 10.12(a) illustrates a Multiplication Array with lines through a 10 by 10 array to show fives (known facts). Students can use this hint to derive multiplication facts. For example, to see 7×7 as $(5 \times 7) + (2 \times 7)$, or $35 + 14$ (Figure 10.12(b)).

There are numerous games that use arrays that can help students derive facts. Activity 10.14 is one example of a game using arrays.

Activity 10.14

CCSS-M: 3.OA.A.1; 3.OA.B.5; 3.OA.C.7

Strive to Derive

You will need Multiplication Array Cards (e.g., for 3s, 4s, 6s, and 9s), a straight thin stick (like uncooked spaghetti), and two dice, one labeled with 3, 3, 6, 6, 9, 9; one with 0, 1, 4, 6, 7, 8. To make Multiplication Array Cards, use 2-Centimeter Grid Paper (Blackline Master 5) and cut out each possible size. In marker, write the product both ways (e.g., cut out a 5-by-6 array and write 5×6 and 6×5 on the array). Spread the cards on the table so they can be seen. Player 1 rolls the dice and selects the related array card. Player 1 then places the stick to partition the array into known facts. If Player 1 rolled a 3 and a 6, she would pick the 3-by-6 array. She can partition it as 2×6 and 1×6 or as 3×5 and 3×1. If Player 1 can solve the fact using a derived fact, she scores 1 point. Return array card to the collection. Player 2 repeats the process. Continue to 10 points. Initially, or to modify for students who struggle, focus on one foundation set of facts, for example, Strive to Derive from 5.

STUDENTS with SPECIAL NEEDS

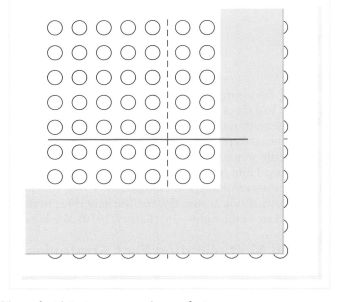

FIGURE 10.12 A multiplication array can illustrate how to partition a fact into two or more known facts.

This game (and others like it) helps students look for known facts in an unknown fact problem. The more they play, the better students become at partitioning unknown facts into known facts.

Doubling. Doubling is a very effective reasoning strategy in helping students learn the difficult facts (Flowers & Rubenstein, 2010/2011). The Double and Double Again strategy shown in Figure 10.13(a) is applicable to all facts with 4 as one of the factors. Remind students that the idea works when 4 is the second factor as well as when it is the first. For 4×8, double 16 is also a difficult addition. Help students with this by noting, for example, that $15 + 15$ is 30, and $16 + 16$ is 2 more, or 32. Adding $16 + 16$ on paper defeats the development of reasoning.

The Double and One More Set strategy shown in Figure 10.13(b) is a way to think of facts with one factor of 3. With an array or a set picture, the double part can be circled, and it is clear that there is one more set. Two facts in this group involve more difficult mental additions: 8×3 and 9×3. Using doubling and one more, you can generate any fact. For the fact 6×7, think of 2×7 (14), then double it to get 4×7 (28), then add two more sets of 7 ($28 + 14 = 42$).

If either factor is even, a Half Then Double strategy as shown in Figure 10.13(c) can be used. Select the even factor and cut it in half. If the smaller fact is known, that product is doubled to get the new fact.

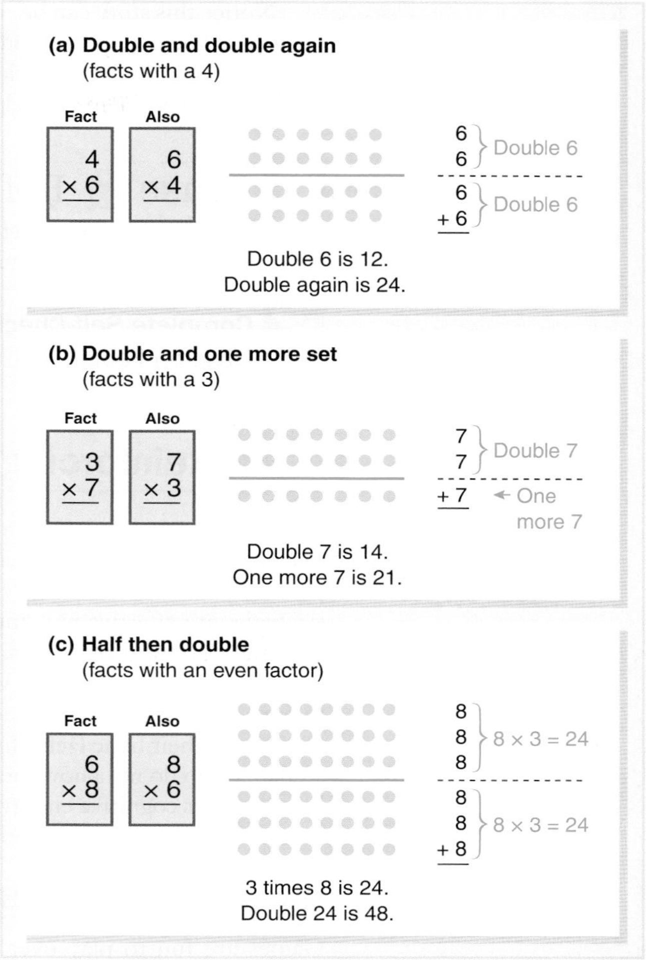

Close Facts. Many students prefer to go to a fact that is "close" and then add one more set to this known fact, as shown in Figure 10.14.

For example, think of 6×7 as 6 sevens. Five sevens is close: That's 35. Add one more seven to get 42. Using set language "5 sevens" is helpful in remembering that one more 7 is needed (not one more 5). This "close" fact reasoning strategy is critically important because it reinforces number sense and it can be used to derive any unknown fact.

Division Facts

Mastery of multiplication facts and connections between multiplication and division are key elements of division fact mastery. For example, to solve $36 \div 4$, we tend to think, "Four times what is thirty-six?" In fact, because of this, the reasoning facts for division are to (1) think multiplication and then (2) apply a multiplication reasoning fact, as needed. Missing factor stories can assist in making this connection.

Analea is creating bags of mini muffins for a bake sale. She puts four in a bag and fills up bags until she has all 36 mini muffins in bags. How many bags did she fill?

(a) Double and double again
(facts with a 4)

Fact   Also

$\begin{array}{c}4\\ \times 6\end{array}$ $\begin{array}{c}6\\ \times 4\end{array}$

6
6 } Double 6
———
6
+ 6 } Double 6

Double 6 is 12.
Double again is 24.

(b) Double and one more set
(facts with a 3)

Fact   Also

$\begin{array}{c}3\\ \times 7\end{array}$ $\begin{array}{c}7\\ \times 3\end{array}$

7
7 } Double 7
———
+ 7 ← One more 7

Double 7 is 14.
One more 7 is 21.

(c) Half then double
(facts with an even factor)

Fact   Also

$\begin{array}{c}6\\ \times 8\end{array}$ $\begin{array}{c}8\\ \times 6\end{array}$

8
8 } $8 \times 3 = 24$
8
———
8
8 } $8 \times 3 = 24$
+ 8

3 times 8 is 24.
Double 24 is 48.

FIGURE 10.13   Using doubles (known facts) to derive unknown facts.

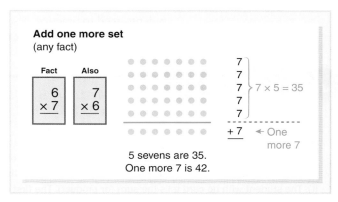

Add one more set
(any fact)

Fact   Also

$\begin{array}{c}6\\ \times 7\end{array}$ $\begin{array}{c}7\\ \times 6\end{array}$

7
7
7 } $7 \times 5 = 35$
7
7
———
+ 7 ← One more 7

5 sevens are 35.
One more 7 is 42.

FIGURE 10.14   Using a close (known) fact to derive an unknown fact.

Notice this story can be represented as 4 × ___ = 36 (missing factor) or as 36 ÷ 4 = ___ (division). The double and double again reasoning strategy can be used to solve the missing factor (What number doubled and doubled again equals 36?). Seeing a situation as both a multiplication and a division problem can help students to think multiplication when encountering division facts.

 Pause & Reflect

Select what you consider a difficult fact to remember and see how many of the derived fact strategies you can use to derive the fact. •

 Complete Self-Check 10.3c: Reasoning Strategies for Multiplication and Division Facts

 Reinforcing Basic Fact Mastery

When students "just know" a fact, or can apply a reasoning strategy so fast they almost don't realize they have done it (e.g., Making 10), they have reached phase 3: mastery. CCSS-M uses the phrase "know from memory" (CCSS0, 2010, pp. 19, 23). Repeated experiences with reasoning strategies are effective in committing facts to memory; memorizing is not. Therefore, games or activities that focus on reasoning strategies are more effective than drilling with flash cards (and more palatable for students). We must use these effective strategies to ensure all students become fluent with facts and abandon long-existing strategies that do not work! If students do not become fluent with their basic facts, they will certainly struggle with multidigit computation. In addition, students who do not know their facts often struggle to understand higher mathematics concepts because their cognitive energy must focus too much on computation when it should be focusing on the more sophisticated concept being developed (Forbringer & Fahsl, 2010).

Games to Support Basic Fact Fluency

Games are fun to play over and over again and therefore are an excellent way to provide repeated experiences for students to learn their facts. Playing games that infuse reasoning strategies helps students be able to flexibly select strategies, decide which strategy is most appropriate for the given problem, and become more efficient and accurate in finding the answer. This is what it takes to become *fluent* with the basic facts! In addition, games increase student involvement, encourage student-to-student interaction, and improve communication—all of which are related to improved academic achievement (Bay-Williams & Kling, 2014; Forbringer & Fahsl, 2010; Kamii & Anderson, 2003; Lewis, 2005).

As you use games, remember to focus on related clusters of facts and on what individual students need to practice. Also, encourage students to self-monitor—they can create their own game board/game, including the facts they are working on (their personal "toughies").

Activity 10.15

CCSS-M: 1.OA.B.4; 1.OA.C.6; 2.OA.B.2; 3.OA.B.5; 3.OA.B.6; 3.OA.C.7

Salute!

Place students in groups of three, and give each group a deck of cards (omitting face cards and using aces as ones). Two students draw a card without looking at it and place it on their forehead facing outward (so the others can see it). The student with no card tells the sum (or product). The first of the other two to correctly say what number is on their forehead "wins" the card set. For ELLs, students with disabilities, and reluctant learners, speed can inhibit participation and increase anxiety. Speed of response can be removed as a variable by having students write down the card they think they have (within five seconds) and getting a point if they are correct. This can be differentiated by including only certain cards (e.g., addition facts using only the numbers 1 through 5).

ENGLISH LANGUAGE LEARNERS

STUDENTS with SPECIAL NEEDS

Activity 10.16

CCSS-M: 1.OA.B.4; 1.OA.C.6; 2.OA.B.2; 3.OA.B.5; 3.OA.B.6; 3.OA.C.7

What's Under My Thumb?

Create a set of circle cards with fact families for each pair of students or have students create their own based on the facts they need to be practicing (see Figure 10.15(a)). You can begin this activity as a whole class and then move to partners. Hold up a card with your thumb over one number. Ask, "What is under my thumb?" Call on a student to share the answer and how they reasoned to get the answer. Place students in partners with their sets of cards and play. Groups can switch decks with other groups for more experiences. Individuals can explore cards like the ones in Figure 10.15(b), with the answer on the back. Alternatively, you can use strips rather than circles (see Figure 10.15(c)).

A Missing-Part Worksheet can be used as a follow-up to Activity 10.16. Fill in two of the three numbers for a set of facts, differentiated for students. An example for addition is shown in Figure 10.16. Have students write an equation for each missing-number card. This is important because students need to connect the missing addend to subtraction.

Table 10.2 offers some ideas for how classic games can be adapted to focus on basic fact mastery (reflects ideas from Forbringer & Fahsl, 2010, and Kamii & Anderson, 2003). Also included are ideas for differentiating the games.

When all facts are learned, continued reinforcement through occasional games and activities is important. Consider the following activity that engages students in creatively applying all four operations.

Standards for Mathematical Practice

MP4. Model with mathematics.

Activity 10.17

CCSS-M: 2.OA.B.2; 3.OA.C.7; 5.OA.A.1

Bowl a Fact

In this activity (suggested by Shoecraft, 1982), you draw circles placed in triangular fashion to look like bowling pins, with the front circle labeled 1 and the others labeled consecutively through 10. Visit the companion website for an activity page that includes lines for recording equations. For culturally diverse classrooms, be sure that students are familiar with bowling. (If they are not, consider showing a YouTube clip or photographs.)

ENGLISH LANGUAGE LEARNERS

Take three dice and roll them. Students use the numbers on the three dice to come up with equations that result in answers that are on the pins. For example, if you roll 4, 2, and 3, they can "knock down" the 5 pin with $4 \times 2 - 3$. If they can produce equations to knock down all 10 pins, they get a strike. If not, roll again and see whether they can knock the rest down for a spare. After doing this with the whole class, students can work in small groups.

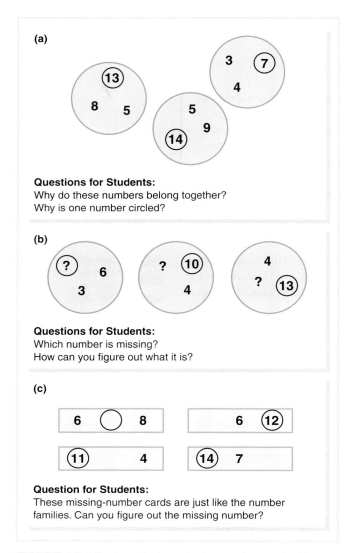

(a)

Questions for Students:
Why do these numbers belong together?
Why is one number circled?

(b)

Questions for Students:
Which number is missing?
How can you figure out what it is?

(c)

Question for Students:
These missing-number cards are just like the number families. Can you figure out the missing number?

FIGURE 10.15 Introducing missing-number cards. Note: These are shown for addition/subtraction but work well for multiplication/division, too.

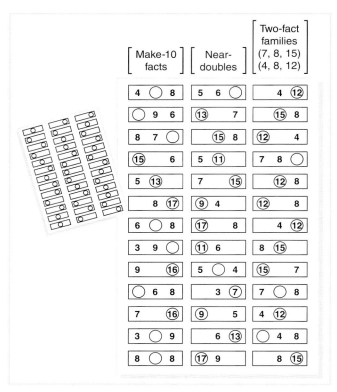

FIGURE 10.16 Example missing-number worksheets. Labels (in brackets) are not included on student pages.

TABLE 10.2   CLASSIC GAMES ADAPTED TO BASIC FACT MASTERY

Classic Game	How to Use It with Basic Fact Mastery	Suggestions for Differentiation
Bingo	Each bingo card has a fact problem (e.g., 2×3) in each box. The same fact will be on multiple bingo cards but in different locations on each card. You will call out an answer (e.g., 6), and the students will find a matching problem (or more than one problem) on their card.	Create bingo boards that focus on different clusters of facts (e.g., doubles or doubles +1 on some boards, and Making 10 on other boards). Be sure that the answers you call out are an even mix of the clusters so that everyone has the same chance to win.
Concentration	Create cards that have a fact problem (e.g., 3×5) on one half and the answers (e.g., 15) on the other half. Shuffle the cards and turn them face-down in a 6×4 grid. (If you like, you can make the grid larger to use more cards.)	Select cards that focus on a particular cluster of facts (e.g., +1 and $\times$ 5 facts) for each round of the game. Multiple groups can play the game simultaneously—each group will use the parts of the deck that contain the facts they are working on. Also, consider making cards that show the ten-frames below the numbers to help provide a visual for students.

(Continued)

TABLE 10.2   *(Continued)*

Classic Game	How to Use It with Basic Fact Mastery	Suggestions for Differentiation
Dominoes	Create (or find online) dominoes that have a fact on one side and an answer (not to that fact) on the other. Each student gets the same number of dominoes (around eight). On his or her turn, they can play one of the dominoes in their hand only if they have an answer or a fact that can connect to a domino on the board.	As with other games, select the dominoes that focus on a particular clusters of facts.
Four in a Row	Create a 6 × 6 square game board with a sum (or product) written on each square. Below, list the numbers 0 through 9. Each of the two players has counters of a different color to use as their game pieces. On the first turn, Player 1 places a marker (paper clip) on two addends/factors and then gets to place his or her colored counter on the related answer. (If you have repeated the same answer on different squares of the board, the player only gets to cover one of them.) Player 2 can only move one paper clip and then gets to place his or her colored counter on the related answer. The first player to get four in a row wins.	Rather than list all the values below the chart, just list the related addends or factors. For example, use 1, 2, 6, 7, 8, 9 if you want to work on +1 and +2, or use 3, 4, 5, 6 if you are working on these multiplication facts.
Old Maid (retitled as Old Dog)	Create cards for each fact and each answer. Add one card that has a picture of an old dog (or use your school mascot). Shuffle and deal cards. On each player's turn, they draw from the person on their right, see whether that card is a match to a card in their hand (a fact and its answer), and, if so, lay down the pair. Then the person to their left draws from them. Play continues until all matches are found and someone is left with the Old Dog. Winner can be the person with (or not with) the Old Dog, or the person with the most pairs.	See Concentration (above).

Source: Based on ideas from Forbringer & Fahsl, 2010, and Kamii & Anderson, 2003.

FORMATIVE ASSESSMENT Notes. As students are engaged in games and activities, interview students to find out whether they are using counting strategies, reasoning strategies, or quick recall. Ask students to tell what strategy they just used. If you observe counting, ask the student to try a reasoning strategy. If many students are counting, more experiences (with ten-frames, for example) are needed. ■

About Drill

Drill—repetitive non-problem-based activity—in the absence of reasoning has repeatedly been demonstrated as ineffective. However, drill can strengthen memory and retrieval capabilities (Ashcraft & Christy, 1995). Drill is only appropriate after students know strategies and have moved from phase 2 to phase 3. Drill should also be low-stress and engaging. The many games and activities in this chapter can continued to be played even after students know the facts from memory. Students will smile when they see cards coming out for another game of *Salute!*

Too often, drill includes too many facts too quickly, and students become frustrated and overwhelmed. Also, students progress at different paces—gifted students tend to be good memorizers, whereas students with intellectual disabilities have difficulty memorizing (Forbringer & Fahsl, 2010). Rather than work on all facts, identify a group of facts (e.g, 3s) and look at patterns within that set. Students can create their own cards with each fact written both ways (e.g., 3 × 7 and 7 × 3), create a dot array, and record the answer on the back. They can work on these at home, with a partner, and keep track of the ones they "just know" and the ones for which they use a strategy.

A plethora of websites and software programs provide opportunities to drill on the basic facts (see Figure 10.17). Though currently none exist that work on strategy development, these programs can support students who are near mastery or maintaining mastery. One disadvantage of most of these sites is that they focus on all the facts at one time. Two exceptions (sites that organize drill by fact family) are *Fun 4 the Brain* and *Math Fact Café*.

 Standards for Mathematical Practice
MP8. Look for and express regularity in repeated reasoning.

Online Resources for Mastery of Basic Math Facts	
Name	**Description**
Fun 4 the Brain: Math Games	This site offers over a dozen games for addition facts and ten for multiplications facts. Pick a game (e.g., Snowy's Friend) and then pick the fact families you would like to explore.
Math Fact Café	Here you will find a lot of downloadable practice: pre-made fact sheets, flashcards, and practice pages, or create your own practice pages, selecting the number of practice problems, the level of difficulties, and which fact families.
NCTM Illuminations *Deep Sea Duel*	Play this applet: The first person to choose a set of digit cards with a specified sum wins. You can choose how many cards, what types of numbers, and the level of strategy.
NCTM Illuminations *Factorize*	In this applet, students visually explore the concept of factors by creating rectangular arrays. Choose your own number or one randomly selected.
NCTM Illuminations *Let's Learn Those Facts*	Six complete lessons for addition facts are provided, including links to resources and student recording sheets.
NCTM Illuminations *Multiplication: It's in the Cards Lessons*	These four lessons, including links to resources and student recording sheets, use the properties of multiplication to help students master the multiplication facts. See also "Six and Seven as Factors."
NCTM Illuminations *The Product Game*	Four lessons provide guidance on using the engaging and effective games "Factor Game" and "Product Game" to help students see the relationship between products and factors.
NCTM's Calculation Nation *Factor Dazzle and Times Square*	These multiplication games are among a number of interactive, fun games to play. Registered players can play against others from all over the world.
BBC *Cross the Swamp*	This British applet asks students to supply a missing operation ($+/-$ or $\times/\div$) and a number to complete an equation (e.g., 4 __ __ = 12). There are five questions in a set, each with three levels of difficulty.
NLVM *Diffy*	Diffy is a classic mathematics puzzle that involves finding the differences of given numbers. Here it is presented as an applet.
IXL Learning	IXL contains interactive practice tools to monitor student progress toward basic fact mastery. Connections with the Common Core State Standards, Department of Defense Education Activity standards, and existing state standards are provided.

FIGURE 10.17 Websites and applets for support in teaching the basic facts.

Fact Remediation

Students who have not mastered their addition facts by third grade or their multiplication facts by fourth grade (or beyond) are in need of interventions that will help them master the facts. More drill is not an intervention! Students who do not know their facts may be stuck back in phase 1 (counting strategies) and likely lack number sense and reasoning strategies (phase 2). Effective remediation first requires figuring out which facts a student knows and which ones he or she does not. Second, effective remediation requires a focus on the three phases—determining where a student is and explicitly teaching reasoning strategies (phase 2) in order to reach mastery (phase 3). Review the ideas offered in the Assessing Basic Facts section to figure out what students do and do not know. Then, use these ideas to help students master all of their facts.

1. *Explicitly teach reasoning strategies.* Students' fact difficulties are due to a failure to develop or connect concepts and relationships such as those that have been discussed in this chapter. They need instruction focused at phase 2, not phase 3. In a remediation program,

students may not have the benefit of class discussion. Share with them strategies that you have "seen other students use." Be certain that they have a conceptual understanding of the strategy and are able to use it.

For example, if a student knows his addition facts within 10, but struggles with the ones that sum to 11–19, then you know which facts to target. Determine if he knows the Combinations of 10 strategy. Practice it until he is fluent with it. Then, explicitly teach the Making 10 strategy. For multiplication, you might notice that a student is very good at doubling. Help her write the way to solve her "toughies" using doubles. For example, to multiply by 4, she can double and double again. For 8, she can double, double, double. Doubling has been found to be very effective in helping middle school students master multiplication facts, increasing their reasoning skills as well as their confidence (Flowers & Rubenstein, 2010/2011).

2. *Provide hope.* As noted in the discussion of timed tests, students' confidence can be affected. Students may feel they are doomed to use finger counting forever. Let these students know that they will explore strategies that will help them with the facts. Turn off the timers. Shorten (or eliminate) the quizzes.

3. *Inventory the known and unknown facts.* Find out which facts are known quickly and comfortably and which are not (see assessment ideas discussed previously). Invite students to do this for themselves as well. Provide sheets of mixed multiplication facts and ask students to answer the ones they "just know" and circle the facts where they have to pause to count or use a strategy. Review the results with them and discuss which strategies and facts you will work on.

4. *Build in success.* Begin with easier and more useful reasoning strategies like Combinations of 10 for addition. Success builds success! Have students find all the facts that can be solved with a newly learned strategy. Use fact charts to show the set of facts you are working on. It is surprising how the chart quickly fills up with mastered facts.

5. *Provide engaging activities.* Use the many games and activities in this chapter to work on phase 2 and phase 3. As students play, ask which strategies they are using. Deemphasize competition and emphasize collaboration. Prepare take-home versions of a game and assign students to play the game at home at least once. Invite parents in for a Math Night and teach them games that they can enjoy (e.g., *Salute!*) and teach families to focus on reasoning strategies over memorization as they play the games.

What to Do When Teaching Basic Facts. We close this chapter with some important reminders in effectively teaching the basic facts. This is such an important life skill for all learners that it is important that we, as teachers, use what research suggests are the most effective practices. The following list of recommendations can support the development of quick recall.

1. *Ask students to self-monitor.* The importance of this recommendation cannot be overstated. Across all learning, having a sense of what you don't know and what you need to learn is important. It certainly holds true with memorizing facts. Students should be able to identify their "toughies" and continue to work on reasoning strategies to help them derive those facts.

2. *Focus on self-improvement.* Help students notice that they are getting quicker or learning new facts or strategies. For example, students can keep track of how long it took them to go through their "fact stack" and then, two days later, pull out the same stack and see whether they are quicker (or more accurate or use a new strategy) compared to the last time.

Standards for Mathematical Practice
MP1. Make sense of problems and persevere in solving them.

3. *Limit practice to short time segments.* You can project numerous examples of double ten-frames in relatively little time. Or you can do a story problem a day—taking five minutes to share strategies. You can also have each student pull a set of flash cards, pair with another student, and go through each other's set in two minutes. Long periods (ten minutes or more) are not effective. Using the first five to ten minutes of the day, or extra time just before lunch, can provide continued support on fact development without taking up mathematics instructional time better devoted to other topics.

4. *Work on facts over time.* Rather than do a unit on fact memorization, work on facts over months and months, working on one reasoning strategy or set of facts until it is learned, then moving on. Be sure foundational facts come first and are down pat before teaching derived fact strategies.

5. *Involve families.* Share the big plan of how you will work on learning facts over the year. One idea is to let parents or guardians know that during the second semester of second grade (or third grade), for example, you will have one or two "Take Home Facts of the Week." Ask family members to help students by using reasoning strategies when they don't know a fact.

6. *Make fact practice enjoyable.* There are many games (including those in this chapter) designed to reinforce facts that are not competitive or anxiety inducing.

7. *Use technology.* When students work with technology, they get immediate feedback and reinforcement, helping them to self-monitor.

8. *Emphasize the importance of knowing their facts.* Without trying to create pressure or anxiety, emphasize to students that in real life and in the rest of mathematics, they will be recalling these facts all the time—they really must learn them and learn them well.

What Not to Do When Teaching Basic Facts. The following list describes strategies that may have been designed with good intentions but work against student recall of the basic facts.

1. *Don't use timed tests.* As we have mentioned, little insight is gained from timed tests and they can potentially negatively affect students. Turn the timers off!

2. *Don't use public comparisons of mastery.* You may have experienced the bulletin board that shows which students are on which step of a staircase to mastering their multiplication facts. Imagine how the student who is on the step 3 feels when others are on step 6. It is great to celebrate student successes, but avoid comparisons between students.

3. *Don't proceed through facts in order from 0 to 9.* Work on foundational facts first, then move to the tougher facts.

4. *Don't work on all facts all at once.* Select a strategy (starting with easier ones) and then work on memorization of that set of facts (e.g., doubles). Be sure these are really learned before moving on. Differentiation is needed!

5. *Don't expect quick recall too soon.* This has been addressed throughout the chapter but is worth repeating. Quick recall or mastery can be obtained only after significant time has been spent on reasoning strategies.

6. *Don't use facts as a barrier to good mathematics.* Mathematics is not solely about computation. Mathematics is about reasoning, using patterns, and making sense of things. Mathematics is problem solving. There is no reason that a student who has not yet mastered all basic facts should be excluded from real mathematical experiences (allow calculators so that students don't get bogged down on computation while working on more complex tasks).

7. *Don't use fact mastery as a prerequisite for calculator use.* Requiring that students master the basic facts before they can use a calculator has no foundation. Calculator use should be based on the instructional goals of the day. If your lesson goal is for students to discover the pattern (formula) for the perimeter of rectangles, then students might be recording the length, width, and perimeter for different rectangles and looking for patterns. Using a calculator can quicken the computation in this lesson and keep the focus on measurement.

 Complete Self-Check 10.4: Reinforcing Basic Fact Mastery

REFLECTIONS ON CHAPTER 10

WRITING TO LEARN

1. Why is memorization not considered a good approach to learn basic facts?

2. How might you decide which addition facts a student only solves by counting, for which ones they are using reasoning strategies, and which ones they just know?

3. What remedial strategies should be applied to students who have not mastered basic facts despite having moved to a higher grade?

4. For the fact 6 × 7, describe two derived fact strategies a student might use (assume the student knows their foundation facts).

5. Why are games and interactive software important in supporting basic fact fluency?

6. This chapter suggests an approach to teaching the basic facts that may be quite different than your own experience. Describe three things that are highlighted in this chapter that were new to you and that you hope to remember to use.

FOR DISCUSSION AND EXPLORATION

◆ Explore a web-based program for drilling basic facts. What features does the program have that are good? Not so good? How would you use such programs in a classroom with only one or two available computers? How would you differentiate it to address those who are working on different fact strategies?

◆ Assume you are teaching a grade that expects mastery of facts (grade 2 for addition and subtraction or grade 3 or 4 for multiplication and division). How will you design fact mastery across the semester or year? Include timing, strategy development, involvement of families, use of games, and so forth.

RESOURCES FOR CHAPTER 10

LITERATURE CONNECTIONS

The children's books described in Chapters 8 and 9 are also good choices when working on the basic facts. In addition to those, consider these opportunities to develop and practice basic facts.

One Less Fish *Toft and Sheather (1998)*

This beautiful book with an important environmental message starts with 12 fish and counts back to zero fish. On a page with 8 fish, ask, "How many fish are gone?" and "How did you figure it out?" Encourage students to use the Down Over 10 strategy. Any counting-up or counting-back book can be used in this way!

The Twelve Days of Summer *Andrews and Jolliffe (2005)*

You will quickly recognize the style of this book with five bumblebees, four garter snakes, three ruffed grouse, and so on. The engaging illustrations and motions make this a wonderful book. Students can apply multiplication facts to figure out how many of each item appear by the end of the book. (For example, three ruffed grouse appear on days 3, 4, 5, and so on.)

RECOMMENDED READINGS

Articles

Baroody, A. J. (2006). Why children have difficulties mastering the basic fact combinations and how to help them. *Teaching Children Mathematics, 13*(1), 22–31.

Baroody suggests that basic facts are developmental in nature and contrasts "conventional wisdom" with a number-sense view. Great activities are included as exemplars.

Boaler, J. (2014). Research suggests that timed tests cause math anxiety. *Teaching Children Mathematics 20*(8), 469–474.

This is a wonderful article to challenge the longstanding practice of timed-tests. Just because we have always done this, doesn't mean it's a good idea!

Buchholz, L. (2004). Learning strategies for addition and subtraction facts: The road to fluency and the license to think. *Teaching Children Mathematics, 10*(7), 362–367.

A second-grade teacher explains how her students developed and named their strategies and even extended them to work with two-digit numbers. She found her "lower ability" students were very successful using reasoning strategies.

Crespo, S., Kyriakides, A. O., & McGee, S. (2005). Nothing "basic" about basic facts: Exploring addition facts with fourth graders. *Teaching Children Mathematics, 12*(2), 60–67.

This article provides evidence of the critical importance of addressing remediation through a focus on reasoning strategies and number sense.

Kling, G. (2011, September). Fluency with basic addition. *Teaching Children Mathematics, 18,* 80–88.

Kling offers many research-based ideas for developing fluency. She emphasizes the need to begin with doubles and combinations of 10 and build from there.

Developing Whole-Number Place-Value Concepts

LEARNER OUTCOMES

After reading this chapter and engaging in the embedded activities and reflections, you should be able to:

11.1 Identify the pre-base-ten understandings based on a count-by-ones approach to quantity.

11.2 Recognize the foundational ideas of place value as an integration of three components: base-ten concepts through groupings and counting, numbers written in place-value notation, and numbers that are spoken aloud.

11.3 Demonstrate how to develop children's skills in place value through the use of base-ten models.

11.4 Explain how students can use grouping activities to deepen their understanding of place-value concepts.

11.5 Explain strategies to support students' ability to write and say numbers.

11.6 Recognize that there are patterns in our number system that provide the foundation for computational strategies.

11.7 Describe how the place-value system extends to large numbers.

Number sense is linked to a complete understanding of place value, including extensions to decimal numeration as it develops across the elementary and middle grades. In first grade, students count and are exposed to patterns in numbers up to 120 and they learn to think about groups of ten objects as a unit. By second grade, these initial ideas of patterns and groups of ten are formally connected to three-digit numbers, and in grade 4 students extend their understanding to numbers up to 1,000,000 in a variety of contexts. In fourth and fifth grades, the ideas of whole numbers are extended to decimals (CCSSO, 2010). A significant part of this development includes students putting numbers together (composing) and taking them apart (decomposing) in a wide variety of ways as they solve addition and subtraction problems with two- and three-digit numbers. Place value is a way for students to think about larger quantities (Mix, Prather, Smith, & Stockton, 2013) and to enhance their ability to invent their own computation strategies. Without a firm foundation and understanding of place value, students may face chronic low levels of mathematics performance (Chan & Ho, 2010; Moeller, Martignon, Wessolowski, Engel, & Nuerk, 2011). The following big ideas are the foundational concepts that will lead students to a full understanding of place value.

BIG IDEAS

◆ Sets of 10 (and tens of tens) can be perceived as single entities or units; for example, three sets of 10 and two singles is a base-ten method of describing 32 single objects. This is the major principle of base-ten numeration.

◆ The positions of digits in numbers determine what they represent and which size group they count. This is the major organizing principle of place-value numeration and is central for developing number sense.

◆ There are patterns to the way that numbers are formed. For example, each decade has a symbolic pattern reflective of the 0-to-9 sequence (e.g., 20, 21, 22 . . . 29).

◆ The groupings of ones, tens, and hundreds can be taken apart in different but equivalent ways. For example, beyond the typical way to decompose 256 of 2 hundreds, 5 tens, and 6 ones, it can be represented as 1 hundred, 14 tens, and 16 ones, or 250 and 6. Decomposing and composing multidigit numbers in flexible ways is a necessary foundation for computational estimation and exact computation.

◆ "Really big" numbers are best understood in terms of familiar real-world referents. It is difficult to conceptualize quantities as large as 1000 or more. However, the number of people who will fill the local sports arena is, for example, a meaningful referent for those who have experienced that crowd.

Pre-Place-Value Understandings

Children know a lot about numbers with two digits (10 to 99) as early as kindergarten. After all, kindergartners learn to count to 100 and count out sets with as many as 20 or more objects. They count students in the room, turn to specific page numbers in their books, and so on. However, initially their understanding is quite different from yours. It is based on a count-by-ones approach to quantity, so the number 18 to them means 18 ones. They are not able to separate the quantity into place-value groups—after counting 18 teddy bears, a young child might tell you that the 1 stands for 1 teddy bear and the 8 stands for 8 teddy bears. Such students have not had enough experiences to realize we are always grouping by tens. Recall Wright and his colleagues' three levels of understanding: (1) children understand ten as ten ones; (2) children see ten as a unit; and (3) children easily work with units of ten. Let's look at a way to assess where students are in this trajectory.

FORMATIVE ASSESSMENT Notes. In a diagnostic interview, ask first or second graders to count out 53 tiles. Watch closely to note whether they count out the tiles one at a time and push them aside without any type of grouping or if they group them into tens. Have the students write the number that tells how many tiles they just counted. Some may write "35" instead of "53," a simple reversal. You may find that early on students count the tiles one by one and are not yet thinking of ten as a unit (level 1), and are therefore in a pre-place-value stage.

The students just described know that there are 53 tiles "because I counted them." Writing the number and saying the number are usually done correctly, but their understanding of 53 derives from the count-by-ones approach. Without your help, students may not easily or quickly develop a meaningful use of groups of ten to represent quantities.

Even if students can tell you that in the numeral 53, the 5 "is in the tens place" or that there are "3 ones," they might just know the name of the positions without understanding that the "tens place" represents how many groups of ten. Similarly, if students use base-ten blocks, they may name a rod of ten as a "ten" and a small cube as a "one" but may not be able to tell how many ones are required to make a ten. Students may attach words to both materials and groups without realizing what the materials or symbols represent.

Students do know that 53 is "a lot" and that it's more than 47 (because you count past 47 to get to 53). They think of the "53" that they write as a single numeral. In this stage, they do not know that the 5 represents five groups of ten things and the 3 represents three single things (Fuson, 2006). Fuson and her colleagues refer to students' pre-base-ten understanding of number as *unitary*. That is, there are no groupings of ten, even though a two-digit number is associated with the quantity. They initially rely on unitary counts to understand quantities. ■

 Complete Self-Check 11.1: Pre-Place-Value Understandings

 # Developing Whole-Number Place-Value Concepts

Place-value understanding requires an *integration* of new and sometimes difficult-to-construct concepts of grouping by tens (the base-ten concept) with procedural knowledge of how groups are recorded in our place-value system and how numbers are written and spoken. Importantly, learners must understand the word *grouping*, especially English language learners (ELLs) who may become confused because the root word *group* is frequently used for instructing students to work together.

Integrating Base-Ten Groupings with Counting by Ones

Once students can count out a set of 53 by ones, help them see that making groupings of tens and leftovers is a way of counting that same quantity. Each of the sets in Figure 11.1 has 53 tiles, yet students move through three distinct grouping stages to construct the idea that all of these sets are the same.

Your foremost objective should be helping students integrate the grouping-by-tens concept with what they already know about numbers from counting by ones. If they only count by ones, ask them, "What will happen if we count these by groups and singles (or by tens and ones)?" If a set has been grouped into tens and singles and counted, then ask, "How can we be really certain that there are 53 things here?" or "How many do you think we will get if we count by ones?" You cannot just *tell* students that these counts will all be the same and hope that will make sense to them—it is a relationship they must construct themselves.

There is a subtle yet profound difference between students at these stages: Some know that base-ten stage is 53 because they understand the idea that 5 groups of ten and 3 more is the same amount as 53 counted by ones; others simply say, "It's 53," because they have been told that when things are grouped this way, it's called 53. The students who understand place value will see no need to count the base-ten grouping by ones. They understand the "fifty-threeness" of the unitary and base-ten grouping to be the same. The students in the pre-place-value stage may not be sure how many they will get if they count the tiles in the base-ten grouping by ones or if the groups were "ungrouped" how many there would then be.

Standards for Mathematical Practice

MP7. Look for and make sense of structure.

 ## Pause & Reflect

What are some defining characteristics of "pre-place-value" students and those who understand place value? ●

Groupings with fewer than the maximum number of tens are referred to as *equivalent groupings*. Understanding the equivalence of the base-ten grouping and the equivalent grouping indicates that grouping by tens is not just a rule that is followed, but also that any grouping by tens, including all or some of the singles, can help tell how many. Many computational techniques (e.g., regrouping in addition and subtraction) are based on equivalent representations of numbers.

Grouping Stage	Visual Representation	Counting Approach	Students Can:
UNITARY Count by ones	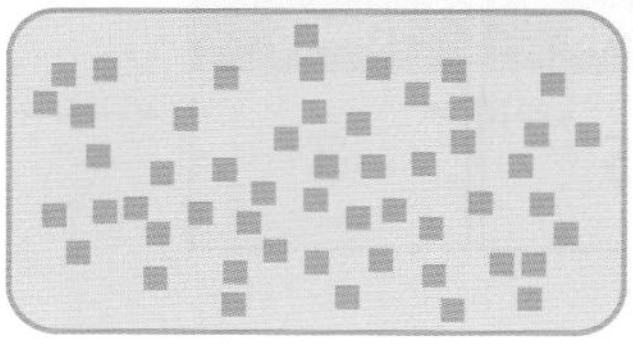	1, 2, 3, 4, 5, 6, 7, 8, 9, 10, 11, and so on	• Name a quantity or "tell how many" by counting each piece. • Are not yet able to think of 10 as a single unit. • Use counting by ones as the only way they are convinced that different sets have the same amount.
BASE TEN Count by groups of tens and ones	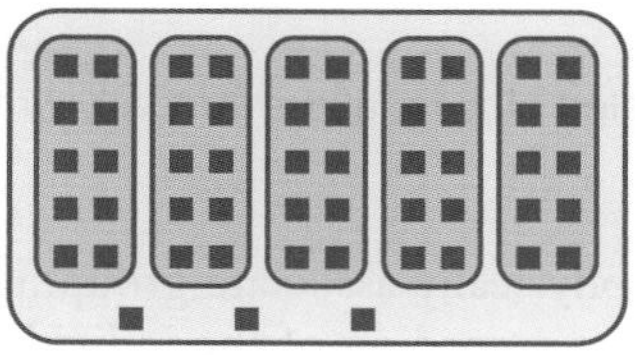	1, 2, 3, 4, 5 groups of 10 and 1, 2, 3, ones (singles) or 10, 20, 30, 40, 50, 51, 52, 53	• Count a group of 10 objects as a single item (unitizing). • Coordinate the base ten approach with a count by ones to as a means of telling "how many." • Use the second version of the count and explicitly state the number of items.
EQUIVALENT Non-standard base ten	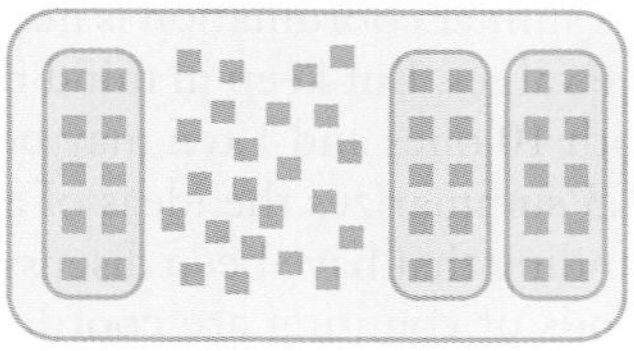	Before counting students would trade and then count 10, 20, 30, 40, 50, 51, 52, 53	• Group the pieces flexibly into versions that include tens and ones but all trades have not been carried out. • Use these alternate groupings to relate to computation by being able to trading or regroup numbers in a variety of ways.

FIGURE 11.1 Three stages of the grouping of 53 objects.

Integrating Base-Ten Groupings with Words

The way we say a number such as "fifty-three" must also be connected with the grouping-by-tens concept. The counting methods provide a connection. The count by tens and ones results in saying the number of groups and singles separately: "five tens and three." Saying the number of tens and singles separately in this fashion can be called base-ten language. Students can associate the base-ten language with the standard language: "five tens and three—fifty-three."

There are several variations of the base-ten language for 53: 5 tens and 3, 5 tens and 3 ones, 5 tens and 3 singles, and so on. Each may be used interchangeably with the standard name, "fifty-three." But if you have ELLs, it is best to select one base-ten approach (e.g., 5 tens and 3 ones) and consistently connect it to the standard approach. Other languages often use the base-ten format (e.g., 17 in Spanish is *diecisiete*, literally meaning "ten and seven"), so this can be a good cultural connection.

It is important to be precise in your language. Whenever you refer to a number in the tens, hundreds, or thousands (or beyond), make sure you do not just say "six," but instead refer to it with its place value location, such as 6 tens (or 60). Students are often confused when numbers are discussed as digits rather that describing their actual value.

CCSS Standards for Mathematical Practice
MP6. Attend to precision.

Integrating Base-Ten Groupings with Place-Value Notation

The symbolic scheme that we use for writing numbers (ones on the right, tens to the left of ones, and so on) must be coordinated with the grouping scheme. Activities can be designed so

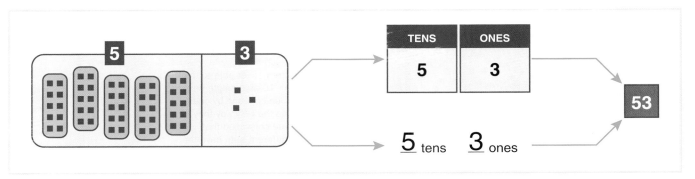

FIGURE 11.2 Groupings by 10 are matched with numerals, recorded in labeled places, and eventually written in standard form.

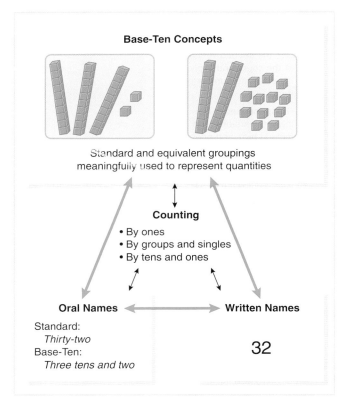

FIGURE 11.3 Relational understanding of place value integrates three components shown as the corners of the triangle.

that students physically associate groupings of tens and ones with the correct recording of the individual digits, as Figure 11.2 indicates.

Language again plays a key role in making these connections. The explicit count by groups and singles matches the individual digits as the number is written in the usual left-to-right manner. A similar coordination is necessary for hundreds and other place values. But keep in mind that having students see "ten" as both 10 ones and 1 ten may be a challenge.

Figure 11.3 summarizes the ideas of an integrated place-value understanding that have been discussed so far. Note that all three methods of counting are coordinated as the principal method of integrating the base-ten concepts, the written names, and the oral names.

 **Complete Self-Check 11.2: Developing Whole-Number Place-Value Concepts**

Base-Ten Models for Place Value

Physical models for base-ten concepts play a key role in helping students develop the idea of "a ten" as both a single entity and as a set of 10 units. Remember, though, that the models do not "show" the concept to the students; the students must mentally construct the "ten makes one relationship" and impose it on the model.

An effective base-ten model for ones, tens, and hundreds is one that is *proportional*. That is, a model for ten is physically 10 times larger than the model for a one, and a hundred model is 10 times larger than the ten model. Proportional materials allow students to check that ten of any given piece is equivalent to one piece in the column to the left (10 tens equals 1 hundred, and so on). Base-ten proportional models can be categorized as *groupable* or *pregrouped*.

Groupable Models

Models that most clearly reflect the relationships of ones, tens, and hundreds are those for which the ten can actually be made or grouped from the single pieces. When students put 10 beans in a cup, the cup of 10 beans literally *is the same as* the 10 single beans. Plastic connecting cubes also provide a good transition to pre-grouped rods because they form a similar shape. Bundles of wooden craft sticks or coffee stirrers can be grouped with rubber bands. Examples of these groupable models are shown in Figure 11.4(a).

As students begin to make groupings of ten, start introducing the language of "tens" by matching the objects, such as "cups of tens and ones" or "bundles of tens and singles." Then graduate to a general phrase, such as "groups of tens and ones." Eventually you can abbreviate this simply to "tens." There is no hurry to use the word "ones" for the leftovers. Language such as "four tens and seven" works very well.

When students become more familiar with these models, collections of tens can be made in advance by the students and kept as ready-made tens (e.g., craft sticks can be left prebundled, connecting cubes left connected). This is a good transition to the pregrouped models described next.

Pregrouped Models

Models that are pregrouped are commonly shown in textbooks and are often used in instructional activities. Pregrouped models, such as those in Figure 11.4(b) and the Base-Ten Materials, cannot be taken apart or put together. When 10 single pieces are accumulated, they must be exchanged or traded for a ten, and likewise, tens must be traded for hundreds. With pre-grouped models, make an extra effort to confirm that students understand that a ten piece really is the same as 10 ones. Students combine multiplicative understanding (each place is 10 times the value of the place to the right) with a positional system (each place has a value)—something hard to do prior to multiplication being taught! Although there is a pregrouped cube to represent 1000, it is important to group 10 hundred pieces and attach them together as a cube to show how it is formed. Otherwise, some students may only count the square units they see on the surface of the six faces and may think the cube represents 600.

The Little Ten-Frames effectively link to the familiar ten-frames students used early on to think about numbers, and as such, may initially be more meaningful than paper strips and squares of base-ten materials. This model has the distinct advantage of always showing the distance to the next decade. For example, when 47 is shown with 4 ten cards and a seven card, a student can see that three more will make five full cards, or 50.

A significant challenge with using the pregrouped physical models occurs when students have not had adequate experiences with groupable models first. Then there is the potential for students to use them without reflecting on the ten-to-one relationships. For example, if students are just *told* to trade 10 ones for a ten, it is quite possible for them to make this trade without attending to the "ten-ness" of the piece they call a ten. Similarly, students can "make the number 42" by simply picking up 4 tens and 2 ones pieces without understanding that if all the pieces were broken apart there would be 42 ones.

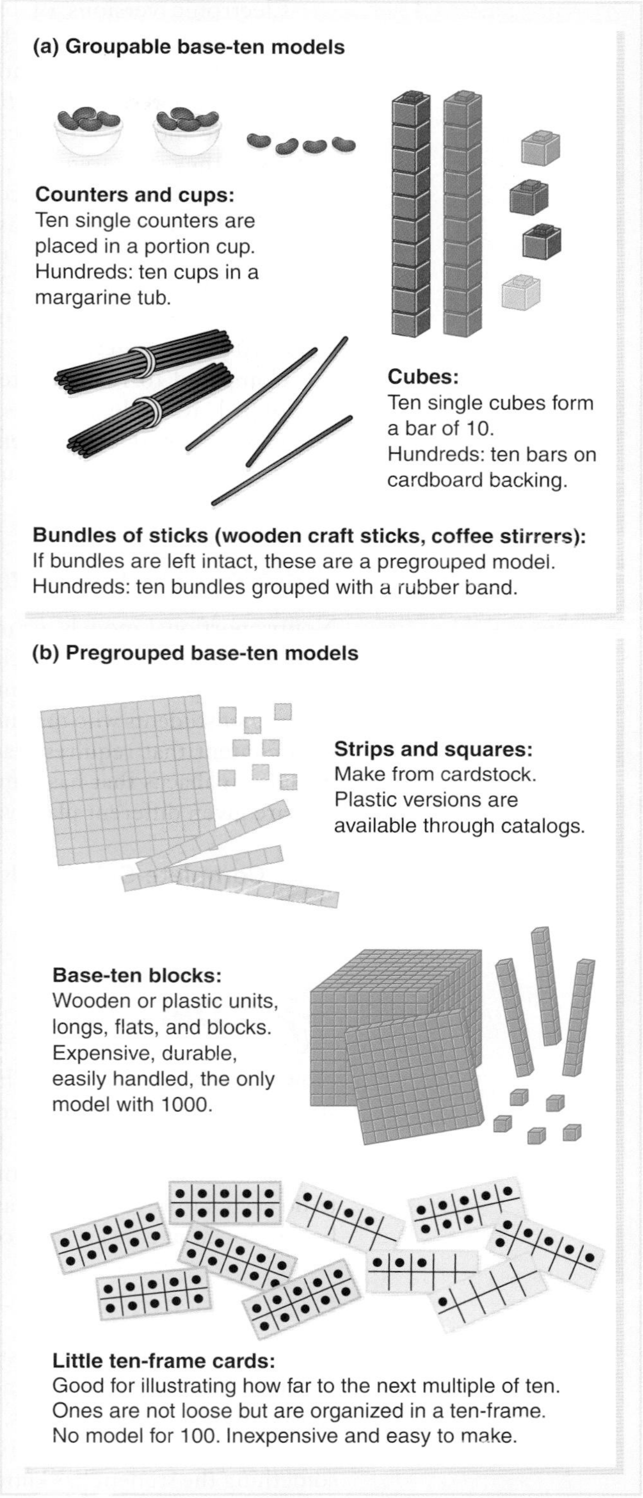

(a) Groupable base-ten models

Counters and cups:
Ten single counters are placed in a portion cup.
Hundreds: ten cups in a margarine tub.

Cubes:
Ten single cubes form a bar of 10.
Hundreds: ten bars on cardboard backing.

Bundles of sticks (wooden craft sticks, coffee stirrers):
If bundles are left intact, these are a pregrouped model.
Hundreds: ten bundles grouped with a rubber band.

(b) Pregrouped base-ten models

Strips and squares:
Make from cardstock.
Plastic versions are available through catalogs.

Base-ten blocks:
Wooden or plastic units, longs, flats, and blocks. Expensive, durable, easily handled, the only model with 1000.

Little ten-frame cards:
Good for illustrating how far to the next multiple of ten.
Ones are not loose but are organized in a ten-frame.
No model for 100. Inexpensive and easy to make.

FIGURE 11.4   Groupable and pregrouped base-ten models.

Electronic versions of base-ten manipulatives are computer representations of the three-dimensional base-ten blocks, including the thousands piece. With simple mouse clicks, students (including those with disabilities) can place ones, tens, hundreds, or thousands on the screen. In the *Base Blocks* applets at the National Library of Virtual Manipulatives, the models are placed on a place-value mat. If 10 of one type are lassoed by a rectangle, they snap together; if a piece is dragged one column to the right, the piece breaks apart into 10 of that unit. Scott Foresman's *eTools* has a similar place-value tool with a bit more flexibility. Select the base-ten blocks of your choice and add ones, tens, or hundreds. Place-value columns can be turned on and off, and the "odometer" option can show the number 523 as *5 hundreds + 2 tens + 3 ones*, as *500 + 20 + 3*, or as *five hundred twenty-three*. A hammer icon will break a piece into 10 smaller pieces, and a glue bottle icon is used to group 10 pieces together.

Compared to real base-ten blocks, these digital materials are free, easily grouped and ungrouped, available in endless supply, and can be manipulated by students and displayed by projector or smart board. Remember though, virtual models are no more conceptual than physical models and as such are only a representation for students who understand the relationships involved.

Nonproportional Models

Nonproportional models, or models where the ten is not physically 10 times larger than the one, are *not* used for introducing place-value concepts. They are used when students already have a conceptual understanding of the numeration system and need additional reinforcement, or by older students who may need to return to place-value concepts because they are struggling with content that requires place-value understanding. Examples of nonproportional models include an abacus that has same-sized beads in different columns (on wires), money, or chips that are given different place values by color.

 Complete Self-Check 11.3: Base-Ten Models for Place Value

 # Developing Base-Ten Concepts

Now that you have a sense of the important place-value concepts, we turn to activities that assist students in developing these concepts. This section focuses on base-ten concepts or grouping by tens (see the top of Figure 11.3). Connecting this important idea with the oral and written names for numbers (the rest of Figure 11.3) is discussed separately to help you focus on how to do each. However, in the classroom, the oral and written names for numbers can and should be developed in concert with conceptual ideas.

Grouping Activities

Reflect for a moment on how strange it must sound to say "seven ones." Certainly students have never said they were "seven ones" years old. The use of the word *ten* as a singular group name can be even more mysterious. Consider the phrase "Ten ones makes one ten." The first *ten* carries the usual meaning of 10 things, but the other *ten* is a singular noun, a thing. How can something the student has known for years as the name for a lot of things suddenly become one thing? And if you think this is confusing for native speakers, imagine the potential difficulty for ELLs.

Because students come to their development of base-ten concepts with a count-by-ones idea of number, you must begin there. You cannot arbitrarily impose grouping by ten on students. Students need to experiment with showing amounts in groups of like size and perhaps come to an agreement that ten is a very useful size to use. The following activity could be done in late first grade as an example of a first effort at developing grouping concepts.

Activity 11.1

CCSS-M: K.NBT.A.1; 1.NBT.B.2a

Counting in Groups

Find a collection of items between 25 and 100 that students might be interested in counting—perhaps the number of shoes in the classroom, a jar of cubes, a long chain of plastic links, or the number of crayons in the classroom crayon box. Then pose the question, "How could we count our shoes in some way that would be easier than counting by ones?" Whatever suggestions you get, try them. After testing several methods, you can have a discussion of what worked well and what did not. If no one suggests counting by tens, you might casually suggest that as an idea to try.

One teacher challenged her students to find a good way to count all the connecting cubes being held by the students after the children collected a cube for each of their pockets. The first suggestion was to count by sevens. That was tried but did not work very well because none of the students could easily count by sevens. In search of a more efficient way, the next suggestion was to count by twos. This did not seem to be much better than counting by ones. Finally, they settled on counting by tens and realized that this was a pretty good method.

This and similar activities provide you with the opportunity to suggest that materials actually be arranged into groups of tens before the "fast" way of counting is begun. Remember that students may count "ten, twenty, thirty, thirty-one, thirty-two" but not fully realize the "thirty-two-ness" of the quantity. To connect the count-by-tens method with their understood method of counting by ones, the students need to count both ways and discuss why they get the same result.

The idea in the next activity is for students to make groupings of ten and record or say the amounts. Number words are used so that students will not mechanically match tens and ones with individual digits. It is important that students confront the actual quantity in a manner meaningful to them.

Activity 11.2

CCSS-M: K.NBT.A.1; 1.NBT.B.2a; 1.NBT.B.2b; 1.NBT.B.2c

STUDENTS with SPECIAL NEEDS

Groups of Ten

Prepare bags of different types of objects such as toothpicks, buttons, beans, plastic chips, connecting cubes, craft sticks, or other items. Students should use the Bag of Tens Activity Page similar to the top left of Figure 11.5. The bags can be placed at stations around the room or given to pairs of students. Students empty the bags and count the contents. The amount is recorded as a number word. Then the objects are grouped in as many tens as possible. The groupings are recorded on the form. After returning the objects to the bags, bags are traded, or students move to another station. Note that students with disabilities may initially need to use a ten-frame to support their counting. Then the use of the ten-frame should eventually fade.

Variations of the "Groups of Ten" activity are suggested by the three other recording sheets in Figure 11.5. On Get This Many Activity Page, students count the dots and then count out the corresponding number of counters. Provide small cups to put the groups of ten in. Notice that the activity requires students to first count the set in a way they understand (e.g., count by ones), record the amount in words, and then make the place-value groupings. The Fill the Tens and Loop This Many Activity Pages begin with a verbal name (number word), and students must count the indicated amount and then make groups.

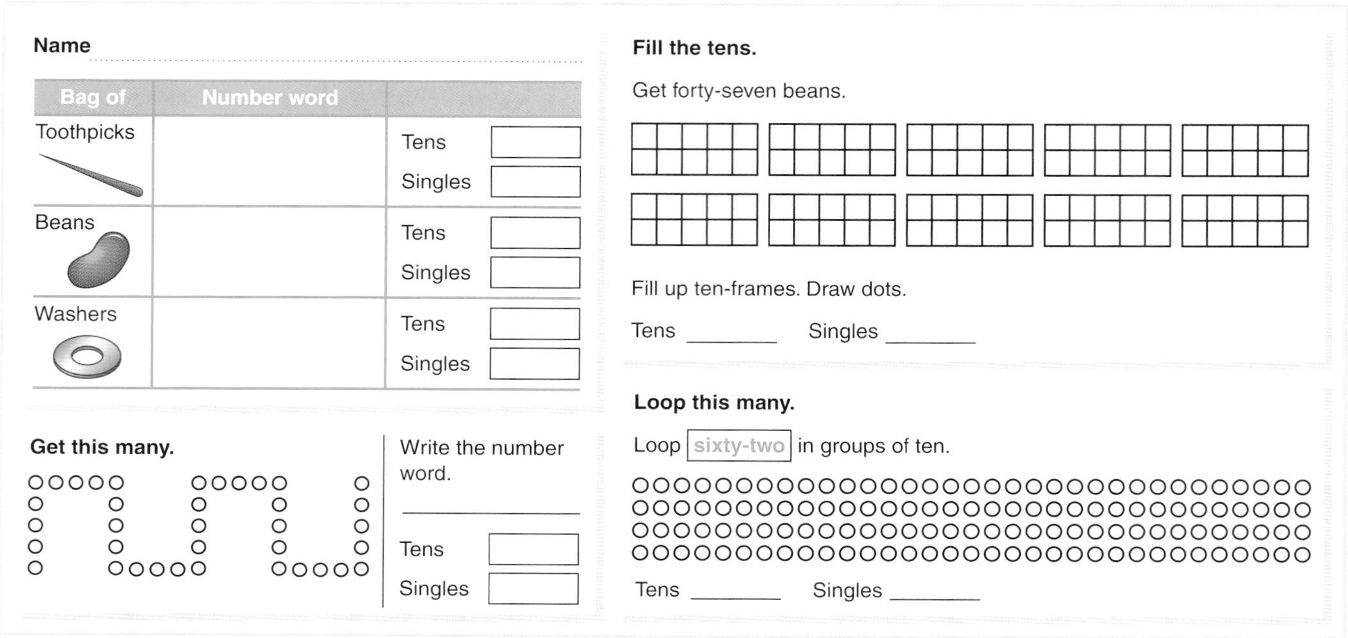

Name ....

Bag of	Number word		
Toothpicks		Tens	
		Singles	
Beans		Tens	
		Singles	
Washers		Tens	
		Singles	

Get this many.

○○○○○   ○○○○○   ○
○   ○   ○   ○   ○
○   ○   ○   ○   ○
○   ○   ○   ○   ○
○   ○○○○○   ○○○○○

Write the number word.

_____

Tens [ ]

Singles [ ]

Fill the tens.

Get forty-seven beans.

Fill up ten-frames. Draw dots.

Tens _____   Singles _____

Loop this many.

Loop [sixty-two] in groups of ten.

○○
○○
○○
○○

Tens _____   Singles _____

FIGURE 11.5 Activities involving number words and making groups of ten.

Activity 11.3

CCSS-M: K.NBT.A.1; 1.NBT.B.2a; 1.NBT.B.2b

Estimating Groups of Tens and Ones

Give students a length that they are going to measure—for example, the length of a child lying down or the distance around a sheet of newspaper. At one end of the length, line up 10 units (e.g., 10 linking cubes, toothpicks, rods, or blocks). On a recording sheet (see Figure 11.6 and the How Long? Activity Page), students record an estimate of how many groups of 10 and ones they think will match the length. Next they find the actual measure, placing units along the full length. These are counted by ones and also grouped in tens. Both results are recorded. Estimating the groups of ten requires children to pay attention to the ten as a group or unit. Notice that all three place-value components are included. Visit the companion website to see an Expanded Lesson for this activity.

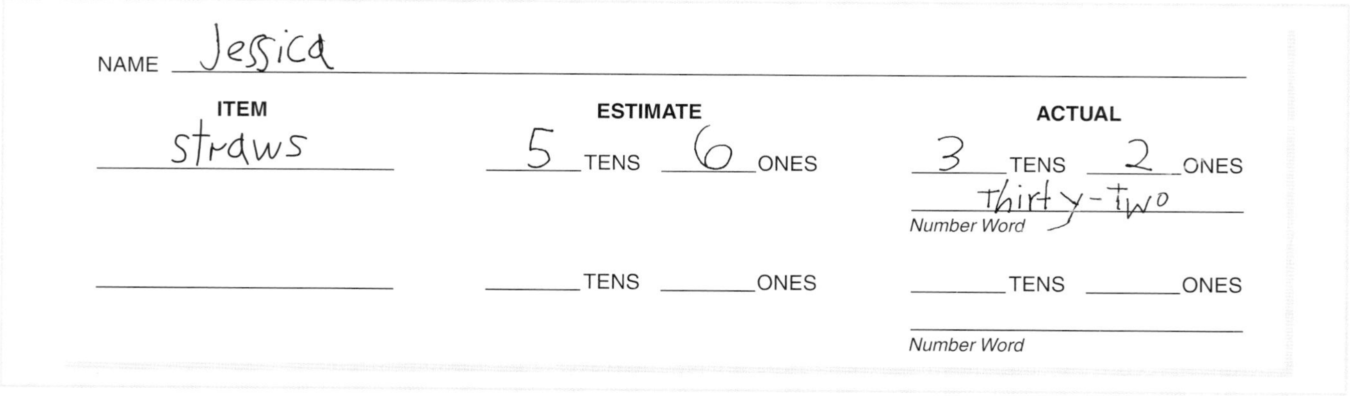

NAME _Jessica_

ITEM	ESTIMATE	ACTUAL
Straws	_5_ TENS _6_ ONES	_3_ TENS _2_ ONES
		Thirty-two
		Number Word
_____	_____ TENS _____ ONES	_____ TENS _____ ONES
		_____
		Number Word

FIGURE 11.6 Recording sheet for estimating groups of tens and ones.

FORMATIVE ASSESSMENT Notes. Use a Class Observational Checklist to record observations about how students do these activities to learn a lot about their base-ten concept development. For example, how do students count out the objects? Do they make groupings of ten? Do they count to 10 and then start again at 1? Students who do that are already using the base-ten structure. But what you may likely see early on is students counting a full set without stopping at tens and without any effort to group the materials in piles. If you notice that behavior, use a diagnostic interview and ask the student to count a jar of beans (with between 30 and 50 beans) and record the number. Ask the student, "If you were to place each group of 10 beans in a small cup, how many cups would you need?" If the student has no idea or makes random guesses, what would you know about the student's knowledge of place value? ■

Grouping Tens to Make 100

In second grade, numbers up to 1000 become important (CCSSO, 2010). Here the issue is not just connecting a count-by-ones concept to a group of 100, but rather seeing it in multiple ways, including as 100 single objects, as 10 tens, and as a singular thing. In textbooks, this connection is often presented on one page showing how 10 rods of ten can be put together to make 1 hundred piece. This quick demonstration may be lost on many students. Additionally, the word *hundred* is equally strange and can get even less attention. These word names are not as simple as they seem!

As a means of introducing hundreds as groups of 10 tens and also 100 singles, consider the estimation activity Too Many Tens.

Activity 11.4

CCSS-M: 2.NBT.A.1

Too Many Tens

Show students any quantity with 150 to 1000 items. For example, you might use a jar of lima beans, a long chain of connecting links or paper clips, a box of Styrofoam packing peanuts, or a grocery bag full of straws. First, have students make and record estimates of how many beans, for example, are in the jar. Discuss how students determined their estimates. Then distribute portions of the beans to pairs or triads of students to put into cups of 10 beans. Collect leftover beans and put these into groups of ten as well. Now ask, "How can we use these groups of ten to tell how many beans we have? Can we make new groups from the groups of ten? What is 10 groups of ten called?" Be prepared with some larger containers or baggies into which 10 cups (or other collections of 10 tens) can be placed. When all groups are made, count the hundreds, the tens, and the ones separately. Record the total as 4 hundreds + 7 tens + 8 ones. This activity can be extended to third graders with amounts more than 1000.

In this activity, it is important to use a groupable model so that students can see how the 10 groups are the same as the 100 individual items. At first you may think this activity will take too much time. But this activity helps cement the connection that is often lost in the rather simple display of a hundreds flat or a paper hundreds square in the pregrouped base-ten models.

Visit the companion website to watch video of a student playing a Race to 100 game with a teacher. This game will also help students carry out the equal trades that reinforce the use of pregrouped base-ten models.

 **Standards for Mathematical Practice**
MP8. Look for and express regularity in repeated reasoning.

Equivalent Representations

An important variation of the grouping activities is aimed at the equivalent representations of numbers. For example, pose the following task to students who have just completed the Groups of Ten activity.

What is another way you can show 42 besides 4 groups of ten and 2 singles? Let's see how many ways you can find.

Interestingly, most students will go next to 42 singles. The following activities focus on creating other equivalent representations.

Activity 11.5

CCSS-M: 1.NBT.B.2; 1.NBT.C.5

Can You Make the Link?

Show a collection of materials that are only partly grouped in sets of ten. For example, you may have 5 chains of 10 links and 17 additional unconnected links. Be sure the students understand that each chain has 10 links. Have students count the number of chains and the number of singles in any way they wish to count. Ask, "How many in all?" Record all responses and discuss how they got their answers. Next, before their very eyes, change the groupings (make a ten from the singles, or break apart one of the tens) and repeat. Do not change the total number from one time to the next. Once students begin to understand that the total does not change, ask in what other ways the items could be grouped if you use tens and ones.

If you are teaching in second grade, equivalent representations for hundreds as groups of tens can help with the concept of a hundred as 10 tens. The next activity is similar to "Can You Make the Link?" but is done using pregrouped materials and includes hundreds.

Activity 11.6

CCSS-M: 2.NBT.A.1; 2.NBT.A.3; K.CC.B.5

Three Other Ways

Students work in groups or pairs. First, they show 463 on their desks with base-ten materials in the standard representation. Next, they find and record at least three other ways of representing this quantity. A variation is to challenge students to find a way to show an amount with a specific number of pieces. "Can you show 463 with 31 pieces?" (There is more than one way to do this.)

When students have sufficient experiences with pregrouped materials, a semi-concrete square-line-dot notation can be used for recording ones, tens, and hundreds (see Figure 11.7 and Square Line Dot Activity Page). When needed, students can use small squares for hundreds. Use the drawings as a means of suggesting what materials students should get out to solve the problems and ways for students to record results.

The next activity begins to incorporate oral language with equivalent representation ideas.

Activity 11.7

CCSS-M: 1.NBT.A.1; 2.NBT.A.1; 2.NBT.A.3

Base-Ten Riddles

Base-ten riddles can be presented orally or in written form (see Base-Ten Riddle Cards). In either case, students should use base-ten materials to help solve them. The examples here illustrate a variety of different levels of difficulty. Have students write new riddles when they complete these.

I have 23 ones and 4 tens. Who am I?

I have 4 hundreds, 12 tens, and 6 ones. Who am I?

I have 30 ones and 3 hundreds. Who am I?

I am 45. I have 25 ones. How many tens do I have?

I am 341. I have 22 tens. How many hundreds do I have?

I have 13 tens, 2 hundreds, and 21 ones. Who am I?

If you put 3 more tens with me, I would be 115. Who am I?

I have 17 ones. I am between 40 and 50. Who am I? How many tens do I have?

Complete Self-Check 11.4: Developing Base-Ten Concepts

 # Oral and Written Names for Numbers

In this section, we focus on helping students connect oral and written names for numbers (see bottom of Figure 11.3) with their emerging base-ten concepts of using groups of 10 or 100 as efficient methods of counting. Note that the ways we say and write numbers are conventions, not concepts. Students must learn these by being told the convention rather than through problem-based activities. It is also worth remembering that for ELL students, the convention or pattern in our English number words is probably not the same as it is in their native language. This is especially true of the numbers 11 to 19.

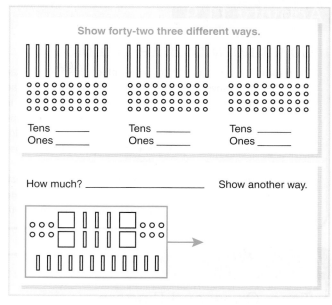

FIGURE 11.7 Equivalent representations using square-line-dot pictures.

Two-Digit Number Names

In kindergarten and first grade, students need to connect the base-ten concepts with the oral number names they have repeatedly used. They know the words but have not thought of them in terms of tens and ones. In fact, early on they may want to write twenty-one as 201.

Almost always use base-ten materials while teaching oral names. Initially, rather than using standard number words, use the more explicit base-ten language (e.g., "4 tens and 7 ones" instead of "forty-seven"). Base-ten language is rarely misunderstood. When it seems appropriate, begin to pair base-ten language with standard language. Emphasize the teens as exceptions. Acknowledge that they are formed "backward" and do not fit the patterns. The next activity helps introduce oral names for numbers.

Activity 11.8   CCSS-M: 1.NBT.B.2c

Counting Rows of Ten

ENGLISH LANGUAGE LEARNERS

Project the 10 × 10 Multiplication Array of dots. Cover up all but two rows, as shown in Figure 11.8(a). "How many tens? [2.] Two tens is called twenty." Have the class repeat. Show another row. "Three tens is called thirty. Four tens is forty. Five tens could have been fivety but is just fifty. How many tens does sixty have?" The names sixty, seventy, eighty, and ninety all fit the pattern. Slide the cover up and down the array, asking how many tens and the name for that many. ELLs may not hear the difference between fifty and fifteen, sixty and sixteen, and so on, so explicitly compare these words and clearly enunciating—even overemphasizing the word endings.

Use the same 10 × 10 multiplication array to work on names for tens and ones. Show, for example, four full lines: "forty." Next, expose one dot in the fifth row. "Four tens and one. Forty-one." Add more dots one at a time. "Four tens and two. Forty-two." "Four tens and three. Forty-three." This is shown in Figure 11.8(b). When that pattern is established, repeat with other decades from 20 through 90.

The next activity shows how this basic approach might be done with other base-ten models.

Activity 11.9

CCSS-M: 1.NBT.B.2; 1.NBT.C.5

Counting with Base-Ten Models

Show some tens on a projector, or just place them on the carpet in a mixed arrangement. Ask, "How many tens?" Add or remove a ten and repeat the question. Next, add some ones. Always have students give the base-ten name and the standard name (for many students, including ELLs and students with disabilities, it is helpful to post examples of base-ten names and the corresponding standard names on the math word wall). Continue to make changes in the materials displayed by adding or removing 1 or 2 tens and by adding and removing ones. Avoid the standard left-to-right order for tens and ones; the emphasis is on the names of the materials, not the order they are in.

Reverse the activity by having students use base-ten blocks at their desks. For example, say, "Make seventy-eight." The students make the number with the models and then give the base-ten name (7 tens and 8 ones) and standard name (78). Students can also record their work (see Figure 11.9).

ENGLISH LANGUAGE LEARNERS

STUDENTS with SPECIAL NEEDS

Activity 11.10

CCSS-M: 1.NBT.B.2a; 1.NBT.B.2b; 1.NBT.B.2c

Tens, Ones, and Fingers

Ask your class, "Can you show 6 fingers [or any amount less than 10]?" Then ask, "How can you show 37 fingers?" Some students will figure out that at least four students are required. Line up four students, and have three hold up 10 fingers while the last student holds up 7 fingers. Have the class count the fingers by tens and ones. Ask for other students to show different numbers. Emphasize the number of sets of ten fingers and the single fingers (base-ten language), and pair this with standard language.

Activities 11.8, 11.9 and 11.10 will be enhanced by having students explain their thinking. If you don't require students to reflect on their responses, they soon learn how to give the response you want, matching number words to models without actually thinking about the total quantities.

Three-Digit Number Names

CCSS **Standards for Mathematical Practice**

MP3. Construct viable arguments and critique the reasoning of others.

The approach to three-digit number names starts by showing mixed arrangements of base-ten materials and have students give the base-ten name (4 hundreds, 3 tens, and 8 ones) and the standard name (438). Vary the arrangement from one example to the next by changing only one type of piece; that is, add or remove only ones or only tens or only hundreds. It is important for students with disabilities to see counterexamples, so actively point out that some (anonymous!) students wrote 200803 for two hundred eighty-three, and ask them whether that is correct. The connection between oral and written numbers is not straightforward, with some researchers suggesting these early expanded number writing attempts are an early milestone on the route to full understanding (Byrge, Smith, & Mix, 2013). These discussions allow students to explore their fledgling steps or clear up any misunderstandings.

The major challenge with three digit numbers is with numbers involving no tens, such as 702 (or later with numbers such as 1046). As noted earlier, the use of base-ten language is quite helpful here. The difficulty of zero-tens (or more generally the internal zero) is more pronounced when writing numerals. Students frequently incorrectly write 7002 for seven hundred two. The emphasis on the meaning in the oral base-ten language will be a significant help. At first, students do not see the importance of zero in place value and do not understand that zero helps us distinguish between such numbers as 203, 23, and 230 (Dougherty, Flores, Louis, & Sophian, 2010). Carefully avoid calling zero a "placeholder," as it is a number with a value. ELLs may need additional time to think about how to say and write the numerals, because they are translating all the terms within the number.

Researchers note that there are significantly more errors with four-digit number names than three-digit numbers, so do not think that students will easily generalize to larger numbers without actually exploring examples and tasks (Cayton & Brizuela, 2007).

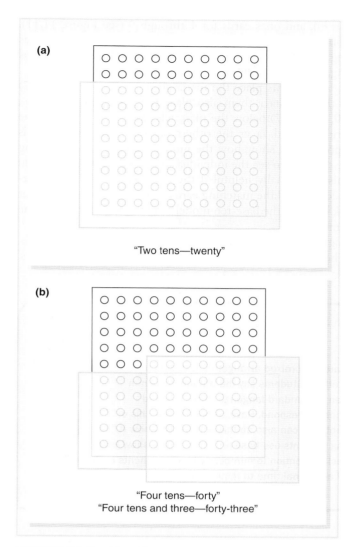

FIGURE 11.8 10 × 10 dot arrays are used to model sets of tens and ones.

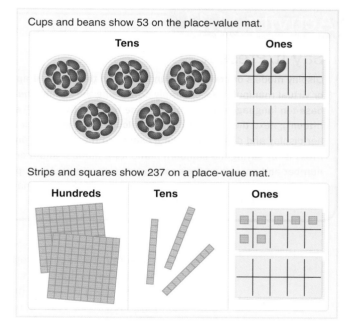

FIGURE 11.9 A student's recording of 78 with models and the base-ten name.

Cups and beans show 53 on the place-value mat.

Strips and squares show 237 on a place-value mat.

FIGURE 11.10 Place-value mats with two ten-frames in the ones place promote the concept of groups of ten.

Written Symbols

Place-value mats are simple mats divided into two or three sections to hold ones and tens or ones, tens, and hundreds pieces, as shown in Figure 11.10. You can suggest to your students that the mats are a good way to organize their materials when working with base-ten blocks. Explain that the standard way to use a place-value mat is with the space for the ones on the right and the tens and hundreds places to the left.

Although not commonly seen in textbooks, it is strongly recommended that two ten-frames be drawn in the ones place as shown on the Place-Value Mat. That way, the amount of ones on the ten-frames is always clearly evident, eliminating the need for repeatedly counting the ones. The ten-frame also makes it very clear how many additional ones would be needed to make the next set of ten. If students are modeling two numbers at the same time, one ten-frame could be used for each number.

As students use their place-value mats, they can be shown how the left-to-right order of the pieces is also the way that numbers are written. To show how the numbers are "built," have a set of 27 Place-Value Cards—one for each of the hundreds (100–900), one for each of the tens

FIGURE 11.11 Building numbers with a set of place-value cards.

(10–90), and ones cards for 1 through 9 (see Figure 11.11). Notice that the cards are made so that the tens card is twice as long as the ones card and the hundreds card is three times as long as the ones card.

As students place the materials for a number (e.g., 457) on the mat, have them also place the matching cards (e.g., 400, 50, and 7) below the materials. Then, starting with the hundreds card, layer the others on top, right aligned. This approach will show how the number is built while allowing the students to see the individual components of the number. This is especially helpful if there are zero tens. The place-value mat and the matching cards demonstrate the important link between the base-ten models and the written form of the numbers.

The next two activities are designed to help students make connections between models, oral language, and written forms. The activities can be done with two- or three-digit numbers, depending on students' needs.

Activity 11.11

CCSS-M: 2.NBT.A.1a; 2.NBT.A.1b; 2.NBT.A.3

Say It/Press It

Display models of ones, tens, hundreds (and thousands, if appropriate) in a mixed arrangement. Use a projector or virtual manipulatives or simply draw using the square-line-dot method. Students say the amount shown in base-ten language ("four hundreds, one ten, and five ones") and then in standard language ("four hundred fifteen"); next, they enter it on their calculators or use paper and pencil to respond. Have someone share his or her display and defend it. Make a change in the materials and repeat. You can also do this activity as "Show It/ Press It" by saying the standard name for a number and then having students use base-ten materials to show that number and enter it on their calculators (or write it). Again, pay special attention to numbers with components in the teens (e.g., 317) and those with internal zeros (e.g., 408). ELLs may need additional time to think of the words that go with the numbers, especially as the numbers get larger.

ENGLISH LANGUAGE LEARNERS

To support students struggling with reading a number with an internal zero you may want to show (or say) 7 hundreds and 4 ones. Then the class says, "Seven hundreds, zero tens, and four ones, which is—seven hundred (*slight pause*) four." The pause and the base-ten language support the correct reading of the three-digit number.

The next activity is also a good assessment to see whether students really understand the value of digits in two-, three- or four-digit numbers.

Activity 11.12

CCSS-M: 1.NBT.B.2; 1.NBT.C.5; 1.NBT.C.6; 2.NBT.A.1; 2.NBT.A.3; 2.NBT.B.5; 2.NBT.B.8

Digit Change

Have students enter a specific two-, three-, or four-digit number on the calculator. The task is to change one of the digits in the number without simply entering the new number. For example, change 48 to 78. Change 315 to 305 or to 295. Changes can be made by adding or subtracting an appropriate amount. Students should write or discuss explanations for their solutions. Students with disabilities may need the visual support of having cards that say "add ten" or "add one" first to explore how the number changes. They may also need support with materials to be able to conceptualize the number and then move to more abstract work using only the calculator.

STUDENTS with SPECIAL NEEDS

FORMATIVE ASSESSMENT Notes. Students are often able to disguise their lack of understanding of place value by following directions, using the tens and ones pieces in prescribed ways, and using the language of place value.

The diagnostic interviews presented here are designed to help you look more closely at students' understanding of the integration of the three components of place value. Designed as interviews rather than full-class activities, these tasks have been used by several researchers and are adapted primarily from Labinowicz (1985), Kamii (1985), and Ross (1986).

The first interview is referred to as the Digit Correspondence Task. Take out 36 blocks. Ask the student to count the blocks, and then have the student write the number that tells how many there are. Circle the 6 in 36 and ask, "Does this part of your 36 have anything to do with how many blocks there are?" Then circle the 3 and repeat the question. As with all diagnostic interviews, do not give clues. Based on responses to the task, Ross (1989, 2002) has identified five distinct levels of understanding of place value:

1. *Single numeral.* The student writes 36 but views it as a single numeral. The individual digits 3 and 6 have no meaning by themselves.
2. *Position names.* The student correctly identifies the tens and ones positions but still makes no connections between the individual digits and the blocks.
3. *Face value.* The student matches 6 blocks with the 6 and 3 blocks with the 3.
4. *Transition to place value.* The 6 is matched with 6 blocks and the 3 with the remaining 30 blocks but not as 3 groups of 10.
5. *Full understanding.* The 3 is correlated with 3 groups of ten blocks and the 6 with 6 single blocks.

For the second interview, write the number 342. Have the student read the number. Then have the student write the number that is 1 more. Next, ask for the number that is 10 more. You may wish to explore further with models. One less and 10 less can be checked the same way. Observe whether the student is counting on or counting back or whether he immediately knows that ten more is 352. This interview can also be done with a two-digit number.

A third interview can also provide interesting evidence of depth of understanding. Ask the student to write the number that represents 5 tens, 2 ones, and 3 hundreds. Note that the task does not give the places in order. What do you think will be a common misunderstanding? If the student doesn't write 352, then ask them to show you the number with base-ten materials. Ask them what number they have with the materials. Compare to what they wrote previously, if different. What information can you get from the results of this interview?

Visit the companion website to watch a video clip relating to place value. ■

 Complete Self-Check 11.5: Oral and Written Names for Numbers

Patterns and Relationships with Multidigit Numbers

In this section, the focus will be on the patterns in our number system and how numbers are related. We are interested in the relationships of numbers to important special numbers called *benchmark numbers* and ten-structured thinking—that is, flexibility in using the structure of tens in our number system. These ideas begin to provide a basis for computation.

The Hundreds Chart

The Hundreds Chart (see Figure 11.12) is such an important tool in the development of place-value concepts that it deserves special attention. K–2 classrooms should have a hundreds chart displayed prominently.

1	2	3	4	5	6	7	8	9	10
11	12	13	14	15	16	17	18	19	20
21	22	23	24	25	26	27	28	29	30
31	32	33	34	35	36	37	38	39	40
41	42	43	44	45	46	47	48	49	50
51	52	53	54	55	56	57	58	59	60
61	62	63	64	65	66	67	68	69	70
71	72	73	74	75	76	77	78	79	80
81	82	83	84	85	86	87	88	89	90
91	92	93	94	95	96	97	98	99	100

FIGURE 11.12 A hundreds chart.

A useful version of a hundreds chart can be made of transparent pockets into which each of the 100 numeral cards can be inserted. Using colored paper inserts, number patterns such as skip counting by 2 (even numbers), 5, and 10 (2.NBT.A.2) can be highlighted easily for second graders. You can also have students skip count by threes and fours and color in each number they count. Discuss the pattern shown on the chart as well as the patterns in the numbers.

In the first grade, students can recognize two-digit numbers on the hundreds chart including the decade numbers from 10 to 100. Additionally, they can use the hundreds chart to develop a base-ten understanding of adding two-digit numbers with multiples of 10, noticing that jumps up or down are jumps of ten (1.NBT.C.4), while already recognizing that jumps to the right or left are jumps of one.

There are lots of patterns on the hundreds chart, and in discussions, different students will describe the same pattern in several ways. Accept all ideas. Here are some of the important place-value-related patterns students may point out:

- The numbers in a column all end with the same number, which is the same as the number at the top of the chart.
- In a row, the first number (tens digit) stays the same and the "second" number (ones digit) counts 1, 2, 3, . . . 9, 0) changes as you move across.
- In a column, the first number (tens digit) "counts" or goes up by ones as you move down.
- You can count by tens going down the far right-hand column.
- Starting at 11 and moving down on the diagonal, you can find numbers with the same digit in the tens and ones (e.g., 11, 22, 33, 44, and so on).

For students, these patterns are not obvious or trivial. For example, one student may notice the pattern in the column under the 4—every number ends in a 4. Two minutes later, another student will "discover" the parallel pattern in the column headed by 7. That there is a pattern like this in every column may not be completely obvious.

Once you've discussed some of the patterns, try the Missing Numbers activity.

Activity 11.13

CCSS-M: K.CC.A.1; K.NBT.A.1; 1.NBT.A.1; 1.NBT.B.2; 1.NBT.C.5

STUDENTS with SPECIAL NEEDS

Missing Numbers

Provide students with a hundreds chart on which some of the number cards have been removed. Use the classroom pocket hundreds chart or a projection. The students' task is to replace the missing numbers. To begin, have only a random selection of individual numbers removed. Later, remove sequences of several numbers from three or four different rows. Finally, remove all but one or two rows or columns. Eventually, challenge students to replace all of the numbers on the Blank Hundreds Chart. **For students with disabilities, model the placement of a missing number using a "think-aloud" to describe how you make your decision and what key features of the number you think about as you place the number properly on the chart.**

FORMATIVE ASSESSMENT Notes. Replacing the number cards or tiles on a blank chart is a good station activity for two students to try. By listening to how students go about finding the correct places for numbers, you can assess how well they have constructed an understanding of the 1-to-100 sequence. ∎

Activity 11.14

CCSS-M: K.CC.A.1; K.NBT.A.1; 1.NBT.A.1; 1.NBT.B.2; 1.NBT.C.5

Finding Neighbors on the Hundreds Chart

Begin with a blank or nearly Blank Hundreds Chart (project it on a screen or give individual students copies). Then, circle a particular missing number. Students should fill in the designated number and its "neighbors," the numbers to the left, right, above, and below. After students become comfortable naming the neighbors of a number, ask what they notice about the neighboring numbers. The numbers to the left and right are one less and one more than the given number. Those above and below are ten less and ten more, respectively. What about those on the diagonal? By discussing these relationships on the chart, students begin to see how the sequence of numbers is related to numerical relationships.

Notice that students will first use the hundreds chart to learn about the patterns in the sequence of numbers.

In the following activity, number relationships on the chart are made more explicit by modeling the numbers with base-ten materials.

CCSS Standards for Mathematical Practice

MP7. Look for and make use of structure.

Activity 11.15

CCSS-M: K.CC.A.1; K.NBT.A.1; 1.NBT.A.1; 1.NBT.B.2; 1.NBT.C.5

Models with the Hundreds Chart

Use any base-ten model for two-digit numbers with which the students are familiar. Access Base-Ten Materials or the Little Ten-Frame Cards.

- Give students one or more numbers to first make with the models and then find on the chart. Use groups of two or three numbers in either the same row or the same column.

- Indicate a number on the chart. What would you have to change to make each of its neighbors (the numbers to the left, to the right, above, and below)?

As a first step in moving to larger numbers, continue your hundreds charts to 200. Then extend the hundreds chart to a thousands chart.

TECHNOLOGY Note. Several web-based resources include hundreds charts that allow students to explore patterns. Learning about Number Relationships is an example from NCTM's *e-Standards* that has a calculator and hundreds chart and allows for a variety of explorations. (There are extensions to thousands charts, too.) Students can skip-count by any number and also begin their counts at any number. ABCya's Interactive Number Chart (0-99 or 1-100) allows the students to find and document patterns using by coloring the squares that contain the numbers. ■

Activity 11.16

CCSS-M: 2.NBT.A.1; 2.NBT.A.2; 2.NBT.A.3; 2.NBT.B.8

The Thousands Chart

Provide students with several Blank Hundreds Charts. Assign groups of three or four students the task of creating a 1-to-1000 chart. The chart is made by taping 10 hundreds charts together in a long strip. Students should decide how they will divide up the task, with different students taking different parts of the chart. The thousands chart should be discussed as a class to examine how numbers change as you count from one hundred to the next, what the patterns are, and so on. In fact, all of the earlier hundreds chart activities can be extended to thousands charts.

Relationships with Benchmark Numbers

One of the most valuable features of both the hundreds chart and the little ten-frame cards is how clearly they illustrate the distance to the next multiple of 10—the end of the row on the chart or the blank spaces on the ten-frame card. Multiples of 10, 100, and occasionally other special numbers, such as multiples of 25, are referred to as *benchmark* numbers. Students learn to use this term as they work with informal methods of computation. When finding the difference between 74 and 112, a student might say, "First, I added 6 onto 74 to get to 80, which is a benchmark number. Then I added 2 more tens onto 80 to get to 100 because that's another benchmark number." Whatever terminology is used, understanding how numbers are related to these special numbers is an important step in students' development of number sense and place value.

In addition to the hundreds chart, the number line is an excellent way to explore these relationships. The next two activities are suggestions for using the Number Lines Activity Page as a student recording sheet.

Activity 11.17

CCSS-M: 1.NBT.A.1; 1.NBT.B.2; 1.NBT.B.3; 2.NBT.A.1; 2.NBT.A.2; 2.NBT.A.4

Who Am I?

Sketch a long line (or use cash register tape) and label 0 and 100 at opposite ends. Mark a point with a "?" that corresponds to your secret number. (Estimate the position the best you can.) Have students try to guess your secret number. For each guess, place and label a mark at that number on the line until your secret number is discovered. As a variation, the end points can be different from 0 and 100. For example, try 0 and 1000, 200 and 300, or 500 and 800.

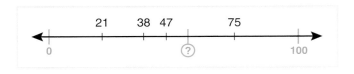

Activity 11.18

CCSS-M: 1.NBT.A.1; 1.NBT.B.2; 1.NBT.B.3; 2.NBT.A.1; 2.NBT.A.2; 2.NBT.A.4

Who Could They Be?

Label two points on a number line (not necessarily the ends) with benchmark numbers. Show students different points labeled with letters and ask what numbers they might be and why they think that. In the example shown here, B and C are less than 100 but probably more than 60. E could be about 180. You can also ask where 75 might be or where 400 is. About how far apart are A and D? Why do you think D is more than 100? For ELLs, rather than just saying the numbers, also write them on a card or ask students to write them.

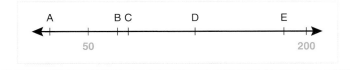

The next activity has students apply some of the same ideas about benchmark numbers that we have been exploring.

Activity 11.19

CCSS-M: 1.NBT.A.1; 1.NBT.B.2; 1.NBT.B.3; 2.NBT.A.1; 2.NBT.A.2; 2.NBT.A.4

ENGLISH LANGUAGE LEARNERS

Close, Far, and In Between

Put any three numbers on the board. If more appropriate for your students, use two-digit numbers.

With these three numbers as referents, ask questions such as the following, encouraging discussion of all responses:

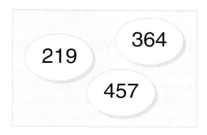

Which two numbers are closest? How do you know?

Which is closest to 300? To 250?

Name a number between 457 and 364.

Name a multiple of 10 between 219 and 364.

Name an even number that is greater than all of these numbers.

About how far apart are 219 and 500? 219 and 5000?

If these are "big numbers," what are some small numbers? Numbers that are about the same? Numbers that make these seem small?

For ELLs, this activity can be modified by using prompts that are similar to each other (rather than changing the prompts each time, which increases the linguistic demand). Also, ELLs will benefit from using a visual, such as a number line, and from writing the numbers rather than just hearing/saying them.

Look at the corresponding Expanded Lesson, where students estimate the relative size of a number between 0 and 100, and strengthen their conceptual understanding of number size and place value.

Connections to Real-World Ideas

We should not permit students to study place-value concepts without encouraging them to see numbers in the world around them. You do not need a prescribed activity to bring real numbers into the classroom.

Students in the second grade should be thinking about numbers up to 1000 (CCSSO, 2010). Where are numbers like this in the school? You might use the number of children in the third grade, the number of minutes devoted to mathematics each week, or the number of days since school has started. And then there are measurements, numbers discovered on a field trip, numbers in books in other subject areas, and so on. What do you do with these numbers? Turn them into interesting graphs, write stories using them, and make up problems. For example, how many cartons of chocolate and plain milk are served in the cafeteria each month? Can students estimate how many cartons will be sold in a year? Collecting data and then grouping into tens and hundreds (or thousands) will help cement the value of grouping in situations when you need to count and compare.

As students get more skilled, the interest in numbers can expand beyond the school to the home and the community. The particular way you bring number and the real world together in your class is up to you. But do not underestimate the value of connecting the real world to the classroom.

Complete Self-Check 11.6: Patterns and Relationships with Multidigit Numbers

Numbers beyond 1000

For students to have good concepts of numbers beyond 1000, the place-value ideas that have been carefully developed must be extended. This is sometimes difficult to do because physical models for thousands are not readily available, or you may just have one large cube to show. At the same time, number-sense ideas must also be developed. In many ways, it is these informal ideas about very large numbers that are the most important.

Extending the Place-Value System

Two important ideas developed for three-digit numbers should be extended to larger numbers as students move to thinking about 1,000,000 in fourth grade (CCSS0, 2010). First, the multiplicative structure of the number system should be generalized. That is, ten in any position makes a single thing (group) in the next position to the left, and vice versa. Second, the oral and written patterns for numbers in three digits are duplicated in a clever way for every three digits to the left. These two related ideas are not as easy for students to understand as adults seem to believe. Because models for large numbers are so difficult to demonstrate or visualize, textbooks must deal with these ideas in a predominantly symbolic manner. That is not sufficient!

Activity 11.20   CCSS-M: 2.NBT.A.1; 2.NBT.A.3

What Comes Next?

Use paper models of Base-Ten Materials. The unit or ones piece is a 1-centimeter (cm) square. The tens piece is a 10–cm × 1–cm strip. The hundreds piece is a square, 10 cm × 10 cm. What is next? Ten hundreds is called a thousand. What shape would a thousand be? Tape together a long strip made of 10 paper hundreds squares. What comes next? (Reinforce the idea of "10 makes 1" that has progressed to this point.) Ten one-thousand strips would make a square measuring 1 meter (m) on each side, making a paper ten-thousands model. Once the class has figured out the shape of each piece, the problem posed to them is, "What comes next?" Let small groups work on the dimensions of a hundred-thousand piece.

If your students become interested in seeing the big pieces from "What Comes Next?" engage them in measuring them out on paper. Ten ten-thousand squares (100,000) go together to make a huge strip. Draw this strip on a long sheet of brown paper and mark off the 10 squares that make it up. You will have to go out in the hall.

How far you want to extend this square-strip–square-strip sequence depends on your class. The idea that 10 in one place makes 1 in the next can be brought home dramatically and memorably. It is quite possible with older students to make the next 10-m × 10-m square using chalk lines on the playground. The next strip is 100 m × 10 m. This can be measured out on a large playground with students marking the corners. By this point, the payoff includes an appreciation of both the increase in size of each successive amount and the 10-makes-1 progression. The 10-m × 10-m square models 1 million, and the 10-m × 10-m strip is the model for 10 million. The difference between 1 million and 10 million is dramatic. Even the concept of 1 million tiny centimeter squares is impressive.

Try the "What Comes Next?" discussion in the context of three-dimensional models. The first three shapes are distinct: a *cube*, a *long*, and a *flat*. What comes next? Stack 10 flats and they make a cube—the same shape as the first one, only 1000 times larger. What comes next?

Standards for Mathematical Practice

MP7. Look for and make sense of structure.

(See Figure 11.13.) Ten cubes make another long. What comes next? Ten big longs make a big flat. The first three shapes have now repeated! Ten big flats will make an even bigger cube, and the trio of shapes begins again. The pattern of "10 of these makes 1 of those" is "infinitely extendable" (Thomas, 2004, p. 305). Note that students with disabilities may have difficulty interpreting spatial information, which plays into their challenges with interpreting the progression of place-value materials (Geary & Hoard, 2005). Although we are using the terms *cube*, *long*, and *flat* to describe the shape of the materials, students will see the shape pattern made as each gets 10 times larger. In fact, it is still critical to call these representations "ones, tens, and hundreds," particularly for students with disabilities. We need to consistently name them by the number they represent rather than their shape. This reinforces conceptual understanding and is less confusing for students who may struggle with these concepts.

Each cube has a name. The first one is the *unit* cube, the next is a *thousand*, the next a *million*, then a *billion*, and so on. Each long is 10 cubes: 10 units, 10 thousands, 10 millions. Similarly, each flat shape is 100 cubes.

To read a number, first mark it off in triples from the right. The triples are then read, stopping at the end of each to name the unit for that triple (see Figure 11.14). Leading zeros in each triple are ignored. If students can learn to read numbers like 059 (fifty-nine) or 009 (nine), they should be able to read any number. To write a number, use the same scheme. If first mastered orally, the system is quite easy. Remind students not to use the word "and" when reading a whole number. For example, 106 should be read as "one hundred six," not "one hundred *and* six." The word "and" will be needed to signify a decimal point. Please make sure you read numbers accurately.

It is important for students to realize that the system does have a logical structure, is not totally arbitrary, and can be understood.

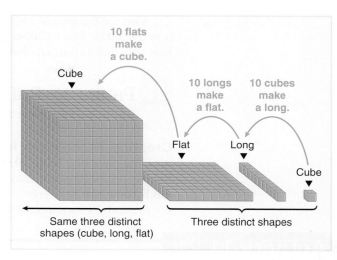

FIGURE 11.13 With every three places, the shapes repeat. Each cube represents a 1, each long represents a 10, and each flat represents a 100.

Conceptualizing Large Numbers

The ideas just discussed are only partially helpful in thinking about the actual quantities involved in very large numbers. For example, in extending the paper square-strip-square-strip sequence, some appreciation for the quantities of 1000 or of 100,000 is acquired. But it is hard for anyone to translate quantities of small squares into quantities of other items, distances, or time.

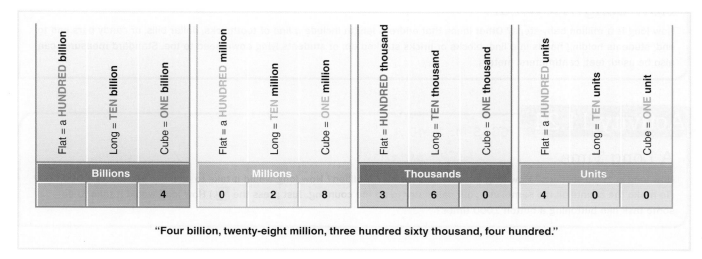

"Four billion, twenty-eight million, three hundred sixty thousand, four hundred."

FIGURE 11.14 The triples system for naming large numbers.

Visit the companion website to watch a video clip of a teacher discussing with her students how 192,000 is also 19,200 tens. These are important discussions to consider and you will see how they link to computational skills.

 Pause & Reflect

How do you think about 1000 or 100,000? Do you have any real concept of a million? ●

Creating References for Large Benchmark Numbers. In the following activities, numbers like 1000, 10,000 (see 10,000 Grid paper), or even 1,000,000 are translated literally or imaginatively into something that is easy or fun to think about. Interesting quantities become lasting reference points or benchmarks for large numbers and thereby add meaning to numbers encountered in real life.

Activity 11.21

CCSS-M: 2.NBT.A.2; 2.NBT.A.3

Collecting 10,000

As a class or grade-level project, collect some type of object with the objective of reaching some specific quantity—for example, 1000 or 10,000 bread tabs or soda can pop tops. If you begin aiming for 100,000 or 1,000,000, be sure to think it through. One teacher spent nearly 10 years with her classes before amassing a million bottle caps. It takes a small dump truck to hold that many!

Activity 11.22

CCSS-M: 2.NBT.A.2; 2.NBT.A.3

Showing 10,000

Sometimes it is easier to create large amounts than to collect them. For example, start a project in which students draw 100 or 200 or even 500 dots on a sheet of paper. Each week, different students contribute a specified number. Another idea is to cut up newspapers into pieces the same size as dollar bills to see what a large quantity would look like. Paper chain links can be constructed over time and hung down the hallways with special numbers marked. Let the school be aware of the ultimate goal.

Activity 11.23

CCSS-M: 2.NBT.A.1a; 2.NBT.A.3

How Long?/How Far?

How long is a million baby steps? Other ideas that address length include a line of toothpicks, dollar bills, or candy bars end to end; students holding hands in a line; blocks or bricks stacked up; or students lying down head to toe. Standard measures can also be used: feet, centimeters, meters.

Activity 11.24

CCSS-M: 3.MD.A.1

A Long Time

How long is 1000 seconds? How long is a million seconds? A billion? How long would it take to count to 10,000 or 1,000,000? (To make the counts all the same, use your calculator to do the counting. Just press the = .) How long would it take to do some task like buttoning a button 1000 times?

Estimating Large Quantities. Activities 11.21 through 11.24 focus on specific numbers. The reverse idea is to select a large quantity and find some way to measure, count, or estimate how many.

Activity 11.25   CCSS-M: 2.MD.A.3; 3.MD.A.1; 3.MD.C.5

Really Large Quantities

Ask how many:

- Candy bars would cover the floor of your classroom
- Steps an ant would take to walk around the school building
- Grains of rice would fill a cup or a gallon jug
- Quarters could be stacked in one stack from floor to ceiling
- Pennies can be laid side by side down the entire hallway
- Pieces of notebook paper would cover the gym floor
- Seconds you have lived

Big-number projects need not take up large amounts of class time. They can be explored over several weeks as take-home projects, done as group projects, or, perhaps best of all, translated into great schoolwide estimation events.

 Complete Self-Check 11.7: Numbers beyond 1000

REFLECTIONS ON CHAPTER 11

WRITING TO LEARN

1. Name the three ways one can count a set of objects. Explain how these methods of counting can be used to coordinate concepts and oral and written names for numbers.

2. Describe the three types of physical models for base-ten concepts. What is the significance of the differences between these models?

3. How can students learn to write two- and three-digit numbers in a way that is connected to the base-ten meanings of ones and tens or ones, tens, and hundreds?

4. Describe some ways you can develop the concepts of large numbers in students.

5. What are benchmark numbers? Describe the relationships you want students to develop concerning benchmark numbers. Describe an activity that addresses these relationships.

FOR DISCUSSION AND EXPLORATION

- Based on the suggestions in this chapter, conduct a diagnostic interview with a student. If possible invite a colleague to act as an observer or to use a video recorder to document the interview. Analyze the student's understanding of the concepts, and suggest your next instructional steps.

RESOURCES FOR CHAPTER 11

LITERATURE CONNECTIONS

Books that emphasize groups of things, even simple counting books, are a good beginning to the notion of ten things in a single group. Many books have wonderful explorations of large quantities and how the numbers can be composed and decomposed.

100th Day Worries *Cuyler (2005)*

The 100th Day of School from the Black Lagoon
Thaler, 2014

Both of these books focus on the 100th day of school, which is one way to recognize the benchmark number of 100. Through a variety of ways to think about 100 (such as collections of 100 items), students will be able to use these stories to think about the relative size of 100 or ways to make 100 using a variety of combinations.

How Much Is a Million? *Schwartz (2004)* (https://www.youtube.com/watch?v=MKkK87E46I4)

If You Made a Million *Schwartz (1994)* (https://www.youtube.com/watch?v=N8cNRB_VWJI)

On Beyond a Million: An Amazing Math Journey *Schwartz (2001)*

The Magic of a Million Activity Book—
Grades 2–5 *Schwartz & Whitin (1999)*

David Schwartz has generated a series of entertaining and conceptually sound children's books about the powers of ten or what makes a million—from visual images of students standing on one another's shoulders in a formation that reaches the moon to various monetary collections. In addition, the activity book by Schwartz and Whitin provides a series of powerful activities to help students interpret large numbers.

If I Had a Million Bucks *Johnson (2012)*

This story is about Ada, a girl who likes to plan. Ada is thinking about what she could do if she had one million dollars.

This is a fun way to have students think about what could be purchased with large amounts of money.

RECOMMENDED READINGS

Articles

Burris, J. T. (2013). Virtual place value. *Teaching Children Mathematics, 20*(4), 228–236.

This is an interesting study that explored teaching place value using several activities with technology. Students worked with both concrete base-ten materials and virtual versions to help reinforce conceptual structures, particularly for showing equivalent representations.

Kari, A. R., & Anderson, C. B. (2003). Opportunities to develop place value through student dialogue. *Teaching Children Mathematics, 10*(2), 78–82.

Two teachers describe a mixed first-/second-grade classroom, illustrating in vivid detail how students' understanding of two-digit numbers can at first be quite mistaken, but can be developed conceptually with the aid of discussion. Much of the conversation revolves around a student's belief that any 1 in a number stands for ten. The student in the article is convinced that 11 + 11 + 11 is 60. Reading this article emphasizes the wide range of student ideas and the value of classroom discourse.

Book

Richardson, K. (2003). *Assessing math concepts: Grouping tens.* Bellingham, WA: Mathematical Perspectives.

This is one of a nine-part series on using diagnostic interviews and other assessment tools to understand students' grasp of a concept—in this case, grouping by tens. Tips are shared about conducting careful observations, with suggestions for instruction. Blackline Masters are included to support the assessments.

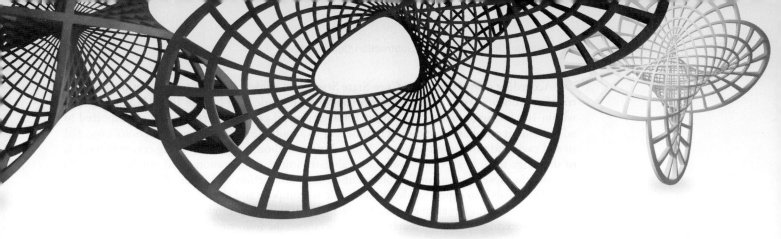

12

Developing Strategies for Addition and Subtraction Computation

LEARNER OUTCOMES

After reading this chapter and engaging in the embedded activities and reflections, you should be able to:

12.1 Recognize the interplay between understanding place value and learning addition and subtraction computational strategies.

12.2 Identify three types of computational strategies.

12.3 Demonstrate how to develop a classroom environment for supporting students' use of invented strategies with a variety of models.

12.4 Explain multiple invented strategies for addition and subtraction with multidigit numbers.

12.5 Explain the development of the standard algorithm and ways to record students' thinking.

12.6 Identify ways to teach computational estimation as a way to develop students' flexibility and ability to recognize reasonable answers.

12.7 Describe three computational estimation strategies for addition and subtraction.

Much of the public sees computational skills as the hallmark of what it means to know mathematics at the elementary school level. Although that is far from the whole story, learning computational skills with whole numbers is, in fact, a very important part of the curriculum. Expectations for competency in today's workforce as well as in daily life mean that changes are warranted in how computation is taught.

Rather than presenting a single method of adding or subtracting, the most appropriate method can and should change flexibly as the numbers and the context change. In the spirit of the Common Core State Standards (CCSSO, 2010) and the Principles and Standards for School Mathematics (NCTM, 2000), the goal is no longer just a matter of "knowing how to subtract three-digit numbers," rather, it is the development over time of an assortment of flexible skills that will best serve students as they prepare for college and careers. *Adding It Up* (National Research Council, 2001) describes it this way:

> More than just a means to produce answers, computation is increasingly seen as a window on the deep structure of the number system. Fortunately, research is demonstrating that both skilled performance and conceptual understanding are generated by the same kinds of activities. (p. 182)

According to the Common Core State Standards, students should solve addition and subtraction problems with numbers appropriate for their grade level (within 10 for kindergartners, within 100 for first graders, and within 1000 for second graders). First graders are expected to add two-digit numbers to one-digit numbers or to a multiple of 10. Second graders are expected to add two- and three-digit numbers. The solution methods range from using concrete models or drawings to strategies based on place value, meanings of operations, and number sense. To support the development of flexible addition and subtraction strategies, the Common Core State Standards also expect students to be able to compose and decompose numbers (numbers less than 20 for kindergartners, numbers less than 100 for first graders, and numbers less than 1000 for second graders). To reach these expectations the following big ideas are essential.

 BIG IDEAS

◆ Flexible methods of addition and subtraction computation involve taking apart (decomposing) and combining (composing) numbers in a wide variety of ways. Most of the decomposing of numbers is based on place value or compatible numbers—which are number pairs that work easily together, such as 25 and 75.

◆ Invented strategies provide flexible methods of computing that vary with the numbers and the situation. Successful use of the strategies requires that they be understood by the one who is using them—hence the term *invented*.

◆ Flexible methods for computation require a deep understanding of the operations and properties of the operations (the commutative property and the associative property). How addition and subtraction are related as inverse operations is also important.

◆ The standard algorithms are elegant strategies for computing that are based on performing the operation on one place value at a time with transitions to an adjacent position (trades or regrouping). Standard algorithms tend to cause students to think in terms of digits rather than the composite number that the digits make up, so students often lose track of the actual place value of a digit.

◆ Multidigit numbers can be built up or taken apart in a variety of ways to make the numbers easier to work with. These parts can be used to estimate answers in calculations rather than using the exact numbers involved. For example, 36 is the same as 30 and 6 or 25 and 10 and 1. Also, 483 can be thought of as $500 - 20 + 3$.

◆ Computational estimations involve using easier-to-handle parts of numbers or substituting difficult-to-handle numbers with close compatible numbers so that the resulting computations can be done mentally.

 Toward Computational Fluency

Addition and subtraction strategies that build on decomposing and composing numbers in flexible ways contribute to students' overall number sense. In most everyday instances, these alternative strategies for computing are easier and faster than the standard algorithms (procedures for computing) and can often be done mentally. Therefore, it is best to have students learn a variety of methods that they can select from as needed. Did you learn a single way to add or subtract or were you encouraged to use a collection of flexible approaches?

Consider the following problem:

Mary has 114 spaces in her photo album. So far, she has placed 89 photos in the album. How many more photos can she put in before the album is full?

❚❚ Pause & Reflect

Try solving the photo album problem using a method other than the one you were taught in school. If you are tempted to begin with the 9 and the 4, try a different approach. Can you solve it mentally? Can you solve it in more than one way? Work on this before reading further. ●

Here are just four of many methods that have been used by students in the primary grades to solve the computation in the photo album problem:

89 + 11 is 100. 11 + 14 is 25.

90 + 10 is 100 and 14 more is 24 plus 1 (because we should have started at 89, not 90) is 25.

Subtract 14 and then subtract 10 more to get 90, and then 1 more to get to 89, which is 25 in all.

89, 99, 109 (that's 20), 110, 111, 112, 113, 114 (keeping track on fingers) is 25.

Strategies such as these can be done mentally, are generally faster than standard algorithms, and make sense to the person using them. Every day, students and adults resort to often error-prone standard algorithms that they don't fully understand when other, more meaningful methods would be faster and more accurate. For a closer look at several of the standard algorithms, go to the University of Chicago's Everyday Mathematics website and search "Algorithms." This site provides video examples of various computational algorithms including the research base, advice for use, and other information. "In addition, early work with reasoning strategies is related to algebraic reasoning. As students learn how quantities can be taken apart and put back together in different ways (i.e., decomposition and composition of numbers), they establish a basis for understanding properties of the operations" (NCTM, 2014, p. 39). Flexibility with a variety of computational strategies is an important tool for a mathematically literate citizen to be successful in daily life. It is time to broaden our perspective of what it means to compute. Watch this video (https://www.youtube.com/watch?v=ZFUAV00bTwA) in which William McCallum and Jason Zimba, lead writers of the Common Core State Standards for Mathematics, describe the relationship between developing understanding and fluency in computation. If you haven't developed these strategies on your own, you will learn them as you read this chapter and as you teach! Let's connect to where we just left off—place value.

Connecting Addition and Subtraction to Place Value

One important shift has been to blend instruction on numeration and place value with computation with two- and three-digit (and beyond) numbers. This emerges from research that shows that learning place value is a prerequisite for learning operations with those numbers (Baroody, 1990) and other research that suggests that problems involving addition and subtraction are a good context for learning place-value concepts (Wright, Martland, Stafford, & Stanger, 2008). If students only understand computation as a digit-by-digit exercise and not the value of the numbers involved, they make many errors and are often unable to judge the reasonableness of their answers. So here we will connect place value to addition and subtraction. The key component in the following activities is whether students can apply their emerging understanding of place value to computation. Remember, place value is not only a basis for computation; students also develop place-value understanding as a *result* of finding their own methods of computing.

For example, Jerrika, in January of the first grade, solves a story problem for 10 + 13 + 22 using connecting cubes. Her written work (Figure 12.1) shows she is still at a pre-place-value stage. We can observe that she is beginning to use the idea of "1 ten" but most likely counted on the remaining 35 cubes by ones. Her classmate, Monica, solved the same problem but has clearly utilized more base-ten ideas (Figure 12.1). Ideas such as these continue to grow with additional problem solving and sharing of ideas during class discussions.

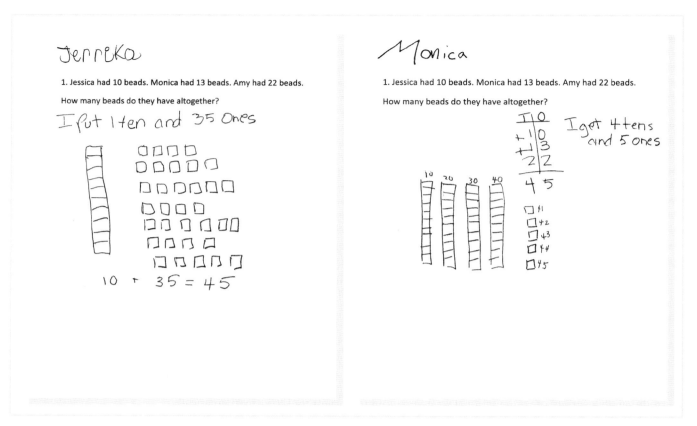

FIGURE 12.1 The work of two first graders in January. They both solved the problem $10 + 13 + 22$.

The activities in this section are designed to further students' understanding of place value concepts while engaging them in addition and subtraction. The first of these bridging activities involves counting with a constant using the calculator. By adjusting the numbers, it can be made appropriate for almost any ability level.

Activity 12.1
CCSS-M: 1.NBT.C.5

Calculator Challenge Counting

STUDENTS with SPECIAL NEEDS

Students press any number on the calculator (e.g., **17**) and then ⊞ **10**. They say the sum before they press ⊟. Then they continue to add **10** mentally, challenging themselves to say the sum before they press ⊟. Students should see how far they can go without making a mistake.

You can differentiate this activity for students by adjusting the numbers. You may want to begin with a starting number less than **10** for students with disabilities or with a number such as **327** for students who need a challenge. Also, the constant addend (⊞ **10** in the preceding example) can be any number with one, two, or three digits. Some students will even find jumps of **5** can be fairly challenging if the starting number is not a multiple of **5**. Skip counting by **20** or **25** will be easier than counting by **7** or **12** and will help develop important patterns and relationships.

Also try the reverse. That is, enter a number such as **53** (or **123**) in the calculator and press ⊟ **10** (or for more of a challenge, try ⊟ **6**). As before, students say the result before pressing ⊟. Each successive press will subtract **10** or **6** or whatever constant was entered. Have students share strategies for determining the sum or difference and discuss patterns that appear.

The flexibility of this activity allows for it to be used over and over at various skill levels, always challenging students and improving their mental skills with numbers.

The key purpose of the following activities is to provide opportunities for students to apply their emerging understanding of place value to computation using benchmark numbers.

Activity 12.2   CCSS-M: 1.NBT.B.4

50 and Some More

Say or write a number between 50 and 100. Students respond with "50 and ____." For 63, the response is "50 and 13." Any benchmark number can be used instead of 50. For example, you could use any number that ends in 50 for the first part, such as "450 and some more." Or you can use numbers such as 70 or 230 as starting points.

The benchmark numbers we explored in our discussions of place value are also used in computational strategies to make the calculations easier. The next activity is aimed at what may be one of the most important benchmark numbers: 100.

Activity 12.3   CCSS-M: 1.NBT.B.4; 2.NBT.B.5

The Other Part of 100

Two students work together with a set of Little Ten-Frames. One student makes a two-digit number. Then both students work mentally to determine what goes with the ten-frame amount to equal 100. They write their solutions on paper and then check by making the other part with the cards to see whether the total is 100. Students take turns making the original number (see Other Part of 100 Activity Page). Figure 12.2 shows three different thought processes that students might use.

Have students take a look at Maurice's Chart. Have them decide whether Maurice is right or wrong and, if needed, describe how to correct the mistake.

If your students are adept at finding parts of 100, you can change the whole from 100 to other multiples of 10 such as 70 or 80 or extend the whole to any number less than 100.

⏸ Pause & Reflect

Suppose that the whole is 83. Sketch four little ten-frame cards showing 36. Looking at your cards, what goes with 36 to equal 83? How did you think about it? ●

What you might have done in finding the other part of 83 was subtract 36 from 83. Or you might have added up from 36 to 83. Notice that you did not regroup. Most likely you did it in your head, possibly using benchmark numbers and place value. With more practice you (and students as early as second grade) can do this without the aid of the cards.

Compatible numbers for addition and subtraction are numbers that easily combine to equal benchmark numbers. Numbers that equal tens or hundreds are the most common examples. Compatible sums also include numbers that end in 5, 25, 50, or 75, because these numbers are easy to work with as well. Your task is to get students accustomed to looking for combinations that work together and then looking for these combinations in computational situations.

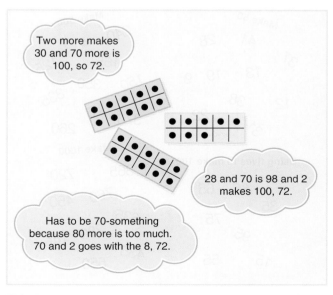

Two more makes 30 and 70 more is 100, so 72.

28 and 70 is 98 and 2 makes 100, 72.

Has to be 70-something because 80 more is too much. 70 and 2 goes with the 8, 72.

FIGURE 12.2   Thinking about the "other part of 100."

Activity 12.4 CCSS-M: 2.NBT.B.5

Compatible Pairs

Searching for compatible pairs can be done as an activity with the full class. One at a time, project the 4 suggested searches in Figure 12.3. The possible searches are at different difficulty levels. Have students name or connect the compatible pairs as they see them.

The next activity combines base-ten representations with symbolism.

Activity 12.5 CCSS-M: 2.NBT.B.7

Numbers, Squares, Lines, and Dots

As illustrated in Figure 12.4, share some base-ten pieces and the Number, Squares, Lines, and Dots Activity Page as handouts or displays. Use small squares (hundreds), lines (tens), and dots (ones) to represent base-ten materials with simple drawings. Students then mentally compute the totals or the differences. Note that the subtraction problems with the removed amount represented by the numeral will be easiest to start with.

If this activity is done with the whole class, discuss each task before moving to the next. If you use the activity sheet, you can display individual problems or cut the handout and have students write how they went about solving each. But it is still important to have a discussion with the class. Students can also show these representations as a way to calculate or check answers, as shown in the work of a second grader in Figure 12.5.

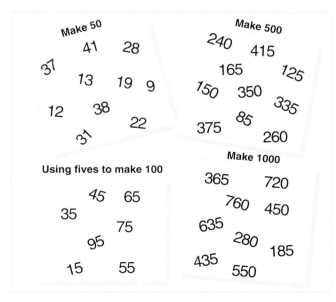

FIGURE 12.3   Compatible-pair searches.

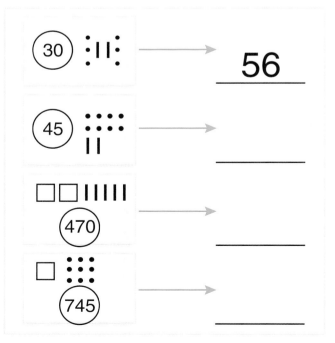

FIGURE 12.4   Flexible counting on or addition using both models and numerals.

The next activity extends the use of the hundreds chart by using it for addition (https://www.youtube.com/watch?v=cNLP8JylBvY).

The hundreds chart can be thought of as a stacked number line—one that highlights the distance from any number to the next multiple of 10. A jump down a row is the same as adding 10, and a jump up a row is 10 less. As illustrated in Figure 12.6(a), you will see that a student added 13 + 12 by just counting by ones. Many students like this one will simply count on 12 individual squares from 13—an indication that they may not understand how to count by tens from any starting value (an important place-value concept). Consider how a student might use the hundreds chart to help think about the sum of 27 and 12. This next student's approach (Figure 12.6(b)) is to begin at 27, jump down one row, and count over 2 to 39. Figure 12.6(c) shows a subtraction problem with a drawing of part of a hundreds chart, beginning at 39, jumping up one row, and backing off 2. Notice how the student checked her answer by using an equation.

The following activity is similar to Hundreds Chart Addition but explores the idea of "think-addition" as a method of subtraction.

Your choice of the two numbers will have an impact on the strategies students will use. The easiest pairs are in the same column on the hundreds chart, such as 24 and 64, which is a good place to begin. When the larger number is in a different column from the smaller number (e.g., 24 and 56), students can add on tens to get to the target number's row and then add or subtract ones. Of course, this is also a reasonable strategy for any two numbers. But consider 17 and 45, where the column that 45 is in on the chart is to the left of the column that 17 is in. A student might count by tens and go down 3 rows (+ 30) to 47 and then count back 2 (− 2) to 45. The total count is now 30 − 2 or 28. There are also other possible approaches. The next activity uses little ten-frame cards instead of the hundreds chart.

FORMATIVE ASSESSMENT Notes. Students who exhibit difficulty with any of these activities may be challenged with invented computation strategies. Therefore, conduct a diagnostic interview to find how students strategize the exercises in Activity 12.5, "Numbers, Squares, Lines, and Dots." That activity requires that students have sufficient understanding of base-ten concepts to use them in meaningful counts. If students are still counting by ones, perhaps on their fingers, then back up and consider additional counting activities in which students have opportunities to see the value of grouping by ten before moving on. ■

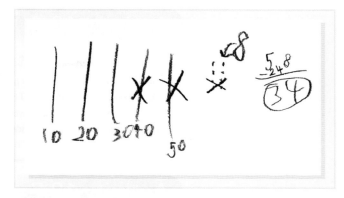

FIGURE 12.5   A student shows subtraction using a line and dot model.

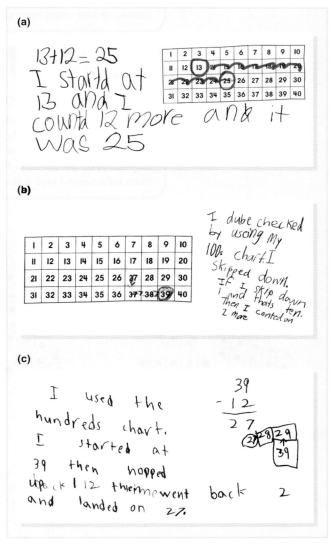

FIGURE 12.6   Three students use the hundreds chart to add or subtract.

Activity 12.6
CCSS-M: 2.NBT.B.5

Hundreds Chart Addition

Display a hundreds chart (or a thousands chart) for all students to see or, alternatively, give students their own individual hundreds charts from the Four Small Hundreds Charts. Students use the hundreds chart to add two numbers (e.g., 38 and 14). There are many ways that students can use the hundreds chart for addition, so the value is in the class discussions. Have students work on one sum at a time and then have a discussion to compare the different methods students used.

Activity 12.7
CCSS-M: 2.NBT.B.5

How Much Between?

Provide students a blank Hundreds Chart. Give the students two numbers. Their task is to determine how much from one number to the next.

Activity 12.8
CCSS-M: 2.NBT.B.5

Little Ten-Frame Sums

Provide pairs of students with two sets of Little Ten-Frames. Each student chooses a number. An example (47 + 36) is shown in Figure 12.7. Partners work to find the total number of dots recording the pair of numbers and the sum. The activity can also be done by showing the two ten-frames on the projector for 10–15 seconds and asking the students to give the total. Show them for a second look if students request another look.

How much in all?

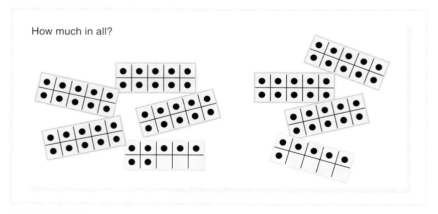

FIGURE 12.7 Using little ten-frame cards to add.

 Complete Self-Check 12.1: Connecting Addition and Subtraction to Place Value

Three Types of Computational Strategies

Figure 12.8 lists a general instructional sequence that includes three types of computational strategies. The direct modeling methods can, with guidance, develop into an assortment of more flexible and useful invented strategies, many of which can be carried out mentally. The standard algorithms remain an important part of what students need to learn. However, reinforce that, just like the other strategies, the standard algorithm is more useful in some instances than in others. Discuss which methods seem best in which situations.

Direct Modeling

The developmental step that usually precedes invented strategies and takes place in the primary grades for addition and subtraction and in grades 3 and 4 for multiplication and division is called *direct modeling*. This is the use of manipulatives or drawings along with counting to directly represent the meaning of an operation or story problem (see Figure 12.9).

Students who consistently count by ones in additive situations most likely have not developed base-ten grouping concepts. That does not mean that they should not continue to solve problems involving two-digit numbers. As you work with students who are still struggling with seeing ten as a unit, suggest that they consider a tool to help them think, such as grouping counters by tens as they count or making bars of 10 from connecting cubes. Some students will initially use the base-ten rod of 10 as a counting device to keep track of counts of ten, even though they are counting each 10 rod by ones. Have students write down the corresponding numbers for memory support (perhaps as they complete each intermediate step).

Students will soon move from direct modeling to invented strategies derived from number sense and the properties of operations. But direct modeling is a necessary phase for students to work through. These developmental strategies are also important because they provide students who are not ready for more efficient methods a way to explore the same problems as classmates who have progressed beyond this stage. It is important not to push students to prematurely abandon concrete approaches using materials. However, some students may need encouragement to move away from direct modeling. Here are some ideas to promote the fading of direct modeling:

- Record students' verbal explanations on the board in ways that they and others can follow.
- Ask students who have just solved a problem with models if they can do it mentally.
- Ask students to make a written numeric record of how they solved the problem with models. Then have them try the same written method on a new problem.

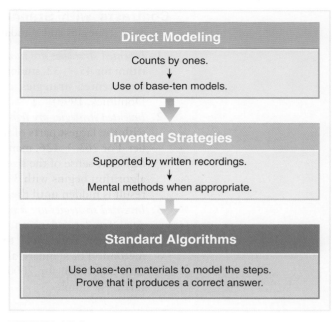

FIGURE 12.8 Three types of computational strategies.

FIGURE 12.9 A possible direct modeling of 36 + 27 using base-ten models.

Invented Strategies

Carpenter and colleagues (1998) refer to any strategy other than the standard algorithm or that does not involve the use of physical materials or counting by ones as an *invented strategy*. In the Common Core State Standards (CCSSO, 2010) they describe these in their expectations for first and second graders as "strategies based on place value, properties of operations, and/or the relationship between addition and subtraction" (pp. 16, 19). More specifically, students are expected to "develop, discuss, and use efficient, accurate, and generalizable methods to compute sums and difference of whole numbers in base-ten notation, using their understanding of place value and the properties of operations" (p. 17). At times, invented strategies become mental methods after the ideas have been explored, used, and understood. For example, after some experience, students may be able to do 75 + 19 mentally (75 + 20 is 95, less 1 is 94). For 847 + 256, students may need to write down intermediate steps (i.e., add 3 more) to support their memory as they work through the problem. (Try that one yourself.) In the classroom, written support is often encouraged as strategies develop because they are more easily shared and help students focus on the ideas. Distinctions among written, partially written, and mental computation are not important, especially in the development period.

A number of research studies have focused attention on how students of a variety of ages handle computational situations when they have been given options for multiple strategies (Keiser, 2010; Lynch & Star, 2014; Rittle-Johnson, Star, & Durkin, 2010; Verschaffel, Greer, & De Corte, 2007). "There is mounting evidence that students both in and out of school can construct methods for adding and subtracting multi-digit numbers without explicit instruction" (Carpenter et al., 1998, p. 4). One of the best ways for students to grow their repertoire is to listen to the strategies invented by classmates as they are shared, explored, and tried out by others. However, students should not be permitted to use any strategy without understanding it (Campbell, Rowan, & Suarez, 1998).

Contrasts with Standard Algorithms. There are significant differences between invented strategies and standard algorithms.

1. *Invented strategies are number oriented rather than digit oriented.* Using the standard algorithm for 45 + 32, students think of 4 + 3 instead of 40 and 30. Kamii, longtime advocate for invented strategies, claims that standard algorithms "unteach" place value (Kamii & Dominick, 1998).
2. *Invented strategies are left-handed rather than right-handed.* Invented strategies often begin with the largest parts of numbers (leftmost digits) because they focus on the entire number. For 263 + 126, many invented strategies will begin with "200 + 100 is 300," providing some sense of the size of the eventual answer in just one step. In contrast, the standard algorithm begins with 3 + 6 is 9. By beginning on the right with a digit orientation, the result is hidden until the end. The exception is the standard long-division algorithm.
3. *Invented strategies are a range of flexible options rather than "one right way."* Invented strategies are dependent on the numbers involved so that students can make the computation easier. Try each of these mentally: 465 + 230 and 526 + 98. Did you use the same method? The standard algorithm suggests using the same tool on all problems. The standard algorithm for 7000−25 typically leads to student errors, yet a mental strategy is relatively simple.

Benefits of Invented Strategies. The development and use of invented strategies deliver more than computational proficiency. The positive benefits are:

- *Students make fewer errors.* Research reveals that students using methods they understand make many fewer errors because they understanding their own methods (Gravemeijer & van Galen, 2003). Maybe students do not understand the underlying concepts of standard algorithms. Not only do these students make errors, but the errors are often systematic and difficult to remediate. Errors with invented strategies are less frequent and rarely systematic.
- *Less reteaching is required.* Teachers often are concerned when students' early efforts with invented strategies are slow and time consuming. But the productive struggle in these early stages builds a meaningful and well-integrated network of ideas that is robust and long lasting and significantly decreases the time required for reteaching.
- *Students develop number sense.* Students' development and use of number-oriented, flexible algorithms offers them a rich understanding of the number system through strategies they understand. In contrast, students who frequently use standard algorithms are unable to explain why they work.
- *Invented strategies are the basis for mental computation and estimation.* When invented strategies are the norm for computation, there is no need to talk about mental computation as if it were a separate skill. As students become more proficient with these flexible methods, they find they are able to use them mentally or sometimes need to jot down intermediate steps.
- *Flexible methods are often faster than standard algorithms.* Consider 76 + 46. A simple invented strategy might involve 70 + 40 = 110 and 6 + 6 = 12. The sum of 110 and 12 is 122. This is easily done mentally, or even with some recording, in much less time than the steps of the standard algorithm.
- *Algorithm invention is itself a significantly important process of "doing mathematics."* Students who invent a strategy for computing, or who adopt a meaningful strategy shared by a classmate, are both involved in the process of sense making and building confidence. This development of procedures is a process that was often hidden from students (possibly yourself included). By engaging in this aspect of mathematics, a significantly different and valuable view of "doing mathematics" is revealed to learners.
- *Invented strategies serve students well on standardized tests.* Evidence suggests that students using invented strategies do as well or better than students using standard algorithms in computation on standardized tests (Fleischman, Hopstock, Pelczar, & Shelley, 2010; Fuson, 2003).

Mental Computation. A mental computation strategy is simply any invented strategy that is done mentally. What may be a mental strategy for one student may require written support by another. Initially, students may not be ready to do computations mentally, as they may still be at the direct modeling stage or need to notate parts of the problem as they think it through. As your students become more adept, they can and should be challenged to do appropriate computations mentally. You may be quite amazed at the ability of students (and at your own ability) to do mental mathematics. Visit the companion website and watch Connor use two different invented strategies to solve the same two-digit addition problem mentally.

Try mental computation with this example:

$$342 + 153 + 481$$

 Pause & Reflect

For this addition task, try the following method: Begin by adding the hundreds, saying the totals as you go—*3 hundred, 4 hundred, 8 hundred.* Then add on to this the tens in successive manner and finally the ones. Give it a try. ●

Standard Algorithms

More than a century of tradition combined with pressures from families who were taught only the standard algorithm may result in thinking that there is only one best approach and one "right" algorithm. Arguments for a single algorithm generally revolve around efficiency and the need for methods that will work with all numbers. For addition and subtraction, however, well-understood and practiced invented strategies are more than adequate and sometimes more efficient and accurate.

The main focus in teaching the standard algorithm should not be as a memorized series of steps, but as making sense of the procedure as a process. The Common Core State Standards (CCSSO, 2010) require that students eventually have knowledge of the standard algorithms (addition and subtraction with multidigit whole numbers in grade 4, multiplication with multidigit whole numbers in grade 5, and division of multidigit whole numbers in grade 6). Notice that the grades in which this knowledge of standard algorithms is required is long after the time where the topic is introduced. This timeline points to the need for full conceptual development to take place first. Importantly, the Common Core State Standards recognize that starting by teaching only the standard algorithm doesn't allow students to explore other useful approaches. Understanding how algorithms work and when they are the best choice (over an invented approach) is central to development of procedural proficiency.

Standard Algorithms Must Be Understood. Students may pick up the standard algorithms from siblings and other family members while you are still trying to teach a variety of invented strategies. Some of these students may resist learning more flexible strategies thinking that they already know the "right" approach. What do you do then?

First and foremost, apply the same rule to standard algorithms as to all strategies: *If you use it, you must understand why it works and be able to explain it.* In an atmosphere that says, "Let's figure out why this works," students can profit from making sense of standard algorithms just as they should be able to reason about other approaches. But the responsibility for the explanations should be theirs, not yours. Remember, "Never say anything a kid can say!" (Reinhart, 2000).

The standard algorithm (once it is understood) is one more strategy to put in the students' "toolbox" of methods. But reinforce the idea that just like the other strategies, it may be more useful in some instances than in others. Pose problems in which a mental strategy is useful, such as 504−498 or 4568 + 12,813. Discuss whether a mental strategy or the standard algorithm seems best. Visit the companion website and watch the video clip of Estephania, who compares the use of a mental strategy with the standard subtraction algorithm.

FIGURE 12.10 The "equal addition" algorithm.

Delay! Delay! Delay! Students are unlikely to invent the standard algorithms. You will need to introduce and explain each algorithm to them and help them understand how and why it works. No matter how carefully you introduce these algorithms into your classroom as simply another alternative, students are likely to sense that this is the "one right way." So spend a significant amount of time with invented strategies—months, not weeks. Again, note that the Common Core State Standards (CCSSO, 2010) require that students learn a variety of strategies based on place value and properties of the operations one or two years before the standard algorithms are expected to be mastered. The understandings students gain from working with invented strategies will make it easier for you to meaningfully teach the standard algorithms. If you think you are wasting precious time by delaying, just be reminded of how many years you and others teach the same standard algorithms over and over to students who still make errors with them and are still unable to explain them. Visit the companion website and watch the video clip of Gretchen who uses the standard algorithm incorrectly but still thinks that answer is correct—even when other approaches lead to a different answer.

Cultural Differences in Algorithms. Some people falsely assume that mathematics is easier than other subjects for students who are not native English speakers. In fact, there are many international differences in notation, conventions, and algorithms. Knowing more about the diverse algorithms students might bring to the classroom and their ways of recording symbols for "doing mathematics" will assist you in supporting students and responding to families. What the United States calls the "standard algorithm" may not be customary in other countries, so encouraging a variety of algorithms is important in valuing the experiences of all students.

For example, equal addition is a subtraction algorithm used in many Latin and European countries. It is based on the knowledge that adding the same amount to both the minuend and the subtrahend will not change the difference (answer). Therefore, if the expression to be solved is $15 - 5$, there is no change to the answer (or the difference) if you add 10 to the minuend and subtrahend and solve $25 - 15$. There is still a difference of 10. Let's look at $62 - 27$ to think about this. Using the familiar algorithm that you may think of as "standard," you would likely regroup by crossing out the 6 tens, adding the 10 with a small "1" to the 2 in the ones column (making 12), and then subtracting the 7 from the 12 and so forth. In the "equal addition" approach (see Figure 12.10), you add 10 to 62 by just mentally adding a small "1" (to represent 10) to the 2 in the ones column and thereby having 12, and then counteract that addition of 10 to the minuend by mentally adding 10 to the 27 (subtrahend), by increasing the tens column by one and subtracting 37. This may sound confusing to you—but try it. Especially when there are zeros in the minuend (e.g., $302 - 178$), you may find this a productive option. More important, your possible confusion can give you the sense of how your students (and their families) may react to a completely different procedure from the one they know and find successful.

Another key component to understanding cultural differences in algorithms is the emphasis on mental mathematics in other countries (Perkins & Flores, 2002). In fact, some students pride themselves on their ability to do math mentally. Don't be surprised if students from other countries can produce answers without showing work.

✓ **Complete Self-Check 12.2: Three Types of Computational Strategies**

Development of Invented Strategies

You will not be surprised to hear that students do not spontaneously invent wonderful computational methods while you sit back and watch. Students tend to develop or gravitate toward different strategies, suggesting that teachers and programs do have an effect on the methods students develop (Verschaffel et al., 2007). The following section discusses pedagogical methods that support students' development of invented strategies for multidigit addition and subtraction.

Creating a Supportive Environment

Invented strategies are developed out of a strong understanding of numbers. The development of place-value concepts begins to prepare students for the challenges of inventing computational strategies. For example, the CCSSO (2010) suggests that second graders should be able to use mental computation to find a number that is 10 or 100 more (or less) than a given number between 100 and 900. This standard calls for young learners to publicly share emerging ideas. Therefore, students need a classroom environment where they can act like mathematicians and explore ideas without fear. When students in your classroom attempt to investigate new ideas such as invented strategy use, they should find your classroom a safe and nurturing place for expressing naive or rudimentary thoughts.

Some of the characteristics described previously regarding the development of a problem solving environment need to be reiterated here to establish the climate for taking risks, testing conjectures, and trying new approaches. Students also need to know that they will need to persevere and be ready for productive struggle; as that is when learning takes place. Hiebert and Grouws (2007) stated, "We use the word *struggle* to mean that students expend effort to make sense of mathematics, to figure something out that is not immediately apparent. . . . We do not mean the feelings of despair that some students can experience when little of the material makes sense" (p. 387). We need to encourage students to persist with material that is challenging but within their grasp and understandable.

Here are some factors to keep in mind:

- Avoid immediately identifying the right answer when a student states it. Give other students a chance to consider whether they think the answer and approach are correct.
- Expect and encourage student-to-student interactions, questions, discussions, and conjectures. Allow plenty of time for discussions.
- Encourage students to clarify previous knowledge and make attempts to construct new ideas.
- Promote curiosity and openness to trying new things.
- Talk about both right and wrong ideas in a nonevaluative and nonthreatening way.
- Move unsophisticated ideas to more sophisticated thinking through coaching and strategic questioning.
- Use familiar contexts and story problems to build background and connect to students' experiences. Avoid using "naked numbers" as a starting point, as they do not encourage strategy development.
- Show samples of anonymous students' work and allow students to critique the reasoning of others.

Models to Support Invented Strategies

The Common Core State Standards require that students "fluently add and subtract within 1000" (https://www.youtube.com/watch?v=ymVYmiSXdMQ&list=PLnIkFmW0ticPvtvPU lAaLdvRQ1JkaVe5C) using strategies based on "place value, properties of operations and the relationship between addition and subtraction" (CCSSO, 2010, p. 24). Try seeing how you would do these without using the standard algorithms: 487 + 235 and 623 − 247. For subtraction, a counting-up strategy is usually the easiest. Occasionally, other strategies appear with larger numbers. For example, "chunking off" multiples of 50 or 25 is often a useful method. For 462 + 257, pull out 450 and 250 to equal 700. That leaves 12 and 7 more, for 719.

There are three common types of invented strategies to solve addition and subtraction situations that can be extended to higher numbers: split strategy (https://www.youtube.com/ watch?v=XjRiQpMMI-k) (also called decomposition), jump strategy (https://www.youtube .com/watch?v=w9haFFL-AMs) (similar to counting on or counting back), and shortcut strategy (https://www.youtube.com/watch?v=_v9Kb-qFVxY) (sometimes known as compensation) (Torbeyns, De Smedt, Ghesquiere, & Verschaffel, 2009). The notion of "splitting" a number into parts (often by place value) is a useful strategy for all operations. Both the word *split* and the use of a visual diagram help students develop strategies (Verschaffel et al., 2007). When recording students' ideas, try using arrows or lines to explicitly indicate how two computations are joined together, as shown in Figure 12.11(a).

(a) **How much is 86 and 47?**

S: I know that 80 and 20 more is 100.

T: Where do the 80 and the 20 come from?

S: I split the 47 into 20 and 20 and 7 and the 86 into 80 and 6.

T: (illustrates the splitting with lines)
So then you added one of the 20s to 80?

S: Yes, 80 and 20 is 100. Then I added the other 20 and got 120.

T: (writes the equations on the board)

S: Then I added the 6 and the 7 and got 13.

T: (writes this equation)

S: Then I added the 120 to the 13 and got 133.

T: Indicates with joining lines.

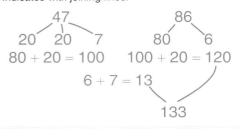

(b) **What is 84 minus 68?**

S: I started at 84. First, I jumped back 4 to make 80.

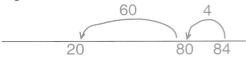

T: Why did you subtract 4 first? Why not 8?

S: It was easier to think about 80 than 84. I will save the other part of 8 until later. Then I jumped back 60 to get 20.

S: Then I jumped back 4.

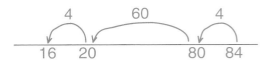

T: Why 4?

S: That was how much I still had left over from 68.

FIGURE 12.11   Two methods of recording students' thought processes so that the class can follow the strategy.

The empty number line (also known as an *open number line*) shown in Figure 12.11(b) is a number line with no prewritten numbers. Students can use it to incorporate a sequential jump strategy that is very effective for thinking about addition and subtraction situations (Caldwell, Kobett, & Karp, 2014; Gravemeijer & van Galen, 2003; Verschaffel et al., 2007). The empty number line is much more flexible than the usual number line because it can be jotted down anywhere, works with any numbers, and eliminates confusion with hash marks and the spaces between them. It is also found less prone to computational errors (Gravemeijer & van Galen, 2003).

Initially, the empty number line is a good way to help you model a student's thinking for the class, especially when you link to their early understanding of a unit. They need to be reminded that the number line is a length marked off into particular units—and in this case, they are creating their own units with jumps. Students determine the start and result numbers based on the problem they are solving. Then they often use "friendly numbers" to make their jumps and then calculate the total of the jumps (Barker, 2009). The jumps on the line can be recorded as the students share or explain each step of their solution counting up or down from an initial number. With time and practice, students will find the empty number line to be an effective tool to use in supporting their thinking.

Activity 12.9   CCSS-M: 2.OA.A.1

Exploring Subtraction Strategies

Use the set of problems on the Looking at Collections Activity Page. Ask students, "How can you use strategies, bar diagrams, or open number lines to show how you are solving these problems?" See the Expanded Lesson for more details on how to adapt this activity for students with disabilities and English language learners.

STUDENTS
with
SPECIAL
NEEDS

ENGLISH
LANGUAGE
LEARNERS

Bar diagrams can also be used to support students' thinking and help them explain their ideas to others. Bar diagrams work particularly well for contexts that fit a subtraction comparison situation and a part-part-whole model. See Figure 12.12 for a sample of each.

The *shortcut strategy* involves the flexible adjustment of numbers. For example, just as students used 10 as an anchor in learning their facts, they can move from numbers such as 38 or 69 to the nearest 10 (in this case 40 or 70) and then take the 2 or 1 off to compensate later. As another example, $51-37$ can be thought of as $37 + 10 = 47$ and $47 + 4$ more equals 51.

In each case, as these examples suggest, the numbers in the problem and the type of problem will influence the strategies students use. Therefore, it is important to think carefully about the type of story problem you pose as well as the numbers you use!

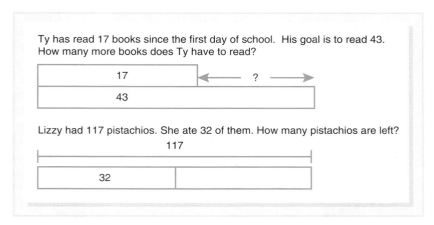

FIGURE 12.12   Using bar diagrams to help think about two problems.

 Complete Self-Check 12.3: Development of Invented Strategies

Development of Invented Strategies for Addition and Subtraction

Students should use strategies that they understand and can use efficiently and effectively. Your goal might be that each of your students has at least one or two methods that are reasonably efficient, mathematically correct, and useful with lots of different numbers. Expect different students to settle on different strategies that play to their strengths. The following sections suggest a variety of invented strategies that students often use.

Single-Digit Numbers

When adding or subtracting small amounts or finding the difference between two reasonably close numbers, many students will use counting to solve the problems. One goal should be to extend students' knowledge of basic facts and the ten-structure of the number system so that counting is not required. When the calculation crosses a ten (e.g., $58 + 6$), using the decade number (60) and thinking $58 + 2 + 4$, for example, extends students' use of the Make 10 strategy (e.g., add on to equal 10 and then add the rest).

Activity 12.10   CCSS-M: 1.NBT.C.4; 2.OA.A.2

Crossing a Decade

Quickly review the Make 10 and Down Under 10 Strategies from basic facts (from Chapter 10) using little ten-frames. Then have Little Ten-Frames, and Base-Ten Materials, a Place-Value Mat, or Hundreds Chart available for children's use. Pose an addition or subtraction story problem that crosses a decade number and involves a change or difference of less than 10. Here are some example problems:

- Tommy was on page 47 of his book. Then he read 8 more pages. What page did he end up on?
- How far is it from 68 to 75?
- Ruth had 52 cents. She bought a small toy for 8 cents. How much does she have left?

Two students can partner to determine how to quickly find the total.

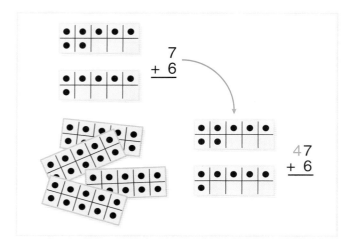

FIGURE 12.13 Students extend the Up Over 10 strategy to larger numbers.

Listen for students who are counting on or counting back without paying attention to the ten and suggest they use either the hundreds chart or the little ten-frames as shown in Figure 12.13. Also, find out how they solve fact combinations such as 8 + 6 and 13 − 5. The use of tens for these facts is essentially the same as for the higher-decade problems. Have students using the strategy share their ideas with others. They might say, for 47 + 6, "I added 3 from the 6 to the 47 to get to 50. Then I added the remaining 3 to get to 53."

As you transition students from single-digit to two-digit numbers, adding and subtracting tens and hundreds is an important intermediate step. Sums and differences involving multiples of 10 or 100 are easily computed mentally. Write a problem such as the following:

$$300 + 500 + 20$$

Challenge students to solve it mentally. Ask students to share how they did it. Listen for the use of place-value words: "3 *hundred* and 5 *hundred* is 8 *hundred*, and 20 is 820." Start with problems that do not require regrouping and then evolve to more difficult problems such as 70 + 80. Continue to use base-ten models to help students think in terms of units of tens and hundreds.

Activity 12.11 — CCSS-M: 1.NBT.C.4; 1.NBT.C.5; 1.NBT.C.6

I Am, but Who Is?

Have students practice their mental calculations and prepare for multidigit computation by adding or subtracting multiples of tens (or other familiar combinations) with two-digit numbers. Use the I Am/Who Is? Game Cards for a class up to 30 students. If you have fewer than 30 students, give students who need a challenge two cards. There are also some easier combinations, so find the answer to those combinations and give those cards to students with disabilities. Start the game by calling out any number you see on a card, such as "Who is 22?" The student should respond with "I am 22, who is . . ." and then read the rest of the card. The game will loop all the way around through the thirty problems.

STUDENTS
with
SPECIAL
NEEDS

Adding Two-Digit Numbers

In the CCSS-M the development of fluency with multidigit addition and subtraction begins in grade 1 with the addition of multiples of ten (1.NBT.C.5) and continues through grade 4, when students are expected to "Fluently add and subtract multi-digit whole numbers using the standard algorithm" (4.NBT.B.4) (CCSSO, 2010). This fluency must be built with years of explorations using concrete models or drawings and strategies based the inverse relationship between addition and subtraction, place value, and the properties of operations. Although double-digit addition is a focus in second grade, students in grades 3 and 4 may still be challenged by these computations. Problems involving the sum of 2 two-digit numbers will usually produce a wide variety of invented strategies and it is those strategies that are the foundation for adding three-digit numbers (and beyond). Some strategies will involve starting with one or the other number and working from that point, either by adding on to get to the next ten or by adding tens from one number to the other.

Let's start by looking at the following story problem.

Two Scout troops went on a field trip. There were 46 Girl Scouts and 38 Boy Scouts. How many Scouts went on the trip?

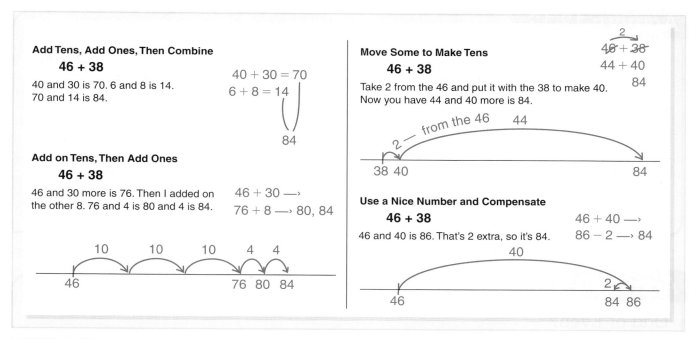

FIGURE 12.14 Four different invented strategies for addition with two-digit numbers.

Figure 12.14 illustrates four different invented strategies for the addition of these 2 two-digit numbers. The ways that the solutions are recorded are suggestions, but note the frequent use of the empty number line.

The move to the shortcut strategy and compensation strategies focusing on making ten is useful when one of the numbers ends in 8 or 9. To promote that strategy, present problems with addends like 39 or 58. Note that it is only necessary to adjust one of the two numbers.

⏸ Pause & Reflect

Try adding 367 + 155 in as many different ways as you can. How many of your ways are like those in Figure 12.14? ●

FORMATIVE ASSESSMENT Notes. Periodically you will want to focus on a student to determine his or her strategy use. Try the following problem with a student in a diagnostic interview: 46 + 35. See if the student begins by splitting the numbers. That is, for 46 + 35, a student may add on 4 to the 46 to get to 50 and then add the remaining 31. Or first add 30 to 46 to get to 76, then add 4 to get to 80 and then add the remaining 1. In either case, you can see whether they are taking advantage of the utilization of tens. Some students may use an open number line and count up with jumps of ten saying "46, 56, 66, 76." as they draw corresponding arc and numbers such as + 10 and so on. Many students will count past these multiples without stopping at ten. Another approach they may use involves splitting the numbers into parts and adding the easier parts separately. Usually the split will involve tens and ones, or students may use other parts of numbers such as 50 or 25 as an easier "compatible number" to work with.

Students will often use a counting-by-tens-and-ones technique. That is, instead of "46 + 30 is 76," they may use an open number line and count up "46, 56, 66, 76." These jumps can be written down to help keep track. If they are not seeing the ten as a unit, you may need more work on place-value activities. ■

The following activity supports students' thinking about adjusting numbers by using 10 as an anchor.

Activity 12.12

CCSSM-M: 2.NBT.B.5; 2.NBT.B.9

STUDENTS
with
**SPECIAL
NEEDS**

Just Adjust It

Create a series of problems using numbers that will increase the likelihood that students will gravitate toward the idea of using 10, but do not require them to do so. The point is to try to help students become more aware of different ways to adjust numbers. Consider using this series of problems:

$$50 + 30 \qquad 48 + 30 \qquad 50 + 32 \qquad 51 + 28 \qquad 53 + 29$$

Project one problem at a time and give students time to solve it before you ask for answers and then for explanations of their approaches. Record students' strategies so that you can refer back to them when appropriate. If no student suggests the idea of using 50 + 30 to help solve the subsequent related problems, you may want to challenge them to determine how they could use that problem to help them solve all the others. By listening to classmates, other students, particularly students with disabilities, can become more aware of different ways to adjust numbers.

This activity helps students determine whether a sum of two numbers has an odd or even sum.

Activity 12.13

CCSS-M: 2.OA.C.3

Odd or Even?

Start the class off with a two-digit addition problem that looks at two consecutive numbers. Have them write the problem on the top line of the Odd or Even Activity Page. Is the sum odd or even? How do you know? Try other two- or three-digit addends. Are the sums odd or even? Do you think the sum will always be that way? Why or why not?

Subtraction as "Think-Addition"

CCSS Standards for
Mathematical
Practice

MP2. Reason abstractly
and quantitatively.

Students who know the think-addition strategy for their basic facts can also use the same concept for solving problems with multidigit numbers. This is an amazingly powerful way to subtract and is particularly successful with students with disabilities (Peltenburg, van den Heuvel-Panhuizen, & Robitzsch, 2012). For 38−19, the idea is to think, "How much do I add to 19 to get to 38?" Notice that this strategy is probably not as efficient for 42−6. Using *join with change unknown* problems or *missing-part* problems (discussed in Chapter 9) will encourage the use of the think-addition strategy. Here is an example of each.

Sam had 46 baseball cards. He went to a card show and got some more cards for his collection. Now he has 73 cards. How many cards did Sam buy at the card show?

Juanita counted all of the teacher's pencils. Some were sharpened and some not. She counted 73 pencils in all; 46 pencils were not sharpened. How many were sharpened?

Figure 12.15 shows invented strategies that use addition to solve subtraction story problems. As you can see, using tens is also an important part of these strategies. Simply asking for the difference between two numbers may also prompt these strategies.

Take-Away Subtraction

Using a take-away action is considerably more difficult to do mentally. However, take-away strategies are common, probably because many textbooks emphasize "take away" as the meaning of subtraction (even though there are other meanings). Four different strategies are shown in Figure 12.17 for the following story problem.

There were 73 students on the playground. The 46 second-grade students came in first. How many students were still on the playground?

Add Tens to Get Close, Then Ones

73 − 46

46 and 20 is 66. (30 more is too much.) Then 4 more is 70 and 3 is 73. That's 20 and 7 or 27.

$46 + 20 = 66$
$66 + 4 = 70$
$70 + 3 = 73$
$20 + 4 + 3 = 27$

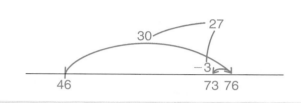

Add Tens to Overshoot, Then Come Back

73 − 46

46 and 30 is 76. That's 3 too much, so it's 27.

$46 + 30 \longrightarrow 76 - 3 \longrightarrow 73$
$30 - 3 = 27$

Add Ones to Make a Ten, Then Tens and Ones

73 − 46

46 and 4 is 50. 50 and 20 is 70 and 3 more is 73. The 4 and 3 is 7 and 20 is 27.

$46 + 4 \longrightarrow 50$
$50 + 20 \longrightarrow 70$
$70 + 3 \longrightarrow 73$
$4 + 20 + 3 = 27$

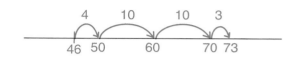
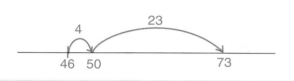

Similarly, 46 and 4 is 50. 50 and 23 is 73. 23 and 4 is 27.

$46 + 4 \longrightarrow 50$
$50 + 23 \longrightarrow 73$
$23 + 4 = 27$

FIGURE 12.15 Three different invented strategies for subtraction by "think addition."

Activity 12.14   CCSS-M: 2.NBT.B.5; 2.NBT.B.9

How Far to My Number?

Students work in pairs with a single set of Little Ten-Frames. One student uses the cards to make a number less than 50 while the other student writes a number greater than 50 on pieces of paper, as shown in Figure 12.16. For students with a disability or students who need a challenge you may choose to suggest the size of the second number (e.g., less than 100, less than 500). The task is for the students work together to find out how much more must be added to the number shown with the ten-frames to get to the larger number and write the corresponding equation. Once an answer is determined, they should demonstrate how their answer combined with the smaller number matches the larger number. Then students can fade the use of the cards.

STUDENTS
with
SPECIAL NEEDS

The two methods that begin by taking tens from tens are reflective of what most students do with their base-ten pieces. The other two methods leave one of the numbers intact and subtract from it. When the subtracted number is a multiple of 10 or close to a multiple of 10, take-away can be an easy method to use. Try $83 - 29$ in your head by first taking away 30 and adding 1 back. Some students will become confused when they hear a classmate describe this strategy for $83 - 29$. In particular they do not understand why you add 1 back. They think because you added 1 to 29 to equal 30, you should subtract 1 from the answer. Let them act it out with Base-Ten Materials so they can see that when they take away 30, they took 1 too many away and that is why they need to add 1 back.

TECHNOLOGY Note. Virtual Base-Ten Blocks for Addition and Subtraction are available at the National Library of Virtual Manipulatives. These two similar applets use base-ten blocks on a

How far from 48 to 73?

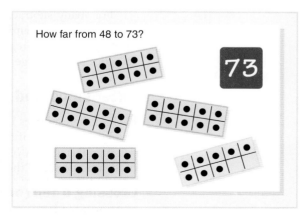

FIGURE 12.16 Use think-addition to solve How Far? problems.

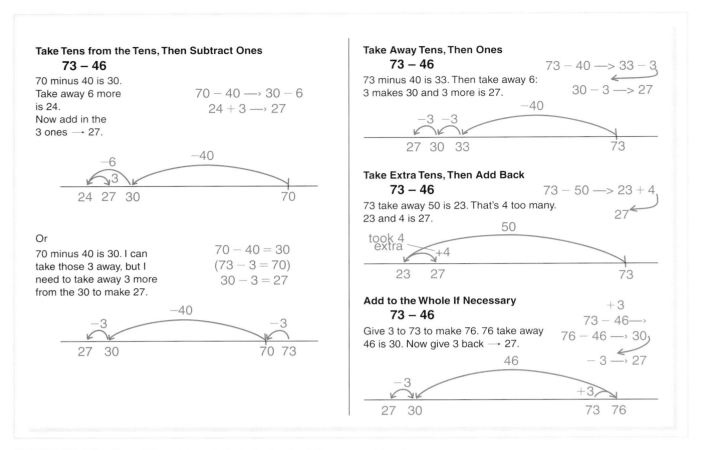

FIGURE 12.17 Four different invented strategies for take-away subtraction.

place-value chart. You can form any problem you wish up to four digits. The subtraction model shows the bottom number in red instead of blue. When the top blocks are dragged onto the red blocks, they disappear. Although you can begin in any column, the model forces a regrouping strategy as well as a take-away model for subtraction. These digital versions of physical base ten materials are useful for reinforcing the standard algorithm. ■

 Pause & Reflect

Try computing 82 − 57. Use both take-away and counting-up methods. Can you use all of the strategies in Figures 12.15 and 12.17 without looking? •

For many subtraction problems, especially those with three digits, the think-addition approach is significantly easier than a take-away approach. For students who could benefit from an add-on strategy but are not using it, you may want to return to simple missing-part activities to encourage that type of thinking.

Extensions and Challenges

Each of the examples in the preceding sections involved sums less than 100, and all involved *crossing a ten;* that is, if done with a standard algorithm, they required regrouping or trading. As you plan instruction you should consider whether a problem requires crossing a ten, the size of the numbers, and the potential for doing problems mentally.

Crossing a Ten (or More). For most of the strategies, it is easier to add or subtract when crossing a ten is not required. Try each strategy with 34 + 52 or 68−24 to see how it works.

Easier problems build confidence. They also permit you to challenge your students by asking, "Would you like a harder one?" There is also the issue of crossing 100 or 1000. Try 58 + 67 with different strategies. Crossing across hundreds is also an issue for subtraction. Problems such as 128−50 or 128−45 are more difficult than problems that do not cross a hundred.

Larger Numbers. The Common Core State Standards recommend that second graders add and subtract three-digit numbers using a variety of strategies. Try seeing how you would do these problems without using the standard algorithms: 487 + 235 and 623−247. Again, for subtraction, a think-addition strategy is usually the easiest. Occasionally, students will use other strategies with larger numbers. For example, "chunking off" multiples of 50 or 25 is often a useful method. For 462 + 257, pull out 450 and 250 to equal 700. That leaves 12 and 7 more, which equals 719.

 Complete Self-Check 12.4: Development of Invented Strategies for Addition and Subtraction

Standard Algorithms for Addition and Subtraction

Students are not likely to invent the standard algorithms because they are less intuitive, so your instruction will necessarily be more directed. Given that, it is critical that you teach algorithms in a conceptual manner, helping students understand the tens and ones as they work.

The standard algorithms require an understanding of regrouping, exchanging 10 in one place-value position for 1 in the position to the left—or the reverse, exchanging 1 for 10 in the position to the right. The corresponding terms *carrying* and *borrowing* are obsolete and conceptually misleading. The word *regroup* may initially have little meaning for young students, so start with the term *trade*. Ten ones are *traded* for a ten. A hundred is *traded* for 10 tens. Notice that none of the invented strategies involves regrouping.

Standard Algorithm for Addition

Two things to remember in teaching the standard algorithm for addition: (1) Be sure students continue to view it as one possible algorithm that is a good choice in some situations (just as invented strategies are good choices in some situations), and (2) as with any procedure (algorithm), it must begin with the concrete, and then explicit connections must be made between the concept (regrouping) and the procedure.

Begin with Models Only. In the beginning, focus on regrouping without recording the numerical process. Provide students with Place-Value Mats and Base-Ten Materials. Have students use the base-ten materials to make one number at the top of the mat and a second beneath it, as shown in the top portion of Figure 12.18. Point out this one procedure: *Begin in the ones column.* Then let students solve the problem on their own. Allow plenty of time and then have students explain what they did and why. Let students

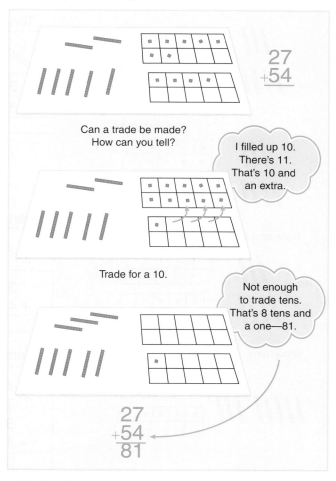

FIGURE 12.18 Working from right to left in addition.

display their work on the projector or use interactive whiteboard models to help with their explanations. One or two problems in a lesson with lots of discussion are more productive than a lot of problems based on rules that are poorly understood.

Develop the Written Record. Use the Addition and Subtraction Recording Sheets to help students record numerals in columns as they model each step of the procedure they do with the base-ten models. The first few times you do this, guide each step carefully through questioning, as shown in Figure 12.19. A similar approach would be used for three-digit problems. Have students work in pairs with one responsible for the models and the other recording the steps. They can reverse roles with each problem.

A common error students make is to record their answers in this way:

$$
\begin{array}{r}
57 \\
+69 \\
\hline
1116
\end{array}
$$

As you can see, this student has lost her connection to the place value and is treating the ones and tens as two separate problems. The student should try to use another way to check her answer—in this case, suggest manipulatives, such as base-ten blocks, to help her model the problem and estimate a reasonable answer. You can ask, "Do you think your answer will be

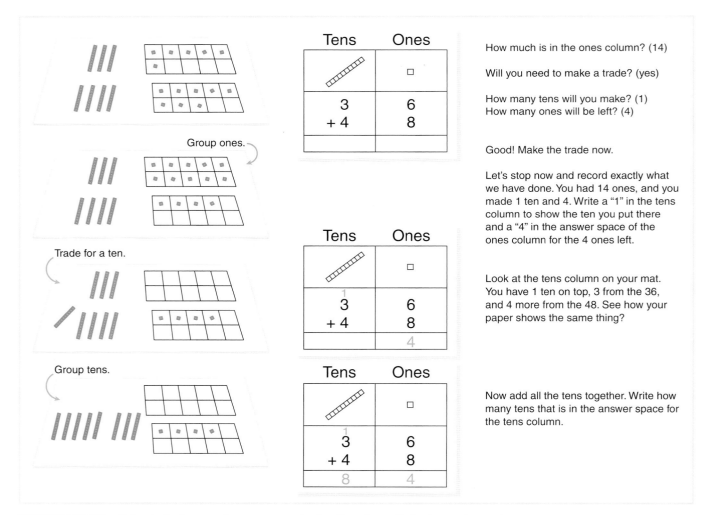

FIGURE 12.19   Help students record on paper each step they do on their place-value mats.

between 100 and 200 or 200 and 300?" to help the student see that an answer in the thousands is not logical. Visit the companion website and take a look at Talecia as she too loses her connection to the real value of the numbers she is recording when she adds 34 + 57.

Figure 12.20 shows a variation of the traditional recording scheme that is very valuable, at least for up to three digits. This is known as the partial sums approach. Partial sums avoids the "carried ones" and focuses attention on the actual value of the digits. If students start adding on the left as they are inclined to do, this would just be a vertical recording scheme for the invented strategy "add tens, add ones, then combine" (Figure 12.14). This adaptation is particularly effective with students with disabilities.

Standard Algorithm for Subtraction

The general approach to developing the subtraction algorithm is the same as for addition. When the procedure is completely understood with models, a do-and-record approach connects it with a written form.

Begin with Models Only. Start by having students model the top number (minuend) in a subtraction problem on the top half of their place-value mats. For the amount to be subtracted, have students write each digit on a small piece of paper and place these pieces near the bottom of their mats in the respective columns, as in Figure 12.21. To avoid errors, suggest making all trades first. That way, the full amount on the paper slip can be taken off at once. Also explain to students that they are to begin working with the ones column first, as they did with addition.

Anticipate Difficulties with Zeros. Exercises in which zeros are involved anywhere in the problem tend to cause special difficulties. Give extra attention to these cases while still using models.

The very common errors that emerge when students "regroup across zero" are best addressed at the modeling stage. For example, in 403 − 138, students must make a double trade: trading a hundreds piece for 10 tens and then a tens piece for 10 ones.

Develop the Written Record. The process of recording each step as it is done is the same as was suggested for addition using the Addition and Subtraction Recording Sheets.

When students can explain the use of symbols involved in the recording process, move them away from the use of the physical materials toward the complete use of symbols. Again, be attentive to problems with zeros.

If students are permitted to follow their natural instincts and begin with the biggest pieces (from the left instead of the right), recording schemes similar to that shown in Figure 12.22 are possible. The trades are made from the pieces remaining *after* the subtraction in the column to the left has been done. A "regroup across zero" difficulty will still occur in problems like 462 − 168. Try it.

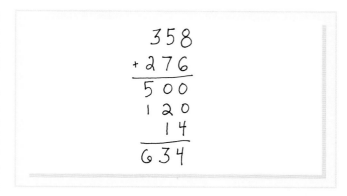

FIGURE 12.20 The partial sums approach can be used from left to right as well as from right to left.

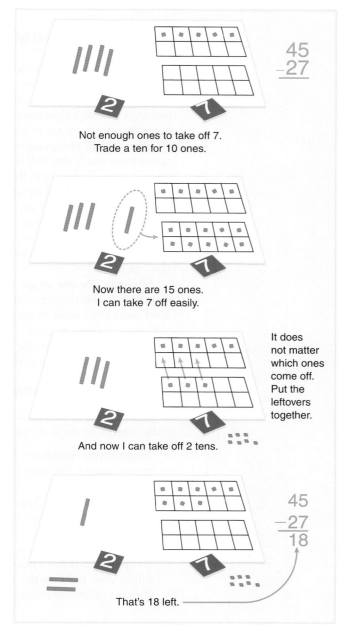

FIGURE 12.21 Two-digit subtraction with models.

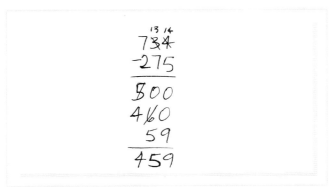

FIGURE 12.22   A left-hand recording scheme for subtraction.

 **Pause** & **Reflect**

Contrast teaching students to regroup in subtraction, especially regrouping across zero, with think-addition. For example, try solving this: 428 and how much equals 703? Now think about teaching students to regroup across zero to solve 703−428. Which is easier? Why? •

✓ **Complete Self-Check 12.5: Standard Algorithms for Addition and Subtraction**

 ## Introducing Computational Estimation

Whenever we are faced with a computation in real life, we have a variety of choices to make concerning how we will find a reasonable answer. A first decision is: "Do we need an exact answer, or will an approximation be okay?" If precision is called for, we can use an invented strategy, a standard algorithm, or even a calculator. How close an estimate must be to the actual computation is a matter of context, as was the original decision to use an estimate.

The goal of computational estimation is to be able to flexibly and quickly produce an approximate result that will work for the situation and be reasonable. However, computational estimation is a higher-level thinking skill that requires many decisions. The NCTM Standards state, "Teachers should help students learn how to decide when an exact answer or an estimate would be more appropriate, how to choose the computational methods that would be best to use, and how to evaluate the reasonableness of answers to computations" (NCTM, 2000, p. 220). The Common Core State Standard in Mathematical Practice 5 states that students should "detect possible errors by strategically using estimation and other mathematical knowledge" (p. 7)*.

Students are not as good at computational estimation as they are at producing exact answers and sometimes find computational estimation uncomfortable (Siegler & Booth, 2005). Good estimators tend to employ a variety of computational strategies they have developed over time. As early as grade 2, we teach strategies to help students develop an understanding of what it means to estimate a computation. From then on through middle school, students should continue to develop and add to their estimation strategies and skills.

Understanding Computational Estimation

An *estimate* refers to a number that is a suitable approximation for an exact number given the particular context. In the K–8 mathematics curriculum, *estimation* refers to three quite different ideas:

- *Measurement estimation*: Determining an approximate measure without making an exact measurement. For example, we can estimate the length of a room or the weight of a watermelon.
- *Quantity estimation*: Approximating the number of items in a collection. For example, we might estimate the number of students in the auditorium or jelly beans in the "estimation jar."
- *Computational estimation*: Determining a number that is an approximation of a computation that we cannot or do not need to determine precisely. For example, we might want to know the approximate amount we are spending at a store and need to add the cost of several items to see whether $20.00 will cover the amount.

---

*Reprinted with permission from *Principles and Standards for School Mathematics*, copyright 2000 by the National Council of Teachers of Mathematics. All rights reserved.

Many students confuse the idea of estimation with guessing. None of the three types of estimation involves guessing. Each involves reasoning and sense making. Computational estimation, for example, involves actually computing. Therefore, it's important to (1) avoid using the words *guess* and *guessing* when working on estimation activities and (2) explicitly help students see the difference between a guess and a reasonable estimate.

Computational estimation may be underemphasized in situations where the focus is on the standard algorithm. But, if you recall the problem solving process, the last of the four steps is to look back. If students practice estimating when they are computing and "look back" at the end of a computation, they should be able to see whether the answer is in the ballpark. Take 403 − 138, mentioned previously. At a glance, this answer has to be more than 200, so an incorrect answer of 175 (a common error) would be recognized as impossible.

Suggestions for Teaching Computational Estimation

Here are some general principles that are worth keeping in mind as you help your students develop computational estimation skills.

Use Real Examples. Discuss real-life situations in which computational estimations are used. Some common examples include comparative shopping (which store has the item for less); adding up distances in planning a trip; determining approximate monthly totals (school supplies, lawn-mowing income, time playing video games); and figuring the cost of going to a sporting event or movie, including transportation, tickets, and snacks. Look at newspaper headlines to find where numbers are the result of estimation and where they are the result of precision (e.g., "Hundreds of Students Leave School Ill" versus "Fourteen Students Injured in Bus Accident"). Students are more motivated with real examples—for example, asking older students, "Are you a million seconds old? How can you find out?"

Use the Estimation Language. Words and phrases such as *about*, *close*, *just about*, *a little more* (or *less*) *than*, and *between* are part of the language of estimation. Students should understand that they are trying to get as close as possible using efficient methods, but there is no "one correct" or "winning" estimate. Language can help convey that idea.

Use a Context. Situations play a role in estimation. For example, it is important to know whether the cost of a car would be $950 or $9500. Could attendance at the school play be 30 or 300 or 3000? A simple computation can provide the important digits, with knowledge of the context providing the rest.

Accept a Range of Estimates, Offer a Range as an Option. Because estimates are based on computation, how can there be different answers? The answer, of course, is that any particular estimate depends on the strategy used and the kinds of adjustments made in the numbers. Estimates also vary with the need for the estimate. Estimating someone's age from an approximate year they were born is quite different from trying to decide whether your last $5 will cover three items you need at Fast Mart.

What estimate would you give for 270 + 325? If you use 200 + 300, you might say 500. Or you might use 250 for the 270 and 350 for the 325, making 600. You could also use 300 for 270 and add 325, getting 625. Is only one of these "right"? By sharing students' estimates and letting them discuss how and why different estimates resulted, they can begin to see that estimates generally fall in a range around the exact answer.

Important teacher note: Do not reward or overemphasize the estimate that is the closest. It is already very difficult for students to handle "approximate" answers; worrying about accuracy and pushing for the one closest answer exacerbates this problem. Instead, focus on whether the answers given are *reasonable* for the situation or problem at hand. Offer ranges for answers that are estimates. Ask whether the answer will be between 300 and 400, 450 and 550, or 600 and 700.

Focus on Flexible Methods, Not Answers. Remember that having students reflect on the strategies used by classmates will lead to additional strategy development. Class discussions are just as important as they were for the development of invented strategies of computation. For any given estimation, there are often several very good but different methods of estimation. Here is an activity in which a specific number is not required to answer the questions.

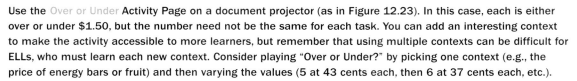

Activity 12.15

CCSS-M: 3.OA.C.8

ENGLISH
LANGUAGE
LEARNERS

Over or Under?

Use the Over or Under **Activity Page on a document projector (as in Figure 12.23). In this case, each is either over or under $1.50, but the number need not be the same for each task. You can add an interesting context to make the activity accessible to more learners, but remember that using multiple contexts can be difficult for ELLs, who must learn each new context. Consider playing "Over or Under?" by picking one context (e.g., the price of energy bars or fruit) and then varying the values (5 at 43 cents each, then 6 at 37 cents each, etc.).**

Here are some addition examples for the "Over or Under?" activity:

$$37 + 75 \qquad \text{(over/under 100)}$$
$$712 - 458 \qquad \text{(over/under 300)}$$

 Complete Self-Check 12.6: Introduction to Computational Estimation

Computational Estimation Strategies

There are numerous strategies that are helpful in computing estimates in addition and subtraction. Here are a few to present to students.

Front-End Methods

A front-end approach is reasonable for addition or subtraction when all or most of the numbers have the same number of digits. Figure 12.24 illustrates this idea. Notice that when a number has fewer digits than the rest, that number may be ignored initially. Also note that only the front (leftmost) number is used and the computation is then done as if there were zeros in the other positions.

After adding or subtracting the front digits, an adjustment is made to correct for the digits or numbers that were ignored. Making an adjustment is actually a separate skill. For young students, practice first just using the front digits.

The front-end strategy can be easy to use because it does not require rounding or changing numbers. You do need to be sure that students pay close attention to place value and only consider digits in the largest place, especially when the numbers vary in the number of digits.

Rounding Methods

In the Common Core State Standards (3.OA.D.8) third graders are expected to "assess the reasonableness of answers using mental computation and estimation strategies including rounding." In grades 3 and 4 (3.NBT.A.1 and 4.NBT.A.3) students use place-value understanding to round whole numbers. When several numbers are to be added, it is usually a good idea to round them to the same place value. Keep a running sum as you round each number. Figure 12.25 shows an example of rounding.

$1.50

(a)

5 energy bars
at 43¢ apiece

(b)

17¢
89¢
39¢

one of
each

(c)

$0.23
$0.05
$0.49
$0.35
$0.15

FIGURE 12.23 Over or Under? is a good beginning estimation activity.

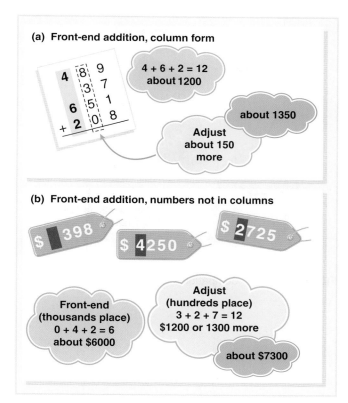

(a) **Front-end addition, column form**

4 + 6 + 2 = 12
about 1200

about 1350

Adjust
about 150
more

4 | 8 | 9
  | 3 | 7
6 | 5 | 1
+ 2 | 0 | 8

(b) **Front-end addition, numbers not in columns**

$ ■ 398

$ 4250

$ 2725

Front-end
(thousands place)
0 + 4 + 2 = 6
about $6000

Adjust
(hundreds place)
3 + 2 + 7 = 12
$1200 or 1300 more

about $7300

FIGURE 12.24   Front-end estimation in addition.

What is the approximate value of this coin collection?

$ 4827

$ 710

$ 85

I'll round to thousands:
5000 + 0 + 1000,
so about 6000.

FIGURE 12.25   Rounding using place value.

Activity 12.16

CCSS-M: 3.NBT.A.1

Round Up?

Create a number line on the floor with painter's tape, a rope, or cash register tape. Use sticky notes or pieces of paper to label the benchmark numbers of the tens (10, 20, 30, . . .), hundreds (100, 200, 300, . . .) or whatever range of numbers you are considering as a class. Have the numbers far apart so that 3 to 4 students can stand facing forward between each number. Then distribute numbers for students to round. For example, give 53. The student stands on the line where 53 should be, then rounds to the nearest ten (50). Talk about the case of a 5 in the ones position (or in other halfway positions for larger numbers) as a convention—we all agree that we round up when we are midway between numbers.

For addition and subtraction problems involving only two numbers, one strategy is to round only one of the two numbers. For example, you can round only the subtracted number such as 6724−1863 becomes 6724−2000, resulting in 4724. You can stop here, or you can adjust. Adjusting might go like this: Because you subtracted a bigger number, the result must be too small. Adjust to about 4800.

Compatible Numbers

It is sometimes useful to look for two or three compatible numbers that can be grouped to equal benchmark values (e.g., 10, 100, 500). If numbers in the list can be adjusted slightly to equal these amounts, that will make finding an estimate easier. This approach is illustrated in Figure 12.26.

In subtraction, it is often possible to adjust only one number to produce an easily observed difference, as illustrated in Figure 12.27.

The following activity (adapted from Coates & Thompson, 2003) is a blend of mental computation and estimation. Figuring out where the numbers go to create the exact solution involves estimation.

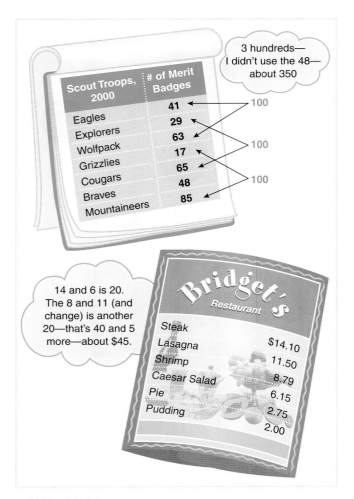

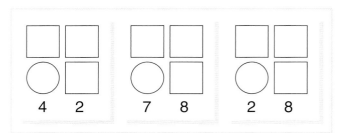

FIGURE 12.26 Compatible numbers used in addition.

FIGURE 12.27 Compatibles can help find the difference.

Activity 12.17

CCSS-M: 2.NBT.B.5

Box Math

Give students three digits to use (e.g., 3, 5, 7) and two operations ($+$ and $-$), using the Number Cards cut out from card stock so they can manipulate them easily. Give students a set of equations with answers only and ask them to use their number cards (in the squares) and operations (in the circle) to get to the answers shown.

STUDENTS
with
SPECIAL
NEEDS

4   2   7   8   2   8

For students who have disabilities, you may want to have the operation signs built into the displays of answers (such as an addition box and a subtraction box that generate the answer 42). These fixed problems will reduce the amount of decision making needed and allow for a focus on the numbers.

FORMATIVE ASSESSMENT **Notes.** In a diagnostic interview, ask a student to solve the following: "Charlie wants to estimate how much he needs to save to buy two video games. One game is $99 and the other is $118. How much should he save to purchase the two games?" Ask the student how he came up with his estimate. If the student is trying to mentally carry out the standard algorithm in the air or on the table with a finger, he likely has a limited ability with estimation strategies. Because $99 is so close to $100, it would be important for the student to use that fact in combining the two prices. If the student is unclear whether to change 99 to 100 or to 98 (as it is equally as close), that would pinpoint a lack of understanding of the purpose of estimation. Estimation cannot be easily assessed with paper-and-pencil tasks, so interviews that require explanations give more substantial evidence of student performance. ■

✔ **Complete Self-Check 12.7: Computational Estimation Strategies**

REFLECTIONS ON CHAPTER 12

WRITING TO LEARN

1. What are invented strategies and what are their benefits?

2. List three different invented strategies for adding 46 + 38. What models might work best in combination with the mental mathematics?

3. Use two different adding-up strategies for 93−27 and for 545−267. Make up a story problem that would encourage an adding-up strategy.

4. Why is an assessment that gets at student understanding so important when teaching standard algorithms?

5. What is a measurement estimation? How is it different from guessing?

6. Why might computational estimation be uncomfortable for students?

7. What are some important considerations for teaching computational estimation?

8. What is the rounding method of estimation? Why does this method produce a good approximation?

FOR DISCUSSION AND EXPLORATION

◆ What is the importance of mental mathematics and computational estimation for daily living? What are the advantages of being able to estimate in public situations and settings?

RESOURCES FOR CHAPTER 12

LITERATURE CONNECTIONS

Children's literature plays a valuable role in helping you develop problems that lead to invented strategies and mental computation.

The Great Math Tattle Battle *Bowen (2006)*

This entertaining book is largely about correcting errors in double-digit addition calculations. You can share a "student worksheet" that contains lots of mistakes and see whether your class can find errors and correct the paper. There's also an important message about tattling!

The Breakfast Cereal Gourmet *Hoffman (2005)*

National Geographic Kids Almanac 2015 *National Geographic (2014)*

These nonfiction books include interesting facts that can be used to create a variety of word problems. Hoffman's book provides data about breakfast eating habits; for example, the average person eats 160 bowls of cereal a year. The *National Geographic Kids Almanac* combines information with numerical data. For example, if Felix Baumgartener did a 24-mile free fall from space, how long would two jumps be? Explore your local newspaper to get students thinking about calculations that naturally emerge from real situations.

RECOMMENDED READINGS

Articles

O'Loughlin, T. A. (2007). Using research to develop computational fluency in young mathematicians. *Teaching Children Mathematics*, *14*(3), 132–138.

This article describes a second-grade teacher's journey to improve students' computational fluency through the use of invented strategies. The interesting collection of student work and related thought-provoking debriefing by the teacher will demonstrate various methods, such as split and jump strategies.

Russell, S. J. (2000). Developing computational fluency with whole numbers. *Teaching Children Mathematics*, 7, 155–158.

In just four pages, you will find an articulate description of computational fluency with each point illuminated by examples from students. The author explains that teaching for fluency is complex and requires that teachers understand mathematics, select appropriate tasks, and recognize when to capitalize on students' ideas.

Wentick, M., Behrand, J. L., & Mohs, L. C. (2013) A pathway for mathematical practices, *Teaching Children Mathematics*, *19*(6), 354–362.

In this article students examine the commutative property of addition, the decomposing of numbers, number relationships, and the meaning of the equal sign. Invented strategies are shared as students describe their thinking. The importance of carefully selecting problems is highlighted.

Book

Caldwell, J., Kobett, B., & Karp, K. (2014). *Essential understanding of addition and subtraction in practice, grades K–2.* Reston, VA: NCTM.

This book emphasizes the pedagogical content knowledge needed to teach the big ideas of addition and subtraction. There are many tasks to try and samples of students' work to share in class discussions!

13 Developing Strategies for Multiplication and Division Computation

LEARNER OUTCOMES

After reading this chapter and engaging in the embedded activities and reflections, you should be able to:

13.1 Recognize how understanding place value and the properties of operations support the learning of a variety of computational strategies in multiplication.

13.2 Identify a variety of models and recording approaches for developing the multiplication algorithm.

13.3 Explain invented strategies for division with multidigit numbers.

13.4 Explain the development of the standard algorithm for division and ways to record students' thinking.

13.5 Identify ways to teach computational estimation for multidigit multiplication and division as a way to develop students' flexibility and ability to recognize reasonable answers.

As students enter the intermediate grades, they begin to focus on computation strategies with multiplication and division. In fact, at least half of the grade 3 standards in the Common Core State Standards involve understanding multiplication (Kinzer & Stanford, 2013/2014). However, researchers suggest that invented strategies for multiplication and division are less well documented (Verschaffel et al., 2007) and the relationship between the operations more difficult to grasp than addition and subtraction (Robinson & LeFevre, 2012). The way to counter these challenges is to create an instructional environment that rewards flexibility so that students will successfully explore and test new ideas. As it was with addition and subtraction, students who only have knowledge of the standard multiplication and division algorithms often have difficulty following steps they do not fully understand (Biddlecomb & Carr, 2011). When students can compute multidigit multiplication and division problems in a variety of ways, complete written records of their work, explain their thinking, and discuss the merits of one strategy over another, they are developing as independent learners.

BIG IDEAS

◆ Flexible methods of computation in multiplication and division involve decomposing and composing numbers in a wide variety of ways.

◆ Flexible methods for multiplication and division require a strong understanding of the commutative property, the associative property, and the distributive property of multiplication over addition. How multiplication and division are related as inverse operations is also critical knowledge.

◆ Invented strategies provide flexible methods of computing that vary with the numbers and the situation. Successful use of the strategies requires that they be understood by those who are using them—hence, they must grasp that the process and the outcome of that process are related.

◆ The standard algorithms are clever strategies for computing that have been developed over time. Each is based on performing the operation on one place value at a time with transitions to an adjacent position.

◆ Nearly all computational estimations involve using easier-to-handle parts of numbers or substituting difficult-to-handle numbers with close compatible numbers so that the resulting computations can be done mentally.

Student-Invented Strategies for Multiplication

CCSS Standards for Mathematical Practice
MP7. Look for and make use of structure.

For multiplication, students' ability to break numbers apart in flexible ways is even more important than in addition or subtraction. This skill hinges on the full understanding of the distributive property of multiplication over addition. For example, to multiply 43 × 5 one might think about breaking 43 into 40 and 3, multiplying each by 5, and then adding the results. Students require ample opportunities to develop these concepts by making sense of their own ideas and those of their classmates. Visit the companion website to watch a video of Andrew as he uses the distributive property to solve 7 × 12

Useful Representations

The problem 6 × 34 may be represented in a number of ways, as illustrated in Figure 13.1. Often the choice of a model is influenced by a story problem. To determine how many oranges 6 classes need if there are 34 students in each class, students may model 6 sets of 34. If the problem is about a rectangle's area 6 cm × 34 cm, then some form of an array is likely. But each representation is appropriate for thinking about 6 × 34 regardless of the context, and students should get to a point at which they select meaningful ways to think about multiplication and use tools strategically.

How students represent a product is directly related to their methods for determining answers. At first, the equal groups of 34 students in a class might suggest repeated additions, but rather than adding one group at a time, suggest they take the groups at least two at a time. Double 34 is 68 and there are three of those, so 68 + 68 + 68 = 204. Remember, you want to move them away from repeated addition and to thinking multiplicatively. Another option is to think about how the six groups of base-ten pieces might be broken into tens and ones: 6 times 3 tens or 6 × 30 and 6 × 4. Or some students use the tens individually: 6 tens make 60. So that's 60 and 60 and 60 (180); then add on the 24 to make 204.

All of these ideas should be part of students' repertoire of models for multidigit multiplication computation.

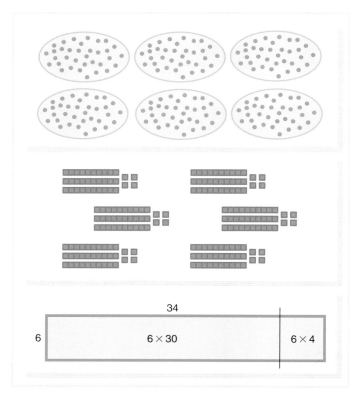

FIGURE 13.1   Different ways to model **6 × 34** may support different computational strategies.

Introduce different representations as ways to explore multiplication until you are comfortable that students' have a collection of useful ideas. Although teachers may worry that presenting multiple methods to solve problems will overwhelm and confuse students, researchers found that comparing a variety of methods from the start helped students gain flexibility and enhanced learning (Rittle-Johnson et al., 2010).

Multiplication by a Single-Digit Multiplier

As with addition and subtraction, it is helpful to place multiplication tasks in context. Let students model the problems in ways that make sense to them. The three categories described here are strategies grounded in student reasoning, as described in research on multiplicative reasoning (Baek, 2006; Confrey, 2008; Petit, 2009).

Complete-Number Strategies (Including Doubling). Students who are not yet comfortable decomposing numbers into parts will approach the numbers in the sets as single groups. Often, these early strategies will be based on repeated addition, which in the long term is neither efficient (234 × 78) nor useful (think about multiplication of fractions) (Devlin, 2011). Initially students may list long columns of numbers and add them up. In an attempt to fade this process, encourage students to recognize that if they add two numbers, the next two will have the same sum and so on. This doubling can become the principal approach for many students (Flowers & Rubenstein, 2010/2011). Doubling capitalizes on the distributive property, whereby doubling 47 is double 40 + double 7, and the associative property, in which doubling 7 tens—or 2 × (7 × 10)—is the same as doubling 7 and then multiplying by 10 or (2 × 7) × 10. Figure 13.2 illustrates two methods students may use.

Partitioning Strategies. Students break numbers up in a variety of ways that reflect an understanding of place value, at least four of which are illustrated in Figure 13.3. The "by decades" partitioning strategy (which can be extended to by hundreds, by thousands, etc.) is the same as the standard algorithm except that students always begin with the largest values. This is

Complete-Number Strategies for Multiplication

63 × 5

$$
\begin{array}{r}
63 \\
+\,63 \\
\hline
126 \\
+\,63 \\
\hline
189 \\
+\,63 \\
\hline
252 \\
+\,63 \\
\hline
315
\end{array}
$$

FIGURE 13.2 Students who use a complete-number strategy do not break numbers apart into decades or tens and ones.

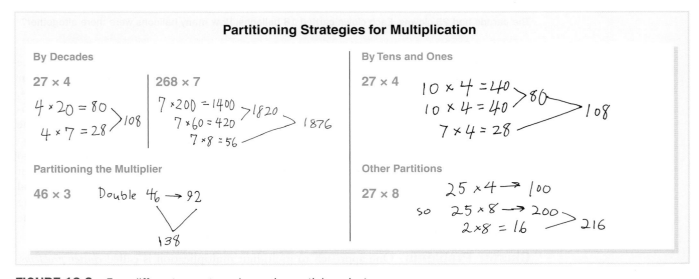

Partitioning Strategies for Multiplication

By Decades

27 × 4

$4 \times 20 = 80$
$4 \times 7 = 28$ ⟩ 108

268 × 7

$7 \times 200 = 1400$
$7 \times 60 = 420$ ⟩ 1820
$7 \times 8 = 56$ ⟩ 1876

By Tens and Ones

27 × 4

$10 \times 4 = 40$
$10 \times 4 = 40$ ⟩ 80
$7 \times 4 = 28$ ⟩ 108

Partitioning the Multiplier

46 × 3   Double 46 → 92

138

Other Partitions

27 × 8

$25 \times 4 → 100$
so $25 \times 8 → 200$
$2 \times 8 = 16$ ⟩ 216

FIGURE 13.3 Four different ways to make easier partial products.

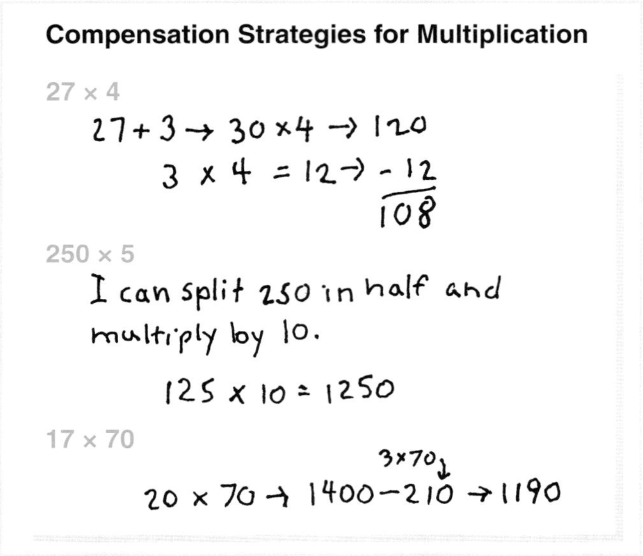

Compensation Strategies for Multiplication

27 × 4

$$27 + 3 \rightarrow 30 \times 4 \rightarrow 120$$
$$3 \times 4 = 12 \rightarrow -12$$
$$\overline{108}$$

250 × 5

I can split 250 in half and multiply by 10.

$$125 \times 10 = 1250$$

17 × 70

$$3 \times 70$$
$$20 \times 70 \rightarrow 1400 - 210 \rightarrow 1190$$

FIGURE 13.4 A compensation is made in the answer, or one factor is changed to compensate for a change in the other factor.

a very powerful mental math strategy. Another valuable strategy is to compute mentally with multiples of 25 and 50 and then add or subtract a small adjustment. All partitioning strategies rely on knowledge of the distributive property. Visit the companion website to watch a video of Rachel as she uses partitioning to solve 45 × 36.

Compensation Strategies. Students and adults look for ways to manipulate numbers so that the calculations are easy. In Figure 13.4, the problem 27 × 4 is changed to an easier one, and then an adjustment or compensation is made. The second example shows the "half-then-double strategy," in which one factor is cut in half and the other factor doubled. This is often used when a 5 or a 50 is involved. Because these strategies are dependent on the numbers involved, they can't be used for all computations. However, they are valuable approaches, especially for mental math and estimation.

Multiplication of Multidigit Numbers

As you move students from single-digit to two-digit factors, there is a value in exposing them to products involving multiples of 10 and 100. This supports the importance of place value and an emphasis on the number rather than the separate digits. Consider the following problem:

A Scout troop wants to package 400 battery packs as a fundraising project. If each pack will have 12 batteries inside, how many batteries are the Scouts going to need?

Students can use 4 × 12 = 48 to figure out that 400 × 12 is 4800. Make sure you discuss how to say and write "forty-eight hundred." Be aware of students who simply tack on zeros without understanding why. They may say "to multiply by 10, just add a zero on the end of the number." But very soon this rule will "expire" (Karp, Bush, & Dougherty, 2014) as students try to solve 2.5 × 10, a problem for which this rule will not work. Try problems in which tens are multiplied by tens, such as 30 × 60 or 210 × 40.

Then students should move to problems that involve any two-digit numbers, not just those that are multiples of 10. A problem such as this one can be solved in many different ways:

The parade had 23 clowns. Each clown carried 18 balloons. How many balloons were there altogether?

Some students might look for smaller products such as 6 × 23 and then add that result three times. Another method is to do 20 × 23 and then subtract 2 × 23. Others will calculate four separate partial products: 10 × 20 = 200, 8 × 20 = 160, 10 × 3 = 30, and 8 × 3 = 24. Two-digit multiplication is both complex and challenging. But students can solve these problems in a variety of interesting ways, many of which will contribute to the development of the standard algorithm. Figure 13.5 shows three fourth-grade students' work prior to instruction on the standard algorithm. Kenneth's work shows how he is *partitioning* the factor 12 into 3 × 2 × 2. Briannon is using a *complete-number strategy*. She may need to see and hear about strategies other classmates developed to move toward a more efficient approach. Nick's method is conceptually very similar to the standard algorithm. As students like Nick begin partitioning numbers by place value, their strategies are often like the standard algorithm but without the traditional recording schemes.

Cluster Problems. One approach to multidigit multiplication is called *cluster problems*. This approach encourages students to use facts and combinations they already know in order

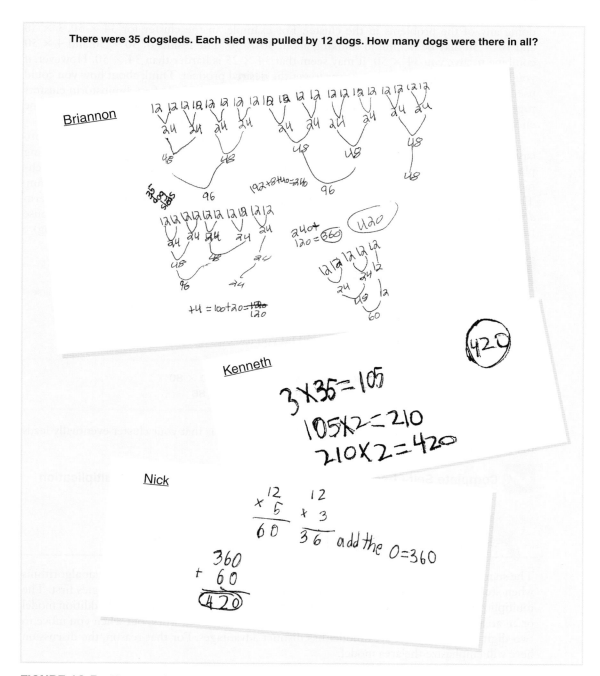

FIGURE 13.5 Three students solve a multiplication problem using invented strategies.

to figure out more complex computations. For example, to find 34×50, students might record the following cluster of known facts:

3×50

10×50

34×25

30×50

Using these problems as support, students can analyze to see which ones can be used in finding the product (there are multiple options). They can also consider adding other problems that might be helpful. In this case, have students make an estimate of the final product before doing any of the problems in the cluster. For example, in the cluster for 34 × 50, 3 × 50 and 10 × 50 may be helpful in thinking about 30 × 50. The results of 30 × 50 and 4 × 50 combine to give you 34 × 50. It may seem that 34 × 25 is harder than 34 × 50. However, if you know 34 × 25, double the answer to get the desired product. Think about how you could use 10 × 34 (and some other related problems) to find 34 × 25. At first, brainstorm clusters together as a class, but when students become familiar with the approach, they should be encouraged to make up their own cluster of problems for a given product.

Cluster problems help students think about ways that they can decompose numbers into easier parts. The strategy of breaking the numbers apart and multiplying the parts—using place-value knowledge coupled with the distributive property—is an extremely valuable technique for flexible computation and prepares students for understanding the standard algorithm. The Common Core State Standards state that students do not have to use the formal term *distributive property*, but they expect students to understand why this property works because that knowledge is critical to understanding multiplication (and its ties to algebraic thinking).

 Pause & Reflect

Try making up a cluster of problems for 86 × 42. Include all possible problems that you think might be helpful. Then use your cluster to find the product. Is there more than one way? •

Were these problems in your cluster? Did you use others?

2 × 80   4 × 80   2 × 86   40 × 80

6 × 40   10 × 86   40 × 86

All that is required to begin the cluster problem approach is that your cluster eventually leads to a solution.

 Complete Self-Check 13.1: Student-Invented Strategies for Multiplication

 Standard Algorithms for Multiplication

The standard multiplication algorithm is probably the most challenging of the four algorithms when students have not had plenty of opportunities to explore their own strategies first. The multiplication algorithm can be meaningfully developed using either a repeated-addition model or an area model. For one-digit multipliers, either approach will work, but when you move to two-digit multipliers, the area model has distinct advantages. For that reason, the discussion here will emphasize the area model.

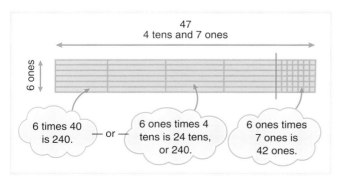

FIGURE 13.6 A rectangle covered with base-ten pieces is a useful model for two-digit-by-one-digit multiplication.

Begin with Models

As with the other algorithms, as much time as necessary should be devoted to the conceptual development of the algorithm using concrete or semi-concrete models, with the recording or written part coming later.

Area Model. Start with a context and give students a drawing of a rectangular garden 47 cm by 6 cm. What is the area of the garden? Let students solve the problem in groups using base-ten materials before discussing it as a class.

As shown in Figure 13.6, the rectangle can be sliced or separated into two parts so that one part will be 6 ones by 7 ones, or 42 ones, and the other will be 6 ones by 4 tens, or 24 tens. Notice that the base-ten language "6 ones times 4 tens equals 24 tens" tells how many tens pieces are in the big section. To say "6 times 40 equals 240" is also correct and tells how many units or square centimeters are in the section. What you wish to avoid is saying "6 times 4" when the 4 actually represents 40. Each section is referred to as a *partial product.* By adding the two partial products, you get the total product or area of the rectangle.

This is called the *area model* (can be thought about as a connected array) and it is an important visual representation that can support students' multiplicative understanding and reasoning (Barmby, Harries, Higgins, & Suggate, 2009; Izsák, 2004). The area model uses a row and column structure to automatically organize equal groups and offer a visual demonstration of the commutative and distributive properties (unlike the number line). The area model can also be linked to successful representations of the standard multiplication algorithm and to future topics such as multiplication of fractions and binomials (Lannin, Chval, & Jones, 2013).

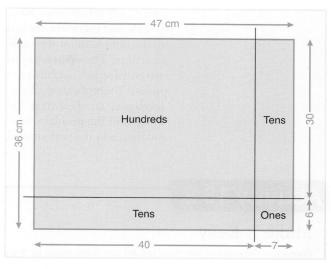

FIGURE 13.7 Ones, tens, and hundreds pieces fit exactly into the four sections of this 47 × 36 rectangle.

A valuable exploration with the area model uses large rectangles that have been precisely prepared with dimensions between 25 cm and 60 cm and square corners. Each group of students uses one of these rectangles to determine how many small ones pieces (base-ten materials) will fit inside the rectangle. Later, students can simply be given a tracing of a rectangle on grid paper or be asked, "What is the area of a rectangle that is 47 cm by 36 cm?"

CCSS Standards for Mathematical Practice
MP5. Use appropriate tools strategically.

For a rectangle that is 47 cm by 36 cm, most students will cover the rectangle with as many hundreds pieces as possible. One approach is to put the 12 hundreds in one corner. This will leave narrow regions on two sides that can be covered with tens pieces and a final small rectangle that will hold ones. Especially if students have had earlier experiences with finding products in arrays, figuring out the size of each subrectangle and combining them to find the size of the whole rectangle is relatively straightforward. The sketch in Figure 13.7 shows the four regions. Visit the companion website to watch a very brief video to see how students label the products of the subrectangles in their area models of two-digit by two-digit multiplication by marking sections with sticky notes.

Activity 13.1   CCSS-M: 4.NBT.B.5

Build It and Break It

Select a problem such as 23 × 18. Use base-ten blocks or grid paper to build the corresponding area model. Then, have students show and record as many ways as possible to "slice" the array into pieces. For example, they could cut the array into 23 × 10 + 23 × 8. What other vertical or horizontal slices can be made? What property does this link to? Before launching this activity, provide students, particularly ELLs and students with disabilities, a labeled visual of an array (or area model) that includes the terms *array, area model, slice, vertical,* and *horizontal.* In a wrap-up discussion, be sure to focus on the vocabulary of the key concepts (*distributive property, decompose, strategy,* etc.).

STUDENTS with SPECIAL NEEDS

ENGLISH LANGUAGE LEARNERS

Open Array. The open array (Fosnot & Dolk, 2001; NCTM, 2014) is a semi-concrete representation of the area model and can be successfully used after students actually experience several constructions of area models with base-ten materials. Starting with a blank rectangle, students can mark off areas (the number of subdivisions depends on the digits in the factors) that align with the use of the distributive property. Then they can record partial products inside each subdivision. Note that the dimensions of the open array are not necessarily drawn to scale and therefore are often not precisely proportional. But the model can be productively used to think about the multiplication as an area of a rectangle, which aligns to the standard algorithm. The open array will also connect to future work with multiplication with fractions, two polynomials, and also to the history of mathematics through looks at Egyptian and Russian peasant multiplication (Lee, 2014). Look at Figure 13.8 to see four steps in the process of developing an open array for the problem 36 × 72: Create an array according to the number of digits in the problem, label the sides with the factors broken down by place value, multiply, and then add the partial products.

Activity 13.2

CCSS-M: 4.NBT.B.5

Make It Easy

Computer versions of the area model can ease some of the difficulties of physically covering rectangular grids with base-ten blocks. Go to the NLVM website and find the Rectangle Multiplication applet. Model a multiplication problem of your choice up to 30 × 30. See how the rectangle is split into two parts rather than four, corresponding to the tens and ones digits in the multiplier. How does this representation correlate to the standard algorithm? For students with disabilities, you may need to have a set of base-ten blocks nearby to show how the concrete version corresponds to the computer illustration.

STUDENTS with **SPECIAL NEEDS**

Research analyzed sixth graders' varied strategies for solving multiplication problems on the factors of flexibility, accuracy, and efficiency. Given the problem 13 × 7, only 11 percent of the students used the standard algorithm. When multiplying 2 two-digit numbers, 20 percent used the standard algorithm, with less than half of the 20 percent reaching the correct answer (Keiser, 2010). Interestingly, this work confirmed the researcher's prior observations that the standard algorithm for multiplication was not the most popular approach for multiplying two-digit factors when students were taught other options. The array or area model was most often selected.

Move from having students draw large rectangles and arrange base-ten pieces using the Base-Ten Grid Paper. On the grid paper, students can draw accurate rectangles showing all of the pieces. Do not impose any recording technique on students until they understand how to use the two dimensions of a rectangle to get a product.

Develop the Written Record

To help with a recording scheme, provide sheets with base-ten columns on which students can record problems. When the two partial products are written separately and added together, there is little new to learn. But, as illustrated in Figure 13.9(a), it is possible to teach students how to write the first product with a regrouped digit so that the combined product is written on one line. This recording scheme is known to be a source of errors. The little digit representing the regrouping is often the difficulty—it often gets added in before the subsequent multiplication or is forgotten. To avoid errors, encourage students to record partial products. Then it makes no difference in which order the products are written. Figure 13.9(b) show how students can record partial products, which mirrors how this computation can be done mentally.

Partial Products. With the area model, the progression to a two-digit multiplier is relatively straightforward. Rectangles can be drawn on base-ten grid paper, full-sized rectangles can be covered with base-ten pieces, or an open array can be used. Now there will be four partial products, corresponding to four different sections of the rectangle.

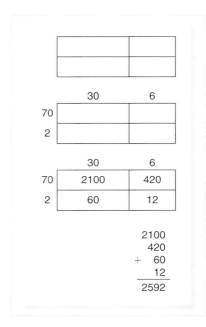

FIGURE 13.8 The open array is a means to record multidigit multiplication.

Several variations in language might be used. Consider the product 47 × 36, as illustrated in Figure 13.10. In the partial product 40 × 30, if base-ten language is used—*4 tens times 3 tens is 12 hundreds*—the result tells how many hundreds pieces are in that section. Avoid saying "four times three," which promotes thinking about digits rather than numbers. It is important to stress that a product of *tens times tens is hundreds*.

Figure 13.10 also shows the recording of four partial products in the traditional order and how these can be collapsed to two lines if digits representing the regrouping are used. Here the second exchange or trade technically belongs in the hundreds column but is often written elsewhere, which is again a source of errors. The lower left of the figure shows the same computation with all four products written in a different order. This is also acceptable. Using this approach, multiplying numbers such as 538 × 29 results in six partial products, but far fewer errors!

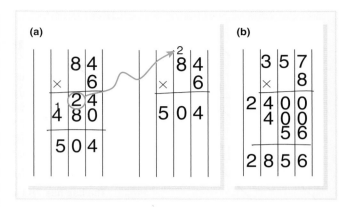

FIGURE 13.9 In the standard algorithm, the product of ones is recorded first (a). The tens digit of this first product is written as a regrouped digit above the tens column. In (b) partial products can be recorded in any order.

Lattice Multiplication. Another approach for recording multidigit multiplication is known as *lattice multiplication*. Historically this method has been used in a variety of cultures. Here students use a grid with squares split by diagonal lines to organize their thinking along diagonally organized place-value columns. Watch this video (http://www.youtube.com/watch?v=x2UG0YzT2UA) on how the lattice model (called the Gelosia model in the video) is set up, filled in, and calculated. Note that the instructor in the video incorrectly uses the word *and* when reading numbers and also uses the outdated word *carry* to discuss recording a regrouping. Look at Figure 13.11 to see the final recording for the problem 36 × 72.

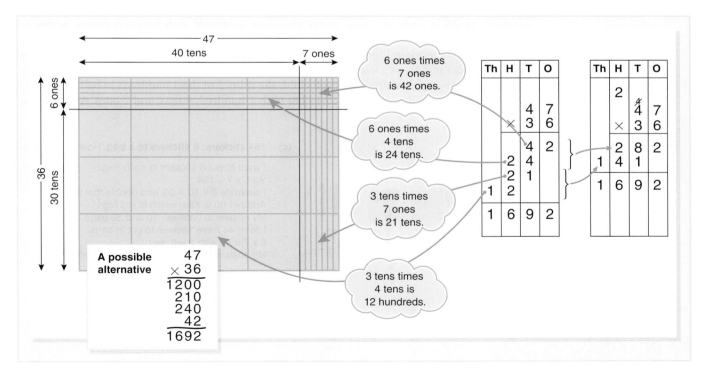

FIGURE 13.10 47 × 36 rectangle covered with base-ten pieces. Base-ten language connects the four partial products to the written format of the standard algorithm.

 Complete Self-Check 13.2: Standard Algorithms for Multiplication

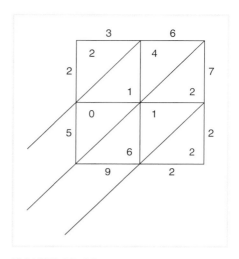

FIGURE 13.11   36 × 72 shown using a lattice multiplication technique.

Student-Invented Strategies for Division

Even though many adults think division is the most onerous of the computational operations, students may find it easier than multiplication. Division computation strategies with whole numbers are developed in third through fifth grade (CCSSO, 2010).

Recall that there are two concepts of division. First, there is the partition, or fair-sharing idea, illustrated by this story problem:

The bag has 783 jelly beans, and Eileen and her 4 friends want to share them equally. How many jelly beans will Eileen and each of her friends get?

Then there is the measurement, or repeated subtraction, concept:

Jumbo the elephant loves peanuts. His trainer has 625 peanuts. If he gives Jumbo 20 peanuts each day, how many days will the peanuts last?

Students should be challenged to solve both types of problems. However, the fair-share problems are often easier to solve with base-ten pieces, and they mirror the idea of partitioning in the standard algorithm. Eventually, students will develop strategies that they will apply to both types of problems.

Figure 13.12 shows strategies that three fourth graders used to solve division problems. The first example (a) illustrates 72 ÷ 3 using base-ten blocks and a sharing process. When no more tens can be distributed, a ten is traded for ten ones. Then the 12 ones are distributed, resulting in 24 in each set. This direct modeling approach with base-ten pieces is easy to understand and use.

The student work in Figure 13.12(b) shows that for the problem 342 ÷ 4, she sets out the base-ten pieces and draws a four-column recording chart to match the divisor. After noting that there are not enough hundreds for each child, she splits 2 of the 3 hundreds in half, putting 50 in each of the four columns. That leaves her with 1 hundred, 4 tens, and 2 ones. After trading

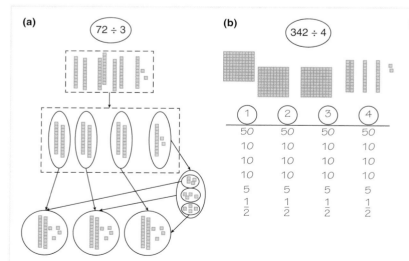

(c)   **164 stickers; 6 stickers to a bag. How many bags?**

I want to put 6 stickers in each bag.
So 6 x ? = 164
I estimate 6 x 10 = 60, and double that is 120.
Another 60 is 180, which is too high.
My answer is between 20 and 30 bags.
I have 44 more stickers to put in bags.
6 x 7 = 42 with 2 left over.
My answer is 27 bags with 2 stickers left over.

FIGURE 13.12   Students use both models and symbols to solve division tasks.

the one hundred for tens (now 14 tens), she gives 3 (tens) to each child, recording a total of 30 in each column. Now she is left with 2 tens and 2 ones, or 22. She knows that 4×5 is 20, so she gives each child 5, leaving 2. Then she splits the 2 into halves and writes $\frac{1}{2}$ in each column.

The student in Figure 13.12(c) solves a division problem that involves a measurement situation: How many bags with 6 stickers in each can be made if there are 164 stickers? She wants to find out how many groups of six are in 164. As a first step she estimates and tries 6×20. She actually does this by multiplying 6×10 and doubling the answer. Then she tries adding another group of 10 and recognizes that is too high. So she knows the answer is more than 20 and less than 30. Then she thinks about how many sixes in 44, which she knows is 7 with 2 left over. So her answer is 27 bags with 2 stickers left over.

Missing-Factor Strategies. In Figure 13.12(c), the student is using a multiplicative approach. She is trying to find out, "What number times 6 will be close to 164 with less than 6 remaining?"

 Pause & Reflect

Before reading further, think about the quotient of 318 ÷ 7 by trying to figure out *what number times 7* (or *7 times what number*) is close to 318 without going over. Do not use the standard algorithm.

There are several places to begin solving this problem. For instance, because 10×7 equals 70 and 100×7 equals 700, the answer is between 10 and 100. You might start with multiples of 10. Forty sevens are 280. Fifty sevens are 350. So 40 is not enough and 50 is too many. The answer has to be forty-something. At this point, you could test numbers between 40 and 50 or add on groups of seven. Or you could notice that 40 sevens (280) leaves you with 20 plus 18 or 38. Five sevens will be 35 of the 38 with 3 remaining. In all, that's $40 + 5$ or 45 with a remainder of 3.

This missing-factor approach is likely to be invented by some students if they are solving measurement problems such as the following:

Grace can put 6 pictures on one page of her photo album. If she has 82 pictures, how many pages will she need?

Alternatively, you can simply pose a task such as $82 \div 6$ and ask students, "What number times 6 would be close to 82?"

Cluster Problems. Another approach to developing missing-factor strategies is to use cluster problems, as discussed for multiplication. Here are examples of two clusters for two different division problems (in bold at the bottom of the columns):

Cluster 1	Cluster 2
100×4	10×72
$500 \div 4$	5×70
25×4	2×72
6×4	4×72
$527 \div 4$	5×72
	$381 \div 72$

Notice that the missing-factor strategy works equally well for one-digit divisors as for two-digit divisors. Also notice that it is okay to include division problems in the cluster. In the first example, $400 \div 4$ could easily have replaced 100×4, and 125×4 could replace $500 \div 4$. The idea is to capitalize on the inverse relationship between multiplication and division.

Cluster problems provide students with a sense that problems can be solved in different ways and with different starting points. Therefore, rather than cluster problems, you can provide students with a variety of first steps for solving a problem.

Pause & Reflect

Solve 514 ÷ 8 in two different ways beginning with different first steps. Do your approaches converge before you reach your solution? •

For example, here are four possible starting points for 514 ÷ 8:

10 × 8   400 ÷ 8   60 × 8   80 ÷ 8

When you first ask students to solve problems using two different strategies, they often use an inefficient method for their second approach (or revert to a standard algorithm). For example, to solve 514 ÷ 8, a student might perform a very long string of repeated subtractions (514 − 8 = 506, 506 − 8 = 498, 498 − 8 = 490, and so on) and count how many times he or she subtracted 8. Others will actually draw 514 tally marks and loop groups of 8. These students have not developed sufficient flexibility to think of other, more efficient methods. Posing a variety of starting points can nudge students into other, more profitable alternatives, as will class discussions where flexible approaches are shared. Visit the companion website to watch a video of a class discussion involving a variety of student strategies for solving 251 × 12. What questions does the teacher ask that encourage students to share their methods? Why do you think the teacher asks the students how the strategies are different and how they are the same?

 Complete Self-Check 13.3: Student-Invented Strategies for Division

Standard Algorithm for Division

The Common Core State Standards (CCSSO, 2010) suggest that the division algorithm with one-digit divisors is developed in the fourth grade, and it should provide the basis for the extension to two-digit divisors in the fifth grade. Students who are still struggling in grades 5 and beyond with single-digit divisors can also benefit from the following conceptual development.

Begin with Models

Long division is the one standard algorithm that starts with the left-hand or biggest pieces. The conceptual basis for the algorithm most often taught is the partition or fair-share method, the method we will explore in detail here.

Partition or Fair-Share Model. Traditionally, if the problem 4)583 was posed, we might hear someone say, "4 goes into 5 one time." Initially, this is quite mysterious to students. How can you just ignore the "83" and keep changing the problem? Preferably, you want students to think of the 583 as 5 hundreds, 8 tens, and 3 ones, not as the independent digits 5, 8, and 3. One idea is to use a context such as candy bundled in boxes of ten with 10 boxes (100 pieces) to a carton. Then the problem becomes as follows: *We have 5 cartons, 8 boxes, and 3 pieces of candy to share evenly between 4 schools.* In this context, it is reasonable to share the cartons first until no more can be shared. Those remaining cartons are "unpacked," and the boxes shared, and so on.

 Pause & Reflect

Try the distributing or sharing process yourself using base-ten pieces, four paper plates, and the problem 583 ÷ 4. Try to talk through the process without using "goes into." Think about sharing equally. Language plays an enormous role in thinking conceptually about the standard division algorithm. Most adults are so accustomed to the "goes into" language that it is hard for them to let it go. For the problem 583 ÷ 4, here is some suggested language:

- I want to share 5 hundreds, 8 tens, and 3 ones among these four sets. There are enough hundreds for each set to get 1 hundred. That leaves 1 hundred that I can't share.
- I'll trade the remaining hundred for 10 tens. That gives me a total of 18 tens. I can give each set 4 tens and have 2 tens left over. Two tens are not enough to go around the four sets.
- I can trade the 2 tens for 20 ones and put those with the 3 ones I already had. That makes a total of 23 ones. I can give 5 ones to each of the four sets. That leaves me with 3 ones as a remainder. In all, I gave out to each group 1 hundred, 4 tens, and 5 ones with 3 left over. •

Activity 13.3

CCSS-M: 4.NBT.B.6

Left Overs

STUDENTS
with
**SPECIAL
NEEDS**

Use the Left Over Game Board **and have students work in pairs and place their game pieces at the "start" point of the path. The first player uses the** Left Over Spinner **and spins. The amount on the spinner is used as the divisor for the number on the start square. If there are left overs after the division, the player moves the number of spaces that equals the remainder. If there is no remainder, the player stays in the same position. If they move the amount of the remainder, they get a bonus turn. The winner is the first to reach the end of the path. You can differentiate the game by using easier (or harder) divisors (see blank spinners on the Left Over Spinner Activity Page).**

Partial Quotients Using a Visual Model. You can look at division with an eye to partial quotients by using a version of a bar diagram model blended with the repeated subtraction approach. Take a look at the problem 1506 ÷ 3. If we use multiplication facts we know as a guide, then we can repeatedly subtract partial products and record them through an approach that uses measurement division (see Figure 13.13).

Develop the Written Record

The recording scheme for the standard long-division algorithm is not completely intuitive. You will need to be quite directive in helping students learn to record the fair sharing with models. There are essentially four steps:

1. *Share* and record the number of pieces put in each group.
2. *Record* the number of pieces shared in all. Multiply to find this number.
3. *Record* the number of pieces remaining. Subtract to find this number.
4. *Trade* (if necessary) for smaller pieces, and combine with any of the same-sized pieces that are there already. Record the new total number in the next column.

When students model problems with a one-digit divisor, steps 2 and 3 seem unnecessary. Explain that these steps really help when you don't have the pieces there to count.

Explicit-Trade Method. Figure 13.14 details each step of the recording process just described. On the left, you see the standard algorithm. To the right is an explicit-trade method that matches the actual action with the models by explicitly recording the trades. Instead of the "bring-down" step of the standard algorithm, the traded pieces are crossed out, as is the number of existing pieces in the next column. The combined number of pieces is written in this column using, in this case, a two-digit number. In the example, 2 hundreds are traded for 20 tens, combined with the 6 that were there for a total of 26 tens. The 26 is, therefore, written in the tens column.

$$200 + 200 + 100 + 2 = 502$$

	1506	906	306	6
3	−600	−600	−300	−6
	906	306	6	0

FIGURE 13.13 Using a bar diagram to show partial quotients.

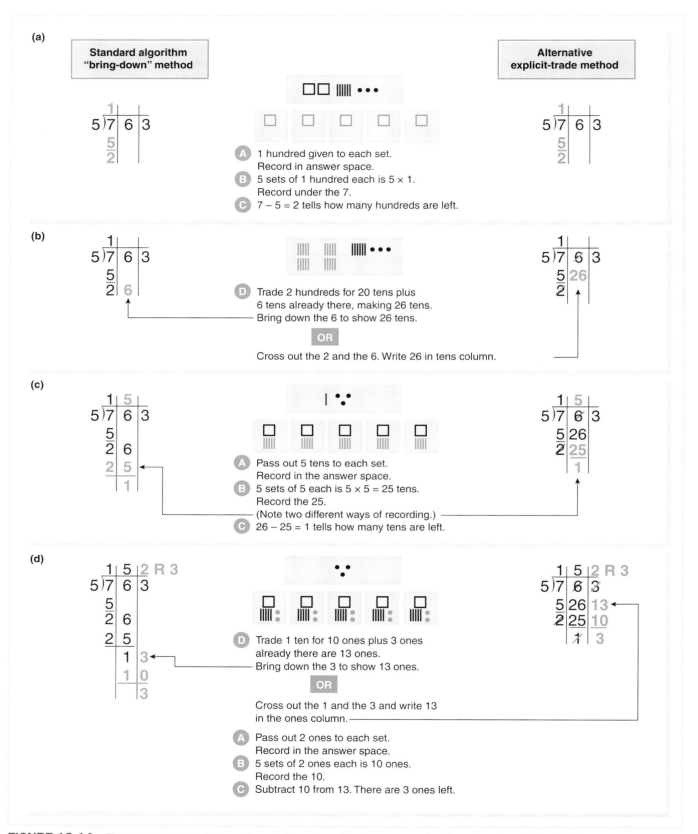

FIGURE 13.14 The standard algorithm and explicit-trade method are connected to each step of the division process.

Students often find this Explicit-Trade Method easier to follow. (The explicit-trade method is a successful approach invented by of John Van de Walle and tested with students in grades 3 to 8. You will not find it in other textbooks.) Blank Multiplication and Division Recording Charts with wide place-value columns are highly recommended for this method. By spreading out the digits in the dividend when writing down the problem, you help students avoid the common problem of leaving out a middle zero in a problem (see Figure 13.15).

Repeated Subtraction.
Another well-known algorithm is based on repeated subtraction and the measurement model of division. This approach may be viewed as a good way to record the missing-factor approach with partial products recorded in a column to the right of the division computation (see Figure 13.16). Students may prefer this strategy, especially students who bring this approach from other countries and students with learning disabilities who can select facts they already know and work from that point. This method is also useful with multidigit divisors. Explore Quotient Café on the NCTM Illuminations website for a way to explore a repeated subtraction approach in a variety of story situations.

Two-Digit Divisors

The Common Core State Standards states that fifth-grade students should be able to find "whole-number quotients of whole numbers with up to four-digit dividends and two-digit divisors, using strategies based on place value, the properties of operations, and/or the relationship between multiplication and division." The CCSSO goes on to state that the student should "[i]llustrate and explain the calculation by using equations, rectangular arrays, and/or area models" (CCSSO, 2010 p. 35). In the past, a large part of fourth, fifth, and sometimes sixth grade was spent on "long division," with the result that many students did not master the skill and instead some students came away with negative attitudes toward mathematics.

An Intuitive Idea.
Suppose that you were sharing a large pile of candies with 36 friends. Instead of passing them out one at a time, you conservatively estimate that each person could get at least 6 pieces. So you give 6 to each of your friends. Now you find there are more than 36 pieces left. Do you have everyone give back the 6 pieces so you can then give them 7 or 8? That would be silly! You simply pass out more.

The candy example gives us two good ideas for sharing in long division. First, always underestimate how much can be shared. You can always pass out some more. To avoid overestimating, always pretend there are more sets to share than there really are. For example, if you are dividing 312 by 43 (sharing among 43 sets or "friends"), pretend you have 50 sets instead. Round *up* to the next multiple of 10. You can easily determine that 6 pieces can be shared among 50 sets because 6 × 50 is an easy product. Therefore, since there are really only 43 sets, clearly you can give *at least* 6 to each.

Using the Idea Symbolically.
Using these ideas, both the standard algorithm and the explicit-trade method of recording are illustrated in Figure 13.17. The rounded-up divisor, 70, is written in a little "think bubble." Rounding up has another advantage: It is easy to use the multiples of 70 and compare them to 374. Think about sharing base-ten pieces (thousands, hundreds, tens, and ones). Work through the problem one step at a time, saying exactly what each recorded step stands for.

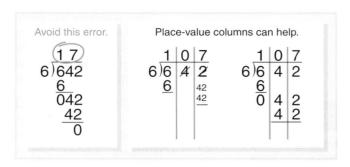

FIGURE 13.15 Using lines to mark place-value columns can help students remember to record zeros.

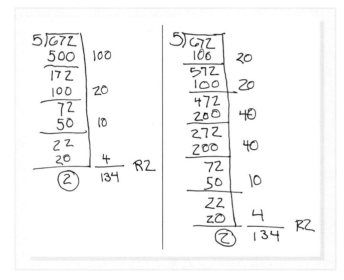

FIGURE 13.16 The numbers on the side indicate the quantity of the divisor being subtracted from the dividend. The divisor can be subtracted from the dividend in groups of any amount.

This approach has proved successful with students in the fourth grade who are learning division for the first time, with students in the sixth to eighth grades in need of remediation, and with students with disabilities. It reduces the mental strain of making choices and essentially eliminates the need to erase. If an estimate is too low, that's okay. And if you always round up, the estimate will never be too high. The same is true of the explicit-trade notation.

A Low-Stress Approach. With a two-digit divisor, it is hard to come up with the right amount to share at each step. First, start by thinking about place value by asking students to consider whether their answer will be in the thousands, hundreds, tens, and so on. Then create a "doubling" sidebar chart (Martin, 2009) that starts with a benchmark multiple of the divisor and then doubles each subsequent product. So, for the problem $3842 \div 14$, decide first whether the answer is in the thousands, hundreds, or tens. Selecting hundreds in this case, the students will then develop a chart of 100, 200, 400, and 800 times 14 (see Figure 13.18). Can you see how knowing 100 times 14 can help you figure out 200 and other products? Using this doubling sidebar chart can help students with the products of the divisor multiplied by 100 through 900 by adding the products in combinations. For example, to know 300 times 14, add the products of 100 times and 200 times the divisor or subtract 100 times 14 from 400 times 14. Knowing these products will logically help the student also know what 10 through 90 times the divisor is! Then the division becomes focused on the equal groups within the dividend and,

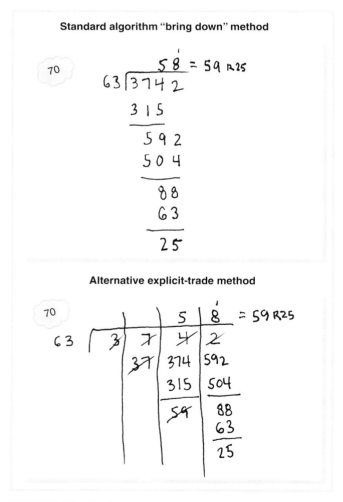

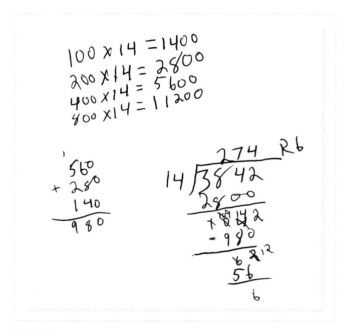

FIGURE 13.18 A student uses doubling to generate useful estimates in a sidebar chart.

FIGURE 13.17 Round the divisor up to 70 to estimate, but multiply what you share by 63. In the ones column, share 8 with each set. Oops! 88 left over so just give 1 more to each set.

FIGURE 13.19 An empty number line can be labeled in different ways to help students round to numbers that are close.

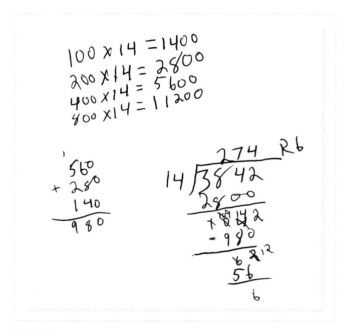

CCSS **Standards for Mathematical Practice**
MP5. Reasoning abstractly and quantitatively.

Activity 13.4

Double, Double—No Toil or Trouble!

Select a division problem with a two-digit divisor, such as 936 ÷ 18. Display a corresponding sidebar chart (Martin, 2009) of the products of the divisor (in this case, 10, 20, 40, and 80 × 18). Then try to think about the division using a missing factor approach and repeated subtraction. See if this helps in the estimation process. When working with students with learning disabilities, you may need to progress in a structured way by first supplying them with the appropriate sidebar chart with the products filled in. Then, on the next day, supply them with the chart and have them fill in the products, moving toward their independent creation and completion of the chart. This fading of support moves students in an organized and systematic way to more responsibility for their learning.

STUDENTS with SPECIAL NEEDS

as such, lowers stress. This scaffolding will help students (particularly students who are struggling) estimate more successfully while allowing them to concentrate on the division process.

Research analyzed middle school students' strategies for solving division problems within a context and as naked numbers (Keiser, 2012). Given two problems with double-digit divisors, only 4 of 91 students used the standard algorithm and of those 4 students only 2 were correct. Largely, students relied on a repeated subtraction approach or a missing-factor strategy. The teachers often found that errors occurred when students misapplied mathematical properties. For example, students solving 95 ÷ 16 broke it into 95 ÷ 10 + 95 ÷ 6, demonstrating a common misunderstanding. Students thought that when using the distributive property you can break apart the divisor, when instead you need to split the dividend into components.

 FORMATIVE ASSESSMENT Notes. To assess understanding for algorithms, call on different students to explain individual steps using the appropriate terminology that connects to the concept of division. Use a checklist to record students' responses, indicating how well they seem to understand the algorithm. For struggling students, you may want to conduct a short diagnostic interview to explore their level of understanding in more detail. Begin by having the student complete 115 ÷ 9 and ask them to talk about what they are thinking as they carry out specific steps in the process. If there is difficulty explaining, have the student use base-ten blocks to perform the computation. Then ask them to make connections between what was done with the models and what was done symbolically. ■

 Complete Self-Check 13.4: Standard Algorithm for Division

Computational Estimation in Multiplication and Division

Particularly in multiplicative situations, computational estimation is useful in daily events such as calculating a tip or figuring out miles per gallon of gasoline. As students move to a more technological world where calculations are frequently carried out by devices, never before has judging reasonableness been more important. Those who can estimate well will rarely be tricked by a mistake in using a calculator.

Computational estimation skills in multiplication and division round out a full development of flexible and fluent thinking with whole numbers. The Common Core State Standards state that fourth graders should "assess the reasonableness of answers using mental computation and estimation strategies including rounding" (CCSSO, 2010, p. 29).

Suggestions for Teaching Computational Estimation

What estimate would you give for 27 × 325? If you use 20 × 300, you might say 6000. Or you might use 25 for the 27, noting that four 25s make 100. Because 325 ÷ 4 is about 81, that would make 8100. If you use 30×300, your estimate is 9000, and 30×320 gives an estimate of 9600. Is one of these "right"?

The more strategies students experience, the better they can select one that best suits the situation at hand. In contrast, if you tell students to use a given strategy (e.g., round each number to one significant digit and multiply), they won't develop the skills to pick different strategies for different situations. Sometimes rounding is cumbersome and other strategies are quicker or more accurate.

Ask for Information, But No Answer. Consider the risk a student perceives when you ask for an estimate of the product $7 \times \$89.99$. Students commonly try to quickly calculate an exact answer and then round it (Hanson & Hogan, 2000). To counter this, ask questions that provide a focus on the result, using prompts like "Is it more than or less than 1000?" or "Will $500 be enough to pay for the tickets?" The question "About how much?" is quite different from "Is it more than $600?" Another option is to ask students to choose if the answer is between $100 and $400, $500 and $800, or $900 and $1200. Narrow your ranges as students become more adept.

Each activity that follows suggests a format for estimation in which a specific numeric response is not required.

Activity 13.5   CCSS-M: 4.NBT.A.3; 4.NBT.B.5

High or Low?

Display a computation and three or more possible computations that might be used to create an estimate. The students' task is to decide whether the estimation will be higher or lower than the actual computation. For example, present the computation 736×18. For each of the following, decide whether the result will be higher or lower than the exact result and explain why you think so.

$$750 \times 10 \qquad 730 \times 15$$
$$700 \times 20 \qquad 750 \times 20$$

Also explore the High or Low Activity Page for additional problems and the Expanded Lesson for an instructional plan for this activity.

Activity 13.6   CCSS-M: 4.OA.A.3

That's Good Enough

Present students with a computation that is reasonably difficult. For example: T-shirts with the school logo cost $6 wholesale. The Pep Club has saved $257. How many shirts can they buy for a fundraiser? The task is to describe the steps they would take to get an exact answer but not do them. For students with disabilities, you may give them a series of examples and counterexamples of the steps that they must choose from and put in order. Share students' ideas. Next, have students actually do one or two steps. Stop and see whether they come up with good estimates.

Computational Estimation Strategies

Mental calculations using estimations are more complex than just the application of a procedure in that they require a deep knowledge of how numbers work (Hartnett, 2007). The CCSS suggest that for all four operations, students in grades 3 and 4 should "assess the reasonableness of answers using mental computation and estimation strategies including rounding" (CCSSO, 2010, pp. 23, 29). See Table 13.1 for more information on estimation strategies.

TABLE 13.1 ESTIMATION STRATEGIES

Estimation Strategy	Description and Strategies	Examples
Front End	• This method focuses on the leading, or left-most, digits in numbers. Once the first digit it identified, then students think about the rest of the number as if there were zeros in the other positions. Adjustments are made to correct for the digits or numbers that were ignored. This method has been shown to be one of the easiest for students to learn (Star & Rittle-Johnson, 2009). • When estimating, avoid presenting division problems using the computational form 7)3482 because this format suggests a computation rather than an estimate. Present problems in context or use the algebraic form: 3482 ÷ 7.	• 480 × 7 is 400 × 7, or 2800. • 452 × 23, consider 400 × 20, or 8000. Adjust in a second step to 9000. • 3482 ÷ 7, first decide the correct place value of the estimate (100 × 7 is too low, 1000 × 7 is too high, so the estimate will be in the hundreds). There are 34 hundreds in the dividend, so because 34 ÷ 7 is between 4 and 5, the front-end estimate is 400 or 500. In this example, because 34 ÷ 7 is almost 5, the more precise estimate is 500.
Rounding	• This method is a way of changing the numbers in the problem to others that are easier to compute mentally. In multiplication, students can either round one number or both. • Use a number line marked by a scale of 5, 10, 100, etc. The ends can be labeled 0 and 100, 100 and 200, 100 and 1000, or a range of your choice. If given a factor such as 463 and asked to round to the nearest 100, the answer is 500; if rounding to the nearest 50 then 450 would be a possible estimate (see Figure 13.18).	• If one factor can be rounded to 10, 100, or 1000, the resulting product is easy to determine without adjusting the other factor (see Figure 13.20(a)). • When one factor is a single digit, round the other factor—so for 7 × 485, round 485 to 500, and the estimate is 3500. That is too high by the amount of 7 × 15 so, if more precision is required, subtract about 100 (an estimate of 7 × 15) (see Figure 13.20(b)). • Another option is to round one factor up and the other down. So for 86 × 28, 86 is between 80 and 90, but 28 is very close to 30. Round 86 down to 80 and 28 up to 30. The estimate of 2400 is only slightly off from the actual product of 2408 (see Figure 13.20(c) for another example).
Compatible Numbers	• This method refers to changing the number to one that would make the problem easier to compute mentally. This is usually used in division by adjusting the divisor or dividend (or both) to close numbers. Many percent, fraction, and rate situations involve division, and the compatible numbers strategy is quite useful.	• 413 × 24 can be thought of as 400 × 25. Because 4 × 25 is 100, a good estimate is 10,000. • 497 ÷ 48 is approximately 500 ÷ 50, so 10 is a reasonable estimate. • See other examples in Figure 13.21.

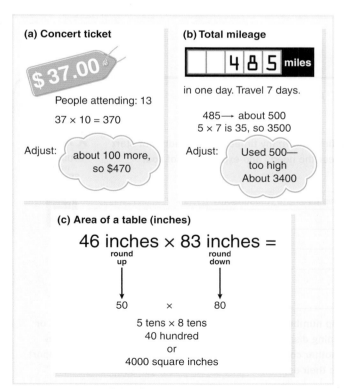

FIGURE 13.20 Rounding in multiplication.

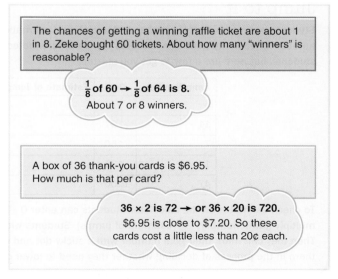

FIGURE 13.21 Using compatible numbers in division.

Estimation strategies are specific approaches that produce approximate results. As you work through the strategies in this section, you may recognize many of the same approaches students developed from their invented methods. It is also likely that some of the strategies in this section will not have been developed, and you will need to introduce these to your students.

FORMATIVE ASSESSMENT Notes. Teachers often wonder how they can assess computational estimation so that they can identify if students are computing on paper and then just rounding the answer to make it look like an estimate. One method is to prepare performance-based tasks that include about three estimation exercises for display on a projection device. Briefly show one exercise at a time, perhaps for 20 seconds, depending on the task. Students write their estimate immediately and indicate whether they think their estimate is "low" or "high"—that is, lower or higher than the exact computation. They are not to do any written computation. Continue until you are finished. Then show all the exercises and have students write down how they did each estimate. They should indicate why they think the estimate was reasonable or not. By only doing a few estimates but having the students reflect on them in this way, you receive more information than you would with just the answers to a longer list. ■

Activity 13.7
CCSS-M: 4.NBT.A.3; 4.NBT.B.5

What Was Your Method?

Select a problem with an estimation given. For example, say, "Juan estimated that 139 × 43 is about 6000. How do you think he came up with 6000? Was that a good approach? Is the estimate larger or smaller than the actual answer, and how do you know? How should it be adjusted? Why might someone select 150 instead of 140 as a substitute for 139?" Almost every estimate can involve different choices and methods. Alternatives make for good discussion points, helping students see different methods and learn that there is no single correct estimate.

Activity 13.8
CCSS-M: 4.NBT.B.5; 4.NBT.A.3

Jump to It

Students begin with a start number and use mental estimation to find how many times they will add that start number to reach the goal. The numbers can be differentiated to meet the needs and experiences of your students, but here are a few to get you started:

STUDENTS
with
SPECIAL
NEEDS

Jump Number	Goal	Estimate of Jumps	Was Estimate Reasonable?
5	72		
11	97		
7	150		
14	135		
47	1200		

To check estimates on the calculator, students can enter 0 ⊞ [jump number] and press ⊟ once for every estimated jump, or multiply [jump number] ⊠ [estimate of jumps]. Students with learning disabilities may need to have a number line close by. Then they can mark their goal number with a sticky dot and use another color dot to mark their first estimate. This will support them in the process of deciding whether they need to lower or raise their estimation of the number of jumps.

Activity 13.9

CCSS-M: 4.NBT.B.5

Hit the Target

This is an estimation game using a calculator that can be used for any of the four operations. First, pick a start number and an operation. Pairs of students (or the whole class with a projection device) take turns entering the start number, ×, a number of choice, and = to try to make the result land in the stated target. The following example for multiplication illustrates the activity:

Start Number: 17
Target: 800–830

If the first number tried is 25, pressing 17 ⊗ 25 gives 425, which is not in the range. Then the calculator is passed to the partner, who clears the screen and picks a different number—for example, a number close to 50 because the first product was about half of numbers in the target range. A second guess might be 17 ⊗ 45, or 765. This is closer, but still not in the target range. The calculator goes back to the first person. Continue to clear each guess and try again until someone gets a product that hits the target range. Figure 13.22 gives examples for all four operations. Prepare a list of start numbers and target ranges.

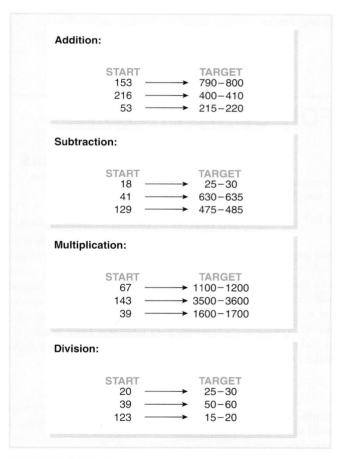

FIGURE 13.22   Possible starting numbers and targets for the Hit the Target game.

 Complete Self-Check 13.5: Computational Estimation in Multiplication and Division

REFLECTIONS ON CHAPTER 13

WRITING TO LEARN

1. Draw pictures showing how 4×57 could be modeled in two ways using base-ten blocks, an open array, or an area on a grid.

2. What would you do if your students seemed to persist in using repeated addition for multiplication problems without really doing any multiplication?

3. Which division concept, measurement or partition, is easier for direct modeling? Which is the one used to develop the standard long-division algorithm? Make up an appropriate word problem to go with $735 \div 6$.

4. Use the standard algorithm for $735 \div 6$, then repeat the process using the text's suggestion of recording trades explicitly. With the two algorithms side by side, explain every recorded number in terms of what it stands for when sharing base-ten blocks.

5. Describe each of these estimation strategies and include an example.

FOR DISCUSSION AND EXPLORATION

♦ You notice a student is estimating by doing the computation and rounding the answer. Why might the student be using this strategy? What experiences might you plan to improve the student's ability to estimate?

RESOURCES FOR CHAPTER 13

LITERATURE CONNECTIONS

Literature often provides excellent contexts for computation and estimates, as in the following two engaging examples.

Is a Blue Whale the Biggest Thing There Is?
Wells (2005)

This is an intriguing book about large objects and large distances. Blue whales look small next to Mount Everest, which in turn looks small next to the earth. The data in the book allow students to make other comparisons, such as the number of fourth graders who would have the same weight or volume as a blue whale or would fill the gymnasium. These comparisons are the perfect place for estimations and discussions about how much precision is necessary to make a meaningful comparison.

Counting on Frank *Clement (1991)*

This book's narrator uses his dog, Frank, as a counting reference. For example, he explains that 24 Franks would fit in his bedroom. Because the book offers approximations, there are limitless opportunities to do computational estimation. For example, how many Franks would fit in five rooms? If there were 24 Franks, how many cans of dog food (discussed on a later page) might be knocked over? The back of the book offers a helpful series of estimation questions.

RECOMMENDED READINGS

Articles

Benson, C., Wall, J., & Malm, C. (2013). The distributive property in grade 3? *Teaching Children Mathematics*, *19*(8), 498–506.

> *Don't let the title influence you; this is not just a reading for those who work with third graders! This article links the numerical and geometrical interpretations of multiplication through the connection with the distributive property. Through a collection of visual representations using area of rectangular regions (sometimes highlighted by the use of color), the authors move students from what they know to what they don't know while building their understanding of the power of the distributive property.*

Book

Fosnot, C. T., & Dolk, M. (2001). *Young mathematicians at work: Constructing multiplication and division.* Portsmouth, NH: Heinemann.

> *One in a series, this book is the product of a collaborative effort of researchers and teachers. Together they examine how students learn and how to support that learning. The authors show students' work constructing ideas about number, operations, and computation in ways not found elsewhere.*

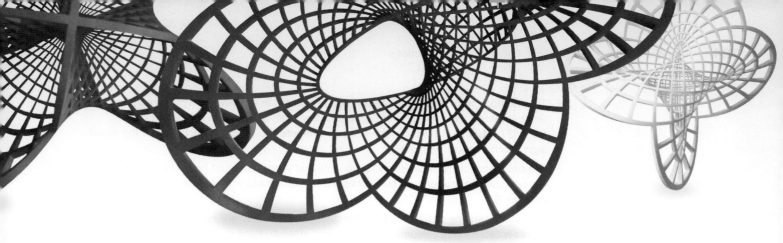

CHAPTER 14

Algebraic Thinking, Equations, and Functions

LEARNER OUTCOMES

After reading this chapter and engaging in the embedded activities and reflections, you should be able to:

14.1 Summarize each area of algebraic thinking

14.2 Describe connections between number and algebraic thinking.

14.3 Explore ways to engage students in applying properties of the operations to number and algebra.

14.4 Illustrate and describe patterns and functions and describe how to engage students in learning about functions in K–8.

14.5 Analyze challenges students have with symbols (e.g., equal sign, variables) and identify strategies that can avoid or undo these limited conceptions.

14.6 Define mathematical modeling and describe ways to infuse modeling into instruction across mathematics.

Algebraic thinking (also called algebraic reasoning) begins in Kindergarten as young students "represent addition and subtraction with objects, fingers, mental images, drawings, sounds (e.g., claps), acting out situations, verbal explanations, expressions, or equations" (CCSSO, 2010, p. 11) Similar connections between arithmetic and algebra are noted in every grade from kindergarten through fifth grade, where number and algebra are combined in the discussions of clusters and standards under the domain of Operations and Algebraic Thinking. In middle school, students begin to study algebra in more abstract and symbolic ways, focusing on understanding and using variables, expressions, and equations. CCSS-M introduces *functions* as a domain in grade 8, but *functional thinking* begins in the early grades as students consider situations that co-vary, such as the relationship between number of T-shirts purchased and the cost of those T-shirts. Algebraic thinking is present across content areas and is central to mathematical reasoning, as can be seen from the strong connections to the Standards for Mathematical Practice.

BIG IDEAS

♦ Algebra is a useful tool for generalizing arithmetic and representing patterns in our world. Explaining the regularities and consistencies across many problems gives students the chance to generalize (Mathematical Practice 8).

 ◆ The methods we use to compute and the structures in our number system can and should be generalized. For example, the generalization that $a + b = b + a$ tells us that $83 + 27 = 27 + 83$ without the need to compute the sums on each side of the equal sign (Mathematical Practice 7).

 ◆ Symbols, especially those involving equality and variables, must be well understood conceptually for students to be successful in mathematics (Mathematical Practice 6).

 ◆ The understanding of functions is strengthened when they are explored across representations (e.g., equations, tables, and graphs). Each mathematical model provides a different view of the same relationship (Mathematical Practice 4).

Strands of Algebraic Thinking

It is human to try to make sense of the world (and to see how things are related) (Fosnot & Jacob, 2010). Algebraic thinking is used to generalize arithmetic, to notice patterns that hold true in algorithms and with properties, and to reason quantitatively about such things as whether expressions are equivalent or not. Algebra must be presented in a way that students see it is a useful tool for making sense of all areas of mathematics and real-world situations.

Algebraic thinking involves forming generalizations from experiences with number and computation and formalizing these ideas with the use of a meaningful symbol system. Far from being a topic with little real-world use, algebraic thinking pervades all of mathematics and is essential for making mathematics useful in daily life.

Researchers suggest three strands of algebraic reasoning, all infusing the central notions of generalization and symbolization (Blanton, 2008; Kaput, 2008):

1. The study of structures in the number system, including those arising in arithmetic.
2. The study of patterns, relations, and functions.
3. The process of mathematical modeling, including the meaningful use of symbols.

Algebra is a separate strand of the mathematics curriculum but is also embedded in all areas of mathematics. This chapter is organized around these three strands, though we split 1 and 3 into two parts. In each section we share how these ideas develop across grades K–8.

Structure in the Number System: Connecting Number and Algebra

Algebra is often referred to as generalized arithmetic. For students to generalize an operation or pattern, they must look at several examples and notice what is happening in the problem, in other words, gain insights into the structure of the number system. Here we share three ways to connect arithmetic to algebra.

Number Combinations

Looking for generalizations in sets of problems can begin in the early grades, with decomposing numbers (CCSS-M K.NBT.A.1) and continue through the early grades as students use strategies to add and subtract (CCSS-M 1.OA.B.3 and 2.OA.B.2). The following task, based on Neagoy (2012), uses the context of birds to focus on decomposing numbers.

Seven birds have landed in your backyard, some landed on a tree, and some are at your feeder. How many birds might be in the tree and how many at the feeder?

 Pause & Reflect

If there are 2 birds at the feeder, how many are in the tree? If there are 6 birds at the feeder how many birds are in the tree? How can you find how many in the tree if you know how many birds are at the feeder? •

Generalizations can be analyzed when data is recorded in a table. Visit the companion website for the Birds in the Backyard Activity Page. Students can describe the pattern with symbols, something that elementary students can do and that middle school students must do. In CCSS-M variables are introduced in grade 3 and 4 as they solve for missing unknowns (3.OA.D.8 and 4.OA.A.3), and are emphasized across grades 6–8 in the Expressions and Equations Domain. For example, in the Birds in the Backyard problem, after students answer the questions in the Pause and Reflect, ask "If I have t birds in the tree, how might you describe how many birds are at the feeder?" Students might answer, "Seven minus t." Write $7 - t$. If the students answer "f" (for the variable to represent the number of birds at the feeder), then ask how t and f are related in an equation. Three equations could describe this situation: $t + f = 7$, $7 - f = t$, and $7 - t = f$.

Place-Value Relationships

Fundamental to mental mathematics is generalizing place-value concepts. Consider the sum $49 + 18$. How would you add it in your head? Many people will move one over to make a 10 and think $50 + 17$ (or move two over to get $47 + 20$). Many of these strategies have been addressed in the previous four chapters.

The hundreds chart helps students to generalize the relationship between tens and ones. Ask students, "What did we add to get from 72 to 82? From 5 to 15? From 34 to 44?" Students notice across these examples (and more like them) that they are adding 10 and moving down exactly one row. Moves on the hundreds chart can be represented with arrows (for example, → means right one column or plus 1, and ↑ means up one row or less 10). Consider asking children to complete these problems:

14 →→←←   63 ↑↑↓↓   45 →↑←↓

Some students may count up or back using a count-by-ones approach. Others may jump 10 or 1 (up or down). Still others may recognize that a downward arrow "undoes" an upward arrow– an indication that these children are moving toward generalizations (Blanton, 2008). In other words, they recognize that $+10$ and -10 results in a zero change. Students can also write the equations for the arrow moves with numbers or with variables—for example, for the first problem, $n + 1 + 1 - 1 - 1 = n + (1 - 1) + (1 - 1) = n$. The more variables and numbers are used in looking at generalizations, the better able students become at using symbols.

CCSS Standards for Mathematical Practice
MP4. Model with mathematics.

FORMATIVE ASSESSMENT Notes. As students work on such tasks, you can observe while using a **checklist** to note which students are solving by counting by ones, by jumping, or by noticing the "doing" and "undoing." What you observe can help your discussion as you can have students start by first sharing the more basic strategies and then have students who have generalized the situation share how they think about it. ∎

Activity 14.1 provides an engaging context for students to explore patterns involving place value and addition.

Activity 14.1

CCSS-M: 1.NBT.C.4; 2.NBT.B.9; 3.OA.D.9

STUDENTS
with
SPECIAL
NEEDS

Diagonal Sums

Provide each student with a hard copy of a Hundreds Chart, Blackline Master 3, or you can use an interactive virtual hundreds chart (numerous options are available on the Web). Students select any four numbers in the hundreds chart that form a square. Ask students to add the two numbers on each diagonal as in the example shown here. For younger students or students who struggle, use calculators so that they can explore the pattern without getting bogged down in computations.

13	14
23	24

Have students share their diagonal sums with a partner. Compare what happened. Together invite students to find another square. Ask them to describe why this pattern works. Allow time for each pair to share why the pattern works. To extend this activity, use diagonals of rectangles; for example, the numbers 15, 19, 75, and 79.

⏸ Pause & Reflect

Before reading further, stop and explore why the diagonal sums described in the previous activities are the same. What questions might you ask students to be sure they are noticing the relationship between tens and ones? ●

Here are some additional tasks you might explore on a hundreds chart. With each one, notice how the first aspect of the task is about number and the latter questions focus on generalizations (algebraic thinking).

- Pick a number. Move down two and over one. What is the relationship between the original number and the new number? What algebraic expression describes this move?
- Pick a number. Add it to the number to its left and to its right. Divide by 3. What answer do you get? Can you explain why this works? Can you explain using variables?
- Skip count by different values (e.g., 2, 4, 5). Which numbers make diagonal patterns? Which make column patterns? What is true about all numbers that make a column pattern?
- Find two skip-count numbers in which one number lands "on top of" the other (that is, all of the shaded values for one pattern are part of the shaded values for the other)? How are these two skip-count numbers related?

Asking questions such as "When will this be true?" and "Why does this work?" requires children to generalize and consequently, strengthen their understanding of the number concepts they are learning.

Algorithms

When studying the operations, students are often asked to explain how they solved a problem, for example, 504−198. As you listen to students' strategies, record their ideas using symbols. For this problem, you might record a student's mental strategy like this: 504 − 200 + 2. Ask, "Does this show how you solved it?" or "Is this equivalent to the original expression?" Such questions to the class can lead to rich discussions about the properties (Blanton et al., 2011).

Slight shifts in how arithmetic problems are presented can open up opportunities for generalizations (Blanton, 2008). For example, instead of a series of unrelated computation problems, consider a list that can lead to a discussion of a generalization:

$$3 \times 7 = ? \qquad 6 \times 7 = ?$$

In discussing the relationship, students notice that 6 is twice 3 and therefore the answer is twice as much. This strategy can be applied to any of the $\times$ 6 basic facts, helping students with what is often some of the more challenging facts to learn.

Sets of problems are good ways for students to look for and describe patterns across the problems, patterns that build an understanding for the operation and related algorithms:

$$\frac{1}{2} \times 12 = \qquad \frac{1}{4} \times 12 = \qquad \frac{1}{8} \times 12 = \qquad \frac{3}{4} \times 12 = \qquad \frac{3}{8} \times 12 =$$

 Standards for Mathematical Practice
MP8. Look for and express regularity in repeated reasoning.

Once students have solved sets of related problems, focus attention on what you want students to generalize: What do you notice? How are the problems alike? Different? How does the difference in the problem alter the answer? Why? In this set of problems, such a discussion can help students understand the relationship between the numerator and the denominator and what that means in multiplication situations.

 Complete Self-Check 14.1: Structure in the Number System: Connecting Number and Algebra

Structure in the Number System: Properties

The importance of the properties of the operations cannot be overstated. Table 14.1 provides a list of the ones students must know, including how students might describe the property. In the CCSS-M, properties of the operations are one of the only things mentioned in the standards for each grade, grades 1 to 8. Importantly, the emphasis is on *using* and *applying* the properties (not identifying them); for example, in grade 2, one standard states, "Explain why addition and subtraction strategies work, using place value and the properties of operations" (CCSSO, 2010, p. 19).

The properties are essential to computation (Blanton, Levi, Crites, & Dougherty, 2011). Traditionally, instruction on the properties has been on matching equations to which property they illustrate. That is not sufficient and should not be the focus of your instruction on the properties. Instead, focus on helping students recognize and understand these important generalizations— and use them to generate equivalent expressions in order to solve problems efficiently and flexibly (for example, understanding the commutative property for both addition and multiplication reduces substantially reduces the number of facts to be memorized). The properties of the operations have been discussed in several chapters in this book, in particular Chapter 9 and Chapter 10. In this chapter the focus is on exploring the properties as generalizations of number.

Making Sense of Properties

Students begin to notice equivalent expressions as they engage in their work with numbers. For example, young students might be asked to solve this pair of equations: 3 + 7 = ____ and 7 + 3 = ____ . Some students may say that these equal the same, but it is important to discuss why this is true. A young student might explain that it could be beans on two plates and you moved the plates to trade places. Using or applying this same property means that in an

TABLE 14.1   PROPERTIES OF THE NUMBER SYSTEM

Properties of the Operations		
Name of Property	**Symbolic Representation**	**How a Student Might Describe the Pattern or Structure**
Addition		
Commutative	$a + b = b + a$	"When you add two numbers in any order you will get the same answer."
Associative	$(a + b) + c = a + (b + c)$	"When you add three numbers you can add the first two and then add the third or add the last two numbers and then add the first number. Either way you will get the same answer."
Additive Identity	$a + 0 = 0 + a = a$	"When you add zero to any number you get the same number you started with."
	$a - 0 = a$	"When you subtract zero from any number you get the number you started with."
Additive Inverse	$a - a = a + (-a) = 0$	"When you subtract a number from itself you get zero."
Inverse Relationship of Addition and Subtraction	If $a + b = c$ then $c - b = a$ and $c - a = b$	"When you have a subtraction problem you can 'think addition' by using the inverse."
Multiplication		
Commutative	$a \times b = b \times a$	"When you multiply two numbers in any order you will get the same answer."
Associative	$(a \times b) \times c = a \times (b \times c)$	"When you multiply three numbers you can multiply the first two and then multiply the answer by the third or multiply the last two numbers and then multiply the answer by the first number. Either way you will get the same answer."
Multiplicative Identity	$a \times 1 = 1 \times a = a$	"When you multiply one by any number you get the same number you started with."
Multiplicative Inverse	$a \times \dfrac{1}{a} = \dfrac{1}{a} \times a = 1$	"When you multiply a number by its reciprocal, you will get one."
Inverse Relationship of Multiplication and Division	If $a \times b = c$ then $c \div b = a$ and $c \div a = b$	"When you have a division problem you can 'think multiplication' by using the inverse."
Distributive (Multiplication over Addition)	$a \times (b + c) = a \times b + a \times c$	"When you multiply two numbers, you can split one number into two parts (7 can be 2 + 5), multiply each part by the other number, and then add them together."

equation such as $394 + 176 = n + 394$, a student recognizes the commutative property and uses it to efficiently solve the problem. She may say that n must be 176 because $394 + 176$ is the same as $176 + 394$.

To ensure the property is generalized, ask students to share their generalization in symbols (e.g., $a + b = b + a$). This makes the connection from number to algebra explicit, while helping students understand how to write the properties symbolically. Using such letters to describe the properties can be used as early as first grade (Blanton et al., 2011; Carpenter, Franke, & Levi, 2003).

Just as sets of tasks can be used to generalize an algorithm, sets of tasks can be used to focus on the properties:

35	52	23	46
$\times 52$	$\times 35$	$\times 46$	$\times 23$
$\dfrac{1}{6} \times 12 =$	$12 \times \dfrac{1}{6} =$	$\dfrac{2}{3} \times 12 =$	$12 \times \dfrac{2}{3} =$

Standards for Mathematical Practice

MP7. Look for and make use of structure.

Although students may understand the commutative property of multiplication with whole numbers, they may not recognize that the property also applies to fractions (in fact, all real numbers). Ask students "Is this true for fractions?" "Is it true for other types of numbers?" "All numbers?" Activity 14.2 provides a creative way for students to understand the identity for addition and/or multiplication, as well as other properties.

Activity 14.2

CCSS-M: 1.0A.B.3; 1.0A.C.6; 1.0A.D.7; 2.0A.B.2; 3.0A.D.9

Five Ways to Zero

Place students in partners. Give each pair a number (you can use a deck of cards). If they get a 7, they are to write 5 different ways to get to 0 using number sentences. For example, they could write 7−5−2 or it could be 7 + 3−10. Be sure students are using correct notation and grouping so that their statements are true. As a follow-up, ask students to find five ways to get their own number as the answer. All students might benefit from using counters or a number line in exploring the possibilities. After they find five ways, ask students what was true about all of the problems they wrote.

Discussing problem sets such as these, and others, helps students to make sense of the properties. In this first grade vignette, the teacher is helping students to reason about the commutative property.

Teacher: [*Pointing at* 5 + 3 = 3 + 5 *on the board.*] Is it true or false?
Carmen: True, because 5 + 3 is 8 and 3 + 5 is 8.
Andy: There is a 5 on both sides and a 3 on both sides and nothing else.
Teacher: [*Writing* 6 + 9 = 9 + 6 *on the board.*] True or false?
Class: True! It's the same!
Teacher: [*Writing* 25 + 48 = 48 + 25 *on the board*] True or false?
Children: True!
Teacher: Who can describe what is going on with these examples?
Rene: If you have the same numbers on each side, you get the same thing.
Teacher: Does it matter what numbers I use?
Class: No
Teacher: [*Writing a* + 7 = 7 + *a on the board*] What is *a*?
Michael: It can be any number because it's on both sides.
Teacher: [*Writing a* + *b* = *b* + *a on the board*] What are *a* and *b*?
Children: Any number!

Notice how the teacher is developing the commutative property of addition in a conceptual manner—focusing on exemplars to guide students to generalize, rather than asking them to memorize or identify the properties, which can be a meaningless, rote activity.

The structure of numbers can sometimes be illustrated geometrically. For example, 8×43 can be illustrated as a rectangular array. That rectangle can be partitioned (symbolically this is $8(40 + 3)$) and then represented as two rectangles [e.g., $(8 \times 40) + (8 \times 3)$], preserving the quantity:

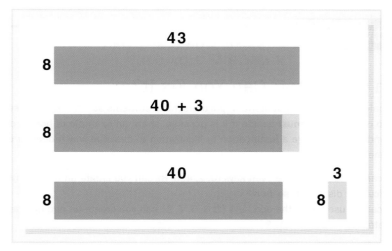

Challenge students to think about this idea *in general*. This may be described in words (at first) and then as symbols: $a \times b = (c \times b) + (d \times b)$, where $c + d = a$. Be sure students can connect the examples to general ideas and the general ideas back to examples. This is the distributive property, and it is perhaps the most important central idea in arithmetic (Goldenberg, Mark, & Cuoco, 2010).

Applying the Properties of Addition and Multiplication

Noticing generalizable properties and attempting to prove that they are true is a significant form of algebraic reasoning and is at the heart of what it means to do mathematics (Ball & Bass, 2003; Carpenter et al., 2003; Schifter, Monk, Russell, & Bastable, 2007). Students can make conjectures about properties as early as first or second grade, and this must be encouraged by the teacher. For example, as first graders are exploring addition, a student might suggest that the order you add two numbers does not matter ($1 + 6 = 6 + 1$). This idea can be presented to the group. Students can test the idea with other numbers and eventually try to explain why this is true. They can write it in symbols: $a + b = b + a$ (yes, first graders can understand and benefit from using variables). It is important to ask, how can this help us do math problems? For a first grader, recognizing that when they see $1 + 6$ that they can start with 6 and add on 1 is an important step toward learning how to add efficiently (as well as learn the basic facts).

The distributive property is central to basic facts and the algorithms for the operations. For example, in learning the multiplication facts, students learn derived fact strategies. For 6×8, they can split up the 6 however they like, multiply its parts by 8 and then put it back together (e.g., $(5 \times 8) + (1 \times 8) = 6 \times 8$). They may justify this with the following rectangles:

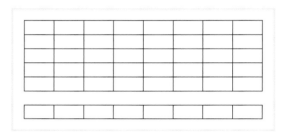

Beyond the properties in Table 14.1, students can apply the properties to make other conjectures, the focus of Activities 14.3 and 14.4.

Activity 14.3

CCSS-M: 1.OA.B.3; 2.OA.C.3; 2.NBT.B.5; 3.OA.D.9

Broken Calculator: Can You Fix It?

Distribute calculators to every student. In partners, have students select one of these two problems to explore. They must decide if it is possible, share an example of how to do it (if it is possible), and finally prepare a justification or illustration to describe why it does or doesn't work (in general).

1. If you cannot use any of the even keys (0, 2, 4, 6, 8), can you create an even number in the calculator display? If so, how?
2. If you cannot use any of the odd keys (1, 3, 5, 7, 9), can you create an odd number in the calculator display? If so, how?

Invite early finishers to take on the other problem or to write their justifications using variables. In the follow-up discussion, ask students for other patterns or generalizations they notice about odd and even numbers.

Activity 14.4 CCSS-M: 1.OA.B.3; 2.NBT.B.9; 3.OA.B.5; 5.OA.A.1

Convince Me Conjectures

To begin, offer students a conjecture to test (see Conjecture Cards Activity Page for ideas for the four operations). For example, "If you add one to one addend and take one away from the other addend, the answer will be the same." Ask students to (1) test the conjecture and (2) prove it is true for any number. Point out the difference between testing and proving. Then, invite students to create their own conjecture (in words) that they believe is always true. Then they must prepare a visual or explanation to convince others that it is true. All students, particularly ELLs, may struggle with correct and precise terms. You can "revoice" their ideas using appropriate phrases to help them learn to communicate mathematically, but be careful to not make this the focus—the focus should be on the ideas presented. Students with disabilities benefit from the presentation and discussion of counterexamples.

ENGLISH LANGUAGE LEARNERS

STUDENTS with SPECIAL NEEDS

Odd and even numbers provide an excellent context for exploring structure of the number system. Students will often observe that the sum of two even numbers is even, that the sum of two odd numbers is even, or that the sum of an even and an odd number is always odd. To explain why two odds make an even, a student might explain that when you divide an odd number by two, there will be a leftover. If you do this with the second odd number, it will have a leftover also. The two leftovers will go together so there won't be a leftover in the sum. Students should also use manipulatives such as connecting cubes to show their reasoning.

Figure 14.1 shows a fourth grader's "Convince Me Conjecture" illustration for the conjecture: *For a product, you can take half of the one factor and double the other factor and you will get the same answer.* Although the student's work only shows two examples, the student is illustrating that this process of cutting the array and moving it down below, can be generalized for other numbers. Ask students how they might write the conjecture in symbols. For the example above, students might write "If $a \times b = c$, then $\frac{1}{2}a \times 2b = c$." In addition, the Expanded Lesson One Up, One Down focuses on a conjecture, starting with trying out numbers, which then generalizing using tools or reasoning (see discussion in Chapter 2 for this activity).

Using and *applying* the properties is central to mathematical proficiency—it is not only emphasized in the CCSS-M content, but also in the Mathematical Practices (CCSSO, 2010). An explicit focus on seeking generalizations and looking for structure is also important in supporting the range of learners in the classroom, from those who struggle to those who excel (Schifter, Russell, & Bastable, 2009). Doing so requires planning—deciding what questions you can ask to help students think about generalized characteristics within the problems they are doing—across the mathematical strands (not just when they are in an "algebra" unit).

 Complete Self-Check 14.2: Structure in the Number System: Properties

 ## Study of Patterns and Functions

Patterns are found in all areas of mathematics. Learning to look for patterns and how to describe, translate, and extend them is part of thinking algebraically. Two of the eight Standards for Mathematical Practice begin with the

FIGURE 14.1 A student justifies a conjecture.

phrase "look for," implying that students who are mathematically proficient pay attention to patterns as they do mathematics. Functional thinking begins in pre-K–2 when students make observations like, "Each person we add to the group we add 2 more feet" (Blanton et al., 2011). Let's look at a modified version of the *Birds in the Backyard* problem:

Five birds have landed in your backyard, some at the feeder and some in the tree. How many ways might the birds be in the tree and at the feeder?

 Pause & Reflect

Can you list all the ways in which this can occur with 5 birds? With 7 birds? With 10 birds? Is there a rule to describe the number of ways in which 10 birds can be sitting in the tree and at the feeder? •

There are 6 ways for 5 birds to be in the tree and at the feeder, 8 ways for 7 birds, and 11 ways for 10 birds. Upper elementary and middle school students should be able to explain why this is the case: For any number of birds (n), there are $n + 1$ ways because there can be 0, 1, 2, n birds at the feeder. Using a problem that is concrete and that begins with listing numeric possibilities is a way to help students learn to generalize a pattern. To extend the discussion, ask students questions such as these: "What if there were 340 birds? Would the rule still hold? If you knew there were 20 different ways in which the birds could be in the backyard, how many birds are there? Is there a rule for that?"

The study of patterns and functions is infused throughout the CCSS-M, and explicitly addressed in these standards:

- Identify arithmetic patterns (https://www.youtube.com/watch?v=1X-RWOTsHQw&list= PLnIkFmW0ticNxpCDlb7vOE7j4qrZtXrX8) (including patterns in the addition table or multiplication table). (grade 3)
- Generate a number or shape pattern that follows a given rule. (https://www.youtube .com/watch?v=vKcXncMARu4&list=PLnIkFmW0ticOLvcMb6M3YyFBsGRMB_zLs) Identify apparent features of the pattern that were not explicit in the rule itself. (grade 4)
- Generate two numerical patterns using two given rules. Identify apparent relationships between corresponding terms. (grade 5)
- Represent and analyze quantitative relationships between dependent and independent variables. (grade 6)
- Solve real-life and mathematical problems using numerical and algebraic expressions and equations. (grade 7)
- Understand the connections between proportional relationships, lines, and linear equations. (grade 8)
- Define, evaluate, and compare functions. (https://www.youtube.com/watch?v= Jq-1RjEIulA) (grade 8)
- Use functions to model relationships between quantities. (grade 8)

This list is an indication of the importance of focusing on patterns and functions for many years before students reach the formal algebra course.

Repeating Patterns

Repeating patterns are those patterns that have a core that repeats. For example, red-blue could the core and a string of beads continues to repeat this pattern: red-blue-red-blue-red. . . . Repeating patterns is not mentioned in the CCSS-M, but looking for patterns in operations and in numbers (place value) is found across the grades. Non-number patterns can build a foundation for later noticing odd-even-odd-even patterns. Physical materials provide a trial-and-error approach and allow patterns to be extended beyond the few spaces provided on a page. By using a variety of materials such as colored blocks, buttons, and connecting cubes to create and extend their patterns, students begin to generalize ideas of patterns. These can be recorded symbolically, for example red-blue is an AB pattern because the core has two different elements, A and B. Figure 14.2 provides some illustrations.

An important concept in working with repeating patterns is for students to identify the *core* of the pattern (Warren & Cooper, 2008). One possible way to emphasize the core is to place shape patterns under a document camera, say aloud what is there and ask what comes next. After a few add-ons, ask students what the pattern is. Label the pattern with letters (i.e., an ABC pattern has three different shapes that repeat).

Repeating patterns are everywhere! The seasons, days of the week, and months of the year are just a beginning. Ask students to think of real-life AB patterns—for example, "to school, home from school" or "set table before eating, clear table after eating." Children's books often have patterns in repeating rhymes, words, or phrases. *Pattern Fish* (Harris, 2000) and *My Mom and Dad Make Me Laugh* (Sharratt, 1994) are two great choices. A very long repeating pattern can be found in *If You Give a Mouse a Cookie* (Numeroff, 1985) (or any of this series), in which each event eventually leads back to giving a mouse a cookie, with the implication that the sequence would be repeated.

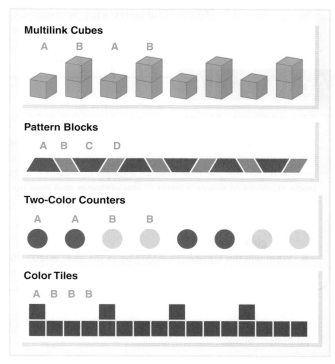

FIGURE 14.2 Examples of repeating patterns with various manipulatives.

Oral patterns can be recited. For example, "do, mi, mi, do, mi, mi" (ABB) is a simple singing pattern. Body movements such as waving the arm up, down, and sideways can make patterns: up, side, side, down, up, side, side, down (ABBC). There are numerous sites on the Web for exploring repeating patterns. For example, NLVM has several explorations with repeating (and growing) patterns, including Attribute Trains, Block Patterns, Color Patterns, Pattern Blocks, and Space Blocks. Repeating patterns can be used to strengthen students understanding of number, for example multiples and division with remainders, as in Activity 14.5.

Activity 14.5
CCSS-M: 2.OA.C.3; 4.OA.B.4

Predict Down the Line

Provide students with a pattern to extend (e.g., ABC pattern made with colored links). Before students begin to extend the pattern, have them predict exactly what elements (links) will be in, say, the twelfth position. (Notice that in an ABC pattern the third, sixth, ninth, and twelfth terms are the C element because they are multiples of 3.) After students predict, have them complete the pattern to check. Ask them how they knew. You can differentiate this lesson by starting with a more basic AB pattern or by having different groups of students work on different types of patterns based on their readiness. Students should be required to provide a reason for their prediction in writing supported with visuals.

In fourth grade, connect to the idea of remainders connecting the repeating patterns to division. Ask students to predict the 100th term for ABC pattern. Because $100 \div 3 = 33$ remainder 1, it would be the A element in the pattern.

Predicting has some interesting real-world contexts appropriate for upper elementary and middle school students. One context is the Olympics (Bay-Williams & Martinie, 2004b). The Summer Olympics are held in 2016, 2020, and every four years after that. The Winter Olympics are held in 2014, 2018, and so on. This pattern can be described using variables.

The years with Summer Olympics are in the form $4n$ and Winter Olympics in the form $4n + 2$. Hurricanes, the focus of Activity 14.6, are also in a repeating pattern (Fernandez & Schoen, 2008).

Activity 14.6

CCSS-M: 4.OA.A.3; 4.OA.B.4; 5.OA.B.3; 6.EE.B.2a

Hurricane Names

Ask students what they know about hurricanes and hurricane names. Hurricanes are named such that the first one of the year has a name starting with A, then B, and so on. For each letter, there are six names in a six-year cycle using an ABCDEF pattern (except those that are retired when a major hurricane has that name). The gender of the names alternate in an AB pattern. Invite students to select a letter of the alphabet and look up the list of six names. Ask students to answer questions such as these (assume the names do not get retired):

- What years will the hurricanes be named after the first name on your list? The last name? What years will the hurricanes be a girl's name?
- What will the hurricane's name be in the year 2020? 2030? 2050?
- Can you describe in words how to figure out the name of a hurricane, given the year?

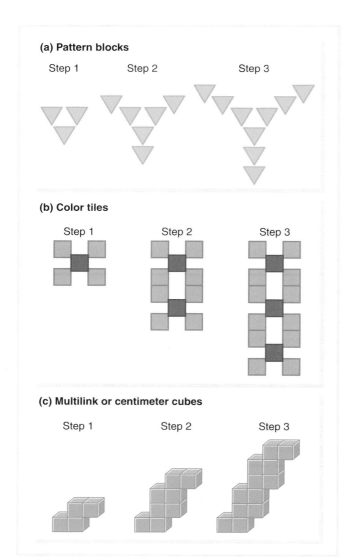

(a) Pattern blocks
Step 1   Step 2   Step 3

(b) Color tiles
Step 1   Step 2   Step 3

(c) Multilink or centimeter cubes
Step 1   Step 2   Step 3

FIGURE 14.3 Geometric growing patterns using manipulatives.

Growing Patterns

Beginning in the primary grades and extending through the middle school years, students can explore patterns that involve a progression from step to step. In technical terms, these are called *sequences*; we will simply call them *growing patterns*. With these patterns, students not only extend or identify the core but also look for a generalization or an algebraic relationship that will tell them what the pattern will be at any point along the way (e.g., the nth term). Figure 14.3(a) is a growing pattern in which design 1 requires three triangles, design 2 requires six triangles, and so on—so we can say that the number of triangles needed is a function of which design it is (in this case, number of triangles $= 3 \times$ design number).

Geometric patterns make good exemplars because the pattern is easy to see and because students can manipulate the objects. Figure 14.3 shows three different growing patterns, though the possibilities for visuals and patterns are endless. The questions in Activity 14.7, mapped to the pattern in Figure 14.3(a), can be adapted to any growing pattern and help students begin to reason about functional situations.

Analyzing growing patterns should include the developmental progression of reasoning by looking at the visuals, then reasoning about the numerical relationships, and then extending to a larger (or nth) case (Friel & Markworth, 2009). Students' experiences with growing patterns should start with fairly straightforward patterns (such as in Figure 14.3) and continue with patterns that are more complicated (such as the Dot Pattern in Figure 14.4).

Activity 14. 7

CCSS-M: 5.OA.B.3; 6.EE.C.9; 7.EE.B.4a; 8.F.A.1

**ENGLISH
LANGUAGE
LEARNERS**

Predict How Many

Distribute Predict How Many Windows or Predict How Many Dot Arrays. **Working in pairs or small groups, have students explore a pattern and respond to these questions:**

● Complete a table that shows the number of triangles for each step.

Step Number	1	2	3	4	5 ⋯	10	20
Number of Triangles (Element)							

● How many triangles are needed for step 10? Step 20? Step 100? Explain your reasoning.
● Write a rule (in words) that gives the total number of pieces to build any step number.
● Write a rule in symbols using the variable *n* for step number.

See Expanded Lesson Exploring Functions through Geometric Growing Patterns **for more details.**

Keep in mind that ELLs need clarification on the specialized meanings of *step* **and** *table* **because these words mean something else outside of mathematics.**

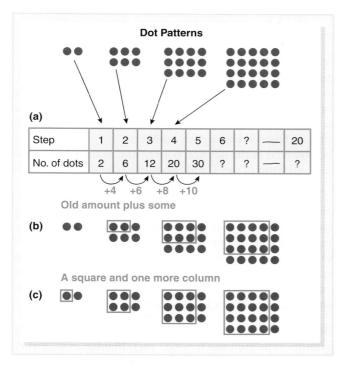

FIGURE 14.4 Analyzing relationships in the "Dot Pattern."

Term	1	2	3	4
Fraction	$\frac{1}{2}$	$\frac{2}{3}$	$\frac{3}{4}$	$\frac{4}{5}$

If the list of fractions above continues in the same pattern, which term will be equal to 0.95?

Ⓐ The 100th
Ⓑ The 95th
Ⓒ The 20th
Ⓓ The 19th
Ⓔ The 15th

FIGURE 14.5 NAEP item for 13-year-olds.

Source: Lambdin, D. V., & Lynch, K. (2005). "Examining Mathematics Tasks from the National Assessment of Educational Progress." *Mathematics Teaching in the Middle School, 10*(6), 314–318. Reprinted with permission. Copyright © 2005 by the National Council of Teachers of Mathematics. All rights reserved.

It is also important to include fractions and decimals in working with growing patterns. In 2003, the National Assessment of Educational Progress (NAEP) tested 13-year-olds on the item in Figure 14.5. Only 27 percent of students answered correctly (Lambdin & Lynch, 2005).

Relationships in Functions

When students are exploring a growing pattern, there are three types of patterns they might notice. And, noticing the types of patterns is developmental (Blanton et al., 2011; Tanish, 2011). Each is shared here, connected to the growing T:

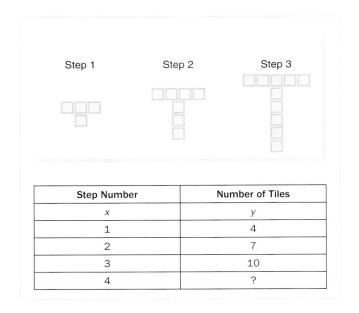

Step Number	Number of Tiles
x	y
1	4
2	7
3	10
4	?

Recursive Patterns. The description that tells how a pattern changes from step to step is known as a *recursive* pattern (Bezuszka & Kenney, 2008; Blanton, 2008). For most students, it is easier to see the patterns from one step to the next, seeing the increase (or decrease). For the T pattern, this is noticing that the right column goes up by 3 each time. In the Dot Pattern (Figure 14.4(a)), the recursive pattern is adding successive even numbers.

The recursive pattern can also be observed in the physical pattern and in the table. In the T pattern, we see that one tile is added to the top of the T and two tiles to the stem. In the dot Pattern, notice that in each step, the previous step has been outlined (Figure 14.4(b)).

Standards for Mathematical Practice

MP2. Reason abstractly and quantitatively.

Covariational Thinking. Covariational thinking involves noticing how two quantities vary in relation to each other and being explicit in making that connection (Blanton et al., 2011). In the T pattern, a student might say, "As the step number grows by 1, the number of tiles needed goes up by 3." Notice that developmentally this is more developmentally sophisticated than just noticing a skip pattern, as the student is connecting how the change in one quantity affects the change in the other quantity (i.e., how they covary). Students in grades 3–5 can employ covariational thinking (Tanish, 2011), and doing so is important in building their algebraic thinking.

Correspondence Relationship. A *correspondence relationship* (also known as the *explicit rule*) is a correlation between two quantities expressed as a function rule (Blanton et al., 2011). In other words, it is begin able to look across the table to see how to use the input (x) to generate the output (y). In the T pattern, the rule is $3x + 1$. Imagine that you needed to find the number of tiles needed for the hundredth T. If you use recursive thinking, you will need to find all of the prior 99 entries in the table. If you notice how x and y correspond (the explicit rule), you can use that rule to find how many tiles are needed for the hundredth T.

 Pause & Reflect

Can you determine the correspondence relationship (explicit rule) for the dot pattern in Figure 14.4? Where do you see the relationship in the table? In the dots? •

You might analyze the table and notice that if they multiply the step number by the next step number, they will get the number of dots for that step. This leads to the explicit rule or function: $d = n(n + 1)$, where d is number of dots and n is the step number. Or, you might analyze the dots to see what is changing. In Figure 14.4(c), a square array is outlined for each step. Each successive square is one larger on a side and the side of each square is the same as the step number. The column to the right of each square is also the step number. The numeric expression is $1^2 + 1$, $2^2 + 2$, $3^2 + 3$, and $4^2 + 4$. The explicit rule or function is therefore $d = n^2 + n$.

Input-output activities can begin with young children. The book *Two of Everything* (Hong, 1993) works well because the Haktaks put things "in the pot" and then take things "out of the pot." The book tells of the pot doubling, but that rule can be changed. Shoeboxes or large refrigerator boxes can be turned into input-output boxes. Decorate the box to look like a machine and add buttons for "easy," "medium," and "hard," and design functions that are appropriate for the grade of your students (Fisher, Roy, & Reeves, 2013). Virtual function machines can be found at NLVM, Math Playground, and Shodor Project Interactive, among others.

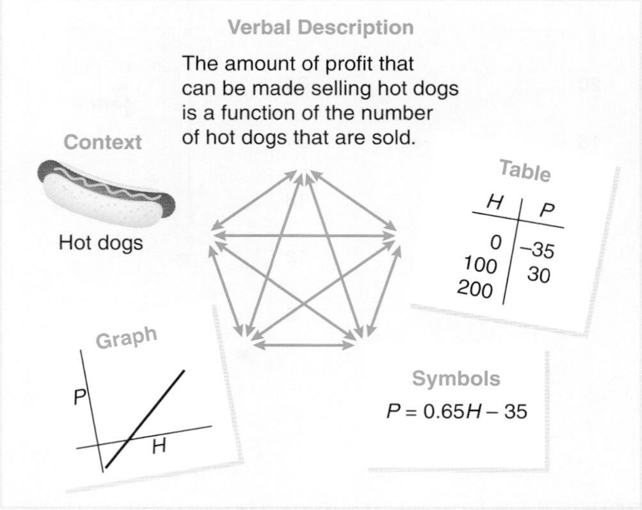

Regardless of whether students use the table or the manipulatives, they will likely be able to describe the explicit formula in words before they can write it in symbols. If the goal of your lesson is to find the "rule," then stopping with the verbal formula is appropriate. In this case, you may have some students who are ready to represent the formula in symbols, and they can be challenged to do so as a form of differentiating your instruction. If your instructional goal is to write formulas using symbols, then ask students to first write the rule in words and then think about how they can translate that statement to numbers and symbols.

FIGURE 14.6 Five representations of a function for the situation of selling hotdogs.

TECHNOLOGY Note. There are several websites that focus on relationships in functions. NCTM's Illuminations website has a lesson titled, "The Crow and the Pitcher: Investigating Linear Functions Using a Literature-Based Model." PBS Kids' CyberChase has a fun game called "Stop That Creature" in which students figure out the rule that runs the game to shut down the creature-cloning machine. ∎

Graphs of Functions

So far, growing patterns have been represented by (1) the physical materials or drawings, (2) a table, (3) words, and (4) symbols. A graph adds a fifth representation, and one that illustrates covariation. Figure 14.6 illustrates what these five representations look like with the context of selling hotdogs. Importantly, given any one of these representations, students need to be able to generate the others and understand how they are related.

Figure 14.7 shows the graph for the T pattern and the dot pattern. Notice that the first is a straight-line (linear) relationship and the other is a curved line that would make half of a parabola if the points were joined.

Activity 14.8   CCSS-M: 6.EE.C.9; 7.EE.B.4a; 8.F.A.1; 8.F.A.2

Perimeter Patterns

Using a document camera or interactive white board, show rows of same-shape pattern blocks (see Figure 14.8). Working in pairs or small groups, have students build each pattern and explore what patterns they notice about how the perimeter grows. Ask: What is the perimeter of a row with 6 squares? 10 squares? Any number of squares? Repeat the process with trapezoids and hexagons (or have different groups of students working on different shapes). Distribute a Coordinate Graph, **Blackline Master** 22). Ask students to create a graph to illustrate the relationship between the number of pattern blocks in the row and the perimeter.

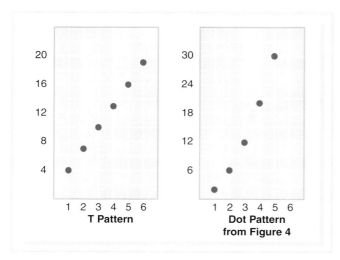

FIGURE 14.7 Graphs of two growing patterns.

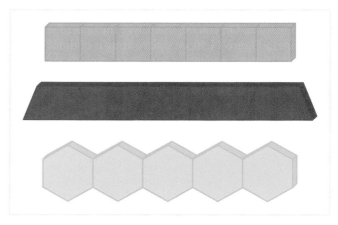

FIGURE 14.8 Same-color strings of pattern blocks. Can you determine the perimeter for *n* pattern blocks in a string?

⏸ Pause & Reflect

Which representations do you find most useful in determining the explicit rule or function? Which representation do you think students new to exploring patterns will use? ●

Having graphs of three related growing patterns offers the opportunity to compare and connect the graphs to the patterns and to the tables (see Figure 14.9). For example, ask students to discuss how to get from one coordinate to the next (e.g., up six, over one for the hexagon), and then ask how that information can be found in the table.

A graph encourages covariational thinking, which can lead to identifying the function. Pose the following questions to students to support covariational thinking and help students:

• How does each graph represent each of the row patterns?
• Why is there not a line connecting the dots?
• Why is one line steeper than the others?
• What does this particular point on the graph match up to in the model and the table?

TECHNOLOGY Note. Function graphing tools permit users to create the graph of almost any function very quickly. Multiple functions can be plotted on the same axis. It is usually possible to trace along the path of a curve and view the coordinates at any point. The dimensions of the viewing area can be changed easily so that it is just as easy to look at a graph for x and y between -10 and $+10$ as it is to look at a portion of the graph thousands of units away from the origin. By zooming in on the graphs, it is possible to find points of intersection without algebraic manipulation or to confirm an algebraic manipulation. Similarly, the point where a graph crosses the axis can be found to as much precision as desired.

Digital programs can also be used for these purposes, and add speed, color, visual clarity, and a variety of other interesting features to help students analyze functions. Graphsketch is an online demonstration tool for making graphs of equations. For the teacher, Modeling Middle School Mathematics (MMSMath) offers video clips, such as "V-Patterns, Beans,

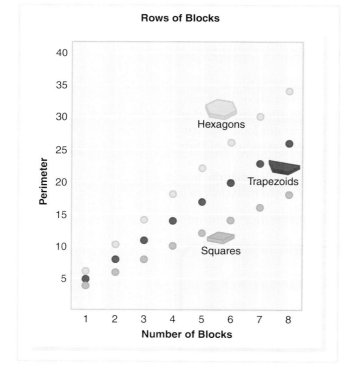

FIGURE 14.9 Graphs of the perimeters of three different pattern-block strings.

Hair & Nails," where students explore patterns with formulas and represent solutions using linear equations, graphs, and tables. ■

FORMATIVE ASSESSMENT Notes. Being able to make connections across representations is important for understanding functions, and the only way to know if a student is seeing the connections is to ask. In a **diagnostic interview,** ask questions like the ones just listed and check to see whether students are able to link the graph to the context, to the table, and to the formula. ■

Students also need opportunities to estimate with graphs. Exploring situations without exact values focuses students' attention on covariation relationships, the focus of Activity 14.9.

Activity 14.9

CCSS-M: 6.EE.D.9; 8.F.B.5

Sketch a Graph

Sketch a graph for each of these situations. No numbers or formulas are to be used.

**ENGLISH
LANGUAGE
LEARNERS**

a. The temperature of a frozen dinner from 30 minutes before it is removed from the freezer until it is removed from the microwave and placed on the table. (Consider time 0 to be the moment the dinner is removed from the freezer.)

b. The value of a 1970 Volkswagen Beetle from the time it was purchased to the present. (It was kept by a loving owner and is in top condition.)

c. The level of water in the bathtub from the time you begin to fill it to the time it is completely empty after your bath.

**STUDENTS
with
SPECIAL
NEEDS**

d. Profit in terms of number of items sold.

e. The height of a thrown baseball from when it is released to the time it hits the ground.

f. The speed of the same baseball.

Be sure that the contexts you pick are familiar to students, including ELLs. If they are not, change the context or illustrate what it is. Have students sketch their graphs without identifying which situation they selected (no labels on the graphs). Then display them on a projector. Let students examine the graph to see whether they can determine the matching situation.

Rather than sketch-a-graph, you can do match-a-graph (see illustrations in Figure 14.10). Match a graph can be a first experience as a scaffold, or as an alternative for students with disabilities.

Finally, it is also worthwhile to have students look at a graph and write a story to match (see Create a Journey Story **Activity Page**).

Describing Functions

Discrete and Continuous. Even in elementary school, the discussion of functions, especially graphical representations, should include a discussion of whether the points plotted on the graph should be connected or not and why. In the pattern blocks perimeter problem, the answer is no; the points should not be connected because you will only use whole-number values for counting blocks. When isolated or selected values are the only ones appropriate for a context, the function is *discrete*. If all values along a line or curve are solutions to the function, then it is *continuous*. The Sketch a Graph situations are all continuous, with the independent variable of time.

Domain and Range. The *domain* of a function comprises the possible values for the independent variable. If it is discrete, like the pattern blocks perimeter problem, it may include all positive whole numbers. For the 24-meter rectangular pen, the domain is all real numbers between 0 and 12.

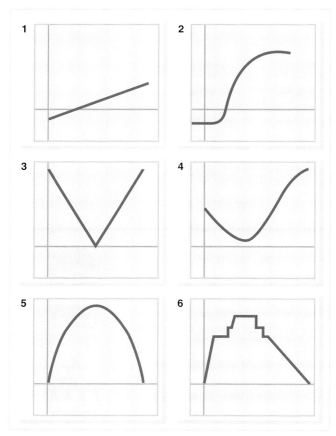

FIGURE 14.10 Match each graph with the situations described in Activity 14.9. Talk about what change is happening in each case.

The *range* is the corresponding possible values for the dependent variable. In the pattern blocks perimeter problem, the range is the positive whole numbers. In the rectangular pen, the range for the length is the same as the domain—real numbers between 0 and 12.

Linear Functions

Linear functions are a subset of functions, which can be linear or nonlinear. But because linearity is a major focus of middle school mathematics, and because growing patterns in elementary school tend to be linear situations, it appears here in its own section. *Curriculum Focal Points* and the Common Core State Standards emphasize the importance of linear functions across the middle grades, with a strong focus on linearity in seventh and eighth grade (CCSSO, 2010; NCTM, 2006).

⏸ Pause & Reflect

Think back to example tasks shared in this chapter. Which are linear functions? Which are not linear, but are still functions? ●

The examples that involved linear functions include the birds (how many ways they could be on the bush and in the tree), the geometric growing patterns, the T pattern, and the pattern block perimeters. The dot pattern is nonlinear (it is quadratic). For linear functions, the key is to focus on the idea that the recursive pattern has a constant rate of change—this is a central concept of linearity (Smith, 2008; Tanish, 2011).

In middle school, students are to notice if situations are linear or not (CCSSO, 2010). Consider the following example.

You are asked to build a rectangular pen with **24 yards of fence. (1)** Write an equation to describe the relationship between the width and the area. **(2)** Write an equation to describe the relationship between the length and width.

An explicit formula for the width is $w = 12 - l$ (*l* is the length), which decreases at a constant rate, therefore looking like a line. By contrast, the explicit formula for area of the pen is $a = l(12 - l)$—it rises in a curve, reaches a maximum value, and then goes back down (see Figure 14.11).

Linear (and nonlinear) situations should be analyzed across representations (picture/objects, equation, graph, table, and situation). In a graph, this can be established by seeing that the plotted points lie on one line. In a table, the change will be constant (e.g., a recursive pattern is +4 each time). In the equation, linearity can be determined by looking at the part of the expression that changes and seeing if it represents constant change or not.

Rate of Change and Slope. Rate, whether constant or varying, is a type of change associated with how fast something is traveling. Rates can be seen in a wide range of contexts, such as the geometric model of the pattern block perimeters or the rate of growth of

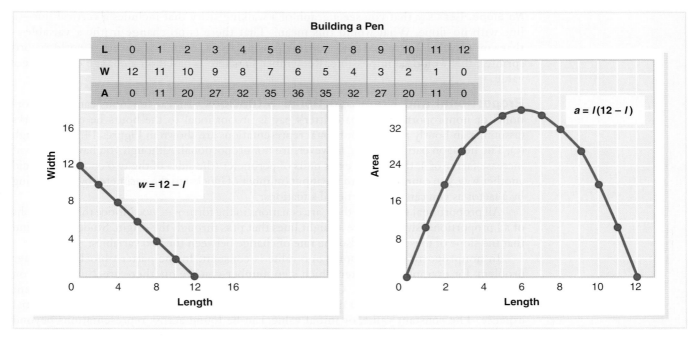

FIGURE 14.11   The width and area graphs as functions of the length of a rectangle with a fixed perimeter of 24 units.

a plant. Other rate contexts include hourly wages, gas mileage, profit, and cost of an item, such as a bus ticket.

Explorations of linear rate situations develop the concept of *slope*, which is the numeric value that describes the rate of change for a linear function. For example, one of the explicit formulas for the hexagon perimeter growing pattern is $y = 4x + 2$. Note that the rate of change is 4 because the perimeter increases by 4 with each new piece. All linear functions can be written in this form: $y = mx + b$ (including $y = mx$ when $b = 0$).

Conceptually, then, slope signifies how much y increases when x increases by 1. If a line contains the points $(2,4)$ and $(3,-5)$, you can see that as x increases by 1, y decreases by 9. So the rate of change, or slope, is -9. For the points $(4,3)$ and $(7,9)$, you can see that when x increases by 3, y increases by 6. Therefore, an increase of 1 in x results in a change of 2 in y (dividing 6 by 3). The slope is 2. After further exploration and experiences, your students will begin to generalize that you can find the rate of change or slope by finding the difference in the y values and dividing by the difference in the x values. Exploring this first through reasoning is important for students if they are to be able to make sense of and remember the formula for calculating slope when given two points. For an interactive tool that connects linear equations in the form $y = mx + b$ to graphs, try "Interactive Linear Equation" at Math Warehouse.

Zero Slope. Understanding these two easily confused slopes requires contexts, such as walking rates. Consider this story:

You walk for 10 minutes at a rate of 1 mile per hour, stop for 3 minutes to watch a nest of baby birds, then walk for 5 more minutes at 2 miles per hour.

What will the graph look like for the 3 minutes when you stop? What is your rate when you stop? In fact, your rate is 0, and because you are at the same distance for 3 minutes, the graph will be a horizontal line.

No Slope. Let's say that you see a graph of a walking story that includes a vertical line—a line with no slope. What would this mean? That there is no change in the x variable—that you traveled a distance with no time passing! Now, even if you were a world record sprinter, this would be impossible. Remember that rate is based on a change of 1 in the x value.

Proportional and Nonproportional Situations. Linear functions can be proportional or nonproportional. A babysitter's pay is proportional to the hours he or she works (assuming an hourly rate). Proportional representations are shown in Figures 14.3(a) through (c). The hexagon pattern blocks, however, are nonproportional. Although you have a constant increase factor of 4, there are 2 extra units of perimeter (the sides of the two end blocks). Said another way, you cannot get from the input (number of blocks) to the perimeter by multiplying by a factor as you can in proportional situations.

All proportional situations, then, are equations in the form $y = mx$. Notice that the graphs of all proportional situations are straight lines that pass through the origin. Students will find that the slope of these lines is also the rate of change between the two variables.

In nonproportional situations, one value is constant. In the pattern blocks perimeter problem, for example, no matter which step number you are on, there are 2 units (one on each end) that must be added. Other examples include if you were walking at a constant rate but had a head start of 50 meters or if you were selling something and had an initial expense. The constant value, or initial value, can be found across representations beyond the contexts described here. In the table, it is the value when $x = 0$, which means it is the point where the graph crosses the y-axis. Context is important. The Grocery Store task, for example, asks students to figure out how long grocery carts are when they are pushed together. Students can see that it grows at a constant rate, but that there is a little extra on the end.

Nonproportional situations are more challenging for students to find the correspondence relationship or explicit rule. Students want to use the recursive value (e.g., +4) as the factor (×4). Also, in proportional situations it is true that there are twice as many in the twentieth term than in the tenth term, because the relationship is multiplicative only. But when there is a constant involved, this shortcut does not work, though students commonly make this error. Mathematics education researchers have found that having students analyze errors such as these is essential in helping support their learning of mathematics concepts (Lannin, Arbaugh, Barker, & Townsend, 2006).

Parallel, Same, and Perpendicular Lines. Students in eighth grade should be comparing different linear situations that result in parallel, same, or perpendicular lines (CCSSO, 2010). Using a context is necessary to build understanding.

Larry and Mary each earn $30 a day for the summer months. Mary starts the summer $50 dollars in debt, and Larry already has $20. In week 3, how much more money does Larry have? How much more does he have in week 7? When will Mary and Larry have the same amount of money?

The rates for Larry's and Mary's earnings are the same—and the graphs therefore go up at the same rate—that is, the slopes are the same. The graphs of Larry's earnings ($y = 30x + 20$) and Mary's earnings ($y = 30x - 50$) are parallel. We know this without even making the graphs because the rates (or slopes) are the same. Can you think of what change in Larry's and Mary's situations might result in the same line? Their initial value must be the same (and their rate).

Slopes can also tell us when two lines are perpendicular, but it is less obvious. A little bit of analysis with similar triangles will show that for perpendicular lines, the slope of one is the negative reciprocal of the other.

 Complete Self-Check 14.3: Study of Patterns and Functions

Meaningful Use of Symbols

One reason students are unsuccessful in algebra is that they do not have a strong understanding of the symbols they are using. Symbols represent real situations and should be seen as useful tools for representing situations and solving real-life problems (e.g., calculating how many cookies we need to sell to make *x* dollars or at what rate do a given number of employees need to work to finish the project on time). Students cannot make sense of such situations without a strong understanding of mathematical symbols.

Standards for Mathematical Practice

MP4. Model with Mathematics.

Looking at equivalent expressions that describe a context is an effective way to bring meaning to numbers and symbols. The classic task in Activity 14.10 involves such reasoning.

Activity 14.10

CCSS-M: 6.EE.A.1; 6.EE.A.2a; b, c, 6.EE.A.3; 6.EE.A.4

ENGLISH LANGUAGE LEARNERS

Border Tiles

Ask students to build an 8×8 square array representing a swimming pool with colored tiles such that tiles of a different color are used around the border (Figure 14.12). Challenge students to find at least two ways to determine the number of border tiles used without counting them one by one. Students should use their tiles, words, and number sentences to show how they counted the squares. Ask students to illustrate their solution on centimeter grid paper. For ELLs, the drawing will be a useful support, but be sure the instructions are clear. There are at least five different methods of counting the border tiles around a square other than counting them one at a time.

A great online tool for this problem is the site titled "Plan Your Room." Input your dimensions (e.g., 8 feet 0 inches $\times$ 8 feet 0 inches) and click "Start with a Room."

 Pause & Reflect

See whether you can find four or five different counting schemes for the "Border Tiles" problem. Can you see how the different expressions are equivalent? What questions might you pose to students in order to help them focus on these equivalent expressions? ●

Let's look at the various ways to count the border tiles. First, you may notice there are 10 squares across the top and across the bottom, leaving 8 squares on either side. This might be written as follows:

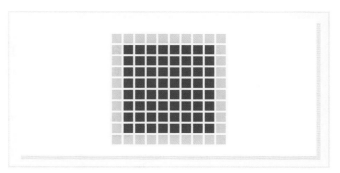

FIGURE 14.12 How many different ways can you find to count the border tiles of an 8×8 pool?

$$10 + 10 + 8 + 8 = 36 \text{ or } (2 \times 10) + (2 \times 8) = 36$$

Each of the following expressions can likewise be traced to looking at the squares in various groupings:

$$4 \times 9$$

$$4 \times 8 + 4$$

$$4 \times 10 - 4$$

$$100 - 64$$

Standards for Mathematical Practice

MP3. Construct viable arguments and critique the reasoning of others.

More equivalent expressions are possible because students may use addition instead of multiplication. Once the generalizations are created, ask students to justify how the elements in the expression map to the physical representation. Ask students to compare the different expressions and discuss whether they are all correct (and therefore equivalent) expressions for describing the general rule.

Notice that the task just completed involved numeric expressions—a good place to start. These expressions did not involve the two types of symbols that are perhaps the most important to understand—and, unfortunately, among the least well understood by many middle-school students. The equal sign ($=$) and inequality signs ($<$, $\leq$, $>$, $\geq$) are the first type. Variables are the second type. The sections that follow provide strategies for helping students understand these symbols.

Equal and Inequality Signs

The equal sign is one of the most important symbols in elementary arithmetic, in algebra, and in all mathematics. At the same time, research dating from 1975 to the present suggests that $=$ is a very poorly understood symbol (Kieran, 2007; RAND Mathematics Study Panel, 2003) and rarely represented in U.S. textbooks in a way to encourage students to understand the equivalence relationship—an understanding that is critical to understanding algebra (McNeil et al., 2006). The Common Core State Standards explicitly address developing an understanding of the equal sign as early as the first grade.

Why is it so important that students correctly understand the equal and inequality signs? First, it is important for students to understand and symbolize relationships in our number system. These signs are how we mathematically represent quantitative relationships. Conversely, when students fail to understand the equal sign, they typically have difficulty with algebraic expressions (Knuth, Stephens, McNeil, & Alibali, 2006). Consider the equation $5x + 24 = 54$. It requires students to see both sides of the equal sign as equivalent expressions. It is not possible to "do" the left-hand side. However, if both sides are understood as being equivalent, students will see that $5x$ must be 24 less than 54 or $5x = 30$. Therefore, x must equal 6.

‖ Pause & Reflect

In the following expression, what number do you think belongs in the box?

$$8 + 4 = \Box + 5$$

How do you think students in the early grades or in middle school typically answer this question? ●

In one study, no more than 10 percent of students from grades 1 to 6 put the correct number (7) in the box. The common responses were 12 and 17. (How did students get these answers?) In grade 6, not one student out of 145 put a 7 in the box (Falkner, Levi, & Carpenter, 1999).

Where do such misconceptions come from? A large majority of equations that students encounter in elementary school look like this: $5 + 7 = \_\_\_$ or $8 \times 45 = \_\_\_\_$. Naturally, students come to see $=$ as signifying "and the answer is" rather than a symbol to indicate equivalence (Carpenter et al., 2003; McNeil & Alibali, 2005; Molina & Ambrose, 2006).

Subtle shifts in the way you approach teaching computation can alleviate this major misconception. For example, rather than always asking students to solve a problem (like $45 + 61$ or 4×26), ask them to instead find an equivalent expression (Blanton, 2008). So, for $45 + 61$, students might write $45 + 61 = 40 + 66$. For a multiplication problem, students might write $4 \times 26 = 4 \times 25 + 4$ or $4 \times 26 = 2 \times (2 \times 26)$. Activity 14.11 is a way to work on equivalent expressions, while supporting the development of Making 10 strategy for learning the basic facts.

Activity 14.11

CCSS-M: 1.OA.C.6; 1.OA.D.7; 2.OA.B.2

Capture Ten

In this activity (based on Fosnot & Jacob, 2010), each pair of students will need eight note cards with the equations from $10 + 1$ to $10 + 8$ (see Equation Cards Activity Page). Students lay the cards out on their desks.

The partners will also need a deck of cards from which all face cards, aces, and ten cards have been removed. Together the partners each draw one playing card from the deck. They decide which note card is equivalent to the sum of their playing cards and place their cards behind the note card (e.g., if partners drew 8 and 5, they place their cards behind the $10 + 3$ card). If the sum of the playing cards is less than 10, place the cards back in the deck. Note that the students do not need to actually add their cards; they just find an equivalent expression. Students can also play independently.

As an alternative to using note cards, you can prepare a game board whose spaces are all the equations from $10 + 1$ to $10 + 8$. The partners then place the sum of the playing cards drawn below the space on the game board.

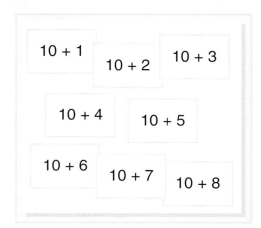

Another way to support a stronger understanding of symbols is to encourage students to write their mental math strategies symbolically. For example, a student might explain that they solve $0.25 \times n$ by finding one-half of the number and then one-half again. In symbols, this might be written as: $0.25 \times 26 = \frac{1}{2}(\frac{1}{2} \times 26)$. This practice increases student understanding of the equal sign *and* the relationships among numbers and forms of numbers (e.g., $\frac{1}{2} \times \frac{1}{2} = \frac{1}{4}$, so $0.5 \times 0.5 = 0.25$). Finally, as students are exploring the operations across the different situations, engage students in writing missing-addend and missing-factor equations, as well as equations with the result (answer) on the left (e.g., $50 = 5 \times 10$).

Inequalities are also poorly understood and have not received less attention than the equal sign, likely because inequalities are not as prevalent in the curriculum or in real life. In the CCSS-M standards, they are first mentioned in grade 6. Understanding and using inequalities is important and can be introduced earlier as a way for students to compare quantities: Are these two quantities equal or is one greater than the other?

The number line is a valuable tool for understanding inequalities. For example, students can be asked to show $x < 5$ on the number line:

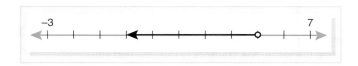

A context such as money can provide a good way to make sense of inequalities, as in the following example.

You have $100 for purchasing gift cards for your 5 friends. You want to spend the same on each, and you will also need to spend $10 to buy a package of card-holders for the gift cards. Describe this situation with symbols.

 Pause & Reflect

How would you write this inequality? How might students write it? What difficulties do you anticipate? And, importantly, what questions will you pose to help students build meaning for the inequality symbols? •

Students might record the situation in any of the following ways (using *a* for the amount of money for the gift):

$$5a + 10 \leq 100 \qquad 10 + 5a \leq 100 \qquad 100 \geq 10 + 5a \qquad 100 \geq 5a + 10$$

They may also make these inequalities without the equal signs: $<$ and $>$. Discuss with students what it means to say "less than" or "less than or equal to." Invite students to debate which signs make more sense given the situation. Graph the result and see if the graph makes sense given the situation.

Deciding whether to use the less than or greater than sign can be confusing for students. Invite students to say in words what the inequality means. For example, the first statement directly translates to 5 gift cards and $10 for a package of holders must be less than or equal to $100. The final example directly translates to I have $100, which must be more than or the same as the cost of 5 cards and the holders. Ask questions that help students analyze the situation quantitatively, such as, "Which has to be more, the amount you have or the amount you spend?"

FORMATIVE ASSESSMENT Notes. Ask students to **write** a real-life story problem that involves an inequality. You can add expectations such as "It must be multi-step" and "you must illustrate the solution on a number line" (for more details see Whaley, 2012, for a full lesson, examples, rubric and discussion). Writing helps students connect representations and helps you see what misconceptions they might have. ■

Conceptualizing the Equal Sign as a Balance. Helping students understand the idea of equivalence can and must be developed concretely. The next two activities illustrate how kinesthetic approaches, tactile objects, and visualizations can reinforce the "balancing" notion of the equal sign.

Activity 14.12   CCSS-M: 1.OA.D.7; 2.NBT.A.4

Seesaw Students

STUDENTS with **SPECIAL NEEDS**

Ask students to raise their arms to look like a seesaw. Explain that you have big juicy oranges, all weighing the same, and tiny little apples, all weighing the same. Ask students to imagine that you have placed an orange in each of their left hands (students should bend to lower left side). Ask students to imagine that you place another orange on the right side (students level off). Next, with oranges still there, ask students to imagine an apple added to the left. Finally, say you are adding another apple, which is going on the left (again). Then ask them to imagine the apple moving over to the right. This is a particularly important activity for students with disabilities, who may be challenged with the abstract idea of balancing values of expressions.

After acting out several seesaw examples, ask students to write Seesaw Findings (e.g., "If you have a balanced seesaw and add something to one side, it will tilt to that side," and "If you take away the same object from both sides of the seesaw, it will still be balanced").

Activity 14.13

CCSS-M: 6.EE.A.2a; 6.EE.B.5; 6.EE.B.6; 7.EE.B.4a, b

What Do You Know about the Shapes?

Present a scale with objects on both sides. Here is an example:

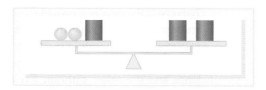

Ask students what they know about the shapes: "The red cylinders weigh the same. The yellow spheres (balls) weigh the same. What do you know about how the weights of the spheres and the cylinders compare?" Figure 14.13 illustrates how a third grader explained what she knew. (Notice that these tasks, appropriate for early grades, are good beginnings for the more advanced balancing tasks later in this chapter.)

For more explorations like this, see "Pan Balance—Shapes" on NCTM's Illuminations website.

After students have experiences with these shapes, they can then explore numbers, eventually moving on to variables. Figure 14.14 offers examples that connect the balance to the related equation. This two-pan balance model also illustrates that the expressions on each side represent a number.

Activity 14.14

CCSS-M: 2.NBT.A.4; 4.NBT.A.1; 5.NBT.A.3a, b; 6.EE.A.4

Tilt or Balance

Draw or project a simple two-pan balance. In each pan, write a numeric expression and ask which pan will go down or whether the two will balance (see Figure 14.14(a)). Select expressions appropriate for the grade level of students (e.g., sums within 100 for grade 2 and sums of fractions for grade 5). Challenge students to write expressions for each side of the scale to make it balance. For

STUDENTS
with
SPECIAL NEEDS

each, write a corresponding equation to illustrate the meaning of $=$. Note that when the scale "tilts," either a "greater-than" or "less-than" symbol ($>$ or $<$) is used, and if it is balanced, an equal sign ($=$) is used. Include examples (like the third and fourth balances in the figure) for which students can make the determination by analyzing the relationships on the two sides rather than by doing the computation. For students with disabilities, instead of having them write expressions for each side of the scale, share a small collection of cards with expressions and have them identify the ones that will make the scale balance.

As an alternative or extension, use missing-value expressions. Ask students to find a number that will result in one side tilting downward, a number that will result in the other side tilting downward, and one that will result in the two sides being balanced (see Figure 14.14(b)). (See Expanded Lesson Tilt or Balance for more details on teaching this activity.)

The balance is a concrete tool that can help students understand that if you add or subtract a value from one side, you must add or subtract a like value from the other side to keep the equation balanced.

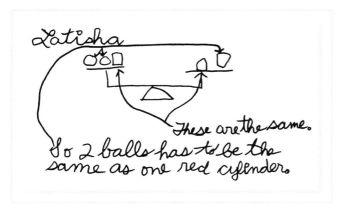

FIGURE 14.13 Latisha's work on the problem.

There are several excellent activities online:

- PBS Cyberchase Poddle Weigh-in: Shapes are balanced with numbers between 1 and 4.
- Agame Monkey Math Balance: Students select numbers for each side of a balance to make the two sides balance (level of difficulty can be adapted).
- NCTM Illuminations Pan Balance—Numbers or Pan Balance—Expressions provide a virtual balance where students can enter what they believe to be equivalent expressions (with numbers or symbols).

Figure 14.15 shows solutions for two equations, one in a balance and the other without. Even after you have stopped using the balance, it is a good idea to refer to the two-pan balance concept of equality and the idea of keeping the sides balanced. This use of concrete (an actual balance) or semi-concrete (drawings of a balance) representations helps students develop a strong understanding of the abstract concept of equality.

The notion of preserving balance also applies to inequalities—but what is preserved is imbalance. In other words, if one side is more than the other side and you subtract 5 from both, the one side is still more.

In middle school, students begin to manipulate equations so that they are easier to graph and/or to compare to other equations. These experiences help ground a student's understanding of how to preserve equivalence when moving numbers or variables across the equal sign.

True/False and Open Sentences. Carpenter and colleagues (2003) suggest that a good starting point for helping students with the equal sign is to explore equations as either true or false. Clarifying the meaning of the equal sign is just one of the outcomes of this type of exploration, as seen in the following activity.

Activity 14.15

CCSS-M: 1.OA.B.3; 1.OA.D.7; 1.NBT.B.4; 2.NBT.B.5; 3.OA.B.5; 4.NBT.B.5; 5.NF.A.1

True or False?

Introduce true/false sentences or equations with simple examples to explain what is meant by a true equation and a false equation. Then put several simple equations on the board, some true and some false. The following are appropriate for primary grades:

$$7 = 5 + 2 \qquad 4 + 1 = 6$$
$$4 + 5 = 8 + 1 \qquad 8 = 10 - 1$$

Your collection might include other operations, but keep the computations simple. Ask students to talk to their partners and decide which of the equations are true equations (and why) and which are not (and why not).

For older students, use fractions, decimals, and larger numbers.

$$120 = 60 \times 2 \qquad\qquad 318 = 318$$
$$\frac{1}{2} = \frac{1}{4} + \frac{1}{4} \qquad 1 = \frac{3}{4} + \frac{2}{1}$$
$$\qquad\qquad\qquad\qquad\qquad 345 + 71 = 70 + 344$$
$$1210 - 35 = 1310 - 45 \qquad 0.4 \times 15 = 0.2 \times 30$$

Listen to the types of reasons that students use to justify their answers, and plan additional equations accordingly. ELLs and students with disabilities will benefit from first explaining (or showing) their thinking to a partner (a low-risk speaking opportunity) and then sharing with the whole group. "Pan Balance—Numbers" on NCTM's Illuminations website can be used to explore and/or verify equivalence.

ENGLISH LANGUAGE LEARNERS

STUDENTS *with* **SPECIAL NEEDS**

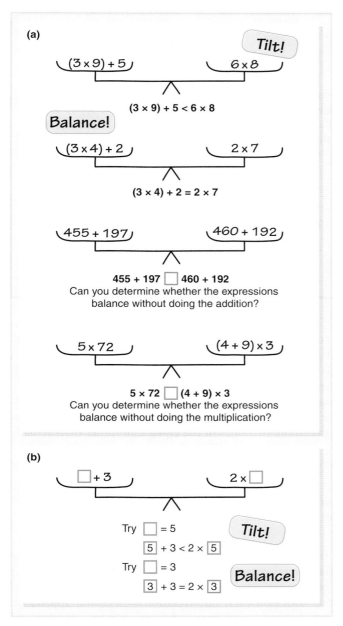

FIGURE 14.14 Using expressions and variables in equations and inequalities.

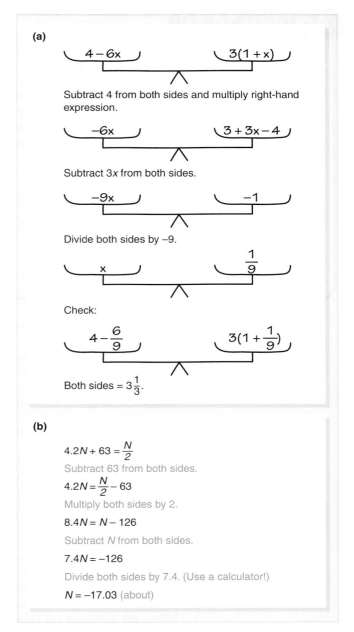

FIGURE 14.15 Using a balance scale to think about solving equations.

Students will generally agree on equations when there is an expression on one side and a single number on the other, although initially the less familiar form of $7 = 5 + 2$ may generate discussion. For an equation with no operation ($8 = 8$), the discussion may be lively. Reinforce that the equal sign means **"is the same as"** by using that language when you read the symbol. Inequalities should be explored in a similar manner.

After students have experienced true/false sentences, introduce an open sentence—one with a box to be filled in or a variable. As early as first grade students can understand and benefit from using variables (Blanton et al., 2011). To develop an understanding of open sentences, encourage students to look at the number sentence holistically and discuss in words what the equation represents.

Activity 14.16

CCSS-M: 1.OA.D.7; 1.OA.D.8; 2.OA.A.1; 3.OA.A.4; 5.OA.A.2; 6.EE.A.3; 6.EE.B.5

What's Missing?

Prepare a set of missing-value equations, using numbers appropriate for the grade level. A sampling across the grades is provided below. Ask students to figure out what is missing and how they know. Notice that the equations are set up so that students do not always have perform the operations to figure out what is missing. Encourage them to look at the equation and see if they can figure out what is missing without solving it. Probe to see if there is more than one way to find what is missing.

Here is a sampling of ideas across the grades:

$4 + \square = 6$	$4 + 5 = \square - 1$	$\square + 5 = 5 + 8$	$3 \times 7 = 7 \times \square$
$15 + 27 = n + 28$	$12 \times n = 24 \times 5$	$6 \times n = 3 \times 8$	$15 \times 27 = n \times 27 + 5 \times 27$
$0.5 + a = 5$	$4.5 + 5.5 = a + 1$	$a \times 4 = 4.8$	$2.4 \div a = 4.8 \div 6$
$3.6 - n = 3.7 - 4$	$n + 0.5 = 0.5 + 4.8$	$15 \times 27 = n \times 27 + 5 \times 27$	$1 = 0.5 \div n$

Relational Thinking. Students may think about equations in three ways, each developmental in nature (Stephens et al., 2013). First, as noted previously, they may have an *operational view*, meaning that the equal sign means "do something." Second, students develop a *relational–computational* view. At this phase, students understand that the equal sign symbolizes a relation between answers to two calculations, but they only see computation as they way to determine if the two sides are equal or not. Finally, students develop a *relational–structural view* of the equal sign (we will refer to this as relational). In this thinking, a student uses numeric relationships between the two sides of the equal sign rather than actually computing the amounts.

Consider two distinctly different explanations for placing an 8 in the box for the open sentence $7 + n = 6 + 9$.

a. Since $6 + 9$ is 15, I need to figure out 7 plus what equals 15. It is 8, so n equals 8.
b. Seven is one more than the 6 on the other side. That means that n should be one less than 9, so it must be 8.

The first student computes the result on one side and adjusts the result on the other to make the sentence true (relational–*computational* approach). The second student uses a relationship between the expressions on either side of the equal sign. This student does not need to compute the values on each side (relational–*structural* approach). When the numbers are large, a relational-structural approach is much more efficient and useful.

Pause & Reflect

How are the two students' correct responses for $7 + n = 6 + 9$ different? How would each of these students solve this open sentence?

$$534 + 175 = 174 + \underline{\quad\quad}$$

The first student will do the computation and will perhaps have difficulty finding the correct addend. The second student will reason that 174 is one less than 175, so the number in the box must be one more than 534.

FORMATIVE ASSESSMENT Notes. As students work on these types of tasks, you can **interview** them one on one (though you may not get to everyone). Listen for whether they are using relational-structural thinking. If they are not, ask, "Can you find the answer without actually doing any computation?" This questioning helps nudge students toward relational thinking and helps you decide what instructional steps are next. ■

Students need many and ongoing opportunities to explore problems that encourage relational thinking (Stephens et al., 2013). Explore increasingly complex true/false and open sentences with your class, perhaps as daily problems, warm-ups, enrichment, or at stations. Use large numbers that make computation difficult (not impossible) and multistep equations as a means to encourage relational-structural thinking. Here are some examples:

True/False

$$674 - 389 = 664 - 379 \qquad 42 = 0.5 \times 84$$

$$\frac{2}{5} = \frac{1}{2} + \frac{1}{3} \qquad\qquad 64 \div 14 = 32 \div 28$$

Open Sentences

$$126 - 37 = n - 40 \qquad 7.03 + 0.056 = 7.01 + n$$

$$20 \times 48 = n \times 24 \qquad 4800 \div 25 = n \times 48$$

Multistep Sentences

$$512 \times 5 \times 20 = n \qquad 68 + 58 = 57 + 69 + n$$

$$\frac{3}{10} + n + \frac{1}{10} = \frac{2}{5} + \frac{1}{5} \qquad 37 \times 18 \div 37 = n$$

⏸ Pause & Reflect

Look at each of the multistep sentences and think about the order in which you can solve it. Can relational-structural thinking help make the problem easier to solve? ●

Notice that the careful construction of these equations encourages relational thinking. Each of the mulistep problems can be solved mentally if the first step of solving is chosen carefully. Selecting equations such as this encourage students to look at equations in their entirety rather than just jumping right into a series of computations, an important aspect of algebraic thinking (Blanton et al., 2011).

Molina and Ambrose (2006), researchers in mathematics education, used the true/false and open-ended prompts with third graders who did not have a relational understanding of the equal sign. For example, all 13 students answered $8 + 4 = \underline{\quad} + 5$ with 12. They found that asking students to write their own open sentences was particularly effective in helping students solidify their understanding of the equal sign (see Activity 14.17).

Activity 14.17

CCSS-M: 1.OA.D.7; 1.OA.D.8; 2.OA.A.1; 3.OA.A.4; 4.NF.B.3a; 5.OA.A.2

Make a Statement!

Ask students to write their own true/false and open sentences that they can use to challenge their classmates. This works for both equations and inequalities! To support student thinking, provide dice with numerals on them. They can turn the dice to different faces to try different possibilities.

STUDENTS
with
SPECIAL NEEDS

Ask students to write three equations (or inequalities) with at least one true and at least one false sentence. For students who need additional structure, in particular students with disabilities, consider providing frames such as these:

$$\_\_\_ + \_\_\_ = \_\_\_ + \_\_\_ \qquad\qquad \_\_\_ + \_\_\_ > \_\_\_ + \_\_\_$$
$$\_\_\_ - \_\_\_ = \_\_\_ - \_\_\_ \qquad\qquad \_\_\_ + \_\_\_ < \_\_\_ - \_\_\_$$
$$\_\_\_ + \_\_\_ = \_\_\_ - \_\_\_ \qquad\qquad \_\_\_ + \_\_\_ \geq \_\_\_ - \_\_\_$$

(or use multiplication and division)

Students can trade their set of statements with other students to find the False Statement. Interesting equations/inequalities can be the focus of a follow-up full-class discussion.

When students write their own true/false sentences, they often are intrigued with the idea of using large numbers and lots of numbers in their sentences. This encourages them to create sentences involving relational-structural thinking.

The Meaning of Variables

Variables can be interpreted in many ways. Variables are first mentioned in the CCSS-M standards in grade 6, but researchers suggest starting much earlier so that students are more adept at using variables when they encounter more complex mathematical situations in middle school (Blanton et al., 2011). Variables can be used to represent a unique but unknown quantity or represent a quantity that varies. Unfortunately, students often think of the former (the variable is a placeholder for one exact number) and not the latter (the a variable could represent multiple, even infinite values). As discussed in functions, variables are also used to describe a pattern. Experiences in elementary and middle school should focus on building meaning for both, as delineated in the next two sections.

Variables Used as Unknown Values. In the open sentence explorations, the □ is a precursor of a variable used in this way. Even in the primary grades, you can use letters instead of a box in your open sentences, such as an *n* standing for the missing number.

Many story problems involve a situation in which the variable is a specific unknown, as in the following basic example:

Gary ate 5 strawberries and Jeremy ate some, too. The container of 12 was gone! How many did Jeremy eat?

Although students can solve this problem without using algebra, they can begin to learn about variables by expressing it in symbols: $5 + s = 12$. These problems can grow in difficulty over time.

With a context, students can even explore three variables, each one standing for an unknown value, as in the following activity (adapted from Maida, 2004).

Activity 14.18
CCSS-M: 6.EE.A.4; 7.EE.A.2; 8.EE.C.8b

Ball Weights

Students will figure out the weight of three balls, given the following three facts:

Ask students to look at each fact and make observations that help them generate other facts. For example, they might notice that the soccer ball weighs 0.1 pound more than the football. Write this in the same fashion as the other statements. Continue until these discoveries lead to finding the weight of each ball. Encourage students to use models to represent and explore the problem.

One possible approach: Add equations 1 and 2:

Then take away the football and soccer ball, reducing the weight by 1.9 pounds (based on the information in equation 3), and you have two baseballs that weigh 0.7 pound. Divide by 2, so one baseball is 0.35 pounds.

You may recognize this last example as a system of equations presented in a visual. In this format, it can be solved by reasoning, making it accessible to upper elementary and middle school students.

Another concrete way to work on systems of equations is through balancing. Notice the work done in building the concept of the equal sign is now applied to understanding and solving for variables.

In Figure 14.16, a series of examples shows problems in which each shape on the scales represents a different value. Two or more scales for a single problem provide different information about the shapes or variables. Problems of this type can be adjusted in difficulty for students across the grades. The NLVM applet Algebra Balance Scales and Algebra Balance Scales—Negative is an excellent tool for learning about balancing equations.

When no numbers are involved, as in the top two examples of Figure 14.16, students can find combinations of numbers for the shapes that make all of the balances balance. If an arbitrary value is given to one of the shapes, then values for the other shapes can be found accordingly.

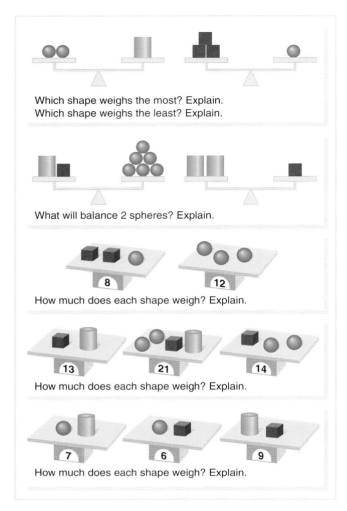

Which shape weighs the most? Explain.
Which shape weighs the least? Explain.

What will balance 2 spheres? Explain.

8   12
How much does each shape weigh? Explain.

13   21   14
How much does each shape weigh? Explain.

7   6   9
How much does each shape weigh? Explain.

FIGURE 14.16 Examples of problems with multiple variables and multiple scales.

In the second example, if the sphere equals 2, then the cylinder must be 4 and the cube equals 8. If a different value is given to the sphere, the other shapes will change accordingly.

⏸ Pause *&* Reflect

How would you solve the last problem in Figure 14.16? Can you solve it in two ways? ●

You (and your students) can tell whether you are correct by checking your solutions against the original scale positions. Believe it or not, you have just solved a system of equations, a skill generally found in a formal algebra class.

Simplifying Expressions and Equations. Simplifying equations and solving for x have often been meaningless tasks, and students are unsure of why they need to know what x is or what steps to do and in what order. This must be taught in a more meaningful way! Knowing how to simplify and recognizing equivalent expressions are essential skills for working algebraically. Students are often confused about what the instruction "simplify" means. (Imagine an ELL wondering why the teacher is asking students to change the original problem to an easier one.) The Border Tiles problem provides a good context for thinking about simplifying and equivalence. Recall that there are at least 5 possibilities for finding the number of border tiles. If the pool had dimensions other than 8×8, those equations would be structurally the same, but with different values. If the square had a side of length p, the total number of tiles could be found in similar ways:

$$10 + 10 + 8 + 8 \qquad (2 \times 10) + (2 \times 8) \qquad 4 \times 9 \qquad 100-64$$
$$(p+2)+(p+2)+p+p \qquad 2 \times (p+2) + (2 \times p) \qquad 4 \times (p+1) \qquad (p+2)^2 - p^2$$

Invite students to enter these expressions into the Table function on their graphing calculator and graph them to see whether they are equivalent (Brown & Mehilos, 2010). Looking at these options, the connection can be made for which one is stated the most simply (briefest or easiest to understand).

Students need an understanding of how to apply mathematical properties and how to preserve equivalence as they simplify. (This is one of the Common Core State Standards in grade 7.) In addition to the ideas that have been offered (open sentences, true/false sentences, etc.), one way to do this is to have students look at simplifications that have errors and explain how to fix the errors (Hawes, 2007). Figure 14.17 shows how three students have corrected the simplification of $(2x + 1) - (x + 6)$. You can create your own examples of simplified expressions that have an error in them—select an error that is commonly made in your classroom so that the class can discuss why the expression is not correct.

Activity 14.19 provides an engaging way for students to explore properties and equivalent expressions.

Activity 14.19

CCSS-M: 5.OA.A.2; 6.EE.A.2a; 7.EE.A.2

Solving the Mystery

STUDENTS
with
SPECIAL
NEEDS

Begin by having students do the following sequence of operations:

Write down any number.

Add to it the number that comes after it.

Add 9.

Divide by 2.

Subtract the number you began with.

Now, you can "read their minds." Everyone ended up with 5! Ask students, "How does this trick work? [Start with n. Add the next number: $n + (n + 1) = 2n + 1$. Adding 9 gives $2n + 10$. Dividing by 2 leaves $n + 5$. Now, subtract the number you began with, leaving 5.] See also a second Solving the Mystery task. For students with disabilities or students who struggle with variables, suggest that instead of using an actual number they use an object, such as a cube, and physically build the steps of the problem, as illustrated in Figure 14.18. In this Mystery, the result is a two-digit number where the tens place is the first number selected and the second digit is the second number selected (ask students to explain how this happened). As a follow-up or for enrichment, students can generate their own number tricks.

Explain how to fix this simplification. Give reasons.
$(2x + 1) - (x + 6) = 2x + 1 - x + 6$

Gabrielle's solution

IF X=3 then the order of operations would take place, so the problem would look like $(2 \cdot 3 + 1) - (3 + 6) = 2 \cdot 3 + 1 - 3 + 6$ you would have to do 1 - 3 instead of 1 + 6. But its actually 3 + 6. So that's the mistake.

Prabdheep's solution

The problem will look like this in its correct form $(2x + 1) - (x + 6) = 2x + ^-1x + ^-6$ because there is a minus sign right outside of the () On the left side it means its -1. So if you times -1 by x its -1x not 1-x. When you times -1 by 6 its ⁻6 not 6.

Briannon's solution

Explain how to fix this problem. Give Reasons
$(2x + 1) - (x + 6) = 2x + 1 - x(+)6$
you are subtracting x and 6 not subtracting x and adding 6
correctly simplified the problem is
$(2x + 1) + ^-(x + 6)$ — distribute negative
$2x + 1 + ^-x + ^-6$
$\boxed{x + ^-5}$

FIGURE 14.17 Three students provide different explanations for fixing the flawed simplification.

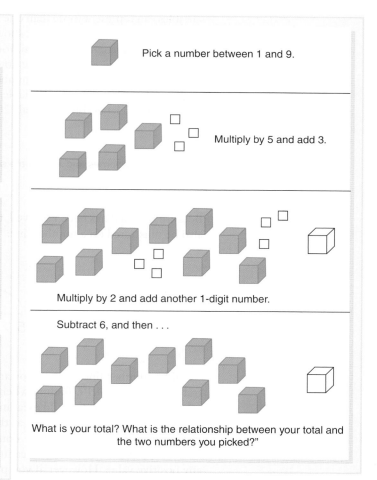

Pick a number between 1 and 9.

Multiply by 5 and add 3.

Multiply by 2 and add another 1-digit number.

Subtract 6, and then . . .

What is your total? What is the relationship between your total and the two numbers you picked?"

FIGURE 14.18 Cubes can illustrate the steps in "Solving the Mystery."

Solving systems of equations has also been presented in a way that includes a series of procedures with little attention to meaning (e.g., by graphing, by substitution, and simultaneously). Mathematically proficient students should have access to multiple approaches, including these three (CCSSO, 2010). However, rather than learn one way by rote each day or be tested on whether they can use each approach, they should encounter a system and be guided by the question when you ask, "How can we determine the point of intersection of this system?" Just as they did with the operations, students should *choose* a method for solving a system of equations that fits the situation, using appropriate tools.

Graphing calculators make the choice of using a graph to determine the point of intersection an efficient option, whereas graphing by hand used to be one of the most tedious methods. Also among the strategies that students must try is observation. Too often, students leap into solving a system algebraically without stopping to observe the values in the two equations. Look at the systems of equations here, and see which ones might be solved for x or y by observation.

$$x + y = 25 \text{ and } x + 2y = 25 \qquad 3x + y = 20 \text{ and } x + 2y = 10$$

$$8x + 6y = 82 \text{ and } 4x + 3y = 41 \qquad \frac{y}{3} = 5 \text{ and } y + 5x = 60$$

Variables Used as Quantities That Vary. As noted earlier, the important concept that variables can represent more than one missing value is not well understood by students and is not as explicit in the curriculum as it should be. Students need experiences with variables that vary early in the elementary curriculum. Young students can begin to describe patterns using variables. For example, when describing the how many legs for any number of dogs, students might write $L = 4 \times D$, meaning that the number of legs is four times the number of dogs. Importantly, you must emphasize that the variable stands for *the number of* because students can confuse the variable to be a label (Blanton et al., 2011). Let's revisit the previous story above, but remove the result:

Gary ate 5 strawberries and Jeremy ate some, too. How might you describe the total number of strawberries eaten?

Because the total has been removed, the goal becomes writing the expression $(5 + s)$. This can also be illustrated on a number line:

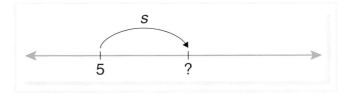

The number line is an important model in developing the concept of variable. As illustrated in Figure 14.19, finding where variables are in relation to numbers and in relation to other variables helps to build meaning (Darley, 2009).

When students are looking at the number line, ask questions like, "What is the value of x? Can it be any number? If we don't know what x is, how can we place $\frac{1}{3}x$ on the number line?" "Think of a value that x cannot be." Notice that in the two examples, x really can be any positive value. However, if you place $x + 2$ on the number line somewhere close to x, the space between these is 2, and you can use this distance as a "measure" to approximate the size of x. Because students use the number line extensively with whole numbers, it is a good way to bridge to algebra. Having an algebra number line posted in your room where you can trade out what values are posted can provide many opportunities to think about the relative value of variables.

Context is important in writing equations with variables. Compare the two problems here (Blanton, 2008):

1. Annie has $10. Noah has $3 more than Annie. How much money does Noah have?
2. Annie has some money. Noah has $3 more than Annie. How much money does Noah have?

Primary grade students can list possible ways in a table and eventually represent the answer as *Annie + 3 = Noah* or more briefly, *A + 3 = N*.

The following example is appropriate for middle school students as a context for exploring variables that vary:

If you have $10 to spend on $2 granola bars and $1 fruit rolls, how many ways can you spend all your money without receiving change?

To begin exploring this problem, students record data in a table and look for patterns. They notice that when the number of granola bars changes by 1, the number of fruit rolls changes by 2. Symbolically, this representation is $2g + f = \$10$, where g is the number of granola bars and f is the number of fruit rolls.

It is also important to include decimal and fraction values in the exploration of variables. As any algebra teacher will confirm, students struggle most with these numbers—again resulting from the lack of earlier, more concrete, and visual experiences mixing fractions and decimals with variables. For example, if you were buying $1.75 pencils and $1.25 erasers from the school store and spent all of $35.00, how many combinations are possible? What equation represents this situation?

For students with special needs or students who might be unfamiliar with using a table, it is helpful to adapt the table to include both how many and how much, as shown in Figure 14.20. Reinforce the two elements with each entry (how many and how much). In addition, calculators can facilitate exploration of possible solutions. To increase the challenge for advanced or gifted students, ask students to graph the values or to consider more complex situations.

Once students have the expression in symbols (in this case, $1.75x + 1.25y = 35.00$), ask students to tie each number and variable back to the context. In this way, students can make sense of what is normally poorly understood and really develop a strong foundation for the algebra they will study in secondary school.

Independent and Dependent Variables. Although the meanings of *independent variables* and *dependent variables* are implied by the words themselves, the concepts can still be challenging for students. The independent variable is the step number, or the input, or whatever value is being used to find another value. For example, in the case of the strings of pattern blocks, the independent variable is the number of blocks in the string. The dependent variable is the number of objects needed, the output, or whatever value you get from using the independent variable. In the pattern blocks problem, it is the perimeter. You can say that the perimeter of the block structure depends on the

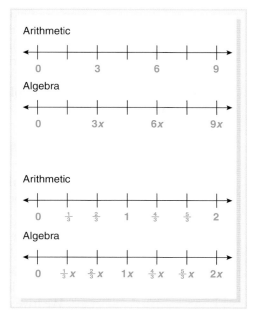

FIGURE 14.19   Using the number line to build meaning of variables.

$1.75 item		$1.25 item	
			Total $35.00
	$35.00		$0
20		0	
	$0		$35
0		28	

FIGURE 14.20   A table adapted to include how many and how much for each row.

Source: Hyde, A., George, K., Mynard, S., Hull, C., Watson, S., and Watson, P. (2006). "Creating Multiple Representations in Algebra: All Chocolate, No Change," *Mathematics Teaching in the Middle School*, 11(6), 262–268.

number of blocks. Recall the two equations and graphs representing a pen of 24 meters in Figure 14.11. In this case, the length has been selected as the independent variable (though it could have as easily been the width), and the dependent variable is width. What are the independent and dependent variables for the Border Tiles (Figure 14.12)?

 Complete Self-Check 14.4: Meaningful Use of Symbols

 Mathematical Modeling

Modeling with mathematics is one of the eight Standards for Mathematical Practice in the Common Core State Standards.

> Modeling links classroom mathematics and statistics to everyday life, work, and decision-making. Modeling is the process of choosing and using appropriate mathematics and statistics to analyze empirical situations, to understand them better, and to improve decisions. (CCSSO, 2010, p. 72)

Mathematical models are not to be confused with visual models such as manipulatives or drawings for building a pattern (such as pattern blocks or centimeter grid paper).

We have already seen many examples of mathematical models (e.g., the model or equation for describing the number of tiles required for a pool of various dimensions). The equation, or mathematical model, allows us to find values that cannot be observed in the real phenomenon.

Activity 14.20 provides another context appropriate for developing a mathematical model.

Activity 14.20 CCSS-M: 7.EE.A.2; 7.EE.B.4a; 8.F.B.4

How Many Gallons Left?

Ask students to create equations to describe the gallons left for given miles traveled (assuming that you started the trip with a full tank of gasoline).

For example:

A car gets 27 miles per gallon of gas. It has a gas tank that holds 15 gallons.

A van gets 18 miles per gallon and has a tank that holds 20 gallons.

The mathematical model or equation in the first situation is $g = 15 - \frac{m}{27}$. After students write an equation, use it to answer questions about the trip. For example, "How can you tell from the model how much gas will be left after driving 300 miles?" "How many miles can you drive before the gas tank has only 3 gallons left?" ELLs may be more familiar with kilometers per liter, which means you can adapt the problem to those units or connect the meaning of the two.

 ENGLISH LANGUAGE LEARNERS

---

1. Pleasant's Hardware buys widgets for $4.17 each, marks them up 35 percent over wholesale, and sells them at that price. Create a mathematical model to relate widgets sold (*w*) to profit (*p*). The manager asks you to determine the formula if she were to put the widgets on sale for 25 percent off. What is your formula or mathematical model for the sale, comparing widgets sold (*s*) to profit (*p*)?

2. In Arches National Park in Moab, Utah, there are sandstone cliffs. A green coating of color, called cyanobacteria, covers some of the sandstone. The cyanobacteria grow by splitting into two (or doubling) in a certain time period. If the sandstone started with 50 bacteria, create a mathematical model for describing the growth of cyanobacteria on the sandstone. (See Buerman, 2007, for more on exploring Arches National Park mathematically.)

Creating equations to describe situations is a very important skill and students need multiple opportunities to translate situations into equations where the goal is the mathematical model (and not a solution). Two more engaging contexts are provided in Figure 14.21.

Sometimes a model is provided, and the important task is for students to understand and use the formula. Consider the following classic pumping water problem based on the Michigan Algebra Project task (Herbel-Eisenmann & Phillips, 2005):

FIGURE 14.21 Mathematical modeling problems for further exploration.

You turn on a pump to empty the water from a swimming pool. The amount of water in the pool (*W*, measured in gallons) at any time (*T*, measured in hours) is given by the following equation: $W = -350(T-4)$.

Pause & Reflect

What questions might you pose to middle school students to help them make sense of this equation? Try to think of three. ●

In the Michigan Algebra Project, students were asked to solve several problems and explain how the equation was used to find the answer. Those questions and one student's responses are provided in Figure 14.22.

 Complete Self-Check 14.5: Mathematical Modeling

 # Algebraic Thinking across the Curriculum

One reason the phrase "algebraic thinking" is used instead of "algebra" is that the practice of looking for patterns, regularity, and generalizations goes beyond curriculum topics that are usually categorized as algebra topics. You have already experienced some of this integration—the strong connection between number and algebra (e.g., properties and generalizations), geometric growing patterns. Here we briefly share a few more.

Geometry, Measurement and Algebra

Soares, Blanton, and Kaput (2006) describe how to "algebraify" the elementary curriculum. One measurement example they give uses the children's book *Spaghetti and Meatballs for All* (https://www.youtube.com/watch?v=jN_GmgeU5cw) by Marilyn Burns looking at the increasing number of chairs needed given the growing number of tables.

Geometric formulas relate various dimensions, areas, and volumes of shapes. Each of these formulas involves at least one functional relationship. Consider any familiar formula for measuring a geometric shape. For example, the circumference of a circle is $c = 2\pi r$. The radius is the independent variable and circumference is the dependent variable. We can say that the circumference is dependent on the radius. Even nonlinear formulas like volume of a cone ($V = \frac{1}{3}\pi r^2 h$) are functions. Here the volume is a function of both the height of the cone and the radius. If the radius is held constant, the volume is a function of the height. Similarly, for a fixed height, the volume is a function of the radius.

The following activity explores how the volume of a box varies as a result of changing the dimensions.

Activity 14.21
CCSS-M: 5.MD.C.5b; 6.EE.A.2c; 6.G.A.2

Designing the Largest Box

Give each student or pair of students a piece of card stock. Explain that they are to cut out a square from each corner using an exact measurement. All four squares must be the same size. Assign different lengths for the squares that are cut out (e.g., 2 cm, 2.5 cm, 3 cm, and so on). Explain to students that after they cut out their four squares, they will fold up the four resulting flaps, and tape them together to form an open box. Have students calculate the volume of their box. Then, have students trade boxes and determine the volume of other boxes. The volume of the box will vary depending on the size of the squares (see Figure 14.23). Ask students to record their data in a table.

After they have recorded the data for several boxes, challenge students to write a formula that gives the volume of the box as a function of the size of the cutout squares. Use the function to determine what size the squares should be to create the box with the largest volume. Alternatively, make origami boxes using squares with various side lengths and see what the relationship is between the side length and the volume of the open box. (See DeYoung, 2009, for instructions for making the box and more on this idea. Or look on the Internet.)

A. How many gallons of water are being pumped out each hour?

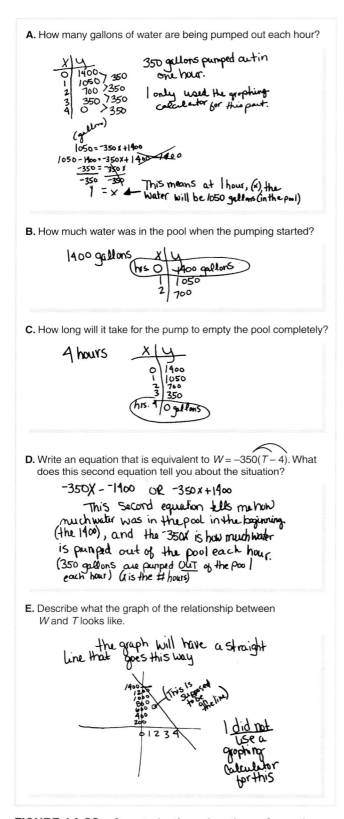

B. How much water was in the pool when the pumping started?

C. How long will it take for the pump to empty the pool completely?

D. Write an equation that is equivalent to $W = -350(T - 4)$. What does this second equation tell you about the situation?

E. Describe what the graph of the relationship between W and T looks like.

FIGURE 14.22 One student's explanations of questions regarding what a mathematical model means.

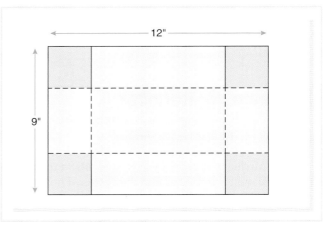

FIGURE 14.23 Cutting squares from cardstock. What size squares will result in an open box with the largest volume?

Data and Algebra. Data can be obtained from sports records, census reports, the business section of the newspaper, and many other sources. Students can gather data such as measurement examples or survey data. The Internet also has many sites where data can be found.

Experiments. There are many experiments that students can explore to see the functional relationships, if any, that exist between two variables. Gathering real data is an excellent way to engage a range of learners and to see how mathematics can be used to describe phenomena.

Data should be collected and then represented in a table or on a graph. The goal is to determine whether there is a relationship between the independent and dependent variables, and if so, whether it is linear or nonlinear, as in the following engaging experiments:

- How long would it take for 100 students standing in a row to complete a wave similar to those seen at football games? Experiment with different numbers of students from 5 to 25. Can the relationship predict how many students it would take for a given wave time?
- How far will a Matchbox car roll off of a ramp, based on the height the ramp is raised?
- How is the flight time of a paper airplane affected by the number of paper clips attached to the nose of the plane?
- What is the relationship between the number of dominoes in a row and the time required for them to fall over? (Use multiples of 100 dominoes.)
- Make wadded newspaper balls using different numbers of sheets of newspaper and a constant number of rubber bands to help hold the paper in a ball. What is the relationship between the number of sheets and the distance the ball can be thrown?
- What is the relationship between the number of drops of colored water dropped on a paper towel and the diameter of the spot? Is the relationship different for different brands of towels?

- How much weight can a toothpick bridge hold? Lay toothpicks in a bunch to span a 2-inch gap between two boards. From the toothpicks, hang a bag or other container into which weights can be added until the toothpicks break. Begin with only one toothpick (McCoy, 1997).

Experiments like these are fun and accessible to a wide range of learners. They also provide an opportunity for students to engage in experimental design—a perfect blend of mathematics and science.

Scatter Plots. Often in the real world, phenomena are observed that seem to suggest a functional relationship, but they are not necessarily as clean or as well defined as some of the situations we have described so far. In such cases, the data are generally plotted on a graph to produce a scatter plot of points. Two very good scatter plot generators can be found online at NLVM and NCES Kids' Zone.

A visual inspection of the scatter plot may suggest what kind of relationship, if any, exists. If a linear relationship seems to exist, for example, students can approximate a line of best fit or use graphing technology to do a linear regression to find the line of best fit (along with the equation).

 Complete Self-Check 14.6: Algebraic Thinking across the Curriculum

REFLECTIONS ON CHAPTER 14

WRITING TO LEARN

1. What is functional thinking? How is it expressed?
2. What misconceptions or limited conceptions do students have regarding the equal sign? What causes these misconceptions, and how can instruction clear these up?
3. What misconceptions or limited conceptions do students have regarding variables? What causes these misconceptions, and how can instruction clear these up?
4. How does a graph of a pattern help develop algebraic thinking in students?
5. What is a recursive relationship? A correspondence relationship (explicit rule)? Where in a table for a growing pattern would you look for the recursive relationship?
6. What is mathematical modeling?

FOR DISCUSSION AND EXPLORATION

- The idea of having students make connections from arithmetic to algebra is the emphasis of algebra in the elementary grades. What examples can you find in the curriculum for taking an algorithm and presenting it in a way that it becomes a process for generalizing a rule?

- Try to understand the connections between algebraic thinking and functional thinking. How can you develop functional thinking in young students? What kind of models may be useful for this?

RESOURCES FOR CHAPTER 14

LITERATURE CONNECTIONS

The following three examples of books are excellent beginnings for patterns and chart building.

Anno's Magic Seeds *Anno (1994)*

Anno's Magic Seeds has several patterns. A wise man gives Jack two magic seeds, one to eat and one to plant. The planted seed will produce two new seeds by the following year. Several years later, Jack decides to plant both seeds. Then he has a family and starts to sell seeds. At each stage of the story, there is an opportunity to develop a chart and extend the current pattern into the future. Austin and Thompson (1997) describe how they used the story to develop patterns and charts with sixth- and seventh-grade students.

Bats on Parade *Appelt and Sweet (1999)*

This story includes the pattern of bats walking 1 by 1, then 2 by 2, and so on. One activity from this enjoyable book is determining the growing pattern of the number of bats given the array length (e.g., 3 for the 3 $\times$ 3 array). There is also one mouse, so this can be included in a second investigation. Activity Pages for these two ideas and two others can be found in Roy and Beckmann (2007).

Equal Shmequel *Kroll (2005)*

This story is about a mouse and her friends who want to play tug-of-war. To do so, they must determine how to make both sides equal so that the game is fair. In the end, they use a teeter-tooter to balance the weight of the friends. This focus on equal sides and balance make this a great book for focusing on the meaning of the equal sign.

Two of Everything: A Chinese Folktale *Hong (1993)*
(https://www.youtube.com/watch?v=TY_NP528ph4)

The magic pot discovered by Mr. Haktak doubles whatever goes in it, including his wife! This idea of input–output is great for exploring functions from grades 2 through 8; just vary the rule of the magic pot from doubling to something more complex. For more details and handouts, see Suh (2007a) and Wickett and colleagues (2002).

RECOMMENDED READINGS

Articles

Kalman, R. (2008). Teaching algebra without algebra. *Mathematics Teaching in the Middle School, 13*(6), 334–339.

This article includes three contexts that involve simplifying equations and effectively explains how to make sense of the simplification by relating it to the context. An excellent resource for helping middle school students make sense of symbols and properties.

Leavy, A., Hourigan, M., & McMahon, A. (2013). Early understanding of equality. *Teaching Children Mathematics, 20*(4), 247–252.

Nine strategies are shared for helping students strengthen their understanding of the equal sign. Each suggestion includes specific activity suggestions.

Molina, M., & Ambrose, R. C. (2006). Fostering relational thinking while negotiating the meaning of the equals sign. *Teaching Children Mathematics, 13*(2), 111–117.

This article helps us understand the conceptual considerations related to the equal sign while simultaneously illustrating the value of errors and misconceptions in creating opportunities for learning.

Books

Essential Understandings Series (*Expressions, Equations, and Functions: Grades 6–8* (2011) and *Algebraic Thinking: Grades 3–5* (2011)). Reston, VA: NCTM.

Each of these books provides a teacher-friendly discussion of the big ideas of algebra. Interwoven are excellent tasks to use with students.

Blanton, M. L. (2008). *Algebra and the elementary classroom.* Portsmouth, NH: Heinemann.

This is an excellent book for teachers at all levels—full of rich problems to use and helpful for expanding the reader's understanding of algebra. Great for book study.

Carpenter, T. P., Franke, M. L., & Levi, L. (2003). *Thinking mathematically: Integrating arithmetic and algebra in elementary school.* Portsmouth, NH: Heinemann.

This book is a detailed look at helping students in the primary grades develop the thinking and create the generalizations of algebra. The included CD shows classroom-based examples of the ideas discussed.

Fosnot, C. T., & Jacob, B. (2010). *Young mathematicians at work: Constructing algebra.* Portsmouth, NH: Heinemann.

Like the other books in the series, this is a gem. Full of classroom vignettes and examples that will enrich your understanding of how algebra can support arithmetic (and vice versa).

Greenes, C. E., & Rubenstein, R. (Eds.). (2008). *Algebra and algebraic thinking in school mathematics.* NCTM 70th Yearbook. Reston, VA: NCTM.

NCTM yearbooks are always excellent collections of articles for grades pre-K–12. This one is no exception, offering a wealth of thought-provoking and helpful articles about algebraic thinking.

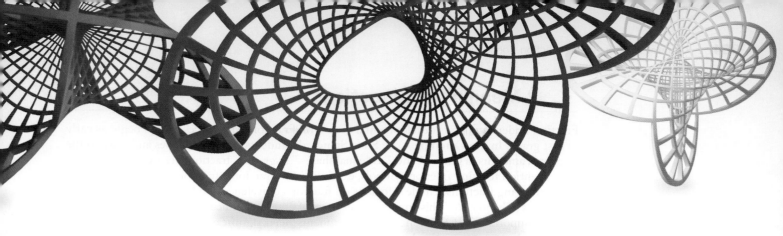

CHAPTER 15

Developing Fraction Concepts

LEARNER OUTCOMES

After reading this chapter and engaging in the embedded activities and reflections, you should be able to:

15.1 Describe and give examples for fractions constructs.

15.2 Name the types of fractions models and describe activities for each.

15.3 Explain foundational concepts of fractional parts, including iteration and partitioning, and connect these ideas to CCSS-M expectations.

15.4 Illustrate examples across fraction models for developing the concept of equivalence.

15.5 Compare fractions in a variety of ways and describe ways to teach this topic conceptually.

15.6 Synthesize how to effectively teach fraction concepts.

Fractions are one of the most important topics students need to understand in order to be successful in algebra and beyond, yet it is an area in which U.S. students struggle. NAEP test results have consistently shown that students have a weak understanding of fraction concepts (Sowder & Wearne, 2006; Wearne & Kouba, 2000). This lack of understanding is then translated into difficulties with fraction computation, decimal and percent concepts, and the use of fractions in other content areas, particularly algebra (Bailey, Hoard, Nugent, & Geary, 2012; Brown & Quinn, 2007; National Mathematics Advisory Panel, 2008). Therefore, it is absolutely critical that you teach fractions well, present fractions as interesting and important, and commit to helping students understand the big ideas.

BIG IDEAS

- For students to really understand fractions, they must experience fractions across many constructs, including part of a whole, ratios, and division.

- Three categories of models exist for working with fractions—area (e.g., $\frac{1}{3}$ of a garden), length (e.g., $\frac{3}{4}$ of an inch), and set or quantity (e.g., $\frac{1}{2}$ of the class).

- Partitioning and iterating are ways for students to understand the meaning of fractions, especially numerators and denominators.

- Equal sharing is a way to build on whole-number knowledge to introduce fractional amounts.

- Equivalent fractions are ways of describing the same amount by using different-sized fractional parts.

- Fractions can be compared by reasoning about the relative size of the fractions. Estimation and reasoning are important in teaching understanding of fractions.

Meanings of Fractions

Fraction understanding is developmental in nature. Fraction experiences should begin as early as first grade. In the Common Core State Standards students partition shapes and refer to the fractional amounts in grades 1 and 2 as "equal shares." In grade 3, fractions are a major emphasis, with attention to using fraction symbols, exploring unit fractions (fractions with numerator 1), and comparing fractions. Grade 4 focuses on fraction equivalence and begins work on fraction operations (Chapter 16). This emphasis over years of time is an indication of both the complexity and the importance of fraction concepts. Students need significant time and experiences to develop a deep conceptual understanding of this important topic.

Understanding a fraction is much more than recognizing that $\frac{3}{5}$ is three shaded parts of a shape partitioned into five sections. Fractions have numerous constructs and can be represented as areas, quantities, or on a number line. This section describes these big ideas. The next sections describe how to teach the concepts of fractions.

Fraction Constructs

Understanding fractions means understanding all the possible concepts that fractions can represent. One of the commonly used meanings of fraction is part-whole. But many who research fraction understanding believe students would understand fractions better with more emphasis across other meanings of fractions (Clarke, Roche, & Mitchell, 2008; Lamon, 2012; Siebert & Gaskin, 2006).

 Pause Reflect

Beyond shading a region of a shape, how else are fractions represented? Try to name three ideas. ●

Part-Whole. Using the part-whole construct is an effective starting point for building meaning of fractions (Cramer & Whitney, 2010). Part-whole can be shading a region, part of a group of people ($\frac{3}{5}$ of the class went on the field trip), or part of a length (we walked $3\frac{1}{2}$ miles).

Measurement. Measurement involves identifying a length and then using that length as a measurement piece to determine the length of an object. For example, in the fraction $\frac{5}{8}$, you can use the unit fraction $\frac{1}{8}$ as the selected length and then count or measure to show that it takes five of those to reach $\frac{5}{8}$. This concept focuses on how much rather than how many parts, which is the case in part-whole situations (Behr, Lesh, Post, & Silver, 1983; Martinie, 2007).

Division. Consider the idea of sharing $10 with 4 people. This is not a part-whole scenario, but it still means that each person will receive one-fourth ($\frac{1}{4}$) of the money, or $2\frac{1}{2}$ dollars. Division is often not connected to fractions, which is unfortunate. Students should understand and feel comfortable with the example here written as $\frac{10}{4}$, $4\overline{)10}$, $10 \div 4$, $2\frac{2}{4}$, and $2\frac{1}{2}$ (Flores, Samson, & Yanik, 2006).

Operator. Fractions can be used to indicate an operation, as in $\frac{4}{5}$ of 20 square feet or $\frac{2}{3}$ of the audience was holding banners. These situations indicate a fraction of a whole number, and students may be able to use mental math to determine the answer. This construct is not emphasized enough in school curricula (Usiskin, 2007). Just knowing how to represent fractions doesn't mean students will know how to operate with fractions, which occurs in various other areas in mathematics (Johanning, 2008).

Ratio. Discussed at length in Chapter 18, the concept of ratio is yet another context in which fractions are used. For example, the fraction $\frac{1}{4}$ can mean that the probability of an event is one in four. Ratios can be part-part or part-whole. For example, the ratio $\frac{3}{4}$ could be the ratio of those wearing jackets (part) to those not wearing jackets (part), or it could be part-whole, meaning those wearing jackets (part) to those in the class (whole).

Why Fractions Are Difficult

Students build on their prior knowledge, meaning that when they encounter situations with fractions, they naturally use what they know about whole numbers to solve the problems. Based on the research, there are a number of reasons students struggle with fractions. They include:

- There are many meanings of fractions (see later section "Fraction Constructs").
- Fractions are written in a unique way.
- Students overgeneralize their whole-number knowledge (McNamara & Shaughnessy, 2010).

It is important for a teacher to help students see how fractions are alike and different from whole numbers. An explanation of common misapplications of whole-number knowledge to fractions follows, along with ways you can help.

Misconception 1. Students think that the numerator and denominator are separate values and have difficulty seeing them as a single value (Cramer & Whitney, 2010). It is hard for them to see that $\frac{3}{4}$ is one number.

How to Help: Find fraction values on a number line. This can be a fun warm-up activity each day, with students placing particular values on a classroom number line or in their math journals. Measure with various levels of precision (e.g., to the nearest eighth-inch). Avoid the phrase "three *out of* four" (unless talking about ratios or probability) or "three over four." Instead, say "three *fourths*" (Siebert & Gaskin, 2006).

Misconception 2. Students do not understand that $\frac{2}{3}$ means two equal-sized parts (although not necessarily equal-shaped objects). For example, students may think that the following shape shows $\frac{3}{4}$ green, rather than $\frac{1}{2}$ green:

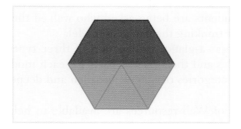

How to Help: Ask students to create their own representations of fractions across various manipulatives and on paper. Provide problems like the one illustrated here, in which all the partitions are not already drawn.

Misconception 3. Students think that a fraction such as $\frac{1}{5}$ is smaller than a fraction such as $\frac{1}{10}$ because 5 is less than 10. Conversely, students may be told the reverse—the bigger the denominator, the smaller the fraction. Teaching such rules without providing the reason may lead students to overgeneralize that $\frac{1}{5}$ is more than $\frac{7}{10}$.

How to Help: Use many visuals *and* contexts that show parts of the whole. For example, ask students if they would rather go outside for $\frac{1}{2}$ of an hour, $\frac{1}{4}$ of an hour, or $\frac{1}{10}$ of an hour. Use the idea of fair shares: Is it fair if Mary gets one-fourth of the pizza and Laura gets one-eighth? Ask students to explain why this is not fair and who gets the larger share.

Misconception 4. Students mistakenly use the operation "rules" for whole numbers to compute with fractions—for example, $\frac{1}{2} + \frac{1}{2} = \frac{2}{4}$.

How to Help: Use many visuals *and* contexts. Emphasize estimation (see later section in this chapter) and focus on whether answers are reasonable or not.

Students who make these errors do not understand fractions. Until they understand fractions meaningfully, they will continue to make errors by overapplying whole-number concepts (Cramer & Whitney, 2010; Siegler et al., 2010). The most effective way to help students reach higher levels of understanding is to use multiple representations, multiple approaches, and explanation and justification (Harvey, 2012; Pantziara & Philippou, 2012). This chapter is designed to help you help students deeply understand fractions.

 Complete Self-Check 15.1: Meanings of Fractions

 ## Models for Fractions

There is substantial evidence to suggest that the effective use of visuals in fraction tasks is important (Cramer & Henry, 2002; Siebert & Gaskin, 2006). Unfortunately, textbooks rarely incorporate manipulatives, and when they do, they tend to be only area models (Hodges, Cady, & Collins, 2008). This means that students often do not get to explore fractions with a variety of models and/or do not have sufficient time to connect the visuals to the related concepts. In fact, what appears to be critical in learning is that the use of physical tools leads to the use of mental models, which builds students' understanding of fractions (Cramer & Whitney, 2010; Petit, Laird, & Marsden, 2010).

Properly used, tools can help students clarify ideas that are often confused in a purely symbolic model. Sometimes it is useful to do the same activity with two different representations and ask students to make connections between them. Different representations offer different opportunities to learn. For example, an area model helps students visualize parts of the whole. A linear model shows that there is always another fraction to be found between any two numbers—an important concept that is underemphasized in the teaching of fractions. Some students are able to make sense of one representation, but not another. Importantly, students need to experience fractions in real-world contexts that are meaningful to them (Cramer & Whitney, 2010). These contexts may align well with one representation and not as well with another. For example, if students are being asked who walked the farthest, a linear model is more likely to support their thinking than an area model.

Table 15.1 provides an at-a-glance explanation of three types of models—area, length, and set—defining the wholes and their related parts for each model. Using appropriate representations and different categories of models broaden and deepen students' (and teachers') understanding of fractions.

An increasing number of Web resources are available to help represent fractions. One excellent source, though subscription based, is Conceptua Fractions (https://www.youtube .com/watch?v=7OJTjYxWCIU), developed by Conceptua Math. This site offers free tools that help students explore various fraction concepts using area, set, and length models (including the number line). The activities can be prescribed by the teacher and contain formative assessment resources.

CCSS **Standards for Mathematical Practice**
MP5. Use appropriate tools strategically.

TABLE 15.1 **MODELS FOR FRACTION CONCEPTS AND HOW THEY COMPARE**

Model	What Defines the Whole	What Defines the Parts	What the Fraction Means
Area	The area of the defined region	Equal area	The part of the area covered as it relates to the whole unit
Length or number line	The unit of distance or length	Equal distance/length	The location of a point in relation to 0 and other values on the number line
Set	Whatever value is determined as one set	Equal number of objects	The count of objects in the subset as it relates to the defined whole

Source: Based on Petit, Laird, & Marsden (2010).

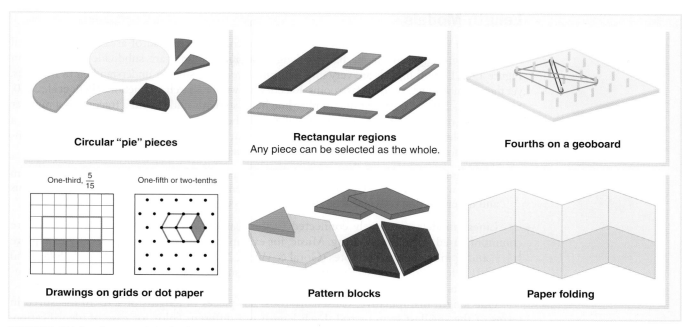

FIGURE 15.1 Area models for fractions.

Area Models

With these visuals, fractions are based on parts of an area. See Figure 15.1 for examples. Area is a good place to begin fraction explorations because it lends itself to equal sharing and partitioning.

Circular Fraction Pieces are the most commonly used area model. One advantage of the circular model is that it emphasizes the part-whole concept of fractions and the meaning of the relative size of a part to the whole (Cramer, Wyberg, & Leavitt, 2008). Other area models in Figure 15.1 demonstrate how different shapes can be the whole. Grid or Dot Paper provides flexibility in selecting the size of the whole and the size of the parts (see Blackline Masters 5–11 for a selection). Many commercial versions of area manipulatives are available, including circular and rectangular pieces, pattern blocks, geoboards, and tangrams. Activity 15.1 (adapted from Roddick & Silvas-Centeno, 2007) uses pattern blocks to help students develop concepts of partitioning and iterating.

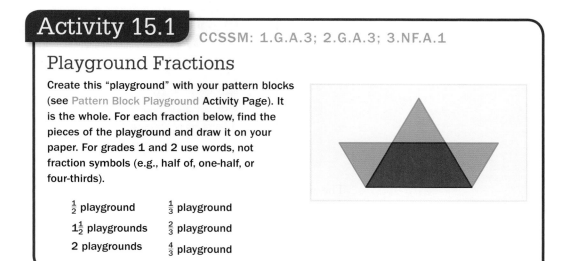

Activity 15.1

CCSSM: 1.G.A.3; 2.G.A.3; 3.NF.A.1

Playground Fractions

Create this "playground" with your pattern blocks (see Pattern Block Playground **Activity Page**). It is the whole. For each fraction below, find the pieces of the playground and draw it on your paper. For grades 1 and 2 use words, not fraction symbols (e.g., half of, one-half, or four-thirds).

$\frac{1}{2}$ playground $\frac{1}{3}$ playground

$1\frac{1}{2}$ playgrounds $\frac{2}{3}$ playground

2 playgrounds $\frac{4}{3}$ playground

Length Models

With length models, lengths or measurements are compared instead of areas. Either physical materials are compared on the basis of length or number lines are subdivided, as shown in Figure 15.2. Length models are very important in developing student understanding of fractions, yet they are not widely used in classrooms. Recent reviews of research on fractions (Petit et al., 2010; Siegler et al., 2010) report that the number line helps students understand a fraction as a number (rather than one number over another number) and helps develop other fraction concepts. In a report completed by the Institute of Educational Sciences (IES), the researchers prepared recommendations for supporting the learning of fractions (Siegler et al., 2010), advising teachers to:

> Help students recognize that fractions are numbers and that they expand the number system beyond whole numbers. Use number lines as a central representational tool in teaching this and other fraction concepts from the early grades on. (p. 1)

Linear models are closely connected to the real-world contexts in which fractions are commonly used, such as measuring. Music, for example, is an excellent opportunity to explore $\frac{1}{2}, \frac{1}{4}, \frac{1}{8}$, and $\frac{1}{16}$ in the context of notes (Goral & Wiest, 2007). In fact, Courey, Balogh, Siker, and Paik (2012) found that connecting fractions to measures in music significantly improved student understanding of fractions.

One length manipulative, Cuisenaire rods, has pieces in lengths of 1 to 10 measured in terms of the smallest strip or rod. Each length is a different color for ease of identification. Strips of paper or adding-machine tape, also a length model, can be folded to produce student-made fraction strips.

TECHNOLOGY Note. Virtual Cuisenaire rods and accompanying activities can be found at online at various websites such as the University of Cambridge's NRICH Project. ■

Rods or strips provide flexibility because any length can represent the whole. For example, if you wanted students to work with $\frac{1}{4}$ and $\frac{1}{8}$, select the brown Cuisenaire rod, which is 8 units long. Therefore, the four rod (purple) becomes $\frac{1}{2}$, the two rod (red) becomes $\frac{1}{4}$, and the one rod (white) becomes $\frac{1}{8}$. For exploring twelfths, put the orange rod and red rod together to make a whole that is 12 units long.

Cuisenaire rods consist of the following colors and lengths:

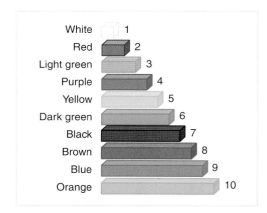

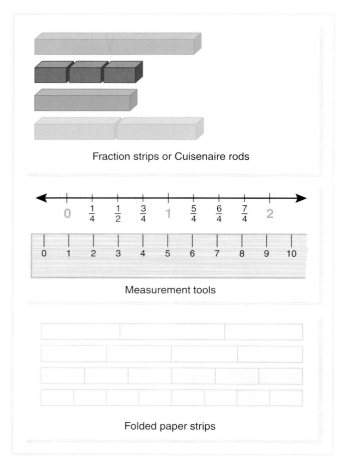

Fraction strips or Cuisenaire rods

Measurement tools

Folded paper strips

FIGURE 15.2 Length or measurement models for fractions.

The number line is a significantly more sophisticated length model than the physical tools described previously (Bright, Behr, Post, & Wachsmuth, 1988), but it is an essential model that needs be emphasized more in the teaching of fractions (Clarke et al., 2008; Flores et al., 2006; Siegler et al., 2010; Usiskin, 2007; Watanabe, 2006).

Like with whole numbers, the number line is used to compare the relative size of numbers. Importantly, the number line reinforces that fact that there is always one more fraction to be found between two fractions. The following activity (based on Bay-Williams & Martinie, 2003) is a fun way to use a real-world context to engage students in thinking about fractions through a linear model.

Activity 15.2

CCSSM: 3.NF.A.2a, b; 3.NF.A.3a, b, d

Who Is Winning?

ENGLISH LANGUAGE LEARNERS

STUDENTS *with* **SPECIAL NEEDS**

Use Who Is Winning? **Activity Page and give students paper strips or ask them to draw a number line. This activity can be done two ways (depending on your lesson goals). First, ask students to use reasoning to answer the question "Who is winning?" Students can use reasoning strategies to compare and decide. Second, students can locate each person's position on a number line. Explain that the friends below are playing "Red Light, Green Light." The fractions tell how much of the distance they have already moved. Can you place these friends on a line to show where they are between the start and finish? Second, rather than place them, ask students to use reasoning to answer the question "Who is winning?"**

Mary: $\frac{3}{4}$ Harry: $\frac{1}{2}$ Larry: $\frac{5}{6}$

Han: $\frac{5}{8}$ Miguel: $\frac{5}{9}$ Angela: $\frac{2}{3}$

This game can be differentiated by changing the value of the fractions or the number of friends (fractions). The game of "Red Light, Green Light" may not be familiar to ELLs. Modeling the game with people in the class and using estimation are good ways to build background and support students with disabilities.

Set Models

In set models, the whole is understood to be a set of objects, and subsets of the whole make up fractional parts. For example, 3 objects are one-fourth of a set of 12 objects. The set of 12 in this example represents the unit, the whole or 1. The idea of referring to a collection of counters as a single entity makes set models difficult for some students. Putting a piece of yarn in a loop around the objects in the set to help students "see" the whole. Figure 15.3 illustrates several set models for fractions.

A common misconception with set models is to focus on the size of a subset rather than the number of equal sets in the whole. For example, if 12 counters make a whole, then a subset of 4 counters is one-*third*, not one-fourth, because 3 equal sets make the whole. However, the set model helps establish important connections with many real-world uses of fractions and with ratio concepts.

Two color counters are an effective set manipulative. Counters can be flipped to change their color to model various fractional parts of a whole set. Any countable objects (e.g., a box of crayons) can be a set model (with one box being the unit or whole). The following activity uses your students as the whole set. It can be done as an energizer, warm-up, or full lesson.

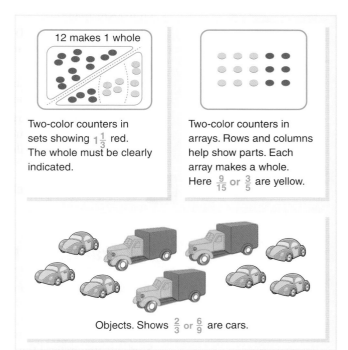

12 makes 1 whole

Two-color counters in sets showing $1\frac{1}{3}$ red. The whole must be clearly indicated.

Two-color counters in arrays. Rows and columns help show parts. Each array makes a whole. Here $\frac{9}{15}$ or $\frac{3}{5}$ are yellow.

Objects. Shows $\frac{2}{3}$ or $\frac{6}{9}$ are cars.

FIGURE 15.3   Set models for fractions.

Activity 15.3

CCSSM: 3.NF.A.1; 3.NF.A.3b

Class Fractions

Use a group of students as the whole—for example, six students if you want to work on halves, thirds, and sixths. Invite them to come to the front of the room. Say to the group, "If you [are wearing tennis shoes, have brown hair, etc.], move to the right. If not, move to the left." Ask everyone, "What fraction of our friends [are wearing tennis shoes]?" Invite them to whisper to a partner, then share with the class.

Change the number of selected students in the whole. You can also ask, "How many friends in one-half of this group? One-fourth of this group?" Connect to the symbols for fractions (e.g., $\frac{1}{2}$, $\frac{1}{3}$, and $\frac{1}{6}$), asking students to write the fraction that tells how many students [are wearing tennis shoes]. Also, if you have six students in your group, and you have three in your subgroup, then students are likely to say "three-sixths" and "one-half." Discuss that these values are equivalent.

Students must be able to explore fractions across the three area, length, and set models. As a teacher, you will not know whether they really understand the meaning of a fraction such as $\frac{1}{4}$ unless you have seen a student represent one-fourth using all three models.

 FORMATIVE ASSESSMENT Notes. A straightforward way to assess students' knowledge of a fractional amount is to give them a piece of paper folded into thirds. Write *area*, *length*, and *set* at the top of each section and give them a fractional value (e.g., $\frac{3}{4}$). Observe as they (1) draw a picture and (2) write a sentence describing a context or example for the selected fraction. This can be done exactly for commonly used fractions or can be an estimation activity with fractions like $\frac{31}{58}$. ■

 TECHNOLOGY Note. Virtual manipulatives are available for all three models. Virtual manipulatives have been found to positively affect student achievement, especially when they are paired with using the actual manipulatives (Moyer-Packenham, Ulmer, & Anderson, 2012). Recommended sites include:

Cyberchase (PBS): *Cyberchase* is a popular television series. Their website offers videos that model fractions with real-world connections and activities such as "Thirteen Ways of Looking at a Half" (fractions of geometric shapes) and "Make a Match" (concept of equivalent fractions).

Illuminations (NCTM) Fractions Model: Explore length, area, region, and set models of fractions, including fractions greater than one, mixed numbers, decimals, and percentages.

Math Playground Fraction Bars: On this site you can explore fractional parts, the concepts of numerator and denominator, and equivalence.

National Library of Virtual Manipulatives: This site offers numerous models for exploring fractions, including fraction bars and fraction pieces. There is also an applet for comparing and visualizing fractions. ■

✓ **Complete Self-Check 15.2: Models for Fractions**

Fractional Parts

The first goal in the development of fractions should be to help students construct the idea of *fractional parts of the whole*—the parts that result when the whole or unit has been partitioned into *equal-sized portions or fair shares*. (Recall that Table 15.1 describes the meanings of parts and wholes across each type of model.)

Students understand the idea of separating a quantity into two or more parts to be shared fairly among friends. This is the beginning of understanding fractions and in the CCSS-M occurs in grades 1 and 2. In grade 3 and beyond, students make connections between the idea of fair (equal) shares and fractional parts. The next three sections describe ideas foundational to finding equal shares.

Fraction Size Is Relative

A fraction by itself does not describe the size of the whole or the size of the parts. A fraction tells us only about the *relationship between* the part and the whole. Consider the following situation:

Pizza Fallacy: Mark is offered the choice of a third of a pizza or a half of a pizza. Because he is hungry and likes pizza, he chooses the half. His friend Jane gets a third of a pizza but ends up with more than Mark. How can that be?

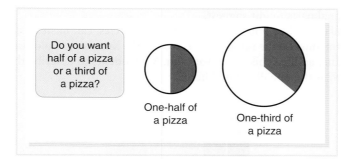

The visual illustrates how Mark got misdirected in his choice. The point of the "pizza fallacy" is that whenever two or more fractions are discussed in the same context, one cannot assume (as Mark did) that the fractions are all parts of the same size whole. Teachers can help students understand fractional parts if they regularly ask, "What is the whole?" or "What is the unit?"

Comparing two fractions with any representation can be made only if both fractions are parts of the same size whole. For example, when using Cuisenaire rods, $\frac{2}{3}$ of a light green strip cannot be compared to $\frac{2}{3}$ of an orange strip.

Partitioning

Sectioning a shape into equal-sized parts is called *partitioning*. When a brownie (or other area) has been partitioned into four equal shares, the parts are called *fourths*. Explain to students, "We call these *fourths*. The whole is cut into four parts. All of the parts are the same size—fourths." The words for fractional parts (e.g., *halves, thirds, fourths, eighths*, and so on) are introduced before the symbols. In the CCSS-M the words for fractional parts (as they relate to equal shares) are introduced in grades 1 and 2; the symbols for fractions are introduced in grade 3. Figure 15.4 illustrates sixths across area, length, and set models.

Partitioning with Area Models. When partitioning an area into fractional parts, students need to be aware that (1) the fractional parts must be the same size, though not necessarily the same shape; and (2) the number of equal-sized parts that can be partitioned within the unit determines the fractional amount (e.g., partitioning into 4 parts means each

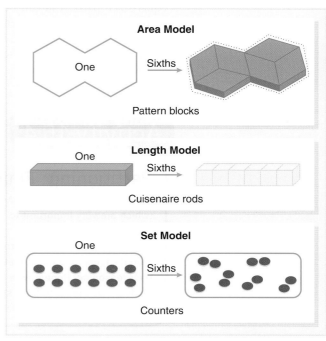

FIGURE 15.4 Which of these shapes are partitioned into sixths? Explain why or why not for each.

part is *one-fourth* of the unit). It is important for students to understand, however, that sometimes visuals do not *show* all the partitions. For example, consider the following picture:

Referring back to the two criteria, a student might think, "If I partitioned this so that all pieces were the same size, then there will be four parts; therefore, the smaller partitioned region represents one-fourth"—not one-third, as many students without a conceptual understanding of fractional parts might suggest.

Some manipulatives, like fraction bars or fraction circles, can mislead students to believe that fractional parts must be the same *shape* as well as the same size. Color tiles can be used to create rectangles that address this misconception. Ask students to describe the fractional parts in a rectangle, such as the one illustrated here:

Students who recognize that each color represents thirds understand that fractional parts must be the same size, and that the shape of the thirds may be different.

Area models are the first types of models to use in teaching fractional parts. Young students, in particular, tend to focus on shape, when the focus should be on equal-*sized* parts. Activity 15.1 is an example of how you can use pattern blocks to focus on partitioning into equal-sized parts. You can build on this activity by building other shapes that use different pattern block pieces and then have students figure out how much each piece is of the whole. Visit the companion website to watch how a classroom teacher helps his students understand parts of the whole using pattern blocks.

Activity 15.4 uses partitioned drawings to develop the concept of fractional parts.

Activity 15.4   CCSSM: 1.G.A.3; 2.G.A.3; 3.NF.A.1

Partitioning: Fourths or Not Fourths?

STUDENTS
with
SPECIAL
NEEDS

Use Fourths or Not Fourths **Activity Page** showing examples and nonexamples (which are very important to use with students with disabilities) of fourths (see Figure 15.5).

Ask students to identify the wholes that are correctly divided into fourths (equal shares) and those that are not. For each response, have students explain their reasoning. Repeat with other fractional parts, such as thirds or eighths. To challenge students, ask them to draw shapes that fit each of the four categories listed on the next page for other fractional parts, such as sixths. (See Sixths or Not Sixths **Activity Page.**)

In the preceding activity, the shapes fall in each of the following categories:

1. Same shape, same size: (a) and (f) [equivalent]
2. Different shape, same size: (e) and (g) [equivalent]
3. Different shape, different size: (b) and (c) [not equivalent]
4. Same shape, different size: (d) [not equivalent]

FORMATIVE ASSESSMENT Notes. Activity 15.4 is a good diagnostic interview to assess whether students understand that it is the *size* that matters, not the shape. If students get all correct except (e) and (g), they hold the misconception that parts should be the same shape. Future tasks are needed that focus on equivalence. For example, you can ask students to take a square and subdivide a picture themselves, as in Activity 15.5. ■

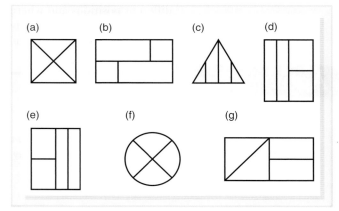

FIGURE 15.5 Given a whole, find fractional parts.

Activity 15.5

CCSSM: 1.G.A.3; 2.G.A.3; 3.NF.A.1

Finding (All the) Fair Shares

Give students dot paper and ask them to enclose a region that lends itself to partitioning with a particular fractional part. For example, they might enclose a 3-by-6 rectangle if they are going to partition into thirds. Ask students to find a way to partition the rectangle into thirds. Then redraw another rectangle that is the same size whole and partition it a different way to show thirds. Ask students to find a way to show thirds where the thirds are different shapes. See how many ways they can find. For ELLs, fraction parts sound like whole numbers (e.g., *fourths* and *fours*). Be sure to emphasize the *th* on the end and explicitly discuss the difference between four areas and a *fourth of* an area.

ENGLISH LANGUAGE LEARNERS

Partitioning with Length Models. The explanation of partitioning in the CCSS-M may be difficult to interpret. For example:

> 3.NF.A.2b: Represent a fraction a/b on a number line diagram by marking off a lengths $1/b$ from 0. Recognize that the resulting interval has size a/b and that its endpoint locates the number a/b on the number line. (CCSSO, 2010, p. 24)

Put more simply, students need to be able to partition a number line into fourths and realize that each section is one-fourth:

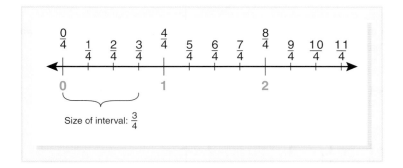

Number lines are difficult for students. Students may ignore the size of the interval (McNamara & Shaughnessy, 2010; Petit et al., 2010). Students can develop an understanding of the number line by folding paper strips. Provide examples where the shaded sections are in different positions and where partitioning isn't already shown to strengthen students' understanding of equal parts. Activity 15.6 and Activity 15.7 provide such opportunities, one with paper strips and one with number lines.

Activity 15.6

CCSSM: 3.NF.A.1; 3.NF.A.2a, b

What Fraction Is Colored?

Prepare a set of paper strips prior to doing this activity (you can cut 1-inch wide pieces of 8.5" by 11" paper and shade, or cut pieces of adding machine tape). Color the strips so that they have a fractional amount shaded in various positions (not just left justified!) (Sarazen, 2012). Here are a few examples:

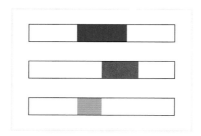

Explain that the strip represents one whole. Give each student a paper strip. Ask students to explain what fraction is colored and explain how they know. A common misconception is for students to count parts and call each of these one-third. If a student makes this error, ask if the parts are the same-sized and if not to partition to make same-sized parts. Use toothpicks or uncooked spaghetti to illustrate the partitions:

Students can also justify their reasoning by measuring the length of each partition.

Using paper strips can help students better understand the number line, the focus of the next activity.

Activity 15.7

CCSSM: 3.NF.A.1; 3.NF.A.2a, b

How Far Did Nicole Go?

Give students number lines partitioned such that only some of the partitions are showing. Use a context such as walking to school. For each number line, ask, "How far has Nicole gone? How do you know?"

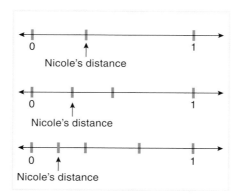

Students can justify their reasoning by measuring the length of each partition.

Locating a fractional value on a number line is particularly challenging but very important for students to be able to do. Shaughnessy (2011) found four common errors students make in working with the number line: They use incorrect notation, change the unit (whole), count the tick marks rather than the space between the marks, and count the ticks marks that appear without noticing any missing ones. This is evidence that we must use number lines more extensively in exploring fractions (most real-life contexts for fractions are measurement related).

Partitioning is a strategy commonly used in Singapore (a high-performing country on international mathematics assessments) as a way to solve story problems. Consider the following story problem (Englard, 2010):

A nurse has 54 bandages. Of those, $\frac{2}{9}$ are white and the rest are brown. How many of them are brown?

A bar diagram can be used as a tool for solving the problem. A student first partitions a strip into nine parts and then figures out the equal shares of bandages for each partition:

Did you notice that this is an example of fraction as operator? These types of partitioning tasks are good building blocks for multiplying with fractions.

Partitioning with Set Models. Students can partition sets of objects such as coins, counters, or baseball cards. When partitioning sets, students may confuse the number of counters in a share with the name of the share. In the example in Figure 15.4, the 12 counters are partitioned into 6 sets—*sixths*. Each share or part has two counters, but it is the number of shares that makes the partition show *sixths*. As with the other models, when the equal parts are not already figured out, then students may not see how to partition. Students seeing a picture of two cats and four dogs might think $\frac{2}{4}$ are cats (Bamberger, Oberdorf, & Schultz-Ferrell, 2010). Consider the following problem:

Eloise has 6 trading cards, Andre has 4 trading cards, and Lu has 2 trading cards. What fraction of the trading cards does Lu have?

A student who answers "one-third" is not thinking about equal shares but about the number of people with trading cards.

Understanding that parts of a whole must be partitioned into equal-sized parts across different models is an important step in conceptualizing fractions and provides a foundation for exploring sharing and equivalence tasks, all of which are prerequisites to performing fraction operations (Cramer & Whitney, 2010).

Sharing Tasks

An important recommendation by the IES research team on ways to help students learn fractions states, "Build on students' informal understanding of sharing and proportionality to develop initial fraction concepts" (Siegler et al., 2010, p. 1). In particular, they suggest using equal-sharing activities to develop the concepts of fraction, equivalence, and ordering of fractions. See Equal Sharing Stories Expanded Lesson for a lesson designed for grades 1 or 2.

Students in the early grades partition by thinking about fair shares (division). Sharing tasks are generally posed in the form of a simple story problem. *Four friends are sharing two cookies. How many cookies will each friend get?* Then problems become slightly more difficult: *Suppose there are four cookies to be shared fairly among three children. How much will each child get?* Visit the companion website to watch how Eduardo reasons about this sharing situation. Students initially perform sharing tasks by distributing items one at a time. When this process leaves leftover pieces, students must figure out how to subdivide so that every group (or person) gets a fair share. Contexts that lend to subdividing an area include cookies, brownies, sandwiches, pizzas, and so on.

Pattern blocks are a good tool to focus on equal shares because each piece is *not* an equal share, so creating shapes with pattern blocks and asking about equal shares helps students focus on the important idea of fair (equal) shares. Ask students to create a "cookie" using the six different pattern block shapes and ask, "Can this cookie be shared fairly with 6 people?" (Ellington & Whitenack, 2010). The answer is "no." Then, ask students to build a cookie that can be shared fairly.

Sharing brownies is a classic activity that focuses on partitioning to make equal shares (see, for example, Empson, 2002). Using concrete tools such as dough can make sharing accessible even to kindergartners (Cwikla, 2014).

Activity 15.8   CCSSM: 1.G.A.3; 2.G.A.3

Cookie Dough: Cut Me a Fair Share!

Give students a ball of dough and a plastic knife. Explain that they are going to be finding a way to share each group of cookies fairly with a group of students. Start with an example that is not too difficult. For example:

Four friends want to share ten brownies so that each friend gets the same amount of brownies. How much will each friend get?

Invite students to shape their dough into squares for brownies and then show how to share them fairly with four friends, using a paper knife if necessary. Encourage students to share their ways of thinking about this problem. A strategy many students will use for this problem is to deal out two brownies to each child and then halve each of the remaining brownies (see Figure 15.6).

Then, offer a selection of other sharing tasks with different numbers of brownies and different number of sharers (see additional examples below).

"Kids and Cookies" is an excellent online tool for sharing cookies (both round and rectangular). Display the situations on an interactive whiteboard and ask for different ways to share fairly (you can begin with whole numbers and increase in difficulty) (Center for Technology and Teacher Education, n.d.).

The relationship between the number of things to be shared and the number of sharers determines problem difficulty. Students' initial strategies for sharing involve halving, so a good place to begin is with two, four, or even eight sharers. Here are some examples:

5 brownies shared with 2 children

5 brownies shared with 4 children

7 brownies shared with 4 children

2 brownies shared with 4 children

4 brownies shared with 8 children

3 brownies shared with 4 children

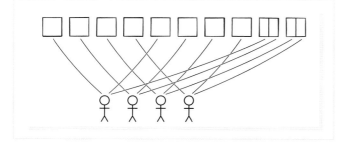

FIGURE 15.6 Ten brownies shared with four children.

These can be prepared as Brownie Sharing Cards. The last example, three brownies shared with four children, is more challenging because there are more sharers than items, and it involves more than just finding halves. One strategy is to partition each brownie into four parts and give each child one-fourth from each brownie—a total of three-fourths. Students (even adults) are surprised at the relationship between the problem and the answer. On the companion website, Felisha explains the fractional amount each of 5 children get when sharing 2 cookies, but loses track of what the whole is in determining each person's share.

Tier 1 task: For students who still need experience with halving	Tier 2 task: For students comfortable with halving and ready to try other strategies	Tier 3 task: For students ready to solve tasks in which students combine halving with new strategies
How can 2 people share 3 brownies?	How can 4 people share 3 brownies?	How can 3 people share 5 brownies?
How can 2 people share 5 brownies?	How can 3 people share 4 brownies?	How can 3 people share 2 brownies?
How can 4 people share 3 brownies?	How can 3 people share 5 brownies?	How can 6 people share 4 brownies?
How can 3 people share 4 brownies?	How can 6 people share 4 brownies?	How can 5 people share 4 brownies?

FIGURE 15.7 Example of a tiered lesson for the brownie-sharing problem.

▐▐ Pause & Reflect

Is this pattern (that three brownies shared among four children means each gets three-fourths) true for any sharing tasks? Why is this true? ●

Because the level of difficulty of these sharing tasks varies, it is useful for creating a tiered lesson. In a tiered lesson, the goal (sharing) is the same, but the specific tasks vary in their challenge. Figure 15.7 shows how one teacher offers these three tiers for her lesson on sharing brownies (Williams, 2008).

Sharing into thirds or sixths is more challenging because students cannot rely on halving to get to the answer. Here are some examples:

4 pizzas shared with 3 children

7 pizzas shared with 6 children

5 pizzas shared with 3 children

4 pizzas shared with 6 children

Figure 15.8 shows how a student partitioned to solve "5 pizzas shared with 3 children." This took much guess and check, at which point the teacher asked, "Can you see a pattern in how you have divided the pizza and how many people are sharing?" At this point, the student noticed a pattern: If there are three people, the remaining pizzas need to be partitioned into thirds.

As students report their answers, it is important to emphasize the equivalence of different representations (Flores & Klein, 2005). For example, in the case of three people sharing four pizzas, the answer might be noted on the board this way:

$$\frac{4}{3} = 1\frac{1}{3} = 1 + \frac{1}{3}$$

Iterating

In whole-number learning, counting precedes and helps students to add and later subtract. This is also true with fractions. Counting fractional parts, or *iterating*, helps students understand the relationship between the parts (the numerator) and the whole (the denominator). The iterative concept is most clear when focusing on these two ideas about fraction symbols:

• The top number (numerator) *counts.*
• The bottom number (denominator) tells *what is being counted.*

Each of the children gets 1 and 2/3 of a pizza.

I think that however many children there are, that is how many peices you have to split the item into.

Each child gets 1 and 1/4 of a pizza.

FIGURE 15.8 Elizabeth explains a pattern for finding equal shares of a pizza.

Students need to understand that $\frac{3}{4}$, for example, can be thought of as a count of three parts called *fourths* (Post, Wachsmuth, Lesh, & Behr, 1985; Siebert & Gaskin, 2006; Tzur, 1999).

If you know the kind of part you are counting, you can tell when you get to one, when you get to two, and so on. Students should be able to answer the question, "How many fifths are in one whole?" just as they know how many ones are in ten. However, the 2008 National Assessment of Education Progress (NAEP) results indicated that only 44 percent of students answered this question correctly (Rampey, Dion, & Donahue, 2009). This is the focus of Activities 15.9 through 15.11.

Activity 15.9
CCSSM: 3.NF.A.1; 3.NF.A.2a, b

More, Less, or Equal to One Whole

Give students a collection of fractional parts (all the same-size pieces) and indicate the kind of fractional part they have. For example, if done with Cuisenaire rods, the collection might have seven light green rods/strips with a caption or note indicating "each piece is $\frac{1}{8}$." The task is to decide if the collection is less than one whole, equal to one whole, or more than one whole. Ask students to draw pictures or use symbols to explain their answer. As students count each collection of parts, discuss the relationship to one whole. Ask questions that help students focus on the meaning of the numerator and denominator, such as "Why did we get almost two wholes with seven-fourths, and yet we don't even have one whole with ten-twelfths?"

After exploring Activity 15.9 with same-sized pieces, try Activity 15.10, which returns to using the pattern blocks to help students focus on the size of the parts, not the number of pieces or partitions (Champion & Wheeler, 2014; Ellington & Whitenack, 2010).

Activity 15.10
CCSSM: 3.NF.A.1; 3.NF.A.2a, b

Pattern Block Creatures

Ask students to build a Pattern Block Creature that fits with a set of rules (a creature represents one-whole). These rules can begin with just stating a fractional quantity for a color, such as "The red trapezoid is one-fourth of the creature." But, more constraints can be added to the rules. For example:

The blue parallelogram is one-sixth of the creature. Use at least two colors to build your creature.

The yellow hexagon is one-half of the creature. Use three colors to build your creature.

Green triangles are one-third of your creature. Use four different colors to build your creature.

After a student creates their creature, they can sketch the creature on paper and write the rule below it. Other students can critique the creature to see if it follows the rules it was given. Alternatively, the student can write their rule as "The red trapezoid is _____ of my creature" and trade it with another student to see if they can figure out the fractional amount.

Activity 15.11
CCSSM: 3.NF.A.1; 3.NF.A.3a, c

STUDENTS
with
SPECIAL
NEEDS

Calculator Fraction Counting

Many calculators, like the TI-15, display fractions in correct fraction format and offer a choice of showing results as mixed numbers or simple fractions. Ask students to type in a fraction (e.g., $\frac{1}{4}$) and then $+$ and the fraction again. To count, press 0 Op1, Op1, Op1, repeating to get the number of fourths wanted. The display will show the counts by fourths and also the number of times that the Op1 key has been pressed. Ask students questions such as the following: "How many fourths to get to 3?" "How many fifths to get to 2?" These can get increasingly more challenging: "How many fourths to get to $4\frac{1}{2}$?" "How many two-thirds to get to 6? Estimate and then count by two-thirds on the calculator." Students, particularly students with disabilities, should coordinate their counts with fraction models, adding a new fourths piece to the pile with each count.

The TI-15 display can be switched back and forth from mixed number to fractions, reinforcing the equivalence of values such as $1\frac{2}{3}$ and $\frac{5}{3}$. A variation on Activity 15.11 is to show students a mixed number such as $3\frac{1}{8}$ and ask how many counts of $\frac{1}{8}$ on the calculator it will take to count that high. The students should try to stop at the correct number, $\frac{25}{8}$, before pressing the mixed-number key.

Iterating applies to all models but is particularly connected with length models because iteration is much like measuring. Consider that you have $2\frac{1}{2}$ yards of ribbon and are trying to figure out how many fourths you can cut. You can draw a strip and start counting (iterating) the fourths:

Using a ribbon that is $\frac{1}{4}$ of a yard long as a measuring tool, a student marks off ten fourths:

Students can participate in many tasks that involve iterating lengths, including ones where they are asked to find what the whole or unit is.

Activity 15.12

CCSSM: 3.NF.A.1; 3.NF.A.2a, b

A Whole Lot of Fun

Use A Whole Lot of Fun **Activity Page** and a strip of paper like the one here:

Tell students that this strip is three-fourths of one whole (unit). Ask students to sketch strips of the other lengths on their paper (e.g., $\frac{5}{2}$). You can repeat this activity by selecting other values for the starting amount and selecting different fractional values to sketch. A context, such as walking, is effective in helping students make sense of the situation. Be sure to use fractions less than and greater than 1 and mixed numbers.

Notice that to solve the task in Activity 15.12, students first partition the piece into three sections to find $\frac{1}{4}$ and then iterate the $\frac{1}{4}$ to find the other lengths.

Iterating can be done with area models. Display some circular fractional pieces in groups as shown in Figure 15.9. For each collection, tell students what type of piece is being shown and simply count them together: "*One*-fourth, *two*-fourths, *three*-fourths, *four*-fourths, *five*-fourths." Ask, "If we have five-fourths, is that more than one whole, less than one whole, or the same as one whole?" To reinforce the piece size even more, you can slightly alter your language to say, "One one-fourth, two one-fourths, three one-fourths," and so on.

Iteration can also be done with set models. For example, show a collection of two-color counters and ask questions such as, "If 5 counters is one-fourth of the whole, how much of the whole is 15 counters?" These problems can be framed as engaging puzzles for students.

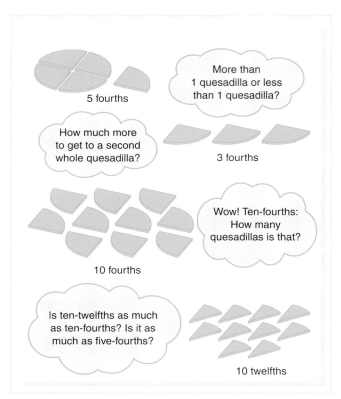

FIGURE 15.9 Iterating fractional parts in an area model.

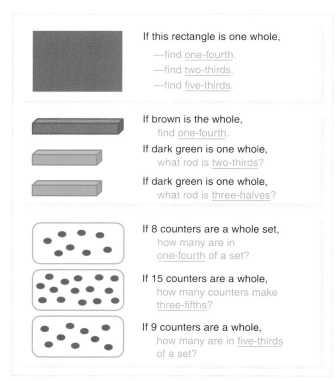

FIGURE 15.10 Given the whole and the fraction, find the part.

For example: "Three counters represent $\frac{1}{8}$ of my set; how big is my set?" If the fraction is not a unit fraction, then students first partition and then iterate. For example, "Twenty counters represents $\frac{2}{3}$ of my set; how big is my set?" first requires finding find $\frac{1}{3}$ (10 counters), then iterating that three times to get 30 counters in three-thirds (one whole). Counting Counters: Find the Part Activity Page and Counting Counters: Find the Whole Activity Page provides such problems for students to solve.

Pause & Reflect

Work through the exercises in Figures 15.10 and 15.11. If you do not have access to Cuisenaire rods or counters, just draw lines. What can you learn about student understanding of partitioning and iterating if they are able to solve problems in Figure 15.10 but not 15.11? If students are stuck, what contexts for each model can be used to support their thinking? ●

The partitioning and iterating questions are challenging yet very effective at helping students reflect on the meanings of the numerator and denominator and understand the meaning of fractions.

FORMATIVE ASSESSMENT Notes. The tasks in Figures 15.10 and 15.11 can be used as performance assessments. If students are able to solve these types of tasks, they can partition and iterate. That means they are ready to do equivalence and comparison tasks. If they are not able to solve problems such as these, provide a range of similar tasks, using real-life contexts and involving area, length, and set models. ■

Fraction Notation

The way that we write fractions with a top and a bottom number and a bar between is a convention—an arbitrary agreement for how to represent fractions. However, understanding of the convention can be clarified by giving explicit attention to the meaning of the numerator and the denominator as part of iterating activities. Students can understand the idea of halves and fourths, yet not understand the meaning of the symbols $\frac{1}{2}$ and $\frac{1}{4}$. In the CCSS-M, understanding the symbols for fractions is an emphasis in grade 3. Fractions should include examples that are less than 1, equal to one (e.g., $\frac{4}{4}$), and greater than 1 (e.g., $\frac{4}{8}$ and $\frac{4}{3}$). Engage students in iterating tasks and using symbols, then pose questions to make sense of the symbols, such as:

What does the numerator in a fraction tell us?

What does the denominator in a fraction tell us?

What might a fraction equal to 1 look like?

How do you know if a fraction is greater than or less than 1? Greater than or less than 2?

Here are some likely explanations for the top and bottom numbers from third graders:

- The numerator is the counting number. It tells how many shares or parts we have. It tells how many have been counted.
- The denominator tells what size piece is being counted. For example, if there are four parts in a whole, then we are counting *fourths*.

Making sense of symbols requires connections to visuals. Illustrating what $\frac{5}{4}$ looks like in terms of pizzas (area), on a number line (length), or connected to filling bags with objects (set) will help students make sense of this value.

One of the best things we can do for students is to emphasize equivalence and different ways to write fractional amounts.

❙❙ Pause & Reflect

What fraction notation might you use for the visual here (the large square represents one unit)? ●

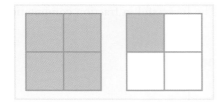

There are (at least) three ways to notate this quantity:

$$\frac{5}{4} \qquad 1\frac{1}{4} \qquad \frac{1}{4} + \frac{1}{4} + \frac{1}{4} + \frac{1}{4} + \frac{1}{4}$$

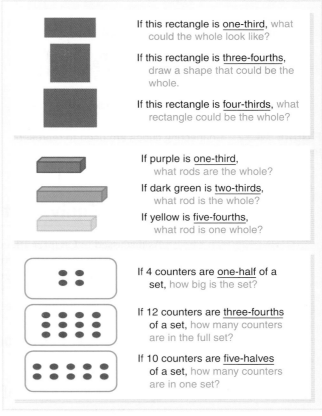

FIGURE 15.11 Given the part and the fraction, find the whole.

Do you think that students would be able to describe this quantity in all three ways? In the fourth National Assessment of Educational Progress (NAEP), fewer than half of the seventh graders assessed knew that $5\frac{1}{4}$ was the same as $5 + \frac{1}{4}$ (Kouba et al., 1988).

Throughout this chapter we have been including fractions less than 1 and fractions greater than 1. This helps students develop understanding of fractions as values that come between whole numbers (or can be equivalent to whole numbers). Too often, students aren't exposed to numbers equal to or greater than 1 (e.g., $\frac{6}{6}$, $\frac{5}{2}$ or $4\frac{1}{4}$), so when these values are added into the mix (no pun intended!), students find them confusing.

The term *improper fraction* is used to describe fractions that are greater than one, such as $\frac{5}{2}$. This term can be a source of confusion as the word *improper* implies that this representation is not acceptable, which is not the case at all—in fact, it is often the preferred representation in algebra. Instead, try not to use this phrase and instead use "fraction" or "fraction greater than 1." Note that the word *improper* is not used in the CCSS-M content standards.

If you have counted fractional parts beyond a whole, as discussed in the previous section, your students already know how to write $\frac{13}{6}$ or $\frac{13}{5}$. Ask students to use a model to illustrate these values and find equivalent representations using wholes and fractions (mixed numbers). Using connecting cubes was the most effective way to help students see both forms for recording fractions greater than 1 (Neumer, 2007) (see Figure 15.12). Students identify one cube as the unit fraction ($\frac{1}{5}$) for the problem ($\frac{12}{5}$). They count out 12 fifths and build wholes. Conversely, they could start with the mixed number, build it, and find out how many total cubes (or fifths) were used. Repeated experiences in building and solving these tasks will help students to notice a pattern that actually explains the algorithm for moving between mixed numbers and fractions greater than 1.

Help students move from physical models to mental images. Challenge students to figure out the two equivalent forms by just picturing the stacks in their heads. A good explanation for

CCSS Standards for Mathematical Practice
MP1. Make sense of problems and persevere in solving them.

CCSS Standards for Mathematical Practice
MP8. Look for and express regularity in repeated reasoning.

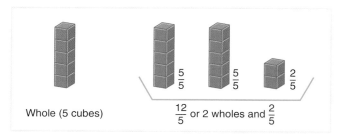

Whole (5 cubes) $\frac{12}{5}$ or 2 wholes and $\frac{2}{5}$

FIGURE 15.12 Connecting cubes are used to represent the equivalence of $\frac{12}{5}$ and $2\frac{2}{5}$.

$3\frac{1}{4}$ might be that there are 4 fourths in one whole, so there are 8 fourths in two wholes and 12 fourths in three wholes. The extra fourth makes 13 fourths in all, or $\frac{13}{4}$. (Note the iteration concept playing a role.)

Do not push the standard algorithm (multiply the bottom by the whole number and add the top), as it can interfere with students making sense of the relationship between the two and their equivalence.

 Complete Self-Check 15.3: Fractional Parts

Equivalent Fractions

As discussed in Chapter 14, equivalence is a critical but often poorly understood concept. This is particularly true with fraction equivalence. In the CCSS-M, fraction equivalence and comparisons are emphasized in grade 3 and applied in grade 4 (and beyond) as students engage in computation with fractions. Students cannot be successful in fraction computation without a strong understanding of fraction equivalence.

Conceptual Focus on Equivalence

Pause & Reflect

How do you know that $\frac{4}{6} = \frac{2}{3}$? Before reading further, think of at least two different explanations.

Here are some possible answers to the preceding question:

1. They are the same because you can simplify $\frac{4}{6}$ and get $\frac{2}{3}$.
2. If you have a set of 6 items and you take 4 of them, that would be $\frac{4}{6}$. But you can make the 6 into 3 groups, and the 4 would be 2 groups out of the 3 groups. That means it's $\frac{2}{3}$.

3. If you start with $\frac{2}{3}$, you can multiply the top and the bottom numbers by 2, and that will give you $\frac{4}{6}$, so they are equal.
4. If you had a square cut into 3 parts and you shaded 2, that would be $\frac{2}{3}$ shaded. If you cut all 3 of these parts in half, that would be 4 parts shaded and 6 parts in all. That's $\frac{4}{6}$, and it would be the same amount.

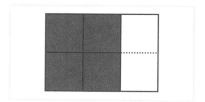

All of these answers are correct. But let's think about what they tell us. Responses 2 and 4 are conceptual, although not as efficient. The procedural responses, 1 and 3, are efficient but do not indicate conceptual understanding. All students should eventually be able to write an equivalent fraction for a given fraction. At the same time, the procedures should never be taught or used until the students understand what the result means. Consider how different the procedure and the concept appear to be:

Concept: Two fractions are equivalent if they are representations for the same amount or quantity—if they are the same number.

Procedure: To get an equivalent fraction, multiply (or divide) the top and bottom numbers by the same nonzero number.

Rushing too quickly to the algorithm can impede students' conceptual understanding of fractions and fraction equivalence. Be patient!

Equivalent Fraction Models

The general approach to helping students create an understanding of equivalent fractions is to have them use contexts and models to find different names for a fraction (see Figure 15.13 for examples). This is the first time in students' experience that they are seeing that a fixed quantity can have more than one name (actually an infinite number of names). Area models are a good place to begin understanding equivalence.

Activity 15.13   CCSSM: 3.NF.A.1; 3.NF.3a, b, c

Making Stacks

Select a manipulative that is designed for exploring fractions (e.g., pattern blocks, tangrams, fraction strips, or fraction circles). Prepare fraction cards with different fractional amounts, such as $\frac{2}{3}, \frac{1}{2}, \frac{3}{4}, 1, \frac{3}{2}, \frac{4}{3}$, and 2. (Note: you may want to begin with fractions less than 1, then move to fractions equal to and greater than 1.) Working individually or with a partner, students first identify the whole. Then they see how many stacks they can make on top of the whole. A stack must use the same-sized piece. Ask students to record all the possibilities they find (they can color the shapes and write the fraction). After completing several examples, have students look at the fractions they wrote for a stack and describe or write about the patterns they notice.

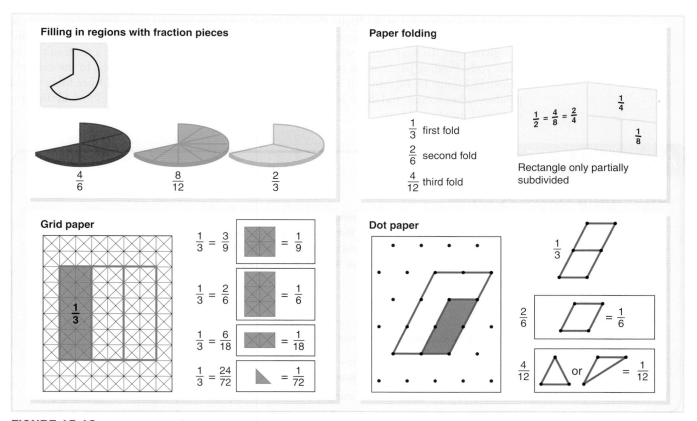

FIGURE 15.13   Area models for equivalent fractions.

Standards for Mathematical Practice

MP3. Construct viable arguments and critique the reasoning of others.

In a classroom discussion following this activity, you can help students reason about equivalent fractions by asking them to consider what other equivalencies are possible (and justify their thinking). For example, ask, "What equivalent fractions could you find if we had sixteenths in our fraction kit? If you could have a piece of any size at all, what other fraction names are possible?"

The following activity moves from using manipulatives to sketches on paper.

Activity 15.14

CCSSM: 3.NF.A.1; 3.NF.3a, b, c

Dot Paper Equivalences

Use Fraction Names Activity Page, which includes three different grids with a fraction shaded (each enclosed area represents one whole). Ask students how many fraction names they think the first problem has. Then ask them to see how many they can find (working individually or in partners). Invite students to share and explain the fraction names they found for problem 1. Repeat for the next two problems. Alternatively, cut this page into three task cards, laminate the cards, and place each at a station along with an overhead pen. Have students rotate in partners to a station and see how many fraction names they can find for that shape (using the pen as needed to show their ways). Rotate to the next station. You may also want to refer to the Dot Paper Equivalences Expanded Lesson.

To make additional pictures, create your own using your choice of Grid or Dot Paper (see Blackline Masters 5–11). (Figure 15.13 includes an example drawn on an isometric grid). The larger the size of the whole, the more names the activity will generate.

The Dot Paper Equivalences activity involves what Lamon (2012) calls "unitizing"—that is, given a quantity, finding different ways to chunk the quantity into parts in order to name it. She points out that this is a key ability related not only to equivalent fractions but also to proportional reasoning, especially in the comparison of ratios.

Length models should be used in activities similar to the Making Stacks task. Asking students to locate $\frac{2}{5}$ and $\frac{4}{10}$ on a number line, for example, can help them see that the two fractions are equivalent (Siegler et al., 2010). Rods or paper strips can be used to designate both a whole and a part, as illustrated in Figure 15.14. Students use smaller rods to find fraction names for the given part. To have larger wholes or values greater than one whole, use a train of two or three rods. Folding paper strips is another method of creating fraction names. In the example shown in Figure 15.14, one-half is subdivided by successive folding in half. Other folds would produce other names, and these possibilities should be discussed if no one tries to fold the strip in an odd number of parts.

Activity 15.15

CCSSM: 3.NF.A.3a, b, d; 4.NF.A.2

Stretching Number Lines

Using elastic strips has been effective in helping students understand equivalence of fractions and compare fractions (Harvey, 2012).

Cut strips of elastic (about 1 meter or yard in length). Hold the elastic taut and mark off ten partitions on each. Hand one out to each pair of students. Ask students to use their stretching number line to find the place on a table that represents the fraction of the distance across the table. For each pair, ask: Ask "Which distance is greater, or are they equal?"

a. $\frac{5}{10}$ of the distance across.
b. $\frac{1}{2}$ of the distance across.

a. $\frac{3}{10}$ of the distance across.
b. $\frac{3}{8}$ of the distance across. (Note: they have to rethink the whole as 8 sections.)

a. $\frac{3}{4}$ of the distance across. (Note: they have to rethink the whole as 8 sections.)
b. $\frac{6}{8}$ of the distance across. (Note: they have to rethink the whole as 8 sections.)

For early finishers, invite them to find their own equivalencies using their elastic to test their ideas.

Set models can also be used to develop the concept of equivalence. Legos, a highly motivating manipulative, can help students learn to write fraction equivalencies (for an excellent elaboration on this idea, see Gould, 2011). Lego bricks and can be viewed as an area (array) or as a set (students can count the studs).

Two color counters are an effective tool for fraction equivalencies. Visit the companion website to listen to John Van de Walle discuss fractions equivalencies with two color counters. Activity 15.17 uses the context of apples, which can be modeled using two color counters.

In the activities so far, there has only been a hint of a rule for finding equivalent fractions. Activity 15.18 moves a bit closer, but should still be done before developing an algorithm.

Students who have learning disabilities and other students who struggle with mathematics may benefit from using clocks to do equivalence; for example, to find equivalent fractions for $\frac{10}{12}$, $\frac{3}{4}$, $\frac{4}{6}$, and so on (Chick, Tierney, & Storeygard, 2007).

NCTM's Illuminations website offers an excellent set of three units called "Fun with Fractions." Each unit uses one of the model types (area, length, or set) and focuses on comparing and ordering fractions and equivalences. The five to six lessons in each unit incorporate a range of manipulatives and engaging activities to support student learning.

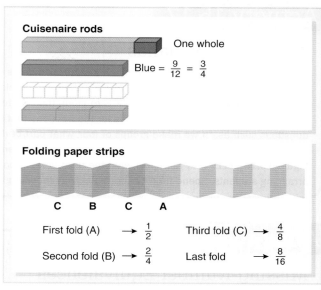

FIGURE 15.14 Length models for equivalent fractions.

Activity 15.16

CCSSM: 2.G.A.3; 3.NF.A.1; 3.NF.3a, b, c; 4.NF.B.3a, b

Lego Land: Building Options

Hand out one 2-by-6 Lego to each student. Ask them to describe it (there are 12 studs, two rows of 6). For second grade or as a warm-up, ask students what same-colored pieces could cover their land (e.g., 6 of the 2-by-1 pieces). Ask students to imagine that 12 pieces of Legos represents one plot of land. It can be covered with various smaller pieces as shown here:

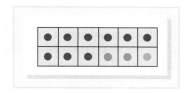

Ask students to build the plot of land using different Lego pieces (1-by-2, 1-by-3, 2-by-2, 1-by-1, 2-by-6, etc.). After they have completed their plot of land, ask students to tell the fraction of their land that is represented by a particular piece (e.g., the 2-by-6 is $\frac{6}{12}$ as well as $\frac{1}{2}$ and $\frac{2}{4}$).

To focus on iteration and to build connections to addition (grade 4), students can write equations to describe their Lego Land. In the one pictured here, that would be

$$\frac{6}{12} + \frac{3}{12} + \frac{2}{12} + \frac{1}{12} \quad \text{OR} \quad \frac{1}{2} + \frac{1}{4} + \frac{1}{6} + \frac{1}{12}.$$

Note that students have misconceptions about how to name fractions parts, naming the blue part as $\frac{1}{3}$ rather than $\frac{1}{4}$ because they see three pieces (Wilkerson, Bryan, & Curry, 2012). This becomes a good topic for a classroom discussion: What is the fractional value of the blue pieces (simplified)?

Activity 15.17

CCSSM: 3.NF.A.1; 3.NF.3a, b, c

Apples and Bananas

ENGLISH LANGUAGE LEARNERS

Use Apples and Bananas Activity Page or just have students set out a specific number of counters in two colors—for example, 24 counters, with 16 of them red (apples) and 8 of them yellow (bananas). The 24 counters make up the whole. The task is to group the counters into different fractional parts of the whole and use the parts to create fraction names for the fractions that are apples and fractions that are bananas. Ask questions such as, "If we make groups of four, what part of the set is red?" to encourage students to think of different ways to form equal-sized groups. In Figure 15.15, 24 counters are arranged in different groups. You might also suggest arrays (see Figure 15.16). ELLs may not know what the term *group* means because when used in classrooms, the word usually refers to arranging students. Spend time before the activity modeling what it means to group objects.

Activity 15.18

CCSSM: 3.NF.3a, b, c; 4.NF.A.1

Missing-Number Equivalences

Use Missing-Number Equivalences Activity Page or give students an equation expressing an equivalence between two fractions, but with an unknown value. Ask students to use counters or rectangles to illustrate and find the equivalent fraction. Example equations:

$$\frac{5}{3} = \frac{}{6} \qquad \frac{2}{3} = \frac{6}{} \qquad \frac{8}{12} = \frac{}{3} \qquad \frac{9}{12} = \frac{3}{}$$

The missing value can be in a numerator or a denominator; the missing number can be either larger or smaller than the corresponding part of the equivalent fraction. (All four possibilities are represented in the examples.) Figure 15.17 illustrates how Zachary represented the equivalences with equations and partitioning rectangles. The examples shown involve simple whole-number multiples between equivalent fractions. Next, consider pairs such as $\frac{6}{8} = \frac{}{12}$ or $\frac{9}{12} = \frac{6}{}$. In these equivalences, one denominator or numerator is not a whole-number multiple of the other. In addition, include equivalencies for whole numbers and fractions greater than one: $\frac{8}{x} = \frac{6}{6} \qquad \frac{10}{3} = \frac{x}{9}$

CCSS Standards for Mathematical Practice

MP1. Make sense of problems and persevere in solving them.

Developing an Equivalent-Fraction Algorithm

When students understand that fractions can have different (but equivalent) names, they are ready to develop a method for finding equivalent names for a particular value. An area model is a good visual for connecting the concept of equivalence to the standard algorithm for finding equivalent fractions (multiply both the top and bottom numbers by the same number to get an equivalent fraction). The approach suggested here is to look for a pattern in the way that the fractional parts in both the part and the whole are counted. Activity 15.21 is a beginning, but a good class discussion following the activity will also be required.

Activity 15.19

CCSSM: 3.NF.3b; 4.NF.A.1

Garden Plots

Have students draw a square "garden" on blank paper, or give each student a square of paper (like origami paper). Begin by explaining that the garden is divided into rows of various vegetables. In the first example, you might illustrate four rows (fourths) and designate $\frac{3}{4}$ as corn. Ask students to partition their square into four rows and shade three-fourths as in Figure 15.18. Then explain that the garden is going to be shared with family and friends in a way that each person gets a harvest that is $\frac{3}{4}$ corn. Show how the garden can be partitioned horizontally to represent two people sharing the corn (i.e., $\frac{6}{8}$). Ask what fraction of the newly divided garden is corn. Next, tell students to come up with other ways that friends can share the garden (they can choose how many friends, or you can). For each newly divided garden, ask students to record an equation showing the equivalent fractions.

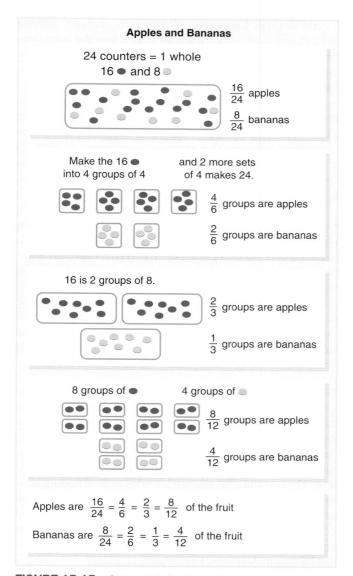

FIGURE 15.15   Set models for illustrating equivalent fractions.

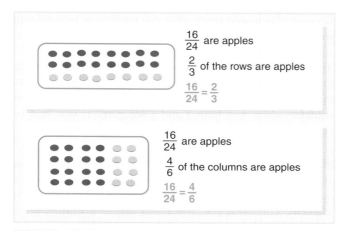

FIGURE 15.16   Arrays for illustrating equivalent fractions.

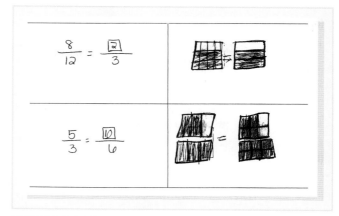

FIGURE 15.17   A student illustrates equivalence fractions by partitioning rectangles.

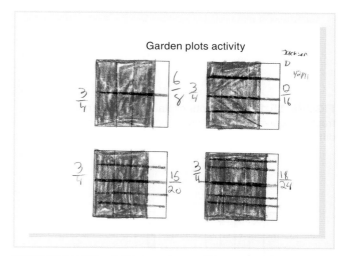

FIGURE 15.18   A third grader partitions a garden to model fraction equivalences.

(a)

I noticed that on number 3 on both numbers you can multiply by 2 to get the new fraction.

(b)

you can multiply the numerater and the denominator wich will create an equivalent fraction.

(c)

What do you notice?
I notice if you multiply the top you also multiply it to the bottom by the same number.

FIGURE 15.19 Students explain what they notice about fraction equivalences based on partitioning "gardens" in different ways.

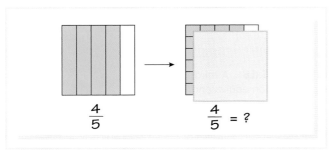

$$\frac{4}{5} \qquad \frac{4}{5} = ?$$

FIGURE 15.20 How can you count the fractional parts if you cannot see them all?

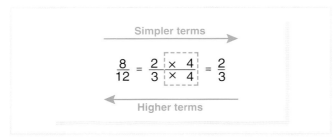

Simpler terms →

$$\frac{8}{12} = \frac{2 \times 4}{3 \times 4} = \frac{2}{3}$$

← Higher terms

FIGURE 15.21 Using the equivalent-fraction algorithm to write fractions in simplest terms.

After students have prepared their own examples, provide time for them to look at their fractions and gardens and notice patterns about the fractions and the diagrams. Once they have time to do this individually, ask students to share. Figure 15.19 provides student explanations that illustrate the range of "noticing."

As you can see, for some of these students more experiences are needed. You can also assist in helping students make the connection from the partitioned square to the procedure by displaying a square (for example, partitioned to show $\frac{4}{5}$) (see Figure 15.20). Then, partition the square vertically into six parts, covering most of the square as shown in the figure. Ask, "What is the new name for my $\frac{4}{5}$?"

The reason for this exercise is that it helps students see the connection to multiplication. With the covered square, students can see that there are four columns and six rows to the shaded part, so there must be 4×6 parts shaded. Similarly, there must be 5×6 parts in the whole. Therefore, the new name for $\frac{4}{5}$ is $\frac{4 \times 6}{5 \times 6}$, or $\frac{24}{30}$.

Examine examples of equivalent fractions that have been generated with other visuals (e.g., a number line) and see if the rule of multiplying top and bottom numbers by the same number holds. Ask students to explain why. Ask students, "If the rule is correct, how can $\frac{6}{8}$ and $\frac{9}{12}$ be equivalent?"

Writing Fractions in Simplest Terms. The multiplication scheme for equivalent fractions produces fractions with larger denominators. But creating equivalent forms for $\frac{6}{8}$ might involve multiplication to get $\frac{12}{16}$ or division to get $\frac{3}{4}$. To write a fraction in *simplest terms* means to write it so that numerator and denominator have no common whole-number factors. One meaningful approach to this task of finding simplest terms is to reverse the earlier process, as illustrated in Figure 15.21. The search for a common factor or a simplified fraction should be connected to grouping. Texas Instruments offers a comparing fractions activity using the number line on their Classroom Activities Exchange.

Two additional things should be noted regarding fraction simplification:

1. Notice that the phrase *reducing fractions* was not used. Because this would imply that the fraction is being made smaller, this terminology should be avoided. Fractions are simplified, *not* reduced.
2. Teachers sometimes tell students that fraction answers are incorrect if not in simplest or lowest terms. This also misinforms students about the equivalence of fractions. When students add $\frac{1}{6} + \frac{1}{2}$, both $\frac{2}{3}$ and $\frac{4}{6}$ are correct. It is best to reinforce that they are both correct and are equivalent.

Multiplying by One. Mathematically, equivalence is based on the multiplicative identity (any number multiplied by 1 remains unchanged). Any fraction of the form $\frac{n}{n}$ can be used as the identity element. Therefore, $\frac{3}{4} = \frac{3}{4} \times 1 = \frac{3}{4} \times \frac{2}{2} = \frac{6}{8}$. Furthermore, the numerator and denominator of the identity element can also be fractions. In this way, $\frac{6}{12} = \frac{6}{12} \times \left(\frac{1/6}{1/6}\right) = \frac{1}{2}$. Understanding this idea is an expectation in the CCSS-M in grade 4.

***TECHNOLOGY* Note.** Developing the concept of equivalence can be supported with the use of technology. In the NCTM e-Examples, there is a fraction game (Fraction Track) for two players (Applet 5.1, *Communicating about Mathematics Using Games*). The game uses a number-line model, and knowledge of equivalent fractions plays a significant role. The Equivalent Fractions tool from NCTM's Illuminations website is designed to help students create equivalent fractions by dividing and shading square or circular regions and then matching each fraction to its location on a number line. Students can use the computer-generated fraction or build their own. Once the rectangular or circular shape is divided, the student fills in the parts or fractional region and then builds two models equivalent to the original fraction. The three equivalent fractions are displayed in a table and in the same location on a number line. ■

✔ **Complete Self-Check 15.4: Equivalent Fractions**

 # Comparing Fractions

When students are looking to see whether two or more fractions are equivalent, they are comparing them. If they are not equivalent, then students can determine which ones are smaller and which ones are larger. As illustrated in Ally's interview about comparing fractions on the companion website, students often have misconceptions about fractions and therefore are not able to compare—for example, thinking that bigger numbers in the denominator mean the fraction is bigger. The ideas described previously for equivalence across area, length, and set models are appropriate for comparing fractions. The use of contexts, models, and mental imagery can help students build a strong understanding of the relative size of fractions (Bray & Abreu-Sanchez, 2010; Petit et al., 2010). The next section offers ways to support students' understanding of the relative size of fractions.

Comparing Fractions Using Number Sense

In the National Assessment of Educational Progress (NAEP) test, only 21 percent of fourth-grade students could explain why one unit fraction was larger or smaller than another—for example, $\frac{1}{5}$ and $\frac{1}{4}$ (Kloosterman et al., 2004). For eighth graders, only 41 percent were able to correctly put in order three fractions given in simplified form (Sowder, Wearne, Martin, & Strutchens, 2004).

Comparing Unit Fractions. As noted earlier, whole-number knowledge can interfere with comparing fractions. Students think, "Seven is more than four, so sevenths should be bigger than fourths" (Mack, 1995). The inverse relationship between number of parts and size of parts cannot be "told" but must be developed in each student through many experiences, including ones that were described earlier related to partitioning, iterating, estimation, and equivalence.

Activity 15.20   CCSSM: 3.NF.A.3d; 4.NF.A.2

Ordering Unit Fractions

List a set of unit fractions such as $\frac{1}{3}$, $\frac{1}{8}$, $\frac{1}{5}$, and $\frac{1}{10}$ (assume same size whole for each fraction). Ask students to use reasoning to put the fractions in order from least to greatest. Challenge students to explain their reasoning with an area model (e.g., circles) *and* on a number line. Ask students to connect the two representations. ("What do you notice about $\frac{1}{3}$ of the circle and $\frac{1}{3}$ on the number line?") Students with disabilities may need to use clothespins with the fractions written on them and place them on the line first.

Repeat with all numerators equal to some number other than 1.

Repeat with fractions that have different numerators and different denominators. You can vary how many fractions are being compared to differentiate the task.

STUDENTS
with
**SPECIAL
NEEDS**

Students may notice that larger bottom numbers mean smaller fractions (this is an important pattern to notice), but it only holds true when the numerators are the same. Still, it is conjecture that can be posed to the class for testing. Eventually they will find cases where it is not true (e.g., $\frac{1}{8} < \frac{1}{4}$ but $\frac{3}{8} > \frac{1}{4}$).

Standards for Mathematical Practice

MP2. Reason abstractly and quantitatively.

Comparing Any Fractions. You have probably learned rules or algorithms for comparing two fractions. The usual approaches are finding common denominators and using cross-multiplication. These rules can be effective in getting correct answers but require no thought about the size of the fractions. If students are taught these rules before they have had the opportunity to think about the relative sizes of various fractions, they are less likely to develop number sense about fraction size. The goal is to select an efficient strategy for determining the larger fraction, and these two methods are not always the most efficient (CCSSO, 2010).

❚❚ Pause & Reflect

Assume for a moment that you do not know the common-denominator or cross-multiplication techniques. Now examine the pairs of fractions in Figure 15.22 and select the largest of each pair using a reasoning approach that a fourth grader might use. ●

The Which Is Greater? Activity Page can be used to do this activity with students. Figure 15.23 provides explanations from two students on the first column (A–F). Both students are able to reason to determine which is larger, though one student is better able to articulate those ideas.

The following list summarizes ways that the fractions in Figure 15.22 might have been compared:

1. *Same-size whole (same denominators).* To compare $\frac{3}{8}$ and $\frac{5}{8}$, think about having 3 parts of something and also 5 parts of the same thing. (This method can be used for problems B and G.)
2. *Same number of parts (same numerators) but different-sized wholes.* Consider the case of $\frac{3}{4}$ and $\frac{3}{7}$. If a whole is divided into 7 parts, the parts will certainly be smaller than if divided into only 4 parts. (This strategy can be used with problems A, D, and H.)
3. *More than/less than one-half or one.* The fraction pairs $\frac{3}{7}$ versus $\frac{5}{8}$ and $\frac{5}{4}$ versus $\frac{7}{8}$ do not lend themselves to either of the previous thought processes. In the first pair, $\frac{3}{7}$ is less than half of the number of sevenths needed to make a whole, and so $\frac{3}{7}$ is less than a half. Similarly, $\frac{5}{8}$ is more than a half. Therefore, $\frac{5}{8}$ is the larger fraction. The second pair is determined by noting that one fraction is greater than 1 and the other is less than 1. (This method could be used on problems A, D, F, G, and H.)
4. *Closeness to one-half or one.* Why is $\frac{9}{10}$ greater than $\frac{3}{4}$? Each is one fractional part away from one whole, and tenths are smaller than fourths. Similarly, notice that $\frac{5}{8}$ is smaller than $\frac{4}{6}$ because it is only one-eighth more than a half, wheras $\frac{4}{6}$ is a sixth more than a half. Can you use this basic idea to compare $\frac{3}{5}$ and $\frac{5}{9}$? (*Hint:* Each is half of a fractional part more than $\frac{1}{2}$.) Also try $\frac{5}{7}$ and $\frac{7}{9}$. (This is a good strategy for problems C, E, I, J, K, and L.)

How did your reasons for choosing fractions in Figure 15.22 compare to these ideas? It is important that you are comfortable with these informal comparison strategies as a major component of your own number sense as well as for helping students develop theirs. Notice that some of the comparisons, such as problems D and H, could have been solved using more than one of the strategies listed.

Tasks you design for your students should assist them in developing these methods of comparing two fractions. The ideas should emerge from your students' reasoning. To teach "the four ways to compare fractions" defeats the purpose of encouraging

Which fraction in each pair is greater?
Give one or more reasons. Try not to use drawings or models.
Do <u>not</u> use common denominators or cross-multiplication.

A. $\frac{4}{5}$ or $\frac{4}{9}$ G. $\frac{7}{12}$ or $\frac{5}{12}$

B. $\frac{4}{7}$ or $\frac{5}{7}$ H. $\frac{3}{5}$ or $\frac{3}{7}$

C. $\frac{3}{8}$ or $\frac{4}{10}$ I. $\frac{5}{8}$ or $\frac{6}{10}$

D. $\frac{5}{3}$ or $\frac{5}{8}$ J. $\frac{9}{8}$ or $\frac{4}{3}$

E. $\frac{3}{4}$ or $\frac{9}{10}$ K. $\frac{4}{6}$ or $\frac{7}{12}$

F. $\frac{3}{8}$ or $\frac{4}{7}$ L. $\frac{8}{9}$ or $\frac{7}{8}$

FIGURE 15.22 Comparing fractions using reasoning strategies.

students to apply their number sense. Instead, select pairs of fractions that will likely elicit desired comparison strategies. On one day, for example, you might have pairs of fractions with the same numerators. Ask students to tell which is greater and why they think so. Ask them to give an example to convince you. On another day, you might pick fraction pairs in which each fraction is exactly one part away from a whole. Try to build strategies over several days by the strategic choice of fraction pairs.

The use of an area or number-line model may help students who are struggling to reason mentally. Place greater emphasis on students' reasoning and connect it to the visual models.

Using Equivalent Fractions to Compare

Equivalent-fraction concepts can be used in making comparisons. Smith (2002) suggests that the comparison question to ask is, "Which of the following two (or more) fractions is greater, or are they equal?" (p. 9). He points out that this question leaves open the possibility that two fractions that may look different can, in fact, be equal.

In addition to this point, with equivalent-fraction concepts, students can adjust how a fraction looks so that they can use ideas that make sense to them. Burns (1999) describes how fifth graders compared $\frac{6}{8}$ to $\frac{4}{5}$. (You might want to stop for a moment and think how you would compare these fractions.) One child changed the $\frac{4}{5}$ to $\frac{8}{10}$ so that both fractions would be two parts away from the whole and he reasoned from there. Another changed both fractions to a common *numerator* of 12.

Be absolutely certain to revisit the comparison activities and include pairs such as $\frac{8}{12}$ and $\frac{2}{3}$ in which the fractions are equal but do not appear to be.

Estimating with Fractions

Number sense with fractions means that students have some intuitive feel about the relative size of fractions (knowing "about" how big a particular fraction is). As students are deciding about how big something is, they are comparing that fraction to benchmark numbers, such as 0, $\frac{1}{2}$, or 1. As with whole numbers, students are less confident and less capable of estimating than they are at computing exact answers and a focus on estimation can strengthen their understanding of fractions (Clarke & Roche, 2009). Therefore, you need to provide many opportunities for students to estimate with fractions. In daily classroom discussions, ask questions like "About what fraction of your classmates are wearing sweaters?" Or after tallying survey data about a topic like favorite dinner, ask, "About what fraction of our class picked spaghetti?" Activity 15.13 offers examples of visual estimating activities with area and number lines.

(a)

A. 4/5 is larger because it is 1/5 from a whole + 4/9 is close to being 1/2.
B. The denominator is the same but the NUMERATOR of 5/7 is greater, making it a bigger fraction.
C. 4/10 is greater because they are both 1 away from half, but tenths are smaller, therefore 4/10 is closer + bigger.
D. Because 5/3 is greater than whole but 5/8 is an eighth bigger than only half.
E. 9/10 is bigger because they are both 1 away from whole but tenths are smaller, making it closer + larger
F. 4/7 is greater because it's denominator is smaller, + it's numerator is bigger.

(b)

a. $\frac{4}{5}$ is only one away from being a whole. $\frac{4}{9}$ is closer to $\frac{1}{2}$.
B. $\frac{5}{7}$ is greater than $\frac{4}{7}$ because $\frac{5}{7}$ is closer to a whole.
C. $\frac{4}{10}$ is greater than $\frac{3}{8}$ because $\frac{4}{10}$ would have smaller slices.
D. $\frac{5}{3}$ is greater than $\frac{5}{8}$ because $\frac{5}{3}$ is greater than one whole.
E. $\frac{9}{10}$ is greater than $\frac{3}{4}$ because $\frac{9}{10}$ would have smaller slices.
F. $\frac{4}{7}$ is greater than $\frac{3}{8}$ because $\frac{4}{7}$ is closer to a whole.

FIGURE 15.23   Two students explain how they compared the fractions in problems A through F from Figure 15.22.

Activity 15.21

CCSSM: 3.NF.A.1; 3.NF.A.2a, b

About How Much?

Draw a picture like one of those in Figure 15.24 (or prepare some ahead of time for the overhead). Have each student write down a fraction that he or she thinks is a good estimate of the amount shown (or the indicated mark on the number line). Listen to the ideas of several students, and ask them whether a particular estimate is a good one. There is no single correct answer, but estimates should be in the "ballpark." If students have difficulty coming up with an estimate, ask whether they think the amount is closer to 0, $\frac{1}{2}$, or 1. For students with disabilities, you may want to give them a set of cards showing possible options for estimates. Then they can match the card to one of the pictures.

STUDENTS
with
SPECIAL NEEDS

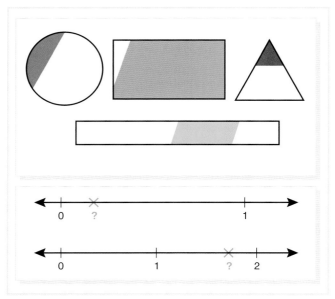

FIGURE 15.24 About how much? Name a fraction for each drawing and explain why you chose that fraction.

The number line is a good model for helping students develop a better understanding for the relative size of a fraction (Petit, Laird, & Marsden, 2010). For example, if students think about where $\frac{3}{20}$ might be by partitioning a number line between 0 and 1, they will see that $\frac{3}{20}$ is close to 0, whereas $\frac{9}{10}$ is quite close to 1. Number lines should also go beyond 1, asking students to tell a nearby benchmark fraction—for example, explaining that $3\frac{3}{7}$ is almost $3\frac{1}{2}$.

After students have experience with visuals, they should continue to reason about the relative size of fractions using mental strategies or creating their own visuals to reason about the fractions.

Finally, comparing fractions can include finding fractions that fall between two given fractions. An important idea in fractions that there is always one more fraction between any two given numbers. Fraction Find is an activity that focuses on this idea. The fractions selected can be varied to meet individual students' needs.

Activity 15.22

CCSSM: 3.NF.A.3d; 4.NF.A.2

Zero, One-Half, or One

On a set of cards, write a collection of 10 to 15 fractions, one per card. A few should be greater than $1\frac{9}{8}$ or $\frac{11}{10}$, with the others ranging from 0 to 1. Let students sort the fractions into three groups: those close to 0, close to $\frac{1}{2}$, and close to 1. For those close to $\frac{1}{2}$, have them decide whether the fraction is more or less than half. The difficulty of this task largely depends on the fractions you select. The first time you try this, use fractions that are very close to the three benchmarks, such as $\frac{1}{20}$, $\frac{53}{100}$, or $\frac{9}{10}$. On subsequent days, mostly use fractions with denominators less than 20. You might include a few fractions that are exactly in between the benchmarks, such as $\frac{2}{8}$ or $\frac{3}{4}$. Ask students to explain how they are using the numerator and denominator to decide. For ELLs, be sure the term **benchmark** is understood and encourage illustrations as well as explanations.

As an extension or alternative to differentiate this activity, ask students to create their own fractions close to each benchmark fraction.

✓ **Complete Self-Check 15.5: Comparing Fractions**

Teaching Considerations for Fraction Concepts

Because the teaching of fractions is so important, and because fractions are often not well understood even by adults, a recap of the big ideas is needed. Hopefully you have recognized that one reason fractions are not well understood is that there is a lot to know about them, from part-whole relationships to division constructs, and understanding includes representing across area, length, and set models and includes contexts that fit these models. Many of these strategies may not have been part of your own learning experience, but they must be part of your teaching experience so that your students can fully understand fractions and be successful in algebra and beyond.

Iterating and partitioning must be a significant aspect of fraction instruction. Equivalence, including comparisons, is a central idea for which students must have sound understanding and skill. Connecting visuals with the procedure and not rushing the algorithm too soon are important aspects of the process.

Clarke and colleagues (2008) and Cramer and Whitney (2010), researchers of fraction teaching and learning, offer research-based recommendations that provide an effective summary of this chapter:

1. Give a greater emphasis to number sense and the meaning of fractions, rather than rote procedures for manipulating them.
2. Provide a variety of models and contexts to represent fractions.
3. Emphasize that fractions are numbers, making extensive use of number lines in representing fractions.
4. Spend whatever time is needed for students to understand equivalences (concretely and symbolically), including flexible naming of fractions.
5. Link fractions to key benchmarks and encourage estimation.

 Complete Self-Check 15.6: Teaching Considerations for Fraction Concepts

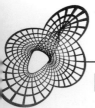

REFLECTIONS ON CHAPTER 15

WRITING TO LEARN

1. What is the goal of activities involving the concept of sharing? When would you implement sharing activities?

2. Give examples of manipulatives and contexts that fall into each of the three categories of fraction models (area, length, and set).

3. What do equivalent fractions mean? Explain and illustrate.

4. How would you teach children to compare fractions?

5. What are two ways to build the conceptual relationship between $\frac{11}{4}$ and $2\frac{3}{4}$?

6. Describe two ways to compare $\frac{5}{12}$ and $\frac{5}{8}$ (not using common denominator or cross-product methods).

FOR DISCUSSION AND EXPLORATION

◆ A common error that students make is to write $\frac{3}{5}$ for the fraction represented here:

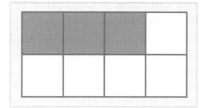

◆ Why do you think they do this? What activity or strategy would you use to try to address this misconception?

◆ Fractions are often named by adults (and depicted in cartoons) as a dreaded math topic. Why do you think this is true? How might your fraction instruction alter this perception for your students?

RESOURCES FOR CHAPTER 15

LITERATURE CONNECTIONS

Context takes students away from rules and encourages them to explore ideas in a more open and meaningful manner. The way that students approach fraction concepts in these contexts may surprise you.

How Many Snails? A Counting Book *Giganti (1988)*

Each page of this book has a similar pattern of questions. For example, the narrator wonders how many clouds there are, how many of them are big and fluffy, and how many of them are big and fluffy and gray. Students can look at the pictures and find the fraction of the objects (e.g., clouds) that have the particular characteristic (big and fluffy). Whitin and Whitin (2006) describe how a class used this book to write their own stories in this pattern and record the fractions for each subset of the objects.

The Doorbell Rang *Hutchins (1986)*

Often used to investigate whole-number operations of multiplication and division, this book is also an excellent early introduction to fractions. The story is a simple tale of two children preparing to share a plate of 12 cookies. Just as they have figured out how to share the cookies, the doorbell rings and more children arrive. You can change the number of children to create a sharing situation that requires fractions (e.g., 5 children).

The Man Who Counted: A Collection of Mathematical Adventures *Tahan (1993)*

This book contains a story, "Beasts of Burden," about a wise mathematician, Beremiz, and the narrator, who are traveling together on one camel. They are asked by three brothers to solve an argument. Their father has left them 35 camels to divide among them: half to one brother, one-third to another, and one-ninth to the third brother. The story provides an excellent context for discussing fractional parts of sets and how fractional parts change as the whole changes. However, if the whole is changed from 35 to, say, 36 or 34, the problem of the indicated shares remains unresolved. The sum of $\frac{1}{2}$, $\frac{1}{3}$, and $\frac{1}{9}$ will never be one whole, no matter how many camels are involved. Bresser (1995) describes three days of activities with his fifth graders.

Apple Fractions *Pallotta (2002)*

This book offers interesting facts about apples while introducing fractions as fair shares (of apples, a healthier option than books that focus on chocolate and cookies!). In addition, the words for fractions are used and connected to fraction symbols, making it a good connection for fractions in grades 1–3.

RECOMMENDED READINGS

Articles

Clarke, D. M., Roche, A., & Mitchell, A. (2008). Ten practical tips for making fractions come alive and make sense. *Mathematics Teaching in the Middle School, 13*(7), 373–380.

Ten excellent tips for teaching fractions are discussed and favorite activities are shared. An excellent overview of teaching fractions.

Flores, A., & Klein, E. (2005). From students' problem-solving strategies to connections in fractions. *Teaching Children Mathematics, 11*(9), 452–457.

This article offers a very realistic view (complete with photos of student work) of how children develop initial fraction concepts and an understanding of notation as they engage in sharing tasks like those described in this chapter.

Books

Burns, M. (2001). *Teaching arithmetic: Lessons for introducing fractions, grades 4–5.* Sausalito, CA: Math Solutions Publications.

This book offers well-designed lessons with lots of details, sample student dialogue, and blackline masters. These are introductory ideas for fraction concepts. Five lessons cover one-half as a benchmark. Assessments are also included.

Lamon, S. (2012). *Teaching fractions and ratios for understanding: Essential content knowledge and instructional strategies.* New York, NY: Taylor & Francis Group.

As the title implies, this book has a wealth of information to help with better understanding fractions and teaching fractions well. Many rich tasks and student work are provided throughout.

McNamara, J., & Shaughnessy, M. M. (2010). *Beyond pizzas and pies: 10 essential strategies for supporting fraction sense (grades 3–5).* Sausalito, CA: Math Solutions Publications.

This book has it all—classroom vignettes, discussion of research on teaching fractions, and many activities, including student work.

Website

Rational Number Project (website housed at the University of Minnesota).

This project offers numerous readings, activities for students, and other materials—a great collection of high quality resources for teaching fractions for understanding.

CHAPTER 16

Developing Fraction Operations

LEARNER OUTCOMES

After reading this chapter and engaging in the embedded activities and reflections, you should be able to:

16.1 Describe a process for teaching fraction operations with understanding.

16.2 Illustrate and explain how to add and subtract fractions with different fraction models.

16.3 Connect whole-number multiplication to fraction multiplication, including connecting fraction multiplication to meaningful contexts.

16.4 Connect whole-number division to fraction division using both measurement and partitive real-life examples.

A fifth-grade student asks, "Why is it when we times 29 times two-ninths that the answer goes down?" (Taber, 2002, p. 67). Although generalizations to fraction computation from whole-number computation can confuse students, they can also help students make sense of operations involving fractions. We must build on students' prior understanding of the whole-number operations to give meaning to fraction computation. This, combined with a firm understanding of fractions (including relative size and equivalence), provides the foundation for understanding fraction computation (Petit et al., 2010; Siegler et al., 2010). Fraction computation is too often taught without any meaning. Instead, fraction operations instruction must help students be able to answer questions like, "When might we need to multiply by fractions?" and "Why do we invert and multiply when dividing fractions?" Students will be able to answer these questions when these big ideas are the focus of teaching operations involving fractions.

BIG IDEAS

◆ The meanings of each operation with fractions are the same as the meanings for the operations with whole numbers. Operations with fractions should begin by applying these same meanings to fractional parts.

◆ For addition and subtraction, the numerator tells the number of parts and the denominator the unit. The parts are added or subtracted.

◆ Repeated addition and area models support development of concepts and algorithms for multiplication of fractions.

◆ Partition and measurement models lead to two different thought processes for division of fractions.

◆ Estimation should be an integral part of computation development to keep students' attention on the meanings of the operations and the expected sizes of the results.

 # Understanding Fraction Operations

Success with fractions, in particular computation, is closely related to success in Algebra I. If students enter formal algebra with a weak understanding of fraction computation (in other words, they have only memorized the four procedures but do not understand them), they are at risk of struggling in algebra, which in turn can limit college and career opportunities. Building such understanding takes time! The Common Core State Standards (CCSSO, 2010) recognize the importance and time commitment required to teach fraction operations well and suggest the following developmental process:

> Grade 4: Adding and subtracting of fractions with like denominators, and multiplication of fractions by whole numbers (p. 27).
>
> Grade 5: Developing fluency with addition and subtraction of fractions, and developing understanding of the multiplication of fractions and of division of fractions in limited cases (unit fractions divided by whole numbers and whole numbers divided by unit fractions) (p. 33).
>
> Grade 6: Completing understanding of division of fractions (p. 39).
>
> Grade 7: Solve real-world and mathematical problems involving the four operations with rational numbers (p. 48).

Teaching fraction operations with understanding may be a significant point of departure from what you may have experienced as a student—learning only one designated (standard) algorithm and not knowing why it worked or when it might be needed. Some teachers may argue that they can't or don't need to devote so much time to fraction operations, that sharing one algorithm is quicker and leads to less confusion for students. This approach does not work! First, none of the algorithms helps students think conceptually about the operations and what they mean. When students follow a procedure they do not understand, they have no means for knowing when to use it and no way of assessing whether their answers make sense. Second, mastery of poorly understood algorithms in the short term is quickly lost, particularly with students who struggle in mathematics. All too soon the different algorithms become a meaningless jumble. Students ask, "Do I need a common denominator, or do I just add or multiply the bottom numbers?" "Which one do you invert, the first or the second number?" Third, students can't adapt to slight changes in the fractions. For example, if a mixed number appears, students don't know how to apply the algorithm. Commit to teaching fraction operations with understanding and avoid these ineffective practices of the past.

A Problem-Based Number-Sense Approach

Students should understand and have access to a variety of ways to solve fraction computation problems. In many cases, a mental or invented strategy can be applied, and a standard algorithm is not needed. Procedural fluency includes being *flexible* in how students approach fraction operations (CCSSO, 2010).

In a report that summarizes findings on fraction learning, researchers suggest that teachers "help students understand why procedures for computations with fractions make sense"

(Siegler et al., 2010). They suggest four steps to effective fraction computation instruction. Each is briefly described here and then elaborated within the discussion of each operation throughout the chapter:

1. *Use contextual tasks.* This should seem like déjà vu, as this recommendation applies to nearly every topic in this book. Huinker (1998) makes an excellent case for using contextual problems and letting students develop their own methods of computation with fractions. Problem contexts need not be elaborate. What you want is a context that fits both the meaning of the operation and the fractions involved.

2. *Explore each operation with a variety of models.* Have students defend their solutions using models, including simple student drawings. Importantly, the models must be connected to the symbolic operations. The visuals will help students make sense of the symbols and related operations, but only when they are explicitly connected through repeated experiences.

3. *Let estimation and invented methods play a big role in the development of strategies.* "Should $2\frac{1}{2} \times \frac{1}{4}$ be more or less than 1? More or less than 2?" Estimation keeps the focus on the meanings of the numbers and the operations, encourages reflective thinking, and helps build number sense with fractions. Can you reason to get an exact answer without using the standard algorithm? One way is to apply the distributive property, splitting the mixed number and multiplying both parts by $\frac{1}{4}$: $(2 \times \frac{1}{4}) + (\frac{1}{2} \times \frac{1}{4})$. Two $\frac{1}{4}$s are $\frac{2}{4}$ or $\frac{1}{2}$ and a half of a fourth is $\frac{1}{8}$. So add an eighth to a half and you have $\frac{5}{8}$.

4. *Address common misconceptions regarding computational procedures.* Students apply their prior knowledge—in this case whole-number computation—to new knowledge. Using whole-number knowledge can be a support to learning. For example, ask, "What does 2×3 mean?" Follow this with "What might $2 \times 3\frac{1}{2}$ mean?" The concepts of each operation are the same, but the procedures are different. This means that whole-number knowledge also leads to errors (e.g., adding denominators when adding fractions). Teachers should present common misconceptions and discuss why some approaches lead to right answers and why others do not (Siegler et al., 2010).

Following this process helps students understand the meaning of fraction operations. Ongoing connections must be made between the contexts, models, and processes. It takes multiple experiences and time for these relationships to be well understood.

Finally, although this chapter is separated by operation, students need opportunities to solve story problems to determine *which* operation fits the story. Too often students are given subtraction story problems on a day they are learning how to subtract, which removes the central question of "Which operation is a match to this story situation?"

⏸ Pause & Reflect

Which operation can be used to solve the story situations in Figure 16.1? ●

CCSS Standards for Mathematical Practice
MP2. Reason abstractly and quantitatively.

Let's look at Jeremy's situations in Figure 16.1 (area situation). In (a) the answer is in the problem—Jeremy at $\frac{1}{8}$ of the cake. In the second case, you must figure out $\frac{1}{8}$ of $\frac{1}{4}$, which is $\frac{1}{32}$ of the

---

a. Jeremy's friends eat $\frac{3}{4}$ of his birthday cake. Jeremy eats $\frac{1}{8}$ of the cake. How much did Jeremy eat?

b. Jeremy's friends eat $\frac{3}{4}$ of his birthday cake. Jeremy ate $\frac{1}{8}$ of the leftover cake. How much of the cake did Jeremy eat?

c. Jeremy's friends ate $\frac{3}{4}$ of one birthday cake and $\frac{1}{8}$ of another cake. How much cake was eaten?

d. Jessica walked $\frac{1}{8}$ of a mile. Her goal is $\frac{3}{4}$ of a mile. How much further to reach her goal?

a. Jessica walks $\frac{1}{8}$ of a mile to school. How many trips to and from school are needed for her to reach her goal of walking $\frac{3}{4}$ of a mile?

FIGURE 16.1 Mixed story problems involving fractions.

cake. In the third case, it is not clear if the cakes are the same-sized whole, so there is no way to solve this problem. If it is adapted to clarify that the cakes are the same-size, then it could be solved using addition. In Jessica's first situation (linear), subtraction is needed to compare how far she has walked to how much she needs to walk. In the latter case, the question is "How many trips?" or "How many eighths are in three-fourths?" This can be solved by counting eighths or by division: $\frac{3}{4} \div \frac{1}{8}$. A story problem like any one of these can be posted as a warm-up problem throughout year with the focus on what is happening in the story and then discussing which operation makes sense (and why).

 Complete Self-Check 16.1: Understanding Fraction Operations

 # Addition and Subtraction

Here we describe how the four steps described earlier are used to develop a strong understanding of addition and subtraction (usually both are taught together). Students should find a variety of ways to solve problems with fractions, and their invented approaches will contribute to the development of the standard algorithms (Huinker, 1998; Lappan & Mouck, 1998; Schifter, Bastable, & Russell, 1999b).

Contextual Examples and Invented Strategies

Just like with whole numbers, invented strategies are important for students because they build on student understanding of fractions and fraction equivalence, and they can eventually be connected to the standard algorithm in such a way that the standard algorithm makes sense. Recall also that the CCSS content standards outline addition situations, which are connected to whole-number operations, but that also should be applied to fraction addition and subtraction. Those situations are join, separate, part-part-whole, and compare (CCSSO, 2010; Chval, Lannin, & Jones, 2013). See Chapter 9 for more on whole-number addition and subtraction situations.

Consider the real-life example of measuring something in inches (sewing, cutting molding for a doorway, hanging a picture, etc.). One inch is one unit or one whole. Measurements include halves, fourths, eighths, and/or sixteenths—fractions that can be added mentally by considering the relationship between the sizes of the parts (e.g., $\frac{1}{2} = \frac{2}{4} = \frac{4}{8} = \frac{8}{16}$). If you can easily find the equivalent fraction (e.g., that one-fourth of an inch is also two-eighths), then you can add like-sized parts mentally.

Contexts should vary and be interesting to students. Here are several good examples. As you read, think about how they differ from each other (beyond the story context):

Jacob ordered 3 pizzas. But before his guests arrived he got hungry and ate $\frac{3}{8}$ of one pizza. How much was left for the party?

On Friday, Lydia ran $1\frac{1}{2}$ miles, on Saturday she ran $2\frac{1}{8}$ miles and on Sunday she ran $2\frac{3}{4}$ miles. How many miles did she run over 3 days?

Sammy gathered $\frac{3}{4}$ pounds of walnuts and Chala gathered $\frac{7}{8}$ pounds. Who gathered the most? How much more?

In measuring the wood needed for a picture frame, Elizabeth figured that she needed two pieces that were $5\frac{1}{4}$ inches and two pieces that were $7\frac{3}{4}$ inches. What length of wood does she need to buy to build her picture frame?

Notice that these story problems (1) incorporate different addition situations (join, compare, etc.); (2) use a mix of area and linear contexts; (3) use a mix of whole numbers, mixed numbers, and fractions; (4) include both addition and subtraction situations; and (5) sometimes involve more than two addends. With each story you use, it is very important to ask students to select a picture or tool to illustrate it and write the symbols that accurately model the situation.

A fifth-grade class was asked to solve the problem of Jacob's pizza in two ways. Many students attempted or correctly used a standard subtraction algorithm for mixed numbers as one method. They used pictures as their second method.

> **FORMATIVE ASSESSMENT Notes.** A simple problem like any of the preceding ones can be used as a formative assessment with an observation checklist. On the checklist would be such concepts as: (1) Can determine a reasonable estimate; (2) Selects and accurately uses a manipulative or picture; (3) Recognizes equivalences between fourths and eighths; and (4) Can connect symbols to a model. Students may be able to illustrate but then not find equivalences, or students may select a circle to illustrate and find it does not help them think about the situation. The next steps in instruction could include explicit attention to connecting the picture to the symbols, or to use other manipulatives or pictures to represent the situation. ■

CCSS Standards for Mathematical Practice
MP4. Model with mathematics.

Models

Recall that there are area, length, and set models for illustrating fractions (see Chapter 15). Set models can be confusing in adding fractions, as they can reinforce the adding of the denominator. Therefore, instruction should initially focus on area and linear models. Visit the companion website for a video that shows how to add and subtract fractions with like denominators using rectangles and number lines, and a video that uses fraction bars to illustrate how to add fractions with unlike denominators.

Area Models. Students seem to have a preference for drawing circles to represent fractions. Perhaps that says something about an overuse of circles. The drawings in Figure 16.2 are not carefully drawn—the partitioning does not show equal parts. However, the students are not making conclusions based on the size of the pieces, but rather drawing to count sections.

Circles can be a highly effective visual for adding and subtracting fractions because they allow students to develop mental images of the sizes of different pieces (fractions) of the circle (Cramer, Wyberg, & Leavitt, 2008). Figure 16.2 shows how students estimate first (including marking a number line) and then explain how they added the fraction using fraction circles.

How you ask students to solve a problem can make a difference in what occurs in the classroom. For example, consider this problem:

Jack and Jill ordered two medium pizzas, one cheese and one pepperoni. Jack ate $\frac{5}{6}$ of a pizza, and Jill ate $\frac{1}{2}$ of a pizza. How much pizza did they eat together?

$$\frac{1}{5} + \frac{1}{10} =$$

Estimate first by putting an **X** on the number line.

Solve with Fraction Circles. Draw pictures of what you did with the circles below.

Record what you did with the circles with symbols.

$$\frac{1}{5} + \frac{1}{10}\left(\frac{2}{10} + \frac{1}{10}\right) = \frac{3}{10}$$

FIGURE 16.2 A student estimates and then adds fractions using a fraction circle.

Source: Cramer, K., Wyberg, T., & Leavitt, S. (2008). "The Role of Representations in Fraction Addition and Subtraction." *Mathematics Teaching in the Middle School, 13*(8), p. 495. Reprinted with permission. Copyright © 2008 by the National Council of Teachers of Mathematics. All rights reserved.

⏸ Pause & Reflect

Try to think of two ways that students might solve this problem without using a common-denominator symbolic approach. ●

If students draw circles as in the earlier example, some will try to fill in the $\frac{1}{6}$ gap in the pizza. Then they will need to figure out how to get $\frac{1}{6}$ from $\frac{1}{2}$. If they can think of $\frac{1}{2}$ as $\frac{3}{6}$, they can use one of the sixths to fill in the gap. Another approach, after drawing the two pizzas, is to notice that there is a half plus two more sixths in the $\frac{5}{6}$ pizza. Put the two halves together to make one whole, and there are $\frac{2}{6}$ more—$1\frac{2}{6}$. These are certainly good solutions that represent the type of reasoning you want to encourage.

There are many other area models that can be used. Pattern blocks, for example, have pieces such that the hexagon can be one whole, the blue parallelogram $\frac{1}{3}$, the green triangle $\frac{1}{6}$, and the red trapezoid $\frac{1}{2}$. Rectangles can be drawn for any fractional value, depending on how it is partitioned. In fact, partitioning a rectangle can be easier and more accurate. The key is to select manipulatives that align with the contexts so that students make connections among the situation, the visual, and the symbols. Activity 16.1 works with a rectangular illustration.

Activity 16.1

CCSS-M: 4.NF.B.3a, d; 5.NF.A.1; 5.NF.A.2

Gardening Together

Give each student a blank piece of paper (or a piece of paper with a large empty rectangle on it). Explain the situation and ask each student to design the garden to illustrate these quantities:

Al, Bill, Carrie, Danielle, Enrique, and Fabio are each given a portion of the school garden for spring planting. Here are the portions:

Al $= \frac{1}{4}$	Bill $= \frac{1}{8}$	Carrie $= \frac{3}{16}$
Danielle $= \frac{1}{16}$	Enrique $= \frac{1}{4}$	Fabio $= \frac{1}{8}$

Then, explain that these students decide to work together and combine their parts. 'What fraction of the garden will each of the following groups have if they combine their portions of the garden? Show your work.'

Bill and Danielle	Al and Carrie
Fabio and Enrique	Carrie, Fabio, and Al

To challenge students, ask them to solve puzzle-type questions like: 'Which two people could work together and have the least amount of the garden? The most? Which combinations of friends could combine to work on one-half of the garden?'

Linear Models. Cuisenaire rods are linear models. Suppose that you had asked the students to solve the Jack and Jill pizza problem but changed the context to submarine sandwiches (linear context), suggesting students use Cuisenaire rods or fraction strips to model the problem. The first decision that must be made is what strip to use as the whole. That decision is not required with a circular model, where the whole is already established as the circle. The whole must be the same for both fractions. In this case, the smallest rod that will work is the 6-rod or the dark green strip, because it can be partitioned into sixths (1 rod/white) and into halves (3 rod/light green). Figure 16.3(a) illustrates a solution.

What if you instead asked students to compare the quantity that Jack and Jill ate? Figure 16.3(b) illustrates lining up the "sandwiches" to compare their lengths. Recall that subtraction can be thought of as "separate" where the total is known and a part is removed, "comparison" as two amounts being compared to find the difference, and "how many more are needed" as starting with a smaller value and asking how much more to get to the higher value (think-addition). This sandwich example is a comparison—be sure to include more than "take away" examples in the stories and examples you create.

An important model for adding or subtracting fractions is the number line (Siegler et al., 2010). One advantage of the number line is that it can be connected to the ruler, which is a familiar context and perhaps the most common real context for adding or subtracting fractions. The number line is also a more challenging model than an area model, because it requires that the student understand $\frac{3}{4}$ as 3 parts of 4, and also as a value between 0 and 1 (Izsák, Tillema, & Tunc-Pekkam, 2008). Using the number line in addition to area representations

Activity 16.2

CCSS-M: 4.NF.B.3a, d; 5.NF.A.1; 5.NF.A.2

ENGLISH
LANGUAGE
LEARNERS

Jumps on the Ruler

Use Jumps on the Ruler Activity Page. Tell students to model the given examples on the ruler. A linear context can be added (length of grass in the yard, hair growing/getting cut), but if students have been doing many contextual tasks, it is important to see whether they can also add and subtract without a context. Use the ruler as a visual and find the results of these three problems without applying the common-denominator algorithm. ELLs may not be as familiar with inches, because most countries measure in metric. In this case, be sure to spend time prior to the activity discussing how the inch is partitioned and/or add labels for fourths as a reminder that it is different from the metric system.

$$\frac{3}{4} + \frac{1}{2} \qquad 4\frac{1}{2} - 3\frac{3}{4} \qquad 4\frac{1}{8} - \frac{1}{2}$$

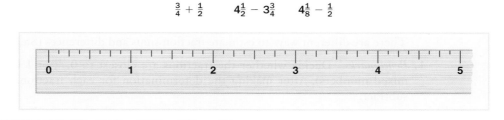

can strengthen student understanding (Clarke et al., 2008; Cramer et al., 2008; Petit et al., 2010).

Encourage students to use different strategies as they compute. In the first problem, students might use 1 as a benchmark (in the way that 10 or 100 is used as a benchmark with whole numbers). They use $\frac{1}{4}$ from the $\frac{1}{2}$ to get to one whole and then have $\frac{1}{4}$ more to add on—so $1\frac{1}{4}$. Similarly, they could take the $\frac{1}{2}$ from the $\frac{3}{4}$ to make a whole with the $\frac{1}{2}$ and then add on the $\frac{1}{4}$, or they might just know that $\frac{1}{2}$ is $\frac{2}{4}$ and then count to get $\frac{5}{4}$ (or $1\frac{1}{4}$). Compare the two subtraction problems and picture them on the number line. The first subtraction situation has two fractions close together. It is easier to think about this as a difference situation rather than a take-away situation. In other words, "What is the difference between $4\frac{1}{2}$ and $3\frac{3}{4}$?" The third problem lends itself to a take-away interpretation.

The selected context and quantities can be adapted to steer students toward specific strategies (difference or take-away). For example, consider two ways to pose the subtraction problem:

1. Desmond runs $2\frac{1}{2}$ miles a day. If he has just passed the $1\frac{1}{4}$ mile marker, how far does he still need to go?
2. Desmond is at mile marker $2\frac{1}{2}$, and James is at mile marker $1\frac{1}{4}$. How much farther has Desmond gone?

With many experiences with area and linear models, students are ready to connect those visuals to algorithms.

TECHNOLOGY Note. Conceptua Fractions, developed by Conceptua Math has free tools that help students explore various fraction concepts using area, set, and length models (including the number line). Some of the newer tools allow students to explore multiplication, measurement division, the commutative and distributive properties of multiplication, and division using equal shares. ■

(a) $\dfrac{5}{6} + \dfrac{1}{2}$

Find a strip for a whole that allows both fractions to be modeled.

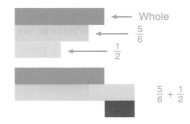

The sum is 1 whole and a red rod more than a whole. A red is $\frac{1}{3}$ of a dark green. So $\frac{5}{6} + \frac{1}{2} = 1\frac{1}{3}$.

(b) $\dfrac{5}{6} - \dfrac{1}{2}$

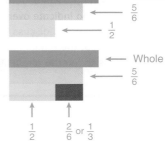

Compare the lengths of the two fractions. $\frac{5}{6}$ is $\frac{2}{6}$ longer than $\frac{1}{2}$, so the difference is $\frac{2}{6}$ or $\frac{1}{3}$.

FIGURE 16.3 Using rods to add and subtract fractions.

Estimation and Informal Methods

Do you think students are better at computing with fractions or estimating? If you said computing, you are correct! Think about how you would answer the following:

Estimate the answer to $\frac{12}{13} + \frac{7}{8}$. You will not have time to solve the problem using paper and pencil.

Nearly two-thirds of middle school students could find the exact answer to this problem, but only one-fourth could correctly estimate (Reys, 1998). Notice that computing this answer requires finding the common denominator of thirteenths and eighths, but to estimate requires no computation whatsoever—only a realization that each fraction is close to 1, so the answer is close to 2.

There are different ways to estimate fraction sums and differences (Siegler et al., 2010):

1. *Benchmarks.* Decide whether the fractions are closest to 0, $\frac{1}{2}$, or 1 (or 3, $3\frac{1}{2}$, or 4 for mixed numbers). After making the determination for each fraction, mentally add or subtract.

Example: $\frac{7}{8} + \frac{1}{10}$. Think, "$\frac{7}{8}$ is close to 1, $\frac{1}{10}$ is close to 0, the sum is about 1 + 0 or close to 1."

Example: $5\frac{1}{3} \div \frac{3}{5}$. Think, "$5\frac{1}{3}$ is close to five, and $\frac{3}{5}$ is close to $\frac{1}{2}$. How many halves in five? Ten."

---

2. *Relative size of unit fractions.* Decide how big the fraction is, based on its unit (denominator), and apply this information to adding or subtracting.

Example: $\frac{7}{8} + \frac{1}{10}$. Think, "$\frac{7}{8}$ is just $\frac{1}{8}$ away from a whole (one) and $\frac{1}{8}$ is close to (but bigger than) $\frac{1}{10}$, so the sum will be close to, but less than, 1."

Example: $\frac{1}{3} \times 3\frac{4}{5}$. Think, "I need a third of this value. A third of 3 is 1 and $\frac{1}{3}$ of $\frac{4}{5}$ is going to be just over $\frac{1}{5}$ (since there are four parts), so about $1\frac{1}{5}$."

The following activity can be done frequently as a warm-up or be a focus activity for a full lesson.

Activity 16.3
CCSS-M: 4.NF.B.3a; 5.NF.A.2

Over or Under 1

Tell students that they are going to estimate a sum or difference of two fractions. They are to decide only whether the exact answer is more than 1 or less than 1. Project a sum or difference for no more than 10 seconds. Then hide or remove it. Ask students to write down on paper or a mini whiteboard their choice of "over" or "under" one. You can also ask students to show you "thumbs up" and "thumbs down" to indicate over or under. Do several problems. (Figure 16.4 offers several possible problems.) Then return to each problem and discuss how students decided on their estimates. Students with disabilities should use a number line to try to think about the amounts. They may also need more than 10 seconds to think about the amounts. During the discussion, ask students to refer to a real-life example, a number line, or an area model (e.g., rectangular region) to justify their decision.

Over time, Activity 16.3 can include tasks that are more challenging, or it can be differentiated with different groups of students working on different over/under values. Consider the following variations:

- Use a target answer that is different from 1. For example, estimate more or less than $\frac{1}{2}$, $1\frac{1}{2}$, 2, or 3.
- Adapt to multiplication or division problems.

- Choose fraction pairs that are both less than 1 or both greater than 1. Estimate sums or differences to the nearest half.
- Ask students to create equations that are slightly less than or slightly more than 1 (or other values). They can trade equations with other students, who in turn need to decide whether the sum or difference is over 1 or under 1 (or other value).

❚❚ Pause & Reflect

Test your own estimation skills with the sample problems in Figure 16.4. Look at each computation for only about 10 seconds and write down an estimate. After writing down all six of your estimates, look at the problems and decide whether your estimate is higher or lower than the actual computation. ●

Estimate

1. $\frac{1}{8} + \frac{4}{5}$

2. $\frac{9}{10} + \frac{7}{8}$

3. $\frac{3}{5} + \frac{3}{4} + \frac{1}{8}$

4. $\frac{3}{4} - \frac{1}{3}$

5. $\frac{11}{12} - \frac{3}{4}$

6. $1\frac{1}{2} - \frac{9}{10}$

Number your papers 1 to 6. Write only answers.

Estimate!
   Use whole numbers
   and benchmark fractions.

FIGURE 16.4   Example of fraction estimation expressions.

An engaging estimation activity is shared in Activity 16.4, based on Fung and Latulippe (2010) and Hynes (1996).

Activity 16.4   CCSS-M: 4.NF.B.3a; 5.NF.A.2

Cups of Milk

Ask students to fill in the missing numerator and denominator with something that makes the equation approximately true. They cannot use any of the numbers already in the problem. The context of milk can help students reason about the quantities. Four examples are provided here:

$$\frac{\square}{4} + \frac{3}{\square} \approx \frac{1}{2} \qquad \frac{3}{\square} + \frac{\square}{4} \leq \frac{1}{2}$$

$$\frac{\square}{2} - \frac{2}{\square} > 2 \qquad \frac{1}{\square} - \frac{\square}{2} \approx 1$$

Keep in mind that these are estimates, so many values are possible. In some cases, however, there are no solutions (can you spot the impossible one in the list here?).

Developing the Algorithms

The algorithms develop side by side with the visuals and situations. The way fractions are notated can lead to errors when students compute fractions in isolation. The way to prevent this is to ensure students are connecting fraction symbols with contexts and visuals. As discussed in Chapter 15, having a strong conceptual foundation of equivalence is critical to operations of fractions. Students who have a level of fluency in moving between $\frac{1}{2}, \frac{2}{4}, \frac{4}{8},$ and $\frac{8}{16}$ or $\frac{3}{4}, \frac{6}{8},$ and $\frac{12}{16}$ can adjust the fractions as needed to add or subtract fractions. For example, ask students to think about how far a person has walked, if the following equation represents their walking: $\frac{3}{8} + \frac{1}{2}$. Given sufficient concrete experiences, a student should be able to readily trade out one-half for four-eighths to solve:

$$\frac{3}{8} + \frac{1}{2} = \frac{3}{8} + \frac{4}{8} = \frac{7}{8}$$

Like Denominators. Fraction addition and subtraction begin with situations using like denominators. In the Common Core State Standards (CCSSO, 2010), this is suggested for grade 4. When working on adding with like denominators, however, it is important to be sure that students are focusing on the key idea—the units are the same, so they can be combined (Mack, 2004). This is the iteration idea discussed in Chapter 15. In other words, the problem $\frac{3}{4} + \frac{2}{4}$ is asking, "How many fourths altogether?" The equation $3\frac{7}{8} - 1\frac{3}{8}$ is counting back (taking away) eighths or finding the number of eighths between the two quantities (comparing). Iteration connects fraction operations to whole-number operations and explains why the denominator stays the same.

FORMATIVE ASSESSMENT Notes. The ease with which students can or cannot add like-denominator fractions should be viewed as an important concept assessment before moving students to an algorithm. A diagnostic interview that asks students to (1) explain the meaning of the numerators and denominators, (2) connect the addition problems to a situation, and (3) illustrate with a model can help you determine whether they have a deep understanding of the numerator and denominator. If student responses are rule oriented and not grounded in understanding parts and wholes, then encourage students to focus on the meaning of the fractions by emphasizing the unit: "Three *fifths* plus one *fifth* is how many *fifths*?" This must be well understood before moving to adding with unlike denominators. Otherwise, any further symbolic development will almost certainly be without understanding. ■

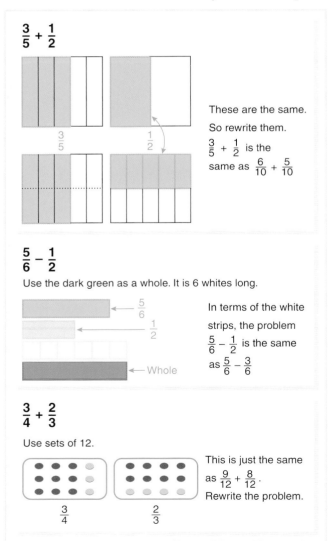

FIGURE 16.5 Illustrating common denominators with different tools.

Unlike Denominators. Begin adding and subtracting fractions with unlike denominators with tasks where only one fraction needs to be changed, such as $\frac{5}{8} + \frac{1}{4}$. A situation might be amount of pizza eaten. Ask students to estimate whether they think one or more pizzas were eaten altogether. Then, invite students to draw or select a tool to illustrate a solution, recording fractions to go with their drawings or manipulatives. As students explain how they solved it, write equivalent expressions on the board and ask if they are equal:

$$\frac{5}{8} + \frac{1}{4} = \frac{5}{8} + \frac{2}{8}$$

Continue with examples in which both fractions need to be changed—for example, $\frac{2}{3} + \frac{1}{4}$ (or $\frac{2}{3} - \frac{1}{4}$), still using contexts, visuals, and student explanations. In the discussion of student solutions, focus attention on the idea of *rewriting an equivalent problem* to make it possible to add or subtract *equal-sized parts*. If students express doubt about the equivalence of the two problems ("Is $\frac{8}{12} + \frac{3}{12}$ really the answer to $\frac{2}{3} + \frac{1}{4}$?"), that should be a cue that the concept of equivalent fractions is not well understood, and more experience using examples, visuals, or concrete tools is needed.

The three examples in Figure 16.5 show how tools might be used. Note that each tool requires students to think about the size of a whole that can be partitioned into the units of both fractions (e.g., fifths and halves require tenths).

As students continue to explore solutions to sums and differences of fractions, the equations may be given without situations or visuals, but students should be able to create stories or visuals for any problem.

As you may recall in the discussion of whole numbers and in algebra, it is important to not always have the result unknown. The parts can also be unknown. This helps students relate addition to subtraction. Any of the stories provided earlier can be adapted to have a part unknown. For example:

Sammy gathered some walnuts and Chala gathered $\frac{7}{8}$ pounds. Together they gathered $1\frac{1}{2}$ pounds. How much did Sammy gather?

Activity 16.5 provides an engaging opportunity to reason about fractions when the result is known.

Activity 16.5
CCSS-M: 4.NF.B.3a; 5.NF.A.2

Can You Make It True?

Use the Can You Make It True? **Activity Page, which includes a list of equations with missing values, such as the ones here:**

$$\frac{\square}{6} + \frac{\square}{3} = 1 \text{ and } \frac{4}{\square} - \frac{\square}{2} = \frac{1}{2}$$

To begin, post one example and invite students to share possible whole number solutions. If they have found one way, ask "Is there more than one way to make that equation true?" Include examples that are impossible for whole number missing values, such as:

$$\frac{1}{\square} - \frac{1}{\square} = 1$$

As students work, ask them to explain the reasoning they are using. Encourage students to use visuals (e.g., number line or fraction pieces) to support their thinking.

Equations such as the ones in Activity 16.5 require reasoning and thinking about the role of the numerator and denominator, as well as reinforcement of why the numerators are added and the denominators are not.

Are Common Denominators "Required"? No. Teachers and websites often explain, "To add or subtract fractions, you have to find common denominators." Using their own invented strategies, students will see that many correct solutions are found without ever finding a common denominator (Taber, 2009). Consider these expressions:

$$\frac{3}{4} + \frac{1}{8} \qquad \frac{1}{2} - \frac{1}{8} \qquad \frac{2}{3} + \frac{1}{2} \qquad 1\frac{1}{2} - \frac{3}{4} \qquad 1\frac{2}{3} + \frac{3}{4}$$

Working with the ways different fractional parts are related one to another often provides solutions without common denominators. For example, halves, fourths, and eighths are easily related because $\frac{1}{8}$ is half of $\frac{1}{4}$ and $\frac{1}{4}$ is half of $\frac{1}{2}$.

As noted, the number line is also a tool that can be used to mentally solve addition and subtraction situations without finding a common denominator. Students instead may start by finding one fraction on the number line or ruler and then "jump" the value of the other fraction. For example, in $3\frac{1}{4} - 1\frac{1}{2}$, students can find $3\frac{1}{4}$, jump down one to $2\frac{1}{4}$, and then jump $\frac{1}{2}$, which takes them to $1\frac{3}{4}$.

Fractions Greater Than One

A separate algorithm for mixed numbers in addition and subtraction is not necessary even though mixed numbers are often treated as separate topics in traditional textbooks and in some lists of objectives (note that mixed numbers have been integrated throughout the previous discussion). Include mixed numbers in all of your stories and examples and encourage students to solve them in ways that make sense to them. Students tend to naturally add or subtract the whole numbers and then the fractions. Sometimes this is all that needs to be done, but in other cases, regrouping across the whole number and fraction is needed. In subtraction, this happens when the second fraction is larger than the first, and it occurs in addition when the answer of the fraction sum is more than 1.

Dealing with the whole numbers first makes sense. Consider this problem: You had $5\frac{1}{8}$ yards of fabric and used $3\frac{5}{8}$ yards. How much do you have left? What equation describes this situation? $5\frac{1}{8} - 3\frac{5}{8}$. It is a linear situation, so a number line is a good way to think about this problem. Given the context students are likely to subtract 3, leaving $2\frac{1}{8}$, and then need to subtract $\frac{5}{8}$. Students may count down (iterate), stopping at $1\frac{1}{2}$. Another approach is to take $\frac{5}{8}$ from the whole part, 2, leaving $1\frac{3}{8}$, and then add the $\frac{1}{8}$ back on to get $1\frac{4}{8}$ or $1\frac{1}{2}$.

The "standard" algorithm, which is not as intuitive, is to trade one of the wholes for $\frac{8}{8}$, add it to the $\frac{1}{8}$ to get $1\frac{9}{8}$ and then take away $\frac{5}{8}$.

Students tend to make many errors when such regrouping is needed. An excellent alternative is to change the mixed numbers to single, or improper, fractions. You may have been taught that this was the process used for multiplication, but that is part of the "rules without reason" approach of having one way to do one procedure. Let's revisit $5\frac{1}{8} - 3\frac{5}{8}$. This can be rewritten as $\frac{41}{8} - \frac{29}{8}$. (See Chapter 15 for conceptual ways for helping students do this.) Because 41 – 29 is 12, the solution is $\frac{12}{8}$ or $1\frac{1}{2}$. This is certainly efficient and will always work. Provide both options to students and encourage them to decide which strategy works the best in different situations. To develop mathematically proficient students, they must pick the strategy that is most efficient given the situation or the numbers in the problem.

TECHNOLOGY Note. The National Library of Virtual Manipulatives (NLVM) has three different activities that can help reinforce fraction addition and subtraction across different models:

Fractions—Adding: Two fractions and an area model for each are given. The user must find a common denominator to rename and add the fractions.

Fraction Bars: This applet places bars over a number line on which the step size can be adjusted, providing a flexible model that can be used to illustrate addition and subtraction.

Diffy: This puzzle asks you to find the differences between the numbers on the corners of a square, working to a desired difference in the center. This activity encourages students to consider equivalent forms of fractions to solve the puzzle. ■

Addressing Misconceptions

It is important to explicitly talk about common misconceptions with fraction operations because students naturally overgeneralize what they know about whole-number operations.

Adding Both Numerators and Denominators. The most common error in adding fractions is to add both numerators and denominators. Consider the following task:

Ms. Rodriguez baked a pan of brownies for the bake sale and cut the brownies into 8 equal-sized parts. In the morning, three of the brownies were sold; in the afternoon, two more were sold. What fractional part of the brownies had been sold? What fractional part is still for sale?

Students solving this task are able to effectively draw a rectangle partitioned into eighths and are able to shade $\frac{3}{8}$ and $\frac{2}{8}$, as shown here.

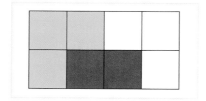

However, about half of students will write $\frac{3}{8} + \frac{2}{8} = \frac{5}{16}$, even after drawing the model correctly. And they won't seem to be bothered that the two answers ($\frac{5}{8}$ and $\frac{5}{16}$) are different (Bamberger et al., 2010). In such a case, ask students to decide whether both answers could be right. Ask them to defend which is right and why the other answer is not right. You cannot just tell students which is right—the key is for students to connect the situation to the fraction symbols.

Even after students have more experience with adding and subtracting, they can forget about the meaning of the denominator, so it is important to challenge potential misconceptions. For example, one teacher asked her fifth graders if the following were correct: $\frac{3}{8} + \frac{2}{8} = \frac{5}{16}$. A student correctly replied, "No, because they are eighths (*holds up one-eighth of a fraction circle*). If you put them together you still have eighths (*shows this with the fraction circles*). See, you didn't make them into sixteenths when you put them together. They're still eighths" (Mack, 2004, p. 229).

Failing to Find Common Denominators. Less common, but still prevalent, is the tendency to just ignore the denominator and add the numerators (Siegler et al., 2010). For example, $\frac{4}{5} + \frac{4}{10} = \frac{8}{10}$. This is an indication that students do not understand that the different denominators indicate different-sized pieces. Using a number line or fraction strip, where students must pay attention to the relative size of the fraction, can help develop a stronger understanding of the role of the denominator in adding. NCTM's Illuminations has a useful lesson on "Making and Using Fraction Strips." Also, the online FractionStrip tool is a digital version of physical fractions strips.

Difficulty Finding Common Multiples. Many students have trouble finding common denominators because they are not able to quickly come up with common multiples of the denominators. This skill requires having a good command of multiplication facts. Activity 16.6 is aimed at the skill of finding least common multiples or common denominators. Least common denominators are preferred because the computation is more manageable with smaller numbers, but *any* common denominator will work, whether it is the smallest or not. As students' skills improve, they will see that finding the smallest multiple is more efficient.

Activity 16.6   CCSS-M: 4.OA.B.4; 5.NF.A.1

Common Multiple Flash Cards

Make flash cards with pairs of numbers that are potential denominators. Most should be less than 12 (see Figure 16.6). Place students in partners and give them a deck of cards. On a student's turn, he or she turns over a card and states a common multiple (e.g., for 6 and 8, a student might suggest 48). The partner gets a chance to suggest a smaller common multiple (e.g., 24). The student suggesting the least common multiple (LCM) gets to keep the card. Be sure to include pairs that are prime, such as 9 and 5; pairs in which one is a multiple of the other, such as 2 and 8; and pairs that have a common divisor, such as 8 and 12. Start students with disabilities with the card where one member of the pair is a multiple of the other. Color code the cards so that they are easily located.

STUDENTS
with
SPECIAL NEEDS

A context can help in finding common multiples. The activity Interference engages students in determining how often two orbiting satellites will cross paths.

Difficulty with Mixed Numbers. Too often, instruction with mixed numbers is not well integrated into fraction instruction, and therefore students find these values particularly troubling. Here are three misconceptions described in the research (Petit et al., 2010; Siegler et al., 2010; Spangler, 2011):

1. When given a problem like $3\frac{1}{4} - 1\frac{3}{8}$, students subtract the smaller fraction from the larger ($\frac{3}{8} - \frac{1}{4}$). Though this occurs with whole-number subtraction, it is more prevalent with mixed numbers.

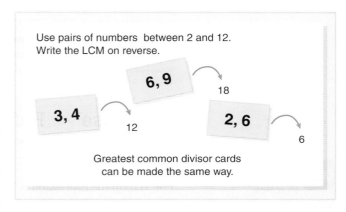

Use pairs of numbers between 2 and 12. Write the LCM on reverse.

6, 9   18

3, 4   12

2, 6   6

Greatest common divisor cards can be made the same way.

FIGURE 16.6 Least common multiple (LCM) flash cards.

2. When given a problem like $4 - \frac{7}{8}$, students don't know what to do with the fact that one number is not a fraction. They will tend to place an 8 under the $4(\frac{4}{8} - \frac{7}{8})$ in order to find a solution.

3. When given a problem like $14\frac{1}{2} - 3\frac{1}{8}$, students focus only on the whole-number aspect of the problem and don't know what to do with the fractional part.

How do you prevent these misconceptions? Include more mixed numbers with fractions. Use models and contexts. And, importantly, take on these misconceptions by making them part of public discussions.

 Complete Self-Check 16.2: Addition and Subtraction

 Multiplication

Can you think of a situation that requires using multiplication of whole numbers? Multiplication of fractions? For many, the answer to the first is yes but to the second is no. This is a result of not knowing what fraction multiplication is. As you will see in the sections that follow, the foundational ideas of iterating (counting) fractional parts and partitioning are at the heart of understanding multiplication of fractions. If students have not had sufficient experiences with these two ideas, you must find ways to engage them in iterating and partitioning so that they are ready to apply these ideas to multiplication.

Contextual Examples and Models

When working with whole numbers, we would say that 3×5 means "3 sets of 5" (equal sets) or "3 rows of 5" (area or array) or "5 three times" (number line). Notice the set, area, and linear models fitting with the multiplication structures. Different models must be used and aligned with contexts so that students get a comprehensive understanding of multiplication of fractions. The story problems that you use to pose multiplication tasks to students need not be elaborate, but it is important to think about the numbers and contexts that you use in the problems. A possible progression of problem difficulty is developed in the sections that follow.

Multiply a Fraction by a Whole Number. These problems look like this: $5 \times \frac{1}{2}$, $6 \times \frac{1}{8}$, $10 \times \frac{3}{4}$, and $3 \times 2\frac{1}{3}$ and in the CCSS-M are introduced in grade 4. Look again at the wording of this subsection—because the word *fraction* preceded *whole number*, there is sometimes confusion over what this means, but to multiply a fraction by a whole number means examples such as the ones provided here. Students' first experiences should be of this type because conceptually it is a close fit to multiplication of whole numbers using the idea of equal sets. Consider the following two situations:

Marvin ate 3 pounds of meat every day. How much meat did Marvin eat in one week?

Murphy ate $\frac{1}{3}$ pounds of meat every day. How much meat did Murphy eat in one week?

 Pause & Reflect

What expressions represent each situation? What reasoning strategies would you use to solve each? ●

CCSS **Standards for Mathematical Practice**
MP2. Reason abstractly and quantitatively.

For Marvin the expression is 7 (groups of) 3 pounds, or 7×3. You can solve this by skip counting $3 + 3 + 3 + 3 + 3 + 3 + 3$ to get the answer of 21 pounds (but if you know your facts, you just *multiplied*). Murphy similarly ate $7 \times \frac{1}{3}$ pounds, and it can similarly be solved by skip counting, this time by his portion size of thirds: $\frac{1}{3} + \frac{1}{3} + \frac{1}{3} + \frac{1}{3} + \frac{1}{3} + \frac{1}{3} + \frac{1}{3}$, which in total is seven-thirds $\left(\frac{7}{3}\right)$. Notice the skip counting, called *iterating*, is the meaning behind a whole number times a fraction.

Activity 16.7

CCSS-M: 4.NF.B.4a, b

Hexagon Wholes

ENGLISH LANGUAGE LEARNERS

Distribute a set of hexagons to students. To start, designate the yellow hexagon as the whole. Ask students the fractional value of the green, blue, and red pieces. Ask students to find how many wholes for different quantities:

5 blue pieces?　　10 green pieces?

Ask students to write a fraction equation to represent their problem. For the two examples here:

$$5 \times \frac{1}{3} = 1\frac{2}{3} \text{ or } \frac{5}{3} \qquad 10 \times \frac{1}{6} = \frac{10}{6} \text{ or } 1\frac{4}{6} \text{ or } 1\frac{2}{3}$$

Create a variety of tasks. Other wholes can be used—for example, using two hexagons as one whole to vary the types of fractions that can be used. ELLs may benefit from having the shapes labeled with their names and the fraction symbols written with fraction words (e.g., $\frac{1}{6}$ is "one-sixth")

Circular Fraction Pieces can be used in addition to or instead of pattern blocks to do Activity 16.7. Notice that in the answers given, the fraction (improper fraction) shows a pattern that can be generalized as $a \times \frac{1}{b} = \frac{a}{b}$, an important pattern for students to discover from having explored many examples that follow this pattern. Linear examples are also important to include. Jumps on the Ruler (see Activity 16.2) can be readily adapted to be jumps of equal length.

Multiply a Whole Number by a Fraction. Students' second experiences with multiplication should involve finding fractions of whole numbers. Although multiplication is commutative, the thinking involved in this type of multiplication involves partitioning (not iterating). The fraction construct is fraction as operator (Lamon, 2012). Examples look like this: $\frac{1}{2} \times 8, \frac{1}{2} \times 5, \frac{1}{5} \times 8, \frac{3}{4} \times 24$, and $2\frac{1}{2} \times 3$. Notice this is a compare or *scaling* situation (think of creating a scale drawing that is $\frac{1}{5}$ of the actual size). In the CCSS-M, this type of fraction multiplication is introduced in grade 5. Visit the companion website to watch a video that provides examples and illustrations.

These stories can be paired with manipulatives to help students understand this type of fraction operation:

1. The walk from school to the public library takes 25 minutes. When Anna asked her mom how far they had gone, her mom said that they had gone $\frac{1}{2}$ of the way. How many minutes have they walked? (Assume a constant walking rate.)
2. There are 15 cars in Michael's Matchbox car collection. Two-thirds of the cars are red. How many red cars does Michael have?

For a full lesson using multiplication stories, use Expanded Lesson: Multiplication-of-Fractions Stories.

Notice that the thinking in these situations is partitioning (finding a parts of the whole). How might students think through each problem? For problem 2, students might partition 15 into three groups (or partition a line into three parts) and then see how many are in two parts. Recording this in symbols ($\frac{2}{3}$ of 15) gives the following result: $15 \div 3 \times 2$.

Counters (a set model) is an effective tool for finding parts of a whole. Recall that in Chapter 15 two-color counters were used to develop the concept of partitioning and iterating with prompts such as, "If the whole is 45, how much is $\frac{1}{5}$ of the whole?" and "If the whole is 24, what is $\frac{3}{8}$ of the whole?" These can be slightly adapted to make the connection to multiplication more explicit by having students write the equations that match the question. Counting Counters: Fraction of a Whole Activity Pages 1 and 2 are designed to do this.

An area model, such a rectangle, provides an excellent visual tool for illustrating and making generalizations (Witherspoon, 2014), as can be seen in Activity 16.8.

Activity 16.8

CCSS-M: 5.NF.B.4a, b

STUDENTS with SPECIAL NEEDS

How Big Is the Banner?

To begin, explain to (or show) students that you have a roll of paper you will be using to make banners. The roll is one foot wide (you can also use one yard or one meter) and you are going to roll out several feet. The first banner you cut is 1 ft. by 6 ft.:

Ask students, "What is the area of this banner?" ($1 \times 6 = 6$ square feet). You can ask additional questions of banners of other lengths (with a width of 1 foot).

Then, explain to students that you want to cut the banners long-wise. Ask students to use this rectangle to show banners that are $\frac{1}{2}$ ft. $\times$ 6 ft. Then ask them to tell you the square feet of the new banner:

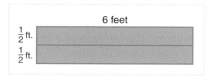

Students fill in the strips to show that there are 3 feet in each half-strip:

Repeat the process by asking how big the banners will be if the 6 feet is is cut into three strips (one-third ft. each). Repeat with fourths (note that the area for one-fourth of 6 is $1\frac{1}{2}$ ft.). After exploring this 6-foot banner, use a variety of lengths (e.g., **12 feet, 15 feet**) and various widths (e.g., halves, fourths, thirds). For thirds and fourths, ask, "What if the banner was one-fourth foot wide? Three-fourths wide?" Encourage students to notice patterns that help them determine the area of the banners, considering how the banner is scaled based on the values involved in the problem. For students with disabilities or students who benefit from using physical materials, you can cut out paper strips in advance and have them fold the paper to show the partitions.

FORMATIVE ASSESSMENT Notes. These "fraction of a whole" problems can be used as a performance assessment. From their written solutions and from what you observe as students work, record your insights on a checklist about which of these models (area, linear, and set) are easy or challenging for different learners. This will provide valuable insights in terms of planning instruction that builds on student strengths, because you can select examples and models that make sense to students. Also, you can identify which models need more attention so that they are better understood. ■

Fractions of Fractions—No Subdivisions. Once students have had experiences with wholes of fractions (15 groups of $\frac{2}{3}$) and fractions of a whole ($\frac{2}{3}$ of 15), a next step is to introduce fraction of a fraction. Be careful to pick tasks where no additional partitioning is required. See if you can mentally answer the next three problems:

You have $\frac{3}{4}$ of a pizza left. If you give $\frac{1}{3}$ of the leftover pizza to your brother, how much of a whole pizza will your brother get?

Someone ate $\frac{1}{10}$ of the loaf of bread, leaving $\frac{9}{10}$. If you use $\frac{2}{3}$ of what is left of the loaf to make French toast, how much of a whole loaf will you have used?

Gloria used $2\frac{1}{2}$ tubes of blue paint to paint the sky in her picture. Each tube holds $\frac{4}{5}$ ounce of paint. How many ounces of blue paint did Gloria use?

These values do not need to be subdivided: The first problem is $\frac{1}{3}$ of three things, the second is $\frac{2}{3}$ of nine things, and the last is $2\frac{1}{2}$ of four things. Figure 16.7 shows how problems of this type might be modeled. However, it is important for students to model and solve these problems in their own way, using whatever models or drawings they choose as long as they can explain their reasoning. In fact, there is more than one way to partition. In $\frac{3}{4} \times \frac{1}{3}$, for example, you can find one-third of the three-fourths (as in Figure 16.7), or you could find $\frac{1}{3}$ of *each* fourth and then combine the pieces (Izsák, 2008).

Subdividing the Unit Parts. When the pieces must be subdivided into smaller unit parts, the problems become more challenging.

Zack had $\frac{2}{3}$ of the lawn left to cut. After lunch, he cut $\frac{3}{4}$ of the lawn he had left. How much of the whole lawn did Zack cut after lunch?

The zookeeper had a huge bottle of the animals' favorite liquid treat, Zoo Cola. The monkey drank $\frac{1}{5}$ of the bottle. The zebra drank $\frac{2}{3}$ of what was left. How much of the bottle of Zoo Cola did the zebra drink?

Task	Finding the starting amount	Showing the fraction of the starting amount	Solution
Pizza Find $\frac{1}{3}$ of $\frac{3}{4}$ (of a pizza) or $\frac{1}{3} \times \frac{3}{4}$	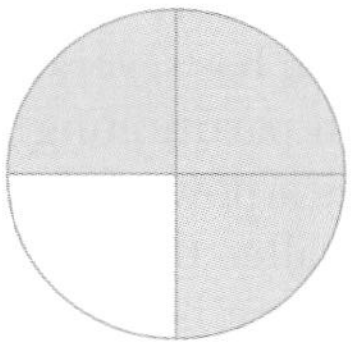	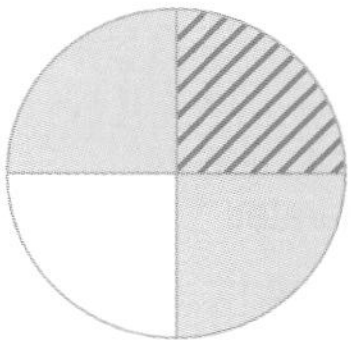	$\frac{1}{3}$ of the $\frac{3}{4}$ is $\frac{1}{4}$ of the original pizza. $\frac{1}{3} \times \frac{3}{4} = \frac{1}{4}$
Bread Find $\frac{2}{3}$ of $\frac{9}{10}$ (of a loaf of bread) or $\frac{2}{3} \times \frac{9}{10}$	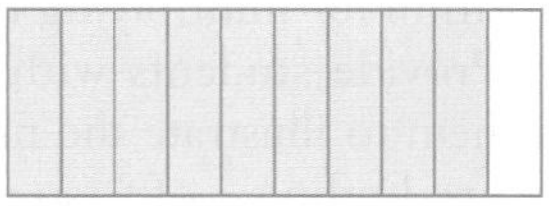	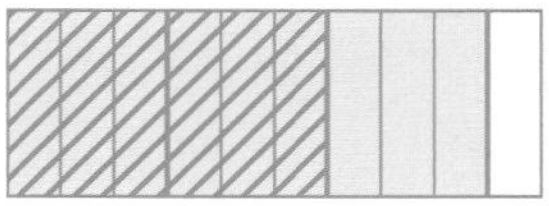	$\frac{2}{3}$ of the $\frac{9}{10}$ is 6 slices of the loaf or $\frac{6}{10}$ of the whole. $\frac{2}{3} \times \frac{9}{10} = \frac{6}{10}$
Paint Find $2\frac{1}{2}$ of $\frac{4}{5}$ (ounces of paint) or $2\frac{1}{2} \times \frac{4}{5}$		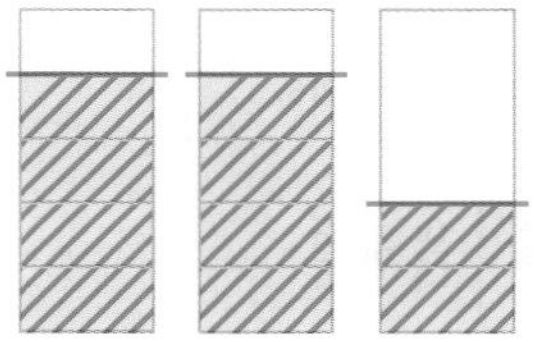	$2\frac{1}{2}$ of the $\frac{4}{5}$ is $\frac{4}{5} + \frac{4}{5} + \frac{2}{5} = \frac{10}{5}$

FIGURE 16.7   Connecting representation to the procedure for three problems involving multiplication.

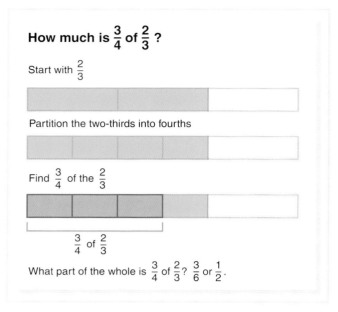

How much is $\frac{3}{4}$ of $\frac{2}{3}$?

Start with $\frac{2}{3}$

Partition the two-thirds into fourths

Find $\frac{3}{4}$ of the $\frac{2}{3}$

$\frac{3}{4}$ of $\frac{2}{3}$

What part of the whole is $\frac{3}{4}$ of $\frac{2}{3}$? $\frac{3}{6}$ or $\frac{1}{2}$.

FIGURE 16.8 Solutions to a multiplication problem when the parts must be subdivided.

Pause & Reflect

Pause for a moment and figure out how you would solve each of these problems. Draw pictures to help you, but do not use a computational algorithm. ●

In Zack's lawn problem, it is necessary to find fourths of two things, the two-*thirds* of the grass left to cut. In the Zoo Cola problem, you need thirds of four things, the four-*fifths* of the cola that remains. Again, the concepts of the top number counting and the bottom number naming what is counted play an important role. Figure 16.8 shows a possible solution for Zack's lawn problem. A similar approach can be used for the Zoo Cola problem. You may have used different drawings, but the ideas should be the same.

Using a paper strip and partitioning is an effective way to solve multiplication problems, especially when they require additional partitioning (Siebert & Gaskin, 2006). As illustrated in Figure 16.8, paper is folded or partitioned to show thirds first, then shaded to show two-thirds. Next, the two-thirds must be partitioned (subdivided) to show fourths, then three-fourths is re-shaded. Finally the re-shaded part is compared back to the whole. What fraction of the whole is three-fourths of $\frac{2}{3}$? One-half.

The NLVM website has a nice collection of fraction applets. *Number Line Bars—Fractions* allows the user to place bars of any fractional length along a number line. The number line can be adjusted to have increments from $\frac{1}{2}$ to $\frac{1}{15}$, but the user must decide. For example, if bars of $\frac{1}{4}$ and $\frac{1}{3}$ are placed end to end, the result cannot be read from the applet until the increments are in twelfths.

Multiplication of fractions can be modeled with counters (see Figure 16.9). Do not discourage students from using counters, but be prepared to help them find ways to determine the whole.

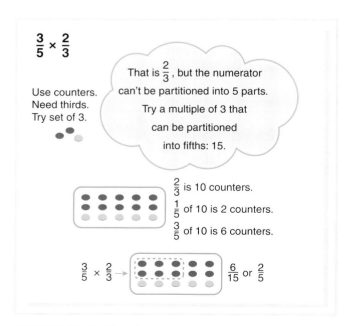

$\frac{3}{5} \times \frac{2}{3}$

Use counters. Need thirds. Try set of 3.

That is $\frac{2}{3}$, but the numerator can't be partitioned into 5 parts. Try a multiple of 3 that can be partitioned into fifths: 15.

$\frac{2}{3}$ is 10 counters.
$\frac{1}{5}$ of 10 is 2 counters.
$\frac{3}{5}$ of 10 is 6 counters.

$\frac{3}{5} \times \frac{2}{3} \rightarrow$ $\frac{6}{15}$ or $\frac{2}{5}$

FIGURE 16.9 Modeling multiplication of fractions with counters.

Area Model. The area model for modeling fraction multiplication has several advantages. First, it works for problems in which partitioning a length can be challenging. Second, it provides a powerful visual to show that a result can be quite a bit smaller than either of the fractions used or that if the fractions are both close to 1, then the result is also close to one. Third, it is a good model for connecting to the standard algorithm for multiplying fractions.

Provide students with a square as in Figure 16.10 and ask them to illustrate the first fraction. For example, in $\frac{3}{5} \times \frac{3}{4}$, you are finding $\frac{3}{5}$ of $\frac{3}{4}$, so you first must show $\frac{3}{4}$ (see Figure 16.10(a)). To find fifths of the $\frac{3}{4}$, draw four horizontal lines through the $\frac{3}{4}$ (see Figure 16.10(b)) or all the way across the square so that the whole is in the same-sized partitions (see Figure 16.10(c)).

Using a context and building on whole-number knowledge can support student reasoning about a fraction of a fraction. Quilting is a good context, because quilts are rectangles and the individual rectangles (or squares) within the quilt are a fraction of the whole quilt. Activity 16.9 provides a two-step activity with quilts adapted from Tsankova & Pjanic (2009/2010).

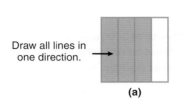 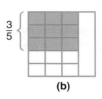 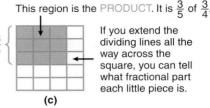

$\frac{3}{5} \times \frac{3}{4}$ This means "$\frac{3}{5}$ of a set of $\frac{3}{4}$." To get the product, make $\frac{3}{4}$, and then take $\frac{3}{5}$ of it.

This region is the PRODUCT. It is $\frac{3}{5}$ of $\frac{3}{4}$.

Draw all lines in one direction.

$\left.\frac{3}{5}\right\{$ $\left.\frac{3}{5}\right\{$

If you extend the dividing lines all the way across the square, you can tell what fractional part each little piece is.

    (a)   **(b)**   **(c)**

There are three rows and three columns in the PRODUCT, or 3 × 3 parts.

The WHOLE is now five rows and four columns, so there are 5 × 4 parts in the whole.

PRODUCT $= \frac{3}{5} \times \frac{3}{4} = \dfrac{\boxed{\text{Number}}\text{ of parts in product}}{\boxed{\text{Kind}}\text{ of parts}} = \dfrac{3 \times 3}{5 \times 4} = \dfrac{9}{20}$.

FIGURE 16.10   Development of the standard algorithm for multiplication of fractions.

Activity 16.9   CCSS-M: 5.NF.B4b; 5.NF.B.5b

Quilting Pieces

Have students use grid paper to sketch a drawing of a quilt that will be 8 feet by 6 feet—or create a full-sized one for your class! Explain that each group will prepare a picture that is 3 feet by 2 feet for the quilt. Ask students to tell you what fraction of the quilt a group will provide.

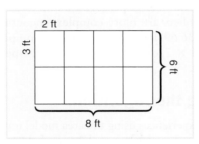

Second, rephrase the task. Explain that in the quilt, each group is to prepare a section of the quilt that is $\frac{1}{4}$ of the length and $\frac{1}{2}$ of the width. Ask students to sketch the quilt and the portion that their group will prepare.

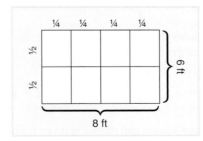

Help students make the connection that $\frac{1}{4}$ the length $\times$ $\frac{1}{2}$ the width $= \frac{1}{8}$ of the area ($\frac{1}{4} \times \frac{1}{2} = \frac{1}{8}$).

    The following activity (based on Imm, Stylianou, & Chae, 2008, p. 459) engages students in exploring multiplication of fractions and the commutative property.

Activity 16.10

CCSS-M: 5.NF.B.4b; 5.NF.B.6

Playground Problem

Show students the following problem.

Two communities, A and B, are building playgrounds in grassy lots that are 50 yards by 100 yards. In community A, they have been asked to convert $\frac{3}{4}$ of their lot to a playground, and $\frac{2}{5}$ of that playground should be covered with blacktop. In community B, they are building their playground on $\frac{2}{5}$ of the lot, and $\frac{3}{4}$ of the playground should be blacktop. In which park is the grassy playground bigger? In which lot is the blacktop bigger? Illustrate and explain.

Ask students to predict which community will have the bigger playground. Record predictions. Place students in partners and ask one to solve the problem for community A and the other to solve for community B. Once they have completed their illustrations and solutions, ask students to compare their responses and to be ready to report to the class what they decided.

Area models can also be found at the NLVM site. The Fractions Rectangle Multiplication applet allows you to explore multiplication of any two fractions up to 2×2.

Estimation and Invented Strategies

In the real world, there are many instances when whole numbers and fractions must be multiplied and mental estimates or even exact answers are quite useful. For example, sale items are frequently listed as "half off," or we read of a "one-third increase" in the number of registered voters. Also, fractions are excellent substitutes for percents, as you will see in the next chapter. To get an estimate of 75 percent of $36.69, it is useful to think of 75 percent as $\frac{3}{4}$, finding one-fourth (about $9) and then three-fourths ($27). This example illustrates a process for mentally multiplying a large number by a fraction: First determine the unit fractional part, and then multiply by the number of parts you want.

When numbers are more complex, encourage students to use compatible numbers. To estimate $\frac{3}{5}$ of $36.69, for example, a useful compatible number is $35. One-fifth of 35 is 7, so three-fifths is 3×7, or 21. Now adjust a bit—perhaps add an additional 50 cents, for an estimate of $21.50.

Developing the Algorithms

With enough experiences using the area model (or the linear model), students will start to notice a pattern. Remember that "enough" is probably a lot more than is usually provided—in other words, this does not mean two or three examples, but several weeks working with different examples and representations. These exercises will lead students to focus on how the denominators relate to how the grid (or line) is partitioned and how the numerator affects the solution to the problem.

When students are ready to start using the standard algorithm, ask them to solve three examples such as the following:

$$\frac{5}{6} \times \frac{1}{2} \qquad \frac{3}{4} \times \frac{1}{5} \qquad \frac{1}{3} \times \frac{9}{10}$$

For each one, use a square and partition it vertically and horizontally to model the problems. Ask, "How did you figure out what the unit of the fraction [the denominator] was?" Or more specifically, on the first problem, you can ask, "How did you figure out that the denominator would be twelfths? Is this a pattern that is true for the other examples?" Then ask students to see whether they can find a similar pattern for how the number of parts (the numerator) is determined.

As you help students focus on the pattern and learn to use the algorithm, do not forget to emphasize the meaning of what they are doing. Ask students to estimate how big they think the answer will be and why. In the first example here, a student might note that the answer will be slightly less than $\frac{1}{2}$ because $\frac{5}{6}$ is close to, but less than, 1.

Factors Greater Than One

As students explore multiplication, begin to include tasks in which one of the factors is a mixed number—for example, $\frac{3}{4} \times 2\frac{1}{2}$. The more these are integrated into multiplication with fractions less than one, the more it will help students think about the impact of multiplying by a number less than one and a number more than one. Activity 16.11 (based on Thompson, 1995) is a way to focus on this reasoning.

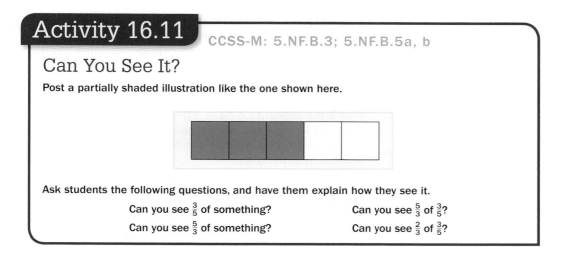

Activity 16.11

CCSS-M: 5.NF.B.3; 5.NF.B.5a, b

Can You See It?

Post a partially shaded illustration like the one shown here.

Ask students the following questions, and have them explain how they see it.

Can you see $\frac{3}{5}$ of something?   Can you see $\frac{5}{3}$ of $\frac{3}{5}$?

Can you see $\frac{5}{3}$ of something?   Can you see $\frac{2}{3}$ of $\frac{3}{5}$?

Many textbooks have students change mixed numbers to fractions (often referred to as *improper fractions*) in order to multiply them. Changing to improper fractions is an efficient way to solve these types of problems, but it is not the only way. In fact, students can multiply either way. Area representations can be used to model the problem in both cases, as illustrated in Figure 16.11. Students who understand that $2\frac{1}{2}$ means $2 + \frac{1}{2}$ might multiply $\frac{3}{4} \times 2$ and $\frac{3}{4} \times \frac{1}{2}$ and add the results—the distributive property. When both factors are mixed numbers, there are four partial products, just as there are when multiplying 2 two-digit numbers.

⏸ Pause & Reflect

Find the four partial products in this multiplication: $3\frac{2}{3} \times 2\frac{1}{4}$. ●

Figure 16.12 shows how this product might be worked out by multiplying the individual parts. In most cases, the partial products can be solved mentally. More importantly, the process is more conceptual and also lends itself to estimation—either before the partial products are determined or after. Notice that the same four partial products of Figure 16.12 can be found in the rectangle in Figure 16.11.

Addressing Misconceptions

When students begin working with fraction multiplication, they already have internalized concepts of whole-number multiplication and fraction addition and subtraction that can lead to confusion. This is exacerbated when students are not given adequate time to explore multiplication of fractions conceptually and when they are too quickly pressed to memorize rules, such as "multiply both the bottom and the top." The result of memorizing rules that don't make sense is an inability to solve multiplication problems. This becomes a significant barrier for solving proportions and algebraic expressions.

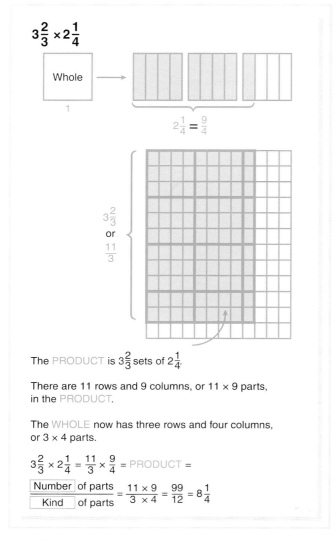

The PRODUCT is $3\frac{2}{3}$ sets of $2\frac{1}{4}$.

There are 11 rows and 9 columns, or 11 × 9 parts, in the PRODUCT.

The WHOLE now has three rows and four columns, or 3 × 4 parts.

$$3\frac{2}{3} \times 2\frac{1}{4} = \frac{11}{3} \times \frac{9}{4} = \text{PRODUCT} =$$

$$\frac{\boxed{\text{Number}} \text{ of parts}}{\boxed{\text{Kind}} \text{ of parts}} = \frac{11 \times 9}{3 \times 4} = \frac{99}{12} = 8\frac{1}{4}$$

FIGURE 16.11 The approach used to develop the algorithm for fractions less than 1 can be expanded to mixed numbers.

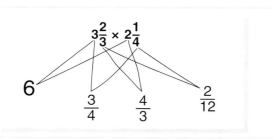

FIGURE 16.12 When multiplying two mixed numbers, there will be four partial products. These can then be added to get the total product, or an estimate may be enough.

Treating the Denominator the Same as in Addition/Subtraction Problems. Why does the denominator stay the same when adding fractions and get multiplied when multiplying fractions? Do you have a conceptual explanation for this? You need one. In adding, the process is counting parts of a whole, so those parts must be the same size. In multiplication, you are actually finding a part of a part, so the part may change size. Compare the two operations with a rectangle, circle, or number line to see how these are conceptually different.

Inability to Estimate Approximate Size of the Answer. Some students have been told that multiplication makes bigger. So they have difficulty deciding whether their answers make sense. On one hand, they may never even think about fraction size, so any answer looks good to them (e.g., $\frac{1}{2} \times 6\frac{1}{4} = 12\frac{1}{8}$). On the other hand, they might actually notice the answer ($\frac{1}{2} \times 6\frac{1}{4} = 3\frac{1}{8}$) but become concerned that this can't be right because the answer should be bigger. Estimation, contexts, and visuals are needed to better understand fraction multiplication.

Matching Multiplication Situations with Multiplication (and Not Division). Multiplication and division are closely related, and our language is sometimes not as precise as it needs to be. In the question, "What is $\frac{1}{3}$ of \$24?" students may correctly decide to divide by 3 or multiply by $\frac{1}{3}$. But they may (incorrectly) divide by $\frac{1}{3}$, confusing the idea that they are finding a fraction of the whole. This is more evident when the numbers are more complex or the story is more involved. Estimation can help students. This is particularly true for ELLs, who become confused by language such as "divide it *in* half" and "divide it *by* half" (Carr et al., 2009). Ask, "Should the result be larger or smaller than the original amount?" Also, having students rewrite a phrase to more clearly state the problem can help them determine whether the appropriate operation is multiplication or division.

 Complete Self-Check 16.3: Multiplication

 Division

Can you think of a real-life example for dividing by a fraction? Few people can, even though we conceptually use division involving fractions in many real-life situations. Do you know the "invert and multiply" algorithm? Have you used it in real situations? Division of fractions remains one of the most mysterious algorithms in elementary mathematics. We want to avoid this mystery at all costs and help students really understand when and how to divide with situations involving fractions.

Partitioning and iterating, both discussed in Chapter 15, are absolutely essential prior knowledge to begin exploring division involving fractions. Division should follow a developmental progression that focuses on four types of problems:

a. A whole number divided by a whole number: $14 \div 5$ OR $22 \div 7$

b. A fraction divided by a whole number: $\frac{1}{2} \div 4$ OR $\frac{7}{8} \div 2$

c. A whole number divided by a fraction: $4 \div \frac{1}{3}$ OR $4 \div \frac{2}{3}$

d. A fraction divided by a fraction: $\frac{7}{8} \div \frac{1}{8}$ OR $2\frac{1}{4} \div \frac{1}{2}$

These types of problems are each described in the following section. In the CCSS-M standards, division involving fractions begins in fifth grade but is limited to the first three types, and only with unit fractions. In sixth grade, all types are explored, and in seventh grade, all types are explored using both positive and negative fractions.

Contextual Examples and Models

Begin by building on students' prior knowledge of division with whole numbers. As with whole numbers, there are two meanings of division: partitive (sharing) and measurement (equal subtraction) (Gregg & Gregg, 2007; Kribs-Zaleta, 2008; Tirosh, 2000). These meanings are both needed to develop the different types of fraction problems, as you will see in these examples.

Whole Number Divided by Whole Number. A partitive or sharing context is helpful in interpreting division of a whole number by a whole number (Lamon, 2012). Very young children can understand sharing (e.g., 3 cookies shared with 2 people). Because it is a foundational concept closely tied to partitioning, sharing tasks are a major topic in Chapter 15. Here we limit the discussion to developing a progression for division involving fractions.

Sharing tasks can result in each person receiving a fractional part: 5 sandwiches shared with 4 friends ($5 \div 4$). If you partition each sandwich into fourths, you see that each friend will have five-fourths (friend 1 takes the gold section from each sandwich, friend 2 takes the red section, etc.):

Notice that $5 \div 4 = \frac{1}{4} \times 5 = \frac{5}{4}$. The first expression means five sandwiches shared with 4 friends; the second expression means find one-fourth of 5 sandwiches (that is one person's fair share); and the final expression means five-fourths is one person's share—a fourth from each of 5 sandwiches. Students must be able to see the connections and meanings of each of these equivalent expressions.

This concept applies, no matter how messy the numbers. Think of 92 sandwiches shared with 11 people ($92 \div 11$). Still, each person would receive $\frac{1}{11}$ of each of 92 sandwiches, and so have $\frac{92}{11}$ of the sandwiches.

Having seen that division of a whole number by a whole number is the same as multiplying the number by a unit fraction, students are ready to extend the same reasoning to division of a unit fraction by a whole number.

Fraction Divided by a Whole Number. These problem types are introduced in the CCSS-M in grade 5 as unit fractions ($\frac{1}{4} \div 3$) and in sixth grade for non-unit fractions ($\frac{9}{10} \div 3$ OR $2\frac{1}{2} \div 6$). Notice that in partitive (sharing) problems, you are asking, "How much is the share for *one* friend?" Questions could also be "How many miles are walked in *one* hour?" or "How much ribbon for *one* bow?"

Standards for Mathematical Practice
CCSS
MP7. Look for and make use of structure.

Pause & Reflect

What situation might fit $\frac{1}{4} \div 3$? ●

There are many situations that can fit this equation. Activity 16.12 provides three different situations for exploring this situation.

Activity 16.12

CCSS-M: 5.NF.B.7a, c

Fractions Divided by Whole-Number Stories

Provide students with different situations to explore the same problem. Here are three stories (one area, one linear, and one set):

- **Garden Plots.** Three gardeners are equally sharing $\frac{1}{4}$ of an acre for their plots. What part of an acre is each gardener's plot?
- **Water Bottles.** There is $\frac{1}{4}$ of a gallon of water that is poured equally into three water bottles. How much is poured into each?
- **Cheese Sticks.** Arlo buys a bag of cheese sticks (24 in the bag). He takes $\frac{1}{4}$ of the cheese sticks to a picnic. At the picnic he decides to share the cheese sticks equally with 2 friends (and himself). What fraction of the bag does each person get?

After they finish, compare their different visuals and connect the meaning of the operation to the visuals. Ask students to write an expression for each (they should be the same!). Emphasize the notion of "How much for *one*?" After exploring this initial task, students can be challenged to create their own stories to match problems like $\frac{1}{4} \div 3$.

Once students have explored a unit fraction divided by a whole number, they need experiences dividing any fraction (or mixed number) by a whole number, using contexts. Ribbon provides a good linear model:

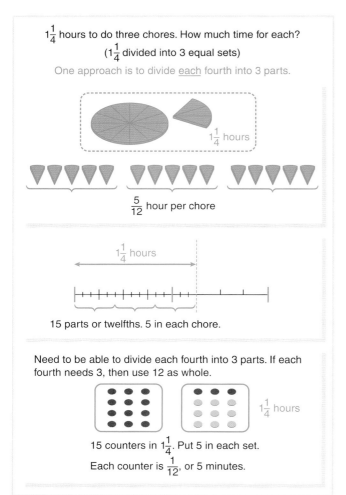

FIGURE 16.13 Three models of partitive division with a whole-number divisor.

Cassie has $5\frac{1}{3}$ yards of ribbon to make four bows for birthday packages. How much ribbon should she use for each bow if she wants to use the same length of ribbon for each?

When the $5\frac{1}{3}$ is thought of as fractional parts, there are 16 thirds to share, or 4 thirds for each bow. Alternatively, one might think of allotting 1 yard per bow, leaving $1\frac{1}{3}$ yards. These 4 thirds are then shared, one per bow, for a total of $1\frac{1}{3}$ yards for each bow. The unit parts (thirds) required no further partitioning in order to do the division. Students need numerous experiences with sharing tasks that come out evenly before exploring tasks that do not.

In the following problem, the parts must be split into smaller parts:

Mark has $1\frac{1}{4}$ hours to finish his three chores. If he divides his time evenly, how many hours can he give to each chore?

Note that the question is, "How many hours for one chore?" The 5 fourths of an hour that Mark has do not split neatly into three parts. So some or all of the parts must be partitioned. Figure 16.13 shows how to model these with each type of model (area, linear, and set). In each case, all of the fourths are subdivided into three equal parts, producing twelfths. There are a total of 15 twelfths, or $\frac{5}{12}$ hour for each chore. (Test this answer against the solution in minutes: $1\frac{1}{4}$ hours is 75 minutes, which divided among 3 chores is 25 minutes per chore. $\frac{25}{60} = \frac{5}{12}$.) See Expanded Lesson Division-of-Fraction Stories for a complete lesson using Cassie and Mark's stories.

Whole Numbers Divided by Fractions. This problem type lends to a measurement interpretation (also called *repeated subtraction* or *equal groups*). In these situations, an equal group is taken away from the total repeatedly. For example, *If you have 13 quarts of lemonade, how many canteens holding 3 quarts each can you fill?* Notice that this is not a sharing situation but rather an equal subtraction situation. In this case, the question we ask is "How many 3s are in 13?"

The measurement interpretation is a good way to explore division by a fraction because students can draw illustrations to show the measures (Cramer et al., 2010). There are numerous ways to illustrate how to divide whole numbers by fractions. And measurement interpretation will be used to develop an algorithm for dividing fractions, so it is important for students to explore this idea in contextual situations. A good context for a measurement interpretation is counting servings of a particular size.

Activity 16.13 uses a context of serving sandwiches to build a foundation for division by unit fractions.

Activity 16.13

CCSS-M: 5.NF.B.7b, c

Sandwich Servings

Super Sub Sandwiches is starting a catering business. A child's serving is $\frac{1}{6}$ of a Super Sub and an adult serving can be either $\frac{1}{3}$ or $\frac{1}{2}$ of a Super Sub, depending on whether the catering customer requests small or medium. The employees must be quick at deciding the number of subs for an event based on serving size. See how you do—make a decision without computing.

1. Which portion size serves the most people—child-size $\frac{1}{6}$, small $\frac{1}{3}$, or medium $\frac{1}{2}$? Why?

$$6 \div \frac{1}{6} \qquad 6 \div \frac{1}{3} \qquad 6 \div \frac{1}{2}$$

2. Describe what is happening in each sandwich situation below (how many sandwiches and which kind of serving size).
   Estimate: Which situation serves the most people? Explain your reasoning.

$$8 \div \frac{1}{3} \qquad 5 \div \frac{1}{2} \qquad 6 \div \frac{1}{6}$$

Notice that question 1 provides the opportunity to compare the impact of unit divisors and discuss *why* you get more servings when you have smaller fractions as divisors. This helps to build the relationship between multiplication and division and students may notice the general case: $1 \div \frac{1}{n} = n$ and therefore, $a \div \frac{1}{n} = a \times n$ (Cavey & Kinzel, 2014). The second prompt provides the opportunity for students to test their conjectures from question 1 on new examples. Both prompts can be illustrated using various visuals.

After students have explored unit divisors, they are ready to explore measurement situations with non-unit fraction divisors, such as this task:

CCSS **Standards for Mathematical Practice**

MP8. Look for and express regularity in repeated reasoning.

Les & Colin's Smoothies Shop has just bought a machine that blends 6 pints of smoothies for one batch. Their Smoothie Cups hold $\frac{3}{4}$ of a pint. How many smoothies can be served from one batch?

A visual that fits this context might be a vertical number line or bar diagram, or it could be six rectangles partitioned into fourths. Students may be able to readily count the total number of fourths (24), but not be sure on how to count servings of *three*-fourths. Encourage students to use visuals and to group three of the fourths together as one serving.

A sharing or partitioning interpretation can (and should) be used in working with whole numbers divided by fractions. At first, it may seem that sharing doesn't make sense when the divisor is a fraction, but remember that the focus question in sharing is "How much for one (e.g., person)?" or "How many for one?" You may recall that in Chapter 15 there were a set of tasks where students are asked to find the whole, given the part (see Figure 15.11). Essentially, these tasks are saying, "How much for one?" and are therefore a good way to build meaning for division by a fraction. Activity 16.14 provides a sampling of such tasks revisited to be more explicit about the connection to division.

Activity 16.14
CCSS-M: 5.NF.B.7a, c

How Much in One Whole Set?

Use Counting Counters: How Much for One Activity Page or give students a collection of counters, such as two-color counters. Ask them to sets of tasks, such as the ones provided here:

1. If 8 counters represents $\frac{1}{4}$ of the whole, how much is one whole set?

   Expression: $8 \div \frac{1}{4}$

2. If 15 counters represents $\frac{3}{5}$ of the whole, how much is one whole set?

   Expression: $15 \div \frac{3}{5}$

3. If 18 counters represents $2\frac{1}{4}$ sets, how much is one whole set?

   Expression: $18 \div 2\frac{1}{4}$

As students are working, ask them to describe their reasoning strategies. Help them to notice that they are finding how many in *one part* (e.g., one-fourth or one-fifth), and then iterating (multiplying) to find out how many in *one whole* (e.g. four-fourths or five-fifths).

Sharing tasks such as this are very closely connected to the meaning of the division by a fraction algorithm, as described in the next section.

Fractions Divided by Fractions. Over time, using various contexts and numbers that vary in difficulty, students will be able to take on problems that are more complex both in the context and in the numbers involved. Using the measurement concept of serving size, Gregg and Gregg (2007) use cookie serving size of $\frac{1}{2}$ to bridge from a whole number divided by a fraction to a fraction divided by a fraction. Examples are illustrated in Figure 16.14, but many more examples can be inserted along this progression from whole number divided by a fraction, to fraction divided by a fraction (that has a remainder). As the examples in this figure illustrate, moving slowly to more complex examples will enable students to use their whole-number concepts to build an understanding of division with fractions.

Though you may think that mixed numbers are more difficult, using mixed numbers early can help students make sense of division of a fraction by a fraction:

Farmer Brown found that he had $2\frac{1}{4}$ gallons of liquid fertilizer concentrate. It takes $\frac{3}{4}$ gallon to make a tank of mixed fertilizer. How many tankfuls can he mix?

Standards for Mathematical Practice
MP6. Attend to precision.

Try solving this problem yourself. Use any model or drawing you wish to help explain what you are doing. Notice that you are trying to find out how many sets of 3 fourths are in a set of 9 fourths. Your answer should be 3 tankfuls (not 3 fourths). It is important to emphasize units with students as it is easy to forget what whole (unit) the fraction describes.

Fractions divided by fractions can also be explained using partitioning/sharing. That is the focus of this next activity.

Activity 16.15
CCSS-M: 5.NF.B.7a, c; 6.NS.A.1

How Much for 1?

Pose contextual problems where the focus question is, "How much for one _____?" Ask students to create bar diagrams or other visuals to illustrate how much for one:

Dan paid $3\frac{3}{4}$ for a $\frac{3}{4}$ pound box of cereal. How much is that per pound?

Andrea found that if she walks quickly during her morning exercise, she can cover $2\frac{1}{2}$ miles in $\frac{3}{4}$ of an hour. She wonders how fast she is walking in miles per hour.

With both problems, first find the amount of one-fourth (partitioning) and then the value of one whole (iterating). Andrea's walking problem is a bit harder because the $2\frac{1}{2}$ miles, or 5 half-miles, do not neatly divide into three parts. Hint: divide each half-mile into three parts.

Answers That Are Not Whole Numbers

Many problems are not going to come out evenly and it becomes very important to make sense of the leftover. If Cassie had 5 yards of ribbon to make bows, and each needs $1\frac{1}{6}$ yards each, she could make only four bows because a part of a bow does not make sense. But other contexts, like the Farmer Brown problem, don't require the student to disregard the leftover. If Farmer Brown begins with 4 gallons of concentrate and makes five tanks of mix, he uses $\frac{15}{4}$, or $3\frac{3}{4}$ gallons, of the concentrate. With the $\frac{1}{4}$ gallon of remaining concentrate, he can make a *partial* tank of mix. He can make $\frac{1}{3}$ of a tank of mix, because it takes *3* fourths to make a whole, and he has *1* fourth of a gallon (he has one of the three parts he needs for a tank).

Here is another problem to try:

John is building a patio. Each patio section requires $\frac{1}{3}$ of a cubic yard of concrete. The concrete truck holds $2\frac{1}{2}$ cubic yards of concrete. If there is not enough for a full section at the end, John can put in a divider and make a partial section. How many patio sections can John make with the concrete in the truck?

⏸ Pause & Reflect

Try to solve this problem in some way that makes sense to *you.* ●

One way to do this is by counting how many thirds there are in $2\frac{1}{2}$.

Here you can see that you get 3 patio sections from the yellow whole and 3 more from the orange whole, and then you get 1 more full section and $\frac{1}{2}$ of what you need for another patio section. So the answer is $7\frac{1}{2}$. Students will want to write the "remainder" as $\frac{1}{3}$ because they were measuring in thirds, but the question is how many sections can be made—$7\frac{1}{2}$.

Will common denominators work for division? Let's see. The problem you just solved, $2\frac{1}{2} \div \frac{1}{3}$ would become $2\frac{3}{6} \div \frac{2}{6}$, or it could be $\frac{15}{6} \div \frac{2}{6}$. The question becomes, *How many sets of 2 sixths are in a set of 15 sixths? Or, How many twos in 15?* This produces the correct answer of $7\frac{1}{2}$. This is as efficient as the standard algorithm, and it may make more sense to students to do it this way.

1. A serving is $\frac{1}{2}$ cookie. How many servings can I make from 2 cookies?

2. A serving is $\frac{1}{2}$ cookie. How many servings can I make from 1 cookie?

3. A serving is $\frac{1}{2}$ cookie. How many servings can I make from $\frac{3}{4}$ cookie?

4. A serving is $\frac{1}{2}$ cookie. How many servings can I make from $\frac{3}{8}$ cookie?

5. A serving is $\frac{1}{2}$ cookie. How many servings can I make from $\frac{5}{8}$ cookie?

FIGURE 16.14 Tasks that use the measurement interpretation of "How many servings?" to develop the concept of division.

Source: Gregg, J., & Gregg, D. W. (2007). "Measurement and Fair-Sharing Models for Dividing Fractions." *Mathematics Teaching in the Middle School, 12*(9), p. 491. Reprinted with permission. Copyright © 2007 by the National Council of Teachers of Mathematics. All rights reserved.

Figure 16.15 shows two division problems solved this way, each with a different representation. That is, both the dividend or given quantity and the divisor are expressed in the same type of fractional parts. This results in a whole-number division problem.

 FORMATIVE ASSESSMENT Notes. For all operations with fractions, using a mathematical adaptation of the Frayer Model, such as the Procedure—Illustration—Concept—Situation Activity Page can be used as a pre- or postassessment or as a performance assessment to see if students can represent the operation using visuals and symbols and explain connections between procedures and concepts. ■

Estimation and Invented Strategies

Understanding division can be greatly supported by using estimation. What does $\frac{1}{6} \div 4$ mean? Will the answer be greater than 1? Greater than $\frac{1}{2}$? Greater than $\frac{1}{6}$? The answer to each of these questions is "no." The answer should be obvious to someone who understands the meaning of this operation (that one-sixth is being shared four ways, resulting in even smaller parts). Conversely, consider what $12 \div \frac{1}{4}$ means. Will the answer be greater than 1? Greater than 12? The answer to these questions is "yes" and again it should be obvious, because you are actually answering the question, "How many fourths in 12?" (there are 48 fourths in 12 wholes).

Ask students to estimate by asking questions such "*About* how many halves in $4\frac{1}{3}$?" Reinforce answers of 8 and 9. The following activity encourages estimation because an exact answer is not needed.

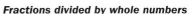

Activity 16.16

CCSS-M: 5.NF.B.7a, b, c; 6.NS.A.1

The Size Is Right: Division

Start with either fractions divided by whole numbers or whole numbers divided by fractions, but then mix up the tasks. Have each of these problems ready to flash and cover on a document camera or Smartboard projection. Leave up for a few seconds, then remove. Ask students to pick one of the options from the dashboard (illustrated below). Then invite students to pair-compare their selections and decide if they are reasonable.

ENGLISH LANGUAGE LEARNERS

STUDENTS with SPECIAL NEEDS

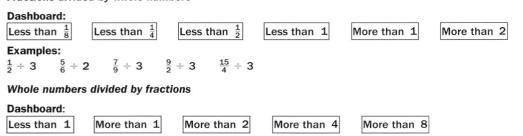

Fractions divided by whole numbers

Dashboard:

| Less than $\frac{1}{8}$ | Less than $\frac{1}{4}$ | Less than $\frac{1}{2}$ | Less than 1 | More than 1 | More than 2 |

Examples:

$\frac{1}{2} \div 3$ $\frac{5}{6} \div 2$ $\frac{7}{9} \div 3$ $\frac{9}{2} \div 3$ $\frac{15}{4} \div 3$

Whole numbers divided by fractions

Dashboard:

| Less than 1 | More than 1 | More than 2 | More than 4 | More than 8 |

Examples:

$3 \div \frac{1}{3}$ $1 \div \frac{2}{3}$ $2 \div \frac{1}{3}$ $4 \div \frac{7}{8}$ $4 \div \frac{3}{8}$

For English language learners, provide sentence starters to support the speaking opportunities: "I think the answer is [dashboard choice] because. . . . " For students with disabilities or students who benefit from visuals, have tools available such as Cuisenaire Rods or fraction circles so that they can more readily see the relative size of each fraction.

Activity 16.16 can also be used for fractions divided by fractions, with dashboards such as Quotient < 1, Quotient = 1 and Quotient > 1 (Johanning & Mamer, 2014). Students can write division expressions that fit in each of these categories. The more estimation students do, the more they begin to develop a much-needed number sense for fraction division.

Developing the Algorithms

There are two different algorithms for division of fractions. Methods of teaching both algorithms are discussed here.

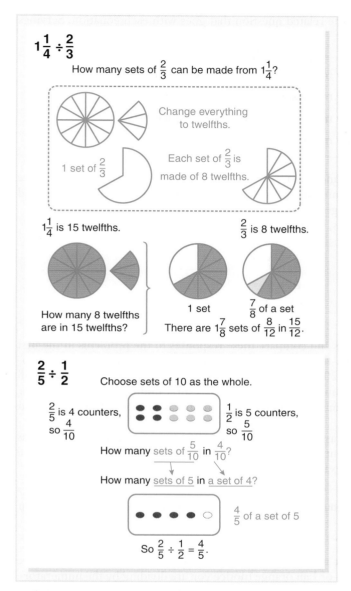

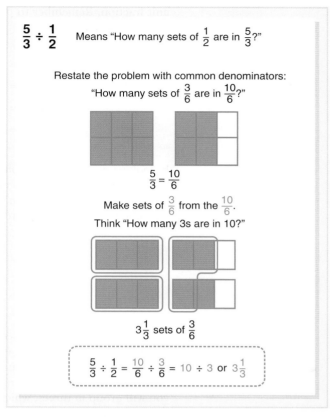

FIGURE 16.16 Models for the common-denominator method for fraction division.

FIGURE 16.15 Common denominators can be used to solve division of fraction problems.

Common-Denominator Algorithm. The common-denominator algorithm relies on the measurement or repeated subtraction concept of division. Consider the problem $\frac{5}{3} \div \frac{1}{2}$. As shown in Figure 16.16, once each number is expressed in terms of the same fractional part, the answer is exactly the same as the whole-number problem $10 \div 3$. The name of the fractional part (the denominator) is no longer important, and the problem is one of dividing the numerators. The resulting algorithm, therefore, is as follows: *To divide fractions, first get common denominators, and then divide numerators.* For example, $\frac{5}{3} \div \frac{1}{4} = \frac{20}{12} \div \frac{3}{12} = 20 \div 3 = \frac{20}{3} = 6\frac{2}{3}$.

Try using circular fraction pieces, fraction strips, and then sets of counters to model $1\frac{2}{3} \div \frac{3}{4}$ using a common-denominator approach.

Invert-and-Multiply Algorithm. Providing a series of tasks and having students look for patterns in how they are finding the answers can help students discover this poorly understood and commonly taught algorithm. For example, consider this first set, in which the divisor is a unit fraction. Remember to pose the related question that goes with each equation. Servings of food can be the context.

$$3 \div \tfrac{1}{2} = \text{(How many servings of } \tfrac{1}{2} \text{ in 3 containers?)}$$
$$5 \div \tfrac{1}{4} = \text{(How many servings of } \tfrac{1}{4} \text{ in 5 containers?)}$$
$$8 \div \tfrac{1}{5} = \text{(How many servings of } \tfrac{1}{5} \text{ in 8 containers?)}$$
$$3\tfrac{3}{4} \div \tfrac{1}{8} = \text{(How many servings of } \tfrac{1}{8} \text{ in } 3\tfrac{3}{4} \text{ containers?)}$$

In looking across these problems (and others) and looking for a pattern, students will notice they are multiplying by the denominator of the second fraction. For example, in the third example, a student might say, "You get five for every whole container, so 5×8 is 40."
    Then move to similar problems, but with a second fraction that is not a unit fraction:

$$5 \div \tfrac{3}{4} =$$
$$8 \div \tfrac{2}{5} =$$
$$3\tfrac{3}{4} \div \tfrac{3}{8} =$$

Have students solve these problems and compare these responses to the problems in the first set. Notice that if there are 40 one-fifths in 8, then when you group the fifths in pairs (two-fifths), you will have half as many—20. Stated in servings, if the serving is twice as big, you will have half the number of servings. Similarly, if the fraction is $\tfrac{3}{4}$, after finding how many fourths, you will group in threes, which means you will get $\tfrac{1}{3}$ the number of servings. You can see that this means you must divide by 3.
    The examples given were measurements because the size of the group (serving) was known, but not the number of groups. Partitioning or sharing examples nicely illustrate the standard algorithm. Consider this example:

You have $1\tfrac{1}{2}$ oranges, which is $\tfrac{3}{5}$ of an adult serving. How many oranges (and parts of oranges) make up 1 adult serving? (Kribs-Zaleta, 2008)

You may be thinking that you first need to find what one-fifth would be—which would be one-third of the oranges you have—or $\tfrac{1}{2}$ an orange (notice you are dividing by the numerator). Then, to get the whole serving, you multiply $\tfrac{1}{2}$ by 5 (the denominator) to get $2\tfrac{1}{2}$ oranges in 1 adult serving.
    In either the measurement or the partitive interpretations, the denominator leads you to find out how many fourths, fifths, or eighths you have, and the numerator tells you the size of the serving, so you group according to how many are in the serving. So the process is *multiply by the denominator and divide by the numerator*. At some point, someone reasoned that just flipping the fraction would be more straightforward—multiplying by the top and dividing by the bottom—and that is why we have learned to "invert and multiply."

Addressing Misconceptions

The biggest misunderstanding with division of fractions is just not knowing what the algorithm means. Once students realize the meaning of division, they are able to begin thinking of different ways to approach problems and decide whether their answers make sense. Within division, there are some common misconceptions that need to be addressed.

Thinking the Answer Should Be Smaller. Based on their experiences with whole-number division, students think that when dividing by a fraction, the answer should be smaller. This is true if the divisor is a fraction greater than one (e.g., $\tfrac{5}{3}$), but it is not true if the fraction is less than one. One way to help students address the misconception is to ask them to estimate. Estimation can be a final product, as in Activity 16.16, or it can just be a beginning to doing a computation as a way to help students decide whether their answer is reasonable.

Connecting the Illustration with the Answer. Students may understand that $1\frac{1}{2} \div \frac{1}{4}$ means "How many fourths are in $1\frac{1}{2}$?" So they may set out to count how many fourths and get 6. But in recording their answer, they can confuse the fact that they were using fractions and instead record $\frac{6}{4}$ (Cramer et al., 2010).

Knowing What the Unit Is. Students might get an answer such as $\frac{3}{8}$, but when you say "$\frac{3}{8}$ of what?" they just don't know. To make sense of division, students must know what the unit is. Errors occur less frequently when units (e.g., servings, feet, or quesadillas) are emphasized (Dixon & Tobias, 2013).

Writing Remainders. Knowing what the unit is (the divisor) is critical and must be understood in giving the remainder (Coughlin, 2010/2011; Lamon, 2006; Sharp & Welder, 2014). In the problem $3\frac{3}{8} \div \frac{1}{4}$, students are likely to count 4 fourths for each whole (12 fourths) and one more for $\frac{2}{8}$ but then not know what to do with the extra eighth. It is important to be sure they understand the measurement concept of division. Ask, "How much of the next piece do you have?" Context can also help—in particular, servings. In this case, if this problem were about pizza servings, there would be 13 full servings and $\frac{1}{2}$ of the next serving.

 Complete Self-Check 16.4: Division

REFLECTIONS ON CHAPTER 16

WRITING TO LEARN

1. Why is it important to include estimation with fractions?

2. A student adds $\frac{4}{5} + \frac{2}{3}$ and gets $\frac{6}{8}$. How will you help the student understand that this is incorrect? How would you redirect him or her to do it correctly?

3. For the problem $3\frac{1}{4} - 1\frac{1}{2}$, think of a story problem that would be a "take-away" situation and one that would be a "compare" situation.

4. Explain at least one mental method (estimation or mental computation) for each of these:

$$\frac{3}{4} \times \frac{1}{2} \qquad 1\frac{1}{8} \text{ of } 40$$

5. Make up a word problem with a fraction as a divisor. Is your problem a measurement problem or a partition problem? Make up a second word problem with fractions of the other type (measurement or partition).

FOR DISCUSSION AND EXPLORATION

◆ Imagine you are about to start teaching fraction computation. You quickly find that your students have a very weak understanding of fractions. Your textbook primarily targets the algorithms. Some teachers argue that there is no time to reteach the concepts of fractions. Others would argue that it is necessary to teach the meanings of numerators and denominators and equivalent fractions or else all the computation will be meaningless rules. How will you plan for instruction? Justify your approach.

◆ Several calculators are now available that do computations in fractional form as well as in decimal form. If you have access to such a calculator, discuss how it might be used in teaching fraction operations. If such calculators become commonplace, should we continue to teach fraction computation?

RESOURCES FOR CHAPTER 16

LITERATURE CONNECTIONS

Alice's Adventures in Wonderland *Carroll and Gray (1865/1992)*

This well-known children's story needs no introduction. Because Alice shrinks in the story, there is an opportunity to explore multiplication by fractions. Taber (2007) describes in detail how she used this story to engage students in understanding the meaning of multiplication of fractions. She begins by asking how tall Alice would be if she were originally 54" tall but was shrunk to $\frac{1}{9}$ of her height. What height will Alice be if she is later restored to only $\frac{5}{6}$ her original height? The students write their own Alice multiplication-of-fractions equations.

The Man Who Made Parks *Wishinsky and Zhang (1999)*

This nonfiction book explains the remarkable story of Frederick Olmsted, who designed Central Park in New York City. Creating a park design, students can be given fractional amounts for what needs to be included in the park—for example, $\frac{2}{5}$ gardens, $\frac{1}{10}$ playgrounds, $\frac{1}{2}$ natural habitat (streams and forest), and the rest special features (like a zoo or outdoor theater). Students can build the plan for their park on a rectangular grid. To include multiplication of fractions, include guidelines such as that $\frac{3}{4}$ of the park is natural habitat, with $\frac{1}{3}$ of that to be wooded and $\frac{1}{6}$ to be water features, and so on.

RECOMMENDED READINGS

Articles

Cavey, L. O., & Kinzel, M. T. (2014). From whole numbers to invert and multiply. *Teaching Children Mathematics, 20*(6), 375–383.

An excellent progression of teaching division of whole numbers to division of fractions in a way that makes strong connections between multiplication and division. CCSS-M included, this article helps with content knowledge and teaching ideas.

Cramer, K., Wyberg, T., & Leavitt, S. (2008). The role of representations in fraction addition and subtraction. *Mathematics Teaching in the Middle School, 13*(8), 490–496.

Illustrations and student work are used to show how to teach addition and subtraction using the fraction circle. Essential considerations of effective instruction are emphasized.

Gregg, J., & Gregg, D. U. (2007). Measurement and fair-sharing models for dividing fractions. *Mathematics Teaching in the Middle School, 12*(9), 490–496.

These authors provide a series of tasks to develop the concept of division of fractions—a must-read for a teacher needing more experiences exploring division or trying to plan a good instructional sequence.

Imm, K. L., Stylianou, D. A., & Chae, N. (2008). Student representations at the center: Promoting classroom equity. *Mathematics Teaching in the Middle School, 13*(8), 458–463.

Using a park context, these authors explain how to model multiplication of fractions. Equity and a culture for learning are emphasized.

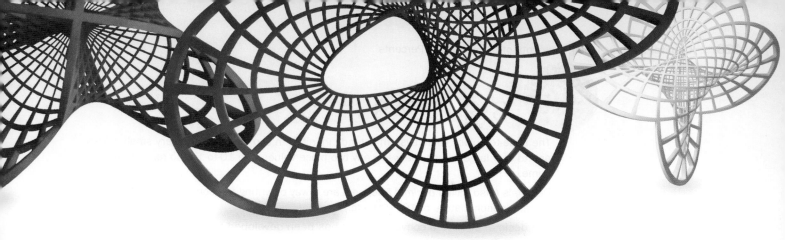

CHAPTER

17

Developing Concepts of Decimals and Percents

LEARNER OUTCOMES

After reading this chapter and engaging in the embedded activities and reflections, you should be able to:

17.1 Describe how the place-value system links to the understanding of decimal fractions.

17.2 Identify three models that can be used to connect fractions to decimals.

17.3 Demonstrate how to compare and order decimal fractions.

17.4 Explain multiple strategies for computing with decimals.

17.5 Explain how percents are related to fractions and decimals.

People need to be able to interpret decimals for such varied needs as reading precise metric measures, calculating distances, interpreting output on a calculator, and understanding sports statistics such as those at the Olympics, where winners and losers are separated by hundredths of a second. Decimals are critically important in many occupations: For nurses, pharmacists, and workers building airplanes, for example, precision affects the safety of the general public. Because students and teachers have been shown to have greater difficulty understanding decimals than fractions (Martinie, 2007; Helme & Stacey, 2000; Vamvakoussi, Van Dooren, & Verschaffel, 2012), conceptual understanding of decimals and their connections to fractions must be carefully developed.

In the Common Core State Standards, students in fourth grade should "understand decimal notation [to hundredths] for fractions and compare decimal fractions" (CCSSO, 2010, p. 31). In the fifth grade the document highlights one of the critical areas as performing operations with decimals (to hundredths), expanding comparisons of decimals to thousandths, and rounding decimals. In the sixth grade, students extend this work with tenths and hundredths to all decimals as they develop standard algorithms for all four operations. In the seventh grade, they develop a "unified understanding of number" (CCSSO, 2010, p. 46) so as to be able to move fluently between decimals, fractions, and percents.

Fractions with denominators of 10, 100, 1000, and so on—for example, $\frac{7}{10}$ or $\frac{63}{100}$, which can also be written as 0.7 and 0.63—will be referred to as *decimal fractions*. The phrase *decimal fractions* is often shortened to *decimals*, and in this chapter we will use these terms interchangeably.

Explicitly linking the ideas of fractions to decimals can be extremely useful, both from a pedagogical view as well as a practical view. Many of the big ideas focus on that connection.

BIG IDEAS

- ◆ The base-ten place-value system extends infinitely in two directions: to very small values and to very large values. Between any two place values, the 10-to-1 ratio remains the same.

- ◆ Decimals (also called *decimal fractions*) are a way of writing fractions within the base-ten system (denominators of 10, 100, etc.).

- ◆ The decimal point is a convention that has been developed to indicate the unit's position. The position to the left of the decimal point marks the location of the units place.

- ◆ Addition and subtraction with decimals are based on the fundamental concept of adding and subtracting the numbers in like position values—an extension from whole numbers.

- ◆ Multiplication and division of two numbers will produce the same digits, regardless of the positions of the decimal point. As a result, multiplicative computations with decimal fractions can be performed as whole numbers with the decimal placed by way of estimation, as well as by identifying patterns.

- ◆ Percents are simply hundredths and as such are a third way of writing both fractions and decimals.

 ## Extending the Place-Value System

Before exploring decimal numerals with students, it is advisable to review ideas of whole-number place value. One of the most basic of these ideas is the 10-to-1 multiplicative relationship between the values of any two adjacent positions. In terms of a base-ten model such as paper strips and squares, 10 of any one piece will make 1 of the next larger (to the immediate left), and movement of a piece to the immediate right involves division by 10 (1 divided by 10 is one-tenth).

The 10-to-1 Relationship—Now in Two Directions!

As you learned in the study of place value, the 10-makes-1 rule continues indefinitely to larger and larger pieces or positional values. If you are using the paper strip-and-square base-ten models, for example, the strip and square shapes alternate in an infinite progression as they get larger. Likewise, we can move in the other direction as we explore decimal fractions, where each adjacent piece to the right in this continuum gets smaller by one-tenth. The critical question becomes "Is there ever a smallest piece?" In the students' prior experience, the smallest piece is the centimeter square or unit piece. But couldn't that piece be divided into 10 small strips? And couldn't those small strips be divided into 10 very small squares, and so on?

The goal of this discussion is to help students see that a 10-to-1 relationship can extend infinitely in two directions. There is no smallest piece and no largest piece. The symmetry of the system is around the ones place (tens to the left of the ones place, tenths to the right, and so on)—not the common misconception that it is symmetrical around the decimal point. The relationship between adjacent pieces is the same regardless of which two adjacent pieces are being considered. Figure 17.1 illustrates this idea.

Even at this stage, students need to be reminded of the powerful concept of regrouping. Flexible thinking about place values should be practiced prior to exploring decimals. Have students revisit not only making 1 ten from 10 units, but think about regrouping 2,451 into

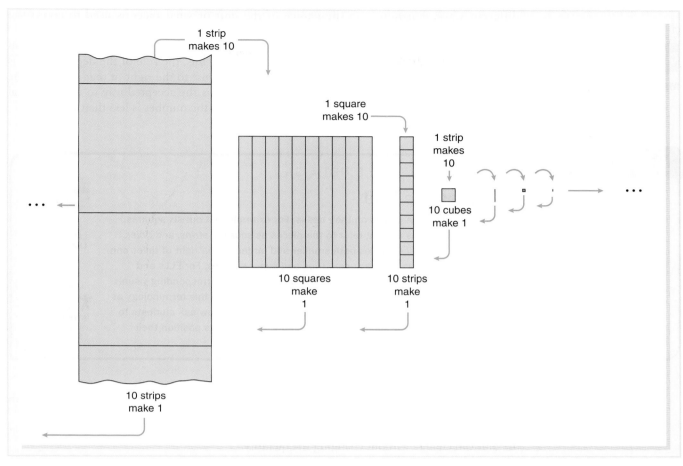

FIGURE 17.1 Theoretically, the strips and squares extend infinitely in both directions.

24 hundreds, 5 tens and 1 unit; or 245 tens and 1 unit; or 2,451 ones. As you can see, this process will be essential in thinking about 0.6 as 6 tenths, as well as 60 hundredths and so on.

The Role of the Decimal Point

Students must know that the decimal point marks the location of the ones (or units) place. That is why on a calculator, when there is a whole-number answer, no decimal point appears. Only when the ones place needs to be identified will the decimal point show in the display. Students also need to see that adding zeros to the left of a whole number or to the right of a decimal fraction will not change the value of number.

An important idea to be realized in this discussion is that there is no built-in reason why any one position (or base-ten piece) should be chosen to be the unit or ones position. In terms of strips and squares, for example, which piece is the ones piece? The small centimeter square? Why? Why not a larger or a smaller square? Why not a strip? *Any piece could effectively be chosen as the ones piece.* As shown in Figure 17.2, a given quantity can be written in

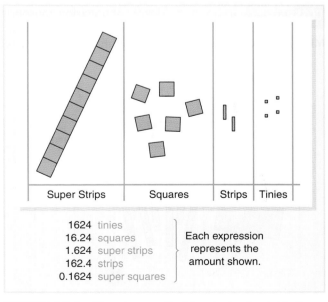

| Super Strips | Squares | Strips | Tinies |

1624 tinies	
16.24 squares	Each expression
1.624 super strips	represents the
162.4 strips	amount shown.
0.1624 super squares	

FIGURE 17.2 The placement of the decimal point indicates which position is the units.

different ways, depending on the choice of the unit or what piece is used to count the entire collection.

The decimal point is placed between two positions with the convention that the position to the left of the decimal is the units or ones position. Thus, the role of the decimal point is to designate the units position, and it does so by sitting just to the right of that position. The decimal notation of a 0 in the ones place, such as 0.60, is the accepted way to write decimal fractions. This is a convention and a way to indicate that the number is less than 1.

Activity 17.1

CCSS-M: 4.NF.C.6; 5.NBT.A.3a

The Decimal Point Names the Unit

Have students display a certain number of base-ten pieces on their desks. For example, put out six squares, two strips, and four tinies as in Figure 17.2. For this activity, refer to the pieces as *squares, strips,* and *tinies,* and reach an agreement on names for the theoretical pieces both smaller and larger. To the right of tinies can be *tiny strips* and *tiny squares.* To the left of squares can be *super strips* and *super squares.* For ELLs and students with disabilities it is particularly important that you write these labels with the corresponding visuals in a prominent place in the classroom (and in student notebooks) so that they can refer to this terminology as they participate in the activity. Each student should also have a "smiling" decimal point. Now ask students to write and say how many squares they have, how many super strips, and so on. The students position their decimal point accordingly and both write and say the amounts.

ENGLISH LANGUAGE LEARNERS

STUDENTS with SPECIAL NEEDS

A reminder to help students think about the decimal point is shown in Figure 17.3, with the "eyes" focusing up toward the name of the units or ones.

Activity 17.1 illustrates the convention that the decimal indicates the named unit and that the unit can change without changing the quantity.

Measurement and Monetary Units. The notion that the decimal point identifies the units place is useful in a variety of contexts. For example, in the metric system, seven place values have names. As shown in Figure 17.4, the decimal point can be used to designate any of these places as the unit without changing the actual measure. The CCSS Mathematical Practices state, "[Mathematically proficient students] express numerical answers with a degree of precision appropriate for the problem context" (CCSSO, 2010, p. 7). Consider the two measurements 0.06 and 0.060. They are equivalent in terms of numerical value, but the latter communicates a greater level of precision. By adding the additional zero, it signals that the measurement was done to the nearest thousandth and that there were 60 thousandths. In the first case, the measurement was completed only to the nearest hundredth, so it might have been 0.058 or 0.063, not necessarily exactly 0.060.

Our monetary system is also a decimal system. In the amount $172.95, the decimal point designates the dollars position as the unit. There are 1 hundred (dollars), 7 tens, 2 singles, 9 dimes (one-tenth of a dollar), and 5 pennies (one-hundredth of a dollar) in this amount of money, regardless of how it is written. If pennies were the designated unit, the same amount would be written as 17,295 cents or 17,295.0 cents. It could just as correctly be 0.17295 thousands of dollars or 1729.5 dimes.

In the case of measures such as metric lengths or weights or the U.S. monetary system, the name of the unit is written after the number rather than above the digit as on a place-value chart. In the paper, we may

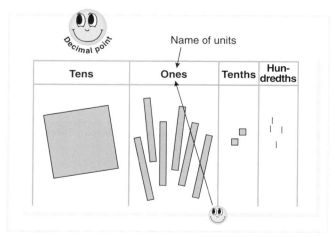

FIGURE 17.3 The decimal point always "looks up at" the name of the units position. In this case, we have 16.24.

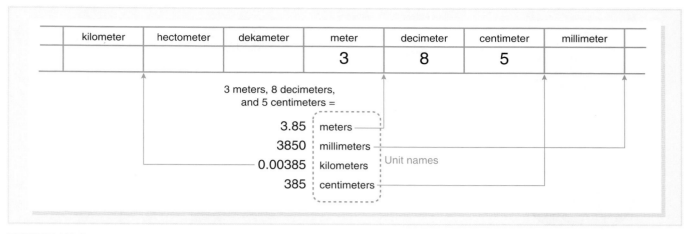

kilometer	hectometer	dekameter	meter	decimeter	centimeter	millimeter	
			3	8	5		

3 meters, 8 decimeters,
and 3 centimeters =

3.85 meters
3850 millimeters
0.00385 kilometers
385 centimeters

Unit names

FIGURE 17.4   In the metric system, each place-value position has a name. The decimal point can be placed to designate which length is the unit length. Any of the metric positions can be the unit length, as illustrated here.

read about Congress spending $7.3 billion. Here the units are billions of dollars, not dollars. A city may have a population of 2.4 million people. That is the same as 2,400,000 individuals.

 Complete Self-Check 17.1: Extending the Place-Value System

 ## Connecting Fractions and Decimals

The symbols 3.75 and $3\frac{3}{4}$ represent the same quantity, yet on the surface they appear quite different. For students, the world of fractions and the world of decimals are very distinct. Even adults tend to think of fractions as sets or areas (e.g., three-fourths of something), but decimals as values or numbers (e.g., weight). When we tell students that 0.75 is the same as $\frac{3}{4}$, this can be confusing because the denominators are hidden in decimal fractions. Even though there are different ways of writing the numbers, the amounts are equal. A significant goal of instruction in decimal and fraction numeration should be to help students see that both systems represent the same concepts.

Say Decimal Fractions Correctly

You must make sure you are reading and saying decimals in ways that support students' understanding and links to fraction numeration. Always say "five and two-tenths" instead of "five point two." Using the point terminology results in a disconnect to the fractional part that exists in every decimal. This is not unlike the ill-advised reading of fractions as "two over ten" instead of correctly saying "two-tenths." This level of precision in language will provide your students with the opportunity to hear the connections between decimals and fractions, so that when they hear "two-tenths," they think of both 0.2 and $\frac{2}{10}$.

Use Visual Models for Decimal Fractions

Many fraction manipulatives are not useful for depicting decimal fractions because they cannot show hundredths or thousandths. It is important to provide visual models for decimal fractions using the same conceptual approaches that were used for fractions such as thirds and fourths.

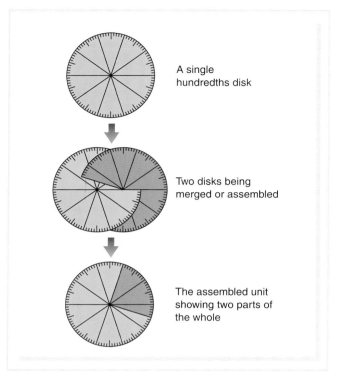

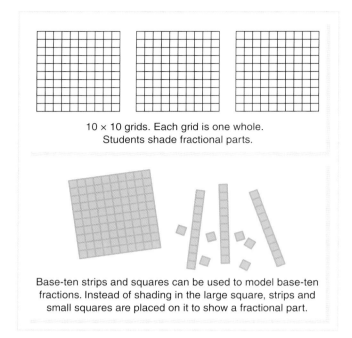

A single
hundredths disk

Two disks being
merged or assembled

The assembled unit
showing two parts of
the whole

FIGURE 17.5 Rational number wheel. For example, rotate the disks to show $\frac{25}{100}$ of the blue plate (also $\frac{1}{4}$ of the circle).

10 × 10 grids. Each grid is one whole.
Students shade fractional parts.

Base-ten strips and squares can be used to model base-ten fractions. Instead of shading in the large square, strips and small squares are placed on it to show a fractional part.

FIGURE 17.6 10 × 10 grids model decimal fractions.

Area Models. Two area models that can be used as representations of decimal fractions are circular disks and a square grid. A Rational Number Wheel shown in Figure 17.5, is marked with 100 equal intervals on the circumference and is cut along one radius. Two disks of different colors, slipped together as shown, can be used to model fractions less than 1. Fractions modeled on this rational number wheel can be read as decimal fractions by noting the units marked around the circumference but can also be stated as simple fractions (e.g., $\frac{3}{4}$), helping students further make the connection between fractions and decimal fractions.

The most common area model for decimal fractions is a 10 × 10 square (see Figure 17.6 and 10 × 10 Grids). Base-ten blocks are often used for this, with the 10-cm square that was used as the "hundreds" now representing the whole, or 1. Each rod (strip) is then 1 tenth, and each small cube ("tiny") is 1 hundredth. With base-ten blocks, the thousands block can also represent the whole, and consequently the flats (squares) are then tenths, the rods hundredths, and small cubes thousandths. 10,000 Grid Paper provides a large square that is subdivided into 10,000 tiny squares. Students can identify how many squares are needed for 0.1, 0.01, 0.001, and 0.0001, using appropriate names for the values. Notice that any one of the base-ten pieces can be assigned the value of 1, which affects the values of the other pieces. A digital version of these blocks, "Base Blocks–Decimals" is available at the National Library of Virtual Manipulative's website.

Because students may be accustomed to a particular piece being used as the unit (e.g., the little square or cube being 1), they can benefit from activities in which the unit changes, such as Activity 17.2. Remember to call the pieces by their place-value name (e.g., hundredths) rather than by their shape (e.g., rod) to reinforce the precise language and the value of the materials. Also highlight the "ths" at the end of the words as both you and the students talk about decimal fractions. Exaggerate the "ths" in your pronunciations as initially students are not accustomed to the small differences in such word as tens and tenths.

Activity 17.2

CCSS-M: 4.NF.C.6; 5.NBT.A.1; 5.NBT.A.2; 5.NBT.A.3a

Shifting Units

Give students a collection of paper base-ten pieces created from Base-Ten Materials, or base-ten blocks. Ask them to pull out a particular mix—for example, a student might have three squares, seven strips, and four "tinies." Tell students that you have the unit behind your back; when you show it to them, they are to figure out how much they have and to record the value. Hold up one of the units. Observe what students record as their value. Ask students to accurately say their quantity aloud. For ELLs and students with disabilities, it is particularly important that you write these labels with the visuals in a prominent place in the classroom (and in student notebooks) so that they can refer to the terminology and illustrations as they participate in the activity. Repeat several times. Be sure to include examples in which a piece is not represented so that students will understand decimal values like 3.07. Continue playing in partners with one student selecting a mix of base-ten pieces and the other student deciding which one is the unit and writing and saying the number.

ENGLISH LANGUAGE LEARNERS

STUDENTS with SPECIAL NEEDS

Length Models. One of the best length models for decimal fractions is a meter stick. Each decimeter is one-tenth of the whole stick, each centimeter is one-hundredth, and each millimeter is one-thousandth. Any number-line model broken into 100 subparts is likewise a useful model for hundredths.

Empty number lines like those used in whole-number computation are also useful in helping students compare decimals and think about scale and place value (Martinie, 2014). Given two or more decimals, students can use an empty number line to position the values, revealing what they know about the size of these decimals using zero, one-half, one, other whole numbers, or other decimal values as benchmarks. A large number line stretched across a wall or on the floor can be an excellent tool for exploring decimals.

Set Models. Many teachers use money as a model for decimals, and to some extent this is helpful. However, for students, money is almost exclusively a two-place system and is nonproportional (e.g., one-tenth, a dime, does not physically compare to a dollar in that proportion.). Numbers like 3.2 or 12.1389 do not relate to money and can cause confusion (Martinie, 2007). Students' initial contact with decimals should be more flexible, and so money is not recommended as an initial model for decimals, although it is certainly an important application of decimal numeration.

Multiple Names and Formats

We acquaint students with the various visual models to help students flexibly think of quantities in terms of tenths and hundredths, and to learn to read and write decimal fractions in different ways. Have students model a decimal fraction, say $\frac{65}{100}$, and then explore the following ideas:

- Is this fraction more or less than $\frac{1}{2}$? Than $\frac{2}{3}$? Than $\frac{3}{4}$? Some familiarity with decimal fractions can be developed by comparison with fractions that are easy to think about.
- What are some different ways to say this fraction using tenths and hundredths? ("6 tenths and 5 hundredths," "65 hundredths") Include thousandths when appropriate.
- Show two ways to write this fraction ($\frac{65}{100}$ or $\frac{6}{10} + \frac{5}{100}$).

Notice that decimals are usually read as a single value. That is, 0.65 is read "sixty-five hundredths." But to understand them in terms of place value, the same number must be thought of as 6 tenths and 5 hundredths. A mixed number such as $5\frac{13}{100}$ is usually read the same way as a decimal: 5.13 is "five and thirteen-hundredths." Please note that it is accurate to use the word "and," which represents the decimal point. For purposes of place value, it should also be understood as $5 + \frac{1}{10} + \frac{3}{100}$. Making these expanded forms with base-ten materials will be helpful in translating fractions to decimals, which is the focus of Activity 17.3.

Activity 17.3

CCSS-M: 4.NF.C.6; 5.NBT.A.1

Build It, Name It

For this activity, have students use their paper Base-Ten Materials. **Agree that the large square represents one.** Have students cover a decimal fractional amount of the square using their strips and tinies (remember to call the pieces "tenths" and "hundredths"). For example, have them cover $2\frac{35}{100}$ of the square. Whole numbers require additional squares. The task is to decide how to write and say this fraction as a decimal and demonstrate the connection using their physical models. **For students with disabilities, you may want to have the amount shaded rather than have the students try to cover the exact amount;** then ask them to name and write the decimal fraction.

STUDENTS
with
SPECIAL
NEEDS

In Activity 17.3, $2\frac{35}{100}$ is the same as 2.35 because there are 2 wholes, 3 tenths, and 5 hundredths. It is important to see this physically. The same materials that are used to represent $2\frac{35}{100}$ of the square can be rearranged or placed on a place-value chart with a paper decimal point used to designate the units position, as shown in Figure 17.7.

The calculator can also play a significant role in developing decimal concepts.

Activity 17.4

CCSS-M: 4.NF.C.6; 5.NBT.A.1

Calculator Decimal Counting

Recall how to make the calculator "count" by pressing ⊞ 1 ⊟ ⊟. and so on. Now have students press ⊞ 0.1 ⊟ ⊟ and so on. When the display shows 0.9, stop and discuss what this means and what the display will look like with the next count. Many students will predict 0.10 (thinking that 10 comes after 9). This prediction is even more interesting if, with each press, the students have been accumulating base-ten strips as models for tenths. One more press would mean one more strip, or 10 strips. Why doesn't the calculator show 0.10? When the tenth press produces a display of 1 (calculators are not usually set to display trailing zeros to the right of the decimal), the discussion should revolve around trading 10 tenths for one whole. Continue to count to 4 or 5 by tenths. How many presses to get from one whole number to the next? **For students with disabilities and ELLs, counting out loud along with the calculator "one tenth, two tenths, . . . " supports the concept** (e.g., 10 tenths as being the same as 1 whole) **while reinforcing appropriate mathematical language.** Students may need to be reminded that a place is "full" when it has 9 of any unit and the addition of another unit will push to the position that is one unit to the left (like the mileage in a car). Once students are working well with tenths, try counting by 0.01 or by 0.001, which dramatically illustrates how small one-hundredth and one-thousandth really are. It requires 10 counts by 0.001 to get to 0.01 and 1000 counts to reach 1.

ENGLISH
LANGUAGE
LEARNERS

STUDENTS
with
SPECIAL
NEEDS

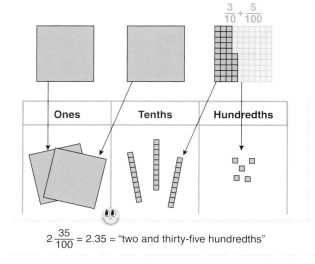

$2\frac{35}{100}$ = 2.35 = "two and thirty-five hundredths"

FIGURE 17.7 Translation of a fraction to a decimal using physical models.

Calculators that permit entry of fractions also have a fraction-decimal conversion key, making them valuable tools for connecting fraction and decimal symbolism. On some calculators, a decimal such as 0.25 will convert to the fraction $\frac{25}{100}$ and allow for either manual or automatic simplification. But challenge students to explain why 0.25 and $\frac{25}{100}$ are equivalent rather than relying on the calculator to do the conversion.

✓ **Complete Self-Check 17.2: Connecting Fractions and Decimals**

Developing Decimal Number Sense

So far, the discussion has largely focused on the connection of decimals to fractions with denominators of 10 and 100. Number sense implies more—having intuition about, or a flexible understanding of, decimal numbers. To this end, it is useful to connect decimals to the fractions with which students are familiar, to be able to compare and order decimals, and to approximate decimals using useful benchmarks.

Results of NAEP exams reveal that students have difficulties with the fraction-decimal relationship. When high school students were asked to translate 0.029 to a fraction, given the choice of $\frac{29}{1000}$ only 30 percent were successful (Kloosterman, 2010). In 2009, Shaughnessy found that more than 46 percent of the sixth graders she studied could not write $\frac{3}{5}$ as a decimal. Instead many wrote $\frac{3}{5}$ as 3.5, 0.35, or 0.3. She also found that more than 25 percent could not write $\frac{3}{10}$ as a decimal. This misconception was also reversed when students wrote the decimal 4.5 as the fraction $\frac{4}{5}$. Division of the numerator by the denominator may be a means of converting fractions to decimals, but it contributes little to understanding the resulting equivalence.

Familiar Fractions Connected to Decimals

Students should extend their conceptual familiarity with common fractions such as halves, thirds, fourths, and eighths to the same concepts expressed as decimal fractions. One way to do this is to have them translate familiar fractions to decimals in a conceptual manner, which is the focus of the next two activities.

Activity 17.5
CCSS-M: 4.NF.C.7

Familiar Fractions to Decimals

Students are given a familiar fraction (e.g., $\frac{3}{5}$) to convert to a decimal. Ask students to shade 10 × 10 Grids to illustrate that value (or build it with base-ten materials). Referring to their shaded grid or the base-ten pieces, ask students to write the decimal equivalent. A good sequence is to start with halves and fifths, then fourths, and possibly eighths. Thirds are a possibility for a student who needs a challenge, as they will result in a repeating decimal. For ELLs, make sure you connect the word decimal to the fact that *deci-* means tens. For students with disabilities, have some preshaded 10 × 10 grids with different fractions shaded and ask the student to find the grid that shows $\frac{1}{2}$. Have them skip count the squares that are shaded to identify the equivalent of $\frac{50}{100}$. Explore an Expanded Lesson for this activity.

ENGLISH LANGUAGE LEARNERS

STUDENTS with SPECIAL NEEDS

Figure 17.8 shows how translations in the last activity might work with a 10 × 10 grid. For fourths, students will often shade a 5 × 5 section (half of a half). The question then becomes how to translate this to a decimal. Ask these students how they could think about each half strip as 0.05 and then use the models to reason that 2 of the half strips (0.05 + 0.05) equal 0.1. So then you would have 0.1 + 0.1 + 0.05, or 0.25, and if they counted the shaded squares they would find $\frac{25}{100}$. This approach starts where the students' prior knowledge is and works toward a solution. The fraction $\frac{3}{8}$ represents a wonderful challenge. A hint might be to find $\frac{1}{4}$ first and then notice that $\frac{1}{8}$ is half of a fourth. Remember that the next smaller pieces are tenths of the "tinies" (or thousands). Therefore, a half of a "tiny" is $\frac{5}{1000}$. Note how the student found that $\frac{2}{8} + \frac{1}{8} = \frac{37}{100} + \frac{5}{1000} = 0.375$.

Because the circular model carries such a strong mental link to fractions, it is worth the time to do some fraction-to-decimal conversions with the rational number wheel shown in Figure 17.5 and used in the next activity.

CCSS Standards for Mathematical Practice
MP2. Reason abstractly and quantitatively.

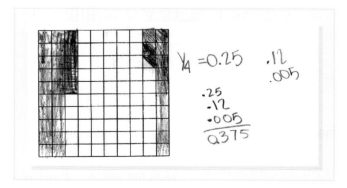

FIGURE 17.8 A student uses a 10 × 10 grid to convert $\frac{3}{8}$ to a decimal.

Activity 17.6

CCSS-M: 4.NF.C.7

Estimate, Then Verify

With the blank side of the Rational Number Wheel **facing them, direct students to adjust the wheel to show a given fraction, for example $\frac{3}{4}$. Next, ask students to estimate how many hundredths they think are equivalent. Then, ask students to justify how they decided their estimate and the corresponding decimal equivalent. Repeat with other fractions. For students with disabilities, cut up some rational number wheels into tenths and hundredths so that these parts can be used as a comparison tool (see Figure 17.9).**

The number line is a good model to connect decimals and fractions. The following activity continues the development of fraction-decimal equivalences.

Activity 17.7

CCSS-M: 4.NF.C.6

Decimals and Fractions on a Double Number Line

Give students five decimal numbers that have familiar fraction equivalents. Keep the numbers between two consecutive whole numbers. For example, use 3.5, 3.125, 3.4, 3.75, and 3.66. Show a number line starting at 3.0 and going to 4.0 as either an empty number line or with subdivisions of only fourths, thirds, or fifths, but without labels. The students' task is to locate each of the decimal numbers on the fraction number line and to provide the fraction equivalent for each.

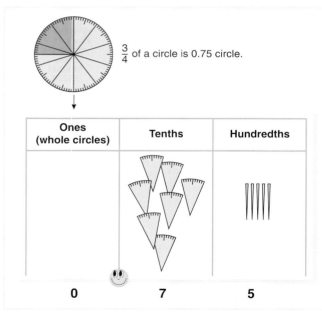

$\frac{3}{4}$ of a circle is 0.75 circle.

Ones (whole circles)	Tenths	Hundredths
0	7	5

FIGURE 17.9 Fraction models could be decimal models.

The exploration of modeling $\frac{1}{3}$ as a decimal is a good introduction to the concept of an infinitely repeating decimal, which is a standard for seventh grade (CCSSO, 2010). Try to partition the whole 10 × 10 Grid into 3 parts using strips and tinies. Each part receives 3 strips with 1 strip left over. To divide the leftover strip, each part gets 3 tinies with 1 left over. To divide the tiny, each part gets 3 tiny strips with 1 left over. (Recall that with base-ten pieces, each smaller piece must be $\frac{1}{10}$ of the preceding size piece.) It becomes apparent that this process is never-ending. As a result, $\frac{1}{3}$ is the same as 0.333333 . . . or 0.$\overline{3}$. For practical purposes, $\frac{1}{3}$ is about 0.333. Similarly, $\frac{2}{3}$ is a repeating string of sixes, or about 0.667. Later, students will discover that many fractions cannot be represented by a finite decimal.

FORMATIVE ASSESSMENT Notes. A simple yet powerful performance assessment to evaluate decimal understanding has students represent two related decimal numbers, such as 0.5 and 0.05, using multiple representations: an empty number line, a 10 × 10 grid, and place value concepts (Martinie, 2014). Ask students to describe their representations. If students have significantly more difficulty with one model over another, this may mean that they have not developed full conceptual understanding of decimal fractions. Placement of decimals on an empty number line is perhaps the most interesting task—and provides the most revealing information (see Figure 17.10). ■

Approximation with a Compatible Fraction. In the real world, decimal fractions are rarely those with exact equivalents to common fractions. What fraction would you say approximates the decimal 0.52? In the sixth NAEP exam, only 51 percent of eighth graders selected $\frac{1}{2}$. The other choices were $\frac{1}{50}$ (29 percent), $\frac{1}{5}$ (11 percent), $\frac{1}{4}$ (6 percent), and $\frac{1}{3}$ (4 percent) (Kouba, Zawojewski, & Strutchens, 1997). Again, students need to wrestle with the size of decimal fractions and begin to develop a sense of familiarity with them.

As with fractions, the first benchmarks that should be developed are 0, $\frac{1}{2}$, and 1. For example, is 7.3962 closer to 7, $7\frac{1}{2}$, or 8? Why? How would you respond to these answers: "Closer to 7 because 3 is less than 5"? or "It is closer to $7\frac{1}{2}$ than 7?" Often the 0, $\frac{1}{2}$, or 1 benchmarks are good enough to make sense of a situation. If more precision is required, encourage students to consider other common fractions (thirds, fourths, fifths, and eighths). In this example, 7.3962 is close to 7.4, which is $7\frac{2}{5}$. A good number sense with decimals entails the ability to think of a fraction that is a close equivalent, a skill needed in the next activity.

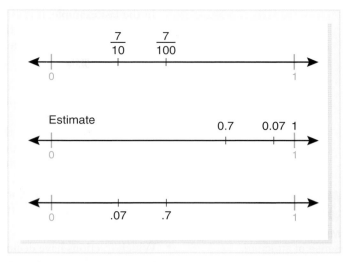

FIGURE 17.10 Three different students attempt to draw a number line and show the numbers 0.7 and 0.07.

Activity 17.8

CCSS-M: 4.NF.C.6

Best Match

STUDENTS
with
SPECIAL NEEDS

Create a deck of Fraction-Decimal Cards of familiar fractions on half of the set of cards and decimals that are close to the fractions but not exact on the other half. In this game students are to pair each fraction with the decimal that best matches it. The difficulty is determined by how close the various fractions are to one another. Some students might select one pairing and then realize there is a better match. For students with disabilities you may need to have them reflect each time on whether what they've turned over is close to 0, close to $\frac{1}{2}$, or close to 1 to help support their matchmaking. Have students share their thinking as the rationales provide strategies that the others will find useful.

FORMATIVE ASSESSMENT Notes. You can find out if your students have a flexible understanding of the connections between models and the two symbol systems for rational numbers—fractions and decimals—with a diagnostic interview. Provide students with a number represented as a fraction, a decimal, or a physical model, and then have them provide the other two representations along with an explanation. Here are a few examples:

- Write the fraction $\frac{5}{8}$ as a decimal. Use a drawing or a physical model (meter stick or 10×10 grid) and explain why your decimal equivalent is correct.
- What fraction is represented by the decimal 2.6? Use a physical model and words to explain your answer.
- Use both a fraction and a decimal to tell what point might be indicated on this number line. Explain your reasoning.

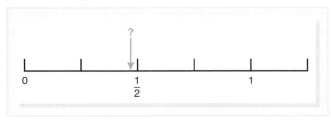

In the last example, it is especially interesting to see which representation students select first—fraction or decimal. Furthermore, do they then translate this number to the other representation or make a second independent estimate?. ∎

Other Fraction-Decimal Equivalents. Recall that the denominator is a divisor and the numerator is a multiplier. For example, $\frac{3}{4}$ means the same as $3 \times (1 \div 4)$ or $3 \div 4$. So how would you express $\frac{3}{4}$ on a simple four-function calculator? Simply enter $3 \div 4$. The display will read 0.75.

Too often, students think that dividing the denominator into the numerator is simply an algorithm for converting fractions to decimals, and they have no understanding of why this might work. Use the opportunity to help students develop the idea that in general $\frac{a}{b} = a \div b$, where b is not 0.

The calculator is an important tool when developing familiarity with decimal concepts. Finding decimal equivalents with a calculator can produce interesting patterns. Here are some questions to explore:

- Which fractions have decimal equivalents that terminate? Is the answer based on the numerator, the denominator, or both?
- For a given fraction, how can you tell the maximum length of the repeating part of the decimal? Try dividing by denominators of 7 and 11 and 13 and then make a conjecture.
- Explore all of the ninths: $\frac{1}{9}, \frac{2}{9}, \frac{3}{9}, \ldots \frac{8}{9}$. Remember that $\frac{1}{3}$ is $\frac{3}{9}$ and $\frac{2}{3}$ is $\frac{6}{9}$. Use only the pattern you discover to predict what $\frac{9}{9}$ should be. But doesn't $\frac{9}{9} = 1$?
- How can you find what fraction produces this repeating decimal: $3.454545\ldots$?

The last question can be generalized for any repeating decimal, illustrating that every repeating decimal is a rational number.

Standards for Mathematical Practice
CCSS
MP7. Look for and make sense of structure.

Comparing and Ordering Decimal Fractions

Comparing decimal fractions and putting them in order from least to greatest is a skill closely related to comparing fractions and decimals. But comparing decimal fractions (particularly "ragged" decimals with unequal length) has important distinctions from comparing whole numbers. These differences can be initially confusing and cause student errors.

FORMATIVE ASSESSMENT Notes. Consider the following list: 0.36, 0.058, 0.375, 0.97, 0, 2.0, and 0.4. Ask students to order these decimals from least to greatest. Use Table 17.1 to identify if the students are exhibiting any of the six common errors and misconceptions that students often demonstrate when comparing and ordering decimals (Desmet, Gregoire, & Mussolin, 2010; Muir & Livy, 2012; Steinle & Stacey, 2004a, 2004b). Knowing these common errors will help you pinpoint ways to improve their conceptual understanding. ∎

TABLE 17.1 **ERRORS AND MISCONCEPTIONS WITH COMPARING AND ORDERING DECIMALS**

Common Error or Misconception	Description	Example
Longer is larger	Students select the number with more digits as largest. This is an overgeneralization of whole-number ideas, as students just look at the number beyond the decimal point and judge it as they would a whole number. This is the most common initial error.	Under this misconception, students would say that 0.375 is greater than 0.97.
Shorter is larger	The student thinks that because the digits far to the right represent very small numbers, hence, longer numbers are smaller because "a tenth is larger than a hundredth." So with this thinking, any amount of tenths is larger than any amount of hundredths.	They would choose 0.4 as larger than 0.97.
Internal zero	In this case, students are confused by a zero in the tenths position, like 0.078, thinking that "zero has no impact" when written to the left, as is the case with a whole number. This has also shown to be a cause for confusion when placing decimals on the number line.	Here they would see 0.58 as less than 0.078.

Common Error or Misconception	Description	Example
Less than zero	When some students compare a decimal to zero, because zero is a whole number positioned in the ones column (to the left of the decimal point), it is therefore greater than a decimal fraction (to the right of the decimal point).	When given 0.36 and 0, they choose 0 as larger.
Reciprocal thinking	This error usually takes teachers by surprise. Using their knowledge that decimals are fractions, they connect 0.4 to $\frac{1}{4}$ and 0.6 to $\frac{1}{6}$ and erroneously decide 0.4 is greater.	When asked to compare 0.4 and 0.6, students incorrectly select 0.4 as larger.
Equality	Another surprise is that students don't integrate the idea of regrouping decimals and that 4 tenths is equal to 40 hundredths or 400 thousandths.	Students think that the 0.4 is not close to 0.375 and/or that 0.3 is smaller than 0.30.

All of these common errors reflect a lack of conceptual understanding of how decimal numbers are constructed. Watch the videos of Vanessa and of Sean comparing decimals at the companion website. Which of the common errors or misconceptions do you think they are exhibiting? Note that Sean can correctly add, but do you think he fully understands what he is adding?

The following activities can help promote discussion about the relative sizes of decimal numbers.

Activity 17.9

CCSS-M: 4.NF.C.6; 4.NF.C.7; 5.NBT.A.1; 5.NBT.A.3a; 5.NBT.A.3b

STUDENTS with SPECIAL NEEDS

Line 'Em Up

Prepare a list of four or five decimal numbers that students might be challenged to put in order between the same two consecutive whole numbers. Use a context such as the height of plants. First, have students predict the order of the numbers, from least to greatest. Then, require students to use a model of their choice to defend their ordering. With the context of plant height, a large, empty number line, shown in Figure 17.11, is useful. As students wrestle with representing the numbers with a model (perhaps a number line or 10,000 Grid Paper), they will necessarily confront the idea of which digits contribute the most to the size of a decimal. For students who are struggling, some explicit instruction might be helpful. Write one of decimals on the board—3.0917, for example. Start with the whole numbers: "Is it closer to 3 or 4?" Then go to the tenths: "Is it closer to 3.0 or 3.1?" Repeat with hundredths and thousandths. At each answer, challenge students to defend their choices with the use of a model or other conceptual explanation.

Density of Decimals

When students only see decimals rounded to two places, this may reinforce the notion that there are no numbers between 2.37 and 2.38 (Steinle & Stacey, 2004b). But an important concept is that there is always another number between any two numbers. Finding the decimal located between any two decimals requires that students understand the density of decimals.

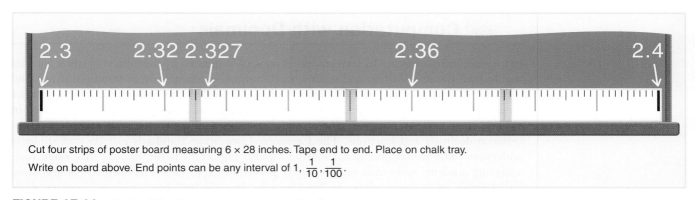

Cut four strips of poster board measuring 6 × 28 inches. Tape end to end. Place on chalk tray.
Write on board above. End points can be any interval of 1, $\frac{1}{10}$, $\frac{1}{100}$.

FIGURE 17.11 Decimal fractions on an empty number line.

Using a linear model helps to show that there is always another decimal to be found between any two decimals—an important concept that is emphasized in the following activities.

Activity 17.10

CCSS-M: 5.NBT.A.3b

Close Decimals

Have your students name a decimal between 0 and 1.0. Next, have them name another decimal that is even closer to 1.0 than the first. Continue for several more decimals in the same manner, each one being closer to 1.0 than the previous decimal. Similarly, try close to 0 or close to 0.5. Let students with disabilities use models or a number line to help them with their decision making. Later, confirm if they can explain their thinking without representations.

STUDENTS
with
SPECIAL NEEDS

Activity 17.11

CCSS-M: 5.NBT.C3b; 6.NS.C.6

Zoom

Stretch a number line (e.g., clothesline or cash register tape) across the front of the room. Ask students to mark where 0.75 and 1.0 are on the line. Then ask students to "zoom in" to find and record three more values between those two values. Ask students to share their thinking strategies. Make sure ELLs are clear of the meaning of the word *between,* even demonstrating this relationship with students in the front of the room. For students with disabilities, you may need to give them a set of choices of decimals and ask them to select three that are between 0.75 and 1.0. See the Expanded Lesson for a full set of procedures, assessment ideas, and questions to pose.

ENGLISH LANGUAGE LEARNERS

STUDENTS
with
SPECIAL NEEDS

Confusion over the density of decimals also plays out when students try to find the nearest decimal (Ubuz & Yayan, 2010). Many times when having students find which decimal is closer to a given decimal, students revert to thinking that tenths are comparable to tenths and that there are no hundredths between. When asked which decimal is closer to 0.19—0.2 or 0.21—they select 0.21 (ignoring the decimal point). They also are unsure if 0.513 is near 0.51. They may also think that 0.3 is near 0.4 but far away from 0.31784. These examples are evidence that students are in need of additional experiences focused on the density of decimals and are probably not yet ready for operations with decimals.

 Complete Self-Check 17.3: Developing Decimal Number Sense

 ## Computation with Decimals

In the past, instruction on decimal computation was dominated by the following rules: Line up the decimal points (addition and subtraction), count the decimal places (multiplication), and shift the decimal point in the divisor and dividend so that the divisor is a whole number (division). Some textbooks continue to emphasize these rules, but specific procedures are not always necessary if computation is built on a firm understanding of place value and a connection between decimals and fractions. The Common Core State Standards expects that students understand why procedures make sense. And also important is the finding that when low-achieving students were only taught highly procedural approaches to decimal computation, initial levels of understanding declined rapidly. In only ten days, students' average daily performance levels of approximately 80 percent dropped to a mean of 34 percent (Woodward, Baxter, & Robinson, 1999).

Addition and Subtraction

There is much more to adding and subtracting decimals than knowing to "line up the decimal points." The Common Core State Standards say that fifth graders should "apply their understandings of models for decimals, decimal notation, and properties of operations to add and subtract decimals to hundredths. They develop fluency in these computations, and make reasonable estimates of their results" (CCSSO, 2010, p. 33) .

Estimating Decimal Sums and Differences. Estimation is important, as often an estimate is all that is needed. Students should become adept at estimating decimal computations before they learn to compute with the standard algorithm. This thinking is aligned with the CCSS (2010), where fifth graders start a focus on decimal computation but the standard algorithm is not required until the sixth grade. As with fractions, until students have a sound understanding of place value, equivalence, and relative size of decimals, they are not ready to develop understanding of the operations (Cramer & Whitney, 2010). An emphasis on estimation is very important, especially for students who have learned the rules for decimal computation yet cannot decide whether their answers are reasonable. A minimum goal should be to have the estimate contain the correct number of digits to the left of the decimal—the whole-number part.

 Pause & Reflect

Before continuing, try making whole-number estimates of the following computations.

1. 4.907 + 123.01 + 56.1234
2. 459.8 − 12.345
3. 0.607 + 0.18
4. 89.1 − 0.998

Your estimates might be:

1. Between 175 and 200
2. A little less than 450
3. Close to 0.8
4. About 88

In these examples, an understanding of decimal numeration and basic whole-number estimation skills (e.g., front-end, rounding, and compatibles) can produce reasonable estimates. When encouraging students to estimate, do not use rigid rules; instead focus on the size of the numbers and the operations and on using a variety of strategies.

Visit the companion website and watch the video of a fourth-grade class playing a game with decimals, called Fill Two, that capitalizes on students' ability to use an area model with a 10 × 10 grid to represent and add decimal fractions. By understanding the size of the decimals, they are better able to estimate how much more they need to fill two wholes.

Developing Addition and Subtraction Algorithms. Invented strategies receive significant attention when developing whole-number computation skills, but there is often less focus on them with fraction and decimal computation. However, invented strategies are grounded in place value, are efficient, and are often more conceptual for students than standard algorithms. This is certainly true for adding and subtracting decimal fractions. Even after the standard algorithm is learned and understood, students should be encouraged to pick the best method given the situation. This is what mathematically proficient students do.

Consider this problem:

Jessica and Sumiko each timed their own quarter-mile run with a stopwatch. Jessica says that she ran the quarter mile in 74.5 seconds. Sumiko was more accurate in her timing, reporting that she ran the quarter mile in 81.34 seconds. Who ran it the fastest and how much faster was she?

CCSS Standards for Mathematical Practice

MP7. Make sense of problems and persevere in solving them.

Students who understand decimal numeration should be able to tell approximately what the difference is—close to 7 seconds. Then they should be challenged to figure out the exact difference using a variety of strategies. The estimate will help them avoid the common error of lining up the 5 under the 4. Instead, students might note that 74.5 and 7 more is 81.5, then figure out how much extra that is (0.16) and subtract the extra to get the difference of 6.34. Other students may count on from 74.5 by adding 0.5, which equals 75, and then add 6 more seconds to get to 81, and finally add on the remaining 0.34 seconds. This strategy can be effectively represented on an empty number line, which aligns with the context of the problem. Another strategy is to change 74.5 to 74.50 and subtract using their prior knowledge regarding regrouping. Similar story problems for addition and subtraction, some involving different numbers of decimal places, will help develop students' understanding.

After students have had several opportunities to solve addition and subtraction story problems, it is important to see if they can flexibly think about a problem through multiple representations, as in the next activity.

Activity 17.12

CCSS-M: 5.NBT.B.7

Representing Sums and Differences

Give students a copy of the Translation Task Activity Page with a problem involving different numbers of decimal places, such as 73.46 + 6.2 + 0.582, in the upper left quadrant. Students should estimate and then calculate the answer. The second task is to write a situation that fits the problem. In the third quadrant they can illustrate the operation using an empty number line or base-ten pieces. Finally, they explain how they solved the problem in the last box, sharing their strategy for adding decimal numbers. The same task can be done with subtraction.

FORMATIVE ASSESSMENT Notes. As students complete Activity 17.12, use a checklist to record whether they are showing evidence of having an understanding of decimal concepts and the role of the decimal point in computation. Note whether students get a correct sum by using a rule they learned but are challenged to give an explanation, or if they are unable to describe a situation that matches the computation or create a corresponding illustration. If there are difficulties in several areas of the task, shift attention to the foundational decimal concepts until those are understood. ■

As students become more proficient in adding and subtracting with the standard algorithm, continue to provide opportunities for them to estimate, illustrate by using one of the two models discussed here, use invented strategies, and explain a context to fit the situation. For example, the NLVM game "Circle 3" is a great reasoning experience that challenges students to use logic as they combine decimals to add to 3 (it is not as easy as it sounds!). These types of continued experiences will ensure that students develop procedural proficiency for decimal addition and subtraction.

Multiplication

Multiplication of decimals tends to be poorly understood. Students (and adults) blindly count over how many decimal places they have in the problem to decide where the decimal point will be placed in the answer. Often little attempt is made to assess if the answer is reasonable. But being mathematically proficient means having a much deeper understanding of multiplication of decimals. Students need to be able to use concrete models or drawings, choose strategies based on place value (invented strategies) and properties of operations, and explain the reasoning used (CCSSO, 2010). Estimation is essential in building that understanding.

Estimating Products. It might be argued that much of the estimation in the real world involves fractions, decimals, and percents. A key consideration in estimating is using whole numbers to estimate rational numbers.

Decide what numbers you would use in each case as you estimate the problems listed below. Which ones were easy to estimate? Difficult?

1. 5.91 × 6.1
2. 145.33 × 0.109
3. 0.58 × 9.67023

A student's reasoning might be similar to the following:

1. This is about 6 times 6, so the answer is about 36.
2. This is like 145 dimes, so divide by 10 and it is about 14.50. *Or*, this is about one tenth of 145, so 14.5.
3. The first value is about one-half, so half of about 10 is about 5.

When problems involve two very small decimals, estimation is difficult, but it is still possible to look at the answer to see if it is relatively smaller than what the initial factor was (taking a small part of a small part results in an even smaller part).

Activity 17.13

CCSS-M: 5.NBT.B.7; 6.NS.B.3

Hit the Target: Continuous Input

Select a target range. Next, enter the starting number in the calculator and hand it to the first player. For multiplication or division, only one operation is used through the whole game. After the first or second turn, decimal factors are usually required. This variation provides excellent understanding of multiplication or division by decimals. A sequence for a target of 262 to 265 might be like this:

Start with 63.

Player 1	☒ 5 ☰ ⟶	315 (too high)
Player 2	☒ 0.7 ☰ ⟶	220.5 (too low)
Player 1	☒ 1.3 ☰ ⟶	286.65 (too high)
Player 2	☒ 0.9 ☰ ⟶	257.985 (too low)
Player 1	☒ 1.03 ☰ ⟶	265.72455 (very close!)

(What would you press next?)

This game can be played using division. Adapt the game for addition and subtraction; the first player then presses either ⊞ or ⊟ followed by a number and then ☰.

Developing Multiplication Algorithms. Explore multiplication of decimals by using problems in a context and by returning to physical models that were useful in thinking about whole-number multiplication. Estimation should play a significant role in developing a multiplication algorithm. As a beginning, consider this problem:

The farmer fills each jug with 3.7 liters of cider. If you buy 4 jugs, how many liters of cider is that?

Ask students, "Is it more than 12 liters? What is the most it could be?" Once an estimate of the result is decided on, let students use their own methods for determining an exact answer (based on place value and properties). One strategy might be to double 3.7 (which equals 7.4), double it again, and total. Another is to multiply 3 × 4, then count on 0.7 four times. Or, students may double 3.7 (getting 7.4) and double it again. Eventually, students will agree on the exact result of 14.8 liters. Connect these strategies to the number line, showing how jumps on the decimal number line match the invented strategies.

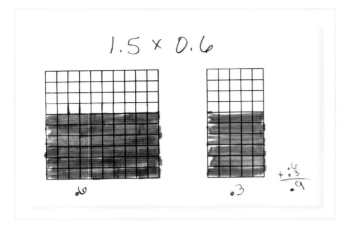

1.5 × 0.6

FIGURE 17.12 A student's use of 10 × 10 grids to reason about 1.5 × 0.6.

The area model is particularly useful in illustrating decimal multiplication (Rathouz, 2011). Use a scenario such as this one that aligns with the rectangular array:

A gardener has 1.5 m² of her garden where she can plant flowers. She decides to plant bluebells on an area that is 0.6 of the garden. On how many total square meters did she plant bluebells?

See a student's solution (Figure 17.12) using a grid diagram to model the problem 0.6 × 1.5. Each large square represents 1 m² with each row of 10 small squares as 0.1 m² and each small square as 0.01 m². The shaded section shows 0.6 m² + 0.3 m² = 0.9 m². Notice that this is a proportional model, allowing students to "see" the values of the factors.

Also use problems that can be illustrated with an empty number line such as:

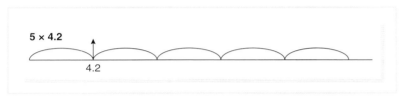

FIGURE 17.13 A number line is used to illustrate multiplication of decimals.

A frog hops 4.2 inches at every hop. How far away is she from her starting point after 5 hops?

Figure 17.13 provides illustrations of a line to illustrate the frog leaps. This illustration should remind students of the multiplication strategies they already know; this connection can be used in developing meaning for the standard algorithm for decimal multiplication.

Ask students to compare a decimal product with one involving the same digits but no decimal. For example, how are 23.4 × 6.5 and 234 × 65 alike? Interestingly, both products have exactly the same digits: 15210. (The zero may be missing from the decimal product.) Have students use a calculator to explore other products that are alike except for the location of the decimals points involved. The digits in the answer are always alike. After seeing how the digits remain the same for these related products, do the following activity.

Activity 17.14 CCSS-M: 5.NBT.B.7; 6.NS.B.3

ENGLISH LANGUAGE LEARNERS

Where Does the Decimal Go? Multiplication

Have students compute the following product: 24 × 63. Using only the result of this computation (1512) and estimation, have them give the exact answer to each of the following:

0.24 × 6.3   24 × 0.63   2.4 × 63   0.24 × 0.63

For each computation, they should write a rationale for how they placed the decimal point. For examples, on the first one a student might explain that 0.24 is close to one-fourth and one-fourth of 6 is less than two, so the answer must be 1.512. They can check their results with a calculator. ELLs may apply a different mental strategy that is common in their country of origin. Even if they have trouble articulating their reasoning, it is important to consider alternative ways to reason through the problem. Discussing errors and how to avoid them is also an important class discussion.

❚❚ Pause & Reflect

What is the value in having students explain how they placed the decimal point? How does that compare to having students count over the number of places? ●

Another way to support full understanding of the algorithm is to rewrite the decimals in their fraction equivalents. So if you are multiplying 3.4 × 1.7, that is the same as $\frac{34}{10} \times \frac{17}{10}$.

When multiplied, you would get $\frac{578}{100}$, which rewritten as a decimal fraction is 5.78, which corresponds to moving the decimal two places to the left (Rathouz, 2011).

The method of placing the decimal point in a product by way of estimation is more difficult as the product gets smaller. For example, knowing that 37×83 is 3071 does not make it easy to place the decimal in the product 0.037×0.83. But the standard algorithm can be developed from this problem, all the while helping students understand the properties of multiplication. Here is the process:

$$0.037 \times 0.83 = (37 \times \tfrac{1}{1000}) \times (83 \times \tfrac{1}{100})$$

$$(37 \times \tfrac{1}{1000}) \times (83 \times \tfrac{1}{100}) = 37 \times 83 \times \tfrac{1}{1000} \times \tfrac{1}{100}$$

$$37 \times 83 \times \tfrac{1}{1000} \times \tfrac{1}{100} = (37 \times 83) \times (\tfrac{1}{1000} \times \tfrac{1}{100})$$

$$(37 \times 83) \times (\tfrac{1}{1000} \times \tfrac{1}{100}) = 3071 \times \tfrac{1}{100,000} = 0.03071$$

This may look complicated, but if you just follow what is happening with the decimal fractions, you can see why you count the number of values to the right of each factor, and then place the decimal in the product so that it has the same number of decimal places. The standard algorithm for multiplication is the following: Do the computation as if all numbers were whole numbers. When finished, place the decimal by reasoning or estimation if possible. If not, count the decimal places, as illustrated previously. Even if students have already learned the standard algorithm, they need to know the conceptual rationale centered on place value and the powers of ten for "counting" and shifting the decimal places. By focusing on rote applications of rules, students lose out on opportunities to understand the meaning and effects of operations and are more prone to misapply procedures (Martinie & Bay-Williams, 2003).

Questions such as the following keep the focus on number sense and provide useful information about your students' understanding.

1. Consider these two computations: $3\frac{1}{2} \times 2\frac{1}{4}$ and 2.27×3.18. Without doing the calculations, which product do you think is larger? Provide a reason for your answer that can be understood by someone else in this class.
2. How much larger is 0.26×8 than 0.25×8? How can you tell without doing the computation?

Student discussions and explanations as they work on these or similar questions can provide insights into their decimal and fraction number sense and the connections between the two representations.

CCSS Standards for Mathematical Practice
MP2. Reason abstractly and quantitatively.

CCSS Standards for Mathematical Practice
MP3. Construct viable arguments and critique the reasoning of others.

Division

In the same way multiplication of decimals is often carried out rotely, division of decimals can be poorly understood. Returning to whole-number understanding of the meaning of the operation of division can help students make sense of decimal division. Watch as John A. Van de Walle at the companion website discusses patterns with and teaching division of decimals in a problem-based manner.

Estimating Quotients. Division can be approached in a manner exactly parallel to multiplication. In fact, the best approach to a division estimate generally comes from thinking about multiplication rather than division. Consider the following problem:

The trip to Washington was 282.5 miles. It took exactly 4.5 hours to drive. What was the average miles per hour?

To make an estimate of this quotient, think about what times 4 or 5 is close to 280. You might think $60 \times 4.5 = 240 + 30 = 270$. So maybe about 61 or 62 miles per hour.

Here is a second example without context.

Make an estimate of $45.7 \div 1.83$. Think only of what times $1\frac{8}{10}$ is close to 46.

Pause & Reflect

Will the answer be more or less than 46? Why? Will it be more or less than 20? Now think about 1.8 being close to 2. What times 2 is close to 46? Use this to produce an estimate. •

Because 1.83 is close to 2, the estimate is near 23. And because 1.83 is less than 2, the answer must be greater than 23—say, 25 or 26. (The actual answer is 24.972677.)

Developing the Division Algorithm. Although estimation can produce a reasonable result, you may still require a standard algorithm to produce an exact answer in the same way it was done for multiplication. Figure 17.14 shows division by a whole number and how that can be carried out to as many places as you wish. (The explicit-trade method described in Chapter 13 is shown on the right.)

Activity 17.15

CCSS-M: 5.NBT.B.7; 6.NS.B.3

Where Does the Decimal Go? Division

ENGLISH LANGUAGE LEARNERS

Provide a quotient such as 146 ÷ 7 = 20857—correct to five digits but without the decimal point. The task is to use only this information and estimation to give a fairly precise answer to each of the following:

   146 ÷ 0.7   1.46 ÷ 7   14.6 ÷ 0.7   1460 ÷ 70

For each computation, students should write a rationale for their answers and then check their results with a calculator. Any errors should be acknowledged, and the rationale that produced the error adjusted. As noted in multiplication, ELLs may apply a different mental strategy, and it is important to value alternative approaches. Again, engage students in explicit discussions of common errors or misconceptions and how to fix them.

23.5 ÷ 8

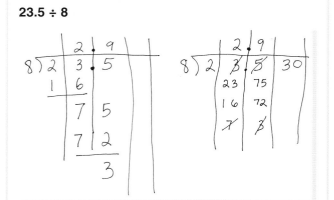

Trade 2 tens for 20 ones, making 23 ones.
Put 2 ones in each group, or 16 in all.
That leaves 7 ones.

Trade 7 ones for 70 tenths, making 75 tenths.
Put 9 tenths in each group, or 72 tenths in all.
That leaves 3 tenths.

Trade the 3 tenths for 30 hundredths.

(Continue trading for smaller pieces as long as you wish.)

FIGURE 17.14 Extension of the division algorithm.

An algorithm for division is parallel to that for multiplication: Ignore the decimal points and do the computation as if all numbers were whole numbers. When finished, place the decimal using estimation. This is reasonable for divisors greater than 1 or close to a familiar value (e.g., 0.1, 0.5, 0.01). If students have a method for dividing by 45, they can divide by 0.45 and 4.5.

✓ **Complete Self-Check 17.4: Computation with Decimals**

Introducing Percents

The term *percent* is simply another name for *hundredths* and as such is a standardized ratio with a denominator of 100. If students can express fractions and decimals as hundredths, the term *percent* can be substituted for the term *hundredth*. Consider the fraction $\frac{3}{4}$. As a fraction expressed in hundredths, it is $\frac{75}{100}$. When $\frac{3}{4}$ is written in decimal form, it is 0.75. Both 0.75 and $\frac{75}{100}$ are read in exactly the same way, "seventy-five hundredths." When used as operators, $\frac{3}{4}$ of something is the same as 0.75 or 75 percent of that same thing. Thus, percent is merely a new notation and terminology, not a new concept.

The results of the 2005 NAEP exam reveals that only 37 percent of eighth graders could determine the new amount when given a percent of increase. A common error was that many students believe the increased amount is calculated by adding the percent itself to the original amount. That is, for a 10 percent increase, they would select an answer that was 10 more than starting value. In another question, only 30 percent could accurately calculate the percent of the tip when given the cost of the meal and the amount of the tip left by the diners. In this book, we explore percentages twice; here connected to fractions and decimals and in Chapter 18 as we explore percent as a ratio.

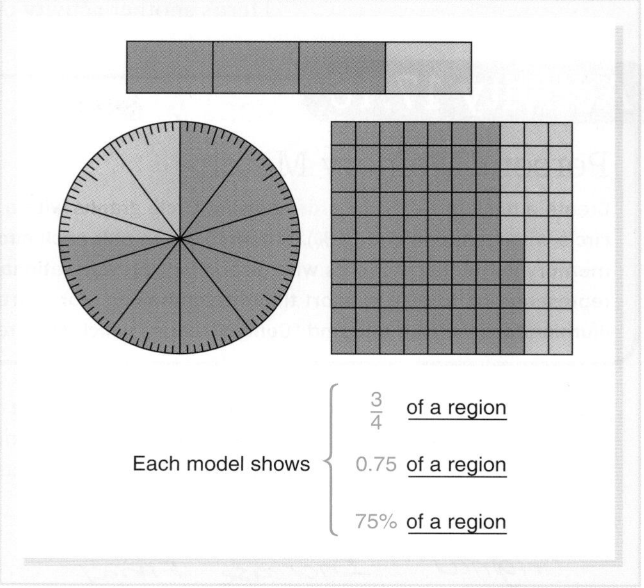

Physical Models and Terminology

Physical models provide the main link between fractions, decimals, and percents, as shown in Figure 17.15, the Rational Number Wheel, and 10 × 10 Grid. Base-ten models are suitable for fractions, decimals, and percents, because they all represent the same idea. The rational number wheel (Figure 17.5) with 100 markings around the circumference is a model for percents as well as a fraction model for hundredths. The same

Each model shows:
- $\frac{3}{4}$ of a region
- 0.75 of a region
- 75% of a region

FIGURE 17.15   Models connect three different notations.

is true of a 10 × 10 grid where each little square inside is 1 percent of the grid. Each row or strip of 10 squares is not only a tenth but also 10 percent of the grid.

Zambo (2008) suggests linking fractions to percent using a 10 × 10 grid. By marking one out of every four squares on the chart or shading a 5 × 5 region in the corner of the grid, students can discover the link between $\frac{1}{4}$ and $\frac{25}{100}$ or 25 percent. Zambo goes on to suggest that even more complex representations, such as $\frac{1}{8}$, can lead to interesting discussions about the remaining squares left at the end resulting in $12\frac{1}{2}$ out of 100 squares or $12\frac{1}{2}$ percent (or 12.5 percent).

Similarly, the common fractions (halves, thirds, fourths, fifths, and eighths) should become familiar in terms of percents as well as decimals. Three-fifths, for example, is 60 percent as well as 0.6. One-third of an amount is frequently expressed as $33\frac{1}{3}$ percent instead of 33.3333 . . . percent. These ideas should be explored with base-ten models and with contexts rather than poorly understood rules about moving decimal points.

One representation that can be used to link percentages with data collection is a percent necklace. Using fishing cord or sturdy string, link 100 beads and knot them in a tight, circular necklace. Anytime a circle graph is displayed in class, the percent necklace can provide an estimation tool. Given any circle graph, even a human circle graph as shown in Figure 21.9 on page 564, place the necklace in a circle so that its center coincides with the center of the circle graph (don't try to align the necklace with the outside edge of the circle graph). If the necklace makes a wider concentric circle, students can use a straight edge to extend the lines distinguishing the different categories straight out to meet the necklace. If the circle graph is larger than the necklace, as it would be in Figure 21.9, merely use the radial lines marking off the categories. Have students count the number of beads between any two lines that represent a category. For example, they might find that 24 beads are in the section of the circle graph that shows how many students selected blue as their favorite color. That becomes an estimate that approximately 24 percent of the students favor blue. Counting the beads in a given category gives students an informal approach to estimating percent while investigating a meaningful model for thinking about the concept of per-one-hundred.

TECHNOLOGY Note. The activity "Fraction Models" on the NCTM Illuminations website explores equivalence of fractions, mixed numbers, decimals, and percents. You select the fraction and pick the type of model (length, area [rectangle or circle], or set), and it shows the corresponding visual and all the equivalences. ∎

Here's another activity that focuses just on representations of percent:

Activity 17.16

CCSS-M: 6.RP.A.3c

Percent Memory Match

Create a deck of Percent Cards showing circle graphs with a percentage shaded in and matching percents (like a circle with $\frac{1}{2}$ shaded and 50%). Students are to pair each circle graph with the percent that best matches it in a memory game. For students with disabilities, provide rational number wheels (Figure 17.5) as a movable representation to help support their matchmaking. For a virtual game that has the same goal, go to the NCTM Illuminations website and find "Concentration," which uses representations of percents and fractions and a regional model.

STUDENTS
with
SPECIAL
NEEDS

Percent concepts can be developed through other powerful visual representations that link to proportional thinking. One option is the use of a three-part model to represent the original amount, the decrease/increase, and the final amount (Parker, 2004). Using three rectangles that can be positioned and divided, students can analyze components and consider each piece of the model. The rectangles can be a particularly useful representation for the often confusing problems that include a percentage increase to find an amount greater than the original. In a 2005 NAEP item, students were asked to calculate how many employees there were at a company whose workforce increased by 10 percent over the previous level of 90. Using Parker's approach, you can see in Figure 17.16 how a student used this proportional model to come up with a correct solution.

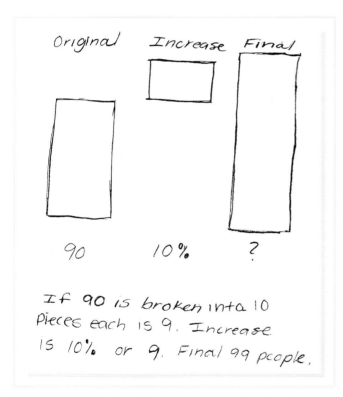

FIGURE 17.16 A student uses a proportional model for reasoning about percent.

Another helpful approach to the terminology involved with percentages is through the role of the decimal point. Recall that the decimal point identifies the units position. When the unit is ones, a number such as 0.659 means a little more than 6 tenths of 1. The word *ones* is understood (6 tenths of 1 one or one whole). But 0.659 is also 6.59 tenths and 65.9 hundredths and 659 thousandths. The name of the unit must be explicitly identified. Because *percent* is another name for hundredths, when the decimal point identifies the hundredths position as the units, the word *percent* can be specified as a synonym for hundredths. Thus, 0.659 (of some whole or 1) is 65.9 hundredths or 65.9 percent of that same whole. As illustrated in Figure 17.17, the notion of placing the decimal point to identify the percent position is conceptually more meaningful than the rule: "To change a decimal to a percent, move the decimal two places to the right." A more conceptually focused idea is to equate hundredths with percent both orally and in notation.

Percent Problems in Context

Some teachers may talk about "the three percent problems." The sentence "_____ is _____ percent of _____" has three spaces for numbers—for example, "20 is 25 percent of 80." The classic three percent problems come from this sterile expression; two of the numbers are given, and the students are asked to produce the third. Students tend to set up proportions but are not quite sure which numbers to put where. In other words, they are not connecting understanding with the procedure. Furthermore, commonly encountered percent

		Percent	
Ones	Tenths	Hundredths	Thousandths
	3	6	5

0.365 (of 1 whole) = 36.5 percent (of 1 whole)

FIGURE 17.17 Hundredths are also known as percents.

situations, such as sales figures, taxes, food composition (% of fat), and economic trends are almost never in the " _____ is _____ percent of _____" format.

Though students must have some experience with the noncontextual situations in Figure 17.18, it is important to have them explore percent relationships in real contexts. Find or make up percent problems, and present them in the same way that they appear in newspapers, on television, and in other real contexts. In addition to realistic problems and formats, follow these guidelines for your instruction on percents:

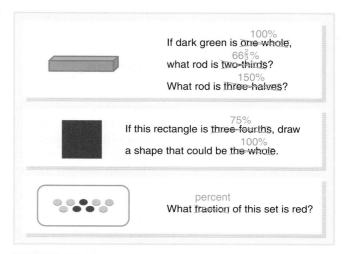

FIGURE 17.18 Part-whole fraction exercises can be translated into percent exercises.

- Emphasize percents to familiar fractions (halves, thirds, fourths, fifths, and eighths) or easy percents ($\frac{1}{10}, \frac{1}{100}$), and use numbers compatible with these fractions. The focus of these exercises is the relationships involved, not complex computations.
- Do not rush to developing rules or procedures for different types of problems—encourage students to notice patterns.
- Use the terms *part*, *whole*, and *percent* (or *fraction*). *Fraction* and *percent* are interchangeable. Help students see these percent exercises as the same types of exercises they did with simple fractions.
- Require students to use models, drawings, and contexts to explain their solutions. It is wiser to assign three problems requiring a drawing and an explanation than to give 15 problems requiring only computation and answers. Remember that the purpose is the exploration of relationships, not computational skill.
- Encourage mental computation.

The following problems meet these criteria for familiar fractions and compatible numbers. Try working each problem, identifying each number as a part, a whole, or a fraction. Draw bar diagrams to explain or work through your thought process. Examples of student reasoning using bar diagrams are illustrated in Figure 17.19.

1. The PTA reported that 75 percent of the total number of families were represented at the meeting. If students from 320 families go to the school, how many were represented at the meeting?
2. The baseball team won 80 percent of the 25 games it played this year. How many games were lost?
3. In Mrs. Carter's class, 20 students, or $66\frac{2}{3}$ percent, were on the honor roll. How many students are in her class?
4. Zane bought his new computer at a $12\frac{1}{2}$ percent discount. He paid $700. How many dollars did he save by buying it at a discount?
5. If Nicolas has read 60 of the 180 pages in his library book, what percent of the book has he read so far?
6. The hardware store bought widgets at 80 cents each and sold them for $1 each. What percent did the store mark up the price of each widget?

FORMATIVE ASSESSMENT Notes. These context-based percent problems are an effective performance assessment to evaluate students' understanding. Assign one or two, and have students explain why they think their answer makes sense. You might take a percent problem and substitute fractions for percents (e.g., use $\frac{1}{8}$ instead of $12\frac{1}{2}$ percent) to see how students handle these problems with fractions compared to percents.

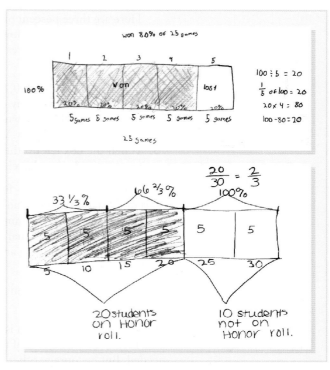

FIGURE 17.19 Students use bar diagrams to solve percent problems.

If your focus is on reasoning and justification rather than number of problems correct, you will be able to collect all the assessment information you need. ∎

Estimation

Many percent problems do not have simple (familiar) numbers. Frequently, in real life an approximation or estimate in percent situations is enough to help one think through the situation. Even if a calculator will be used to get an exact answer, an estimate based on an understanding of the relationship confirms that a correct operation was performed or that the decimal point was positioned correctly.

To help students with estimation in percent situations, two ideas that have already been discussed can be applied. First, when the percent is not a simple one, substitute a close percent that is easy to work with. Second, select numbers that are compatible with the percent involved to make the calculation easy to do mentally. In essence, convert the complex percent problem into one that is more familiar. Here are some examples.

1. The 83,000-seat stadium was 73 percent full. How many people were at the game?
2. The treasurer reported that 68.3 percent of the dues had been collected, for a total of $385. How much more money could the club expect to collect if all dues are paid?
3. Max McStrike had 217 hits in 842 at bats. What was his batting average?

 Pause & Reflect

Use familiar percents, fractions, and compatible numbers to estimate solutions to each of these last three problems. ●

Your estimates might be similar to the following:

1. (Use $\frac{3}{4}$ and 80,000) → about 60,000
2. (Use $\frac{2}{3}$ and $380; will collect $\frac{1}{3}$ more) → about $190
3. ($4 \times 217 > 842$; $\frac{1}{4}$ is 25 percent, or 0.250) → a bit more than 0.250

Here are three percent problems with two sets of numbers. The first number in the set is a compatible number that allows the problem to be worked mentally using fraction equivalents. The second number requires a substitution with an approximation or estimation as in the last activity.

1. The school enrolls {480, 547} students. Yesterday { $12\frac{1}{2}$ percent, 13 percent} of the students were absent. How many came to school?
2. Mr. Carver sold his lawn mower for {$45, $89}. This was {60 percent, 62 percent} of the price he paid for it new. What did the mower cost when it was new?
3. When the box fell off the shelf, {90, 63} of the {720, 500} widgets broke. What percentage was lost in the breakage?

The first problem asks for a part (whole and fraction given), the second asks for a whole (part and fraction given), and the third asks for a fraction (part and whole given).

There are several common uses for estimating percentages in real-world situations. As students gain full conceptual understanding and flexibility, there are ways to think about percents that are useful as you are shopping or in situations that bring thinking about percents to the forefront.

Tips. To figure a tip, you can find 10 percent of the amount and then half of that again to make 15 percent.

Taxes. The same approach is used for adding on sales tax. Depending on the tax rate, you can find 10 percent, take half of that, and then find 1 percent and add or subtract that amount as needed. But encourage other approaches as well. Students should realize that finding percents is a process of multiplication; therefore, finding 8 percent (tax) of $50 will generate the same result as finding 50 percent (half) of 8, or $4.

Discounts. A 30 percent decrease is the same as 70 percent of the original amount, and depending on the original amount, using one of those percents may be easier to use in mental calculations than the other. If a $48 outfit is 30 percent off, for example, you are paying 70 percent. Round $48 to $50 and you have .70 × 50 (think 7 × 5), so your cost is less than $35.

Again, these are not rules to be taught, but reasoning activities to develop that require a full understanding of percent concepts and the commutative property.

 Complete Self-Check 17.5: Introducing Percents

REFLECTIONS ON CHAPTER 17

WRITING TO LEARN

1. List three different models that help support students' exploration of decimals.

2. How can we help students think about very small place values such as thousandths and millionths in the same way we get students to think about very large place values such as millions and billions?

3. Use an example involving base-ten pieces to explain the role of the decimal point in identifying the units position. Relate this idea to changing units of metric measurement.

4. Explain how the line-up-the-decimals rule for adding and subtracting can be developed through practice with estimation.

5. Explain how the line-up-the-decimals rule for adding and subtracting decimals can be developed through practice with estimation.

6. Give an example explaining how, in many problems, multiplication and division with decimals can be replaced with estimation and whole-number methods.

FOR DISCUSSION AND EXPLORATION

◆ A way you may have learned to order a series of decimals is to annex zeros to each number so that all numbers have the same number of decimal places. For example, rewrite

0.34 as 0.3400

0.3004 as 0.3004

0.059 as 0.0590

Now ignore the decimal points and any leading zeros, and order the resulting whole numbers. This method was found to detract from students' conceptual understanding (Roche & Clarke, 2004). Why do you think that was the case? What should you try instead?

RESOURCES FOR CHAPTER 17

LITERATURE CONNECTIONS

In newspapers and magazines, you will find decimal and percent situations with endless real-world connections. Money-related increases and decreases are interesting to project over several years. If the consumer price index rises approximately 3 percent a year, how much will a $100 shopping cart of groceries cost by the time your students are 21 years old?

The Phantom Tollbooth *Juster (1961)*

Mathematical ideas abound in this story about Milo's adventures in Digitopolis, where everything is number-oriented. There, Milo meets a half of a boy, appearing in the illustration as the left half of a boy cut from top to bottom. As it turns out, the boy is actually 0.58 because he is a member of the average family: mother, father, and 2.58 children. The boy is the 0.58. One advantage, he explains, is that he is the only one who can drive 0.3 of a car, as the average family owns 1.3 cars. This story can lead to a great discussion of averages that result in decimals.

An extension is to explore averages that are interesting to the students (average number of siblings, etc.) and see where these odd decimal fractions come from. Illustrating an average number of pets can be very humorous!

Piece = Part = Portion: Fraction = Decimal = Percent *Gifford & Thaler (2008)*

Illustrated with vivid photos, this book shows how fractions relate to decimals and percents. Written by a teacher, connections are made through common representations, such as one sneaker representing $\frac{1}{2}$ or 0.50 or 50 percent of a pair of shoes. Real-world links such as one-seventh of a week and one-eleventh of a soccer team will connect with students.

RECOMMENDED READINGS

Articles

Cramer, K., Monson, D., Wyberg, T., Leavitt, S., & Whitney, S. B. (2009). Models for initial decimal ideas. *Teaching Children Mathematics, 16*(2), 106–116.

This article describes ways of using 10 × 10 grids and decimal addition and subtraction boards to enhance students' understanding. Several diagnostic interviews and an emphasis on having students use words, pictures, and numbers are included.

Martinie, S. (2014). Decimal fractions: An important point. *Mathematics Teaching in the Middle School, 19*(7), 420–429.

By offering assessment tasks for decimals that include using multiple representations, the author taps into common misconceptions and confusions faced by students learning about decimals. A summary of student responses and samples of work help pinpoint common problems and implications. Next instructional steps are shared.

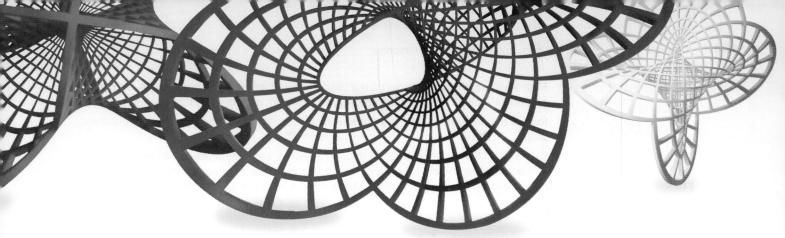

18

Ratios, Proportions, and Proportional Reasoning

LEARNER OUTCOMES

After reading this chapter and engaging in the embedded activities and reflections, you should be able to:

18.1 Describe the essential features of a ratio, including how it relates to fractions, and articulate ways to help students understand and be able to use ratios.

18.2 Contrast proportional and nonproportional situations using additive and multiplicative examples.

18.3 Illustrate the different ways to solve proportional problems and describe a developmental progression for these ways.

18.4 Compare traditional methods of teaching proportional reasoning to research-based methods.

In their book describing the essential understandings of ratios, proportions, and proportional reasoning, Lobato and Ellis (2010) write that it is really all one big idea: "When two quantities are related proportionally, the ratio of one quantity to the other is invariant as the numerical values of both quantities change by the same factor" (p. 11).

Proportional reasoning goes well beyond the notion of setting up a proportion to solve a problem—it is a way of reasoning about multiplicative situations. In fact, proportional reasoning, like equivalence, is considered a unifying theme in mathematics. It is estimated that more than half the population of adults are not proportional thinkers (Lamon, 2012). This is a direct result of mathematics experiences that exclusively focused on solving missing-value proportions. Such rote practice is particularly troubling in the area of proportional reasoning because it is at the core of so many important concepts, including "similarity, relative growth and size, dilations, scaling, pi, constant rate of change, slope, speed, rates, percent, trigonometric ratios, probability, relative frequency, density, and direct and inverse variations" (Heinz & Sterba-Boatwright, 2008, p. 528). Wow!

BIG IDEAS

♦ A ratio is a multiplicative comparison of two quantities or measures. A key developmental milestone is the ability of a student to think of a ratio as a distinct entity, different from the two measures that made it up.

- Ratios and proportions involve multiplicative rather than additive comparisons. This means that equal ratios result from multiplication or division, not from addition or subtraction.
- Rate is a way to represent a ratio, and in fact represents an infinite number of equivalent ratios.
- Proportional thinking is developed through activities and experiences involving comparing and determining the equivalence of ratios. This means solving proportions in a wide variety of problem-based contexts and situations through reasoning, not rigid use of formulas.

 # Ratios

A *ratio* is a number that relates two quantities or measures within a given situation in a multiplicative relationship (in contrast to a difference or additive relationship). Reasoning with ratios involves paying attention to two quantities that covary. Ratios and rates are described as one of the four critical areas in grade 6 (CCSSO, 2010). These concepts grow out of students' prior understanding of multiplicative reasoning, in particular multiplicative comparisons.

Types of Ratios

Part-to-Part Ratios. A ratio can relate one part of a whole (9 girls) to another part of the same whole (7 boys). This can be represented as $\frac{9}{7}$, meaning "a ratio of nine to seven," not nine-sevenths (the fraction). In other words, part-to-part ratios are not fractions, though they can be written using the fraction bar; the context is what tells you it is a part-to-part ratio.

Part-to-part ratios occur across the curriculum. In geometry, corresponding parts of similar geometric figures are part-to-part ratios. The ratio of the diagonal of a square to its side is $\sqrt{2}$. In algebra, the slope of a line is a ratio of rise to one unit of horizontal distance (called the *run*). The probability of an event is a part-to-whole ratio, but the *odds* of an event is a part-to-part ratio.

Part-Whole Ratios. Ratios can express comparisons of a part to a whole—for example, the ratio of the number of girls in a class (9) to the number of students in the class (16). This can be written as the ratio $\frac{9}{16}$, or can be thought of as nine-sixteenths of the class (a fraction). Percentages and probabilities are examples of part-whole ratios.

Ratios as Quotients. Ratios can be thought of as quotients. For example, if you can buy four kiwis for $1.00, the ratio of money for kiwis is $1.00 to 4 kiwis. The cost per kiwi ($0.25) is the rate.

Ratios as Rates. Miles per gallon, square yards of wall coverage per gallon of paint, passengers per busload, and roses per bouquet are all rates. A rate is a ratio between two measurements with different units. Relationships between two units of measure are also rates—for example, inches per foot, milliliters per liter, and centimeters per inch. A rate represents an infinite set of equivalent ratios (Lobato & Ellis, 2010), for example if a person's rate of exercise is 10 miles in 3 days, it could mean they walk 20 miles in 6 days, 30 miles in 9 days, and so on. Click here (https://www.youtube.com/watch?v=bIt87I--z48&list=PLnIkFmW0ticN6e7HXn0uj5dMb4oy58kIg) for an explanation of the relationship between ratios and rates.

Ratios Compared to Fractions

Ratios are closely related to fractions, but should be thought of as overlapping concepts with important distinctions (Lobato & Ellis, 2010). Because they are represented symbolically with a fraction bar, it is important to help students see that fractions and ratios are related. Here are three examples to make this point:

1. The ratio of cats to dogs at the pet store is $\frac{3}{5}$. This ratio is not a fraction, as fractions are not part-to-part.
2. The ratio of cats to pets at the pet store is $\frac{3}{8}$. This can be adapted to say three-eighths of the pets are cats. Because this is part-whole, this is both a ratio and a fraction.
3. Mario walked three-eighths of a mile ($\frac{3}{8}$ miles). This is a fraction of a length and not a ratio, as there is not a multiplicative comparison.

Unfortunately, ratios are often addressed in a superficial manner, with students recording the symbols (3:5) to tell the ratio of girls to boys. Instead, ratios should be taught as relations that involve multiplicative reasoning.

Two Ways to Think about Ratio

As Lobato and colleagues (2010) state, "forming a ratio is a **cognitive task**—not a **writing task**" (p. 22, emphasis added). What they mean is that ratio is a relationship, and that relationship can be thought of in different ways, regardless of whether it is notated as $\frac{2}{5}$ or 2:5 or 2 ÷ 5. It is important to understand two ways to think about ratios: as multiplicative comparisons and as composed units.

Standards for Mathematical Practice
MP1. Make sense of problems and persevere in solving them.

Multiplicative Comparison. Multiplicative comparisons, introduced in grade 4 in the CCSS, serve as an important foundation to understanding ratios (see Chapter 9). A ratio represents a multiplicative comparison, and that comparison can go either way. Consider the following relationship: Wand A is 8 inches long, and Wand B is 10 inches long. The ratio of the two wands is 8 to 10. But this statement does not necessarily communicate the *relationship* between the measures. There are two ways to compare the relationship multiplicatively:

The short wand is eight-tenths as long as the long wand (or four-fifths the length).
The long wand is ten-eighths as long as the short wand (or five-fourths or $1\frac{1}{4}$).

The questions related to multiplicative comparisons can be worded in two ways: "How many times greater is one thing than another?" Or "What fractional part is one thing of another?" (Lobato et al., 2010, p. 18). When two different units are compared (e.g., 6 wands per 2 magicians or 3 wands per magician), the ratio is a rate. Understanding this relationship is a grade 6 expectation in the CCSS-M (6.RP.A.2). Also in grade 6 in the CCSS-M is the expectation to solve real-world problems involving ratios. These problems should include multiplicative comparisons, and those problems should increase in their difficulty (Cohen, 2013).

Activity 18.1   CCSS-M: 6.RP.A.1; 6.RP.A.2; 6.RP.A.3

ENGLISH LANGUAGE LEARNERS

Stocking the Pond

Use Stocking the Pond Activity Page or simply pose each of the three problems, one at a time, for students to solve. Ask students to use tape diagrams (also referred to as *strip diagrams*) as a tool to represent each problem. The first task is included here:

For every 3 bass that are put in a pond, Environmental Edwin puts in 8 bluegill. If Edwin puts 24 bluegill in the pond, how many bass does he need to put in the pond?

After students have solved the problem, ask questions such as, "What fractional part is the bass compared to the bluegill?" (three-eighths) and "What fractional part is the bluegill compared to the bass?" (eight-thirds). Continue to more questions that vary what information is unknown in the story. For ELLs, it is helpful to keep the same context to reduce the linguistic load and to point out the four types of fish names. Also, be sure that the word "if" is understood in the situation to mean "assume."

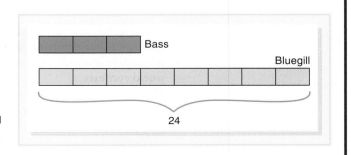

Activity 18.2

CCSS-M: 6.RP.A.1; 6.RP.A.2; 6.RP.A.3

Birthday Cupcakes

Explain to students that they are going to be icing cupcakes and selling them at school. In a recipe for icing, the instructions say that to ice one batch of cupcakes with aqua-colored icing, you will need 2 drops of green food coloring and 5 drops of blue food coloring. Ask students to figure out how many drops of food coloring will be needed for 1 batch of cupcakes, 2 batches, 5 batches, and so on (composed unit thinking). Students may want to record their data in a table.

Next, ask students to figure out how many blue drops for one drop of green, and how much green for one drop of blue (multiplicative comparison). Ask students to think about how this information helps them determine the number of color drops for various numbers of batches. Students—particularly students with disabilities—may benefit from visualizing this comparison, which can be done by lining up green and blue color tiles or counters (or use drawings).

STUDENTS *with* **SPECIAL NEEDS**

Composed Unit. *Composed unit* refers to thinking of the ratio as one unit. For example, if kiwi are 4 for $1.00, then you can think of this as a unit, and then think about other multiples that would also be true, like 8 for $2.00, 16 for $4.00, and so on. (Each of these would be a unit composed of the original ratio.) This is *iterating*, a foundational idea in working with rational numbers, as discussed in Chapters 15 and 16. Composed units can also be *partitioned*: 2 for $0.50 and 1 for $0.25. Any number of kiwis can be priced through using these composed units.

It is important that students can apply both types of ratios. Activity 18.2 provides a context for thinking of a composed unit and then a multiplicative comparison.

 Complete Self-Check 18.1: Ratios

 Proportional Reasoning

Ratios are extended to understanding and applying proportional reasoning—for example, investigating contexts such as interest, taxes, and tips as well as connecting to work with similar figures, graphing, and slope. Developing understanding of and applying proportional relationships is a focus in grade 7 (CCSSO, 2010; NCTM, 2006). But reasoning proportionally doesn't begin in middle school; one-to-one correspondence, place value, fraction concepts, and multiplicative reasoning are all topics that involve early ideas of proportional reasoning (Seeley & Schielack, 2007).

Proportional reasoning is difficult to define in a simple sentence or two. It is not something that you either can or cannot do. According to Lamon (2012), proportional thinkers:

* Understand *ratios as distinct entities* representing a relationship different from the quantities they compare (see earlier discussion about composed units)
* Recognize *proportional relationships as distinct from nonproportional relationships* in real-world contexts
* Have a sense of *covariation* (that is, they understand relationships in which two quantities vary together and are able to see how the variation in one coincides with the variation in another)

- Develop *a wide variety of strategies* for solving proportions or comparing ratios, most of which are based on informal strategies rather than prescribed algorithms.

Each of these last three areas is addressed in the sections that follow.

Proportional and Nonproportional Situations

Students should be able to compare situations and discuss whether the comparison is due to an *additive, multiplicative,* or *constant* relationship (Van Dooren, De Bock, Vleugels, & Verschaffel, 2010). Importantly, a ratio is a number that expresses a multiplicative relationship (part-part or part-whole) that can be applied to a second situation in which the relative quantities or measures are the same as in the first situation. For example, in the kiwi problem, the first situation was 4 kiwis for $1.00, and this relative quantity (4 for $1.00, or 1 for $0.25) is also true.

Standards for Mathematical Practice
MP2. Reason abstractly and quantitatively.

 Pause & Reflect

Solve each of the following problems.

1. Janet and Jeanette were walking to school, each walking at the same rate. Jeanette started first. When Jeanette has walked 6 blocks, Janet has walked 2 blocks. How far will Janet be when Jeanette is at 12 blocks?
2. Lisa and Linda are planting corn on the same farm. Linda plants 4 rows and Lisa plants 6 rows. If Linda's corn is ready to pick in 8 weeks, how many weeks will it take for Lisa's corn to be ready?
3. Kendra and Kevin are baking cookies using the same recipe. Kendra makes 6 dozen and Kevin makes 3 dozen. If Kevin is using 6 ounces of chocolate chips, how many ounces will Kendra need?

Can you figure out which of the three problems above is an *additive, multiplicative,* and *constant* relationship? What are the differences in the wording of these situations that make them *additive, multiplicative,* or *constant* relationships? How can you help students distinguish between these types? ●

Let's review each situation. The first situation is additive. Janet will still be 4 blocks behind, so 8 blocks. If incorrectly solved through multiplicative reasoning, however, you would have gotten 4 blocks. The second situation is constant. It will still take 8 weeks for the corn to grow, regardless of how many rows were planted. If solved through multiplicative reasoning, the incorrect answer would be 12 weeks. The final situation is multiplicative, and the answer is 12 ounces. How did you do?

The way to get students to distinguish between these types of reasoning is to provide opportunities for them to make the distinction between these problem types. Consider the following sample problem suggested by Cai and Sun in their discussion of how teachers in Chinese classrooms introduce the concept of ratio (2002, p. 196):

Mr. Miller's 25 students are asked if they are basketball fans (yes or no). Twenty of them say "yes" and five say "no." Describe as many relationships as you can about those who are basketball fans and those who are not.

Students should report several different relationships:

- There are 20 more fans than nonfans.
- There are four times as many fans as nonfans.
- For every four students who like basketball, there is one who does not.

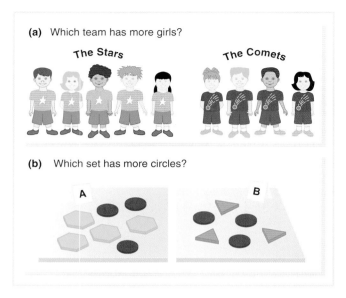

(a) Which team has more girls?

The Stars

The Comets

(b) Which set has more circles?

A

B

FIGURE 18.1 Two pictorial situations that can be interpreted with either additive or multiplicative comparisons.

Of these, the first is an additive relationship—focusing on the difference between the two numbers. The other two are variations of the multiplicative relationship, each expressing the 3-to-1 ratio of fans to nonfans in a slightly different way. A discussion helps to contrast the multiplicative relationship with the additive one.

The following problem, adapted from the book *Adding It Up* (National Research Council, 2001), involves a comparison.

Two weeks ago, two flowers were measured at 8 inches and 12 inches, respectively. Today they are 11 inches and 15 inches tall. Did the 8-inch or 12-inch flower grow more?

Additive reasoning would lead to the response that they both grew the same amount—3 inches. Reasoning multiplicatively leads to a different conclusion: The first flower grew $\frac{3}{8}$ of its height whereas the second grew $\frac{3}{12}$ of its height. So the first flower grew more. This is a proportional view of this change situation. Here, both the additive reasoning and multiplicative reasoning produce valid, albeit different, answers. As students critique these different approaches, they are able to better understand the difference between additive and multiplicative comparisons.

The following activities provide more opportunities for students to make the distinction between additive reasoning and multiplicative reasoning.

Activity 18.3
CCSS-M: 6.RP.A.1

Which Has More?

Provide students with situations similar to those in Figure 18.1. Ask students to decide which has more and share a rationale for their thinking. As students share their reasoning, help students see the difference between looking at the difference (additive reasoning) and looking at the ratio (multiplicative reasoning). For ELLs, take time to build meaning for what these terms mean—connect *additive* with the word *add,* and *multiplicative* with *multiple* and *multiply*. Reasoning can be modeled through illustrations or explanations. If no one suggests one of the options, introduce it. For example, say, "Amy says it is the second group. Can you explain why she made that choice?" or "Which class team has a larger proportion of girls?"

ENGLISH LANGUAGE LEARNERS

Activity 18.4
CCSS-M: 6.RP.A.1

Weight Loss

Show students the data in the following chart:

Week	Max	Moe	Minnie
0	210	158	113
2	202	154	107
4	200	150	104

Max, Moe, and Minnie are each on a diet and have recorded their weight at the start of their diet and at two-week intervals. After four weeks, which person is the most successful dieter?

Ask students to make three different arguments, each favoring a different dieter. (The argument for Moe is that he is the most steady in his loss.)

Additive and Multiplicative Comparisons in Story Problems

When comparisons are embedded in a story situation, they may be additive *or* multiplicative. Using additive reasoning in a situation that calls for multiplicative, or vice versa, leads to incorrect answers. Solve the five-item assessment shown in Figure 18.2, devised to examine students' appropriate use of additive or multiplicative reasoning (Bright, Joyner, & Wallis, 2003). Which ones are multiplicative situations? Additive? What is the difference between items 2 and 4?

Notice that the items involving rectangular representations (1, 2, and 5) cannot be answered correctly using additive reasoning. Students are often challenged to determine which type of reasoning to use. When these questions were posed to 132 eighth- and ninth-grade students, scores on items 1 through 4 ranged from 45 percent to 67 percent correct. Item 5 proved very difficult (37 percent correct for most square, 28 percent correct for least square).

 FORMATIVE ASSESSMENT Notes. All five of these items could be used as a performance assessment, or a few of these (at least one additive) can be used as a diagnostic interview. For example, item 5 was given to an eighth grader, who first solved it incorrectly using an additive strategy (subtracting the sides). When asked if a very large rectangle 1,000,000 feet by 1,000,050 feet would look less square, he replied, "No—*oh*, this is a proportional situation." He then solved it using a novel strategy (see Figure 18.3). ■

Return for a moment to item 3 in Figure 18.2. This item has been used in other studies showing that students try to solve this as a proportion problem, though it is an additive situation (The two runners will end up six laps apart, which is how they began). Watson and Shaughnessy (2004) note that often the way that we word problems is a clue that a proportion is involved. Students become accustomed to this wording being related to proportions and automatically arrange four quantities (three known and one unknown) into a proportion without paying attention to whether there is a multiplicative relationship between the numbers. They are focused on the structure of the proportion, not the concept of the proportion (Heinz & Sterba-Boatwright, 2008).

For each problem, circle the correct answer.

1. Mrs. Allen took a 3-inch by 5-inch photo of the Cape Hatteras Lighthouse and made an enlargement on a photocopier using the 200% option. Which is "more square," the original photo or the enlargement?

   a. The original photo is "more square."
   b. The enlargement is "more square."
   c. The photo and the enlargement are equally square.
   d. There is not enough information to determine which is "more square."

2. The Science Club has four separate rectangular plots for experiments with plants:

1 foot by 4 feet	7 feet by 10 feet
17 feet by 20 feet	27 feet by 30 feet

   Which rectangular plot is most square?

   a. 1 foot by 4 feet
   b. 7 feet by 10 feet
   c. 17 feet by 20 feet
   d. 27 feet by 30 feet

3. Sue and Julie were running equally fast around a track. Sue started first. When Sue had run 9 laps. Julie had run 3 laps. When Julie completed 15 laps, how many laps had Sue run?

   a. 45 laps
   b. 24 laps
   c. 21 laps
   d. 6 laps

4. At the midway point of the basketball season, you must recommend the best free-throw shooter for the all-star game. Here are the statistics for four players:

Novak: 8 of 11 shots	Peterson: 22 of 29 shots
Williams: 15 of 19 shots	Reynolds: 33 of 41 shots

   Which player is the best free-throw shooter?

   a. Novak   b. Peterson   c. Williams   d. Reynolds

5. Write your answer to this problem.
   A farmer has three fields. One is 185 feet by 245 feet, one is 75 feet by 114 feet, and one is 455 feet by 508 feet. If you were flying over these fields, which one would seem most square? Which one would seem least square? Explain your answers.

FIGURE 18.2 Five items to assess proportional reasoning. For each problem, circle the correct answer.

Source: Reprinted with permission from Bright, G. W., Joyner, J. J., & Wallis, C. (2003). "Assessing Proportional Thinking." *Mathematics Teaching in the Middle School, 9*(3), p. 167. Copyright © 2003 by the National Council of Teachers of Mathematics. All rights reserved.

Activity 18.5

CCSS-M: 6.RP.A.3a; 7.RP.2b

Pencil-to-Pencil

If possible, read a children's book about giants (see the end-of-chapter Literature Connections for ideas of books to connect to this activity). Hold up a cutout of a very large pencil (e.g., 30 inches in length). Explain to students that this is the exact size of a pencil used by a giant. Ask, "If this is her pencil, what else can you tell me about her?" For students (particularly those with disabilities) who need more structure or guidance, ask specific questions like "How tall is the giant?" "How long would her hand be?" After students have found out things about the giant, have them post their findings on posters, and have them illustrate or explain how they found the measures. ELLs are likely to be more familiar with centimeters, so have students choose what measurement system they use, or have all students use centimeters. As an alternative, and to use fractional measurements, begin with a tiny pencil and consider the size of the tiny person.

ENGLISH LANGUAGE LEARNERS

STUDENTS *with* SPECIAL NEEDS

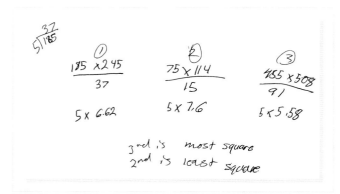

FIGURE 18.3 Jacob noticed that each length was divisible by 5; therefore, he simplified each ratio to have a side of 5 and then compared the widths.

CCSS Standards for Mathematical Practice

MP1. Makes sense of problems and persevere in solving them.

Activity 18.5 describes an activity (based on Che, 2009) that can help students move from additive to multiplicative reasoning.

When students first engage in this activity, they may focus on the (additive) difference of the pencil they are shown and a real pencil they have. If they reason about this difference, then they will find that the giant is only 24 inches taller than they are. Thinking about this should raise some doubt about this line of reasoning, because there are real people who are two feet taller, and a 30-inch pencil would still be too big for them to manage. They might then start thinking of how many of their pencils would equal the extra large pencil. By counting (iterating), they may notice it takes about 5 of their pencils. In debriefing this activity with students, discuss their thought processes and why the situation is a multiplicative comparison and not an additive comparison. Ask students to write examples of additive differences and multiplicative differences. This can help them distinguish between these ideas, which they must be able to do in order to reason with ratios (which is multiplicative).

Contrasting two very similar problems can also support students' emerging skills at reasoning proportionally. Consider these two tasks and how they are the same and how they are different:

1. A red car and a silver car are traveling at the same constant rate. When the red car has traveled 20 miles, the silver car has traveled 12 miles. How far will the red car be when the silver car has traveled 32 miles?

2. A red and a silver car are traveling at different but constant rates. They pass Exit 95 at the same time. When the red car has traveled 20 miles past exit 95, the silver car has traveled 16 miles. How far will the red car be when the silver car has traveled 32 miles?

Consider the situation using equations. Writing the relationships in variables can further help students see the differences between additive and multiplicative situations (Lim, 2009). In the first case, the relationship is red = silver + 8 because the red car is 8 miles in front of the silver car. In the latter case, the relationships is red = $\frac{5}{4}$ silver because for every five miles the red car travels, the silver car travels four.

Covariation

Covariation can sound like a high school or college concept, but it simply means that two different quantities (a ratio) vary together. For example, five mangos cost $2.00 (two quantities in a multiplicative relationship); as the number of mangos varies (for example, to 10 mangos), so does the cost. And as the cost changes, so does the number of mangos you will get. Once you know either a new price or a new number of mangoes, you can determine the missing variable.

Within and Between Ratios. A ratio of two measures in the same setting is a *within* ratio. For example, in the case of the mangos, the ratio of mango to money is a within ratio; that is, it is "within" the context of that example.

A *between* ratio is a ratio of two corresponding measures in different situations. In the case of the mangos, the ratio of the original number of mangos (5) to the number of mangos in a second situation (10) is a between ratio; that is, it is "between" the two situations.

The drawing in Figure 18.4 is an effective way of looking at two ratios and determining whether a ratio is between or within. A drawing similar to this will be very helpful to students in setting up proportions, especially students who struggle with abstract representations.

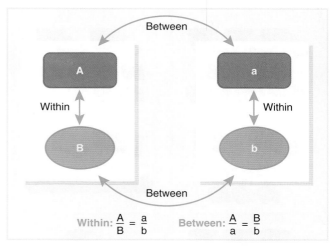

$$\text{Within: } \frac{A}{B} = \frac{a}{b} \qquad \text{Between: } \frac{A}{a} = \frac{B}{b}$$

FIGURE 18.4 In a proportional situation, the two between ratios will be equivalent, as will the two within ratios.

CCSS Standards for Mathematical Practice

MP4. Model with mathematics.

Activity 18.6

CCSS-M: 6.RP.A.1; 6.RP.A.2

Different Objects, Same Ratios

Prepare cards with distinctly different objects, as shown in Figure 18.5. Given one card, students are to select a card on which the ratio of the two types of objects is the same. This task moves students toward a numeric approach rather than a visual one and introduces the notion of ratios as rates. In this context, it makes the most sense to find the boxes per truck as the rate (rather than trucks per box). Finding the rate (amount for 1 unit) for pairs of quantities facilitates comparisons (just as the unit prices provided in grocery stores allow you to compare different brands).

Covariation in Measurement and Geometry. Within and between ratios apply to measurement conversions. Consider that the capital A and B in Figure 18.4 is the conversion of inches to feet. How might you use within and between ratios to determine the number of feet in 60 inches?

$$\frac{12 \text{ inches}}{1 \text{ foot}} = \frac{60 \text{ inches}}{? \text{ feet}}$$

You might notice that the between ratio is $\times 5$ (left to right), or you might notice that the within ratio is $\div 12$ (inches to feet). Measurement conversions are difficult even for adults, and are a goal in grade 6 in the CCSS-M. Setting up a between and within equation such as this one and analyzing the relationships can help students see the options they have for finding the conversion.

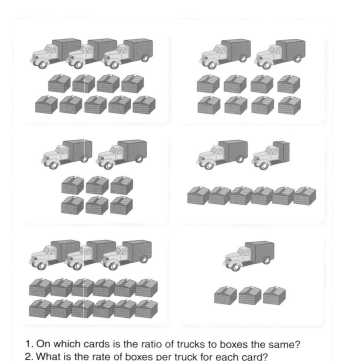

1. On which cards is the ratio of trucks to boxes the same?
2. What is the rate of boxes per truck for each card?

FIGURE 18.5 Ratio cards for exploring ratios and rates.

Within and between ratios are particularly relevant in exploring similarity with geometric shapes, a topic in grade 8 in the CCSS-M. Students often struggle to determine which features to compare to which features. Activity 18.7 can help students begin to analyze which features to compare.

The connection between proportional reasoning and the geometric concept of similarity is very important. Similar figures provide a visual representation of proportions, and proportional thinking enhances the understanding of similarity. Discussion of the similar figures should focus on the ratios between and within the figures.

 TECHNOLOGY Note. Dynamic geometry software such as *GeoGebra* (a free download) offers a very effective method of exploring festthe idea of ratio. In Figure 18.6, two lengths are drawn on a grid using the software's "snap-to-grid" option. The lengths are measured, and two ratios are computed. As the length of either line is changed, the measures and ratios are updated instantly. A screen similar to Figure 18.6 could be used to discuss ratios of lengths as well as inverse ratios with your class. In this example, notice that the difference between the first pair and second pair of lines is the same but the ratios are not the same.

Activity 18.7

CCSS-M: 6.RP.A.1; 6.RP.A.3a; 7.RP.A.2a

Look-Alike Rectangles

Provide students with cutouts of the rectangles provided in Look-Alike Rectangles **Activity Page** or have students cut out a set for themselves. (Rectangles A, I, and D have sides in the ratio of 3 to 4. Rectangles C, F, and H have sides in the ratio of 5 to 8. Rectangles J, E, and G have sides in the ratio of 1 to 3. Rectangle B is a square, so its sides are in the ratio of 1 to 1.)

Ask students to group the rectangles into three sets that "look alike." If your students know the word *similar* from geometry, use that term instead of *look alike*. To explain what of *look alike.* means, draw three rectangles on the board, with two that are similar and one that is clearly dissimilar to the other two, as in the following example. Have students use ratio language to explain why rectangles 1 and 3 are alike.

When students have decided on their groupings, stop and discuss the reasons they classified the rectangles as they did. Be prepared for some students to try to match sides or look for rectangles that have the same amount of difference between them. Next, have the students measure and record the sides of each rectangle to the nearest half-centimeter. Use the Look-Alike Rectangles Recording Sheet to record the data. Discuss these results and ask students to offer explanations of how the ratios and groupings are related. If the groups are formed of proportional (similar) rectangles, the ratios within each group will be equivalent. Students with disabilities may need to have examples of one rectangle from each grouping as a starting point for the groupings.

STUDENTS
with
SPECIAL
NEEDS

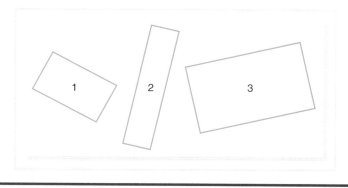

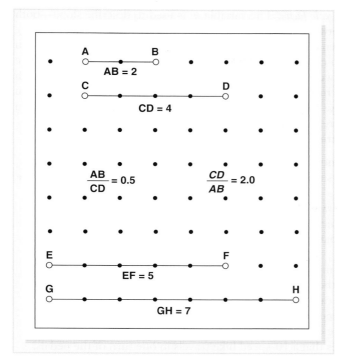

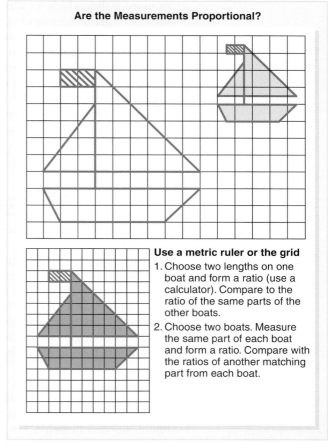

Are the Measurements Proportional?

Use a metric ruler or the grid

1. Choose two lengths on one boat and form a ratio (use a calculator). Compare to the ratio of the same parts of the other boats.

2. Choose two boats. Measure the same part of each boat and form a ratio. Compare with the ratios of another matching part from each boat.

FIGURE 18.6 Dynamic software can be used to draw line segments or geometric shapes to see if a proportional relationship exists. You can also use dynamic geometry software to explore dilations (i.e., similar figures) and corresponding measures. Figures can be drawn and then dilated (reduced or enlarged proportionally) according to any scale factor. The ratios of beginning and ending measures (lengths and areas) can then be compared to the scale factor. ■

FIGURE 18.7 Comparing similar figures drawn on grids.

Creating *scale drawings* is an application of similarity. Multiplication *is* scaling (making something three times bigger or one-half the size, for example). Scale drawings, then, are an important way for students to see the connection between multiplicative reasoning and proportional reasoning. ■

Activity 18.8   CCSS-M: 6.RP.A.1; 7.RP.A.3a

Scale Drawings

On 1-Centimeter Grid Paper, 0.5-Centimeter Grid Paper, or on Dot Paper (see Blackline Masters 6, 7, and 8), have students draw a simple shape using straight lines with vertices on the dots. After one shape is complete, have students draw a larger or smaller shape that looks similar to the first. This can be done on a grid of the same size or a different size, as shown in Figure 18.7. First compare ratios within (see 1 in Figure 18.7), then compare ratios between the figures (see 2 in Figure 18.7).

   Corresponding sides from one figure to the next should all be in the same ratio. The ratio of two sides within one figure should be the same as the ratio of the corresponding two sides in another figure. With ELLs, be sure the term *scale* is understood, as it may be confused with the machine that weighs things and/or what fish have.

ENGLISH LANGUAGE LEARNERS

Comparisons of corresponding lengths, areas, and volumes in proportional figures lead to some interesting patterns. If we know the length of a figure, we can create the ratio of 1 to k, for example, to represent the relationship to a proportional figure. The variable k is the constant of proportionality, which is called the *scale factor*. The variable *m* is used to describe slope—both variables refer to the rate or ratio between two values.) If two figures are proportional (similar), then any corresponding linear dimensions will have the same scale factor. Now, imagine you have a square that is 3 by 3 and you create a new square that is 6 by 6. The ratio between the lengths is 1:2. What is the ratio between the two areas? Why is it 1:4? Try the same idea with the volume of a cube—what is the relationship of the original to the new volume when you double the length of the edges? Why? Returning to the sailboat in Figure 18.7, what would you conjecture is the ratio between the areas of the two sailboats? Measure and test your hypothesis.

Here are some interesting situations to consider for scale drawings:

- If you wanted to make a scale model of the solar system and use a ping-pong ball for the earth, how far away should the sun be? How large a ball would you need to represent the sun?
- What scale should be used to draw a scale map of your city (or some region of interest) so that it will nicely fit onto a standard piece of posterboard?
- Use the scale on a map to estimate the distance and travel time between two points of interest.
- Roll a toy car down a ramp, timing the trip with a stopwatch. How fast was the car traveling in miles per hour? If the speed is proportional to the size of the car, how fast would this have been for a real car?
- Your little sister wants a table and chair for her doll. Her doll is 14 inches tall. How big should you make the table? The chair?
- Determine the various distances that a 10-speed bike travels in one turn of the pedals. You will need to count the sprocket teeth on the front and back gears.

TECHNOLOGY Note. Google Earth (available in online and App formats) is a great resource for doing authentic scaling activities (Roberge & Cooper, 2010). If you get a Google Earth diagram that includes something for which the measure is known, students can figure out other measures. For example, you know that a standard football field is 100 yards from end zone to end zone (120 yards if you include the end zone), so zoom in on your school football field. By zooming to different levels, students can build an understanding of scale factor in an interesting context. You can even do some interdisciplinary teaching by exploring regions that align with what is being studied in social studies! Scale City, available for free through PBS Learning Media and aligned to the CCSS-M, features fun and engaging videos and interactive simulations for exploring scale drawings. ■

Covariation in Algebra. Proportional situations are linear situations. Graphing equivalent ratios is a powerful way to illustrate this concept. The CCSS-M has emphasized the need to connect ratios and proportions to graphs (CCSSO, 2010). Ratios are a special case of linear situations that will always go through the origin, because they are multiplicative relationships. The ratio or rate is the slope of the graph.

Activity 18.9

CCSS-M: 7.RP.A.2a,b,c,d

Rectangle Ratios: Graph It!

This activity is connected to Activity 18.7. Using the Look-Alike Rectangles: Graph It! Activity Page, have students select one set of "alike" rectangles and record the measures in the ratio table, then create their three of their own examples of "alike" rectangles using their knowledge of equivalent ratios. Also, see if students can find a rectangle that has a noninteger side (e.g., $4\frac{1}{2}$ cm).

Next, ask students to graph the data for their 6 rectangles. The graph in Figure 18.8 is based on the ratios of two sides of similar rectangles. After the ratios have been graphed, challenge students to use their graph to determine a seventh look-alike rectangle. Also, ask questions to help students understand the graph, such as: What does a point on the graph mean (even if it is not one of the rectangles)? What is the length for a look-alike rectangle with a width of 1 cm? (This is the unit rate.) Challenge students to find the unit rate each way (also finding the width if the length is 1). The, ask students how, if they know the short side, they could find the long side (and vice versa).

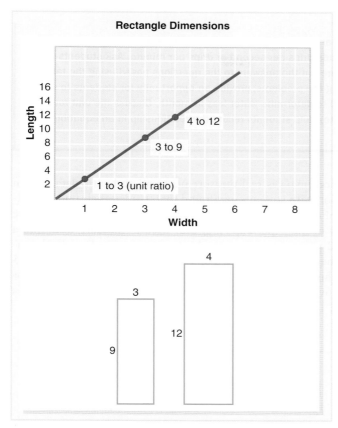

FIGURE 18.8 Graph shows ratios of sides in similar rectangles.

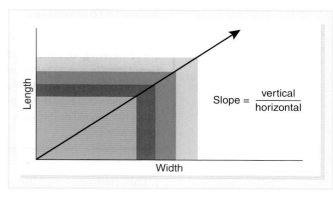

FIGURE 18.9 The slope of a line through a stack of proportional rectangles is equal to the ratio of the two sides.

A great geometry/algebra connection is to actually stack the look-alike rectangles so that they are aligned at one corner, as in Figure 18.9. Place a straight edge across the diagonals, and you will see that opposite corners also line up. If the rectangles are placed on a coordinate axis with the common corner at the origin, the slope of the line joining the corners is the ratio of the sides. A great connection to algebra!

Graphing ratios can be challenging for students. For example, students can struggle to decide what points to graph, deciding which axes to use for the two measures, and making sense of what the graph means (Kastberg, D'Ambrosio, Lynch-Davis, Mintos, & Krawczyk, 2014). With ratios, the choice of which variable is on the *x*-axis and which variable goes on the *y*-axis is arbitrary. All graphs of equivalent ratios fall along straight lines that pass through the origin. If the equation of one of these lines is written in the form $y = mx$, the slope *m* is always one of the equivalent ratios.

Using real-life contexts and gathering data, for example about dripping faucets, can help students make sense of unit rates and proportional reasoning (Williams, Forrest, & Schnabel, 2006). That is the focus of Activity 18.10.

Activity 18.10

CCSS-M: 6.RP.A.1; 6.RP.A.3a, b; 7.RP.A.2b, c

Dripping Faucet

Pose the following problem to students:

> *If you brush your teeth twice a day and leave the water running when you brush, how many gallons of water will you waste in one day? In two days? In a week? A month? Any number of days?*

continued

Activity 18.10 (continued)

Have students actually gather data and record it in a ratio table. Ask students what ratio they are considering. Options might include drips per second or drips per minute. Ask students to record data in a ratio table and figure out the answers to the questions posed using the table or a reasoning strategy. After solving the problems, provide an opportunity for students to share their results and how they reasoned to determine water loss in month. Discuss the unit rate (drips per second or drips per minute) Help students record the relationship in an equation in the form $y = kx$.

This environmental investigation involves real measurement and authentic data. Stemn (2008) implemented this investigation with students and found that it aided their understanding of the difference betwee multiplicative and additive situations. Students in her class were challenged to figure out how many of the paper cups that they used to measure would fill a gallon. The class figured out that 2 paper cups were equal to one-quarter gallon. Each student reasoned how many gallons they wasted in a day. For example, a student who wasted 5 paper cups of water reasoned that this would be two-fourths, plus a half of another fourth (or one-eighth). So, in total, there are five-eighths of a gallon of water wasted per day. The class recorded what they knew in a table:

Paper cups of water wasted	1	2	3	4	5
Gallons of water wasted	$\frac{1}{8}$	$\frac{1}{4}$	$\frac{3}{8}$	$\frac{2}{4}$	$\frac{5}{8}$

The teacher encouraged them to rewrite the table with common denominators. Students recognized that the ratio of paper cups to gallons was $1 : \frac{1}{8}$. Notice the connection to algebraic reasoning and to measurement. The formula $y = \frac{1}{8}x$ describes the number of paper cups (x) to gallons (y). This investigation also showed the students how to reason through measurement conversions with a nonstandard measure (the paper cup), which is a very challenging concept for students.

 TECHNOLOGY Note. For a good selection of challenging ratio and proportion problems using work and everyday life situations, go the NCTM website and check out Figure This! Math Index: Ratios and Proportions. ■

 Complete Self-Check 18.2: Proportional Reasoning

Strategies for Solving Proportional Situations

To be mathematically proficient, students must be flexible, efficient, accurate, and able to choose appropriate strategies. Nowhere is that more true than in solving proportional situations. Sometimes the numbers in the situation lend themselves to simple reasoning strategies, and sometimes they require a more sophisticated strategy. The most commonly known strategy is cross products, but as the most abstract and least intuitive strategy, it should only be introduced after students have solved proportional problems through reasoning and by using drawings such as a tape diagram or double number line. Posing problems that have multiple solution strategies can help students to reason proportionally (Berk, Taber,

Gorowara, & Poetzl, 2009; Ercole, Frantz, & Ashline, 2011). Strategies for solving proportional situations include:

- Rate
- Scaling up or down
- Scale factors (within or between measures)
- Ratio tables
- Graphs
- Equations

Which of these are familiar to you? All of these are important in implementing the CCSS-M vision for ratios and proportions in middle school! As you read about each type, keep in mind that *all* of these involve reasoning abstractly and quantitatively and any one of them may be useful in a particular situation. The first three are the most intuitive, and therefore ones students might invent, and a good place to begin.

Rates and Scaling Strategies

Unit rate and scale factor can be used to mentally solve many proportional situations. The key is to know both strategies and pick the one that best fits the particular numbers in the problem, as the next examples illustrate.

Tammy bought 3 widgets for $2.40. At the same price, how much would 10 widgets cost?
Tammy bought 4 widgets for $3.75. How much would a dozen widgets cost?

 Pause & Reflect

Before reading further, solve these two problems using an approach other than the cross-product algorithm. ●

 Standards for Mathematical Practice
MP1. Make sense of problems and persevere in solving them.

In the first situation, it is perhaps easiest to determine the cost of one widget—the unit rate or unit price. This can be found by dividing the price of three widgets by 3. Multiplying this unit rate of $0.80 per widget by 10 will produce the answer. This approach is referred to as the *unit-rate* method of solving proportions. Notice that the unit rate is a within ratio. This approach applies the ratio as a multiplicative comparison.

In the second problem, a unit-rate approach could be used, but the division does not appear to be easy. Because 12 is a multiple of 4, it is easier to notice that the cost of a dozen is 3 times the cost of 4, or that the scale factor between the ratios is 4. This is called a *buildup strategy*. (This strategy could have been used on the first problem but would have been more difficult because the scale factor between 3 and 10 is $3\frac{1}{3}$.) Notice that the buildup approach applies the ratio as a composed unit. Although using scale factors (the buildup strategy) is a useful way to think about proportions, it is most frequently used when the numbers are compatible (i.e., the scale factor is a whole number). Be sure to give students problems in which the numbers work easily with both approaches so that they will explore (and compare) both methods.

Try using the unit-rate method or scale factors to solve the next two problems.

At the Office Super Store, you can buy 4 pencils for 59 cents, or you can buy the same pencils in a large box of 5 dozen for $7.79. How much will you save per pencil if you buy the large box?
The price of a box of 2 dozen gumballs is $4.80. Bridget wants to buy 5 gumballs. What will she have to pay?

To solve the pencil problem, you might notice that the between ratio of pencils to pencils is 4 to 60 (5 dozen), or 1 to 15. If you multiply the 59 cents by 15, the factor of change, you will get the price of the box of 60 if the pencils were sold at the same price. In the gumball problem, the within ratio of 24 to $4.80 lends to finding the unit rate of $0.20 per gumball, which can then be multiplied by 5. See Expanded Lesson: It's a Matter of Rates for a full lesson using stories to develop strategies for reasoning about ratios and rates.

It is important to follow these tasks with problems that have more difficult numbers, asking students to apply the same strategies to reason to an answer. For example, try to apply both strategies to the next problem.

Standards for Mathematical Practice

MP2. Reason abstractly and quantitatively.

Brian can run 5 km in 18.4 minutes. If he keeps running at the same speed, how far can he run in 23 minutes?

Selecting problems that can be solved many ways is important. The following activity has been used in various studies and curricula because it can be approached in so many ways.

Activity 18.11

CCSS-M: 6.RP.A.1; 6.RP.A.3a, b; 7.RP.1; 7.RP.A.2a

Comparing Lemonade Recipes

Show students a picture of two lemonade pitchers, as in Figure 18.10. The little squares indicate the recipes used in each pitcher. In this case the recipes are:

3 cups water	4 cups water
2 cups concentrate	3 cups concentrate

A yellow square is a cup of lemonade concentrate and a blue square is a cup of water. Ask which pitcher will have the stronger lemon flavor or whether they will both taste the same. Recipes can be adapted to include fractional values. For example, ask students to reason about which of these has a stronger lemon flavor:

$\frac{3}{4}$ cup water	$\frac{3}{2}$ cup water
$\frac{1}{8}$ cup of concentrate	$\frac{1}{4}$ cup of concentrate

Look at the between and within ratios in this second example. What do you notice? The within ratio for both recipes is $\times$ 6 (or $\div$ 6). The between ratio for both water and concentrate is $\times$ 2 or $\div$ 2. These recipes will taste the same! Watch a video of John A Van de Walle and others discussing this problem on the companion website.

= 1 cup of water   = 1 cup of lemonade concentrate

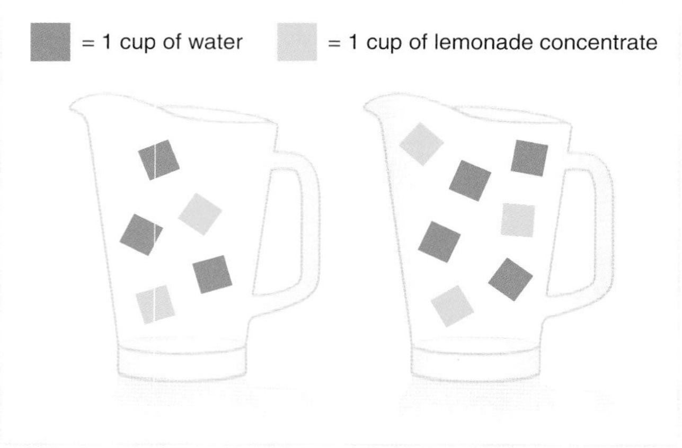

FIGURE 18.10 A comparing ratios problem: Which pitcher will have the stronger lemon flavor, or will they be the same?

A fun, hands-on adaptation to mixing juice is to mix paint shades, creating a paint swatch. You can ask students to write 5 different shades using two primary colors (e.g., use red and yellow to make recipes for shades of orange). Ask students to order them (e.g., from the reddest to the yellowest), and try to include some that are equivalent ratios. Use real paint drops and have students test their ratios and create their own paint chart (see Beswick, 2011, for details).

⏸ Pause & Reflect

Solve the lemonade problem and write down your reasoning. Is there more than one way to justify the answer? •

The task in "Comparing Lemonade Recipes" is interesting because of how many ways there are to make the comparison. A common method is to figure out how much water goes with each cup of concentrate. As we will see later, this is using a unit rate: cups of water per cup of lemonade concentrate ($1\frac{1}{2}$ vs. $1\frac{1}{3}$). Other approaches use fractions instead of unit rates and attempt to compare the fractions: concentrate compared to water ($\frac{2}{3}$ vs. $\frac{3}{4}$) or the reverse, and also lemonade concentrate as a fraction of the total ($\frac{2}{5}$ vs. $\frac{3}{7}$). This can also be done with water as a fraction of the total. Some students may also use percentages instead of fractions, creating the same arguments. Another way to justify their answer is to use multiples of one or both of the pitchers until either the water or the lemonade concentrate is equal in both.

The lemonade task can be adjusted for difficulty or to encourage students to look at between and within ratios. As given, there are no simple relationships between the two pitchers. If the solutions are 3 to 6 and 4 to 8 (equal flavors), the task is much simpler. For a 2-to-5 recipe versus a 4-to-9 recipe, it is easy to double the first and compare it to the second. When a 3-to-6 recipe is compared to a 2-to-5 recipe, the unit rates are perhaps more obvious (1 to 2 vs. 1 to $2\frac{1}{2}$).

The following problem provides another context for comparing ratios using a variety of approaches.

Two camps of Scouts are having pizza parties. The Bear Camp ordered enough so that every 3 campers will have 2 pizzas. The leader of the Raccoons Camp ordered enough so that there would be 3 pizzas for every 5 campers. Did the Bear Campers or the Raccoon Campers have more pizza?

When the pizzas are sliced up into fractional parts as in Figure 18.11(a), the approach is to look for a unit rate—pizzas per camper. A partitioning approach has been used for each ratio (as in division). But notice that this problem does not say that the camps have only 3 and 5 campers, respectively. Any multiples of 2 to 3 and 3 to 5 can be used to make the appropriate comparisons. This scaling approach is illustrated in Figure 18.11(b). Three "clones" of the 2-to-3 ratio and two clones of the 3-to-5 ratio are made so that the number of campers getting a like number of pizzas can be compared. This is like getting common numerators to compare fractions. There are more campers in the Raccoon Camp ratio (larger denominator), so there is less pizza for each camper.

Hopefully you have noticed that the problems in this section are quite varied. Some have missing values, some have all the values, but you were asked to compare. Some lend themselves more easily to a unit-rate strategy, some to a buildup strategy, and some to other strategies. The more experiences students have in comparing and solving situations that are proportional in nature, the more they will be able to reason proportionally.

Ratio Tables

Ratio tables or charts that show how two variable quantities are related are good ways to organize information. They serve as a tool for applying the buildup strategy but can be used to determine unit rate. Consider the following table:

Acres	5	10	20	60	
Pine trees	75	150	300	?	

If the task is to find the number of trees for 60 acres of land, students can proceed by using addition—that is, they can add fives along the top row until they reach 60. This is a recursive pattern, or repeated addition strategy. Or, they might notice that 60 acres will have 6 times the number of pine trees as 10 acres, and therefore multiply 150 by 6. The between relationship here (the relationship between acres and pine trees) is $\times$ 15. In algebra this is called a *generative pattern* and it describes the multiplicative relationship between the two units. This is the rate (15 pine trees per acre). The equation for this situation is $y = 15x$, where x is number of

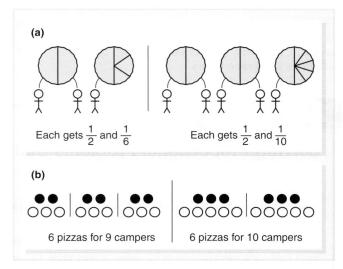

(a)

Each gets $\frac{1}{2}$ and $\frac{1}{6}$ Each gets $\frac{1}{2}$ and $\frac{1}{10}$

(b)

6 pizzas for 9 campers   6 pizzas for 10 campers

FIGURE 18.11   Rate and scaling methods for comparing pizzas per camper.

acres and *y* is the number of pine trees. Ratio tables do not use variables or equations, making it less abstract than using proportions.

Ratio tables can be used to find a specific equivalent ratio. For example, Factory Ratios Activity Page provides an interesting factory context and connects ratio tables to graphs to explore production ratios.

Because different ratios are represented in the ratio table, those ratios can be compared, or a missing value found. Therefore, they are a strategy for solving missing-value proportions. Activity 18.12 provides examples, and Figure 18.12 gives illustrations of this use of a ratio table (ideas based on Dole, 2008, and Lamon, 2012).

You may recognize these tasks as typical "solve the proportion" tasks. One ratio and part of a second are given, with the task being to find the fourth number. Figure 18.12 shows three different ways to solve the Jupiter weight task using ratio tables. As this example illustrates, the ratio table has several advantages over the missing-value proportion. Students label each row and are more successful at placing the values appropriately, and therefore they are able to compare. Also, working within the ratio table is more directly connected to the concept of seeking an equivalent ratio than solving a missing value proportion. Therefore, the ratio table should be introduced prior to using the cross-product approach. In connecting the ratio table to an equation, students are able to better understand the meaning of ratios and rates.

In applying this technique, students are using multiplicative relationships to transform a given ratio into an equivalent ratio. They are also able to see that there are infinitely many equivalent ratios, an important concept of ratio and rate.

FORMATIVE ASSESSMENT Notes. Because there are many ways to reason about proportional situations, it is important to capture *how* students are reasoning. Writing is an effective way to do this. You can simply ask students to explain how they solved a problem or used the ratio table, or you can provide more structure by using specific writing prompts or sentence starters or asking students to describe two different ways they could arrive at the solution. ■

CCSS Standards for
Mathematical
Practice
MP4. Model with
mathematics.

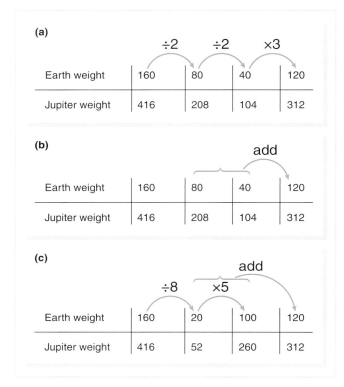

FIGURE 18.12 Something weighing 160 pounds on Earth is 416 pounds on Jupiter. If something weighs 120 pounds on Earth, how many pounds would it weigh on Jupiter? Three solutions using ratio tables.

Tape or Strip Diagram

Tape or strip diagrams are a nice visual that helps students visual the multiplicative relationships. CCSS-M defines a tape diagram as "drawings that look like a segment of tape,

---

Activity 18.12

CCSS-M: 6.RP.A.3a, b; 7.RP.A.1; 7.RP.A.2b, c; 7.RP.A.3

Solving Proportional Problems Using Ratio Tables

Use the Proportional Problems Task Cards Activity Page to create task cards. The activity sheet includes tasks such as:

If you run at the constant rate of $\frac{1}{2}$ mile in $\frac{1}{10}$ of an hour, how long will it take you to run a half-marathon (13 miles)?

**ENGLISH
LANGUAGE
LEARNERS**

You can give a set of cards to each pair of students, or select different cards for different groups to differentiate the activity. For each task card, ask students to (1) make a ratio table, (2) solve the problem, and (3) represent the proportional relationship as an equation ($y = kx$). Note: These contexts may have language that needs to be reinforced with ELLs. Posting visuals or translations can support their reading comprehension.

used to illustrate number relationships. Also known as strip diagrams, bar models or graphs, fraction strips, or length models" (CCSSO, 2010). Consider this statement: The ratio of boys to girls in the class is 3 to 4. This can be set up in strips as shown here, or a similar diagram that looks more like a partitioned line segment. These can be drawn on 1-Centimeters Grid Paper, 0.5-Centimeters Grid Paper, or Dot Paper (see Blackline Masters 6, 7, and 8), or created by folding and cutting paper strips:

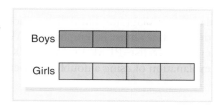

Once this basic ratio is provided, students use this sketch to solve problems. Let's look at three different ways these might be asked and sketched:

1. If there are 12 girls, how many boys? (One part is given, the other part requested)

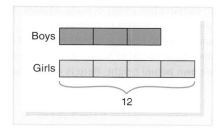

In observing the girls tape, students "see" the need to divide 12 by 4, placing 3 in each partition. Therefore, there will be 9 boys.

2. If there are 21 children, how many are boys? (The whole is given, a part is requested)

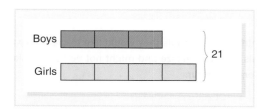

This second situation is harder for students to solve (Cohen, 2013). In particular it can be difficult for students to set up proportions to represent these situations.

3. There are 5 more girls than boys. How many girls are there? (The difference between the parts is given, a part is requested)

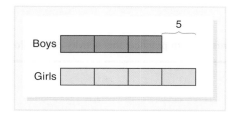

Notice how the tape diagram makes this situation much more accessible. We can see that the five represents one-fourth of the girls, so there are 20 girls. Solving this type of problem by setting up a proportion is a much more difficult task. The tape diagrams provide a more concrete strategy that can be done first and then connected to the related equations.

TECHNOLOGY **Note.** For a nice virtual model of a tape or strip diagram, go to Math Playground and scroll down to "Thinking Blocks—Model and Solve Ratio and Proportion Word Problems." This site has instructions and practice that connects the two strips to different types of proportional situations. ■

Double Number Line Diagrams

Double number lines are similar to tape diagrams, but may not show partitions. Importantly, like with tape diagrams, labeling the two lines must be emphasized. Watch this video (https://www.youtube.com/watch?v=rnAcwJLsbcI&list=PLnIkFmW0ticP00KNrtYkbJYwpGuF12lo8&index=2) for illustrations and explanation of using a double number line to solve story problems.

Activity 18.13

CCSS-M: 6.RP.A.3a, d; 7.RP.A.2b; 7.RP.A.3

You and the Zoo

In this activity, you will need plastic animals that are several inches long (approximate) and are in scale with each other. This activity works well with play dough but can also be done with construction paper cutouts. Explain to students that they will use double number lines to prepare a zoo scene—starting with preparing a replica of themselves!

Each pair or group of students is given a plastic animal and asked to make a representation of themselves that is in proportion to the animals. The first task is for them to determine the actual height of the animal (they may look it up online, or you may prepare this data in advance and post it), as well as their own actual height. Here is an example:

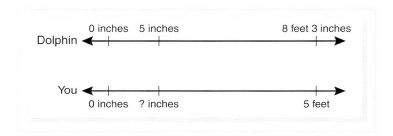

Once the "You" number line is known, students can identify other animals they would like to create for their zoo. Challenge students to select two favorite animals, or assign animals that vary in size and might not be hard to sketch or mold. Examples include: bald eagle, tree frog, boa constrictor, panda, tiger, and lemur.

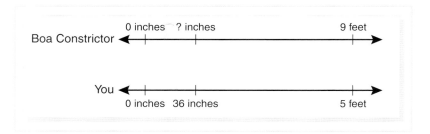

Note: Consider which measurement conversions your students need to practice; this activity can be done with metric or U.S. units.

Percents

Percent problems can be solved using any of the strategies in this section (e.g., a ratio table). A series of videos (https://www.youtube.com/watch?v=gg27-FRbaIs&index=3&list=PLnIkFmW0ticPm5BvVZc7_ZIZpSIrT7q14) illustrates the different ways to apply these strategies to ratios. The double number line just described is an excellent tool for solving percent situations. It is particularly helpful in helping students to figure out which part is unknown. Once the double number line is created, students can use this diagram to set up as a proportion. The values of one number line correspond to the numbers or measures in the problem. On the second number line, the values indicate the corresponding values in terms of percents (with a whole of 100).

Activity 18.14

CCSS-M: 6.RP.3c; 7.RP.A.2c; 7.RP.A.3

Making Sense of Percent Stories

This activity can be done with any set of traditional missing value percent problems. You can post a story or create a set of cards, each with its own problem on it. Three such stories are provided in Figure 18.13, along with how they can be illustrated on a double number line. In order to make the activity interactive and to connect representations, follow these steps: (1) hand out different problems to each group; (2) have each group set up their double number line on a note card (don't solve it); (3) trade the double number line sketch with another pair of students; (4) write a proportion that matches the double number line and solve it; (5) return the cards to the original pair to check to see if the answer makes sense.

Notice how flexible this double number line representation is for different types of percent problems (https://www.youtube.com/watch?v=uocsyPZhR0U&list=PLnIkFmW0tic Pm5BvVZc7_ZIZpSIrT7q14). It allows modeling of not only part-whole scenarios but also increase–decrease situations and those in which there is a comparison between two distinct quantities. Another advantage of a linear model is that it does not restrict students from thinking about percents greater than 100, because the line could represent more than 100 percent, unlike a circle model (Parker, 2004).

Equations

Traditional textbooks show students how to set up an equation of two ratios, a proportion, and then solve for the unknown (x) by cross-multiplying and solving for x. "The central challenge of developing students' capacity to think with ratios (to reason proportionally) is to teach ideas and restrain the quick path to computation" (Smith, 2002, p. 15). Even when using cross products, students should be encouraged to reason in order to find the missing value, rather than just applying the cross-product algorithm. Here we share how to help students how to understand how to use equations to solve proportions problems.

Create a Visual Model. Rather than start by telling students to set up their proportion, ask them to illustrate the problem in a way that shows what is covarying. Figure 18.14(a) shows a simple sketch, which then leads to proportions. Figure 18.14(b) shows a sketch that reflects the context. Both examples include two equations, one that focuses on within ratios and one that focuses on between ratios. Providing visual cues to set up proportions is a very effective way to support a wide range of learners.

Solve the Proportion. Look at the situations in Figure 18.14. As students (and adults) often do naturally, you can determine the *unit rate* or the price for 1 pound by dividing the 80 cents by 4 and then multiplying this result by 6 to determine the price of 6 pounds. The equation is $(0.80 \div 4) \times 6 = 1.20$. Or you can examine the *scale factor* from 4 to 6 pounds (within ratio), which is 1.5. Multiply 0.80 by the same scale factor to get $1.20. The equation is $([6 \div 4] \times .80) = 1.20$. One equation uses 80 in a multiplication and the other equation uses 80 in division. These are exactly the two devices we employed in the line segment and picture approaches: (1) *scale factor* and (2) *unit rate*. If you cross-multiply the between ratios, you get exactly the same result. Furthermore, you get the same result if you had written the two ratios inverted—that is, with the reciprocals of each fraction. Try it!

The cross product is not the only way to solve proportions, but if it is used, it should be understood. This strategy, when understood, is useful when numbers are more challenging and finding unit rate or scale factor is not as easy to calculate.

 Complete Self-Check 18.3: Strategies for Solving Proportional Situations

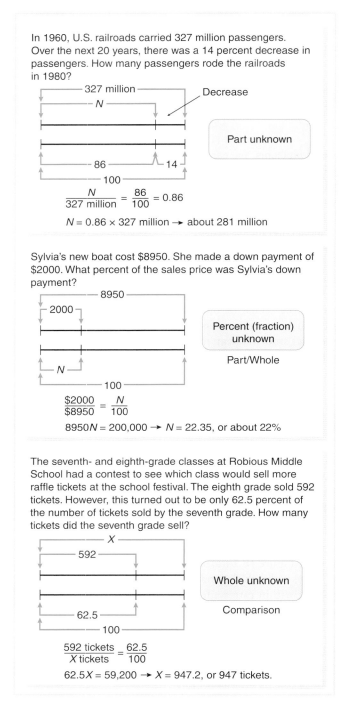

In 1960, U.S. railroads carried 327 million passengers. Over the next 20 years, there was a 14 percent decrease in passengers. How many passengers rode the railroads in 1980?

327 million
N
Decrease
Part unknown
86   14
100

$$\frac{N}{327 \text{ million}} = \frac{86}{100} = 0.86$$

N = 0.86 × 327 million → about 281 million

Sylvia's new boat cost $8950. She made a down payment of $2000. What percent of the sales price was Sylvia's down payment?

8950
2000
Percent (fraction) unknown
N
Part/Whole
100

$$\frac{\$2000}{\$8950} = \frac{N}{100}$$

8950N = 200,000 → N = 22.35, or about 22%

The seventh- and eighth-grade classes at Robious Middle School had a contest to see which class would sell more raffle tickets at the school festival. The eighth grade sold 592 tickets. However, this turned out to be only 62.5 percent of the number of tickets sold by the seventh grade. How many tickets did the seventh grade sell?

X
592
Whole unknown
62.5
Comparison
100

$$\frac{592 \text{ tickets}}{X \text{ tickets}} = \frac{62.5}{100}$$

62.5X = 59,200 → X = 947.2, or 947 tickets.

FIGURE 18.13 Percentage problems represented as double number lines and equations.

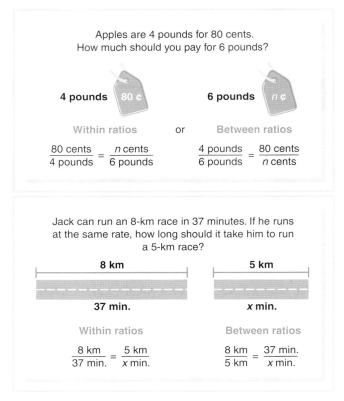

Apples are 4 pounds for 80 cents. How much should you pay for 6 pounds?

4 pounds 80 ¢   **6 pounds** n ¢

Within ratios   or   Between ratios

$$\frac{80 \text{ cents}}{4 \text{ pounds}} = \frac{n \text{ cents}}{6 \text{ pounds}} \qquad \frac{4 \text{ pounds}}{6 \text{ pounds}} = \frac{80 \text{ cents}}{n \text{ cents}}$$

Jack can run an 8-km race in 37 minutes. If he runs at the same rate, how long should it take him to run a 5-km race?

8 km   **5 km**

37 min.   **x min.**

Within ratios   Between ratios

$$\frac{8 \text{ km}}{37 \text{ min.}} = \frac{5 \text{ km}}{x \text{ min.}} \qquad \frac{8 \text{ km}}{5 \text{ km}} = \frac{37 \text{ min.}}{x \text{ min.}}$$

FIGURE 18.14 Drawings can help in setting up proportion equations.

Teaching Proportional Reasoning

Considerable research has been conducted to determine how students reason in various proportionality tasks and to determine whether developmental or instructional factors are related to proportional reasoning (for example, see Bright et al., 2003; Lamon, 2007, 2012; Lobato et al., 2010; Siegler et al., 2010). The findings are shared here as a way to summarize the chapter.

1. Use composed unit and multiplicative comparison ideas in building understanding of ratio. Learning more about multiplicative comparisons should lead to an understanding of rate, which is a strategy to be applied to proportions.
2. Help students distinguish between proportional and non-proportional comparisons by providing examples of each and discussing the differences.
3. Provide ratio and proportion tasks in a wide range of contexts, including situations involving measurements, prices, geometric and other visual contexts, and rates of all sorts.
4. Engage students in a variety of strategies for solving proportions. In particular, use ratio tables, visuals (e.g., tape diagrams and double number lines), equations, and graphs to solve problems—always expecting students to apply reasoning strategies.
5. Recognize that symbolic or mechanical methods, such as the cross-product algorithm, for solving proportions do not develop proportional reasoning and should not be introduced until students have had many experiences with intuitive and conceptual methods.

 Complete Self-Check 18.4: Teaching Proportional Reasoning

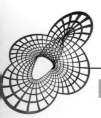

REFLECTIONS ON CHAPTER 18

WRITING TO LEARN

1. Describe the idea of a ratio in your own words. Explain how your idea fits with each of the following statements:
   a. A fraction is a ratio.
   b. Ratios can compare things that are not at all alike.
   c. Ratios can compare two parts of the same whole.
   d. Rates such as prices or speeds are ratios.

2. Describe a situation in which the comparison involved could be interpreted both additively and multiplicatively. Why is it important to include both types of reasoning when introducing ratios?

3. What is covariation? Give an algebraic and geometric example of covariation.

4. Make up a realistic proportional situation that can be solved mentally by a scale-factor approach and another that can be solved mentally by a unit-rate approach.

5. Consider this problem: *If 30 eggs are required to make 2 cakes, how many eggs will be required to make 5 cakes?*

Draw a sketch to illustrate the proportion and set up the equation in two different ways.

FOR DISCUSSION AND EXPLORATION

- Proportional reasoning is a unifying theme in mathematics. For each of the content strands (number, algebra, measurement, geometry, and data analysis and probability), think about content that involves proportional reasoning and explain the connections among all of these ideas.

- In Chapter 17, the percentage problems were developed around the theme of which element was missing—the part, the whole, or the fraction that related the two. In this chapter, percent is related to proportions, an equality of two ratios with one of these ratios a comparison to 100. How are these two approaches alike? How are they different?

RESOURCES FOR CHAPTER 18

LITERATURE CONNECTIONS

Literature brings an exciting dimension to the exploration of proportional reasoning. Many books and stories discuss comparative sizes, concepts of scale as in maps, giants and miniature people who are proportional to regular people, comparative rates (especially rates of speed), and so on. For example, Beckman, Thompson, and Austin (2004) explore the popular *Harry Potter* stories, *The Lord of the Rings*, and *The Perfect Storm* for exciting contexts for proportional reasoning activities. Here are a few more, but many more exist beyond this list! And, check YouTube where you can sometimes find audio versions of these stories.

If You Hopped Like a Frog *Schwartz (1999)*

David Schwartz compares features of various creatures to humans. For example, in the title comparison, Schwarts deduces that if a person had a frog's jumping ability, he could jump from home plate to first base in one hop. This short picture book contains 12 more fascinating comparisons. Schwartz also provides the factual data on which the proportions are based. Students can figure out how strong or tall they would be if they were one of the featured animals.

Holes *Sachar (1998)*

A popular book and movie, this novel tells the story of boys in a camp digging holes every day, which provides an opportunity to look at daily rates of dirt removal. Pugalee and colleagues (2008) describe an excellent activity with this book that involves not only proportional reasoning but also measurement and algebra.

Literature with Large and/or Small People

There is a plethora of literature involving very little or very big people (or animals). With any of these books, body parts can be compared as a way to explore within and between ratios. The following list of some great literature can lead to wonderful lessons on proportional reasoning:

Alice's Adventures in Wonderland *Carroll (1865/1982)*
(https://www.youtube.com/watch?v=9MBf3XhZuPA)

In this classic, Alice becomes very small and very tall, opening doors to many ratio and proportion investigations.

The Borrowers *Norton (1953)*

In a classic tale of little folk living in the walls of a house, furnishings are created from odds and ends of the full-sized human world.

Gulliver's Travels *Swift and Winterson (1726/1999)*

Yet another classic story—in this case, Gulliver first visits the Lilliputians, where he is 12 times their size, and then goes to Brobdingnag, where he is a tenth the size of the inhabitants.

Jim and the Beanstalk *Briggs (1970)*

What happened to the giant after Jack? Jim comes along. Jim wants to help the poor, pessimistic giant. This heartwarming story is great for multiplicative or proportional reasoning.

Kate and the Beanstalk *Osborne and Potter (2000)*

This version of the traditional "Jack and the Beanstalk" tale includes a giantess. The giantess falls to earth, and Kate finds out that the castle belongs to her family.

"One Inch Tall" in Where the Sidewalk Ends *Silverstein (1973)*

Shel Silverstein is a hit with all ages. This poem asks what it would be like if you were one inch tall.

Swamp Angel *Isaacs and Zelinsky (1994)*

A swamp angel named Angelica grows into a giant. Students can explore birth height to current height or compare Angelica's measurements to their own.

RECOMMENDED READINGS

Articles

Ercole, L. K., Frantz, M., & Ashline, G. (2011). Multiple ways to solve proportions. *Mathematics Teaching in the Middle School*, 16(8), 482–490.

This article shares the many ways of reasoning to solve proportions: unit rate, factor of change, building up, ratio tables, and cross-multiplication. Student work is shared throughout.

Langrall, C. W., & Swafford, J. (2000). Three balloons for two dollars. *Mathematics Teaching in the Middle School*, 6(4), 254–261.

The authors describe and give examples of four levels of proportional reasoning using examples from the classroom. A good article on a difficult topic.

Books

Litwiller, B. (Ed.). (2002). *Making sense of fractions, ratios, and proportions: 2002 yearbook.* Reston, VA: NCTM.

Eleven of the 26 short chapters discuss explicitly the issue of multiplicative relationships and/or proportional reasoning. Accompanying the yearbook is a book of classroom activities complete with blackline masters.

Lobato, J., Ellis, A. B., Charles, R. I., & Zbiek, R. M. (2010). *Developing essential understanding of ratios, proportions, and proportional reasoning: Grades 6–8.* Reston, VA: NCTM.

If you want to really understand the important nuances of ratios and proportions, this is a phenomenal resource. Ten essential understandings are explained, along with excellent activities for students and teaching suggestions.

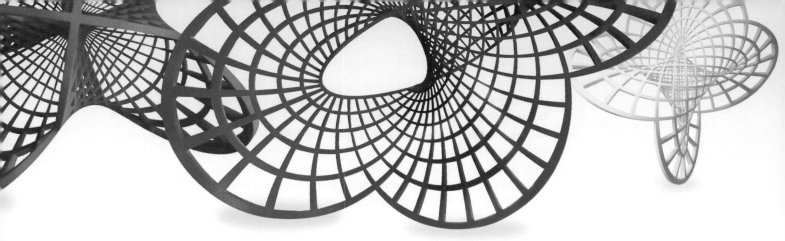

CHAPTER 19

Developing Measurement Concepts

LEARNER OUTCOMES

After reading this chapter and engaging in the embedded activities and reflections, you should be able to:

19.1 Describe the measurement process, including the identification and use of nonstandard and standard units, and demonstrate how to estimate measurements.

19.2 Demonstrate how to measure the length of objects.

19.3 Explain the development of area formulas.

19.4 Explain how volume is measured in standard and nonstandard units.

19.5 Demonstrate a way to compare weights of objects.

19.6 Explain how angles are measured.

19.7 Describe the best model for teaching elapsed time.

19.8 Explain strategies for counting the value of coins.

Measurement is the process of describing a continuous quantity with a numerical value. It is one of the most useful mathematics content strands, as it is an important component in everything from occupational tasks to life skills for the mathematically literate citizen. From gigabytes that measure amounts of information to font size on computers, to miles per gallon, to recipes for a meal, people are surrounded with measurement concepts that apply to many real-world contexts and applications. However, measurement is not an easy topic for students to understand. Data from international studies consistently indicate that U.S. students are weaker in the area of measurement than any other topic in the mathematics curriculum (Thompson & Preston, 2004).

 BIG IDEAS

- ◆ Measurement involves a comparison of an attribute of an item or situation with a unit that has the same attribute. Lengths are compared to units of length, areas to units of area, time to units of time, and so on.

- ◆ Estimation of measures and the development of benchmarks for frequently used units of measure help students increase their familiarity with units, preventing errors and aiding in the meaningful use of measurement.

◆ Measurement instruments (e.g., rulers) group multiple units so that you do not have to iterate a single unit multiple times.

◆ Area and volume formulas provide a method of measuring these attributes by using only measures of length.

◆ Area, perimeter, and volume are related. For example, as the shapes of regions or three-dimensional objects change while maintaining the same areas or volumes, there is an effect on the perimeters and surface areas.

The Meaning and Process of Measuring

Suppose that you asked your students to measure an empty bucket as in Figure 19.1. The first thing they would need to know is *what* about the bucket is to be measured. They might measure the height, diameter (distance across), or circumference (distance around). All of these are length measures. The surface area of the side could be determined. A bucket also has volume (or capacity) and weight. Each aspect that can be measured is an *attribute* of the bucket.

Once students determine the attribute to be measured, they then choose a unit that has the attribute being measured. Length is measured with units that have length, volume with units that have volume, and so on.

Technically, a *measurement* is a number that indicates a comparison between the attribute of the object (or situation, or event) being measured and the same attribute of a given unit of measure. We commonly use small units of measure to determine a numeric relationship (the measurement) between what is measured and the unit. For example, to measure a length, the comparison can be done by lining up copies of the unit directly against the length being measured. For most attributes measured in schools, we can say that *to measure* means that the attribute being measured is "filled" or "covered" or "matched" with a unit of measure with the same attribute.

In summary, to measure something, one must perform three steps:

1. Decide on the attribute to be measured.
2. Select a unit that has that attribute.
3. Compare the units—by filling, covering, matching, or using some other method—with the attribute of the object being measured. The number of units required to match the object is the measure.

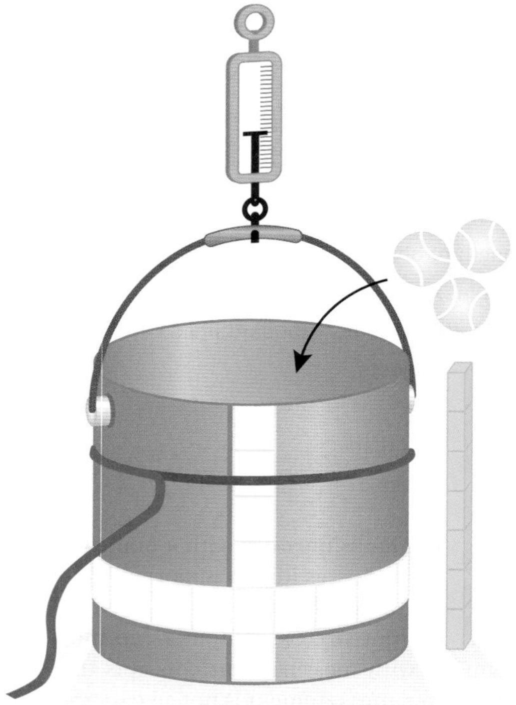

Concepts and Skills

If a typical group of young students attempt to measure the length of their classroom by laying strips 1 meter long end to end, the strips sometimes overlap and the line can weave in a snakelike fashion. Do they understand the concept of length as an attribute of the classroom? Do they understand that each 1-meter strip has this attribute of length? They most likely understand that they are counting a line of strips stretching

Attribute: Weight
Units: objects that <u>stretch</u> the spring in the scale
How many units will pull the spring as far as the bucket will?

Attribute: Volume/Capacity
Units: cubes, balls, cups of water
How many units will <u>fill</u> the bucket?

Attribute: Length
Units: rods, toothpicks, straws, string
How many units are <u>as tall as</u> the bucket?
How much string is needed to <u>go around</u> the bucket?

Attribute: Area
Units: index cards, squares of paper, tiles
How many cards will <u>cover</u> the surface of the bucket?

FIGURE 19.1 Measuring different attributes of a bucket.

TABLE 19.1   MEASUREMENT INSTRUCTION: A SEQUENCE OF EXPERIENCES

Step	Goal	Type of Activity	Notes
1. Make comparisons	Students will understand the attribute to be measured.	Make comparisons based on the attribute (for example, longer/shorter, heavier/lighter). Use direct comparisons whenever possible.	When it is clear that the attribute is understood, there is no further need for comparison activities.
2. Use physical models of measuring units	Students will understand how filling, covering, matching, or making other comparisons of an attribute with measuring units produces a number called a *measure*.	Use physical models of measuring units to fill, cover, match, or make the desired comparison of the attribute with the unit.	Begin with nonstandard units. Progress to the direct use of standard units before using formulas or measuring tools.
3. Use measuring instruments	Students will use common measuring tools with understanding and flexibility.	Make measuring instruments (grouped units) and compare them with the individual unit models to see how the measurement tool is performing the same function. Make direct comparisons between the student-made tools and the standard tools. Standard measuring instruments such as rulers, scales, and protractors make the filling, covering, or matching process easier.	Without a careful comparison of the nonstandard (or informal) tools with the standard tools, much of the value in making the tools can be lost.

from wall to wall. The skill of measuring with a unit must be explicitly linked to the concept of measuring as a process of comparing attributes, using measuring units and using measuring instruments as outlined in Table 19.1.

Making Comparisons.
Sometimes with a measure such as length, a direct comparison can be made where one object can be lined up and matched to another. But often an indirect method using a third object must be used. For example, if students compare the volume of one box to another, they must devise an indirect way to compare. They may fill one box with beans and then pour the beans into the other box. Another example using length would use a string to compare the height of a wastebasket to the distance around. The string is the intermediary, as it is impossible to directly compare these two lengths.

Remember to use precise language when helping students make comparisons. Avoid using the phrases "bigger than" and "smaller than"; instead use more precise language such as "longer than" or "holds more than."

Standards for Mathematical Practice
MP6. Attend to precision.

Using Physical Models of Measuring Units.
For most attributes measured in elementary schools, it is possible to have physical models of the units of measure. Time and temperature are exceptions. Many other attributes not commonly measured in school also do not have physical units of measure, such as light intensity, speed, and loudness. Unit models can be found for both nonstandard (sometimes referred to as *informal*) units and standard units. For length, for example, drinking straws (nonstandard) or 1-foot-long paper strips (standard) might be used as units.

To help make the notion of the unit explicit, use as many copies of the unit as are needed to fill or match the attribute measured (this is called *tiling* and it involves equal partitioning). To measure the area of the desktop with an index card (nonstandard) as your unit, you can literally cover the entire desk with index cards. Somewhat more difficult is to use a single copy of the unit (this is called *iteration*). That means measuring the same desktop with a single index card by repeatedly moving the card from position to position and keeping track of which areas the card has covered.

It is useful to measure the same object with units of different size to help students understand that the unit used is important. For each different-sized unit, estimate the measure in advance and discuss the estimate afterward. They also must start to observe that smaller units produce larger numeric measures, and vice versa. This is a concept related to converting units and it is hard for some students to understand. This inverse relationship can only be mentally constructed by estimating, then experimenting, and finally reflecting on the measurements.

FIGURE 19.2 *"How long is this crayon?"*

Using Measuring Instruments. In the 2003 NAEP exam (Blume, Galindo, & Walcott, 2007), only 20 percent of fourth graders could give the correct measure of an object not aligned with the end of a ruler, as in Figure 19.2. At the eighth grade, only 56 percent answered the same situation accurately (Kloosterman, Rutledge, & Kenney, 2009a). These results point to the difference between using a measuring device and understanding how it works. Students on the same exam also experienced difficulty when the increments on a measuring device were not one unit.

When students construct simple measuring instruments using unit models with which they are familiar, they are more likely to understand how an instrument measures. A ruler is a good example. If students line up individual physical units along a strip of card stock and mark them off, they can see that it is the *spaces* on rulers and not the hash marks or numbers that are important. It is essential that students discuss how measurement with iterating individual units compares with measurement using an instrument. Without this comparison and discussion, students may not understand that these two methods are essentially the same. Then they are ready to compare their "ruler" with standard rulers (or other instruments such as scales) and can compare the use of these devices.

Introducing Nonstandard Units

It is common in primary grades to use nonstandard units to measure length, but unfortunately, measurement activities in the upper grades, where other attributes are measured, often do not begin with this important first step. The use of nonstandard units for beginning measurement activities is beneficial at all grade levels for the following reasons:

- Nonstandard units focus directly on the attribute being measured. For example, when discussing how to measure the area of an irregular shape, units such as square tiles or circular counters may be suggested. Each unit covers area, and each will give a different result. The discussion can focus on what it means to measure area.
- The use of nonstandard units avoids conflicting objectives in introductory lessons. Is your lesson about what it means to measure area or about understanding square centimeters?
- Nonstandard units provide a good rationale for using standard units. The need for a standard unit has more meaning when your students have measured the same objects with their own collections of nonstandard units and arrived at different and sometimes confusing answers.

The amount of time that should be spent using nonstandard units varies with students' age and level of understanding and with the attributes being measured. Some students need many experiences with a variety of nonstandard units of length, weight, and capacity. Conversely, the benefits of nonstandard units may last only a day or two when, for example, fourth graders learn to measure angles. When nonstandard units have served their purpose, move on.

Introducing Standard Units

Measurement sense demands that students be familiar with standard measurement units, able to make estimates in terms of these units, and able to meaningfully interpret measures depicted with standard units.

Perhaps the biggest error in measurement instruction is the failure to recognize and separate two types of objectives: (1) understanding the meaning and technique of measuring a particular attribute, and (2) learning about the standard units commonly used to measure that attribute.

Teaching standard units of measure can be organized around three broad goals:

1. *Familiarity with the unit.* Students should have a basic idea of the size of commonly used units and what they measure. Knowing approximately how much 1 liter of water is or

being able to estimate a shelf as 5 feet long is as important as measuring either of these accurately.

2. *Ability to select an appropriate unit.* Students should know both what is a reasonable measurement unit in a given situation and the required level of precision. (Would you measure your lawn to purchase grass seed with the same precision as you would use in measuring a window to buy a pane of glass?) Students need practice in selecting appropriate standard units and judging the level of precision.

3. *Knowledge of relationships between units.* Students should know the relationships that are commonly used, such as those between inches, feet, and yards or milliliters and liters.

Developing Unit Familiarity. Two types of activities can develop familiarity with standard units: (1) comparisons that focus on a single unit and (2) activities that develop personal referents or benchmarks for single units or easy multiples of units.

Activity 19.1

CCSS-M: 1.MD.A.2; 2.MD.A.1; 3.MD.B.4

Familiar References

ENGLISH LANGUAGE LEARNERS

Read *Measuring Penny* (Leedy, 2000) to get students interested in the variety of ways familiar items can be measured. In this book, the author bridges between nonstandard units (e.g., dog biscuits, swabs, etc.) and standard units (inches, centimeters, etc.) to measure Penny, the pet dog. Have students use the idea of measuring Penny to find something at home (or in class) to measure in as many ways as they can think of using standard units. The measures can be rounded to whole numbers or to a fractional unit depending on the grade level. Discuss in class the familiar items chosen and their measures so that different ideas and benchmarks are shared.

Of special interest for length are benchmarks found on our bodies. These become quite familiar over time and can be used in many situations as approximate rulers.

Activity 19.2

CCSS-M: 2.MD.A.1; 3.MD.B.4; 4.MD.B.4

Personal Benchmarks

Measure your body. About how long are your foot, your stride, your hand span (stretched or with fingers together), the width of your finger, your arm span (finger to finger and finger to nose), and the distance around your wrist and around your waist? Data can be graphed in a line plot. (There are wonderful proportional relationships to be found between these measures too!) Some may prove to be useful benchmarks for standard units, and some may be excellent models for single units. (The average child's fingernail width is about 1 cm, and most people can find a 10-cm length somewhere on their hands.)

Choosing Appropriate Units. Should the room be measured in feet or inches? Should the concrete blocks be weighed in grams or kilograms? The answers to questions such as these involve more than simply knowing how big units are, although that is certainly required. Another consideration involves the need for precision. If you were measuring your wall in order to cut a piece of molding to fit, you would need to measure it very precisely. The smallest unit would be an inch or a centimeter, and you would also use small fractional parts. But if you were determining how many 8-foot molding strips to buy, the nearest foot would probably be sufficient.

Standards for Mathematical Practice

MP6. Attend to precision.

Activity 19.3

CCSS-M: 3.MD.A.2; 3.MD.C.5; 4.MD.A.1; 5.MD.C.3

Guess the Unit

STUDENTS with SPECIAL NEEDS

Find examples of a variety of measurements in newspapers, on signs, or in other everyday situations. Present the context and measures, but without units. For example, you may consider ads for carpeting, articles about gas prices, and so forth. You can also use the Measurement Cards. The task is to predict what units of measure were used. Have students discuss their choices. For students with disabilities, you may want to provide the possible units so they can sort the real-world measures into groups (i.e., area, capacity, weight, time, length).

Important Standard Units and Relationships. Countries worldwide have passed laws stating that international commerce must use metric units. So, if U.S. students are going to be prepared for the global workplace, they must be knowledgeable about and comfortable with metric units. Yet results of the 2004 NAEP reveal that only 40 percent of fourth graders were able to identify how many kilograms a bicycle weighed given the choices of 1.5, 15, 150, and 1500 kg. Even among eighth graders, only 37 percent knew how many milliliters were in a liter (Perie, Moran, & Lutkus, 2005). Surprisingly, U.S. students do better on metric units than customary units (Preston & Thompson, 2004).

NCTM (2011) takes a strong position on the metric system, as it is a globally used system and therefore all students need to understand metric units and their relationships. The statement goes on to say that because we are still using customary measures in day-to-day life, students must work in that system as well. The Common Core State Standards (2010) introduce centimeters in second grade, with further expectations for units such as meters, cubic centimeters, grams, kilograms, and liters.

The relationships between units within either the metric or customary systems are conventions. As such, students must simply be told what the relationships are, and instructional experiences must be devised to reinforce them. It can be argued that initially knowing about how much liquid makes a liter, or being able to pace off 3 meters—unit familiarity—is more important than knowing how many cubic centimeters are in a liter. Another approach to unit familiarity is to begin with common items and use their measures as references or benchmarks. A doorway is a bit more than 2 meters high, and a doorknob is about 1 meter from the floor. A bag of flour is a good reference for 5 pounds. A paper clip weighs about a gram and is about 1 centimeter wide. A gallon of milk weighs a little less than 4 kilograms. However, in the intermediate grades, knowing basic relationships becomes more important in making conversions between units in the same system.

The customary system has few patterns or generalizable rules to guide students in converting units. In contrast, the metric system was systematically created around powers of ten. Understanding of the role of the decimal point as indicating the units position is a powerful concept for making metric conversions (see Figure 17.4). As students grasp the structure of decimal notation, develop the metric system with all seven places: three prefixes for smaller units (*deci-*, *centi-*, *milli-*) and three for larger units (*deka-*, *hecto-*, *kilo-*). Avoid mechanical rules such as "To change centimeters to meters, move the decimal point two places to the left." Instead create conceptual, meaningful methods for conversions rather than rules that are often misused and forgotten.

The Role of Estimation and Approximation

Measurement estimation is the process of using mental and visual information to measure or make comparisons without using measuring instruments. People use this practical skill almost every day. Do I have enough sugar to make cookies? Can you throw the ball 15 meters? Is this suitcase over the weight or size limit? Will my car fit into that parking space? Here are several reasons for including estimation in measurement activities:

- Estimation helps students focus on the attribute being measured and the measuring process. Think how you would estimate the area of the cover of this book using playing cards as the unit. To do so, you have to think about what area is and how the units might be placed on the book cover.
- Estimation provides an intrinsic motivation for measurement activities. It is interesting to see how close you can come in your estimate to the actual measure.
- When standard units are used, estimation helps develop familiarity with the unit. If you estimate the height of the door in meters before measuring, you must think about the size of a meter.
- The use of a benchmark to make an estimate promotes multiplicative reasoning. The width of the building is about one-fourth of the length of a football field—perhaps 25 yards.

In all measuring activities, emphasize the use of approximate language. The desk is *about* 15 orange rods long. The chair is *a little less than* 4 straws high. Approximate language is very useful for students because many measurements do not result in whole numbers. As they develop, students will begin to search for smaller units or use fractional units to try to be more precise, which is an opportunity to develop the idea that all measurements include some error. Acknowledge that each smaller unit or subdivision produces a greater degree of *precision*. For example, a length measure can never be more than one-half unit in error.

For example, suppose you are measuring a length of ribbon with a ruler that only shows quarter inches—so the unit is a quarter of an inch. If the length of ribbon falls between $3\frac{3}{4}$ and 4 inches, we would usually round to whichever number is closer to the length of ribbon. If the length of ribbon is more than halfway towards the 4-inch mark, we would say it's 4 inches long. However, if the length of ribbon is less than halfway from $3\frac{3}{4}$, we say it is closer to $3\frac{3}{4}$ inches long. In either case, we are within $\frac{1}{8}$ of an inch or one-half of the unit and are essentially ignoring the difference, and this constitutes our "error." If we need more precision in our measurement, we use smaller units to ensure that our measurement rounding or error is within an acceptable range.

Because mathematically there is no "smallest unit," there is always some error. The Standards for Mathematical Practice in the Common Core State Standards (CCSSO, 2010) include, "Attend to precision." Within that standard, they expect students to be "careful about specifying units of measure" and to "express numerical answers with a degree of precision appropriate for the problem context" (p. 7)[*].

Strategies for Estimating Measurements. Always begin a measurement activity with students making an estimate. This is true with both nonstandard and standard units. Just as for computational estimation, specific strategies exist for estimating measures. Here are four strategies:

1. *Develop benchmarks or referents.* Research shows that students who acquire mental benchmarks or reference points for measurements *and* practice using them in class activities are much better estimators than students who have not learned to use benchmarks (Joram, 2003). Students must pay attention to the size of the unit to estimate well (Towers & Hunter, 2010). Referents should be things that are easily envisioned by the student. One example is the height of a child (see Figure 19.3). Students should have a good referent for single units and also for useful multiples of standard units.
2. *Use "chunking" or subdivisions.* Figure 19.3 shows an example of chunking using windows, bulletin boards, and spaces between as chunks. It may be easier to estimate the shorter chunks along the wall than to estimate the whole length. The weight of a stack of books is easier to estimate if some referent is given for the weight of an "average" book. But,

---

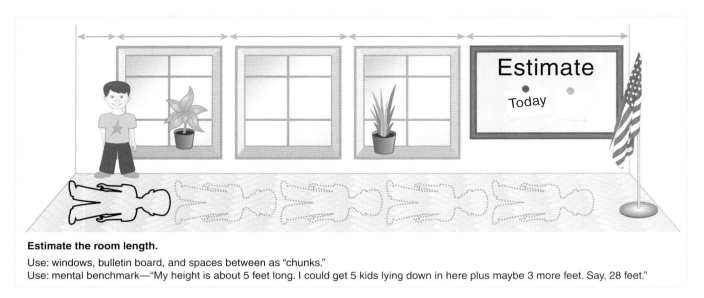

Estimate the room length.

Use: windows, bulletin board, and spaces between as "chunks."

Use: mental benchmark—"My height is about 5 feet long. I could get 5 kids lying down in here plus maybe 3 more feet. Say, 28 feet."

FIGURE 19.3 Estimating measures using benchmarks and chunking.

if the wall length to be estimated has no useful chunks, it can be mentally subdivided in half and then in fourths or even eighths by repeated subdivisions until a manageable length is found. Length, volume, and area measurements all lend themselves to subdivisions.

3. *Iterate units.* For length, area, and volume, it is sometimes easy to mark off single units mentally or physically. You might use your hands or make marks to keep track as you go. If you know, for example, that your stride is about $\frac{3}{4}$ meter, you can walk off a length and then multiply to get an estimate. Hand and finger widths are useful for shorter measures.

Each strategy just listed should be explicitly taught and discussed with students. Suggested benchmarks for useful measures can be developed and recorded on a class chart. Include items found at home. But the best approach to improving estimation skills is to have students do a lot of estimating. Keep these teaching tips in mind:

1. *Help students learn strategies by having them first try a specified approach.* Later activities should permit students to choose whatever techniques they wish.
2. *Discuss how different students made their estimates.* This will confirm that there is no single right way to estimate while reminding students of other useful approaches.
3. *Accept a range of estimates.* Think in relative terms about what is a good estimate. Within 10 percent for length is reasonable. Even 30 percent "off" may be reasonable for weights or volumes.
4. *Do not promote a "winning" estimate.* This discourages estimation and promotes only seeking the exact answer.
5. *Encourage students to give a range of estimates that they believe includes the actual measure.* For example, the door is between 7 and 8 feet tall. This not only is a practical approach in real life but also helps focus on the approximate nature of estimation.
6. *Make measurement estimation an ongoing activity.* Post a daily measurement to be estimated. Students can record their estimates and discuss them in a five-minute period. Older students can take turns determining the daily measurements to estimate, with individuals or a team assigned this task each week.
7. *Be precise with your language.* Do not use the word *measure* interchangeably with the word *estimate* (Towers & Hunter, 2010). Randomly substituting one word for the other will cause uncertainty and possibly confusion in students.

Measurement Estimation Activities. Estimation activities need not be elaborate. Any measurement activity can have an "estimate first" component. For more emphasis on the process of estimation itself, simply think of measures that can be estimated, and have students estimate. Here are two suggestions.

Activity 19.4

CCSS-M: K.MD.A.1; K.MD.A.2; 1.MD.A.1; 1.MD.A.2; 2.MD.A.3

ENGLISH LANGUAGE LEARNERS

Estimation Quickie

Select a single object such as a box, a pumpkin, a painting on the wall of the school, or even the principal. Each day, select a different attribute or dimension to estimate. For a pumpkin, for example, students can estimate its height, circumference, weight, volume, and surface area. If you have ELLs, then be sure to include metric measures or help students connect the centimeter to the inch. Watch this short video (http://www.youtube.com/watch?v=ygeIbA4TJNk) about a class exploring various measures of a pumpkin.

Activity 19.5

CCSS-M: 1.MD.A.2; 2.MD.A.1; 2.MD.A.3

Estimation Scavenger Hunt

Conduct estimation scavenger hunts. Give teams a list of either nonstandard or standard measurements, and have them find things that are close to having those measurements. Do not let them use measuring instruments at first. Look at the Estimation Scavenger Hunt Activity Page for some possible ideas. Let students suggest how to judge results in terms of accuracy.

 FORMATIVE ASSESSMENT Notes. Estimation tasks are a good way to assess students' understanding of both measurement and units. Use an Observation Checklist to take notes about students' estimates and measures of a variety of real objects and distances. Prompt students to explain how they arrived at their estimates to get a more complete picture of their measurement knowledge. Asking only for a numeric estimate can mask a lack of understanding and will not give you the information you need to provide next instructional steps. ■

✓ **Complete Self-Check 19.1: The Meaning and Process of Measuring**

Length

Length is usually the first attribute students learn to measure. Length is an attribute of an object that is found by locating two endpoints and examining how far it is between those points. We measure lengths by selecting a unit (that has length) and repeatedly matching that unit to the object.

Length measurement is not immediately understood by young students and there are several common misconceptions and difficulties students might exhibit. Here are a few:

- Measuring from the wrong end of the ruler or beginning at 1 instead of 0
- Counting the hash marks rather than the spaces (units)
- Not aligning two objects when comparing them

Comparison Activities

Students in pre-K and kindergarten should begin with direct comparisons of two or more lengths and then move to indirect comparisons by the first grade (CCSSO, 2010; NCTM, 2006).

Activity 19.6   CCSS-M: K.MD.A.2; 1.MD.A.1; 2.MD.A.3

Longer, Shorter, Same

Create learning stations where students can explore which objects in a group are longer, shorter, or about the same as a specified "target" object. Change the target object and students will find the shorter item is now longer than the target. A similar task can involve putting a set of objects in order from shortest to longest.

Activity 19.7   CCSS-M: K.MD.A.2; 1.MD.A.1; 1.MD.A.2; 2.MD.A.3

Length (or Unit) Hunt

STUDENTS *with* **SPECIAL NEEDS**

Give pairs of students a strip of card stock, a stick, a length of rope, or some other object with an obvious length dimension. The task is to find five things in the room that are shorter than, longer than, or about the same length as their target unit. They can record what they find in pictures or words. Allow students with disabilities to have a copy of the "target" to carry with them as they make actual comparisons. By making the target length a standard unit (e.g., a meter stick or a 1-meter length of rope), the activity can be repeated to provide familiarity with important standard units.

Also compare lengths that are not in straight lines. One way to do this is by using indirect comparisons, which means using another object to help make the measure, as in the next activity.

Activity 19.8   CCSS-M: 1.MD.A.1; 2.MD.A.3; 2.MD.A.4

Crooked Paths

STUDENTS *with* **SPECIAL NEEDS**

Make some crooked or curvy paths on the floor (or outside) with masking tape or chalk. Ask students to determine which path is longest, next longest, and so on. The students should suggest ways to measure the crooked paths so that they can be compared easily. If you wish to offer a hint, provide pairs of students with a long piece of string (at first make it longer than the path). Have students explain how they solved the problem. For students with disabilities, you may need to tape the end of the string to the beginning of the path and help them mark the final measurement on the string with a marker. Use another string for the other path in the same way. Then compare the string lengths. Students who argue that the straight path "looks longer" than the more compact crooked path may need to explore an example of these two paths on the floor. Have students walk each to see which takes longer to walk. See Expanded Lesson: Crooked Paths for an enhanced version of this activity.

Using Physical Models of Length Units

There are four important principles of iterating units of length, whether they are nonstandard or standard (Dietiker, Gonulates, Figueras, & Smith, 2010):

- Units must be equal in length or you cannot iterate them by counting.
- Units must align with the length being measured or a different quantity is measured.
- Units must be placed without gaps or a part of the length is not measured.
- Units must be placed without overlaps or the length has portions that are measured more than one time.

Students can begin to measure length using a variety of nonstandard units, including these:

- *Giant footprints:* Cut out about 20 copies of a large footprint about $1\frac{1}{2}$ to 2 feet long on posterboard.
- *Measuring ropes:* Cut rope into lengths of 1 m. These can measure the perimeter and the circumference of objects such as the teacher's desk, a tree trunk, or the class pumpkin.
- *Drinking straws:* Straws provide large quantities of a useful unit as they are easily cut into smaller units or linked together with a long string. The string of straws can be a bridge to a ruler or measuring tape.
- *Short units:* Connecting cubes and paper clips are useful nonstandard units for measuring shorter lengths. Cuisenaire rods are also useful, as they are easy to place end to end and are also metric (centimeters) and thus make an excellent bridge to a ruler.

The following activity encourages students to develop their own approach to measuring lengths.

Activity 19.9

CCSS-M: 1.MD.A.2; 2.MD.A.1; 2.MD.A.2; 2.MD.A.3

How Long Is the Teacher?

Explain that you have received an important request from the principal. She needs to know exactly how tall each teacher in the building is. The students are to decide how to measure the teachers and write a note to the principal explaining how tall their teacher is and detailing the process that they used. If you wish to give a hint, have students make marks at your feet and head and draw a straight line between these marks.

Explain that the principal says they can measure using any nonstandard or standard unit (provide choices). For each choice of unit, supply enough units to more than cover your length. Put students in pairs and allow them to select one unit with which to measure. Ask students to estimate first and then use their unit to measure. For a challenge, have students measure with two different units.

After students complete their measuring, follow up with questions like "How did you get your measurement?" "Did students who measured with the same unit get the same answers? Why or why not?" "How could the principal make a line that was as long as the teacher?" Focus on the value of carefully lining units up end to end. Discuss what happens if you overlap units, have a gap in the units, or don't follow in a straight line.

The following activity adds an estimation component.

Activity 19.10

CCSS-M: 1.MD.A.2; 2.MD.A.1; 2.MD.A.3

STUDENTS
with
SPECIAL
NEEDS

Estimate and Measure

Make lists of items in the room to measure (see Figure 19.4) or use the Estimating and Measuring with Nonstandard Units Activity Page. For younger students, run a piece of masking tape along the dimension of objects to be measured. Include curves or other distances that are not straight lines. Have students estimate before they measure. Young students and students with disabilities may find it difficult to come up with a reasonable estimate, so provide possible strategies. For example, make a row or chain of exactly 10 of the units to help them visualize. They first lay 10 units against the object and then make their estimate.

Standards for
CCSS **Mathematical**
Practice
MP3. Construct viable arguments and critique the reasoning of others.

FORMATIVE ASSESSMENT Notes. Observation and discussion during activities such as those just described provide evidence of how well your students understand length measurement. Additional tasks that can be used as assessments in a diagnostic interview format are:

- Ask students to draw a line or mark off a distance of a prescribed number of units. Observe whether students know to align the units in a straight line without overlaps or gaps.
- Demonstrate in the classroom how a fictitious student used a ruler to measure the length of an object. Make many errors such as showing gaps, overlaps, and a wavy line of alignment in the placement of the ruler. The students' task is to explain why these measurement may be inaccurate.
- Have students measure two different objects. Then ask how much longer the longer object is. Observe whether students can use the two measurements they have to answer or whether they need to make a third measurement to find the difference.
- Have students measure a length with small paper clips and then again with large paper clips. Can they identify the inverse relationship between the measures they find and the size of the units?

If your assessment indicates that there is some confusion about how length is measured, use the class discussion of these results to help students self-assess and come to a deeper understanding. ■

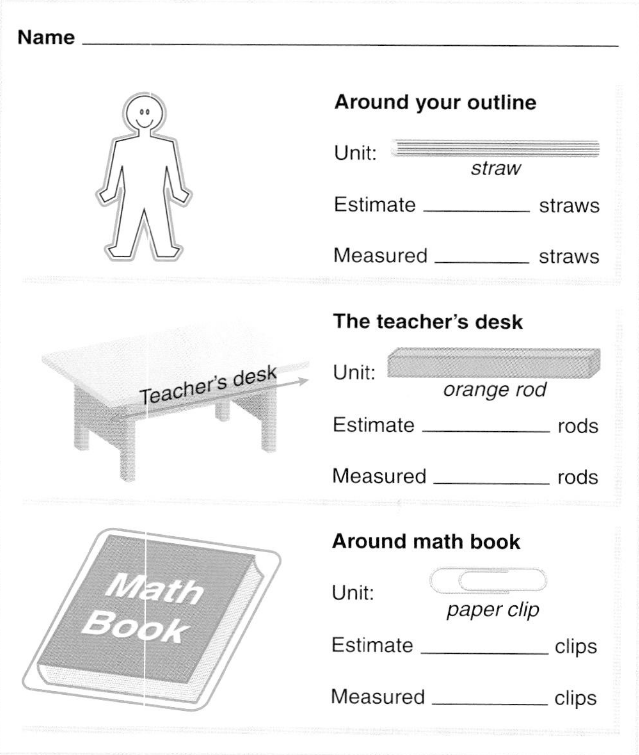

Name _____

Around your outline

Unit: _____ straw

Estimate _____ straws

Measured _____ straws

Teacher's desk

The teacher's desk

Unit: _____ orange rod

Estimate _____ rods

Measured _____ rods

Math Book

Around math book

Unit: _____ paper clip

Estimate _____ clips

Measured _____ clips

FIGURE 19.4 Example of a recording sheet for measuring with nonstandard length units.

Conversion

Linked to the last item of the formative assessment, as required in the standards (CCSSO, 2010), students must be able to convert measures in the same system to larger or smaller units. However, it is a challenge to explain to students that larger units will produce a smaller measure and vice versa. Instead, engage students in activities like the following, where this issue is emphasized.

Activity 19.11   CCSS-M: 2.MD.A.2; 2.MD.A.3

Changing Units

Have students measure a length with a specified unit. Then provide them with a different unit that is either twice as long or half as long as the original unit. Their task is to predict the measure of the same length using the new unit. Students should write down and discuss how they made their estimations, then determine the actual measurement. Cuisenaire rods are excellent for this activity. Some students can be challenged with units that are more difficult multiples of the original unit.

In this activity, you are reinforcing the basic idea that when the unit is longer, the measure is smaller and when the unit is smaller, the measure is larger. This is a good activity to do just to introduce unit conversion with standard units (this is in the Common Core State Standards in grades 4 and 5), and is an excellent proportional reasoning task for middle school students. After completing activities like the one that follows, encourage students to draw conclusions that you multiply to convert a larger unit to a smaller unit. What do you predict is the process to go from a smaller unit to a larger unit?

Activity 19.12   CCSS-M: 4.MD.A.1; 5.MD.A.1

Conversion Please

Give students a copy of the Two-Column Conversion Table. Select several items around the classroom and have students measure the items in feet and then again in inches. Only have them complete half of the page. Ask them to describe the relationship between the two measurements. They are likely to notice that the longer the unit chosen, the fewer units needed and vice versa. For the second half of the table, give them the item to measure only with feet and have them convert to find how many inches. When complete, they can confirm their answers by measuring. Try other units.

Making and Using Rulers

The jump from measuring with actual units to using standard rulers is challenging. One method to help students understand rulers is to have them make their own rulers.

Activity 19.13   CCSS-M: 1.MD.A.2; 2.MD.A.1; 2.MD.A.3

Make Your Own Ruler

Use two colors of precut narrow strips of construction paper, 5 cm long and about 2 cm wide. Discuss how the strips could be used to measure by laying them end to end. Provide long strips of card stock about 3 cm wide. Have students make their own ruler by gluing the units onto the card stock. Have students use their new rulers to measure items on a list that you provide. Discuss the results. It is possible that there will be discrepancies due to rulers that were not made properly or to a failure to understand how a ruler works.

Also consider using larger nonstandard units, such as tracings of students' footprints glued onto strips of cash register tape (without gaps or overlaps). Older students can use standard units (centimeter, inch, foot) to make marks on the strips and color in the spaces with alternating colors.

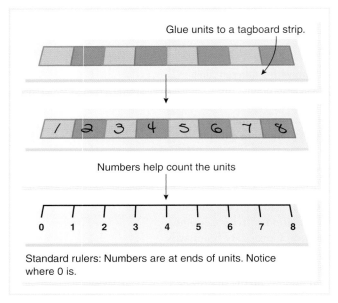

Glue units to a tagboard strip.

Numbers help count the units

Standard rulers: Numbers are at ends of units. Notice where 0 is.

FIGURE 19.5 Give meaning to numbers on rulers.

Students should use their rulers to measure lengths that are longer than their rulers and discuss how that can be done. Another challenge is to find more than one way to measure a length with a ruler. Do you have to begin at the end? What if you begin at another unit in the center? Students can eventually put numbers on their handmade rulers, as shown in Figure 19.5. For students who struggle, numbers can be written in the center of each unit to make it clear that the numbers are a way of precounting the units. When numbers are written in the standard way, at the ends of the units, the ruler becomes a number line.

Be explicit in making this connection from the handmade rulers to standard rulers. Give students a standard ruler, and discuss how it is alike and how it differs from the ones they have made. What are the units? Could you make a ruler with units the same as this? What do the numbers mean? What are the other marks for? Where do the units begin?

FORMATIVE ASSESSMENT Notes. Research indicates that when students see standard rulers with the numbers on the hash marks, they often believe that the numbers are counting the marks rather than indicating the units or spaces between the marks. This is an incorrect understanding of rulers that can lead to wrong answers. As a performance assessment, provide students a ruler with hash marks but no numbers. Have students use the ruler to measure an item that is shorter than the ruler. Use an Observation Checklist to record whether students count spaces between the hash marks.

Another good performance assessment of ruler understanding is to have students measure with a "broken" ruler, one with the first two units broken off. Use your Observation Checklist to note whether students say that it is impossible to measure with such a ruler because there is no starting point. Also note those who match and count the units meaningfully. The dynamic GeoGebra worksheet is a good tool for this.

Observing how students use a ruler to measure an object that is longer than the ruler is also informative. Students who simply read the last mark on the ruler may struggle because they do not understand how a ruler is a representation of a continuous row of units. ■

Activity 19.14 CCSS-M: 1.MD.A.2; 2.MD.A.1; 2.MD.A.3

About One Unit

Give students a model of a standard unit and have them search for objects that measure about the same as that one unit (see About One Meter Activity Page). For example, to develop familiarity with the meter, give students a piece of rope 1 meter long. Have them make lists of familiar things in their life that are about 1 meter. Keep separate lists for things that are a little less (or a little more) or twice as long (or half as long). Be sure to include curved or circular lengths. Later, students can try to predict whether a particular object is more than, less than, or close to 1 meter.

The same activity can be done with other unit lengths. Families can be enlisted to help students find familiar distances that are about 1 mile or about 1 kilometer. Suggest in a take-home letter that families check the distances around the neighborhood, to the school or shopping center, or along other frequently traveled paths. If possible, send home (or use in class) a 1-meter or 1-yard trundle wheel to measure distances. For other interesting looks at measuring places, go online to Google Earth's Measuring Tools, where students can measure distances in centimeters, inches, feet, yards, kilometers, and miles. Watch this video (http://www.youtube.com/watch?v=6iK5b2uA2Ac) of a class estimating while using a trundle wheel to measure the length of the school hallway.

Other measures of length, such as perimeter and circumference, will be discussed in subsequent sections.

 Complete Self-Check 19.2: Length

 # Area

Area is the measure of two-dimensional space inside a region. As with other attributes, students must first understand the attribute of area before measuring. Data from the 2011 NAEP suggest that fourth-grade students have an incomplete understanding of area, with only 24 percent able to find the area of a square given a perimeter of 12 units and including a drawing of the square with hash marks around the sides. Instead, 44 percent merely counted the eight hash marks around the edge (National Center for Educational Statistics, 2014). Estimating and measuring area begin in third grade, as students connect to multiplication, and continue in grade 4 with finding the area of rectangles using formulas and real-world problems. In fifth grade students explore area problems with fractional measures and use area to find volumes of three-dimensional shapes. By grade 6, students explore area of a wide range of polygons and learn surface area. In grade 7, students explore area of circles.

Comparison Activities

Comparing area measures is a bigger conceptual challenge than comparing length measures because areas come in a variety of shapes. Comparison activities with areas should help students distinguish between size (or area) and shape, length, and other dimensions. A long, skinny rectangle may have less area than a triangle with shorter sides. Many students do not understand that rearranging areas into different shapes does not affect the amount of area (although the perimeter can change).

Direct comparison of two areas is frequently impossible except when the shapes involved have some common dimension or property. For example, two rectangles with the same width can be compared directly (see Rectangle Comparison Activity Page), as can any two circles. Comparison of these special shapes, however, fails to deal with the attribute of area. Instead, activities in which one area is rearranged (conservation of area) are suggested. The following activity can support this purpose.

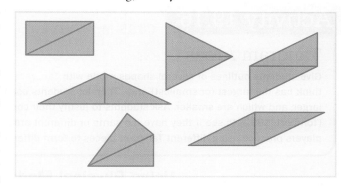

FIGURE 19.6   Different shapes, same area.

Activity 19.15   CCSS-M: 3.MD.C.5

Two-Piece Shapes

Cut a large number of Rectangles of the Same Area, about 3 inches by 5 inches. Each pair of students will need six rectangles. Have students fold and cut the rectangles on the diagonal, making two identical triangles. Next, have them rearrange the triangles into different shapes, including back into the original rectangle. The rule is that only sides of the same length can be matched up and they must be matched exactly. Have students work in pairs to find all the shapes that can be made this way, gluing the triangles on paper as a record (see Figure 19.6). Discuss the area and shape of each response. Does one shape have a greater area than the rest? How do you know? Help students conclude that although each figure is a different shape, all the figures have the same *area*.

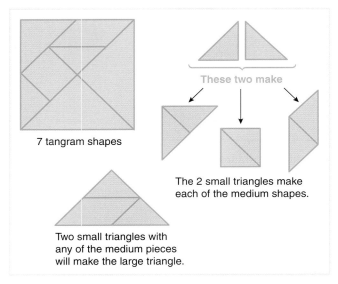

FIGURE 19.7 Tangrams provide an opportunity to investigate area concepts.

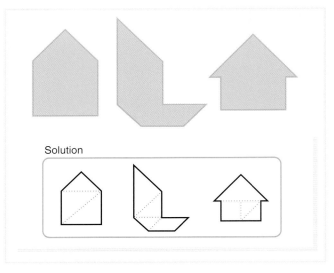

FIGURE 19.8 Compare the area of shapes made of tangram pieces.

Tangrams, an ancient puzzle, can be used for the same purpose. The standard set of seven Tangram Pieces is cut from a square, as shown in Figure 19.7 or in the online version at the National Library of Virtual Manipulatives. The two small triangles can be used to make the parallelogram, the square, and the medium triangle. This permits a similar discussion about the pieces having the same area but different shapes.

Activity 19.16   CCSS-M: 3.MD.C.5; 3.MD.C.6

Tangram Areas

Give students outlines of several shapes made with Tangram Pieces, as in Figure 19.8. Ask groups to estimate which one they think has the largest (or smallest) area. Then let students use tangrams to decide which shapes are the same size, which are larger, and which are smaller. Ask students to justify their conclusions. Use the animal shapes from *Grandfather Tang's Story* (Tompert, 1997) to see if they have the same or different areas. PBS Kid's Cyberchase website has a Tangram game in which players practice using different Tangram pieces to form different pictures (e.g., rabbit, duck, space ship, sailboat, etc.).

Using Physical Models of Area Units

Prior to learning formulas, students need multiple opportunities to "cover the surface" of two-dimensional shapes. Although squares are the most common area units, any tile that conveniently fills up a plane region can be used, such as index cards, sheets of newspaper, notebooks, two-color counters or playing cards. Eventually move to models of standard units such as color tiles (1-inch sides) or Cuisenaire rods or base-ten blocks (1-cm sides). Students can use units to measure surfaces in the room such as desktops, bulletin boards, or books. Large regions can be outlined with masking tape on the floor. Small regions can be duplicated on paper so that students can work at stations.

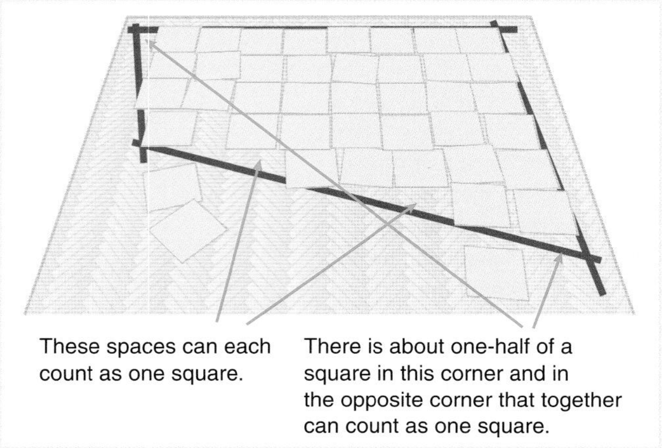

In area measurements, there are typically units that only partially fit. You may wish to begin with shapes in which the units fit by building a shape with units and drawing the outline. According to the Common Core State Standards (CCSSO, 2010), in third grade, students should begin to wrestle with partial units and mentally put together two or more partial units to count as one unit which prepares them for the use of fractional units in fifth grade. Figure 19.9 shows one possible measurement exercise.

These spaces can each count as one square.

There is about one-half of a square in this corner and in the opposite corner that together can count as one square.

FIGURE 19.9 Measuring the area of a large shape with card stock squares.

The following activity is a good starting point.

Activity 19.17

CCSS-M: 3.MD.C.5; 3.MD.C.6

Cover and Compare

Draw two rectangles and a blob shape on a sheet of paper. Make it so that the three areas are not the same but with no area that is clearly largest or smallest. Ask students to estimate which is the smallest and the largest area of the three shapes. After recording their estimate, they should trace or glue the same two-dimensional unit on the shapes, or cut the shapes out and place them on grid paper. Students should explain in their strategy and justification in writing.

Your initial objective in the beginning is to develop the idea that area is measured by covering or tiling. Do not introduce formulas yet. Groups are likely to come up with different measures for the same region. Discuss these differences with the students, and point to the difficulties involved in making estimates around the edges.

Students should begin to apply the concept of multiplication using arrays to the area of rectangles. The following comparison activity is a good step in that direction.

Activity 19.18

CCSS-M: 3.MD.C.5; 3.MD.C.6; 3.MD.C.7

STUDENTS with SPECIAL NEEDS

Rectangle Comparison: Square Units

Give students a pair of rectangles that are the same or very close in area. Also supply them with a model of a single square unit and a ruler that measures the appropriate unit. Students are not permitted to cut out the rectangles, but they may draw on them if they wish. The task is to use their rulers to determine, in any way that they can, which rectangle is larger or whether they are the same. They should use words, pictures, and numbers to explain their conclusions. Some suggested pairs are as follows:

4×10 and 5×8 5×10 and 7×7 4×6 and 5×5

Some students with disabilities may need to have modified worksheets of the figures on grid paper that matches the square units to be used.

The goal of this activity is to apply students' developing concepts of multiplication to the area of rectangles without introducing a formula. In order to count a single row of squares along one edge and then multiply by the length of the other edge, the first row must be thought of as a single unit that is then replicated to fill in the rectangle (Outhred & Mitchelmore, 2004) (see Figure 19.10). Many students will attempt to draw in all the squares. By having students share strategies, more students can be exposed to the use of multiplication in this context as they move toward learning the formula.

Grids of various types can be thought of as "area rulers." A grid of squares does for area what a ruler does for length: It lays out the units for you. Square grids on transparencies can be made from several kinds of Grids of the Unit of Your Choice. Have students place the clear grid over a region to be measured and count the units inside. An alternative method is to trace around a region on a paper grid.

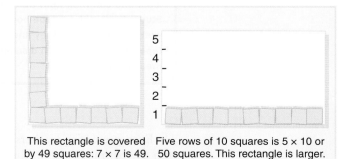

This rectangle is covered by 49 squares: 7×7 is 49.

Five rows of 10 squares is 5×10 or 50 squares. This rectangle is larger.

FIGURE 19.10 Students use multiplication to tell the total number of square units.

The Relationship between Area and Perimeter

Area and perimeter are a continual source of confusion for students. Although perimeter is a standard at grade 3 (CCSSO, 2010), of the eighth graders given an illustration of a rectangle with only the two side lengths on the NAEP exam, only 71 percent accurately identified the perimeter. Perhaps confusion emerges because both area and perimeter involve regions to be measured or because students are taught formulas for both concepts at about the same time. Teaching these two concepts during a close timeframe is particularly challenging for students with disabilities (Parmar, Garrison, Clements, & Sarama, 2011).

Perimeter is a length measure of the distance around a region and, as such, it is additive. Students should be able to calculate perimeter given side measures as well as identify missing side lengths. A good hint for helping students remember the concept of perimeter is that the word "rim" is in the word pe**rim**eter.

What is the perimeter of this figure?

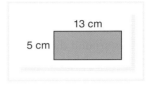

The perimeter of the rectangle below is 32. What is the length of the side marked A?

Activity 19.19
CCSS-M: 3.MD.D.8

What's the Rim?

STUDENTS
with
SPECIAL NEEDS

Have students select objects with a perimeter that they would like the whole class to measure (like the top of a book) or more challenging (the top of a wastebasket). First, students estimate the perimeter on the What's the Rim? Activity Page. They also need to choose tools strategically (given rulers, cash register tape, or nonstretching string) and record their choice. Then they measure the actual amount, including noting the unit. The discussion should include class comparisons of at least one common item that will provide a basis for exploring any measurement errors. Students should describe how they measured objects that were larger than the tool they were using and how they knew when to use a flexible measuring tool (i.e., string or paper tape). For students with disabilities, have them trace the perimeter with their finger prior to measuring.

Even preservice teachers were confused as to whether the area of a rectangle increases with the perimeter (Livy, Muir, & Maher, 2012). An interesting approach to alleviating this confusion is to contrast area and perimeter, as in the next two activities.

Activity 19.20

CCSS-M: 3.MD.D.8; 4.MD.A.3

Fixed Perimeters

Give students a loop of nonstretching string that is 24 centimeters in circumference and 1-Centimeter Grid Paper, or just use the grid paper alone. The task is to decide what different-sized rectangular gardens can be made with a perimeter of 24 cm. Each different rectangle can be recorded on the 1-cm grid paper with the area noted inside the sketch of the garden ($A = 20 \text{ cm}^2$). Then record all of the results on the Fixed Perimeter Recording Sheet.

Activity 19.21

CCSS-M: 3.MD.C.6; 3.MD.C.7; 4.MD.A.3

Fixed Areas

Provide students with 1-Centimeter Grid Paper. The task is to see how many rectangular gardens can be made with an area of 36—that is, to make filled-in rectangles, not just borders. Each new rectangle should be recorded by sketching the garden and the dimensions on grid paper. For each rectangle, students should determine and record the perimeter inside the figure ($P = 24$ cm). Then record all the results on the Fixed Area Recording Sheet. You might also use the Expanded Lesson for this activity.

 Pause & Reflect

Let's think about the two preceding activities. For "Fixed Areas," will all of the perimeters be the same? If not, what can you say about the shapes with longer or shorter perimeters? For "Fixed Perimeters," will the areas remain the same? Why or why not? •

Activity 19.22

CCSS-M: 3.MD.C.6; 3.MD.C.7; 4.MD.A.3

Sorting Areas and Perimeters

Students must complete Activities 19.20 and 19.21 first and cut out all the figures. Then have two charts or locations labeled with "Perimeter" and "Area." Teams should place their figures (left to right) from smallest perimeter (or area) to largest perimeter (or area) on the appropriate chart. Ask students to write down observations, make conjectures, and draw conclusions. Students may be surprised to find out that rectangles having the same areas do not necessarily have the same perimeters and vice versa. And, of course, this fact is not restricted to rectangles.

When students complete these activities they will notice an interesting relationship. When the area is fixed, the shape with the smallest perimeter is "square-like," as is the rectangle with the largest area. If you allowed for any shapes whatsoever, the shape with the smallest perimeter for a fixed area is a circle. Also, they will notice that the "fatter" a shape, the shorter its perimeter; the skinnier a shape, the longer its perimeter. (These relationships are also true in three dimensions—replace perimeter with surface area and area with volume.)

As students move to thinking about formulas, they can consider exploring how the perimeter of rectangles can be put into a general form. Begin by having students generate ways that perimeter problems can be solved. As in the rectangle shown previously, it is common

Standards for Mathematical Practice

MP8. Look for and express regularity in repeated reasoning.

for students to be given a perimeter problem in which only one length and one width are included. So if students are only considering adding these two numbers, discussing the formula $P = l + w + l + w$ for a rectangle will help point out that there are four length dimensions that should be added. This connection to the equation will help avoid the common error of only adding the two given dimensions. An alternative perimeter formula for rectangles that might emerge from the conversations would be $P = 2(l + w)$, which will reinforce the multiplication of the pair of sides, or $P = 2l + 2w$, which emphasizes that the perimeter involves combining lengths. When you have triangles or shapes that are more complex, the perimeter formula is adjusted to reflect the number of sides.

TECHNOLOGY Note. Shodor's Project Interactivate has a tool called "Perimeter Explorer." This online tool allows the user to calculate the perimeter of a random shape. A random shape is displayed and the user enters a value for the perimeter. The applet then informs the student whether or not the value is correct. The user may continue trying until he or she gets the correct answer. An option to compare the perimeters with corresponding areas is given. ■

Developing Formulas for Area

When students *develop* formulas, they gain conceptual understanding of the ideas and relationships involved, and they engage in "doing mathematics." Students form general relationships when they see how all area formulas are related to one idea: length of the base times the height. And students who understand where formulas come tend to remember them or are able to derive them, which reinforces the idea that mathematics makes sense.

The results of NAEP testing indicate clearly that students do not have a very good understanding of area formulas. For example, in the 2007 NAEP, only 39 percent of fourth-grade students were able to give the area of a carpet 15 feet long and 12 feet wide. Such results may be due to an overemphasis on formulas with little or no conceptual background. Two major misconceptions are:

1. *Confusing linear and square units.* The shift in third grade (CCSSO, 2010) to multiplicative thinking links to difficulty of moving from length measurement to the more abstract measurement of area. Putrawangsa, Lukito, Amin, and Wijers (2013) suggest that one of the major issues with area measurement is thinking about area as the length of two lines (length and width), rather than the measure of a surface. A focus on the formula and the use of a ruler to measure the sides confuses the unit as well as the tool for measuring area (as the use of the ruler is indirect). This confusion can cause some students to believe that if there are no sides to measure (no length and width), the shape doesn't have an area (Zacharos, 2006).

   The tasks in Figure 19.11 cannot be solved with simple formulas; they require an understanding of concepts and how formulas work. "Length times width" is not a definition of area; instead, area is a measure of a two-dimensional surface enclosed by a boundary.

2. *Difficulty in conceptualizing the meaning of height and base.* The shapes in Figure 19.12 each have a slanted side and a height given. Students tend to confuse these two. Any side of a figure can be called a *base*. For each base that a figure has, there is a corresponding height. If the figure were to slide into a room on a selected base, the *height* would be the height of the shortest door it could pass through without tipping—that

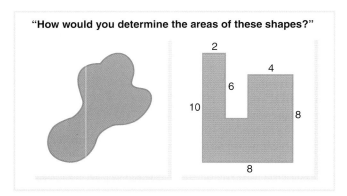

"How would you determine the areas of these shapes?"

FIGURE 19.11 Understanding the attribute of area.

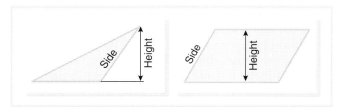

FIGURE 19.12 Heights of two-dimensional figures are not always measured along an edge.

is, the perpendicular distance to the base. The confusion may be because students have a lot of early experiences with the length-times-width formula for rectangles, in which the height is exactly the same as the length of a side.

Areas of Rectangles, Parallelograms, Triangles, and Trapezoids

The formula for the area of a rectangle is one of the first that is developed and is usually given as $A = L \times W$, or "area equals length times width." Thinking ahead to other area formulas, an equivalent but more unifying idea might be $A = b \times h$, or "area equals *base* times *height*." The base-times-height formulation can be generalized to all parallelograms (not just rectangles) and is useful in developing the area formulas for triangles and trapezoids. Furthermore, the same approach can be extended to three dimensions—volumes of cylinders are given in terms of the *area of the base* times the height. Therefore, base times height connects a large family of formulas that otherwise must be mastered independently.

Standards for Mathematical Practice
MP8. Look for and express regularity in repeated reasoning.

Rectangles. Research suggests that it is a significant leap for students to move from counting squares inside of a rectangle to a conceptual development of a formula. Battista (2003) found that students often try to fill in empty rectangles with drawings of squares and then count the result one square at a time.

An important concept to review is the meaning of multiplication as seen in arrays with an emphasis on the structure of rows and columns of squares. When we multiply a length times a width, we are not multiplying "squares times squares." Rather, the *length* of one side indicates how many squares will fit on that side. If this set of squares is taken as a unit, then the *length* of the other side (not a number of squares) will determine how many of these *rows of squares* can fit in the rectangle. Then the amount of square units covering the rectangle is the product of the length of a row and the number of rows (column × row = area). Revisit Activity 19.18 and note whether students draw in all of the squares and count them. They have not yet thought about a row of squares as a single unit that can be replicated.

Now, explain to students that you like the idea of measuring one side to tell how many squares will fit in a row along that side. You would like students to call or think of this side as the *base* of the rectangle even though some people call it the *length* or the *width*. Then the other side can be called the *height*. Be sure that students conclude that either side could be the base. If you use the formula $A = b \times h$, then the same area will result using either side as the base.

Standards for Mathematical Practice
MP1. Make sense of problems and persevere in solving them.

From Rectangles to Other Parallelograms. Once students understand the base-times-height formula for rectangles, the next challenge is to determine the areas of parallelograms. Rather than provide a formula, use the following activity, which asks students to devise their own formula, building on what they know about rectangles.

Activity 19.23   CCSS-M: 6.G.A.1

Area of a Parallelogram

Give students two or three parallelograms either drawn on grid paper or, for a slightly harder challenge, drawn on plain paper with all dimensions—the lengths of all four sides and the height. Ask students to use what they have learned about the area of rectangles to determine the areas of these parallelograms. Students should find a method that will work for any parallelogram, even if not drawn on a grid.

If students are stuck, ask them to examine ways that the parallelogram is like a rectangle or how it can be changed into a rectangle by decomposing and recomposing the shape. As shown in Figure 19.13, a parallelogram can always be transformed into a rectangle with the same base, the same height, and the same area. Thus, the formula for the area of a parallelogram is exactly the same as for a rectangle: *base* times *height*.

From Parallelograms to Triangles. With that background, the area of a triangle can logically follow. Again, use a problem-based approach, as in the next activity.

Activity 19.24

CCSS-M: 6.G.A.1

Area of a Triangle

STUDENTS
with
SPECIAL
NEEDS

Provide students with at least two triangles drawn on grid paper. Avoid right triangles because they are an easier special case. Challenge the students to use what they have learned about the area of parallelograms to find the area of each of the triangles and to develop a method that will work for any triangle. They should be sure that their method works for all the triangles given to them as well as at least one more that they draw. For students with disabilities or those that need more structure, ask, "Can you find a parallelogram that is related to your triangle?" Then suggest that they fold a piece of paper in half, draw a triangle on the folded paper, and cut it out, making two identical copies. Use the copies to fit the triangles together into a parallelogram. This provides a nice visual of how a triangle is related to a parallelogram.

As shown in Figure 19.14, two congruent triangles can always be arranged to form a parallelogram with the same base and the same height as the triangle. The area of the triangle will, therefore, be one-half as much as that of the parallelogram. Have students further explore all three possible parallelograms, one for each triangle side that serves as a base. Will the computed areas always be the same?

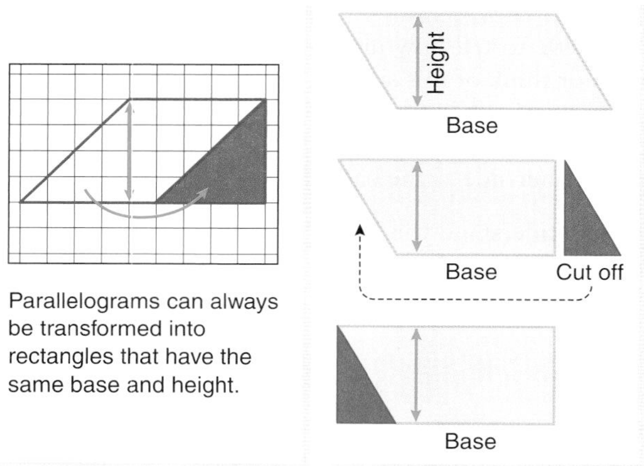

From Parallelograms to Trapezoids. After developing formulas for parallelograms and triangles, your students may be interested in tackling trapezoids. There are many methods of arriving at an area formula for trapezoids, each related to decomposing the trapezoid into a simpler shape or combination of shapes where ways to find these areas are already known. Then the area of the trapezoid is the sum of the areas of these shapes. One method uses the same approach that was used for triangles, except students work with two identical trapezoids. Figure 19.15 shows how this method results in the formula.

Here are a few suggestions, each leading to a different approach to finding the area of a trapezoid:

- Make a parallelogram inside the given trapezoid using three of the sides.
- Make a parallelogram using three sides that surround the trapezoid.
- Draw a diagonal forming two triangles.
- Draw a line through the midpoints of the nonparallel sides. The length of that line is the average of the lengths of the two parallel sides.
- Draw a rectangle inside the trapezoid, leaving two triangles, then put those two triangles together.

Students can also use transformational geometry or enclose the trapezoid in a larger shape (Manizade & Mason, 2014).

Parallelograms can always be transformed into rectangles that have the same base and height.

FIGURE 19.13 Transforming a parallelogram into a rectangle.

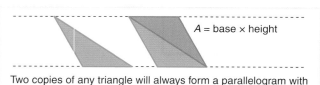

$A = \text{base} \times \text{height}$

Two copies of any triangle will always form a parallelogram with the same base and height; therefore, the triangle has an area of half of the parallelogram, $A = \frac{1}{2}(\text{base} \times \text{height})$.

FIGURE 19.14 Two congruent triangles always make a parallelogram.

TECHNOLOGY Note. The relationship between the areas of rectangles, parallelograms, and triangles can be dramatically illustrated using dynamic geometry programs such as *The Geometer's Sketchpad* (Key Curriculum Press) or *GeoGebra* (free public domain software). Draw two congruent segments on two parallel lines, as shown in Figure 19.16. Connect the segment end points to form a parallelogram and two triangles. The height is indicated by a segment perpendicular to the parallel lines. Either of the two line segments can be dragged left or right to slant the parallelogram and triangle without changing the base or height. All area measures remain fixed! Also, explore the applets at NCTM Illuminations to test how changes in the base and height of these shapes affect the area. ■

Surface Area. According to the Common Core State Standards (CCSSO, 2010), sixth-grade students begin a study of surface area by exploring prisms and pyramids, which extends to more complex shapes in seventh grade. Build on the knowledge students have of the areas of two-dimensional figures. If they think of each solid as its two-dimensional components (nets), they can find the area of each face and add the areas. One of the best approaches to teaching the surface area of three-dimensional figures is to create several rectangular prisms, cubes, or cylinders on card stock with the sides held together by small pieces of Velcro. In this way, students can think about the components or the "net" of the figure as they consider the individual faces and calculate the surface area.

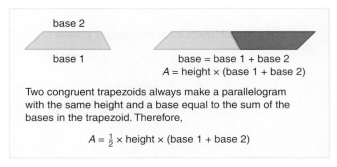

Two congruent trapezoids always make a parallelogram with the same height and a base equal to the sum of the bases in the trapezoid. Therefore,

$$A = \tfrac{1}{2} \times \text{height} \times (\text{base 1} + \text{base 2})$$

FIGURE 19.15 Two congruent trapezoids always form a parallelogram.

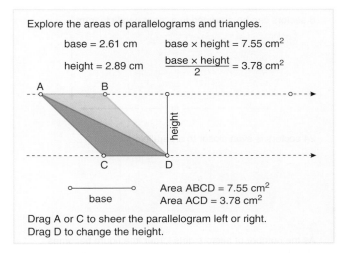

FIGURE 19.16 Dynamic geometry software demonstrates that figures with the same base and height maintain the same area.

Activity 19.25

Making Boxes

Joan's Dine & Dessert Shop orders take-out boxes in three sizes (dinner, pie, and cake) and Joan wants an estimate of how much cardboard is used for each so that she can decide whether she should make her own boxes. Find how much cardboard is used for these boxes (assume they are taped and there is no overlap of cardboard).

- **Dinner box: 7 in. × 7 in. × 3 in.**
- **Pie box: 5 in. × 4 in. × 3 in.**
- **Cake box: 8 in. × 8 in. × 5 in.**

Have grid and blank paper for students to create their net for each box. Students should compare their diagrams and surface areas. They may have picked different bases, and the illustrations may look different, but this is an opportunity to talk about why these different nets have equal surface areas.

Circumference and Area of Circles

The relationship between the *circumference* of a circle (the distance around or the perimeter) and the length of the *diameter* (a line through the center joining two points on the

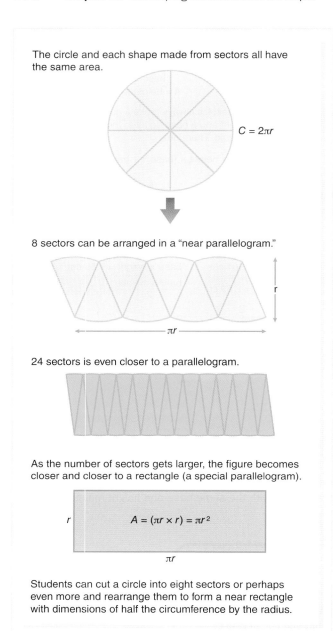

The circle and each shape made from sectors all have the same area.

$C = 2\pi r$

8 sectors can be arranged in a "near parallelogram."

r

πr

24 sectors is even closer to a parallelogram.

As the number of sectors gets larger, the figure becomes closer and closer to a rectangle (a special parallelogram).

r

$A = (\pi r \times r) = \pi r^2$

πr

Students can cut a circle into eight sectors or perhaps even more and rearrange them to form a near rectangle with dimensions of half the circumference by the radius.

FIGURE 19.17 Development of the circle area formula.

circle) is one of the most interesting that students can discover and is a Common Core State Standards expectation for seventh grade (CCSSO, 2010). The circumference of every circle is about 3.14 times as long as the diameter. The exact ratio is an irrational number close to 3.14 and is represented by the Greek letter π. So $\pi = \frac{C}{D}$, the circumference divided by the diameter. In equivalent forms, $C = \pi D$ or $C = 2\pi r$. (Activity 20.14 in Chapter 20 will discuss the concept of π and how students can discover this important ratio.)

Students should be challenged to figure out the area formula for circles on their own. For example, give a hint by showing students how to cut a circle into sectors and arrange them into an approximate parallelogram. You may need to help them notice that the smaller the sectors used, the closer the arrangement gets to a rectangle. Figure 19.17 presents a common development of the area formula $A = \pi r^2$.

 Complete Self-Check 19.3: Area

 ## Volume and Capacity

Volume and *capacity* are both terms for measures of the "size" of three-dimensional regions—a topic beginning in the fifth grade, with continuing emphasis in grades 6 and 8, according to the Common Core State Standards (CCSSO, 2010). The term *capacity* is generally used to refer to the amount that a container will hold. Standard units of capacity include quarts, gallons, liters, and milliliters. The term *volume* can be used to refer to the capacity of a container but is also used for the amount of space occupied by three-dimensional objects. Standard units of volume include cubic inches or cubic centimeters. Here is a brief video (http://www.youtube.com/watch?v=Dzcn qT7YZPg) that explores the appropriate units and tools.

Comparison Activities

A simple method of comparing capacity is to fill one container with something and then pour the same amount into the comparison container. The apparent volumes of solid objects are sometimes misleading, and a method of comparison is also difficult. To compare volumes of solids such as a ball and an apple, a displacement method must be used. Have students predict which object has the smaller or greater volume and then place it in a measuring cup or beaker filled with water to see how much the water rises.

Young children should compare the capacities of different containers as in the following activity.

Activity 19.26

CCSS-M: K.MD.A.2; 3.MD.A.2; 5.MD.C.3

Capacity Sort

Provide a variety of containers, with one marked as the "target." Ask students to sort the collection into those that hold more than, less than, or about the same amount as the target container. Then use the Capacity Sort Activity Page to circle the estimate of "holds more," "holds less," or "holds about the same." Provide a filler (such as beans, rice, or Styrofoam peanuts), scoops, and funnels. Working in pairs, have students measure and record results under "Actual Measure" on the recording sheet. Discuss what students noticed (e.g., that fatter/rounder shapes hold more).

Try the following activity yourself as well as with students.

Activity 19.27

CCSS-M: 5.MD.C.3

Which Silo Holds More?

Give pairs of students two sheets of equal-sized paper. With one sheet they make a tube shape (cylinder) by taping the two long edges together. They make a shorter, fatter cylinder from the other sheet by taping the short edges together. Then ask, "If these were two silos, would they hold the same amount, or would one hold more than the other?" To test the conjectures, use a filler such as beans or pasta. Place the skinny cylinder inside the fat one. Fill the inside tube and then lift it up, allowing the filler to empty into the fat cylinder.

The goal of this activity and the next is for students to realize that surface area (the size of the paper) does not determine the volume and there that there is a relationship between surface area and volume, just as there is between perimeter and area.

Activity 19.28

CCSS-M: 5.MD.C.3; 5.MD.C.4; 5.MD.C.5

ENGLISH LANGUAGE LEARNERS

Fixed Volume: Comparing Prisms

Give each pair of students a supply of centimeter or inch cubes. Ask students to use 64 or 36 cubes to build different rectangular prisms with that volume and record the surface area for each in a table. If you have ELLs, provide a visual of a rectangular prism, labeling key words such as *length, width, height, surface area, cube, volume,* and *side.* Ask students to describe any patterns that they notice as they compare the dimensions of each prism to its surface area. What happens as the prism becomes less like a tall, skinny box and more like a cube? Explore the Expanded Lesson for this activity.

CCSS Standards for Mathematical Practice

MP8. Look for and express regularity in repeated reasoning.

The eventual goal is for students to realize that volume does not dictate surface area and to recognize that the pattern between surface area and volume is similar to the one found

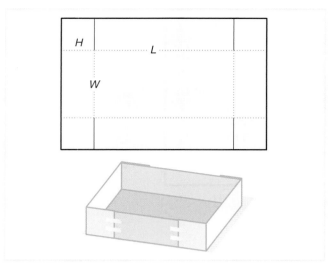

FIGURE 19.18 Make boxes by starting with a rectangle and drawing a square on each corner. Cut on the solid lines, fold the box up, wrap the corner squares to the outside, and tape them to the sides.

between area and perimeter. Namely, prisms that are more cubelike have less surface area than prisms with the same volume that are long and narrow.

Using Physical Models of Volume and Capacity Units

Two types of units can be used to measure volume and capacity: solid units and containers. Solid units are objects like wooden cubes that can be used to fill the container being measured. The other unit model is a small container that is filled with liquid and poured repeatedly into the container being measured. The following examples are of units that you might want to collect:

- Liquid medicine cups
- Plastic jars and containers of almost any size
- Wooden cubes or same-sized blocks of any shape
- Styrofoam packing peanuts (produces conceptual measures of volume despite not packing perfectly)

The following activity explores volume of two boxes.

Activity 19.29
CCSS-M: 5.MD.C.3, 5.MD.C.4, 5.MD.C.5

Box Comparison: Cubic Units

Provide students with a pair of small boxes that you have made from card stock (see Figure 19.18). Use unit dimensions that match the cubes that you have for units. Students are given two boxes, one cube, and a corresponding ruler. (If you use 2-cm cubes, make a ruler with the unit equal to 2 cm.) Ask students to decide which box has the greater volume or if they have the same volume.

Here are some suggested box dimensions ($L \times W \times H$):

$$6 \times 3 \times 4 \qquad 5 \times 4 \times 4 \qquad 3 \times 9 \times 3 \qquad 6 \times 6 \times 2 \qquad 5 \times 5 \times 3$$

Students should use words, drawings, and numbers to explain their conclusions.

A useful hint in the last activity is to first figure out how many cubes will fit on the bottom of the box. Some students will discover a multiplicative rule for the volume. The boxes can be completely filled with cubes to confirm conclusions.

Instruments for measuring capacity are generally used for small amounts of liquids or pourable materials such as rice or water. These tools are commonly found in kitchens and laboratories. Students should use measuring cups to explore recipes such those in the *Better Homes and Gardens New Junior Cookbook* (2012), which provide student-friendly opportunities to use units of capacity.

The following two activities focus on liquid volume.

Activity 19.30
CCSS-M: 3.MD.A.2

That's Cool

Give teams of students beakers marked in milliliters. Tell the students they will receive three ice cubes. First, they must estimate how many milliliters of water will be in the beaker when the ice melts. Then the ice is placed in each team's container, and students wait until the ice warms and turns to water. What was the difference between their estimates and their actual answers? Students can use a line plot to record and discuss the different measures.

Activity 19.31

CCSS-M: 3.MD.A.2

Squeeze Play

Students work in teams, with each team having access to a measuring cup or beaker marked in milliliters. Have several stations set up with buckets and different-sized sponges. Have students first estimate how much water they can squeeze from each sponge using the hand they do not write with. Does a sponge that is two times larger than another sponge provide two times the water? What do the students notice?

Developing Formulas for Volumes of Common Solid Shapes

A common error that repeats from two- to three-dimensional shapes is that students confuse the meaning of height and base in their use of formulas. Note that the shapes in Figure 19.19 each have a slanted side and a height given. The base of the figure can be any flat surface of a figure. As mentioned before, to visualize the height, have students think of the figure sliding under a doorway: The *height* would be the height of the shortest door it could pass through. Keep this in mind as you use precise language to develop formulas for volume.

The relationships between the formulas for volume are completely analogous to those for area. As you read, notice similarities between rectangles and prisms, between parallelograms and slanted (oblique) prisms, and between triangles and pyramids. Not only are the formulas related, but the processes for developing the formulas are similar.

Volumes of Cylinders. A *cylinder* is a solid with two congruent parallel bases and sides with parallel elements that join corresponding points on the bases. There are several special classes of cylinders, including *prisms* (with polygons for bases), *right prisms, rectangular prisms,* and *cubes* (Zwillinger, 2011). Interestingly, all of these solids have the same volume formula, and that one formula is analogous to the area formula for parallelograms.

The development of the volume formula (see Activity 19.29) is parallel to the development of the formula for the area of a rectangle, as shown in Figure 19.20. The *area* of the base (instead of *length* of the base for rectangles) determines how many *cubes* can be placed on the base, forming a single unit—a layer of cubes. The *height* of the box then determines how many of these *layers* will fit in the box, just as the height of the rectangle determined how many *rows* of squares would fill the rectangle.

Recall that a parallelogram can be thought of as a slanted rectangle, as was illustrated with dynamic geometry software (see Figure 19.16). Show students a stack of three or four decks of cards (or a stack of books). When stacked straight, they form a rectangular solid. The volume, as just discussed, is $V = A \times h$, with A equal to the area of one playing card (the base). Now, if the stack is slanted to one side, as shown in Figure 19.21, what will the volume be? Students should be able to argue that this figure has the same volume (and same volume formula) as the original stack.

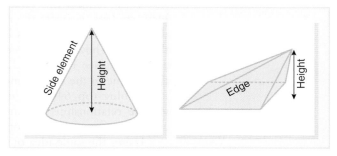

FIGURE 19.19   Heights are not always measured along an edge or surface.

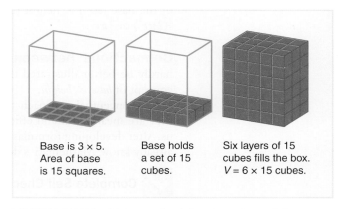

FIGURE 19.20   Volume of a right prism: *Area* of the base × height.

Base is 3 × 5. Area of base is 15 squares.

Base holds a set of 15 cubes.

Six layers of 15 cubes fills the box. $V = 6 \times 15$ cubes.

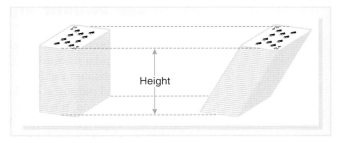

FIGURE 19.21   Two prisms with the same base and height have the same volume.

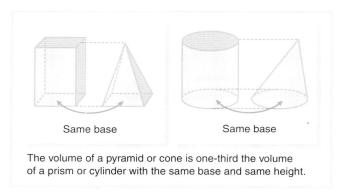

The volume of a pyramid or cone is one-third the volume of a prism or cylinder with the same base and same height.

FIGURE 19.22 Comparing volumes of pyramids to prisms and cones to cylinders.

What if the cards in this activity were some other shape? If they were circular, the volume would still be the area of the base times the height; if they were triangular, still the same. The conclusion is that the volume of *any* cylinder is equal to *area of the base* × *height*.

Volumes of Cones, Pyramids and Spheres.

Knowing these formulas are a part of grade 8 expectations (CCSSO, 2010). Recall that when parallelograms and triangles have the same base and height, the areas are in a 2-to-1 relationship. Interestingly, the relationship between the volumes of cylinders and cones with the same base and height is 3 to 1. That is, *area* is to *two*-dimensional figures what *volume* is to *three*-dimensional figures. Furthermore, triangles are to parallelograms as cones are to cylinders.

To investigate this relationship, use translucent plastic models of these related shapes. Have students estimate the number of times the pyramid will fit into the prism. Then have them test their predictions by filling the pyramid with water or rice and emptying it into the prism. They will discover that exactly three pyramids will fill a prism with the same base and height (see Figure 19.22), making the volume of a cone or pyramid exactly one-third the volume of the corresponding cylinder. Watch this video (http://mediaplayer.pearsoncmg .com/_blue-top_640x360_ccv2/ab/streaming/myeducationlab/mathmethods/modeling_ volume_relationships_iPad.mp4) of a teacher demonstration of the displacement method in an exploration of this relationship.

Using the same idea of area of the base times height, it is possible to explore the volume of a sphere ($\frac{2}{3}$ of the volume of a cylinder with the same height and base as identified through pouring water into the cylinder with the same height and base). The height of the matching cylinder is the sphere's radius doubled. The volume of the cylinder is the area of the base (πr^2) × height ($2r$). So we find that the volume of the corresponding sphere is $\frac{2}{3}(2\pi r^3)$ or $\frac{4}{3}\pi r^3$.

Connections between Formulas.

The connectedness of mathematical ideas can hardly be better illustrated than with the connections of all of these formulas to the single concept of *base* × *height*.

A conceptual approach to the development of formulas helps students understand that they are meaningful and efficient ways to measure different attributes of the objects around us. After developing formulas in conceptual ways, students can derive formulas from what they already know. Mathematics does make sense!

 Complete Self-Check 19.4: Volume and Capacity

 ## Weight and Mass

Weight is a measure of the pull or force of gravity on an object. *Mass* is the amount of matter in an object and a measure of the force needed to accelerate it. On the moon, where gravity is much less than on earth, an object has a smaller weight than on earth but the identical mass. For practical purposes, on the earth, the measures of mass and weight will be about the same. In this discussion, the terms *weight* and *mass* will be used interchangeably.

Although the concept of heavier and lighter begins to be explored in kindergarten, the notion of units of weight or mass appears in third-grade standards (CCSSO, 2010). At any grade level, experiences with informal unit weights are good preparation for standard units and scales.

Comparison Activities

The most conceptual way to compare weights of two objects is to hold one in each hand, extend your arms, and experience the relative downward pull on each—effectively communicating to a pre-K through grade 1 student what "heavier" or "weighs more" means. This personal experience can then be transferred to one of two basic types of scales—balances and spring scales. Visit the companion website to watch a brief video that shows a child acting as a human balance scale.

When students place the objects in the two pans of a balance, the pan that goes down can be understood to hold the heavier object. Even a relatively simple balance will detect small differences. If two objects are placed one at a time in a spring scale, the heavier object pulls the pan down farther. Both balances and spring scales have real value in the classroom. (Technically, spring scales measure weight and balance scales measure mass. Why?)

Using Physical Models of Weight or Mass Units

Any collection of uniform objects with the same mass can serve as nonstandard weight units. For very light objects, large paper clips, wooden blocks, or plastic cubes work well. Coins also can be used (e.g., U.S. nickels weigh 5 grams and pennies weigh 2.5 grams). Large metal washers found in hardware stores are effective for weighing slightly heavier objects. You will need to rely on standard weights to weigh things as heavy as a kilogram or more.

Weight cannot be measured directly. Either a two-pan balance or a spring scale must be used. In a balance scale, place an object in one pan and weights in the other pan until they balance. In a spring scale, first place the object in and mark the position of the pan on a piece of paper taped behind the pan. Remove the object and place just enough weights in the pan to pull it down to the same level. Discuss how equal weights will pull the spring with the same force.

 Complete Self-Check 19.5: Weight and Mass

 # Angles

Understanding the concept (or attribute) of angle and measuring angles is one of the mathematical standards in the Common Core State Standards (CCSSO, 2010), beginning at grade 4 and developing in middle school. Angle measurement can be a challenge for two reasons: The attribute of angle size is often misunderstood, and protractors are commonly introduced and used without students understanding how they work.

Comparison Activities

The attribute of angle size might be called the "spread of the angle's rays." Angles are composed of two rays that are infinite in length with a common vertex. The only difference in their size is how widely or narrowly the two rays are spread apart or rotated around the vertex.

To help students conceptualize the attribute of the spread of the rays, two angles can be directly compared by tracing one and placing it over the other. Be sure to have students compare angles with rays of different lengths. A student may think a wide angle with short rays is smaller than a narrow angle with long rays. This is a common misconception among students (Munier, Devichi, & Merle, 2008). As soon as students can differentiate between a large angle and a small one, regardless of the length of the rays, you can move on to measuring angles.

Using Physical Models of Angular Measure Units

A unit for measuring an angle must be an angle. Nothing else has the same attribute of spread that we want to measure. (Contrary to what many people think, you do not need to use degrees to measure angles.)

Activity 19.32

CCSS-M: 4.MD.C.5

A Unit Angle

Give each student an index card. Have students draw a narrow angle on the card using a straightedge and cut it out or use wedges. The resulting wedge can then be used as a unit of angular measure by counting the number of wedges that will fit in a given angle (see Figure 19.23). Distribute an Angles Activity Page and have students use their angle unit to measure the angles. Because students made different unit angles, the results will differ and can be discussed in terms of unit size.

Activity 19.32 illustrates that measuring an angle is the same as measuring length or area; unit angles are used to fill or cover the spread of an angle just as unit lengths fill or cover a length. Once this concept is well understood, move on to the use of measuring instruments.

Using Protractors

The tool commonly used for measuring angles is the protractor. According to the Common Core State Standards, fourth-grade students should begin to learn to accurately use protractors. Yet, the protractor is one of the most poorly understood measuring instruments. Part of the difficulty arises because the units (degrees) are so small. It would be physically impossible for students to cut out and use a single degree to measure an angle accurately. In addition, the numbers on protractors run clockwise and counterclockwise along the edge, making the scale hard to interpret without a strong conceptual foundation. Note that the units of degrees are based on an angle where the vertex of the rays is located at the midpoint of a circle, creating an arc. A "one degree" angle is one where the arc is $\frac{1}{360}$ of the circle (degrees). These small angles are used to measure.

Students can make nonstandard waxed-paper protractors (see Figure 19.24) but should soon move to standard instruments. To understand measures on a protractor (see Figure 19.25), students need an approximate mental image

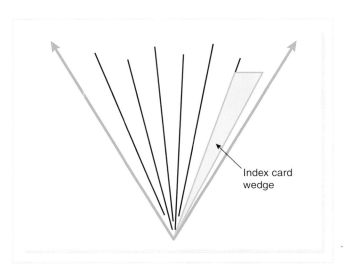

FIGURE 19.23 Using a wedge as a unit angle, this angle measures about $7\frac{1}{2}$ wedges.

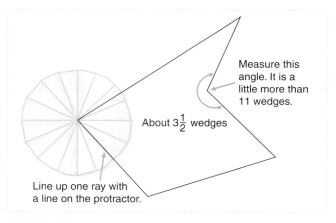

FIGURE 19.24 Measuring angles in a polygon using a waxed-paper protractor.

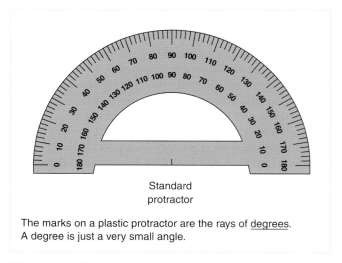

The marks on a plastic protractor are the rays of <u>degrees</u>. A degree is just a very small angle.

FIGURE 19.25 A protractor measures angles.

of angle size. Then false readings of the protractor scale will be eliminated. One approach is to use an angle maker. You can cut and merge two different colored paper plates in the same way as the rational number wheel in Figure 17.5 in Chapter 17. You can then rotate the plates to match angles observed or to estimate benchmark angles such as 30, 45, 60, 90, 135, 180, and 270 degrees. If students have a strong grasp of the approximate sizes of angles, this "angle sense" will give them the background needed to move to standard measuring tools.

 Complete Self-Check 19.6: Angles

 # Time

Time is different from most other attributes that are commonly measured in school because it cannot be seen or felt and because it is more difficult for students to comprehend units of time or how those units are matched against a given time period or duration.

Comparison Activities

Time can be thought of as the duration of an event from its beginning to its end. For students to adequately understand the attribute of time, they should make comparisons of events that have different durations. If two events begin at the same time, the shorter duration will end first and the other last longer—for example, which top spins longer? However, this form of comparison focuses on the ending of the duration rather than the duration itself. In order to think of time as something that can be measured, it is helpful to compare two events that do not start at the same time. This requires that some form of measurement of time be used from the beginning.

Students need to learn about seconds, minutes, and hours and develop some concept of how long these units are. You can help by making a conscious effort to note the duration of short and long events during the day. Have students time familiar events in their daily lives: brushing teeth, eating dinner, riding to school, doing homework.

Timing small events of $\frac{1}{2}$ minute to 2 minutes is fun and useful and can be adapted from the following activity.

Activity 19.33   CCSS-M: 1.MD.B.3

Ready for the Bell

Give students a recording sheet with a set of Clock Faces. **Secretly set a timer to go off at the hour, half hour, or minute. When the bell rings, students should look up and record the time on the clock face and in numerals on the recording sheet. This highly engaging activity motivates students not only to think about telling time but also to consider the relationship between the analog clock reading and digital recording. Elapsed time can also be explored by discussing the time between timer rings.**

Reading Clocks

The common instrument for measuring time is the clock. However, learning to tell time has little to do with time measurement and more to do with the skills of learning to read a dial-type instrument. Clock reading can be a difficult skill to teach. Starting in first grade, students are usually taught first to read clocks to the hour, then the half hour, and finally to 5- and 1-minute intervals in second and third grades (CCSSO, 2010). In the early stages of this sequence,

"About 7 o'clock" "A little bit past 9 o'clock" "Halfway between 2 o'clock and 3 o'clock"

FIGURE 19.26 Approximate time with one-handed clocks.

students are shown clocks set exactly to the hour or half hour. Thus, many students who can read a clock at 7:00 or 2:30 are initially challenged by 6:58 or 2:33.

Digital clocks permit students to read times easily, but they do not relate very well to benchmark times. To know that a digital reading of 7:58 is nearly 8:00, the student must know that there are 60 minutes in an hour, that 58 is close to 60, and that 2 minutes is not a very long time. The analog clock shows "close to" times visually without the need for understanding large numbers or how many minutes in an hour.

The following suggestions can help students focus on the actions and functions of the minute and hour hands.

1. Begin with a one-handed clock by breaking off the minute hand from a regular clock. Use lots of approximate language: "It's about 7 o'clock." "It's a little past 9 o'clock." "It's halfway between 2 o'clock and 3 o'clock" (see Figure 19.26).
2. Discuss what happens to the big hand as the little hand goes from one hour to the next. When the minute hand is at 12, the hour hand is pointing precisely to a number. If the hour hand is about halfway between numbers, about where would the minute hand be? If the hour hand is a little past or before an hour (10 to 15 minutes), where would the minute hand be?
3. Use two clocks, one with only an hour hand and one with two hands. Cover the two-handed clock. Periodically during the day, direct attention to the one-handed clock. Have students predict where the minute hand should be. Uncover the other clock and discuss.

Standards for Mathematical Practice
MP6. Attend to precision.

4. After step 3 has begun, teach intervals by counting by fives going around the clock (grade 2 CCSS). Instead of saying the minute hand is "pointing at the 4," transition to the language "it is about 20 minutes after the hour." As skills develop, suggest that students look first at the hour hand to learn approximately what time it is and then focus on the minute hand for precision.
5. Predict the reading on a digital clock when shown an analog clock and set an analog clock when shown a digital clock. See the Time—Analog and Digital or the Time-Match Clocks applets at the NLVM.
6. Relate the time after the hours to the time before the next hour. This is helpful not only for telling time but for number sense as well.
7. Finally, discuss the issue of A.M. and P.M.

The following activity assesses students' ability to read an analog clock.

Activity 19.34
CCSS-M: 1.MD.B.3; 2.MD.C.7

One-Handed Clocks

Prepare a page of Clock Faces by drawing an hour hand on each. Include placements that are approximately a quarter past the hour, a quarter until the hour, half past the hour, and some that are close to but not on the hour. For each clock face, ask students to write the digital time and draw the corresponding minute hand. If you have ELLs, note that telling time is done differently in different cultures. For example, in Spanish any time past 30 minutes is stated as the next hour minus the time until that hour. For example, 10:45 is thought of as 15 minutes before 11, or eleven minus a quarter. Be explicit that in English it can be said either way: "10:45" or "a quarter til 11."

ENGLISH LANGUAGE LEARNERS

Solving Problems with Time

Solving problems involving addition and subtraction of time intervals is an expectation starting in grade 3 (CCSSO, 2010). If given the digital time or the time after the hour, students must state how many minutes to the next hour. This should certainly be a mental process of counting on for multiples of 5 minutes, possibly using an analog clock face to support the skip count. Avoid having students use pencil and paper to subtract 25 from 60.

This is the foundation for problems involving elapsed time and also a skill that students can find challenging, especially when the period of time spans noon or midnight. Figuring the time from, say, 8:15 A.M. to 11:45 A.M. is a multistep task that requires deciding what to do first and keeping track of the intermediate steps. In this case you could count hours from 8:15 to 11:15 and add on 30 minutes. But students will be challenged by any interval that spans the change from A.M. to P.M.

There is also the task of finding the end time given the start time and elapsed time, or finding the start time given the end time and the elapsed time. In keeping with the spirit of problem solving and the use of models, consider having students sketch an empty timeline (similar to the empty number line, discussed for computation). The number line is also the model suggested in the Common Core State Standards. It is important not to be overly prescriptive in telling students how to use the timeline because there are various alternatives (Dixon, 2008). For example, in Figure 19.27, a student might count by full hours from 10:45 (11:45, 12:45, 1:45, 2:45, 3:45) and then subtract 15 minutes. Watch this video (https://www.youtube.com/watch?v=WPvy4knZ_YY) that uses the Iditarod Sled Dog Race in Alaska as the context for a lesson on elapsed time.

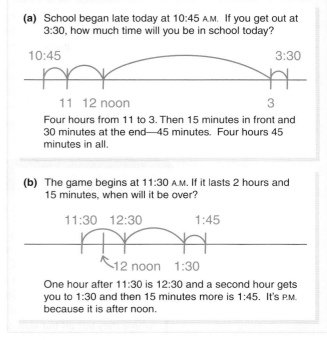

(a) School began late today at 10:45 A.M. If you get out at 3:30, how much time will you be in school today?

Four hours from 11 to 3. Then 15 minutes in front and 30 minutes at the end—45 minutes. Four hours 45 minutes in all.

(b) The game begins at 11:30 A.M. If it lasts 2 hours and 15 minutes, when will it be over?

One hour after 11:30 is 12:30 and a second hour gets you to 1:30 and then 15 minutes more is 1:45. It's P.M. because it is after noon.

FIGURE 19.27 A sketch of an empty timeline can be useful in solving elapsed time problems.

  Complete Self-Check 19.7: Time

Money

Here is a list of the money ideas and skills typically required in the primary grades:

- Recognizing coins
- Identifying and using the values of coins
- Counting and comparing sets of coins
- Creating equivalent coin collections (same amounts, different coins)
- Selecting coins for a given amount
- Making change
- Solving word problems involving money (starting in second grade [CCSSO, 2010])

The following sections support the learning of these ideas and skills.

Recognizing Coins and Identifying Their Values

The names of our coins are conventions of our social system. Students learn these names the same way that they learn the names of physical objects in their daily environment—through exposure and repetition.

The value of each coin is also a convention that students must simply be told. For these values to make sense, students must understand 5, 10, and 25 and think of these quantities without seeing countable objects. Where else do we say, "this is 5," while pointing to a single item? A student who is tied to counting objects by ones will be challenged to understand the values of coins. Coin value lessons should focus on purchase power—a dime can *buy the same thing* that 10 pennies can buy.

Naming the total value of a group of coins is the same as mentally adding their values. Second-grade students can be asked to do the mental math required in counting a collection of different coins. Visit the companion website and watch the video of an interview of a child thinking about a story problem involving money. Should the teacher ask other questions that link the amounts to the money, such as, "What is 100 cents also equal to?" in an effort to get the student to use money denominations such as one dollar or four quarters? Why is that flexibility important?

Make sure students sort their coins and start counting from the highest values. Even though it is mental computation, the numbers are fortunately multiples of 5 and 10 with some ones added at the end. The next activity is a preparation for counting money.

Activity 19.35
CCSS-M: 2.MD.C.8

ENGLISH LANGUAGE LEARNERS

Money Skip Counting

Explain to students that they will start skip counting by one number, and at your signal they will shift to a count by a different number. Use any two of these numbers: 100, 50, 25, 10, 5, 1. Begin with two different amounts—say, 25 and 10—and write them on the board. Always start with the largest number (25) and have students begin to skip count. After three or more counts, raise your hand to indicate a pause in the counting. Then point to 10. Students continue the skip count from where they left off but now count by tens. If you have ELLs who are recent immigrants, invite them to share the coins from their country and see how they compare to our coins.

Activity 19.36
CCSS-M: 2.MD.C.8

Hundreds Chart Money Count

Give students a Hundreds Chart and a collection of play money. Begin with two different coins—say, a quarter and a dime. Represent the 25 cents in the same way students have previously used the chart (count two rows down and over five spaces to the right). Place the quarter on the 25 space and then count 10 more (down one row) and place the dime on 35. The total of the two coins is 35 cents. Use other coin collections and what students already know about patterns on the hundreds chart to calculate the value of larger collections.

Because adding on to find a difference is such a valuable skill, it makes sense to give students experiences with "think-addition" to make change. As students become more skillful at adding on, they can see the process of making change as an extension of a skill already acquired.

✓ **Complete Self-Check 19.8: Money**

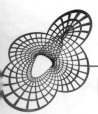

REFLECTIONS ON CHAPTER 19

WRITING TO LEARN

1. Explain what it means to measure something. Does your explanation work equally well for length, area, weight, volume, and time?

2. A general instructional plan for measurement has three steps. Explain how the type of activity used at each step accomplishes the instructional goal.

3. Three reasons were offered for using nonstandard units instead of standard units in instructional activities. Which of these seem most important to you and why?

4. Describe a few strategies for estimating measurements. Explain the process of estimation by means of an activity.

5. Explain how the area of a parallelogram can be determined using the basic formula for the area of a rectangle.

FOR DISCUSSION AND EXPLORATION

♦ Examine a textbook for any grade level and look at the chapters on measurement. How well does the book cover metric measurement ideas? How would you modify or expand on the lessons found there?

RESOURCES FOR CHAPTER 19

LITERATURE CONNECTIONS

How Big Is a Foot? *Myller (1991)* (https://www.youtube .com/watch?v=bWhWL1MET7A)

This is a fun story for young students. The king measures the queen using his feet and orders a bed that is 6 feet long and 3 feet wide. The carpenter's apprentice, who is very small, makes the bed according to his own feet, demonstrating the need for standard units. (Another tale of nonstandard units is *Twelve Snails to One Lizard* [Hightower, 1997].)

Just a Second *Jenkins (2011)*

This beautifully illustrated book is not just about the concept of time. The author provides fascinating facts about what can happen in a second, a minute, an hour, a day, a month, and a year. Did you know a bumblebee beats its wings 200 times a second? Students can use the facts provided to explore and discuss many mathematical problems.

RECOMMENDED READINGS

Articles

Austin, R., Thompson, D., & Beckmann, C. (2005). Exploring measurement concepts through literature: Natural links across disciplines. *Mathematics Teaching in the Middle School, 10*(5), 218–224.

This article includes almost 30 children's books that emphasize length, weight, capacity, speed, area, perimeter, and volume. Three books are described in detail as the authors share how to link measurement to science, history, geography, and economics.

Whitin, D. (2008). Learning our way to one million. *Teaching Children Mathematics, 14*(8), 448–453.

Through exploration of one million, Whitin suggests ways for students to investigate length, area, and money. Activities emphasize the need for problem solving in real-world contexts.

CHAPTER 20

Geometric Thinking and Geometric Concepts

LEARNER OUTCOMES

After reading this chapter and engaging in the embedded activities and reflections, you should be able to:

20.1 Summarize the four major geometry goals for students.

20.2 Describe the van Hiele levels of geometric thinking.

20.3 Analyze strategies for teaching students about shapes and properties.

20.4 Describe geometric transformations.

20.5 Explore ways to engage students in thinking about location.

20.6 Illustrate approaches that are used to develop students' imagery and visualization skills.

Geometry is a "network of concepts, ways of reasoning and representation systems" used to explore and analyze shape and space (Battista, 2007, p. 843). This critical area of mathematics appears in everything from global positioning systems to computer animation. In their *Principles and Standards* (2000) document, the National Council of Teachers of Mathematics cites geometry as at the core of early mathematics, alongside the strand of number. Unique to the Common Core State Standards, geometry appears as a domain across grades kindergarten through 8.

 BIG IDEAS

- What makes shapes alike and different can be determined by geometric properties. Shapes can be classified into a hierarchy of categories according to the properties they share.

- Transformations provide a significant way to think about the ways properties change or do not change when a shape is moved in a plane or in space. These changes can be described in terms of translations, reflections, rotations, and dilations.

- Shapes can be described in terms of their location in a plane or in space. Coordinate systems can be used to describe these locations precisely. In turn, the coordinate view of shape offers ways to understand certain properties of shapes, changes in position (transformations), and how they appear (visualization).

◆ Three-dimensional shapes can be seen from different viewpoints, which help us understand relationships between two- and three-dimensional figures and mentally change the position and size of shapes.

 ## Geometry Goals for Students

For too long, geometry curricula emphasized the learning of terminology. Geometry is much more than vocabulary and naming shapes. First, it involves developing spatial sense. *Spatial sense* is an intuition about shapes and the relationships between them and is considered a core area of mathematical study, like number (Sarama & Clements, 2009). Spatial sense includes the ability to mentally visualize objects and spatial relationships—to turn things around in one's mind. It also includes a familiarity with geometric descriptions of objects and position. People with well-developed spatial sense appreciate geometric form in art, nature, and architecture and they use geometric ideas to describe and analyze their world.

Second, geometry has a number of significant content goals that apply to all grade levels. Let's look at four major geometry strands:

- *Shapes and properties* includes a study of the properties of shapes in two and three dimensions, as well as the relationships built on properties.
- *Transformation* includes a study of translations, reflections, rotations, dilations, the study of symmetry and the concept of similarity.
- *Location* includes a study of coordinate geometry or other ways of specifying how objects are located in the plane or in space.
- *Visualization* includes the recognition of shapes in the environment, developing relationships between two- and three-dimensional objects, and the ability to draw and recognize objects from different viewpoints.

The content in this chapter is divided according to these four categories, with each category beginning with foundational experiences and moving through more challenging experiences using van Hiele's levels of geometric thought as a guidepost.

 Complete Self-Check 20.1: Geometry Goals for Students

 ## Developing Geometric Thinking

All learners are capable of growing and developing the ability to think and reason in geometric contexts, but this ability requires ongoing and significant experiences across a developmental progression. Recently there has been an emphasis in mathematics education on identifying learning progressions and trajectories as a way to move students forward logically on different mathematics topics. Fortunately, in geometry such a progression has been well documented. The research of two Dutch educators, Pierre van Hiele and Dina van Hiele-Geldof, provides insights into the differences in geometric thinking through the descriptions of different levels of thought. The van Hiele theory (1984) significantly influences geometry curricula worldwide and can help all teachers understand developmentally appropriate next steps for their students' geometry instruction.

The van Hiele Levels of Geometric Thought

The van Hiele model is a five-level hierarchy of understanding spatial ideas (see Figure 20.1). Each level describes the thinking processes used in geometric contexts. Specifically, the levels

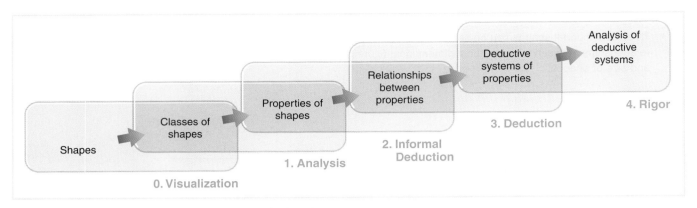

FIGURE 20.1 The van Hiele theory of geometric thought.

TABLE 20.1 CHARACTERICS OF THE VAN HIELE LEVELS

Characteristic	Implication
1. Sequential	To arrive at any level above 0, students must move through all prior levels. The products of thought at each level are the same as the objects of thought at the next level, as illustrated in Figure 20.1. The objects (ideas) must be created at one level so that relationships between these objects of thought can become the focus of the next level.
2. Developmental	When instruction or language is at a level higher than that of the students, students will be challenged to understand the concept being developed. A student can, for example, memorize a fact (such as all squares are rectangles) but not mentally construct the actual relationship of how the properties of a square and rectangle are related.
3. Age independent	A third grader or a high school student could be at level 0.
4. Experience dependent	Advancement through the levels requires geometric *experiences*. Students should explore, talk about, and interact with content at the next level while increasing experiences at their current level.

describe how we think and what types of geometric ideas we think about (called *objects of thought*) and what students can do (*products of thought*). The levels are developmental—learners of any age begin at level 0 and progress to the next level through experiences with geometrical ideas. Characteristics of the van Hiele levels are provided in Table 20.1.

Level 0: Visualization

The objects of thought at level 0 are shapes and what they "look like."

Students at level 0 recognize and name figures based on the global visual characteristics of the figure. For example, a square is defined by a level 0 student as a square "because it looks like a square." Appearance is dominant at level 0 and can therefore overpower students' thinking about the properties of a shape. A level 0 thinker, for example, may see a square with sides that are not horizontal or vertical (it appears tilted) and believe it is a "diamond" (not a mathematical term for a shape) and no longer a square. Students at this level will sort and classify shapes based on their appearance—"I put these together because they are all pointy." Students are able to see how shapes are alike and different and as a result, they can create and begin to understand classifications of shapes.

The products of thought at level 0 are classes or groupings of shapes that seem to be "alike."

The emphasis at level 0 is on shapes that students can observe, feel, build (compose), take apart (decompose), or work with in some manner. The general goal is to explore how shapes are alike and different and use these ideas to create classes of shapes (both physically and mentally). Some of these classes of shapes have names—rectangles, triangles, prisms, cylinders, and so on. Properties of shapes, such as parallel sides, symmetry, right angles, and so on, are included at this level but only in an informal, observational manner.

The following activity is a good representation of an experience for level 0 learners as it focuses on how shapes are alike or different.

Activity 20.1

CCSS-M: K.G.B.4; 1.G.A.1; 2.G.A.1; 3.G.A.1

Shape Sorts

Have students work in groups of four with a set of 2-D shapes (see Figure 20.2) to do the following related activities in order:

- Each student selects a shape. In turn, the students tell one or two things they find interesting about their shape.
- Students each randomly select two shapes and try to find something that is alike about their two shapes and something that is different.
- The group selects one target shape at random and places it in the center of the workspace. Their task is to find all other shapes that are like the target shape according to the same rule. For example, if they say "This shape is like the target shape because it has a curved side and a straight side," then all other shapes that they put in the collection must have these properties. Challenge students to do a second sort with the same target shape but using a different property.
- Do a "secret sort." You (or one of the students) create a collection of about five shapes that fit a secret rule. Leave others that belong in your set in the pile. Students try to find additional pieces that belong to the set and/or guess the secret rule.

Also explore the Expanded Lesson for this activity.

These find-a-rule activities will elicit a wide variety of ideas as students examine the shapes. They may start describing the shapes with ideas such as "curvy" or "looks like a rocket" rather than typical geometric properties. But as students notice more sophisticated properties, you can attach appropriate names to them. For example, students may notice that some shapes have corners "like a square" (explain that those are called *right angles*) or that "these shapes are the same on both sides" (explain that that is called *line symmetry*).

What clearly makes this a level 0 activity is that students are operating on the shapes that they see in front of them and are beginning to see similarities and differences in shapes. By forming groups of shapes, they begin to imagine shapes belonging to classes that are not present in their collection.

Level 1: Analysis

The objects of thought at level 1 are classes of shapes rather than individual shapes.

Students at the analysis level are able to consider all shapes within a class rather than just the single shape on their desk. Instead of talking about *this* particular rectangle, they can talk about properties of *all* rectangles. By focusing on a class of shapes, students are able to think about what makes a rectangle a rectangle (four sides, opposite sides parallel, opposite sides same length, four right angles, congruent diagonals, etc.). The irrelevant features (such as size or orientation) fade into the background, and students begin to understand that if a shape belongs to a particular class such as cubes, it has the corresponding properties of that class: "All cubes have six congruent faces, and each of those faces is a square." These properties were unspoken at level 0. Students operating at level 1 may be able to list all the properties of squares, rectangles, and parallelograms but may not see that these are subclasses of one another—that all squares are rectangles and all rectangles are

FIGURE 20.2 A collection of shapes for sorting.

parallelograms. In defining a shape, level 1 thinkers are likely to list as many properties of a shape as they know.

The products of thought at level 1 are the properties of shapes.

Although level 1 students will continue to use physical models and drawings of shapes, they begin to see these individual shapes as representatives of classes of shapes. Their understanding of the properties of shapes, such as symmetry, perpendicular and parallel lines, and so on, continues to be refined. The identification of properties is an important cognitive activity (Yu, Barrett, & Presmeg, 2009).

In the following activity, level 1 students use the properties of shapes such as symmetry, angle classification (right, obtuse, acute), parallel and perpendicular, and the concept of congruent line segments and angles.

Activity 20.2

CCSS-M: 2.G.A.1; 3.G.A.1; 4.G.A.2; 4.G.A.3

Property Lists for Quadrilaterals

ENGLISH LANGUAGE LEARNERS

Prepare handouts for parallelograms, rhombuses, rectangles, **and** squares (see Figure 20.3). Assign groups of three or four students to work with one type of quadrilateral (for ELLs and students with disabilities, post labeled shapes as a reference). Ask students to list as many properties as they can that apply to all of the shapes on their sheet. They will need tools such as index cards (to check right angles, compare side lengths, and draw straight lines), mirrors (to check line symmetry), and tracing paper (for identifying angle congruence). Encourage students to use the words "at least" when describing how many of something: for example, "rectangles have at least two lines of symmetry," because squares—included in the rectangles category—have four.

Have students prepare their property lists under these headings: Sides, Angles, Diagonals, and Symmetries. Groups then share their lists with the class, and eventually a class list for each category of shape will be developed. For ELLs, placing emphasis on these words, having students say the words aloud, and having students point to the word as you say it are ways to reinforce meaning and support their participation in discussions.

STUDENTS
with
SPECIAL NEEDS

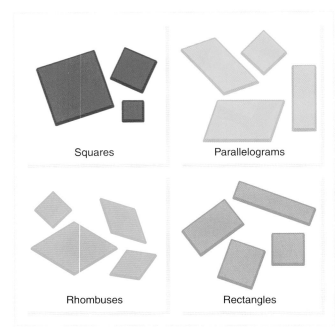

FIGURE 20.3 Shapes for the "Property Lists for Quadrilaterals" activity.

Notice that students must assess whether the properties apply to all shapes in the category. If they are working on the squares, for example, their observations apply to a square mile as well as a square centimeter.

Level 2: Informal Deduction

The objects of thought at level 2 are the properties of shapes.

As students begin to think about properties of geometric objects without focusing on one particular object (shape), they are able to develop relationships between these properties. "If all four angles are right angles, the shape must be a rectangle. If it is a square, all angles are right angles. If it is a square, it must be a rectangle." Once students have a greater ability to engage in if–then reasoning, students can classify shapes using only a minimum set of defining characteristics. For example, four congruent sides and at least one right angle are sufficient to define a square. Rectangles are parallelograms with a right angle. Observations go beyond properties themselves and begin to focus on logical arguments about the properties. Students at level 2 will be able to follow and appreciate informal deductive arguments about shapes and their properties. "Proofs" may be more intuitive than deductive; however, there is the ability to follow a logical argument. An understanding of a formal deductive system (an agreed-on set of rules), however, remains under the surface.

The products of thought at level 2 are relationships between properties of geometric objects.

The signature characteristic of a level-2 activity is the inclusion of informal logical reasoning. Because students have developed an understanding of various properties of shapes, it is now time to encourage conjecture and to ask "Why?" or "What if?"

Activity 20.3

CCSS-M: 4.G.A.2; 5.G.B.3

Minimal Defining Lists

This activity is a sequel to Activity 20.2. Once property lists for the parallelogram, rhombus, rectangle, and square (and possibly the kite and trapezoid) have been generated, post the lists. Have students work in groups to find "minimal defining lists," or MDLs, for each shape. An MDL is a subset of the properties for a shape that is defining and minimal. The term "defining" here means that any shape with all the properties on the MDL must be that shape. The term "minimal" means that if any single property is removed from the list, it is no longer defining. For example, one MDL for a square is a quadrilateral with (1) four congruent sides and (2) four right angles (two items on the list). If a shape has these two properties it must be a square. Another minimal defining list for a square is (1) is has four sides of the same length and (2) perpendicular diagonals. Challenge students to find more than one MDL for their shape. A proposed list is not defining if a counterexample—a shape other than one being described— can be produced by using only the properties on the list.

The hallmark of this and other level 2 activities is the emphasis on logical reasoning: "*If* a quadrilateral has these properties, *then* it must be a square." Logic is also involved in proving that a proposed list is faulty—either not minimal or not defining. Here students begin to learn the nature of a definition and the value of counterexamples. In fact, any minimal defining list (MDL) is a potential definition. The other aspect of this activity that clearly involves level 2 thinking is that students focus on analyzing the relationships between properties (for example, if a quadrilateral has four right angles, it also has diagonals of the same length).

Level 3: Deduction

The objects of thought at level 3 are relationships between properties of geometric objects.

At level 3, students analyze informal arguments; the structure of a system complete with axioms, definitions, theorems, corollaries, and postulates begins to develop and can be appreciated as the necessary means of establishing geometric truth. The student at this level is able to work with abstract statements about geometric properties and make conclusions based on logic. A student operating at level 3 is not only aware that the diagonals of a rectangle bisect each other (level 2) but has an appreciation of the need to prove this from a series of deductive arguments.

The products of thought at level 3 are deductive axiomatic systems for geometry.

Level 4: Rigor

The objects of thought at level 4 are deductive axiomatic systems for geometry.

At the highest level of the van Hiele hierarchy, the objects of thought are axiomatic systems themselves, not just the deductions within a system. This is generally the level of a college mathematics major who is studying geometry as a branch of mathematical science.

The products of thought at level 4 are comparisons and contrasts among different axiomatic systems of geometry.

Levels 3 and 4 are beyond the scope of this book.

FORMATIVE ASSESSMENT **Notes.** How do you discover the van Hiele level of each student? Once you know, how will you select the right activities to match your students' levels? As you conduct an activity, listen to the types of observations that students make and record them on an Observation Checklist. Can your students talk about shapes as classes? Do they refer, for example, to "rectangles" or do they base their discussion on a particular rectangle? Do they generalize that certain properties are attributable to a type of shape or simply the shape at hand? Do they understand that shapes do not change when the orientation changes? With simple observations such as these, you will soon be able to distinguish between levels 0 and 1. If by middle school students are not able to understand logical arguments, are not comfortable with conjectures, and are unsure of if–then reasoning, they are likely still at level 1 or below and will need interventions to prepare them for level 2 thinking. To prepare students for the deductive geometry of high school (primarily level 3) and beyond, reaching the van Hiele level 2 by the end of the eighth grade is critically important. ■

Implications for Instruction

All teachers should be aware that the collection of geometric experiences they provide are the single most important factor in moving students up this developmental ladder to higher levels of geometric thought. The van Hiele theory and the developmental perspective of this book highlight the necessity of teaching at the student's level of thought. However, almost any activity can be modified to span two levels of thinking, helping students move from one level to the next.

Consider Clements and Sarama's (2014) four features of effective early geometry instruction:

1. Show a variety of shapes and have students compare both examples and nonexamples with a focus on critical characteristics.
2. Facilitate student discussions about the properties of shapes, having them develop essential language along the way.
3. Encourage the examination of an array of shape classes that goes beyond the traditional, allowing students to explore relationships and recognize different categories, orientations, and sizes.
4. Provide students with a range of geometric experiences at every level, having them use physical materials, drawings, and computer models.

Watch (https://www.youtube.com/watch?v=v2D75Va_3Y) as Douglas Clements talks about activities that correspond with some of the early levels of geometric thinking.

Moving from Level 0 to Level 1. Very young students are usually at level 0, but so are older students who need interventions to prepare them for grade-level material. Instructional considerations that support students moving from level 0 to level 1 are as follows:

- *Focus on the properties of figures rather than on simple identification.* As new geometric concepts are learned, students should be challenged to use these attributes to classify shapes.
- *Challenge students to test ideas about shapes using a variety of examples from a particular category.* Say to them, "Let's see if that is true for other rectangles," or "Can you draw a triangle that does not have a right angle?" In general, question students to see whether observations made about a particular shape apply to other shapes of a similar kind.
- *Provide ample opportunities to draw, build, make, put together (compose), and take apart (decompose) shapes in both two and three dimensions.* These activities should be built around understanding and using specific attributes or properties.
- *Apply ideas to entire classes of figures* (such as *all* rectangles or *all* prisms) *rather than to individual models.* For example, find ways to sort all possible triangles into groups. From these groups, define types of triangles.

Moving from Level 1 to Level 2. Level 2 thinking should begin in grade 5 (CCSSO, 2010), when students are to classify shapes based on their properties (attributes) in categories and subcategories. Instructional considerations that support students moving from level 1 to level 2 are as follows:

- *Challenge students to explore and test examples.* Ask questions that involve reasoning, such as "If the sides of a four-sided shape are all congruent, will you always have a square?" and "Can you find a counterexample?"
- *Encourage the making and testing of hypotheses or conjectures.* "Do you think that will work all the time?" "Is that true for all triangles or just equilateral ones?"
- *Examine properties of shapes to determine necessary and sufficient conditions for a shape to be a particular shape.* "What properties must diagonals have to guarantee that a quadrilateral with these diagonals will be a square?"
- *Use the language of informal deduction.* Say: *all, some, none, if . . . then, what if,* and so on.
- *Encourage students to attempt informal proofs.* As an alternative, require them to make sense of informal proofs that you or other students have suggested.

 Standards for Mathematical Practice
MP3. Construct viable arguments and critique the reasoning of others.

The remainder of this chapter offers a sampling of activities organized around the four content goals of the NCTM *Principles and Standards for Mathematics* (2000): Shapes and Properties, Location, Transformations, and Visualization. Understand that all of these subdivisions are quite fluid; the content areas overlap and build on each other. Activities in one section may help develop geometric thinking in another content area.

 Complete Self-Check 20.2: Developing Geometric Thinking

Shapes and Properties

This is the content area most often associated with geometry in pre-K through grade 8 classrooms; students are working with both two- and three-dimensional shapes. This is the time when young students begin to "perceive, say, describe/discuss and construct objects in 2-D space" (National Research Council Committee, 2009, p. 177). Students need experience with a wide variety of two- and three-dimensional shapes. Triangles should be shown in more than just equilateral forms and not always with the vertex at the top. (If students say a triangle is upside down, it may be because they have rarely seen triangles illustrated differently.) Shapes should have curved sides, straight sides, and combinations of these. As students describe the shape or property, the terminology can be introduced, as in the next activity.

Activity 20.4   CCSS-M: K.G.A.1; K.G.A.2; K.G.B.4

Shape Show and Hunt

Use masking tape to create a large target shape that students can walk around on the community rug or floor. Ask students if they can name the shape or any attributes (such as straight or curved sides, number of sides, right angles, etc.). Make sure students, especially ELLs, understand the terms you use. You can also have students draw the shape in the air or on paper. Then, ask students to find one or two items in the classroom, on the playground, or somewhere else at school that have this same shape. Take photos of the examples students find so they can be used later for discussion. Ask students to talk about how they know the example is like the target shape. For students with disabilities, provide a cutout of the target shape that they can take with them as they search for an example.

 ENGLISH LANGUAGE LEARNERS

 STUDENTS with SPECIAL NEEDS

Sorting and Classifying

As young students work at classification of shapes, be prepared for them to notice features that you do not consider to be "real" geometric attributes, such as "dented" or "looks like a tree." Students at this level will also attribute to shapes ideas that are not part of the shape, such as "points up" or "has a side that is the same as the edge of the board."

For variety in two-dimensional shapes, use materials like a set of Assorted Shapes. Make multiple copies so that groups of students can all work with the same shapes. Once you have your sets constructed, try Activity 20.1, "Shape Sorts."

In any sorting and classifying activity, the students—not the teacher—should decide how to group the shapes. By listening to the kinds of attributes that they use in their sorting, you will be able to tell what properties they know and use and how they think about shapes. Figure 20.4 illustrates a few of the possible ways a set might be sorted.

The secret sort in Activity 20.1 is one option for introducing a new property. For example, sort the shapes so that all have at least one right angle or "square corner." When students discover your rule, you have an opportunity to talk more about that property and name the property "right angle."

The following activity also uses the two-dimensional shapes.

Activity 20.5

CCSS-M: 1.G.A.1; 2.G.A.1; 3.G.A.1; 4.G.A.2

What's My Shape?

Cut out a double set of 2-D shapes on card stock. Glue each shape from one set inside a file folder to make "secret-shape" folders. The other set of shapes should be glued on cards and placed on the table for reference. Designate one student as the leader; he or she holds the secret-shape folder. The other students are to find the shape that matches the shape in the folder by asking the leader only "yes" or "no" questions. The group can eliminate shapes (turning over the cards) as they get answers about the properties that narrow down possibilities. They are not allowed to point to a piece and ask, "Is it this one?" Rather, they must continue to ask questions about properties or characteristics that reduce the choices to one shape. The final shape card is checked against the one in the leader's folder. Students with disabilities may need a list of possible properties and characteristics (such as number of sides) to help support their question asking.

STUDENTS *with* **SPECIAL NEEDS**

The difficulty of Activity 20.5 largely depends on the shape in the folder. The more shapes in the collection that share properties with the secret shape, the more difficult the task.

FORMATIVE ASSESSMENT Notes. Using three-dimensional shapes, adapt "Shape Sorts" (Activity 20.1) for a diagnostic interview. Make sure you have a collection of solids that has a lot of variation (curved surfaces, etc.). Collections of 3-D shapes are available commercially, or collect real objects such as cans, boxes, balls, and Styrofoam shapes. Figure 20.5 illustrates some classifications of solids.

The ways students describe these three-dimensional shapes is good evidence of their level of geometric thinking. The classifications made by level 0 thinkers are generally limited to the shapes that they have in front of them. Level 1 thinkers will begin to create categories based on properties, and their language will indicate that they know there are more shapes in the group than those present. Students may say things like "These shapes have square corners sort of like rectangles," or "These look like boxes. All the boxes have square [rectangular] sides." ■

Composing and Decomposing Shapes

Students need to freely explore how shapes fit together to form larger shapes (compose) and how larger shapes can be made of smaller shapes (decompose). This ability to compose and decompose shapes supports geometric measurement such as finding area, surface area, and volume.

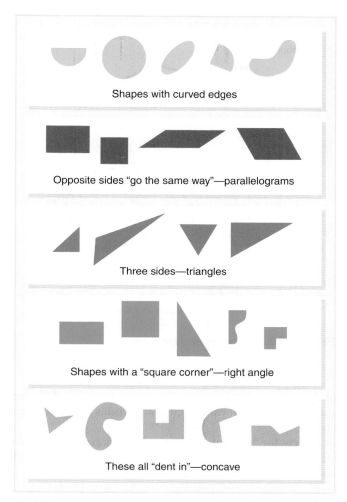

Shapes with curved edges

Opposite sides "go the same way"—parallelograms

Three sides—triangles

Shapes with a "square corner"—right angle

These all "dent in"—concave

FIGURE 20.4 By sorting shapes, students begin to recognize properties.

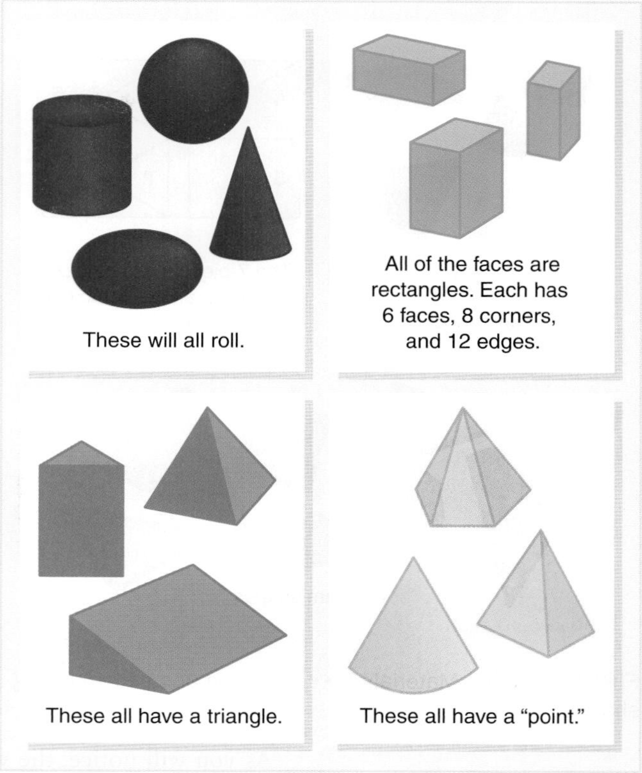

These will all roll.

All of the faces are rectangles. Each has 6 faces, 8 corners, and 12 edges.

These all have a triangle.

These all have a "point."

FIGURE 20.5 Early classifications of three-dimensional shapes.

Among two-dimensional shapes for these activities, pattern blocks and tangrams are the best known. Pierre van Hiele (1999) also describes an interesting set of tiles he calls the Mosaic Puzzle (see Figure 20.6).

Activity 20.6

CCSS-M: K.G.B.6; 1.G.A.2; 2.G.A.1

Tangram Puzzles

TECHNOLOGY

Using a set of Tangram Pieces, have students explore the Tangram Puzzles Activity Page where they compose shapes to create a larger figure. The National Library of Virtual Manipulatives also has a tangram applet with a set of fourteen puzzle figures that can be made using all seven tangram pieces.

Activity 20.7

CCSS-M: K.G.B.6; 1.G.A.2; 2.G.A.1; 3.G.A.1; 4.G.A.2

Mosaic Puzzle

Give pairs of students a copy of the Mosaic Puzzle and have them use the Mosaic Puzzle Questions Activity Page to explore using what they know about a shape's properties to compose and decompose other shapes.

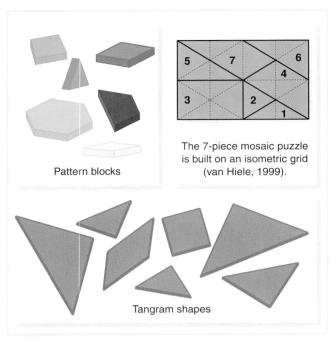

Pattern blocks

The 7-piece mosaic puzzle is built on an isometric grid (van Hiele, 1999).

Tangram shapes

FIGURE 20.6 Materials for composing and decomposing shapes.

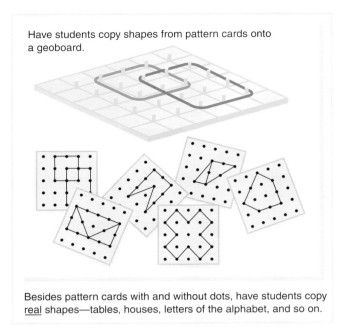

Have students copy shapes from pattern cards onto a geoboard.

Besides pattern cards with and without dots, have students copy <u>real</u> shapes—tables, houses, letters of the alphabet, and so on.

FIGURE 20.7 Shapes on geoboards.

As you will notice, the value of the mosaic puzzle is that the set contains five different angles (which could lead to discussions of types of informal angle comparisons and groupings of angle measures such as right, acute, and obtuse).

The geoboard is one of the best devices for "constructing" two-dimensional shapes. Following are a few of the many possible activities appropriate for thinking about composing and decomposing shapes using a geoboard.

Activity 20.8

CCSS-M: 1.G.A.2; 2.G.A.1; 4.G.A.1; 4.G.A.2; 4.G.A.3

Geoboard Copy

Prepare Geoboard Design Cards **(see Figure 20.7). Project the shapes onto a screen and have students copy them on geoboards (or** Geoboard Patterns **or** Geoboard Recording Sheet**). Begin with designs using one band, then create more complex designs, including those that show a shape composed of other smaller shapes. Discuss properties such as number of sides, parallel lines, or line symmetry, depending on the grade level. Students with disabilities may need to have a copy of the design card at their desk for closer reference.**

STUDENTS
with
SPECIAL
NEEDS

Teach students from the very beginning how to record their designs on geoboard recording sheets. To help students who struggle with this transfer, suggest that they first mark the dots for the corners of their shape ("second row, end peg"). With the corners identified, it is much easier for them to draw lines between the corners to make the shape. These drawings can be placed in groups for classification and discussion or sent home to families to showcase what students are learning.

Activity 20.9

CCSS-M: 1.G.A.2; 1.G.A.3; 2.G.A.1; 2.G.A.3; 3.G.A.2

Decomposing on the Geoboard

Show students a shape from the Decomposing Shapes **Activity Page and ask them to copy it on their geoboards or** Geoboard Recording Sheet**. Then specify the number of smaller shapes they should decompose each large shape into, as in Figure 20.8. Also specify whether the smaller shapes are all to be congruent or simply of the same type.**

Allow students to choose the tool (geoboard, grid paper, or dot paper) that best supports their thinking on a given problem. There are also excellent digital versions of the geoboard. One is found at National Library of Virtual Manipulatives and includes the instant calculation of perimeter and area by clicking the "measures" button.

Categories of Two- and Three-Dimensional Shapes

As students' attention shifts to properties of shapes (moving to level 1 thinking), they learn the proper names for shapes and their properties. You will notice that the definitions of shapes support the exploration of the relationships between shapes.

Two-Dimensional Shapes. Table 20.2 lists some important categories of two-dimensional shapes. Examples of these shapes can be found in Figure 20.9.

In the classification of quadrilaterals and parallelograms, some subsets overlap. For example, a square is a rectangle and a rhombus. All parallelograms are trapezoids, but not all trapezoids are parallelograms.* Students often have difficulty seeing this type of subcategory. They may quite correctly list all the properties of a square, a rhombus, and a rectangle and still might classify a square as a "nonrhombus" or a

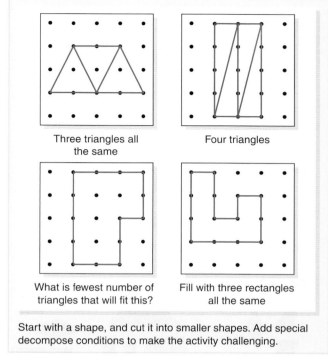

Three triangles all the same

Four triangles

What is fewest number of triangles that will fit this?

Fill with three rectangles all the same

Start with a shape, and cut it into smaller shapes. Add special decompose conditions to make the activity challenging.

FIGURE 20.8   Decomposing shapes.

TABLE 20.2   CATEGORIES OF TWO-DIMENSIONAL SHAPES

Shape	Description
Simple Closed Curves	
Concave, convex	An intuitive definition of concave might be "having a dent in it." If a simple closed curve is not concave, it is convex. A more precise definition of concave may be interesting to explore with older students.
Symmetrical, nonsymmetrical	Shapes may have one or more lines of symmetry.
Regular	All sides and all angles are congruent.
Polygons	Simple closed curves with all straight sides.
Triangles	
Triangles	Polygons with exactly three sides.
Classified by sides	
Equilateral	All sides are congruent.
Isosceles	At least two sides are congruent.
Scalene	No two sides are congruent.
Classified by angles	
Right	One angle is a right angle.
Acute	All angles are smaller than a right angle.
Obtuse	One angle is larger than a right angle.
Convex Quadrilaterals	
Convex quadrilaterals	Convex polygons with exactly four sides.
Kite	Two opposing pairs of congruent adjacent sides.
Trapezoid	At least one pair of parallel sides.
Isosceles	A pair of opposite sides is congruent.
Parallelogram	Two pairs of parallel sides.
Rectangle	Parallelogram with a right angle.
Rhombus	Parallelogram with all sides congruent.
Square	Parallelogram with a right angle and all sides congruent.

*Some definitions of trapezoid specify *only one* pair of parallel sides, in which case parallelograms would not be trapezoids. The University of Chicago School Mathematics Project (UCSMP) uses the "at least one pair" definition, meaning that parallelograms and rectangles are trapezoids. Some regions mandate one definition over another, so consult your local curriculum (Manizade & Mason, 2014).

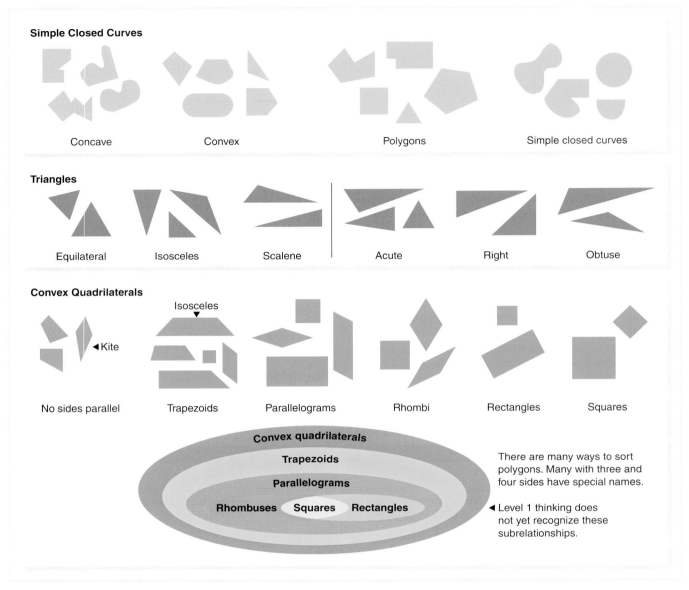

FIGURE 20.9 Classification of two-dimensional shapes.

"nonrectangle." To help learners think about this, suggest that a student can be on two different sports teams. A square is an example of a quadrilateral that belongs to two other "teams."

By third grade, students must think about subcategories of quadrilaterals, and by fifth grade, they must "understand that attributes belonging to a category of two dimensional figures also belong to all subcategories of that category" (CCSSO, 2010, p. 38)

Three-Dimensional Shapes. Important and interesting shapes and relationships also exist in three dimensions. Table 20.3 describes classifications of solids. Figure 20.10 shows examples of cylinders and prisms. Note that prisms are defined here as a special category of cylinder—a cylinder with a polygon for a base (Zwillinger, 2011). Figure 20.11 shows a comparable grouping of cones and pyramids.

Some textbooks may limit the definition of cylinders to just circular cylinders. These books do not have special names for other cylinders. Under that definition, the prism is not a special case of a cylinder. This points to the fact that definitions are conventions, and not all conventions are universally agreed on. If you return to the volume formulas in Chapter 19, you will find that the more inclusive definition of cylinders and cones allows one formula for any type of cylinder—hence, prisms (with a similar statement that is true for cones and pyramids).

TABLE 20.3   CATEGORIES OF THREE-DIMENSIONAL SHAPES

Shape	Description
Sorted by Edges and Vertices	
Spheres and "egglike" shapes	Shapes with no *edges* and no *vertices* (corners).
	Shapes with *edges* but no *vertices* (for example, a flying saucer).
	Shapes with *vertices* but no *edges* (for example, a football).
Sorted by Faces and Surfaces	
Polyhedron	Shapes made of all faces (a face is a flat surface of a solid). If all surfaces are faces, all the edges will be straight lines.
	Some combination of faces and rounded surfaces (circular cylinders are examples, but this is not a definition of a cylinder).
	Shapes with all curved surfaces.
	Shapes with and without edges and with and without vertices.
	Faces can be parallel. Parallel faces lie in planes that never intersect.
Cylinders	
Cylinder	Two congruent, parallel faces called *bases*. Lines joining corresponding points on the two bases are always parallel. These parallel lines are called *elements* of the cylinder.
Right cylinder	A cylinder with elements perpendicular to the bases. A cylinder that is not a right cylinder is an oblique cylinder.
Prism	A cylinder with polygons for bases. All prisms are special cases of cylinders.
Rectangular prism	A cylinder with rectangles for bases.
Cube	A square prism with square sides.
Cones	
Cone	A solid with exactly one face and a vertex that is not on the face. Straight lines (elements) can be drawn from any point on the edge of the base to the vertex. The base may be any shape at all. The vertex need not be directly over the base.
Circular cone	Cone with a circular base.
Pyramid	Cone with a polygon for a base. All faces joining the vertex are triangles. Pyramids are named by the shape of the base: *triangular* pyramid, *square* pyramid, *octagonal* pyramid, and so on. All pyramids are special cases of cones.

Applying Definitions and Categories. Using these definitions and categories helps students focus more deeply on the properties that make the shape what it is (not just that it looks like the others in its group). The next activity provides a good way to introduce a category of shapes.

Activity 20.10

CCSS-M: 1.G.A.1; 2.G.A.1; 3.G.A.2; 4.G.A.2

Mystery Definition

Give students the Mystery Definition **Activity Page**, or project a grade-level-appropriate logic problem on the board (such as the format of the example in **Figure 20.12**). At the top of your sheet, for your first collection, be certain that you have allowed for all possible variables. For example, in the first grouping a square is included in the set of rhombuses. Also, choose nonexamples to be as close to the positive examples as is necessary to help with a precise definition. The third or mixed set should also include those nonexamples with which students are most likely to be confused. Students should justify their choices in a class discussion. Note that the use of nonexamples is particularly important for students with disabilities.

STUDENTS
with
SPECIAL NEEDS

The value of the "Mystery Definition" activity is that students develop ideas and informal definitions based on their own concept development. After their definitions have been discussed, compared, and refined, you can contrast their ideas to the conventional definition for that shape.

Determining types of triangles is introduced in grade 4 with the concept of right triangles. Then in seventh grade, students focus on the properties based on the measures of the sides and angles (CCSSO, 2010). For defining types or categories of triangles, the next activity is an especially good starting place.

CCSS Standards for Mathematical Practice

MP6. Attend to precision.

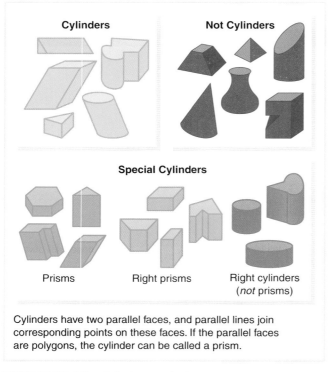

Cylinders have two parallel faces, and parallel lines join corresponding points on these faces. If the parallel faces are polygons, the cylinder can be called a prism.

FIGURE 20.10 Cylinders and prisms.

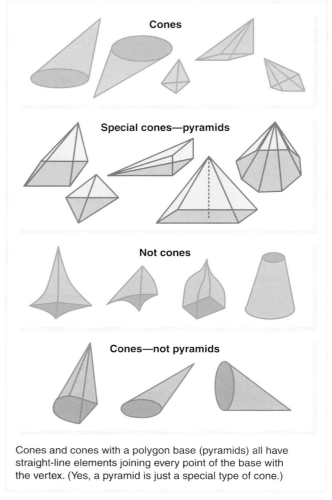

Cones and cones with a polygon base (pyramids) all have straight-line elements joining every point of the base with the vertex. (Yes, a pyramid is just a special type of cone.)

FIGURE 20.11 Cones and pyramids.

Activity 20.11

CCSS-M: 2.G.A.1; 3.G.A.2; 4.G.A.2; 5.G.B.3; 5.G.B.4

Triangle Sort

Give teams the triangles from the Assorted Triangles Activity Page, which includes examples of right, acute, and obtuse triangles; examples of equilateral, isosceles, and scalene triangles; and triangles that represent every possible combination of these categories. Ask the teams to sort the entire collection into three discrete groups so that no triangle belongs to two groups. When this is done and descriptions of the groupings have been written, students should then find a second criterion for creating three different groupings. Students with disabilities may need a hint to look only at angle sizes or only at the issue of congruent sides, but delay giving these hints if you can. Once the groups have been determined, provide appropriate terminology. For ELLs and other students who may struggle with the vocabulary, focus on the specialized meaning of these terms (such as contrasting "acute pain" and "acute angle"), and root words (*equi-* meaning *equal* and *-lateral* meaning *side*). As a follow-up, challenge students to sketch a triangle in each of the nine cells of the Triangle Sort Chart. Extend the activity by repeating the process using kites and trapezoids or introduce three-dimensional shape definitions.

ENGLISH LANGUAGE LEARNERS

STUDENTS with SPECIAL NEEDS

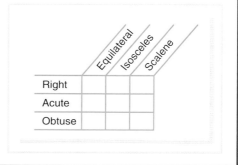

⏸ Pause & Reflect

Of the nine cells in the Triangle Sort chart, two of them are impossible to fill. Can you tell which ones and why? ●

Quadrilaterals (polygons with four sides) are a rich source of investigations. Once students are familiar with the concepts of right, obtuse, and acute angles, congruence of line segments and angles, and line symmetry, Activity 20.2, "Property Lists for Quadrilaterals," is a good way to bring these ideas together.

The class must agree with everything that is put on the property list. As new relationships come up in this presentation-and-discussion period, introduce proper terminology. For example, if two diagonals intersect in a square corner, then they are perpendicular. Other terms such as *parallel*, *congruent*, *bisect*, *midpoint*, and so on can be clarified as you help students write their descriptions. This is also a good time to introduce symbols such as ≅ for *congruent* or ‖ for *parallel*.

In the next activity, students examine the diagonals of various classes of quadrilaterals.

Standards for Mathematical Practice

MP3. Construct viable arguments and critique the reasoning of others.

Activity 20.12 CCSS-M: 4.G.A.2; 5.G.B.3; 5.G.B.4

Diagonals of Quadrilaterals

Give each student three card stock Diagonal Strips. Punch the nine holes as marked. Use a brass fastener to join two strips. A quadrilateral is formed by joining the four end holes as shown in Figure 20.13. Provide students with the list of possible relationships for angles, lengths, and proportional comparisons of parts (ratios). Have students use the strips to determine the properties of diagonals that will produce different quadrilaterals. Have students make drawings on 1-Centimeter Dot Paper to test the various hypotheses and record their findings on the Properties of Quadrilateral Diagonals Activity Sheet. See the Expanded Lesson of this activity for the full description of this instructional experience.

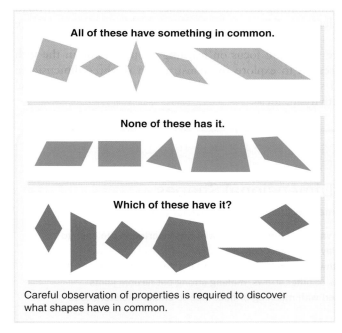

Careful observation of properties is required to discover what shapes have in common.

FIGURE 20.12 A mystery definition.

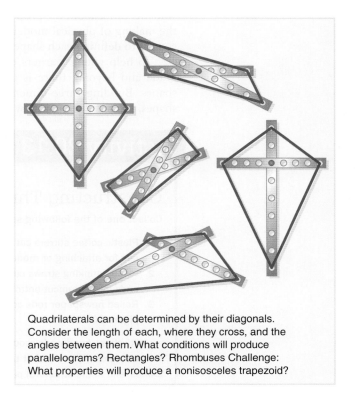

Quadrilaterals can be determined by their diagonals. Consider the length of each, where they cross, and the angles between them. What conditions will produce parallelograms? Rectangles? Rhombuses Challenge: What properties will produce a nonisosceles trapezoid?

FIGURE 20.13 Diagonals of quadrilaterals.

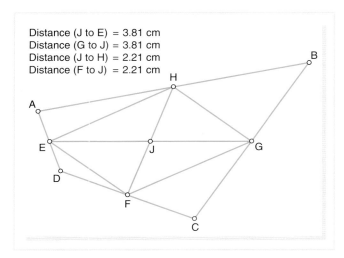

Distance (J to E) = 3.81 cm
Distance (G to J) = 3.81 cm
Distance (J to H) = 2.21 cm
Distance (F to J) = 2.21 cm

FIGURE 20.14 A construction made with dynamic geometry software illustrating an interesting property of quadrilaterals.

Every type of quadrilateral can be uniquely described in terms of its diagonals using only the conditions of length, proportional comparison of parts, and whether they are perpendicular. This activity can also be explored with a dynamic geometry program where points, lines, and geometric figures are easily constructed on the computer using only a mouse or a stylus.

The best known dynamic geometry programs are *The Geometer's Sketchpad* (Key Curriculum Press) and *GeoGebra* (open source software). To appreciate the potential (and the fun) of dynamic geometry software, you need to experience it because the geometric objects can be moved about and manipulated in an endless variety.

One of the most significant ideas is that when a geometric object is created with a particular relationship to another object, that relationship is maintained no matter how either object is moved or changed. For example, in Figure 20.14, the midpoints of a freely drawn quadrilateral ABCD have been joined. The diagonals of the resulting quadrilateral (EFGH) are also drawn and measured. No matter how the points A, B, C, and D are dragged around the screen, even inverting the quadrilateral, the other lines will maintain the same relationships (joining midpoints and diagonals), and the measurements will be instantly updated.

With a dynamic geometry program, if a quadrilateral is drawn, only one shape is observed, as would be the case on paper or on a geoboard. But now that quadrilateral can be stretched and altered in endless ways, students actually explore not one shape but an enormous number of examples from that *class* of shapes. If a property does not change when the figure changes on the dynamic geometry program, the property is attributable to the class of shapes rather than any particular shape.

Construction Activities. Building or drawing shapes is an important activity to help students think about the properties and defining attributes of shapes (CCSSO, 2010). Through the making of physical models, students can focus on the attributes and components that are central to defining each shape.

To help young learners explore solids and focus on learning about volume in the fifth grade and beyond, there is good reason to explore the construction of three-dimensional shapes. Building three-dimensional shapes is more difficult than building two-dimensional shapes, so consider the following activity for ideas.

Activity 20.13

CCSS-M: K.G.A.3; K.G.B.5; 1.G.A.2; 2.G.A.1; 6.G.A.4

Constructing Three-Dimensional Shapes

Collect one of the following sets of materials for students to use for construction:

1. Plastic coffee stirrers cut into a variety of lengths with twist ties inserted in the ends to use for attaching or modeling clay to connect corners
2. Plastic drinking straws cut lengthwise from the top down to the flexible joint—insert the slit ends into the uncut bottom ends of other straws, making strong but flexible joints
3. Rolled newspaper rods connected with masking or duct tape to create skeletons (see Figure 20.15)

With these handmade models, discuss the strength and rigidity of triangular components in the structures. Point out that triangles are used in many bridges, in the long booms of construction cranes, and in the structural parts of buildings. They can also be used to explore surface area.

Circles. Many interesting relationships can be observed among measures of different parts of the circle. One of the most astounding and important is the ratio between measures of the circumference and the diameter.

Activity 20.14   CCSS-M: 7.G.B.4

Discovering Pi

Have groups of students carefully measure both the circumference and diameter of a collection of circular items such as jar lids, cans, and wastebaskets. To measure circumference, wrap string once around the object and then measure that length of string. Also measure the circumference of large circles marked on gym floors and playgrounds with a trundle wheel or rope. circles marked on gym floors and playgrounds with a trundle wheel or rope.

   Students gather the circumference and diameter from a variety of circular items and enter the measures in a Circle Table Activity Page. Note that they also should divide to find the ratio of the circumference to the diameter for each circle. The exact ratio is an irrational number, about 3.14159, represented by the Greek letter π (pi).

What is most important in Activity 20.14 is that students develop a clear understanding of π as the ratio of circumference to diameter in any circle regardless of size. The quantity π is not some mystical number that appears in mathematics formulas; it is a naturally occurring and universal ratio.

Investigations, Conjectures, and the Development of Proof

As students develop an understanding of various geometric properties and attach these properties to categories of shapes, it is essential to encourage conjecture and to explore informal deductive arguments to develop logical reasoning. Students should begin to attempt—or at least follow—simple proofs and explore ideas that connect directly to algebra.

To understand the difference between level 1 and level 2 of the van Hiele theory, let's revisit the pair of activities "Property Lists for Quadrilaterals" (Activity 20.2), and "Minimal Defining Lists" (Activity 20.3). The parallelogram, rhombus, rectangle, and square each have at least four MDLs. One of the most interesting MDLs for each shape consists only of the properties of its diagonals. For example, a quadrilateral with diagonals that bisect each other and are perpendicular (intersect at right angles) is a rhombus.

Notice that the MDL activity is actually more involved with logical thinking than with examining shapes. Students say, "If we specify only this list of properties, will that guarantee this particular shape?" A second feature is the opportunity to discuss what constitutes a definition. In fact, any MDL could be the definition of the shape. We usually choose MDLs based on the ease with which we can understand them. A quadrilateral with diagonals that bisect each other does not immediately call to mind a parallelogram, even though that is a defining property.

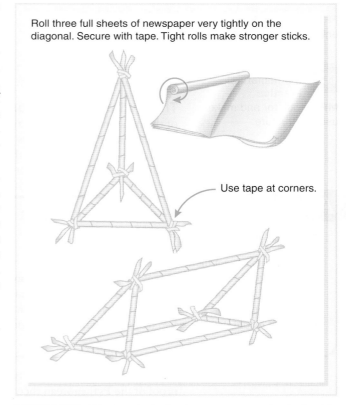

Roll three full sheets of newspaper very tightly on the diagonal. Secure with tape. Tight rolls make stronger sticks.

Use tape at corners.

FIGURE 20.15   Large skeletal structures can be built with tightly rolled newspaper.

❚❚ Pause & Reflect

Use the property list for squares and rectangles to prove "all squares are rectangles." Notice that you must use logical reasoning to understand this statement. It does little good to simply force definitions on students who are not ready to develop the relationship. ●

The next activity supports logical reasoning and is a good follow-up to Activities 20.2 and 20.3, because it is not restricted to quadrilaterals and can include three-dimensional shapes as well.

Activity 20.15

CCSS-M: 4.G.A.2; 5.G.B.3; 5.G.B.4

True or False?

Prepare a set of true/false statements of the following forms: "If it is a _____, then it is also a _____." "All _____ are _____." "Some _____ are _____ " or use the True/False Statements Activity Page. Ask students to determine whether the statements are true or false and present an argument to support the decision (see Figure 20.16). Four or five true/false statements will make a good lesson. Once this format is understood, let students challenge their classmates by making their own lists of a mixture of true/false statements.

1. If it is a square, then it is a rhombus.

TRUE .. A Square can be a rhombus Beacuse they are both parallelograms and all the sides are the exact. Also if you rotate a square than it becums a mombus.

2. If it is a pyramid, then it must have a square base.

FALSE ... To be a pyramid it does not have to have square base. I think this beacuse thair can be tryangular pyramids.

Net ...

FIGURE 20.16 True or false? A fifth-grade student presents an argument to support her decision.

CCSS **Standards for Mathematical Practice**

MP7. Look for and make use of structure.

FORMATIVE ASSESSMENT Notes. The "True or False?" activity is also a good diagnostic assessment. Note how the student's work shown in Figure 20.16 gives insights into her ideas and representations. She also reveals her emerging conceptions as she attempts to make arguments for her choices. ∎

Remember, if you write a theorem on the board and ask students to prove it, you have already "told" them that it is true. If, by contrast, a student makes a statement about a geometric situation the class is exploring, it can be written with a question mark as a conjecture—a statement whose truth has not yet been determined. You can ask, "Is it true? Always? Can we prove it? Can we find a counterexample?"

On the path to more formal deduction, students should construct diagrams and consider pertinent definitions (Sinclair, Pimm, & Skelin, 2012). You will see in the following sections that the students will begin to notice evidence of a pattern and then check it with multiple approaches based on mathematical properties and structure.

The Pythagorean Theorem. The *Pythagorean theorem*, explored in eighth grade, is one of the most important mathematical relationships and warrants in-depth conceptual investigation. In geometric terms, this relationship states that if a square is constructed on each side of a right triangle, the areas of the two smaller squares will together equal the area of the square on the longest side, the hypotenuse.

Activity 20.16

CCSS-M: 8.G.B.6; 8.G.B.7

The Pythagorean Relationship

Have students draw a right triangle on 0.5-Centimeter Square Grid Paper. Assign each student a different triangle by specifying the lengths of the two legs. Students are to draw a square on each leg and the hypotenuse and find the areas of all three squares. For the square on the hypotenuse, the exact area can be found by making each of the sides the diagonal of a rectangle (see Figure 20.17). Have students record their own data on the Table of the Areas Activity Page and then them collect and record data from two teams with different triangles. Ask students to look for a relationship between the squares of a particular triangle.

What about proof? The two large congruent squares in Figure 20.18 together show a visual proof of the Pythagorean theorem (Nelson, 2001). Note that both large squares are decomposed into squares and triangles—and that the four triangles in each large square are the same but arranged differently. By adding up the areas of the squares and the triangles in each large square and setting them equal to each other, the Pythagorean relationship can be found by subtracting

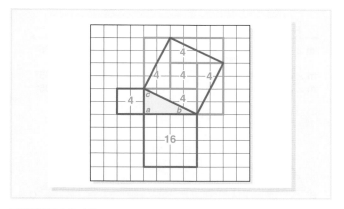

FIGURE 20.17 The Pythagorean relationship. Here $4 + 16 = 20$, the area in square units of the square on the hypotenuse.

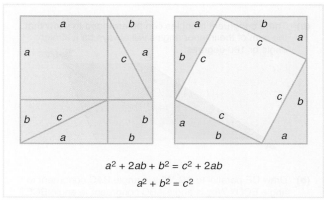

$$a^2 + 2ab + b^2 = c^2 + 2ab$$
$$a^2 + b^2 = c^2$$

FIGURE 20.18 The two large squares together are a "proof without words." Can you supply the words?

out the common areas in both squares (the areas of the triangles). An algebraic recording of the thinking process is shown below the drawings. The applet at Illuminations entitled "Proof without Words: Pythagorean Theorem" is a dynamic proof that is worth sharing with your students. Here's an interesting video (https://www.youtube.com/watch?v=gjSAE8_FahM) titled, "Pythagorean Theorem—Proof without Words" that explores this concept using paper cutouts of triangles and a square.

Standards for Mathematical Practice
MP2. Reason abstractly and quantitatively.

 Pause & Reflect

Use the two drawings in Figure 20.18 to create a proof of the Pythagorean relationship. •

Interior Angles of a Triangle. As middle school students move to focus more intently on reasoning and deductive thinking, dynamic geometry software programs help develop deductive arguments to support the relationships students come to believe through inductive reasoning. For example, suppose that you have students use a dynamic geometry program to draw a triangle, measure all of the angles, and add them up. As the triangle vertices are dragged around, the sum of the angles would remain steadfast at 180 degrees. Students can conjecture that the sum of the interior angles of a triangle is always 180 degrees, and they would be completely convinced of the truth of this conjecture based on this inductive experience. (They can be led to the same conclusion by tearing off the angles of paper triangles and combining them to create a straight line.) However, the experience just described fails to explain why it is so. Consider the following activity to support the conjecturing that will lead to more formal proofs.

Standards for Mathematical Practice
MP3. Construct viable arguments and critique the reasoning of others.

Activity 20.17   CCSS-M: 8.G.A.5

Angle Sum in a Triangle

Ask students to cut out Three Congruent Triangles and label each triangle with angles A, B, and C making sure the corresponding angles on the same triangles have the same letters. Place one triangle on a line and the second directly next to it in the same orientation. Place the third triangle in the space between the triangles as shown in Figure 20.19(a). Ask, "How are the three angles shown in the bottom of the figure, where the three congruent triangles meet, related to the angles in the red triangle? Will this relationship be true for any kind of triangle? Based on this experience, what conjecture can you make about the sum of the angles in a triangle?" For students with disabilities, have them label the angles on each of their congruent triangles with A, B, and C before they assemble the figure. This will support their ability to see how the three angles sum to 180 degrees.

STUDENTS with SPECIAL NEEDS

(a) Three congruent triangles can be arranged to show that the sum of the interior angles will always be a straight angle or 180 degrees.

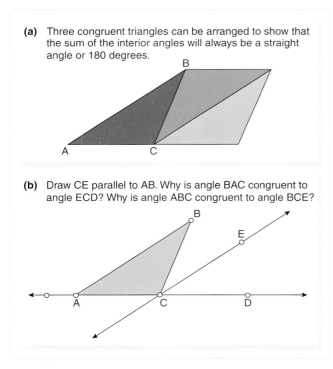

(b) Draw CE parallel to AB. Why is angle BAC congruent to angle ECD? Why is angle ABC congruent to angle BCE?

FIGURE 20.19 Deductive, logical reasoning is necessary to prove relationships that appear true from observations.

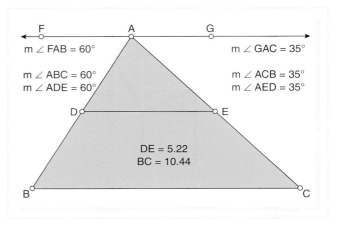

m ∠ FAB = 60°   m ∠ GAC = 35°

m ∠ ABC = 60°   m ∠ ACB = 35°
m ∠ ADE = 60°   m ∠ AED = 35°

DE = 5.22
BC = 10.44

FIGURE 20.20 The midsegment of a triangle is always parallel to the base and half as long.

The same idea can be examined through technology tools. Using a dynamic geometry program, the three triangles in Figure 20.19(a) can be drawn by starting with one triangle, translating it to the right the length of AC, and then rotating the same triangle about the midpoint of side BC. When vertices of the original triangle are dragged, the other triangles will change accordingly and remain congruent. Although this exploration demonstrates to students that the angle sum is always a straight angle, it does not show them why. In Figure 20.19(a), there are lines parallel to each side of the original triangle. By using facts about supplementary, complementary, vertical, and adjacent angles formed by cutting parallel lines with a transversal, it is straightforward to argue that the sum of the angles will always be a straight line. See Figure 20.19(b) to explore a proof involving exterior angles.

Midsegments of a Triangle. The following activity further illustrates a way to help students move from observation of geometric relationships to making and testing conjectures that explore why relationships hold.

Activity 20.18   CCSS-M: 7.G.A.2; 8.G.A.5

Triangle Midsegments

Using a dynamic geometry program, draw a triangle and label the vertices A, B, and C. Draw the segment joining the midpoints of AB and AC, and label this segment DE, as in Figure 20.20. Measure the lengths of DE and BC. Also measure angles ADE and ABC. Drag points A, B, and C. What conjectures can you make about the relationships between segment DE (the *midsegment* of triangle ABC) and BC (the base of ABC)? Explore the Expanded Lesson for this activity.

The midsegment is half the length of the base and parallel to it, but why is this so? If needed, suggest that students draw a line through A parallel to BC. List all pairs of angles that they know are congruent. Why are they congruent? Note that triangle ABC is similar to triangle ADE. Why is it similar? With hints such as these, many students can begin to make logical arguments for why the things they observe to be true are in fact true.

 Complete Self-Check 20.3: Shapes and Properties

Transformations

Transformations are changes in position or size of a shape and are a major focus of eighth grade in the *Common Core State Standards*. Interestingly, the study of line symmetry (introduced in fourth grade in CCSS) is also included under the study of transformations. Do you know why?

Line Symmetry

If a shape can be folded on a line so that the two halves match exactly, then it is said to have *line symmetry* (sometimes called *reflectional* or *mirror symmetry*). Notice that the fold line is actually a line of *reflection*—the portion of the shape on one side of the line is reflected onto the other side. Again, that is the connection between line symmetry and transformations.

One way to introduce line symmetry to students is to show examples and nonexamples using an all-of-these/none-of-these approach, as in Figure 20.12. Here's another possibility:

Fold a sheet of paper in half and cut out a shape of your choosing on the side with the fold. When you open the paper, what do you notice?

Another approach is to use mirrors. When you place a mirror on a picture or design so that the mirror is perpendicular to the table, you see a shape with symmetry when you look in the mirror. Explore the "Mirror Tool" symmetry activity on the NCTM Illuminations website where students can investigate symmetry with a virtual mirror.

Activity 20.19   CCSS-M: 4.G.A.3

STUDENTS with SPECIAL NEEDS

Pattern Block Mirror Symmetry

Give students a plain sheet of paper with a straight line drawn through the middle. Ask students to use about six to eight pattern blocks to make a design completely on one side of the line that touches the line in some way. Once one side is finished, then students try to make the mirror image of their design on the other side of the line. After the design is complete, have students use a mirror to check their work. They place the mirror on the line and look into it from the side of the original design. With the mirror in place they should see exactly the same image as they see when they raise the mirror. For students with disabilities, make sure the line of reflection is vertical with a left and right side. The task is harder if the line is oriented horizontally or diagonally. You can also challenge students to make designs with more than one line of symmetry.

The same task can be done with tangram pieces or created on a geoboard. If students wish to try the geoboard, first they stretch a band down the center or from corner to corner. Then they make a design on one side of the line and its mirror image on the other. Check with a mirror. This can also be done with dynamic geometry software or on either isometric or rectangular dot grids, as described in the following activity.

Activity 20.20   CCSS-M: 4.G.A.3

Dot Grid Line Symmetry

Give students a piece of either 1-Centimeter Isometric Dot Paper or 1-Centimeter Dot Paper. Students should draw a line through several dots. This line can be horizontal, vertical, or diagonal. Students make a design completely on one side of the drawn line that touches the line, as in the figures shown on the left in Figure 20.21. Have students make the mirror image of their design on the other side of the line or have them exchange their partial design with a peer who must finish it. When finished they can check by placing a mirror on the line and looking into the mirror. They should see exactly the same image as they see when they lift the mirror.

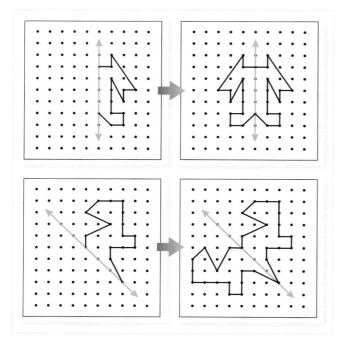

FIGURE 20.21 Exploring symmetry on dot grids.

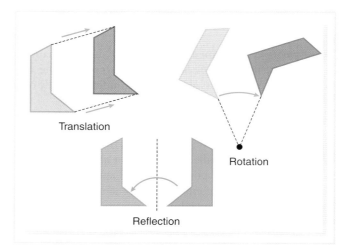

FIGURE 20.22 Translation (slide), reflection (flip), rotation (turn).

FIGURE 20.23 A parallelogram is rotated 180 degrees.

Have students try these two problems:

A shape with one line of symmetry has exactly 6 sides and two 90-degree angles. Can you draw the shape?

A quadrilateral has diagonals that do not form lines of symmetry, but the quadrilateral is symmetrical (one line). Can you draw the quadrilateral?

These exercises combine several key areas of geometry such as line symmetry, properties of shapes, and visualization with reasoning. Try to have students come up with other problems for their classmates to draw.

Rigid Motions

Movements that do not change the size or shape of the object moved are called "rigid motions." *Translations* (or slides), *reflections* (or flips), and *rotations* (or turns) are rigid transformations that result in congruent shapes (Figure 20.22).

Here are the definitions of the rigid motions:

Translation: A translation (slide) requires a *direction* and a *distance*. In a translation, every point on the preimage moves in the same direction for the same distance to form the image. This may be described on a coordinate grid as moving "up 2 and over 3" for each of the points in the figure.

Reflection: A reflection (flip) requires a *line of reflection*. A reflection is a transformation in which an object is flipped across a line of reflection. The line of symmetry can be the *x*-axis, the *y*-axis, or any other line. If a shape is reflected over the *x*-axis, for example, the *x*-values of the preimage are the opposite of the *x*-values of the image, and the *y*-values in both images are the same.

Rotation: A rotation (turn) requires a *center of rotation* (point) and a *degree of rotation* (see Figure 20.23). The point can be any point on the coordinate axis, although in middle school, rotation around the origin is most common. A figure can be rotated up to 360 degrees.

The Motion Man activity described next can also be used to introduce students to the terms *slide, flip,* and *turn.* In the activity, rotations are restricted to $\frac{1}{4}$, $\frac{1}{2}$, and $\frac{3}{4}$ turns in a clockwise direction. The center of the turn will be the center of the figure. Reflections will be flips over vertical or horizontal lines. These restrictions are for simplicity. In the general case, the center of rotation can be anywhere on or off the figure. Lines of reflection can also be anywhere. Beginning work with rigid motions can involve sketches on paper prior to using coordinate axes, as in Activity 20.21.

Activity 20.21   CCSS-M: 8.G.A.1a, b, c

ENGLISH LANGUAGE LEARNERS

Motion Man

Make copies of the first Motion Man Activity Page and then copy the mirror image on the back, as in Figure 20.24. You want the back image to match the front image when held to the light. Give all students a two-sided Motion Man.

Demonstrate each of the rigid motions. A slide is simply that—Motion Man moves over a particular distance (such as 4 inches right and 2 inches down). A reflection requires a line so Motion Man can reflect over a vertical or horizontal line. So, demonstrate a horizontal flip (top goes to bottom) and a vertical flip (left goes to right). The figure rotates clockwise around a center point on the figure, so demonstrate turns by giving a degree measure (such as "rotate Motion Man 90 degrees") and making the clockwise motion. For all students, ELLs in particular, ensure that these demonstrations include explicit practice with the vocabulary and that visuals are posted for reference. Practice by having students start with their Motion Man in the same orientation. As you announce one of the moves, students slide, flip, or turn Motion Man accordingly.

Then display two Motion Men side by side in any orientation. The task is to decide what motion or combination of motions will get the man on the left to match the man on the right. Students use their own man to work out a solution. Test the solutions that students offer. If both men are in the same position, call that a slide.

Composition of Transformations. One transformation can be followed by another. For example, a figure can be reflected over a line, and then that figure can be rotated about a point. A combination of two or more transformations is called a *composition.*

⏸ Pause & Reflect

Begin with the Motion Man in the left position shown in Figure 20.24. Now place a second Motion Man next to the first. How did he get there? Will it take one move or more than one move (transformation) to get from the first to the second Motion Man? Are there any positions that require more than two moves? ●

At first, students who try this same challenge will be confused when they can't get their Motion Man into the new position with one transformation. This causes an excellent problem—but don't be too quick to suggest that it may take two moves. There are often numerous ways to get him to the new position.

Have students experiment with compositions of two or even three transformations using a simple shape on a rectangular dot grid as a step toward using coordinates on the coordinate axis. For example, have students draw an L shape on a dot grid and label it L_1 (Figure 20.25). Reflect it through a line, then rotate the image $\frac{1}{4}$ turn clockwise about a point not on the shape. Call this image L_2, the image of a composition

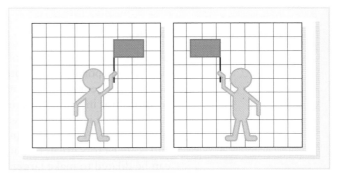

FIGURE 20.24   Motion Man is used to show slides, flips, and turns.

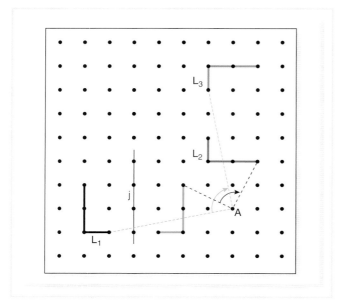

FIGURE 20.25 Shape L_1 was reflected across line j and rotated $\frac{1}{4}$ turn about point A, resulting in L_2. L_1 was also rotated $\frac{1}{4}$ turn about point A, resulting in L_3. How are L_2 and L_3 related? Will this always work?

of a reflection followed by a rotation. Notice that if L_1 is rotated $\frac{1}{4}$ turn clockwise about the same point used before (the result of which we will call L_3), there is a relationship between L_2 and L_3. Continue to explore different combinations of transformations. Don't forget to include translations (slides) in the compositions.

Compositions do not have to involve different types of transformations. For example, a reflection can be followed by another reflection. NCTM's e-Example, "Understanding Congruence, Similarity, and Symmetry" (Applet 6.4) on their website is one of the best applets to support students' understanding of all three rigid motions. In the last two parts, students explore compositions of reflections and then other compositions of up to three transformations.

Congruence

Congruent shapes are defined in terms of transformations. Two shapes are considered congruent if you can apply rigid transformations from one shape to the other. The Common Core State Standards for eighth grade state that students should "understand that a two dimensional figure is congruent to another if the second can be obtained from the first by a sequence of rotations, reflections, and translations; given two congruent figures, describe a sequence that exhibits the congruence between them" (CCSSO, 2010, p. 55).

Having explored foundational experiences like Motion Man and transformations on dot paper, students are ready to explore transformations and compositions of transformations on the coordinate axis. A focus on congruence helps connect these two related ideas, as in Activity 20.22.

Activity 20.22
CCSS-M: 8.G.A.1; 8.G.A.2

Are They Congruent?

Draw various triangles on the coordinate grid, some congruent and some not. Ask students to find a match of two congruent triangles and prove they are congruent by stating the transformations that they applied in order to get one shape to exactly cover the one they selected as a match.

The coordinate axis is addressed in detail in a later section, "Location," in which transformations will continue to be explored.

Similarity

Two figures are *similar* if all of their corresponding angles are congruent and the corresponding sides are proportional. As noted in Chapter 18, proportional reasoning activities are good connections to geometry, such as Activity 18.7, which involves scale drawings and proportional relationships in similar figures.

A *dilation* is a nonrigid (can change size) transformation that produces similar two-dimensional figures. A dilation requires a *scale factor*. Scale factors less than 1 produce smaller figures and scale factors greater than 1 produce larger figures. Figure 20.26 shows how a given figure can be dilated to make larger or smaller figures.

If different groups of students use the same scale factor to dilate the same figure, they will find that the resulting figures are all congruent, even with each group using different dilation points. Dynamic geometry software makes the results of this exercise quite dramatic. The software allows for the scale factors to be set at any value. Once a dilation is made, the dilation point can be dragged around the screen and the size and shape of the image clearly stay unchanged.

Using Transformations and Symmetries

Tessellations are a motivating and artistic application of transformations. A *tessellation* is a tiling of the plane using one or more shapes in a repeating pattern with no gaps or overlaps (see Figure 20.27). Tessellations are based on a circle—if the angle measures add up to 360 degrees, the shapes will fit together at a vertex with no overlaps or gaps. A *regular tessellation* is made of a single polygon (all sides and angles congruent).

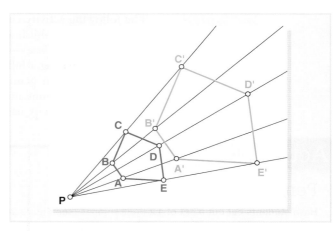

FIGURE 20.26 Begin with figure ABCDE and place point P anywhere. Draw lines from P through each vertex. Place point A' twice as far from P as A is from P (scale factor of 2). Do similarly for the other points. ABCDE is similar to A'B'C'D'E'.

 **Pause & Reflect**

Which regular polygons can be used to form regular tessellations? •

An equilateral triangle has angles of 60 degrees, so six triangles can form a regular tessellation. Likewise, a square can form a regular tessellation and a checkerboard is a simple example of what that looks like. So too can regular hexagons, as seen in a bee hive.

A *semiregular tessellation* is made of two or more different regular polygons. At each vertex of a semiregular tessellation, the same collection of regular polygons comes together in the same order. Students can figure out which polygons are possible at a vertex and design their own semiregular tessellations. Have them use either transformations or combining compatible polygons on 2-Centimeter Grid Paper to create tessellations that are artistic and quite complex (see Figure 20.27). NCTM's Illuminations website also has a tool called "Tessellation Creator" that allows shapes to be combined to make patterns that repeat and cover the plane with no gaps or overlaps.

The Dutch artist M. C. Escher is well known for his tessellations, where the tiles are very intricate and are often shaped like birds, horses, or lizards. Escher took a simple shape such as a triangle, parallelogram, or hexagon and performed transformations on the sides. For example, draw a shape on 1-Centimeter Dot Paper. Then a curve drawn along one side might be translated (slid) to the opposite side. Another idea is to draw a curve from the midpoint of a side to the adjoining vertex. This curve is then rotated about the midpoint to form a totally new side of the tile. These two ideas are illustrated in Figure 20.28. Once a tile has been designed, it can be traced over and over again.

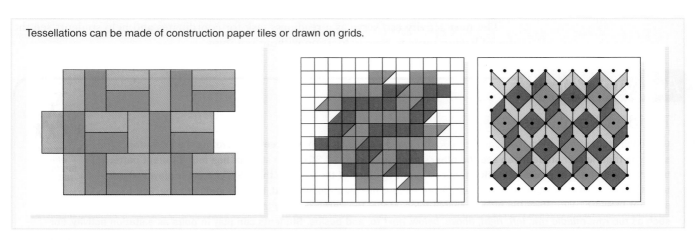

Tessellations can be made of construction paper tiles or drawn on grids.

FIGURE 20.27 Tessellations.

The following activity challenges students to use their understanding of symmetries and transformations to establish an interesting relationship between these two ideas. The shapes used are called *pentominoes*—shapes made from 5 squares, each square touching at least one other square by sharing a full side. A well-known geometry investigation is to have students see how many different pentominoes they can find (see Activity 20.31). For our purposes in discussing transformations and symmetries, the 12 pentominoes serve as a collection of shapes, as in the following activity based on Walter (1970).

Activity 20.23

CCSS-M: 8.G.A.1

Pentomino Positions

Have students cut out a set of **12** Pentominoes (see Figure 20.29). **Mark one side of each piece to help remember whether it has been flipped over. The first part of the task is to determine how many different ways can you position each pentomino piece on** 2-Centimeter Grid Paper. **A position is considered "different" if a reflection or a rotation is required to make them match. Therefore, the cross-shaped piece has only one position. The strip of five squares has two positions (a vertical one and a horizontal one). Some pentomino pieces have as many as eight positions—can you find them?**

 Complete Self-Check 20.4: Transformations

 Location

In pre-K and kindergarten, students learn about everyday positional descriptions—*above*, *below*, *beside*, *in front of*, *behind* and *next to* (CCSSO, 2010). These "place learnings" (Sarama & Clements, 2014) are useful for helping students begin to specify locations. However, helping students refine the way they think and reason about direction, distance, and location enhances spatial understandings. Geometry, measurement, and algebra are all supported by the use of a grid system with numbers or coordinates attached that can specify location. Students at the primary level can begin to think in terms of a grid system to identify location. After early development of terms for how objects are located with respect to other objects (for example, "the ball is under the table"), location activities involve analysis of paths from point to point as on a map, as well as the use of coordinate systems. The first quadrant of the coordinate plane in introduced in grade 5 as students should "Graph points on the coordinate plane to solve real-world and mathematical problems" (CCSSO, 2010, p. 34). Then in grade 6 all quadrants are included, scale drawing and constructions are added in grade 7, and the coordinate axis is used in grade 8 for graphing lines and performing transformations.

The next activity can serve as a readiness task for coordinates and help students see the value of having a way to specify location without pointing.

Activity 20.24

CCSS-M: K.G.A.1; 5.G.A.1

Hidden Positions

STUDENTS
with
SPECIAL
NEEDS

Give each student a Hidden Positions Gameboard. **Two students sit with a "screen" separating their desktop space so that neither student can see the other's grid (see Figure 20.30). Each student has four different pattern blocks. The first player places a block on four different sections of the grid. He then tells the other player where to put blocks on her grid to match his own. When all four pieces are positioned, the two grids are checked to see that they are alike. Then the players switch roles. Model the game once by taking the part of the first student. Use words such as** *top row, middle row, left, right, above, below, next to,* **and** *beside.* **Students can play in pairs as a station activity. For students with disabilities, consider starting with just one shape. then move to two, and so on. For gifted students, extend the grids up to 6 × 6. As the grid size increases, notice how the need for a system of labeling positions increases.**

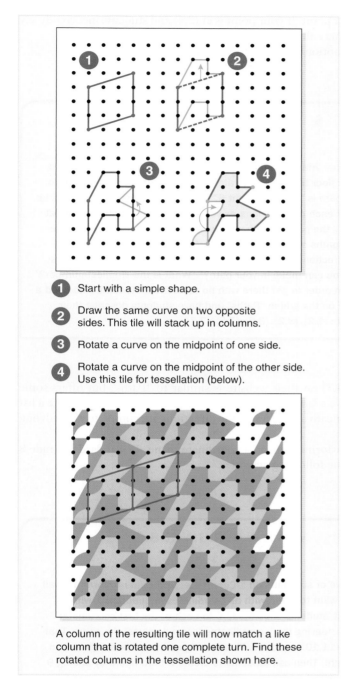

① Start with a simple shape.

② Draw the same curve on two opposite sides. This tile will stack up in columns.

③ Rotate a curve on the midpoint of one side.

④ Rotate a curve on the midpoint of the other side. Use this tile for tessellation (below).

A column of the resulting tile will now match a like column that is rotated one complete turn. Find these rotated columns in the tessellation shown here.

FIGURE 20.28 Creating an Escher-type tessellation.

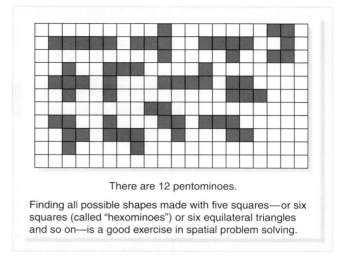

There are 12 pentominoes.

Finding all possible shapes made with five squares—or six squares (called "hexominoes") or six equilateral triangles and so on—is a good exercise in spatial problem solving.

FIGURE 20.29 There are 12 different pentomino shapes.

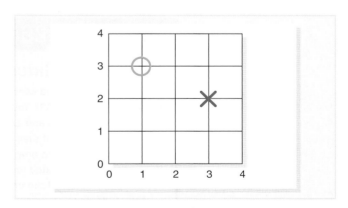

FIGURE 20.30 The "Hidden Positions" game.

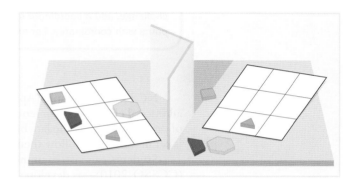

FIGURE 20.31 A simple coordinate grid. The X is at (3,2) and the O is at (1,3). Use the grid to play "Three in a Row" (like Tic-Tac-Toe). Put marks on intersections, not spaces.

As the grid size increases, the need for a system of labeling positions increases. Students can begin to use a simple coordinate system as early as the first grade. Use a Coordinate Grid like the one shown in Figure 20.31 and explain how to use two numbers to designate an intersection point on the grid. The first number tells how far to move to the right. The second number tells how far to move up. Initially use words along with the numbers: 3 right and 0 up. Be sure to include 0 in your introduction. Then select a point on the grid and have students decide what two numbers name that point. If your point is at (2,4) and students incorrectly say "four, two," then simply indicate where the point is that they named.

The next activity explores the notion of different paths on a grid.

Activity 20.25
CCSS-M: K.G.A.1; 5.G.A.1

Paths

On a sheet of 2-Centimeter Grid Paper, mark two different points A and B as shown in Figure 20.32. Using a projection display or floor tiles, demonstrate how to describe a path from A to B. For the points in the figure, one path is "up 5 and right 6." Another path might be "right 2, up 3, right 4, up 2." Count the length of each path. As long as you always move toward the target point (in this case either right or up), the path lengths will always be the same. Here they are 11 units long. Students draw three paths on their papers from A to B using different-colored crayons. For each path they write directions that describe their paths. Ask students, "What is the greatest number of turns that you can make in your path?" "What is the smallest number?" "Where would A and B have to be in order to get there with no turns?" For students who need a challenge, add a coordinate system on the grid in "Paths" and have students describe their paths with coordinates: For example: (1,2), (3,2), (3,5), (7,5), (7,7).

NCTM's e-Example (Applet 4.3) on their website is similar to "Paths" but offers some additional challenges. Students move a ladybug by issuing directions. The task is to make a list of directions to hide the ladybug beneath a leaf. When the directions are complete, the ladybug is set in motion to follow them.

Students can also examine transformations on a coordinate plane—a standard in grade 8 (CCSSO, 2010)—as developed in the following activities.

Activity 20.26
CCSS-M: 6.G.A.3; 8.G.A.1; 8.G.A.3

Coordinate Slides

Ask students to plot and connect five or six points on 1-Centimeter Grid Paper to form a small shape (see Figure 20.33). You may want to begin with all coordinates in quadrant 1 with coordinates between 5 and 12. Next, students should add 6 to each of the first coordinates (called *x*-coordinates) of their shape, leaving the *y*-coordinates (second values) the same. That is, for the point (5,10), a new point (11,10) is plotted. This new figure should be congruent to the original and translated to the right. Then ask students to create a third figure by adding 9 to each *y*-coordinate of the original coordinates.

Ask students to conjecture and test what could be done to the coordinates to move the figure along a diagonal line up and to the right. Figure 20.33 shows a slide created by adding 6 to all of the first coordinates and adding 9 to all of the second coordinates, thus translating the figure without distortion. Challenge students to figure out how to change the coordinates to make the figure slide down and to the left. (Subtract from the coordinates instead of add.)

Ask students, "What does adding (or subtracting) a number from the first coordinates cause? What if the number is added or subtracted from the second coordinates? From both coordinates?" Have students draw lines connecting corresponding points in the original figure with one of those where both coordinates were changed. What do they notice? (The lines are parallel and the same length.)

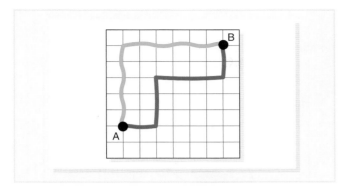

FIGURE 20.32   Different paths from A to B on a grid.

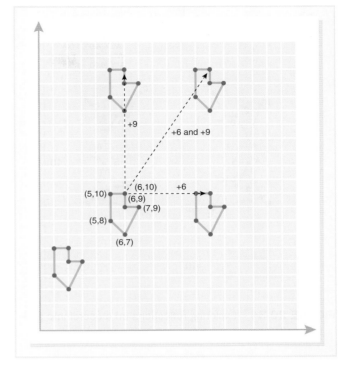

FIGURE 20.33   By adding or subtracting from the coordinates, new shapes are found that are translations (slides) of the original.

In "Coordinate Slides," the figure did not twist, turn, flip over, or change size or shape. The shape "slid" along a path that matched the lines between the corresponding points. Reflections can be explored on a coordinate grid just as successfully as translations. Begin with using the x- or y-axis as the line of reflection, as in the following activity.

Activity 20.27   CCSS-M: 8.G.A.1; 8.G.A.3

Coordinate Reflections

Ask students to draw a five-sided shape in the first quadrant on Coordinate Grid Paper. Label the Figure ABCDE and call it Figure 1 (see Figure 20.34). Use the y-axis as a line of symmetry and draw the reflection of the shape in the second quadrant. Label the reflected points A′B′C′D′E′ and call it Figure 2. Now use the x-axis as the line of reflection and create Figure 3 (in quadrant III) and Figure 4 (in Quadrant IV). Label the points of these figures with double and triple primes A″ and A‴, and so on). Write in the coordinates for each vertex of all four figures.

● How is Figure 3 related to Figure 4? How else could you have gotten Figure 3? How else could you have found Figure 4?
● How are the coordinates of Figure 1 related to its image in the y-axis, Figure 2? What can you say about the coordinates of Figure 4?
● Make a conjecture about the coordinates of a shape reflected in the y-axis and a different conjecture about the coordinates of a shape reflected in the x-axis.
● Draw lines from the vertices of Figure 1 to the corresponding vertices of Figure 2. What can you say about these lines? How is the y-axis related to each of these lines?

In the following activity, multiplying a constant times the coordinates is a transformation that is not a rigid motion.

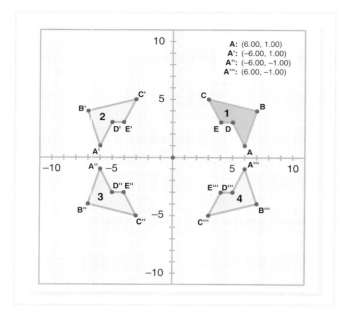

FIGURE 20.34 Exploring reflections on a coordinate grid.

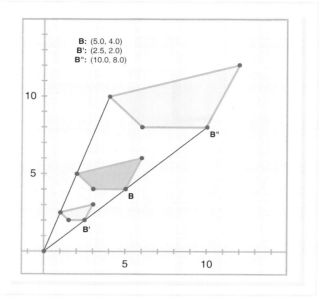

FIGURE 20.35 Dilations of a trapezoid when the scale factor is 2.0 and 0.5.

Activity 20.28   CCSS-M: 7.G.A.1; 8.G.A.1; 8.G.A.3

Coordinate Dilations

Ask students to create a four-sided shape in the first quadrant of a Coordinate Grid. They then make a list of the coordinates, make a new set of coordinates by multiplying each of the original coordinates by 2, and plot the resulting shape. What is the result? Now have students multiply each of the original coordinates by $\frac{1}{2}$ and plot that shape. What is the result? Next, students draw a line from the origin to a vertex of the largest shape on their paper. Repeat for one or two additional vertices and ask for observations. (An example is shown in Figure 20.35.)

⏸ Pause & Reflect

How do the lengths of sides and the areas of the shapes compare when the coordinates are multiplied by 2? What if they are multiplied by 3? By $\frac{1}{2}$? ●

When the coordinates of a shape are multiplied as in the last activity, each by the same factor, the new shape is *similar* to the old shape. This is called a *dilation*, a transformation that is not rigid because the shape changes.

Your students may enjoy exploring dilations a bit further, including the connection to scale drawings. If they start with a drawing of a simple face, boat, or some other shape drawn with straight lines connecting vertices, they will create an interesting effect by multiplying just the first coordinates, just the second coordinates, or using a different factor for each. When only the second coordinate is multiplied, the vertical dimensions alone are dilated, so the figure is proportionately stretched (or shrunk) vertically. Students can explore this process to see how an arithmetic operation can control a figure. Imagine being able to control slides, flips, turns, and dilations, not just in the plane but also for three-dimensional figures. The process is identical to computer animation techniques.

While exploring the transformation activities in the last section, students might be challenged with questions that deepen their understanding of transformations, such as the following:

- How should the coordinates be changed to cause a reflection if the line of reflection is not the *y*-axis but is parallel to it?
- Can you discover a single rule for coordinates that would cause a reflection across one of the axes followed by a rotation of a quarter turn? Is that rule the same for the reverse order—a quarter turn followed by a reflection?
- If two successive slides are made with coordinates and you know what numbers were added or subtracted, what number should be added or subtracted to get the figure there in only one move?
- What do you think will happen if different factors are used for different coordinates in a dilation?

Measuring Distance on the Coordinate Plane

Measuring in the coordinate plane begins in grade 6 with students measuring vertical and horizontal lines and moves in grade 8 to student exploration of distance—eventually leading to the distance formula. The following activity has students use the coordinate grid and the Pythagorean relationship to develop a formula for the distance between points.

Activity 20.29   CCSS-M: 6.G.A.3; 8.G.B.8

Finding Distance Using the Pythagorean Theorem

To start, students should draw a line between two points in the first quadrant (on Coordinate Grid Paper or using dynamic geometry software) that are not on the same horizontal or vertical line. What is the length of this line? Then, ask students to draw a right triangle using the line as the hypotenuse (the vertex at the right angle will share one coordinate with each end point). Students then apply the Pythagorean theorem to find the distance. Ask students to do two to four more examples, asking them to look for patterns across their examples.

   Next, have them look through all of their calculations and see how the coordinates of the two end points were used. Challenge students to use the same type of calculations to get the distance between two new points without drawing any pictures.

Eighth graders do not need to construct proofs independently but should be able to follow the rationale if shown proofs. By using the Pythagorean theorem to find the length of one line (or the distance between the end points), you provide the opportunity for students to make an important connection between two big mathematical ideas.

 Complete Self-Check 20.5: Location

 ## Visualization

Visualization might be called "geometry done with the mind's eye." It involves being able to create mental images of shapes and then turn them around mentally, thinking about how they look from different viewpoints and predicting the results of various transformations. It includes the mental coordination of two and three dimensions—in sixth grade, for example, by determining the net (a two-dimensional drawing) for a three-dimensional shape. Any activity that requires students to think about, manipulate, or transform a shape mentally or to represent a shape as it is seen visually will contribute to the development of students' visualization skills.

Two-Dimensional Imagery

At first students are thinking about shapes in terms of the way they look, so visualization activities will challenge students to think about two-dimensional shapes in different orientations.

Activity 20.30   CCSS-M: K.G.B.4; 1.G.A.2; 2.G.A.1

Can You Remember?

STUDENTS *with* SPECIAL NEEDS

Display one of these simple Sketches of Figures (see Figure 20.36) for about 5 seconds. Then have students attempt to reproduce it on their own. Show the same figure again for a few more seconds and allow students to modify their drawings. Repeat with additional figures.

Have a class discussion where students are asked to describe how they thought about the figure or give examples of attributes of the figure that helped them remember what they saw. As students learn to verbally describe what they see, their visual memory will improve. Another option is to have students with disabilities identify the displayed figure from a set of figures that look alike.

Finding out how many different shapes can be made with a given number of simple tiles demands that students mentally flip and turn shapes in their minds and find ways to decide whether they have found them all. That is the focus of the next activity.

Activity 20.31   CCSS-M: 1.G.A.2; 2.G.A.1

Pentominoes

A pentomino is a shape formed by joining five squares as if cut from a square grid. Each square must have at least one side in common with another. Provide students with five square tiles and a sheet of 1-cm grid paper for recording. Challenge them to see how many different pentomino shapes they can find. Shapes that are flips or turns of other shapes are not considered different. Do not tell students how many pentomino shapes there are. Good discussions will come from deciding whether some shapes are really different and if all shapes have been found.

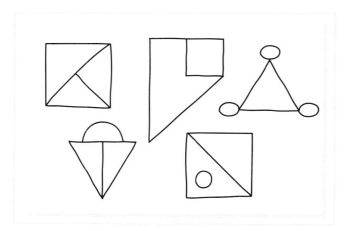

FIGURE 20.36   Examples to use in the "Can You Remember?" activity.

Once students have decided that there are just 12 pentominoes (revisit Figure 20.29), the 12 pieces can then be used in a variety of activities. For example, try to fit all 12 pieces into a 6 × 10 or 5 × 12 rectangle. Another task is to examine each of the 12 pentominoes and decide which will fold up to make an open box. This two-dimensional representation of a three-dimensional object is called a *net*. For those pentominoes that are "box makers," which square is the bottom?

The following are extensions of pentomino activities that are appropriate visualization tasks for students who need a challenge (moving toward level 2):

• How many *hexominoes* are there? A hexomino is made of six squares following the same rule as for pentominoes. Because there are quite a few hexominoes (35), devising a logical scheme for categorizing the shapes is one of the few ways students will know all the hexominoes have been found.

- Instead of putting together five squares, students can find all of the arrangements of five cubes. These shapes are called *pentominoids*. In general, shapes made of cubes in which adjoining cubes share a complete face are called *polyominoids*.

Three-Dimensional Imagery

Another aspect of visualization for young students is to be able to think about three-dimensional shapes in terms of their two-dimensional representations—focusing on faces.

Activity 20.32   CCSS-M: 1.G.A.2; 2.G.A.1; 3.G.A.1; 4.G.A.2

Face Matching

Provide students with Find a Shape Activity Page and sets of Face Matching Cards (see Figure 20.37). There are two versions of the task: Given a Find a Shape card, find the corresponding solid, or given a solid, find the matching Find a Shape card. With a collection of individual face matching cards, students can select the cards that go with a particular solid. For another variation, stack all of the single-face cards for one solid face down. Turn the cards up one at a time as clues to identifying the solid. Use the Face Matching Card Questions Activity Page and collect student responses.

One of the main goals of the visualization strand is to be able to identify and draw two-dimensional images of three-dimensional figures and to build three-dimensional figures from two-dimensional images, which falls in level 1.

Activity 20.33   CCSS-M: 6.G.A.4; 7.G.A.1

Building Views

For this activity, students will need 1-Centimeter Grid Paper for drawing a building plan and 1-inch blocks for constructing a building.

- Version 1: Students begin with a building made of the blocks and draw the left, right, front, and back views (these are called elevations). In Figure 20.38, the building plan shows a top view of the building and the number of blocks in each position. After students build a building from a plan like this, they draw the elevations (views) of the front, right, left, and back as shown in the figure.
- Version 2: Students are given right and front elevations. Ask students to build the corresponding building. To record their solution, they draw a building plan (top elevation with numbers).

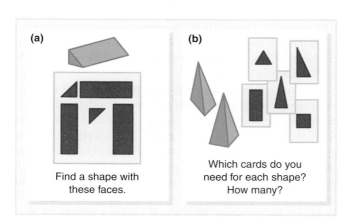

FIGURE 20.37   Matching face cards with solid shapes.

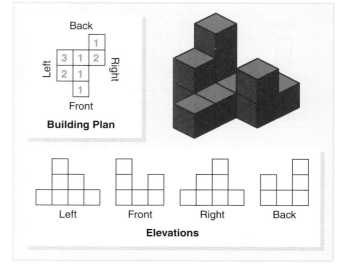

FIGURE 20.38   "Building Views" task.

Notice that front and back elevations are symmetric, as are the left and right elevations. That is why only one of each is given in the second part of the activity. To make "Building Views" significantly more challenging, students can draw 3-D drawings (isometric) of these block buildings or match 3-D drawings with a building use 2-Centimeter Isometric Dot Paper or 1-Centimeter Isometric Dot Paper to create these drawings). Isometric grids allow an *axonometric* drawing where the scale is preserved in all dimensions (height, depth, width). The next activity provides a glimpse at this form of visualization.

Activity 20.34
CCSS-M: 6.G.A.4; 7.G.A.1

Three-Dimensional Drawings

STUDENTS with SPECIAL NEEDS

- Version 1: Students begin with an isometric 3-D drawing of a building created by the teacher on Isometric Grid Paper or Isometric Dot Paper. The assumption is that there are no hidden blocks. From the drawing, the students build the actual building with their blocks. To record the result, they draw a building plan (top view) indicating the number of blocks in each position.
- Version 2: Students are given the four elevation views and a building plan (top view) (see Figure 20.39). They build the building accordingly and draw two or more of the elevation views. There are four possible views: the front left and right and the back left and right. For students who struggle, have them build the building on a sheet of paper with the words "front," "back," "left," and "right" written on the edges to keep them from confusing the different views.

An amazing computer tool for drawing two-dimensional views of block buildings is the Isometric Drawing Tool, available at the NCTM Illuminations website. This applet uses mouse clicks to draw either whole cubes, any single face of a cube, or just lines. The drawings, however, are actually "buildings" and can be viewed as three-dimensional objects. They can be rotated in space so that they can be seen from any vantage point. Prepared investigations lead students through the features of the tool.

Watch this video clip (http://www.youtube.com/watch?v=CtmXu2yt5SE) that shows components of two lessons on imagery in a seventh-grade classroom. One explores the building activities just described and the lessons end with slicing solids which will be our next investigation.

Slicing solids in different ways is an interesting connection between two and three dimensions. This is a standard for grade 7 (CCSSO, 2010). When a solid is sliced into two parts, a two-dimensional figure is formed on the slice faces. Slices from solids made of clay that have been cut with potter's wire can be explored. Figure 20.40 shows a cube being sliced off at the corner, leaving a triangular face. Ask students, "Can you slice the solid you have to create a trapezoid face? A triangle face? A square face?"

Another engaging method is to partially fill a translucent or clear plastic solid (such as Power Solids) with water. The surface of the water simulates a slice and models the face of the solid as if it were cut at that location. By tilting the shape in different ways, every possible "slice" can be observed. Given a particular solid, prior to testing with water, students might use a list of possible triangles and quadrilaterals to predict which can be made and which are impossible. In each case, they should offer a reason for that hypothesis.

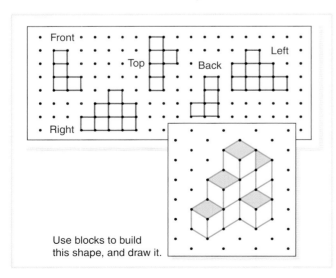

Use blocks to build this shape, and draw it.

FIGURE 20.39 Block "buildings" on isometric grids.

The Platonic Solids

A *polyhedron* is a three-dimensional shape with polygons for all faces. Among the various polyhedra, *Platonic solids* is the name given to the set of completely regular polyhedrons. "Completely regular" means that each face is an identical regular polygon and every vertex has exactly the same number of faces joining at that point. An interesting visualization task appropriate for this level is to find and describe all of the Platonic solids.

Activity 20.35   CCSS-M: 7.G.A.2

Search for the Platonic Solids

Provide students with a supply of paper equilateral triangles, squares, regular pentagons, and regular hexagons or pieces from one of the plastic sets for building solids (such as Polydron or Geofix). Explain what a completely regular solid is. Ask students to find as many different completely regular solids as possible. For students with disabilities, share the following explicit structure to support their search. The smallest number of sides a face can have is three, so begin with triangles, then squares, then pentagons, and so on. Furthermore, because every vertex must have the same number of faces, try three faces at a point, then four, and so on. They will find that it is impossible to have only two faces at a point.

STUDENTS with SPECIAL NEEDS

Students will find they can have three, four, or five triangles coming to a point. For each, they can begin with a "tent" of triangles and then add more triangles so that each vertex has the same number. With three at a point, you get a four-sided solid called a *tetrahedron* (*tetra* is Greek for "four"). With four at each point, you get an eight-sided solid called an *octahedron* (*octa* = eight). It is really exciting to build the solid with five triangles at each point. It will have 20 sides and is called an *icosahedron* (*icosa* = twenty).

In a similar manner, students will find that there is only one solid made of squares—three at each point and six in all—a *hexahedron* (*hex* = six), also called a *cube*. And there is only one solid with pentagons—three at each point, and 12 in all. This is called a *dodecahedron* (*dodeca* = twelve). At that point they have identified the five Platonic solids. A fantastic (and sturdy) skeletal version of each can be built out of the newspaper rods described earlier (see Figure 20.15).

✓ **Complete Self-Check 20.6: Visualization**

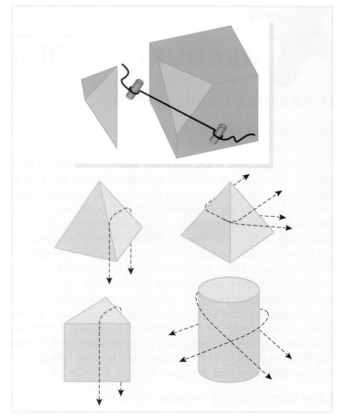

FIGURE 20.40   Predict the shape of the slice face, then cut the clay model with potter's wire.

REFLECTIONS ON CHAPTER 20

WRITING TO LEARN

1. Describe in your own words the first three van Hiele levels of geometric thought (levels 0, 1, and 2), including the object of thought and product of thought. How would activities aimed at levels 0, 1, and 2 differ?

2. Briefly describe the nature of the content in each of the four geometric strands discussed in this chapter: shapes and properties, transformations, location, and visualization.

3. What can you do when the students in your classroom are at different van Hiele levels of thought?

4. Find one of the suggested applets or explore GeoGebra and explain how it can be used. What are the advantages of using the computer instead of hands-on materials or drawings?

5. How can you use van Hiele's theory to assess your students' geometric growth or spatial sense?

FOR DISCUSSION AND EXPLORATION

◆ Examine the teacher's edition of a textbook and select a geometry lesson. How might the lesson be adapted for students who may be at several different van Hiele levels?

RESOURCES FOR CHAPTER 20

LITERATURE CONNECTIONS

The Greedy Triangle *Burns (1995)* (https://www.youtube.com/watch?v=kPuI4XyyZUE)

This delightful book is the story of a triangle that is very busy being a sail or a roof or fitting into the crook of the arm of someone standing with hand on hip. Soon he becomes bored and travels to the local shape-shifter with a request for one more side and one more angle. Now a quadrilateral, there are new things to try as he fits into different four-sided figures in the environment. There are several other shape-shifts with interesting results. Using a meter-long loop of yarn for every pair of students (or three ace bandages tied in a loop for a demonstration), have students follow and discuss events in the book by creating appropriate shapes with the loop (holding it in the air between their hands). First they can explore different triangles, and eventually they can investigate properties as they shift from one shape to the next. They can also move to level 2 thinking—by providing proof that they have a square, for example.

I Spy Shapes in Art *Micklethwait (2007)*

Museum Shapes *Metropolitan Museum of Art (2005)*

Using artwork from such masters as Matisse and Warhol, you can challenge students to look for particular shapes in paintings through an "I spy" approach. This activity can be extended to postcards of artwork from local museums or act as a catalyst for budding "mathematical" artists in the classroom.

Color Farm *Ehlert (1990)*

Color Zoo *Ehlert (1989)*

These visually motivating books engage students in thinking about shapes. Using cutout overlays of circles, rectangles, triangles, and other familiar shapes, images of either farm or zoo animals are created. The reader turns the page to remove a shape, transforming the image into a new animal. Because these books reinforce shapes, animals, and colors, they can engage English language learners and their families.

Cubes, Cones, Cylinders and Spheres *Hoban (2000)*

Shapes, Shapes, Shapes *Hoban (1996)*

So Many Circles, So Many Squares *Hoban (1998)*

These wordless books contain dramatic photographs of geometric shapes in the environment. Using digital cameras to create Hoban-like books invites students to seek and identify two- and three-dimensional shapes in the world around them. Send the books home for students to share with families or have students in upper grades make books for younger students.

RECOMMENDED READINGS

Articles

Edwards, M. T., & Harper, S. R. (2010). Paint bucket polygons. *Teaching Children Mathematics, 16*(7), 420–428.

To advance students' understanding of polygons, examples and nonexamples are used to help refine definitions. Using the "paint bucket" feature found in many graphics programs or Microsoft Word's "fill color" feature, students are able to define attributes of polygons.

Koester, B. A. (2003). Prisms and pyramids: Constructing three-dimensional models to build understanding. *Teaching Children Mathematics, 9*(8), 436–442.

Explorations with third to fifth graders include using straws and pipe cleaners to build models. The activities involve classification and definitions of shapes and seeking patterns in the number of faces, vertices, and edges.

Renne, C. G. (2004). Is a rectangle a square? Developing mathematical vocabulary and conceptual understanding. *Teaching Children Mathematics, 10*(5), 258–263.

Examples in this article provide clear descriptions of the difficulty that students at level 1 have in attempting to make logical conclusions about geometric properties and relationships.

Developing Concepts of Data Analysis

LEARNER OUTCOMES

After reading this chapter and engaging in the embedded activities and reflections, you should be able to:

21.1 Explain differences between statistics and mathematics, including what is meant by "doing statistics."

21.2 Compare questions to determine which ones are statistical questions.

21.3 Describe techniques for collecting data, including sampling, as well as quality sources for finding data.

21.4 Show how to use manipulatives to teach young children to classify data.

21.5 Contrast different graphical displays, including which are developmentally appropriate for students in K–8 and what each display can and cannot illustrate.

21.6 Illustrate and explain the meaning of measures of center and measures of variability.

21.7 Compose questions that help students focus on interpreting data.

Graphs and statistics bombard the public in areas such as advertising, opinion polls, population trends, health risks, and progress of children in schools. We hear that the average amount of rainfall this summer is more than it was last summer or that the average American family consists of 3.19 people. In April 2014 the median price of a home was $275,800, and the mean was $320,100. Knowing these statistics should raise an array of questions: How were these data gathered? What was the purpose? Why are the median and the mean for home sales so different and which one makes more sense?

Statistical literacy is critical to understanding the world around us, essential for effective citizenship, and vital for developing the ability to question information presented in the media (Shaughnessy, 2007). Misuse of statistics occurs even in trustworthy sources like newspapers, where graphs are often designed to exaggerate a finding. Students in pre-K through grade 8 should have meaningful experiences with basic concepts of statistics throughout their school years. The first Mathematical Practice, for example, states, "Mathematically proficient students can explain correspondences between equations, verbal descriptions, tables, and graphs or draw diagrams of important features and relationships, graph data, and search for regularity or trends" (CCSSO, 2010, p. 6). The following are the big ideas that help students become statistically literate.

BIG IDEAS

- ◆ Statistics is its own field different from mathematics; one key difference is focus on variability of data in statistical reasoning.
- ◆ Doing statistics involves a four-step process: formulating questions, collecting data, analyzing data, and interpreting results.
- ◆ Data are gathered and organized in order to answer questions about the populations from which the data come. With data from only a sample of the population, inferences are made about the population.
- ◆ Different types of graphs and other data representations provide different information about the data and, hence, the population from which the data were taken. The choice of graphical representation can affect how well the data are understood.
- ◆ Measures that describe data with numbers are called *statistics*. The use of a particular graph or statistic can mediate what the data tell about the population.
- ◆ Both graphs and statistics can provide a sense of the shape of the data, including how spread out or how clustered they are. Having a sense of the shape of data is having a big picture of the data rather than a collection of numbers.

What Does It Mean to Do Statistics?

Doing statistics is, in fact, a different process from doing mathematics—a notion that has recently received much attention in standards documents and research (Burrill & Elliott, 2006; Franklin et al., 2005; Shaughnessy, 2003). As Richard Scheaffer, past president of the American Statistics Association, notes,

> Mathematics is about numbers and their operations, generalizations and abstractions; it is about spatial configurations and their measurement, transformations, and abstractions. . . . Statistics is also about numbers—but numbers in context: these are called data. Statistics is about variables and cases, distribution and variation, purposeful design or studies, and the role of randomness in the design of studies, and the interpretation of results. (2006, pp. 310–311)

Statistical literacy is needed by all students to help interpret the world. This section describes some of the big ideas and essential knowledge regarding statistics and explains a general process for doing statistics. Each of the four steps in the process is used as a major section in the organization of this chapter.

The CCSS-M includes data across the grades. At the pre-K–grade 1 level (CCSSO, 2010), students can begin this understanding by learning how data can be categorized and displayed in various graphical forms. In grades 2–5, students should collect and organize sets of data as well as represent data in frequency tables, bar graphs (scaled with one-to-many), line (dot) plots (including fractional units), and picture graphs (CCSSO, 2010). As they enter middle school, students are introduced to new data representations such as histograms, box plots, scatter plots, and stem-and-leaf plots. Students should also study measures of center—for example, median and mean and measures of variability.

Is It Statistics or Is It Mathematics?

Statistics and mathematics are two different fields; however, statistical questions are often asked in assessments with questions that are mathematical in nature rather than statistical. The harm in this is that students are not focusing on statistical reasoning, as shown by the following excellent exemplars from Scheaffer (2006).

Read the following questions and label each as "doing mathematics" or "doing statistics."

1. The average weight of 50 prize-winning tomatoes is 2.36 pounds. What is the combined weight, in pounds, of these 50 tomatoes? (NAEP sample question)

   a. 0.0472
   b. 11.8
   c. 52.36
   d. 59
   e. 118

2. Joe had three test scores of 78, 76, and 74, whereas Mary had scores of 72, 82, and 74. How did Joe's average (mean) compare to Mary's average (mean) score? (TIMSS eighth-grade released item)

   a. Joe's was one point higher.
   b. Joe's was one point lower.
   c. Both averages were the same.
   d. Joe's was 2 points higher.
   e. Joe's was 2 points lower.

3. Table 21.1 gives the times each girl has recorded for seven trials of the 100-meter dash this year. Only one girl may compete in the upcoming track meet. Which girl would you select for the meet and why?

TABLE 21.1 RACE TIMES FOR THREE RUNNERS

Runner	1	2	3	4	5	6	7
Suzie	15.2	14.8	15.0	14.7	14.3	14.5	14.5
Tanisha	15.8	15.7	15.4	15.0	14.8	14.6	14.5
Dara	15.6	15.5	14.8	15.1	14.5	14.7	14.5

Which of these involves statistical reasoning? All of them? None of them? As explained by Schaeffer, only the last is statistical in nature. The first requires knowing the formula for averages, but the task required is to work backwards through a formula—mathematical thinking, not statistical thinking. Similarly, in the second problem, one must know the formula for the mean, but the question is about the computational process of using the formula. In both of these, you might notice that the context is irrelevant to the problem. The final question is statistical in nature because the situation requires analysis—graphs or averages might be used to determine a solution. The mathematics here is basic; the focus is on statistics. Notice the context is central to responding to the question, which is an indication that it is statistical reasoning.

In statistics, the context is essential to analyzing and interpreting the data (Franklin & Garfield, 2006; Franklin et al., 2005; Langrall, Nisbet, Mooney, & Jansem, 2011; Scheaffer, 2006). Looking at the spread, or shape, of data and considering the meaning of unusual data points (outliers) are determined based on the context.

The Shape of Data

A big conceptual idea in data analysis can be referred to as the *shape of data:* a sense of how data are spread out or grouped, what characteristics about the data set as a whole can be described, and what the data tell us in a global way about the population from which they are taken. Graphs, such as dot plots, can illustrate the distributions of data (Kader & Jacobbe, 2013). Figure 21.1 shows four different dot plots (line plots that use dots instead of Xs), each showing a different shape to the data.

Different graphing techniques or types of graphs can provide a different snapshot of the data as a whole. For example, bar graphs and circle graphs (percentage graphs) each show how the data cluster in different categories. The circle graph focuses more on the relative values of this

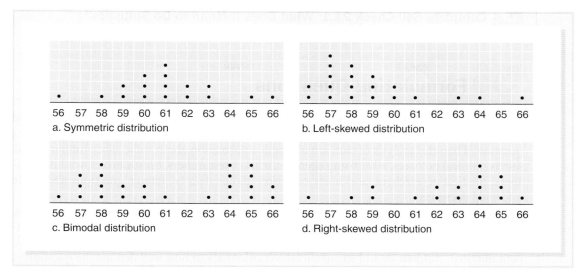

FIGURE 21.1   Dot plots showing different distributions (shape) of data.

clustering, whereas the bar graph adds a dimension of quantity. The choice of which and how many categories to use in these graphs will result in different pictures of the shape of the data.

Part of understanding the shape of data is being aware of how spread out or clustered the data are. In the early grades, this can be discussed informally by looking at almost any graph. For numeric data, there are statistics that tell us how data are spread or dispersed. The simplest of these is the range. Averages (the mean and the median) tell us where the "center" of the data is. In high school, students will learn about the standard deviation statistic, which is also a measure of spread. At the middle school level, a simple graphical technique called the *box plot* is designed to give us visual information about the spread of data.

The Process of Doing Statistics

Just as learning addition involves much more than the procedure for combining, doing statistics is much more than being able to create a graph or a computational procedure for finding the mean. To engage students *meaningfully* in learning and doing statistics, they should be involved in the full process, from asking and defining questions to interpreting results. This broad approach provides a framework and purpose under which students learn how to create graphs, compute the mean, and analyze data in other ways. This chapter is organized around this process, which is presented in Figure 21.2.

I. Formulate Questions
- Clarify the problem at hand
- Formulate one (or more) questions that can be answered with data

II. Collect Data
- Design a plan to collect appropriate data
- Employ the plan to collect the data

III. Analyze Data
- Select appropriate graphical and numerical methods
- Use these methods to analyze the data

IV. Interpret Results
- Interpret the analysis
- Relate the interpretation to the original question

FIGURE 21.2   Process of doing statistics.

Source: Franklin, C., Kader, G., Mewborn, D., Moreno, J., Peck, R., Perry, M., & Scheaffer, R. (2005, August) *Guidelines for Assessment and Instruction in Statistics Education (GAISE) Report: A Pre-K–12 Curriculum Framework*, p. 11.

Complete Self-Check 21.1: What Does It Mean to Do Statistics?

 Formulating Questions

Statistics is about more than making graphs and analyzing data. It includes both asking and answering questions about our world. Data collection should be for a purpose, to answer a question. Then the analysis of data actually adds information about some aspect of our world, just as political pollsters, advertising agencies, market researchers, census takers, wildlife managers, medical researchers, and hosts of others gather data to answer questions and make informed decisions.

Students, even young students, should have opportunities to generate their own questions, decide on appropriate data to help answer these questions, and determine methods of collecting the data (CCSSO, 2010; NCTM, 2006). Whether the question is teacher initiated or student initiated, children should engage in conversations about how well defined the question is. For example, if the teacher asks, "How many brothers and sisters do you have?" there may be a need to discuss half siblings. If students want to know how many shoes each classmate owns, questions may arise as to whether they should count bedroom slippers and flip-flops.

When students formulate the questions, the data they gather become more meaningful. How they organize the data and the techniques for analyzing them have a purpose. Often questions will come naturally in the course of discussion or from questions arising in other content areas. The next two sections suggest many ideas.

CCSS **Standards for Mathematical Practice**

MP1. Make sense of problems and persevere in solving them.

Classroom Questions

Students want to learn about themselves (what does the "typical" student look like or have an interest in?), their families and pets, measures such as arm span or time to get to school, their likes and dislikes, and so on. The easiest questions are those that can be answered by each class member contributing one piece of data. Here are a few ideas:

- *Favorites:* TV shows, games, movies, ice cream, video games, sports teams, music (when there are lots of possibilities, start by restricting the number of choices)
- *Numbers:* Number of pets or siblings, hours watching TV or hours of sleep, bedtime, time spent on the computer
- *Measures:* Height, arm span, area of foot, long-jump distance, shadow length, seconds to run around the track, minutes spent traveling to school

Beyond One Classroom

The questions in the previous section are designed for students to contribute data about themselves. These questions can be expanded by asking, "How would this compare to another class?" Comparison questions are a good way to help students focus on the data they have collected and the variability within that data (Russell, 2006). As students get older, they can begin to think about various populations and differences between them. For example, how are fifth graders similar to or different from middle school students? Students might examine questions where they compare responses of boys versus girls, adults or teachers versus students, or categories of full-time workers compared to college students. These situations involve issues of sampling and making generalizations and comparisons. In addition, students can ask questions about things beyond the classroom. Discussions about communities provide a good way to integrate social studies and mathematics.

The newspaper suggests all sorts of data-related questions. For example, how many full-page ads occur on different days of the week? What types of stories are on the front page? Which comics are really for kids and which are not?

Activity 21.1

CCSS-M: 2.MD.D.10; 3.MD.B.3; 6.SP.A.1; 7.SP.B.3

Who Is in Our Village?

The picture book *If the World Were a Village: A Book about the World's People* (2nd ed.) (Smith, 2011) provides an excellent opportunity to compare class data or school data to the wider population in the world. It explores global wealth, culture, language, and other influences, providing the statistics in the adapted case of the world being a village of 100 people. Read the book or several of the comparisons to the class. Ask students if they think our class (or school) will represent the data in the book for particular topics. Gather and compare class data to world data. Then ask students what else they think might be interesting data about our world that could be added to the pages of this book. (See Riskowski, Olbricht, & Wilson, 2010, for details on a project exploring concepts of statistics using 100 students.)

Science is about inquiry and therefore statistics is an excellent time for interdisciplinary planning. For example, consider this short list of ideas:

- How many plastic bottles or aluminum cans are placed in the school's recycling bins over a given week?
- How many days does it take for different types of bean, squash, and pea seeds to germinate when kept in moist paper towels?
- Which brand of bubble gum will give you the largest bubble?
- Do some liquids expand more than others when frozen?
- Does a plant grow faster when watered with water, soda, or milk?

Observations on a zoo field trip can be preceded with the development of questions that are used to gather data on the trip (Mokros & Wright, 2009).

As noted earlier, a distinguishing feature of statistics is that the context is front and center. Therefore it is particularly important that the context be culturally meaningful. Culturally meaningful contexts create a supportive classroom environment (McGlone, 2008). This can be as simple as asking about favorite family meal or game, or can include an exploration of family customs. The key to having such questions lead to a supportive classroom environment is sharing the results in a way that helps others in the class appreciate the unique lives of their classmates.

Activity 21.2

CCSS-M: 1.MD.C.4; 2.MD.D.10; 6.SP.A.1; 6.SP.B.4; 6.SP.B.5

What Can We Learn about Our Community?

This activity plays out over several days. First, ask students to turn in a note card with three statistical questions they would like to investigate during the year. This could be assigned as homework, with students' families helping to brainstorm ideas. Collect these ideas. When you have time to start the investigation, take one question from the set. As a class, refine the question to one that can be answered using statistics. Examples of questions include:

- How many different kinds of restaurants or stores are in our community (fast food restaurants versus "sit down" restaurants; Italian, Mexican, or American; convenience stores, grocery stores, clothing stores, variety stores)?
- How many responses are made by local firefighters each month? How many different types of responses are made by local firefighters each month (fire, medical, hazardous, public service)? (Data can usually be found on websites of local institutions.)
- How many state and local government officials do voters elect?

Discuss ways to gather the data. Set up a plan and deadline for gathering the data. When students bring in the data, encourage students to select and use data displays (e.g., circle graph/pie chart, line plot, etc.). Invite students to share. Return to the question and ask, "What does our data tell us about _____?" Consider how the different data displays communicate the answer to this question. See Expanded Lesson: Using Data to Answer a Question for a full lesson of this activity.

Students will need help in designing questions that can be answered using statistics. These are questions that include variability and for which data can be gathered. Providing examples and nonexamples can help students, in particular students with disabilities, focus on the elements of an appropriate statistical question. For example, in the questions below, some can be answered by statistics and some are not appropriate.

1. How much change do I have in my pocket?
2. What is the typical amount of loose change a person carries in their pocket?
3. What cereal is most healthy?
4. What reasons do people use in selecting gum (e.g., taste, cost, bubble-making quality, long lasting, good breath)?
5. How long do different kinds of gum keep their flavor?
6. Which store has the best prices?
7. Where will you buy shampoo?

 Pause & Reflect

Which of the previous questions are statistical and which ones are not statistical in nature?

Questions 1, 3, and 7 are *not* statistical in nature. Question 3 could be adapted to a statistical question with a more specific focus on what is meant by healthy. Similarly, question 7 is very broad and will need to be focused in order to collect the data needed to answer it. Facilitating discussions with students about examples and nonexamples as well as questions they develop improves their ability to generate appropriate statistical questions.

 Complete Self-Check 21.2: Formulating Questions

 Data Collection

How to collect good data is an important (and sometimes skipped) part of the discussion as students learn statistics. Students may start by just hand raising or counting events, then move to using a ballot with limited and then unlimited response options (Hudson, Shupe, Vasquez, & Miller, 2008). In addition to surveys, data can be collected through observations. For example, set up a bird feeder outside the classroom window and collect data at different times during the day to count the number or type of birds. Students can also conduct observational data collection events on field trips (Mokros & Wright, 2009) and in evening or weekend activities with their families.

Collecting Data

Gathering data is not easy for students, especially young students. In a first-grade class, a teacher asked students to gather data on "Are you 6?" Upon receiving the prompt, 18 eager students began asking others in the class if they were 6 and tallying the yes and no responses. The problem? They had no idea whom they had asked more than once and whom they had not asked at all. This provided an excellent entry into a discussion about how statisticians must gather data. Carolyn Cook, a kindergarten teacher, asked her students to help think of an organized manner to gather the data from their classmates on favorite ice cream flavors. These students decided a class list (see Figure 21.3) would allow them to keep track (Cook, 2008).

There are two types of data that can be collected—categorical and numerical. Categorical data is (as the name implies) data grouped by labels (categories) such as favorite vacations, colors of cars in the school parking lot, and the most popular suggestion for a mascot for the middle school team. Numerical data, on the other hand, counts things or measures on a continuous scale. Numerical data are ordered numerically, like a number line, and can include fractions and decimals. This kind of data includes how many miles to school, the temperature in your town over a one-week period, or the weight of the students' backpacks. Students need to explicitly explore the idea that statistical measures such as mean or median involve using numerical data (Leavy, Friel, & Mamer, 2009).

Sampling. When asking a question about a small population, like your class, data can be gathered on everyone. But statistics generally does not involve gathering data from the whole population and instead uses a representative sample. CCSS-M identifies learning about sample populations in order to make inferences as a critical area for seventh graders (CCSSO, 2010).

Sampling must take into consideration variability. For example, a poll on favorite TV shows will produce different answers from a survey of seventh graders than a group of teachers or third graders. It may also vary for girls and for boys or culturally. Answers also may vary based on the day the question is asked or whether a particular show has been recently discussed. To help students determine if they have identified a representative sample, ask, "What is the population for your question?" or "Who or what is the subject of your question?"

Then ask students to consider how they will gather data that will include representatives across that population. For example, if they are hoping to learn the movie choice for a seventh-grade movie night at your school, they need to poll girls and boys across the seventh-grade teams within the middle school. Provide opportunities for students to justify if the data is representative and to critique the explanation of others as they describe what is a representative sample.

Even when it may appear that a sample is representative, it may not be. Unintentional biases can occur, and we cannot always know what subsets might exist within a population. Therefore, *random sampling* is used in statistics. It increases the validity of the results, and therefore gives more confidence in being able to make inferences. Seventh graders who begin informal work with random sampling start to consider the importance of representative samples for drawing inferences (CCSSO, 2010). Activity 21.3 can help students develop an awareness of the importance of sampling.

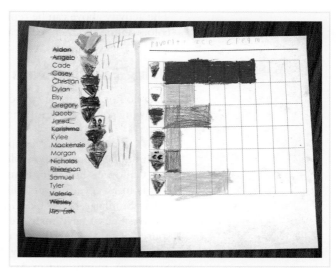

FIGURE 21.3 Kindergartners collect data on favorite ice cream flavors, tally the data, and create a horizontal bar graph.

Source: Cook, C. D. (2008). "I Scream, You Scream: Data Analysis with Kindergartners." *Teaching Children Mathematics, 14*(9), p. 539. Reprinted with permission. Copyright © 2008 by the National Council of Teachers of Mathematics. All rights reserved.

CCSS Standards for Mathematical Practice
MP3. Construct viable arguments and critique the reasoning of others.

Activity 21.3

CCSS-M: 6.SP.A.1; 6.SP.A.2; 7.SP.A.1; 7.SP.B.3

How Do We Compare?

Using *Book of Lists: Fun Facts, Weird Trivia, and Amazing Lists on Nearly Everything You Need to Know!* by James Buckley and Robert Stremme, or a similar book or online resource, find a list that includes sampling a group of people. Use the How Do We Compare? Activity Page. Read the question to the students and gather data using the class as the sample. Ask students, "Do you think our class will be a representative sample of the population targeted in this question?" Ask students to offer why the class might be or might not be a representative sample. Gather data from the class. Compare the two data sets. If appropriate, create a circle graph/pie chart, line/dot plot, or stem-and-leaf plot to compare the two data sets. After displaying the two sets, ask students what technique they think the authors might have used to sample the population.

Although this activity involved people, "population" in statistics is used broadly to mean "group or subject of study." So the population could be a species of a plant, an insect, or a type of car.

The activity above can be replicated with other data. For example, you can look up favorite car colors online and then see if cars that drive by the school form a representative sample of all cars.

Using Existing Data Sources

Data do not have to be collected by survey; existing data abound in various places, such as the following sources of print and Web data.

Print Resources. Newspapers, almanacs, sports record books, maps, and various government publications are possible sources of data that may be used to answer student questions.

Children's literature is another excellent and engaging resource. Young students can tally words in a repeating verse like "Hickory, Dickory, Dock" (Niezgoda & Moyer-Packenham, 2005). Similarly, books like *Goodnight Moon* (by Margaret Wise Brown) or *Green Eggs and Ham* (by Dr. Seuss) have many repeated words or phrases. Nonfiction literature can be another source of data, especially for older students. For example, *Book of Lists: Fun Facts, Weird Trivia, and Amazing Lists on Nearly Everything You Need to Know!* (by James Buckley and Robert Stremme), mentioned in Activity 21.3, reports on various statistics and includes surveys at the end of every section. Books on sports, such as *A Negro League Scrapbook* (by Carole Boston Weatherform), can have very interesting statistics about historic periods that students can explore and compare.

Web Resources. The Internet provides seemingly limitless data that are often accessed by simply typing the related question into a search. Students may be interested in facts about another country as a result of a social studies unit or a country in the news. Olympic records in various events over the years or data related to environmental issues are other examples of topics around which student questions may be formulated. For these and hundreds of other questions, data can be found on the Internet. Below are several websites with a lot of interesting data.

- The **USDA Economic Research Service Food Consumption** site offers wonderful data sets on the availability and consumption of hundreds of foods. Annual per capita estimates often go back to 1909.
- **Google Public Data Explorer** makes large data sets available to explore, visualize, and interpret.
- **Better World Flux** provides data related to the progress of countries and the world over the years, highlighting interesting trends and patterns.
- **NCTM Illuminations State Data Map** is a source that displays state data on population, land area, political representation, gasoline use, and so on.
- **The Central Intelligence Agency (CIA) World Fact Book** provides demographic information for every nation in the world: population, age distributions, death and birth rates, and information on the economy, government, transportation, and geography.
- **U.S. Census Bureau** has copious statistical information by state, county, or voting district.

 Complete Self-Check 21.3: Data Collection

 Data Analysis: Classification

Classification involves making decisions about how to categorize things, a basic activity that is fundamental to data analysis. In order to formulate questions and decide how to represent data that have been gathered, decisions must be made about how things might be categorized. Young students might group farm animals, for example, by number of legs; by type of product they provide; by those that work, provide food, or are pets; by size or color; by the type of food they eat; and so on. Each of these groupings is based on a different attribute of the animals.

CCSS-M places classification by attributes as a kindergarten topic. Attribute activities are explicitly designed to develop flexible reasoning about the characteristics of data.

Attribute Materials

Attribute materials can be any set of objects that lend themselves to being sorted and classified in different ways—for example, seashells, leaves, the students themselves, or the students' shoes. The *attributes* are the ways that the materials can be sorted. For example, hair color, height, and gender are attributes of students. Each attribute has a number of different *values:* for example, blond, brown, black, or red (for the attribute of hair color); tall or short (for height); male or female (for gender).

Commercially available attribute blocks come in sets of 60, with each piece having four attributes: color (red, yellow, blue), shape (circle, triangle, rectangle, square, hexagon), size (big, little), and thickness (thick, thin). The specific values, number of values, or number of attributes that a set may have is not important. At least initially, attribute activities are best done by sitting in a large circle on the floor where all students can see and have access to the materials to be sorted. Digital versions of attribute blocks can be found by visiting the National Library of Virtual Manipulatives or Glencoe's Virtual Manipulatives website.

Activity 21.4
CCSS-M: K.MD.3; 1.MD.C.4

What about "Both"

Give students two large loops of string and attribute blocks. Direct them to put all the red pieces inside one string and all triangles inside the other. Let the students try to resolve the difficulty of what to do with the red triangles. When the notion of overlapping the strings to create an area common to both loops is clear, more challenging activities can be explored. Students with disabilities will need to use labels on each loop of string.

Instead of attribute blocks, or in addition to attribute blocks, use Woozle Cards (see Figure 21.4). To make, copy the Woozle Cards Activity Page on white cardstock. Color all the Woozles on one page the same color, then another page in another color, etc., to have color as an attribute for sorting Woozles. Select two attributes (e.g., shape and number of dots) and follow the same steps described for the attribute blocks.

STUDENTS with SPECIAL NEEDS

As shown in Figure 21.5, the labels need not be restricted to single attributes. If a piece does not fit in any region, it is placed outside all of the loops.

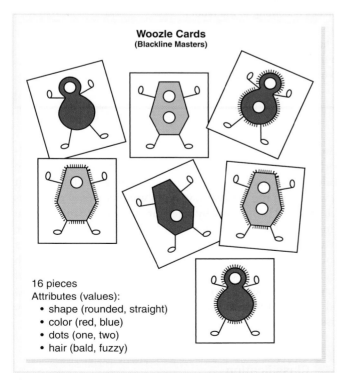

FIGURE 21.4   Sample set of Woozle Cards and list of attributes.

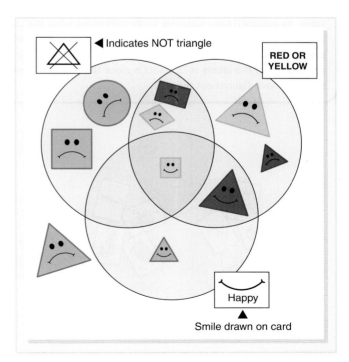

FIGURE 21.5   A Venn diagram activity with attribute pieces. A rule is written on a card for each Venn diagram circle.

As students progress, it is important to introduce labels for negative attributes such as "not red" or "not small." Also important is the eventual use of *and* and *or* connectives, as in two-value rules such as "red and square" or "big or happy." This use of *and*, *or*, and *not* significantly widens students' classification schemes.

An engaging and challenging activity is to infer how things have been classified when the loops are not labeled. The following activities require students to make and test conjectures about how things are being classified.

Activity 21.5

CCSS-M: K.MD.3; 1.MD.C.4

Guess My Rule

For this activity, try using students instead of shapes as attribute "pieces." Decide on an attribute such as "wearing blue jeans" or "stripes on clothing," but do not tell your rule to the class. Silently look at one student at a time, and move the student to the left or right according to this secret rule. After a number of students have been sorted, have the next student come up and ask students to predict which group he or she belongs in. Before the rule is articulated, continue the activity for a while so that others in the class will have an opportunity to determine the rule. This same activity can be done with virtually any materials that can be sorted, such as students' shoes, shells, or buttons. Encourage ELLs to use their native language and English to describe the rule.

ENGLISH LANGUAGE LEARNERS

Activity 21.6

CCSS-M: K.MD.3; 1.MD.C.4

Hidden Labels

Use attribute blocks or Woozle Cards, as illustrated in Figure 21.4. Select label cards for the loops of string used to make Venn diagrams. Place the cards facedown. Ask students to select a piece for you to place. For ELLs and students with disabilities, provide a list of the labels with pictures and/or translations for each as a reference. Begin to sort pieces according to the hidden rules. As you sort, have students try to determine what the labels are for each of the loops. Let students who think they have guessed the labels try to place a piece in the proper loop, but avoid having them guess the labels aloud. Students who think they know the labels can be asked to "play teacher" and respond to the guesses of the others. Point out that one way to test an idea about the labels is to select a piece that you think might go in a particular section. Wait to turn the cards up until most students have figured out the rule.

ENGLISH LANGUAGE LEARNERS

STUDENTS *with* **SPECIAL NEEDS**

FIGURE 21.6 Can you guess the rule that was used to sort these bugs?

"Hidden Labels" can and should be repeated with real-world materials connected to other content areas and to students' experiences. For example, if you were doing a unit on wildlife in the backyard, you can use pictures of creatures (see Figure 21.6) to sort by relevant attributes. Students can bring in things they can recycle and these objects can be sorted by type (English, 2013). The class can "graph" data about themselves by first placing information in loops with labels. A graph of "Our Pets" might consist of a picture of each student's pet or favorite stuffed animal (in lieu of a pet) and be affixed to a wall display showing how the pets were classified.

 Complete Self-Check 21.4: Data Analysis: Classification

Data Analysis: Graphical Representations

Graphs summarize the data that were collected. In the CCSS-M (2010), representing and interpreting data begins in grade 1 and is included at each grade thereafter, with increasingly complex representations and analysis expected. How data are organized should be directly related to the question that caused you to collect the data in the first place. For example, suppose students want to know how many pockets they have on their clothing (Russell & Economopoulos, 2008). Data collection involves each student counting his or her pockets. Or, middle school students may wonder how many songs their friends listen to in one day. The question might be, "How many songs do students in our class listen to in one day?" For data collection, you might decide to have students keep track on a school day (Tuesday, for example) and come to class on Wednesday with their own totals. Each student records the number on a Post-it and places the Post-it on the board.

 Pause & Reflect

If your second-grade class had collected pocket data or your sixth-grade class had collected song data, what methods might you suggest they use for organizing and graphing them? Which methods are better? ●

In second grade a picture or bar graph can be made with one bar per student. However, is it the best way to showcase the data in order to analyze it? If the data were instead categorized by number of pockets, then a graph showing the number of students with two pockets, three pockets, and so on will illustrate which number of pockets is most common and how the number of pockets varies across the class.

In sixth grade, a *dot plot* (also called a *line plot*) could be used to illustrate the spread and shape of the data. Or a histogram can be created to capture how many students fall within a range of songs listened to (e.g., between 0 and 10, 11 and 20, etc.). Or a box plot can be created, boxing in the middle 50 percent to focus attention on the center of the data as well as the range. Each of these displays gives a different snapshot of the data and provides different insights into the question posed.

Creating Graphs

Students should be involved in deciding how they want to represent their data, but they will need to be introduced to what the options are and when each display can and cannot be used.

The value of having students actually construct their own graphs is not so much that they learn the techniques, but that they are personally invested in the data and that they learn how a graph conveys information. Once a graph is constructed, the most important activity is discussing what it tells the people who see it. Analyzing data that are numerical (number of pockets) versus categorical (color of socks) is an added challenge for students as they struggle to make sense of the graphs (Russell, 2006). If, for example, the graph has seven stickers above the five, students may think that five people have seven pockets or seven people have five pockets.

Creating graphs requires care and precision, including determining appropriate scales and labels. But the reason for the precision is so that an audience is able to see at a glance the summary of the data gathered on a particular question.

 Standards for Mathematical Practice
MP6. Attend to precision.

 TECHNOLOGY Note. Computer programs and graphing calculators can provide a variety of graphical displays. Use the time saved by technology to focus on the discussions about the information that each display provides! Students can make their own selections from among different graphs and justify their choice based on their own intended purposes. The graphing calculator puts data analysis technology in the hands of every student. The TI-73 calculator is designed for middle-grade students. It will produce eight different kinds of plots or graphs, including pie charts, bar graphs, and picture graphs, and will compute and graph lines of best fit. The Internet also offers opportunities to explore different graphs. Create a Graph (NCES Kids

Standards for Mathematical Practice
MP5. Use appropriate tools strategically.

Zone) provides tools for creating five different graphical displays. Illuminations Data Grapher and Advanced Data Grapher allow students to enter data, select which set(s) to display, and choose the type of representation (e.g., bar graph, pie charts, line graph, etc.). ■

Analyzing Graphs

Once a graph has been constructed, engage the class in a discussion of what information the graph tells or conveys—the analysis. Questioning and assessment should focus on how effectively the graph communicates the findings of the data gathered. For example, ask, "What can you tell about our class by looking at this graph of the number of songs listened to in one day?" Graphs convey factual information (e.g., there is a wide variability in the number of songs sixth graders listen to in one day) and also provide opportunities to make inferences that are not directly observable in the graph (e.g., most sixth graders listen to between 20 and 30 songs a day).

Discussions about graphs the students have created help them analyze and interpret other graphs and charts that they see in newspapers and on TV. For example, you can select graphs from newspapers or websites and ask students "What can you learn from this graph?" "What do you not know that you wish you knew?" These questions help students focus on what different graphs can and cannot illustrate.

The difference between *actual facts* and the *inferences that go beyond the data* is an important idea in data analysis. Students can examine graphs found in newspapers or magazines and discuss the facts in the graphs and the message that may have been intended by the person who made the graph. Students' conceptual ability to analyze data and draw conclusions and interpretations is often weak (Tarr & Shaughnessy, 2007); discussing and analyzing data is a way to support this higher-level thinking skill.

Bar Graphs

Bar graphs include object graphs (real objects used in the graph), picture graphs (also called pictographs), and regular bar graphs and are appropriate for categorical and numerical data.

Object Graphs. An object graph uses the actual objects being graphed. Examples include types of shoes, favorite apple, energy bar wrappers, and books. Each item can be placed in a square or on a floor tile so that comparisons and counts are easily made. Notice that an object graph is a small step from sorting. If real objects are sorted into groups, those groups can be lined up for comparison—an object graph! Visit the companion website for a video that illustrates how preschoolers are able to create object graphs (and transition to picture graphs).

Picture Graphs. Picture graphs (also called pictographs) move up a level of abstraction by using a drawing or picture of some sort that represents what is being graphed. The picture can represent one piece of data or it can represent a designated quantity. For example, a picture of a book can be assigned to mean five books in a graph of how many books were read each day. When students view the graph and see four books for Monday, they skip count to determine that twenty books were read on Monday.

Children can make their own drawings, but this can often become time consuming and tedious. There are various ways to make the creation of picture graphs easier to create, and thereby keep the focus on the meaning of the graph rather than the creation of it. For, example you can use stickers, objects cut out with a die-cut, or clip art (copied repeatedly on a page that can then be cut out).

Bar Graphs. After object and picture graphs, bar graphs are among the first ways used to group and present data with children in pre-K–2. To help transition from object and picture graphs to bar graphs, have children use something to represent the pieces of data or the things being counted. An easy idea is to use sticky notes to represent the individual pieces of data. These can be stuck directly to the board or to a chart and rearranged if needed.

Figure 21.7 illustrates a few techniques that can be used to make a graph quickly with the whole class.

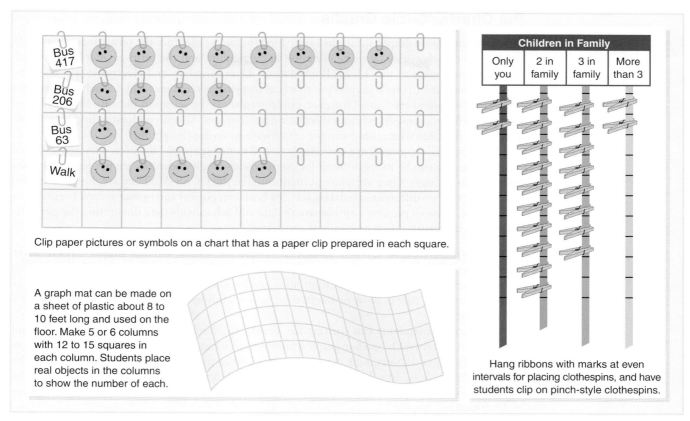

Clip paper pictures or symbols on a chart that has a paper clip prepared in each square.

A graph mat can be made on a sheet of plastic about 8 to 10 feet long and used on the floor. Make 5 or 6 columns with 12 to 15 squares in each column. Students place real objects in the columns to show the number of each.

Hang ribbons with marks at even intervals for placing clothespins, and have students clip on pinch-style clothespins.

FIGURE 21.7 Some ideas for quick graphs that can be used again and again.

Activity 21.7

CCSS-M: 2.MD.D.4; 3.MD.B.3

Picture Graphs to Bar Graphs

Determine a question that lends itself to pre-set categories and is of interest to students (e.g., favorite sport). Ask students draw a picture of the ball that goes with the sport on a Post-it note, place their Post-it in a "row" on the white board (or wall) so that there is a little space between the post-its. Invite students to make observations about their picture graph. Discuss with students how they might make a bar graph to illustrate their data. Move the post-its so there is no space between them and they look like a bar. Discuss ways to know how long the bar is and add a scale next to the bars to show the height of each bar. This activity can be done with a scaled situation, too. For example, they might decide to use one picture of a baseball to represent 3 students. In the bar graph, the scale will skip count by 3s. Be sure students record their scale (e.g., 1 ball = 3 students).

Once a graph has been constructed, engage the class in a discussion of what information the graph tells or conveys. Students' conceptual ability to analyze data and draw conclusions and interpretations is often weak (Tarr & Shaughnessy, 2007). Ask questions such as, "What can you tell about our class by looking at this shoe graph?" Graphs convey factual information (more students wear sneakers than any other kind of shoe) and also provide opportunities to make inferences that are not directly observable in the graph (kids in this class do not like to wear leather shoes). Students can examine graphs found in newspapers or magazines and discuss the facts in the graphs and the message that may have been intended by the person who made the graph.

Pie Charts/Circle Graphs

Pie charts and circle graphs mean the same thing (in fact, sometimes the term *pie graph* is used); the term *circle graph* may be more common in curriculum and the term *pie chart* is used with graphing tools such as the TI-73, Illuminations Data Grapher, and electronic spreadsheets. Typically, we think of circle graphs/pie charts as showing percentages and, as such, they are not accessible for young students. However, circle graphs can be set up to indicate the number of data points from a total set, without calculating percentages. Also, an understanding of percentages is not required when using computer software to create the graph.

Pie charts/circle graphs are commonly found in newspapers. However, they are less used in statistics, as it can be more difficult for comparisons (angle measures are harder to compare than lengths of bars). They are also not mentioned in the CCSS-M. They are, however, useful for comparing two different-sized data sets, for both categorical and numeric data. Figure 21.8, for example, shows a pie chart for classroom data and schoolwide data illustrating the percentages of students with different numbers of siblings.

Easily Constructed Circle Graphs. There are several fun and simple ways to make a pie chart. For example, students can first form lines for their response to, "What is your favorite after school activity?" and then lines can be joined end-to-end to make a circle. See Expanded Lesson: Bar Graphs to Circle Graphs for a full lesson on this idea and Figure 21.9 for an illustration.

Alternatively, students can convert bar graphs to pie charts by cutting out the bars and taping them together. Once a bar graph is complete, cut out the bars themselves and tape them together end to end. Next, tape the two ends together to form a circle. Estimate where the center of the circle is, draw lines to the points where different bars meet, and trace around the full loop. You can estimate percentages using the rational number wheel or percent necklace as described in Chapter 17.

Determining Percentages. The concrete circle-making helps make sense of the mathematics of a circle graph. The numbers in each category are added to form the total or whole. The percent of one section is computed by dividing each of parts by the whole (and multiplying by 100). It is an interesting proportional problem for students to convert between percents and degrees because one is out of 100 and the other out of 360. It is helpful to start with

CCSS **Standards for Mathematical Practice**
MP2. Reason abstractly and quantitatively.

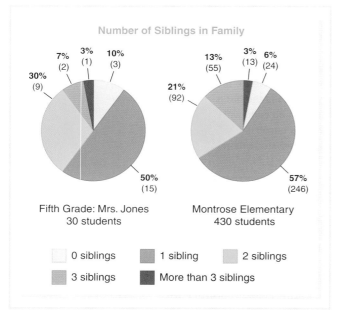

FIGURE 21.8 Pie charts show ratios of part to whole and can be used to compare ratios.

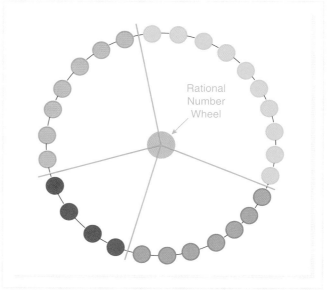

FIGURE 21.9 A human circle graph: Students are arranged in a circle, with string stretched from the center to show the pie pieces.

common values like 50 percent, 25 percent, and 10 percent before moving to more difficult values. A table with one row for percent and one row for degrees can serve as an important tool to help students reason.

FORMATIVE ASSESSMENT Notes. Students should write in a journal about their graphs, explaining what the graph tells and why they selected that type of graph to illustrate the data. As you evaluate students' responses, it is important not to focus undue attention on the skills of constructing a graph, but instead to focus on whether they chose an appropriate representation and have provided a good rationale for its selection that connects back to their question (step 1). ■

Continuous Data Graphs

Bar graphs or picture graphs are useful for illustrating categories of data that have no numeric ordering—for example, favorite colors or TV shows. On the other hand, when data are grouped along a continuous scale, they should be ordered along a number line. Examples of such information include temperatures that occur over time, height or weight over age, and percentages of test takers' scoring in different intervals along the scale of possible scores.

Stem-and-Leaf Plots. Stem-and-leaf plots (sometimes called *stem plots*) are a form of bar graph in which numeric data are graphed and displayed as a list. By way of example, consider the National League baseball teams total wins for the 2013 season:

East Division Teams	Number of Wins	Central Division Teams	Number of Wins	West Division Teams	Number of Wins
Atlanta Braves	96	St. Louis Cardinals	97	Los Angeles Dodgers	92
Washington Nationals	86	Pittsburgh Pirates	94	Arizona Diamondbacks	81
New York Mets	74	Cincinnati Reds	90	San Diego Padres	76
Philadelphia Phillies	73	Milwaukee Brewers	74	San Francisco Giants	76
Miami Marlins	62	Chicago Cubs	66	Colorado Rockies	74

If the data are to be grouped by tens, list the tens digits to form the stem, as shown in Figure 21.10(a). Next, write the ones digits next to the appropriate tens digit, as shown in Figure 21.10(b), ordered from smallest to largest, forming the "leaves." The result shows the shape of data, indicating where the data clusters and where the outliers are. Furthermore, every piece of data can be retrieved from the graph.

Stem-and-leaf plots are not limited to two-digit data. For example, if the data ranged from 600 to 1300, the stem could be the numerals from 6 to 13 and the leaves made of two-digit numbers separated by commas.

Figure 21.11 shows how to illustrate two sets of data with the leaves extending in opposite directions from the same stem. In this example, notice that the data are grouped by fives instead of tens.

Notice that stem-and-leaf plots show the shape of the data. You can observe how the data spread and how they cluster, and students can describe the shape numerically using range, median, mean, mode, and outliers.

Line Plots and Dot Plots. Line and dot plots are counts of things along a numeric scale on a number line. Both terms are used in the CCSS-M standards, with line plots introduced in grade 2 using whole-number units and progressing to displaying data in fractions of a unit in grade 5. In middle school the term *dot*

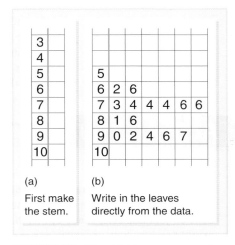

FIGURE 21.10 Making a stem-and-leaf plot.

Test Scores

			Mrs. Day						Mrs. Knight					
				4	**5**									
					•	9								
			2	3	**6**									
		7	7	8	**•**	5								
3	0	4	2	4	**7**	1	0							
		7	9	5	**•**	8	6	9	9					
	3	4	1	**8**	4	0	1	3	1	2				
	5	8	7	**•**	9	5								
				9	3	1	0							
		9	6	**•**	7									
		0	0	**10**	0									

FIGURE 21.11 Stem-and-leaf plot can be used to compare two sets of data.

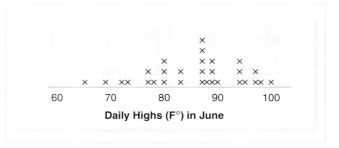

FIGURE 21.12 Line plot of temperatures in June.

plot replaces *line plot*, but the only difference is that line plots use Xs to represent each data point and dot plots use dots (CCSSO, 2010). To make a line or dot plot, a number line is drawn and an X or dot is made above the corresponding value on the line for every corresponding data element. One advantage of a line or dot plot is that every piece of data is shown on the graph. They can therefore be a good first step to then creating a box plot or histogram, which are more difficult graphical representations because they do not illustrate each data point (Groth & Bargagliotti, 2012). An example of a line plot is shown in Figure 21.12.

To introduce line plots in a concrete manner, connect to picture graphs, but use a numeric scale rather than a categorical scale. That is the focus in Activity 21.8.

Activity 21.8

CCSS-M: 1.MD.C.4; 2.MD.D.10; 3.MD.B.4

ENGLISH LANGUAGE LEARNERS

Stand by Me

Use masking tape to create a bar graph or line plot on the floor of the classroom or gymnasium. Label it with numbers ranging from 0 minutes to 20 minutes (or whatever is appropriate for your children). Have students write on a sticky note how many minutes it takes them to travel to school. By groups, ask students to stand on the location above that number on the line. Encourage peers to confirm they are standing in the correct place. Then, ask students to leave their Post-it where they were standing and sit down. Recreate the line plot on the interactive whiteboard and have students create one on their own paper. Ask students questions about their data (e.g., how many more or less are in one category). In summary, ask students to write one observation. ELLs will benefit from sentence starters like, "I notice that _____ students walk _____ ."

Having children be "in the graph" is an important experience and will enable them to better understand the more abstract graphical representation.

Line and dot plots can and should represent rational numbers, and measurement is an appropriate context for incorporating fractions. Students might measure and plot, for example, their foot length, their cubit (length of forearm from elbow to finger tips), height of the stack of books they happen to have brought to class, and so on. Data can also be gathered from plants growing, time passing, or weather, as in the next activity.

Activity 21.9

CCSS-M: 3.MD.B.4; 4.MD.B.4; 5.MD.B.2; 6.SP.B.4; 7.SP.B.3

Storm Plotter

Create a class line plot (grades 2 and 5) or dot plot (middle school) and chart the amount of rain (or snow) that falls with each storm (install a rain gauge or access the information online). Place the data from each storm on the line/dot plot. This can be done all year and color-coded by month. As more data is gathered, you can ask, "What do we notice about rain fall in our area?" Focus on both variability and center. If you don't want to take months gathering data, instead look up the rain/snow fall in various cities/towns after a storm has passed through and use that to create a storm plot. Seventh graders can explore and compare two different locations.

Line and dot plots work well for comparisons. For example, if data is gathered from two different groups, separate dot plots can be created, providing a great visual to see the difference in the shape of the data.

Histograms. Though line and dot plots are widely used for small data sets, in many real data sets, there is a large amount of data and many different numbers. A dot plot would be too tedious to create and not illustrate the spread of data as effectively. In this case, a histogram is an excellent choice as data are grouped in appropriate intervals. A histogram is a form of bar graph in which the categories are consecutive equal intervals along a numeric scale. The number of data elements falling into that particular interval determines the height or length of each bar. Histograms differ from the other types of bar graphs, which are used for categorical data, and for which the order of the bars doesn't matter. (Metz, 2010).

Histograms are not difficult in concept but can be challenging to construct: What is the appropriate interval to use for the bar width? What is a good scale to use for the length of the bars? The need for all of the data to be grouped and counted within each interval causes further difficulty. Figure 21.13 shows a histogram for the same temperature data used in Figure 21.12. Notice how similar the two displays are in illustrating the spread and clustering of data. Histograms can be created with graphing calculators, computer software, or the NCTM Illuminations Advanced Data Grapher.

Box Plots. Box plots (also known as *box and whisker plots*) are a method for visually displaying not only the center (median) but also the range and spread of data. Sixth graders should be able to create and analyze box plots (CCSSO, 2010). In Figure 21.14, the ages in months for 27 sixth-grade students are given, along with stem-and-leaf plots for the full class and the boys and girls separately. The stem-and-leaf is a good way to prepare for creating a box plot. To find the two quartiles, find the medians of the upper and lower halves of the data. Mark the two extremes, the quartiles, and the median. Then create the box plot on a number line. Box plots for the same data are shown in Figure 21.15.

Each box plot has these three features:

1. A box that contains the "middle half" of the data, one-fourth to the left and right of the median. The ends of the box are at the *lower quartile*, the median of the lower half of the data, and the *upper quartile*, the median of the upper half of the data.
2. A line inside the box at the median of the data.
3. A line (sometimes known as the *whisker*) extending from the end of each box to the *lower extreme* and *upper extreme* of the data. Each line, therefore, covers the upper and lower fourths of the data.

Look at the information these box plots provide at a glance! The box and the lengths of the lines provide a quick indication of how the data are spread out or bunched together. Because the median is shown, this spreading or bunching can be determined for each quarter of the data. The entire class in this example is much more spread out in the upper half than the lower half. The girls are much more closely grouped in age than either the boys or the class as a whole. The range of the data (the difference between upper and lower extremes) is represented by the length of the plot, and the extreme values can be read directly. The mean is indicated by the small

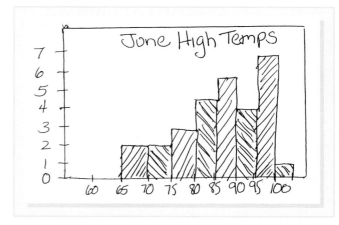

FIGURE 21.13 Histogram of June high temperatures.

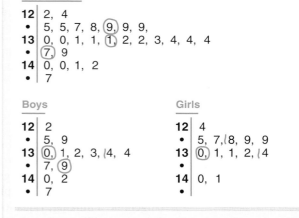

The following numbers represent the ages in months of a class of sixth-grade students.

Boys		Girls	
132	122	140	131
140	130	129	128
133	134	141	131
142	125	134	132
134 Joe B.	147	124	130
137	131	129 Whitney	127
139	129	125 Whitney	

All students

```
12 | 2, 4
 • | 5, 5, 7, 8, (9), 9, 9,
13 | 0, 0, 1, 1, (1) 2, 2, 3, 4, 4, 4
 • | (7), 9
14 | 0, 0, 1, 2
 • | 7
```

Boys   **Girls**

```
12 | 2                 12 | 4
 • | 5, 9               • | 5, 7,|8, 9, 9
13 | (0), 1, 2, 3, |4, 4    13 | (0), 1, 1, 2, |4
 • | 7, (9)             • |
14 | 0, 2              14 | 0, 1
 • | 7                  • |
```

FIGURE 21.14 Stem-and-leaf plots of for sixth graders' ages in months. Medians and quartiles are circled or marked by a vertical bar if they fall between two elements.

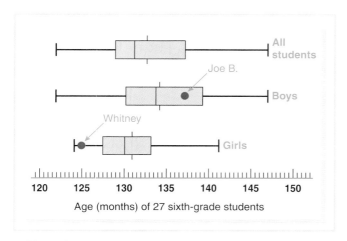

FIGURE 21.15 Box plots for the sixth graders' ages in months data. In addition to showing how data are distributed, data points of particular interest can be shown.

marks above and below each box. A box plot provides useful visual information to help understand the shape of a data set. Therefore, it is a great choice for looking at data from different disciplines. For example, consider creating a box plot for the age of each president at inauguration (Patterson & Patterson, 2014). This can teach interesting history lessons and the value of using a box plot to analyze data.

To make a box plot, put the data in order. Next, find the median. This can be done on stem-and-leaf plots. To find the two quartiles, ignore the median itself, and find the medians of the upper and lower halves of the data. Mark the two extremes, the two quartiles, and the median above an appropriate number line. Draw the box and the lines. See also Illuminations Advanced Data Grapher to create box plots.

Because box plots have so much information and proportional thinking, students may be challenged to interpret box plots (Bakker, Biehler, & Konold, 2004). Support in making these connections can be done by using contexts that are meaningful and asking questions about the various statistics that are shown on the plot. Understanding the proportional relationships can be supported through use of percent strips or ratio tables. (See Chapter 18 for more on models to support proportional thinking.)

Remember that a box plot, like any graph, is a tool for learning about the question posed, not an end in itself (McClain, Leckman, Schmitt, & Regis, 2006). Because a box plot offers so much information on the spread and center of the data, much can be learned from careful examination, and particularly from comparing two box plots with related data.

Graphing calculators and several computer programs draw box plots, making this process even more accessible. The TI-73, TI-84, and TI-Nspire calculators can draw box plots for up to three sets of data on the same axis.

 Pause & Reflect

Notice that in Figure 21.15 the box for the boys is actually a bit longer than the box for the whole class. How can that be when there are clearly more students in the full class than there are boys? How would you explain this apparent discrepancy to a class of seventh graders? •

Bivariate Graphs

In eighth grade, the focus of statistics is to analyze *bivariate data* (CCSSO, 2010). The phrase *bivariate data* may be new to eighth-grade curriculum, but the concept is not. Stated simply, *bivariate* means that two things are varying together (e.g., number of people attending, the number of hot dogs sold). Concepts and activities related to covariation are addressed in Chapter 14 (Algebraic Thinking, Equations, and Functions) and in Chapter 18 (Ratios, Proportions, and Proportional Reasoning). In statistics, the focus of bivariate data is on the distribution and related patterns in the covariation. Graphs and tables are effective in displaying these distributions so that patterns or trends are more observable (Kader & Jacobbe, 2013).

Line Graphs. A coordinate axis allows for the plotting of bivariate data. When that data is continuous, a line connects the data points and illustrates the trend in the data. For example, a line graph might be used to show how the length of a flagpole shadow changed from one hour to the next during the day. The horizontal scale would be time, and the vertical scale would be the length of the shadow. Data can be gathered at specific points in time (e.g., every 15 minutes), and these points can be plotted. A straight line can be drawn to connect these points because time is continuous and data points do exist between the plotted points. See the example in Figure 21.16 for a line graph on temperature change.

Scatter Plots. Scatter plots are an emphasis in grade 8 (CCSSO, 2010). Bivariate data can be plotted on a scatter plot, a graph of points on a coordinate grid with each axis representing one of the two variables. Each pair of numbers from the two sets of data, when plotted, produces a visual image of the data as well as a hint concerning any possible relationships.

For example, you might gather data from 25 eighth-grade boys on their height in inches, weight in pounds, and number of letters in their last name and ask, "Is there a relationship between their height and weight?" and "Is there a relationship between name length and weight?" The two graphs in Figure 21.17 show (a) a scatter plot of height to weight, and (b) a scatter plot of name length to weight.

The scatter plots indicate that there is a relationship in the boys' weights and heights, though there is some variation. But there is no relationship between name length and weight. Encourage students to plot many data sets and look for relationships in the scatter plots, including data sets that suggest linear relationships and those that indicate no apparent relationship between the variables. Activity 21.10 provides engaging ways to explore the relationship between bivariate data.

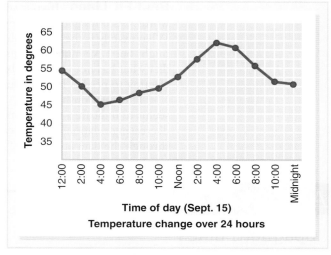

FIGURE 21.16   Line graph of one day's temperatures.

Activity 21.10   CCSS-M: 8.SP.A.1

ENGLISH
LANGUAGE
LEARNERS

Is There a Relationship?

Prepare cards with different questions on them about bivariate situations. For example, is there a relationship between:

- Distance a toy car rolls and its weight?
- Distance a toy car rolls and height of ramp?
- Distance a toy car rolls and how high it starts on the ramp?
- Foot length and height?
- Shoulder width and height?
- Nose length and hand span?
- Months of age and height?
- Head circumference and wrist circumference?
- Minutes watching TV and minutes doing homework?

Distribute cards to groups of four students and a coordinate axis (see Blackline Master 22). Ask students to (1) predict if they think there is a relationship and (2) determine how they will gather data. Have students gather data and create a scatter plot on paper that they will display to the class. ELLs may be more familiar with metric measures and will benefit from seeing what is being measured through gestures or demonstration. Each group reports on their findings and explains whether they think there is a relationship or not. Other groups listen and determine whether they agree that there is a relationship, and what that relationship is. As an extended experience, have students generate their own questions where they wonder, "Is there a relationship between x and y?"

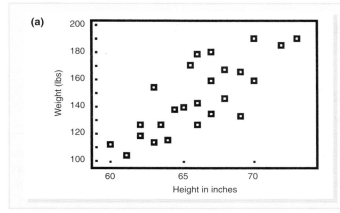

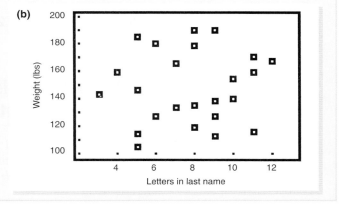

FIGURE 21.17   Scatter plots show potential relationships or lack of relationships.

Best-Fit Lines. If your scatter plot indicates a relationship, it can be simply described in words. "As boys get taller, they get heavier." This may be correct but is not particularly useful. What exactly is the relationship? If I knew the height of a boy, could I predict what his weight might be? Like much of statistical analysis, the value of a statistic is to create a model to predict what has not yet been observed. (For example, we poll a small sample of voters before an election to predict how the full population will vote.)

The relationship in this case is a ratio between the two measures. If the scatter plot seems to indicate a steadily increasing relationship (as in the height–weight graph) or steadily decreasing relationship, you can find the ratio between the variables by drawing a straight line through the data points that "best" represent the pattern or shape of all of the dots.

Activity 21.11

CCSS-M: 8.SP.A.1; 8.SP.A.2

Spaghetti Lines

Engage students in gathering bivariate data (see list in Activity 21.10). For example, ask students to measure foot length and height, and record the data in a class table. Give students a copy of a Coordinate Axis (Quadrant I) (see Blackline Master 22). Ask students to plot the coordinates on their own graph, then place a piece of uncooked spaghetti until they feel it is the "best fit" for the data and tape it down. Then, ask students to write an equation to represent their line. Invite students to compare and discuss the different equations. For example, ask students to use their equation or line to tell how big Big Foot might be (e.g., if his foot is 25 inches long).

What determines best fit? From a strictly visual standpoint, the line you select defines the observed relationship and could be used to predict other values not in the data set. The more closely the dots in the scatter plot cluster around the line you select, the greater the confidence you would have in the predictive value of the line. Certainly you could try to draw a straight line somewhere in the name length–weight graph, but you would not have much confidence in its predictive capability because the dots would be quite dispersed from the line.

Encourage students to use a "mathematical" reason for why a line might be best. Because a good line is one around which most dots cluster, a good-fitting line is one where the distances from all of the dots to the line are minimal. This general notion of least distance to the line for all points is the basis for an algorithm that will always produce a unique line for a given set of points, which is introduced in high school.

 TECHNOLOGY Note. Graphing calculators can be directed to locate the best-fit line. These techniques are programmed into graphing calculators. Students can enter their data into the table feature, plot it on the graph, and then find the line of best fit. If students have already drawn a line by hand, then the calculator provides a good opportunity to compare equations to see whether they are both reasonable. ■

✔ **Complete Self-Check 21.5: Data Analysis: Graphical Representations**

 ## Data Analysis: Measures of Center and Variability

Although graphs provide visual images of data, measures of center and variability of the data are also important ways to summarize, analyze, and describe the data. Measures of center include *mean*, *median*, and *mode* and measures of variability include *range* and *mean absolute*

deviation. This is a critical area in grade 6 of the CCSS-M, and a review of the CCSS-M summary reveals that the emphasis of mean, median, and mode is *not* on how to find each (or which one is which), but on selecting the appropriate measure based on the context and the population. Students can get an idea of the importance of these statistics by exploring the ideas informally.

Measures of Center

The term *average* is heard quite frequently in everyday usage. Sometimes it refers to an exact arithmetic average, as in "the average daily rainfall." Sometimes it is used quite loosely, as in "She is about average height." In either situation, an average is a single number or measure that is describes a set of numbers. Students' understanding of average may be any of the following: average as mode (what is there most of?), average as something reasonable, average as the standard algorithm for finding mean, and average as mathematical equilibrium (Garcia & Garret, 2006).

Mode. The mode is the most frequently occurring value in the data set. The mode is the least frequently used as a measure of center because data sets may not have a mode, may have more than one mode, or the mode may not be descriptive of the data set.

Median. The median is the middle value in an ordered set of data. Half of all values lie at or above the median and half at or below. The median is easier to understand and to compute and is not affected, as the mean is, by one or two extremely large or extremely small values outside the range of the rest of the data. The most common misconception using the median emerges when students neglect to order the numbers in the data set from least to greatest. The median and the mean first appear as standards in the sixth grade in the CCSS-M (CCSSO, 2010).

Mean. Ask an adult what the mean is, and they are likely to tell you something like, "The mean is when you add up all the numbers in the set and divide the sum by the number of numbers in the set." This is not what the mean *is*, this is how you calculate the mean. This is a reminder of the procedurally driven curriculum in our history and the need to shift to a more conceptually focused approach. Another limited conception about the mean is that it is considered *the* way to find a measure of center regardless of the context (McGatha, Cobb, & McClain, 1998). In fact, in the CCSS-M, sixth graders are expected to determine when the mean is appropriate and when another measure of center (e.g., the median) is more appropriate: "Students recognize that a data distribution may not have a definite center and that different ways to measure center yield different values" (CCSSO, 2010, p. 39). The next section focuses on developing the concept of the mean.

Understanding the Mean: Two Interpretations

There are actually two different ways to think about the mean. First, it is a number that represents what all of the data items would be if they were leveled off. In this sense, the mean represents all of the data items. Statisticians prefer to think of the mean as a central balance point. This concept of the mean is more in keeping with the notion of a measure of the "center" of the data or a measure of central tendency. Both concepts are discussed in the following sections.

Leveling Interpretation. Suppose that the average number of family members for the students in your class is 5. One way to interpret this is to think about distributing the entire collection of moms, dads, sisters, and brothers to each of the students so that each would have a "family" of the same size. To say that you have an average score of 93 for the four tests in your class is like spreading the total of all of your points evenly across the four tests. It is as if each student had the same family size and each test score were the same, but the totals matched the actual distributions. An added benefit of this explanation of the mean is that it connects to the algorithm for computing the mean.

Activity 21.12

CCSS-M: 6.SP.A.2; 6.SP.A.3; 6.SP.B.5

Mean Cost of Games

Post a copy of Games Costs Activity Page. Have students make a bar graph of the data using connecting cubes (one cube per dollar). Choose a situation with 5 or 6 values. For example, Figure 21.18(a) shows cube stacks for the price of each game. The task for students is to use the stacks of cubes (bars) to determine what the price would be if all of the games were the same price. Encourage students to use various techniques to rearrange the cubes to "level" the prices, or make the price the same for each item (See Figure 21.18(b).) Be sure that ELLs understand the meaning of "leveling" the bars.

ENGLISH LANGUAGE LEARNERS

Explain to students that the size of the leveled bars is the mean of the data—the amount that each item would cost if all items cost the same amount but the total of the prices remained fixed.

Follow "Mean Cost of Games" with the next activity to help students develop an algorithm for finding the mean.

Activity 21.13

CCSS-M: 6.SP.A.2; 6.SP.A.3; 6.SP.B.5

The Mean Foot

Pose the following question: "What is the mean length of our feet in inches?" This context needs to be clear to ELLs because *foot* is not being used as a measurement unit, but as an object. Also, consider measuring in centimeters rather than inches. Have each student cut a strip of cash register tape that matches the length of his or her foot. Students record their names and the length of their feet in inches on the strips. Suggest that before finding a mean for the class, you will first get means for smaller groups. Put students into groups of four, six, or eight students (use even numbers). In each group, have the students tape their foot strips end to end. The task for each group is to come up with a method of finding the mean without using any of the lengths written on the strips. They can only use the combined strip. Each group will share their method with the class. From this work, they will devise a method for determining the mean for the whole class. For students with disabilities, help them fold the strip to see how to divide the cash register strip into equal lengths.

ENGLISH LANGUAGE LEARNERS

STUDENTS *with* **SPECIAL NEEDS**

Pause Reflect

Before reading on, what is a method that the students could use in "The Mean Foot"? ●

To evenly distribute the inches for each student's foot among the members of the group, they can fold the strip into equal parts so that there are as many sections as students in the group. Then they can measure the length of any one part.

How can you find the mean for the whole class? Suppose there are 23 students in the class. Using the strips already taped together, make one very long strip for the whole class. It is not reasonable to fold this long strip into 23 equal sections. But if you wanted to know how long the resulting strip would be, how could that be done? The total length of the strip is the sum of the lengths of the 23 individual foot strips. To find the length of one section if the strip were actually folded in 23 parts, simply divide by 23. In fact, students can mark off "mean feet" along the strip. There should be very close to 23 equal-length "feet." This dramatically illustrates the algorithm for finding the mean.

Balance Point Interpretation. Statisticians think about the mean as a point on a number line where the data on either side of the point are balanced. To help think about the mean in this way, it is useful to think about the data placed on a line plot. Notice that what is important includes how many pieces of data are on either side of the mean *and* their distances from the mean.

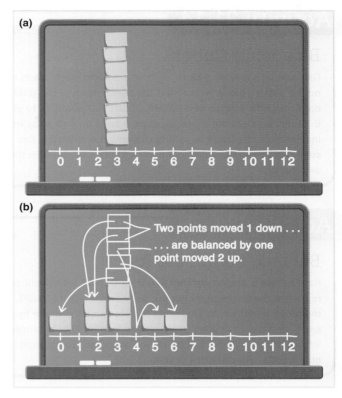

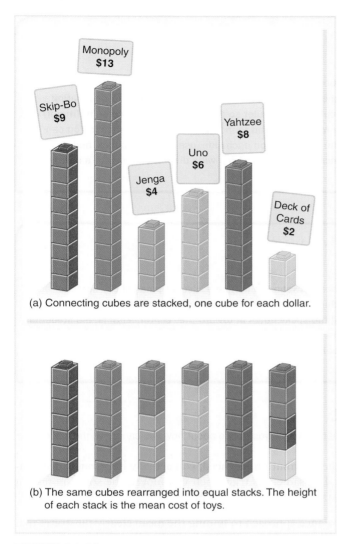

(a) Connecting cubes are stacked, one cube for each dollar.

(b) The same cubes rearranged into equal stacks. The height of each stack is the mean cost of toys.

FIGURE 21.18 Understanding the mean as a leveling of the data.

FIGURE 21.19 (a) If all data points are the same, the mean is that value. (b) By moving data points away from the mean in a balanced manner, different distributions can be found that have the same mean.

To illustrate, draw a number line on the board and arrange eight sticky notes above the number 3, as shown in Figure 21.19(a). Each sticky note represents one family. The notes are positioned on the line to indicate how many pets the family owns. Stacked like this indicates that all families have the same number of pets. The mean is three pets. But different families are likely to have different numbers of pets. So we could think of eight families with a range of numbers of pets. Some may have zero pets, and some may have ten pets or even more. How could you change the number of pets for these eight families so that the mean remains at 3? Students will suggest moving the sticky notes in opposite directions, probably in pairs. This will result in a symmetrical arrangement. But what if one of the families has eight pets, a move of five spaces from the 3? This might be balanced by moving two families to the left, one three spaces to the 0 and one two spaces to the 1. Figure 21.19(b) shows one way the families could be rearranged to maintain a mean of 3. To help them reason about the balancing of the mean, ask students, "Can you find at least two other distributions of the families, each having a mean of 3?"

Use the next activities to find the mean or balance point given the data.

Activity 21.14

CCSS-M: 6.SP.A.2; 6.SP.A.3; 6.SP.B.5

Balancing Cubes

Give students a ruler, a block such as a pattern block piece, and cubes, such as Unifix cubes. Have students balance the ruler on the pattern block. Notice that the 6-inch mark of the ruler is at the center. Explain that students are going to be creating data sets with a mean of 6 (O'Dell, 2012). Ask students to place 4 cubes on the ruler so that there is a balance point (mean) of 6. Students might, for example, place a cube on 4 (2 away from the mean of 6) and then one on the 8 to balance it. You can increase the challenge by asking students the following: Use only one data point on each side, use exactly 5 cubes, add one cube that keeps the balance, move two cubes to maintain the balance, place cubes with a wide distribution or with a narrow distribution.

Activity 21.15

CCSS-M: 6.SP.A.2; 6.SP.A.3; 6.SP.B.5

Balance Point Post-Its

Have students draw a number line from 0 to 13 with about two inches between the numbers. Use six small sticky notes to represent the prices of six games, as shown in Figure 21.20. Have them place a light pencil mark on the line where they think the mean might be. Ask students to determine the mean by moving the sticky notes in toward the "center." That is, the students are to find out what price (point on the number line) balances out the six prices. For each move of a sticky one space to the left, a different sticky must be moved one space to the right. Eventually, all sticky notes should be stacked above the same number, the balance point or mean.

 ## Pause & Reflect

Stop and try this exercise yourself. What do you notice about how you can move the values? ●

After any pair of moves that keep the distribution balanced, you actually have a new distribution of prices with the same mean. The same was true when you moved the sticky notes out from the mean when they were all stacked on the same point.

Changes in the Mean. The balance approach to finding the mean clearly illustrates that different data distributions can have the same mean. Especially for small sets of data, the mean is significantly affected by extreme values. For example, suppose another game with a price of $20 is added to the six we have been using in the examples.

FORMATIVE ASSESSMENT Notes. Consider using a diagnostic interview to assess whether students are able to determine the best measure of center to use in a given situation, such as the average height of students in the class. You can begin with general questions

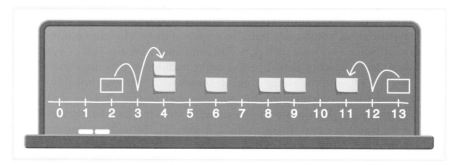

FIGURE 21.20 Move data points in toward the center or balance point without changing the balance around that point. When you have all points at the same value, that is the balance or the mean.

such as these: What is an average? What does the mean represent? What does the median represent? What is the difference between the mean and the median? What is each useful for? Then move to more analytical questions: Which should we use for this set of data? Might we use a different measure of center in another class? When you've found the average height of the students in our class, is it possible that no one is that height? Why? ■

Choosing a Measure of Center

As mentioned earlier, the context in statistics is important. The context of a situation will determine whether the mean or median is the measure you want to use. For example, in reporting home prices (see first page of this chapter), the median is quite different from the mean, with the mean being higher. Which better portrays the cost of housing? Activities 21.16 and 21.17 provide strategies for engaging students in selecting a measure of center.

Activity 21.16

CCSS-M: 6.SP.A.2; 6.SP.A.3; 6.SP.B.5

Which Measure the Center Makes Sense?

STUDENTS
with
SPECIAL
NEEDS

Prepare possible questions to investigate using available data sets like the ones listed here:

- How many pencils does a sixth grader have?
- What is the cost of used cars in our area?
- What is the height of a typical cereal box?
- What is the average monthly cost of a mobile phone?

Students' task is to decide which measure of center makes the most sense and be able to justify their decision. The first question can be explored by gathering classroom data (Johnson, 2011), and then selecting and justifying which measure of center makes sense. For the other situations, you can assign a topic to a group. Each group does the following: (a) selects which measure of center they think makes the most sense for their topic, (b) prepares a data set that illustrates their point, and (c) prepares a justification of why they picked their measure. Students with special needs may benefit from being given several sets of data for their topic as a way to consider which measure might be best. Also discuss the spread and overall shape of the data gathered (e.g., Does the height of cereal crowd the center? Is there a lot of variation in the phone bills?).

Exploring how new data affect each measure of center provides valuable insights to students in comparing the pros and cons of each. Let's revisit the cost of games activity.

Activity 21.17

CCSS-M: 6.SP.A.2; 6.SP.A.3; 6.SP.B.5

Average Cost of More Games

Distribute copies of Average Game Costs Activity Page and post the Games Costs Activity Page. Ask students to predict how the mean, median, and mode will change if a new game costing $20 is part of the game set. What if the $2 game is removed? Then, ask students to figure out the price of a game that was added that increased the mean to $9. For a full lesson, see Expanded Lesson: Playing with Measures of Central Tendency.

Having to make decisions using statistics is an authentic reason for choosing a measure of center, the focus of the next activity.

Activity 21.18

CCSS-M: 6.SP.A.2; 6.SP.A.3; 6.SP.B.5

You Be the Judge

The gymnastics coach can only send one person on to the all-star state competition. She wants to select the student with the best average and most consistency this season. The following table gives overall scores for the eight most recent competitions. Whom should she pick?

Meet	Jenna	Miah	Leah
1	9	9	5
2	3	9	6
3	10	7	7
4	9	8	6
5	7	7	9
6	5	9	8
7	10	9	10
8	9	8	10

Ask students questions such as the following: Which measure of center seems to be the fairest way to judge the competition? What variability do you notice for each person? Which person would you pick and why?

In addition to selecting the measure that makes sense, students need to understand how characteristics of a data set (e.g., distribution of data, outliers) affect the mean, median, and mode. In seventh grade and beyond, students must be able to compare the characteristics of one data set to another (CCSSO, 2010). For example, students can gather data on the time it takes fizz to die down for two different brands of soda (repeated trials for each brand) (Kader & Jacobbe, 2013).

TECHNOLOGY Note. Data can be found online and used for comparison with class data. For example, CNN recently reported that the average youth owns 7 pairs of jeans. Mooney and Bair (2011) used this data to compare to data gathered by their class, which varied from the reported average, and discussed what might cause the deviation. Also, students can efficiently investigate how the mean and median are affected by each piece of data using the Mean and Median applet on NCTM Illuminations. ■

Variability

Although measures of center are a long-standing topic, measures of variability also need explicit attention in the curriculum (Franklin et al., 2005; Kader & Jacobbe, 2013; Scheaffer, 2006). Increased attention to variability is needed, and this may not be adequately addressed in textbooks that have tended to focus on measures of center. In CCSS-M, variability is introduced in grade 6 and becomes a major focus in seventh grade (CCSSO, 2010). Shaughnessy (2006) summarized the findings on what students should know about variability in the following list, starting with basic notions and progressing to more sophisticated ideas:

1. Focusing only on outliers or extremes (but not on the full distribution of the data)
2. Considering change over time (which can lead into discussions of other types of variation)
3. Examining variability as the full range of data (range is everything that occurs, but it doesn't reveal the frequency of different events within the range)
4. Considering variability as the likely range or expected value
5. Looking at how far data points are from the center (e.g., the mean)
6. Looking at how far off a set of data is from some fixed value

In order to be prepared to teach students variability beyond outliers and extremes, it is important to know about the way that variability occurs in statistics.

The Guidelines for Assessment and Instruction in Statistics Education (GAISE) report (Franklin et al., 2005) discusses three levels of statistical thinking that, although developmental in nature, can be roughly mapped to elementary, middle, and high school curricula. This report elaborates on what is in the CCSS-M, providing guidance on how to teach statistics, make meaningful connections, and chart appropriate learning trajectories (Groth & Bargagliotti, 2012). At the first level, the focus is on variability within a group—for example, the varying lengths of students' names, varying family sizes, and so on. When students create a bar graph of class data and compare the data collected, they are discussing the variability within a group.

At the second level, variability within a group continues, but groups of data are also considered. Students might compare the variability of fifth graders' favorite music choices with eighth graders' music choices, an example of variability between groups. In addition, middle school students study how the change in one variable relates to change in another variable— yes, algebra! Students also explore sampling variability (Franklin et al., 2005). When students flip a coin 10 times as a sample, they may get 5 heads and 5 tails, but they also may get many other results (even 0 heads and 10 tails).

At the third level, students examine natural and induced variability. For example, plants grow at different rates (natural variability). But, experiments might compare two groups of plants are in two different gardens, comparing the impact of various factors, such as fertilization, amount of sunlight, amount of water (induced variation). This is at the heart of doing statistics (Franklin & Garfield, 2006).

Variability can be analyzed by looking at data in a table—for example, looking at the frequency of occurrences of categorical data (Kader & Jacobbe, 2013). Figure 21.21 shows the frequency and relative frequency of fourth graders' favorite Saturday activity. Students first submitted their favorite activity on a Post-it note and stuck them to the whiteboard. These were sorted into six categories.

One way to help students understand variability is to ask questions about variability in the discussion of data. Friel, O'Conner, and Mamer (2006), using the context of heart rates, suggest the following questions as examples of how to get students to focus on data and variability:

- If the average heart rate for 9- to 11-year-olds is 88 beats per minute, does this mean every student this age has a heart rate of 88 beats per minute? (Note that the range is actually quite large—from 60 to 110 beats per minute.)
- If we found the heart rate for everyone in the class (of 30), what might the distribution of data look like?
- If another class (of 30) was measured, would their distribution look like the one for our class? What if they just came in from recess?
- Would the distribution of data from 200 students look like the data from the two classes?

Comparing different data sets or playing a game repeatedly provides the opportunity for students to analyze the spread of data and think about variation in data (Franklin & Mewborn, 2008; Kader & Mamer, 2008).

Activity	Frequency	Relative Frequency
Play a sport	7	$\frac{7}{28} = .25 = 25\%$
Go to the movies	3	$\frac{3}{28} = .107 = 11\%$
Read	3	$\frac{3}{28} = .107 = 11\%$
Play outside	6	$\frac{6}{28} = .214 = 21\%$
Hang out with friends	4	$\frac{4}{28} = .143 = 14\%$
Play with electronics	5	$\frac{5}{28} = .178 = 18\%$
TOTAL	28	100%

FIGURE 21.21 Frequency and relative frequency describe the variability in the data.

Range. Range is a *measure* of variability. Range of a data set is the difference between the highest and lowest data points, or it can be expressed by simply stating the minimum and maximum values. The *interquartile range* of the data is connected to the box plot described earlier. It is the difference between the lower and upper quartiles (Q3 – Q1), or the range of the middle 50 percent of the data. A small interquartile range means that there is a lot of clustering around the median.

Let's look at an example.

The data set below is the number of hours seventh graders spent playing sports or playing outside over the weekend (data has already been placed in order).

0 0 0 1 3 4 4 4 5 5 5 5 6 6 7 8 8 9 10 10

Find the interquartile range. What does the result tell you about the variation in the data set?

In this case, the median is 5 (because the tenth and eleventh values of the 20 values are both 5). This is also referred to as quartile 2. Quartile 1 is the median of the lower half of the data. This median is the average of the fifth and sixth value in the data set, which is 3.5. Quartile 3 (Q3) is the median of the upper half of the data set, which in this case falls between 7 and 8, so it is 7.5. The interquartile range is 7.5 – 3.5, or 4. For hours spent exercising, the interquartile range is fairly small, showing there is a lot of clustering around the center of the data.

Mean Absolute Deviation. Whereas the range relates to the median, the mean absolute deviation (MAD) relates to the mean and tells how spread out the data is (Kader & Jacobbe, 2013). In other words, a large MAD means that there is a lot of deviation (difference) between data points and the mean, so the data are spread out. In the CCSS, MAD is introduced in sixth grade, with the intent being that it is explored in an informal manner to develop a deeper understanding of variability. Let's use the previous data set to explore mean absolute variation.

Use the following data set to find the mean absolute deviation:

0 0 0 1 3 4 4 4 5 5 5 5 6 6 7 8 8 9 10 10

What does the result tell you about the variation in the data set?

Figure 21.22 places that data in a dot plot. Dot plots can be used to illustrate absolute deviations from the mean (Hudson, 2012/2013). Students draw a vertical line at the mean (in this case 5), and draw or observe how far away each data point is (absolute deviation).

The first step in finding the mean absolute deviation is to find the deviation (difference) of each data point from the mean. Figure 21.23(a) illustrates these differences in a dot plot. The *absolute* deviation is the distance from the mean, which means the positive difference (see Figure 21.23(b)). Finally, the mean of the absolute deviation is the mean of all these differences (see Figure 21.23(c))—in this case, 2.4. Did you notice that you started with the end of the phrase "mean absolute deviation" by first finding the deviation, then finding absolute deviation, and finally the mean absolute deviation? Pointing this out can help students, in particular students with disabilities, focus on the meaning of what they are doing and why.

In context, this value indicates that the average distance from the mean hours of exercise is around two and a half hours, not much variability. A good way to have students focus on variability is to have two data sets, one that will have a very small absolute mean deviation, and one that will have a large one. Focus attention on how this measure helps students interpret the data set.

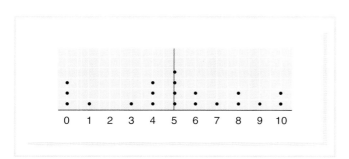

FIGURE 21.22 A dot plot illustrates the data on hours spent exercising over the weekend.

(a) Deviation (from the mean)

					0					
−5				−1	0					
−5				−1	0	1		3		5
−5	−4		−2	−1	0	1	2	3	4	5
0	**1**	**2**	**3**	**4**	**5**	**6**	**7**	**8**	**9**	**10**

(b) Absolute deviation (from the mean)

					0					
5				1	0					
5				1	0	1		3		5
5	4		2	1	0	1	2	3	4	5
0	**1**	**2**	**3**	**4**	**5**	**6**	**7**	**8**	**9**	**10**

(c) Mean absolute deviation (from the mean)

$$\frac{5+5+5+4+2+1+1+1+0+0+0+0+1+1+2+3+3+4+5+5}{20} = \frac{48}{20} = 2.4$$

FIGURE 21.23 Dot plots illustrate the differences from the mean for each data point for hours spent exercising over the weekend.

 Complete Self-Check 21.6: Data Analysis: Measures of Center and Variability

 Interpreting Results

Interpretation is the fourth step in the process of doing statistics. As seen in the sample test items shown earlier, sometimes questions focus on mathematical ideas rather than statistical ideas. Although it is helpful to ask mathematical questions, it is essential to ask questions that are statistical in nature. That means the questions focus on the context of the situation and seeing what can be learned or inferred from the data. This final activity, based on Wilburne and Kulbacki (2014), is an engaging way to involve students in designing their own data analysis and then interpreting their results.

Activity 21.19 CCSS-M: 6.SP.A.1; 6.SP.A.2; 6.SP.B.5

How Many Words on the Page?

Select a book that is very popular with students. Project a picture of a page where most of the page is covered up, showing only about 7–10 lines of text. Ask students to use their statistical reasoning skills to explore this problem and determine how many words are on this page. Explain that in the end, they will have to argue for their result, explaining what methods they used to determine their answer. Debrief by talking about the variability in data, and about the pros and cons of different measures of center.

Interpreting data questions should not just focus on the specific question under investigation, but also focus on key ideas of statistics, such as variability, center of the data, and the shape of the data. During interpretation, students might want to create a different data display to get a different look at the data or gather data from a different population to see whether their results are representative.

Different researchers have recommended questions that focus on statistical thinking (Franklin et al., 2005; Friel, O'Conner, & Mamer, 2006; Russell, 2006; Shaughnessy, 2006). Here are some ideas from their lists to get you started on having meaningful discussions about interpreting data:

- What do the numbers (symbols) tell us about our class (or other population)?
- If we gathered the same kind of data from another class (population), how would that data look? What if we asked a larger group, how would the data look?
- How do the numbers in this graph (population) *compare* to this graph (population)?
- Where are the data "clustering"? How much of the data are in the cluster? How much are *not* in the cluster? About what percent is or is not in the cluster?
- What kinds of variability might need to be considered in interpreting these data?
- Would the results be different if . . . [change of sample/population or setting]? (Example: Would gathered data on word length in a third-grade book be different from a fifth-grade book? Would a science book give different results from a reading book?)
- How strong is the association between two variables (scatter plot)? How do you know? What does that mean if you know *x*? If you know *y*?
- What does the graph *not* tell us? What might we infer?
- What new questions arise from these data?
- What is the maker of the graph trying to tell us?

These prompts apply across many data displays. It certainly should be a major focus of your instruction. Consider it the *after* phase of your lesson, though some of these questions will be integrated in the *during* phase as well.

Our world is inundated with data, from descriptive statistics to different graphs. It is essential that we prepare students to be literate about what can be interpreted from data and what cannot be interpreted from data, what is important to pay attention to and what can be discarded as misleading or poorly designed statistics. This is important for success in school, as well as for being a mathematically literate citizen.

 Complete Self-Check 21.7: Interpreting Results

REFLECTIONS ON CHAPTER 21

WRITING TO LEARN

1. How is statistics different from mathematics? In a lesson on the mean, what mathematical questions and what statistical questions might you ask?

2. What does the "shape of data" mean?

3. Data should be collected to answer questions. What are some examples of questions that students might explore with data at the K–2 level? 3–5? 6–8?

4. What kind of graph will be the most suitable to represent the marks distribution of a class of 200 students on a test of 100 marks?

5. Why are pie graphs less suitable for statistics? How can they be made easy for young students?

6. Describe two measures of variability. How are they connected to the measures of center? How would you explain the difference between these measures to the students?

7. What kind of questions should be posed to students to help them interpret data? Give an example of a problem that can be used to explain data analysis.

FOR DISCUSSION AND EXPLORATION

- Select a popular news magazine such as *Time* or *Newsweek*. Look through at least one issue carefully to find graphs and statistical information a typical reader would be expected to understand. Note that you will not be able to do this by simply looking for graphs. Statistics are frequently used without any corresponding graphs.

◆ The process of doing statistics must be clear to students, even when they are working on a piece (e.g., pie charts)

within the process. Pick a grade and consider possibilities for authentic and engaging (and researchable) questions. Then discuss how you would plan instruction in order to include the four-step process and engage students in statistical thinking.

RESOURCES FOR CHAPTER 21

LITERATURE CONNECTIONS

Literature is full of situations in which things must be sorted, compared, or measured. As noted earlier in this chapter, books of lists also are fruitful beginnings for data explorations. Students can use the data in the books and/or compare similar data collected themselves.

The Best Vacation Ever *Murphy (1997)*

In this book, appropriate for first or second grade, a little girl gathers data from her family on what is important to them to decide where the family would have the best vacation. This book nicely introduces the concept of gathering data to answer a question.

Frog and Toad Are Friends *Lobel (1970)*

When Frog and Toad go walking, Frog loses a button. As they search to find the button, they find many buttons. Whenever Frog's friends ask, "Is this your button?" Frog responds (with a touch of frustration), "No, that is not my button! That button is _____, but my button was _____."

This classic story is a perfect lead-in to sorting activities as described in this chapter. Young students can model the story directly with sets of buttons, shells, attribute blocks, Woozle Cards (see Woozle Cards Activity Page), or other objects with a variety of attributes.

200% of Nothing: An Eye-Opening Tour through the Twists and Turns of Math Abuse and Innumeracy *Dewdney (1993)*

This middle school–friendly book has explanations of the many ways that "statistics are turned" to mislead people. Because the examples are real, provided by readers of *Scientific American*, this book is an excellent tool for showing how important it is to be statistically literate in today's society. Reading the examples can launch a mathematics project into looking for errors in advertisements and at how overlapping groups (as in a Venn diagram) can be reported separately to mislead readers. (See Bay-Williams & Martinie, 2009, for more ways to use this book.)

If the World Were a Village: A Book about the World's People **(2nd ed.)** *Smith (2011)* (https://www.youtube.com/watch?v=QrcOdLYBlw0)

This book explores global wealth, culture, language, and other influences. Each beautiful two-page spread shares the

statistics for the topic (e.g., language). This book can give rise to other questions about the world, which can be researched and interpreted into the village metaphor. An article that links this idea to a project exploring concepts of statistics using 100 students is a great follow up (Riskowski, Olbricht, & Wilson, 2010).

RECOMMENDED READINGS

Articles

Harper, S. R. (2004). Students' interpretations of misleading graphs. *Mathematics Teaching in the Middle Grades, 9*(6), 340–343.

Harper explores some types of misleading graphing techniques that are often seen in the popular press and discusses how she used these graphs with students. This examines the kind of ideas found in the classic book How to Lie with Statistics *(Huff, 1954/1993).*

Franklin, C. A., & Mewborn, D. S. (2008). Statistics in the elementary grades: Exploring distribution of data. *Teaching Children Mathematics, 15*(1), 10–16.

Kader, G., & Mamer, J. (2008). Statistics in the middle grades: Understanding center and spread. *Mathematics Teaching in the Middle Grades, 14*(1), 38–43.

Both of these articles use the process of doing statistics as a launching point to frame effective statistics instruction. Both include excellent examples of activities, including questions and data displays.

Books

Curcio, F. (2010). *Developing data-graph comprehension in grades K–8*. Reston, VA: NCTM.

This NCTM book shares 30 graphing activities on exploring, investigating, reasoning, and communicating about data. Each activity includes procedures, discussion questions, writing and reading prompts, and ways to use technology.

Franklin, C., Kader, G., Mewborn, D., Moreno, J., Peck, R., Perry, M., & Scheaffer, R. (2005). *Guidelines for assessment and instruction in statistics education* (GAISE Report). Alexandria, VA: American Statistical Association.

This excellent framework provides examples for teaching statistics, including great tasks to use with students in pre-K–8.

22

Exploring Concepts of Probability

LEARNER OUTCOMES

After reading this chapter and engaging in the embedded activities and reflections, you should be able to:

22.1 Describe the probability continuum, including examples that help elementary and middle school students understand what it means for an event to be on the continuum from impossible to certain.

22.2 Contrast theoretical probability and experiments, including how to integrate both into instruction to better develop a strong understanding of probability.

22.3 Illustrate and explain strategies for determining sample space for compound events in a developmental manner.

22.4 Explain what a simulation is and how to set up such experiences for middle school students.

22.5 Identify common student misconceptions and how to avoid or address such misconceptions.

References to probability are all around us: The weather forecaster predicts a 60 percent chance of snow, medical researchers predict that people with certain diets have a high chance of heart disease, investors calculate the risks of specific investments, and so on. Simulations of complex situations are frequently based on probabilities and then used in making decisions about such situations as airplane safety under different weather circumstances, highway traffic patterns after new housing has been built, and disaster plans.

Realistic concepts of chance require considerable development before students are ready to construct formal ideas about the probability of an event. Optimally, this development occurs as students consider and discuss the outcomes of a wide variety of probabilistic situations. The emphasis should be on exploration rather than on rules and formal definitions. These informal experiences will provide a useful background from which more formal ideas can be developed in middle and high school.

BIG IDEAS

◆ Chance has no memory. The occurrence of six heads in a row has no effect on whether another head will occur on the next toss of the coin. That chance remains fifty-fifty.

◆ The probability that a future event will occur can be characterized along a continuum from impossible (0) to certain (1). A probability of $\frac{1}{2}$ indicates an even chance of the event occurring.

◆ The relative frequency of outcomes (of *experiments*) can be used as an estimate of the probability of an event. The larger the number of trials, the better the estimate will be. The results for a small number of trials may be quite different from those obtained in the long run.

◆ For some events, the exact probability can be determined by an analysis of the event itself. A probability determined in this manner is called a *theoretical probability*.

◆ *Simulation* is a technique used for answering real-world questions or making decisions in complex situations in which an element of chance is involved. To see what is likely to happen in the real event, a model must be designed that has the same probabilities as the real situation.

Introducing Probability

Probability does not appear in the Common Core State Standards expectations until seventh grade. Notions of chance and fairness, however, should be developed early in school and through playing games, and students should have developed some intuition about how likely an outcome might be. Although such intuition can be a positive thing, in probability it can also be a preconception that works against understanding the randomness of events (Abu-Bakare, 2008). Probability is a ratio that compares the desired outcomes to the total possible outcomes.

Likely or Not Likely

Probability is about how likely an event is. Therefore, a good place to begin is with a focus on possible and not possible (Activity 22.1) and later impossible, possible, and certain (Activity 22.2). In preparation for these activities, discuss the meaning of *impossible* and *certain*. These experiences can be woven into discussions across the curriculum, as in Activity 22.1, which is an idea for connecting to children's literature, as in Activity 22.2, which connects to science and social studies.

Activity 22.1
CCSS-M: 7.SP.C.5

Literature Events: Possible or Not Possible?

Create a table, labeling one column "Impossible" and the other "Possible." Use literature or poems that include either possible or impossible occurrences. Nursery rhymes, such as "Hey, Diddle, Diddle" can be fun even for middle school students as they debate whether something is possible. Songs and raps are also engaging. Record each statement in the appropriate column.

Activity 22.2

CCSS-M: 7.SP.C.5

Is It Likely?

Ask students to judge various events as *certain, impossible,* or *possible* ("might happen"). Consider these examples:

ENGLISH LANGUAGE LEARNERS

STUDENTS with SPECIAL NEEDS

- It will rain tomorrow.
- Drop a rock in water and it will sink.
- A sunflower seed planted today will bloom tomorrow.
- The sun will rise tomorrow morning.
- A hurricane/tornado will hit our town.
- In an election, candidate A will be elected.
- If you ask someone who the first U.S. president was, they will know.
- You will have two birthdays this year.
- You will be in bed by 9:00 P.M.

For each event, students should justify their choice of how likely they think it is. Notice that the last two ideas are about the students. This is an opportunity to bring in students' identities and cultures. Ask students to work with their families to write down family events that are certain, impossible, or possible. Encourage native language use, as appropriate, for ELLs. For students with disabilities, use a strip of cash register tape and label the ends with the words *impossible* and *certain* to assist them in organizing their thinking. Write the events on cards so that students can place them along the strip.

CCSS Standards for Mathematical Practice

MP5. Use appropriate tools strategically.

The key idea to developing chance or probability on a continuum is to help students see that some of these possible events are more likely or less likely than others. For instance, if Erik is a very fast runner and is in a race, the chance of being in first is not certain but is very likely.

The use of random devices (tools) that can be analyzed (e.g., spinners, number cubes, coins to toss, colored cubes drawn from a bag) can help students make predictions about how likely a particular occurrence is. Begin with the use of random devices with which students can count the outcomes. Colored dots can be stuck on the sides of a wooden cube to create different color probabilities. Color tiles (e.g., eight red and two blue) can be placed in opaque bags. Students draw a tile from the bag and then return it after each draw.

TECHNOLOGY Note. Science NetLinks offers an interactive tool, Marble Mania, for exploring probability of different colored marbles in a bag. You can determine how many and what color marbles to place in a virtual marble bag. An advantage of such digital resources is that you can run a large number of different trials in a short amount of time. In addition, the National Library of Virtual Manipulatives (NLVM) has a large collection of probability tools in their Data Analysis and Probability Manipulatives, organized across grade bands. There are also a number of apps for generating random numbers (e.g., Randomness for iOS and numerous dice-rolling apps for iOS/Android). ∎

The process of exploring how likely an event is maps to the *before, during, after* lesson plan model. In the *before* phase, students make predictions of what they think will be likely; in the *during* phase, students experiment to explore how likely the event is; and in the *after* phase, students compile and analyze the experimental results to determine more accurately how likely the event is.

The following dice activities have unequal outcomes. However, students may not initially connect that having more of something means it is more likely. A common initial misconception is that there is a one-in-three chance of each of the values (1, 2, and 3), because each one is possible.

Activity 22.3

CCSS-M: 7.SP.C.5; 7.SP.C.6

1-2-3 How Likely?

Make number cubes with sides labeled as follows: 1, 1, 2, 3, 3, 3. Ask students to predict what number they might get when they roll the cube and record the results in a bar graph. What is likely? What is impossible? Or, more specifically, which row will fill the fastest or will the rows fill at equal rates? (See 1-2-3 How Likely? Activity Page.) Students mark an X in the column for 1, 2, or 3 each time the cube shows that value and stop when one row is full. After they stop, students reflect on how likely each number is.

Activity 22.4

CCSS-M: 7.SP.C.5; 7.SP.C.6; 7.SP.C.8a

1-2-3 How Likely Are Sums?

This game requires two cubes labeled as in Activity 22.3. It is a more difficult task because it considers the probability of two events (two dice rolls). Students take turns rolling the two cubes and recording the sums of the two numbers. Before the game begins, ask students to predict which row will fill the fastest or if the rows will fill at equal rates. Ask students to keep track of their data on 1-2-3 How Likely Are Sums? Activity Page. Students roll the cubes until one of the rows is full. Then discuss with their partner what happened and how likely they now think each number is.

After exploring either 1-2-3 activity, ask, "Which numbers 'won' the most and the least often?" and "If you play again, which number would you pick to win and why?" In Activity 22.4, all outcomes 2 through 6 are possible. 1 is impossible. A sum of 4 is the most likely. Sums of 2 or 6 are not likely.

Area representations, such as spinners, are more challenging because students cannot count the possible outcomes as readily (Abu-Bakare, 2008). Activity 22.5 uses spinners and counting spins to build this connection.

Activity 22.5

CCSS-M: 7.SP.C.6; 7.SP.C.7a, b

Race to Ten

Use the Race to Ten Activity Page. Refer to the spinner and ask: "If we count spins that land on red and ones that land on blue, which one will reach ten first?" Two players take turns spinning the spinner, each time placing an X in the matching column. The Activity Sheet includes a spinner that is three-fourths red and one-fourth blue (give students a paperclip to use as a pointer), but this activity can be played with different spinners (see Figure 22.1). Before playing, each student predicts which color will win, red or blue (or gold). Play continues until one color reaches ten. After the activity, discuss which color won and why. Ask students to explain how likely it is for red to win or for blue to win.

Repeat this activity with a variety of spinners, ones that have two colors with the same area, and colors covering different areas, as shown Figure 22.1.

Students do not always see that the first spinner, last spinner, or a spinner partitioned into just two sections (50% blue, 50% red), have the same chance of getting blue (Cohen, 2006;

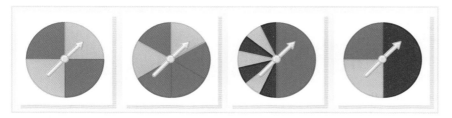

FIGURE 22.1 Possible spinners for Race to Ten.

Nicolson, 2005). Therefore, it is important to use spinners that are partitioned in different ways. Spinner faces can easily be made to adjust the chances of different outcomes. For virtual spinners, NCTM Illuminations "Adjustable Spinner" can be adjusted to have any number of sections of any size.

An effective way to connect the idea that the larger area or region on the spinner is more likely to have a spin land there is to have students use frequency charts to record data. In Figure 22.2, a student explains how she knows which frequency table goes with which circle graph.

Standards for Mathematical Practice

MP2. Reason abstractly and quantitatively.

FORMATIVE ASSESSMENT Notes. Diagnostic interviews can uncover student misconceptions or preconceptions about the probability of an event. Ask students about the probability using color tiles or dice (countable objects). For example, ask, "If there are 3 red and 1 blue tile in this bag and I draw one out, what do you think I will get?" and "If I draw four times and put the tile back each time, what do you think I will get?" Ask about the chance of rolling certain outcomes on a die. Some students may think 5 is a more likely outcome on a die than a 2 because 5 is bigger than 2. Or students may think a 1 is not as likely as rolling a 5 on a die, perhaps because they are familiar with a game in which 1 is desirable. The 1 is not likely compared to the combined possibility of the other 5 choices, but it is as likely as any other number (Nicolson, 2005; Watson & Moritz, 2003). Finally, ask about how likely outcomes are in an area representation such as a spinner. These questions will help you know whether you need to focus on counting or area representations, and what kinds of questions or experiences to prepare in order to help students understand that probability is based on knowing all the possible outcomes and how likely each one is. ∎

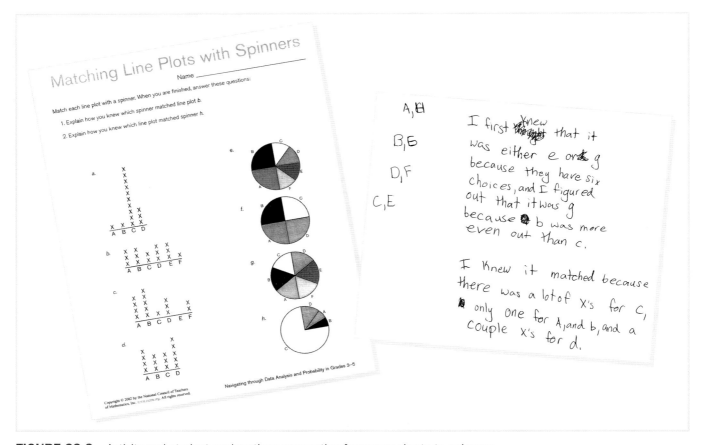

FIGURE 22.2 Activity and student explanations connecting frequency charts to spinners.

Source: Matching Line plots with Spinners page adapted from Chapin, S., Kozial, A., MacPherson, J., & Rezba, C. (2002). *Navigating through Data Analysis and Probability in Grades 3–5.* Reston, VA: NCTM, p. 116. Copyright © 2002 by the National Council of Teachers of Mathematics. All rights reserved.

The Probability Continuum

The number line is an important representation across mathematical concepts, and it is emphasized across the content strands in the CCSS-M (CCSSO, 2010). Probability is no exception. Presenting probability on a number line from 0 (impossible) to 1 (certain) provides a visual representation of how likely an event can be. The number line can be connected to spinners, as illustrated in Figure 22.3. Post the probability continuum in the classroom, where it can be used as a reference for other opportunities to talk about how likely something is (see the questions in Activity 22.2 for a start to the many things you could ask). Some things change in their probability; for example, the chance of a snow day could be posted and moved from day to day.

In order to deepen students' understanding of the probability continuum, select a particular mark along the continuum—for example, $\frac{1}{4}$—and have students create a spinner with a color that is about that likely to occur. This can also be done with counters, as in Activity 22.6.

Activity 22.6

CCSS-M: 7.SP.C.6

Design and Test Bags

Provide each pair or group of students with a copy of the Design a Bag Activity Page and give each group a value on the probability continuum (e.g., $\frac{1}{3}$, $\frac{3}{4}$, $\frac{1}{6}$). Ask each group to choose a designated color for their tiles so that the probability of selecting that color is the probability they have been assigned. Once they have colored the tiles on the Activity Page to match their fraction (e.g., $\frac{1}{3}$ are red), the students trade papers. With the new Activity Page students do the following:

ENGLISH LANGUAGE LEARNERS

1. Mark the probability line at the point they think matches the number of tiles colored red.
2. Place actual colored tiles into brown paper bags based on what is colored on the "Design a Bag" they received. They draw tiles from this bag (with replacement) 50 times. Remind students to shake their bag each time to ensure random sampling.
3. Determine the fraction of times they have drawn a red tile.
4. Return the papers to the group that colored the Design a Bag and find out what the original probability was. (They will have to decide if their fraction is close to the assigned fraction.) For example, is $\frac{17}{30}$ close to $\frac{1}{3}$?

STUDENTS with SPECIAL NEEDS

At the end of the activity, have students explain (on the back of the handout or in their journals) how they decided where to place their mark on the probability line. ELLs and students with disabilities can benefit from sentence starters, such as, "In the bag we received, there were _____ red and _____ blue tiles. We first thought _____. After we did our experiment, we thought_____. We picked this probability because_____."

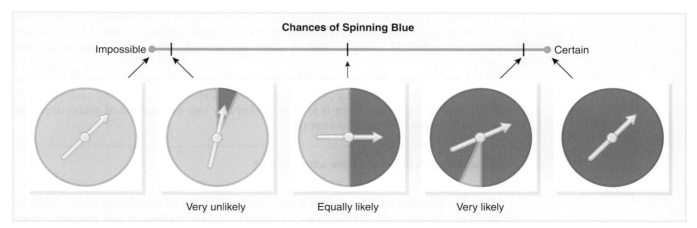

FIGURE 22.3 The probability continuum. Use these spinner faces to help students see how chance can be at different places on a continuum between impossible and certain.

Standards for
Mathematical
Practice

MP3. Construct viable arguments and critique the reasoning of others.

This activity engages students in conjecturing about how likely an event is, experimenting, and comparing their predictions with experimental outcomes as they continue to explore and refine their conjectures about theoretical probability. This builds a strong foundation for the more advanced probability techniques they will develop in seventh grade and beyond.

Activity 22.7

CCSS-M: 7.SP.C.6; 7.SP.C.7a, b

Mystery Bags

This activity builds from Activity 22.6. Ask each original group to select a probability (e.g., $\frac{1}{4}$, $\frac{1}{6}$, $\frac{3}{4}$, $\frac{3}{8}$) and design an opaque bag using **24** two different colored cubes or tiles, such that $\frac{1}{6}$ of the tiles are red if they selected the probability of $\frac{1}{6}$. Students need to give their bag a name so they can get it back! On a secret card, they record the probability they selected and tuck it away. Groups trade bags. The new group cannot look in the bag. The second group conducts 10 draws (with replacement) and on paper write the name of the bag, a prediction for how many tiles they think are red, and what they think the probability is of drawing red. Trade bags again. This time, each group conducts 30 draws (with replacement) and again records the name of their bags and their prediction for how many tiles they think are red and what they think the probability is of drawing red. Return bags to original owners. During share time, each group holds up their bag, hears the prediction from the group that drew 10 times and from the group that drew 30 times, and then reveals the answer. As a whole class, discuss the connection between probability and number of counters, and how many draws are needed to make a good prediction of what is in the bag.

You may notice that probability is closely connected to fractions. Although probability is not explicitly discussed in the grades 3–5 curriculum, fractions are heavily emphasized (CCSSO, 2010). Activities such as Design and Test Bags and Mystery Bags are excellent for thinking about relative size of fractions, comparing fractions, equivalence of fractions, and multiplication of a whole number by a fraction.

 Complete Self-Check 22.1: Introducing Probability

 Theoretical Probability and Experiments

The *probability* of an event is a measure of the chance of that event occurring (Franklin et al., 2005). Students to this point have only been asked to place events on a continuum from impossible to certain or to compare the probability of one event with another. So how do you measure chance of an event? In many situations, there are actually two ways to determine this measure.

Probability has two distinct types. The first type involves any specific event whose probability of occurrence is known (e.g., that a fair die has a $\frac{1}{6}$ chance of producing each number). When the probability of an event is known, probability can be established theoretically by examining all the possibilities. For example:

What is the probability of rolling a three with a fair die?

When the probability of an event is known, probability can be established theoretically by examining all the possibilities. In this case, probability can be established only through empirical data or evidence from past experiments or data collection (Colgan, 2006; Nicolson, 2005). Examples include:

What is the probability that Jon V. will make his free throws (based on his previous record)?

What is the chance of rain (based on how often it has rained under similar conditions)?

Although this type of probability is less common in the school curriculum, it is the most applicable to fields that use probability and therefore important to include in your teaching (Franklin et al., 2005).

In both cases, experiments or simulations can be designed to explore the phenomena being examined. (Sometimes in the K–12 curriculum this is referred to as *experimental probability*, but because this terminology is not employed by statisticians, it is not used here.) Some experiments have outcomes that are equally likely, whereas other experiments do not. With coin flips, there are two possible outcomes that are equally likely, so each has a probability of $\frac{1}{2}$. Hence, the theoretical probability of obtaining a head is $\frac{1}{2}$. When all possible outcomes of a simple experiment are equally likely, the probability of an event can be expressed as follows:

$$\frac{\text{Number of outcomes in the event}}{\text{Number of possible outcomes}}$$

Consider the shift in meaning of the question, "Is this coin fair?" This is a statistics problem that can only be answered by doing an experiment and establishing the frequency of heads and tails over the long run (Franklin et al., 2005). The answer requires empirical data and the probability will be as follows:

$$\frac{\text{Number of observed occurrence of the event}}{\text{Number of trials}}$$

Because it is impossible to conduct an infinite number of trials, we can only consider the relative frequency for a very large number of trials as an approximation of the theoretical probability. This emphasizes the notion that probability is more about predictions over the long term than predictions of individual events.

Theoretical Probability

A problem-based way to introduce theoretical probability is to engage students in an activity with an unfair game. In the following activity, the results of the game will likely be contrary to students' intuitive ideas. This in turn will provide a real reason to analyze the game in a logical manner and find out why things happened as they did—theoretical probability.

Activity 22.8

CCSS-M: 7.SP.C.6; 7.SP.C.7a

ENGLISH LANGUAGE LEARNERS

Fair or Unfair?

Three students toss 2 like coins (e.g., 2 pennies or 2 nickels) and they record points according to the following rules: Player A gets 1 point if the coin toss results in two heads, player B gets 1 point if the toss results in two tails, and player C gets 1 point if the toss results are mixed (one head, one tail). The game is over after 20 tosses. The player who has the most points wins. Have students play the game at least two or three times. After each game, the players are to stop and discuss whether they think the game is fair and make predictions about who will win the next game.

When the full class has played the game several times, conduct a discussion on the fairness of the game. Challenge students to make an argument based on the data and game rules as to whether the game is fair or not. For ELLs, discuss the meaning of *fair* prior to beginning the game and review the term when asking students to create an argument.

A common analysis of the game in Activity 22.8 might go something like this: At first students think that because there are three outcomes—two tails, one head and one tail, or two heads—that each has an equal chance. The game should be fair. However, after playing, students find that player C (the player who gets points for a mixed result) appears to have an unfair advantage (especially if they have played several games or the class pooled its data). This observation seems to contradict the notion that the outcomes are equally likely. As a follow-up to Activity 22.8, challenge students to design their own fair game. See Expanded Lesson: Design a Fair Game for details.

When students from fifth through eleventh grades performed a similar two-coin task and were asked for the probability of getting a head and a tail with two coins, similar misconceptions were found (Rubel, 2006, 2007). About 25 percent of the students said the probability was $\frac{1}{3}$ because one of three things could happen: two heads, one of each, or two tails. Although about half answered correctly, many of these students used faulty reasoning, explaining that they picked that answer because there is a fifty-fifty chance in any experiment. See, for example, Figure 22.4.

In order to help students connect how likely an event is to the possible outcomes, encourage students to analyze the situation and generate all the possible outcomes; for example, use a table such as in Figure 22.5. Getting a head and a tail happens in two out of the four possible outcomes. Figure 22.6 provides an example of a strong student argument for "Fair or Unfair." This theoretical probability is based on a logical analysis of the experiment, not on experimental results.

"Rock-paper-scissors" is a great context for exploring fair games and possible outcomes. It can be played in the normal way or adapted so that "same" scores 1 point for one player and "different" scores 1 point for the other player. Challenge students to determine whether this is a fair game (Ellis, Yeh, & Stump, 2007–2008).

CCSS **Standards for Mathematical Practice**

MP2. Reason abstractly and quantitatively.

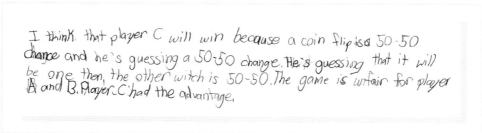

I think that player C will win because a coin flip is a 50-50 chance and he's guessing a 50-50 change. He's guessing that it will be one then, the other witch is 50-50. The game is unfair for player A and B. Player C had the advantage.

FIGURE 22.4 Correct conclusion but incomplete reasoning on "Fair or Unfair?"

First Coin	Second Coin
Head	Head
Head	Tail
Tail	Head
Tail	Tail

FIGURE 22.5 Four possible outcomes of flipping two coins.

I think this game is unfair because it is more likley to get a mix than two of the same sides. This is true because there are more possibilitys for a mix such as heads tails, and tails heads, but the only possibility for player A is two heads, and the only possibility for player B is 2 tails. So for player C they have a 1/2 chance for geting a point, but for the other two they only have a 1/4 chance of geting a point.

FIGURE 22.6 Student reasoning for "Fair or Unfair?" that connects outcomes to probability.

Area has important connections to probability. In the CCSS-M, students explore both area of circles and probability in grade 7. The following activity is an excellent way to integrate these two important ideas.

Activity 22.9   CCSS-M: 7.G.B.4; 7.SP.C.6; 7.SP.C.7b

Chance of Hitting the Target?

Project a target such as the one illustrated here with concentric circles having radii of 2, 6, 8, and 10 inches. Ask students to determine the fraction and percent of the circle that each color is.

Ask students to discuss what the probability for landing on the center (assuming all throws land on the circle and are thrown randomly!). Ask students to discuss why data may or may not match the percent of the area that is covered (e.g., people with good aim will be able to hit the smaller areas more often). Then, have students propose what point values they would assign to each section.

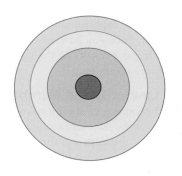

Dartboards can be made many different ways, not just in the traditional way (Williams & Bruels, 2011). For example, using a 10-by-10 grid, any combination of shapes can be drawn in such a way that the area can be calculated. Students can determine the area of various regions and use the areas to determine the probability of different outcomes, an excellent connection between geometry and probability.

Experiments

As noted previously, some probabilities cannot be determined by the analysis of possible outcomes of an event; instead, they can be determined only through gathering empirical data. The data may be preexisting or may need to be established through an experiment, with a sufficiently large number of trials conducted to become confident that the resulting relative frequency is an approximation of the theoretical probability. For example, the probability of a hurricane is based on historical data. The United States Landfalling Hurricane Web Project has a link called Interactive Landfall Probability Display (a hurricane predictor) that provides such probabilities for hurricanes (by state and county).

The following activities are examples of situations in which the only way to establish how likely an outcome is, is to do an experiment and use the results of a large number of trials.

Activity 22.10

CCSS-M: 7.SP.C.7b

Drop It!

In this activity, students drop an object to explore the likelihood of various outcomes. The number of possible outcomes varies with the different objects. Any object can be used. Here are a few ideas to try:

1. *Cup Toss.* Provide a small plastic cup to each pair of students. Ask them to list the possible ways that the cup could land if they tossed it in the air and let it fall on the floor. Which of the possibilities (upside down, right side up, or on the side) do they think is most likely and which least likely? Why? Have students toss the cup 20 times, each time recording how it lands. Students should agree on a uniform method of tossing the cups to ensure unbiased data (e.g., dropping the cups from the same height). Record each pair's data in a class chart. Discuss the differences and generate reasons for them. Have students predict what will happen if they pool their data. Pool the data and compute the three ratios: one for each type of landing (upside down, right side up, or on the side). The relative frequency of the combined data should approximate the actual probability.

2. *Toy Animal Drop.* Bring in small plastic toys that can land in different ways. Repeat the activity above. (See Nelson & Williams, 2009, for an exploration with toy pigs.)

3. *Falling Kisses.* Using Hershey's Kisses, conduct an experiment to see how often they land directly on their base (Gallego, Saldamando, Tapia-Beltran, Williams, & Hoopingarner, 2009). Alternative foods include Hershey's Rolo Caramels, or for more healthful options, consider fish crackers (the direction in which they face).

In these experiments, there is no practical way to determine the results before you start. However, once you have results for 200 tosses (empirical data), you will feel more confident in predicting the results of the next 100 tosses. After gathering data for 1000 trials, you will feel even more confident.

The Law of Large Numbers. The phenomenon in which the relative frequency of an event becomes a closer approximation of the actual probability or the theoretical probability as the size of the data set (sample) increases is referred to as the *law of large numbers*. The larger the size of the data set, the more representative the sample is of the population. In thinking about statistics, a survey of 1000 people provides more reliable and convincing data about the larger population than does a survey of 5 people. The larger the number of trials (people surveyed), the more confident you can be that the data reflect the larger population. The same is true when you are attempting to determine the probability of an event through data collection.

Although critical to understanding probability, this concept is difficult for students to grasp. Students commonly think that a probability should play out in the short term, a misconception sometimes referred to as "the law of small numbers" (Flores, 2006; Tarr, Lee, & Rider, 2006). Comparing small data sets to large data sets is one way to help students think more deeply about the fact that the size of the trial matters. The next two activities are designed with this purpose in mind.

Activity 22.11

CCSS-M: 7.SP.C.6

Get All 6!

Ask students to list the numbers 1 through 6 at the bottom of a frequency table. Students should roll a die and mark an X over each number until they have rolled each number at least once. Repeat five or six times. Discuss how the frequency charts compare in each case. Students will see that in some cases there were many fours, for example, or that it took 25 rolls before all numbers were rolled, whereas in other cases they got all the numbers in only 10 rolls. Now, pool all the data and discuss the relative frequencies for the numbers that emerge. Focus discussion on the fact that in the short run, data varies a lot—it is over the long run that the data "evens out." This activity can also be done on a graphing calculator (see Flores, 2006, for details).

Truly random events often occur in unexpected groups; a fair coin may turn up heads five times in a row. A 100-year flood may hit a town twice in 10 years. Using random devices such as spinning spinners, rolling dice, or drawing cubes from a bag gives students an intuitive feel for the imperfect distribution of randomness. The next activity is designed to help students with this difficult idea.

Activity 22.12
CCSS-M: 7.SP.C.6

What Are the Chances?

Use a copy of What Are the Chances? Activity Page. Provide pairs of students with a spinner face that is half red and half blue. Discuss the chances of spinning blue. Mark the halfway point on the continuum of impossible to certain and draw a vertical line down through all of the lines below this point. Then have the students in each pair spin their spinner 10 times, tallying the number of red and blue spins. Mark the number of blue spins on the second line. For example, if there are 3 blue and 7 red spins, place a mark at about 7 on the 0-to-10 number line. If the result of the 10 spins is not exactly 5 and 5, discuss possible reasons why this may be so.

Repeat 10 more times. Add the tallies for the first 10 spins and again mark the total in the right-hand box of the third line. Repeat at least two more times, continuing to add the results of new spins to the previous results. Using a graphing calculator or applet, even 1000 trials are possible in a short amount of time. Ask students to reflect on what they notice in each number line.

The successive number lines used in "What Are the Chances?" each have the same length and each represent the total number of trials. When the results are plotted on any one number line, the position shows the fraction of the total spins as a visual portion of the whole line. With more trials, the marks will get closer and closer to the $\frac{1}{2}$ mark. Note that 240 blue spins out of 500 is 48 percent, or very close to one-half. This is so even though there are 20 more red spins (260) than blue.

The What Are My Chances? Activity Page and process of accumulating data in stages can and should be used for other experiments. For example, try using this approach with the cup toss experiment in Activity 22.10. Rather than drawing a vertical line before collecting data, decide on the best guess at the actual probability after the number of trials has become large, and then draw the vertical line in the appropriate position. Observe and record on the number lines 10 additional trials, 20 additional trials, and 50 additional trials. Compare these smaller data sets with the larger data set. Write the probabilities as fractions and as percents to show the connection between these representations.

FORMATIVE ASSESSMENT Notes. Pose the following performance assessment to assess students' ideas about long-run results versus short-run results. Have students write about their ideas.

Margaret spins the spinner 10 times. Blue turns up on three spins. Red turns up on seven spins. Margaret says that there is a 3-in-10 chance of spinning blue. Carla then spins the same spinner 100 times. Carla records 53 spins to blue and 47 spins to red. Carla says that the chance of spinning blue on this spinner is about even.

Who do you think is more likely to be correct: Margaret or Carla? Explain. Draw a spinner that you think they may have been using.

Look for evidence that students understand that the result of 10 spins is not very good evidence of the probability and that the result of 100 spins tells us more about how likely each color is, and therefore what percent of the spinner might be blue or red. Also, to assess whether students understand the big idea that chance has no memory, have students write in their journal about the following:

Duane has a lucky coin that he has tossed many, many times. He is sure that it is a fair coin with an even chance of heads or tails. Duane tosses his coin six times and heads come up six times in a row. Duane is sure that the next toss will be tails because he has never been able to toss heads seven times in a row. What do you think the chances are of Duane tossing heads on the next toss? Explain your answer.

In this case, you are looking for the idea that each toss of the coin is independent of prior tosses. ■

Why Use Experiments?

Standards for Mathematical Practice
MP1. Make sense of problems and persevere in solving them.

Actually conducting experiments and examining outcomes in teaching probability are important in helping students address common misconceptions and build a deeper understanding for why certain things are more likely than others.

Specifically, experiments:

- Model real-world problems that are actually solved by conducting experiments (doing simulations)—see, for example, "Undersea Treasure" at the Futures Channel website, which provides a probability map used to locate sunken ships that contained gold treasure
- Provide a connection to counting strategies (lists, tree diagrams) to increase confidence that the probability is accurate
- Provide an experiential background for examining the theoretical model (when you begin to sense that the probability of two heads is $\frac{1}{4}$ instead of $\frac{1}{3}$ through experiments, the analysis in Figure 22.5 seems more reasonable)
- Help students see how the ratio of a particular outcome to the total number of trials begins to converge to a fixed number (for an infinite number of trials, the relative frequency and theoretical probability would be the same)
- Help students learn more than students who do not engage in doing experiments (Gurbuz, Erdem, Catlioglu, & Birgin, 2010)

Try to use an experimental approach whenever possible, posing interesting problems to investigate. If a theoretical analysis is possible (e.g., as in the two-coin experiment in "Fair or Unfair?"), it should also be examined and the results compared with the expected outcomes.

Use of Technology in Experiments

Random outcomes can be generated by computer applications, notebook apps, and calculators. Calculators, for example, produce random numbers that can then be interpreted relative to the possible outcomes in the experiment. Random numbers can be related to the possible outcomes in an experiment. For example, if the final digit is odd, you can assign it to represent one outcome, and if it is even to represent a second outcome. If there are four outcomes, you can look at the remainder when the last two digits are divided by 4 (i.e., the remainder will be 0, 1, 2, or 3) and assign a remainder to each outcome. In addition, some calculators, like the TI-73, TI-83, and TI-84, can run the free Probability Simulation App, an interactive tool that simulates tossing coins, rolling number cubes, using spinners, and generating random numbers.

Computer applets can be used to virtually flip coins, spin spinners, or draw numbers from a hat. NCTM's Illuminations website has a series of lessons in which students explore probability through virtual experiments, including graphing the results.

Standards for Mathematical Practice
MP5. Use appropriate tools strategically.

As long as students accept the results generated by the technology as truly random or equivalent to the hands-on device, these virtual devices have the advantages of being quicker, more motivating to some students, and accessible when the actual devices (e.g., spinners with various partitions) are not. Web-based tools such as the National Library of Virtual Manipulatives' Spinners have the advantage of generating many more trials in much less time. Due to the speed at which an experiment can be done, these digital devices afford the opportunity for teachers to explore probability across a variety of tools (virtual dice, coins, cards, etc.), including the use of graphical displays of the trials. Also, in a virtual world, dice can be "loaded" and used to challenge students' thinking ("Are these fair dice? How can you find out?") (Beck & Huse, 2007; Phillips-Bey, 2004).

 Complete Self-Check 22.2: Theoretical Probability and Experiments

 ## Sample Spaces and the Probability of Compound Events

Understanding the concepts *sample space* and *event* is central to understanding probability. The *sample space* for an experiment or chance situation is the set of all possible outcomes for that experiment. For example, if a bag contains two red, three yellow, and five blue tiles, the sample space consists of all ten tiles. An *event* is a subset of the sample space. The event of drawing a yellow tile has three elements or outcomes in the sample space, and the event of drawing a blue tile has five elements in the sample space. For rolling a single common die, the sample space consists of the numbers 1 through 6. A two-event experiment requires two (or more) actions to determine an outcome. Examples include rolling two dice, drawing two tiles from a bag, and the combination of the occurrence of rain and forgetting your umbrella.

When two-event experiments are explored, there is another factor to consider: Does the occurrence of the event in one stage have an effect on the occurrence of the event in the other? In the following sections, we will consider two-event experiments of both types—those with independent events and those with dependent events. You can watch a lesson in which sixth graders do simulations of dependent and independent events using bags of objects at the companion website.

Independent Events

In Activity 22.8, students explored the results of tossing two coins. The toss of one coin had no effect on the toss of the other. Tossing a coin twice is an example of *independent events;* the occurrence or nonoccurrence of one event has no effect on the other.

Let's explore rolling two dice and adding the results. Suppose that your students gather data on the sums that they get for rolling two dice. The results might be recorded in a dot plot, as in Figure 22.7(a). These events (sums) do not appear to be equally likely, and in fact the sum of 7 appears to be the most likely outcome. To explain this, students might look for the combinations that make 7: 1 and 6, 2 and 5, and 3 and 4. But there are also three combinations for 6 and for 8. It seems as though 6 and 8 should be just as likely as 7, and yet they are not.

Now suppose that the experiment is repeated. This time, for the sake of clarity, suggest that students roll two dice of different colors and that they keep the tallies in a chart like the one in Figure 22.7(b). The results of a large number of dice rolls indicate what one would expect—namely, that all 36 cells of this chart are equally likely. (However, the sums are not equally likely. Why?) Compare the sums of 6, 7, and 8, the most common sums. There are six outcomes that result in a sum of 7 out of a total of the sample space (36), for a probability of $\frac{6}{36}$, or $\frac{1}{6}$. Notice that 3 red, 4 green is different from 4 red, 3 green. Both 6 and 8 have doubles, and therefore only five outcomes, for a probability of $\frac{5}{36}$. Students often do not see 3, 4 and 4, 3 as separate events and therefore don't count each possibility separately. The color-coded dice can help address this misconception.

To create the sample space for two independent events, use a chart or diagram that keeps the two events separate and illustrates all possible combinations. The matrix in Figure 22.7(b) is effective when there are only two events. A tree diagram (Figure 22.8) is another method of creating sample spaces that can be used with any number of events. For example, consider the context of creating an ice cream cone. You can choose a waffle cone or a regular cone, ice cream that is dipped or not dipped, and then any of three single flavors. This can be simulated with coins and a spinner, as illustrated in Figure 22.8.

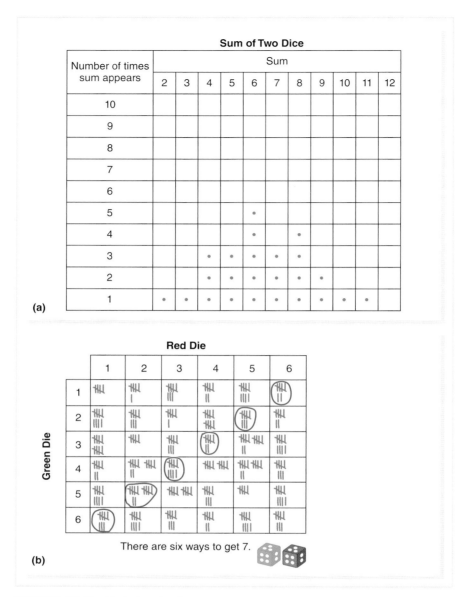

FIGURE 22.7 Exploring the frequencies (dot plot) and possible outcomes (matrix) for the sum of two dice.

⏸ Pause & Reflect

Use a chart and/or tree diagram to analyze the sum of two number cubes each with sides 1, 1, 2, 3, 3, and 3. (These were the cubes used in Activities 22.3 and 22.4.) What is the probability of each sum, 1 through 6? How might these tools support student understanding of sample space and the probability of independent events? ●

A common process to help students connect sample space with probability is to ask them first to make a prediction of the probability of the event, second to conduct an experiment with a large number of trials, and third to compare the prediction with what happened. Then ask students to create the sample space and see how it compares with the prediction and the results of the experiment. Games provide an excellent context for such explorations, as described in Activity 22.13.

Activity 22.13

CCSS-M: 7.SP.C.7a; 7.SP.C.8a

Lu-Lu

This Hawaiian game involves taking turns tossing four stones and calculating the resulting score. The first player to reach fifty wins. (You can create stones like the ones pictured here by getting glass stones from a craft store and marking dots on one side.)

ENGLISH LANGUAGE LEARNERS

 After the students have played, ask what they notice about the sums they are getting. Ask questions about probability: "What sums are possible?" "What sums were common?" "What scores are possible in a single turn?" "What are all the outcomes (possible combinations of stones)?" and "What is the probability of each score?" ELLs may have games from their native countries. These can be used to explore probability; ask questions like the ones posed here. (See McCoy, Buckner, & Munley, 2007, for more on this game.)

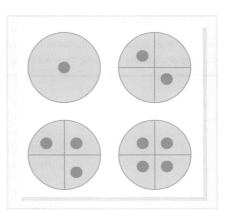

The following are additional examples of probabilities of independent events. Any one of these could be explored as part of a full lesson.

- Rolling an even sum with two dice
- Spinning blue twice on a spinner
- Having a tack *or* a cup land up when each is tossed once
- Getting at *least* two heads from tossing four coins
- Rolling two dice and getting a difference that is *no more than* 3

 Words and phrases such as *and, or, at least,* and *no more than* may cause students some confusion and therefore require explicit attention. Of special note is the word *or* because its meaning in everyday usage is generally not the same as its strict logical meaning in mathematics. In mathematics, *or* includes the case of both. So in the tack and cup example, the event includes tack up, cup up, and both tack and cup up.

Area Representation

One way to determine the theoretical probability of a multi-stage event is to list all possible outcomes and count the number of outcomes that make up the event. This is effective but has some limitations. First, a list implies that all outcomes are equally likely. Second, lists can get tedious when there are many possibilities. Third, students can lose track of which possibilities they have included in the list and may leave off some of the possibilities. For all of these reasons, an area representation is a good option for determining probability, the focus of Activity 22.14.

CCSS Standards for Mathematical Practice

MP6. Attend to precision.

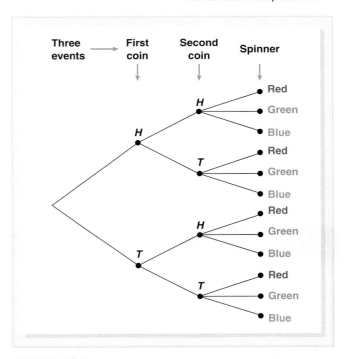

FIGURE 22.8   A tree diagram showing all possible outcomes for two coins and a spinner that is $\frac{1}{3}$ red, $\frac{1}{3}$ green, and $\frac{1}{3}$ blue.

Activity 22.14 CCSS-M: 7.SP.C.8a,b

Are You a Spring Dog?

Before doing this activity, determine which Chinese birth year animals are likely to be represented in the classroom (e.g., the dog and the rooster). Spend some time discussing the Chinese birth year animals with students. (This would be particularly timely at the Chinese New Year!). Begin by finding out what percentage of the class is represented by each animal. Ask, "If I name one of the Chinese birth year animals, what is the probability it will be *your* birth year animal?" Illustrate this percentage by partitioning a rectangle, as in Figure 22.9(a). (This particular illustration finds that 64 percent of the students in the class were born in the year of the dog, and 36 percent were born in the year of the rooster.) Ask, "If I name one of the seasons, what is the probability it will be *your* season?" Ask students to illustrate their response by partitioning and shading a rectangle (Figure 22.9(b)). Then ask, "What is the probability of being both a spring and a dog?"

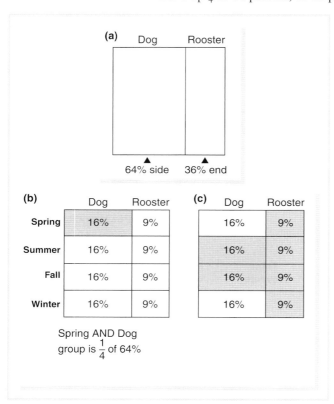

FIGURE 22.9 An area representation for determining probabilities.

In Figure 22.9(b), you can visually see that students in the year of the dog and spring groups make up $\frac{1}{4}$ of 64 percent, or 16 percent of the population. This should look very familiar, as the same process is used for multiplying fractions. The area representation is also effective in solving "or" situations. Consider the question, "What is the probability you were born in fall or summer, or that you are a rooster?" The shading for this example is illustrated in Figure 22.9(c). Half of the students are born in summer or fall, and 36 percent are born in the year of the rooster. Students can add up the percentages in the boxes, or they can think about the two situations separately: 50 percent are born in summer or fall and 36 percent are born in the year of the rooster. The combination of these results is 86 percent, but some students are both and have therefore been double-counted (see overlap in diagram). In this example, the overlap is 18 percent. Therefore, the population that is born in summer or fall or born in the year of the rooster is 50 + 36 − 18 = 68 percent of the population. Challenge students to generalize the patterns they are noticing in their problems and help students connect the area representation to the following model for the probability of two independent events:

$$P(A \text{ or } B) = P(A) + P(B) - P(A \text{ and } B)$$

The area representation is accessible to a range of learn as it is less abstract than equations or tree diagrams.

Designing a spinner is a challenging and engaging way for students to think about the probability of independent events (Ely & Cohen, 2010). The following activity is challenging and an area representation can be used to help students reason about how to design their spinner.

Activity 22.15 CCSS-M: 7.SP.C.6; 7.SP.C.7a; 7.SP.C.8a, b

Design a Winning Spinner

Explain that each student is going to create a winning spinner, which means that when it is spun twice, the sum will be on a number strip with values 2, 3, 4, 5, 6, 7, and 8. Students create their own spinner, partitioning the circle however they like and writing a number in each sector. Once students have their spinner, they pair with someone else and play the game with their own spinner: Student A spins twice and adds the two values. If the sum is 5, student A covers 5 on his or her number strip. Student B takes a turn. The first partner to cover all numbers on his or her strip wins. Play three rounds. Next, ask students to redesign their spinner, find a new partner, and play three more rounds. If possible, repeat a third time. Afterwards, discuss how they designed a winning spinner.

In going backwards (from the desired outcome to the spinner), students can build a deeper understanding of how to determine the probability of independent events.

CCSS Standards for Mathematical Practice

MP8. Look for and express regularity in repeated reasoning.

Dependent Events

A dependent event is a second event whose result depends on the result of a first event. For example, suppose that there are two identical boxes. One box contains one genuine dollar bill and two counterfeit bills, and the other box contains one genuine and one counterfeit bill (you do not know which box is which). You may choose one box and from that box select one bill without looking. What are your chances of getting a genuine dollar bill? Here there are two events: selecting a box and selecting a bill. The probability of getting a dollar in the second event depends on which box is chosen in the first event. These events are *dependent*, not independent.

Activity 22.16   CCSS-M: 7.SP.C.8a, b

Keys to a New Car

Pose the following problem: In a game show, you can win a car—if you make it through the maze to the room where you have placed the car key. You can place the keys in either Room A or Room B (see maze in Figure 22.10). At the start and at each fork in the path, you must spin the indicated spinner and follow the path that it points to. Once you've reached Room A or Room B, the game is over—there is no going back through the maze. In which room should you place the key to have the best chance of winning the car?

You can use the area representation to determine the probability for dependent events. Figure 22.11 illustrates the "Keys to a New Car" task.

 Pause & Reflect

How would the area representation for the car problem be different if the spinner at Forks I and II were $\frac{1}{3}$ A and $\frac{2}{3}$ B spinners? What questions like this one can you ask students in order to help them think about how one event depends on the next? ●

Figure 22.12 shows a tree diagram for the "Keys to a New Car" problem, with the probability of each path in the maze written on the "branch" of the tree. The tree diagram is more abstract than the area approach, but it applies to a wider range of situations. Each branch of the tree diagram in Figure 22.12 shows a section of the square in Figure 22.11. Use the area representation to explain why the probability for each complete branch of the tree is determined by multiplying the probabilities along the branch. Having students describe the connection between the area and the tree diagram representations can help build meaning for the tree diagram approach, which can be used in any multiple-events probability task.

 Complete Self-Check 22.3: Sample Spaces and the Probability of Compound Events

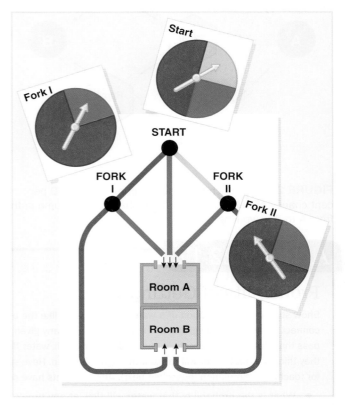

FIGURE 22.10   Should you place your key in Room A or Room B to have the best chance at winning?

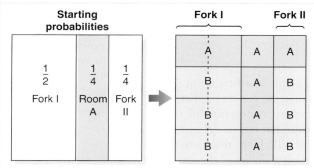

At Fork I, $\frac{3}{4}$ of the time you will go to Room B.

(<u>Note:</u> Not $\frac{3}{4}$ of the square but $\frac{3}{4}$ of the times you go to Fork I.)

At Fork II, $\frac{3}{4}$ of <u>these</u> times (or $\frac{3}{16}$ of <u>total</u> time) you will go to Room B.

Therefore, you will end up in Room A $\frac{7}{16}$ of the time and Room B $\frac{9}{16}$ of the time.

FIGURE 22.11 Using the area representation to solve the maze problem.

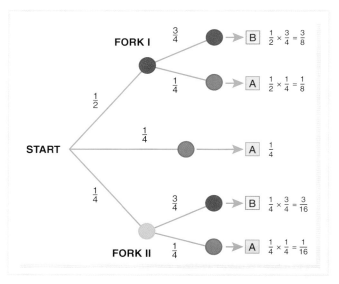

FIGURE 22.12 A tree diagram is another way to representation the outcomes of two or more dependent events.

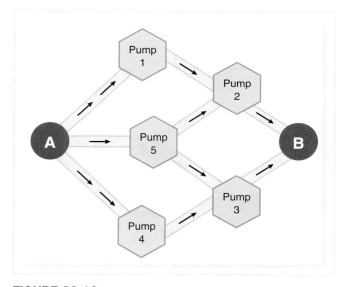

FIGURE 22.13 Each of these five pumps has a 50 percent chance of failure. What is the probability that some path from A to B is working?

Simulations

Simulation is a technique used for answering real-world questions or making decisions in complex situations where an element of chance is involved. Many times simulations are conducted because it is too dangerous, complex, or expensive to manipulate the real situation. To see what is likely to happen in the real event, a model must be designed that has the same probabilities as the real situation. For example, in the designing of a rocket, a large number of related systems all have some chance of failure that might cause serious problems with the rocket. Knowing the probability of serious failures will help determine whether redesign or backup systems are required. It is not reasonable to make repeated tests of the actual rocket. Instead, a model that simulates all of the chance situations is designed and run repeatedly with the help of a computer. The computer model can simulate thousands of flights, and an estimate of the chance of failure can be made.

Activity 22.17   CCSS-M: 7.SP.C.8b,c

Probability of Getting Water

Show students an illustration of a water pump system like the one illustrated in Figure 22.13. Explain that the five pumps that connect A and B are aging, and it is estimated that at any given time, the probability of pump failure is $\frac{1}{2}$. If a pump fails, water cannot pass that station. For example, if pumps 1, 2, and 5 fail, water flows only through pumps 4 and 3. Ask students to discuss how likely they think it is that water will make it through the pump. Have students mark how likely on a probability continuum. Follow the steps for teaching a simulation (described next). After students have completed their simulation, revisit the important probability questions:

- What is the probability that water will flow at any time?
- On the average, about how many stations need repair at any time?

Shodor's Project Interactivate offers a realistic simulation of actual forest fires. The simulation, titled "A Better Fire," uses a virtual "die" to see whether a tree should be planted for each square. Then the fire is set and allowed to burn.

For any simulation, the following steps can serve as a useful guide. Here the steps are explained for use with Activity 22.17.

1. *Identify key components and assumptions of the problem.* The key component in the water problem is the condition of a pump. Each pump is either working or not working. In this problem, the assumption is that the probability that a pump is working is $\frac{1}{2}$.
2. *Select a random device for the key components.* Any random device can be selected that has outcomes with the same probability as those of the key component—in this case, the pumps. Here a simple choice might be tossing a coin, with heads representing a working pump.
3. *Define a trial.* A *trial* consists of simulating a series of key components until the situation has been completely modeled one time. In this problem, a trial could consist of tossing a coin five times, each toss representing a different pump (heads for pump is working and tails for pump is not working).
4. *Conduct a large number of trials and record the information.* For this problem, it would be useful to record the number of heads and tails in groups of five because each set of five is one trial and represents all of the pumps.
5. *Use the data to draw conclusions.* There are four possible paths for the water, each flowing through two of the five pumps. As they are numbered in the drawing, if any one of the pairs 1-2, 5-2, 5-3, and 4-3 is open, it makes no difference whether the other pumps are working. By counting the number of trials in which at least one of these four pairs of coins both come up heads, we can estimate the probability of water flowing. To answer the second question, the number of tails (pumps not working) per trial can be averaged.

Here are a few more examples of problems for which a simulation can be used to gather empirical data.

In a true/false test, what is the probability of getting 7 out of 10 questions correct by guessing alone? (*Key component:* Answering a question. *Assumption:* Chance of getting it correct is $\frac{1}{2}$.)

    Simulation option: Flip a coin 10 times for one trial.

In a group of five people, what is the chance that two were born in the same month? (*Key component:* Month of birth. *Assumption:* All 12 months are equally likely.)

    Simulation option: Use 12-sided die or 12 cards. Draw/roll one, replace, and draw/roll again.

Casey's batting average is .350. What is the chance he will go hitless in a complete nine-inning game? (*Key component:* Getting a hit. *Assumptions:* The probability of a hit for each at-bat is .35. Casey will get to bat four times in the average game.)

    Simulation option: Use a spinner that is 35 percent shaded. Spin four times for one trial.

Krunch-a-Munch cereal packs one of five games in each box. About how many boxes should you expect to buy before you get a complete set? (*Key component:* Getting one game. *Assumption:* Each game has a $\frac{1}{5}$ chance.)

    Simulation option: Use a spinner with five equal sections. Spin until all sections occur at least once. Record how many spins it took (this is one trial). Repeat. The average length of a trial answers the question. Extension: What is the chance of getting a set in eight or fewer boxes?

Students often have trouble selecting an appropriate random device for simulations. Spinners are a good choice because areas can be adjusted to match probabilities. Coins or two-colored counters are useful for probabilities of $\frac{1}{2}$. A standard die can be used for probabilities that are multiples of $\frac{1}{6}$. There are also dice available online and on smartphones with 4, 8, 12, and 20 sides. Many calculators include a key that will produce random numbers that can be used to simulate experiments (e.g., 1 means true and 2 means false). Usually, the random numbers generated are between 0 and 1, such as 0.8904433368. How could a list of decimals like this replace flipping a coin or spinning a spinner? Suppose each was multiplied by 2. The results would be between 0 and 2, as shown here:

$$0.8904433368 \times 2 = 1.7808866736$$

$$0.0232028877 \times 2 = 0.0464057754$$

$$0.1669322714 \times 2 = 0.3338645428$$

If you focus on the ones column, you have a series of zeros and ones that could represent heads and tails, boys and girls, true and false, or any other pair of equally likely outcomes. For three outcomes, the same as a $\frac{1}{4}/\frac{1}{4}/\frac{1}{2}$ spinner, you might decide to look at the first two digits of the number and assign values from 0 to 24 and from 25 to 49 to the two one-quarter portions and values 50 to 99 for the one-half portion. The NCTM Illuminations Adjustable Spinners can be set up for such simulations. Alternatively, each randomly generated number could be multiplied by 4 and the decimal part ignored, resulting in random numbers 0, 1, 2, and 3. These could then be assigned to the desired outcomes.

In this activity, consider how you would design a simulation.

Activity 22.18 CCSS-M: 7.SP.C.8b,c

Chance of Triplet Girls

Ask students, "What is the chance that a woman having triplets will end up with all girls?" Record estimates. Ask students to create a simulation to model this problem using the five steps previously described. Encourage students to use various tools to simulate (flipping three coins, using a random number generator, spinning a two-color spinner three times, etc.). After examining the results, ask questions to relate the predictions to the results. This may lead to creating a tree diagram of the options to make sense of the results.

 Complete Self-Check 22.4: Simulations

 Common Misconceptions about Probability

Tasks like "Chance of Triplet Girls" can lead to interesting follow-up questions: "Are three girls less likely or more likely than two girls and a boy?" and "If a family already has two girls, what do you think they will have for their third child?" (Tillema, 2010). These questions connect to two of the common misconceptions students have related to probability: the commutativity confusion and gambler's fallacy. These misconceptions, and two shared earlier, are discussed briefly here.

1. *Commutativity confusion.* Students may think two girls and one boy is one possible outcome. But notice that if you list the eight possible combinations for three children, you have three girls only once (GGG), but two girls and one boy three times (GGB, GBG, BGG). Two girls and one boy is three times as likely. We refer to this as *commutativity*

confusion because students, knowing that 3 + 4 is the same as 4 + 3, think that that one boy and two girls is one event, not three. Students need to think about all the ways an event can occur when they try to determine how likely an event is.

2. *Gambler's fallacy.* The gambler's fallacy is the notion that what has already happened (two girls) influences the event. Students will argue a boy is more likely because there are already two girls. Similarly, students think that if a coin has had a series of 4 heads, it is more likely on the fifth flip to be tails (Ryan & Williams, 2007). But a coin has no memory, and the probability of heads or tails is still fifty-fifty, just as the probability of a girl is still fifty-fifty.

3. *Law of small numbers.* This misconception is like the gambler's fallacy in that it relates to small samples but, with this misconception, students expect small samples to be like the greater population (Flores, 2006; Tarr, Lee, & Rider, 2006). This is discussed previously in the section "The Law of Large Numbers" (see Activities 22.11 and 22.12). So in the case of the three girls, it is not so unusual—it is just a very small data set, so it is not likely to resemble the larger population.

4. *Possibility counting.* In this case, students see what the possibilities are and assume each is equally likely. If a dice has a 1, 2, 3, then each has a $\frac{1}{3}$ chance of occurring. Similarly, if a spinner has a red and blue section, then each has a fifty-fifty chance of occurring, even if there is more red on the spinner than blue. Activities 22.3, 22.4, and 22.5 are designed to help students focus on frequency rather than possible outcomes in determining probability of an event.

Whether doing simulations, experiments, or theoretical probability, it is important for students to use many representations (lists, area, tree diagrams) and discuss developing conceptions and misconceptions explicitly. In addition to being more interesting, teaching probability in this way allows students to understand important concepts that have many real-world implications. This final activity is designed to apply different representations as well as simulations.

Activity 22.19
CCSS-M: 7.SP.C.8a, b, c

Money in Two Piggy Banks

Use the Money in Two Piggy Banks **Activity Page or post the following problem for students:**

Use an area representation and a tree diagram to determine the probability for the following situation:

In a game at the County Fair, the game leader puts one $5 bill and three $1 bills in the Piggy Bank 1. In Piggy Bank 2, he puts one $5 bill and one $1 bill. To play the game, you get to take one bill from Piggy Bank 1 (without looking) and put it in Piggy Bank 2. After mixing Piggy Bank 2, you get to take one bill from that bank. The game costs $2 to play. Should you spend your money?

Ask students to illustrate the theoretical probability using (1) an area representation and (2) a tree diagram. This can be done by having some pairs work on one and other pairs work on the other, then compare and share their diagrams. Or, everyone can create both. After these illustrations are complete, ask students how they might design a simulation to test this game. Invite students to explain their simulation and present it. Ask other students to determine if the simulation accurately models the game.

 Complete Self-Check 22.5: Common Misconceptions about Probability

REFLECTIONS ON CHAPTER 22

WRITING TO LEARN

1. What are the first ideas about probability that students should develop? How can you help students with these ideas?

2. Activities 22.3, 22.4, 22.5 are designed to help students see that some outcomes are more likely than others. What are the similarities and differences between these two activities? Why might this difference be useful in helping students gain insights about how likely an event is?

3. What are the advantages of having students conduct experiments even before they attempt to figure out a theoretical probability?

4. Explain the law of large numbers. Describe an activity that might help students appreciate this idea.

5. Describe the difference between an independent and dependent event. Give an example of each.

6. What are some misconceptions and challenges students have with learning probability?

FOR DISCUSSION AND EXPLORATION

♦ The classic "Monty Hall Problem" is a favorite for studying probability. In the game show, one of three doors has a big prize. The contestant guesses one door, but before revealing what is behind that door, Monty shows the contestant a goat behind one of the doors not selected. Then he offers the contestant the opportunity to switch doors. Does the contestant have a better chance of winning the big prize by *switching* or by *staying* with the original choice (or does it not matter)? There are numerous methods of answering this question. Make a convincing argument for your own answer based on the ideas and techniques in this chapter.

♦ Go to the Illuminations website and explore one of the virtual experiments. Discuss (a) the advantages and disadvantages of virtual experiments and (b) the content within this chapter that could be discussed following student exploration of this experiment.

RESOURCES FOR CHAPTER 22

LITERATURE CONNECTIONS

The books described here offer both fanciful and real-life data for investigating probability. These books can also be paired with activities in this chapter.

Go Figure! A Totally Cool Book about Numbers
Ball (2005)

This wonderful book could be placed in every chapter of this text. About 40 different topics are covered, one of which is called "Take a Chance." This two-page spread is full of interesting contexts for probability, including a match-dropping experiment and genetics.

Harry Potter and the Sorcerer's Stone *Rowling (1998)*

The game of Quidditch can lend itself to creating a simulation to explore the probability of winning. Wagner and Lachance (2004) suggest that sums of two dice be linked to Quidditch actions. For example, a roll of 7 means a player scores a Quaffle, which is worth 10 points. Rolls of 2 or 12 mean the player catches the Snitch and the game ends, 150 points; 3, 5, 9, 11 means hit by Bludger, lose a turn; 4, 6, 8, 10 means dodge a

Bludger, no points. Students play and then explore the probability of winning.

Do You Wanna Bet? Your Chance to Find Out about Probability *Cushman (2007)*

The two characters in this book, Danny and Brian, become involved in everyday situations both in and out of school. Each situation involves an element of probability. For example, two invitations to birthday parties are for the same day. What is the chance that two friends would have the same birthday? In another situation, Danny flips heads several times and readers are asked about Brian's chances on the next flip. Students can create simulations to examine some of the ideas.

My Little Sister Ate One Hare *Grossman (1996)*

This counting book will appeal to the middle school set as well as to young students due to the somewhat gross thought of a little girl eating one rabbit, two snakes, three ants, and so on, including bats, mice, worms, and lizards. Upon eating ten peas, she throws up everything she ate.

Bay-Williams and Martinie (2004b) used this tale to explore probability. If one of the things the little sister "spilled" on the floor is picked up at random in the process of cleaning up, what is the probability of getting a polliwog (or other animal or category of animal)? Students can use cards representing things eaten and approach the task experimentally.

RECOMMENDED READINGS

Articles

Coffey, D. C., & Richardson, M. G. (2005). Rethinking fair games. *Mathematics Teaching in the Middle School, 10*(6), 298–303.

Students explore the fairness of a matching game both experimentally and using a theoretical model. They then set out to create a variation of the game that would be fair by assigning points to a match and to a mismatch. A TI-73 program is included that simulates the revised game.

Edwards, T. G., & Hensien, S. M. (2000). Using probability experiments to foster discourse. *Teaching Children Mathematics, 6*(8), 524–529.

Fifth-grade students experiment with outcomes of flipping a coin, spinning a spinner, and rolling a die. The discourse is directed to the disparity between the observed outcomes and the theoretical probabilities. For example, is it reasonable that there are 77 heads out of 150 tosses?

McCoy, L. P., Buckner, S., & Munley, J. (2007). Probability games from diverse cultures. *Mathematics Teaching in the Middle School, 12*(7), 394–402.

As the title suggests, this article includes games from African, Hawaiian, Jewish, Mexican, and Native American cultures. Games include probability connections, handouts, and questions to pose to students.

McMillen, S. (2008). Predictions and probability. *Teaching Children Mathematics, 14*(8), 454–463.

This article provides a series of high-quality probability lessons—various contexts and representations are used, as well as calculators. The lessons include a number of key concepts discussed in this chapter, and two handouts are provided.

Book

Shaughnessy, J. M. (2003). Research on students' understanding of probability. In J. Kilpatrick, W. G. Martin, & D. Schifter (Eds.), *A research companion to Principles and Standards for School Mathematics* (pp. 216–226). Reston, VA: NCTM.

Shaughnessy's chapter offers interesting insights from research and makes useful recommendations about successful ways to teach probability concepts.

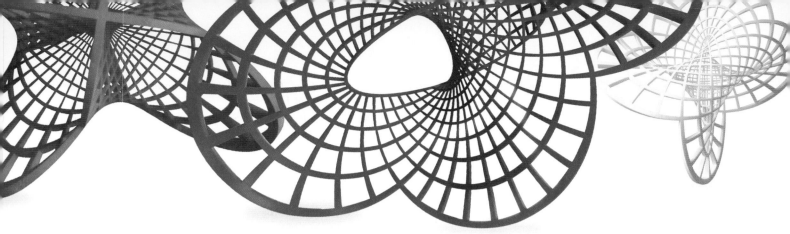

CHAPTER 23

Developing Concepts of Exponents, Integers, and Real Numbers

LEARNER OUTCOMES

After reading this chapter and engaging in the embedded activities and reflections, you should be able to:

23.1 Describe strategies to meaningfully engage students in understanding exponents, order of operations, scientific notation, and very large and very small numbers.

23.2 Compare quantity and number line visuals for teaching integers, and contrast the different contexts for teaching about positive and negative numbers.

23.3 Illustrate and explain conceptual approaches to teaching operations with positive and negative numbers.

23.4 Construct a visual that illustrates the relationships among different types of numbers (irrational, whole, etc.) and describe conceptual ways to introduce irrational numbers.

In elementary school, students explore whole numbers and positive fractions and decimals; in middle school students explore an expanded number system and learn new ways to represent numbers, including scientific and exponential notation, negative numbers, and irrational numbers. The ideas presented in this chapter build on ideas that have been developed throughout this book. Exponents are used in algebraic expressions and add to the operations. Scientific notation expands how large and small numbers are represented, building on place-value concepts. Integers move beyond the positive counting numbers to numbers less than 0 and therefore extend the number line (as well as operations) to include negative values. As students expand their knowledge of how to represent numbers and explore new types of numbers, it is important that the following big ideas are at the center of that instruction.

 BIG IDEAS

- Our number system includes whole numbers, fractions, decimals, and integers, all of which are rational numbers. Every rational number can be expressed as a fraction.

- Integers are the negative and positive counting numbers and 0. Positive and negative numbers describe quantities having both magnitude and direction (e.g., temperature above or below zero).

♦ Exponential notation is a way to express repeated products of the same number. Specifically, powers of 10 express very large and very small numbers in an economical manner.

♦ Many numbers are not rational; the irrationals can be expressed only symbolically or approximately using a close rational number. Examples include $\sqrt{2} \approx 1.41421\ldots$ and $\pi \approx 3.14159\ldots$.

Exponents

As numbers in our increasingly technological world get very small or very large, expressing them in standard form can be cumbersome. Exponential notation is more efficient for conveying numeric or quantitative information. In the CCSS, exponents are first introduced in fifth grade related to powers of ten and place value. In sixth grade, students learn to write and evaluate numerical expressions involving whole-number exponents. In eighth grade, students work with radicals and integer exponents.

Exponents in Expressions and Equations

The "rules" of exponents may be confusing for students. For example, with only a rule-based background they may not remember whether you add or multiply the exponents when you raise a number to a given power. This is an indication that students lack a conceptual understanding of the operations and notation. Students need to explore exponents with whole numbers before they use exponents with variables. By looking at whole-number exponents, they are able to notice patterns in solving problems and are able to generate (and understand) the rules themselves.

A whole-number exponent is simply shorthand for repeated multiplication of a number times itself; for example, $3^4 = 3 \times 3 \times 3 \times 3$.

At first, symbols for exponents are abstract and unfamiliar and thereby require explicit attention. First, an exponent applies to its immediate base. For example, in the expression $2 + 5^3$, the exponent 3 applies only to the 5, so the expression is equal to $2 + (5 \times 5 \times 5)$. However, in the expression $(2 + 5)^3$, the 3 is an exponent of the quantity $2 + 5$ and is evaluated as $(2 + 5) \times (2 + 5) \times (2 + 5)$, or $7 \times 7 \times 7$. Notice that the process follows the order of operations. As with any topic, start with what is familiar and concrete. With exponents, this means beginning with exploring powers of 2 and 3—operations that can be represented geometrically.

Minia knows that square animal pens are the most economical for the amount of area they provide (assuming straight sides). Can you provide a table for Minia that shows the areas of square pens that have between 4 meters and 10 meters of fence on each side?

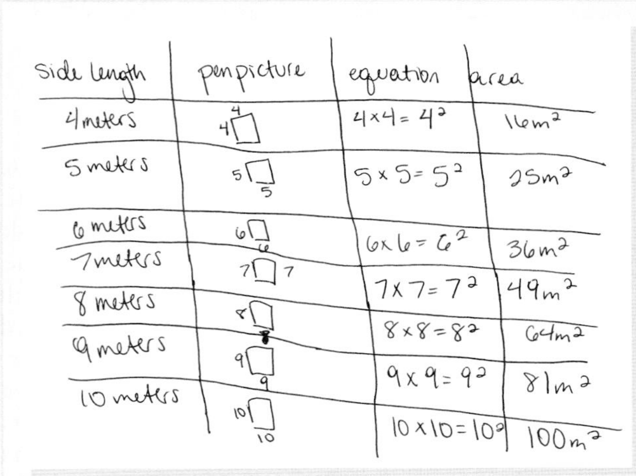

Students may set up a table similar to Figure 23.1, showing possible areas for the square pens.

Another way to explore exponents is to explore algebraic growing patterns involving squares and/or cubes. The classic Painted Cube Problem prepared on the Painted Cube Activity Page and illustrated in Figure 23.2 is an excellent way to explore squares and cubes. The painted cube is made up of centimeter cubes (called blocks here

CCSS **Standards for Mathematical Practice**

MP8. Look for and express regularity in repeated reasoning.

FIGURE 23.1 A student records possibilities for making a square pen.

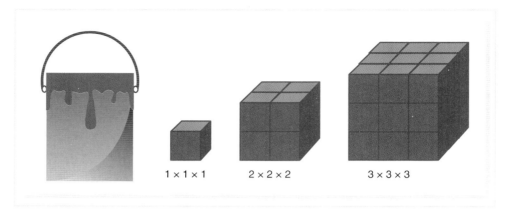

FIGURE 23.2 The Painted Cube Problem asks students to figure out how many sides of the little cubes are painted when the larger cubes are dipped in paint.

for clarity); each face of the cube is painted. As the painted cube grows, so does the size of each face, as well as the number of blocks hidden inside the large painted cube. In a $2 \times 2 \times 2$ painted cube, the faces are 2×2; in a $3 \times 3 \times 3$ painted cube the faces are 3×3. Note that while each face is 3×3, the blocks in the center of each face, get only one side painted, while the blocks on the edges get more sides painted. Consider what is happening with blocks in the middle of the painted cube. In a $2 \times 2 \times 2$ there are 0 inside blocks; in the $3 \times 3 \times 3$ there is a $1 \times 1 \times 1$ "hidden" centimeter block inside that will not get painted on any face. In a $4 \times 4 \times 4$, there will be $2 \times 2 \times 2(8)$ hidden blocks. As students explore, they will see that the number of blocks with one side painted grows at a quadratic rate and the number of hidden blocks grows at a cubic rate. In exploring the pattern, students get experience with algebraic rules that are linear, squared, and cubed.

TECHNOLOGY **Note.** Exponential growth is very interesting to explore in real-world contexts. The site called "Otherwise" offers an applet that can engage students in experiments with population (exponential) growth. Another powerful exploration of exponential growth is to look at Powers of 10 on the Florida State University Molecular Expressions website. This interactive starts way out in the universe (10^{23}), then continues to zoom in until it reaches earth (with real screenshots), ending with zooming in on cells to a quark at 10^{-14}! ■

Order of Operations

Working with exponents extends the *order of operations*. As early as third grade, students need to know the order of operations for addition, subtraction, multiplication, and division, and in sixth grade, exponents are added to the order of operations (CCSSO, 2010). An exponent indicates the number of times the base is used as a factor, so it indicates repeated multiplication and therefore precedes other multiplication and division, as well as addition and subtraction. In the expression $5 \times 4^2 - 6$, 4^2 is done first because in expanded form this would be $5 \times 4 \times 4 - 6$. Order of operations is not just a convention; it is based on the meaning of the operations. Pose a problem like the one here and ask students to explain why exponents are computed prior to multiplication. Then students can see why multiplying before computing the exponent changes the meaning of the problem (and the answer), while doing exponents first results in the same quantity. When we want to communicate that operations are to be computed in a different order, we have to use parentheses.

Though part of the order of operations is due to convention (e.g., working from left to right, using parentheses), the order of the computations are due to the meanings of these operations. A context can make this point clearer, which is the focus of Activity 23.1.

Activity 23.1

CCSS-M: 3.OA.D.8; 6.EE.A.2c

Stacks of Coins

Select a story situation that includes such things as stacks of coins, bricks, or notebooks. If you have the book *Two of Everything* by Lily Hong, you can use the Haktaks' stacks of coins from their magic pot as the context. Tell stories and ask students to (1) write an expression and (2) tell you how many. For example: "Mrs. Haktak had one stack with seven coins and four stacks with ten coins. How many coins did she have?" (Students should write $7 + 4 \times 10$ or $4 \times 10 + 7$ for the expression.) Ask "Could we write it either way? Why or why not?" and "Could we add the seven to the four and then multiply by 10? Why or why not?" Then write expressions with addition and multiplication and ask students to tell their own stories as they solve the problem.

Another way to illustrate why the order is true is to write an expression, such as $4^2 + 3 + 2 \times 5$, as *all* addition: $4^2 + 3 + 2 \times 5 = 4 + 4 + 4 + 4 + 3 + 5 + 5$. How would you combine? Add up all the fours $(4 \times 4 = 4^2)$ then add $5 + 5 (2 \times 5)$, and add on 3.

The phrase "Please excuse my dear Aunt Sally" or more simply, "PEMDAS" or "PEDMAS" is sometimes used in the United States to help students remember the order of operations. In other countries (including Canada, the United Kingdom, and other English-speaking countries), different mnemonics are used, including BODMAS, BEDMAS, and BIDMAS, with the word *bracket* replacing *parentheses*, and *order* or *indices* sometimes used for *exponents* (Bay-Williams & Martinie, 2015). Although a mnemonic may be helpful, it may lead students to think that addition is done before subtraction and multiplication comes before division (Ameis, 2011; Jeon, 2012). A visual can more effectively illustrate that multiplication and division are at the same level and addition and subtraction are at the same level. Two such possible posters are pictured in Figure 23.3. Notice the pyramid has only three levels. These are the three categories of operations (parentheses are used to change the order) (Ameis, 2011).

Another important point about the order of operation is that it is not as rigid as the list might imply. For example, consider the expression $14 \times 7 - 5 \times 7$. It doesn't matter which product is figured first. In fact, the CCSS-M describes mathematically proficient students as those who will look closely to notice the structure of a problem—for example, noticing that in this case that it doesn't matter which product is determined first, and even recognizing that they could apply the distributive property and factor out a 7, then first subtract $14 - 5$.

TECHNOLOGY Note. Math-Play has the Order of Operations Millionaire Game, which engages students in practicing the order of operations in a game format, similar to "Who Wants to Be a Millionaire." You can also strengthen students' understanding of order of operations by having them record expressions, using appropriate symbols, as in the following activity. ■

Standards for Mathematical Practice

MP7. Look for and make use of structure.

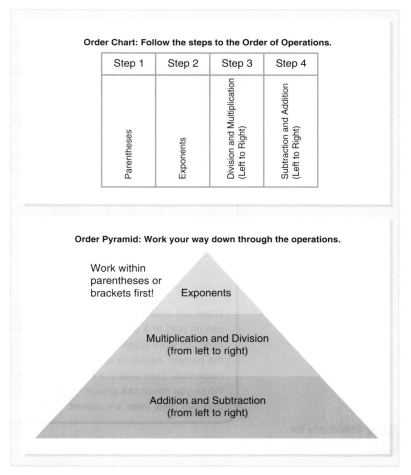

FIGURE 23.3 Two possible posters for illustrating the Order of Operations.

Activity 23.2

CCSS-M: 6.EE.A.2a, b, c; 6.EE.B.6

Guess My Number

In this activity you give hints about a number and students think backwards to find it (using logical reasoning). For ELLs and students with disabilities, provide the statements in writing and verbally. Students create equations, using parentheses appropriately to reflect the clues you give, as in the following three examples:

ENGLISH LANGUAGE LEARNERS

- I am thinking of a number; I add 5, double it, and get 22. $[(n + 5) \times 2 = 22]$
- I am thinking of a number; I subtract 2, square it, and get 36. $[(n - 2)^2 = 36]$
- I am thinking of a number; I double it, add 2, cube it, and get 1000. $[(2n + 2)^3 = 1000]$

STUDENTS with SPECIAL NEEDS

For students with disabilities, you may want to start with a known number rather than an unknown number—for example, start with 5, square it, add 11, divide by 6. They should write $(5^2 + 11) \div 6 = n$.

FORMATIVE ASSESSMENT Notes. Give students an expression that includes all the operations and the use of parentheses—for example, $(4 + 2)^2 \times 2 \div 4$—and ask them to write a story to fit the expression using a context of their choice. Writing these stories in journals provides an excellent assessment of students' understanding of the order of operations. As you review students' stories, see if they realize that multiplication and division (and addition and subtraction) are equal in the hierarchy of order and should therefore be solved left to right. ■

Another way to engage students or assess their understanding of exponents and order of operations is to determine if given equations are true or false. This is the focus of Activity 23.3.

Activity 23.3

CCSS-M: 3.OA.D.8; 6.EE.A.3; 6.EE.A.4

True or False Equations

Write an equation that addresses one or more aspects of the order of operations. For example: $24 \div (4 \times 2) = 24 \div 4 \times 2$. If students think that multiplication comes before division, or if they are not aware of the left-to-right prioritizing, they will write "true." Examples (at various grade levels) include:

$$17 \times 3 = 15 + 2 \times 3$$
$$2 + 5^3 = 7^3$$
$$3.2^2 + 3.2^2 = 3.2^4$$
$$4(2 + x) = 8 + 4x$$
$$4y - y = 4$$

$$3.2 - 1.2 + 0.04 = (3.2 - 1.2) + 0.04$$
$$(3.6 + 0.4)^2 = 4^2$$
$$6 \cdot 2^4 = 12^4$$
$$x + x^2 = x^3$$
$$3z + z = z + z + z + z$$

There are several ways to incorporate true/false equations. First, one or two of these equations can be part of a daily warm-up routine. Second, equations can be written on cards and partners can work together. Both partners think of the answer, one student says true or false, and the partner agrees or disagrees. If they disagree, they try to convince each other of the correct responses. They create a stack of their true equations and a stack of their false equations. When you check the groups' progress, you can formatively assess by seeing if the cards in their true and false piles are correct.

CCSS **Standards for Mathematical Practice**

MP3. Construct viable arguments and critique the reasoning of others.

The true/false statements can address commonly misunderstood aspects of the order of operation. Such tasks make explicit what misconceptions students might have (for example, that multiplication always precedes division). True/false tasks set up an excellent opportunity for students to debate, justify, and critique the justifications of their peers.

Exponent Notation on the Calculator. Most simple four-function calculators do not use algebraic logic, so operations are processed as they are entered. On calculators without algebraic logic, the following two keying sequences produce the same results:

Key: →	3	**+**	2	**×**	7	**=**
Display →	3		2	5	7	35

Key: →	3	**+**	2	**=**	**×**	7	**=**
Display →	3		2	5		7	35

Whenever an operation sign is pressed, the effect is the same as pressing $=$ and then the operation. Of course, neither result is correct for the expressions $3 + 2 \times 7$, which should be evaluated as $3 + 14$, or 17.

Calculators designed for middle grades often use algebraic logic (follow the order of operations) and include parentheses keys so that both $3 + 2 \times 7$ and $(3 + 2) \times 7$ can be keyed in the order that the symbols appear. See the difference in the following displays:

Key: →	3	**+**	2	**×**	7	**=**
Display →	3		2		7	17

Notice that the following display does not change when $\times$ is pressed and a right parenthesis is not displayed. Instead, the expression that the right parenthesis encloses is calculated and that result displayed.

Key: →	**(**	3	**+**	2	**)**	**×**	7	**=**
Display →	[	3		2	5		7	35

Some basic calculators and graphing calculators show the expression $3 + 2 \times (6^2 - 4)$. Nothing is evaluated until you press Enter Enter or EXE EXE . Then the result appears on the next line to the right of the screen:

$3 + 2 * (6^2 - 4)$	
	67

The last expression entered can be recalled and edited so that students can see how different expressions are evaluated. Only minimum key presses are required.

$3 + 2 * (6^2 - 4)$	
	67
$(3 + 2) * (6^2 - 4)$	
	160
$(3 + 2) * 6^2 - 4$	
	176
$3 + 2 * 6^2 - 4$	
	71

Calculators remain a powerful tool for exploring impact of operations. For example, to evaluate 3^8, press 3 $\times$ $=$ $=$ $=$ $=$ $=$ $=$ $=$. (The first press of $=$ will result in 9, or 3×3.) Students will be fascinated by how quickly numbers grow. Enter any number, press $\times$, and then repeatedly press $=$. Try two-digit numbers. Try 0.1.

Give students many opportunities to explore expressions involving exponents and the order of operations.

Activity 23.4

CCSS-M: 6.EE.A.3; 6.EE.A.4

Entering Expressions

Provide students with numeric expressions to evaluate with simple four-function calculators. Ask, "How will you have to enter these to correctly apply the order of operations?" Rewrite the expression the way it will be entered. For the boxes with two expressions, compare how they will be entered differently (or if they are entered the same). Here are some examples of expressions:

$3 + 4 \times 8$ $4 \times 8 + 3$	$3^6 + 2^6$ $(3 + 2)^6$	$3^4 \times 7 - 5^2$ $(3 \times 7)^4 - 5 \times 2$	$3^4 \times 5^2$ $(3 \times 5)^6$

$\dfrac{5^3 \times 5^2}{5^6}$	$4 \times 3 - 2^3 \times 5 + 23 \times 9$	$\dfrac{4 \times 3^5}{2}$ $\quad 4 + \dfrac{3^5}{2}$

A common misconception with exponents is to think of the two values as factors, so 5^3 is thought of as 5×3, rather than the correct equivalent expression of $5 \times 5 \times 5$. This is further problematic when students hear things like "It is five three times," since the word "times" indicates multiplication. Avoid confusing language and spend significant time having students state and write the equivalent expressions. Students should write equivalent expressions without exponents or include parentheses to indicate explicit groupings. For example:

$$
\begin{aligned}
(7 \times 2^3 - 5)^3 &= (7 \times (2 \times 2 \times 2) - 5) \\
&\times (7 \times (2 \times 2 \times 2) - 5) \\
&\times (7 \times (2 \times 2 \times 2) - 5) \\
&= ((7 \times 8) - 5) \times ((7 \times 8) - 5) \times ((7 \times 8) - 5) \\
&= (56 - 5) \times (56 - 5) \times (56 - 5) = 51 \times 51 \times 51
\end{aligned}
$$

For many expressions, there is more than one way to proceed, and sharing different ways is important. Activity 23.3 can be adapted to focus on equivalence of simplified and expanded forms.

Even though calculators with algebraic logic will automatically produce correct results (i.e., follow the order of operations), students must know the order of operations, including when they have to do one operation before another, and when it doesn't matter which goes first. This flexibility and awareness become the foundation for symbolic manipulation in algebra.

Integer Exponents

CCSS Standards for Mathematical Practice

MP8. Look for and express regularity in repeated reasoning.

What does 2^{-4} mean? This is a good question to ask students who have been working with positive exponents. The following two related options can help students explore the possibilities of negative exponents. First, looking for patterns as the power of 10 changes directly relates to place value and helps students see the regularity in the base 10 system.

First, have students consider 10^N as follows:

$10^4 = 10{,}000$

$10^3 = 1000$

$10^2 = 100$

$10^1 = 10$

$10^0 = ?$

$10^{-1} = ?$

To continue the pattern, 10^0 would be 1, which it is! (In fact, it is the definition of 10^0.) If the pattern is to continue, the next value would be one-tenth of 1. And each successive number is one-tenth of the one that comes before it:

$$10^{-1} = 0.1 = \tfrac{1}{10}$$

$$10^{-2} = 0.01 = \tfrac{1}{100} = \tfrac{1}{10^2}$$

$$10^{-3} = 0.001 = \tfrac{1}{1000} = \tfrac{1}{10^3}$$

Here students might notice that the negative exponent is the reciprocal of the value it would be without the negative sign.

Second, students can explore negative exponents on a calculator. For example, ask students to figure out what 4^{-3} or 2^{-5} equal. If the calculator has the decimal-to-fraction conversion feature, suggest that students use that feature to help develop the meaning of negative exponents. Figure 23.4 gives an example of how this might look on a graphing calculator. Ask students to notice patterns that they think are generalizable and test those conjectures.

Students often confuse exponent rules. Identifying a mistake in someone else's work is another effective way to help students think about the correct (and incorrect) order in a problem, as illustrated in Activity 23.5.

Standards for Mathematical Practice
MP3. Construct viable arguments and critique the reasoning of others.

Activity 23.5

CCSS-M: 8.EE.A.1

Find the Error

Make a copy of the Find the Error Activity Page for each student, or create your own set of problems that are solved incorrectly and ask students to explain what the student did wrong and how to correct it. Two examples are provided here:

Wilma: $\frac{20x^8}{5x^2} = 4x^4$ *Yoli*: $3^3 \times 3^{-5} = 3^{-2} = -9$

Examples can be increasingly more challenging and can be mixed with correct solutions. For additional activity pages, see Johnson and Thompson (2009).

Scientific Notation

The more common it becomes to find very large or very small numbers in our daily lives, the more important it is to have convenient ways to represent them. Numbers can be written in common form, but when this becomes cumbersome a better option is scientific notation. In the CCSS, scientific notation is an eighth-grade expectation within the domain of Expressions and Equations (CCSSO, 2010). Scientific notation means a number is changed to be the product of a number greater than or equal to 1 and less than 10 multiplied by a power of 10. For example, 3,414,000,000 can also be written as 3.414×10^9.

Different notations have different purposes and values. For example, the population of the world on 6/11/14 was estimated to be 7,171,919,206 (U.S. Census Bureau, n.d.) (You can go to the go to the U.S. Census Bureau Population Clock to get actual data for the day you do this activity!). This can be expressed in various ways:

7,172 million

7.2×10^9

Nearly 7 billion

Each way of stating the number has value and purpose in different contexts. Rather than spend time with exercises converting numbers from standard form to scientific notation, consider large numbers found in newspapers, magazines, and atlases. How are they written? How are they said aloud? When are they rounded and why? What forms of the numbers seem best for the purposes? What level of precision

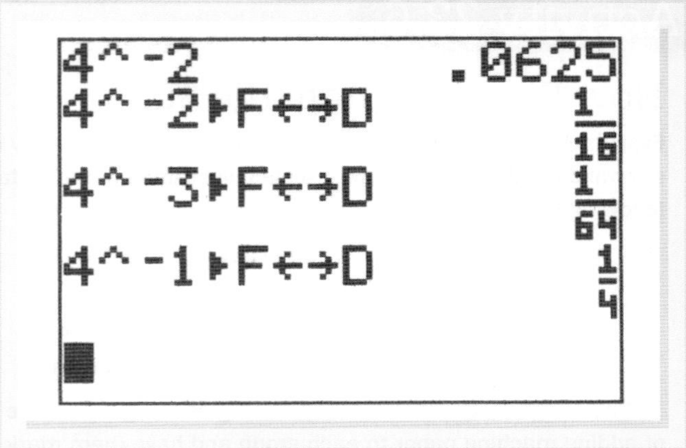

FIGURE 23.4 Graphing calculators evaluate expressions as decimals. This figure shows the screen of a TI-73 calculator. The F-D key converts fractions to decimals as shown here.

is appropriate for the situation? And how do these numbers relate to other numbers? How does the population of the world relate to the population in your state or your continent?

TECHNOLOGY Note. Websites like the U.S. Census Bureau (www.census.gov) make population data readily available. The NCTM Illuminations lesson titled "The Next Billion" provides a high-quality lesson for exploring when the world population will reach 8 billion. Students discuss their predictions, past trends in population growth, and social factors—a good interdisciplinary opportunity. ■

Contexts for Very Large Numbers. The real world is full of very large quantities and measures. We see references to huge numbers in the media all the time. Unfortunately, most of us have not developed an appreciation for extremely large numbers, such as the following examples:

- A state lottery with 44 numbers from which to pick 6 has over 7 million possible combinations of 6 numbers. There are $44 \times 43 \times 42 \times 41 \times 40 \times 39$ possible ways that the balls could come out of the hopper (5,082,517,440). But generally the order in which they are picked is not important. Because there are $6 \times 5 \times 4 \times 3 \times 2 \times 1 = 720$ different arrangements of 6 numbers, each collection appears 720 times. Therefore, there are *only* 5,082,517,440 ÷ 720 possible lottery numbers, or 1 out of 7,059,052 chances to win.
- The estimated size of the universe is 40 billion light-years. One light-year is the number of miles light travels in *one year*. The speed of light is 186,281.7 miles per *second*, or 16,094,738,880 miles in a single day.
- The human body has about 100 billion cells.
- The distance to the sun is about 150 million kilometers.
- The population of the world in 2011 was about 6.96 billion. (Various population estimates can be found by seeking out worldometers on the Internet.)

Connect large numbers to meaningful points of reference to help students get a handle on their true magnitude. For example, suppose students determine the population in their city or town is about 500,000 people. They can then figure that it would take approximately 13,300 cities of the same population size to generate the population of the world. Or suppose students determine that it is about 4600 km between San Francisco, California, and Washington D.C. This would mean that it would take over 32,000 trips back and forth between these two cities to equal the distance between the earth and the sun. Building from such familiar or meaningful reference points helps students develop benchmarks to work with and make sense of large numbers.

The following activity uses real data to develop an understanding of scientific notation and the relative size of numbers.

Activity 23.6

CCSS-M: 8.EE.A.4

How Far Away from the Sun?

Explain to students that they are going to research planetary distances from the sun (in km), record the data in scientific notation, and create a scaled illustration of the distances. If data gathering is not practical, provide the following figures or use the How Far Away? Activity Page:

ENGLISH LANGUAGE LEARNERS

Mercury	57,909,000	Jupiter	778,400,000
Venus	108,200,000	Saturn	1,423,600,000
Earth	149,600,000	Uranus	2,867,000,000
Mars	227,940,000	Neptune	4,488,400,000

Encourage students to develop strategies to figure out the relative distance between each planet. You can give a long strip of adding machine paper to each group and have them mark the sun on one end and Neptune on the other. For ELLs, reinforce the names of thousands, millions, and billions. (Note that billion can mean one million millions in some countries, not one thousand millions as it does in the United States.)

Contexts for Very Small Numbers. It is also important to use real examples of very small numbers. As with large numbers, connecting very small numbers to points of reference can help students conceptualize how tiny these numbers really are, as shown by the following real-world examples:

- The length of a DNA strand in a cell is about 10^{-7} m. This is also measured as 1000 *angstroms*. (Based on this information, how long is an angstrom?) For perspective, the diameter of a human hair is about 2.54×10^{-5} m.
- Human hair grows at the rate of 10^{-8} miles per hour.
- Garden snails have been clocked at about 3×10^{-2} mph.
- The chances of winning the Virginia lottery, based on selecting six numbers from 1 to 44, is 1 in 7.059 million. That is a probability of less than 1.4×10^{-7}.
- The mass of one atom of hydrogen is 0.000 000 000 000 000 000 000 001 675 g. The mass of one paper clip is about 1 g.
- It takes sound 0.28 second (2.8×10^{-1}) to travel the length of a football field. In contrast, a TV signal travels a full mile in about 0.000005368 second, or 5.3×10^{-6} second. A TV viewer at home hears the football being kicked before the receiver on the field does.

Finding real data that are very, very small or very, very large can build meaning of small and large numbers *and* insights into the world.

Activity 23.7
CCSS-M: 8.EE.A.4

At a Snail's Pace

Garden snails have been clocked at about 3×10^{-2} mph. Ask students to estimate how long it will take a snail to cover one mile. To explore, have them record the decimal equivalent of 3×10^{-2} (0.03). In the calculator, they can use the counting function (enter .03 + .03 =). On most calculators, when you hit = repeatedly, the calculator counts by the last value entered (.03). Each = represents one hour. Ask students figure it out mathematically or by counting. Share strategies. When students have shared their results, ask what it would mean if the rate would have been 3×10^{-3}. They can explore this problem, too, and should conclude that it would take ten times longer.

Performing operations with numbers in scientific notation can be less cumbersome than when they are written in standard form. Compare these two examples:

$$30{,}000{,}000 \times 900{,}000 \qquad 3 \times 10^7 \times 9 \times 10^5$$

The answer is 27×10^{12} or 2.7×10^{13}. It is important that students are able to confidently use either form to efficiently solve.

Scientific Notation on the Calculator. Students may learn how to multiply by 10, by 100, and by 1000 by simply moving the decimal point. Help students expand this idea by examining powers of 10 on a calculator that handles exponents.

Activity 23.8
CCSS-M: 8.EE.A.3

Exploring Powers of 10

Have students use any calculator that permits entering exponents to explore some or all of the following:

- Explore 10^N for various values of N. What patterns do you notice? What does 1E15 mean? (1E15 is the typical calculator form of 1×10^{15}.) What does 1E-09 mean?
- What does 4.5E10 mean? 4.5E-10?
- What does 5.689E6 mean? Can you enter this another way?
- Try sums like $(4.5 \times 10^N) + (27 \times 10^K)$ for different values of N and K. What can you find out? Does it hold true when N and K are negative integers?
- What happens with products of numbers like those in the previous item?

Students need to become familiar with the power-of-ten expressions in written forms and the calculator form. For example, on some calculators, the product of $45,000,000 \times 8,000,000$ is displayed as 3.6E14, meaning 3.6×10^{14}, or 360,000,000,000,000 (360 trillion). Visit the companion website to watch a video to learn more.

One misconception students can develop is that the exponent tells the numbers of zeros to add onto the number. Address this explicitly in discussions. For example, ask students, "Why are there 13 zeros and not 14? Is there a relationship between the exponent and the number of zeros?" (No, it depends on how many nonzero digits are in the number.)

 ## Pause Reflect

With each factor in the product expressed in scientific notation—$(4.5 \times 10^7) \times (8 \times 10^6)$ or 4.5E7 $\times$ 8.0E6—can you compute the result mentally? ●

Notice the advantages of scientific notation, especially for multiplication. Here the significant digits can be multiplied mentally ($4.5 \times 8 = 36$) and the exponents added to produce almost instantly 36×10^{13} or 3.6×10^{14}.

Complete Self-Check 23.1: Exponents

 # Positive and Negative Numbers

Generally, negative numbers are introduced with integers—the whole numbers and their negatives or opposites—instead of with fractions or decimals. However, it is a mistake to only focus on integer values, because students must understand where numbers like $^-4.5$ and $^-1\frac{1}{4}$ are positioned on the number line in relation to integer values. In fact, because noninteger negative numbers are not addressed adequately in middle school, students have misconceptions about where noninteger negative numbers belong on the number line. For example, students will place $^-1\frac{1}{4}$ between $^-1$ and 0 instead of between $^-2$ and $^-1$. In the CCSS-M, positive and negative numbers are introduced and developed in sixth grade, and in seventh grade students "Solve multi-step real-life and mathematical problems posed with positive and negative rational numbers in any form (whole numbers, fractions, and decimals), using tools strategically" (p. 49). But students may encounter and make sense of integers at a much younger age.

Every day, students have interactions with numbers less than 0, as shown in the following list:

Temperature

Altitude (above and below sea level)

Golf (above and below par)

Money

Timelines (including B.C.)

Football yardage (gains/losses)

Yet when students encounter negative numbers, they can struggle to adapt their understanding of whole numbers. Students face obstacles in developing an understanding of negative numbers. These include understanding the relative size of a negative number, thinking of a number as something that can be counted, not understanding that they can remove more than are there (e.g., $5 - 8$), and adapting their generalizations that addition always makes larger/subtraction always makes smaller (Bishop et al., 2014).

Standards for Mathematical Practice

MP7. Look for and make use of structure.

Learning about negative numbers is developmental, just as any topic. Initially, students may ignore the negative sign (minus sign), but through experiences students formalize their understanding of negative numbers, seeing the number line as symmetric around 0 (Bofferding, 2014). Looking for and making use of underlying structures to reason about positive and negative numbers is important in supporting students' understanding of integers and integer operations (Bishop et al., 2014).

Contexts for Exploring Positive and Negative Numbers

As with any new topic or type of number, it is important to start with familiar contexts so that students can use prior knowledge to build meaning. For ELLs, it is important to include visuals with the contexts to support language development (Swanson, 2010). As students learn to compare and compute, they can use the contexts to ground their thinking and justify their answers. In CCSS-M, grade 6, students must "Understand that positive and negative numbers are used together to describe quantities having opposite directions or values (e.g., temperature above/below zero, elevation above/below sea level, credits/debits, positive/negative electric charge); use positive and negative numbers to represent quantities in real-world contexts, explaining the meaning of 0 in each situation" (p. 43). A series of videos at the companion website provide explanations of different contexts.

Item	Payments or Deposits	Balance
Mowing lawn	+12.00	$34.00
Phone bill	−55.00	−21.00
iTunes downloads	−9.00	−30.00
Paycheck	+120.00	90.00

FIGURE 23.5 A checkbook as a context for adding and subtracting positive and negative numbers.

Quantity Contexts. Quantity contexts provide an opportunity for students to match opposites (4 and ⁻4) to equal zero. Quantity contexts can be illustrated with two-color counters or other counting objects.

Golf Scores. In golf, scores are often written in relationship to a number considered par for the course. So, if par is 70 for the course, a golfer who ends the day at 67 has a score of ⁻3, or 3 strokes under par. Consider a player in a four-day tournament with day-end scores of ⁺5, ⁻2, ⁻3, ⁺1. What would be his or her final result for the tournament? How did you think about it? You could match up the positive and the negatives (in this case, ⁺5 with ⁻2 and ⁻3 to get a net score of 0), and then see what is left (in this case, ⁺1). The notion that opposites (5 and ⁻5) equal zero is an important concept in teaching of positive and negative numbers. You can post a mixed-up leaderboard of golf scores and ask students to order the players from first through tenth place. Emphasize that first place is the *lowest* score—and therefore the *smallest* number.

Money: Payments and Deposits. Suppose that you have a bank account. At any time, your records show how many dollars are in your account. The difference between the payments and deposit totals tells the amount of money in the account. If there is more money deposited than paid out, the account has a positive balance, or "in the black." If there are more payments than deposits, the account is in debt, showing a negative cash value, or is "in the red." This is a good context for exploring addition and subtraction, as in the example illustrated in Figure 23.5. Net worth is a similar way to look at positive and negative numbers (assets and debts). Considering the net worth of famous people can engage students in making sense of positive and negative numbers (Stephan, 2009) and students can successfully draw on their experiences with assets, debts, and net worths to create meaning for integer addition and subtraction (Stephan & Akyuz, 2012).

Activity 23.9
CCSS-M: 6.NS.C.5

What Is Her Net Worth?

On the Internet, look up the net worth of someone interesting to your students (i.e., popular movie star or singer). Make up two to three assets and two to three debts, and ask your students to figure out her net worth. Then, with students, look up the net worth of other people of their choice. Have them suggest possible assets and debts for that person. One clever way to do this is to have a net worth page filled out with two to three assets and two to three debts, but include a smudge on the paper so that all students can see the total net worth (Stephan, 2009). This visual is particularly important for students with disabilities.

STUDENTS with SPECIAL NEEDS

FIGURE 23.6 Thermometers provide an excellent tool for exploring positive and negative numbers.

Eventually debts can be represented as negative values, and a connection is made to integer addition and subtraction.

Linear Contexts. Many of the real contexts for negative numbers are linear. The number line provides a good tool for understanding the ordering of negative numbers and can support reasoning in doing operations with positive and negative numbers (Bishop et al., 2014). CCSS-M emphasizes the need for sixth graders to be able to represent integers on a number line as well as a coordinate axis (CCSSO, 2010). See the Math Goodies website for a good introduction to integers on a number line.

Temperature. The "number line" measuring temperature is vertical. This context demonstrating negative numbers may be the most familiar to students, as they have either experienced temperatures below zero or know about temperatures at the North or South Pole. A good starting activity for students is finding where various temperatures belong on a thermometer. For example, Figure 23.6 displays a thermometer marked in increments of five degrees, and students are asked to place on the number line the following temperatures from a week in North Dakota: 8°, −2°, −12°, 4°, −8°. Ask students to order the temperatures from the coldest to the warmest (least to greatest). Temperatures as a context have the advantage that you can also use fractional and decimal values.

Altitude. Another vertical number line model, altitude, is also a good context for positive and negative numbers. The altitudes of sites below sea level are negative, such as the town of Dead Sea, Israel (with an altitude of ⁻1371 feet), and Badwater, California, in Death Valley (which has an altitude of ⁻282 feet). Positive values for altitude include Mount McKinley (the tallest mountain in North America) at 20,322 feet. Students can order the altitudes of various places around the world (data easily found through the Internet) or find the difference between the altitudes of two different places—a good context for subtraction of integers (interpreting subtraction as *difference* rather than as take-away).

Timelines. Asking students to place historical events on a timeline is an excellent interdisciplinary opportunity. The timeline is useful for examples with larger values (e.g., 1950) as well as negative values (e.g., ⁻3000 or 3000 B.C.). Or students can explore their own personal timeline (Weidemann, Mikovch, & Hunt, 2001), in which students find out key events that happened before they were born (e.g., the birth of an older sibling) and since they have been alive (e.g., the move to a new house). Students place these events on a number line with 0 representing the day they were born. By partitioning a year into months, students can gain experience with rational numbers (halves, fourths, or twelfths) on the number line. Continue to reinforce the connection to the size of numbers, asking students, "Which number (year) is the smallest (earliest)?"

Football. A statistic reported on every play in a football game is yards gained and yards lost, which provides a good context for exploring integers, especially when it comes to comparing and adding integers. Students can be asked questions like "If the Steelers started their drive on the 20 yard line and the first three plays were recorded as ⁻4, ⁺9, ⁺3, did they get a first down?" or "On the Ravens' first play, the yardage is ⁻4. Where are they in relation to the line of scrimmage (using negatives, if behind the line of scrimmage, in this case ⁻4), and where are they in relation to the first down marker (⁻14)?"

Activity 23.10

CCSS-M: 6.NS.C.5; 6.NS.C.6a

Football Statistics

ENGLISH LANGUAGE LEARNERS

Look up the average yards gained for some of the best running backs in the NFL or from college teams popular with your students. Ask students to use average yards gained per down to create a possible list of yardage gains and losses for that player. For example, if a player had an average of 4 yards per carry in a game, the following could have been his data:

$$10, \ ^-3, \ ^-2, 21, \ ^-5, 3, \ ^-1, 5, \ ^-1, 13$$

You may want to do one like this together and then have students create their own. The football context provides an excellent way to use integers meaningfully, integrated with the important concept of averages. ELLs may not be familiar with American football, because football in most countries is what is called *soccer* in the United States. Modeling the game using students is a fun way to be sure the game is understood by all. Also, a yard is a U.S. measurement that may not be familiar and could be confused with the other meaning of *yard*. Comparing a yard to a meter can provide a point of reference that will help build meaning for this activity.

Meaning of Negative Numbers

Negative numbers are defined in relation to their positive counterparts. For example, the definition of negative 3 is the solution to the equation $3 + ? = 0$. In general, the *opposite of n* is the solution to $n + ? = 0$. If n is a positive number, the *opposite of n* is a negative number. The set of integers, therefore, consists of the positive whole numbers, the opposites of the whole numbers (or negative integers), and 0, which is neither positive nor negative.

Absolute Value. Absolute value is introduced in sixth grade in the CCSS. The *absolute value of a number* is defined as the distance between that number and zero. Knowing the distance between two points, either on a number line or on a plane, is often needed in applications of mathematics. For example, we need to be able to determine how far a helicopter is from a hospital, regardless of its direction. The notation for absolute value consists of two vertical bars on either side of the number. Thus, the absolute value of a number n is $|n|$. Opposites, such as $^-12$ and 12, are the same distance from zero, and therefore have the same absolute value.

When students' absolute value experiences are limited to simplifying expressions like $|^-8|$ or $|6 - 10|$ they do not connect the procedure with the meaning of absolute value or see real purpose for doing this. Add in a context to make it meaningful. For example, $|6 - 10|$ can be the distance between the 10-mile marker and the 6-mile marker. In this example you can see that both $10 - 6$ or $6 - 10$ can lead to the answer, and distance is positive (absolute value), so the answer is 4.

Notations. Students often have a limited understanding of the minus sign, which can interfere with their ability to solve equations and to make sense of variables (Lamb et al., 2012). There are three meanings of the minus symbol (Bofferding, 2014; Lamb et al., 2012). Each is illustrated with examples here:

Subtraction: $25 - 12 = $ ___ OR $9 - $ ___ $= 4.5$

Negative number: $25 + \ ^-12 = $ ___ OR $9 - $ ___ $= \ ^-4.5$

The opposite of: $^-(^-5) = 5$ OR ^-x

To further the challenge of the minus sign, it can switch meanings in the middle of simplifying an equation. For example, consider the equation $3.5 - x = \ ^-1.6$. A step in simplifying might be to add $^-3.5$ to both sides, leaving $^-x = \ ^-4.1$. Here, the equation reads, "The opposite of x

is equal to negative 4.1 (or the opposite of 4.1)." The different heights at which the negative sign may appear (e.g., -7 and $^-7$) may also be confusing. Parentheses are placed around the number so that it is separate from the operation—for example, $8 - (^-5)$. Students have not seen parentheses used in this way and may think they should multiply. It is important to connect to their prior knowledge and explicitly build meaning for the new use of the minus sign and parentheses. The following activity, based on Lamb and colleagues (2012), is designed to do this.

Activity 23.11

CCSS-M: 6.NS.C.5; 6.NS.C.6a

Greater, Less, Equal, or Don't Know?

ENGLISH LANGUAGE LEARNERS

Use the Greater, Less, Equal or Don't Know **Activity Page or write an equation on the board that addresses different meanings of the minus symbol and/or parentheses. Have students "vote" on whether it is equal or not equal. Encourage students to work with a partner to prepare a rationale for whether they think it is equal or not equal. Facilitate a debate, as appropriate. Examples include:**

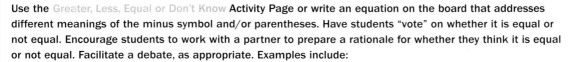

$$2-(^-3)\_\_\_1 \qquad -x\_\_\_x \qquad -(^-8)\_\_\_8$$

In this case, you might ask students, "When do we use parentheses in mathematics?" Students might say they are used for grouping a series of computations to show what to do first and that it can also mean multiplication. Point out that parentheses are also used to make a number sentence more readable—separating the negative number from the operation.

Models for Teaching Positive and Negative Numbers

Two models, one denoted by quantity and the other by linear operations, are popular for helping students understand comparisons and the four operations $(+, -, \times,$ and $\div)$ with negative and positive numbers. Counters can be used for integer values (counting numbers, including 0), and number lines are needed to illustrate positive and negative noncounting numbers.

Counters. Two-color counters are a great fit for showing positive and negative integers because one side (color) can represent positive counts and one side (color) can represent negative counts. One counter of each type results in zero $(^+1 + {}^-1 = 0)$, illustrating that they are opposites. Consider money: If yellow counters are credits and red counters are debits, 5 yellows and 7 reds is the same as 2 reds or 2 debits and is represented as $^-2$ (see Figure 23.7). It is important for students to understand that it is always possible to add to or remove from a collection of any number of pairs consisting of one positive and one negative counter without changing the value. (like adding equal quantities of debits and credits.) Annenberg Learner's website has a nice teacher tutorial titled, "Colored-Chip Models," which teaches how to use chip counters to help explore concepts related to integer operations.

Number Lines. The number line is the second visual tool for modeling computation with negative numbers. A number line has several advantages. Importantly, it is familiar to students from their computation with whole numbers, fractions, and decimals (see Chapters 12, 13, 16 and 17). Second, it is an excellent tool for representing the operations conceptually in terms of increase or decreasing amounts. To add a context, consider using small cutouts of grasshoppers that jump up and down the line (Swanson, 2010). Students can see that as the grasshopper moves to

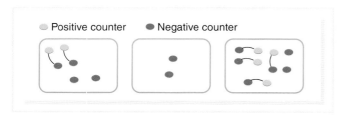

○ Positive counter　● Negative counter

FIGURE 23.7　Each collection is a representation of $^-2$.

the left it goes to smaller numbers and as it moves to the right it goes to larger numbers. Third, the number line shows the distance from 0 (or the absolute value of the number). Fourth, the number line allows students to explore noninteger negative and positives values (e.g., $^-4\frac{1}{4} + 3\frac{1}{3}$ or $-9.2 - 4.5$) that cannot be modeled very well with counters. Finally, the number line is an important connection to the coordinate axis, which involves two perpendicular number lines.

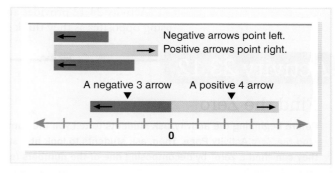

Arrows can be used to show distance and direction. For example, 4 can be modeled with an arrow four units long starting at any location on the number line and pointing to the right, and $^-3$ can be modeled with an arrow three units long starting at any location on the number line and

FIGURE 23.8 Number line visual for negative and positive numbers.

pointing to the left (see Figure 23.8). The arrows help students think of integer quantities as directed distances. A positive arrow never points left, and a negative arrow never points right. Furthermore, each arrow is a quantity with both length (magnitude or absolute value) and direction (sign). These properties are constant for each arrow regardless of its position on the number line.

Which Model to Use. Although the counters and the number line appear quite different, they are alike mathematically. Integers involve two concepts—magnitude and direction. Magnitude is modeled by the number of counters or the length of the arrows. Direction is represented as different colors or directions. Seeing how positive and negative numbers are represented across these two tools while making connections between the visuals can help students extract the intended concepts. The context should also decide the representation: if the context is height, the number line is a better fit.

 Complete Self-Check 23.2: Positive and Negative Numbers

 ## Operations with Positive and Negative Numbers

Once your students understand how integers are represented by each of the models, you can present the operations for the integers in the form of story problems.

Addition and Subtraction

Introduce negative values using one of the contexts discussed earlier such as golf scores. Personalize the story by telling students that each weekend you golf a round on Saturday and on Sunday. The first weekend your results were $^+3$ and $^+5$, the next weekend you scored $^+3$ and $^-5$, and on the last weekend you scored $^-6$ and $^+2$. How successful was your game each weekend? Overall? Because this is a quantity model, counters are a good choice for modeling (though number lines can also be used). A linear context could be used with football yards gained and lost on two plays.

Conversely, ask students to create their own stories for integer operations. One way to scaffold this is to ask students the following three prompts: "Where did you start? How far did you go? Where are you now?" (Swanson, 2010). So, for example, a student might write, "I was 3 feet under water, then dove down 5 feet. Where am I now?"

Contexts are an important place to begin, but students also need to be able to reason about the numbers themselves. It is important to focus on the meaning of opposites.

 **Standards for Mathematical Practice**

MP2. Reason abstractly and quantitatively.

Activity 23.12 provides an excellent way to explore integers quantitatively with a focus on using opposites as they think about integer addition (Friedmann, 2008).

Activity 23.12
CCSS-M: 7.NS.1a, b, c

STUDENTS
with
SPECIAL NEEDS

Find the Zero

Before beginning the activity, ask students to tell you the sums of several opposites (e.g., 4 + ⁻4). Distribute the Find the Zero Activity Page. Then, ask students to look at a sum that is not opposites (e.g., 7 + ⁻4) and ask if they can "find a zero" by decomposing one of the numbers (e.g., (3 + 4) + ⁻4) and solve. Using a number line, students can find the difference between these numbers. Students, particularly students with disabilities, may benefit from creating a "zero box" below each problem as they solve it, as illustrated below.

$$12 + {}^-5 =$$
Zero Box: $\boxed{5 + {}^-5}$
$$(7 + 5) + {}^-5) = 7 + (5 + {}^-5) = 7 + 0 = 7$$

Students must continue to illustrate what is happening when they are adding and subtracting negative numbers. If they do not, they will get lost in the symbols and which direction to head on the number line. See Expanded Lesson: Find the Zero for details on teaching this activity.

Figure 23.9 provides examples of addition problems that are illustrated using different approaches with the two tools: with positive and negative counters and with the number line

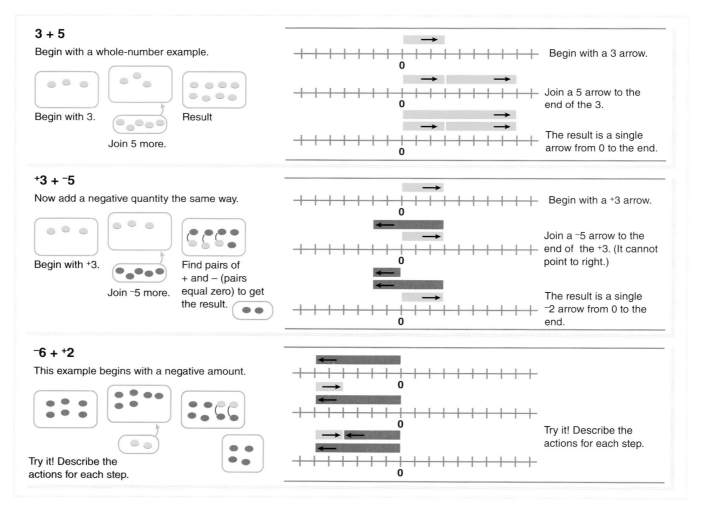

FIGURE 23.9 Addition with counters and number lines.

and arrows. To add using the number line model, note that each added arrow begins at the arrowhead end of the previous arrow.

Subtraction can be used for separate (take-away) situations (e.g., start with 7 and take away 10) or in comparison situations (What is the difference or distance between 7 and ⁻3?). An advantage to the number line model is that it can be used for both separate and comparison situations.

Consider the problem ⁻5 − ⁺2, the second example modeled in Figure 23.10. If using a quantity model, the context could be money, such as, "I start with a debit of $5 and then withdraw (take out) $2 more from my account. What balance will my bank account show (if no fees have been charged yet for my overdrawn account)?" To model this problem, you start with the five red counters. To remove two positive counters from a set that has none, a different representation of ⁻5 must first be made. Because any number of neutral pairs (one positive, one negative) can be added without changing the value of the set, two pairs are added so that two positive counters can be removed. The net effect is to have more negative counters.

With the number line model, subtraction can be illustrated using arrows for separate and comparison situations. Consider take-away as a way to think about the second example in Figure 23.10. Using temperature as a context, the explanation could be: "The day begins at 5 below zero. Then the temperature drops ⁺2°, which means it just got colder and is now −7°. The difficulty in the take-away thinking comes when trying to provide an authentic explanation of subtracting a negative value. For example, for ⁻4 − ⁻7 (see the third example in Figure 23.10) you start with taking away, but because it is negative temperature (or coldness) that is being taken away, you are in fact doing the opposite—warming up by 7 degrees. With

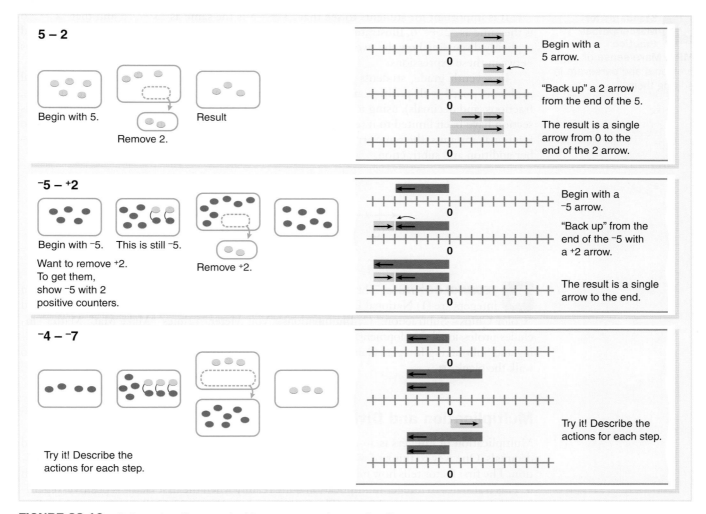

FIGURE 23.10   Subtraction illustrated with counters and a number line.

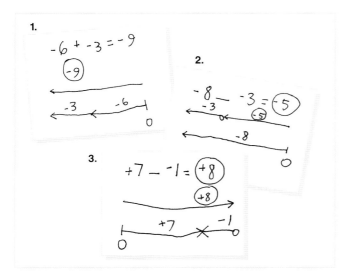

FIGURE 23.11 Students use arrow sketches to represent addition and subtraction.

the number line, you start at ⁻4, then reverse the arrow going left to one going right 7 moves. Number lines can also be used for comparison or distance situations. For subtraction, this can make a lot more sense to students (Tillema, 2012). In this example, the comparison question is "What is the difference from ⁻7 to ⁻4?" In other words, how do you get from ⁻7 to ⁻4? You count up 3. Notice if this were written in reverse (⁻4 − ⁻7) it would be the difference from −4 to −7, still three, but the direction is to the left, so ⁻3 .

⏸ Pause & Reflect

Try to explain the problems in Figures 23.9 and 23.10 using both a quantity and a linear context. For subtraction, explain each using a separate situation and a comparison situation. What kinds of stories or contexts might fit with these different ways to think about addition and subtraction? ●

A significant challenge for students is to connect representations. One way to help students bridge the visual illustrations with the equations is for them to notate basic number line illustrations with their equations. Figure 23.11 illustrates how a student might draw arrows to represent addition and subtraction exercises. You can also have students write story situations as a third representation.

It is important for students to see that ⁺3 + ⁻5 is the same as ⁺3 − ⁺5 and that ⁺2 − ⁻6 is the same as ⁺2 + ⁺6. Illustrating addition and subtraction problems on the number line and explicitly discussing how the two expressions are related will help students see the connections between these expressions.

In seventh grade, students must learn to "Solve multi-step real-life and mathematical problems posed with positive and negative rational numbers in any form (whole numbers, fractions, and decimals), using tools strategically" (CCSSO, 2010, p. 49). The examples in this section have been limited to integers, but by using a ruler or any number line partitioned into fractional amounts, the same arrow illustrations can help students reason about rational number addition and subtraction.

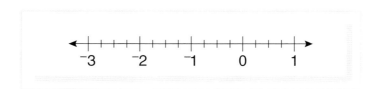

TECHNOLOGY Note. Three quality sites for applets exploring addition and subtraction of integers are (1) National Library of Virtual Manipulatives' "Color Chips—Addition" and "Color Chips—Subtraction," (2) Illuminations' "Volt Meter." iTunes' "Make Math Matter" includes professional development podcasts for operations with integers; and (3) Math-Play Adding and Subtracting Integers Game provides 10 questions to solve mentally as you get a pirate to walk the plank. ■

Multiplication and Division

Multiplication of integers is an extension of multiplication for whole numbers, fractions, and decimals. One way to think of whole-number multiplication is equal groups, or repeated addition. The first factor tells how many sets there are or how many are added in all, beginning with 0. This translates to integer multiplication quite readily when the first factor is positive, regardless of the sign of the second factor. The first example in Figure 23.12 illustrates a positive first

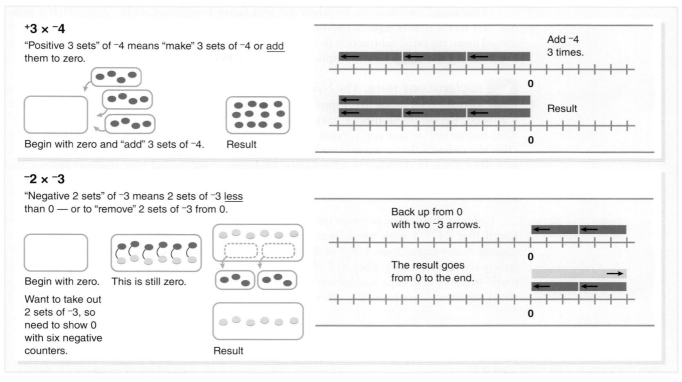

FIGURE 23.12 Multiplication by a positive first factor is repeated addition. Multiplication by a negative first factor is repeated subtraction.

factor and a negative second factor ($3 \times {}^-4$), which translates into the question "If I have three groups of $^-4$, how much do I have?" With a context, this could be "If I lost four dollars three days in a row, how much have I lost?"; "Three days in a row Hans scored $^-4$ in his golf tournament; what is his score?" or, "Three times today the temperature dropped four degrees. How much has the temperature changed?"

Connecting to contexts and looking at repeated examples can then lead to students creating conjectures about the "rules" for multiplying (and dividing) with negative numbers (Choppin, Clancy, & Koch, 2012). That is the focus of the next activity.

Activity 23.13
CCSS-M: 7.NS.A.2a, b

Creating Stories and Conjectures for Operations with Negative Numbers

This activity is described here for multiplication but could be replicated for any of the operations with negative numbers. Ask students to make a conjecture about what they think the sign will be on a product of a positive factor times a negative factor. Invite students to create the stories to match each of the equations. You can display a menu of contexts (see suggested contexts provided in the previous section). Next, give students a set of multiplication problems with a positive times a negative (keep first factor a whole number to better see the pattern), such as:

$$3 \times -10 = \qquad 5 \times -\tfrac{1}{4} = \qquad 8 \times -0.5 =$$

After exploring a small set, ask students to make a generalization about a positive times a negative number.

Repeat this process for a negative times a positive number:

$$-3 \times 4 = \qquad -5 \times \tfrac{1}{2} = \qquad -10 \times 0.25 =$$

Then ask students to revisit and revise (as needed) their conjectures regarding the product of a negative factor times a positive factor.

What could the meaning be when the first factor is negative, as in ⁻2 × ⁻3? If a positive first factor means repeated addition (how many times added to 0), a negative first factor should mean repeated subtraction (how many times subtracted from 0). The second example in Figure 23.12 illustrates how multiplication with the first factor negative can be modeled.

TECHNOLOGY Note. The National Library of Virtual Manipulatives (NLVM) has two virtual explorations that support student understanding of multiplication with negative numbers: "Rectangle Multiplication of Integers" and "Integer Arithmetic." NCTM's Illuminations has an online and app version of "Pick-a-Path," a puzzle game in which players guide Okta the octopus through a maze while performing operations on various types of numbers, including integers. Another good resource for helping understand how students can use the number line when exploring integer multiplication is the "Integer Multiplication" tutorial found at the Braining Camp website. ■

Connect division of negative numbers with what students know about positive numbers. Recall that 24 ÷ 4 with whole numbers has two possible meanings corresponding to two missing-factor expressions: 4 × ? = 24 asks, "Four sets of what sized group equal twenty-four?" (group size is unknown), whereas ? × 4 = 24 asks, "How many groups of four equal twenty-four?" (number of groups is unknown). The latter question is the one that fits well with thinking about negative values because it allows skip counting to 24. The first example in Figure 23.13

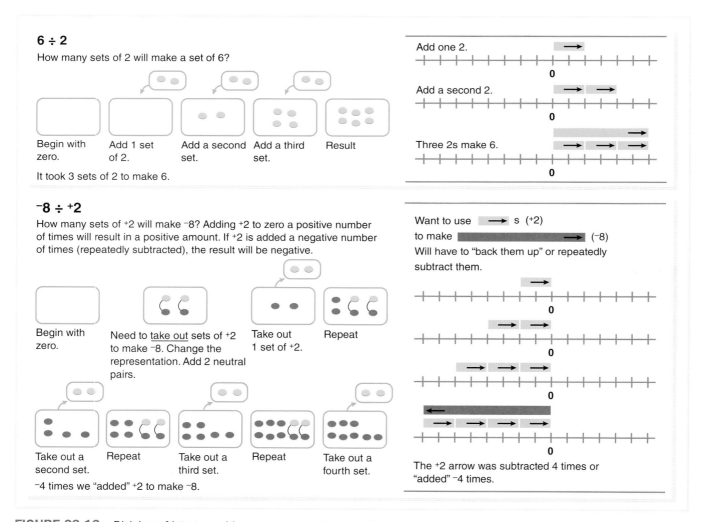

FIGURE 23.13 Division of integers with a measurement approach.

illustrates how the two visual models (two-color counters and number line) work for whole numbers. Following that is an example in which the divisor is positive but the dividend is negative.

 Pause & Reflect

Try talking through examples and drawing pictures for ⁻8 ÷ ⁺2. Check your understanding with the examples in Figure 23.13. Now try ⁺9 ÷ ⁻3 and ⁻12 ÷ ⁻4. What contexts can fit these equations? ●

Understanding division rests on a good conceptual understanding of multiplication problems and knowledge of the relationship between multiplication and division. Encourage students to first think about how to visualize the whole-number situation and then connect that understanding to negative numbers. Extend these explorations to decimal and fraction values and continue to have students draw illustrations to accompany their equations.

 Complete Self-Check 23.3: Operations with Positive and Negative Numbers

 # Real Numbers

Whole numbers, fractions and decimals, and integers are all rational numbers because they can all be written as a fraction with an integer over a nonzero integer. An interesting fact is that there are infinite rational numbers between any two numbers. Exploring this idea can deepen students' understanding of rational numbers.

Find four fractions between $\frac{1}{2}$ and $\frac{9}{10}$.

Students may convert one-half to five-tenths and readily find $\frac{6}{10}, \frac{7}{10}$, and $\frac{8}{10}$, but be challenged to find the fourth equivalence (there are many, e.g., $\frac{2}{3}, \frac{3}{4}, \frac{5}{6}, \frac{7}{8}$, and $\frac{8}{9}$). See Expanded Lesson: How Many In Between for a full lesson exploring rational numbers between two rational numbers.

Irrational numbers are numbers such as $\sqrt{2}$—numbers whose value cannot be written as a fraction and whose exact value can only be estimated. Eighth graders begin to explore irrational numbers and find their rational approximation (CCSSO, 2010). All these numbers are part of the *real numbers*, which are the only types of numbers students explore until high school, where they consider the square roots of negative numbers, called *imaginary numbers*. These sets of numbers are interrelated, and some are subsets of other sets. Figure 23.14 provides an illustration of the types of numbers and how they are interrelated.

 **Standards for Mathematical Practice**
MP7. Look for and make use of structure.

Rational Numbers

Rational numbers comprise the set of all numbers that can be represented as a fraction—or a ratio of an integer to an integer. Even when numbers are written as whole numbers or as terminating decimals, they can also be written as fractions and thus are rational numbers. In fact, in school mathematics the term *rational*

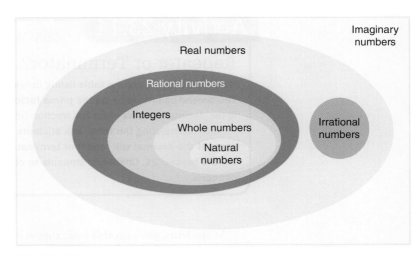
FIGURE 23.14   An illustration of the organization of the real numbers.

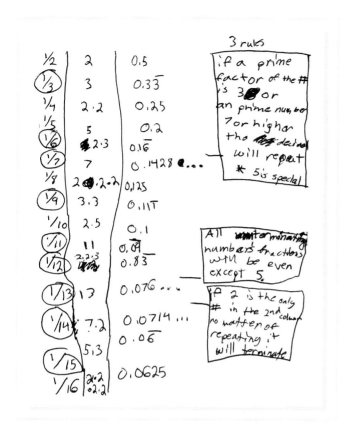

FIGURE 23.15 Jacob notes patterns as he explores the "Repeater or Terminator" activity.

numbers is often used to refer to fractions, decimals (terminating and repeating), and percents. These are rational numbers, but so are integers, including whole numbers.

Moving among Representations. In sixth grade, students should be able to recognize a rational number as a point on a number line (CCSSO, 2010). In seventh grade, "students develop a unified understanding of number, recognizing fractions, decimals (that have a finite or a repeating decimal representation), and percents as different representations of rational numbers" (p. 46). This means that given any value, students are able to think about it and operate it on it across representations, moving flexibly among different representations. In Chapter 17, we explored the idea of the "common" fractions (halves, thirds, fourths, fifths, eighths) in terms of their decimal equivalents. Students should be able to explain equivalence, as noted here:

- $4\frac{3}{5}$ is 4.6 because $\frac{3}{5}$ is six-tenths of a whole, so 4 wholes and six-tenths is 4.6.
- $4\frac{3}{5}$ is $\frac{23}{5}$, and that is the same as $23 \div 5$, or 4.6 if I use decimals.
- 4.6 is read "four and six-tenths," so I can write that as $4\frac{6}{10} = 4\frac{3}{5}$

Similarly, compare these three expressions:

$$\frac{1}{4} \text{ of } 24 \qquad \frac{24}{4} \qquad 24 \div 4$$

This discussion can lead to a general development of the idea that a fraction can be thought of as division of the numerator by the denominator or that $\frac{a}{b}$ is the same as a $\div$ b.

When a fraction is converted to a decimal, the decimal either terminates (e.g., 3.415) or repeats (e.g., 2.5141414 . . .). Is there a way to tell in advance whether a given fraction is a terminating decimal or a repeating decimal? The following activity can be used to discover if that prediction is possible.

Activity 23.14   CCSS-M: 7.NS.A.2d

Repeater or Terminator?

Have students generate a table listing in one column the first 20 unit fractions ($\frac{1}{2}$, $\frac{1}{3}$, $\frac{1}{4}$, . . . $\frac{1}{21}$). The second column is to list the prime factorization of the denominators; and the third column is the decimal equivalent for the fraction (use calculators to get the precise decimal form).

After completing the table, ask students if they can determine a rule that will tell in advance if the decimal will repeat or terminate. They can test the rule with fractions with denominators beyond 21. Challenge students to confirm that their rule applies even if the numerator changes.

As students work on this task, they will notice various patterns, as can be seen in the student work provided in Figure 23.15. As this student has discovered, the only fractions with terminating decimals have denominators that factor with only combinations of twos and fives. Why is this the case?

Middle school students must understand that any rational number, positive or negative, whole or not whole, can be written as a fraction and as a decimal. So, $^-8$ can be written as the fraction $\frac{-8}{1}$ or $\frac{-16}{2}$, or as the decimal $^-8.0$. In fact, there are infinite ways to write equivalencies for $^-8$. This fluency with equivalent representations is critical and requires much more than teaching an algorithm for moving from one representation to another.

TECHNOLOGY Note. "The Weird Number" is a very old but great middle school video that tells a scary, funny story of a village of whole numbers in the mountains that "hear" there are other numbers beyond the hills. ■

Square Roots and Cube Roots

Students encounter *irrational numbers* in seventh grade when they learn about π. However, exploration of irrational numbers occurs in eighth grade (CCSSO, 2010). As noted earlier, *irrational* numbers are not rational, meaning they cannot be written in fraction form. The irrationals together with the rational numbers make up the *real numbers*. The real numbers fill in all the holes on the number line even when the holes are infinitesimally small.

Students' first experience with irrational numbers typically occurs when exploring square roots of whole numbers. The following activity provides a good introduction to square roots and cube roots.

Activity 23.15   CCSS-M: 8.NS.A.1; 8.EE.A.2

Edges of Squares and Cubes

Show students pictures of three squares (or three cubes) as in Figure 23.16. The sides (squares) and edges (cubes) of the first and last figure are consecutive whole numbers. The areas or volumes of all three figures are provided. Ask students to use a calculator to find the length of the sides (squares) or edges (cubes) of the figure in the center. Explain to students that they are not to use the square root or cube root key, but to estimate what they think the side would be and test it by squaring or cubing it. Ask students to continue to estimate until they have found a value to the hundredths place that gets as close to 45 as possible (or 30 in the case of the cube). Solutions will satisfy these equations:

$$\square \times \square = 45, \text{ or } \square^2 = 45$$

and

$$\square \times \square \times \square = 30, \text{ or } \square^3 = 30$$

To solve the cube problem, students might start with 3.5 and find that 3.53 is 42.875, much too large. Through trial and error, they will find that the solution is between 3.1 and 3.2. Continued use of strategic trial and error will lead to a close approximation. Although a calculator can find these square or cube roots quickly, the estimation activity strengthens students' understanding of squares and square roots and the relative sizes of numbers.

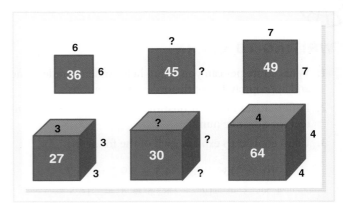

FIGURE 23.16   A geometric interpretation of square roots and cube roots.

 **Pause & Reflect**

Use a calculator to continue getting a better approximation of the cube root of 30 to the hundredths place. ●

From this simple introduction, students can be challenged to find solutions to equations such as ($\Box^2 = 8$). These students are now prepared to understand the general definition of the nth root of a number N as the number that when raised to the nth power equals N. The square and cube roots are simply other names for the second and third roots. It is important to point out that $\sqrt{6}$ is a *number*, not a computation (since it looks so much like a division problem). The cube root of eight is the same as $\sqrt[3]{8}$, which is equivalent to 2.

In middle school, students encounter irrational numbers primarily when working with the Pythagorean theorem ($a^2 + b^2 = c^2$), which is used to find the distance between two points (the distance being the diagonal, or c). If $a = 3$ and $b = 4$, then $c = 5$. All sides are rational numbers. But this case is the exception to the rule. More often sides will be something like 4 and 7 units, in which case $c = \sqrt{16 + 49} = \sqrt{65}$. Although sometimes there is a perfect square that can be simplified, in this case there is not one and the distance is $\sqrt{65}$, an irrational number.

An engaging middle school project applying the Pythagorean theorem and irrational numbers is a Wheel of Theodorus, as described in Activity 23.16. Theodorus was one of the early believers that irrational numbers existed (quite a contentious issue for the Pythagoreans, who were against the idea of irrationals!).

Activity 23.16   CCSS-M: 8.NS.A.2; 8.EE.A.2

Wheel of Theodorus

Ask students to construct a right triangle that measures 1 centimeter on each side adjacent to the right angle, then draw the hypotenuse and record its measure. They then use the hypotenuse as a side and draw a new right triangle with this as side *a* along with a side *b* that is 1 cm. Draw and record the new hypotenuse ($\sqrt{3}$). Create the next triangle, which will have sides of $\sqrt{3}$ and 1 and a hypotenuse of $\sqrt{4}$ or 2, and so on. Doing this about 30 times will form a wheel. (See Bay-Williams & Martinie, 2009, for a complete lesson or search online for instructions and diagrams of a Wheel of Theodorus.)

 TECHNOLOGY Note. The Math Page has a link called *The Evolution of the Real Numbers*, which is an interesting description of many topics related to the real number system. Although mostly text, the pages are filled with interactive questions. ■

✓ **Complete Self-Check 23.4: Real Numbers**

REFLECTIONS ON CHAPTER 23

WRITING TO LEARN

1. What strategies can you use to help students understand and appropriately use the order of operations?

2. Differentiate between quantity context and linear context for negative numbers.

3. Use a context to explain each of the following:

$$^-10 + {}^+13 = {}^+3 \quad {}^-4.5 - {}^-9.2 = {}^+4.7$$
$$4 \times {}^-3 = {}^-12 \quad {}^-82.5 \div 5 = {}^-16.5\,{}^-$$

4. How can you introduce irrational numbers to students? Explain with the help of an activity.

FOR DISCUSSION AND EXPLORATION

♦ Exponents can be easily confused with multiplication. Students often times get the same answer for these three expressions:

$$2^3 \quad 2 \times 3 \quad 3^2$$

♦ For each expression:
   ♦ Explain the meaning of the 2 and the 3.
   ♦ Draw a representation.

◆ Finally, describe what investigation you might plan to help students see the differences in these expressions.

 ◆ Example 1:

◆ A second difficulty for students is understanding the different categories of number. For each of the following numbers, tell all the kinds of numbers it is (real, rational, integer, whole). Discuss how you might use such an activity with students. Describe other activities that might help students understand the different categories of numbers.

$$^-3 \quad 120 \quad \tfrac{4}{5} \quad \sqrt{5}$$

RESOURCES FOR CHAPTER 23

LITERATURE CONNECTIONS

The Number Devil *Enzensberger (1997)*

Full of humor and wit, *The Number Devil* presents a collection of interesting ideas about numbers. Robert, a boy who hates mathematics, meets up with a crafty number devil in each of 12 dreams (one per chapter). On the fourth night's dream, Robert learns about infinitely repeating decimals and the "rutabaga of two" (the square root of two), providing a connection to rational and irrational numbers.

Oh, Yikes! History's Grossest, Wackiest Moments *Masoff and Sirrell (2006)*

In this picture-rich reference book, the authors describe important historical events and people with facts that are interesting to middle schoolers (e.g., "Aztec Antics," "Cruel Constructions," "Humongous Hoaxes"). Selecting a topic, such as brushing teeth, the author describes how this was handled across all of history—an opportunity for timelines that include dates such as 2500 B.C. Students can create a timeline that is proportionally accurate to describe the events related to their topic. This lesson involves integers, measuring, proportional reasoning, and fractions.

RECOMMENDED READINGS

Articles

Reeves, C. A., & Webb, D. (2004). Balloons on the rise: A problem-solving approach to integers. *Mathematics Teaching in the Middle School, 9*(9), 476–482.

 Expanding on a discussion of the possibility of helium balloons making you weigh less if held while on a scale, the fifth-grade students in this article generalize the concepts of integers and use their ideas for addition and subtraction.

Swanson, P. E. (2010). The intersection of language and mathematics. *Mathematics Teaching in the Middle School, 15*(9), 516–523.

 Weaving in many strategies to support ELLs, the author shares how she engaged students in real contexts to learn integer operations. Visuals and language support are used to ensure students understand.

Appendix A
Standards for Mathematical Practice

The Standards for Mathematical Practice found in the *Common Core State Standards* describe varieties of expertise that mathematics educators at all levels should seek to develop in their students. These practices rest on important "processes and proficiencies" with longstanding importance in mathematics education. The first of these are the NCTM process standards of problem solving, reasoning and proof, communication, representation, and connections. The second are the strands for mathematical proficiency specified in the National Research Council's report *Adding It Up*: adaptive reasoning, strategic competence, conceptual understanding (comprehension of mathematical concepts, operations, and relations), procedural fluency (skill in carrying out procedures flexibly, accurately, efficiently, and appropriately), and productive disposition (habitual inclination to see mathematics as sensible, useful, and worthwhile, coupled with a belief in diligence and one's own efficacy).

1. Make sense of problems and persevere in solving them.

Mathematically proficient students start by explaining to themselves the meaning of a problem and looking for entry points to its solution. They analyze givens, constraints, relationships, and goals. They make conjectures about the form and meaning of the solution and plan a solution pathway rather than simply jumping into a solution attempt. They consider analogous problems and try special cases and simpler forms of the original problem in order to gain insight into its solution. They monitor and evaluate their progress and change course if necessary. Older students might, depending on the context of the problem, transform algebraic expressions or change the viewing window on their graphing calculator to get the information they need. Mathematically proficient students can explain correspondences between equations, verbal descriptions, tables, and graphs or draw diagrams of important features and relationships, graph data, and search for regularity or trends. Younger students might rely on using concrete objects or pictures to help conceptualize and solve a problem. Mathematically proficient students check their answers to problems using a different method, and they continually ask themselves, "Does this make sense?" They can understand the approaches of others to solving complex problems and identify correspondences between different approaches.

2. Reason abstractly and quantitatively.

Mathematically proficient students make sense of quantities and their relationships in problem situations. They bring two complementary abilities to bear on problems involving quantitative relationships: the ability to *decontextualize*—to abstract a given situation and represent it symbolically and manipulate the representing symbols as if they have a life of their own, without necessarily attending to their referents—and the ability to *contextualize*, to pause as needed during the manipulation process in order to probe into the referents for the symbols involved.

Quantitative reasoning entails habits of creating a coherent representation of the problem at hand; considering the units involved; attending to the meaning of quantities, not just how to compute them; and knowing and flexibly using different properties of operations and objects.

3. Construct viable arguments and critique the reasoning of others.

Mathematically proficient students understand and use stated assumptions, definitions, and previously established results in constructing arguments. They make conjectures and build a logical progression of statements to explore the truth of their conjectures. They are able to analyze situations by breaking them into cases and can recognize and use counterexamples. They justify their conclusions, communicate them to others, and respond to the arguments of others. They reason inductively about data, making plausible arguments that take into account the context from which the data arose. Mathematically proficient students are also able to compare the effectiveness of two plausible arguments, distinguish correct logic or reasoning from that which is flawed, and—if there is a flaw in an argument—explain what it is. Elementary students can construct arguments using concrete referents such as objects, drawings, diagrams, and actions. Such arguments can make sense and be correct, even though they are not generalized or made formal until later grades. Later, students learn to determine domains to which an argument applies. Students at all grades can listen or read the arguments of others, decide whether they make sense, and ask useful questions to clarify or improve the arguments.

4. Model with mathematics.

Mathematically proficient students can apply the mathematics they know to solve problems arising in everyday life, society, and the workplace. In early grades, this might be as simple as writing an addition equation to describe a situation. In middle grades, a student might apply proportional reasoning to plan a school event or analyze a problem in the community. By high school, a student might use geometry to solve a design problem or use a function to describe how one quantity of interest depends on another. Mathematically proficient students who can apply what they know are comfortable making assumptions and approximations to simplify a complicated situation, realizing that these may need revision later. They are able to identify important quantities in a practical situation and map their relationships using such tools as diagrams, two-way tables, graphs, flowcharts, and formulas. They can analyze those relationships mathematically to draw conclusions. They routinely interpret their mathematical results in the context of the situation and reflect on whether the results make sense, possibly improving the model if it has not served its purpose.

5. Use appropriate tools strategically.

Mathematically proficient students consider the available tools when solving a mathematical problem. These tools might include pencil and paper, concrete models, a ruler, a protractor, a calculator, a spreadsheet, a computer algebra system, a statistical package, or dynamic geometry software. Proficient students are sufficiently familiar with tools appropriate for their grade or course to make sound decisions about when each of these tools might be helpful, recognizing both the insight to be gained and their limitations. For example, mathematically proficient high school students analyze graphs of functions and solutions generated using a graphing calculator. They detect possible errors by strategically using estimation and other mathematical knowledge. When making mathematical models, they know that technology can enable them to visualize the results of varying assumptions, explore consequences, and compare predictions with data. Mathematically proficient students at various grade levels are able to identify relevant external mathematical resources, such as digital content located on a website, and use them to pose or solve problems. They are able to use technological tools to explore and deepen their understanding of concepts.

6. Attend to precision.

Mathematically proficient students try to communicate precisely to others. They try to use clear definitions in discussion with others and in their own reasoning. They state the meaning of the symbols they choose, including using the equal sign consistently and appropriately. They are careful about specifying units of measure and labeling axes to clarify the correspondence with quantities in a problem. They calculate accurately and efficiently, express numerical answers with a degree of precision appropriate for the problem context. In the elementary grades, students give carefully formulated explanations to each other. By the time they reach high school, they have learned to examine claims and make explicit use of definitions.

7. Look for and make use of structure.

Mathematically proficient students look closely to discern a pattern or structure. Young students, for example, might notice that three and seven more is the same amount as seven and three more, or they may sort a collection of shapes according to how many sides the shapes have. Later, students will see 7×8 equals the well-remembered $7 \times 5 + 7 \times 3$, in preparation for learning about the distributive property. In the expression $x^2 + 9x + 14$, older students can see the 14 as 2×7 and the 9 as $2 + 7$. They recognize the significance of an existing line in a geometric figure and can use the strategy of drawing an auxiliary line for solving problems. They also can step back for an overview and shift perspective. They can see complicated things, such as some algebraic expressions as single objects or as being composed of several objects. For example, they can see $5 - 3(x - y)^2$ as 5 minus a positive number times a square and use that to realize that its value cannot be more than 5 for any real numbers x and y.

8. Look for and express regularity in repeated reasoning.

Mathematically proficient students notice if calculations are repeated and look both for general methods and for shortcuts. Upper elementary students might notice when dividing 25 by 11 that they are repeating the same calculations over and over again, and conclude they have a repeating decimal. By paying attention to the calculation of slope as they repeatedly check whether points are on the line through $(1, 2)$ with slope 3, middle school students might abstract the equation $(y - 2)/(x - 1) = 3$. Noticing the regularity in the way terms cancel when expanding $(x - 1)(x + 1), (x - 1)(x^2 + x + 1)$, and $(x - 1)(x^3 + x^2 + x + 1)$ might lead them to the general formula for the sum of a geometric series. As they work to solve a problem, mathematically proficient students maintain oversight of the process while attending to the details. They continually evaluate the reasonableness of their intermediate results.

Source: Council of Chief State School Officers. (2010). *Common Core State Standards.* Copyright © 2010 National Governors Association Center for Best Practices and Council of Chief State School Officers. All rights reserved.

NCTM Mathematics Teaching Practices: from *Principles to Actions*

Establish mathematics goals to focus learning.

Effective teaching of mathematics establishes clear goals for the mathematics that students are learning, situates goals within learning progressions, and uses the goals to guide instructional decisions.

Implement tasks that promote reasoning and problem solving.

Effective teaching of mathematics engages students in solving and discussing tasks that promote mathematical reasoning and problem solving and allow multiple entry points and varied solution strategies.

Use and connect mathematical representations.

Effective teaching of mathematics engages students in making connections among mathematical representations to deepen understanding of mathematics concepts and procedures and as tools for problem solving.

Facilitate meaningful mathematical discourse.

Effective teaching of mathematics facilitates discourse among students to build shared understanding of mathematical ideas by analyzing and comparing student approaches and arguments.

Pose purposeful questions.

Effective teaching of mathematics uses purposeful questions to assess and advance students' reasoning and sense making about important mathematical ideas and relationships.

Build procedural fluency from conceptual understanding.

Effective teaching of mathematics builds fluency with procedures on a foundation of conceptual understanding so that students, over time, become skillful in using procedures flexibly as they solve contextual and mathematical problems.

Support productive struggle in learning mathematics.

Effective teaching of mathematics consistently provides students, individually and collectively, with opportunities and supports to engage in productive struggle as they grapple with mathematical ideas and relationships.

Elicit and use evidence of student thinking.

Effective teaching of mathematics uses evidence of student thinking to assess progress toward mathematical understanding and to adjust instruction continually in ways that support and extend learning.

Appendix C
Guide to Blackline Masters

This Appendix has images of all 33 Blackline Masters (BLM) that you and your students will find useful to engage in many math activities. You can create full-sized masters from these images or print them from the links at the companion website.

Blackline Master	Number
0.5-Centimeter Grid Paper	7
10 × 10 Grids	25
10 × 10 Multiplication Array	16
10,000 Grid Paper	19
1-Centimeter Dot Paper	8
1-Centimeter Grid Paper	6
1-Centimeter Isometric Dot Paper	10
1-Centimeter Square/Diagonal Grid Paper	11
2-Centimeter Isometric Grid Paper	9
2-Centimeter Grid Paper	5
Addition and Subtraction Recording Sheets	20
Base-Ten Grid Paper	18
Base-Ten Materials	32
Blank Hundreds Chart	2
Clock Faces	31
Coordinate Grid—4 Quadrants	23
Coordinate Grid—Quadrant I	22
Degrees and Wedges	30
Double Ten-Frame	15
Five-Frame	12
Four Small Hundreds Charts	4
Geoboard Pattern (10 by 10)	28
Geoboard Pattern (5 by 5)	26
Geoboard Recording Sheets (10 by 10)	29
Geoboard Recording Sheets (5 by 5)	27
Hundreds Chart	3
Multiplication and Division Recording Sheets	21
Number Cards 0–10	1
Observation Checklist	33
Place-Value Mat (with Ten-Frames)	17

Suggestions for Use and Construction of Materials

Card Stock Materials

A good way to have many materials made quickly and easily for students is to have them duplicated on card stock, laminated, and then cut into smaller pieces if desired. Once cut, materials are best kept in clear freezer bags with zip-type closures. Punch a hole near the top of the bag so that you do not store air.

The following list is a suggestion for materials that can be made from card stock using the masters in this section. Quantity suggestions are also given.

Five-Frames and Ten-Frames—12–14

Five-frames and ten-frames are best duplicated on light-colored card stock. Do not laminate; if you do, the mats will curl and counters will slide around.

10 × 10 Multiplication Array—16

Make one per student in any color. Lamination is suggested. Provide each student with an L-shaped piece of card stock to frame the array.

Base-Ten Materials—32

Run copies on white card stock. One sheet will make 4 hundreds and 10 tens or 4 hundreds and 100 ones. Cut into pieces with a paper cutter. It is recommended that you not laminate the base-ten pieces. A kit consisting of 10 hundreds, 30 tens, and 30 ones is adequate for each student or pair of students.

Place-Value Mat (with Ten-Frames)—17

Mats can be duplicated on any pastel card stock. It is recommended that you not laminate these because they tend to curl and counters slide around. Make one for every student.

Rational Number Wheel—24

These disks should be made on card stock. Duplicate the master on two contrasting colors. Laminate and cut the circles and also the slot on the dotted line. Make a set for each student.

Many masters lend themselves to demonstration purposes. The 10 × 10 array, the blank hundreds board, and the large geoboard are examples. The place-value mat can be used with strips and squares or with counters and cups directly on the document camera. The missing-part blank and the record blanks for the four algorithms are pages that you may wish to write on as a demonstration.

The 10,000 grid is the easiest way there is to show 10,000 or to model four-place decimal numbers.

The degrees and wedges page is the very best way to illustrate what a degree is and also to help explain protractors.

All of the line and dot grids are useful for modeling. You may find it a good idea to have several copies of each easily available.

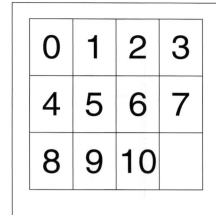

Number Cards 0–10—1

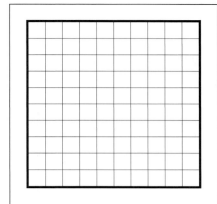

Blank Hundreds Chart—2

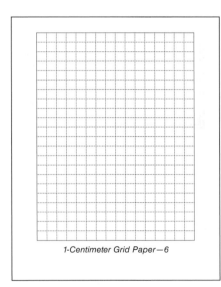

Hundreds Chart—3

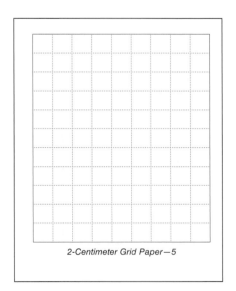

Four Small Hundreds Charts—4

2-Centimeter Grid Paper—5

1-Centimeter Grid Paper—6

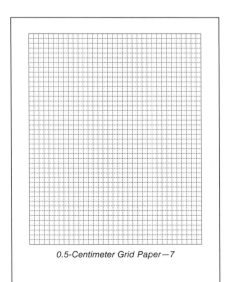

0.5-Centimeter Grid Paper—7

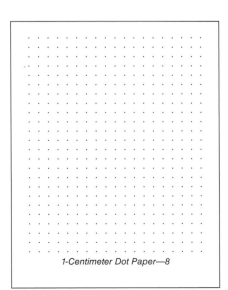

1-Centimeter Dot Paper—8

2-Centimeter Isometric Grid Paper—9

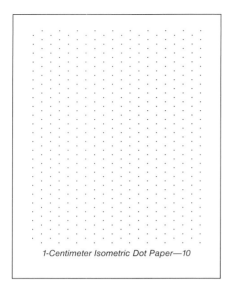

1-Centimeter Isometric Dot Paper—10

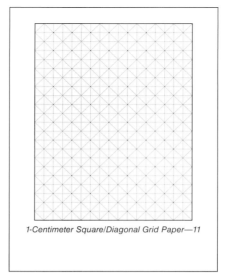

1-Centimeter Square/Diagonal Grid Paper—11

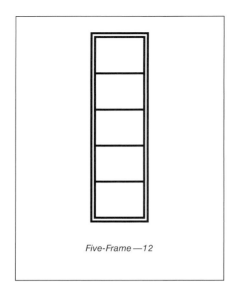

Five-Frame—12

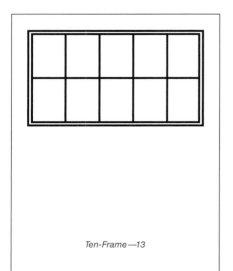

Ten-Frame—13

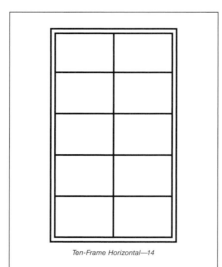

Ten-Frame Horizontal—14

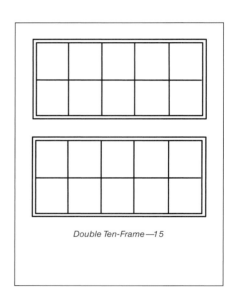

Double Ten-Frame—15

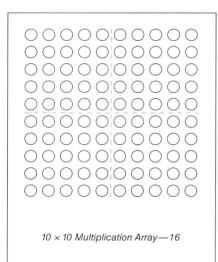

10 × 10 Multiplication Array—16

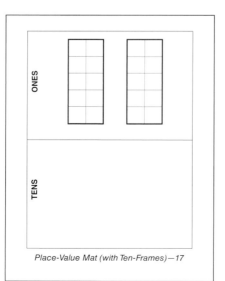

Place-Value Mat (with Ten-Frames)—17

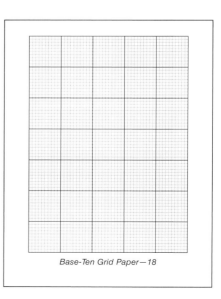

Base-Ten Grid Paper—18

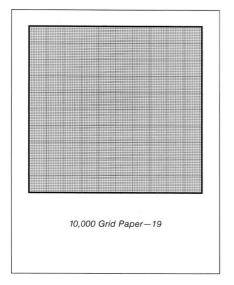

10,000 Grid Paper—19

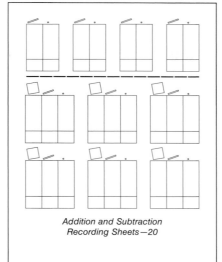

Addition and Subtraction
Recording Sheets—20

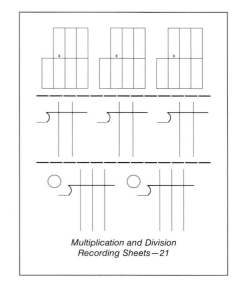

Multiplication and Division
Recording Sheets—21

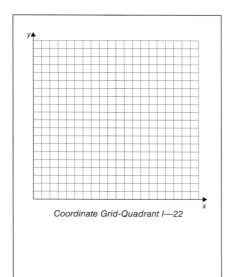

Coordinate Grid-Quadrant I—22

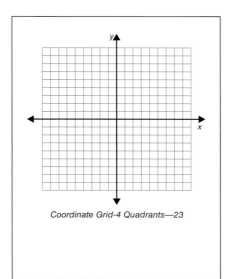

Coordinate Grid-4 Quadrants—23

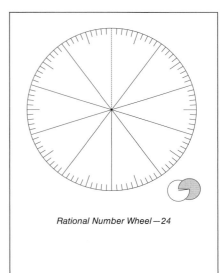

Rational Number Wheel—24

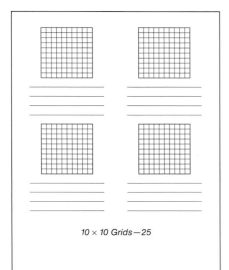

10 × 10 Grids—25

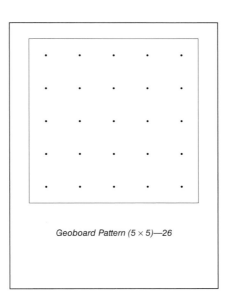

Geoboard Pattern (5 × 5)—26

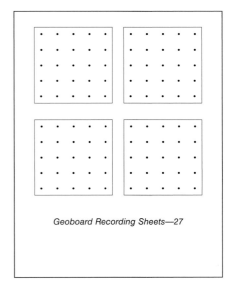

Geoboard Recording Sheets—27

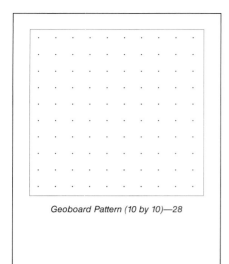

Geoboard Pattern (10 by 10)—28

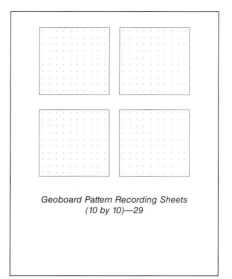

*Geoboard Pattern Recording Sheets
(10 by 10)—29*

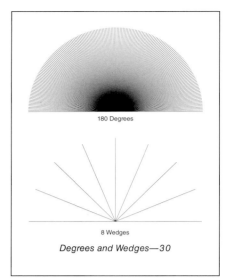

Degrees and Wedges—30

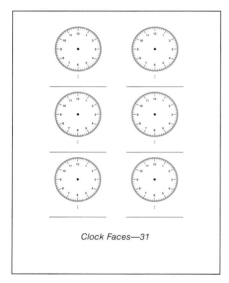

Clock Faces—31

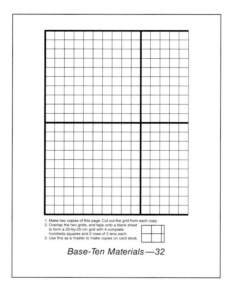

Base-Ten Materials—32

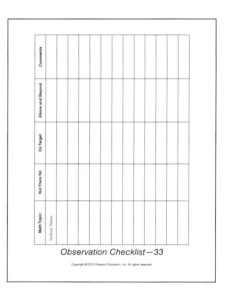

Observation Checklist—33

This table lists the named and numbered activities in Section II of the book. In addition to providing an easy way to find an activity, the table provides the main mathematics content stated as succinctly as possible and the related Common Core State Standards. Remember that this is a book about teaching mathematics and not a book of activities. It is extremely important not to take any activity as a suggestion for instruction without reading the full text in which it is embedded.

Chapter 8   Developing Early Number Concepts and Number Sense

Activity		Mathematics Content	CCSS-M	Page
8.1	Learning Patterns	Develop instant recognition of an amount in a dot pattern	K.CC.B.4	145
8.2	Dot Plate Flash	Practice recognition of amounts without counting	K.CC.B.4a, b	145
8.3	Fill the Towers	Develop one-to-one counting skills	K.CC.B.5	147
8.4	Number Necklaces	Practice number matching and develop basic addition	K.CC.A.3	148
8.5	Number Tubs	Develop counting skills and need for number names	K.CC.B.4; K.CC.B.5	148
8.6	Line Them Up!	Practice number sequence and the use of the number line	K.CC.B.4c; K.CC.A.2	148
8.7	Up and Back Counting	Practice skill of counting forward and backward	K.CC.A.1; K.CC.A.2	149
8.8	Counting On with Counters	Practice counting on	K.CC.A.2; K.CC.B.5	149
8.9	Real Counting On	Practice counting on to tell all	K.OA.A.1; 1.OA.B.5	149
8.10	Make Sets of More/Less/Same	Develop relational concept of more/less/same	K.CC.C.6	150
8.11	Find the Same Amount	Identify sets with more/less/same	K.CC.A.3; K.CC.C.6	151
8.12	More, Less or the Same	Develop concept of 1-more, 2-more, 1-less, 2-less, zero	K.CC.A.3; K.CC.C.6; K.OA.A.1	151
8.13	Make a Two-More-Than Set	Develop concept of 1-more, 2-more, 1-less, 2-less	K.OA.A.2; 1.OA.C.5	153
8.14	A Calculator Two-More-Than Machine	Practice 1-more-, 2-more-, 1-less-, 2-less-than relationships	1.OA.C.5	153
8.15	Five-Frame Tell-About	Develop benchmark of 5 for numbers to 10	K.CC.C.7; K.OA.A.5	154
8.16	Number Medleys	Develop the benchmark of 10 for numbers to 10	K.CC.C.6; K.CC.C.7	154
8.17	Ten-Frame Flash	Practice benchmarks of 5 and 10 for numbers to 10	K.CC.B.5	155
8.18	Build It in Parts	Practice part-whole concepts in a symbolic form	K.OA.A.3; 1.OA.C.6	156

(Continued)

Chapter 8 (*Continued*)

Activity		Mathematics Content	CCSS-M	Page
8.19	Two Out of Three	Develop missing part concepts	K.OA.A.3; K.OA.A.5	157
8.20	Covered Parts	Develop missing part concepts	K.OA.A.2	157
8.21	Missing-Part Cards	Practice missing part concepts	K.OA.A.4	157
8.22	I Wish I Had	Practice missing part concepts	K.OA.A.1; K.OA.A.2	157
8.23	Double War	Practice comparison of numbers to 20	K.CC.C.6	159
8.24	Difference War	Practice finding the difference between two sets	K.CC.C.6; K.OA.A.2	159
8.25	Number Sandwiches	Practice missing part concepts	K.OA.A.2; 1.OA.C.6	160
8.26	Ten and Some More	Develop concept of teen numbers	K.NBT.A.1	161
8.27	More and Less Extended	Extend one-more, two-more, one-less, two-less relation-ships to teen numbers	K.CC.C.6; K.NBT.A.1	161
8.28	Add a Unit to Your Number	Connect number to real-world measures	K.MD.A.1	163
8.29	Is It Reasonable?	Connect number to real-world measures	K.MD.A.1	163

Chapter 9 Developing Meanings for the Operations

Activity		Mathematics Content	CCSS-M	Page
9.1	Up and Down the Line	Practice using units on a number line	K.OA.A.2; 1.OA.A.1; 1.OA.A.2; 2.OA.A.1	175
9.2	Missing-Part Subtraction	Develop subtraction as a name for a missing part	K.OA.A.2; 1.OA.A.1; 1.OA.A.2; 2.OA.A.1	176
9.3	Pigs in Cages	Develop strategies for exploring both addends unknown problems	K.OA.A.3; 1.OA.A.1; 1.OA.B.4	176
9.4	More Than Two Addends	Practice adding more than two addends	1.OA.B.2	178
9.5	Factor Quest	Develop the connection between multiplication and division	4.OA.B.4	184
9.6	Factor Patterns	Develop patterns between arrays and factors	4.OA.B.4	185
9.7	Divide and Conquer	Develop measurement and partition concepts of division	3.OA.A.2	185
9.8	The Broken Division Key	Develop division as repeated subtraction and missing factor	4.NBT.B.6	186
9.9	Divide It Up	Develop the distributive property	3.OA.B.5; 5.OA.A.1	187

Chapter 10   Developing Basic Fact Fluency

Activity		Mathematics Content	CCSS-M	Page
10.1	If You Didn't Know	Use known facts to determine unknown facts	1.OA.C.6; 2.OA.B.2; 3.OA.B.5; 3.OA.C.7	199
10.2	How Many Feet in the Bed?	Practice facts for +2 and −2	1.OA.A.1; 1.OA.C.6; 2.OA.B.2	200
10.3	One More Than and Two More Than with Dice and Spinners	Practice addition facts for +1 and +2	1.OA.C.5; 1.OA.C.6; 2.OA.B.2	201
10.4	Double Magic	Practice addition doubles facts	1.OA.C.5; 1.OA.C.6; 2.OA.B.2	202
10.5	Calculator Doubles	Practice addition doubles facts	1.OA.C.6; 2.OA.B.2	202
10.6	How Much to Equal 10?	Practice combinations of 10 facts	1.OA.B.4; 1.OA.C.6; 2.OA.B.2	203
10.7	Move It, Move It	Develop Making 10 strategy	1.OA.B.3; 1.OA.C.6; 2.OA.B.2	204
10.8	Frames and Facts	Develop Making 10 strategy	1.OA.B.3; 1.OA.C.6; 2.OA.B.2	204
10.9	Flash	Practice using 5 and 10 as anchors	1.OA.B.3; 1.OA.C.5; 1.OA.C.6; 2.OA.B.2	205
10.10	On the Double!	Practice near-doubles addition facts	1.OA.B.3; 1.OA.C.6; 2.OA.B.2	205
10.11	Apples in the Trees	Practice subtraction to 20	1.OA.B.4; 1.OA.C.6; 2.OA.B.2	207
10.12	Apples in Two Trees	Develop missing-value concept, relating addition to subtraction	1.OA.B.3; 1.OA.B.4; 1.OA.C.6; 2.OA.B.2	208
10.13	Clock Facts	Develop minute intervals on the clock as a strategy for fives multiplication facts	3.OA.A.1; 3.OA.C.7	209
10.14	Strive to Derive	Use known facts to determine unknown facts	3.OA.A.1; 3.OA.B.5; 3.OA.C.7	212
10.15	Salute!	Identify the missing addend or factor	1.OA.B.4; 1.OA.C.6; 2.OA.B.2; 3.OA.B.5; 3.OA.B.6; 3.OA.C.7	214

(Continued)

Chapter 10   (*Continued*)

Activity		Mathematics Content	CCSS-M	Page
10.16	What's Under my Thumb?	Connect addition and subtraction facts or multiplication and division facts	1.OA.B.4; 1.OA.C.6; 2.OA.B.2; 3.OA.B.5; 3.OA.B.6; 3.OA.C.7	215
10.17	Bowl a Fact	Practice creating equations in addition, subtraction, multiplication, and division	2.OA.B.2; 3.OA.C.7; 5.OA.A.1	215

Chapter 11   Developing Whole-Number Place-Value Concepts

Activity		Mathematics Content	CCSS-M	Page
11.1	Counting in Groups	Develop concept of groups of ten as an efficient method of counting	K.NBT.A.1; 1.NBT.B.2a	229
11.2	Groups of Ten	Develop concept of groups of ten as a method of counting	K.NBT.A.1; 1.NBT.B.2a, b, c	229
11.3	Estimating Groups of Tens and Ones	Developing the concepts of two-digit numbers as ten and some more	K.NBT.A.1; 1.NBT.B.2a, b	230
11.4	Too Many Tens	Estimate and group quantities into hundreds, tens, and ones	2.NBT.A.1	231
11.5	Can You Make the Link?	Develop alternative groupings of ten to represent a number	1.NBT.B.2; 1.NBT.C.5	232
11.6	Three Other Ways	Develop alternative groupings of tens and hundreds to represent a number	2.NBT.A.1; 2.NBT.A.3	232
11.7	Base-Ten Riddles	Develop alternative groupings of tens and hundreds to represent a number	1.NBT.A.1; 2.NBT.A.1; 2.NBT.A.3	232
11.8	Counting Rows of Ten	Develop and connect three oral counting strategies	1.NBT.B.2c	233
11.9	Counting with Base-Ten Models	Develop and connect three oral counting strategies	1.NBT.B.2; 1.NBT.C.5	234
11.10	Tens, Ones, and Fingers	Develop and connect three oral counting strategies	1.NBT.B.2a, b, c	234
11.11	Say It/Press It	Connect oral and symbolic names for numbers to physical representation	2.NBT.A.1a, b; 2.NBT.A.3	236
11.12	Digit Change	Apply place-value concepts to symbolic representations	1.NBT.B.2; 1.NBT.C.5; 1.NBT.C.6; 2.NBT.A.1; 2.NBT.A.3; 2.NBT.B.5; 2.NBT.B.8	236
11.13	Missing Numbers	Practice sequence of numbers to 100	K.CC.A.1; K.NBT.A.1; 1.NBT.A.1; 1.NBT.B.2; 1.NBT.C.5	238
11.14	Finding Neighbors on the Hundreds Chart	Explore patterns in numbers to 100	K.CC.A.1; K.NBT.A.1; 1.NBT.A.1; 1.NBT.B.2; 1.NBT.C.5	239

Activity		Mathematics Content	CCSS-M	Page
11.15	Models with the Hundreds Chart	Develop concepts of 1-more/less and 10-more/less for two-digit numbers	K.CC.A.1; K.NBT.A.1; 1.NBT.A.1; 1.NBT.B.2; 1.NBT.C.5	239
11.16	The Thousands Chart	Extend patterns for 1 to 100 to patterns to 1000	2.NBT.A.1; 2.NBT.A.2; 2.NBT.A.3; 2.NBT.B.8.	239
11.17	Who Am I?	Develop relative magnitude of numbers to 100	1.NBT.A.1; 1.NBT.B.2; 1.NBT.B.3; 2.NBT.A.1; 2.NBT.A.2; 2.NBT.A.4	240
11.18	Who Could They Be?	Develop relative magnitude of numbers to 100	1.NBT.A.1; 1.NBT.B.2; 1.NBT.B.3; 2.NBT.A.1; 2.NBT.A.2; 2.NBT.A.4	240
11.19	Close, Far, and in Between	Explore relative differences between three-digit numbers	1.NBT.A.1; 1.NBT.B.2; 1.NBT.B.3; 2.NBT.A.1; 2.NBT.A.2; 2.NBT.A.4	241
11.20	What Comes Next?	Develop the continuing pattern in the place-value system	2.NBT.A.1; 2.NBT.A.3	242
11.21	Collecting 10,000	Develop an understanding of the size of large numbers	2.NBT.A.2; 2.NBT.A.3	244
11.22	Showing 10,000	Develop an understanding of the size of large numbers	2.NBT.A.2; 2.NBT.A.3	244
11.23	How Long?/How Far?	Develop an understanding of the size of large numbers	2.NBT.A.1a; 2.MD.A.3	244
11.24	A Long Time	Connect units of time to large numbers	3.MD.A.1	244
11.25	Really Large Quantities	Develop ability to estimate large quantities	2.MD.A.3; 3.MD.A.1; 3.MD.C.5	245

Chapter 12   Developing Strategies for Addition and Subtraction Computation (note that Chapter 12 shares activities with Chapter 11)

Activity		Mathematics Content	CCSS-M	Page
12.1	Calculator Challenge Counting	Develop mental addition strategies through skip counting	1.NBT.C.5	250
12.2	50 and Some More	Develop 50 as a part of numbers between 50 and 100	1.NBT.B.4	251
12.3	The Other Part of 100	Develop missing part strategies with a whole of 100	1.NBT.B.4; 2.NBT.B.5	251
12.4	Compatible Pairs	Explore addition combinations that make multiples of 10 or 100	2.NBT.B.5	252

(Continued)

Chapter 12 *(Continued)*

Activity		Mathematics Content	CCSS-M	Page
12.5	Numbers, Squares, Lines, and Dots	Develop invented strategies for addition and subtraction	2.NBT.B.7	252
12.6	Hundreds Chart Addition	Practice adding two-or three-digit numbers	2.NBT.B.5	254
12.7	How Much Between?	Develop strategies to find the difference	2.NBT.B.5	254
12.8	Little Ten-Frame Sums	Develop invented strategies for addition	2.NBT.B.5	254
12.9	Exploring Subtraction Strategies	Practice solving word problems with two-digit numbers	2.OA.A.1	260
12.10	Crossing a Decade	Extend the Making ten strategy to two-digit numbers	1.NBT.C.4; 2.OA.A.2	261
12.11	I Am, But Who Is?	Practice mental math with addition and subtraction of decade numbers	1.NBT.C.4; 1.NBT.C.5; 1.NBT.C.6	262
12.12	Just Adjust It	Practice using algebraic thinking to add related problems	2.NBT.B.5; 2.NBT.B.9	264
12.13	Odd or Even	Develop patterns when adding two-digit numbers	2.OA.C.3	264
12.14	How Far to My Number?	Develop missing-part strategies for two-digit numbers	2.NBT.B.5; 2.NBT.B.9	265
12.15	Over or Under?	Develop strategies to make computational estimations	3.OA.C.8	272
12.16	Round Up?	Develop strategies to round numbers to the nearest ten or hundred	3.NBT.A.1	273
12.17	Box Math	Practice computation and estimation through problem solving	2.NBT.B.5	274

Chapter 13   Developing Strategies for Multiplication and Division Computation

Activity		Mathematics Content	CCSS-M	Page
13.1	Build It and Break It	Develop the distributive property	4.NBT.B.5	283
13.2	Make It Easy	Develop the standard algorithm for multiplication	4.NBT.B.5	284
13.3	Left Overs	Develop the concept of remainders	4.NBT.B.6	289
13.4	Double, Double—No Toil or Trouble!	Develop a division strategy through doubling	5.NBT.B.6	293
13.5	High or Low?	Develop estimates of double digit multiplication	4.NBT.A.3; 4.NBT.B.5	294
13.6	That's Good Enough	Develop estimates of multiplication situations	4.OA.A.3	294
13.7	What Was Your Method?	Develop estimation strategies	4.NBT.A.3; 4.NBT.B.5	296
13.8	Jump to It	Estimate division using a missing factor strategy	4.NBT.B.5; 4.NBT.A.3	296
13.9	Hit the Target	Estimate for any of the four operations on a calculator	4.NBT.B.5	297

Chapter 14   Algebraic Thinking, Equations, and Functions

Activity		Mathematics Content	CCSS-M	Page
14.1	Diagonal Sums	Explore place-value relationships and generalize patterns	1.NBT.C.4; 2.NBT.B.9; 3.OA.D.9	302
14.2	Five Ways to Zero	Apply properties, such as identity for addition and/or multiplication, to creating equations	1.OA.B.3; 1.OA.C.6; 1.OA.D.7; 2.OA.B.2; 3.OA.D.9	305
14.3	Broken Calculator: Can You Fix It?	Explore properties of odd and even numbers	1.OA.B.3; 2.OA.C.3; 2.NBT.B.5; 3.OA.D.9	306
14.4	Convince Me Conjectures	Make and test generalizations about whole number operations (and properties)	1.OA.B.3; 2.NBT.B.9; 3.OA.B.5; 5.OA.A.1	307
14.5	Predict Down the Line	Explore the structure of repeating patterns analytically	2.OA.C.3; 4.OA.B.4	309
14.6	Hurricane Names	Explore the structure of repeating patterns analytically	4.OA.A.3; 4.OA.B.4; 5.OA.B.3; 6.EE.B.2a	310
14.7	Predict How Many	Develop functional relationships in growing patterns	5.OA.B.3; 6.EE.C.9; 7.EE.B.4a; 8.F.A.1	311
14.8	Perimeter Patterns	Generalize and graph geometric growing patterns (functions)	6.EE.C.9; 7.EE.B.4a; 8.F.A.1; 8.F.A.2	313
14.9	Sketch a Graph	Explore graphical representations of functional relationships	6.EE.D.9; 8.F.B.5	315
14.10	Border Tiles	Explore a pattern to develop a generalization	6.EE.A.1; 6.EE.A.2a, b, c; 6.EE.A.3; 6.EE.A.4	319
14.11	Capture Ten	Develop idea of equivalence while supporting basic fact development	1.OA.C.6; 1.OA.D.7; 2.OA.B.2	321
14.12	Seesaw Students	Develop the concept of the equal sign as a balance	1.OA.D.7; 2.NBT.A.4	322
14.13	What Do You Know about the Shapes?	Develop an understanding of the equal sign	6.EE.A.2a; 6.EE.B.5; 6.EE.B.6; 7.EE.B.4a, b	323
14.14	Tilt or Balance?	Develop understanding of the equal sign and the less-than and greater-than symbols	2.NBT.A.4; 4.NBT.A.1; 5.NBT.A.3a, b; 6.EE.A.4	323
14.15	True or False?	Explore the meaning of the equal sign	1.OA.B.3; 1.OA.D.7; 1.NBT.B.4; 2.NBT.B.5; 3.OA.B.5; 4.NBT.B.5; 5.NF.A.1	324

(Continued)

Chapter 14 (*Continued*)

Activity		Mathematics Content	CCSS-M	Page
14.16	What's Missing?	Explore the meaning of the equal sign	1.OA.D.7; 1.OA.D.8; 2.OA.A.1; 3.OA.A.4; 5.OA.A.2; 6.EE.A.3; 6.EE.B.5	326
14.17	Make a Statement!	Create equivalent expressions	1.OA.D.7; 1.OA.D.8; 2.OA.A.1; 3.OA.A.4; 4.NF.B.3a; 5.OA.A.2	328
14.18	Ball Weights	Explore variables in context	6.EE.A.4; 7.EE.A.2; 8.EE.C.8b	329
14.19	Solving the Mystery	Explore properties and equivalent expressions	5.OA.A.2; 6.EE.A.2a; 7.EE.A.2	331
14.20	How Many Gallons Left	Use mathematical modelling to solve a real-world problem	7.EE.A.2; 7.EE.B.4a; 8.F.B.4	334
14.21	Designing the Largest Box	Explore volume and surface area algebraically	5.MD.C.5b; 6.EE.A.2c; 6.G.A.2	335

Chapter 15 Developing Fraction Concepts

Activity		Mathematics Content	CCSS-M	Page
15.1	Playground Fractions	Develop concepts of equal shares using an area model	1.G.A.3; 2.G.A.3; 3.NF.A.1	343
15.2	Who Is Winning?	Develop fractional concepts using a linear model	3.NF.A.2a, b; 3.NF.A.3a, b, d	345
15.3	Class Fractions	Develop concepts of fractions using a set model	3.NF.A.1; 3.NF.A.3b	346
15.4	Partitioning: Fourths or Not Fourths?	Develop understanding of fractional parts	1.G.A.3; 2.G.A.3; 3.NF.A.1	348
15.5	Finding (All the) Fair Shares	Partition regions in different ways and prove they are partitioned accurately	1.G.A.3; 2.G.A.3; 3.NF.A.1	349
15.6	What Fraction Is Colored?	Determine shaded region on number strips where not all partitions are shown	3.NF.A.1; 3.NF.A.2a, b	350
15.7	How Far Did Nicole Go?	Determine shaded region on number strips where not all partitions are shown	3.NF.A.1; 3.NF.A.2a, b	350
15.8	Cookie Dough: Cut Me a Fair Share!	Explore a sharing task and connect to partitioning	1.G.A.3; 2.G.A.3	352
15.9	More, Less, or Equal to One Whole	Develop understanding of fractional parts	3.NF.A.1; 3.NF.A.2a, b	354
15.10	Pattern Block Creatures	Develop understanding of fractional parts	3.NF.A.1; 3.NF.A.2a, b	354

Activity		Mathematics Content	CCSS-M	Page
15.11	Calculator Fraction Counting	Explore counting by a fraction unit	3.NF.A.1 3.NF.A.3a, c	354
15.12	A Whole Lot of Fun	Partition and iterate to determine lengths of paper strips	3.NF.A.1; 3.NF.A.2a, b	355
15.13	Making Stacks	Introduce to equivalent fractions using pattern blocks	3.NF.A.1; 3.NF.3a, b, c	359
15.14	Dot Paper Equivalencies	Develop an understanding of the concept of equivalent fractions	3.NF.A.1; 3.NF.3a, b, c	360
15.15	Stretching Number Lines	Explore equivalence of fractions and comparing fractions	3.NF.A.3a, b, d; 4.NF.A.2	360
15.16	Lego Land: Building Options	Explore fraction equivalencies in model that can be area or set	2.G.A. 3; 3.NF.A.1; 3.NF.3a, b, c; 4.NF.B.3a, b	361
15.17	Apples and Bananas	Explore equivalence using a set model	3.NF.A.1; 3.NF.3a, b, c	362
15.18	Missing-Number Equivalences	Use counters or rectangles to find equivalent fractions	3.NF.3a, b, c; 4.NF.A.1	362
15.19	Garden Plots	Develop an equivalent fraction algorithm	3.NF.3b; 4.NF.A.1	362
15.20	Ordering Unit Fractions	Compare and order unit fractions	3.NF.A.3d; 4.NF.A.2	365
15.21	About How Much?	Estimate size of fractions	3.NF.A.1; 3.NF.A.2a, b	367
15.22	Zero, One-Half, or One	Compare fractions using benchmarks	3.NF.A.3d; 4.NF.A.2	368

Chapter 16　Developing Fraction Operations

Activity		Mathematics Content	CCSS-M	Page
16.1	Gardening Together	Explore addition and subtraction of fractions in an area model	4.NF.B.3a, d; 5.NF.A.1; 5.NF.A.2	376
16.2	Jumps on the Ruler	Explore addition and subtraction of fractions in a linear model	4.NF.B.3a, d; 5.NF.A.1; 5.NF.A.2	377
16.3	Over or Under 1	Develop estimation of sums and differences of fractions	4.NF.B.3a; 5.NF.A.2	378
16.4	Cups of Milk	Estimate addition and subtraction problems using a linear context (measuring cup)	4.NF.B.3a; 5.NF.A.2	379
16.5	Can You Make It True?	Find missing values in addition and subtraction problems	4.NF.B.3a; 5.NF.A.2	381
16.6	Common Multiple Flash Cards	Practice finding common multiples	4.OA.B.4; 5.NF.A.1	383
16.7	Hexagon Wholes	Explore multiplication of a fraction by a whole number (e.g., 3 x ¼)	4.NF.B.4a, b	385
16.8	How Big Is the Banner?	Explore multiplication of a whole number by a fraction (e.g., ½ x 6)	5.NF.B.4a, b; 5.NF.B.4a, b	386
16.9	Quilting Pieces	Develop multiplication of fractions with an area model	5.NF.B4b; 5.NF.B.5b	389

(Continued)

Chapter 16   (*Continued*)

Activity		Mathematics Content	CCSS-M	Page
16.10	Playground Problem	Explore multiplication of fractions and the commutative property	5.NF.B.4b; 5.NF.B.6	390
16.11	Can You See It?	Relate parts to wholes to explore multiplication of fractions greater than 1	5.NF.B.3; 5.NF.B.5a, b	391
16.12	Fractions Divided by Whole-Number Stories	Explore different contexts for understanding division of a fraction by a whole number	5.NF.B.7a, c	394
16.13	Sandwich Servings	Develop meaning for division by a fraction	5.NF.B.7b, c	395
16.14	How Much in One Whole Set?	Explore whole number divided by a fraction	5.NF.B.7a, c	396
16.15	How Much for 1?	Explore fraction divided by a fraction	5.NF.B.7a, c; 6.NS.A.1	396
16.16	The Size Is Right: Division	Estimate division of fraction problems	5.NF.B.7a, b, c; 6.NS.A.1	398

Chapter 17   Developing Concepts of Decimals and Percents

Activity		Mathematics Content	CCSS-M	Page
17.1	The Decimal Names the Unit	Develop an understanding of the purpose of the decimal point	4.NF.C.6; 5.NBT.A.3a	406
17.2	Shifting Units	Practice shifting the unit in place value	4.NF.C.6; 5.NBT.A.1; 5.NBT.A.2; 5.NBT.A.3a	409
17.3	Build it, Name it	Practice connecting the decimal notation to a physical model	4.NF.C.6; 5.NBT.A.1	410
17.4	Calculator Decimal Counting	Develop an understanding of the patterns in decimal notation	4.NF.C.6; 5.NBT.A.1	410
17.5	Familiar Fractions to Decimals	Develop a conceptual connection between fractions and decimal notations	4.NF.C.7	411
17.6	Estimate, Then Verify	Develop a conceptual connection between fractions and decimal notations	4.NF.C.7	412
17.7	Decimals and Fractions on a Double Number Line	Develop a conceptual connection between fractions and decimal notations	4.NF.C.6	412
17.8	Best Match	Practice estimation of decimal numbers with simple fractions	4.NF.C.6	413
17.9	Line 'Em Up	Develop an understanding of the way that decimal numbers are ordered	4.NF.C.6; 4.NF.C.7; 5.NBT.A.1; 5.NBT.A.3a; 5.NBT.A.3b	415
17.10	Close Decimals	Develop an understanding of the relative size of decimal numbers	5.NBT.A.3b	416
17.11	Zoom	Explore the density of decimals	5.NBT.C.3b; 6.NS.C.6	416
17.12	Representing Sums and Differences	Build the connection between computation, models and context	5.NBT.B.7	418
17.13	Hit the Target: Continuous Input	Estimate for any of the four operations	5.NBT.B.7; 6.NS.B.3	419
17.14	Where Does the Decimal Go? Multiplication	Use estimation to place the decimal point in multiplication	5.NBT.B.7; 6.NS.B.3	420

Activity		Mathematics Content	CCSS-M	Page
17.15	Where Does the Decimal Go? Division	Use estimation to place the decimal point in division	5.NBT.B.7; 6.NS.B.3	422
17.16	Percent Memory Match	Explore the relationship between percents and circle graphs	6.RP.A.3c	424

Chapter 18   Ratios, Proportions, and Proportional Reasoning

Activity		Mathematics Content	CCSS-M	Page
18.1	Stocking the Pond	Solve real-world problems involving ratios	6.RP.A.1; 6.RP.A.2; 6.RP.A.3	431
18.2	Birthday Cupcakes	Develop the concept of a composed unit and multiplicative comparison	6.RP.A.1; 6.RP.A.2; 6.RP.A.3	432
18.3	Which Has More?	Develop the distinction between additive and multiplicative comparisons	6.RP.A.1	434
18.4	Weight Loss	Explore the difference between additive and multiplicative comparison	6.RP.A.1	434
18.5	Pencil-to-Pencil	Develop the distinction between additive and multiplicative comparison	6.RP.A.3a; 7.RP.A.2b	436
18.6	Different Objects, Same Ratios	Explore ratio and proportion concepts in measurement	6.RP.A.1, 6.RP.A.2	437
18.7	Look-Alike Rectangles	Develop the concepts of ratio and proportion in the context of similar rectangles	6.RP.A.1; 6.RP.A.3a; 7.RP.A.2a	438
18.8	Scale Drawings	Develop the concepts of ratio and proportion in the context of similar 2-D figures	6.RP.A.1, 7.RP.A.3a	439
18.9	Rectangle Ratios: Graph It!	Explore proportions through graphs	7.RP.A.2a, b, c, d	440
18.10	Dripping Faucet	Apply algebraic thinking to develop proportional reasoning	6.RP.A.1; 6.RP.A.3a, b; 7.RP.A.2b, c	441
18.11	Comparing Lemonade Recipes	Explore proportional situations and compare ratios	6.RP.A.1; 6.RP.A.3a, b; 7.RP.A.1; 7.RP.A.2a	444
18.12	Solving Proportional Problems Using Ratio Tables	Develop proportional reasoning through scaling	6.RP.A.3a, b; 7.RP.A.1; 7.RP.A.2b, c; 7.RP.A.3	446
18.13	You and the Zoo	Use double number lines to solve situations involving proportions	6.RP.A.3a, d; 7.RP.A.2b; 7.RP.A.3	448
18.14	Making Sense of Percent Stories	Use double number lines to solve situations involving percents	6.RP.A.3c; 7.RP.A.3	449

Chapter 19   Developing Measurement Concepts

Activity		Mathematics Content	CCSS-M	Page
19.1	Familiar References	Explore a variety of real word benchmarks or references	1.MD.A.2; 2.MD.A.1; 3.MD.B.4	457

(Continued)

Chapter 19 *(Continued)*

Activity		Mathematics Content	CCSS-M	Page
19.2	Personal Benchmarks	Explore useful benchmarks using body lengths	2.MD.A.1; 3.MD.B.4; 4.MD.B.4	457
19.3	Guess the Unit	Develop the concept of various units of measure	3.MD.A.2; 3.MD.C.5; 4.MD.A.1; 5.MD.C.3	458
19.4	Estimation Quickie	Practice estimating different attributes	K.MD.A.1; K.MD.A.2; 1.MD.A.1; 1.MD.A.2; 2.MD.A.3	461
19.5	Estimation Scavenger Hunt	Practice measurement estimation in real contexts	1.MD.A.2; 2.MD.A.1; 2.MD.A.3	461
19.6	Longer, Shorter, Same	Practice identifying objects that are longer and shorter or the same as a target length	1.MD.A.2; 2.MD.A.1; 2.MD.A.3	462
19.7	Length (or Unit) Hunt	Develop the concept of length (or familiarity with a standard unit)	K.MD.A.2; 1.MD.A.1; 1.MD.A.2; 2.MD.A.3	462
19.8	Crooked Paths	Develop concept of length along paths that are not straight	1.MD.A.1; 2.MD.A.3; 2.MD.A.4	462
19.9	How Long Is the Teacher?	Develop methods for measuring length	1.MD.A.2; 2.MD.A.1; 2.MD.A.2; 2.MD.A.3	463
19.10	Estimate and Measure	Develop an understanding of length measurement	1.MD.A.2; 2.MD.A.1; 2.MD.A.3	464
19.11	Changing Units	Explore the inverse relationship between unit size and measure	2.MD.A.2; 2.MD.A.3	465
19.12	Conversion Please	Develop the concept of converting from a larger unit to a smaller unit in the same system	4.MD.A.1; 5.MD.A.1	465
19.13	Make Your Own Ruler	Develop understanding of rulers by making a ruler	1.MD.A.2; 2.MD.A.1; 2.MD.A.3	465
19.14	About One Unit	Develop familiarity with standard units (any attribute)	1.MD.A.2; 2.MD.A.1; 2.MD.A.3	466
19.15	Two-Piece Shapes	Develop an understanding of area; equivalent areas with different shapes	3.MD.C.5	467
19.16	Tangram Areas	Develop the concept of area	3.MD.C.5; 3.MD.C.6	468
19.17	Cover and Compare	Develop an understanding of units to measure area	3.MD.C.5; 3.MD.C.6	469
19.18	Rectangle Comparison: Square Units	Develop an understanding of units to measure area; readiness for rectangle area formula	3.MD.C.5; 3.MD.C.6; 3.MD.C.7	469

Activity		Mathematics Content	CCSS-M	Page
19.19	What's the Rim?	Develop the concept of perimeter	3.MD.D.8	470
19.20	Fixed Perimeters	Explore the relationship between area and perimeter of rectangles when the perimeter is constant	3.MD.D.8; 4.MD.A.3	471
19.21	Fixed Areas	Explore the relationship between area and perimeter of rectangles when the area is constant	3.MD.C.6; 3.MD.C.7; 4.MD.A.3	471
19.22	Sorting Areas and Perimeters	Explore the relationship between area and perimeter	3.MD.C.6; 3.MD.C.7; 4.MD.A.3	471
19.23	Area of a Parallelogram	Develop the area formula for parallelograms	6.G.A.1	473
19.24	Area of a Triangle	Develop the area formula for triangles	6.G.A.1	474
19.25	Making Boxes	Explore nets and surface area	6.G.A.4	475
19.26	Capacity Sort	Develop the concept of capacity	K.MD.A.2; 3.MD.A.2; 5.MD.C.3	477
19.27	Which Silo Holds More?	Explore volume of cylinders with non-standard units	5.MD.C.3	477
19.28	Fixed Volume: Comparing Prisms	Explore the relationship between volume and surface area of prisms when the volume is constant	5.MD.C.3; 5.MD.C.4; 5.MD.C.5	477
19.29	Box Comparison: Cubic Units	Develop the concept of volume; readiness for volume formula for prisms	5.MD.C.3; 5.MD.C.4; 5.MD.C.5	478
19.30	That's Cool	Develop estimation with units of liquid capacity	3.MD.A.2	478
19.31	Squeeze Play	Develop estimation with units of liquid capacity	3.MD.A.2	479
19.32	A Unit Angle	Develop an understanding of how units are used to measure angle size	4.MD.C.5	482
19.33	Ready for the Bell	Explore time as the duration of an event	1.MD.B.3	483
19.34	One-Handed Clocks	Develop an understanding of the hour hand in reading a clock	1.MD.B.3; 2.MD.C.7	484
19.35	Money Skip Counting	Develop skill in counting money	2.MD.C.8	486
19.36	Hundreds Chart Money Count	Explore a strategy for counting money	2.MD.C.8	486

Chapter 20   Geometric Thinking and Geometric Concepts

Activity		Mathematics Content	CCSS-M	Page
20.1	Shape Sorts	Develop ways that 2-D shapes are alike and different	K.G.B.4; 1.G.A.1; 2.G.A.1; 3.G.A.1	491
20.2	Property lists for quadrilaterals	Explore all properties attributable to special classes of quadrilaterals	2.G.A.1; 3.G.A.1; 4.G.A.2; 4.G.A.3	492
20.3	Minimal defining lists	Develop logic and reasoning to minimally define shapes	4.G.A.2; 5.G.B.3	493
20.4	Shape Show and Hunt	Explore attributes of two-dimensional shapes and identify their location in the environment	K.G.A.1; K.G.A.2; K.G.B.4	495

(Continued)

Chapter 20 *(Continued)*

Activity		Mathematics Content	CCSS-M	Page
20.5	What's My Shape?	Develop oral descriptions of shapes	1.G.A.1; 2.G.A.1; 3.G.A.1; 4.G.A.2	496
20.6	Tangram Puzzles	Practice composing shapes	K.G.B.6; 1.G.A.2; 2.G.A.1	497
20.7	Mosaic Puzzle	Explore properties of 2-D shapes and compose and decompose shapes	K.G.B.6; 1.G.A.2; 2.G.A.1; 3.G.A.1; 4.G.A.2	497
20.8	Geoboard Copy	Practice representation of shapes	1.G.A.2; 2.G.A.1; 4.G.A.1; 4.G.A.2; 4.G.A.3	498
20.9	Decomposing on the Geoboard	Practice decomposing shapes into other shapes	1.G.A.2; 1.G.A.3; 2.G.A.1; 2.G.A.3; 3.G.A.2	498
20.10	Mystery Definition	Develop defining properties of special classes of shapes	1.G.A.1; 2.G.A.1; 3.G.A.2; 4.G.A.2	501
20.11	Triangle Sort	Develop defining properties of triangles	2.G.A.1; 3.G.A.2; 4.G.A.2; 5.G.B.3; 5.G.B.4	502
20.12	Diagonals of Quadrilaterals	Explore the relationships between diagonals of classes of quadrilaterals	4.G.A.2; 5.G.B.3; 5.G.B.4	503
20.13	Constructing Three-Dimensional Shapes	Explore the construction of 3-D shapes	K.G.A.3; K.G.B.5; 1.G.A.2; 2.G.A.1; 6.G.A.4	504
20.14	Discovering Pi	Develop an understanding of pi as the ratio of circumference to diameter	7.G.B.4	505
20.15	True or False?	Explore informal deductive statements concerning properties of shapes	4.G.A.2; 5.G.B.3; 5.G.B.4	506
20.16	The Pythagorean Relationship	Explore the meaning of the Pythagorean relationship in geometric terms	8.G.B.6; 8.G.B.7	506
20.17	Angle Sum in a Triangle	Draw conjectures for the sum of the angles in a triangle	8.G.A.5;	507
20.18	Triangle Midsegments	Explore geometric relationships and making conjectures	7.G.A.2; 8.G.A.5	508
20.19	Pattern Block Mirror Symmetry	Develop the concept of line symmetry	4.G.A.3	509
20.20	Dot Grid Line Symmetry	Explore relationship between line symmetry and reflection	4.G.A.3	509
20.21	Motion Man	Develop the concepts of slides, flips, and turns	8.G.A.1a, b, c	511

Activity		Mathematics Content	CCSS-M	Page
20.22	Are They Congruent?	Explore congruent triangles using translations on a grid	8.G.A.1; 8.G.A.2	512
20.23	Pentomino Positions	Develop spatial problem solving skills	8.G.A.1	514
20.24	Hidden Positions	Develop a readiness for coordinates	K.G.A.1; 5.G.A.1	514
20.25	Paths	Explore the concept of location using coordinates on a grid	K.G.A.1; 5.G.A.1	516
20.26	Coordinate Slides	Develop the way coordinates are used to control translations	6.G.A.3; 8.G.A.1; 8.G.A.3	516
20.27	Coordinate Reflections	Explore the effect on coordinates when shapes are reflected about an axis	8.G.A.1; 8.G.A.3	517
20.28	Coordinate Dilations	Develop the way coordinates are used to control dilations	7.G.A.1; 8.G.A.1; 8.G.A.3	518
20.29	Finding Distance Using the Pythagorean Theorem	Develop the formula for the distance between two points	6.G.A.3; 8.G.B.8	519
20.30	Can You Remember?	Develop early spatial visualization skills and visual memory	K.G.B.4; 1.G.A.2; 2.G.A.1	520
20.31	Pentominoes	Develop spatial visualization skills	1.G.A.2; 2.G.A.1	520
20.32	Face Matching	Explore solids in terms of their faces or sides	1.G.A.2; 2.G.A.1; 3.G.A.1; 4.G.A.2	521
20.33	Building Views	Develop spatial visualization skills	6.G.A.4; 7.G.A.1	521
20.34	Three-Dimensional Drawings	Develop spatial visualization skills	6.G.A.4; 7.G.A.1	522
20.35	Search for the Platonic Solids	Explore the concept of the five Platonic Solids	7.G.A.2	523

Chapter 21   Developing Concepts of Data Analysis

Activity		Mathematics Content	CCSS-M	Page
21.1	Who Is in Our Village?	Gather and analyze data about members of the class	2.MD.D.10; 3.MD.B.3; 6.SP.A.1; 7.SP.B.3	531
21.2	What Can We Learn about Our Community?	Generate questions about the community, gather data, and analyze it	1.MD.C.4; 2.MD.D.10; 6.SP.A.1; 6.SP.B.4; 6.SP.B.5	531
21.3	How Do We Compare?	Develop an awareness of the importance of sampling	6.SP.A.1; 6.SP.A.2; 7.SP.A.1; 7.SP.B.3	533
21.4	What about "Both"	Classify shapes by attributes on a Venn diagram	K.MD.3; 1.MD.C.4	535

(Continued)

Activity		Mathematics Content	CCSS-M	Page
22.4	1-2-3 How Likely Are Sums?	Explore how likely particular outcomes are with two events	7.SP.C.5; 7.SP.C.6; 7.SP.C.8a	561
22.5	Race to Ten	Use area context for exploring probability	7.SP.C.6; 7.SP.C.7a, b	561
22.6	Design and Test Bags	Explore probability through experiments	7.SP.C.6	563
22.7	Mystery Bags	Explore probability through experiments	7. SP.C.6; 7.SP.C.7a, b	564
22.8	Fair or Unfair?	Explore games theoretically and through experiments	7.SP.C.6; 7.SP.C.7a	565
22.9	Chance of Hitting the Target?	Explore probability in a area model	7.G.B.4; 7.SP.C.6; 7.SP.C.7b	567
22.10	Drop It!	Determine how likely outcomes are based on empirical data	7.SP.C.7b	568
22.11	Get All 6!	Explore impact of size of the trial	7.SP.C.6	568
22.12	What Are the Chances?	Develop the concept of randomness	7.SP.C.6	569
22.13	Lu-Lu	Compare results of game (experiment) with sample space	7.SP.C.7a; 7.SP.C.8a	573
22.14	Are You a Spring Dog?	Use an area model to determine how likely independent events are	7.SP.C.8a, b	574
22.15	Design a Winning Spinner	Find probability of independent events	7.SP.C.6; 7.SP.C.7a; 7.SP.C.8a, b	574
22.16	Keys to a New Car	Find probability of dependent events	7.SP.C.8a, b	575
22.17	Probability of Getting Water	Design a simulation to determine probability of an event	7.SP.C.8b, c	576
22.18	Chance of Triplet Girls	Design a simulation to determine probability of an event	7.SP.C.8b, c	578
22.19	Money in Two Piggy Banks	Find probability of dependent events	7.SP.C.8a, b, c	579

Chapter 23 Developing Concepts of Exponents, Integers, and Real Numbers

Activity		Mathematics Content	CCSS-M	Page
23.1	Stacks of Coins	Explore the order of operations conceptually	3.OA.D.8; 6.EE.A.2c	585
23.2	Guess My Number	Practice writing an expression using order of operations	6.EE.A.2a, b, c; 6.EE.B.6	586
23.3	True or False Equations	Explore order of operations	3.OA.D.8; 6.EE.A.3; 6.EE.A.4	586
23.4	Entering Expressions	Explore expressions using expressions is the order of operations	6.EE.A.3; 6.EE.A.4	588
23.5	Find the Error	Identify errors that involve order of operations	8.EE.A.1	589
23.6	How Far Away from the Sun?	Explore scientific notation and relative size of numbers	8.EE.A.4	590
23.7	At a Snail's Pace	Explore scientific notation of very small numbers in context	8.EE.A.4	591
23.8	Exploring Powers of 10	Develop an understanding of scientific notation and other expressions for powers of 10	8.EE.A.3	591

(Continued)

Chapter 23   (*Continued*)

Activity		Mathematics Content	CCSS-M	Page
23.9	What Is Her Net Worth?	Develop the concept of positive and negative numbers	6.NS.C.5	593
23.10	Football Statistics	Develop the concept of positive and negative numbers	6.NS.C.5; 6.NS.C.6a	595
23.11	Greater, Less, Equal or Don't Know?	Build an understanding for symbols (minus and parenthesis) used in expressions	6.NS.C.5; 6.NS.C.6a	596
23.12	Find the Zero	Develop strategy for adding with negative numbers	7.NS.A.1a, b, c	598
23.13	Creating Stories and Conjectures for Operations with Negative Numbers	Estimate the result of operations involving negative numbers	7.NS.A.2a, b	601
23.14	Repeater or Terminator?	Develop the connection between repeating versus terminating decimal numbers	7.NS.A.2d	604
23.15	Edges of Squares and Cubes	Develop the concepts of square roots and cube roots	8.NS.A.1; 8.EE.A.2	605
23.16	Wheel of Theodorus	Explore irrational numbers through classic art project	8.NS.A.2; 8.EE.A.2	606

References

Abu-Bakare, V. (2008). *Investigating students,' understandings of probability: A study of a grade 7 classroom* (Master's thesis). Retrieved from http://hdl.handle.net/2429/4073

AIMS. (2001). *Looking at lines: Interesting objects and linear functions*. Fresno, CA: AIMS Education Foundation.

Ameis, J. A. (2011). The truth about PEDMAS. *Mathematics Teaching in the Middle School, 16*(7), 414–420.

Anderson, L.W., & Krathwohl, D. R. (Eds.) (2001). *A taxonomy for learning, teaching, and assessing: A revision of Bloom's Taxonomy of educational objectives: Complete Edition*. New York, NY: Addison Wesley, Longman.

Arbaugh, F., Herbel-Eisenmann, B., Ramirez, N., Kranendonk, H., Knuth, E., & Quander, J. R. (2010). *Linking research and practice: Practitioner community priorities for research in mathematics education*. Reston, VA: Report for the National Council of Teachers of Mathematics, Research Agenda Conference.

Ashcraft, M. H., & Christy, K. S. (1995). The frequency of arithmetic facts in elementary texts: Addition and multiplication in grades 1–6. *Journal for Research in Mathematics Education, 26*(5), 396–421.

Assouline, S. G., & Lupkowski-Shoplik, A. (2011). *Developing math talent: A comprehensive guide to math education for gifted students in elementary and middle school* (2nd ed.). Waco, TX: Prufrock Press.

Austin, R., & Thompson, D. (1997). Exploring algebraic patterns through literature. *Mathematics Teaching in the Middle School, 2*(4), 274–281.

Averill, R., Anderson, D., Easton, H., Te Maro, P., Smith, D., & Hynds, A. (2009). Culturally responsive teaching of mathematics: Three models from linked studies. *Journal for Research in Mathematics Education, 40*(2), 157–186.

Backhouse, J., Haggarty, L., Pirie, S., & Stratton, J. (1992). *Improving the learning of mathematics*. Portsmouth, NH: Heinemann.

Baek, J. M. (2006). Children's mathematical understanding and invented strategies for multidigit multiplication. *Teaching Children Mathematics, 12*(5), 242–247.

Baek, J. M. (2008). Developing algebraic thinking through exploration in multiplication. In C. E. Greenes & R. Rubenstein (Eds.), *Algebra and algebraic thinking in school mathematics: 70th NCTM yearbook* (pp. 141–154). Reston, VA: NCTM.

Bailey, D. H., Hoard, M. K., Nugent, L. & Geary, D. C. (2012). Competence with fractions predicts gains in mathematics achievement. *Journal of Experimental Child Psychology, 113*, 447–455.

Bakker, A., Biehler, R., & Konold, C. (2004). Should young students learn about box plots? In *Curricular development in statistics education* (pp. 163–173). Sweden: Curricular Development in Statistics Education.

Ball, D. L. (1992). Magical hopes: Manipulatives and the reform of math education. *American Educator, 16*(2), 14–18, 46–47.

Ball, D. L., & Bass, H. (2003). Making mathematics reasonable in school. In J. Kilpatrick, W. G. Martin, & D. Schifter (Eds.), *A research companion to Principles and Standards for School Mathematics* (pp. 27–44). Reston, VA: NCTM.

Ball, D. L., & Stacey, K. (2005). Teaching strategies for developing judicious technology use. In W. J. Masalski & P. C. Elliott (Eds.), *Technology-supported mathematics learning environments* (pp. 3–15). Reston, VA: NCTM.

Bamberger, H. J., Oberdorf, C., & Schultz-Ferrell, K. (2010). *Math misconceptions: From misunderstanding to deep understanding*. Portsmouth, NH: Heinemann.

Barker, L. (2009). Ten is the magic number! *Teaching Children Mathematics, 15*(6), 336–345.

Barlow, A. T. (2010). Building word problems: What does it take? *Teaching Children Mathematics, 17*(3), 140–148.

Barlow, A. T., & McCrory, M. (2011). Strategies for promoting math disagreements. *Teaching Children Mathematics, 17*(3), 530–539.

Barmby, P., Harries, T., Higgins, S., & Suggate, J. (2009). The array representation and primary children's understanding and reasoning in multiplication. *Educational Studies in Mathematics, 70*, 217–241.

Barnett, R. C. (2007, October). *As the twig is bent: Early and powerful influences on whether girls choose careers in math and science.* Presentation at Boston University.

Barney, L. (1970, April). Your fingers can multiply! *Instructor,* 129–130.

Baroody, A. J. (1985). Mastery of the basic number combinations: Internalization of relationships or facts? *Journal for Research in Mathematics Education, 16*(2), 83–98.

Baroody, A. J. (1987). *Children's mathematical thinking: A developmental framework for preschool, primary, and special education teachers*. New York: Teachers College Press.

Baroody, A. J. (1990). How and when should place value concepts and skills be taught? *Journal for Research in Mathematics Education, 21*, 281–286.

Baroody, A. J. (2006). Why children have difficulties mastering the basic number combinations and how to help them. *Teaching Children Mathematics, 13*(1), 22–31.

Baroody, A. J. (2011). Learning: A framework. In F. Fennell (Ed.), *Achieving fluency: Special education and mathematics* (pp. 15–58). Reston, VA: NCTM.

Baroody, A. J., Bajwa, N. P., & Eiland, M. (2009). Why can't Johnny remember the basic facts? *Developmental Disabilities Research Reviews, 15*, 69–79.

Baroody, A. J., Feil, Y., & Johnson A. R. (2007). An alternative reconceptualization of procedural and conceptual knowledge. *Journal for Research in Mathematics Education, 38*(2), 115–131.

Baroody, A. J., Li, X., & Lai, M. L. (2008). Toddlers' spontaneous attention to number. *Mathematics Thinking and Learning, 10*, 1–31.

Baroody, A. J., Wilkins, J. L., & Tiilikainen, S. H. (2003). The development of children's understanding of additive commutativity: From protoquantitive concept to general concept? In A. J. Baroody & A. Dowker (Eds.), *The development of arithmetic concepts and skills* (pp. 127–160). Mahwah, NJ: Erlbaum.

Battista, M. T. (2003). Understanding students' thinking about area and volume measurement. In D. H. Clements (Ed.), *Learning and teaching measurement* (pp. 122–142). Reston, VA: NCTM.

Battista, M. T. (2007). The development of geometric and spatial thinking. In F. Lester (Ed.), *Second handbook of research on mathematics teaching and learning* (pp. 843–908). Reston, VA: NCTM.

Bay-Williams, J. M., & Kling, G. (2014). Enriching addition and subtraction fact mastery through games. *Teaching Children Mathematics, 21*(4), 239–247.

Bay-Williams, J. M., & Martinie, S. L. (2003). Thinking rationally about number in the middle school. *Mathematics Teaching in the Middle School, 8*(6), 282–287.

Bay-Williams, J. M., & Martinie, S. L. (2009). *Math and nonfiction: Grades 6–8.* Sausalito, CA: Marilyn Burns Books.

Bay-Williams, J. M., & Martinie, S. L. (2004a). What does algebraic thinking look like? *Mathematics Teaching in the Middle School, 10*(4), 198–199.

Bay-Williams, J. M., & Martinie, S. L. (2004b). *Math and literature: Grades 6–8.* Sausalito, CA: Math Solutions Publications.

Bay-Williams, J. M., & Martinie, S. L. (in press). Order of operations: The myth and the math. *Mathematics Teaching in the Middle School, 20*(6).

Beck, S. A., & Huse, V. E. (2007). A virtual spin on probability. *Teaching Children Mathematics, 13*(9), 482–486.

Beckman, C. E., Thompson, D., & Austin, R. A. (2004). Exploring proportional reasoning through movies and literature. *Mathematics Teaching in the Middle School, 9*(5), 256–262.

Behr, M. J., Lesh, R., Post, T. R., & Silver, E. A. (1983). Rational number concepts. In R. Lesh & M. Landau (Eds.), *Acquisition of mathematics concepts and processes* (pp. 91–126). New York: Academic Press.

Beilock, S. L., Gunderson, E. A., Ramirez, G., & Levine, S. C. (2010). Female teachers' math anxiety affects girls' math achievement. *Proceedings of the National Academy of Sciences (PNAS), 107*(5), 1860–1963.

Bell, E. S., & Bell, R. N. (1985). Writing and mathematical problem solving: Arguments in favor of synthesis. *School Science and Mathematics, 85*(3), 210–221.

Benard, B. (1991). *Fostering resiliency in kids: Protective factors in the family, school and community.* Portland, OR: Northwest Regional Educational Laboratory.

Berk, D., Taber, S., Gorowara, C. C., & Poetzl, C. (2009). Developing prospective elementary teachers' flexibility in the domain of proportional reasoning. *Mathematical Thinking and Learning, 11*(3), 113–135.

Beswick, K. (2011). Make your own paint chart. *Australian Mathematics Teacher, 67*(1), 6–11.

Bezuszka, S. J., & Kenney, M. J. (2008). The three R's: Recursive thinking, recursion, and recursive formulas. In C. E. Greenes & R. Rubenstein (Eds.), *Algebra and algebraic thinking in school mathematics: 70th NCTM yearbook* (pp. 81–97). Reston, VA: NCTM.

Biddlecomb, B., & Carr, M. (2011). A longitudinal study of the development of mathematics strategies and underlying counting schemes. *International Journal of Science and Mathematics Education, 9*, 1–24.

Bishop, A. J. (2001). What values do you teach when you teach mathematics? *Teaching Children Mathematics, 7*(6), 346–349.

Bishop, J. P., Lamb, L. L., Philipp, R. A., Whitacre, I., Schappelle, M. P., Lewis, M. L. (2014). Obstacles and affordances for integer reasoning: An analysis of children's thinking and the history of mathematics. *Journal for Research in Mathematics Education, 45*(1), 19–61.

Black, P. J., & Wiliam, D. (1998). Assessment and classroom learning. *Assessment in Education, 5*(1), 7–74.

Blanton, M. L. (2008). *Algebra in the elementary classroom: Transforming thinking, transforming practice.* Portsmouth, NH: Heinemann.

Blanton, M., Levi, L., Crites, T. W., & Dougherty, B. J. (2011). *Developing essential understanding of algebraic thinking for teaching mathematics in grades 3–5.* Essential Understanding Series. Reston, VA: NCTM.

Bley, N. S., & Thornton, C. A. (1995). *Teaching mathematics to students with learning disabilities* (3rd ed.). Austin, TX: Pro-Ed.

Blote, A., Lieffering, L., & Ouwehand, K. (2006). The development of many-to-one counting in 4-year-old children. *Cognitive Development, 21*(3), 332–348.

Blume, G., Galindo, E., & Walcott, C. (2007). Performance in measurement and geometry from the viewpoint of *Principles and Standards for School Mathematics.* In P. Kloosterman & F. Lester, Jr. (Eds.), *Results and interpretations of the 2003 mathematics assessment of the National Assessment of Educational Progress* (pp. 95–138). Reston, VA: NCTM.

Boaler, J. (2002). *Experiencing school mathematics: Traditional and reform approaches to teaching and their impact on student learning.* Mahwah, NJ: Erlbaum.

Boaler, J. (2008, April). Promoting "relational equity" and high mathematics achievement through an innovative mixed ability approach. *British Educational Research Journal, 34*, 167–194.

Boaler, J. (2012, July 3). Timed tests and the development of math anxiety. *Education Week.* Retrieved from http://www.edweek.org/ew/articles/2012/07/03/36boaler.h31.html

Boaler, J. (2014). Research suggests that timed tests cause math anxiety. *Teaching Children Mathematics, 20*(8), 469–474.

Boaler, J., & Humphreys, C. (2005). *Connecting mathematical ideas: Middle school video cases to support teaching and learning.* Portsmouth, NH: Heinemann.

Bofferding, L. (2014). Negative integer understanding: Characterizing first graders' mental models. *Journal for Research in Mathematics Education, 45*(2), 194–245.

Bransford, J., Brown, A., & Cocking, R., Eds. (2000). *How people learn: Brain, mind, experience, and school: Expanded edition.* Washington, DC: National Academies Press.

Bray, W. S. (2009). The power of choice. *Teaching Children Mathematics, 16*(3), 178–184.

Bray, W. S., & Abreu-Sanchez, L. (2010). Using number sense to compare fractions. *Teaching Children Mathematics, 17*(2), 90–97.

Bray, W., & Santagata, R. (2014). Making mathematical errors: Springboards for learning. In K. Karp & A. Roth-McDuffie (Eds.), *Using research to improve instruction* (pp. 239–248). Reston, VA: NCTM.

Bresser, R. (1995). *Math and literature (grades 4–6).* Sausalito, CA: Math Solutions.

Breyfogle, M. L., & Williams, L. E. (2008–2009). Designing and implementing worthwhile tasks. *Teaching Children Mathematics, 15*(5), 276–280.

Bright, G. W., Behr, M. J., Post, T. R., & Wachsmuth, I. (1988). Identifying fractions on number lines. *Journal for Research in Mathematics Education, 19*(3), 215–232.

Bright, G. W., Joyner, J. M., & Wallis, C. (2003). Assessing proportional thinking. *Mathematics Teaching in the Middle School, 9*(3), 166–172.

Brown, A. (2014). The U.S. Hispanic population has increased sixfold since 1970. Pew Research Center. Retrieved from www.pewresearch.org/fact-tank/2014/02/26/the-u-s-hispanic-population-has-increased-sixfold-since-1970/

Brown, G., & Quinn, R. J. (2007). Investigating the relationship between fraction proficiency and success in algebra. *Australian Mathematics Teacher, 63*(4), 8–15.

Brown, S. A., & Mehilos, M. (2010). Using tables to bridge arithmetic and algebra. *Mathematics Teaching in the Middle School, 15*(9), 532–538.

Brownell, W., & Chazal, C. (1935). The effects of premature drill in third grade arithmetic. *Journal of Educational Research, 29*(1), 17–28.

Bruner, J. S., & Kenney, H. J. (1965). Representation and mathematics learning. *Monographs of the Society for Research in Child Development, 30*(1), 50-59.

Burns, M. (1999). *Making sense of mathematics: A look toward the twenty-first century.* Presentation at the annual meeting of the National Council of Teachers of Mathematics, San Francisco.

Burrill, G. F., & Elliot, P. (2006). *Thinking and reasoning with data and chance: 68th NCTM yearbook.* Reston, VA: NCTM.

Buschman, L. (2003). *Share and compare: A teacher's story about helping children become problem solvers in mathematics.* Reston, VA: NCTM.

Byrge, L., Smith, L. B., & Mix, K. (2013). Beginnings of place value: How preschoolers write three-digit numbers. *Child Development 85(2)*, 437-443.

Cai, J. (2003). What research tells us about teaching mathematics through problem solving. In F. K. Lester, Jr. (Ed.), *Research and issues in teaching mathematics through problem solving* (pp. 241–254). Reston, VA: NCTM.

Cai, J. (2010). Helping elementary school students become successful mathematical problem solvers. In D. Lambdin (Ed.), *Teaching and learning mathematics: Translating research to the classroom* (pp. 9–14). Reston, VA: NCTM.

Cai, J., & Sun, W. (2002). Developing students' proportional reasoning: A Chinese perspective. In B. Litwiller (Ed.), *Making sense of fractions, ratios, and proportions* (pp. 195–205). Reston, VA: NCTM.

Caldwell, J., Kobett, B., & Karp, K. (2014). *Essential understanding of addition and subtraction in practice, grades K–2.* Reston, VA: NCTM.

Campbell, P. F., Rowan, T. E., & Suarez, A. R. (1998). What criteria for student-invented algorithms? In L. J. Morrow (Ed.), *The teaching and learning of algorithms in school mathematics* (pp. 49–55). Reston, VA: NCTM.

Carpenter, T. P., Fennema, E., Franke, M. L., Levi, L., & Empson, S. B. (2014). *Children's mathematics: Cognitively guided instruction* (2nd ed.). Portsmouth, NH: Heinemann.

Carpenter, T. P., Franke, M. L., Jacobs, V. R., Fennema, E., & Empson, S. B. (1998). A longitudinal study of invention and understanding in children's multidigit addition and subtraction. *Journal for Research in Mathematics Education, 29*(1), 3–20.

Carpenter, T. P., Franke, M. L., & Levi, L. (2003). *Thinking mathematically: Integrating arithmetic and algebra in elementary school.* Portsmouth, NH: Heinemann.

Carter, S. (2008). Disequilibrium & questioning in the primary classroom: Establishing routines that help students learn. *Teaching Children Mathematics, 15*(3), 134–137.

Cassone, J. D. (2009). Differentiating mathematics by using task difficulty. In D. Y. White & J. S. Spitzer (Eds.), *Mathematics for every student: Responding to diversity, grades Pre-K–5* (pp. 89–98). Reston, VA: NCTM.

Cavey, L. O., & Kinzel, M. T. (2014). From whole numbers to invert and multiply. *Teaching Children Mathematics, 20*(6), 375–383.

Cayton, G. A., & Brizuela, B. M. (2007). First graders' strategies for numerical notation, number reading and the number concept. In J. H. Woo, H. C. Lew, K. S. Park, & D. Y. Seo (Eds.), *Proceedings of the 31st conference of the international group for the psychology of mathematics education* (Vol. 2, pp. 81–88). Seoul, South Korea: Psychology of Mathematics Education.

CCSSO (Council of Chief State School Officers). (2010). *Common core state standards.* Retrieved from http://corestandards.org

Ceci, S. J., & Williams, W. M. (2010). Sex differences in math-intensive fields. *Current Directions in Psychological Science, 19*(5), 275–279.

Celedón-Pattichis, S. (2009). What does that mean? Drawing on Latino and Latina students' language and culture to make mathematical meaning. In M. W. Ellis (Ed.), *Responding to diversity: Grades 6–8* (pp. 59–74). Reston, VA: NCTM.

Celedón-Pattichis, S., & Ramirez, N. G. (2012). *Beyond good teaching: Advancing mathematics education for ELLs.* Reston, VA: NCTM.

Center for Technology and Teacher Education (n.d.) Kids and cookies. Retrieved from http://www.teacherlink.org/content/math/interactive/flash/kidsandcookies/kidcookie.php

Champion, J., & Wheeler, A. (2014). Revisit pattern blocks to develop rational number sense. *Mathematics Teaching in the Middle School, 19*(6), 337–343.

Chan, B. M. Y., & Ho, C. S. H. (2010). The cognitive profile of Chinese children with mathematics difficulties. *Journal of Experimental Child Psychology, 107*, 260–279.

Che, S. M. (2009). Giant pencils: Developing proportional reasoning. *Mathematics Teaching in the Middle School, 14*(7), 404–408.

Checkley, K. (2006). "Radical" math becomes the standard: Emphasis on algebraic thinking, problem solving and communication. *Education Update, 48*(4), 1–2, 8.

Cheryan, S. (2012). Understanding the paradox in math-related fields: Why do some gender gaps remain while others do not? *Sex Roles, 66*, 184–190.

Chick, C., Tierney, C., & Storeygard, J. (2007). Seeing students' knowledge of fractions: Candace's inclusive classroom. *Teaching Children Mathematics, 14*(1), 52–57.

Choppin, J. (2014). Situating expansions of students' explanations in discourse contexts. In K. Karp & A. Roth-McDuffie (Eds.), *Annual perspectives in mathematics education 2014: Using research to improve instruction* (pp. 119–128) Reston, VA: NCTM.

Choppin, J. M., Clancy, C. B., & Koch, S. J. (2012). Developing formal procedures through sense making. *Mathematics Teaching in the Middle School, 17*(9), 552–557.

Chval, K., Lannin, J., & Jones, D. (2013). *Putting essential understanding of fractions into practice: Grades 3–5.* Reston, VA: NCTM.

Civil, M., & Menéndez, J. M. (2010). *NCTM research brief: Involving Latino and Latina parents in their children's mathematics education.* Retrieved from www.nctm.org/uploadedFiles/Research_News_and_ Advocacy/Research/Clips_and_Briefs/Research_brief_17-civil.pdf

Civil, M., & Planas, N. (2010). Latino/a immigrant parents' voices in mathematics education. In E. L. Grigorenko & R. Takanishi (Eds.), *Immigration, diversity, and education* (pp. 130–150). New York, NY: Routledge.

Cirillo, M., Steele, M., Otten, S, Herbel-Eisenmann, B. A., McAneny, K. & Riser, J. Q.. (2014). Teacher discourse moves: Supporting productive and powerful discourse. In K. Karp & A. Roth-McDuffie (Eds.), *Annual perspectives in mathematics education 2014: Using research to improve instruction* (pp. 141–150). Reston, VA: NCTM.

Clarke, B., & Clarke, D. (2004). Mathematics teaching in K–2: Painting a picture of challenging, supportive, and effective classrooms. In R. N. Rubenstein (Ed.), *Perspectives on the teaching of mathematics: Sixty-sixth yearbook* (pp. 67–81). Reston, VA: NCTM.

Clarke, D., Cheeseman, J., Clarke, B., Gervasoni, A., Gronn, D., Horne, M., et al. (2001, July). *Understanding, assessing and developing young children's mathematical thinking: Research as a powerful tool for professional growth.* Keynote paper at the annual conference of the Mathematics Education Research Group of Australia, Sydney.

Clarke, D., & Roche, A. (2009). Students' fraction comparison strategies as a window into robust understanding and possible pointers for instruction. *Educational Studies in Mathematics, 72,* 127–138.

Clarke, D., Roche, A., & Mitchell, A. (2008). 10 practical tips for making fractions come alive and make sense. *Mathematics Teaching in the Middle School, 13*(7), 373–380.

Cleaves, W. P. (2008). Promoting mathematics accessibility through multiple representations: Jigsaws. *Mathematics Teaching in the Middle School, 13*(8), 446–452.

Clement, L., & Bernhard, J. (2005). A problem-solving alternative to using key words. *Mathematics Teaching in the Middle School, 10*(7), 360–365.

Clements, D. H., & Battista, M. T. (1990). Constructivist learning and teaching. *Arithmetic Teacher, 38*(1), 34–35.

Clements, D., Baroody, A., & Sarama, J. (2013). *Background research on early mathematics.* Background Research for the National Governor's Association (NGA) Center Project on Early Mathematics. Washington, DC: NGA.

Clements, D., & Sarama, J. (2014). *Learning and teaching early math: The learning trajectories approach* (2nd ed.). New York, NY: Routledge.

Clifford, P., & Marinucci, S. J. (2008). Voices inside schools: Testing the waters: Three elements of classroom inquiry. *Harvard Education Review, 78*(4), 675–688.

Coates, G. D., & Mayfield, K. (2009). Families Ask: Cooperative learning. *Mathematics Teaching in the Middle School, 15*(4), 244–245.

Coates, G. D., & Thompson, V. (2003). *Family Math II: Achieving success in mathematics.* Berkeley, CA: EQUALS Lawrence Hall of Science.

Cobb, P. (1988). The tension between theories of learning and instruction in mathematics education. *Educational Psychologist, 23*(2), 87–103.

Cobb, P. (1994). Where is the mind? Constructivist and sociocultural perspectives on mathematical development. *Educational Researcher, 23*(7), 13–20.

Cobb, P., Gresalfi, M. S., & Hodge, L. L. (2009). An interpretive scheme for analyzing the identities that students develop in mathematics classrooms. *Journal for Research in Mathematics Education, 40*(1), 40–68.

Cobb, P., & Jackson, K. (2011). Assessing the quality of the Common Core State Standards for mathematics. *Educational Researcher, 40*(4), 183–185.

Cochran-Smith, M., & Lytle, S. L. (2011). Commentary: Changing perspectives on practitioner research. *Learning Landscapes, 4*(2), 17–24.

Cohen, J., & Hollebrands, K. F. (2011). Technology tools to support mathematics teaching. In T. P. Dick & K. F. Hollebrands (Eds.), *Focus in high school mathematics: Technology to support reasoning and sense making* (pp. 105–122). Reston, VA: NCTM.

Cohen, J. S. (2013). Strip diagrams: Illuminating proportions. *Mathematics Teaching in the Middle School, 18*(9), 536–542.

Cohen, R. (2006). How do students think? *Mathematics Teaching in the Middle School, 11*(9), 434–436.

Colgan, M. D. (2006). March math madness: The mathematics of the NCAA basketball tournament. *Mathematics Teaching in the Middle School, 11*(7), 334–342.

Confrey, J. (2008). *Student and teacher reasoning on rational numbers, multiplicative structures, and related topics.* Presentation at ICME–11, Monterrey, Mexico.

Confrey, J., Maloney, A. & Corley, A. (2014). Learning trajectories: A framework for connecting standards to curriculum. *ZDM, 46*(5), 719–733. doi 10.1007/s11858-014-0598-7

Cook, C. D. (2008). I scream, you scream: Data analysis with kindergartners. *Teaching Children Mathematics, 14*(9), 538–540.

Cooper, H. (2007). *The battle over homework: Common ground for administrators, teachers, and parents* (3rd ed.). Thousand Oaks, CA: Corwin Press.

Corcoran, T., Mosher, F., & Rogat, A. (2009). *Learning progressions in science: An evidence-based approach to reform* (Research Report No. RR-63). Philadelphia, PA: Consortium for Policy Research in Education.

Correll, S. J. (2001). Gender and the career choice process: The role of biased self-assessment. *American Journal of Sociology, 106*(6), 1691–1730.

Coughlin, H. A. (2010/2011). Dividing fractions: What is the divisor's role? *Mathematics Teaching in the Middle School, 16*(5), 280–287.

Courey, S. J., Balogh, E., Siker, J. R., & Paik, J. (2012). Academic music: Music instruction to engage third-grade students in learning basic fraction concepts. *Educational Studies in Mathematics, 81,* 251–278.

Cramer, K., & Henry, A. (2002). Using manipulative models to build number sense for addition of fractions. In B. Litwiller (Ed.), *Making sense of fractions, ratios, and proportions* (pp. 41–48). Reston, VA: NCTM.

Cramer, K., Monson, D., Whitney, S., Leavitt, S., & Wyberg, T. (2010). Dividing fractions and problem solving. *Mathematics Teaching in the Middle School, 15*(6), 338–346.

Cramer, K., & Whitney, S. (2010). Learning rational number concepts and skills in elementary school classrooms. In D. V. Lambdin & F. K. Lester, Jr. (Eds.), *Teaching and learning mathematics: Translating research for elementary school teachers* (pp. 15–22). Reston, VA: NCTM.

Cramer, K., Wyberg, T., & Leavitt, S. (2008). The role of representations in fraction addition and subtraction. *Mathematics Teaching in the Middle School, 13*(8), 490–496.

Crespo, S., & Nicol, C. (2006). Challenging preservice teachers' mathematical understanding: The case of division by zero. *School Science and Mathematics, 106*(2), 84–97.

Cummins, J. (1994). Primary language instruction and the education of language minority students. In C. F. Leyba (Ed.), *Schooling and language minority students: A theoretical framework* (pp. 3–46). Los Angeles, CA: California State University, National Evaluation, Dissemination and Assessment Center.

Cwikla, J. (2014). Can kindergartners do fractions? *Teaching Children Mathematics, 20*(6), 354–364.

Danielson, C., & Luke, M. (2006). If I only had one question: Partner-quizzes in middle school mathematics. *Mathematics Teaching in the Middle School, 12*(4), 206–213.

Darley, J. W. (2009). Traveling from arithmetic to algebra. *Mathematics Teaching in the Middle School, 14*(8), 458–464.

Daro, P., Mosher, F., & Corcoran, T. (2011). *Learning trajectories in mathematics: A foundation for standards, curriculum assessment and instruction.* Philadelphia, PA: Consortium for Policy Research in Education.

Davis, R. B. (1986). *Learning mathematics: The cognitive science approach to mathematics education.* Norwood, NJ: Ablex.

Davis, B., & Simmt, E. (2006). Mathematics-for-teaching: An ongoing investigation of the mathematics that teachers (need to) know. *Educational Studies in Mathematics, 61*(3), 293–319.

Davis, B., & Sumara, D. (2012). Fitting teacher education in/to/for an increasingly complex world. *Complicity: An International Journal of Complexity and Education, 9*(1), 30–40.

Davis, B., Sumara, D., & Luce-Kapler, R. (2008). *Engaging minds: Changing teaching in complex times.* New York, NY: Routledge.

Desmet, L. Gregoire, J., & Mussolin, C. (2010). Developmental changes in the comparison of decimal fractions. *Learning and Instruction, 20*, 521–532.

Devlin, K. (2011). *What exactly is multiplication?* Mathematical Association of America. Retrieved from www.maa.org/devlin/devlin_01_11.html

DeYoung, M. J. (2009). Math in the box. *Mathematics Teaching in the Middle School, 15*(3), 134–141.

Dietiker, L., Gonulates, F., Figueras, J., & Smith, J. P. (2010, April). *Weak attention to unit iteration in U.S. elementary curriculum materials.* Presentation at the annual conference of the American Educational Research Association, Denver, CO.

Ding, M. (2010, October 7). Email interaction.

Ding, M., & Li, X. (2010, April). *The associative property: What do teachers know and how do textbooks help?* Paper presented at the annual meeting of the National Council of Teachers of Mathematics, San Diego, CA.

Diversity in Mathematics Education. (2007). Culture, race, power, and mathematics education. In F. Lester, Jr. (Ed.), *Second handbook of research on mathematics teaching and learning* (pp. 405–434). Charlotte, NC: Information Age Publishing and National Council of Teachers of Mathematics.

Dixon, J. (2008). Tracking time: Representing elapsed time on an open timeline. *Teaching Children Mathematics, 15*(1), 18–24.

Dixon, J. K., & Tobias, J. M. (2013). The whole story: Understanding fraction computation. *Mathematics Teaching in the Middle School, 19*(3), 156–163.

Dole, S. (2008). Ratio tables to promote proportional reasonings in the primary classroom. *Australian Primary Mathematics Classroom, 13*(2), 18–22.

Dougherty, B. (2008). Measure up: A quantitative view of early algebra. In J. Kaput, D. Carraher, & M. Blanton (Eds.), *Algebra in the early grades* (pp. 389–412). New York, NY: Erlbaum.

Dougherty, B., Flores, A., Louis, E., & Sophian, C. (2010). *Developing essential understanding of number and numeration for teaching mathematics in prekindergarten–grade 2.* Reston, VA: NCTM.

Drake, J., & Barlow, A. (2007). Assessing students' level of understanding multiplication through problem writing. *Teaching Children Mathematics, 14*(5), 272–277.

Dweck, C. (2006). *Mindset: The new psychology of success.* New York: Random House.

Dweck, C. S. (2007). The perils and promises of praise. *Educational Leadership, 65*(2), 34–39.

Echevarria, J., Vogt, M. E., & Short, D. (2008). *Making content comprehensible for English learners: The SIOP model* (3rd ed.). Boston, MA: Allyn & Bacon.

Ellington, A. (2003). A meta-analysis of the effects of calculators on students' achievement and attitude levels in precollege mathematics classes. *Journal for Research in Mathematics Education, 34*(5), 433–463.

Ellington, A. J., & Whitenack, J. W. (2010). Fractions and the funky cookie. *Teaching Children Mathematics, 16*(9), 532–539.

Ellis, M., Yeh, C., & Stump, S. (2007–2008). Rock-paper-scissors and solutions to the broken calculator problem. *Teaching Children Mathematics, 14*(5), 309–314.

Else-Quest, N. M., Hyde, J. S., Hejmadi, A. (2008). Mother and child emotions during mathematics homework. *Mathematical Thinking and Learning, 10*, 5–35.

Else-Quest, N. M., Hyde, J. S., & Linn, M. (2010). Cross-national patterns of gender differences in mathematics: A meta-analysis. *Psychological Bulletin, 136*(1), 103–127.

Ely, R. E., & Cohen, J. S. (2010). Put the right spin on student work. *Mathematics Teaching in the Middle School, 16*(4), 208–215.

Empson, S. B. (2002). Organizing diversity in early fraction thinking. In B. Litwiller (Ed.), *Making sense of fractions, ratios, and proportions* (pp. 29–40). Reston, VA: NCTM.

Englard, L. (2010). Raise the bar on problem solving. *Teaching Children Mathematics, 17*(3), 156–165.

English, L. (2013). Surviving an avalanche of data. *Teaching Children Mathematics, 19*(6), 364–372.

Ercole, L. K., Frantz, M., & Ashline, G. (2011). Multiple ways to solve proportions. *Mathematics Teaching in the Middle School, 16*(8), 482–490.

Ernst, K., & Ryan, S. (2014). *Success from the start: Your first years teaching elementary mathematics.* Reston, VA: NCTM.

Ethridge, E. A., & King, J. R. (2005). Calendar math in preschool and primary classrooms: Questioning the curriculum. *Early Childhood Education Journal, 32*(5), 291–296.

Fagnant, A., & Vlassis, J. (2013). Schematic representations in arithmetical problem solving: Analysis of their impact on grade

4 students. *Education Studies in Mathematics, 84*, 149–168. doi: 10.1007/s10649-013-9476-4

Falkner, K. P., Levi, L., & Carpenter, T. P. (1999). Children's understanding of equality: A foundation for algebra. *Teaching Children Mathematics, 6*(4), 232–236.

Farmer, J. D., & Powers, R. A. (2005). Exploring Mayan numerals. *Teaching Children Mathematics, 12*(2), 69–79.

Fernandez, M. L., & Schoen, R. C. (2008). Teaching and learning mathematics through hurricane tracking. *Mathematics Teaching in the Middle School, 13*(9), 500–512.

Fey, J. T., Hollenbeck, R. W., & Wray, J. A. (2010). Technology and the teaching of mathematics: In B. Reys, R. Reys, & R. Rubenstein (Eds.), *Curriculum: Issues, trends, and future directions* (72nd Yearbook). Reston, VA: NCTM.

Fillingim, J. G., & Barlow, A. T. (2010). From the inside out. *Teaching Children Mathematics, 17*(2), 80–88.

Fleischman, H. L., Hopstock, P. J., Pelczar, M. P., & Shelley, B. E. (2010). *Highlights from PISA 2009: Performance of U.S. 15-Year-Old Students in Reading, Mathematics, and Science Literacy in an International Context* (NCES 2011–004). Washington, DC: U.S. Government Printing Office.

Flores, A. (2006). Using graphing calculators to redress beliefs in the "law of small numbers." In G.F. Burrill & P. C. Elliott (Eds.), *Thinking and reasoning with data and chance: 68th NCTM yearbook* (pp. 139–149). Reston, VA: NCTM.

Flores, A., & Klein, E. (2005). From students' problem solving strategies to connections with fractions. *Teaching Children Mathematics, 11*(9), 452–457.

Flores, A., Samson, J., & Yanik, H. B. (2006). Quotient and measurement interpretations of rational numbers. *Teaching Children Mathematics, 13*(1), 34–39.

Flores, M., Hinton, V., & Strozier, S. (2014). Teaching subtraction and multiplication with regrouping using the concrete-representational-abstract sequence and strategic instruction model. *Learning Disabilities Research and Practice, 29*(2), 75–88.

Flowers, J. M., & Rubenstein, R. N. (2010–2011). Multiplication fact fluency using doubles. *Mathematics Teaching in the Middle School, 16*(5), 296–301.

Forbringer, L., & Fahsl, A. J. (2010). Differentiating practice to help students master basic facts. In D. Y. White & J. S. Spitzer (Eds.), *Responding to diversity: Grades pre-K–5* (pp. 7–22). Reston, VA: NCTM.

Forman, E. A., & McPhail, J. (1993). A Vygotskian perspective on children's collaborative problem-solving activities. In E. A. Forman, N. Minick, & C. A. Stone (Eds.), *Contexts for learning: Sociocultural dynamics in children's development* (pp. 213–229). New York, NY: Oxford University Press.

Fosnot, C. T. (1996). Constructivism: A psychological theory of learning. In C. T. Fosnot (Ed.), *Constructivism: Theory, perspectives, and practice* (pp. 8–33). New York, NY: Teachers College Press.

Fosnot, C. T., & Dolk, M. (2001). *Young mathematicians at work: Constructing multiplication and division.* Portsmouth, NH: Heinemann.

Fosnot, C. T., & Jacob, B. (2010). *Young mathematicians at work: Constructing algebra.* Reston, VA: NCTM.

Franke, M. L., Kazemi, E., & Battey, D. (2007). Mathematics teaching and classroom practice. In F. K. Lester (Ed.), *Second handbook of research on mathematics teaching and learning* (pp. 225–256). Reston, VA: NCTM.

Franklin, C. A., & Garfield, J. B. (2006). The *GAISE* Project: Developing statistics education guidelines for grades PreK–12 and college courses. In G. F. Burrill & P. C. Elliott (Eds.), *Thinking and reasoning with data and chance: 68th NCTM yearbook* (pp. 345–376). Reston, VA: NCTM.

Franklin, C. A., Kader, G., Mewborn, D., Moreno, J., Peck, R., Perry, M., & Scheaffer, R. (2005). *Guidelines for assessment and instruction in statistics education (GAISE) report.* Alexandria, VA: American Statistical Association.

Franklin, C. A., & Mewborn, D. S. (2008). Statistics in the elementary grades: Exploring distribution of data. *Teaching Children Mathematics, 15*(1), 10–16.

Frayer, D.A., Fredrick, W. C., and Klausmeier, H. J., (April 1969). *A schema for testing the level of concept mastery (Working Paper No. 16),* University of Wisconsin Center for Educational Research.

Friedman, T. (2007). *The world is flat 3.0: A brief history of the twenty-first century.* New York, NY: Picador.

Friedmann, P. (2008). The zero box. *Mathematics Teaching in the Middle School, 14*(4), 222–223.

Friel, S. N., & Markworth, K. A. (2009). A framework for analyzing geometric pattern tasks. *Mathematics Teaching in the Middle School, 15*(1), 24–33.

Friel, S. N., O'Conner, W., & Mamer, J. D. (2006). More than "meanmedianmode" and a bar graph: What's needed to have a statistical conversation? In G. F. Burrill & P. C. Elliott (Eds.), *Thinking and reasoning with data and chance: 68th NCTM yearbook* (pp. 117–138). Reston, VA: NCTM.

Frye, D., Baroody, A. J., Burchinal, M., Carver, S. M., Jordan, N. C., & McDowell, J. (2013). *Teaching math to young children: A practice guide* (NCEE 2014-4005). Washington, DC: National Center for Education Evaluation and Regional Assistance (NCEE), Institute of Education Sciences (IES), U.S. Department of Education. Retrieved from http://whatworks.ed.gov

Fuchs, L. S., & Fuchs, D. (1986). Effects of systematic formative evaluation: A meta-analysis. *Exceptional Children, 53*(3), 199–208.

Fuchs, L. S., & Fuchs, D. (2001). Principles for the prevention and intervention of mathematics difficulties. *Learning Disabilities Research and Practice, 16*(2), 85–95.

Fuchs, L. S., Fuchs, D., Prentice, K., Hamlett, C. L., Finelli, R., & Courey, S. J. (2004). Enhancing mathematical problem solving among third-grade students with schema-based instruction. *Journal of Educational Psychology, 96*(4), 635–647.

Fuchs, L. S., Fuchs, D., Yazdian, L., & Powell, S. R. (2002). Enhancing first-grade children's mathematics development with peer-assisted learning strategies. *School Psychology Review, 31*(4), 569–583.

Fung, M. G., & Latulippe, C. L. (2010). Computational estimation. *Teaching Children Mathematics, 17*(3), 170–176.

Fuson, K. C. (1984). More complexities in subtraction. *Journal for Research in Mathematics Education, 15*(3), 214–225.

Fuson, K. C. (1992). Research on whole number addition and subtraction. In D. A. Grouws (Ed.), *Handbook of research on teaching and learning* (pp. 243–275). Old Tappan, NJ: Macmillan.

Fuson, K. C. (2003). Developing mathematical power in whole number operations. In J. Kilpatrick, W. G. Martin, & D. Schifter

(Eds.), *A research companion to Principles and Standards in School Mathematics* (pp. 68–94). Reston, VA: NCTM.

Fuson, K. C. (2006). Research on whole number addition and subtraction. In D. Grouws (Ed.), *Handbook of research on mathematics teaching and learning* (pp. 243–275). Charlotte, NC: Information Age Publishing.

Fuson, K. C., Kalchman, M., & Bransford, J. D. (2005). *How students learn: History, mathematics, and science in the classroom.* Washington, DC: The National Academies Press.

Fuson, K. C., & Kwon, Y. (1992). Korean children's single-digit addition and subtraction: Numbers structured by ten. *Journal for Research in Mathematics Education, 23*(2), 148–165.

Gagnon, J., & Maccini, P. (2001). Preparing students with disabilities for algebra. *Teaching Exceptional Children, 34*(1), 8–15.

Gallagher, A. M., & Kaufmann, J. C. (2005). *Gender differences in mathematics: an integrative psychological approach.* Cambridge, UK: Cambridge University Press.

Gallagher, J., & Gallagher, S. (1994). *Teaching the gifted child.* Boston, MA: Allyn & Bacon.

Gallego, C., Saldamando, D., Tapia-Beltran, G., Williams, K., & Hoopingarner, T. C. (2009). Math by the month: Probability. *Teaching Children Mathematics, 15*(7), 416.

Garcia, C., & Garret, A. (2006). On average and open-end questions. In A. Rossman & B. Chance (Eds.), *Proceedings of the seventh international conference on teaching statistics.* Salvador, Brazil: International Statistical Institute.

Garrison, L. (1997). Making the NCTM's Standards work for emergent English speakers. *Teaching Children Mathematics, 4*(3), 132–138.

Gavin, M. K., & Sheffield, L. J. (2010). Using curriculum to develop mathematical promise in the middle grades. In M. Saul, S. Assouline, & L. J. Sheffield (Eds.), *The peak in the middle: Developing mathematically gifted students in the middle grades* (pp. 51–76). Reston, VA: NCTM, National Association of Gifted Children, & National Middle School Association.

Geary, D. C., & Hoard, M. K. (2005). Learning disabilities in arithmetic and mathematics: Theoretical and empirical perspectives. In J. Campbell (Ed.), *Handbook of mathematical cognition* (pp. 253–267). New York, NY: Psychology Press.

Gilbert, M. C., & Musu, L. E. (2008). Using TARGETTS to create learning environments that support mathematical understanding and adaptive motivation. *Teaching Children Mathematics, 15*(3), 138–143.

Goldenberg, E. P., Mark, J., & Cuoco, A. (2010). An algebraic-habits-of-mind perspective on elementary school. *Teaching Children Mathematics, 16*(9), 548–556.

Goldenberg, P., & Mason, J. (2008). Shedding light on and with examples spaces. *Educational Studies in Mathematics, 69,* 183–194.

Gómez, C. L. (2010). Teaching with cognates. *Teaching Children Mathematics, 16*(8), 470–474.

González, N., Moll, L. C., & Amanti, C. (Eds.). (2005). *Funds of knowledge: Theorizing practices in households and classrooms.* Mahwah, NJ: Erlbaum.

Goos, M. (2004). Learning mathematics in a classroom community of inquiry. *Journal for Research in Mathematics Education, 35*(4), 258–291.

Goral, M. B., & Wiest, L. R. (2007). An arts-based approach to teaching fractions. *Teaching Children Mathematics, 14*(2), 74–80.

Gould, H. T. (2011). Building understanding of fractions with LEGO® bricks. *Teaching Children Mathematics, 17*(8), 498–503.

Grandgenett, N., Harris, J., & Hofer, M. (2010–2011). An activity-based approach to technology integration in the mathematics classroom. *NCSM Journal of Mathematics Education Leadership, 13*(1), 19–28.

Gravemeijer, K., & van Galen, F. (2003). Facts and algorithms as products of students' own mathematical activity. In J. Kilpatrick, W. G. Martin, & D. Schifter (Eds.), *A research companion to Principles and Standards for School Mathematics* (pp. 114–122). Reston, VA: NCTM.

Gregg, J., & Gregg, D. U. (2007). Measurement and fair-sharing models for dividing fractions. *Mathematics Teaching in the Middle School, 12*(9), 490–496.

Griffin, L., & Lavelle, L. (2010). *Assessing mathematical understanding: Using one-on-one mathematics interviews with K–2 students.* Presentation given at the Annual Conference of the National Council of Supervisors of Mathematics, San Diego, CA.

Groth, R. E., & Bargagliotti, A. E. (2012). GAISEing into the Common Core State Standards. *Mathematics Teaching in the Middle School, 18*(1), 38–45.

Guerrero, S. M. (2010). The value of guess & check. *Mathematics Teaching in the Middle School, 15*(7), 392–398.

Gutierrez, R. (2009). Embracing the inherent tensions in teaching mathematics from an equity stance. *Democracy and Education, 18*(3), 9–16.

Gurbuz, R., Erdem, H., Catlioglu, O., & Birgin, E. (2010). An investigation of fifth grade students' conceptual development of probability through activity-based instruction: A quasi-experimental design. *Educational Sciences: Theory and Practice, 10*(2), 1053–1068.

Gutstein, E., Lipman, P., Hernandez, P., & Reyes, R. (1997). Culturally relevant mathematics teaching in a Mexican American context. *Journal for Research in Mathematics Education, 28*(6), 709–737.

Haas, E., & Gort, M. (2009). Demanding more: Legal standards and best practices for English language learners. *Bilingual Research Journal, 32,* 115–135.

Hamre, B. K., Downer, J. T., Kilday, C. R., & McGuire, P. (2008). *Effective teaching practices for early childhood mathematics.* White paper prepared for the National Research Council. Washington, DC.

Hanson, S. A., & Hogan, T. P. (2000). Computational estimation skill of college students. *Journal for Research in Mathematics Education, 31*(4), 483–499.

Hartnett, J. (2007). Categorisation of mental computation strategies to support teaching and to encourage classroom dialogue. In J. Watson & K. Beswick (Eds.), *Mathematics: Essential research, essential practice: Proceedings of the 30th annual conference of the Mathematics Education Research Group of Australasia* (pp. 345–352). Hobart, Tasmania, Australia: MERGA.

Harvey, R. (2012). Stretching student teachers' understanding of fractions. *Mathematics Education Research Journal, 24,* 493–511.

Hattie, J. (2009). *Visible learning: A synthesis of over 800 meta-analyses relating to achievement.* New York, NY: Routledge.

Hawes, K. (2007). Using error analysis to teach equation solving. *Mathematics Teaching in the Middle School, 12*(5), 238–242.

Heaton, R. M., & Lewis, W. J. (2011). A mathematician–mathematics educator partnership to teach teachers. *Noticias of the American Mathematical Society, 58*(3), 394–400.

Heck, T. (2006). *Team building games on a shoestring.* Retrieved from www.teachmeteamwork.com/teachmeteamwork/files/Team building_on_a_Shoestring_sml.pdf

Heddens, J. (1964). *Today's mathematics: A guide to concepts and methods in elementary school mathematics.* Chicago, IL: Science Research Associates.

Heege, H. T. (1985). The acquisition of basic multiplication skills. *Educational Studies in Mathematics, 16*(4): 375–388.

Heinz, K., & Sterba-Boatwright, B. (2008). The when and why of using proportions. *Mathematics Teacher, 101*(7), 528–533.

Hembree, R., & Dessert, D. (1986). Effects of hand-held calculators in precollege mathematics education: A meta analysis. *Journal for Research in Mathematics Education, 17*(2), 83–99.

Hembree, R., & Dessert, D. (1992). Research on calculators in mathematics education. In J. Fey & C. R. Hirsch (Eds.), *Calculators in mathematics education* (pp. 23–32). Reston, VA: NCTM.

Henry, V. J., & Brown, R. S. (2008). First grade basic facts: An investigation into teaching and learning of an accelerated, high-demand memorization standard. *Journal for Research in Mathematics Education, 39*(2), 153–183.

Herbel-Eisenmann, B. A., & Breyfogle, M. L. (2005). Questioning our patterns of questioning. *Mathematics Teaching in the Middle School, 10*(9), 484–489.

Herbel-Eisenmann, B. A., & Phillips, E. D. (2005). Using student work to develop teachers' knowledge of algebra. *Mathematics Teaching in the Middle School, 11*(2), 62–66.

Heritage, M., Kim, J., Vendlinski, T., & Herman, J. (2009). From evidence to action: A seamless process in formative assessment? *Education Measurement: Issues and Practice, 28,* 24–31.

Hiebert, J. (2003). What research says about the NCTM standards. In J. Kilpatrick, W. G. Martin, & D. Schifter (Eds.), *A research companion to Principles and Standards for School Mathematics* (pp. 5–23). Reston, VA: NCTM.

Hiebert, J., & Carpenter, T. P. (1992). Learning and teaching with understanding. In D. A. Grouws (Ed.), *Handbook of research on mathematics teaching and learning* (pp. 65–97). Old Tappan, NJ: Macmillan.

Hiebert, J., Carpenter, T. P., Fennema, E., Fuson, K., Human, P., Murray, H., et al. (1996). Problem solving as a basis for reform in curriculum and instruction: The case of mathematics. *Educational Researcher, 25*(4), 12–21.

Hiebert, J., Carpenter, T. P., Fennema, E., Fuson, K., Wearne, D., Murray, H., . . . Human, P. (1997). *Making sense: Teaching and learning mathematics with understanding.* Portsmouth, NH: Heinemann.

Hiebert, J., & Grouws, D. A. (2007). The effects of classroom mathematics teaching on students' learning. In F. K. Lester (Ed.), *Second handbook of research on mathematics teaching and learning* (pp. 371–404). Charlotte, NC: Information Age Publishing.

Hodges, T. E., Cady, J., & Collins, R. L. (2008). Fraction representation: The not-so-common denominator among textbooks. *Mathematics Teaching in the Middle School, 14*(2), 78–84.

Hoffman, B. L., Breyfogle, M. L., & Dressler, J. A. (2009). The power of incorrect answers. *Mathematics Teaching in the Middle School, 15*(4), 232–238.

Howden, H. (1989). Teaching number sense. *Arithmetic Teacher, 36*(6), 6–11.

Hudson, P. J., Shupe, M., Vasquez, E., & Miller, S. P. (2008). Teaching data analysis to elementary students with mild disabilities. *TEACHING Exceptional Children Plus, 4*(3), Article 5. Retrieved from http://escholarship.bc.edu/education/tecplus/vol4/iss3/art5

Hudson, R. A. (2012/2013). Finding balance at the elusive mean. *Mathematics Teaching in the Middle School, 18*(5), 301–306.

Huinker, D. (1994, April). *Multi-step word problems: A strategy for empowering students.* Presented at the annual meeting of the National Council of Teachers of Mathematics, Indianapolis, IN.

Hyde, J., Lindberg, S., Linn, M., Ellis, A., & Williams, C. (2008, July 25). Gender similarities characterize mathematics performance. *Science, 321*(5888), 494–495.

Hynes, M. C. (Ed.). (1996). *Ideas: NCTM Standards-based instruction, grades 5–8.* Reston, VA: NCTM.

Imm, K. L., Stylianou, D. A., & Chae, N. (2008). Student representations at the center: Promoting classroom equity. *Mathematics Teaching in the Middle School, 13*(8), 458–463.

Izsák, A. (2004). Teaching and learning two-digit multiplication: Coordinating analyses of classroom practices and individual student learning. *Mathematical Thinking and Learning, 6,* 37–79.

Izsák, A. (2008). Mathematical knowledge for teaching fraction multiplication. *Cognition and Instruction, 26*(1), 95–143.

Izsák, A., Tillema, E., & Tunc-Pekkam, Z. (2008). Teaching and learning fraction addition on number lines. *Journal for Research in Mathematics Education, 39*(1), 33–62.

Jacobs, V. R., & Ambrose, R. C. (2008). Making the most of story problems. *Teaching Children Mathematics, 15*(5), 260–266.

Jacobs, V. R., Lamb, L. L. C., & Philipp, R. A. (2010). Professional noticing of children's mathematical thinking. *Journal for Research in Mathematics Education, 41*(2), 169–202.

Janzen, J. (2008). Teaching English language learners in the content areas. *Review of Educational Research, 78*(4), 1010–1038.

Jaworski, B. (2006). Theory and practice in mathematics teaching development: Critical inquiry as a mode of learning in teaching. *Journal of Mathematics Teacher Education, 9,* 187–211.

Jeon, K. (2012). Reflecting on PEMDAS. *Teaching Children Mathematics, 18*(6), 370-377.

Johanning, D. I. (2008). Learning to use fractions: Examining middle school students' emerging fraction literacy. *Journal for Research in Mathematics Education, 39*(3), 281–310.

Johanning, D. I., & Mamer, J. (2014). How did the answer get bigger? *Mathematics Teaching in the Middle School, 19*(6), 344–351.

Johnson, D. T. (2011). Pencils and crayons. *Teaching Children Mathematics, 18*(2), 73–74.

Johnsen, S., & Sheffield, L. (Eds.). (2014). *Using the Common Core State Standards for mathematics with gifted and advanced learners.* Waco, TX: Prufrock Press, Inc.

Jones, A. (1999). *Team building activities for every group.* Richland, WA: Rec Room Publishing.

Joram, E. (2003). Benchmarks as tools for developing measurement sense. In D. H. Clements (Ed.), *Learning and teaching measurement* (pp. 57–67). Reston, VA: NCTM.

Jordan, N. C., Kaplan, D., Locuniak, M. N., & Ramineni, C. (2007). Predicting first grade math achievement from developmental number sense trajectories. *Learning Disabilities Research & Practice, 22*(1), 36–46.

Kader, G. D., & Jacobbe, T. (2013). *Developing essential understanding of statistics for teaching mathematics in grades 6–8*. Reston, VA: NCTM.

Kader, G., & Mamer, J. (2008). Statistics in the middle grades: Understanding center and spread. *Mathematics Teaching in the Middle Grades, 14*(1), 38–43.

Kamii, C. K. (1985). *Young children reinvent arithmetic*. New York: Teachers College Press.

Kamii, C. K., & Anderson, C. (2003). Multiplication games: How we made and used them. *Teaching Children Mathematics, 10*(3), 135–141.

Kamii, C. K., & Dominick, A. (1998). The harmful effects of algorithms in grades 1–4. In L. J. Morrow (Ed.), *The teaching and learning of algorithms in school mathematics* (pp. 130–140). Reston, VA: NCTM.

Kaput, J. J. (2008). What is algebra? What is algebraic reasoning? In J. J. Kaput, D. W. Carraher, & M. L. Blanton (Eds.), *Algebra in the early grades*. Reston, VA: NCTM.

Karp, K. (1991). Elementary school teachers' attitudes towards mathematics: Impact on students' autonomous learning skills. *School Science and Mathematics, 91*(6), 265–270.

Karp, K., Brown, E. T., Allen, L., & Allen, C. (1998). *Feisty females: Inspiring girls to think mathematically*. Portsmouth, NH: Heinemann.

Karp, K., Bush, S., & Dougherty, B. (2014). Avoiding rules that expire. *Teaching Children Mathematics, 21*(2), 18–25.

Karp, K., & Howell, P. (2004). Building responsibility for learning in students with special needs. *Teaching Children Mathematics, 11*(3), 118–126.

Kastberg, S. E., D'Ambrosio, B. S., Lynch-Davis, K., Mintos, A., & Krawczyk, K. (2014). CCSSM Challenge: Graphing ratio and proportion. *Mathematics Teaching in the Middle School, 19*(5), 294–300.

Keiser, J. M. (2010). Shifting our computational focus. *Mathematics Teaching in the Middle School, 16*(4), 216–223.

Keiser, J. (2012). Students' strategies can take us off guard. *Mathematics Teaching in the Middle School, 17*(7), 418–425.

Kersaint, G., Thompson, D. R., & Petkova, M. (2009). *Teaching mathematics to English language learners*. New York, NY: Routledge.

Khisty, L. L. (1997). Making mathematics accessible to Latino students: Rethinking instructional practice. In M. Kenney & J. Trentacosta (Eds.), *Multicultural and gender equity in the mathematics classroom: The gift of diversity* (pp. 92–101). Reston, VA: NCTM.

Kilic, H., Cross, D. I., Ersoz, F. A., Mewborn, D. S., Swanagan, D., & Kim, J. (2010). Techniques for small-group discourse. *Teaching Children Mathematics, 16*(6), 350–357.

Kingore, B. (2006, Winter). Tiered instruction: Beginning the process. *Teaching for High Potential*, 5–6.

Kinzer, C., & Stanford, T. (2013/2014). Distributive property: The core of multiplication. *Teaching Children Mathematics, 20*(5), 303–308.

Klein, P., Adi-Japha, E., & Hakak-Benizri, S. (2010). Mathematical thinking of kindergarten boys and girls: Similar achievement, different contributing processes. *Educational Studies in Mathematics, 73*, 233–246.

Kliman, M. (1999). Beyond helping with homework: Parents and children doing mathematics at home. *Teaching Children Mathematics, 6*(3), 140–146.

Kline, K. (2008). Learning to think and thinking to learn. *Teaching Children Mathematics, 15*, 144–151.

Kling, G. (2011). Fluency with basic addition. *Teaching Children Mathematics, 18*(2), 80–88.

Kling, G., & Bay-Williams, J. M. (2014). Assessing basic fact fluency. *Teaching Children Mathematics, 20*(8), 488–497.

Kloosterman, P. (2010). Mathematics skills of 17-year-olds in the United States: 1978 to 2004. *Journal for Research in Mathematics Education, 41*(1), 20–51.

Kloosterman, P., Rutledge, Z., & Kenney, P. (2009a). Exploring the results of the NAEP: 1980s to the present. *Mathematics Teaching in the Middle School, 14*(6), 357–365.

Kloosterman, P., Rutledge, Z., & Kenney, P. A. (2009b). A generation of progress: Learning from NAEP. *Teaching Children Mathematics, 15*(6), 363–369.

Kloosterman, P., Warfield, J., Wearne, D., Koc, Y., Martin, W. G., & Strutchens, M. (2004). Fourth-grade students' knowledge of mathematics and perceptions of learning mathematics. In P. Kloosterman & F. K. Lester, Jr. (Eds.), *Results and interpretations of the 1990–2000 mathematics assessments of the National Assessment of Educational Progress* (pp. 71–103). Reston, VA: NCTM.

Knuth, E. J., Stephens, A. C., McNeil, N. M., & Alibali, M. W. (2006). Does understanding the equal sign matter? Evidence from solving equations. *Journal for Research in Mathematics Education, 37*(4), 297–312.

Kohn, A. (1993). *Punished by rewards: The trouble with gold stars, incentive plans, A's, praise, and other bribes*. Boston, MA: Houghton Mifflin.

Kouba, V. L., Brown, C. A., Carpenter, T. P., Lindquist, M. M., Silver, E. A., & Swafford, J. O. (1988). Results of the fourth NAEP assessment of mathematics: Number, operations, and word problems. *Arithmetic Teacher, 35*(8), 14–19.

Kouba, V. L., Zawojewski, J. S., & Strutchens, M. E. (1997). What do students know about numbers and operations? In P. A. Kenney & E. Silver (Eds.), *Results from the sixth mathematics assessment of the National Assessment of Educational Progress* (pp. 87–140). Reston, VA: NCTM.

Kribs-Zaleta, C. (2008). Oranges, posters, ribbons, and lemonade: Concrete computational strategies for dividing fractions. *Mathematics Teaching in the Middle School, 13*(8), 453–457.

Kulm, G. (1994). *Mathematics and assessment: What works in the classroom*. San Francisco, CA: Jossey-Bass.

Labinowicz, E. (1985). *Learning from children: New beginnings for teaching numerical thinking*. Menlo Park, CA: AWL Supplemental.

Lamb, L. L., Bishop, J. P., Philipp, R. A., Schappelle, B. P., Whitacre, I., & Lewis, M. (2012). Developing symbol sense for the minus sign. *Mathematics Teaching in the Middle School, 18*(1), 5–9.

Lambdin, D. V. (2003). Benefits of teaching through problem solving. In Frank K. Lester, Jr., & R. I. Charles (Eds.), *Teaching mathematics through problem solving: Prekindergarten–grade 6* (pp. 3–13). Reston, VA: NCTM.

Lambdin, D. V., & Lynch, K. (2005). Examining mathematics tasks from the National Assessment of Educational Progress. *Mathematics Teaching in the Middle School, 10*(6), 314–318.

Lamon, S. J. (2006). *Teaching fractions and ratios for understanding: Essential content knowledge and instructional strategies for teachers* (2nd ed.). Mahwah, NJ: Erlbaum.

Lamon, S. J. (2007). Rational numbers and proportional reasoning: Toward a theoretical framework for research. In F. Lester (Ed.), *Second handbook of research on mathematics teaching and learning* (pp. 629–666). Reston, VA: NCTM.

Lamon, S. J. (2012). *Teaching fractions and ratios for understanding: Essential content knowledge and instructional strategies* (3rd ed.). New York, NY: Taylor & Francis Group.

Lampe, K. A., & Uselmann, L. (2008). Pen pals: Practicing problem solving. *Mathematics Teaching in the Middle School, 14*(4), 196–201.

Langrall, C., Nisbet, S., Mooney, E., & Jansem, S. (2011). The role of context expertise when comparing data. *Mathematical Thinking and Learning, 13,* 47–67.

Lannin, J. K., Arbaugh, F., Barker, D. D., & Townsend, B. E. (2006). Making the most of student errors. *Teaching Children Mathematics, 13*(3), 182–186.

Lannin, J., Chval, K., & Jones, D. (2013). *Putting essential understanding of multiplication and division into practice in grades 3–5.* Reston, VA: NCTM.

Lannin, J., Ellis, A. B., Elliott, R. (2011). *Developing essential understanding of mathematical reasoning: PreK–Grade 8.* Reston, VA: NCTM.

Lapp, D. (2001). *How do students learn with data collection devices?* Presentation given at the annual International Teachers Teaching with Technology Conference, Columbus, OH.

Lappan, G., & Even, R. (1989). *Learning to teach: Constructing meaningful understanding of mathematical content* (Craft Paper 89–3). East Lansing, MI: Michigan State University.

Lappan, G., & Mouck, M. K. (1998). Developing algorithms for adding and subtracting fractions. In L. J. Morrow (Ed.), *The teaching and learning of algorithms in school mathematics* (pp. 183–197). Reston, VA: NCTM.

Laursen, S., Hassi, M., Kogan, M., & Weston, T. (2014). Benefits for women and men of inquiry-based learning in college mathematics: A multi-institution study. *Journal for Research in Mathematics Education, 45*(4), 406–418.

Leatham K. R., & Hill, D. S. (2010). Exploring our complex math identities. *Mathematics Teaching in the Middle School, 16*(4), 224–231.

Leavy, A., Friel, S., & Mamer, J. (2009). It's a fird! Can you compute a median of categorical data? *Mathematics Teaching in the Middle School, 14*(6), 344–351.

Lee, J. (2014). Deciphering multiplication algorithms with the area model. *Mathematics Teaching in the Middle School, 19*(9), 557–556.

Leeming, C. (2007, November 3). *"Cool Cash" card confusion.* Manchester Evening News, Manchester, England. Retrieved from www.manchestereveningnews.co.uk/news/s/1022757_cool_cash_card_confusion

Leinwand, S. (2007). Four teacher-friendly postulates for thriving in a sea of change. *Mathematics Teacher, 100*(9), 582–584.

Lesh, R. A., Cramer, K., Doerr, H., Post, T., & Zawojewski, J. (2003). Model development sequences. In R. A. Lesh & H. Doerr (Eds.), *Beyond constructivism: A models and modeling perspective on mathematics teaching, learning, and problem solving* (pp. 35–58). Mahwah, NJ: Erlbaum.

Lesh, R. A., & Zawojewski, J. S. (2007). Problem solving and modeling. In F. K. Lester, Jr. (Ed.), *The handbook of research on mathematics teaching and learning* (2nd ed., pp. 763–804).

Reston, VA: NCTM; Charlotte, NC: Information Age Publishing.

Lester, F. K., Jr. (1989). Reflections about mathematical problem-solving research. In R. I. Charles & E. A. Silver (Eds.), *The teaching and assessing of mathematical problem solving* (pp. 115–124). Reston, VA: NCTM.

Levasseur, K., & Cuoco, A. (2003). Mathematical habits of mind. In H. L. Shoen (Ed.), *Teaching mathematics through problem solving: Grade 6–12* (pp. 23–37). Reston, VA: NCTM.

Lewis, K. (2014). Difference not deficit: Reconceptualizing mathematical learning disabilities. *Journal for Research in Mathematics Education, 45*(3), 351–396.

Lewis, T. (2005). Facts + fun = fluency. *Teaching Children Mathematics, 12*(1), 8–11.

Lim, K. H. (2009). Burning the candle at just one end. *Mathematics Teaching in the Middle School, 14*(8), 492–500.

Livy, S. Muir, T. & Maher, N. (2012). How do they measure up? Primary pre-service teachers' mathematical knowledge of area and perimeter. *Mathematics Teacher Education and Development, 14*(2), 91–112.

Lobato, J., & Ellis, A. (2010). *Developing essential understanding of ratios, proportions, and proportional reasoning: Grades 6–8.* Reston, VA: NCTM.

Locuniak, M. N., & Jordan, N. C. (2008). Using kindergarten number sense to predict calculation fluency in second grade. *Journal of Learning Disabilities, 41*(5), 451–459.

Lubienski, S. T., Robinson, J., Crane, C. C., & Ganley, C. M. (2013). Girls' and boys' mathematics achievement, affect, and experiences: Findings from ECLS-K. *Journal for Research in Mathematics Education, 44*(4), 634–645.

Lynch, K., & Star, J. (2014). Views of struggling students on instruction incorporating multiple strategies in algebra I: An exploratory study. *Journal for Research in Mathematics Education, 45*(1), 6–18.

Lynch, S. D., Lynch, J. M., & Bolyard, J. (2013). Informing practice: I-THINK I can problem solve. *Mathematics Teaching in the Middle School, 19*(1), 10–14.

Ma, L. (1999). *Knowing and teaching elementary mathematics: Teachers' understanding of fundamental mathematics in China and the United States.* Mahwah, NJ: Erlbaum.

Mack, N. K. (1995). Confounding whole-number and fraction concepts when building on informal knowledge. *Journal for Research in Mathematics Education, 26*(5), 422–441.

Mack, N. K. (2004). Connecting to develop computational fluency with fractions. *Teaching Children Mathematics, 11*(4), 226–232.

Mack, N. K. (2011). Enriching number knowledge. *Teaching Children Mathematics, 18*(2), 101–109.

Maida, P. (2004). Using algebra without realizing it. *Mathematics Teaching in the Middle School, 9*(9), 484–488.

Maldonado, L. A., Turner, E. E., Dominguez, H., & Empson, S. B. (2009). English language learning from, and contributing to, mathematical discussions. In D. Y. White & J. S. Spitzer (Eds.), *Responding to diversity: Grades pre-K–5* (pp. 7–22). Reston, VA: NCTM.

Maloney, A. Confrey, J., Ng, D. & Nickell, J. (2014). Learning trajectories for interpreting the K-8 Common Core State Standards with a middle-grades statistics example. In Karp, K. & McDuffie, A. (Eds.). *Using Research to Improve Instruction* (pp 23–34). Reston, VA: NCTM.

Maloney, E., Gunderson, E. Ramirez, G., Levine, S., & Beilock, S. (2014). *Teachers' math anxiety relates to girls' and boys' math achievement.* Unpublished manuscript.

Mancl, D. B., Miller, S. P., & Kennedy, M. (2012). Using the concrete-representational-abstract sequence with integrated strategy instruction to teach subtraction with regrouping to students with learning disabilities. *Learning Disabilities Research and Practice, 27*(4), 152–166.

Manizade, A., & Mason, M. (2014). Developing the area of a trapezoid. *Mathematics Teacher, 107*(7), 508–514.

Mann, R. L. (2004). Balancing act: The truth behind the equals sign. *Teaching Children Mathematics, 11*(2), 68.

Mark, J., Cuoco, A., Goldenberg, E. P., & Sword, S. (2010). Developing mathematical habits of mind. *Mathematics Teaching in the Middle School, 15*(9), 505–509.

Martin, J. F. (2009). The goal of long division. *Teaching Children Mathematics, 15*(8), 482–487.

Martinie, S. L. (2007). *Middle school rational number knowledge* (Unpublished doctoral dissertation). Kansas State University.

Martinie, S. L. (2014). Decimal fractions: An important point. *Mathematics Teaching in the Middle School, 19*(7), 420–429.

Martinie, S. L., & Bay-Williams, J. M. (2003). Investigating students' conceptual understanding of decimal fractions using multiple representations. *Mathematics Teaching in the Middle School, 8*(5), 244–247.

Matthews, M. E., Hlas, C. S., & Finken, T. M. (2009). Using lesson study and four-column lesson planning with preservice teachers. *Mathematics Teacher, 102*(7), 504–508.

Mazzocco, M. M. M., Devlin, K. T., & McKenney, S. J. (2008). Is it a fact? Timed arithmetic performance of children with mathematical learning disabilities (MLD) varies as a function of how MLD is defined. *Developmental Neuropsychology, 33*(3), 318–344.

Mazzocco, M. M. M., & Thompson, R. E. (2005). Kindergarten predictors of math learning disability. *Learning Disabilities Research & Practice, 20*(3), 142–155.

McClain, K., Leckman, J., Schmitt, P., & Regis, T. (2006). Changing the face of statistical data analysis in the middle grades: Learning by doing. In G. F. Burrill & P. C. Elliott (Eds.), *Thinking and reasoning with data and chance: 68th NCTM yearbook* (pp. 229–240). Reston, VA: NCTM.

McCoy, L. P. (1997). Algebra: Real-life investigations in a lab setting. *Mathematics Teaching in the Middle School, 2*(4), 220–224.

McCoy, L. P., Buckner, S., & Munley, J. (2007). Probability games from diverse cultures. *Mathematics Teaching in the Middle School, 12*(7), 394–402.

McGatha, M., Cobb, P., & McClain, K. (1998). *An analysis of students' statistical understandings.* Paper presented at the Annual Meeting of the American Educational Research Association, San Diego, CA.

McGlone, C. (2008, July). *The role of culturally-based mathematics in the general mathematics curriculum.* Paper presented at the Eleventh International Congress on Mathematics Education, Monterrey, Mexico.

McNamara, J. C., & Shaughnessy, M. M. (2010). *Beyond pizzas & pies: Ten essential strategies for supporting fraction sense (Grades 3–5).* Sausalito, CA: Math Solutions.

McNeil, N. M., & Alibali, M. W. (2005). Knowledge change as a function of mathematics experience: All contexts are not created equal. *Journal of Cognition and Development, 6,* 285–306.

Metz, M. L. (2010). Using GAISE and NCTM standards as framework for teaching probability and statistics to preservice elementary and middle school mathematics teachers. *Journal of Statistics Education, 18*(3), 1–27.

Midobuche, E. (2001). Building cultural bridges between home and the mathematics classroom. *Teaching Children Mathematics, 7*(9), 500–502.

Miller, S. P., & Kaffar, B. J. (2011). Developing addition with regrouping competence among second graders with mathematics difficulties. *Investigations in Mathematics Learning, 4*(1), 24–49.

Mishra, P., & Koehler, M. J. (2006). Technological pedagogical content knowledge: A new framework for teacher knowledge. *Teachers College Record, 108*(6), 1017–1054.

Mix, K. S., Prather, R. S., Smith, L. B., & Stockton, J. D. (2014). Young children's interpretation of multidigit number names: From emerging competence to mastery. *Child Development 85*(3), 1306–1319.

Moeller, K., Martignon, L., Wessolowski, S., Engel, J., & Nuerk, H. C. (2011). Effects of finger counting on numerical development: The opposing views of neuro-cognition and mathematics education. *Frontiers in Psychology, 2,* 328.

Moffett, G., Malzahn, K., & Driscoll, M. (2014). Multimodal communication: Promoting and revealing students' mathematical thinking. In K. Karp & A. Roth-McDuffie (Eds.), *Annual perspectives in mathematics education 2014: Using research to improve instruction* (pp. 129–139). Reston, VA: NCTM.

Mokros, J., Russell, S. J., & Economopoulos, K. (1995). *Beyond arithmetic: Changing mathematics in the elementary classroom.* Palo Alto, CA: Dale Seymour Publications.

Mokros, J., & Wright, T. (2009). Zoos, aquariums and expanding students' data literacy. *Teaching Children Mathematics, 15*(9), 524–530.

Molina, M., & Ambrose, R. C. (2006). Fostering relational thinking while negotiating the meaning of the equals sign. *Teaching Children Mathematics, 13*(2), 111–117.

Mooney, E. S., & Bair, S. L. (2011). Average jeans. *Mathematics Teaching in the Middle School, 17*(4), 210–211.

Moschkovich, J. N. (1998). Supporting the participation of English language learners in mathematical discussions. *For the Learning of Mathematics, 19*(1), 11–19.

Moschkovich, J. N. (2009, March). *How do students use two languages when learning mathematics? Using two languages during conversations:* NCTM Research Clip. Reston, VA: NCTM.

Moyer-Packenham, P. S., Ulmer, L. A., & Anderson, K. L. (2012). Examining pictorial models and virtual manipulatives for third-grade fraction instruction. *Journal of Interactive Online Learning, 11*(3), 103–120.

Muir, T., & Livy, S. (2012, December 5). What do they know? A comparison of pre-service teachers' and inservice teachers' decimal mathematical content knowledge. *International Journal for Mathematics Teaching and Learning,* 1–15.

Munier, V., Devichi, C., & Merle, H. (2008). A physical situation as a way to teach angle. *Teaching Children Mathematics, 14*(7), 402–407.

Murata, A. (2008). Mathematics teaching and learning as a mediating process: The case of tape diagrams. *Mathematical Thinking and Learning, 10,* 374–406.

Murrey, D. L. (2008). Differentiating instruction in mathematics for the English language learner. *Mathematics Teaching in the Middle School, 14*(3), 146–153.

National Academy Press (1999). *Global perspectives for local action: Using TIMSS to improve U.S. mathematics and science education.* Washington, DC: NAP.

National Association for Gifted Children (NAGC). (2007). What is giftedness? Retrieved from www.nagc.org

National Center for Education Statistics. (2009). *NAEP Questions Tool.* Retrieved from http://nces.ed.gov/nationsreportcard/itmrlsx/detail.aspx?subject=mathematics

National Center for Education Statistics. (2011). Retrieved from http://nces.ed.gov/nationsreportcard/itmrlsx/search.aspx?subject=mathematics

National Center for Education Statistics (2013). *The nation's report card: A first look: 2013 mathematics and reading* (NCES 2014-451). Institute of Education Sciences, U.S. Department of Education, Washington, DC.

National Center for Educational Statistics. (2014). *NAEP questions tool.* Retrieved from http://nces.ed.gov/nationsreportcard/itmrlsx/landing.aspx

National Center for Technology Innovation. (2010). *Techmatrix.* Retrieved from www.techmatrix.org

National Council of Supervisors of Mathematics. (2011). Common Core State Standards (CCSS) mathematics curriculum materials analysis project. Retrieved from http://www.mathedleadership.org/ccss/materials.html

NCTM (National Council of Teachers of Mathematics). (1989). *Curriculum and evaluation standards for school mathematics.* Reston, VA: NCTM.

NCTM (National Council of Teachers of Mathematics). (1991). *Professional standards for teaching mathematics.* Reston, VA: NCTM.

NCTM (National Council of Teachers of Mathematics). (1995). *Assessment standards for school mathematics.* Reston, VA: NCTM.

NCTM (National Council of Teachers of Mathematics). (2000). *Principles and standards for school mathematics.* Reston, VA: NCTM.

NCTM (National Council of Teachers of Mathematics). (2006). *Curriculum focal points for prekindergarten through grade 8 mathematics: A quest for coherence.* Reston, VA: NCTM.

NCTM (National Council of Teachers of Mathematics). (2007a). *Mathematics teaching today.* Reston, VA: NCTM.

NCTM (National Council of Teachers of Mathematics). (2007b). *Research brief: Effective strategies for teaching students with difficulties in mathematics.* Retrieved from www.nctm.org/news/content.aspx?id=8452

NCTM (National Council of Teachers of Mathematics). (2008, March). *The role of technology in the teaching and learning of mathematics.* Retrieved from www.nctm.org/about/content.aspx?id=14233

NCTM (National Council of Teachers of Mathematics). (2009). *Focus in high school mathematics: Reasoning and sense making.* Reston, VA: NCTM.

NCTM (National Council of Teachers of Mathematics). (2011a, July). *Position statement on calculator use in elementary grades.* Reston, VA: NCTM.

NCTM (National Council of Teachers of Mathematics). (2011b, July). *Position statement on interventions.* Reston, VA: NCTM.

NCTM (National Council of Teachers of Mathematics). (2011c). Technology in teaching and learning mathematics. NCTM Position Statement. Retrieved from www.nctm.org/about/content.aspx?id=6330

NCTM (National Council of Teachers of Mathematics). (2011d). Using calculators for teaching and learning mathematics. NCTM Research Brief. Retrieved from www.nctm.org/news/content.aspx?id=31192

NCTM (National Council of Teachers of Mathematics). (2014). *Position statement on access and equity in mathematics education.* Reston, VA: NCTM.

NCTM (National Council of Teachers of Mathematics). (n.d.). Statement of beliefs. Retrieved from www.nctm.org/about/content.aspx?id=210&LangType=1033

National Governors Association & Council of Chief State School Officers. (2010, June). *Common Core State Standards Initiative.* Retrieved from www.corestandards.org

National KIDS COUNT. (2012). Retrieved from http://datacenter.kidscount.org/data/tables/81-children-who-speak-a-language-other-than-english-at-home?loc=1&loct=2#detailed/1/any/false/868,867,133,38,35/any/396,397

National Mathematics Advisory Panel. (2008). *Foundations for success.* Jessup, MD: U.S. Department of Education.

National Research Council. (2001). *Adding it up: Helping children learn mathematics.* J. Kilpatrick, J. Swafford, & B. Findell (Eds.). Washington, DC: National Academies Press.

National Research Council Committee. (2009). *Mathematics learning in early childhood: Paths toward excellence and equity.* Washington, DC: The National Academies Press.

Neagoy, M. (2012). *Planting the seeds of algebra, PreK–2: Explorations for the early grades.* Thousand Oaks, CA: Corwin.

Nebesniak, A. L., & Heaton, R. M. (2010). Student confidence & student involvement. *Mathematics Teaching in the Middle School, 16*(2), 97–103.

Nelson, C. Q., & Williams, N. L. (2009). Mathematical explorations: Exploring unknown probabilities with miniature toy pigs. *Mathematics Teaching in the Middle School, 14*(9), 557.

Nelson, R. (2001). *Proofs without words II: More exercises in visual thinking.* Washington, DC: Mathematical Association of America.

Neumer, C. (2007). Mixed numbers made easy: Building and converting mixed numbers and improper fractions. *Teaching Children Mathematics, 13*(9), 488–492.

Nicolson, C. P. (2005). Is chance fair? One student's thoughts on probability. *Teaching Children Mathematics, 12*(2), 83–89.

Niess, M. (2008). Guiding preservice teachers in developing TPCK. In AACTE Committee on Innovation and Technology (Eds.), *Handbook of technological pedagogical content knowledge (TCPK) for educators* (pp. 223–250). New York, NY: Routledge/Taylor & Francis Group.

Niezgoda, D. A., & Moyer-Packenham, P. S. (2005). Hickory, dickory, dock: Navigating through data analysis. *Teaching Children Mathematics, 11*(6), 292–300.

Norton, A., & D'Ambrosio, B. S. (2008). ZPC and ZPD: Zones of teaching and learning. *Journal for Research in Mathematics Education, 39*(3), 220–246.

Nosek, B., Banaji, M., & Greenwald, A. (2002). Math = male, me = female, therefore me math. *Journal of Personality and Social Psychology, 83*(1), 44–59.

Nyquist, J. B. (2003). *The benefits of reconstruing feedback as a larger system of formative assessment: A metaanalysis.* Unpublished master's thesis. Vanderbilt University, Nashville, TN.

O'Dell, R. S. (2012). The mean as balance point. *Mathematics Teaching in the Middle School, 18*(3), 148–155.

Outhred, L., & Mitchelmore, M. (2004). Students' structuring of rectangular arrays. In M. J. Hoines & A. B. Fuglestad (Eds.), *Proceedings of the 28th PME International Conference, 3,* 465–472.

Pantziara, M., & Philippou, G. (2012). Levels of students' "conception" of fractions. *Educational Studies in Mathematics, 79,* 61–83.

Parker, R., & Breyfogle, L. (2011). Learning to write about mathematics. *Teaching Children Mathematics, 18*(2), 90–99.

Parker, M. (2004). Reasoning and working proportionally with percent. *Mathematics Teaching in the Middle School, 9*(6), 326–330.

Parmar, R., Garrison, R., Clements, D., & Sarama, J. (2011). Measurement. In F. Fennell (Ed.), *Achieving fluency in special education and mathematics* (pp. 197–216). Reston, VA: NCTM.

Partnership for 21st Century Skills. (n.d.). Framework for 21st century learning. Washington, DC: Author. Retrieved from www.p21.org/storage/documents/1.__p21_framework_2-pager.pdf

Patterson, L. G., & Patterson, K. L. (2014). Problem solve with presidential data. *Mathematics Teaching in the Middle School, 19*(7), 406–413.

Peltenburg, M., van den Heuvel-Panhuizen, M., & Robitzsch, A. (2012). Special education students' use of indirect addition in solving subtraction problems up to 100: A proof of the didactical potential of an ignored procedure. *Educational Studies in Mathematics, 79*(3), 351–369.

Perie, M., Moran, R., & Lutkus, A. (2005). *NAEP 2004 trends in academic progress: Three decades of student performance in reading and mathematics.* Washington, DC: National Center for Education Statistics.

Perkins, I., & Flores, A. (2002). Mathematical notations and procedures of recent immigrant students. *Mathematics Teaching in the Middle School, 7*(6), 346–351.

Petersen, J. (2004). *Math and nonfiction: Grades K–2.* Sausalito, CA: Math Solutions Publications.

Petit, M. (2009). *OGAP (Vermont mathematics partnership ongoing assessment project) multiplicative reasoning framework.* Communication with the author (September 2009).

Petit, M., Laird, R. E., & Marsden, E. L. (2010). *A focus on fractions: Bringing research to the classroom.* New York, NY: Taylor & Francis.

Petit, M., & Zawojewski, J. (2010). Formative assessment in elementary school mathematics. In D. Lambdin & F. K. Lester, Jr. (Eds.), *Teaching and learning mathematics: Translating research for elementary school teachers* (pp. 73–79). Reston, VA: NCTM.

Phelps, K. A. G. (2012). The power of problem choices. *Teaching Children Mathematics, 19*(3), 152–157.

Phillips-Bey, C. K. (2004). TI-73 calculator activities. *Mathematics Teaching in the Middle School, 9*(9), 500–508.

Piaget, J. (1976). *The child's conception of the world.* Totowa, NJ: Littlefield, Adams.

Pólya, G. (1945). *How to solve it.* Princeton, NJ: Princeton University Press.

Popham, W. J. (2008). *Transformative assessment.* Alexandria, VA: Association for Supervision and Curriculum Development.

Porter, A., McMaken, J., Hwang, J., & Yang, R. (2011). Common core standards: The new U.S. intended curriculum. *Educational Researcher, 40*(3), 103–116.

Post, T. R., Wachsmuth, I., Lesh, R. A., & Behr, M. J. (1985). Order and equivalence of rational numbers: A cognitive analysis. *Journal for Research in Mathematics Education, 16*(1), 18–36.

Preston, R., & Thompson, T. (2004). Integrating measurement across the curriculum. *Mathematics Teaching in the Middle School, 9*(8), 436–441.

Pugalee, D. K. (2005). *Writing for mathematical understanding.* Norwood, MA: Christopher Gordon.

Pugalee, D. K., Arbaugh, F., Bay-Williams, J. M., Farrell, A., Mathews, S., &. Royster, D. (2008). *Navigating through mathematical connections in grades 6–8.* Reston, VA: NCTM.

Pugalee, D. K., Harbaugh, A., & Quach, L. H. (2009). The human graph project: Giving students mathematical power through differentiated instruction. In M. W. Ellis (Ed.), *Responding to diversity: Grades 6–8* (pp. 47–58). Reston, VA: NCTM.

Putrawangsa, S., Lukito, A., M Amin, S., & Wijers, M. (2013). Educational design research: Developing students' understanding of area as the number of measurement units covering a surface. In Z. Zulkardi (Ed.), *Proceeding the First South East Asia Design/Development Research (SEA-DR) International Conference, Sriwijaya University, Palembang, April 22–23* (pp. 416–426).

Quinn, R., Lamberg, T., & Perrin, J. (2008). Teacher perceptions of division by zero. *Clearing House, 81*(3), 101–104.

Ramirez, G., Gunderson, E. A., Levine, S. C., & Beilock, S. L. (2013). Math anxiety, working memory, and math achievement in early elementary school. *Journal of Cognition and Development, 14*(2), 187–202.

Rampey, B. D., Dion, G. S., & Donahue, P. L. (2009). *NAEP 2008 Trends in Academic Progress* (NCES 2009–479). Washington, DC: National Center for Education Statistics, Institute of Education Sciences, U.S. Department of Education.

RAND Mathematics Study Panel. (2003). *Mathematical proficiency for all students: Toward a strategic research and development program in mathematics education* (Issue 1643). Santa Monica, CA: Rand Corporation.

Rasmussen, C., Yackel, E., & King, K. (2003). Social and sociomathematical norms in the mathematics classroom. In H. L. Schoen & R. I. Charles (Eds.), *Teaching mathematics through problem solving: Grades 6–12* (pp. 143–154). Reston, VA: NCTM.

Rathmell, E. C. (1978). Using thinking strategies to teach the basic skills. In M. N. Suydam (Ed.), *Developing computational skills* (pp. 13–38). Reston, VA: NCTM.

Rathmell, E. C., Leutzinger, L. P., & Gabriele, A. (2000). *Thinking with numbers.* (Separate packets for each operation.) Cedar Falls, IA: Thinking with Numbers.

Rathouz, M. (2011). 3 ways that promote student reasoning. *Teaching Children Mathematics, 18*(3), 182–189.

Rathouz, M. M. (2011). Making sense of decimal multiplication. *Mathematics Teaching in the Middle School, 16*(7), 430–437.

Ravenna, G. (2008). *Factors influencing gifted students' preference for models of teaching.* Doctoral dissertation, University of Southern California.

Read, J. (2014). Who rises to the top? *Peabody Reflector, 83*(1), 19–22.

Reinhart, S. (2000). Never say anything a kid can say. *Mathematics Teaching in the Middle School, 5*(8), 478–483.

Reis, S., & Renzulli, J. S. (2005). *Curriculum compacting: An easy start to differentiating for high potential students.* Waco, TX: Prufrock Press.

Remillard, J.T, Ebby, C., Lim, V., Reinke, L., Hoe, N., & Magee, E. (2014). Increasing access to mathematics through locally relevant curriculum. In K. Karp & A. Roth-McDuffie (Eds.), *Annual perspectives in mathematics education 2014*: *Using research to improve instruction* (pp. 89–96). Reston, VA: NCTM.

Remillard, J. T., & Jackson, K. (2006). Old math, new math: Parents' experiences with standards-based reform. *Mathematical Thinking and Learning, 3*(6), 231–259.

Renzulli, J. S., Gubbins, E. J., McMillen, K. S., Eckert, R. D., & Little, C. A. (Eds.). (2009). *Systems & models for developing programs for the gifted & talented* (2nd ed.). Mansfield Center, CT: Creative Learning Press.

Reys, R. E. (1998). Computation versus number sense. *Mathematics Teaching in the Middle School, 4*(2), 110–113.

Riegle-Crumb, C. (2006). The path through math: Course-taking trajectories and student performance at the intersection of gender and race/ethnicity. *American Journal of Education, 113*(1), 101–122.

Rigelman, N., & Petrick, K. (2014). Student mathematicians developed through formative assessment cycles. In K. Karp & A. Roth-McDuffie (Eds.), *Using research to improve instruction* (pp. 215–227). Reston, VA: NCTM.

Riordan, J. E., & Noyce, P. E. (2001). The impact of two *standards*-based mathematics curricula on student achievement in Massachusetts. *Journal for Research in Mathematics Education, 32*(4), 368–398.

Riskowski, J. L., Olbricht, G., & Wilson, J. (2010). 100 students. *Mathematics Teaching in the Middle School, 15*(6), 320–327.

Rittle-Johnson, B., Star, J. R., & Durkin, K. (2010, April). *Developing procedural flexibility: When should multiple solution methods be introduced?* Paper presented at the Annual Conference of the American Educational Research Association, Denver, CO.

Roberge, M. C., & Cooper, L. L. (2010). Map scale, proportion, and Google™ Earth. *Mathematics Teaching in the Middle School, 15*(8), 448–457.

Robinson, K., & LeFevre, J. (2012). The inverse relationship between multiplication and division: Concepts, procedures and a cognitive framework. *Educational Studies in Mathematics, 79*(3), 409–428.

Roddick, C., & Silvas-Centeno, C. (2007). Developing understanding of fractions through pattern blocks and fair trade. *Teaching Children Mathematics, 14*(3), 140–145.

Rodríguez-Brown, F. V. (2010). Latino families: Culture and schooling. In E. G. Murillo, Jr., S. A. Villenas, R. T. Galván, J. S. Muñoz, C. Martínez, & M. Machado-Casas (Eds.), *Handbook of Latinos and education: Theory, research, and practice* (pp. 350–360). New York, NY: Routledge.

Ross, S. H. (1986). *The development of children's place-value numeration concepts in grades two through five.* Presented at the annual meeting of the American Educational Research Association, San Francisco, CA.

Ross, S. H. (1989). Parts, wholes, and place value: A developmental perspective. *Arithmetic Teacher, 36*(6), 47–51.

Ross, S. R. (2002). Place value: Problem solving and written assessment. *Teaching Children Mathematics, 8*(7), 419–423.

Rotigel, J., & Fellow, S. (2005). Mathematically gifted students: How can we meet their needs? *Gifted Child Today, 27*(4), 46–65.

Roy, J. A., & Beckmann, C. E. (2007). Batty functions: Exploring quadratic functions through children's literature. *Mathematics Teaching in the Middle School, 13*(1), 52–64.

Rubel, L. (2006). Students' probabilistic thinking revealed: The case of coin tosses. In G. Burrill & P. C. Elliott (Eds.), *Thinking and reasoning about data and chance: Sixty-eighth yearbook* (pp. 49–60). Reston, VA: NCTM.

Rubel, L. (2007). Middle school and high school students' probabilistic reasoning on coin tasks. *Journal for Research in Mathematics Education, 38*(5), 531–557.

Russell, S. J. (1997, April). *Using video to study students' strategies for whole-number operations.* Paper presented at the annual meeting of the National Council of Teachers of Mathematics, Minneapolis, MN.

Russell, S. J. (2006). What does it mean that "5 has a lot"? From the world to data and back. In G. F. Burrill & P. C. Elliott (Eds.), *Thinking and reasoning about data and chance: 68th NCTM yearbook* (pp. 17–30). Reston VA: NCTM.

Russell, S. J., & Economopoulos, K. (2008). *Investigations in number, data, and space.* New York, NY: Pearson.

Ryan, J., & Williams, J. (2007). *Children's mathematics 4–15: Learning from errors and misconceptions.* New York, NY: McGraw-Hill Open University Press.

Sadler, P., & Tai, R. (2007). The two pillars supporting college science. *Science, 317*(5837), 457–458.

Sarama, J., & Clements, D. H. (2009). *Early childhood mathematics education research: Learning trajectories for young children.* New York, NY: Routledge.

Sarazen, D. N. (2012). Fractions: Thinking beyond the lines. *Teaching Children Mathematics, 19*(3), 208.

Saul, M., Assouline, S., & Sheffield, L. J. (Eds.). (2010). *The peak in the middle: Developing mathematically gifted students in the middle grades.* Reston, VA: NCTM, National Association of Gifted Children, & National Middle School Association.

Sawchuk, S. (2010, June 23). Three groups apply for race to top test grants. *Education Week.*

Scheaffer, R. L. (2006). Statistics and mathematics: On making a happy marriage. In G. F. Burrill & P. C. Elliott (Eds.), *Thinking and reasoning about data and chance: Sixty-eighth yearbook* (pp. 309–322). Reston, VA: NCTM.

Schielack, J., & Seeley, C. (2007). A look at the development of data representation and analysis in *Curriculum Focal Points: A Quest of Coherence. Mathematics Teaching in the Middle School, 13*(4), 208–210.

Schifter, D., Bastable, V., & Russell, S. J. (1999a). *Developing mathematical understanding: Numbers and operations, Part 2, Making meaning for operations* (Casebook). Parsippany, NJ: Dale Seymour Publications.

Schifter, D., Bastable, V., & Russell, S. J. (1999b). *Developing mathematical understanding: Numbers and operations, Part 2, Making meaning for operations* (Facilitator's Guide). Parsippany, NJ: Dale Seymour Publications.

Schifter, D., Monk, G. S., Russell, S. J., & Bastable, V. (2007). Early algebra: What does understanding the laws of arithmetic mean in the elementary grades? In J. Kaput, D. Carraher, & M. Blanton (Eds.), *Algebra in the early grades.* Mahwah, NJ: Erlbaum.

Schifter, D., Russell, S. J., & Bastable, V. (2009). Early algebra to reach the range of learners. *Teaching Children Mathematics, 16*(4), 230–237.

Schoenfeld, A. H. (1996). In fostering communities of inquiry, must it matter that the teacher knows "the answer"? *For the Learning of Mathematics, 16*(3), 11–16.

Schroeder, T. L., & Lester, F. K., Jr. (1989). Developing understanding in mathematics via problem solving. In P. R. Trafton (Ed.), *New directions for elementary school mathematics* (pp. 31–42). Reston, VA: NCTM.

Schwartz, S. L. (1996). Hidden messages in teacher talk: Praise and empowerment. *Teaching Children Mathematics, 2*(7), 396–401.

Schwartz, S. (2013). *Implementing the Common Core State Standards through mathematical problem solving kindergarten–grade 2.* Reston, VA: NCTM.

Seattle Times News Services. (2008, July 25). In math, girls and boys are equal. *The Seattle Times.*

Seeley, C. L. (2009). *Faster isn't smarter: Messages about math, teaching, and learning in the 21st century.* Sausalito, CA: Math Solutions.

Seeley, C., & Schielack, J. F. (2007). A look at the development of ratios, rates, and proportionality. *Mathematics Teaching in the Middle School, 13*(3), 140–142.

Seidel, C., & McNamee, J. (2005). Teacher to teacher: Phenomenally exciting joint mathematics—English vocabulary project. *Mathematics Teaching in the Middle School, 10*(9), 461–463.

Setati, M. (2005). Teaching mathematics in a primary multilingual classroom. *Journal for Research in Mathematics Education, 36*(5), 447–466.

Sharp, J., & Welder, R. M. (2014). Reveal limitations through fraction division problem posing. *Mathematics Teaching in the Middle School, 19*(9), 541–547.

Shaughnessy, J. M. (2003). Research on students' understanding of probability. In J. Kilpatrick, W. G. Martin, & D. Schifter (Eds.), *A research companion to Principles and Standards for School Mathematics* (pp. 216–226). Reston, VA: NCTM.

Shaughnessy, J. M. (2006). Research on students' understanding of some big concepts in statistics. In G. F. Burrill & P. C. Elliott (Eds.), *Thinking and reasoning about data and chance: 68th NCTM yearbook* (pp. 77–98). Reston, VA: NCTM.

Shaughnessy, J. M. (2007). Research on statistics learning and reasoning. In F. Lester, Jr. (Ed.), *Second handbook of research on mathematics teaching and learning* (pp. 957–1010). Reston, VA: NCTM.

Shaughnessy, M. (2009). *Students' flexible use of multiple representations for rational numbers: Decimals, fractions, parts of area and number lines* (Doctoral dissertation). University of California–Berkeley.

Shaughnessy, M. M. (2011). Identify fractions and decimals on a number line. *Teaching Children Mathematics, 17*(7), 428–434.

Sheffield, L. J. (Ed.). (1999). *Developing mathematically promising students.* Reston, VA: National Council of Teachers of Mathematics.

Sheffield, S., & Gallagher, K. (2004). *Math and nonfiction: Grades 3–5.* Sausalito, CA: Math Solutions Publications.

Shoecraft, P. (1982). Bowl-A-Fact: A game for reviewing the number facts. *Arithmetic Teacher, 29*(8), 24–25.

Shulman, L. (1986). Those who understand: Knowledge growth in teaching. *Educational Researcher, 15*(2), 4–14.

Siebert, D., & Gaskin, N. (2006). Creating, naming, and justifying fractions. *Teaching Children Mathematics, 12*(8), 394–400.

Siegler, R. S., & Booth, J. L. (2005). Development of numerical estimation: A review. In J. I. D. Campbell (Ed.), *Handbook of mathematical cognition* (pp. 197–212). New York, NY: New York Psychology Press.

Siegler, R. S., Carpenter, T., Fennell, F., Geary, D., Lewis, J., Okamoto, Y., et al. (2010). *Developing effective fractions instruction for kindergarten through 8th grade: A practice guide* (NCEE 2010-4039). Retrieved from www.whatworks.ed.gov/publications/practiceguides

Siegler, R. S., & Ramani, G. B. (2009). Playing linear number board games—but not circular ones—improves low-income preschoolers' numerical understanding. *Journal of Educational Psychology, 101*, 545–560.

Sikes, S. (1995). *Feeding the zircon gorilla and other team building activities.* Tulsa, OK: Learning Unlimited Corporation.

Silver, E. A., & Stein, M. K. (1996). The QUASAR project: The "revolution of the possible" in mathematics instructional reform in urban middle schools. *Urban Education, 30*(4), 476–521.

Simon, M. A. (2009). Amidst multiple theories of learning in mathematics education. *Journal for Research in Mathematics Education, 40*(5), 477–490.

Sinclair, N., Pimm, D., & Skelin, M. (2012). *Developing essential understanding of geometry for teaching mathematics in grades 6-8.* Reston, VA: National Council of Teachers of Mathematics.

Skemp, R. (1978). Relational understanding and instrumental understanding. *Arithmetic Teacher, 26*(3), 9–15.

Small, M. (2010). *More good questions: Great ways to differentiate secondary mathematics instruction.* Reston, VA: NCTM.

Small, M. (2012). *Good questions: Great ways to differentiate mathematics instruction.* Reston, VA: NCTM.

Smith, A. (1997). Testing the surf: Criteria for evaluating Internet information resources. *The Public-Access Computer Systems Review, 8*(3), 5–23.

Smith, B. A. (1997). *A meta-analysis of outcomes from the use of calculators in mathematics education* (Doctoral dissertation). Texas A&M University. *Dissertation Abstracts International, 58,* 787A.

Smith, E. (2008). Representational thinking as a framework for introducing functions in the elementary curriculum. In J. J. Kaput, D. W. Carraher, & M. L. Blanton (Eds.), *Algebra in the early grades* (p. 143). Mahwah, NJ: Lawrence Erlbaum Associates/Taylor & Francis Group.

Smith, J. P., III. (2002). The development of students' knowledge of fractions and ratios. In B. Litwiller (Ed.), *Making sense of fractions, ratios, and proportions* (pp. 3–17). Reston, VA: NCTM.

Smith, M. S., Bill, V., & Hughes, E. K. (2008). Thinking through a lesson: Successfully implementing high-level tasks. *Mathematics Teaching in the Middle School, 14*(3), 132–138.

Smith, M. S., Hughes, E. K., Engle, R. A., & Stein, M. K. (2009). Orchestrating discussions. *Mathematics Teaching in the Middle School, 14*(9), 548–556.

Smith, M. S., & Stein, M. K. (1998). Selecting and creating mathematical tasks: From research to practice. *Mathematics Teaching in the Middle School, 3*(5), 344–350.

Smith, M. S., & Stein, M. K. (2011). *5 Practices for orchestrating productive mathematics discussions.* Thousand Oaks, CA: Corwin Press.

Soares, J., Blanton, M. L., & Kaput, J. J. (2006). Thinking alge-braically across the elementary school curriculum. *Teaching Children Mathematics, 12*(5), 228–234.

Sowder, J. T., & Wearne, D. (2006). What do we know about eighth-grade student achievement? *Mathematics Teaching in the Middle School, 11*(6), 285–293.

Sowder, J. T., Wearne, D., Martin, W. G., & Strutchens, M. (2004). What do 8th-grade students know about mathemat-ics? Changes over a decade. In P. Kloosterman & F. K. Les-ter, Jr., *Results and interpretations of the 1990–2000 mathematics assessments of the National Assessment of Educational Progress* (pp. 105–143). Reston, VA: NCTM.

Sowder, L. (1988). Children's solutions of story problems. *Jour-nal of Mathematical Behavior, 7*(3), 227–238.

Spangler, D. B. (2011). *Strategies for teaching fractions: Using error analysis for intervention and assessment.* Thousand Oaks, CA: Corwin.

Spelke, E. S. (2005). *The science of gender and science: Pinker vs. Spelke, a debate.* Retrieved from www.edge.org/3rd_culture/debate05/debate05_index.html

Star, J. R., & Rittle-Johnson, B. (2009). The role of prior knowledge in the development of strategy flexibility: The case of computational estimation. In S. Swars, D. Stin-son, & S. Lemons-Smith (Eds.), *Proceedings of the 31st annual meeting of the North American Chapter of the International Group for the Psychology of Mathematics Education* (pp. 577–584). Atlanta, GA: Georgia State University.

Steele, D. F. (2007). Understanding students' problem solving knowledge through their writing. *Mathematics Teaching in the Middle School, 13*(2), 102–109.

Stein, M. K., & Bovalino, J. W. (2001). Manipulatives: One piece of the puzzle. *Teaching Children Mathematics, 6*(6), 356–359.

Stein, M. K., Remillard, J., & Smith, M. S. (2007). How curricu-lum influences student learning. In F. J. Lester, Jr. (Ed.), *Sec-ond handbook of research on mathematics teaching and learning* (pp. 319–369). Charlotte, NC: Information Age Publishing.

Stein, M. K., & Smith, M. S. (2010). The role of curricular materials in elementary school mathematics classrooms. In Lambdin, D. V., & Lester, F. K., Jr., *Teaching and learning mathematics: Translating research for elementary school teachers* (pp. 61–65). Reston, VA: NCTM.

Steinle, V., & Stacey, K. (2004a). Persistence of decimal miscon-ceptions and readiness to move to expertise. *Proceedings of the 28th conference of the International Groups for the Psychology of Mathematics Education, 4*, 225–232.

Steinle, V., & Stacey, K. (2004b). A longitudinal study of stu-dents' understanding of decimal notation: An overview and refined results. In I. Putt, R. Faragher, & M. McLean (Eds.), *Mathematics Education for the Third Millennium: Towards 2010. Proceedings of the 27th Annual Conference of the Mathematics Education Research Group of Australasia, 2*, 541–548.

Stemn, B. (2008). Building middle school students' understand-ing of proportional reasoning through mathematical investi-gation. *Education, 36*(4), 3–13.

Stenmark, J. K. (1989). *Assessment alternatives in mathematics: An overview of assessment techniques that promote learning.* Berkeley, CA: EQUALS, University of California.

Stenmark, J. K., & Bush, W. S. (Eds.). (2001). *Mathematics assess-ment: A practical handbook for grades 3–5.* Reston, VA: NCTM.

Stephan, M. L. (2009). What are you worth? *Mathematics Teach-ing in the Middle School, 15*(1), 16–24.

Stephan, M., & Akyuz, D. (2012). A proposed instructional the-ory for integer addition and subtraction. *Journal for Research in Mathematics Education, 43*(4), 428–464.

Stephan, M., McManus, G., & Dehlinger, R. (2014). Using research to inform formative assessment techniques. In K. Karp & A. Roth-McDuffie (Eds.), *Using research to improve instruction* (pp. 229–238). Reston, VA: NCTM.

Stephan, M., & Whitenack, J. (2003). Establishing classroom social and sociomathematical norms for problem solving. In F. K. Lester, Jr. & R. I. Charles (Eds.), *Teaching mathematics through problem solving: Grades pre-K–6* (pp. 149–162). Reston, VA: NCTM.

Stephens, A. C., Knuth, E. J., Blanton, M. L., Isler, I., Gar-diner, A. M., & Marum, T. (2013). Equation structure and the meaning of the equal sign: The impact of task selection in eliciting elementary students' understandings. *The Journal of Mathematical Behavior, 32*, 173–182.

Stevens, T., Wang, K., Olivarez, A., Jr., & Hamman, D. (2007). Use of self-perspectives and their sources to predict the math-ematics enrollment intentions of girls and boys. *Sex Roles, 56*(3), 51–63.

Stigler, J., & Hiebert, J. (2009). Closing the teaching gap. *Phi Delta Kappan, 91*(3), 32–37.

Stoessiger, R., & Edmunds, J. (1992). *Natural learning and math-ematics.* Portsmouth, NH: Heinemann.

Storeygard, J. (2010). *My kids can: Making math accessible to all learners K–5.* Portsmouth, NH: Heinemann.

Suh, J. M. (2007a). Developing "algebra-'rithmetic" in the ele-mentary grades. *Teaching Children Mathematics, 14*(4), 246–253.

Suh, J. M. (2007b). Tying it all together: Building mathematics proficiency for all students. *Teaching Children Mathematics, 14*(3), 163–169.

Sulentic-Dowell, M. M., Beal, G., & Capraro, R. (2006). How do literacy experiences affect the teaching propensities of ele-mentary pre-service teachers? *Journal of Reading Psychology, 27*(2–3), 235–255.

Swanson, P. E. (2010). The intersection of language and mathe-matics. *Mathematics Teaching in the Middle School, 15*(9), 516–523.

Taber, S. B. (2002). Go ask Alice about multiplication of frac-tions. In B. Litwiller (Ed.), *Making sense of fractions, ratios, and proportions* (pp. 61–71). Reston, VA: NCTM.

Taber, S. B. (2007). Using *Alice in Wonderland* to teach multipli-cation of fractions. *Mathematics Teaching in the Middle School, 12*(5), 244–250.

Taber, S. B. (2009). Capitalizing on the unexpected. *Mathematics Teaching in the Middle School, 15*(3), 149–155.

Tanish, D. (2011). Functional thinking ways in relation to lin-ear function tables of elementary school students. *Journal of Mathematical Behavior, 30*, 206–223.

Tarr, J. E., Lee, H. S., & Rider, R. L. (2006). When data and chance collide: Drawing inferences from empirical data. In G. Burrill & P. C. Elliott (Eds.), *Thinking and reasoning with data and chance: 68th NCTM yearbook* (pp. 139–149). Res-ton, VA: NCTM.

Tarr, J. E., & Shaughnessy, J. M. (2007). *Data and chance. Results from the 2003 National Assessment of Educational Process.* Res-ton, VA: NCTM.

Thiessen, D. (Ed.). (2004). *Exploring mathematics through literature*. Reston, VA: NCTM.

Thomas, D., & Brown, J. S. (2011). *A new culture of learning: Cultivating the imagination for a world of constant change* (Vol. 219). Lexington, KY: CreateSpace.

Thomas, K. R. (2006). Students THINK: A framework for improving problem solving. *Teaching Children Mathematics, 13*(2), 86–95.

Thomas, N. (2004). The development of structure in the number system. In M. J. Hoines & A. B. Fuglestad (Eds.), *28th conference of the International Group for the Psychology of Mathematics Education* (pp. 305–312). Bergen, Norway: Bergen University College Press.

Thompson, P. W. (1994). Concrete materials and teaching for mathematical understanding. *Arithmetic Teacher, 41*(9), 556–558.

Thompson, P. W. (1995). Notation, convention, and quantity in elementary mathematics. In J. T. Sowder & B. P. Schappelle (Eds.), *Providing a foundation for teaching mathematics in the middle grades* (pp. 199–221). New York, NY: State University of New York Press.

Thompson, T. D., & Preston, R. V. (2004). Measurement in the middle grades: Insights from NAEP and TIMSS. *Mathematics Teaching in the Middle School, 9*(9), 514–519.

Thornton, C. A., & Toohey, M. A. (1984). *A matter of facts: (Addition, subtraction, multiplication, division).* Palo Alto, CA: Creative Publications.

Tillema, E. S. (2010). Math for real: A three-girl family. *Mathematics Teaching in the Middle School, 48*(5), 304.

Tillema, E. S. (2012). What is the difference? Using contextualized problems. *Mathematics Teaching in the Middle School, 17*(8), 473–478.

Tirosh, D. (2000). Enhancing prospective teachers' knowledge of children's conceptions: The case of division of fractions. *Journal for Research in Mathematics Education, 31*(1), 1, 5–25.

Tobias, S. (1995). *Overcoming math anxiety.* New York, NY: Norton.

Tomlinson, C. A. (1999). *The differentiated classroom: Responding to the needs of all learners.* Alexandria, VA: Association for Supervision and Curriculum Development.

Tomlinson, C. A., & McTighe, J. (2006). *Integrating differentiated instruction.* Alexandria, VA: Association for Supervision and Curriculum Development.

Tooke, D. J., & Lindstrom, L. (1998). Effectiveness of a mathematics methods course in reducing math anxiety of preservice elementary teachers. *School Science and Mathematics, 98*, 136–139.

Torbeyns, J., De Smedt, B., Ghesquiere, P., & Verschaffel, L. (2009). Acquisition and use of shortcut strategies by traditionally schooled children. *Educational Studies in Mathematics, 71*, 1–17.

Torgesen, J. K. (2002). The prevention of reading difficulties. *Journal of School Psychology, 40*(1), 7–26.

Tortolani, M. (2007, February). Presentation at the 2007 National Association of Multicultural Engineering Program Advocates National Conference, Baltimore, MD.

Towers, J. (2010). Learning to teach mathematics though inquiry: A focus on the relationship between describing and enacting inquiry-oriented teaching. *Journal of Mathematics Teacher Education, 13*(3), 243–263.

Towers, J., & Hunter, K. (2010). An ecological reading of mathematical language in a grade 3 classroom: A case of learning and teaching measurement estimation. *The Journal of Mathematical Behavior, 29*, 25–40.

Tsankova, J. K., & Pjanic, K. (2009–2010). The area model of multiplication of fractions. *Mathematics Teaching in the Middle School, 15*(5), 281–285.

Turner, E. E., Celedón-Pattichis, S., Marshall, M., & Tennison, A. (2009). "Fijense amorcitos, les voy a contra una historia": The power of story to support solving and discussing mathematical problems among Latino and Latina kindergarten students. In D. Y. White & J. S. Spitzer (Eds.), *Responding to diversity: Grades pre-K–5* (pp. 23–42). Reston, VA: NCTM.

Tzur, R. (1999). An integrated study of children's construction of improper fractions and the teacher's role in promoting learning. *Journal for Research in Mathematics Education, 30*(4), 390–416.

Ubuz, B., & Yayan, B. (2010). Primary teachers' subject matter knowledge: Decimals. *International Journal of Mathematical Education in Science and Technology, 41*(6), 787–804.

U.S. Census Bureau. (n.d.). Population clocks. Retrieved from www.census.gov/population/international

U.S. Census Bureau. (2014). Retrieved from www.census.gov/newsroom/releases/archives/foreignborn_population/cb14-tps44.html

U.S. Department of Education, Office of Educational Research and Improvement. (1997). *Introduction to TIMSS.* Washington, DC: U.S. Government Printing Office.

Usiskin, Z. (2007). Some thoughts about fractions. *Mathematics Teaching in the Middle School, 12*(7), 370–373.

Vamvakoussi, X., Van Dooren, W., & Verschaffel, L. (2012). Naturally biased? In search for reaction time evidence for a natural number bias in adults. *The Journal of Mathematical Behavior, 31*(3), 344–355.

Van Dooren, W., De Bock, D., Vleugels, K., & Verschaffel, L. (2010). Just answering . . . or thinking? Contrasting pupils' solutions and classifications of missing-value word problems. *Mathematical Thinking and Learning, 12*(1), 20–35.

van Hiele, P. M. (1984). A child's thought and geometry. In Geddes, D., Fuys, D. and Tischler, R. (Eds.). *English Translation of Selected Writings of Dina van Hiele-Geldof and Pierre M. van Hiele,* Washington, D.C., National Science Foundation.

van Hiele, P. M. (1999). Developing geometric thinking through activities that begin with play. *Teaching Children Mathematics, 5*(6), 310–316.

Van Tassel-Baska, J., & Brown, E. F. (2007). Toward best practice: An analysis of the efficacy of curriculum models in gifted education. *Gifted Child Quarterly, 51*(4), 342–358.

Verschaffel, L., Greer, B., & DeCorte, E. (2007). Whole number concepts and operations. In F. Lester, Jr. (Ed.), *Second handbook of research on mathematics teaching and learning* (pp. 557–628). Charlotte, NC: Information Age Publishing.

Vygotsky, L. S. (1978). *Mind and society.* Cambridge, MA: Harvard University Press.

Wagner, M. M., & Lachance, A. (2004). Mathematical adventures with Harry Potter. *Teaching Children Mathematics, 10*(5), 274–277.

Wagner, T. (2012). *Creating innovators: The making of young people who will change the world.* New York: Scribner.

Wai, J., Cacchio, M., Putallaz, M. C., & Mackel, M. C. (2010). Sex differences in the right tail of cognitive abilities: A 20 year examination. *Intelligence, 38*(4), 412–423.

Wai, J., Lubinski, D., & Benbow, C. (2009). Spatial ability for STEM domains: Aligning over 50 years of cumulative psychological knowledge solidifies its importance. *Journal of Educational Psychology, 101*, 817–835.

Wallace, A. H. (2007). Anticipating student responses to improve problem solving. *Mathematics Teaching in the Middle School, 12*(9), 504–511.

Wallace, A. H., & Gurganus, S. P. (2005). Teaching for mastery of multiplication. *Teaching Children Mathematics, 12*(1), 26–33.

Walter, M. I. (1970). *Boxes, squares and other things: A teacher's guide for a unit in informal geometry.* Reston, VA: NCTM.

Wareham, K. (2005). *Hand-held calculators and mathematics achievement: What the 1996 national assessment of educational progress eighth-grade mathematics exam scores tell us.* (Unpublished doctoral dissertation). Utah State University.

Warren, E., & Cooper, T. J. (2008). Patterns that support early algebraic thinking in elementary school. In C. E. Greenes & R. Rubenstein (Eds.), *Algebra and algebraic thinking in school mathematics: 70th NCTM yearbook* (pp. 113–126). Reston, VA: NCTM.

Watanabe, T. (2006). The teaching and learning of fractions: A Japanese perspective. *Teaching Children Mathematics, 12*(7), 368–374.

Watson, J. M., & Moritz, J. B. (2003). Fairness of dice: A longitudinal study of students' beliefs and strategies for making judgments. *Journal for Research in Mathematics Education, 34*(4), 270–304.

Watson, J. M., & Shaughnessy, J. M. (2004). Proportional reasoning: Lessons learned from research in data and chance. *Mathematics Teaching in the Middle School, 10*(2), 104–109.

Wearne, D., & Kouba, V. L. (2000). Rational numbers. In E. A. Silver & P. A. Kenney (Eds.), *Results from the seventh mathematics assessment of the National Assessment of Educational Progress* (pp. 163–191). Reston, VA: NCTM.

Weidemann, W., Mikovch, A. K., & Hunt, J. B. (2001). Using a lifeline to give rational numbers a personal touch. *Mathematics Teaching in the Middle School, 7*(4), 210–215.

Whaley, K. A. (2012). Using students' interests as algebraic models. *Mathematics Teaching in the Middle School, 17*(6), 372–378.

White, J. (2014). *Using children's literature to teach problem solving in math: Addressing the Common Core in Grade K–2.* New York, NY: Taylor & Francis.

Whiteford, T. (2009/2010). Is mathematics a universal language? *Teaching Children Mathematics, 16*(5), 276–283.

Whitin, D. J., & Whitin, P. (2004). *New visions for linking literature and mathematics.* Urbana, IL: National Council of Teachers of English; Reston, VA: NCTM.

Whitin, P. (2007). The mathematics survey: A tool for assessing attitudes and dispositions. *Teaching Children Mathematics, 13*(8), 426–433.

Whitin, P., & Whitin, D. J. (2006). Making connections through math-related book pairs. *Teaching Children Mathematics, 13*(4), 196–202.

Wickett, M., Kharas, K., & Burns, M. (2002). *Lessons for algebraic thinking.* Sausalito, CA: Math Solutions Publications.

Wieser, E. T. (2008). Students control their own learning: A metacognitive approach. *Teaching Children Mathematics, 15*(2), 90–95.

Wigfield, A., & Cambria, J. (2010). Expectancy-value theory: Retrospective and prospective. In S. Karabenick & T. C. Urdan (Eds.), *The decade ahead: Theoretical perspectives on motivation and achievement (advances in motivation and achievement)* (Vol. 16, pp. 35–70). Bradford, UK: Emerald Group Publishing Limited.

Wiggins, G. (2013, May 5). Letter to the Editor. *New York Times,* p. 2.

Wilburne, J. M., & Kulbacki, A. (2014). Connecting the "missing words" to the Common Core. *Mathematics Teaching in the Middle School, 19*(7), 430–436.

Wiliam, D. (2007). Content *then* process: Teacher learning communities in the service of formative assessment. In D. B. Reeves (Ed.), *Ahead of the curve: The power of assessment to transform teaching and learning* (pp. 183–204). Bloomington, IN: Solution Tree.

Wiliam, D. (2008). Changing classroom practice. *Educational Leadership, 65*(4), 36–41.

Wiliam, D. (2010, September). *Practical techniques for formative assessment.* Presentation given in Boras, Sweden. Retrieved from www.slideshare.net/BLoPP/dylan-wiliam-bors-2010

Wilkerson, T. L., Bryan, T., & Curry, J. (2012). An appetite for fractions. *Teaching Children Mathematics, 19*(2), 90–99.

Williams, L. (2008). Tiering and scaffolding: Two strategies for providing access to important mathematics. *Teaching Children Mathematics, 14*(6), 324–330.

Williams, M., Forrest, K., & Schnabel, D. (2006). Water wonders (math by the month). *Teaching Children Mathematics, 12*(5), 248–249.

Williams, N. L., & Bruels, C. (2011). Target geometry and probability using a dartboard. *Mathematics Teaching in the Middle School, 16*(6), 375–378.

Wilson, L. D., & Kenney, P. A. (2003). Classroom and large-scale assessment. In J. Kilpatrick, W. G. Martin, & D. Schifter (Eds.), *A research companion to Principles and Standards for School Mathematics* (pp. 53–67). Reston, VA: NCTM.

Witherspoon, T. F. (2014). Using constructed knowledge to multiply fractions. *Teaching Children Mathematics, 20*(7), 444–451.

Witzel, B. S. (2005). Using CRA to teach algebra to students with math difficulties in inclusive settings. *Learning Disabilities—A Contemporary Journal, 3*(2), 49–60.

Wood, T., & Turner-Vorbeck, T. (2001). Extending the conception of mathematics teaching. In T. Wood, B. S. Nelson, & J. Warfield (Eds.), *Beyond classical pedagogy: Teaching elementary school mathematics* (pp. 185–208). Mahwah, NJ: Erlbaum.

Wood, T., Williams, G., & McNeal, B. (2006). Children's mathematical thinking in different classroom cultures. *Journal for Research in Mathematics Education, 37*(3), 222–255.

Woodward, J. (2006). Developing automaticity in multiplication facts: Integrating strategy instruction with timed practice drills. *Learning Disability Quarterly, 29*(4), 269–289.

Woodward, J., Baxter, J., & Robinson, R. (1999). Rules and reasons: Decimal instruction for academically low achieving students. *Learning Disabilities Research and Practice, 14*(1), 15–24.

Wright, R., Martland, J., Stafford, A., & Stanger, G. (2008). *Teaching number: Advancing children's skills and strategies.* London, UK: Sage.

Wright, R. J., Stanger, G., Stafford, A. K., & Martland, J. (2006). *Teaching number in the classroom with 4–8 year olds.* London, UK: Paul Chapman Publications/Sage.

Wu, Z., An, S., King, J., Ramirez, M., & Evans, S. (2009). Second-grade "professors." *Teaching Children Mathematics, 16*(1), 34–41.

Xin, Y. P., Jitendra, A. K., & Deatline-Buchman, A. D. (2005). Effects of mathematical word problem-solving instruction on middle school students with learning problems. *Journal of Special Education, 39*(3), 181–192.

Yackel, E., & Cobb, P. (1996). Sociomathematical norms, argumentation, and autonomy in mathematics. *Journal for Research in Mathematics Education, 27*(4), 458–477.

Ysseldyke, J. (2002). Response to "Learning Disabilities: Historical Perspectives." In R. Bradley, L. Danielson, & D. Hallahan (Eds.), *Identification of learning disabilities: Research to practice* (pp. 89–98). Mahwah, NJ: Erlbaum.

Yu, P., Barrett, J., & Presmeg, N. (2009). Prototypes and categorical reasoning: A perspective to explain how children learn about interactive geometry objects. In T. Craine & R. Rubenstein (Eds.) *Understanding geometry for a changing world.* Reston, VA: NCTM.

Zacharos, K. (2006). Prevailing educational practices for area measurement and students' failure in measuring areas. *Journal of Mathematics Behavior, 25*(3), 224–239.

Zambo, R. (2008). Percents can make sense. *Mathematics Teaching in the Middle School, 13*(7), 418–422.

Zollman, A. (2009). Mathematical graphic organizers. *Teaching Children Mathematics, 16*(4), 222–229.

Zwillinger, D. (Ed.). (2011). *Standard mathematical tables and formulae* (32nd ed.). Boca Raton, FL: CRC Press.

Children's Literature References

Andrews, J., & Jolliffe, S. (2005). *The twelve days of summer.* Victoria, BC: Orca Book Publishers.

Anno, M. (1994). *Anno's magic seeds.* New York, NY: Philomel Books.

Appelt, K., & Sweet, M. (1999). *Bats on parade.* New York, NY: Morrow Junior Books.

Baer, E. (1990). *This is the Way we go to School.* New York: Scholastic.

Ball, J. (2005). *Go figure! A totally cool book about numbers.* New York, NY: DK Publishing.

Better Homes and Gardens. (2012). *New junior cookbook.* Des Moines, IA: Author.

Bowen, A. (2006). *The great math tattle battle.* Park Ridge, IL: Albert Whitman.

Briggs, R. (1970). *Jim and the beanstalk.* New York, NY: Coward-McCann.

Brown, D. (2000). *Alice Ramsey's grand adventure.* Boston, MA: Sandpiper.

Brown, M. W. (1947). *Goodnight moon.* New York, NY: Harper & Row.

Buckley, J., Jr., & Stremme, R. (2006). *Book of lists: Fun facts, weird trivia, and amazing lists on nearly everything you need to know!* Santa Barbara, CA: Scholastic.

Burns, M. (1995). *The greedy triangle.* New York, NY: Houghton Mifflin.

Burns, M., & Tilley, D. (2008). *Spaghetti and meatballs for all! A mathematical story.* New York, NY: Scholastic.

Carroll, L., & Gray, D. J. (1865/1992). *Alice in wonderland.* New York, NY: Norton.

Clement, R. (1991). *Counting on Frank.* Milwaukee, WI: Gareth Stevens Children's Books.

Cushman, R. (1991). *Do you wanna bet? Your chance to find out about probability.* New York, NY: Clarion Books.

Cuyler, M. (2005). *100th day worries.* New York, NY: Simon & Schuster.

Cuyler, M. (2010). *Guinea pigs add up.* New York, NY: Walker.

Dee, R. (1988). *Two ways to count to ten.* New York, NY: Holt.

DiSalvo-Ryan, D. (1994). *City green.* New York, NY: William Morrow.

Drescher, D. (2008). *What's hiding in there?* Edinburgh, Scotland: Floris Books.

Ehlert, L. (1989). *Color zoo.* New York, NY: HarperCollins.

Ehlert, L. (1990). *Color farm.* New York, NY: HarperCollins.

Enzensberger, H. M. (1997). *The number devil.* New York, NY: Metropolitan Books.

Franco, B. (2009). *Zero is the leaves on the tree.* Berkeley, CA: Tricycle Press.

Gifford, S., & Thaler, S. (2008). *Piece = part = portion: Fraction = decimal = percent.* New York: Tricycle Press.

Giganti, P. (1988). *How many snails? A counting book.* New York, NY: Greenwillow.

Grossman, B. (1996). *My little sister ate one hare.* New York, NY: Crown.

Hamm, D. J. (1991). *How many feet in the bed?* New York, NY: Simon & Schuster.

Harris, T. (2000). *100 days of school.* Minneapolis, MN: Millbrook Press.

Henkes, K. (2008). *Chrysanthemum,* Mulberry Books.

Hightower, S. (1997). *Twelve snails to one lizard: A tale of mischief and measurement.* New York, NY: Simon & Schuster.

Himmelman, J. (2010). *Ten little hot dogs.* Tarrytown, NY: Pinwheel Books.

Hoban, T. (1996). *Shapes, shapes, shapes.* New York, NY: HarperTrophy.

Hoban, T. (1998). *So many circles, so many squares.* New York, NY: Greenwillow.

Hoban, T. (2000). *Cubes, cones, cylinders and shapes.* New York, NY: Greenwillow.

Hoffman, D. (2005). *The breakfast cereal gourmet.* Riverside, NJ: Andrews McMeel Publishing.

Hong, L. T. (1993). *Two of everything: A Chinese folktale.* New York, NY: Albert Whitman.

Hoose, P. (2001). *We were there, too! Young people in U.S. history.* New York, NY: Farrar, Straus & Giroux.

Hutchins, P. (1986). *The doorbell rang.* New York, NY: Greenwillow.

Isaacs, A., & Zelinsky, P. O. (1994). *Swamp angel.* New York, NY: Dutton Children's Books.

Jenkins, S. (2011). *Just a second.* New York: HMH Books for Children.

Johnson, P. (2012). *If I had a million bucks.* Wilmington, DE: Five Start Publications.

Juster, N. (1961). *The phantom tollbooth.* New York, NY: Random House.

Krull, K. (2000). *Wilma unlimited.* Boston, MA: Sandpiper.

Kroll, V. (2005). *Equal Shmequal.* Watertown, MA: Charlesbridge Publishing.

Landau, E. (2006). *The history of everyday life.* Minneapolis, MN: Lerner Classroom.

Leedy, L. (2000). *Measuring Penny*. New York, NY: Holt.

Litwin, E. (2012). *Pete the cat and his four groovy buttons*. New York: HarperCollins.

Lobel, A. (1970). *Frog and Toad are friends*. New York, NY: HarperCollins.

Masoff, J., & Sirrell, T. (2006). *Oh, yikes!: History's grossest, wackiest moments*. New York, NY: Workman.

Mathis, S. B. (1986). *The hundred penny box*. New York, NY: Viking Juvenile Books.

McElligott, M. (2007). *Bean thirteen*. New York, NY: Putnam Juvenile.

McKissack, P. (1996). *A million fish . . . more or less*. New York, NY: Dragonfly Books.

Metropolitan Museum of Art. (2005). *Museum shapes*. New York, NY: Little Brown and Company.

Metzger, s. (2008). *We're Going on a Leaf Hunt*. Cartwheel Books.

Micklethwait, L. (2004). *I spy shapes in art*. New York, NY: Greenwillow.

Murphy, S. (1997). *The best vacation ever*. New York, NY: HarperCollins.

Murphy, S. (2003). *3 Little Firefighters*. New York. Harper Collins.

Murrie, S., & Murrie, M. (2007). *Every minute on earth*. New York, NY: Scholastic.

Myller, R. (1991). *How big is a foot?* South Holland, IL: Yearling Books.

National Geographic. (2011). *Kids Almanac 2012*. Washington, DC: National Geographic Children's Books.

Norton, M. (1953). *The borrowers*. New York, NY: Harcourt Brace.

Numeroff, L. J. (1985). *If you give a mouse a cookie*. New York, NY: HarperCollins.

Osborne, M. P., & Potter, G. (2000). *Kate and the beanstalk*. New York, NY: Atheneum Books for Young Readers.

Overdeck, L. (2013). *Bedtime math*. New York: Feiwel and Friends.

Pallotta, J. (2002). *Apple fractions*. New York, NY: Scholastic Cartwheel Books.

Pinczes, E. (1999). *One hundred angry ants*. Boston, MA: Sandpiper.

Pinczes, E. (2002). *Remainder of one*. Boston, MA: Sandpiper.

Portis, A. (2007). *Not a stick*. New York, NY: HarperCollins.

Rowling, J. K. (1998). *Harry Potter and the sorcerer's stone*. New York, NY: A. A. Lewine.

Sachar, L. (1998). *Holes*. New York, NY: Farrar, Straus & Giroux.

Schwartz, D. M. (1985). *How much is a million?* New York, NY: Lothrop, Lee & Shepard.

Schwartz, D. M. (1994). *If you made a million*. New York, NY: Lothrop, Lee & Shepard.

Schwartz, D. M. (1999). *If you hopped like a frog*. New York, NY: Scholastic Press.

Schwartz, D. M. (2004). *How much is a million?* New York, NY: HarperCollins.

Schwartz, D. M., & Whitin, D. (1999). *The magic of a million activity book—Grades 2–5*. New York, NY: Scholastic.

Seuss, Dr. (1960). *Green eggs and ham*. New York, NY: Random House.

Silverstein, S. (1974). One inch tall. In *Where the sidewalk ends* (p. 55). New York, NY: Harper & Row.

Slobodkina, E. (1938). *Caps for sale*. New York, NY: Scholastic Books.

Smith, D. (2011). *If the world were a village: A book about the world's people* (2nd ed.). Tonawanda, NY: Kids Can Press.

Stoeke, J. M. (1999). *Hide and seek*. New York, NY: Dutton Juvenile Books.

Swift, J., & Winterson, J. (1726/1999). *Gulliver's travels*. Oxford, UK: Oxford University Press.

Tahan, M. (1993). *The man who counted: A collection of mathematical adventures* (Trans. L. Clark & A. Reid). New York, NY: Norton.

Thaler, M. (2014). *The 100th day of school from the black lagoon*. New York, NY: Scholastic.

Toft, K. M., & Sheather, A. (1998). *One less fish*. Watertown, MA: Charlesbridge.

Tompert, A. (1997). *Grandfather Tang's story*. New York, NY: Dragonfly Books.

Weatherform, C. B. (2005). *A Negro league scrapbook*. Honesdale, PA: Boyds Mills Press.

Wells, R. E. (1993). *Is a blue whale the biggest thing there is?* Morton Grove, IL: Whitman.

Wishinsky, F., & Zhang, S. N. (1999). *The man who made parks: The story of parkbuilder Frederick Law Olmsted*. Plattsburgh, NY: Tundra Books.

Index

Credits

Chapter 1: p. 3: quote, Steen, Lynn Arthur (1997). Preface: The New Literacy. In L. A. Steen, *Why Numbers Count*. New York: College Entrance Examination Board; p. 7: Table 1.1, Adapted with permission from NCTM (National Council of Teachers of Mathematics). (2000). *Principles and standards for school mathematics*. Reston, VA: NCTM. Copyright 2000 by the National Council of Teachers of Mathematics. All rights reserved; p. 7: quote, Copyright 2010. National Governors Association Center for Best Practices and Council of Chief State School Officers. All rights reserved.

Chapter 2: p. 21: Figure 2.9, John A. Van de Walle, Karen S. Karp, Lou Ann H. Lovin, & Jennifer M. Bay-Williams, *Teaching Student-Centered Mathematics: Developmentally Appropriate Instruction for Grades 6-8*. Pearson Education.

Chapter 4: p. 66: quote, Copyright 2010. National Governors Association Center for Best Practices and Council of Chief State School Officers. All rights reserved.

Chapter 5: p. 85: quote: Wiliam, D. (2010, September). Practical Techniques for Formative Assessment. Presentation given in Boras, Sweden. Retrieved from www.slideshare.net/BLoPP/dylan-wiliam-bors-2010.

Chapter 6: p. 119: list, Based on Whiteford, T. (2009/2010). Is mathematics a universal language? *Teaching Children Mathematics*, 16(5), 276–283.

Chapter 7: p. 127: quote, NCTM (2014). *Principles to actions: Ensuring mathematical success for all. Reston*, VA: NCTM, p. 128: quote, Fey, J. T., Hollenbeck, R. W., & Wray, J. A. (2010). Technology and the teaching of mathematics, p. 275. In B. Reys, R. Reys, & R. Rubenstein (Eds.) *Mathematics curriculum: Issues, trends, and future directions* (72nd Yearbook). Reston, VA: NCTM; p. 131: National Council of Teachers of Mathematics (NCTM). *Using Calculators for Teaching and Learning Mathematics*. NCTM Research Brief, 2011. http://www.nctm.org/news/content.aspx?id=31192.

Chapter 8: p. 146: Table 8.1, Based on Clements, D. H., & Sarama, J. (2009). *Learning and teaching early math: The learning trajectories approach*. New York: Routledge; p. 152, quote, Based on Howden, H. (1989). Teaching number sense. *Arithmetic Teacher*, 36(6), 6–11; p. 161: quote, © Copyright 2010. National Governors Association Center for Best Practices and Council of Chief State School Officers. All rights reserved.

Chapter 9: pp. 168, 170, 173, 177, 178, 182, 189: Common Core Standards, © Copyright 2010. National Governors Association Center for Best Practices and Council of Chief State School Officers. All rights reserved. p. 172: quote, Based on Fosnot, C. T., & Dolk, M. (2001). *Young mathematicians at work: Constructing number sense, addition, and subtraction*. Portsmouth, NH: Heinemann.

Chapter 10: p. 195: list, Based on Baroody, A. J. (2006). Why children have difficulties mastering the basic number combinations and how to help them, p. 22. *Teaching Children Mathematics*, 13(1), 22–31. pp. 197, 198, 209, 210, 212, 215, 217, 219: Common Core Standards, © Copyright 2010. National Governors Association Center for Best Practices and Council of Chief State School Officers. All rights reserved; p. 196: list, Based on Baroody, A. J. (2006). Why children have difficulties mastering the basic number combinations and how to help them. *Teaching Children Mathematics*, 13(1), 22–31. pp. 216–217: Table 10.2, Based on ideas from Forbringer & Fahsl, 2010, and Kamii & Anderson, 2003.

Chapter 11: p. 224, 225, 231, 234, 239, 242: Common Core Standards, © Copyright 2010. National Governors Association Center for Best Practices and Council of Chief State School Officers. All rights reserved; p. 237: list, Based on Ross, S. H. (1989). Parts, wholes, and place value: A developmental perspective. *Arithmetic Teacher*, 36(6), 47–51; Ross, S. R. (2002). Place value: Problem solving and written assessment. *Teaching Children Mathematics*, 8(7), 419–423.

Chapter 12: p. 247: quote, National Research Council. (2001). *Adding It Up: Helping Children Learn Mathematics. National Academy of Sciences*, National Academies Press, Washington, DC; p. 249: quote, NCTM (2014). *Principles to actions: Ensuring mathematical success for all*. Reston, VA: NCTM; p. 255: quote, Based on Carpenter, T. P., Franke, M. L., Jacobs, V. R., Fennema, E., & Empson, S. B. (1998). A longitudinal study of invention and understanding in children's multidigit addition and subtraction. *Journal for Research in Mathematics Education*, 29(1), 3–20; p. 259: quote: Hiebert, J. & Grouws, D. A. (2007). The effects of classroom mathematics teaching on students' learning. In Frank K. Lester, Jr. *Second Handbook of Research on Mathematics Teaching and Learning* (pp. 371-404), Charlotte, NC: Information Age Publishing; p. 262: quote: Copyright 2010. National Governors Association Center for Best Practices and Council of Chief State School Officers. All rights reserved; p. 264: Common Core Standard, Copyright 2010. National Governors Association Center for Best Practices and Council of Chief State School Officers. All rights reserved; p. 272: quote, Copyright 2010. National Governors Association Center for Best Practices and Council of Chief State School Officers. All rights reserved.

Chapter 13: pp. 278, 283, 292: Common Core Standards, Copyright 2010. National Governors Association Center for Best Practices and Council of Chief State School Officers. All rights reserved; p. 291, 293: quote: Copyright 2010. National Governors Association Center for Best Practices and Council of Chief State School Officers. All rights reserved.

Chapter 14: p. 299: quote: Copyright 2010. National Governors Association Center for Best Practices and Council of Chief State School Officers. All rights reserved. pp.301, 303, 304, 312, 319, 320: Common Core Standards, Copyright 2010. National Governors Association Center for Best Practices and Council of Chief State School Officers. All rights reserved; p. 303: quote, Copyright 2010. National Governors Association Center for Best Practices and Council of Chief State School Officers. All rights reserved; p. 307: Figure 14.1, Van de Walle, J. A., Bay-Williams, J., Lovin, L. A. H., & Karp, K. H. (2014). *Teaching Student-Centered Mathematics.* Boston, MA: Pearson; p. 331: Figure 14.18, Van de Walle, J. A., Bay-Williams, J., Lovin, L. A. H., & Karp, K. H. (2014). *Teaching Student-Centered Mathematics: Developmentally Appropriate Instruction for Grades 6-8.* Boston, MA: Pearson; p. 334: quote, Copyright 2010. National Governors Association Center for Best Practices and Council of Chief State School Officers. All rights reserved.

Chapter 15: pp. 342, 357, 360, 362, 366: Common Core Standards, Copyright 2010. National Governors Association Center for Best Practices and Council of Chief State School Officers. All rights reserved; p. 343: unnumbered figure, Based on Roddick, C., & and Silvas-Centeno, C. (2007). "Developing Understanding of Fractions Through Pattern Blocks and Fair Trade." *Teaching Children Mathematics*, 14(3), 140–145; p. 344: quote, Siegler, R. S., Carpenter, T., Fennell, F., Geary, D., Lewis, J., Okamoto, Y., Wray, J. (2010). *Developing effective fractions instruction for kindergarten through 8th grade: A practice guide* (NCEE 2010-4039). Retrieved from www.whatworks.ed.gov/publications/practiceguides, p. 1; p. 349: quote, Copyright 2010. National Governors Association Center for Best Practices and Council of Chief State School Officers. All rights reserved.

Chapter 16: p. 372: list, Based on CCSSO (Council of Chief State School Officers). (2010). Common core state standards. Retrieved from http://corestandards.org; pp. 373, 375, 384, 395, 396: Common Core Standards, Copyright 2010. National Governors Association Center for Best Practices and Council of Chief State School Officers. All rights reserved.

Chapter 17: pp. 403, 406, 417: quotes, Copyright 2010. National Governors Association Center for Best Practices and Council of Chief State School Officers. All rights reserved; pp 406, 411, 414, 418, 421: Common Core Standards, Copyright 2010. National Governors Association Center for Best Practices and Council of Chief State School Officers. All rights reserved.

Chapter 18: pp. 431, 433, 436, 437, 443, 444, 446: Common Core Standards, Copyright 2010. National Governors Association Center for Best Practices and Council of Chief State School Officers. All rights reserved; p. 432: list, Based on Lamon, S. J. (2006). *Teaching fractions and ratios for understanding: Essential content knowledge and instructional strategies for teachers* (2nd ed.). Mahwah, NJ: Lawrence Erlbaum.

Chapter 19: pp. 455, 457, 464, 471, 473, 477, 484: Common Core Standards: Copyright 2010. National Governors Association Center for Best Practices and Council of Chief State School Officers. All rights reserved.

Chapter 20: pp. 495, 501, 503, 506, 507: Common Core Standards: Copyright 2010. National Governors Association Center for Best Practices and Council of Chief State School Officers. All rights reserved; p. 500, 512, 514: quotes, Copyright 2010. National Governors Association Center for Best Practices and Council of Chief State School Officers. All rights reserved.

Chapter 21: p. 526: quote, Copyright 2010. National Governors Association Center for Best Practices and Council of Chief State School Officers. All rights reserved; p. 527: quote, Scheaffer, R. L. (2006). Statistics and mathematics: On making a happy marriage, pp. 310–311. In G. F. Burrill & P. C. Elliott (Eds.), *Thinking and reasoning about data and chance: Sixty-eighth yearbook* (pp. 309–322). Reston, VA: NCTM; p. 530, 533, 537, 540, 544: Common Core Standards: Copyright 2010. National Governors Association Center for Best Practices and Council of Chief State School Officers. All rights reserved.

Chapter 22: pp. 560, 562, 564, 566, 570, 573, 576: Common Core Standards: Copyright 2010. National Governors Association Center for Best Practices and Council of Chief State School Officers. All rights reserved;

Chapter 23: pp. 583, 585, 586, 588, 589, 592, 597, 600, 603: Common Core Standards: Copyright 2010. National Governors Association Center for Best Practices and Council of Chief State School Officers. All rights reserved; pp. 592, 593, 604: quotes, Copyright 2010. National Governors Association Center for Best Practices and Council of Chief State School Officers. All rights reserved.

Pop-Ups

Select Activity Pages, Expanded Lessons, Blackline Masters, and Teacher Resouces from: John A. Van de Walle, Karen S. Karp, Lou Ann H. Lovin, & Jennifer M. Bay-Williams, *Teaching Student-Centered Mathematics for Grades K-2*, vol. I. Pearson Education; John A. Van de Walle, Karen S. Karp, Lou Ann H. Lovin, & Jennifer M. Bay-Williams, *Teaching Student-Centered Mathematics for Grades 3-5*, vol. II. Pearson Education; John A. Van de Walle, Karen S. Karp, Lou Ann H. Lovin, & Jennifer M. Bay-Williams, *Teaching Student-Centered Mathematics for Grades 6-8*, vol. III. Pearson Education; Jennifer M. Bay-Williams, Maggie McGatha, With Beth M. McCord Kobett, With Jonathan A. Wray (2014)*Mathematics Coaching: Resources and Tools for Coaches and Leaders, K-12*. Pearson; Bay-Williams (2013) *Field Experience Guide, Resources for Teachers of Elementary and Middle School Mathematics.*